Grid Parity

The Art of Financing Renewable Energy Projects in the U.S.

Grid Parity

The Art of Financing Renewable Energy Projects in the U.S.

Gene Beck CEM, CLP

River Publishers

Routledge
Taylor & Francis Group
LONDON AND NEW YORK

First published by Fairmont Press in 2014.

Published 2020 by River Publishers
River Publishers
Alsbjergvej 10, 9260 Gistrup, Denmark
www.riverpublishers.com

Distributed exclusively by Routledge
2 Park Square, Milton Park, Abingdon, Oxon OX14 4RN
605 Third Avenue, New York, NY 10017

First issued in paperback 2023

Routledge is an imprint of the Taylor & Francis Group, an informa business

Publisher's Note
The publisher has gone to great lengths to ensure the quality of this reprint but points out that some imperfections in the original copies may be apparent.

Library of Congress Cataloging-in-Publication Data

Beck, Gene
Grid parity : the art of financing renewable energy projects in the U.S. / Gene Beck CEM, CLP.
pages cm
Includes bibliographical references and index.
ISBN 0-88173-734-8 (alk. paper) -- ISBN 978-8-7702-2315-7 (electronic) -- ISBN 978-1-4822-4170-9 (Taylor & Francis distribution : alk. paper) 1. Renewable energy sources--United States--Finance. 2. Renewable energy sources--Government policy--United States. I. Title.

HD9502.U52B43 2014
333.79'4--dc23

2014000210

Grid parity : the art of financing renewable energy projects in the U.S. / by Gene Beck

ISBN 13: 978-87-7022-924-1 (pbk)
ISBN 13: 978-0-88173-734-9 (The Fairmont Press, Inc.)
ISBN 13: 978-1-4822-4170-9 (hbk)
ISBN 13: 978-8-7702-2315-7 (online)
ISBN 13: 978-1-0031-5184-5 (ebook master)

Table of Contents

Foreword

If you are serious about mastering the skills it takes to succeed in the challenging area of financing for renewable energy assets, this is the book for you. It truly is the definitive guide for that subject, and I can think of no better teacher than Gene Beck.

Decades before he was known as a leading expert in renewable energy financing, Gene was already honing his skills as a finance professional. When solar and wind power, and other forms of renewable energy, began to transition from a novelty to a serious competitor for conventional energy sources, Gene was there from the beginning.

In this book, you will get the advantage of a career's worth of knowledge and experience, as if Gene were right beside you, coaching you through all there is to know on this subject. And believe me, as someone who considers Gene at the top in his field of expertise, that kind of insight and guidance will be of tremendous benefit to you.

So, what sets this book apart from other books, or even seminars and classes on the subject? Maybe a good way to explain what *Grid Parity* is all about is to point out what it is not. This book is not "financing 101," and it is not the bullet-point introduction to the subject that you will get at a weekend seminar. There are plenty of excellent resources out there to learn about the basics. In this book, Gene goes way beyond the fundamentals to help professionals who are already in the renewable energy business or who are looking to break into the business fully understand how the financing and economics of these projects work.

Neither is this book a cursory overview of the subject. It's a comprehensive, expertly explained, in-depth study full of real-life examples, text and commentary on pertinent laws and regulations, helpful charts and graphs, equations and other tools, and much more. *Grid Parity* will walk you through the financial structures that are present in the renewable energy market today, provide valuable information on current market practices, and deepen your understanding of the topic with a number of financial models for these types of assets.

You will find, for example, indispensable financial modeling tips that provide tremendous insight into the finer points of the economic factors that shape the success of renewable energy projects. These are not trivial details; they are the subtleties of the process that make the economics work. Building your understanding and expertise in these financial models can, as a result, help you increase project returns.

In fact, I think of *Grid Parity* as a textbook for professionals—an indispensable source of information and guidance on all topics related to renewable energy project financing. It is a resource you will find yourself turning to again and again.

I think it is important to emphasize that I'm not just a cheerleader for Gene and the prodigious body of knowledge he has built over his career; I'm also a student. As I have read *Grid Parity*—and have revisited various sections for additional information and explanation—I have found it to be an incredibly valuable source of information that has increased my understanding of the complex and ever-evolving field of renewable energy asset financing. I believe you will have the same experience as you read through this outstanding volume and apply its many lessons to your work.

Ed Feo, JD
COO, Coronal Management, LLC
Retired Co-Chair, Global Project Finance Group, Milbank, Tweed, Hadley & McCloy, LLP
Managing Director, USRG Renewable Finance
Managing Partner, Seaward Road Capital

Mr. Feo is a pioneer in energy development and finance and a respected authority on the energy industry. He leads an ongoing dialogue on renewable energy by chairing or speaking at top industry conferences. He was named one of the "Five Most Influential People in Renewable Energy" by Euromoney/Institutional Investor and ranked by Project Finance magazine in "Deals of the Year" and "Top Legal Advisors" in the renewable energy industry.

Mr. Feo holds a bachelor's degree from the University of California, Los Angeles, and earned his Juris Doctor degree from the University of California, Los Angeles-School of Law.

Disclaimer

The information contained in this publication is for general purposes only and is not intended, and should not be construed, as legal, accounting, or tax advice or opinion provided by the author or publisher to the reader. This material may not be applicable or suitable for the reader's specific circumstances or needs. Therefore, the information should not be used as a substitute for consultation with professional accounting, tax, legal or other competent advisors. Please contact your professional advisor before taking any action based upon this information.

Any tax advice included in this written or electronic communication was not intended or written to be used, and it cannot be used by a taxpayer, for the purpose of avoiding any penalties that may be imposed on the taxpayer by any governmental taxing authority or agency.

Tax laws change frequently and therefore references to start and ending dates described in this book are likely to be modified at any time. However, the historical context and the likelihood of similar events occurring in the future are realistic and therefore the reader should be aware of the opportunities and limitations of past tax rules and how they may be applicable in the future to renewable energy projects.

Preface

THE "QE" FUNCTION

(MONEY RULES)

QE = E+E+E+E
QUANTUM ECONOMICS = ENERGY + ENGINEERING + EFFICIENCY + ENVIRONMENT

 +  + 

+ 

Acknowledgments

I would like to express my thanks and gratitude to all the many people who have given me guidance and encouragement over my lifetime, including my family, friends, education colleagues, all the many professionals I have worked with over the past decades, and my clients who have always challenged me with finding new ways to get their projects financed. I appreciate the many helpful comments and suggestions they provided and which have been incorporated into this edition. I truly believe that I would not be where I am today and completed this book without all of their help.

Energy, tax, legal, finance, government and sustainability professionals and experts all provided invaluable input as to what should be included in a book that provides a definitive solution to the complex field of financing cleantech renewable energy projects in the U.S. My personal goal was to provide the best textbook on this exciting new industry.

Special thanks go to my mother whose encouragement to pursue my dreams and never let obstacles stand in my way has been my lifetime guidance. Finally, thanks to my two children, Paul and Steph, along with special close personal friends for their patience, support and understanding while I took time away from them to write. I truly appreciate their help to plan, edit, produce and launch *Grid Parity* they provided. I hope that they are pleased with the result.

Gene Beck, CEM, CLP

Introduction

The U.S. Energy Information Administration (EIA) reported on June 30, 2011 that renewable energy has passed another milestone as domestic production from renewable resources is now significantly greater than that of nuclear power—passing nuclear by 17.91%. The challenge for the energy industry is how this continued growth will get financed. *Grid Parity* addresses this challenge head-on. The book is a treatise on the complexities of renewable energy finance and provides many tools and solutions that will make investors, policy makers, lenders and users of renewable energy large and diversified sums of income. The book exposes dozens of creative methods to achieve renewable energy goals for continued growth—achievements that have been historically kept confidential and never presented in a comprehensive book format before. The complex tax and accounting rules combined with massive rebates and incentives from every segment of the government generates opportunities for the reader to cash in on the green energy revolution.

Grid Parity is a complete resource for all readers seeking an in-depth analysis of the business of financing renewable energy projects in the U.S. The analysis includes detailed information of the following components that drive the ultimate solution to implementing clean renewable energy production:

1. Multiple legal financial structures
2. Understanding the technologies
3. Complete historical review of all legislation driving this energy sector
4. Understanding the massive tax incentives in renewable energy
5. How the transactions must meet the accounting rules and regulations
6. Exposing the many IRS regulations that cause project failures
7. Overview of the incentives and rebates that help pay for the projects
8. How to obtain Safe Harbor Treatment from the IRS on energy project financing
9. How energy efficiency components help pay for production facilities
10. The role energy audits play in supporting project finance
11. Multiple financial analysis models that drive energy costs below that of the utilities utilizing diverse monetary leveraging techniques
12. Examining the role that environmental and regulatory compliance considerations play in renewable energy financing
13. Understanding taxation issues with energy projects
14. Correlations between renewable energy production and support for corporate sustainability and greenhouse gas emission reductions
15. Tools for proper legal documentation of investing in renewable energy projects

Since no book has previously been written on the specific subject of the unique parameters used in financing renewable energy projects in the U.S., the audience seeking to purchase *Grid Parity* covers a broad spectrum of readers including those from the following sectors of the renewable energy industry:

Manufacturers of Renewable Equipment
Engineering, Consulting and R&D Firms
Utilities
Energy Developers
Energy Sponsors
Energy System Integrators
Law Firms
Accounting Firms
Sustainability Consultants & Firms
Environmental Advisory Firms
Venture Capital Firms
Investors (public and private)
Commercial Lending Institutions
Universities—Teachers & Students

Non-Profit Grant Providers
Real Property Owners
Energy Users from All Sectors
Incentive & Rebate Program Designers
Project Managers
Technology Developers
Researchers
Selected Elected Officials and Staff
Regulators
Trade Journal Publishers
Trade Associations
Tax Regulators and Auditors
Government—City, County, State and Federal
Individuals and Companies

For readers such as these, purchasing a book that provides sound financial advice on how to safely receive large sums of income over long periods is a must read. Each of these reader groups view renewable energy financing from a different perspective and have distinct financial goals of what they want to achieve from reading *Grid Parity*. The internal and external parameters needed to understand and then to be applied to each renewable energy project the reader embarks on are universal. The only difference between readers is how they will utilize and apply the complex issues inherent in financing renewable energy projects that they view as most important. The context in which the reader will apply the rules, regulations, economic opportunities, and the legal, tax and accounting issues in their projects will result in both challenges and great financial rewards for each of them when they "artfully" apply the multiple topics presented.

This book will give the reader an in-depth overview of the components needed to "artfully" craft a financing mechanism to achieve what was generally thought as un-achievable—financing clean energy projects that can be less costly than that of fossil-fuel driven energy sources. Energy risks are heightened these days. There is fuel risk, regulatory risk, political risk, commodity pricing risk, tax risk, climate risk and the risk of embracing the wrong technology or putting in place energy technology that could soon be outdated. The continuing combination of these forces is hugely complex and vital to understanding the future of financing renewable projects. *Grid Parity* will guide the reader through these challenges.

Many books have been written by authors on the technology and engineering involved in the renewable energy industry but none have addressed the key issue in every project—how are we going to pay for it. Unless there is an acceptable financing mechanism found that brings the energy costs down below what each user now has, the project will not be closed. The renewable energy sector competes directly with the utilities in America when it comes to paying for the energy needed by the user. This book presents many financial ways to lower the cost of energy and beat the utilities at their own game of providing energy at no initial costs and over long periods. It provides the reader tools to apply and monetize the rebates, incentives, tax attributes and accounting options to achieve enormous energy savings and profits to those seeking to invest in renewable energy.

Public policy designers, tax engineering authorities, economic stimulus policy makers, funding sources, environmental and sustainability engineers, project sponsors and developers, tax equity investors, software designers and users of energy will all be educated on the complexities of properly structuring energy finance projects to meet their own goals and needs. A resource such as *Grid Parity* is beneficial to all of these reader groups. The market for renewable energy is vast and continues to grow at compounded annual growth rates never before seen. Globally, clean energy investments have increased 230 percent since just 2005. The readers of *Grid Parity* all want to cash in on this opportunity and this book will guide them through that process.

Gene Beck has over 35 years of commercial financing experience, energy management certification (CEM—Certified Energy Manager), and finance certification (CLP—Certified Lease Professional). He has a history of over 50 industry speaking engagements and has been a moderator on many industry conference panels. He has circulated articles in trade publications as well as published a monthly 20-page environmental newsletter. He has designed and instructed a university level program course at California State University Fullerton and been a guest lecturer in post graduate classes at the University of Southern California. He has been a private sector industry spokesman at government hearings and policy boards, the designer of governmental lending policy manuals, conference chair and co-convener of industry conferences, and many other achievements.

Chapter 1

Introduction to Renewable Energy Financing

"It's like my father once said. There are three reasons we can't do it: The first one is we don't have the money, and it doesn't make a difference about the other two."
T. Boone Pickens

EXECUTIVE SUMMARY

Grid Parity*: A metric regularly used in evaluating the financial viability of renewable energy projects, which have historically been considered as too expensive. Grid parity is the point at which generating electricity from alternative energy produces power is at a cost to the user that is equal to or less than the price of purchasing power from the grid. A wholesale shift in generation from fossil fuels to clean renewable energy will take place when clean renewable energy reaches grid parity.*

The purpose of this book is to provide all participants in a renewable energy project a detailed introduction on financing tools and structures including tax, accounting, legal, policy, regulatory, legislative and options for the acquisition of renewable energy systems in the U.S. The risks and benefits will be explored along with provided examples of different yield analysis methods and sample documents that will help the reader achieve a better understanding of the complexities involved in this sector of our economy. The cost-effective and creative financing of renewable energy projects will help the scaling up of renewable energy as part of a transition by the United States to a low-carbon, high-energy-efficiency economy. It is written not in a "philosophical" manner or as a "dissertation" that delves in to every possible tax, accounting or legislative detail. Rather, it is written for you, the reader who has an interest in the practical application of multiple aspects of financing renewable energy projects in the U.S.

To fully understand how financing of renewable energy projects functions, one must look at all the components of the endeavor much like an artist looks at components in their creation of artwork such as medium that will be used in the production of the art work, whether it will be done with oil or water colors, etc. To accomplish a full understanding of the components that make up a completed renewable energy project that will get financed in the market place, I have broken down the components, processes and policies into ten chapters with Chapter 7 dedicated to providing examples of how each of these ingredients are mixed and matched much like an artist would do to convey their thoughts and message to a viewer of the completed piece of artwork.

The innovative financial structures utilized in the commercial, industrial and governmental sectors of our economy today has been more revolutionary than evolutionary in nature. Many of the structures crossing over into all types of renewable energy had their originations in the wind industry. Federal tax benefits and multiple sources of revenue from rebates and incentives to help pay for the projects have dramatically transformed the market place. The installed costs of the various technologies have come down in some types of renewable energy but have remained level or actually increased in others. Some revenue sources continue to increase such as the solar renewable energy credits (SRECs) in New Jersey but continue to decline in value by program design in other states like they do under the California Solar Initiative (based on predetermined program levels that started several years ago). Yet in other states, including California, there is a great deal of talk and possible modification of incentive programs that were either cash based or performance based initiatives (PBI) to move to a feed-in tariff incentive that would completely change the economics of how a renewable energy project would be financed. Stay tuned—not a single individual component of the energy project analysis is fixed in stone. Everything from equipment costs to rebates, incentives, performance and production, tax benefits and accounting guidelines are in a state of flux and subject to change on a 30-day notice. And change they will. That is precisely why it is so important to understand both the internal and external components of renewable energy project finance structures. If one understands the components and the implications of their application in the project structure, then you can adjust as the market conditions change and the interaction of the various components play out in the financial analysis.

> *"Oil is much too important a commodity to be left in the hands of the Arabs."*
>
> Henry Kissinger,
> U.S. Secretary of State
> (attributed, Ca. 1974)

I start with an overview of the renewable energy industry sector in Chapter 1 and then a high level view of the three pillars driving renewable energy and common structures used to implement them with an in-depth discussion of the factors that contribute most to a successful project. At the end of the first chapter we will look at the general costs of all energy projects since they will need to be taken into consideration as the finance model is developed.

Chapter 2 will take an in-depth review of what the seven different renewable energy technologies (or hybrids of them) are most often used in an energy project. This chapter also will introduce the reader to basic risks inherent in the financing of each technology.

Chapter 3 introduces the historical legislative processes that have forged the industry including both federal and state law promulgations. Without the incentives produced from this process, the renewable energy sector would not exist or be able to compete with energy generated from fossil fuels. It starts with the energy policy act of 2005 (EPAct), followed by the Energy Improvement and Extension Act of 2008 (HR 1424) and ends with a detailed review of The American Recovery and Reinvestment Act of 2009 (ARRA). The reader will gain valuable insight into the principal drivers of renewable energy—tax credits and tax policy. Each of these three acts was a precursor to consecutively enacted federal laws that made every change more valuable for the sector than the previous act. A project developer, investor, lender or end user of the energy cannot possibly understand what drives renewable energy projects and the financing of those assets without a complete understanding of the legislative history providing the incentives. This chapter includes a complete review of the IRS 1603 grant program and its rules, regulations and guidance that has advanced the financial attractiveness of the industry beyond anyone's wildest dreams. Included is a detailed inspection of the section 1705 Loan Guaranty program started under ARRA. The next section of this chapter looks at how the states have complemented the federal government program with incentives and rules of their own. The end of the chapter is devoted to looking at the regulatory compliance framework that has become such a major driver of new energy projects and how the renewable energy sector plays such an important role for companies who have mandates to meet their climate emission reduction obligations.

In Chapter 4 we will review some of the external components that need to be addressed, quantified, monetized and documented when the financial transaction is developed. These components often become the greatest source for many of the creative revenue aspects of an artful financial solution to the proposed energy project. This includes rebates, incentives, energy savings, utility rate escalation assumptions, system degradation issues, O&M and other revenue and expense components. An in-depth presentation of the IRS Section 45 energy tax credits, Clean Renewable Energy Bonds, feed-in tariffs, net metering, renewable energy credits, renewable portfolio standards in various states, white tags, greenhouse gas emissions, sustainability, carbon management, state legislation, LEED green building designs, production tax credits (IRS section 48 energy tax credits), appraised value of completed renewable energy projects, property accessed financing, and commissioning—all can play an pivotal role in the creation of financing techniques on energy projects.

Chapter 5 examines in great detail the internal components of renewable energy project finance. These components focus on the accounting and tax issues that must be addressed in all finance structures. Without a complete understanding of these factors and the proper application of them when modeling a project, would make any attempt at financing fruitless. This is an area where there are many pitfalls for the unwary project developers, equity partners, customers and lenders. There are many rules and regulations—both on the accounting and the tax side—that set forth how projects can and cannot be structured. We look extensively at the AMT implications in renewable energy project finance and analyze the impact of both FASB and the IRS rules as they dictate the proper techniques. Of great importance is the clear understanding of the "safe harbor" aspects provided by the IRS and examples are provided for how this treatment can be achieved. The chapter also looks extensively at the soon to be implemented future of accounting standards and how those changes in the corporate world could dramatically change forever the way customers view the current methods of financing renewable energy projects. The chapter ends by looking at the historical big three risk considerations of investing money in project finance—credit, collateral and capacity.

In Chapter 6, I look at the "hidden jewel" of energy project finance—energy efficiency (EE). EE is defined and analyzed. I look at different EE projects that could be implemented to complement a renewable energy generation system, consider reasons why EE is not seriously looked at, provide details how EE can play such a significant role in public sector projects and how those projects can be financed. No EE project can be undertaken without the energy audit and understanding the components of that audit and the importance they play in getting a project approved by the customer, review the tax aspects in EE projects, review CHP applications in EE, and end with the "proof of success"—measurement and verification (including best practices).

Chapter 7 will take the reader through a comprehensive financial model analysis of applying all of the components of a renewable energy project discussed in Chapters 1 through 6 into sample energy projects. This will include using current software tools to model the projects. We will look at how financial structures could be modified to artfully meet the unique requirements of developers, investors, lenders and customers. The analysis will use multiple yields, assumptions, risks and databases to model that perfect project, get it built, funded, and serviced over the systems expected life. External, internal, legislative and policy components described in prior chapters will be utilized. LCOE, IRR, NPV, pre- and after-tax results, tables and graphs will all come together to provide to provide a variety of ultimate financial solutions to a project.

> *"Making money is art and working is art and good business is the best art of all."*
>
> Andy Warhol (1928 - 1987)

Chapter 8 takes the reader to the next logical step after the structuring has been completed, approved by all parties to the transaction, and now must be documented. Here again, there are many fissures that need to be bridged to meet the needs of all parties if the project is ready for construction, commissioning and final operations. Two important considerations addressed in this chapter are: (i) the at risk rules and (ii) the passive activity rules set by the IRS. New business structures known as "flip partnerships" are explored and business entity taxation is evaluated. Much of this chapter is devoted to actual project documentation—the written memorialization of what the parties have conceptually agreed too. (Appendix 1 will provide an exhaustive set of sample documents referred to in this chapter.) The chapter also includes a detailed analysis of environmental factors and environmental audits needed to complete the legal requirements of all energy projects along with documents needed to provide for the future sale of the renewable energy credits over the life of the agreement. Bankruptcy concerns are addressed, requirements for estimating fair market value of assets at contract termination, product liability issues are discussed, tax audits and options are examined, and requirements needed for the permitting and actual construction of the renewable energy project are reviewed.

Chapter 9, "Investing in Climate Change," explores the aspects of green-house gas emissions and the role of climate change in the financing of energy projects. Concepts of carbon capture and storage, cap-and-trade markets, state and regional regulatory schemes (AB32 in California and RGGI in the Northeast) and the incentives they provide for renewable energy projects are examined.

The future of renewable energy and the opportunities and caveats they present to energy project parties are discussed in Chapter 10. Both short-term and long-term implications are examined. Economic growth implications on energy, world energy demand and the government policies that will shape the future of renewable energy in America are documented.

Over 40 sample renewable energy project forms and legal documents are provided in Appendix 1 along with a detailed listing of 100 software programs available for analysis of energy projects for buildings is presented in Appendix 2.

RENEWABLE ENERGY OVERVIEW

Grid parity is perceived by many as the holy grail of the renewable energy industry in the United States. The U.S. Energy Information Administration (EIA) reported on June 30, 2011 that renewable energy has passed another milestone as domestic production from renewable resources is now significantly greater than that of nuclear power—passing nuclear by 17.91%. It is well known that the cost of generating 1 kilowatt-hour of clean energy is greater than that of generating the same kW of energy from natural gas or coal *if* tax incentives, rebates and other "stimulus" are not applied to a renewable energy project (assuming no associated costs for carbon pollution). This book will give you an in-depth overview of the components needed to "artfully" craft a financing mechanism to achieve the un-achievable—financing clean energy projects that can be less costly than that of fossil-fuel driven energy systems.

The International Energy Agency (IEA) states in its latest study "Deploying Renewables: Principles for Effective Policies" that nearly 50% of global electricity supplies must come from renewable energy sources in order to cut CO_2 emissions in half by 2050. As a result, PV and concentrating solar power (CSP) alone may fulfill as much as 25% of the world's electricity needs by that date (*see Appendix 4 for renewable energy resource maps in the U.S.*). An unprecedented political commitment, effective policy design and implementation, and tremendous amounts of capital will be needed to meet these very ambitious objectives. The IEA recognizes the scale of such an undertaking, stating that "this is a huge challenge and part of the entire energy revolution we need to achieve."

The established electricity infrastructure in the United States that was built in the 20th century continues to perform well but there is widespread concurrence that fundamentally it needs to change in order to meet the needs of the 21st century. The scale of the challenges to the energy sector is significant. As an example, electrical power in the United States is more than 99 percent reliable, but it still experiences power interruptions that cost homes and businesses $150 billion a year.[1] Global growth in energy consumption is expected to increase by more than 40 percent over the next 25 years.[2] These consumption rates will be driven by a shift to more sustainable technologies of distributed and renewable energy generation as a result of concerns about energy security, environmental sustainability and economic competitiveness. The next major shift will come in the use of *energy storage*—enabling the power to be available when it is needed, not just when it is produced. By integrating energy from renewable sources like solar and wind onto the grid, overall impact on the environment can be curtailed, and regions can be more self-sufficient in energy.

The transition from a fossil based energy sector to a renewable based energy sector will be as significant in history as was the industrial revolution or the computer revolution. And, in the world of global climate change, it is one of the best strategies we have. Renewable energy technologies are by their very nature, secure, affordable (with the proper financing structures), easily accessible, and clean. The ability to create large job growth at all levels of our economy and contributing greatly to our nation's economic growth are just additional value-added benefits. Few industries have the ability—or the opportunity—to meet and change the world energy production needs as do the cleantech renewable energy technologies. Clean technology includes recycling, renewable energy (wind power, solar power, biomass, hydropower, biofuels), information technology, green transportation, electric motors, green chemistry, lighting, and many appliances that are now more energy efficient. It is a means to create electricity and fuels, with a smaller environmental footprint and to minimize pollution. Environmental finance, as part of energy project financing, is a contributing component by which new clean technology projects that have proven they are "additional" or "beyond business as usual" can obtain financing through the generation of carbon credits.

> *"The 1,230 gigawatts (GW) of renewable power generating capacity in place at the end of 2009 (worldwide) now constitutes just over 25 percent of total generating capacity worldwide. This is over three times nuclear generating capacity and roughly 38 percent of the capacity of fossil fuel-burning power plants worldwide."*
>
> Christopher Flavin in REN21 (2010), Renewables 2010 Global Status Report

The renewable energy sector in the U.S. is growing at truly epic rates. That exponential growth is not limited to only specific states or regions. Let's look at some of the more significant facts[3]:

- Although renewable energy (excluding hydropower) is a relatively small portion of total energy supply in the United States, the installed renewable energy capacity in the United States more than *tripled* between 2000 and 2009.
- Including hydropower, renewable energy represented nearly 12% of total installed capacity and more than 10% of total generation in the United States in 2009. Installed renewable energy capacity (including hydropower) is more than 130 gigawatts (GW). Not including hydropower, 2009 renewable electricity installed capacity reached about 53 GW in the United States.
- In the United States, growth in sectors such as wind and solar photovoltaics (PV) signify an ongoing

shift in the composition of our electricity supply. In 2009, cumulative wind capacity increased by 39% and cumulative solar PV capacity grew nearly 52% from the previous year.

- The United States experienced dramatic growth in wind power, as installed wind energy capacity increased by a factor of 14 between 2000 and 2009.
- The U.S. solar energy industry installed a record 1,856 MW of PV capacity in 2011, more than doubling the previous annual record and represents a 109 percent growth rate in 2011.[4]
- In the United States, renewable energy has been capturing a growing percent of new capacity additions during the past few years. In 2009, renewable energy accounted for more than 55% of all new electrical capacity installations in the United States—a large contrast from 2004 when all renewable energy captured only 2% of new capacity additions.
- Since 2006, the United States has been the world's leading ethanol producer. Between 2000 and 2009, production of corn ethanol increased by a factor of 6, and biodiesel production increased by a factor of more than 100. Use of ethanol in the United States has also grown substantially, and it accounts for 7.8% of the total U.S. gasoline pool, up from 1% in 2000.
- In 2009, Maine had the largest percentage of non-hydro renewable generation of any state, producing 23% of the state's total generation using non-hydro renewable energy technologies, mostly from bioenergy. The state aims to reach 40% by 2017.
- Iowa produces 14.5% of its state energy generation from renewables. The state implemented the nation's first renewable portfolio standard (RPS) target in 1983 (105 MW of renewable generation), which has long-since been reached. With low population and electricity demand, policymakers in Iowa now focus on implementing policies that develop renewable resources for export. Iowa ranks second only to Texas in wind capacity.
- Texas leads the country in total (non-hydro) installed renewable energy capacity, almost all of which comes from the state's 9,410 MW of wind capacity. This is three times more than Iowa (3,670 MW). Despite a slower start, Indiana has increased installed wind capacity significantly in recent years, jumping from zero to 1,036 MW in two years, with most of this capacity added in 2009.
- California is the leader in solar energy installed capacity, both for photovoltaic technology (738 MW) and concentrating solar power (364 MW). New Jersey installed 57 MW in 2009 to bring its cumulative capacity to 128 MW.
- Geothermal capacity is concentrated in the West, mostly in California (2,566 MW cumulative) and Nevada (426 MW cumulative), as a result of resource availability.
- Bioenergy capacity is spread across the nation—leading states include California (1,271 MW cumulative), Louisiana (768 MW cumulative), Vermont (759 MW cumulative) and Florida (711 MW cumulative).
- Although installed hydropower capacity within the states has remained relatively unchanged during the past decade, actual generation from this resource has fluctuated greatly, both across the country and over time. Some increase in future hydroelectric capacity could be achieved from the addition or upgrade of turbines at existing facilities; however, increasing competition for water resources across the United States could lead to reduced hydropower generation in coming years.
- The most common state-level energy efficiency policies are rebates, loans, and grants. Most states also have some degree of efficiency standard for public buildings. Vermont, Oregon, New York, and New Jersey have the most energy efficiency policies. Oregon, California, Illinois, Iowa, Maine, Montana, New Hampshire, and Pennsylvania have the strictest building codes, which require high efficiency in commercial and residential construction.

Meeting the energy needs of the world and here in the United States and reducing the greenhouse gas emissions to meet the global climate change challenges will likely require over $22 *trillion* in capital asset investments according to Barry Worthington, Executive Director of the U.S. Energy Association and predictions by the IEA. He further states that "never before, on a global basis, has the energy industry been expected to site, finance and manage the construction of infrastructure on this scale."

Renewable energy generation and energy efficiency have never in our own country's history played a more vital role than it does today. Now that renewable energy has become a national priority, industry and leaders from government acknowledge that we must wean ourselves from an oil addiction that threatens not only our national security but also our environment and our economy. Although there is no single solution to this pressing issue, the production of energy—both electrical

> *"A billion here, a billion there,*
> *pretty soon it adds up to real money."*
> Senator Everett Dirksen (1896-1969)

and thermal—and the reduction in demand through energy conservation and efficiency measures will provide a significant solution that will benefit all of America in many ways. The ultimate challenge is the financing of the capital expenditures needed to meet our goals, both in the private sector and in government.

In 2007, the investments in renewable energy worldwide reached $71 billion. Installations of grid-connected photovoltaic (PV) systems in the United States alone have increased dramatically in recent years—growing from less than 20 MW in 2000 to nearly 500 MW at the end of 2007—a compound average growth rate of 59%! A variety of financial structures has made this growth driven by federal tax credits and other stimuli from state and local government (including utilities) in the form of significant and creative financial incentives and rebates. This unprecedented growth in renewable energy projects has occurred despite the fact the capital costs of the underlying technologies has not been appreciably reduced. Because of the financial innovations in renewable energy projects, users no longer face prohibitively high acquisition costs; are not prevented from proceeding with a quality project simply because they are not in a position to utilize the tax attributes derived from the project; no longer need to provide maintenance, insurance or other "ownership" obligations; and don't even have to accept the risk that the system won't produce the energy expected.

The ability to finance a project is the litmus test for any new renewable energy project transaction. If it is financeable, the project developer, investor or creditor will be able to build and operate the project with sufficient revenue sources to repay its capital investment and obtain an adequate return on that capital over a reasonable period of time. If *any* of the key components (described in later chapters) of an energy project is missing, the project will not get financed. There are many components that have interrelationships, and the ability of a project developer to put all the pieces of the project together is paramount. The components are all subject to change at any time as a project is structured, built and commissioned. This can create challenges, opportunities and disappointment. Fortunately, because there are so many components to a successful energy project finance, there can be many alternative ways to solve a problem project component using one or more of the remaining project components. Alternatively, if some components are uncertain, it may translate into risk premiums that could increase the cost of the finance or cause the financing to fail entirely.

> *"Energy? It's quite simple—it's the utilities' money.*
> *Use renewable resources and the energy*
> *(and hence the money) is yours."*
> Gene Beck, Author

Securing a viable finance structure is the critical path to the realization of nearly all renewable energy projects. Project finance will always succeed best when cleantech investors, developers and creditors can find quality credits who desire to enter into long-term finance structures utilizing the key concepts, components and requirements described in this book—including tax incentives and monetization strategies.

The ability of creditors and project developers to extract the most value from a complicated patchwork of federal and state policies combined with multiple external revenue sources is what has made renewable energy, energy efficiency, cleantech and greentech projects become the success seen today. The synchronization of these internal and external components of an energy project from multiple sources and mechanisms drives the value proposition in each and every renewable energy project.

Although many different finance structures can, and are utilized when funding a project, there are two structures that have come to dominate the renewable energy sector—operating leases and energy purchase agreements. Both of these finance structures are able to maximize the utilization of the many components found in all renewable energy financing structures. The two common elements in all projects are tax attributes (in their many incarnations) and multiple revenue sources that are instrumentally in the final repayment of the investment of the energy project. In each case, the final finance structure will attempt to maximize incentives and at the same time reduce risk, thus achieving the most economically viable project for all participants.

Traditionally, energy projects were financed by leveraging the balance sheet of the site host (energy user) by borrowing money and pledging the credit (and in most cases, some type of assets) of the company. Corporate hurdles to utilizing this type of finance has increased over the years for many reasons including:

- High up-front costs that includes design and engineering, construction and financial requirements by lenders in the form of compensating balances, collateral hypothecation, down-payments, etc.

- Short-term financing (usually seven years or less) by traditional funding sources on assets that needed 10- to 25-year terms or longer to make cash flow sense—basically having terms that produced large amounts of negative cash flow (compared to current energy costs provided by the utilities) and having to finance long-term "infrastructure" type capital assets with a useful life of 25 years or more with available finance terms that were much shorter and designed mostly for income-producing assets (printing presses, construction machinery, machine tools, computers, etc.).
- A steep learning curve for a non-core business function
- Technology and performance risk
- Potential inability to make efficient use of the project's tax benefits

> *"Renewable energy is proven technology, the price is dropping, the rest of the world is going that way, that's where our investment should be going as well."*
>
> Bob Brown, Australian Senator

The operating lease finance structure addresses the up-front costs and efficient use of tax benefits but does not provide for the operating and maintenance costs, insurance obligations, future property tax obligations on the asset, and other similar ownership obligations unless a separate agreement to cover these elements is provided by the lessor. The energy purchase agreement will provide these components in the finance structure but obligates the customer for a longer period than the operating lease structure. However, the energy purchase agreement eliminates performance risk associated with the technology, design and installation of the energy system by charging the site host only for the energy produced—no energy, no charges. Thus, the performance burden has been shifted to the energy provider. In most cases, the operating lease will have a fixed type payment schedule for the term of the contract (although it may vary if it is structured to match revenue sources and/or based on an indexed variable rate such as LIBOR). In fact, the percentage of commercial solar transactions completed in California in 2008 utilizing energy purchase agreement structures was over 80%. Additionally, based on reports by the California Public Utilities Commission, commercial solar PV installations represented only 4% of the total number of installations, but 44% of the total PV watts (2008). A "one-size-fits-all" approach doesn't work for most renewable energy projects and therefore to fully understanding the best structure requires a thorough understanding of all of the elements.

Invariably, what drives every renewable energy project success is if the energy costs by a user (site host) will be less than the avoided cost from the utility now providing the energy. If, at inception or soon thereafter and on a permanent basis, the annualized cost of the new systems versus the current energy costs is not less than what is being paid now, the project will most often not move forward. There are some exemptions. There are some projects that will move forward even if they do not have positive cash flow simply because there are alternative reasons that outweigh (to some limited extent) the negative cash flow:

- The user has a "green" or environmental statement reason for doing so
- The user wants the project to meet LEED standards and be a "sustainable" project
- The user needs the emission reductions achieved by the installation of the new energy system to offset emissions from other sources within the facility and thereby meet economic or regulatory mandates imposed on the facility
- The user has stockholder issues that are forcing the company to be a good corporate citizen that is contributing to a higher environmental goal such as global climate change
- The user needs or desires to obtain a public relations bragging point for the company public image—referred to as "green branding"

The general approach to analyze the economic value of a renewable energy project starts with a series of user-defined assumptions about the project, the financial constraints imposed by the various investors and creditors (target hurdle rates, credit and financial risk, term of investment, etc.), regulatory rules (including tax, accounting and legal) and the multiple revenue sources that will be contributing to the cash flow needs imposed by the financing agreement structure being proposed. If the energy bill savings plus any other revenue sources are higher than the debt schedule of the project, the project would be economical and be built. The financial analysis that determines the debt structure must consider all the components of the project, both internal and external and that process requires both an in-depth knowledge of the i) the technology, ii) tax, legal and accounting rules, and iii) knowledge of all the available revenue sources that will help meet the cash flow needs of the project. In most cases, this also requires sophisticated financial modeling techniques that can encompass all these variables that in the end will meet the original goal of the parties—a permanent reduction in the user's energy bill utilizing renewable technology that has an life expectancy of twenty or more years.

This book will define the components, evaluate the options, and present case examples of how project difficulties could be overcome with creative finance structuring by the project developer. We will explore these components as they are independently broken out in their respective categories that are defined as:

- Internal components
- External components
- Legal components
- Market components
- Technology components

The IEA defines renewable energy as energy that is derived from natural processes that are replenished constantly. It its various forms, it derives directly or indirectly from the sun or from heat generated deep within the earth. Included in the definition is energy generated from solar, wind, biomass, geothermal, hydropower and ocean resources. Also included are bio-fuels, energy from waste sources and hydrogen derived from renewable resources.

In the real world, energy efficiency measures are often included in the financial analysis and structuring of most cleantech and renewable energy projects. Chapter 6 will describe typical energy efficiency measures, how they are incorporated into the energy project, and the implications they have on the cash flows in the project. When actual case studies are presented, those measures will be explored and evaluated as part of the energy finance analysis.

Key points to remember as the financing structures are evaluated include:

- Project finance has come to be the leading method of financing large renewable energy infrastructure projects that might not otherwise be done because they are too capital intensive or speculative because of the longer payback periods associated with infrastructure projects in general.
- Using project finance methods described herein will allow the project's risks and future cash flows pay for the large capital costs and give attractive investment returns to the developers and credit extending entities that understand the risks and can adequately evaluate the cash flow opportunities that abound in renewable energy projects.
- Tight credit markets that have developed in recent years create a great deal of competition for long-term financing and hence, even small differences in transactions can impact the availability of financing. For most equity investors—both private sector and institutional—the appeal of properly structured financed projects can maximize equity returns, move significant liabilities off balance sheet (for the debtor), protect key assets and monetize the tax aspects inherent in all cleantech renewable energy projects.

FINANCING STRUCTURES

Cleantech renewable energy is built on three pillars—technology, policy and capital. The growth of all three pillars are essential for the industry to thrive and grow. Never before in the history of industrial finance in America has there been such a perfect alignment of the pillars of growth for an industry. Technology that provides extremely long life expectancy combined with 20+ years of performance warranties by major manufacturers, cash rebates by states that can cover up to 45% or more of the system cost, tax credits or equivalent cash grants from the federal government of up to 30% of the asset costs, and local, state and federal renewable portfolio standards and green-house gas emission regulations, all converge to push the renewable energy industry in America like no other industry has ever experienced before. Government actions on multiple levels have taken center stage and are driving the thriving renewable energy industry to new levels each year—even in the recent challenging economic downturn. The most recent example is the $787 billion American Recovery & Reinvestment Act of 2009 (ARRA). A massive $100 billion of the plan was earmarked for clean technology including renewable energy.

The structures used to finance renewable energy project have far outpaced other types of financing traditionally used. The amount of creativity, terms, repayment resources, monetization of tax credits, variety of lenders and investors, type of incentives and rebates, and shear variety of parties who play a role in the finance process of renewable is remarkable. The motivations and drivers for the participants transcend the traditional reasons which have been focused almost exclusively on yields, current energy costs from utilities and fuel providers, and tax benefits. Although these are principal components, often the parties will elect to proceed with a project solely for other reasons such as green branding, sustainability, environmental mandates, court mandates and settlements that force a party to directly install renewable energy systems or even pay for others to do so, and legislative requirements that provide severe penalties for entities not reducing their carbon footprints.

> *"The U.S. government knows that conventional oil is running out fast. According to a report on oil shales and unconventional oil supplies prepared by the U.S. office of petroleum reserves last year, "world oil reserves are being depleted three times as fast as they are being discovered." Oil is being produced from past discoveries, but the reserves are not being fully replaced. Remaining oil reserves of individual oil companies must continue to shrink. The disparity between increasing production and declining discoveries can only have one outcome: a practical supply limit will be reached and future supply to meet conventional oil demand will not be available."*
>
> John Vidal, environmental editor, *The Guardian*

The final outcome of the reasons to acquire renewable energy systems and maximizing energy efficiency is what can often lead to the finance structures seen today. Although this book focuses on the commercial aspects of renewable energy projects, there are often creative financing programs designed exclusively for residential applications. A good example is the financing of residential solar PV projects now becoming available in progressive thinking cities in California through a concept called "PACE"—Property Assessed Clean Energy. The concept is also known under other acronyms such as Energy Financing Districts, Sustainable Energy Financing, Clean Energy Assessment Districts, Contractual Assessments, or Special Tax Districts.

The municipality borrows funds through a bond offering and then makes those bond proceeds available to residences of the city to install solar PV systems on their homes with no up-front costs. The city pays the solar system provider directly and gets repaid by the homeowner by a new assessment on their property tax bill that fully pays the system cost back over an extended period of time (usually 20 years). If the homeowner moves, the system stays with the home and the new owner gets use of the renewable energy system and continues to pay for its use through the property tax assessment until the system is completely repaid.

The financing is secured with a "tax" lien on the real property, and, like other taxes, is paid before other claims against the property in the case of foreclosure. It is precisely this aspect of the PACE programs that have created a general temporary halt to the programs as described below (see PACE section on page 104).

The City of Berkeley in Northern California was the first city to implement such an innovative financing instrument and call their program "Berkeley FIRST" (they produced a guide on how to institute property tax based financing districts that can be downloaded at: *http://www.ci.berkeley.ca*). Now many other cities in California are implementing their own financing programs using the same procedure including Palm Desert, Solana Beach and also other states such as Boulder, Colorado, where the city has implemented their own "municipal tax assessment financing" scheme to accomplish similar goals. In each of these programs, the city changes a rate of around 25 basis points over the cost of the bonds to the homeowner which pays for the administrative costs of the program. The end result is that the borrower is able to obtain very favorable financing terms—in both rate and term—by leveraging the city's debt ratings for their own account. Obviously, the total payments will eventually exceed the overall cost of the installation, but those payments will be largely offset by savings the owner enjoys in his low electricity bills on a permanent basis. The amount paid for electricity coming from their own solar PV installation is now "fixed" and never again will there be an electric "rate increase" on that portion of their electric bill. The benefit continues to get better and better as time progresses and at the end of the 20-year increased tax assessment, the system has no cost and the increased electric savings can now go entirely into the homeowner's pocket.

The goal for the city was to help meet their stated climate change and sustainability goals. In the end, both the homeowner and the city benefits along with society at large—the public "progressive" goal of the city. The program is a success largely due to the fact that some states (as in California), law allows for special tax fi-

> *"Even though I love solar and love wind, like most people do, I like the renewable sources, they alone are not going to get America energy independent."*
>
> Mitt Romney, American businessman and politician

nancing districts to be created that can fund projects designed to enhance the public good and general welfare of the community. California assembly bill 811 that was passed in July 2008 allowed for the creation of these special tax districts to create long-term payment plans for solar installations. Although the first applications of the bill use was for solar PV projects, it also provides for energy efficiency projects and does not distinguish between residential or commercial property owners. Berkeley and other cities in California are now setting these special financing districts up to accomplish those goals in record numbers. Although not currently available for non-residential applications, it is sure to be expanded in the near future. Berkeley has called their district the "Sustainable Energy Financing District." Doing so allowed the city to put the bond financing in place. The initial $1.5 million, 40 home pilot projects were completely subscribed within nine minutes of becoming available. Based on that success, the city now plans to immediately start much larger bond financing rounds to accommodate the huge demand by homeowners. The benefits of the program that will finance the renewable energy projects are obvious and include:

- Making solar PV projects "affordable" to the resident
- Providing for no up-front cost to the resident
- Guaranteeing full payment to the supplier when the project is complete
- Immediate cash flow savings to the resident
- No impact on the homeowner's credit worthiness
- Little or no budget impact for the city to implement the program

Although California cities have been the first to implement such a municipal financing mechanism, it probably won't be long before the federal government looks at the success stories by the original pioneering municipalities and set up federal guidelines for other states to use.

The remainder of the book will be looking at commercial renewable energy transactions and examining their many components and combinations of them that create the innovative financial structures being employed an America today. That examination however, must be reviewed by remembering the heavy influence that tax rules, regulations and policy have—and will play—in the future of the renewable energy industry. A historical perspective will be examined in detail throughout all the chapters. But it must always be recognized that whatever exists today, particularly in tax laws, will undoubtedly change in the future on short notice and with major implications for the renewable energy financing business. For example, at the time that this book was written, The American Recovery and Reinvestment Act of 2009 (the Bill) was enacted that will again modify many of the assumptions—and therefore the financial analysis—used in structuring the financing of any energy project in the United States (see Chapter three for a more detailed discussion of the Act). Those changes included:

- Permitted Master Limited Partnerships to utilize the ITC for the first time, opening additional financing opportunities to the industry.
- Extended the placed-in-service sunset for wind projects from January 1, 2010 to January 1, 2013, a three-year extension. The Bill also extended the placed-in-service dates for closed-loop biomass, open-loop biomass, trash, geothermal, qualified hydropower, landfill gas and marine hydrokinetic renewable energy facilities from January 1, 2011 to January 1, 2014.
- The Bill permits taxpayers to elect to claim the ITC (Investment Tax Credit) in lieu of the longer earnings period of the PTC (Production Tax Credit) for wind, closed-loop biomass, open-loop biomass, geothermal land fill gas, trash, qualified hydropower, and marine and hydrokinetic renewable energy facilities placed in service in 2009 and 2010. The taxpayer cannot claim both the ITC and PTC however. Historically, those projects could only claim the PTC based on annual energy production output.
- The Bill permits taxpayers to receive grants from the Treasury Department in lieu of claiming the ITC and the PTC (Section 1603 payment) with respect to certain projects placed in service in 2009 and 2010 (and further extended to 2011) that otherwise would qualify for the ITC. Owners of projects for which an election would be allowed to claim the ITC in lieu of the PTC would be eligible for the grants. Federal, state and local governments and tax-exempt entities would not be eligible for the grants.

  The grants function similarly to a refundable tax credit. The amount of the grant is equal to the amount of the ITC for which the owner of the project otherwise would have been eligible (i.e., generally 30% of the qualified cost of the project). Receipt of the grant is not includable in the gross income of the taxpayer. The tax basis of the property for depreciation purposes includes the amount of the grant but is reduced by one-half of the amount of the ITC that would otherwise have been allowable (i.e., the tax basis for depreciation generally would equal 85% of the qualifying costs of the property).

The Bill contained a very important item—the appropriation to ensure that funds would be available to the Treasury Department to pay the grants to the taxpayer. Treasury will be required to pay the grant to a project owner within 60 days of the submission of an application. See page 40 for more details.

- In 2008 bonus depreciation was allowed on all renewable energy projects. Bonus depreciation is allowed on all tangible personal property with a MACRS recovery period of 20 years or less. The bill extends that bonus depreciation to all property placed in service in 2009 and subsequent years. The asset owner will qualify for and be entitled to deduct 50 percent of the adjusted basis of the property as was done in 2008. The bonus depreciation is in addition to the standard 5-year MACRS depreciation allowed in the first year the asset(s) is owned. The remaining 50 percent of the adjusted basis of the property will be depreciated over the ordinary tax depreciation schedule using the standard accelerated MACRS rules. Then, in 2010, congress passed further legislation that allowed 100% bonus depreciation. That bonus ended in 2011 and has now reverted back to the 50% bonus depreciation on qualified property. The taxpayer must purchase or take complete ownership of the property or to enter into a written binding contract to do so in order to receive the bonus. The IRS definition of a "written binding contract" is one that exists only if it is enforceable under State law against the taxpayer and does not limit damages to a specified amount (e.g., by use of a liquidated damages provision).
- The Bill included a provision that would temporarily extend the net operating loss carry back period from two to five years for businesses that have less than $15 million in revenue. However, the bill provided a penalty of the carry back in that if an election is made to increase the period beyond two years, the applicable NOL is permanently reduced by 10 percent. But be careful—the changes to the NOL and section 382 provisions in ARRA may raise issues with provisions that historically have been treated in an inconsistent manner by states whose carryback and carry forward rules differ from the federal rules. In general, most states do not allow NOL carrybacks and many states provide for shorter carry forwards. Also, some states will not conform to the ARRA deferral of income provision in section 108(i), again hampering taxpayers that are being incentivized to complete these transactions from a federal perspective.
- The alternative minimum tax rules provide that a taxpayer's NOL deduction cannot reduce the taxpayer's alternative minimum taxable income by more than 90 percent of the alternative minimum taxable income. Under the Bill, this 90 percent limitation is suspended for carrybacks of a 2008 or 2009 NOL and carryovers of losses to those taxable years.
- The Bill provides a new 20 percent credit for qualified energy research expenses paid or incurred in the 2009 and 2010 tax years. Qualified energy research expenses are qualified research expenses related to fuel cells and battery technology, renewable energy, energy conservation technology, efficient transmission and distribution of electricity, and carbon capture and sequestration.
- The Bill lifts the $4,000 cap on the section 48 investment tax credit for qualified small wind property and repeals the special basis reduction rule that limits the credit amount allowed for property financed by subsidized energy financing or with proceeds from industrial development bonds.
- The Bill authorizes an additional $1.6 billion of new CREBs to finance facilities that generate electricity from wind, closed-loop biomass, open-loop biomass, geothermal, small irrigation, hydropower, landfill gas, marine renewable and trash combustion facilities.
- The Bill also authorizes an additional $2.4 billion of qualified energy conservation bonds to finance state, municipal, and tribal government programs as an initiative designed to reduce greenhouse gas emissions.
- The Bill extends and modifies the tax credits for qualified energy-efficiency improvements to ex-

> *"Rely on renewable energy flows that are always there whether we use them or not, such as, sun, wind and vegetation: on energy income, not depletable energy capital."*
>
> Amory Lovins, American physicist

isting homes. For 2009 and 2010, the bill increases the amount of the tax credit to 30 percent for all qualified residential energy-efficiency property, replaces the existing property-by-property dollar caps on the tax credit with an aggregate $1,500 cap for all qualifying property, and repeals the present-law reduction in the credit for amounts financed through subsidized energy financing.

- For tax years beginning after December 31, 2008, the Bill removes the present-law cap on the credit for residential solar hot water, geothermal, and wind property under section 25D and repeal the present-law reduction in the credit for amounts financed through subsidized energy financing.
- For 2009 and 2010, the Bill increased the 30 percent alternative refueling property credit for businesses (capped at $30,000) to 50 percent (capped at $50,000). The credit for hydrogen refueling pumps would remain at 30 percent; however, the cap for hydrogen refueling pumps would be increased to $200,000. In addition, the bill increases the 30 percent alternative refueling property credit for individuals (currently capped at $1,000) to 50 percent (capped at $2,000).

> *"It's better to do nothing with your money than something you don't understand."*
>
> Suze Orman, *O Magazine*, February 2003

As can be seen from the above, all of the changes will again increase the complexity and the resulting financial analysis of any new proposed renewable energy project completed in 2009 and beyond. Just when the parties thought the negotiations have come to an acceptable end, changes in the federal tax laws can easily force the parties back to the table for modifications to the financing provisions they thought had been completed.

For the past four years, the renewable energy industry has enjoyed the benefits of the Treasury 1603 cash grant. This incentive alone has driven much of the sector's growth over the past decade. Later chapters will describe the particulars of the grant (including the forms to use in Appendix 1). And, although the grant expired at the end of 2011, it is highly likely that there will be an incarnation of the grant in some manner in subsequent years because of the large positive impact it has had on renewable energy projects in the U.S.

Such changes are both good and bad for the parties. Changes can make payments go up or down, residual assumptions to change, length of contract to change, timing of debt payment schedules to change, and in some cases even cause the cancellation of a project that was not yet started.

The remainder of this book will be focusing on the tax, legal and accounting rules and regulations as they exist today. But keep in mind, that any changes to the existing "rules of the road" could mean a renegotiation and re-structuring of the project to meet the new realities.

GENERAL PROJECT FACTORS

All renewable energy projects can be condensed into two primary phases. The first phase is putting all the work into bringing the project from simply a concept to a project that is ready to construct. The second phase is the construction, commissioning and realizing the revenue from the project over the term of the contract or the life of the system.

That renewable energy project requires a basic set of considerations and factors for the successful financing components. Much more detail is provided later in this book on specific key areas but no project can be considered for a financing structure without encompassing the factors shown in Table 1-1.

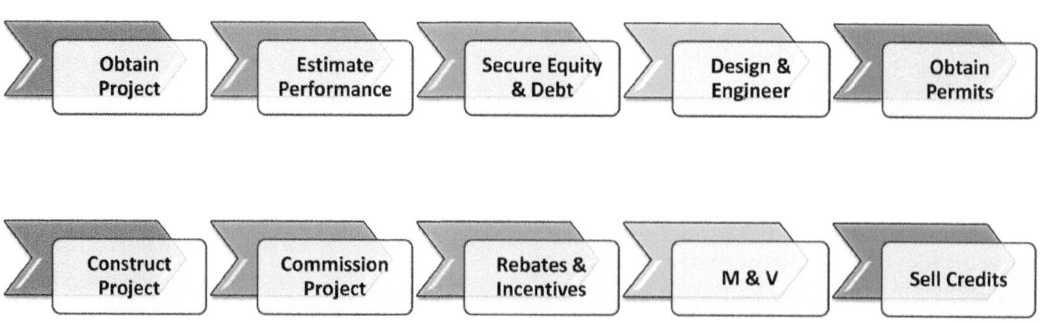

Figure 1-1: Energy Project Phases

RENEWABLE ENERGY PROJECT FINANCE

The basic premise of any project finance is that the entity investing in the project's assets will rely on the return of the investment based on the project's specific risks and future cash flows. Therefore, any project finance—including cleantech and greentech renewable energy technologies—will often employ a finance structure that has no recourse or only limited recourse to the parent company that develops or "sponsors" the project. This is true regardless of whether the investment is directly to the developer or to the end user either through the repayment of a fixed debt obligation or through the long-term commitment to purchase the energy production from the project's assets. Non-recourse means that the investor or lender has no access to the capital or assets of the Sponsor to repay the debt incurred by the entity that actually owns the project. Occasionally, some project financings are *limited* recourse as opposed to truly non-recourse and the Sponsor's capital may be at risk but only for specific purposes and in specific (limited) amounts according the project financing documentation.

Nearly all renewable energy project financings look only to the projected revenue stream the project generates for securing the repayment of the investment or loan. This includes both actual cash revenue sources as well as tax attributes inherent in each of the projects. As will be seen in the subsequent chapters, there are many diversified revenue sources. Not every project will be able to utilize all of them. The goal is to highlight many of the cash and tax revenue aspects (further described in later chapters as "external" and "internal" components of the project) that could be employed in evaluating an investment or extension of credit.

Five general types of financial contracts are employed in renewable energy project financing structures:

Table 1-1: Key Factors in Renewable Energy Projects

FACTOR	DESCRIPTION
Strong underlying credit	No project will succeed without having a principal debtor or host being credit worthy. This is positively rule #1. Don't even think about continuing to structure all the required subsequent steps if the project could in any way not be considered an acceptable credit risk from inception.
Strong EPC contract	High quality engineering, procurement and construction is of paramount importance. All renewable energy projects have assets that must function for a very long time. Since many of the projects will have the principal source of payment the sale of energy, quality design and installation is the only way a creditor or project developer will be able to assure themselves of the ultimate return on their investment plus a profit. The parties providing the EPC must be reliable and be able to be bonded for the full cost of the project. Nothing will kill a project quicker than an un-finished installation that must be completed by another party.
Construction budgets	Detailed budgets including estimated contingencies must accompany every project analysis. This would include suppliers (and alternates), subcontractors, project schedules and milestones, escrow and draw-down provisions, insurance, lien releases, and many other standard construction project standards necessary for a quality built project.
Resource identification and analysis	Detailed financial analysis showing all costs, sources of revenue, leverage positions, tax assumptions, accounting treatments, state and federal tax payments amounts and timing, all cash disbursements and timing, projected cash flows for the entire project term and contingency costs for insurance, asset replacements, O&M contracts, etc. Identify and quantify all components of the project that will be necessary for the project to become fully operational. This would include design, engineering, raw materials, utility interconnections, contract

(*Continued*)

Table 1-1: Key Factors in Renewable Energy Projects (*Continued*)

FACTOR	DESCRIPTION
	documentation (both for construction and the permanent finance structure), permitting, construction, fuel or other energy contracts, rebates and incentives, commissioning, insurance, legal recordings, O&M contracts, decommissioning (if required at termination of the project term), etc.
Permitting & environmental reviews	• Particularly important where the project is large or in an environmentally sensitive area—including local, state and federal compliance • Permitting for the construction • Public reviews of the project when needed and the resulting time to get agency approvals • Allow adequate time for these often time consuming factors
Intellectual property rights and real property negotiations	• Licensing and re-licensing (in case of finance contract default) for the technologies represented in the project • Real property rights of access and use including the public recording of the agreements reached
Energy audits and project performance expectations or contracts	Every energy project should have a full energy audit prior to deciding the scope of the project. It is very difficult to either justify the projected energy savings or energy production projection levels if an accurate measurement of the existing parameters are not carefully measured and verified prior to project implementation. A properly designed, built and operated project can then be measured and compared to projected values to determine the quality and expected performance. Final completed project expectations and disagreements are usually mitigated or eliminated entirely if these precautions are taken by the parties.
Performance contracts	For many renewable energy projects to succeed financially, they require certain performance warranties from manufacturers and installers for an extended length of time. Carefully crafted contracts that include the right of assignment are mandatory. Due diligence is also required on the parties who provide the performance guarantees to back those commitments for the entire time that they are offered. No assurances are worth the paper they are written on if the company is not strong enough financially to back the assurances or worse, are no longer in business should it be necessary to ask for the performance.
Technology assessments	Each project should fully document the technologies to be implemented. Advantages, performances, savings, operational costs, projected asset lives, and potential risk factors need to be identified and explained in detail. This is often critical to justifying financial residual value estimates or future fair market value assumptions in the financial analysis.
Commissioning	Most renewable energy projects will require a defined commissioning prior to final disbursement of proceeds to suppliers and construction companies. In most cases, the utilities or other rebate/incentive sources will also require detailed commissioning to make sure the system is performing according to the design specifications before they will sign off and accept the system.
Equity and/or financing	• Equity (whether tax or debt) sources must be sourced and

(*Continued*)

Table 1-1: Key Factors in Renewable Energy Projects (*Continued*)

FACTOR	DESCRIPTION
sources & commitments	confirmed prior to executing project documentation with a debtor or host • Escrow of funds with a licensed escrow entity is often a good way to be assured that the funds are available when required • Commitment letters and term sheets by lenders that will be contributory to the funding sources must be secured and contracted in writing • Timing of project completion is critical to most tax equity sources since tax benefits only exist when the project is complete—none are available during the construction phase of the project.
Facility and site factors	All factors regarding the integration of the project into a facility and specific site parameters must be accounted for and checked off before construction contracts are entered into. This includes site preparation, soil or water sampling, environmental assessments, hazardous waste stipulations, real property waivers, site lease and license agreements, etc.
Monitoring, reporting and measurement	Nearly all renewable energy projects will require a MM&R (monitoring, measuring and reporting) protocol to substantiate the assumptions made in the financial project structure. This would include support for environmental claims and attributes, energy conservation/reduction targets, and energy production and performance levels needed to realize adequate financial returns to the lender, project developer or investor.
Final documentation & future O&M	Specifications that outline the transfer of final "as built" engineering, design and construction prints, commissioning details and performance specifications, operating manuals, and long-term operating and procedure manuals (and contracts) are all part of a properly planned and built project.
Key staff or third party advisors & contractors	Principal staff needed for the successful completion of the project should be identified. Their background, experience and the role each will play in the project should be itemized and described. This must include professional advisors, suppliers and contractors. Identifying number of new jobs created and thereafter retained from the project is also required for many of the benefits that can be received from the government in the form of tax incentives, grants and loan guarantees to the project.

1. Energy purchase agreements (EPAs) and power purchase agreements (PPAs)—depending upon the type of energy produced by the assets of the project
2. Long-term operating agreement—typically used with energy efficiency rather than energy generation projects
3. Capacity purchase agreement—as found with electrical transmission lines
4. Production sharing agreement—often found where bio-fuels (such as ethanol or algae) are produced
5. Traditional debt obligations—term loans, chattel mortgages, capital leases, etc. used where the debtor wants tax ownership of the underlying project assets

A complete description of many of the possible financial structures that can be used is more fully described later.

A typical project finance structure for renewable energy projects is shown in the following diagram. Keep in mind that there are many different structures that are hybrids of the basic structure but most will have many of the components shown as a starting point before customization.

Figure 1-2: Typical Project Finance Structure

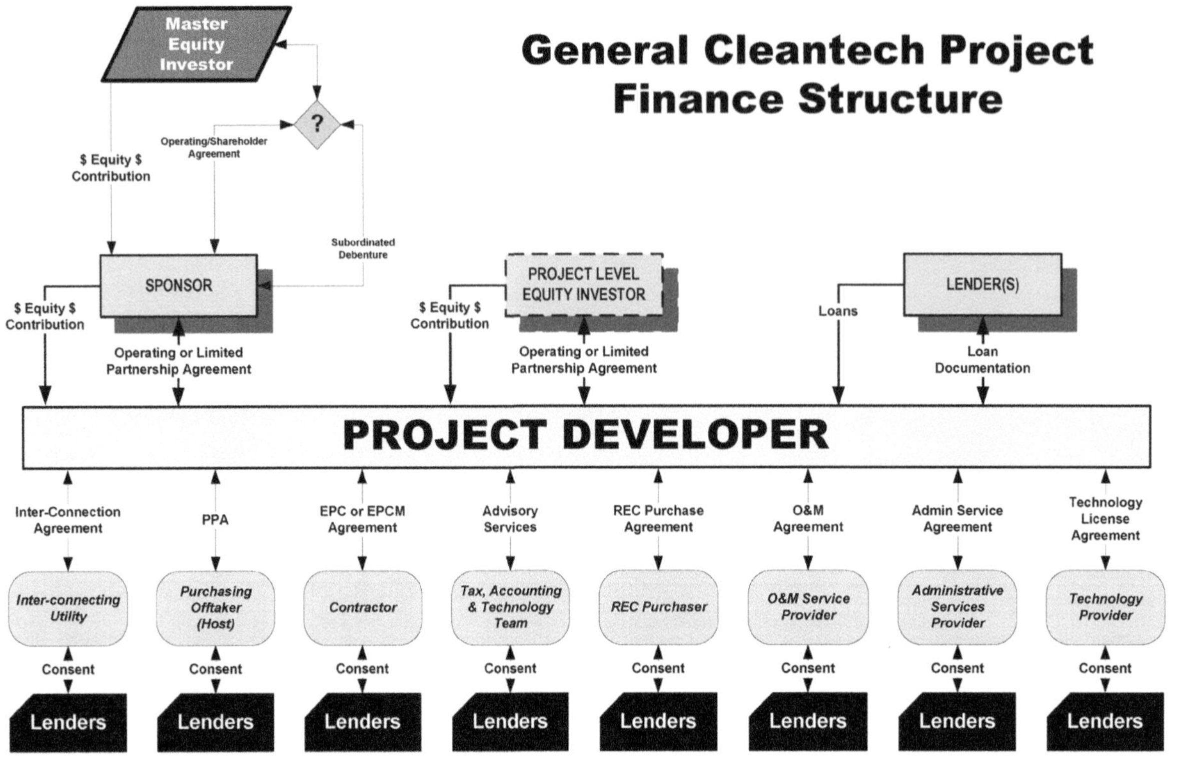

- EPC—Engineering, Procurement & Construction Agreement
- EPCM—Engineering, Procurement, Construction & Maintenance Agreement
- PPA—Power Purchase Agreement
- EPA—Energy Purchase Agreement
- REC—Renewable Energy Credit
- O&M—Operations & Maintenance

> *"We need American sources of resources, we need American energy, brought to you by American ingenuity and produced by American workers."*
>
> Sarah Palin, American politician, commentator and author

In most cleantech renewable energy projects, all of the debt for the project is at the Project Company level, and not the Sponsor level—regardless of whether the debt is recourse or nonrecourse (assuming the project was leveraged with a lender). Most projects do use leverage of some amount to increase the internal rate of return to the Sponsor. The Sponsor's other assets such as investments in other projects, intellectual property and other receivables from other clients are also protected from creditor claims using this model. Using this type of a model also protects the Sponsor from bankruptcy, debt default or foreclosure at the Project Company level. Another term frequently used in that context by some creditors is "bankruptcy remote."

This type of a structure allows for a wide variety of tax structuring opportunities (described more fully in later chapters). To achieve this level of structuring, however, requires a great deal of documentation at all levels of the basic structure shown. Although many companies and investors like a simpler structure to avoid the due diligence required with the resultant large amounts of documentation, it would leave a great deal of opportunities on the table not to do so. It is the complexity of the project that provides the greatest rewards for those willing to accept the challenge. This book will provide you with the core set of components and options to extract the maximum benefits from your investment options—whether as a developer, sponsor, investor, asset owner or lender.

PROJECT COSTS

To achieve the benefits inherent in cleantech projects requires heavy documentation, due diligence costs, tax opinions, administrative fees, project management (including construction and servicing over the term), attorney fees, engineering and design costs, and marketing expenditures that could (in many cases) equal 2-10% of the entire project cost. Many smaller projects cannot absorb these costs and therefore most cleantech renewable energy projects cannot be done cost-effectively for less than $1 million in size. Many of the large players in the market will not entertain a transaction less than $50 million in size.

Table 1-2 gives an example of costs in a project over the entire term of the project finance.

As can be seen, in total these costs can be quite high as a percentage of the asset costs in project finance. Many of them are front-end loaded while others are paid out annually for costs needed to manage the project over the term of the contract. Most projects that involve selling the energy produced such as PPAs in solar PV projects or EPAs in solar thermal projects must carefully structure these costs into the cash flows as a project matures. The good news is that most projects have the ability to carry these costs if the sale of the energy (and other external revenue sources are realized) is priced high enough and at the same time to be low enough to be below the offsetting grid costs from the utility—*Grid Parity*. The bad news is that some neophyte project developers don't take these direct costs into account when pricing the project to the host or borrower. Failure to do so could ultimately present a fatal flaw to the project.

There have been several attempts in recent years to take a portfolio approach to reduce the costs by spreading them over a larger number of transactions that are all identical in nature with varying degrees of success. Many times, the "portfolio promoters" fail to realize the cost of administrating such a large number of individual transactions over the long term. Those costs (see page 270 regarding asset and contract management requirements) will necessarily include that of billing, tax preparations, collections, remarketing and liquidations, and tax audits (from many different jurisdictions include sales, property and income—state and federal—tax regulators).

The Sponsor must also recognize that no cash flow will go up to their level until those levels of participants below them are satisfied. This includes the lender (if the project is leveraged), operating and maintenance of the asset over the term, replacement of components when they fail or start degrading (such as inverters in solar PPAs after ten or more years of a 20-year project contract), IT costs, billing and collections, accounting, tax preparation (both for income taxes and for annual property tax filings in every county and in every state that the underlying project assets are located), legal challenges (e.g., from the borrower/debtor and tax auditors when the principal obligor dies or has a business failure and the project's obligations to you are thrown into an estate or bankruptcy proceeding), change of landlords or mortgage holders on which the project assets are residing, property damage (as in fires, floods or earthquakes), etc. The list of servicing requirements can go on and on. And, since most project financing structures are for 10-20 years or more, the servicing obligations cannot be taken lightly and without a great deal of cash flow planning for the servicing events that could very well occur over the project life. All of these unknown costs will need to be met before any cash flow would flow up to the Sponsor and eventually to the equity participants in the Sponsor level. The following questions should be useful in determining if cleantech renewable energy project financing is right for you:

- Are you competent, or do you have competent advisors, who can properly evaluate the project opportunity?

Table 1-2: Typical Energy Project Costs to Project Developer

Description	% of Project Cost
Marketing costs to sales team and 3rd parties	3.0%
Lending Fees—arranging & structuring	1.0% to 4.0%
Lending Fees—syndication fee with participating lenders	1.0%
Lending Fees—annual administrative fee ($75-250,000 per yr)	2.0% to 10.0%
Lending Fees—annual collateral agency fee ($50,000 per yr)	0.5% to 3.0%
Lending Fees—to each participating lender (.5 to 1.5% each)	0.5% to 5.0%
Professional Fees—for lenders & investors due diligence	0.5% to 3.0%
Annual Insurance Costs (0.25% to 0.75% per year)	5.0% to 15.0%
Annual Servicing Costs (0.25% to 1.0% per year)	5.0% to 20.0%
Annual O&M Costs (0.25% to 1.0% per year)	5.0% to 20.0%
Equipment Replacement Costs (e.g. inverters in solar)	3.0% to 6.0%

- Do you have competent and adequate staff to service the investment over the entire length of the project term (including renewal terms or asset liquidation after the initial contract term has ended)?
- Can you properly document and adequately enforce the transaction?
- Is the project (or portfolio of projects) of sufficient size to warrant the time to be invested in the project and provide the return expected?
- Will the contracts (and hence the revenue stream) be enforceable and also be assured for the entire contract term?
- Would a change in tax, accounting or legislative rules and laws cause your investment to be non-economically rewarding?
- Is the technology and useful life of the underlying assets at least 50% greater than the initial term of the investment?
- Does the obligor under the contract have sufficient (i) cash flow and (ii) sufficient net worth to assure that there will not be a credit risk over at least the original project contract term?
- Are there alternative sources of repayment for the obligation should the primary source of repayment fail?
- Do the physical assets have sufficient liquidation value or, in the alternative, sufficient "in-place" value to assure an orderly liquidation in sufficient amounts to repay the principal investment and provide the projected return envisioned?
- Is there a technology risk in that there is a replacement for the technology that would make the value of the asset diminish so much that a obligor would risk walking away from their obligation at some point in their commitment?
- Is the maintenance factor to keep the assets in top condition affordable—both now and over the term of the contract?
- Is there an established and cohesive team as sponsor or as project developer that can solve any problems that might occur either during the construction of the project or during the repayment term of the project?

If these questions can be answered in the affirmative, then it is time to read on and explore the remaining chapters of this book to determine the best method for you to become an informed investor, project developer, sponsor, owner or lender in a cleantech renewable energy project.

References

1. U.S. Department of Energy, "The Smart Grid: An Introduction," Galvin Electricity Initiative
2. US Energy Information Administration (EIA), International Energy Outlook 2011
3. U.S. D=epartment of Energy, 2009 U.S. State Clean Energy Data Book, October 2010
4. SEIA (Solar Energy Industries Association) 2012 Annual Report, www.seia.org

Chapter 2

Renewable Technologies

Many renewable energy technologies—such as large-scale wind power, solar thermal water heating, and geothermal heat pumps—are already economically competitive with traditional sources of energy, such as fossil fuels. This includes energy efficiency systems.

We are in the midst of the sixth technological revolution since modern man became of age in the agricultural revolution.

		Year
1.	The Industrial Revolution	1771
2.	Age of Steam & Railways	1829
3.	Age of Steel & Electricity	1875
4.	Age of Oil and Automobile	1908
5.	Age of Information	1971
6.	Age of Cleantech & Renewables	Now!

Most of these benefits arise from their virtually inexhaustible nature. Solar and wind resources are replenished on a daily basis. Biomass can be grown through managed agricultural programs to provide continuous sources of fuel. Geothermal power is extracted from the virtually unlimited thermal energy in the earth's crust. Renewable energy resources are broadly available across the U.S. Certain regions, however, tend to have a more accessible resource of one type than another.

The benefits of renewable energy extend beyond abundance and diversity. As indigenous resources, they foster both local control and economic growth. An investment in renewable energy contributes to local economic security. In addition, the incorporation of renewables in a generation portfolio may reduce the risks associated with fluctuating fossil-fuel prices and supplies.

As renewable energy technologies become more cost-competitive, their true economic benefits are being realized. Since many renewable energy plants do not need to be built in large scale to achieve the lowest possible plant costs, they can be built in size increments proportionate to load growth patterns and local needs. This is often referred to as their modularity. Given their smaller size, they can also be located closer to the customer load, reducing infrastructure costs for transmission and distribution, and helping to guarantee local power reliability and quality. Such "distributed" applications appear to have a potentially high economic value beyond just the value of the electricity generated.

> *"We're finally going to get the bill for the Industrial Age. If the projections are right, it's gong to be a big one: the ecological collapse of the planet."*
>
> Jeremy Riftin, *World Press Review*, December 30, 1989

Several of the renewable energy technologies, namely photovoltaics, solar-thermal and wind—produce no emissions during power generation. Biomass plants, with a properly managed fuel cycle and modern emission controls, produce zero net carbon emissions and minimal amounts of other atmospheric effluents. The situation is much the same for geothermal plants. When these technologies displace fossil fuels, they avoid emissions that would otherwise be generated. With the growing concern about climate change and carbon emissions, renewable energy technologies can be significant contributors to global efforts to reduce greenhouse-gas emissions.

The value of renewable-generated electricity is determined in part by the time of day at which the electricity is delivered to the grid and also by the probability that it will be available when needed. For example, solar output tends to follow utility summer-peak loads in many locations. Because power delivered during peak periods is more valuable to the utility system, renewable energy technologies can provide high value electricity and can be significant contributors to a reliable power supply system at critical times in those regions. Biomass, geothermal and fossil-hybrid renewable systems are fully dispatchable and compete most closely with conventional fuel-based systems. In some cases, such as the solar-thermal power tower with hot salt storage, energy storage capability may be included economically. In these cases, the degree of dispatchability achieved depends on the amount of storage included. Intermittent systems, such as wind and solar without storage, will have value as determined primarily by the time of day and year at which electricity output is available.

> *"Evolution is a change from a less coherent form to a more coherent form, consequent on the dissipation of energy and the integration of matter."*
>
> Herbert Spencer,
> British philosopher and sociologist (1880)

The World Resources Institute published a great schematic of describing deployable on-site renewable energy projects[1] and effectively assessing the risks associated with that deployment. Figure 2-1.

In order to choose the best deployment and financing option, a company must define its objectives and understand risk trade-offs. Often, those objectives might include:[2]

- **Reducing Energy Costs**: Either reducing energy costs or creating a hedge against possible future price increases.
- **Improving Energy Reliability**: Although most renewable technologies cannot provide sole back-up power for mission critical needs, an on-side deployment can improve energy reliability if it includes energy storage (such as a battery or thermal storage).
- **Using Tax Appetite**: If a company has sufficient taxable income, it can benefit by taking advantage

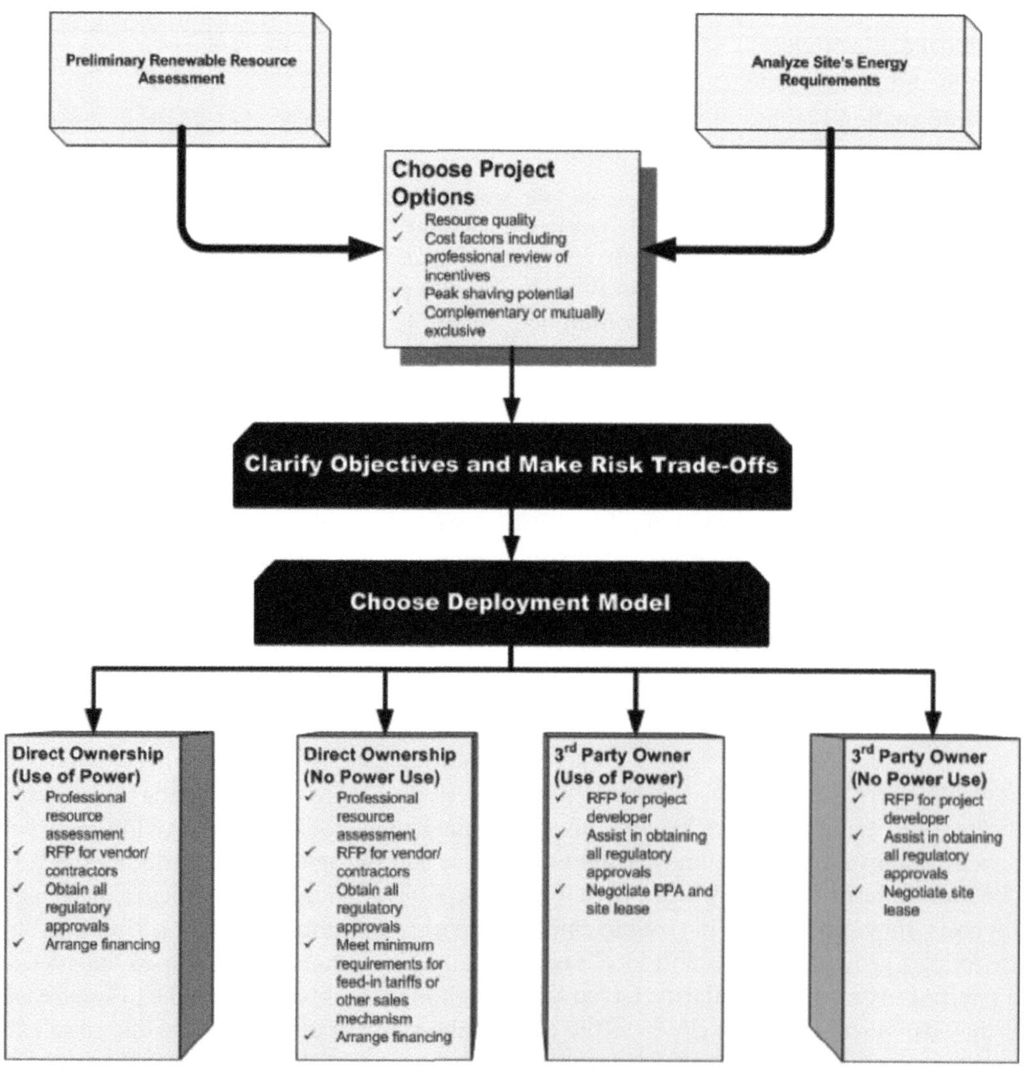

Figure 2-1: Deploying On-site Renewable Energy

of tax-based incentives for deploying renewable energy.

- **Obtaining Rebates, Grants and Other Incentives**: Rebates on many different governmental levels from federal to state and even local communities are often found in addition to rebates and other incentives from utilities.

Risks associated with deploying on-site renewable energy can include:

- **Dispatch Risk**: Power is not generated by an on-site deployment for any reason.
- **Operational Risk**: The system does not perform as anticipated. This risk is typically assumed by the entity responsible for operating and maintaining the system.
- **Technology Risk**: Technological improvement creates an opportunity cost for someone that has already invested in the older technology.
- **Transfer Risk**: Renewable energy assets may have to be redeployed when a company moves or changes business locations.
- **Credit Metrics**: A renewable energy investment may affect the financial ratios that analysts use to assess the credit worthiness of a company.
- **Fuel Risk**: Some technologies utilize renewable fuels that could be highly subject to supply-and-demand market fluctuations.

There are numerous categories and sub-categories of types of renewable energy systems and many of them include a "hybrid" of the renewable energy production technologies on the same project as are "energy efficiency" and "energy storage" components. The general categories include:[3]

- Solar Energy
- Wind Energy
- Geothermal Energy
- Bioenergy
- Hydropower
- Ocean Energy
- Hydrogen & Fuel Cells

Most include multiple sub-categories such as solar: solar PV, concentrating solar PV, flat plate solar thermal, evacuated tube solar thermal and concentrating solar thermal. Fossil fuels are *non-renewable*, that is, they draw on finite resources that will eventually dwindle, becoming too expensive or too environmentally damaging to retrieve. In contrast, the many types of renewable energy resources-such as wind and solar energy-are constantly replenished and will never run out. Renewable energy and energy efficiency technologies are critical to creating a clean energy future for not only the nation, but the world.

Each of the renewable energy technologies described below have positive and negative consequences from their deployment.[4] And, each of the technologies present unique financing structures and financial analysis methods that are subject to all of the details that are described throughout this book.

> *"Renewable energy is derived from natural processes that are replenished constantly. In its various forms, it derives directly from the sun, or from heat generated deep within the earth. Included in the definition is electricity and heat generated from solar, wind, ocean, hydropower, biomass, geothermal resources and biofuels and hydrogen derived from renewable resources."*
>
> Benjamin J. Sovacool, International Energy Agency, *Renewable energy...into the mainstream*

Biomass: The use of forestry and agricultural residues and wastes in direct-combustion systems for cogeneration of electricity and process heat has been a well-established practice in the forest-products industry for many years. Use of these feedstocks in utility electric power plants has also been demonstrated in several areas of the country with access to appropriate fuels, in general with acceptable technical performance and marginal economics. At present, biomass (any plant or animal matter that can be burned or processed to create energy) accounts for 50% of renewable energy used in the U.S. according to the Biomass Power Association (BPA).[5] Factors driving growth include state RPS programs, the availability of low-cost feedstocks

> *"By increasing the use of renewable fuels such as ethanol and bio-diesel, and providing the Department of Energy with a budget to create more energy efficiency options, agriculture can be the backbone of our energy supply as well."*
>
> John Salazar, former congressman from Colorado

and the federal renewable fuels standard, which results in significant biomass cogeneration at plants producing biofuels. This is particularly true in rural areas where feedstock is plentiful. Because biomass projects can use wood waste and other organic materials for fuel, they help prevent overloading of landfills.

Geothermal: Geothermal energy uses heat flowing from the earth's interior as a fuel source. Commercial electricity from geothermal steam reservoirs has been a reality for over 30 years in California and Italy. However, steam reservoirs are rare and have already been exploited, at least in the developed countries. Of greater potential in both developed and developing countries are geothermal-hot-water, or liquid-dominated hydrothermal, resources. A number of hydrothermal plants, perhaps 60 to 80, both developmental and commercial, have been built and are in operation. The U.S. has 3,102 MW of geothermal capacity in operation, more than any other nation, and is expected to be a primary source of industry growth over the next decade according to the Geothermal Energy Association (GEA).[6] California has the most geothermal energy deployed.

There are several different ways that companies use geothermal energy:

- Electricity Generation. Using geothermal heat reservoirs to generate electricity with steam turbines.
- Direct Geothermal Use. Using lower-temperature geothermal resources for district-level heating and in greenhouses or aquaculture. Low-temperature geothermal resources exist throughout the western U.S., and there is tremendous potential for new direct-use applications.
- Geothermal Heat Pumps. Using temperatures just some six feet below ground surface that remain relatively constant throughout the year to assist with heating in winter and cooling in summer.

Photovoltaics: Photovoltaic power systems convert sunlight directly into electricity through a solid-state-electronic process that involves no moving parts, no fluids, no noise and no emissions of any kind. These features are attractive from operating, maintenance and environmental standpoints, and have positioned photovoltaics to be the preferred power technology for many remote applications both in space and on the ground. Relative to conventional grid power, photovoltaic electricity has historically been some five-to-ten-times more expensive. This has changed dramatically over the past decade as 1) component prices have dropped dramatically, 2) utility rates have gone up faster than the historical averages, and 3) tax incentives, rebates, grants and other stimulus have provided cash flow to the transaction that in many parts of the country are now competing directly with the price of electricity from the utilities.

Many parts of the United States—especially in the Southwest—have abundant solar resources. As with wind projects, other issues to consider when planning a solar PV project include zoning and permitting requirements, environmental impacts, grid interconnection, net metering regulations, the ability of the surface to which the system will be attached to withstand the mechanical loads associated with the installation, and the existence of and eligibility criteria for any incentives.

Comparing U.S. potential for solar PV production vs. that which is potentially available in other countries where there have been large amounts of solar PV installed over the past decade can best be shown in the map below from NREL.

> *"The use of solar energy has not been opened up because the oil industry does not own the sun."*
>
> Ralph Nader, U.S. consulter advocate (1980)

Federal policies and incentives play an important role in the commercialization and adoption of solar technologies; they have enabled rapid expansion of solar markets in countries such as Germany, Spain, and Japan where feed-in tariffs have been highly successful in the adoption of both solar PV and concentrating solar PV. Legislation enacted in the United States in 2008 and early 2009 have provided unprecedented levels of federal support for U.S. renewable energy projects, including solar energy projects.

The Emergency Economic Stabilization Act of 2008 (EESA or "bailout bill") became law on October 3, 2008. It contains tax incentives designed to encourage individuals and businesses to invest in renewable energy, including 8-year extensions of the business and residential solar investment tax credits (ITCs). The American Recovery and Reinvestment Act (ARRA or "stimulus bill") was signed into law on February 17, 2009, with an estimated $787 billion overall in tax incentives and spending programs. Many ARRA provisions support solar energy.

Concentrating Solar: Concentrating solar describes two large-scale forms of generation: concentrat-

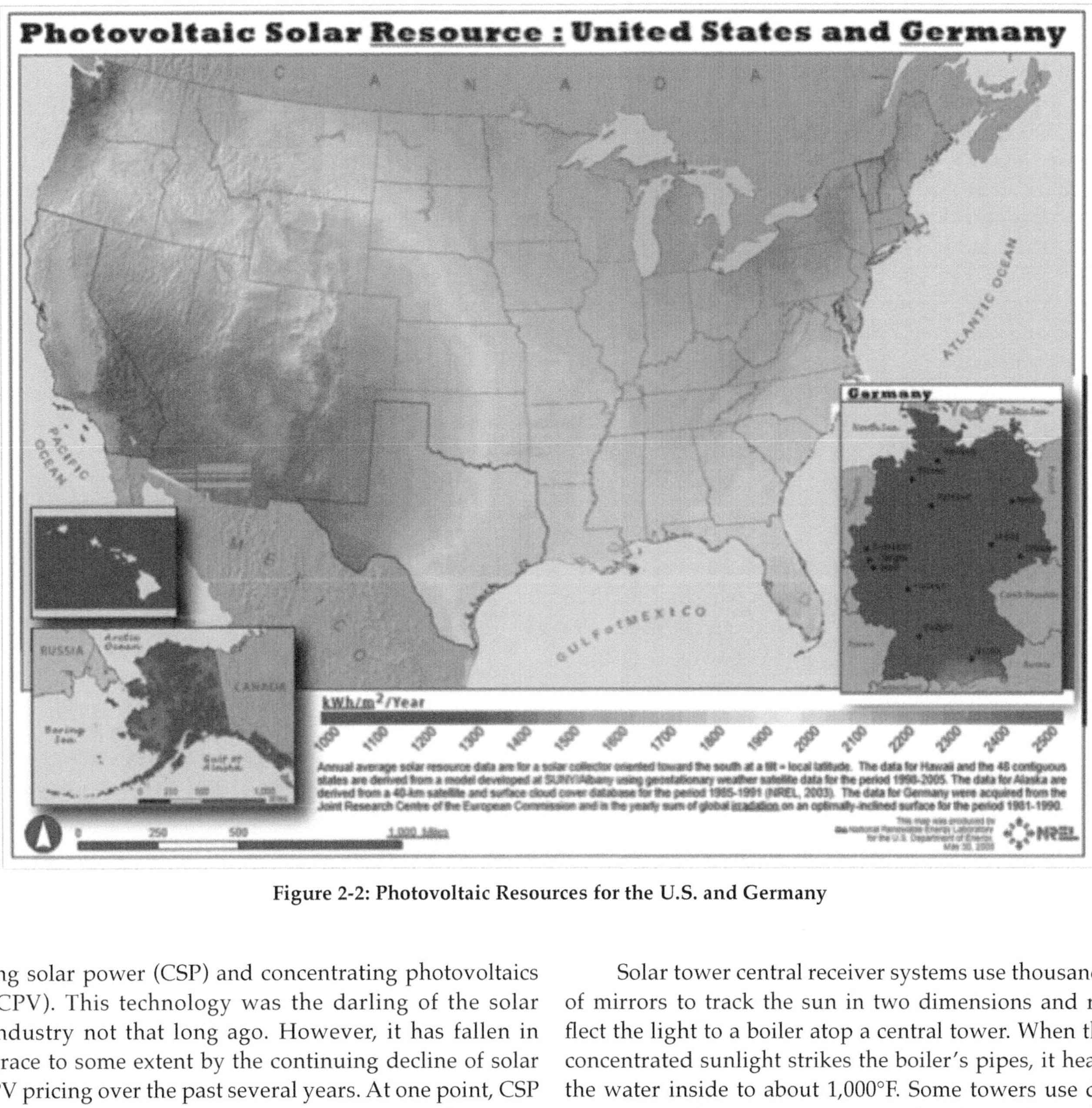

Figure 2-2: Photovoltaic Resources for the U.S. and Germany

ing solar power (CSP) and concentrating photovoltaics (CPV). This technology was the darling of the solar industry not that long ago. However, it has fallen in grace to some extent by the continuing decline of solar PV pricing over the past several years. At one point, CSP plants had a good price point compared to other types of utility-scale solar energy. Its continued growth will be a function of the availability of cost effective financing structures.

The most proven and commonly used CSP technology is the parabolic troughs. Rows of curved mirrors focus the sun's rays on stainless steel tubes that run the length of the trough. The tubes are coated to absorb solar radiation and act as heat collectors. They reach temperatures around 700°F. Water in the tubes is superheated to steam which runs a turbine to produce the electricity. Recently, the medium in the tubes has included molten salt that heats to an even higher temperature.

Solar tower central receiver systems use thousands of mirrors to track the sun in two dimensions and reflect the light to a boiler atop a central tower. When the concentrated sunlight strikes the boiler's pipes, it heats the water inside to about 1,000°F. Some towers use direct saturated steam generation and molten salts as the heat transfer and heat storage medium. After parabolic trough technology, solar towers represent the largest number of new CSP projects underway in the U.S.

Two other technologies are the dish/engine systems and Fresnel collectors. In dish systems, concave central receiver dishes reflect sunlight onto a focal point receiver, while also tracking the sun throughout the day. Most dishes have a small generator at the focal point. They do not require heat transfer fluid or cooling water, and boast the best solar-electric conversion rate amount CSP systems (reaching up to 1,200°F). They are relatively small in size, which means that many dishes must be combined for a large-scale energy production project. The Fresnel collector systems still represent a relatively small portion of the market and consist of long, parallel rows of flat mirrors that track sunlight throughout the day, and reflect to a central receiver in a fixed focal line above the mirrors. Fresnel collectors use water instead of oil or molten salts to transfer heat, so steam can be generated directly inside the receivers.

The final type of concentrating solar is the concentrating PV (CPV). The technology has been around since the 1970s. CPV performs best in high solar radiation areas and works by concentrating sunlight onto a relatively small solar cell. The magnification factor can reach up to several hundred times, allowing a relatively small PV cell to generate a lot of electricity. CPV is already becoming cost-competitive with PV. This is certain to become a leader in the concentrating solar arena of the future.

Solar Thermal: Solar thermal power systems use concentrated sunlight to heat a working fluid that generates electricity in a thermodynamic cycle. The temperatures are extremely high in these types of applications. In lower temperature applications, the technology is used for domestic hot water, industrial steam and HVAC central plant operations using hot and chilled water produced by absorption chillers. Thermal storage adds a great value-added component to solar thermal applications that can defer for days the use of the energy produced.

Solar thermal water heating is not restricted to warm, sunny climates. In fact solar water heating systems can be used effectively throughout the U.S. at any location that has an appropriate near-south facing roof or nearby unshaded grounds of installation of the collectors. In addition to having an appropriate installation surface, the most cost-effective sites for this technology typically have generally constant demand for hot water and relatively high energy prices.

Determining whether a solar water heating system can generate cost savings for a business requires assessing:

- Whether there is an appropriate physical installation site
- The pattern of hot water consumption
- The ability to store the thermal energy in tanks or vessels
- The current cost and type of water heating (electrical vs. natural gas or propane)
- Zoning restrictions or permitting requirements
- Whether any incentives are available.

Wind: Wind power systems progressed substantially as a result of the government incentives over the past 25 years, with a steady trend of cost reductions throughout that time period. Since 1990, the cost of energy from the wind has continued to decline, due to continued deployment and to public-private development programs in the U.S. and, to an even greater extent, in Europe.

The incentive for wind created by congress is the production tax credit (PTC). The problem is that congress tends to approve the PTC for only short periods of time and as a result, the U.S. wind industry goes through periods of boom and bust. Congress has let the PTC lapse three times: in 1999, 2001 and 2003. In the years following expiration, installations dropped by between 73% and 93%, only to revive again once the credit was restored.[7]

> *"Wind projects boost local tax bases, helping to pay for schools, roads and hospitals. Wind projects also revitalize the economy of rural communities by providing steady income to farmers and other landowners. Each wind turbine contributes \$3,000 to \$5,000 or more per year in rental income, while farmers continue to grow crops or graze cattle up to the foot of the turbines."*
>
> American Wind Energy Association (2009)
> Annual Wind Industry Report, Year Ending 2008

Wind energy systems generate electricity by using turbines to capture the wind's energy. Many locations in the U.S. have good wind resources. Evaluating the quality of the wind resource at a specific site is critical to determining if it is suitable. Some thorny issues that could arise with the technology include:

- Zoning restrictions and permitting requirements
- Environmental impacts (including migratory birds)
- Grid interconnection requirements
- Net metering regulations
- Existence of and qualifying criteria for incentives that are constantly changing

The U.S. has not yet built any large-scale offshore wind but in 2011 a handful of projects moved closer to construction as the federal government provided its support. Offshore wind could produce four times the

> *"Because the wind blows during stormy conditions when the sun does not shine and the sun often shines on calm days with little wind, combining wind and solar can go a long way toward meeting demand, especially when geothermal provides a steady base and hydroelectric can be called on to fill in the gaps."*
>
> Mark Z. Jacobson and Mark A. Delucchi.
> *Scientific American*, November 2009

nation's current generation capacity, about 4,150 GW, according to a 2010 report by NREL. Certainly, the low pricing for natural gas the U.S. has seen recently will present economic challenges and competition for large scale deployment of this renewable resource offshore.

Energy Storage: Recent advances in batteries and other storage technologies have resulted in systems that can play a flexible, multi-functional role in the electricity supply network to manage power resources effectively. The current electricity market offers a number of opportunities for energy storage technologies in which storage of a few seconds to a few hours of electricity is valuable. These systems can be located near the generator, transmission line, distribution substation, or the consumer of the energy.

In 2008, about 19% of global final energy consumption came from renewables, with 13% coming from traditional biomass, which is mainly used for heating, and 3.2% from hydroelectricity. New renewables (small hydro, modern biomass, wind, solar, geothermal, and biofuels) accounted for another 2.7% and are growing very rapidly. The share of renewables in electricity generation is around 18%, with 15% of global electricity coming from hydroelectricity and 3% from new renewables.[8]

There is currently a wide disparity in the economic cost of renewable energy technologies. Comparing the costs between the technologies is difficult. The cost of renewable energy generation can be considered in two ways: (1) economic cost, and (2) financial cost.[9]

Economic Cost

Economic cost is the cost of generating power from the underlying renewable energy asset and is a function of the:

- Quality of the available renewable energy resource: For a given renewable energy asset, such as a wind turbine or photovoltaic cell, more power will be generated with a better quality renewable resource. However, better quality does not necessarily just mean stronger. For example, at very high wind speeds, many wind turbines are designed to cut out so as to avoid excessive wear.
- Procurement price: The cost of the renewable energy system has a direct impact on the cost of generating renewable power. For a given renewable energy system and renewable resource, low procurement prices lead to lower power generation costs.
- Operating and maintenance expenses: These are the ongoing costs of operating and maintaining the renewable energy system.
- Warranties: Some technologies such as solar PV provide a standard 25 year warranty on the modules while other technologies provide only a 3-5 year warranty period.
- Fuel: Some technologies require fuel (such as hydrogen in a hydrogen fuel cell) and the cost of that fuel must be calculated into the financial analysis in addition to the supply-and-demand availability of the fuel.

Financial Cost

Financial cost is the actual cost to the company of its renewable energy and is the economic cost adjusted for the impact of:

- Interest expense (financing cost): Although renewable energy systems generally do not require fuel, they can be capital-intensive. As such, the capital charges needed to finance the asset can be a large component of power generation costs.
- Federal, state, and local incentives or rebates: Such financial incentives can reduce the cost of acquiring, financing, or operating a renewable energy system. In particular, this includes the tax implications when a financing structure is selected.

As will be seen throughout this book, incentives

> *"I have long felt that an investment by the Department of Energy of a million dollars a year for next 30 years would pay a higher return than any other investment this country could ever make."*
>
> Wilson Greatbatch,
> American engineer and inventor

that support renewable energy deployment play a very significant role.

References

1. Timothy Hasset, "Harnessing Nature's Power," World Resources Institute, 2009
2. Ibid.
3. Ibid.
4. United States Department of Energy, Office of Budget, Renewable Energy Characterizations, 1997
5. http://www.usabiomass.org
6. http://www.geo-energy.org
7. American Wind Energy Association, www.awea.org
8. Sandia National Laboratories, *Renewables 2010 Global Status Report*, 2010, pp. 15-16
9. Timothy Hasset, *Harnessing Nature's Power*, World Resources Institute, 2009

Chapter 3

Legislative Components

The introduction of current and future legislation into the financial analysis of any renewable energy project can—and will—change all assumptions and will mandate a constant vigilance of changes to federal, state, local, bankruptcy, and accounting laws as the project is documented and completed. Any change could have catastrophic consequences to the finance structure selected and ultimately the return to the lender, investor or project developer.

Entire books have been written and fortunes have been made by professionals on educating their customers and clients on the effects of the changing laws as a result of new tax codes, bankruptcy acts, securities law changes and even accounting rule changes. The effects of federal and state laws on the renewable energy project are immense. If they were static, everyone would be more comfortable. Unfortunately that is not the case. Just about the time that all parties in the renewable energy project have pinned down and ironed out the last of the perceived details, things can change. A project that was not able to move forward because of the current laws, can quickly shift and become a viable project. In an attempt to constantly fine tune the American economy, legislators continually tinker with the tax laws in particular. This chapter will review some of the key pieces of recent legislation that have had a significant effect on how renewable energy projects are structured.

Legislation continues to be a significant driver for change in the energy industry. The grant programs for smart grid and renewable energy outlined in the American Recovery and Reinvestment Act (ARRA) have been initiated, and companies are looking to take advantage of the programs. In addition, President Barack Obama and Congress continue to push forward a legislative agenda focused on promoting alternative energy, reducing greenhouse gas (GHG) emissions, and improving energy efficiency and security.

> *...renewable electricity technologies present policy makers with a superior alternative for minimizing the risk of fuel interruptions and shortages, helping improve the fragile transmission network and reducing environmental harm. These smaller and more environmentally friendly generators cost less to construct, produce power in smaller increments and need not rely on continuous subsidies. They generate little to no waste, have less greenhouse gas emissions per unit of electricity produced and do not contribute significantly to the risk of accidents."*
>
> Benjamin K. Sovacool, *Journal of Contemporary Asia*, 2010

FEDERAL LEGISLATION

Energy Policy Act of 2005

Historically, the 2005 energy tax act—affectionately called EPAct (Energy Policy Act 2005)—was not just a milestone, but the most important single item of legislation ever passed for the clean renewable energy industry in the history of America. It provided many clean energy technologies with the jump start that this sector needed to become a major influence in the energy industry. The Energy Improvement and Extension Act of 2008 (a part of the massive economic rescue package) extended many of the tax credits and allowances that originated in EPAct and created even more incentives that didn't exist in EPAct.

In order to appreciate the impact that the Energy Improvement and Extension Act of 2008, (which is often called EIEA) it is best to look at history.

The *original* Energy Policy Act was passed by Congress on October 24, 1992, with the goal of enhancing our nation's energy security and improving environmental quality. The Act, officially known as Public Law 102-486, included provisions addressing all aspects of energy supply and demand, including energy efficiency, alternative fuels, and renewable energy, as well as more traditional forms of energy such as coal, oil, and nuclear power.

Provisions of EPAct "2005" included benefits for oil and gas production and enhancing refining, electricity reliability and clean coal. Even nuclear power plants got in on the action. Our discussions below, however, will focus primarily on the energy efficiency and conservation and renewable/clean energy incentives. EPAct 2005 provided for three types of funds:

1. Tax credits or deductions for projects that actually come on-line;
2. Direct grants to help projects come to fruition; and
3. Loan guarantees to support project financing.

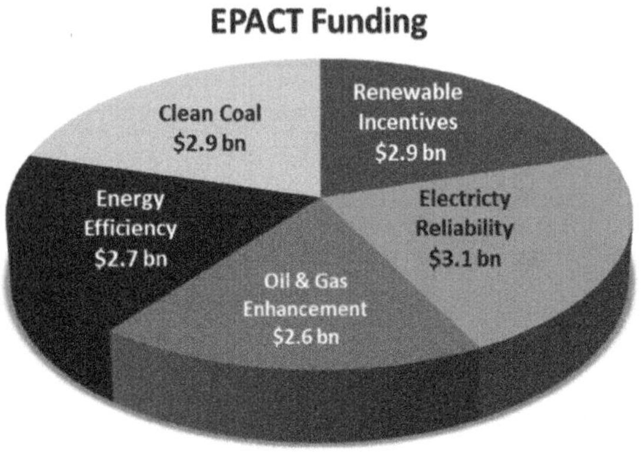

Figure 3-1: EPAct 2005 Funding

EPAct 2005 had many components in the Act. It was signed into law by President Bush on August 8, 2005 and offered consumers and businesses federal tax credits beginning in January 2006 for purchasing fuel-efficient hybrid-electric vehicles and energy-efficient appliances and products. Most of these tax credits would remain in effect through 2007. Further legislation extended those credits for one additional year to the end of 2008. EPAct was the first effort of the United States government to address U.S. energy policy since the Energy Policy Act of 1992. Among many other things, the 1,724 page law provided new tax incentives for a number of solar and energy efficiency measures.

The flexibility of EPAct allowed many creative financial structures to be set up that greatly benefited the financing of the renewable energy generation systems. Traditional lenders including leasing companies were able to very effectively monetize the tax attributes created under the Act and pass the utilization of the tax attributes through to borrowers/debtors in the form of lower payments. Typically, the payments were up to 55% lower than traditional project finance structures using standard terms and without the tax attributes being available. This provided huge savings for businesses—in particular the businesses who wanted to lower their energy costs but were not able to purchase the high cost clean energy generating systems directly.

EPAct 2005 was all about tax credits for the most part and included credits for both consumers and business. A tax credit is generally more valuable than an equivalent *tax deduction* because a *tax credit* reduces tax dollar-for-dollar, while a deduction only removes a percentage of the tax that is owed. There is an important difference between a tax deduction and a tax credit. A tax deduction is subtracted from income before total tax liability is computed. On the other hand, a tax credit is *subtracted directly from the total tax liability*. This means that a deduction and a credit have very different values, with a credit being three or more times more advantageous to the taxpayer than a deduction. For example, a tax credit of $1,000 for someone in the 34% tax bracket (top marginal tax federal bracket) is equivalent to a pre-tax federal deduction of $2,941! Some tax credits on clean energy systems were available prior to EPAct. For example, solar had a 10% tax. This, however, was increased three fold to 30% under EPAct.

The second principal component of EPAct was direct grants. Table 3-1 describes the direct grant provisions of EPAct.

The third component was loan guarantees that were to have been made by the DOE. This component was a complete failure. In the three years following EPAct 2005, the DOE failed to make a single loan guaranty. The attempt failed in every way. An application for a loan guaranty could run over a thousand pages, cost up to 5% of the project cost and the costs were required to be paid up front prior to the actual approval of the guaranty. These requirements were so onerous that very few applicants even tried to get the guaranty. These requirements have been changed substantially as described later in the 2009 American Recovery and Reinvestment Act (ARRA).

The following is a general breakdown of the new tax credits available under EPAct 2005 for both consumers and businesses:

1. **Consumer Tax Credits**
   a. *Automobile Tax Credits*
      i. Individuals and businesses who bought or leased a new hybrid gas-electric car or truck were eligible for, and could receive, an income tax credit of $250 to $3,400—depending on the fuel economy and the weight of the vehicle. Hybrid vehicles that used less gasoline than the average vehicle of similar weight and that met an emissions standard qualified for the credit. "Lean-burn" diesel vehicles could also qualify, but currently available diesel vehicles

Table 3-1: Direct Grant Provisions of EPAct 2005

SUBJECT	EPAct TITLE	COMPONENTS
Energy Efficiency	Title I	• Sustainable building technologies • Weatherization • Energy deliverability and reliability
Renewable Energy	Title II	• Sugar cane/ethanol program • Geothermal, hydropower, solar & wind • Hydrogen technology
Fossil Fuels	Title III-IV	• Natural gas development • Naval petroleum & oil shale reserves • Clean coal power initiative • Carbon capture & sequestration • Futuregen • Gasification & other clean coal development programs
Nuclear Energy	Title VI	• Nuclear Power 2010 • Next generation nuclear power plant • Global nuclear energy partnership • Waste disposal
Clean Vehicles	Title VII	• Project Freedom Car • Clean cities initiative

did not meet the emissions standard. There was a similar credit for alternative-fuel vehicles and for fuel-cell vehicles.

ii. If individuals and businesses bought more than one vehicle, they were eligible to receive a tax credit for each. If a tax-exempt organization bought such a vehicle, the retailer was also eligible to receive another credit. Companies that buy heavy-duty hybrid trucks were also eligible for a larger tax credit. There was a $2,000 tax deduction for hybrid vehicles for the remainder of 2005.

iii. This tax credit was for vehicles "placed-in-service" beginning January 1, 2006, but because there was a waiting list for many hybrids, consumers could receive the tax credit if they arrange to purchase the vehicle in 2005 as long as they do not take possession of the vehicle until January 1, 2006. This tax credit was phased out for each manufacturer once that company had sold 60,000 eligible vehicles. At that point, the tax credit for each company's vehicles was to be gradually reduced over the course of another year.

b. *Home Energy Efficiency Improvement Tax Credits*

i. Consumers who purchased and installed specific products, such as energy-efficient windows, insulation, doors, roofs, and heating and cooling equipment in their home could receive a tax credit of up to $500 beginning in January 2006.

c. *Residential Solar Tax Credits*

The EPAct also provided a credit equal to 30% of qualifying expenditures for purchase of qualified photovoltaic property and for solar water heating property used exclusively for purposes other than heating swimming pools and hot tubs. The credit, however, was limited to a maximum of $2,000.

> *"By reducing our dependence of foreign oil and increasing alternative energy sources such as ethanol, we can begin to bring down prices at the pumps, create thousands of new jobs and bring a much needed boost to our economy."*
>
> Jim Ryun, athlete and politician

2. **Business Tax Credits**

Businesses were also eligible for tax credits for buying hybrid vehicles, for building energy-efficient buildings, and for improving the energy efficiency of commercial buildings. This included:

a. *Biodiesel/Alternative Fuels*

Small producer biodiesel and ethanol credit. This credit benefited small agri-biodiesel producers by giving them a 10 cent per gallon tax credit for up to 15 million gallons of agri-biodiesel produced. In addition, the limit on production capacity for small ethanol producer's increased from 30 million to 60 million gallons. This was effective until the end of 2008.

b. *Credit for Installing Alternative Fuel Refueling Property*
Fueling stations were eligible to claim a 30% credit for the cost of installing clean-fuel vehicle refueling equipment, (e.g. E85 ethanol pumping stations). Under the provision, a clean fuel is any fuel that consists of at least 85% ethanol, natural gas, compressed natural gas, liquefied natural gas, liquefied petroleum gas, or hydrogen and any mixture of diesel fuel and biodiesel containing at least 20% biodiesel. This was effective through December 31, 2010.

c. *Buildings (including energy generating assets)*
Credits were available for business installation of qualified fuel cells, stationary microturbine power plants, and solar equipment. This provided a 30% tax credit for the purchase of qualified fuel cell power plants for businesses, a 10% credit for qualifying stationary microturbine power plants and a 30% credit for qualifying solar energy equipment. To qualify for the credit, fuel cells were required to be 500 watt capacity or greater with a generation efficiency of 30% or greater. Microturbines were required to be of 2,000 kilowatt capacity or less with an efficiency of 26% at International Standards Organization (ISO) conditions. The tax credits and limitations are:
   - For fuel cells, a tax credit of 30% of the expenditure up to a maximum of $500 per 500 watts of capacity.
   - For microturbines, a tax credit of 10% of the expenditure with a credit limitation of $200/kW.

d. *Business Credit of Energy-efficient New Homes*
This provides tax credits to eligible contractors for the construction of qualified new energy-efficient homes. The credit applies to manufactured homes meeting Energy Star® criteria and other homes, saving 50% of the energy compared to the EPAct standard.

e. *Energy-efficient Commercial Building Deduction*
This provision allowed a tax deduction (not a tax credit) for energy-efficient commercial buildings that reduce annual energy and power consumption by 50% compared to the American Society of Heating, Refrigerating, and Air Conditioning Engineers (ASHRAE) 2001 standard. The deduction will equal the cost of energy-efficient property installed during construction, with a maximum deduction of $1.80 per square foot of the building. Additionally, a partial deduction of 60 cents per square foot is provided for building subsystems. An important component of the deduction is that the expense incurred for the energy efficient asset can be written off 100% in the year of installation. The taxpayer does not have to depreciate it over a long time like other components of the building (which could be up to thirty nine years for capital improvements for structures under IRS guidelines). Lighting systems upgrades are often acquired under this provision. The tax deduction is, essentially, an accelerated depreciation of a capital asset investment. The asset must be shown on the books for the increased depreciation to be taken in the first year.
   The tax deduction is only for interior portions of the building, not outdoor space lighting as an example. However, an indoor parking structure would qualify. Remember, you cannot take a deduction for an amount greater than your actual cost.
   To claim the accelerated commercial buildings tax deduction provided by Internal Revenue Code section 179(D) in 2006 or 2007, the tax preparer working for the taxpayer needs a certification document signed by an engineer or contractor who is licensed in the jurisdiction in which the building is located and represents himself as being qualified to do this type of building analysis. The certification document must contain the information stipulated in the IRS June 26th guidance document (Notice 2006-52). This document can be viewed at the following IRS website: *http://www.irs.gov/pub/irs-irbs/irb06-26.pdf*

f. *Energy-efficient Appliances*
This provides a tax credit for the "manufacturer" of energy-efficient dishwashers, clothes washers, and refrigerators. Credits varied depending on the efficiency of the unit. This was effective for appliances manufactured in 2006 and 2007.

Energy Improvement and Extension Act of 2008 (HR 1424)

As 2008 started coming to a close, the entire clean energy industry that had grown so dramatically for three years was on the verge of total collapse. New legislation had been introduced numerous times during the entire year of 2008 to extend the tax credits but had failed to pass both the house and the senate. All clean energy industries tried and tried through their respective trade associations working with congress to get an extension on the books. Every time one arm of congress passed an extender bill, the other would turn it down. In general, there was complete legislative gridlock and that included threats of a veto from then President Bush if whatever came to him didn't meet his own particular requirements.

Then, at the last minute after the senate had turned down the first massive rescue bill that didn't have any "add-ons" to the rescue, the senate came back with its own bill modeled after the house bill, tacked on the "clean energy tax extensions" (mostly in the original form that had been bounced around for all of the earlier part of 2008), added some other "sweeteners" and then sent it back to the house for approval. The house immediately passed the bill and President Bush signed it into law. Politics in this case certainly lived up to two old adages: "politics make strange bedfellows" and "politics is akin to making sausage." That was certainly the case in the creation and passage of the Energy Improvement and Extension Act of 2008 (EIEA).

H.R. 1424, also known as the Energy Improvement and Extension Act of 2008 (the Act), contains a number of tax incentives for renewable energy and other energy activities. The incentives include an extension of the production tax credit (PTC) and the investment-based energy tax credit (ITC) beyond the 2008 sunset date that was set under EPAct 2005. There are many different start dates, ending dates, and total time periods of multiple tax attributes. Therefore, anyone relying on the new, revised or extended tax attributes needs to extremely careful in considering any of those attributes in a project financing scenario. Just some of the more important tax attributes are described below.

PTC Extensions

The Act extended the placed-in-service sunset date for wind and refined coal facilities to December 31, 2009. Unfortunately, congress did not see fit to extend the credit for a longer period so that the "year-to-year" uncertainty of whether the credit will be available when the project is finished puts a real damper on new large projects to move off the drawing boards and into final installation and financing certainty.

The PTC extension for geothermal, biomass, landfill gas, trash and other qualifying facilities extends the placed-in-service sunset date to December 31, 2010.

> *"Improved energy productivity and renewable energy are both available in abundance—and new policies and technologies are rapidly making them more economically competitive with fossil fuels. In combination, these energy options represent the most robust alternative to the current energy system, capable of providing the diverse array of energy services that a modern economy requires. Given the urgency of the climate problem, that is indeed convenient."*
>
> Christopher Flavin
> in Worldwatch Institute (2008)
> Building a Low-Carbon Economy

PTC Modifications

The Act expands the PTC to now include (after October 3, 2008) marine and hydrokinetic renewable energy facilities with a nameplate capacity of at least 150 kilowatts. The credit rate is one-half the general PTC rate and expires in December 31, 2011. The existing credit for small irrigation power is eliminated for any projects placed in service after October 3, 2008.

The Act increases the required emission reductions for refined coal production and eliminates the requirement that refined coal be produced in a manner that increases the market value of the coal (effective for facilities placed in service after December 31, 2008). The Act also amends the definition of "refined coal" to include "steel industry fuel" (generally effective for fuel produced and sold after September 30, 2008, but subject to a limited credit period).

For trash facilities, the Act eliminates the requirement that municipal solid waste be burned to generate electricity and requires only that such waste be "used" to produce electricity. This is effective for electricity produced and sold after October 3, 2008. As said earlier, politics can generate some strange sausage...

The Act provides that new biomass power generation units placed in service in connection with existing qualified open-loop biomass and closed-loop biomass facilities are themselves treated as qualified facilities to the extent of the increased amount of electricity produced by the new units. This provision is also effective for property placed in service after October 3, 2008.

Investment-based Energy Tax Credit Extension

In general, the Act extends all of the placed-in-service sunset dates under EPAct 2005 for solar, fuel cell and microturbine assets to December 31, 2016—an eight year extension. This extension will provide all sellers and users of renewable energy generating assets that are either solar, fuel cells, or microturbines the ability to grow in a stable manner and not have potential energy projects be sidelined because they can't be built and commissioned in time. Nearly all large scale 250 kW and larger solar projects came to a complete halt four to six months prior to year end 2008 because of the uncertainty of the tax credit extension. Now those industries had the ability to plan for a steady growth until year end 2016, train and retain employees and invest in new marketing opportunities.

In addition to the extension of existing tax credits, the new Act provided for additional expansions on the ITC with the following provisions:

- A 10% credit for combined heat and power (CHP) systems. CHP systems are also known as co-generation systems. They provide both heat and power from the same equipment using efficient, clean and reliable energy from a single fuel source—sometimes even renewable fuel such as landfill gas (methane), etc. CHP can greatly enhance the facilities operational efficiency and dramatically reduce the energy costs in the facility. The end result also reduces the GHG emissions, giving rise to emission credit reductions at the facility. The equipment is usually microturbines, turbines, internal combustion engines, steam engines and fuel cells. The energy is generated simultaneously for both heat and power. The credit provisions have some limitations on large projects and are subject to certain reductions.
- A 30% credit for qualified small wind energy assets. This is equipment that uses a wind turbine with a nameplate capacity of 100 kilowatts or less. The credit of the property is capped at $4,000 per year.
- A 10% credit for geothermal heat pump system. This is a system that uses the ground or ground water to heat or cool a structure.

These expansions of the ITC were for property placed in service after October 3, 2008.

They also increase the credit limitation for fuel cell property from $500 per 0.5 kilowatt of capacity to $1,500 per 0.5 kilowatt of capacity.

A major provision of the 2008 Act is that it now allowed any ITC obtained by a taxpayer to fully offset the alternative minimum tax (AMT) liability they might have, subject to certain limitations. This is effective for credits for tax years beginning after October 3, 2008. This is a *significant* departure from EPAct 2005 where the AMT could not be offset with ITC from energy generating property like solar, fuel cells and microturbines. There was a portion of potential energy projects that were not done between 2005 and 2008 because the taxpayer could not offset their AMT liability. This now has changed, and more serious renewable energy projects were committed to because of the Act.

The new 2008 Act also now allows the public utilities to get ITC on renewable energy they purchase for their own use. This was not allowed under EPAct 2005. The in service date is February 13, 2008. Here again, a strange date that got slipped into the Act as part of the political process. In theory this should allow for a large increase of renewable energy property to public utilities by the renewable energy asset providers. Many of the public utilities will now seek to acquire renewable energy generating assets for economic reasons and also to help them satisfy renewable portfolio standards that have been established in states where they operate. Potentially, the size of the systems will also be very large. There are reports of planned projects exceeding 100 megawatts on the drawing boards.

Although the Act did not extend the 50% bonus first year depreciation on any equipment purchased by a taxpayer after 2008, it did extend the provision for a biomass ethanol plant using cellulosic biofuel feedstock placed in service after October 3, 2008. This is another example of a "carve-out" for a particular industry sector.

The Act extends for one year until December 31, 2009 the income tax credit, excise tax credit and excise tax refund provisions applicable to small agri-biodiesel producers to biodiesel, agri-biodiesel, and renewable diesel. Effective for qualifying fuel produced, sold or used after December 31, 2009, the income tax and excise tax credit amounts applicable to biodiesel and biodiesel mixtures were increased from $.50 to $1.00 per gallon, eliminating the disparity under prior law between biodiesel and agri-biodiesel credits. The Act modifies the definition of "renewable diesel" by (1) eliminating the requirement that the fuel be made using a thermal depolymerization process; (2) permitting the Treasury Secretary to identify alternative testing standards to qualify for the credit; (3) including biomass fuel that qualifies as renewable jet fuel (biomass fuel that meets Department of Defense military specifications for jet fuel or ASTM specifications for aviation turbine); and (4) excluding fuel derived from co-processing biomass with a feedstock that is not biomass.

The Act also extends through December 31, 2009 the alternative fuel credit and the alternative fuel mixture credit. Effective for fuel sold or used after October 3, 2008, the alternative fuel credit includes compressed or liquefied biomass gas and all types of qualifying fuels sold for use in aviation. Gasification facilities must meet certain carbon capture requirements to qualify for the credit.

In the transportation sector, the 2008 Act adds a credit for qualified plug-in electric drive motor vehicles purchased between January 1, 2009 and December 31, 2014 (six years). The credit amount is $2,500 plus $417 for each kilowatt hour of traction battery capacity in excess of four kilowatt hours, subject to certain phase-out rules and vehicle weight limitations.

There is an exemption from the heavy vehicle excise tax for the cost of qualifying idling reduction devices (devices or systems certified as providing heat, air conditioning, electricity or similar services to a vehicle with reduced engine idling). This provision is effective for sales or installations after October 3, 2008.

Installation of alternative fuel refueling property wasn't left out either. The Act extended through December 31, 2010 the income tax credit for that property and is effective for property placed in service after October 3, 2008. It also expanded the applicable fuels to include electricity refueling property.

To make sure absolutely everyone is covered in some way, even bicycle commuters weren't left out. The Act adds as a qualified transportation fringe benefit reimbursements for reasonable expenses for the purchase, improvement, repair or storage of a bicycle, capped at $20 per month, but only if the employee does not receive any other qualified transportation fringe benefit and regularly uses a bicycle for a substantial portion of travel between home and work (effective for tax years beginning after December 31, 2008).

Other Provisions

The 2008 Act extends through December 31, 2016 the 30% residential energy credit (thereby matching the commercial side) on qualified solar electric property, qualified solar water heating property and qualified fuel cell property. The Act removed the $2,000 cap that was established for residential energy credit under EPAct 2005 on solar electric property but did not modify the other applicable caps, effective with respect to taxable years beginning after December 31, 2008. The Act expands the credit to apply to qualified small wind energy property and to qualified geothermal heat pump property, subject to certain caps (effective with respect to taxable years beginning after December 31, 2007 for property placed in service on or before December 31, 2016). The act provided that the credit may be used against AMT liability just as it does with the commercial credit for business and is effective with respect to taxable years beginning after December 31, 2007.

The Act generally allowed for a 10 year accelerated depreciation for qualified smart electric meters and qualified smart electric grid systems placed in service after October 32, 2008, unless the property otherwise qualifies for a shorter recovery period.

Interestingly, the only place that the 50% bonus depreciation was applicable to (in general the 50% depreciation was only for tax year 2008) is for certain qualified reuse and recycling property purchases and placed in service after August 31, 2008 (this includes for AMT liability as well).

The Act extended for an additional five years through December 31, 2013 the energy efficient commercial buildings deduction, which generally allows a deduction for the cost of energy efficient commercial building property, subject to a lifetime cap per building of $1.80 per square foot as was explained in more detail above under EPAct 2005.

The Act extended through December 31, 2009 the new energy efficient home credit, which allowed a tax credit of up to $2,000 for the builders of qualified new energy efficient homes. It also extends and makes numerous changes to the credit for the production of qualifying energy-efficient dishwasher, clothes washers and refrigerators effective for appliances produced after December 31, 2007. This credit accrues to the benefit of the company making the product, not the end user.

Clean Renewable Energy Bonds (CREBs) were not left out either. The Act authorizes the issuance of up to $300 million of new CREBs and up to $800 million of Qualified Energy Conservation Bonds. The bill created a new category of tax credit bonds, "Qualified Energy Conservation Bonds" (QECBs) to finance State and local government initiatives designed to reduce greenhouse emissions. QECBs can be issued to finance capital expenditures incurred for: (1) reducing energy consumption by at least 20 percent; (2) implementing green community programs; and (3) rural development involving the production of electricity from renewable resources. The bonds can also be used to finance research facilities and provide research grants for, among other things, technologies to reduce peak use of electricity. The Act extended to September 30, 2012 the sunset date for issuing qualified green building and sustainable design project bonds.

Yolo County, California, made history in July 2011 when officials installed a 1 MW solar PV project to supply power to both a jail and juvenile center. The project is noteworthy because it represents the first known use of QECBs and first known combined use of QECBs and CREBs in the U.S.

As can be seen from the above summary, the 2008 EIEA Act is complex, expansive and has no common starting or ending dates. Each technology is unique and great care needs to be taken when applying these tax benefits to analyzing the renewable energy project financing structure. In most cases, both the lender and the debt obligor will need to work together closely to make sure the application amounts and dates are accurate and also to make sure all attributes that can be monetized or realized by the respective parties and have not been left out.

> *"This curious faith is predicated on the notion that we will soon develop unlimited new sources of energy: domestic oil fields, shale oil, gasified coal, nuclear power, solar energy, and so on. This is fantastical because the basic cause of the energy crisis is no scarcity: it is moral ignorance and weakness of character. We don't know how to use energy or what to use it for. And we cannot restrain ourselves. Our time is characterized as much by the abuse and waste of human energy as it is by the abuse and waste of fossil fuel energy."*
>
> Wendell Berry, author

The American Recovery and Reinvestment Act of 2009

The American Recovery and Reinvestment Act of 2009 (affectionately known as "ARRA") provides "something for everyone" as the authors like to say. However, this is particularly true for the renewable energy sector of the U.S. economy. This Act, signed into law on February 17, 2009 by President Obama, provides more significant changes that are sure to help the renewable energy sector beyond what 2005 EPAct and 2008 EIEA did. Additionally, ARRA provided almost $94 billion of the $787 billion economic stimulus package in direct and indirect spending, through tax incentives, grants and loan guarantees to clean energy companies and projects. Every state was touting the billions of dollars that was coming their way.

The real challenge was to determine which of the provisions are applicable to any given renewable energy project. The problem is made even more difficult by the lack of regulations, rules, guidance and applications that will govern the distribution of many of the funds and tax credits. The rules, regulations and guidance were to be fully developed and implemented during tax year 2009—some were and some were not.

The following is a general breakdown of how the $95 billion was to be allocated:

- Direct investment in:
  - — energy efficiency projects ($26 billion)
  - — smart grid ($17 billion)
  - — green vehicles and transportation ($21 billion)
- Tax incentives on renewable energy projects ($16.5 billion)
- Other ($14.5 billion)

ARRA as a whole can be broken down into the following five categories:

1. Tax incentives
   a. Extension of PTC sunset date
   b. Election to claim ITC rather than utilize PTC
   c. Treasury grant in lieu of ITC
   d. Small wind investment tax credit
   e. Extension of 50% bonus depreciation through 2009
   f. Advanced energy facilities investment tax credit
   g. Clean renewable energy bonds (CREBs)
   h. Qualified energy conservation bonds (QECBs)
2. Federal loan guarantees
3. Federal grant programs
   a. R&D, demonstration and deployment projects
   b. Advanced Research Projects Agency (ARPA) in energy
4. State energy block grants
5. Job training

Without getting into the politics of the Act, the following is a summary of how the bill would affect all parties looking to maximize the benefits associated with the financing of renewable energy projects. The following 13 tax provisions were specifically designed to target renewable energy projects:

1. *Extension of Production Tax Credit Sunset Dates*—For wind facilities, the Act extends the §45 production tax credit to facilities placed in service prior to January 1, 2013. This was a three year extension. Under the current law, the production tax credit applied only to wind facilities placed in service before January 1, 2010. The Act also extended the §45 placed-in-service date for biomass (both closed-loop and open-loop), geothermal, landfill gas, trash and qualified hydropower facilities to January 1, 2014 (previously set to expire on December 31, 2010). This greatly enhanced the ability of larger renewable energy projects to get built since most of them can take several years to engineer and build. Under current law, these facilities would have had to have been placed in service before January 1, 2011. The §45 production tax credit placed-in-service-

date for marine and hydrokinetic renewable energy facilities was extended from January 1, 2012 to December 31, 2013—providing even more time for those projects to be built. This extension removed a significant portion of the uncertainty previously faced by developers and investors in biomass projects with long-term development and construction requirements.

Since its enactment in 1992, the section 45 production tax credit had been allowed to expire three different times: 1999, 2001 and 2003. By granting the extension for these projects, the Act provided more certainty for businesses and investors, and created some near-to-mid-term stability for investment and planning purposes. This is particularly important when trying to structure the correct finance structure on a renewable energy project as can be seen by the components of the project described in this book. This increased stability is particularly beneficial to those projects with long lead times (such as wind), by providing developers with more time to site, plan, engineer, obtain financing, and acquire equipment.

2. *Investment Tax Credit in Lieu of Production Tax Credit*—For certain property that is part of a qualified investment credit facility, the Act provided that a taxpayer may elect a 30 percent investment tax credit in lieu of the §45 production tax credits. Most project developers look at this change positively and started to utilize the new provision using the concept of "a bird in hand is worth two in the bush." Utilizing a tax attribute today is generally better than bringing more in over a longer period of time. Qualified investment credit facilities include wind facilities placed in service before 2012, as well as biomass (both closed-loop and open-loop), geothermal, landfill gas, trash and qualified hydropower, marine and hydrokinetic renewable energy facilities, if those facilities are placed in service before 2013. If this election is made, the affected facilities received the same tax treatment as solar facilities, which were currently eligible for the 30 percent investment tax credit.

An election to claim the investment tax credit in lieu of the production tax credit could provide advantages for projects otherwise eligible only for the production tax credit. For example, this measure provides a higher degree of certainty of cash return since the investment tax credit is based on initial cost instead of the cost and price of electricity production over a 10-year period, which may be variable. Moreover, this election allows wind, geothermal, and biomass developer's access to a larger tax credit equity market made up of regional banks, insurance companies, telecommunications companies, and others more familiar with sale-leaseback and inverted lease tax credit equity structures rather than the partnership-flip structures often seen in the production tax credit equity market.

The entire amount of the ITC is available to the taxpayer in the year in which the qualified asset is placed in service. Any unused portion of the credit from the current year can be carried back one tax year and then carried forward up to 20 tax years. Special rules apply to taxpayers with less than $15 million in gross revenue (see item #8 below). Remember that a taxpayer cannot claim both the PTC and the ITC—it is a one-or-the-other election. Also, the project must be considered to be "placed in service" to qualify for the credits. Generally speaking, a facility is placed in service for tax purposes when it is placed in a state or condition of readiness to fulfill a specifically designated purpose. To be considered place in service, a facility generally need not be operating at full capacity, but must be completed and ready to operate as designed.

Various special rules applicable to investment tax credits under current law continue to apply. For example, if a taxpayer makes the investment tax credit election, the taxpayer may receive the credit even if it leases the facility on which the qualified investment asset is located. Moreover, a lessor may elect to pass through the investment tax credit to its lessee, and the special rule would apply allowing a taxpayer to treat property sold and leased back within three months of its placed-in-service date as new property. Finally, in the case of a disposition within five years, the rules providing for recapture of all or a portion of the investment tax credit would continue to apply.

Property eligible for the investment tax credit is tangible personal property or other tangible property that is used as *an integral part of the qualified facility*. It does not include buildings or structural components not integral to the qualified facility.

Section 48(a)(5) allows taxpayers to irrevocably elect to take the investment tax credit determined under §48 in lieu of the production tax credit under §45 with respect to certain renewable energy facilities. The energy credit for any taxable year is the energy percentage of the basis of each energy property placed in service during the taxable year. The qualified property that is part of a qualified investment credit facility will be treated as energy property for purposes of §48, and that the energy percentage with respect to such property will be 30 percent. The election to take the investment tax credit determined under §48 in lieu of the production tax credit under §45 is available for facilities placed in service after December 31, 2008. The election must be made on a timely filed return (including extensions) for the taxable year in which the facility that is to be treated a qualified investment credit facility is placed in service. Once made, the election is irrevocable.

3. *Grants in Lieu of Tax Credits*—This provision (section 1603) was a much sought after provision by the trade associations of the various renewable energy technologies. For qualified investment assets and facilities, a taxpayer (other than a governmental entity or tax-exempt entity) may, in lieu of production tax credits or investment tax credits, elect to receive a grant from the Secretary of the Treasury equal to the amount of the investment tax credit to which the taxpayer otherwise would have been entitled. This again, is another application of the "bird in hand is worth two in the bush" approach to tax attributes—and cash is king!

For solar, fuel cell assets, wind, biomass (both closed-loop and open-loop), geothermal, landfill gas, trash and qualified hydropower facilities, marine and hydrokinetic renewable energy facilities, the taxpayer may receive a 30% cash grant in lieu of the 30% investment tax credit. For geothermal, microturbine, combined heat and power system property and geothermal heat-pump property, the taxpayer may receive a 10% grant of cash in lieu of the 10% investment tax credit.

By receiving payments for property under section 1603, applicants are electing to forego tax credit under sections 48 and 45 of the IRC with respect to such property for the taxable year in which the payment is made or any subsequent taxable year. The goal of the program was to temporarily fill the gap created by the diminished investor demand for tax credits under sections 48 and 45. In this way, the near term goal of creating and retaining jobs would be achieved, as well as the long-term benefit of expanding the use of clean and renewable energy and decreasing the nations dependency on non-renewable energy sources.

It should be noted that for facilities that are electing to receive this cash grant in lieu of the production tax credit, the calculation of the grant amount follows the same rules applicable to the investment tax credit and therefore is subject to IRS audit for eligibility as well as to the special rules above. This includes the recapture provisions of the ITC.

Under ARRA 2009, the Secretary would be required to make payment of the grant a) within 60 days of the later of the grant application date or b) the date the property is placed in service. For qualified assets to qualify for the grant, it must either be placed in service during 2009 or 2010, or have construction begin in 2009 or 2010, and be placed in service by 2012 (for wind), 2013 (for other facilities electing the grant in lieu of the production tax credit) or 2016 (for energy property electing the cash grant in lieu of the investment tax credit, such as solar). In all cases, the cash grant application must be made no later than October 1, 2011. The cash grant would not itself be includible in the taxpayer's income but, like the investment tax credit, would reduce the depreciable federal tax basis of the property by 50% of the amount of the grant.

> *"We simply must balance our demand for energy with our rapidly shrinking resources. By acting now we can control our future instead of letting the future control us."*
>
> Jimmy Carter, former U.S. President

Any developer, investor or lender of a renewable energy system should be careful to avoid losing the ITC or 1603 grant by having a contract with a tax-exempt entity (see page 149 below). Section 1603(g) of the American Recovery and Reinvestment Act of 2009 specifically provides that the Treasury grants which were available in lieu of ITCs cannot be made to tax-exempt entities, to governments or subdivisions, agencies or instrumentalities thereof, or to any partnership or other pass-through entity any partner or equity holder of which is such an entity. Any leasing of the facility to a tax-exempt entity will cause the facility to deemed "tax-exempt use property" under section 168(h)(1) of the Code and thereby not be eligible for the ITC/grant. This does not mean that you cannot lease a rooftop from the user and sell the energy to the tax-exempt entity as described below (see page 149) under a PPA or service contract.

The principal reason that the treasury grants had become so popular was the transaction costs. It was a lot less expensive to apply for a grant than to try and cover the expenses of forming a tax equity structure. The high costs of tax equity to help fund a renewable energy project are not just the result of higher yields required by the tax equity to monetize a true tax credit, but the tax investor also seeks project ownership after the assumed 20-year life of the facility. Developers, on the other hand, assume cash flows to 25 or 30 years. Passing on project ownership—even after 20 years—alters the developer's return and, in essence, increases the transaction costs associated with the monetization of the tax credits. Administrative costs can also be higher for tax equity deals.

See page 40 later in this chapter for more detailed information on the 1603 grant program process.

4. *Elimination of Basis Reduction for Property Financed by Subsidized Energy Financing or Private Activity Bonds*—For renewable energy property eligible for the §48 investment tax credit, the Act eliminates any basis reduction if the property is financed by subsidized government financing, including tax-exempt financing from a state or local government. Under prior law, this reduction in basis effectively reduced the amount of the investment tax credit by the proportional amount of the project financed with such subsidized government financing.

5. *New Investment Tax Credit for Renewable Energy Manufacturing Facilities or Advanced Energy Project Credit*—The Act creates a new 30% investment tax credit for facilities that manufacture certain property designed to be used in renewable energy projects. This includes any facility which establishes, re-equips or expands a manufacturing facility that produces products used in the production of energy from renewable sources. This will greatly encourage new renewable energy production facilities to be built in the U.S. Facilities will have to apply for these credits under a certification process to be established by the Secretary of Treasury in consultation with the Secretary of Energy. Projects will be selected based upon a reasonable expectation of commercial viability, innovation, job stimulation, and environmental benefits. The credits will be awarded through an application process. Applicants have three years from the date of the award to place the project in service. The Act provides for a total of $2.3 billion of credits that can be allocated by the Secretary of Treasury for these facilities.

This new provision is included in section 48C and operates similar to the "qualifying advanced coal project credit" and the "qualifying gasification credit" (sections 48A and 48B). Before investment tax credits can be claimed on property placed in service, the qualifying advanced energy project must first obtain certification and an award of credit allocation from the Treasury.

A "qualifying advanced energy project" is one that re-equips, expands, or establishes a facility for the production of:

- Property designed to be used to produce energy from the sun, wind, geothermal deposits, or other renewable resource;
- Fuel cells, microturbines, or an energy storage system for use with electric or hybrid-electric motor vehicles;
- Electric grids to support the transmission of intermittent sources of renewable energy, including storage of such energy;
- Property designed to capture and sequester carbon dioxide emissions;
- Property designed to refine or blend renewable fuels or to produce energy conservation technologies (including energy-conserving lighting technologies and smart grid technologies);
- New qualified plug-in electric drive motor vehicles, qualified plug-in electric vehicles, or components designed specifically for use with such vehicles, including electric motors, generators, and power control units; or
- Other advanced energy property designed to reduce greenhouse gas emissions.

Taxpayers must apply for certification within two years of the establishment of the program and provide evidence of compliance with the credit requirements within one year of acceptance to the program. The project for which the credit is made available must be placed-in-service within three years of certification. Only tangible personal property and other tangible property (not buildings or structural components) are eligible for the credit.

Criteria for project selection include: (1) reasonable expectation of commercial viability; (2) domestic job creation; (3) impact avoiding or reducing air pollutants or emissions of greenhouse gases; (4) potential for technological innovation and commercial deployment; (5) low cost of generated or stored energy or measured reduction in energy consumption or greenhouse gas emission; and (6) shortest project time from certification to completion.

Note that if the taxpayer is already receiving the ITC or other project tax credit, they are not eligible nor is it applicable to a project for the manufacture of property used in the refining or blending of any transportation fuel (other than renewable fuels).

6. *Modification of Credit for Carbon Sequestration*—Under current law, taxpayers are eligible for a $10 per ton credit for captured carbon dioxide used as a tertiary injectant in a qualified enhanced oil or natural gas project. ARRA amends this credit to require that carbon dioxide used as a tertiary injectant must also be disposed of in secured geological storage to qualify for the credit. The Act also provides that the Secretary of the Treasury must consult with the Secretary of Energy and Secretary of the Interior, as well as the Administrator of the EPA, in issuing any regulations regarding adequate security measures for secure geological storage.

7. *Extension of Bonus Depreciation*—The Act extended the 50 percent bonus depreciation to apply to property placed in service after December 31, 2008 and before January 1, 2010 (or January 1, 2011 for long-production period property). Under prior law, bonus depreciation expired at the end of 2008 (or would expire at the end of 2009 for long-production period property). The Act thus gave a one year extension. Additionally, the Act allows taxpayers who would otherwise be eligible for this bonus depreciation to claim additional research or minimum tax credits in lieu of the depreciation. There could be interesting applications of this provision on some renewable energy projects.

8. *Five-year Carryback of Operating Losses*—Under current law, net operating losses can only be carried back for two years. For companies with no more than $15 million in gross revenue (therefore limiting the provision to only smaller companies), the Act will allow a net operating loss for 2008 or 2009 to be carried back five years. This provision alone will allow many smaller companies who have paid taxes in the five years prior to the enactment of the Act to get their taxes back that they paid to help pay for the acquisition of a new renewable energy system.

> *"Finally, treat domestic energy production as the economic necessity it is and the job creator it can be. Drill, and frack, and lease, and license, unleash in every way the jobs potential in the enormous energy resources we have been denying ourselves."*
>
> Mitch Daniels, governor of the state of Indiana

9. *Loan Guaranty Program for Renewable Energy and Electric Power Transmission Projects*—The Act authorizes up to $60 billion in DOE loan guarantees (supported by $6 billion in actual funds) under the Title XVII of the EPAct 2005 (42 U.S.C. § 16511 et seq.) for renewable energy systems and facilities that manufacture related components, transmission systems and advanced biofuels that start construction by September 30, 2011. The guarantees may cover up to 80% of a project's costs, with project sponsors contributing the remaining 20% of costs as equity. If 80% of the project cost is guaranteed by the DOE, it is likely that the Federal Financing Bank must provide the guaranteed debt funding. Current loan guarantee programs authorized by Title XVII require that applicants submit materials demonstrating a reasonable prospect of repayment of the guaranteed obligation and satisfy the Department of Energy's underwriting criteria.

10. *CREBs—Clean Renewable Energy Bonds*—The Act increases the new Clean Renewable Energy Bonds limitation from $800 million to $2.4 Billion—a 300% increase! The Act also includes new procedures for the pass-through of CREB tax credits to shareholders of regulated investment companies and requires projects financed with new CREBs to follow certain prevailing wage requirements. The Emergency Economic Stabilization Act of 2008 originally authorized this new allotment of tax credit bonds to finance wind, closed-loop biomass,

open-loop biomass, geothermal, solar, municipal solid waste, small irrigation power and hydropower projects, in addition to existing CREBs created by the Energy Policy Act of 2005. (See Chapter four for a detailed description of the CREBs.) Borrowers are paid interest on the CREBs in the form of federal tax credits by the United States government in lieu of interest paid by the issuer. CREBs, therefore, provide qualified issuers and borrowers with the ability to borrow at a 0% interest rate. The $2.4 billion allotment is divided into thirds among groups of qualified issuers: state, local and tribal governments; public power providers and certain electric cooperatives. To issue CREBs, these qualified issuers must submit applications for a portion of the authorized allotment of bonds through a process administered by the IRS. The Act also includes new procedures for the pass-through of CREBs tax credits to shareholders of regulated investment companies.

In practice, CREBs have frequently proven time consuming and challenging to transact, which has eroded the value for some investors of the federal subsidy. Also, the CREB application process has been a task. Even after a governmental entity has received approval, some have chosen to forgo a CREBs allocation because the cost/benefit comparison of CREBs vs. traditional municipal bonding favored municipal bonds.

11. *Qualified Energy Conservation Bonds*—The Act increases the amount of issuable Qualified Energy Conservation Bonds ("QECBs") under I.R.C. §54D from $800 million to $3.2 billion—a 400% increase! The Act also includes new procedures for the pass-through of QECB tax credits to shareholders of regulated investment companies and requires projects financed with QECBs to follow certain prevailing wage requirements. State and local governments can issue QECBs for a variety of qualified conservation purposes including capital expenditures for reducing energy consumption in publicly owned buildings; implementing green community energy programs; rural development involving production of electricity from renewable energy resources and the construction of wind, solar, geothermal, biomass, landfill gas and hydroelectric projects; research grants and initiatives; mass commuting facilities; demonstration projects that promote green building technology, agricultural waste-to-fuel conversion, electricity demand response programs, advanced batteries, and carbon capture and sequestration; and public education programs. The bonds may be used for capital expenditures to reduce energy use in public buildings by at least 20% and implement green community programs. The total amount of QECBs are allocated to the States and large local governments in proportion to population.

    Initially, qualified tax credit bonds provided a tax credit directly to the bond buyer, which reduced the interest coupon (or payment) required of the government entity. Now there is a direct payment option—allowed through the recent Hiring Incentives to Restore Employment (HIRE) Act (March 18, 2010). With this option, the Treasury reimburses the issuer/borrower at 70% of the interest rate via a refundable tax credit.

    The direct pay option might make CREBs and QECBs more liquid because they do not require buyers to have significant tax liability. Therefore, these mechanisms are expected to have greater appeal to a wider variety of investors.

    - For more information on CREBs, QECBs, and other financing options for state and local governments see *"Solar Powering Your Community: A Guide for Local Governments," U.S. Department of Energy, July 2009.*
    - For more information on CREBs, see *"Financing Public Sector Projects with Clean Renewable Energy Bonds," Fact Sheet Series on Financing Renewable Energy Projects, National Renewable Energy Laboratory (NREL), (NREL Report No. FS-6A2-46605).*
    - For more information on QECBs and CREBs, see the U.S. Department of Energy, Office of Energy Efficiency and Renewable Energy's *"Qualified Energy Conservation Bonds ("QECBs") & New Clean Renewable Energy Bonds ("New CREBs")."*

12. *DOE Energy Efficiency and Renewable Energy Programs*—The Act authorizes $16.8 billion for DOE programs to promote energy efficiency and renewable energy, including:

    - $2 billion for grants for manufacturing advanced batteries and components produced in the U.S. under the program authorized by § 136(b) of the Energy Independence and Security Act of 2007 (42 U.S.C. § 17381 et seq.);

- $3.2 billion for grants to states, local governments, and Indian tribes for improving energy efficiency;
- $3.1 billion for assistance to the states in developing energy conservation programs; and
- $5 billion for assistance to low-income persons for weatherization efforts

13. *Federal Loan Guarantees (Manufacturing)*—ARRA amends EPAct 2005 to provide $6 billion in federal loan guarantees to cover up to 80% of the costs for solar energy projects and facilities that manufacture related components. These projects *will not* be required to meet the "innovative technology" or other requirements of section 1703 of EPAct (which in many cases were difficult to meet for some general renewable projects) and therefore will be available for almost all renewable energy related capital projects that need to be funded with "credit enhancements" to qualify for the granting of credit to the borrower. Eligible projects must commence construction by September 30, 2011. Projects must also pay wages that are in line with the wages paid locally for similar work (Davis Bacon rules) if the project is classified as a "public works" project (generally applicable to most government projects). The program will be administered by the DOE. The $6 billion allocation is expected to generate guarantees on up to $100 billion or more in projects. The guaranty is generally expected to significantly reduce the credit risk in a project and accomplish two things—a lower cost of funding and actual granting of credit on packages that may not have qualified with the guaranty. This alone is one of the most critical components of ARRA for project financiers and developers as well as potential debtors.

At the end of the day, renewable energy companies have received more than $65 billion in tax credits, grants and loans offered through ARRA as of the end of 2011 according to the research company Bloomberg New Energy Finance (BNEF)—an obvious success for the renewable energy sector under anyone's judgment. "Financing for the U.S. renewable sector will look quite different in 2012, compared to the past three years, once the cash grant is gone, but different does not mean dead," according to Michel Di Capua, BNEF's head of North American analysis in New York.

SECTION 1603 TREASURY GRANT

Application Procedures

The application can be completed directly over the internet by going to www.treasury.gov/recovery. A copy of that application is included in Appendix 1 to this book.

For property not placed in service in 2009, 2010 or 2011 but for which construction began in those years, applications must be submitted after construction commences. If the property has been placed in service at the time of the application, Treasury will make payment to the qualified applicant within 60 days from the date the completed application is received. For property not yet placed in service at the time of the application, Treasury will review that application and notify the applicant if all eligibility requirements that can be determined prior to the property being placed in service have been met. If so notified, applicants must then submit, within 90 days after the date the property is placed in service, supplemental information sufficient for Treasury to make a final determination (see below). If an applicant is applying for section 1603 payments for multiple units of property that are going to be treated as a single, larger unit of property, all such units may be included in a single application.

The applicant must also have a DUNS (Data Universal Numbering System) number from Dun and Bradstreet. If you don't have one already, you can request one at no cost by calling the dedicated toll-free DUNS Number request line at (866) 705-5711.

> *"As the economy grows, so will the demand for energy."*
>
> Cliff Stearns, U.S. congressman

When the Treasury determines that an application is approved (having met all the requirements in the application), the applicant will be notified and given 21 days from the date of the notice if additional information needs to be submitted. If the additional information is not received within the 21 day period, the application will be denied. Also, if the application has been denied by the Treasury, the applicant will also be notified and will be given the reason(s) for the termination—the notification will be considered the final agency action on the application.

Remember that the grant is only available for property that is used in a trade or business or held for the production of income (as under a lease or PPA). Therefore, non-business energy property or residential energy efficient property eligible for tax credits under IRS section 25C (non-business energy property) and 25D (residential energy efficiency property) of the IRC do not qualify for the grant.

A copy of the actual application form with the Treasury for the grant (Application for Section 1603 Federal Grant) and an agreement between creditor and debtor (Agreement to Apply Federal Grant to Asset Cost) is found in Appendix 1: Sample Forms.

The application has six principal sections:

1. **Applicant Eligibility**

Remember that certain entities are not eligible for the Grant and this includes: a) federal, state or local governments (or any political subdivision, agency or instrumentality thereof); b) any organization described in section 501 of the Code and exempt from tax under section 501(a) of the Code; c) any entity described in section 54(j)(4) [qualified issuer of Clean Renewable Energy Bonds] of the Code; or d) any partnership or other pass-thru entity which has any of the entities described in (a) through (c) above as a direct or indirect partner, *unless* such ineligible entity owns an indirect interest in the applicant through a taxable C corporation. The guidance clarifies that a foreign person or entity is eligible for a cash payment if at least 50 percent of the income of the person or entity (or shareholder) is subject to US income tax (the exception provided under section 168 (h)(2)(B) of the Code). Those that do qualify are typically entities that are paying taxes and can include a sole proprietorship, joint venture, partnership, domestic C corporation, domestic S corporation, etc. Recognize that the applicant could include the owner of the property or the lessee of the property (would require a waiver from the lessor/owner).

As long as *each* direct and indirect partner in the partnership or shareholder or similar interest holder in any other pass-thru entity is eligible to receive section 1603 payments, the partnership or pass-thru entity is also eligible to receive section 1603 payments. Note also that having as a direct or indirect partner, shareholder, or similar interest holder a taxable C corporation any of whose shareholders are not eligible to receive section 1603 payments does not affect the eligibility of the partnership or pass-thru entity. Neither a Real Estate Investment Trust, nor a cooperative organization described in section 1381(a) of the IRC is a pass-thru entity for this purpose. For an applicant to be eligible to receive a section 1603 payment it must be the owner and must have originally placed the property in service. A foreign person or entity may be eligible for section 1603 payment if the person or entity qualifies for the exception in section 168(h)(2)(B) of the Code. In all cases, the applicant eligibility will be determined as of the time the application is received.

2. **Property Information**

The asset must be depreciable or be property that is public utility property within the meaning of IRC section 168 (i)(10). The application also requires that the physical location of the property be described. Included in the property information section of the application are two critical dates that need to be adhered to:

- "Placed in Service"—The IRS definition of placed in service means *that the property is ready and available for its specific use.* Qualified property must be originally placed in service between January 1, 2009, and December 31, 2011, (regardless of when construction begins) or placed in service after 2011 and before the credit termination date (see table on page 113) if construction of the property begins between January 1, 2009 and December 31, 2011. Qualified *property includes expansions of an existing property* that is qualified property under section 45 or 48 of the IRC.
- "Beginning of Construction"—Construction begins when physical work of a significant nature begins. Physical work of a significant nature begins when the requirement of any one the following options have been met:
  i. **Self Construction**—If an applicant manufactures, constructs, or produces property for use by the applicant in its trade or business (or for its production of income), construction begins when physical work of a significant nature begins (including as described in safe harbor below). Physical work does not include preliminary activities such as planning or designing, securing financing, exploring, or researching.
  ii. **Construction by Contract**—For property that is manufactured, constructed, or produced for the applicant by another person under a written binding contract (as described below) that is entered into prior to the manufacture, construction, or production of the property for use by the applicant in its trade or business (or for its production of income) construction begins when physical work of a significant nature begins under the contract. For example, construction begins when work begins on the excava-

tion for a foundation, the setting of bolts into the ground, installation of support structures on a roof, pouring of concrete foundations, installation of wiring, etc.

A contract is binding *only* if it is enforceable under State law against the applicant or a predecessor, and does not contain damages to a specified amount (for example, by use of a liquidated damages provision). For this purpose, a contractual provision that limits damages to an amount equal *to a least 5 percent* of the total contract price will not be treated as limiting damages to a specified amount. If a contract provides for a full refund of the purchase price in lieu of any damages allowable by law in the event of breach or cancellation, the contract is not considered binding. A contract is binding even if the contract is subject to a condition, as long as the condition is not within the control of either party or a predecessor. A contract will continue to be binding if the parties make insubstantial changes in its terms and conditions or any term is yet to be determined by a standard beyond the control of either party. A contract that imposes significant obligations on the applicant or a predecessor will be treated as binding notwithstanding the fact that certain terms remain to be negotiated by the parties to the contract. An option to either acquire or sell property is not a binding contract. A binding contract does not include a supply, or similar, agreement if the amount and design specifications of the property to be purchased have not been specified.

iii. **Safe Harbor**—An applicant may treat physical work of a significant nature as beginning when the applicant incurs (in the case of an accrual basis applicant) or pays (in the case of a cash basis applicant) more than 5 percent of the total cost of the property (excluding the cost of any land and preliminary activities such as planning or designing, securing financing, exploring, or researching). When property is manufactured, constructed, or produced for the applicant by another person, this test must be met by the applicant, not the other person. For the purpose of determining whether an applicant has incurred more than 5 percent of the total cost of the property, the economic performance standards of IRC section 461(h) apply. Be careful here—rules can vary depending upon whether you are a cash basis tax payer or an accrual basis tax payer.

- "Units of Property"—For purposes of determining the beginning of construction of property or the date property is placed in service, all the components of a larger property are a single unit of property if the components are functionally interdependent. Components of property that are produced by, or for, the applicant are functionally interdependent if the placing in service of one component is dependent on the placing in service of the other component.

  It is important to note that to submit the application for the section 1603 Federal Grant, the project must:

  — have started construction (applicant must state the date that the construction began—this must be after January 1, 2009), and, if the project is not yet complete

  — if the property is not yet placed in service, the anticipated date when the property will be placed in service (see the above table for critical construction completed deadline dates)

  — the applicant must also provide a narrative description of what construction activities have occurred if the project is not already placed in service

3. Applicant Information

The applicant will need to provide their complete contact information including:

- Full address
- Contact person
- DUNS number
- Email address
- Website address (if applicable)

4. Property Description

The applicant will need to select the pre-defined description of the energy property (see Tables 3-2 and 3-3). These are specified properties eligible under section 45 (table 3) or under section 48 (table 4) of the IRC.

In the case of section 48 property (see table below), only the portion of a facility that is described in section 48 of the IRC is taken into account in computing the section 1603 payment. For example, in the case of a building with solar property on its roof, only the cost of the solar property (including the cost of mounting the solar property on the roof, inverters, control panels, monitoring systems, etc.) qualifies for a section 1603 payments—the building does not qualify. Another example would

Table 3-2: Specified Energy Property Eligible for 1603 Grants (Section 45) Energy Property Description (Facility)

Energy Property Description (Facility)
Wind—uses wind to produce electricity (wind turbines with a capacity of 100kW or less may also qualify below as small wind energy property but only one payment is allowed with respect to the property)
Closed-loop Biomass Facility (other than a facility described below)—uses organic material from a plant grown exclusively for purposes of being used to generate electricity. If a portion of fuel is not closed-loop biomass, you will need to give the percentage of fuel, on an annual basis, that is closed-loop biomass.
Facility modified to use closed-loop biomass to co-fire with coal, other biomass, or both—modification must be approved under the *Biomass Power for Rural Development Program* or be part of a pilot project of the *Commodity Credit Corporation*. You will need to give the percentage of fuel, on an annual basis, that is closed-loop biomass.
Open-loop Biomass Facility (cellulosic waste material)—uses solid, non-hazardous, cellulosic waste material or any lignin material derived from qualified sources described in section 45(c)(3)(ii) of the IRC to produce electricity. If a portion of fuel is not open-loop biomass of this type, you will need to give the percentage of fuel, on an annual basis, that is open-loop biomass of this type.
Open-loop Biomass Facility (livestock waste nutrients—uses agricultural livestock waste nutrients to produce electricity and has a nameplate capacity rating of not less than 150 kW. If a portion of fuel is not agricultural livestock waste nutrients, you will need give the percentage of fuel, on an annual basis, that is agricultural livestock waste nutrients.
Geothermal Facility—uses geothermal energy to produce electricity.
Landfill Gas Facility—uses gas derived from the biodegradation of municipal solid waste to produce electricity.
Trash Facility—uses municipal solid waste to produce electricity and is not a landfill gas facility.
Hydropower Facility (incremental hydropower)—produces incremental hydropower production as a result of efficiency improvements and additions to capacity to which the incremental hydropower production is attributable. The baseline and incremental increase in energy production must be certified by FERC (Federal Energy Regulatory Commission).
Marine and Hydrokinetic Renewable Energy Facility—uses marine and hydrokinetic renewable energy to produce electricity and has a nameplate capacity rating of at least 150kW.

be the case of a forklift powered by a fuel cell power plant, the fuel cell may be eligible for a section 1603 payment but the forklift in which it is used is not part of the specified energy property.

Qualified property includes only tangible property that is both used as an integral part of the activity performed by a qualified facility and located at the site of the qualified facility. The qualified property does not include a building *but may include structural components of a building*. Property is an integral part of a qualified property if the property is used directly in the qualified facility, is essential to the completeness of the activity performed in that facility, and is located at the site of the qualified facility. An example would be roadways, paved roads and parking areas located at a qualified biomass facility that is used for transport of material to be processed at the facility or equipment to be used in maintaining and operating the facility and is integral to the activity preformed there. However, roadways or paved parking lots that are provided solely for employee or visitor vehicle traffic are not an integral part of a qualified facility.

In the case of an open-loop biomass, closed-loop biomass, or municipal solid waste facility, an integral part of the qualified facility includes property used at the plant site for unloading, transfer, storage, reclaiming

Table 3-3: Specified Energy Property Eligible for 1603 Grants (Section 48) Energy Property Description

Energy Property Description
Solar Electricity Property—uses solar energy to generate electricity.
Solar Thermal Property—uses solar energy to heat or cool (or provide hot water for use in) a structure, or to provide solar process heat. Note: Property used to generate energy for heating a swimming pool is ineligible under this section.
Solar Lighting Property—uses solar energy to illuminate the inside of a structure using fiber-optic distributed sunlight.
Geothermal Property—equipment used to produce, distribute, or use energy derived from a geothermal deposit.
Fuel Cell Property—fuel cell power plant that has a nameplate capacity of at least 0.5 kW of electricity using an electrochemical process and an electricity-only generation efficiency greater than 30%.
Microturbine Property—stationary microturbine power plant that has a nameplate capacity of less than 2,000 kW and an electricity-only generation efficiency of not less than 26% at ISO conditions.
Combined Heat and Power (CHP) System Property—system that uses the same energy source for the simultaneous or sequential generation of electrical power, mechanical shaft power, or both, in combination with the generation of steam or other form of useful thermal energy and that meets all of the following requirements: 1. System produces at least 20% of total useful energy in the form of thermal energy which is not used for electrical or mechanical power. 2. System produces at least 20% of total useful energy in the form of electrical or mechanical power (or combination). 3. System energy efficiency percentage exceeds 60% (unless system used open or closed loop biomass for at least 90% of the energy source). 4. System does not exceed 50 MW or a mechanical capacity in excess of 67,000 horsepower or an equivalent combination of electrical and mechanical energy capacities.
Small Wind Energy Property—uses a turbine with nameplate capacity of not more than 100 kW to generate electricity.
Geothermal Heat Pump Property—uses the ground or ground water as a thermal energy source to heat a structure or as a thermal energy sink to cool a structure.

from storage, or preparation (shredding, chopping, pulverizing, or screening) of the material to be processed at the plant. However, if the equipment is located away from the plant site, it is not an integral part of the qualified facility.

Property that is integral to a geothermal facility includes equipment that transports geothermal steam or hot water from a geothermal deposit to the site of ultimate use. This includes components of a heating system, such as pipes and ductwork that distribute within a building the energy derived from the geothermal deposit and, if geothermal energy is used to generate electricity, includes equipment that transports hot water from the geothermal deposit to a power plant.

For qualified section 1603 grant property that generates electricity, qualified property includes storage devices, power conditioning equipment, transfer equipment, and parts related to the functioning of those items but does not include any electrical transmission equipment to transport power away from the facility such as transmission lines and towers, or any equipment beyond the electrical transmission stage, such as transformers and distribution lines.

In general, a qualified facility must be capable of operating as an independent unit even though the property is installed at the site of an existing facility. Certain modifications to property installed on an existing facility qualify as specified energy property even if the facility was placed in service before 2009. Be very careful in your documentation and have engineers and design teams clearly show that the equipment is an independent unit and can operate on its own.

Each type of qualified energy specific property has its own unique requirements that are described in the guidance documents. Carefully review the specifications to make sure the renewable energy property subject to the project finance adheres in every way to those requirements. Each type has different criteria. Those specific energy properties include:

- Closed-loop biomass
- Open-loop biomass
- Geothermal
- Landfill gas
- Qualified hydropower
  - Incremental
  - Non-hydroelectric dam
- Marine and hydrokinetic
- Solar
- Qualified fuel cell
- Qualified microturbine
- Combined heat and power systems CHP)
- Qualified small wind energy
- Geothermal heat pump

If the property is to be used predominantly outside the U.S., it would not qualify for the section 1603 payment. The determination of whether property is used predominantly outside the United States is made by comparing the period of time during which the property is physically located outside the U.S. with the period of time during which the property is physically located within the U.S. in a given year. If the property is located outside the U.S. during more than 50% of the year, the property would not qualify since it was used "predominantly" outside the United States.

The original use of the property must begin with the applicant. This means that the property cannot contain more than 20% of the total cost of the project (whether acquired or self-constructed) in used components. If in doubt, it is best to use 100% new parts and components to avoid a project being disqualified. In the applicant narrative describing the property, it is advisable to state that the project contains only new equipment. If it does contain any used parts, state the percentage and describe the reason for the used parts and components keeping in mind the 20% rule.

The applicant must submit supporting documentation demonstrating that the property is eligible property and that it has been placed in service. If placed in service after December 31, 2010, documentation will be required to be submitted to show that construction began in 2009, 2010 or 2011. The documentation that must be provided, as applicable, to demonstrate that the property is eligible would include:

- Design plans (required of all applicants). This would include final engineering design documents, stamped by a licensed professional engineer.

- Documentation demonstrating that the property is designed to have a nameplate capacity that meets required minimums or maximums for properties that have the minimum or maximum nameplate capacities that would include:
  - Open-loop biomass facility (livestock waste nutrients)
  - Marine and hydrokinetic renewable energy facility
  - Fuel cell property
  - Microturbine property
  - Combined heat and power system property
  - Small wind energy property

- The documentation can be included within the required design plans or commissioning report, or with the original equipment manufacturer (OEM)/ equipment vendor specification sheets.

> *"Should you find yourself in a chronically leaking boat, energy devoted to changing vessels is likely to be more productive than energy devoted to patching leaks."*
>
> Warren Buffett, American business

- Documentation demonstrating that the property is designed to meet the electricity-only generation efficiency requirements described in section 4A of the Application (fuel cell property and microturbine property only). The system efficiency is typically calculated as a ratio of the electrical energy output from the device to the amount of fuel consumed to produce the electricity divided by the lower heating value (LHV) of the fuel (if alternating current, be sure to include conversion losses due to parasitic loads). OEM/equipment vendor specification sheets that specify the above values can be used as supporting documentation for nameplate capacity and system efficiency. This documentation can also be included within the required design plans or commissioning report, as long as it specifies the above values.

- For combined heat and power system property only, documentation demonstrating that the system is designed to meet the requirements described in section 4A (*see the forms in the Appendix 1*) of the Application. See IRC section 48 (c)(3) (C) for calculation of the system energy efficiency percentage. This documentation can be included within the required design plans or commissioning report, or with OEM/equipment vendor specification sheets.

- For a closed-loop biomass facility modified to use closed-loop biomass to co-fire with coal, other biomass, or both, documentation demonstrating approval under the Biomass Power for Rural Development Program or documentation demonstrating that the facility is part of a pilot project of the Commodity Credit Corporation.

- FERC (Federal Energy Regulatory Commission) certification (applicable to incremental hydropower production projects only). Certification provided by FERC that certifies the baseline and incremental increase in energy production for incremental hydropower production.

- FERC license (applicable to hydropower facility installed on a qualifying non-hydroelectric dam only).

- To demonstrate that the property has been placed in service (see above), the applicant must provide supporting documentation. There are two principal documents that could be used:
  - Commissioning report—this is required for all projects approved for section 1603 payment anyway. It is generally a report provided by the project engineer, or the equipment vendor, or an independent third party that certifies that the equipment has been installed, tested, and is ready and capable of being used for its intended purpose.
  - Interconnection agreement—generally this agreement is required for property placed in service that is interconnected with a utility. It is a formal document between the applicant and the local utility that established the terms and conditions under which the utility agrees to interconnect with the applicant's system. In many states, the interconnection agreement is also required to be signed off prior to getting any rebates or incentives from the utility or the state under its various renewable energy incentive programs. Applicants must also submit any subsequent documentation to demonstrate that the interconnection agreement has been placed in effect.

- If the project is "under construction" but not yet "placed-in-service," the following documentation must be provided, as applicable, to demonstrate that construction has begun on the property:
  - Paid invoices and/or other financial documents demonstrating that physical work of a significant nature has begun on the property as described earlier. If beginning of construction is based on the safe harbor rule (see above), these documents must demonstrate that *more than 5 percent* of the total cost of the property (excluding the cost of any land and preliminary activities such as planning, designing, securing financing, exploring, or researching) has been incurred or paid by the applicant (IRC section 461(h)). For projects relying on the 5% safe harbor, applicants will need to submit a statement from an authorized representative (or if the property's basis equals $1 million or more, an independent accountant) attesting to the method of accounting used by the applicant including the amount paid/incurred, a description of costs, estimate of total costs, and evidence that costs have actually been paid/incurred (invoices, financial records). If you are relying on costs paid or incurred by a contractor, a copy of the binding written contract and a statement from the contractor explaining the costs paid or incurred and allocated to the applicant's project must be included.

> *"Without passion, you don't have energy, without energy you have nothing."*
>
> Donald Trump,
> American business magnate and author

  - Binding contract (required for property not yet placed in service that is being manufactured, constructed or produced for the applicant by another person). The binding contract required is described earlier.

- If the property is going to be leased, the applicant must provide proof of the written contract with the lessor to demonstrate that the lessor and lessee have entered into the agreement.
- Lastly, the applicant must provide additional information concerning the jobs to be created by the property and the jobs that are retained by the project. This includes both a description of the full time jobs created as well as the part time jobs to be created during the construction stage. The applicant will also be required to declare the amount of full time jobs and part time jobs created over the operational life of the property project. The job tracking is an integral part of ARRA in general. It is one of the ways that will ultimately be used by the government to determine the final impact that the application of the funds under the Act will have had on America.

5. Eligible Cost Basis

The cost basis of the qualified energy property is determined in accordance with the general rules for determining the basis of property for federal income tax purposes. Generally, the basis of property is its cost (see IRC section 1012), unreduced by any other adjustment to basis, such as that for depreciation, and includes all items properly included by the taxpayer in the depreciable basis of the property, such as installation costs, engineering costs, design costs, permit fees and the cost for freight incurred in construction of the specified energy property.

Costs that will be expensed for federal income tax purposes in the year in which they are paid or incurred are not includible in the basis on which the payment is determined. The best example is if the applicant elects to take the IRC section 179 deduction for all or part of the cost of the property, then no payment is allowed for the portion of the cost of the property for which the IRC section 179 deduction has been taken. This is a mistake that could easily be overlooked and therefore the economics of the financing transaction could change dramatically. The regulation is very clear on this issue. Under an IRS audit, the 179 deduction portion of the section 1603 grant payment would have to be refunded to the Treasury if the applicant chose that election. This is a deadly event and should be avoided. It is definitely better to get the cash grant (cash in hand at inception of the project) rather than an additional deduction for half the "net" depreciable basis (taxpayer has a requirement of reducing the depreciable basis of the property by 50 percent of the cash grant received) first year. An example would be for geothermal property. If intangible drilling and development expenses will be expensed by the applicant, no section 1603 payment will be allowed on the costs that will be deducted as intangible drilling and development expenses. On the other hand, if the applicant elects to capitalize and amortize (over the 60 months) the intangible drilling and development expenses, the section 1603 grant payment could include those expenses.

Another structuring point of concern is a limitation on eligible basis on some projects if a portion of the cost of the facility is attributable to a non-qualifying activity. For example, for a biomass facility that burns fuel other than open-loop biomass or closed-loop biomass, the eligible cost basis is the percentage of total eligible costs that is equal to the percentage of the electricity produced at the facility that is attributable to the open-loop biomass and closed-loop biomass. If a portion of the facility that is co-fired with coal or other biomass, it would not qualify. The taxpayer applicant will need to support the request with a detailed breakdown of all costs included in the basis. Other supporting documentation, such as contracts, copies of invoices, and proof of payment will need to be retained and made available to the Treasury upon request.

Any project for which the applicant is requesting a section 1603 payment that has a cost basis in excess of $500,000 must have an independent accountant's certification attesting to the accuracy of all costs claimed as part of the basis of the property. It is easy to forget this requirement and have a request denied or delayed. Moral of the story is to submit an "overabundance" of documentation in every application!

6. Leased Property

A lessor who is eligible to receive a section 1603 payment with respect to a qualified energy property may elect to pass-through the payment to a lessee. The election may only be made with respect to property that would be eligible for the section 1603 payment if owned by the lessee. Therefore, only a taxpaying entity entering into a lease contract with a lessor would qualify. Non-profits and other non-taxpaying entities such as governments and special taxing districts as a lessee would not qualify.

Such an election will treat the lessee as having acquired the property for an amount equal to the independently assessed fair market value of the property on the date the property is transferred to the lessee and will generally follow the rules in the IRC and Treasury regulations governing elections to allow lessees to receive energy tax credits. The lessor and lessee must agree in writing that the lessor waives all right to a section 1603 payment (or a production or investment tax credit) with respect to the eligible property, before the lessee may apply for a section 1603 payment on the property. An interesting effect is that the lessee must agree to include ratably in gross income over the five year recapture period an amount equal to 50% of the amount of the section 1603 payment. This correlates to the fact that the lessor could depreciate the entire asset cost with no reduction in basis for the section 1603 grant payment since the lessor did not directly receive it. This could prove to be a negative for a lessee who wants the right to claim the section 1603 payment. Pricing for the transaction would of course change in the process since the lessor would be giving up a significant amount of cash flow that they would otherwise have received.

In order to make this election, both the lessor and the lessee must be taxpayers eligible to receive a payment under section 1603. Additionally, this election may not be made by a lessor that is a mutual savings bank or similar financial organization, a regulated investment company or a real estate investment trust. This stipulation is a carryover from prior tax law and is not a new concept.

The election of a lessor to allow the lessee to receive a section 1603 payment may be made with respect to each property leased by the lessor to the lessee. The lessee's written consent is required. The lessor's election is made by a written agreement with the lessee that contains all of the following information:

- A waiver of the lessor's right to receive any payment under section 1603 with respect to the property, as well as a waiver of the lessor's right to claim a production or investment tax credit under sections 45 and 48 of the IRC with respect to the same property for the taxable year of the payment or subsequent years—you really didn't think they would let you get by doing so did you?
- All information necessary to determine the amount of lessee's section 1603 payment;
- The name, address, and employer identification number of the lessor and the lessee;
- A description of each property with respect to which the election is being made;
- The date on which possession of the property is transferred to the lessee; and
- The lessee's consent to the election.

A copy of the agreement and election must be included in the lessee's application for the section 1603 payment. The election is irrevocable—no second thoughts allowed.

Grant Guidance and Policy

The grant's economic value to renewable energy projects, relative to the PTC or even the 30% ITC, can be broken down into three non-overlapping components:[1]

1. The grant program reduces the market's dependence on scarce and/or costly third-party tax equity.
2. The grant program also provides significant "direct" or "fact" value to many renewable power projects.
3. The grant also conveys a number of "indirect" or "ancillary" benefits that, although often overlooked, can provide significant economic value to projects. These include full relief from the AMT, elimination of "PTC haircuts" caused by the use of other government grants or subsidized energy financing, the ability to pursue leasing (even to tax-exempt lessees, see page 149) as a viable financing option, compatibility with behind-the-meter projects, relief from passive credit limitations, a reduction in performance risk, and a general preference for cash (a dollar in hand is worth two in the bush...).

As can be seen from Table 3-4 (accurate as of March 1, 2010), the grants have had a positive economic effect across all renewable technologies.[2]

As of October 31, 2011, the Department of Treasury[3] reports that 22,747 projects have been funded by the 1603 grant program for a total of more than $9.6 billion since the program began in 2009! The technology percentages were approximately the same as they were in the prior table above from Lawrence Berkeley National Laboratory in 2009. The state of Texas received the largest total dollar amounts followed closely by California.

Recent documents released from the IRS and the U.S. Department of Treasury show increased scrutiny on the grant program. Disagreements between Treasury and grant recipients regarding the calculation of the 1603 grants appeared shortly after the program be-

Table 3-4: Technologies Receiving 1603 Treasury Grants

Technology	Number of Projects	Grants Awarded ($)	% of Grants Awarded
Biomass	8	$ 72,509,889	2.8%
Combined Heat & Power	2	436,473	0.0%
Fuel Cell	4	2,770,235	.1%
Geothermal Electric (new equipment)	2	2,224,148	.1%
Geothermal Electric (new plant)	4	152,383,474	5.9%
Geothermal Heat Pump	4	54,853	0.0%
Hydropower (incremental)	2	4,078,644	.2%
Landfill Gas	4	12,864,644	.5%
Solar Heat & Hot Water	20	839,906	0.0%
Solar Photovoltaic	280	94,940,363	3.7%
Solar Thermal Electric (new equipment)	1	2,913,273	.1%
Solar Thermal Electric (new plant)	1	19,543,649	.8%
Wind (small)	20	883,009	0.0%
Wind (large)	40	2,225,671,487	85.9%
Total:	392	$ 2,592,114,057	100%

gan. The Treasury department faced legal challenges for refusing to pay part or all of the grants it deemed ineligible. On January 18, 2011, in the case *ARRA Energy Co. I v. United States,* the court ruled that Treasury could not simply refuse to award grants it deemed ineligible. This finding raised the question of how much Treasury is allowed to scrutinize the reported FMV costs of a renewable energy system. Some have argued that the court decision directed the Treasury department not to withhold grants; instead they must determine whether each reported FMV cost should be included or excluded from the eligible basis. This argument is supported by the document released April 13, 2011 by Treasury which provides updated guidance on how it reviews grant applications. Scrutiny of the grants do not end after they are given. Treasury has recently released reports on projects that have received treasury grant awards and been subsequently audited to determine whether the award amount is correct—going back to the issue of "FMV" of the renewable energy assets. Because the Treasury department and the IRS want to make sure that government funds are being distributed legally they are paying particularly close attention to how the cost of systems are calculated.

To be eligible, a property must be placed in service in 2009, 2010, or 2011 or placed in service after 2011 but only if construction of the property began during 2009, 2010, or 2011. Properties placed in service after 2011 must be placed in service by the credit termination date.

Property eligible to receive section 1603 payments is "specified energy property." Specified energy property includes only tangible personal property (not including a building) that is an integral part of the facility. It is further defined in sections 1.48-1(c) and (d) of the IRC. Specified energy property is also defined as property for which depreciation is allowable.

The guidance provides that the original use of the property must begin with the applicant. However, the sale-leaseback rules are applicable—if the property is placed in service by a person, sold to an applicant and then leased back by the applicant to the person that placed the property in service within 90 days of the "placed-in-service date," the original use begins with the applicant/lessor and the property is considered to be placed in service when it is first used under the leaseback. A word of caution: be careful of possible negative effects if state laws prevent such an event without incurring a second sales tax on the transaction.

In a sale-leaseback, the guidance states that the lessee may receive the cash payment if the following three conditions (for federal IRS rules—not necessarily for state rules) are satisfied:

1. The lessee must be the person who originally placed the property in service
2. The property must be sold by and leased back

to the original lessee within three months of the placed-in-service date

3. The lessee and lessor must not make an election out of the sale-leaseback rules

The guidance also permits a lessor (who is eligible to receive the Treasury grant) to pass through the cash payment to a lessee (who is also eligible to receive a Treasury grant). In order to make the election, the property must be eligible to receive a Treasury grant if such property is owned by the lessee. If an election is made (and which must be documented between the lessee and lessor), the lessee will be treated as having acquired the property for an amount equal to the independently assessed fair market value of the property on the date the property is transferred to the lessee. The election will generally follow the rules in the Code and the Treasury regulations governing lessee pass-through elections. The guidance provides additional rules and requirement regarding the election.

> *"The Texas Energy Office's Loan Star Program has reduced building energy consumption and taxpayers' energy costs through the efficient operation of public buildings, saving taxpayers more than $172 million through energy efficiency projects."*
>
> Rosa DeLauro, congresswoman from Connecticut

Taxpayers electing to receive the cash grant in lieu of the tax credit should remember that if the qualified property is disposed of within a five-year recapture period, or otherwise ceases to be specified energy property, or is disposed of to a disqualified person, recapture of the cash grant amount will occur in a manner similar to the operation of the investment tax credit provisions. The recapture percentages are as shown in Table 3-5.

Be careful about to *whom* you sell the property during the recapture period—you may be required to recapture and repay 100% of the section 1603 payment received. Specified energy property is considered to have been disposed of to a "disqualified person" if any interest in the property or in the applicant or in any partnership or pass-thru entity that is a direct or indirect owner of an interest in the applicant is sold to:

- Any Federal, state or local government, including any political subdivision, agency or instrumentality thereof;
- Any organization that is described in section 501(c) of the IRC and is exempt from tax under section 501(a) of the IRC; or
- Any entity referred to in paragraph (4) of section 54(j) of the IRC or any partnership or other pass-thru entity any partner (or other holder of an equity or profits interest) of which is a Federal, state or local government, including any political subdivision, agency or instrumentality thereof.

A taxable corporation, some or all of whose shareholders are disqualified persons, is not a disqualified person and such a corporation's ownership of an interest in a partnership or other pass-thru entity will not cause the partnership or other entity to be treated as a disqualified person.

Additionally, energy property may cease to qualify as a specified energy property if the use of the property changes so that it no longer qualifies as specified energy property. For example, this could occur if the property use changes so that it is used predominantly outside the U.S. (see above). Interestingly, the guidance states that if the property use permanently stops as qualified because of a natural disaster, it will not result in a recapture.

Selling or otherwise disposing of the property to an entity other than a disqualified person does not result in recapture provided the property continues to qualify as a specified energy property and provided the purchaser of the property agrees to be jointly liable with the applicant for any recapture. Recapture would occur, how-

Table 3-5: Recapture of Section 1603 Grant Provisions

If sold or disposed of within:	Recapture Amount
One year from the date placed in service	100%
After year one but before 2 years of being placed in service	80%
After year two but before 3 years of being placed in service	60%
After year three but before 4 years of being placed in service	40%
After year four but before 5 years of being placed in service	20%
After five years of being placed in service	None

ever, in the event the property is resold to a disqualified person or ceases to qualify as a specified energy property. The applicant remains jointly liable to the Treasury for the recapture amount even if the applicant no longer has control over the property. This provision is different than that which has been in place for recapture of the Investment Tax Credit in general. Under the prior IRC, any sale of the property by the original owner (pursuant to the recapture provisions shown in the table above) would result in a recapture regardless of whether the property remained in use in the same manner as used by the original owner or not.

> *"The energy produced by the breaking down of the atom is a very poor kind of thing. Anyone who expects a source of power from the transformation of these atoms is talking moonshine."*
>
> Ernest Rutherford, British Physicist (born New Zealand) (1933)

Applicants are not required to post a bond as a condition of receiving payment under the section 1603 program and receipt of payment does not create a lien on the property in favor of the United States. However, funds that must be repaid to the Treasury under the recapture rules are considered "debts" owed to the United States and if not paid when due, will be collected by all available means against any assets of the applicant, including enforcement by the United States Department of Justice. Debts arising under these rules are not considered tax liabilities. This again is different than under the prior IRC Investment Tax Credit rules.

Applications must be submitted before December 31, 2011. The Treasury Department must pay the grant by 60 days after the later of: (a) the date of the application, or (b) the date the facility is placed in service. In the real world however, payments of the grant by the government can easily exceed 120 days. Remember, the grant is not available to any governmental agency, tax-exempt entity, or rural electric cooperative.

Applicants may submit, along with their request for payment, a Notice of Assignment, assigning the payment to a third party (limited to a single payee, not multiple parties) provided the requirements of the Federal Assignment of Claims Act (31 U.S.C. 3727) are met. The Notice of Assignment will need to include the DUNS number for the third party (see the sample form in Appendix 1). The request must comply with the following requirements:

- Corporation
  - Executed by an authorized representative;
  - Attested by the secretary or the assistant secretary of the corporation; and
  - Impressed with the corporate seal or accompanied by a true copy of the resolution of the corporation's board of directors authorizing the signing representative to execute the assignment.
- Partnership
  - Assignments by a partnership may be signed by one partner, if the assignment is accompanied by adequate evidence that the signer is a general partner of the partnership and is authorized to execute assignments on behalf of the partnership.
- Individual
  - Assignments by an individual shall be signed by that individual and the signature acknowledged before a notary public or other person authorized to administer oaths.

Fortunately, the section 1603 payment does not make the property or project subject to NEPA (National Environmental Protection Act) as many other grants by the government do. Also, the 1603 payment is not subject to the requirement of the Davis-Bacon Act that mandates many prevailing wage requirements for certain projects.

Once the section 1603 payment is received, the applicant has an annual reporting requirement to the Treasury including an annual performance report. Often, this requirement is forgotten about once the grant has been received—particularly on smaller projects. A good example of this is vendors or suppliers who have received the grant through an assignment. They should follow up on each project with the applicant to make sure the reporting is being done to avoid a possible enforcement action by the IRS against them to enforce the requirement. This is a five year requirement (the vesting period for the section 1603 payment). The annual performance reports are due no later than 21 days following the end of the reporting period. The first reporting period begins on the date the property is placed in service (see placed-in-service requirement above). Items that need to be included in the annual report are:

- Name of applicant
- Current owner of property
- Treasury application number
- Name of project

- Location of project: city/county/state/zip
- Number of jobs retained
- Annual production (in kilowatt hours, MMBtus, or horsepower as applicable)
- Installed nameplate capacity (in kilowatts, MMB-tus, or horsepower as applicable)
- Possible other information or reports as mandated by Treasury in the future

The applicant must maintain project, financial, and accounting records on an on-going basis sufficient to demonstrate that section 1603 funds were properly obtained in accordance with the section 1603 program and the terms and conditions thereof. The Treasury (and the authorized representatives) will have the right of physical access to the applicant's facilities and to any pertinent books, documents, papers, or other records (electronic and otherwise) of the applicant and each partnership and pass-thru entity that directly or indirectly owns an interest in the applicant which are pertinent to the section 1603 payment, or order to conduct audits, examinations, and evaluations.

Additionally, the Treasury has the right to publicly release the name of the applicant; the type, location, and description of the property that is the subject of the application; and the amount of funding provided. Therefore, be careful that the information you provide to the Treasury in the documentation does not contain any proprietary data and technical information.

This cash grant provision has the potential to be a very important tool for alternative energy investments. By operation, the cash grants, in effect, are a refundable income tax credit benefiting developers that might not otherwise be able to utilize tax credits or find investors in the tax credit syndication market. Moreover, by providing renewable energy developers the ability to monetize these tax credits directly through an application to the Treasury, presumably fewer transaction costs will be incurred and more subsidy will flow to the project rather than to the transaction underwriters.

> *"We need to become energy independent or at least aspire to that."*
> Thomas Friedman, Pulitzer prize winning author

Tables 3-6 and 3-7 show two very important results. First, it makes very little difference in the underlying yield on a transaction whether the lender/investor elects to take the ITC or cash grant in lieu of the ITC. Secondly, the underlying yield goes up dramatically when the lender/investor leverages the transaction with a loan equal to 50% of the equipment cost in the finance project. The pretax effective MISF yield goes up 48% when a 20 year PPA finance leveraged structure (in this case, 50%) is used on the project. The real eye-opener is when looking at a 10-year operating lease project finance structure. The pretax effective MISF yield goes up an astounding 431% when the transaction is leveraged with 50% debt and the ITC is used rather than the cash grant! Even when using the cash grant option in an operating lease, the yield increase using 50% debt goes up by over 200%.

With both structures, it is assumed that a loan could be obtained for a ten year term for 50% of the project cost, 8% interest, paid monthly and fully amortized over the 10 year term with a fixed payment. The dramat-

Table 3-6: ITC vs. Cash Grant in Lieu of ITC Yields Utilizing a *PPA Structure*

	Pre-Tax MISF Yields (effective)	After-Tax MISF Yields (effective)
Utilizing ITC—No Loan	10.8675%	6.7107%
Utilizing ITC—50% Loan	16.1073%	9.9463%
Cash Grant—No Loan	10.6222%	6.5592%
Cash Grant—50% Loan	16.2697%	10.0465%

Table 3-7: ITC vs. Cash Grant in Lieu of ITC Yields Utilizing an *Operating Lease Structure*

	Pre-Tax MISF Yields (effective)	After-Tax MISF Yields (effective)
Utilizing ITC—No Loan	12.1346%	7.4931%
Utilizing ITC—50% Loan	64.4036%	39.7692%
Cash Grant—No Loan	11.7069%	7.2290%
Cash Grant—50% Loan	37.2196%	22.9831%

ic increase occurs simply because the loan is for 50% of the project term with a PPA and 100% of the project term with the operating lease. In both cases there is adequate cash flow to service the underlying debt from the project receipts.

Because of the difficulty in finding tax equity players in most renewable projects, perhaps the most used basic project finance structure under ARRA will be:

- 30% cash grant (in lieu of the ITC)
- 20% equity
- 50% debt (loans or equity)

This assumes that the debt cost and terms will be acceptable to the owner of the project. For example if the maximum loan available for the project is less than 50%, if the cost of debt would be too high, or most critical—if the debt term would be less than a 10-year amortization time, then the returns shown in the above tables would change considerably and could actually make the project produce a negative return.

- High quality financial modeling is the key to maximizing the benefits available to a taxpayer when selecting the correct financial structure, including:
- Selecting ITC, PTC or cash in lieu of ITC
- Ability to use 100% of the credits or the cash grant in the current tax year
- Ability to allocate tax losses to a non-corporate investor in a project financed with nonrecourse debt—the introduction of cash grants in lieu of ITC are assumed to be not subject to the at-risk and passive activity loss rules that can limit individual investors' ability to benefit from the PTC and the ITC

There have been a number of potential concerns with the section 1603 grant program.[4] The program was created and implemented with great speed and excitement in the renewable energy sector. The perceived problems include free-ridership (and its cost), the fact that the grant rewards "investment" rather than "performance" (which could *potentially* lead to "gold-plating" and/or poor performance), the location of job support (i.e., foreign versus domestic), and a few other concerns surrounding the short window of opportunity, the continued need for tax equity in some cases, and uncertainty over state tax treatment. Free-ridership means that the project would have been built anyway and did not need the grant.

Although the 1603 grants are specifically exempted from Federal taxation by statute, individual states are free to choose whether or not to tax the grant. Many states conform to Federal tax treatment, but some do not. Perhaps most notably, California considers Section 1603 grants to be taxable at the state level, but the legislature there is working on a way to waive such taxes.

SECTION 1705 LOAN GUARANTEES

The new section of the ARRA relating to DOE loan guaranties is section 1705. Title XVII states the guaranty is available for projects that "avoid, reduce, or sequester air pollutants or anthropogenic emissions of greenhouse gas; and employ new or significantly improved technologies as compared to commercial technologies in service in the United States at the time the guarantee is issued." Title XVII section 1702(d) also requires a "reasonable prospect of payment" of any loan or debt obligation issued to a project and the project should be using technology that is mature enough to assure dependable commercial operations and generate sufficient revenues to repay the loan or debt obligation.[5]

"Commercial Technology" means a technology in general use in the commercial marketplace in the U.S. at the time the Term Sheet is issued by DOE. A technology is in general use if it has been installed in and is being used in three or more commercial projects in the U.S., in the same general application as in the proposed project, and has been in operation in each commercial project for a period of at least five years. The five year period is measured, for each project, starting on the in service date of the project or facility employing that particular technology.

Section 1705 under ARRA adds three additional types of technologies to those in section 1703 and they are renewable energy systems, transmission projects and leading edge biofuel projects—regardless of whether they employ "new or significantly improved technology." The original technologies identified ten discrete categories of projects:

1. Renewable energy systems;
2. Advanced fossil energy technology (including coal gasification meeting the criteria in subsection 1703(d));
3. Hydrogen fuel cell technology for residential, industrial, or transportation applications;
4. Advanced nuclear energy facilities;
5. Carbon capture and sequestration practices and

technologies, including agricultural and forestry practices that store and sequester carbon;

6. Efficient electrical generation, transmission, and distribution technologies;
7. Efficient end-use energy technologies;
8. Production facilities for fuel efficient vehicles, including hybrid and advanced diesel vehicles;
9. Pollution control equipment; and
10. Refineries, meaning facilities at which crude oil is refined into gasoline.

As one can see, the "big" ten above generally implies that the projects to be guaranteed under EPAct 2005 (original section 1703 loan guaranty originated under this Act) were going to very large energy projects and not small residential or small commercial project that might cost between $5,000 and $10 million. Rather, they would generally be $10 million or more. The application fees that would need to accompany the application for guarantee also reflected the size of the large projects. In general the fees for the application were broken down into three segments as follows (with 25% of the fee due under the initial application and 75% due after the initial application was approved):

Segment I—Application (First Fee)

Table 3-8: ARRA Guarantee Segment I Fees

Loan Guarantee Amount	Total Fee Amount
$0-$150 million	1% of the Guaranteed Amount
$150 million to $500 million	$375,000 + .75% of the Guaranteed Amount
Above $500 million	$1,625,000 + .50% of the Guaranteed Amount

Segment II—Facility (Second Fee)

Table 3-9: ARRA Guarantee Segment II Fee

Loan Guarantee Amount	Total Application Fee Amount	25% of Application Fee Due When Applying	75% of Application Due Upon DOE Notification
$0-$150 million	$75,000	$18,750	$56,250
$150 million to $500 million	$100,000	$25,000	$75,000
Above $500 million	$125,000	$31,250	$93,750

Segment III—Maintenance (Third Fee)

Maintenance fees are payable to cover DOE's administrative expenses in servicing and monitoring the Loan Guarantee Agreement during the construction, startup, commissioning and operational phases of a project. The amount of such fee is expected to be in the range of $50,000 to $100,000 per year and will be either (i) payable each year in advance, commencing upon the closing date of the Loan Guarantee Agreement, or (ii) if provided for the Loan Guarantee Agreement, payable as a one-time fee at the closing in a lump sum amount equal to the aggregate sum of such annual fees specified in the Loan Guarantee Agreement for the entire term of the loan guarantee, discounted to net present value.

As can be seen, those are some incredibly large sums of money payable to the government and those fees don't even cover the lender's fees, placement fees or legal costs. A twenty year loan guarantee guaranty could easily see fees that reach 25% of the original project cost. No wonder that in the first three years after the program was established, only a handful of applications were received and only one was finally approved. DOE won't state whether it was ever put in place however, since the information is proprietary and did not need to be disclosed to the public.

One final nail in the coffin for fees with the DOE is that on top of the above fees, they will also charge the applicant for other costs and expenses in accordance with section 1702(H). Those costs and expenses are in the form of technical review, financial analysis, credit investigations, legal opinions and other due diligence fees in general incurred. These are administrative expenses to evaluate the Pre-Application and Comprehensive Application, prepare the offering, negotiation and closing of the loan guarantee and to service the loan guarantee and monitoring of the progress of the project over the entire project life covering the loan guarantee.

In keeping with the notion that ARRA funding should only be used for "shovel ready" projects, the DOE is only interested in providing a guarantee for projects that:

- Have received all necessary licenses, permits and local and national environmental clearances necessary to proceed;
- Completed all pre-construction design and prototype testing;
- Engaged all required contractors and ordered all necessary essential equipment and supplies so that physical construction of such project has commenced or may commence on or before September 30, 2011 (last date an application will be considered by the DOE).

This is truly a "catch 22" situation. Most project developers would never proceed to those levels without having all funding arranged and that would include any government guarantees. The biggest risk would be that of the government issuing a guarantee to a lender who in turn would not proceed to a loan commitment without such a guarantee. The costs incurred to that point would be prohibitive for most project developers in the cleantech renewable energy or energy efficiency sector.

Conceptually, ARRA provided for up to $2.5 billion to cover credit subsidy costs of a project that would qualify for funding under ARRA. The requirement is not mandated by statute but reflects an apparent policy decision by DOE which has broad statutory discretion regarding the deployment of ARRA funds. Future guidance and policies will clearly define where and how DOE utilizes these discretionary funds.

The DOE guarantee will become available through a solicitation process with multiple "rounds." In addition, the DOE will evaluate the applications received in each round using Table 3-10 in their weighting criteria.

The guarantee most likely would be for 80% of the project cost (excluding the guarantee subsidy costs) but the DOE would have discretion for either a larger or smaller amount. The guarantee would be issued to eligible lenders and could include any individual or legal entity, approved by DOE, formed for the purpose of, or engaged in the business of, lending money, including, but not limited to, commercial banks, savings and loan institutions, insurance companies, factoring companies, investment banks, institutional investors, venture capital investment companies, trusts, or other entities designed as trustee or agents acting on behalf of bondholders or other lenders.

As currently being applied, there can be only one guarantee issued under the program on a single project from a "Project Sponsor." Guarantees on multiple projects would not be allowed. A project sponsor is defined as any individual, firm, corporation, company, partnership, association, society, trust, joint venture, joint stock company or the like that assumes substantial responsibility for the development, financing, and structuring of a project eligible for a loan guarantee and owns or controls the Applicant. Hence, it appears that the likely format would be to have a Host under an Energy Purchase Agreement, a borrower under a term loan or a lessee under a lease agreement be the applicant so that a project developer or renewable energy lender would not be limited in any way for getting DOE guarantees under ARRA for the various projects that it would be involved in. There is a great deal of confusion on this issue and only time will tell what the end method to be employed for applying for the guarantee will be and who the specific Applicant will be. The DOE is still promulgating rules that will be applied.

Table 3-10: DOE ARRA Guarantee Review Criteria

Factors	Detail	Weighting
Technical	Technical Relevance and Merit	10.0%
	Applicant Capabilities, Technical Approach and Work Plan	20.0%
	Environmental and Energy Security Benefits	20.0%
Financial	Creditworthiness	30.0%
	Construction Factors	10.0%
	Legal and Regulatory Factors	10.0%
	Total	100.0%

The process to obtain the guarantee is a two-step process. The first step is called a "Pre-Application" and if approved by the DOE, the second step is to submit a "Comprehensive Application" that requires a great amount of additional detailed information. As an example, the second step would need to include the following items:

- A detailed description of all material amendments, modifications, and additions made to the information and documentation provided in the Pre-Application, including any changes in the proposed project's financing structure or terms;
- A detailed description of the nature and scope of the proposed project, including key milestones, detailed information on location of the project (including legal description and current use of the facilities), identification and commercial feasibility of the new or significantly improved technologies to be employed in the project, how Applicant intends to employ such technologies in the project, and how the Applicant or others intend to assure the further commercial availability of the technologies in the United States;
- A detailed explanation of how the proposed project qualifies as an Eligible Project;
- An estimate of the amount of the total Subsidy Cost for the project, including a description of the methodology used for this calculation and any supporting documentation;
- A detailed description of the construction contractor(s) and equipment supplier(s), construction schedules for the project including major activity and cost milestones as well as the performance guarantees, performance bonds, liquidated damages provisions, and equipment warranties to be provided;
- A detailed description of the operations and maintenance provider(s), the plant operating plan, estimated staffing requirements, parts inventory, major maintenance schedule, estimated annual downtime, and performance guarantees and related liquidated damage provisions, if any;
- A description of the management plan of operations that Applicant will employ in carrying out the project, and information concerning the management experience of each officer or key person associated with the project;
- A detailed description of the project decommissioning, deconstruction and disposal plan and the anticipated costs associated therewith;
- An analysis of the market for the product(s) to be produced by the project, including relevant economics justifying the analysis, and copies of any contractual agreements for the sale of these products or assurance of the revenues to be generated from sale of these products;
- A detailed description of the overall financial plan for the proposed project, including all sources of funding, equity, and debt, and the liability of parties associated with the project over the lifetime of the requested loan guarantee;
- A copy of all loan documents that Borrower and Lender will sign if the Application for a loan guarantee is approved, containing all of the terms and conditions of the loan or other debt obligations to be guaranteed, including the proposed amount of the loan, interest charges, repayment position, principal repayment schedule, fees, pre-payment and late payment penalties, and cure rights;
- A copy of all material agreements, whether entered into or proposed, relevant to the investment, construction and commissioning of the project;
- A copy of the financial closing checklist for the equity and debt;
- Applicant's business plan on which the project is based and project pro forma statements for the proposed life of the loan guarantee, including income statements, balance sheets, and cash flows. All such statements should include assumptions made in their preparation and the range of revenue, operating cost, and credit assumptions considered;
- Financial statements for the past three (3) years that have been audited by an independent certified public accountant, including all associated notes, as well as interim financial statements and notes for the current fiscal year, of Applicant and parties relevant to Applicant's financial backing, together with business and financial interests of principal organizations, if appropriate, such as parent and subsidiary corporations or partners of Applicant;
- A copy of all legal opinions, engineering reports, and other material reports, analysis, and reviews related to the project;

- Credit history of Applicant and, if appropriate, any party who owns or controls a five percent or greater interest in the project or the Applicant;
- A preliminary credit assessment for the project without a loan guarantee from a nationally recognized rating agency (this requirement is waived for projects of less than $25 million);
- A list of all project-related applications filed and approvals issued by Federal, state and local government agencies for permits and authorizations to site, construct, and operate the project. If still outstanding, the Application should contain an estimation of completion for any required filings and approvals;
- A report containing an analysis of the potential environmental impacts of the project that will enable DOE to assess whether the project will comply with all applicable environmental rules and regulations, including how, and to what measurable extent, the project avoids, reduces, or sequesters air pollutants or anthropogenic emissions of greenhouse gases, including how Borrower intends to verify those benefits;
- A listing of assets associated, or to be associated, with the project and any other asset that will serve as collateral for the guaranteed loan and assure repayment of the loans and other debt obligations of the project, including appropriate data as to the value and useful life of any physical assets and a description of any other associated security and its value. With respect to any ownership interest in a real property asset described above or any pledged asset that is not part of the project, an appraisal should be performed by state licensed or certified appraisers that is consistent with the "Uniform Standards of Professional Appraisal Practice," promulgated by the Appraisal Standards Board of the Appraisal Foundation;
- An analysis demonstrating that at the time of the Application, there is a reasonable prospect that Borrower will be able to repay the loan or other debt obligation to be guaranteed (including interest) according to its terms, and a complete description of the operational and financial assumptions on which this demonstration is based;
- Written affirmation from an officer of the Lender confirming that Lender is an Eligible Lender in good standing with DOE's and other agencies' loan guarantee programs; and
- Such other information requested in the solicitation or invitation to submit an Application necessary for a complete assessment of the loan guarantee application for the project.

As can be seen from the above basic requirements, this would not be a task to be undertaken lightly. There will obviously be a considerable amount of expense involved in the preparation of these items. Although many of these items would normally be undertaken on any significant renewable energy project financing, it could be more than some project developers, lenders and debtors would be willing to undertake just to get a government guarantee that "might" enhance the financing structure. Great care needs to be taken to make sure that time and costs to do so don't become so onerous as to kill the project entirely.

Assuming that the application is completed entirely and reviewed by the DOE based on the factors above, it will be submitted to the "Credit Review Board" of the DOE. If the project is deemed to be suitable for a loan guarantee, because, among other things:

1. It qualifies as an Eligible Project;
2. There exists a reasonable expectation of payment based on the materials provided in the Application;
3. The proposed project will advance the President's Advanced Energy Initiative.

Then the DOE will notify the Borrower and the Lender in writing and provide them with a copy of a proposed "Term Sheet." That term sheet will cover items such as terms and conditions of the loan guarantee and will determine the Subsidy Costs. The term sheet becomes a "conditional" commitment if both DOE and Applicant agree to the proposed terms and conditions and sign the Term Sheet.

This Conditional Commitment will specify the required payment of fees, other documents, availability of authority provided and set a closing date. Then the DOE will enter into a Loan Guarantee Agreement with the Applicant that satisfies the specified conditions precedent if and only if all funding and other contractual, statutory and regulatory requirements have been satisfied. Prior to the issuance of that Loan Guarantee Agreement the DOE will:

- Determine the project qualifies as an Eligible Project under the Act;

- The project will be constructed and operated in the United States and the technology is or is likely to be available in the United States for further commercial application;
- The debt to be guaranteed by DOE is limited to no more than 80 percent of the total Project Costs;
- The amount of the loan guarantee does not exceed 80 percent of the total face value of the loan or other debt obligation of the project, or provides sufficient evidence to support a guarantee exceeding 80 percent (but in no event 100 percent);
- Applicant and other principals involved in the project have made a significant equity investment;
- The prospective Borrower is obligated to make full repayment of the guaranteed loan over a period of up to the lesser of 30 years or 90 percent of the projected useful life of the project's major physical assets, as calculated in accordance with generally accepted accounting principles and practices (also taking into account the engineering reports);
- The loan guarantee does not finance, either directly or indirectly a Federal tax-exempt obligation. Accordingly, the loan guarantee may not be used for a Federal tax-exempt obligation or serve as collateral to secure a tax-exempt obligation;
- The guaranteed portion of a loan must not be separated from or "stripped" from the non-guaranteed portion of the loan and resold in the secondary debt market;
- The amount of the loan guaranteed, when combined with other funds committed to the project, will be sufficient to carry out the project, including adequate contingency funds;
- There is a reasonable prospect of repayment by Borrower of the principal and interest of the Guaranteed Obligations;
- The prospective Borrower has pledged project assets and other collateral or surety, including non-project-related assets, as determined by the Secretary of DOE to be necessary as assurance for the repayment of the loan;
- The Loan Guarantee Agreement and related documents must include detailed terms and conditions as appropriate to protect the interest of the U.S. in the case of default, including ensuring availability of all intellectual property rights, technical data including software, and physical assets necessary for any person selected, including, but not limited to, the Secretary, to be reasonable, taking into account the range of interest rates prevailing in the private sector for similar Federal government guaranteed obligations of comparable risk;
- The guaranteed loan is not subordinate to any loan or other debt obligation for the project, not part of the Guaranteed Obligations and is in a first lien position regarding all assets of the project and all collateral security pledged;
- There is satisfactory evidence that Borrower is willing, competent, and capable of performing the terms and conditions of the loan or the debt obligation and the loan guarantee;
- The Lender is not a Federal entity, possesses sufficient financial wherewithal and expertise, and will exercise the requisite standard of care as deemed necessary by the Secretary and state in DOE's lender eligibility criteria in Section VI of the guidelines;
- Lender or other parties servicing the loan and monitoring the project should be satisfactory to the Secretary. In addition, the Secretary will need to find that the Lender and other appropriate parties will exercise a high level of care and diligence in the establishment and enforcement of the conditions precedent to all loan disbursements and the Borrower covenants throughout the term of the loan and that each Lender will be required to diligently perform its duties in the servicing and collection of the loan as well as in ensuring that the collateral package securing the loan remains uncompromised. The Lender will also provide annual or more frequent periodic financial reports on the status and condition of the loan, and is required to promptly notify DOE if it becomes aware of any problems or irregularities concerning the project or the ability of the Borrower to make payment on the loan or other debt obligations. Even though DOE will rely on Lender (or other servicer) to service and monitor the loan with utmost care and expertise, Lender's responsibilities with respect to the loan are separate from DOE's own monitoring and review of the loan and the project;
- As specified in the Conditional Commitment, the prospective Borrower makes payment of the fee for the Administrative Cost of Issuing a Loan Guarantee pursuant to section 1702(h) of the Act. While covering the other costs included in the Administra-

tive Cost of Issuing a Loan Guarantee, this payment will not include the servicing and monitoring costs identified in the guidelines. These latter costs will be assessed in accordance with the Loan Guarantee Agreement which will require payment of administrative fees to the Federal government by Borrower, either directly or through the Lender, periodically thereafter for the duration of the loan guarantee. DOE intends to use all of the fees mentioned above to defray administrative expenses associated with issuing and monitoring loan guarantees;

- DOE representatives have access to the project site at all reasonable times in order to monitor the performance of the project;
- DOE and Borrower will need to reach an agreement as to what project information will be made available to DOE and which project information will be made publicly available;
- The Borrower will have filed applications for or obtained any required regulatory approvals for the project and is in compliance with all Federal and state regulatory requirements;
- Applicant has no delinquent Federal debt, including tax liabilities, unless the delinquency has been resolved with the appropriate Federal agency in accordance with the standards of the Debt Collection Improvement Act of 1996; and
- The Loan Guarantee Agreement contains such other terms and conditions as the Secretary deems reasonable and necessary to protect the interest of the United States.

The Lender must also meet certain eligibility requirements. Those general requirements are:

- The Lender is a "non-Federal qualified institutional buyer," as defined in 17 CFR 230.144A(a), including qualified retirement plans and governmental plans;
- The Lender is not a party debarred or suspended from participation in a Federal government contract (under 48 CFR 9.4) or participation in a non-procurement activity;
- The Lender is not delinquent on any Federal debt or loan;
- The Lender is duly organized and legally authorized to enter into the transaction;
- The Lender is able to demonstrate experience in originating and servicing loans for commercial deals similar in size and scope with the project under consideration; and
- The Lender is able to demonstrate experience or capability as the lead lender or underwriter of other energy related projects.

Now, let's cover what can be included in the Project Costs. All costs must first of all be recorded in accordance with generally accepted accounting principles and practices. The Applicant should calculate the sum of reasonable and customary costs that it has paid and expects to pay and which are directly related to the project. Those costs include, but are not limited to:

- Costs of acquisition, lease or rental of real property, including engineering fees, surveys, title insurance, recording fees, and legal fees incurred in connection with land acquisition, lease or rental, site improvements, site restoration, access roads, security requirements and fencing;
- Engineering, architectural, energy audits, legal and bond fees, and insurance paid in connection with construction of the facility; and materials, labor, services, travel and transportation for facility construction, startup, tests and final commissioning;
- Equipment purchase and startup testing;
- Costs to provide equipment, facilities, and services related to safety and environmental protection;
- Financial and legal services costs, including other professional services and fees necessary to obtain required licenses and permits and to prepare environmental reports and data;
- Interest costs and other normal charges affixed by Lenders;
- Necessary and appropriate insurance and bonds of all types;
- Costs of startup, commissioning and shakedown;
- A reasonable contingency reserve for cost overruns during construction;
- Capitalized interest necessary to meet market requirements, reasonably required reserve funds and other carrying costs during construction;
- Costs of obtaining licenses to intellectual proper-

ty necessary to design, construct, and operate the project; and

- Other necessary and reasonable costs approved by the Secretary.

> *"Here's what I think the truth is: We are all addicts of fossil fuels in a state of denial, about to face cold turkey. And like so addicts about to face cold turkey, our leaders are now committing violent crimes to get what little is left of what we're hooked on."*
>
> Kurt Vonnegut, American writer

Of course, there are items that are not allowed to be included in the project costs and those include:

- Fees and commissions charged to Borrower, including finder fees, for obtaining Federal funds;
- Parent corporation's general and administrative expenses, and non-project related parent corporation assessments, including organizational expenses;
- Goodwill, franchise, trade, or brand name costs;
- Dividends and profit sharing to stockholders, employees, and officers;
- Research, development, and demonstration costs of readying the energy technology for employment in a commercial project;
- Costs that are excessive or are not directly required to carry out the project, as determined by the Secretary;
- Administrative Cost of Issuing a Loan Guarantee paid by the Borrower;
- The Subsidy Cost of the loan guarantee; and
- Operating expenses incurred after startup, commissioning and shakedown.

The Holder of the guarantee (in most cases the Lender) will have to properly enforce the terms and conditions of the Loan Guarantee Agreement to collect the payments from the Borrower. If those procedures don't produce the required repayment of the loan or debt instrument, the Lender can make demand on the DOE to pay the balance of the Loan Guarantee Agreement and the DOE has 60 days to do so. All obligations from the DOE would be classified as AAA debt obligations with the full faith and backing of the United States Government. The result is that the guarantee would be very marketable in the secondary market should the Holder elect to sell the obligation.

Not mentioned above but required as part of the evaluation by the DOE is an emissions evaluation analysis. The applicant will be required to compile and submit a worksheet (in Excel format) concerning an evaluation of NO_X, SO_2 and greenhouse gas emissions, as well as the avoided emissions, associated with the project. This is done by applying a standardized evaluation methodology employing a comprehensive lifecycle inventory approach and is required irrespective of the Applicant conducting its own project analysis of emissions. The greenhouse gases evaluation section includes not only carbon dioxide (CO_2), but other greenhouse gases (e.g., methane, N_2O, CO, CH_4). The Applicant will also need to quantify other air emissions such as particulate matter (PM10 and PM2.5), SO_2, NO_X, VOCs and Mercury). Other items that will need to be listed and analyzed include types of fuel used, solid wastes (municipal, hazardous, combined wet solids, etc.) and water usage and discharges. This approach will be applied to direct emissions from all processes including combustion, purchased electric power and avoided emissions within the electric power grid. In the case of emissions related to electric power, a region-specific time-matched marginal approach to emissions analysis will be used. The applicant will need to include complete process flow diagrams that details each process involved in the project—from cradle to grave. The diagrams will need to include processes related to all material, chemical and electricity inputs, transportation, manufacturing, fuel processing, distribution, etc. There is a special section of the analysis for biomass and biofuels.

One final item is the requirement for frequent reporting to DOE. Most of the reporting relates to the "Jobs Accountability Act." Not later than 10 days after the end of each calendar quarter, each recipient of a Loan Guarantee from the DOE will need to submit a report that contains:

- The total amount of guarantee received;
- Name of the project;
- The status of the project;
- An estimate of the number of jobs created and the number of jobs retained by the project;
- Other funds received on the project from state and local governments, the purpose, total cost, and rationale of the agency for funding the other portions of the project; and
- Detailed information on any subcontracts or subgrants on the project.

These reports will be made public by posting the information on a website.

Lastly, ARRA provides $3.1 billion for the State Energy Program, designed as a flexible federal-state partnership implemented by state energy offices to provide additional funds that do not need to be matched by state funds. This important change from prior legislation allows the states to leverage federal funds to match state, local and private efforts for funding energy efficiency, renewable energy, and a wide variety of energy measures. The prior program had only $50 million available and hence ARRA increases the amount of funds by over 60 times—and without the usual strings attached to the use of funds (requiring the typical state/local matching fund requirement)! The funds are to be distributed based on high energy consumptions. Therefore, states that have higher energy consumption get a higher percentage of the available funds. The only catch is that the funds will only be available to states that intend to adopt (or have adopted) strict building energy codes and incentivize the utilities to adopt energy efficiency measures.

The energy tax provisions in the Act put into action many of the current administrations promises to implement a "green" economic recovery plan. Historically, current tax laws to promote renewable and alternative energy as well as conservation have generally enjoyed broad bipartisan support. However, they have been enacted in a piecemeal fashion and on a temporary basis. Everyone agrees (and have suggested) that the sporadic nature, frequent lapses, and short term extensions have created uncertainty in the marketplace, limited their relative effectiveness, and impeded long-term investment and development. This Act extends and modifies a number of the existing energy incentives and adds some important new ones.

There is a great deal of information, rules and regulations in ARRA that have not had final treasury comments at the time this book is published. This makes it very important that lenders, investors and project developers stay abreast of the new developments as they occur and remain ready to react as the new guidelines and rules are promulgated (and sure to be redefined and amended over time).

STATE LEGISLATION

The research firm Clean Edge[6] looks annually at how the states compare based on various clean energy metrics. Table 3-11 is their current assessment of the top 10 states for clean energy in the U.S. Not only did California rank as number one in terms of clean energy deployment, but they also ranked number when it came to attracting venture capital.

Table 3-11: Top 10 States for Clean Energy

Rank	State	Score
1	California	95.3
2	Oregon	79.4
3	Massachusetts	71.8
4	New York	63.1
5	Colorado	60.2
6	Washington	60.0
7	New Mexico	57.0
8	Minnesota	57.0
9	Connecticut	56.9
10	Vermont	53.2

State legislative action closely follows the ranking above. Those higher ranking states for clean energy are also the most active when it comes to new legislative actions each year.

In the 2011 legislative sessions alone, states introduced nearly 1000 bills related to renewable energy with more than 140 enacted. These bills include a range of incentives, training for green jobs, directives on the use of federal funds, comprehensive energy policies, net metering, updates to renewable portfolio standards, and more. This number continues to increase each year and so do the complexities with the laws as it relates to renewable energy project financing. Below is a sampling of the state legislation currently under consideration or enacted in 2011:[7]

- *Financing Renewable Energy Projects*
  Financing renewable energy projects was a major trend in 2011 legislation with over 10 states enacting legislation related to financing projects. Most legislation focused on financing tools such as loans, bonds and rebates. Two states repealed certain financing mechanisms for renewable energy projects.

  Loans:
  California, Nevada, Texas, Virginia and Wyoming enacted bills relating to renewable energy loans.
  — California's bill required the Alternative Energy and Advanced Transportation Financing Authority to administer a Clean Energy Upgrade Program to reduce property owner costs of a loan provided by a financial

institution.

- — Nevada's bill authorized the director of the Fund for Renewable Energy, Energy Efficiency and Energy Conservations Loans to provide loans for the construction of renewable energy systems.
- — Texas aimed to promote the use of renewable energy technology in a pilot program under the loanstar revolving loan program.
- — Virginia gave localities the authority to secure loans for the initial acquisition and installation of clean energy programs.
- — Wyoming authorized the adoption of energy improvement programs by local governments to provide energy improvement loans to property owners—many other states have authorized similar property assisted clean energy (PACE) finance programs.

Bonds

New Hampshire and New Mexico enacted bills relating to bonds for renewable energy projects.

> *"Is it a fact—or have I dreamt it—that, by means of electricity, the world of matter has become a great nerve, vibrating thousands of miles in a breathless point of time?"*
>
> Nathaniel Hawthorne, U.S. author (1804 - 1864)

- — New Hampshire's bill established that financing may be provided through issuance of municipal revenue bonds for clean energy districts.
- — New Mexico created the "renewable energy transmission bonding fund" which will pay the interest on bonds issued pursuant to the New Mexico Renewable Energy Transmission Authority Act.

Rebates

Maine provided rebates for cost-effective renewable energy technologies.

Cost-Recovery

- — Hawaii directed the Public Utilities Commission to investigate an On-Bill Financing Program for residential electric utility customers in order to finance renewable energy devices through their utility bills.
- — Indiana allowed for the recovery of renewable energy project costs through rate adjustments of projects undertaken by an energy utility in order to comply with federal clean air requirements.

Financial Assistance

- — California amended an existing law to include thermal energy systems in the definition of renewable energy programs that meet the requirements for financial assistance from the State Alternative Energy and Advanced Transportation Financing Authority.
- — Indiana qualified certain waste and methane as renewable energy resources allowing them to receive financial incentives.
- — Virginia enacted a bill which adds renewable energy projects to those projects which the Virginia Resources Authority may finance.

Finance Authorities

- — California enacted a bill which authorizes community facilities to finance energy improvements to real property and buildings.
- — Virginia created the Universities Clean Energy Development and Economic Stimulus Foundation to identify and administer funding for research and development of clean energy production.

- *Tax Incentives*
  Nine states enacted bills relating to tax incentives for renewable energy projects.
- *Project Siting and Land-Use*
  Nine states enacted legislation relating to renewable energy project siting and land-use.
- *Ownership Rights*
  Kansas, Montana, Oklahoma and Wyoming enacted bills relating to renewable energy ownership rights of surface property.
- *Homeowners Associations*
  Illinois and Texas enacted legislation regarding homeowners associations and renewable energy systems.
- *Exemptions from Regulations*
  California and Hawaii enacted legislation that exempts specific renewable energy projects from certain regulations.

- *Renewable Energy Districts*
  Arizona and Illinois enacted bills relating to renewable energy districts – designated districts that may produce renewable energy.

- *Net Metering*
  Seven states enacted legislation regarding net metering, which allows small renewable energy system owners generate energy and receive credit for the electricity they generate.

  Net metering programs are an important incentive for getting consumers to invest in renewable energy generation. Net metering lets them use their own generation to offset their consumption over a billing period by allowing their electric meters to turn backwards when they generate electricity in excess of their demand. Net metering is viewed as essential to successfully integrating rooftop solar, small wind and other distributed renewable generation systems.

- *Self-generation*
  California and Texas enacted legislation concerning self-generation.

- *Solar Energy*
  Nine states enacted legislation specifically relating to solar energy. Much of this legislation was enacted in order for property owners to be able to install solar devices with less restrictions.

- *Wind Energy*
  Seven states enacted legislation specifically relating to wind energy.

- *Renewable Energy-General*
  - Maine enacted a bill that aims to reduce energy prices for consumers by stating that investor-owned utilities only enter into contracts as agents for their customers.
  - Montana enacted 2 bills that revise their state energy policy and focus on the promotion of alternative energy.
  - Nevada eliminated the Renewable Energy and Energy Efficiency Authority and the position of Energy Commissioner.
  - Oregon assigned ownership of certain renewable energy certificates to the owner of the facility generating the renewable energy.
  - Rhode Island enacted a bill that creates a board to develop and recommend a strategic renewable energy plan for the state and also enacted another bill which facilitates and promotes installation of grid-connected generation of renewable energy.
  - Virginia stated that an electric cooperative is deemed to offer an approved tariff for electric energy that is 100 percent from renewable resources.
  - Vermont enacted a bill titled, "Energy Act of 2011" which is a comprehensive state energy bill focusing on renewable energy.

As can be seen from this very small sampling of actions taken, state legislative actions can play a very vital role in the financing of cleantech renewable energy projects throughout the U.S. Drilling down into each of these individual laws can reveal a great deal about both the process of getting energy legislation passed as well as the impact it could have on any given energy project. It can't be overemphasized enough how important it is to being informed on existing and pending legislation in your state as it relates to the project being financed. Even after a project is built and funded, on-going legislative activity could play a significant role in the ultimate returns and asset management of a renewable energy project.

Although state legislative actions clearly define project issues on a regional basis, don't overlook the federal actions that are described throughout this chapter. Combine the two and a reader can easily see just how complex things can get when considering the salient points in renewable energy project finance.

The first area any project will come face to face though is on the "local" level as project construction permits are applied for or evaluated for costs and compliance. It is beyond the scope of this book to look into the myriad of issues that could arise on just the local level for a single project, yet it is at the local level that most projects are first evaluated for feasibility.

REGULATORY COMPLIANCE

The fear of non-compliance by companies in America is daunting and yet the cost of measuring that fear in quantifiable terms is often difficult. The sources of those fear factors can come from many directions. Those could include the following and often include more than one single source:

- Environmental compliance

- Securities compliance including Sarbanes Oxley, Dodd-Frank, SEC and others
- Industry regulators such as FERC (Federal Energy Regulatory Commission), Public Utilities Commissions, NERC (North American Electric Reliability Corporation), FDA (Food and Drug Administration), OSHA (Occupational Safety and Health Administration), etc.
- Insurance regulators
- Local, State and Federal agencies that issue operating permits on air, water, solid waste, storm water discharge, etc.
- GHG regulations like AB32 in California

Although in some cases these compliance costs can be measured, in others they cannot be or are legislated but not yet clearly enough defined. A good example of the first is in the renewable portfolio standards (RPS) established in some states by which electrical utilities must generate a certain amount of the electricity they sell to their customers from renewable sources.

Let's compare two states—California and New Jersey. California is a "voluntary" compliance RPS state in the sense that there is a requirement that all investor owned utilities (IOUs) in the state get 20% of the energy they sell from renewable sources by 2010—there is no fiscal "penalty" for non-compliance. New Jersey however, has a penalty associated with a similar compliance mandate for their RPS. As a result, a renewable energy certificate (REC) in California is currently selling for $6.00. That same REC if it were generated in New Jersey had reached a value of over $800.00![8] This is a clear example of both the qualitative impact compliance has, as well as the different costs associated with that compliance mandate on a regional level.

> *"I have no doubt that we will be successful in harnessing the sun's energy… If sunbeams were weapons of war, we would have had solar energy centuries ago."*
>
> George Porter, British chemist (1972)

The California utilities, realizing that the California Public Utilities Commission may soon impose a "penalty" for non-compliance, are now taking significant steps to acquire their own renewable energy generation facilities, or will be seeking ways to purchase the RECs attributable to energy generated from renewable energy assets. In March 2010, the CPUC voted unanimously to approve tradable renewable energy credits (T-REC). The new rules said that the REC can be trade separately from the underlying energy produced by a renewable generating facility. These energy credits can then be applied, by the utility, toward their renewable energy compliance goals.

A flurry of controversy erupted immediately. The three large investor owned utilities (IOUs) in the state (SDG&E, SCE and PG&E) filed petitions to modify the decision. Then on January 13, 2011, the CPUC rejected the petitions and reaffirmed the original March 11, 2010 ruling (with some minor modifications). Therefore, the rules going forward all on the use of Tradable RECs, including out-of-state generation, now need to meet compliance requirements under California's RPS. However, there were two restrictions:

1. T-RECs can only be used to meet 25% of a utilities compliance obligation
2. Transactions are capped at $50 per T-REC

Furthermore, California just raised its RPS from 20% renewables by 2020 to 33% *renewables by the same year*. This is a huge challenge for the utilities and, they need to get the electricity generated by those resources to the places where it will be consumed—an even more difficult job. The responsibility for that job rests with the California Independent System Operator Corporation (ISO). The ISO needs to make sure that it has a reliable, cost-effective transmission system with adequate interconnections. The latest iteration of the ISO's annual transmission plan proposes 29 new "reliability-driven transmission projects" that have an estimated cost of nearly $650 million. Currently, California ISO has 25,865 circuit-miles of transmission lines.

In 2011, the number of proposed solar projects in California were 4 ½ times the level needed by the state to meet its 33 percent renewable power target by 2020. California is the biggest U.S. solar market and will likely remain so for the next decade. Could this mean the California will become the "Saudi Arabia" of solar energy? The CPUC (on February 3, 2012) announced that renewable energy efforts in 2011 resulted in the greatest increase in renewable generation since the beginning of the program. They said that more than 830 megawatts of new renewable capacity came on line—all of which was wind and solar PV projects. Collectively, the state's large investor owned utilities served 17 percent of their electricity with renewable energy sources in 2010.

There could be a catch in that scenario however.

According to Timothy Alan Simon who is a commissioner with the California Public Utilities Commission (the CPUC regulates the power utilities in California), only about six percent of new project proposals in 2011 won approval by their agency. A recent glut of solar panels drove prices down by as much as 50 percent in 2011. Those price declines have helped many installers and system integrators to sell more systems into the market. Some bids for large scale solar PV projects in California that are to be built and operational in 2015-2016 were being submitted to the utilities for the sale of the energy as low as 7 cents/KWh. This is a remarkable achievement and likely to compete with wind energy on some new energy projects. It is obvious that competition between solar developers has become fierce and creative financing mechanisms have provided the developers the tools needed to achieve these prices. **GRID PARITY!!**

California also has passed legislation that requires power plants using coastal and estuary waters for cooling be retrofitted, repowered or retired by 2017. The state's two nuclear plants have until 2024 to do this. The legislation affects 11 natural gas plants in addition to the nuclear plants. The implication is that there will be an increase in renewable power supplied over the grid transmission lines in the very near future as some of the plants will be closed resulting in a need for additional renewable energy production to fill the gap. Keeping a reliable transmission system is part and parcel of supporting renewable energy production integration and could have a significant risk to developers and lenders of the renewable technologies.

Rapidly evolving carbon reduction (GHG emissions) requirements and legislation is another example—either on a federal and state level. Mandatory reduction mandates with differing implementation deadlines further complicate the compliance issue. A company with facilities in different regions or states can face different costs and different compliance schedules that are dramatically different, depending on the physical location of each facility. Therefore, a "national" compliance schedule that meets all the company's needs nationwide is almost impossible and the costs attributable to that mandate cannot be equally spread for implementation in a coherent manner.

A final quagmire affecting regulatory compliance as it relates to renewable energy certificates and energy production is the fact that in most states the REC is used in the state for compliance needs whereas the energy that correlates to the REC may have been produced in a nearby state and the bifurcation of the energy from the REC is very difficult. That is, the REC demand is state specific but the supply relating to the energy production may not be.

References

1. M Bollinger, "Preliminary Evaluation of the Impact of the Section 1603 Treasury Grant Program on Renewable Energy Deployment in 2009," Lawrence Berkeley National Laboratory.
2. Ibid
3. U.S. Department of the Treasury, Overview and Status Update of the §1603 Program, October 31, 2011
4. M Bollinger, "Preliminary Evaluation of the Impact of the Section 1603 Treasury Grant Program on Renewable Energy Deployment in 2009," Lawrence Berkeley National Lab.
5. Federal Register, Vol. 71, No. 156, Monday, August 14, 2006
6. http://www.cleanedge.com
7. National Council on State Legislatures, http://www.ncsl.org
8. The price has now dropped to $245 in New Jersey and is $540 in Massachusetts.

Chapter 4

External Components of the Financial Analysis

Parties wishing to structure the ideal financing for a cleantech renewable energy or energy efficiency project need to carefully consider both external and internal components of the structure. In this chapter we will review some of the external components that need to be addressed, quantified, monetized and documented when the finance structure is developed. In many cases, the external components bring a revenue stream to the project and in still other cases the external components only affect policy issues. Whether that revenue source is large, small or aggregated, it becomes a significant ingredient and can play a very large role in the economics of the project. The external components are items like energy savings, efficiency savings, rebates and incentives, projected utility rate increases over the project life, etc. These external components are normally in the form of "revenue" sources that will contribute to the payments scheduled under the project finance agreement. Some of the more significant external components of the financial analysis are highlighted below.

OVERVIEW

The most significant external component to enhancing returns to the parties in the renewable energy project are federal tax credits and to a lesser extent, state tax credits when available. Whether the creditor has used them to increase yield in the finance structure or the debtor has negotiated their use by the creditor and thereby having monetized their value and received a lower cost of financing, their role in the financial analysis and resultant finance structure cannot be underestimated. The government policy for the continued expansion and use of tax credits to stimulate growth by targeting certain segments of the economy are best exemplified by looking at the following tax acts enacted in just the past 6 years—all which have tax credits as a key element:

- Energy Policy Act of 2005
- Katrina/GO Zone Acts of 2005
- Tax Relief and Health Care Act of 2006
- Small Business and Work Opportunity Act of 2007
- Housing and Economic Recovery Act of 2008
- Emergency Economic Stabilization Act of 2008
- American Recovery and Reinvestment Act of 2009 (ARRA)
- The Tax Relief, Unemployment Insurance Reauthorization, and Job Creation Act of 2010

Corporate tax is imposed in the United States at the Federal, most state, and some local levels on the income of entities treated for tax purposes as corporations. Federal tax rates on corporate taxable income vary from 15% to 35%. State and local taxes and rules vary by jurisdiction, though many are based on Federal concepts and definitions (e.g., California top marginal corporate tax rate is 8.84%). Taxable income may differ from book income both as to timing of income and tax deductions and as to what is taxable. Corporations are also subject to a Federal Alternative Minimum Tax and alternative state taxes. Like individuals, corporations must file tax returns every year and they must make quarterly estimated tax payments. Controlled groups of corporations may file a consolidated return.

INTERNAL REVENUE CODE SECTION 45 ENERGY TAX CREDITS

The Energy Policy Act of 2005 (and subsequent "annual" tax code changes) made many changes to section 45 of the Internal Revenue Code of 1986, as amended (the "Code"). The purpose of this section of the components is to set out the requirements for claiming the tax credit, the resources and facilities that qualify for the section 45 energy tax credit (alternatively known as the production tax credit). This section will also discuss the entities eligible for claiming the energy tax credits, the requirements for such entities to be created and passing the energy tax credits on to the investors in the entity. As part of the Energy Improvement and Extension Act of 2008, the ITC, which previously existed for solar power, fuel cells and microturbines, expanded to include small wind, geothermal heat pumps, and combined heat and power (CHP) systems. Under ARRA of 2009, the ITC was further expanded to include wind.

> *"Never spend your money before you have it."*
>
> Thomas Jefferson (1743 - 1826)

The federal tax credits and incentives are integral to project economics and include:

- IRC Section 45 Production Tax Credit (PTC)
- IRC Section 48 Investment Tax Credit (ITC)
- ARRA Section 1603 Treasury Grant
- MACRS tax depreciation deductions

Property is generally not eligible for the ITC or Treasury Grant if it is "used" by a governmental unit or tax-exempt entity. However, a much more detailed section (see page 149) looks carefully at this issue and defines what type of debt contract is needed to avoid this pitfall.

The two types of federal tax credits that create the highest visibility in renewable energy projects are investment tax credits (IRC §48) and energy production tax credits (IRC §45). Investment tax credits are available when an investment in qualified property has been made by acquisition, rehabilitation or construction (e.g. solar, clean coal, etc.) and usually have a 5-year recapture period if the asset is sold before the fifth full year of ownership. This tax credit is sometimes referred to as "going green." Energy credits (IRC §48—commonly referred to as a PTC or Production Tax Credit) are available when an asset owned by a taxpayer is producing energy from a qualified energy resource (or in some cases qualified fuels) and includes energy efficient commercial building property (*see the chapter on Energy Efficiency, page 195*).

Both the PTC and the ITC can be applied directly towards a taxpayer's tax bill. But, unlike the PTC, the ITC is equal to a percentage of the project's qualified capital expenditure, and is not linked to production of energy. To make use of the ITC, projects have to be placed in service by December 31, 2012 for wind, December 31, 2014 for biomass and December 31, 2016 for the remaining energy systems.

Table 4-1. Green Tax Credits

Credit Type	Credit Amount	Credit Period	Extended Through (under 2009 tax act)
Investment Tax Credit	• 30% solar & fuel cell • 10% stationary microturbine	Investment Based	12/31/2016
Production Tax Credit	• 2.2 cents/KWh (wind) and adjusted annually for inflation	10 years	12/31/12 for Wind 12/31/2013-Other
Energy-Efficient Commercial Building Deduction	Up to $1.80 per sq ft	Investment based	12/31/2013
Energy-Efficient Appliance Credit	$45 to $250 with various limitations	Per appliance	12/31/2010
Energy-Efficient New Home	$2,000	Per Dwelling Unit	12/31/2009
Residential Energy-Efficient Property	• 30% solar • $4,000 wind • $2,000 geothermal heat pump	Investment based	12/31/2016
Energy-Efficient Improvements to Existing Homes	• 10% • $50 to $300 various limitations	Investment based	12/31/2009

Table 4-1 highlights the most common tax credits for going green.

Now, let's look more closely at specifically the renewable energy tax credits that are based on the "annual production" from the qualified resource or facility with the following table. All of these credits are based on production levels achieved and are in some cases called "production tax credits" (IRC §45).

Most all types of tax credits will require that their value be reduced if there has been any type of subsidized energy financing, grants, tax-exempt bonds or other such credits as part of the finance structure for the project.

In most cases, the depreciable basis on the assets is reduced by 50% of the ITC taken, must be used in a trade or business, and must meet performance standards. Credits for solar and wind facilities are components of the general business credit. As such, they cannot exceed the taxpayer's net income tax reduced by the taxpayer's tentative minimum tax (or, if greater, by 25% of the taxpayer's regular tax in excess of $25,000). Credits that cannot be used under this limitation can be carried back one year and carried forward up to 20 years.

Transaction Structuring

Under general case law principles in the case of *Sacks v. Commissioner,*[1] the tax court upheld a tax-motivated leveraged-lease program involving solar equipment. In Sacks, an investor (Mr. Sacks) purchased, for cash and a recourse note, solar heating equipment from a company known as BFS Solar. BFS leased back the equipment and then subleased it to homeowners. The Ninth Circuit held that the investor was entitled to claim depreciation deductions for investments in the solar equipment, based on these facts:

1. Mr. Sacks was personally obligated to pay the purchase price.
2. He paid fair market value for the equipment.
3. The tax benefits would have existed for someone, either BFS Solar or Mr. Sacks, so the transaction shifted them but did not create them from thin air.

> *"First, there is the power of the Wind, constantly exerted over the globe… Here is an almost incalculable power at our disposal, yet how trifling the use we make of it!"*
>
> Henry David Thoreau,
> U.S. author and naturalist (1817-1862)

4. The business of putting solar water heaters on homeowners' roofs was genuine.
5. The business consequences of a rise or fall in energy prices and solar energy devices were genuinely shifted to Sacks by the transaction.

The court also held that the absence of a pre-tax profit motive did not make the investment a sham: "if the government treats tax-advantaged transactions as shames unless they make economic sense on a pre-tax basis, then it takes away with the executive hand what it gives with the legislative.

It is also important to note when equipment that is normally eligible for the ITC or PTC becomes ineligible if:

1. **Property used outside the U.S.**
2. **Property is used for lodging**

However, this will not apply to lodging facilities if:

Table 4-2. Production Tax Credits from Renewable Energy Projects

Qualified Renewable Resource/Facility	Credit Amount for 2011**	Credit Period	Extended Through (under 2009 tax act)
Geothermal	$0.022 per kWh*	10 years	12/31/2013
Wind	$0.022 per kWh*	10 years	12/31/2012
Closed-loop Biomass	$0.022 per kWh*	10 years	12/31/2013
Open-loop Biomass	$0.011 per kWh*	10 years	12/31/2013
Small Irrigation Power	$0.011 per kWh*	10 years	12/31/2013
Landfill Gas	$0.011 per kWh*	10 years	12/31/2013
Marine & Hydrokinetic	$0.011 per kWh*	10 years	12/31/2013

*Adjusts for inflation
**Sale of energy production to unrelated person is required

- Non-lodging commercial facilities which are available to persons not using the lodging facilities on the same basis as they are available to persons using the lodging facilities;
- Property used by a hotel or motel in connection with the trade or business of furnishing lodging where the predominant portion of the accommodations is used by transients;
- A certified historic structure to the extent of the portion of the basis which is attributable to qualified rehabilitation expenditures; and
- Any energy property.

3. **Property used by certain tax-exempt organizations**
Unless such property is used predominantly in an unrelated trade or business the income of which is subject to tax under IRC section 511

4. **Property used by governmental units or foreign persons or entities** (*see procedures on page 149*).

OTHER IMPORTANT EXTERNAL COMPONENTS FOR RENEWABLE ENERGY PROJECTS

There are many other important external components available to the renewable energy project (they are applicable in various projects and are very project and region specific) and are described in more detail below.

Clean Renewable Energy Bonds (CREBs)

As part of H.R. 6, the Energy Tax Incentives Act of 2005 (EPAct or simply, the "Act," created in July 2005 and signed into law on August 8, 2005), congress created a number of incentives that have driven the cleantech renewable energy business in the United States. Arguably, many have called that Act the largest stimulus for the renewable energy business ever implemented. One of the little known incentives was that of the creation of CREBs. It permits State and local governments, cooperative electric companies, clean renewable energy bond lenders and tribal Indian governments to issue CREBs for the finance of both renewable energy projects and clean coal facilities. However, almost all of the bonds to date have been used to finance renewable energy projects. In the first year, 610 projects had been approved by the IRS throughout the U.S. Overall, there were 709 total applications from 40 different states and the District of Columbia requesting allocations for authority to issue approximately $2.6 billion in CREBs to finance 786 projects. There were 231 proposed projects in California, 67 in New Mexico, 64 in Minnesota, 41 in New Jersey, 38 in Montana, 27 in Colorado, 24 in Massachusetts, 13 in New York and 12 in Ohio. The size of the proposed projects in the applications ranged from $23,000 to $80 million.

CREBs are a form of tax credit bond, a relatively new type of debt instrument, in which interest on the bonds is paid in the form of federal tax credits by the Federal government in lieu of interest paid by the issuer. End result is that the CREB provides qualified borrowers/issuers with the ability to borrow funds at no interest. The federal tax benefit to the bond holder is greater than the benefit derived from tax-exempt municipal bonds. This is accomplished because the tax credit resulting from the CREB would be used to offset, on a dollar-for-dollar basis, a bond holder's tax liability in the year that the bond was purchased instead of excluding from current income the interest from other tax exempt bonds. The tax credit can be applied by the taxpayer against both the regular and alternative minimum tax liability. As a comparison to another valuable component of the Act, the regular ITC obtained under the Act on renewable energy assets can only be applied against the regular minimum tax liability. Therefore, a CREB provides an excellent tax vehicle for the taxpayer to maximize their leverage from the funding of a renewable energy project.

A complete description of the IRS Code can be found at *http://www.irs.gov/pub/irs-drop/n-06-07.pdf* and *http://www.irs.gov/pub/irs-drop/n-07-26.pdf*.

The CREB Program Mechanics

Initially, section 54 of the Internal Revenue Code of 1986 set up the concept of a CREB that was in the form of Qualified Zone Academy Bonds (QZABs). Section 54 provided tax credits in lieu of interest. QZABs were used mostly by schools and other education agencies.

The CREB is:

- Issued by a qualified issuer
- Issued pursuant to an allocation by the Secretary of the Treasury when CREB funds are available
- At least 95% of the proceeds are to be used for capital expenditures on one or more qualified projects within five years of issuance (issuer must enter into a binding commitment within 6 months of the date of issue with a third party to spend at least 10% of the proceeds of the issue)
- The issuer designates such bond as issued under section 54 and it must be registered

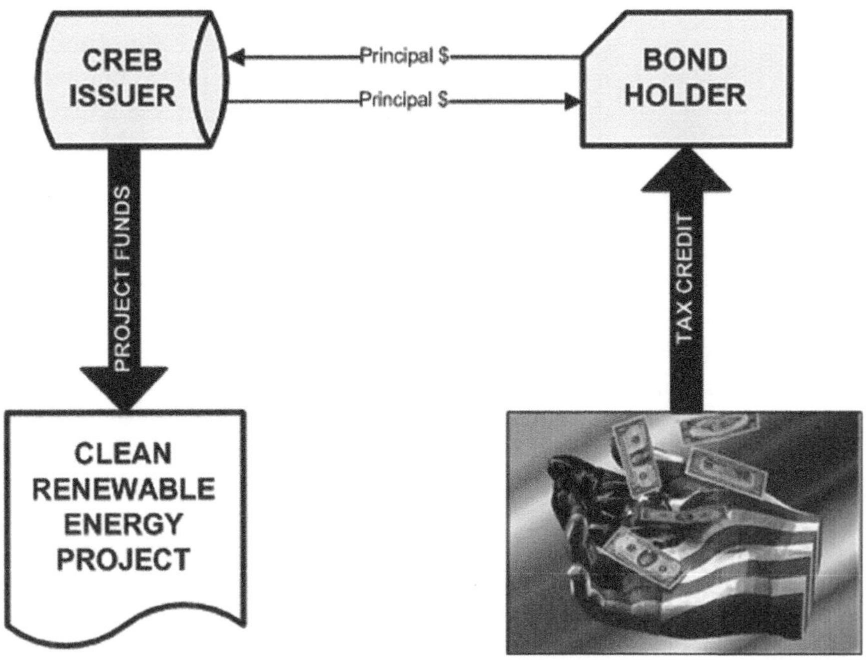

Figure 4-1: CREB Structure

- The issuer must meet applicable spending requirements

A qualified project is a renewable energy facility described in section 45(d) of the Internal Revenue Code of 1986, without regard to the placed-in-service date requirements under that section. These facilities are: wind energy facilities, open-loop and closed-loop biomass facilities, geothermal energy facilities, solar energy facilities, small irrigation power facilities, landfill gas facilities, trash combustion facilities, refined coal production facilities and certain hydropower facilities (incremental hydro or hydropower added to existing dams).

A qualified issuer includes State and local governments, U.S. territories and possessions, the District of Columbia, Indian tribal governments, CoBank, Cooperative electric companies and the National Rural Utilities Cooperative Finance Corporation.

An allocation cap is established periodically by the Secretary of the Treasury. The Act provides no specific guidance to the Secretary regarding the allocation process. Funds that are allocated are then provided to the issuer on a "first-come, first-served" basis. Initially that allocation was set at $800 million. This was subsequently amended in 2006 to an increased level of $1.2 billion. Then under the 2008 Energy Improvement and Extension Act signed into law in August 2008, an additional amount of $300 million was added plus up to $800 million of Qualified Energy Conservation Bonds.

The CREBs program was not left out of the ARRA in 2009 either. ARRA provided another $1.6 billion to the program raising the total to $2.4 billion.

The new deadline was set for August 4, 2009 for submittal of applications and was valid for three years from the date the IRS issued them. Also, the IRS has determined that facilities "functionally related and subordinate" to the generation facility itself are also eligible for CREB financing. Examples would be auxiliary components such as transmission lines and interconnection upgrades. To obtain an allocation, a qualified issuer is required to submit an application to the IRS.

Each application must: 1) identify the qualified borrower expected to own the project, 2) if any of the bonds are expected to be issued as pooled financing bonds (the League of California Cities though its joint power authority has proposed doing just that with its member cities), demonstrate that the qualified issuer will enter into a written loan commitment with each qualified borrower prior to the issue date of the bond issue (e.g., in California, the League of California Cities though its joint power authority), 3) describe in detail the project to be financed with the proceeds of the bonds, 4) demonstrate that the project will constitute a qualified project (certified by an independent, licensed engineer that it will be qualified project and technically viable), and 5) contain a detailed description of the plan of financing. The allocation is done on a project-by-project basis by the IRS staff with no authority to each of the States.

Uniquely, the projects are allocated beginning with the project(s) for which the "smallest" dollar amount has been requested. For purposes of allocation rules, all qualified projects located at the same site and owned by the same qualified borrower are treated as a single project.

Examples of qualified projects would include:

- Wind Facilities
- Closed and Open-Loop Biomass Facilities
- Geothermal Facilities
- Solar Facilities

- Small Irrigation Power Facilities
- Qualified Hydropower Facilities
- Refined Coal Production Facilities
- Landfill Gas Facilities
- Trash Combustion Facilities

Interestingly, a CREB can also be used to refinance a prior debt of a qualified project provided the debt was originally incurred by a qualified borrower after August 8, 2005. There are specific additional requirements, however, that must be adhered to under this provision. The reimbursement rules are more restrictive than those generally applicable to other tax-exempt bonds.

The tax credit rate is set daily by the Treasury Department. The rate can be found at *http://www.publicdebt.treas.gov*. The rate is applied as of the date that there is a written binding contract for the sale. The rate is set such that the CREB can be issued without discount or interest rate cost to the issuer (par) and is based on estimated yields of outstanding AA-rated corporate bonds with similar maturities. The rate is fixed for the duration of the bond.

The Secretary of the Treasury also sets the maximum maturity limitation of the CREB. The maximum maturity is the term that the Secretary estimates will result in the present value of the obligation to repay the principal on the bond being equal to 50% of the face amount of the bonds. The interest rate used for this purpose is determined at least monthly by the Treasury using the average annual interest rate on tax-exempt bonds having a term of 10 years. For example, if an issuer issued $10 million of CREBs and the applicable Treasury discount rate is 6%, the term of the bonds is established by determining how long it will take $5 million invested at 6% to equal $10 million. Under the Act, however, the issuer is required to repay the principal amount of bonds in level annual installments. At the current average interest rate for tax-exempt 10-year bonds, most CREBS would have a maximum term of 11-14 years. Generally, a discount rate of 110% of the long-term adjusted applicable federal rate, compounded semi-annually, for the month in which the bond is sold would be used for this purpose under the IRS guidelines.

Under the IRS Code, CREBs must provide for an equal amount of principal to be paid by the qualified issuer during each calendar year that the issue is outstanding. A single principal due date is not permitted. Often, this can require that the issuer make a principal payment prior to the completion of the project if it takes a period of more than one year to completely build and commission the project. In the real world of project finance, this principal repayment prior to completion of the project could be accomplished by the issuer using their existing lines of credit to fund the interim construction costs and then use the CREB to provide the permanent financing once the project has been completed as described above.

The CREBs may be purchased and held by any taxpayer. If a taxpayer holds a CREB on one or more credit allowance dates during any taxable year, the holder will be allowed a tax credit in that tax year. The amount of any credit received must be included in gross income of the taxpayer, and is required to be treated as interest income. An example of this rule regarding the tax credit calculation and the net tax benefit follows:

Tax Credit Calculation. Assume the credit rate of an issue of CREBs sold on July 1, 2007 is 6%. Further assume that, on June 15, 2009, the principal outstanding amount of the issue is $10,000,000. On June 14, 2009, the taxpayer will receive a tax credit in the amount of $150,000, which is 25% of the tax credit rate of 6%, multiplied by the principal amount of the outstanding CREB of $10,000,000. As described above, the total credit is earned on a quarterly basis and therefore the 6% was divided into four equal installments.

The end result is that as the principal is reduced over the term of the CREB (remember that the principal must be reduced on a straight line basis over the term of the CREB), the amount of the tax credit (and interest deemed received by the holder of the CREB) will decrease.

Net Tax Benefit. Assume a bondholder is in the top 34% federal tax bracket and receives a CREB tax credit in the amount of $150,000 (using the example above). The bondholder has taxable bond income in the amount of $150,000, resulting in a tax liability of $51,000 (34% of $150,000). The net tax benefit, therefore, is a tax credit in the amount of $99,000 ($150,000-$51,000). This credit could then be used to offset either the regular tax or the AMT of the bondholder.

Another way to express the value of the CREB tax attribute using the above example is that the net tax benefit would provide for absolutely no taxes being paid on other income the bondholder receives on $291,176.47 during that period of their tax year. This is calculated by applying the tax credit to the taxes that would have been due on income of $291,176.47 (34% or $99,000). This is a good example of the power that tax credits in general have in increasing the after tax income for taxpayers who invest funds in cleantech renewable energy projects. It is important to note that the tax credits cannot be carried forward or backward into another tax year—you must "use it or lose it."

Feed-in Tariffs

Often, net-metering and feed-in tariffs (FIT) are thought of as the same driver for renewable energy deployment. They are not similar and net-metering will be discussed later. However, both have a direct way of assisting individual states with meeting their Renewable Portfolio Standards (RPS) if monitored and accounted for properly. Some states and even individual utilities are now adopting or considering the adoption of a FIT.

A feed-in tariff is an incentive structure to encourage the adoption of renewable energy generation through government legislation. FIT policies are effectively used to meet a range of state policy goals other than RPS mandates including job creation and economic development. The FIT payment from the utility to the energy producing asset owner can be comprised of electricity alone or of electricity bundled with the renewable energy certificates (REC). Normally, the payments are guaranteed for a period of 15-20 years.

FIT policies are known variously as renewable energy payments, fixed-price policies, production-based incentives, feed laws, and standard offer contracts. They have been implemented in over 40 countries worldwide and have resulted in major market successes.

Europe in particular has chosen to adopt feed-in tariffs as the principal tool in helping individual European countries meet their energy and GHG emission targets that each have adopted. With rare exceptions, feed-in tariffs have not been adopted in North America with two exceptions—New Brunswick and Michigan. Both have only recently passed legislation requiring feed-in tariffs and it is too early to ascertain the results. Results in Europe have been very effective and large quantities of renewable (particularly solar) energy project have been completed and are producing vast quantities of electrical energy.

In 2008, California provided for feed-in tariffs for all customer-generators of Pacific Gas and Electric and Southern California Edison (both major investor owned utilities) for up to 228 MW of renewable generating capacity. To qualify for the feed-in tariff, the facility must be powered by an eligible renewable energy resource (including wind and solar) and have electric generating capacity of no greater than 1.5 MW. By offering standard contract terms (10, 15 or 20 years) including guaranteed pricing mechanisms, it will be easier for small customer generators to sell excess generating capacity from an on-site energy system. To date, only California has enacted FIT legislation on a state-wide basis.

America has been very slow in adopting this tool to meet its future energy needs through the development of new renewable energy production sources. This will probably change in the very near future. As demand for energy increases, costs rise, climate mitigation measures are adopted, and a real acknowledgement that the country must find ways to reduce its reliance on foreign oil imports; this external component will play a much larger role in helping to finance the new renewable energy generation projects of the future.

FIT policies are being experimented with in the United States, though at a smaller scale and less comprehensively than in a number of European countries. To date, several utilities in California, Florida, Oregon, Vermont, Washington, and Wisconsin have implemented initially different variations of FIT policies. There are substantive differences between the FIT policies found in the United States and those currently implemented in Europe.

California, as an example, has a state mandate that the state's investor-owned utilities (the four major ones are Pacific Gas & Electric, Southern California Edison, Southern California Gas and San Diego Gas & Electric), energy service providers, and community choice aggregators to serve 20% of all retail electrical sales with renewable sources by 2010. Public owned utilities such as Los Angeles Department of Water & Power are required to develop RPS programs as well. This requirement increases to 33% by 2020 and is expected to need new policy tools to meet this aggressive target. In addition, it is clear that renewable energy must play a significant role in meeting the state's aggressive carbon-reduction goals. California is not on track to meet these RPS mandates and it is now seriously considering adopting feed-in tariffs as the principal method to do so. Current incentives in California such as the California Solar Initiative (CSI) have not been able to provide sufficient markets to assist the utilities in their mandates.

In September 2008, the California Energy Commission (CEC) came out with a report exploring the use of feed-in tariffs as a mechanism to aid in making California's renewable energy generation a reality. They are considering six different possible feed-in tariff alternatives. The report draws heavily on the experiences in Germany and Spain and the lessons learned by those countries. In real terms, California and other states (and perhaps even on a nationwide federal level) are very close to using this method of incentives to get possible energy providers to invest in the projects needed to meet these aggressive RPS standards that have been adopted or will soon be (see Renewable Portfolio Standards component below). The CEC is carefully examining the options for design issues such as appropriate tariff structure, eligibility and pricing. A complete copy of the report can be obtained at *http://www.energy.ca.gov/2008publications/CEC-300-2008-009/CEC-300-2008-009-D.pdf.*

The six policy paths that are examined in the report are summarized below. These policy paths span a range of policy directions, as well as timing and scope. In addition to the six options identified, there is an implicit seventh choice—maintaining the status quo.

As of March 2009, state representatives in the U.S. have proposed a wide range of FIT policies. These states include Arkansas, California, Florida, Hawaii, Illinois, Indiana, Michigan, Minnesota, New York, New Jersey, Oregon, Rhode Island, Vermont, Washington, and Wisconsin. Throughout this flurry of legislative activity, a trend toward designing FIT policies similarly to those found in Europe can be seen.

The city of Gainesville, Florida, as an example, recently passed a PV feed-in tariff ordinance which became effective on March 1, 2009. Gainesville is the first municipality in the United States to provide a feed-in tariff. Customers of the Gainesville Regional Utilities who install PV equipment for building, pavement mounted systems of any size, or a ground-mounted system below 25 kW are eligible for a $0.32 kWh price for the power the system generates. Customers who install free standing solar electric systems larger than 25 kW receive $0.26 kWh price. Tariffs are guaranteed for a period of 20 years.

At its simplest, a feed-in tariff is an offering of a fixed-price contract over a specified term with specified operating conditions to eligible renewable energy generators. Feed-in tariffs can be either an all-inclusive rate or a fixed premium payment on top of the prevailing

Table 4-3: FIT Policy Options

	Option 1	Option 2	Option 3	Option 4	Option 5	Option 6
Feed-in Tariff Policy Attribute	Full-Market, unlimited size, differentiated cost-based with competitive benchmark, triggered by failure to meet 2010 RPS target	> 20 MW, undifferentiated value-based 3-yr pilot in 1 utility	Differentiated Cost-based CREZ[1]-Only, > 1.5 MW	Solar > net metering pilot in 1 utility, cost-based with competitive benchmark	Sustainable biomass > 1.5 MW only, cost-based	Full market < 20 MW cost-based differentiated by technology & size
Resource Type	All	All	All	Solar	Biomass (sustainable)	All
Vintage	New, separate price for repowering	New + repowering	New	New	New	New, separate price for repowering
Size	No limit	> 20	>1.5	> Net metering threshold	>1.5	<20
Timing	Trigger (RPS < 20 percent under contract by 2010, implement Feed-in Tariff in 2012/13)	Now (available for 3-year duration)	Automatically in 2010/11 (so projects are developed in parallel with transmission)	Now	Now	Now
Scope	Full Market	Pilot (limited time, one utility)	CREZ-Only	Pilot (e.g. within one utility)	Full Market	Full Market
Setting the Price	Cost-based with initial differentiated auction without MPR to set competitive benchmark for subsequent tariff	Value Based (time & peak differentiated with CO_2 & other adders)	Cost-based	Cost-Based w/ Competitive benchmark	Cost-based, calculated to consider sustainable yield of local biomass sources	Cost-based
Contract Duration	Long-term	Long-term	Long-term	Long-term	ST/MT	Long-term
Tariff Differentiation	Differentiation by technology & size	Not applicable	Wind by size, geothermal, biomass by size, solar by technology	By size, type	By fuel and size	Differentiation by technology & size
Limits	Capped at RPS targets; caps on more expensive technologies	Uncapped	Capped at CREZ Transmission limit	Capacity limit will be established for the sponsoring utility.	Uncapped	Uncapped

[1]Competitive Renewable Energy Zone

spot market price for power. The price paid represents estimates of either the cost or value of renewable generation. The tariff is generally offered by the interconnecting utility and sets a standing price for each category of eligible renewable generator; the price is available to all eligible generators. Tariffs are often differentiated based on technology type, resource quality, or project size and may decline on a set schedule over time.

Feed-in tariff payments are most often based on one of three methods:

1. *Levelized RE Project Costs*. The FIT payment is methodologically based on the levelized cost of RE generation plus a target rate of return.
2. *Avoided Utility Costs*. The FIT payment is based on the avoided costs to the utility of producing power from other technologies.
3. *Fixed-price Incentives*. The FIT is awarded as a fixed-price incentive, without regard to avoided cost, of the cost of RE generation.

The FIT payment based on levelized renewable energy costs has been the most successful FIT option in terms of driving the rapid deployment of RE internationally. This is true largely because it provides investors with a price adequate to ensure a reasonable return on investment. It is also the most common FIT design used in Europe. However, in the U.S., the avoided cost and fixed-price incentive options are most common.

FIT policies will most often guarantee grid access that allows both small and large projects to connect to the grid according to uniform interconnection standards. A good comparison is that of a power purchase agreement between the generating asset owner and the utility.

As with other policies, feed-in tariffs provide benefits and limitations, a number of which depend upon the design of the tariff. From the generator's perspective, the benefits of a feed-in tariff include the availability of a guaranteed price, buyer, and long term revenue stream without the cost of solicitation. Market access is enhanced by feed-in tariffs, as project timing is not constrained by periodic scheduled solicitations. In addition, completion dates may not be constrained by contractual requirements, quantities are often uncapped, and interconnection is typically guaranteed. Together, these characteristics can help to reduce or alleviate generator revenue uncertainty, project risk, and associated financing concerns. Feed-in tariffs reduce transaction costs for both buyer and seller and are more transparent to administer than the current system. Because responding to standing tariffs is likely to be less costly and less complex than competitive solicitations, feed-in tariffs may increase the ability of smaller projects or developers to help the state meet its Renewable Portfolio Standard (RPS) and greenhouse gas emission reduction goals. Policy makers can target feed-in tariffs to encourage specific types of projects and technologies if so desired.

The German model of feed-in tariffs that began in 1990 and refined in 2000 when it became a federally managed program has proven to be the world's most effective practice for boosting adoption of renewable energy technologies. Renewable Feed-In Tariffs (REFIT) has been associated with a large growth in wind power in Spain, Germany and Denmark. These countries now boast the supply of 9%, 5% and 20% of their electricity respectively. These systems involve fixed payments that are guaranteed in the long term; 20 years in the cases of Spain and Germany.

It will also soon be realized in America that feed-in tariffs will become the incentive of choice to encourage renewable energy development. A feed-in tariff incentive would probably be the largest commercial incentive of any currently available to rapidly expand the development of large scale deployment of renewables. Therefore, in the near future, this external component of revenue for renewable energy projects will play a much larger role when analyzing and structuring the proper finance structure for the acquisition of renewable energy projects. Feed-in tariff laws were in place in 46 jurisdictions across the world by 2007.

The price that the utility purchases the renewable energy at is substantially larger than what the utility is currently selling the power at. This is the fundamental parameter in feed-in tariffs. The difference is spread over all of the customers of the utility. For example, if $1 million worth of renewable energy costs is purchased in one year by a utility and that cost is amortized over 1 million customers, then each of those customers would have $1.00 added to their electric bill over a period of one year. Thus, a small annual increase in the price of electricity per customer can result in a large incentive for people to install renewable energy systems.

Michigan is an example of where legislation has already been introduced to put a feed-in tariff in place. Like the German law which powered that country to world leadership in wind, solar, and biomass energy—and created nearly one-quarter million new jobs in its booming renewable energy industry—proponents of the bill are hoping the tariff will revive Michigan's flagging economy. The tariffs proposed are equivalent to those in

Germany and would be the highest in North America if the bill is made a law. The feed-in tariffs proposed in Michigan are:

- Hydro less than 500 kW: $0.10 USD/kWh
- Biogas less than 150 kW: $0.145 USD/kWh
- Geothermal less than 5 MW: $0.19 USD/kWh
- Wind: $0.105 USD/kWh
- Wind energy from small wind turbines: $0.25 USD/kWh
- Rooftop solar less than 30 kW: $0.65 USD/kWh
- Solar facade cladding less than 30 kW: $0.71 USD/kWh

> "Energy conservation is the foundation of energy independence."
>
> Thomas H. Allen, former member of the U.S. House of Representatives from Maine

Generally, a second meter would need to be installed under a feed-in tariff structure. One is used for measuring the amount of electricity consumed by the rate payer, and the second meter is used to measure the amount of electricity produced by the renewable energy system which is subsequently sold to the utility—and normally at a price significantly higher than that consumed by the first meter.

FITs offer a long-term guaranty to renewable energy project owners for all the electricity they produce. There are two monetary value components to the FIT—electricity sales and renewable energy certificates or RECs. In some cases they are bundled together and in other cases they are sold separately. The end result of a well-designed FIT program is to provide a cost-efficient method for fostering rapid development of renewable energy resources. The benefits accrue to all interested parties including project owners, utilities, non-government organizations and country as a whole. The FIT offers a long-term certainty of payment terms with minimum barriers to administrative and regulatory mandates. They are flexible and can adapt to many different electricity market structures. There are even discussions taking place as how to best apply a FIT structure to thermal energy production as is now customary in the electricity market. In fact, FIT policies can be implemented to support all renewable technologies including wind, solar photovoltaic (PV), solar thermal, geothermal, biogas, biomass, fuel cells and even tidal and wave power.

The success of feed-in tariffs around the world (most apparent in Europe) suggests that they will continue to grow in importance in the United States and be used as a cost effective measure for the implementation and financing of many renewable energy projects. The fact that there is a fixed long-term source of additional revenue to repay the debt in a project is critical to attractive financing structures.

A well designed feed-in tariff has several advantages over other types of renewable energy incentives. Other RE incentives one could compare a FIT to are upfront rebates, net metering and quota-based policies like renewable portfolio standards. Initial evidence suggests that there are two primary reasons FIT policies are more cost-efficient than other RE policies.[2] First, policies that make use of competitive solicitations like RPSs involve a higher degree of risk for the developer, putting upward pressure on the required returns.[3,4] The reduction of these investment-level risks under FIT policies can also help reduce capital costs, ultimately reducing the cost of renewable electricity.[5] Second, projects vying under the competitive solicitation processes tend to be financed by larger institutional or corporate investors who provide equity as opposed to debt financing. Since equity is more expensive than debt, leading to a higher weighted average cost of capital, further upward pressure is placed on the levelized costs of energy.

Successful FIT policies are generally designed to allow for an adequate recovery of project costs plus a reasonable rate of return, thereby increasing investor security. Furthermore, by offering transparent payment levels and uniform contract terms at the outset, FIT policies help create a framework with low administrative and regulatory barriers for promoting RE deployment (de Jager and Rathmann 2008). A further advantage of FIT policies is that because average citizens and business owners can participate, they tend to reduce the social opposition to RE development. This may prove to be particularly important in the years ahead, and may become an important condition for the broader expansion of RE technologies.

The payment structure for FIT payments can be either fixed or variable (premium-price). One variation of the premium-price FIT design is the "spot-market gap" model, currently implemented in the Netherlands. A spot market is one where energy can be sold for cash and delivered immediately. It may be of particular interest to policy makers in the U.S., because it represents a novel FIT design that may be found to be more compatible with the current U.S. regulatory policy environment. However, most countries with existing FIT policies have chosen the fixed-price approach.

As can be seen in Figure 4-2: Fixed Price Feed-in Tariff Structure below, the fixed pricing model is attractive during the first 60% of the contract term but will turn negative in the later years. However, since the positive cash flow during the early years of the renewable energy project has a greater impact on the net present value analysis and IRR of a project than payments received in later years, it proves to be an attractive investment. The total FIT revenue payment from the project remains independent from the market price of the energy and is a predetermined payment for a guaranteed period of time. Because fixed-price FIT policies offer market-independent payments, they create stable conditions for investors. Often, this structure can lead to low project-financing costs.

FIT payments can also be offered as a premium on top of the spot-market electricity price. One variation is shown in Figure 4-3: Premium Price Feed-in Tariff Structure below. Under a premium-level FIT policy, the project owner receives payment for the total electricity generated (at market prices), as well as a FIT payment.

Although a non-variable premium is a simpler design as shown above, it risks resulting in windfall profits for developers if spot-market prices for electricity increase significantly. Similarly, if electricity prices fall, the investor return would be at risk, which would tend to put upward pressure on project-financing costs. This risk premium method would require proportionally higher payments to obtain the same amount of renewable energy development. Additional models could use a "floor" and a "ceiling" pricing to also mitigate investment yield risk.

It is important to note the main differences between FIT and RPS policies to understand their potential relationship to each other. RPS mandates prescribe how much customer demand must be met with renewable, while properly structured FIT policies attempt to support new supply development by providing investor certainty. FIT policies are typically designed to provide a renewable project with revenue streams sufficient to cover development costs, plus a reasonable return. They are focused on setting the right price to drive RE deployment. In contrast, most RPS policies are focused on the quantity, leaving the price up to competitive bidding.

Under an RPS, the load-serving entities or central procurement agency must determine how they comply with the mandate. Typically, a competitive solicitation is used to secure supply to meet RPS polices in the United States. Utilities issue a request for proposals and select the projects that offer the most promising package of siting, operational expertise, and cost. However, due to the high costs of developing a bid, the high risk of failing to obtain a contract, and the nature of the investors financing projects at this scale, the return on investment requirement in competitive solicitations are generally much higher than in jurisdictions employing feed-in tariffs. Also, the overall market structure that results from a competitive bidding framework limits the investor pool and can lead to a less-dynamic RE market.

A FIT policy can be developed to work in concert with an RPS policy, which sets a goal or mandate of how much customer demand should be provided by renewables. A properly structured FIT policy attempts to provide investor certainty to help support new supply development—playing right into the hands of an astute renewable energy project developer, lender or investor.

Overall, FIT policies also help provide flexibility. When differentiated according to technology type, they can be designed to encourage any RE technology, as well as a particular subset of technologies depending on local resource availability. By differentiating the payment

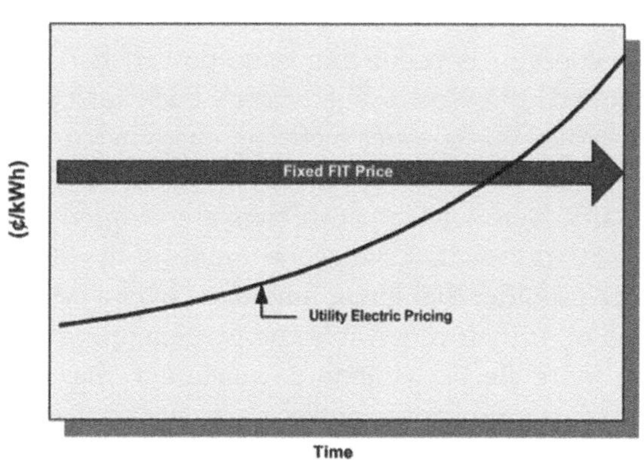

Figure 4-2: Fixed Price Feed-in Tariff Structure

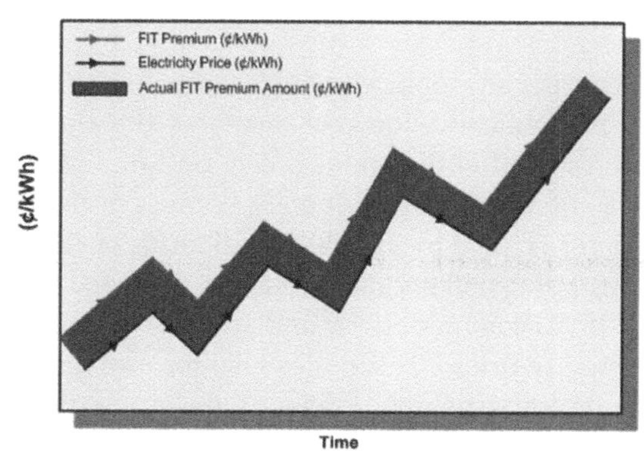

Figure 4-3: Premium Price Feed-in Tariff Structure

levels according to different project variables, including project size, FIT policies allow RE investment to be profitable for citizens, small business owners, and large commercial-scale developers. This flexibility, ensured by the differentiated payment levels, helps leverage capital investment toward renewables and drives rapid RE deployment in a number of different technology classes.

FIT policies face five central challenges.

1. They do not address the barrier posed by the high up-front costs of RE systems. Whereas, other up-front "capacity-based" incentives often do that, and may be provided by utilities, states or other governmental entities.
2. FIT policies can put near-term, upward pressure on electricity rates, particularly if high-cost technologies like solar photovoltaics are included in large amounts (i.e., thousands of MW). The risk of cost impacts grows in proportion to the rate and scale of deployment of these costlier technologies.
3. Well-designed FIT policies require a significant up-front administrative commitment to design the policy and to establish FIT payments based on the levelized cost of RE generation.
4. FIT policies designed to include guaranteed grid interconnection, regardless of location on the grid, could lead to less-than-optimal project siting. Accordingly, if projects are sited far from load centers or transmission or distribution lines, interconnection costs increase, putting upward pressure on policy costs.
5. Due to changes in technology costs and market prices over time, FIT policies must be adjusted periodically to account for these changes. Accounting for changes in technology costs accurately remains a continuous challenge to the policies established under the specific FIT program.

As with any policy, benefits and challenges surround FIT policies. However, many of the challenges can be resolved with careful policy design and proper cost-benefit analysis. Additionally, because of the intrinsic benefits created by FIT policies in terms of RE development, policymakers may accept a tradeoff between the positive economic effects and any near-term impacts on electricity prices. This bodes well for any renewable energy project developer, lender or investor as these FIT policies play out.

There are seven key elements of a successful FIT policy, as identified by leading European Research[6] that would be most applicable to a national FIT policy in American and include:

1. Offer a stable FIT policy.
2. Offer long-term (15-20 years) contract to provide investment security.
3. Base payment levels on the levelized cost of RE generation to ensure a modest profit for developers and investors.
4. Introduce incremental payment decreases (annual tariff degression).
5. Differentiate payment levels by technology type, project size, and resource quality to offer project-appropriate FIT payments.
6. Incorporate the added costs of a FIT policy into the electricity rate base.
7. Streamline approval processes to reduce administrative barriers and transaction costs.

Net Metering

Net metering is an electricity policy for project owners who own renewable energy generation facilities, such as wind or solar power. "Net" is used in the sense of meaning "what remains after deductions"—in this case, the deduction of any energy outflows from metered energy inflows. Under net metering, a system owner receives credit for at least a portion of the electricity they generate. In most cases, net metering has the existing electricity meter spinning backwards, effectively banking excess electricity production for future credit. In reality, the rules vary significantly by country and possibly state/province (including utility by utility)—if net metering is available, if and how long you can keep your banked credits, how much the credits are worth (retail/wholesale), etc.

When a net metering customer's renewable energy generator is producing more power than is being consumed, the electric meter runs backward generating credits. When a net metering customer uses more power than is being produced, the meter runs forward normally. Net metering customers are charged only for the "net" power that they consume from the electricity service provider that has accumulated over a designated period or, if their renewable energy-generating systems make more electricity than is consumed, they may be credited or paid for the excess electricity contributed to the grid over that same period.

Under the Energy Policy Act of 2005 (EPAct or simply the "Act") section 1251, all public electric utilities are now required to make available upon request net metering to their customers. New Jersey and Colorado are widely considered to have the best net-metering policies in the United States as both have no limit on enrollment (less than 2MW each), roll over month to month and pay annually for excess generation at avoided-cost rate (New Jersey) or incremental cost (Colorado). California only allows the "net" generation to be zero. Any excess electricity generated by the system over the period (usually annually) is kept by the utility and no money is due the rate payer (energy producer). Even in Canada, some provinces have net metering regulations. Effective use of net metering can occur on systems wherein the user's demand load may be managed so that there is a net production of electricity during high cost periods. This can be done, for example, by chilling water during off-peak times for air conditioning use during high demand periods, or by pre-cooling the thermal mass of the building during low cost periods.

California also passed new legislation in September of 2008 (AB 2768) that provides for net metering at the same rates as charged by the utilities under "time of use" (TOU) tariffs. The effect is that the solar energy producer is being credited at the same time of use rate that the utility is charging the customer at that time. Prior to passage of AB 2768, the energy generator was only paid the base rate which was substantially lower than that the utility was charging the customer during the same time period. State of the art meters are required to be installed by the energy producer to be eligible under the new tariff rate structures on net metering. Therefore, the systems peak performance time matches that needed by the grid during peak demand periods.

Net metering has the potential to be a bad deal for utilities. If market penetration of solar and other renewable energy-powered buildings becomes substantial, utilities are likely to become concerned with revenue losses. The utility might seek higher rates from its remaining customers to recover fixed costs. Migration away from utility-generated power can leave certain disadvantaged customers holding the bag as rates continue to rise. Additionally, utilities do more than just generate and sell electricity to customers. They also are responsible for transmission (delivering the electricity) and reliability (making sure that the lights work when you flip the switch.)

The potential interplay between existing net metering programs and feed-in tariff programs could possibly lead to some confusion and debate. One is not necessarily exclusive of the other. However, it is generally assumed that a rate payer/energy producer could not do both on the same asset although a second system could be installed to seize the opportunity of the alternate incentive.

Net metering has been adopted in all states with the exception of Alabama, Alaska, Kansas, Mississippi, South Dakota, and Tennessee. Many of the states that have adopted net-metering regulations also may impose limitations on the net metering such as allowing a maximum of 2 megawatts.

Two great resources for determining the net-metering provisions in each state (along with a tremendous amount of other renewable energy rules, regulations, incentives, etc.) can be found at *http://www.dsireusa.org* and *http://www.irecusa.org*. The most recent version of the presentation "Freeing the Grid" outlining state net-metering rules can be found on the web.[7] It was a collaborative effort between IREC, The Vote Solar Initiative, North Carolina Solar Center and Network for New Energy Choices.

Renewable Energy Credit Certificates

Renewable Energy Certificates (RECs) are often referred to as "Green Tags." They are a market-based

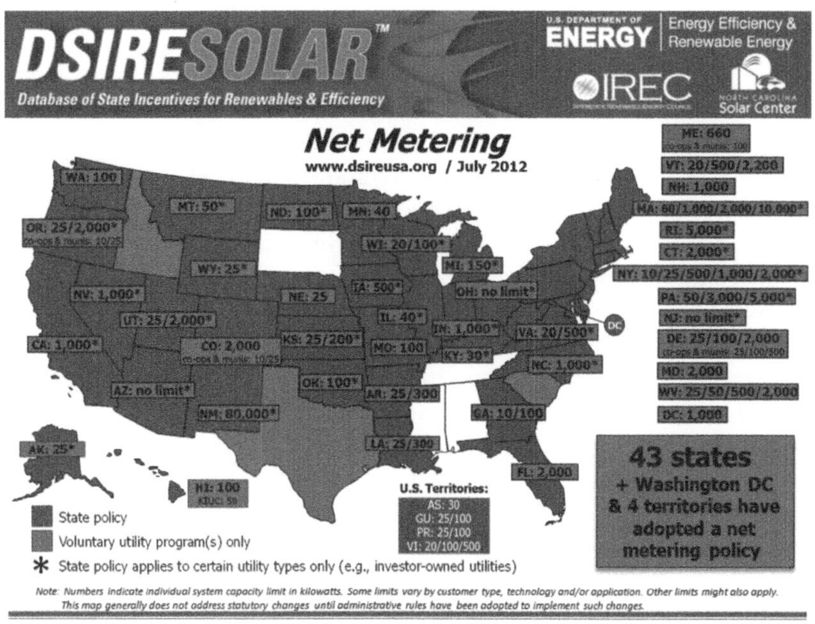

Figure 4-4: Net Metering Map in US

commodity designed to facilitate transactions between buyers and sellers of renewable energy, free from the constraints of the electricity grid. By unbundling the renewable characteristic from the actual electricity commodity, RECs allow renewable energy generators more flexibility in the distribution of their products, and therefore encourages further development of the renewable energy market. In states or regions that have an REC program, one REC represents the environmental attributes generally associated with one megawatt-hour (MWh) of electricity from renewable resources. Commonly, solar RECs are known in the industry as SRECs. Generally, the RE system owner would want to "unbundle" the REC from the energy produced by the system, thereby providing an additional source of revenue from the project.

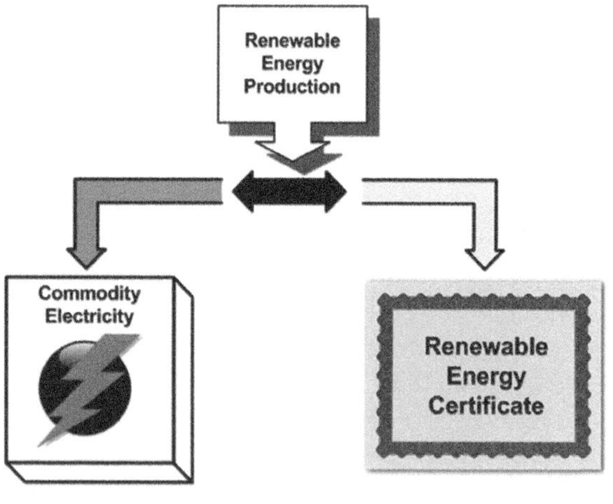

Figure 4-5: Renewable Energy Production Unbundling

Currently, the United States has two distinct REC markets—the compliance market and the voluntary market. The compliance market is driven primarily by the RPS mandates found in many states (see next external component). The compliance market is driven largely by state government regulation, while consumers drive the voluntary market interested in supporting renewable energy or reducing their environmental footprint. Besides having different drivers, these two markets for renewable energy also differ in pricing. Within the voluntary market, pricing typically reflects the additional cost of renewable generation above conventional resources. Additional factors affecting voluntary REC prices are the resource type and location, and whether the generator is new or already exists. Prices within the compliance market reflect the supply-and-demand balance for the commodity value of 1 MWh of renewable energy. There is no assigned value. Because each state designs its own renewables program and corresponding REC market, prices vary across compliance markets. In states, such as New Jersey, where the Solar Alternative Compliance Penalty (SACP) in 2010 was $693, SRECs are worth more than a state with an SACP of $250. The SACP in Massachusetts for year 2012 is $550 and the credits are selling for $540. Most often the RECs are traded through aggregators and brokers since it is too costly for an individual project owner to do the paperwork for a single small project (e.g., a residential home).

A good example of the wide difference between the "compliance" market and that of the "voluntary" market is that between California (a historically voluntary market) and New Jersey (a compliance market). The current price of 1 REC in California is $8-12 while the price in New Jersey for an equal REC was over $300. In 2004, the price of 1 REC in New Jersey was $160. As of October 2008, that same REC is now selling for $308. That is a 94% increase in value over just four years! Subsequently, the price has now dropped to $205 in New Jersey and in Ohio, the same SREC is bringing $285. Hence, in any renewable energy project, it is imperative that the correct assumptions are made when doing the financial analysis and relying on future REC pricing as a significant parameter in the project model.

There are many benefits to a tradable REC market including:

- *Market efficient subsidy*—in a property functioning market, the value of the REC will equal the difference between the cost of a renewable energy certificate and alternative energy sources as it has in Europe with the carbon offset trading mechanisms.
- *Minimal impact on taxpayers*—the burden of a REC market falls primarily on the electricity ratepayers, not the taxpayers. The additional cost to the utility will be diffused across the large ratepayer base that pays for the non-renewable electricity.
- *Provides industry stability*—the REC market has a stabilizing effect for the renewable energy sector in a state. The continual production of RECs by the renewable energy projects in the state provide a market stabilization that will not require grants and other subsidies to promote renewable energy that are currently provided by each state.
- *Provides alternative compliance tool*—utilities are provided with an alternate option to meet the compliance mandates set forth in state legislation for increased power generation from renewable energy sources without paying a financial penalty

Table 4-4: Historical SREC Prices[8]

SREC Prices	Dec-11	Jan-12	Feb-12
Delaware			
2009-10	-	-	-
2010-11	$60.00	-	-
2011-12	$60.10	$65.00	$60.00
Maryland			
In-State			
2010	-	-	$180.00
2011	$210.00	$204.99	205.00
Out-of-State			
2010	-	-	-
2011	-	$35.00	-
Massachusetts			
2011	$530.00	$540.00	-
New Jersey			
2010	-	-	-
2011	$225.00	$245.00	-
2012	$225.00	$245.00	$205.00
Ohio			
In-State			
2010	-	-	-
2011	$370.00	-	$285.00
Out-of-State			
2010	$30.00	$30.00	-
2011	$30.00	$30.00	$40.00
Pennsylvania			
2010	$20.00	-	$9.99
2011	$10.00	$20.00	$30.00
2012	$18.00	$29.99	$35.00
Washington, D.C.			
2010	$176.00	$250.00	-
2011	$201.00	$270.00	$275.00

"-" means that bids and/or offers were not placed for SRECs of that vintage period or the market was unable to determine a clearing price because of the value of bid and offer prices.

if they are not able to achieve the goals set by the state. The utility is provided a choice: pay a penalty if that is less costly than the REC, or purchase RECs if that is a less costly alternative than the penalty.

The most significant force that impacts demand for RECs is the available supply.[9] The relationship between supply and demand is one of the most crucial aspects of a successful REC market. A market that is unable to attract the supply to meet the demand will have above market REC prices until the supply increases. A market that attracts too much supply too quickly could face a collapse in REC pricing. The consensus of many in the renewable energy sector is that over time and as compliance mandates become increasingly more difficult to achieve, the price of RECs may exceed the actual revenue from the sale of the underlying energy being produced. In some time frame between 10 and 15 years from now, it is expected that the REC revenue will start exceeding the energy revenue on a project. Chapter Seven will explore the impact this could have on the rates of return to the investor/lender and what the risks could be priced at. RECs are environmental commodities created by state regulation. Any investor/lender that plans to create and sell RECs from a renewable energy project will run the risk that the political environment might change. Regulations existing today could easily be modified or even rescinded at some time in the future. In most cases, project owners will not rely on current or future REC revenue unless there is a fixed contract in place to support the revenue stream expectations.

Standardization initiatives are developing on the regional and national levels. For example, the California Energy Commission (CEC) and the Western Electricity Coordinating Council (WECC) established the Western Renewable Energy Generation Information System (WREGIS) to issue, register, and track RECs for the territory covered by the Western Interconnection. Other similar regional tracking organizations include the PJM Generation Attribute Tracking System (GATS) and the New England Power Pool Generation Information System (NEPOOL GIS). Each of these organizations issues certificates with unique serial numbers that represent the attributes of the generation for each megawatt-hour produced by qualified generators. States that are parties to the organization may use and exchange certificates within each tracking system.

Many solar advocates are hoping that the California Tradable Renewable Energy Credits (TRECs) program will boost solar development the way SREC markets have in the country's fastest growing solar markets on the East Coast. TRECs are generally defined as renewable energy credits that can be traded separate and apart from the energy associated with their creation, in contrast to bundled transactions in which both the renewable energy credits and the associated power are sold together. The definition of bundled transactions adopted by the CPUC means that any transactions with renewable resources that do not have their first point of interconnection with a California balancing authority, or do not dynamically transfer power to a California balancing authority, would be deemed a TREC transaction subject to the cap of 25% on the use of TRECs on Energy Service Providers (ESPs). This would be true even if the renewable resource delivered power to California under a firming and shaping arrangement.

A TREC, which is equivalent to 1 MWH of renewable energy from a qualified source,[10] is an unbundled purchase of a REC by a load-serving entity (LSE) for RPS compliance, without the accompanying energy. Conversely, a bundled transaction includes both the REC and energy from a renewable energy facility. Prior to this order, only qualified bundled transactions could be used by LSEs for RPS compliance. By permitting the use of TRECs for up to 25% of RPS compliance, IOUs have an additional method for meeting part of their RPS obligations.

The CPUC temporarily capped the price the three largest IOUs can pay for TRECs at $50 per MWH. The CPUC asserted that a temporary cap was required because of the infancy of the TREC market (the cap is set to sunset on December 31, 2013). The cap also matches the penalty for not achieving RPS compliance. This avoids providing IOUs an incentive to pay more for the TREC than the RPS compliance penalty since IOU ratepayers pay for TRECs whereas penalties are paid for by IOU shareholders.

After much delay, the program was finally set to launch in late 2011. Ten months after initially authorizing the use of tradable renewable energy credits, the California Public Utilities Commission lifted its moratorium on approval of TREC transactions. However, the decision retains restriction on TREC transactions that could limit the amount of out-of-state generation that the three major investor-owned utilities can use to meet their RPS obligations. Unfortunately, the odds are stacked against the distributed solar industry and here is why:[11]

> *"The word 'energy' incidentally equates with the Greek word for "challenge." I think there is much to learn in thinking of our federal energy problem in that light. Further, it is important for us to think of energy in terms of a gift of life."*
>
> Thomas Carr, American film director

The first hurdle was whether or not the California Public Utilities Commission (CPUC) would allow distributed generation (DG) projects to be eligible for the state Renewable Portfolio Standard (RPS). For the sake of clarification, DG is often referred to as smaller, commercial size projects, but in California, the technical definition extends to all projects that are considered onsite generation, meaning the electricity produced by the system is used locally, rather than transmitted through the broader electricity grid (think residential, small commercial and community solar projects). Based on recent proposed revisions, the CPUC will likely approve DG projects for RPS eligibility and has already started to layout the process for approving projects.

The next hurdle centers around how DG TRECs are classified within the RPS. There are three categories/buckets used for RPS compliance:

1. **Bucket 1—In-state or In-state Equivalent**: At least 50% of the renewable energy must be sited in California. Beginning in 2013, the majority (increasing to a minimum of 75 percent by 2017), of RECs that may be used for RPS compliance purposes must come from in-state or in-state equivalent products. Thus, the definition of the transactions qualifying as an in-state or in-state equivalent product has significant commercial and policy consequences. Up to 50% of the renewable energy can come from projects outside California that supply electricity to the California grid. Up to 25% of the RPS can be met through the purchase of Tradable Renewable Energy Certificates, a cap that will be reduced to 10% by 2020.
2. **Bucket 2—Firmed and Shaped Products**: The CPUC defines a "firmed and shaped" transaction as having three commercial elements:
   a. The utility purchaser does not sell the electricity back to the generator after making a simultaneous purchase of electricity and associated RECs;
   b. "The purchased energy must not in practice be already committed to consumption by another party;" and
   c. The substitute energy must be acquired at the same time as the RPS-eligible energy, or at least prior to submission of the contract for the firmed and shaped transaction for Commission approval.

In addition, in order for the transaction to provide "incremental electricity" the substitute energy must be "newly procured" by the retail seller for the firming and shaping transaction. The CPUC reasons that this requirement eliminates the possibility of "tagging" unbundled RECs to previously purchased electricity by a retail seller in order to have the unbundled RECs be counted as a Bucket 2 product instead of a Bucket 3 product.

3. **Bucket 3—Unbundled RECs and Other Products:** Bucket 3 captures all other RPS products which fail to qualify for the other two buckets. Bucket 3 thus includes not only so-called unbundled RECs, but also "other" products that were intended to qualify for a more advantageous RPS status but for whatever reason failed to do so. For example, a situation where a firmed and shaped transaction ended up with some substitute electricity that was not scheduled in the same calendar year as the RPS generation would result in a Bucket 3 product.

   Importantly, the CPUC clarifies that Bucket 3 includes all unbundled RECs, even those that were initially associated with, but subsequently separated from, generation that was produced and consumed inside a California balancing authority. The CPUC focuses on the transaction of the buyer that actually retires the RECs for RPS compliance. If that buyer ultimately purchased unbundled RECs only, the buyer will be participating in a Bucket 3 transaction regardless of the provenance of those RECs.

This is a key battle for the relevance of TRECs in supporting DG projects in California. Proponents for DG have argued that TRECs from in-state distributed projects should be included in the 1st bucket. A few reasons supporting this position include the added benefits from reduced transmission costs inherent in DG projects and the fact that the state should favor supporting distributed renewable energy projects sited in California over utility-scale projects outside of California. In a rare occurrence, advocates for the solar industry and the major utilities in California share this opinion. The only opponents are regulators and lawyers choosing a strict interpretation of a poorly written portion of a legislative mandate and unfortunately, it appears the only way to fix this would be to go back to the legislature. It is likely that the legislature envisioned tradable RECs as those coming from systems sited outside of regional territories and/or outside the state of California, without proper consideration for what that meant for legitimate, local, distributed renewable projects.

The impact of these recent decisions will effectively curtail the ability for distributed solar projects to count towards the RPS, while also making TRECs a non-factor in the financing of distributed solar projects. The RPS incentive scheme will first favor utility-scale hydro, wind and solar from within the state borders, followed by counterparts outside California and then, TRECs produced by renewable facilities anywhere in the Western U.S. and a portion of Canada (WREGIS). This means TREC prices will be next to nothing and the market will be dominated by regional utility-scale hydro and wind projects able to produce at a much larger scale than local DG solar. To put that into perspective, the fastest growing solar markets in the U.S. today (SREC states driven by RPS laws such as New Jersey, Pennsylvania and Massachusetts) are made up primarily of DG solar projects. As a result, California will need to find ways outside the RPS to encourage the growth of distributed solar energy. This most likely means a continuation of short-term, taxpayer funded, grant/rebate based programs like the California Solar Initiative (CSI).

Even if the CPUC decides to include DG in the in-state bucket, questions still exist around whether or not the potential TREC values will be enough to impact solar DG development. Compared to other states, California is backward in its approach to DG projects. The solar industry in California is fighting to be on a level playing field with utility-scale renewables, where other states have DG or solar set-asides that recognize the value of distributed generation and favor it in their RPS incentive structure over utility-scale renewables.[12]

State efforts suggesting the creation of a national marketplace likely will become a reality in the near future. Creating a nationwide, perhaps global, fungible REC commodity also could facilitate a national RPS, although significant obstacles remain. Nevertheless, REC advancements also serve as a foundation for national carbon trading. For companies actively engaged today, the desirable benefits of standard contracting, verification, and revenue stability will foster opportunities in regional and global carbon trading markets in the future.

As REC markets develop, key issues are being addressed regarding market interaction. The first involves certificate verification with respect to both verification of the renewable attributes of the power and the ownership of those attributes. Second, developers and utilities focus increasingly on protecting the revenue stream produced by REC sales by directing the revenue toward the expansion of renewable power generation. Finally, utilities and regulators across the country will focus on standardizing the REC programs, to capture the value of consistency and homogeneity for healthy REC trading markets.

California regulators are now moving forward with a new financing technique to stimulate immediate development of medium scale renewable energy projects. These are projects of 1.5 to 20 megawatt size. The so-called renewable auction mechanism or RAM, is expected to bring 1,000 megawatts of green electricity online over a two year period. The program is designed for developers to submit bids to utilities on projects that can be completed within 18 months at the lowest cost possible. There will be two auctions a year for a period of two years (four total). The program is designed as an alternative to a traditional FIT as found in most of Europe. Prices for renewable energy systems under RAM are essentially set by market forces and can respond quickly to changes, such as plummeting prices of solar panels.

Renewable Portfolio Standards (RPS)

A Renewable Portfolio Standard (RPS) is a regulation that requires the increased production of energy from renewable energy sources, such as wind, biomass, solar and geothermal. The RPS mechanism generally places an obligation on electricity supply companies to produce a specified fraction of their electricity from renewable energy sources. Renewable Portfolio Standards have been adopted in the following states: Arizona, California, Colorado, Connecticut, Delaware, Hawaii, Illinois, Iowa, Maine, Maryland, Massachusetts, Minnesota, Missouri, Montana, Nevada, New Hampshire, New Jersey, New Mexico, New York, North Carolina, North Dakota, Ohio, Oregon, Pennsylvania, Rhode Island, South Dakota, Texas, Utah, Vermont, Virginia, Washington, Wisconsin, District of Columbia and Guam. That means that as of May 2011, 29 states and the District of Columbia had set target percentages and dates for integration of renewable sources of energy. Although renewable resource availability varies considerably across wide regions of the United States, some areas are better endowed with renewable resources than others—including the types of renewable resources. For example, the Northwest has an abundance of hydropower and the Southwest has an abundance of solar. In most states, RPS targets usually start low and then gradually increase annually.

On April 12, 2011, Governor Jerry Brown of California signed into law a new RPS mandating all California utility companies to build an energy portfolio with 33% renewables by 2020. Senate Bill 14 raising the RPS from 20% to 33% had already passed the California legislature in September 2010. With the higher RPS of 33%, California is now the state with the most aggressive alternative energy mandate in the U.S. The 33% RPS must be met by 2020. In their 2015 forecast the California Public Utilities Commission (CPUC) expects the solar power portion of the portfolio to grow the biggest share from less than 5% to 30% of all renewables, even bigger than wind power, currently a little above 30%. Utilities which do not meet the 33% RPS will have to pay a penalty of $0.05/kWh. The governor also wants the legislature to implement a system similar to the feed-in tariff for distributed generation projects, without spiking the electricity prices for rate payers.

Compliance with the 20% earlier mandate in California wasn't as distant as it was originally thought. Everyone thought it was going to near-impossible to achieve—particularly the three major investor owned utilities (IOUs) in the state. The three IOUs came in collectively at a shade under 18 percent. As a result, no non-compliance penalties have been levied against the IOUs. However, achieving the 33% RPS could be more problematic unless there a greater use of tradable RECs as an alternative compliance tool (see page 81). The 33% percent requirement will be due in 2020. While that goal has been the subject of an administrative and legislative tug-of-war over the past years, the bill was passed and then signed by the governor and is now in effect.

State-based RPS targets for renewable energy generation targets have been so successful in developing new projects that any current proposals by the federal government for a federal clean energy standard could require little or no additional capacity according to Ryan Wiser, a scientist specializing in electricity markets and policy at Lawrence Berkeley National Laboratory (LBNL). Bipartisan legislation introduced by US senators Jeff Bingaman and Tom Udall to create a national RPS only called for one third of that or 11%. A much smaller amount than California calls for in its 33% RPS.

The state of California is also requiring utilities at the end of 2011 (residential only) that a solar PV generator will be paid for the excess electricity they feed in to the grid. Up until now, the utilities did not have to compensate for the excess over that which the homeowner used. The average rate for the excess energy is generally less than $0.10/kWh. However, the utility PG&E in Northern California has published rates of a contract with a feed-in tariff between $0.88/kWh (under a 10 year contract) and $0.10/kWh (20 year contract) as the nominal amount, which will be multiplied by a time-of-day factor—off and on-peak rates. The factor for peak hours of 11 am and 7 pm from June to September can be as high as 2.2 times that or $.019/kWh.

It is conceivable that RPS standards could be the single largest driver on installing new renewable energy projects in states that support the RPS. The price that utilities may need to pay for acquiring the power from renewables could easily exceed even the highest projected IRR in a typical renewable energy project. Only time will tell, but if there is an "insight" into the possible revenue coming from meeting RPS standards one needs only to look at the carbon pricing results in Europe as industries there have had to find ways to meet their carbon reduction compliance mandates over the past three years. In the real world, RPS mandates and carbon credits are both compliance mechanisms that have a defacto cap and trade underpinning.

The United Kingdom (UK) has come up with its own innovative mandates that are comparable to the RPS mechanisms in America. Called Renewable Obligation Certificates (ROC), a ROC is issued to generators of electricity for each megawatt hour of renewable energy they generate from qualifying forms of renewable energy technologies just like in the U.S. They are used as a financial incentive to encourage renewable energy generation but with a twist. Utilities in the UK can meet its obligations for renewables generation by 1) submitting ROCs for each obligation period; 2) paying a penalty known as the "buy-out" price; or 3) using a combination of these two methods.

Although some states (New Jersey as an example) have carve-outs for specific technologies such as solar (SRECs), they are not weighted differently than other RECs as far as value is concerned. The UK sets different weighted values for different periods on different technologies. The result is reduction values on some technologies could have significant adverse impact on which technologies get developed over others. They refer to this methodology as "banding rates." For example, anaerobic digestion technologies have a ROC per MWh value of 2 that drops to 1.9 in 2014 and to 1.8 in 2016. Compare this to landfill gas renewable technologies that have only a .25 ROC value that doesn't change over time. The technology they most support now is wave/tidal stream with a ROC value of 2 for each megawatt hour of energy produced. Hence, you see a great deal of R&D going into that technology for utilities to meet their renewable goals. As a side note, the UK has also used the principle of "grandfathering" on some of these technologies over others.

This method of meeting renewable portfolio standards could gain some ground in the future either on a federal level in the U.S. or possibly with some states as they look at technologies that provide more benefits than others based on the natural resources in their region. For example, tidal generation technologies could have more value to the state of Washington and solar technologies to the state of Nevada.

White Tags

White Tags are also known as Energy Savings Certificate (ESC) or Energy Efficiency Credit (EEC). The document certifies that a certain reduction of energy consumption has occurred. These certificates are tradable or can be sold to other parties. The certificate can only be issued by a qualifying registration entity. The qualifying registration entity confirms that each certificate is a unique and traceable commodity carrying a property right over a certain amount of additional energy savings and guaranteeing that the benefit of these savings has not been accounted for elsewhere. Twenty two states plus the District of Columbia have adopted Energy Efficiency Portfolio Standards that require regulated utilities to meet a certain percentage of their projected power needs through energy efficiency. Utilities must meet their obligations by either reducing their consumers' energy usage, or by purchasing energy efficiency certificates from others.

The cleanest form of energy is energy *that is not used*. Opportunities for energy savings in this area are very high. The U.S. DOE states that 30% of the energy use in buildings is inefficient or unnecessary. Commercial and industrial buildings generate 45% of the nation's greenhouse gas emissions. If these same buildings increased energy efficiency 10%, the greenhouse gas reduction would compare to removal of 30 million vehicles from the nation's roads.

> "The cheapest energy is the energy
> you don't use in the first place."
>
> Sheryl Crow, American singer-songwriter and actress

Sterling Planet is an example of a certifying company that issues the white tag energy efficiency credits. They introduced the concept to the industry in 2006. Each white tag they issue represents a 1 megawatt-hour of electricity savings. Buyers include electric utilities in mandated markets with portfolio standards and companies in voluntary markets that are looking to meet targets for greenhouse gas emission reduction. Each green tag certificate they issue is serialized and unique.

The white tag certificate is created through the implementation of energy conservation projects—both demand-side and CHP. This normally occurs through equipment upgrades, retrofits and replacement; operational modifications and set point changes; energy management and monitoring systems (EMS); CHP or cogeneration; and high efficiency lighting. Each white tag can be created in one state and sold in another state. Certificates represent the contractual right to claim the environmental and other attributes associated with electricity generated from a renewable energy facility. They are traded independently of the energy.

The key issue for white tags is their certification through an accurate and measurable verification process. There is no meter measuring energy reduction and therefore must be determined through energy reduction calculations in the projects. It is the *owner of the facility* and not the owner of the equipment that has title to the white tags. This creates one of the few instances where the owner of the equipment does not have the title. Therefore, close agreement between the renewable energy project owner and the customer is a must. However, the project itself generates the credit and can therefore be used in producing a monetary value that helps to finance the project.

The regulations limit the availability of the certificates to projects that were completed after January 1, 2006. Mandated markets begin trading on January 1, 2007. CHP projects must achieve 50% efficiency and 20% thermal output and must meet efficiency requirements every quarter. Compliance prices in mandated markets range from $31-50 per MWh. The tags have a "vintage year" and expire the year after they are created (plus three months). Each certification requires the approval of an M&V (measurement and verification) plan.

Greenhouse Gas (GHG) Emissions, Sustainability and Carbon Management

Re-engineering business to meet the GHG emission reduction mandates now before us and a very challenging future of sustainability and carbon management, presents yet another opportunity for all parties seeking to finance cleantech energy projects a tool to achieve future compliance regulations. The sage advice of an old friend and veteran in emissions trading, Josh Margolis formerly with Cantor Fitzgerald, is most appropriate—"you may not believe in the science, but you had better believe in the politics or risk your company's future."

There is probably no component of renewable energy that has less history and more unknowns than this aspect. The role it plays in financing of renewable energy projects could be a very significant driver in all new cleantech projects. Nearly all of that impact focuses on and is a result of pending regulatory changes. These changes will not only mandate the purchase of massive amounts of new renewable energy technologies, but also the purchase of capital equipment that will dramatically lower the carbon footprint of companies across all segments of our economy. No one will be exempt including both for-profit and non-profit entities, public and private entities, large and small, and both the manufacturing and service sectors. The pending regulatory and compliance mandates and new legislation on federal, state, county and local levels will have an effect on anyone doing business in the U.S. From the costs of compliance and reporting requirements, securities disclosures and insurance risk costs, to accounting for the economic impacts of carbon on the income statement and balance sheet, those responsible for the regulated entities will have to lead and execute the alignment of an entity's financial strategy to that of a well-designed carbon management strategy.

Despite the current recession driven economy, the effects of new carbon reduction mandates marches on without regard to the economic costs to society. New reporting requirements beginning in 2011 are best met by having a carbon management strategy in place now. This creates huge opportunities for the renewable energy and cleantech industries that are uniquely positioned to provide solutions to these challenges. The financing of those assets through creative structures present great opportunities for the lender/project developer or asset owners to acquire assets that lower GHG emissions and provide effective manage carbon footprints for their clients and customers.

Just a few of the recent regulatory developments that will be driving this market:

- The "American Clean Energy and Security Act" (also known as the Waxman-Markey legislation) was passed by the House of Representative on June 26, 2009. A similar bill is winding its way through the senate. The bill calls for nearly a 20% carbon emission reduction through cuts of methane and CO_2 by 2020. On top of the mandate, is a detailed plan for a nationwide cap and trade system for those carbon emissions.
- For large users of energy and fossil fuel consuming industries, the Environment Protection Agency (EPA) requires new carbon emissions disclosures for 2010 to be reported in 2011. This is just a precursor for complete "command-and-control" regu-

lations (for which the EPA is well known and very good at). Furthermore, in Massachusetts et al. versus the EPA (Case No. 05-1120), the Supreme Court found that the gases that cause global warming are pollutants under the Clean Air Act. Thus, the EPA can enact new rules to manage carbon emissions under existing law—and odds are that they will.

- The COP15 United Nations Conference on Climate Change in December 2009 in Copenhagen sought to frame a successor to the Kyoto Protocols before they expire in 2012. Since the current Obama administration's strong commitment to a global protocol on GHGs emissions, there is a strong incentive to complete a Federal legislative package on greenhouse gas reductions in advance of the conference or immediately thereafter.
- New disclosure rules by the insurance and securities industries (for proper disclosure of corporate risks associated with carbon emissions), demands by large buyers of products in the supply chain like Wal-Mart or other retailers, and minority shareholder litigation on environmental and social sustainability issues, will all require more investments in measuring, monitoring, accounting and reporting of carbon emissions.

> "I think the environment should be put in the category of our national security. Defense of our resources is just as important as defense abroad. Otherwise what is there to defend?"
>
> Robert Redford, Yosemite National Park dedication. 1985

Even if the U.S. legislature can't agree to a fast track on new emission regulations, the Supreme Court decision clearly creates the framework for the EPA to promulgate new regulations under the Clean Air Act.

More companies will continue in their efforts to "offset" carbon emissions rather than avoid them in the first place. Point Carbon's Market Outlook expects the global carbon offset market to grow 20 percent in terms of volume in 2009. They forecast that 5.9 gigatons (Gt) of carbon dioxide equivalent (CO_2e) will trade in 2009, compared to 4.9 Gt in 2008. Renewable energy projects that create the GHG emission offsets will enjoy a very bright future—whether used directly by the end user or sold to a third party as an additional revenue source for the lender or project developer/energy provider. The carbon offsets can come from both energy efficiency projects that lower the carbon footprint directly or from renewable energy generation projects that produce energy with zero GHG emissions. The McKinsey Quarterly estimated that $170 billion a year will be invested in energy efficiency between now and 2020. This alone could lower global energy demand by substantial amounts from current levels and thereby eliminate the production of the GHG emissions in the first place.

It is now very clear that a company's carbon footprint is a source of liability. However, the reverse side of the coin is that carbon allowances and GHG emission credits can become assets that have a significant effect on the company balance sheet and income statement and therefore, the financial performance of the company's operations to shareholders and the public. Remember, it is the "owner" of the asset that has title to those emission assets (unless those environmental attributes are passed through to the debt obligator with a corresponding source of revenue to the original owner). Senior management has a fiduciary responsibility to find methods of incorporating those assets, liabilities and related risks into the fiscal strategies of the company.

A company must create a corporate wide strategy to manage its carbon footprint with a view towards how those strategies will affect the company balance sheet and income statement of the future. The strategy needs to involve everyone from the corporate board level all the way down to the facility managers. Only when everyone is involved will the opportunities for financing of the ultimate solutions be a viable option. Meeting the corporate carbon strategy goals requires a complete team effort. Often this will not be accomplished if there isn't someone at the senior level of management who is a "champion" for the solutions. Anyone seeking to present solutions to a customer needing cost effective and practical solutions to a carbon management and sustainable strategy need must recognize this challenge if a financing structure is to be a constructive solution. Therefore, a sustainability program, like most strategic initiatives, is much more likely to succeed with strong executive management support from its first stages and with specific resources dedicated to its implementation.

Uncertainty in the regulatory and technology environments is a fertile territory for cleantech technologies and financing groups to present creative financing structure solutions that are explored in the chapters of this book. Most senior corporate level executives want to minimize the risk they face in a carbon constrained environment and will welcome proposals that present techniques that can both save money on energy costs and at the same time present carbon mitigation options for the future.

Legislation

Legislation now plays a significant role in how a renewable energy project will be structured. This includes both existing legislation and new legislation—federal, state and local—that is rapidly accelerating and has a profound effect as creditors and project developers look over the horizon to the implications that future legislation will have on the project currently being financed.

Certainly, no state has been more aggressive in this regard than has California. Therefore, it is important to look at two recently enacted legislative items that will dramatically affect the renewable energy sector—AB32 and SB 1368. The reason California legislation is so important is that "as California goes, so does the rest of the nation" belief. In environmental legislation, no state has played more of a leadership role. In many cases, that state not only implements the federal environmental mandates more quickly, but they always go beyond what the federal government sets as standards and implements even stricter standards.

AB 32

On September 27, 2006, Governor Schwarzenegger signed Assembly Bill 32, the Global Warming Solutions Act of 2006 (Fabian Núñez and Fran Pavley, Chapter 488, Statutes of 2006). The event marked a watershed moment in California's history. By requiring in law a reduction of greenhouse gas (GHG) emissions to 1990 levels by 2020, California set the stage for its transition to a sustainable, clean energy future. This historic step also helped put climate change on the national agenda, and has spurred action by many other states.

The legislation calls for an ambitious but achievable reduction in California's carbon footprint. Reducing greenhouse gas emissions to 1990 levels means cutting approximately 30 percent from business-as-usual emission levels projected for 2020, or about 15 percent from today's levels. On a per-capita basis, that means reducing annual emissions of 14 tons of carbon dioxide equivalent for every man, woman and child in California down to about 10 tons per person by 2020. According to the California Air Resources Board, "this challenge also presents a magnificent opportunity to transform California's economy into one that runs on clean and sustainable technologies, so that all Californians are able to enjoy their rights in the future to clean air, clean water, and a healthy and safe environment."

Getting to the 2020 goal is not the end of the State's effort. According to climate scientists, California and the rest of the developed world will have to cut emissions by 80 percent from today's levels to stabilize the amount of carbon dioxide in the atmosphere and prevent the most severe effects of global climate change. This long range goal is reflected in California Executive Order S-3-05 that requires an 80 percent reduction of greenhouse gases from 1990 levels by 2050!

SB 1368

On September 29, 2006, Governor Arnold Schwarzenegger signed into law Senate Bill 1368 (Perata, Chapter 598, Statutes of 2006). The law limits long-term investments in baseload generation by the state's utilities to power plants that meet an emissions performance standard (EPS) jointly established by the California Energy Commission and the California Public Utilities Commission.

The GHG performance standard established by SB 1368 will help the state to meet its GHG reduction targets under AB 32 while protecting California consumers from the significant financial and reliability risks of high GHG-emitting energy sources. Dozens of new conventional coal-fired power plants were being considered for development throughout the western United States. The utilities that would own these plants were hoping to sell their power to California to meet the state's projected demand for electricity. That all changed with the enactment of SB 1368. The law will now compel electricity generators to comply with the GHG emission performance standards (EPS) to be enforced by the California Energy Commission. The law impacts both in-state power generators and any electricity imported into the state by generators outside the state!

As a result of the enactment of the law, the California Energy Commission designed regulations that:

- Established a standard for baseload generation owned by, or under long-term contract to publicly owned utilities, of 1,100 lbs. CO_2 per megawatt-hour (MWh). The goal was to encourage the development of power plants that meet California's growing energy needs while minimizing their emissions of greenhouse gases;
- Required posting of notices of public deliberations by publicly owned utilities on long-term invest-

ments on the Energy Commission website. This will facilitate public awareness of utility efforts to meet customer needs for energy over the long-term while meeting the State's standards for environmental impact, and;

- Establish a public process for determining the compliance of proposed investments with the EPS. This process includes the following components:
  - — A utility may request that the Commission determine whether or not an investment under consideration is subject to or complies with the EPS (Request for Evaluation of a Proposed Procurement)
  - — A utility may request that an investment be exempted from the requirement that it meet the EPS if the investment is necessary to ensure reliable service to utility customers or to avoid a threat of significant financial harm (Request for Reliability or Financial Exemption), or, if the utility is under a legal obligation to contribute a share of a larger investment (Request for Exemption Due to Pre-existing Multi-Party Commitment).
  - — A utility must submit a compliance filing upon committing to an investment that is required to meet the EPS (Compliance Filing)
  - — Any party may request that the Energy Commission conduct a complaint or investigation proceeding to determine a utility's compliance with the regulations (Request for Compliance Investigation)

This first-of-its-kind Emissions Performance Standard is a facility-based emissions standard requiring that all new long-term commitments for baseload generation to serve California consumers be with power plants that have emissions no greater than a combined cycle gas turbine plant. "New long-term commitment" refers to new plant investments (new construction), new or renewal contracts with a term of five years or more, or major investments by the utility in its existing baseload power plants.

The PUC has jurisdiction over the energy commitments of investor-owned utilities. SB 1368 gives additional authority to the PUC to implement and enforce the EPS for electric service providers (competitive retail providers delivering energy to consumers within the service territories of the investor-owned utilities) as well as any potential community choice aggregators (CCAs) that may form in the future (there are currently no CCAs operating in California, though a number are in the planning stages). SB 1368 also grants specific authority to the California Energy Commission (CEC) to implement and enforce an EPS for the municipal utilities in California.

Leadership in Energy and Environmental Design (LEED™)

One of the first questions asked by anyone thinking of incorporating renewable energy generation technology and energy efficiency components in a new building or the retrofit of an existing building is "what will going green cost?" This generally means—will it cost more? That is, more than comparable buildings in the marketplace, more than the funds I have available to build it, or more than the building would have cost without the sustainable design features. The U.S. Green Building Council (USGBC) has emerged as the leader in addressing this component of a renewable energy project through their LEED™ program.

LEED™ is a registered trademark of the USGBC. The Leadership in Energy and Environmental Design (LEED™) Green Building Rating System™ encourages and accelerates global adoption of sustainable green building and development practices through the creation and implementation of universally understood and accepted tools and performance criteria.

LEED™ is a third-party certification program of the USGBC and the nationally accepted benchmark for the design, construction and operation of high performance green buildings. LEED™ gives building owners and operators the tools they need to have an immediate and measurable impact on their buildings' performance. LEED™ promotes a whole-building approach to sustainability by recognizing performance in five key areas of human and environmental health:

- sustainable site development
- water savings
- energy efficiency
- materials selection
- indoor environmental quality

LEED™ indicates a property's overall sustainability by awarding points for just about any sustainable feature imaginable, from bike racks and rainwater collection and reuse systems, to energy-efficient lighting and low-flow plumbing fixtures. It is comprised of specific programs tailored for new buildings, existing buildings and tenant build-outs, and awards different tiers of certification such as Silver, Gold or Platinum (highest).

LEED™ rating systems include:

- New Construction and Major Renovations—designed to guide and distinguish high-performance commercial and institutional projects
- Existing Buildings: Operations and Maintenance—provides a benchmark for building owners and operators to measure operations, improvements and maintenance
- Commercial Interiors—a benchmark for the tenant improvement market that gives the power to make sustainable choices to tenants and designers
- Core and Shell—aids designers, builders, developers and new building owners in implementing sustainable design for new core and shell construction
- Schools—recognizes the unique nature of the design and construction of K-12 schools and addresses the specific needs of school spaces
- Retail—recognizes the unique nature of retail design and construction projects and addresses the specific needs of retail spaces
- Healthcare—promotes sustainable planning, design and construction for high-performance healthcare facilities
- Homes—promotes the design and construction of high-performance green homes
- Neighborhood Development—integrates the principles of smart growth, urbanism and green building into the first national program for neighborhood design

LEED™ certification provides independent, third-party verification that a building project meets the highest green building and performance measures. There are both environmental and financial benefits to earning LEED™ certification. LEED-certified buildings:

- Lower operating costs and increased asset value.
- Reduce waste sent to landfills.
- Conserve energy and water.
- Are healthier and safer for occupants.
- Reduce harmful greenhouse gas emissions.
- Qualify for tax rebates, zoning allowances and other incentives in hundreds of cities.
- Demonstrate an owner's commitment to environmental stewardship and social responsibility.

Therefore, anytime renewable energy projects can use LEED guidelines to increase savings by lowering energy bills, there is an opportunity for a project owner/lender/developer to get involved in the project. As a result, IRR can increase, payments can be lowered, and capital costs that can be funded by a third party investor and not the building owner, and the building owner benefits. To earn LEED™ certification, a project must satisfy all prerequisites and earn a minimum number of points outlined in the LEED™ Rating System under which it is registered.

Studies performed for the USGBC have found that sustainable "green" buildings outperform their peer non-green assets in key areas such as occupancy, sale price and rental rates, sometimes by wide margins. The results indicate a broader demand by property investors and tenants for buildings that have earned either LEED™ certification or the Energy Star® label and strengthen the "business case" for green buildings, which proponents have increasingly cast as financially sound investments.

According to the study, LEED™ buildings command rent premiums of $11.24 per square foot over their non-LEED peers and have 3.8 percent higher occupancy. Rental rates in Energy Star® buildings represent a $2.38 per square foot premium over comparable non-Energy Star® buildings and have 3.6 percent higher occupancy. And, in a trend that could signal greater attention from institutional investors, Energy Star® buildings are selling for an average of $61 per square foot more than their peers, while LEED™ buildings command a remarkable $171 more per square foot.

A study, performed by the New Buildings Institute for the USGBC, found that on average, LEED-NC buildings are delivering anticipated savings. LEED™ energy use is similar to predictions—25-30% better than the national average. Average savings increase for the higher LEED™ levels, with Gold/Platinum buildings approaching the interim goal of Architecture 2030.

Further, a report done by Davis Langdon[13] and often cited by the USGBC (and further reasserted in an article written by Peter Morris and Lisa Matthiessen in 2007) concludes that the cost per square foot for buildings seeking LEED™ certification falls into the existing range of costs for building of similar program types. Therefore, one can conclude that in nearly all projects seeking LEED™ certification and recognition, any incremental costs are extremely small or don't exist at all. This suggests that building owners are finding ways to incorporate the elements important to the goals and values of the project, regardless of budget, by making choices and value decisions.

The certification fee to obtain LEED™ certification is based on the rating system that the project is certifying under, and the size of the project. This fee is paid when the project team submits documentation for review. Table 4-5 outlines the rates.[14]

Although it is clear that there are higher incremental costs for getting LEED™ certification on a building, economically the net benefits far outweigh the costs. Higher occupancy and rent rates, as well as quicker lease-up and better tenant retention is one of the main earmarks of a LEED™ certified building. This can equate to a substantial revenue enhancement component in the financial analysis of a renewable energy project.

Residential Renewable Energy Tax Credits

The energy tax credits under IRC 45 (the production tax credits) and IRC 48 (the investment tax credits) have had a profound effect on investments in renewable energy systems over the past 10 years. Those energy tax credits are best known for their use in the commercial and industrial sector and much of this book is focused on their rules of use and the applications in financing renewable energy projects. However, there is also an application in the residential sector for individuals as opposed to corporate investors in the use of renewable energy tax credits.

Established by the Energy Policy Act of 2005, the federal tax credit for residential energy property initially applied to solar-electric systems, solar water heating systems and fuel cells. The Energy Improvement and Extension Act of 2008 (H.R. 1424) extended the tax credit to small wind-energy systems and geothermal heat pumps, effective January 1, 2008. Other key revisions included an eight-year extension of the credit to December 31, 2016; the ability to take the credit against the alterna-

Table 4-5: LEED Certification Fees

	Less than 50,000 Square Feet	50,000-500,000 Square Feet	More than 500,000 Square Feet	
	Project Gross Floor Area in Sq Ft (excluding all parking areas)			
	Less than 50,000	50,000 to 500,000	More than 500,000	Expedited Review
Registration				
USGBC members		$900		N/A
Non-members		$1,200		
Precertification Review (Optional, LEED CS only)				
USGBC members		$3,250		$5,000 surcharge
Non-members		$4,250		
Standard Review	Flat Rate	Per Sq Ft	Flat Rate	
Design & Construction Review				
USGBC members	$2,250	$0.045/sf	$22,500	
Non-members	$2,750	$0.055/sf	$27,500	$10,000 surcharge
Split Review	Flat Rate	Per Sq Ft	Flat Rate	
Design Review				
USGBC members	$2,050	$0.040/sf	$20,000	$5,000 surcharge
Non-members	$2,250	$0.045/sf	$22,500	
Construction Review				
USGBC members	$500	$0.010/sf	$5,000	$5,000 surcharge
Non-members	$750	$0.015/sf	$7,500	
Appeals				
Complex credits		$800/credit		$500/credit surcharge
All other credits		$500/credit		
LEED Interpretations				
USGBC members		$180/credit		N/A
Non-members		$380/credit		
Project CIRs		$220/credit		N/A

tive minimum tax; and the removal of the $2,000 credit limit for solar-electric systems beginning in 2009. The credit was further enhanced in February 2009 by The American Recovery and Reinvestment Act of 2009 (H.R. 1: Div. B, Sec. 1122, p. 46), which removed the maximum credit amount for all eligible technologies (except fuel cells) placed in service after 2008.

A residential taxpayer may claim a tax credit of 30% of qualified expenditures for a system that serves a dwelling unit located in the United States and used as a residence by the taxpayer. Expenditures with respect to the equipment are treated as made when the installation is completed. If the installation is at a new home, the "placed in service" date is the date of occupancy by the homeowner. Expenditures include labor costs for on-site preparation, assembly or original system installation, and for piping or wiring to interconnect a system to the home. If the federal tax credit exceeds tax liability, the excess amount may be carried forward to the succeeding taxable year. The excess credit may be carried forward until 2016, but it is unclear whether the unused tax credit can be carried forward after then. The maximum allowable credit, equipment requirements and other details vary by technology. It should be noted however, The American Recovery and Reinvestment Act of 2009 does not allow taxpayers eligible for the residential renewable energy tax credit to receive a U.S. Treasury Department grant instead of taking this credit.

Production Tax Credits

The production tax credit (PTC) is covered under IRC section 45, was established by the 1992 Energy Policy Act, and gives tax credits to the taxpayer who owns the eligible capital asset (primarily wind with some biomass, geothermal power, eligible hydropower, landfill gas, and municipal solid waste.). For each MWh of electricity a qualifying project generates, the owner receives a tax credit that can be applied directly to its tax bill. Today, that credit is roughly $22/MWh. The incentive is production-based. The more hours a project produces power and the more MWh it produces, the more credits it generates. The PTC applies to the first 10 years of the project's life and is indexed to inflation over the 10-year period.

In part as a direct result of the PTC, the U.S. has led the world in wind power. Over the last four years, the U.S. wind industry has attracted an average of $17 billion in private investment each year. Over the last six years, U.S. domestic production of wind turbine components has grown 12-fold to more than 400 facilities in 43 states.[15]

Though the historical impacts of the PTC are well known, somewhat less recognized is the fact that the frequent expiration/extension cycle that we have seen since 1999 has had several negative consequences for the growth of wind power. Due to the series of shorter-term, 1- to 2-year PTC extensions, growing demand for wind power has been compressed into tight and frenzied windows of development. This has led to boom and bust cycles in renewable energy development, under-investment in manufacturing capacity in the U.S., and variability in equipment and supply costs. Recent work at Berkeley Lab suggests that this boom-and-bust cycle has made the PTC less effective in stimulating low-cost wind development than might be the case if a longer term and more stable policy were established.[16] Originally enacted in 1992, the PTC has been renewed and expanded numerous times, most recently by H.R. 1424 (Div. B, Sec. 101 & 102) in October 2008 and again by H.R. 1 (Div. B, Section 1101 & 1102) in February 2009.

The PTC has also sometimes been criticized as being too narrowly applicable, thereby restricting the types of investors that can efficiently make use of it. Most obviously, as a tax credit, the PTC is not available to entities that do not pay taxes (e.g., publicly owned electric utilities, rural electric cooperatives, government bodies, and non-profits), though due to several design features, the PTC is also not easily accessible by certain tax-paying entities as well. This would include individuals who are restricted by the passive income rules of the IRC. These restrictions have led to a concentration of wind project ownership in the hands of relatively few entities with sufficient tax liabilities to make use of the credit.

The American Recovery and Reinvestment Act of 2009 (H.R. 1) allows taxpayers eligible for the federal renewable electricity production tax credit (PTC) to take the federal business energy investment tax credit (ITC) *or* to receive a grant from the U.S. Treasury Department instead of taking the PTC for new installations. The grant is only available to systems where construction began prior to December 31, 2011. The law also allowed taxpayers eligible for the business ITC to receive a grant from the U.S. Treasury Department instead of taking the business ITC for new installations. The Treasury Department issued Notice 2009-52 in June 2009, giving limited guidance on how to take the federal business energy investment tax credit instead of the federal renewable electricity production tax credit. That opportunity expired on December 31, 2011 when the 1603 Treasury grant program expired. There is a lot of effort currently going on to finding ways of extending the grant program into 2012 and beyond. However, the PTC is in place until the end of 2012.

> *"Well, there's no doubt about the fact that, that higher energy prices lead to greater conservation, greater energy efficiency, and they also, of course, play a useful role on the supply side."*
>
> John W. Snow, former U.S. Secretary of Treasury

In the proposed fiscal year 2013 budget, President Barack Obama proposed extending the renewable energy production tax credit. The legislation was passed and extended the production tax credit for wind facilities and the investment tax credit for wind facility property through 2013.

Savings from Renewable Energy Projects

Renewable energy projects involve the installation of devices and/or systems that generate energy (e.g., electricity or heat) or displace energy use thorough the use of renewable energy resources. Examples of technologies that do this include: photovoltaics (PV), active or passive solar systems for space conditioning or production of domestic hot water, biomass conversion systems (e.g., landfill gas methane recovery projects), and wind systems. For additional information on the measurement and verification of renewable energy projects, refer to IPMVP (International Performance Measurement & Verification Protocol) for renewables.

The most notable difference between renewable energy projects and other ECMs is that renewable projects supply energy rather than reduce the amount of energy used. Measuring the energy supplied allows for a simplified approach to measuring savings that is not possible with energy efficiency projects.

Like many projects, the performance of most renewable energy technologies depends on the environmental conditions, such as solar radiation or wind speed. The use of long-term averages of these values is reliable, but any M&V Plan (see Chapter six) should be structured in such a way as to allocate the risk due to short-term variations in environmental conditions. Therefore, it may be appropriate to stipulate these conditions and verify the performance of the equipment using short-term measurements (e.g., the efficiency of a solar hot water heater). Long-term performance typically needs to be verified.

There are two general approaches for calculating energy savings from renewable energy projects:

- Net energy use
- Normalized savings based on typical environmental conditions and actual performance characteristics

For all renewable energy projects, consideration should be given to the impact of parasitic energy use by the renewable system and to increased operations and maintenance costs due to the addition of new equipment. Demand savings from renewable energy technologies may occur, but, depending on the electric utility's rate structure, the energy must be available and uninterrupted during all peak periods. Accounting for demand savings requires more sophisticated metering that aligns measurement intervals with the utility interval.

The first approach—net energy use—involves directly measuring the energy output from the system and quantifying any additional costs incurred or savings realized. This approach is suitable for wind, PV, and other electricity generating equipment. The measurement concept assumes that energy (electrical and/or thermal) produced by the renewable system is used at the project site, and displaces energy that would have been provided by an existing source. Savings are determined by measuring the net amount of energy produced by the renewable system and used at the project site valued at prescribed utility rates. This approach eliminates the need for a baseline and places the risk of weather variations on the project developer when the parties to the project financing have elected to use an energy purchase agreement as the structure for the project finance.

Utility savings from renewable measures that supply thermal energy (e.g., solar hot water heater) are determined by dividing the energy delivered by the efficiency of the original equipment (e.g., conventional water heater). For projects that may sell excess energy or store energy on-site, additional costs and savings may need to be considered. Cost savings using this approach can be calculated using the formula in Equation 4-1.

The second primary approach to calculate energy savings in a renewable energy project involves calculating normalized savings based on typical environmental conditions and actual performance characteristics of the system. Savings are determined by calculating the difference between baseline energy and demand and predicted or metered energy and demand, with both sets of data adjusted to a prescribed set of conditions. Depending on the type of system, this strategy can use any of the M&V options described in Chapter 6.

Normalizing savings in this manner places the risk of weather fluctuations on the customer/debtor, and requires that the project developer/lender periodically demonstrate that specified performance characteristics have been met. These performance characteristics and how they will be determined should be specified in the project-specific M&V Plan. Performance parameters that should be specified include efficiency of PV modules, minimum hot-water temperatures, and the content in landfill gases.

The basic energy savings equation can be modified to determine cost savings, as shown in Equation 4-2.

Equation 4-1

$$\textit{Cost Savings} = (\textit{kWh delivered}) * (\textit{Rate}_{kWh}) + \{\textit{Thermal Energy} / \textit{Efficiency Displaced Equipment}\} * (1\textit{kWh} / 3{,}414\ \textit{Btu}) * (\textit{Rate}_{kWh}) + \{\$_{\textit{Energy Sold}}\} - \{\$_{\textit{Parasitic Loads}}\} - \{\$_{\textit{New O\&M Costs}}\}$$

Where:

kWh Delivered	=	Electrical energy delivered by the system and used at the facility
$Rate_{kWh}$	=	Specified cost of electrical energy
Thermal Efficiency	=	Thermal energy delivered by the system in BTUs during the performance period
Efficiency Displaced Equipment	=	Operating efficiency of the equipment that would have been used
1kWh/3,414 BTU	=	Conversion between thermal energy (BTU) and electrical energy (kWh)
$\$_{Energy\ Sold}$	=	Funds received through the sale of energy produced
$\$_{Parasitic\ Loads}$	=	Cost of operating systems and equipment related to renewable technology
$\$_{New\ O\&M\ Costs}$	=	Additional cost of operations and maintenance due to renewable technology

Equation 4-2

$$\textit{Cost Savings} = [\{(\textit{Baseline Energy}) - (\textit{Performance Period Energy}) \pm \textit{Adjustments}\} * (\textit{Rate}_{\textit{kWh Energy}})] - \{\$_{\textit{Parasitic Loads}}\} - \{\$_{\textit{New O\&M Costs}}\}$$

Where:

Baseline Energy	=	The calculated or measured energy use of a piece of equipment prior to the implementation of the project
Performance Period Energy	=	The calculated or measured energy use of a piece of equipment after the implementation of the project (including electrical and thermal)
Adjustments	=	Routine and non-routine changes made to the baseline or performance period energy use to account for expected and unexpected variations in conditions
$Rate_{kWh\ Energy}$	=	Specified cost of electrical energy
Thermal Energy	=	Thermal energy delivered by the system in BTU during the post-installation period converted to kWh
$\$_{Parasitic\ Loads}$	=	Cost of operating systems and equipment related to renewable technology
$\$_{New\ O\&M\ Costs}$	=	Additional cost of operations and maintenance due to renewable technology

Energy measurement is the critical component to the above formulas. Determining the electrical output of systems is relatively straightforward. This is because electrical output and parasitic loads can be simply measured with many commercially available meters. Measuring thermal output (e.g., hot water from a domestic hot-water solar system displacing an electric water heating system) is also straightforward, but not necessarily inexpensive, using commercial Btu meters, water flow meters, temperature transducers, etc. However, all of the thermal and electrical output from a system does not necessarily displace an equivalent amount of load. This is due to storage, system losses, and differences in time between when useful energy is produced and when it is needed.

Electricity measurements associated with system output, parasitic loads, power to the project site, and power to third parties and the utility may be needed. All electrical meters (and related equipment) are usually provided, installed, owned, and maintained by the project developer/lender or the servicing utility.

When a net metering approach is used, meter(s) will typically show the measure's gross output (in kW and kWh) less parasitic use (e.g., pump motors) and sales to third parties or the local utility, as well as any local transformation and transmission and battery storage losses (the sale of environmental attributes may or may not be included). The goal with this method is usually to measure net generation delivered to the project site. Metering, interconnection (including safety provisions), reporting, and other related issues are to be in accordance with current electrical standards and the requirements of the servicing electric utility.

With the net energy-use M&V approach, deliveries to and from the facility should be separately recorded and treated as separate transactions. For purposes of power delivered to the site, a single meter that records energy supplied to the site is preferred. If a calculated transformer loss value is used, it should be based on certified factory test data for that particular transformer.

The following are some suggested metering requirements:

- kWh and demand metering at the point of delivery
- Time of-delivery metering
- Provisions for remote meter reading

Thermal meters (e.g., Btu meters) are required for measuring the net thermal output of certain renewable energy systems (e.g., hot water generated by an active solar system). Note that metering of thermal energy requires a "net" measurement of flows and enthalpy to and from a system. Measurements of thermal flows may need to take into account any vented or wasted energy that is produced by the system but not used at the site, as well as distribution and storage losses. Also note that small errors in enthalpy measurements (usually determined by temperature) can introduce large errors in the energy calculations; hence, meter precision, accuracy, and calibration are especially important.

Active solar thermal systems include systems for producing industrial process heat, domestic hot water, and space heating and cooling. Useful monitoring includes 1) site inspections and brief temperature and system monitoring for diagnostics, 2) spot, short-term, or long-term monitoring of system key parameters such as temperatures, energy flows, and control status, and 3) utility billing analyses.

Passive solar systems usually involve the performance of a whole building with architectural features such as overhang design and use of thermal mass. As such, this technology is different from other renewable energy measures in that mechanical devices with identifiable energy inputs and outputs are not involved. Thus, passive solar M&V typically involves the analysis of a whole building, and thus it is best to use utility billing analyses or calibrated simulation techniques.

With wind, PV and other renewable energy systems, the performance characteristics of the components are usually well defined, such as the conversion efficiency of the PV modules or the Btu content of landfill gas. In addition, the electrical or thermal flows can usually be easily measured. The complexity of these projects lies in projecting long-term performance due to variation in the resources (e.g., solar insolation, wind resource, or reserve of methane gas in a landfill) and accounting for any variations between when the resource is available and when it is needed (i.e., the interaction of storage systems and their inefficiencies).

Appraisal Value on Real Property

An *Appraisal Journal* article[17] by Rick Nevin and Gregory Watson references a study on the residential real estate markets that shows an increase in home value for energy efficient homes (which includes installation of renewable energy generation technology) that reflect the discounted value of annual fuel savings. They found that the home value increases by about $20 for $1 reduction in annual utility bills (assuming an after-tax mortgage interest rate of about 5%). Another study estimates sales price premiums for PV-equipped California homes at 14-22 times the value of annual energy savings.[18] Regression analysis of American Housing Survey data confirms this hypothesis for national and metropolitan area samples, attached and detached housing, and detached housing subsamples using a specific fuel type as the main heating fuel (could include electrical as well as natural gas, propane or fuel oil). Most professionals agree that the same analysis can be applied to commercial and industrial properties where there is an even higher value given to cap costs. In real terms however, other energy efficiency measures would also have been installed (such as insulation, weatherproofing, double or triple pane windows, solar lighting systems, energy efficient appliances, and lighting retrofit systems) that would have a much lower cost and even faster payback, thus enhancing the appraised value vs. cost approach to more like 50-75% value.

Sandia National Laboratories has just come out with a new tool for estimating the value of a PV system installed on either a residential or commercial property called PV Value™. The model follows the Income Capitalization Approach used by appraisers to determine the value of a PV system as a function of the potential energy produced over the system's lifetime (see Chapter seven for actual application of this model). PV Value™ is intended for use by real estate appraisers, mortgage underwriters, credit analysts, real property assessors, insurance claims adjusters—and of course—renewable energy project owners, investors, credit lenders and system users. The current version of the software was released in December 2012. A web application is currently in development for 2013. It can be downloaded free of charge (including instruction manual) from Sandia at *http://energy.sandia.gov/?page_id=8047*. The program is an Excel™ spreadsheet with real-time links to current mortgage discounts and other data for use in the financial analysis. The program valuation tool was made possible through funding provided by the U.S. Department of Energy's Office of Energy Efficiency and Renewable Energy.

A presentation on Standardizing Appraisals for PV Installations was made at the Photovoltaic Specialist Conference in Tampa, FL on June 21, 2013. (*http://energy.sandia.gov/wp/wp-content/gallery/uploads/SAND2013-5239C.pdf*)

The *income capitalization approach* used by PV Value™ is based on the idea that the value of a property is equal to the capitalized value of the net income stream generated by that property—including energy savings. Applying this approach to PV looks at what a potential buyer may be willing to pay today for the opportunity to receive future cash flows using a discounted cash flow model. The model considers the present value of projected future energy production along with estimated operation and maintenance costs that are anticipated to occur during the solar module power production warranty timeframe. The residential or commercial building owner or purchaser's weighted average cost of capital (WACC) is used along with a risk premium spread to determine a discount rate for the present value calculation. The purchaser's WACC is then calculated based off of a readably available benchmark interest rate such as the Fannie Mae or Freddie Mac 30-year fixed rate 60-day commitment. Regardless of the benchmark chosen, for the purchase of the model it should closely mirror the cost of borrowing for the purchaser of the income stream.

Using the income approach, a reasonable valuation can be arrived at through the observation of visible installed components and a review of the latest system performance test and installation documentation, including a digital shading analysis. The following available parameter fields need to be accurately inserted into the model to obtain accurate results:

- Zip code
- System size in watts
- Derate factor (default is 0.77)
- Module degradation rate (defaulted to 0.5 and reflects a 0.5% annual degradation rate)
- Array type
- Array tilt
- Array azimuth
- Discount rate (defaults to 30 year Fannie Mae fixed rate but can be customized)
- Utility rates (done automatically based on PVWatts™ and can also have custom input)
- Utility escalation rate (based on zip code but can also have custom input)
- O&M expenses (both automatic and customized input options)
- Warranty period
- Age of system
- Remaining life expectancy
- Option to evaluate using a lease purchase input selection

This tool will be used later in Chapter seven covering fundamental structuring techniques and examples.

An additional benefit can come down the road when the homeowner or business facility owner elects to sell the real property. In addition to the increased value in the real property, mortgage lenders are more receptive to lower down payments or lower interest rates on new mortgages when these energy improvements have been added to the property. On the other hand, home appraisals may not always reflect the total cost of energy efficiency and energy production investments because research has never clearly demonstrated or quantified the relationship between energy efficiency and market value in multiple published works, studies or papers. This of course will change over time and become much more important to the valuation process as fossil fuel prices continue to rise or are curtailed in any significant manner. Feed-in tariffs providing significant long term income on a renewable energy production asset could also dramatically increase the value of the property far beyond the examples provided above.

Fannie Mae and Freddie Mac[19] are currently engaged in pilot programs that allow the incremental cost of energy-efficient, cost-effective upgrades to be added to the appraised value of a home. Under these programs, the home buyer must provide only the additional down payment associated with the increase in appraised value in order to maintain the same loan-to-value ratio. Other commercial property mortgage lenders are evaluating the same underwriting determinations on non-residential property.

An additional key factor appraisers will take into consideration is the inflation rate of electric or gas rates in the region where the RE facility will be located. Purchasing a renewable energy system will fix the energy cost and allow it not to escalate with rates from the utility (excluding the maintenance costs which should be very minor). The following table shows the electric rate escalation in one specific region—the state of California—from 1980 to 2005. It shows the retail electric rates from the six major utilities in the state over that period of time.

As can be seen, with the exception of SMUD whose rates went up 400% over that 25 year period (16% per year), the average rate increase was 8.45% per year (a CAGR of 4.08% per year). It is important to remember that these rate escalations do not look at the "tiered" rates that became prevalent starting in 1990 from most California utilities. Those rates (particularly the higher tiers) have gone up dramatically faster than those shown in the chart above. Hence, considering the "inflation" or "escalation" electric rates further supports the higher values for real property values where renewable energy systems have been installed.

A final parameter to take into consideration is the fact that in many states, renewable energy production systems add value to the real estate but the renewable energy system is exempt from property taxes. This fact alone can add substantial value to the real estate on which the RE system is located given that an appraiser could do a net present value analysis on the savings from not paying property taxes on the improvement to the real property to add to the value of a RE system (as in California—other states may be different).

As a result, it can be seen that the installation of renewable energy systems for energy production can substantially increase the value of the real property. As a

Table 4-6. Weighted Average Retail Electric Rates in California 1980 - 2005

Year (Historical)	PG&E	SCE	SDG&E	LADWP	SMUD	BGP
1980	4.76	6.09	8.43	5.61	2.53	6.72
1981	6.05	6.45	9.36	6.16	2.82	6.48
1982	6.24	7.37	11.26	6.11	3.03	7.60
1983	6.42	7.42	11.66	5.85	3.75	7.48
1984	7.86	7.64	11.80	6.08	3.92	7.79
1985	8.73	7.94	12.84	6.54	4.56	7.81
1986	8.72	8.20	11.66	6.74	5.45	7.65
1987	7.56	8.19	10.42	7.09	6.64	8.22
1988	7.85	8.51	9.82	7.57	7.35	9.05
1989	8.79	9.17	9.51	8.06	7.41	9.50
1990	9.24	9.45	9.22	8.39	8.27	9.82
1991	9.87	10.07	9.36	8.23	8.30	9.91
1992	10.42	10.36	9.47	8.62	8.21	10.34
1993	10.59	10.06	9.89	9.13	7.69	10.96
1994	10.71	10.28	9.69	9.53	7.96	11.49
1995	9.89	10.46	9.67	9.14	8.18	11.43
1996	10.20	10.22	10.36	9.12	8.14	11.36
1997	10.30	10.22	10.70	9.36	7.92	10.51
1998	9.74	10.10	10.16	9.76	7.63	10.95
1999	9.81	10.05	10.16	9.75	7.60	10.96
2000	9.82	10.12	13.72	9.79	7.61	10.97
2001	11.74	12.87	13.66	9.79	9.26	13.57
2002	12.72	12.82	14.45	9.80	9.27	12.72
2003	13.18	13.16	14.26	9.80	9.81	12.43
2004	12.72	12.18	14.55	9.66	8.60	11.88
2005	13.07	12.93	14.72	9.31	10.10	11.97

Source: California Energy Commission

PG&E = Pacific Gas & Electric (Investor Owned Utility)
SCE = Southern California Edison (Investor Owned Utility)
SDG&E = San Diego Gas & Electric (Investor Owned Utility)
LADWP = Los Angeles Department of Water & Power (Municipal Owned Utility)
SMUD = Sacramento Municipal Utility District (Municipal Owned Utility)
BGP = Burbank, Glendale Pasadena (Municipal Owned Utility)

component of the real property, in many cases they can provide an attractive vehicle for financial investment. These tangible benefits are financially quantifiable.[20]

Commissioning

Commissioning of installed equipment and systems is considered industry best-practice. Commissioning ensures that systems are designed, installed, functionally tested in all modes of operation, and are capable of being operated and maintained in conformity with the design intent (i.e., energy production levels, appropriate lighting levels, cooling capacity, comfortable temperatures, etc.). Benefits of commissioning include safety tie-in to existing utility interconnection, proper interface (as designed) to load centers in the facility and existing plant processes and systems, increased building comfort, reduced operational problems, lower installation costs, fewer contractor call-backs, and improved energy performance. The commissioning requirements outlined below have been adapted from industry standard procedures detailed in ASHRAE's commissioning guidelines (0-2005).

Commissioning (Cx) is a process that begins at project conception and typically ends after project acceptance. Key activities in the commissioning process include documentation of design intent, design reviews, execution of construction checklists, systematic functional testing of equipment and systems, oversight of training for operations and maintenance staff, and follow-up on any warranty issues.

Commissioning usually requires taking performance measurements to ensure that systems are working properly. Because of the overlap in commissioning and post-installation measurement and verification (M&V—see Chapter six) activities, some people may confuse the two. The difference is that commissioning ensures that systems are functioning properly—post-installation M&V quantifies how well the systems are working from an energy standpoint.

Following the commissioning process will help realize the full potential of the energy conservation measures (ECMs) and renewable energy production projects, but key issues must be anticipated and planned. These issues are discussed below, and include:

- Allocating adequate resources and time to the commissioning process
- Appointing a commissioning agent (CxA), and/or prescribing the affiliation and qualifications required
- Providing an overview of roles and responsibilities for CxA, customer, and project developer/lender
- Making provisions to document the design intent for each energy production system or ECM
- Incorporating a process for design reviews and submittal approvals
- Specify commissioning reporting requirements.

> *"There is too much energy conversation instead of energy conservation. Let us walk the talk. 'Just' energy audits should be outlawed. What comes after is more important. Energy efficiency is a state of mind and not just a love affair with State-of-the-Art Technology. An experienced energy auditor working in tandem with a committed and empowered energy manager is a dream team of intellectual sparring partners to reduce energy consumption and costs. A sustainable national energy management strategy is the sum of energy efficiency + energy modesty + renewable energy. It is not about favoring one over the other."*
>
> A. Kaupp, Famous or Infamous Quotes about Energy Conservation in India

The commissioning contract should outline the project's specific commissioning requirements. The key items that should be specified include:

- The affiliation and qualifications of the Commissioning Agent (CxA)
- Roles and responsibilities of CxA, ESCO and agency, including witnessing of Cx activities
- Process that will be followed to document the design intent or agency's project requirements for each energy conservation measure (ECM) or system
- Requirements for agency or third-party design reviews or submittal approvals
- Schedule for developing and approving a Cx plan, including expected content such as:
  - — Pre-functional inspections
  - — Functional testing procedures
  - — Required use of manufacturer start-up procedures
  - — Plan for seasonal testing and conditional acceptance, if needed
  - — Contents and timing of the Final Cx Report, Systems Manual, and any periodic project report

    — Requirements for CxA oversight of O&M training
    — Plan for warranty walk-through or other follow-up procedures

The contract should designate both the affiliation and qualifications of the CxA that will lead the commissioning process for the project. The key responsibilities of the CxA are: 1) directing the commissioning team in the completion of the commissioning requirements; 2) overseeing or performing the commissioning tests; and 3) verifying the adequacy of the commissioning results.

In the ideal scenario, the CxA will be from an independent third party reporting directly to the project developer/lender and the customer/debtor when appropriate. In some cases the CxA may be a qualified member of the project developers or lenders staff, but sufficient time and resources must be allocated for fulfillment of this role. Key qualifications for the individual acting as CxA include onsite availability, experience executing the Cx process, hands-on experience in testing and troubleshooting applicable systems, familiarity with a variety of testing equipment, and detailed understanding of the systems and equipment affected by the project.

Once the financing contract has been signed, any remaining design and engineering of the project scope is completed. Commissioning related activities performed by the Cx team in the design phase include:

- The project developer/lender completes the project design
- The financing parties and CxA review design and approve equipment submittals
- The project developer/lender and customer/debtor document the design intent for each ECM or energy production system
- The CxA develops a draft Cx Plan, including the specifics of all pre-functional inspections and functional performance tests
- The CxA develops Cx specifications for the project (if needed)
- The parties to the financing agreement review and accept Cx documents
- The CxA issues Final Commissioning Plan and specifications

After the design and commissioning plan have been finalized, construction begins. Cx-related activities that occur during the construction phase include:

- Construction is observed by the parties to the financing contract Cx representatives and the CxA
- Periodic Cx meetings are held with the project team
- Cx progress reports are submitted by the CxA
- Pre-functional inspections are completed and certified by the project developer/lender prior to equipment start-up and functional testing
- Manufacturer start- procedures are completed by the project developer/lender or manufacturer's representative

Once construction has been completed and ready for acceptance by the project developer/lender, the functional performance tests are executed and the procedures are documented by the CxA. The CxA documents the test results, explicitly including how the project developer/lender's and customer/debtor's project requirements or design intent prescribed for each energy production system and ECM were met. Any items that did not pass are tracked and presented to the project team in a deficiency log. The project developer/lender then rectifies the items and performs a retest in the presence of the CxA to confirm that the items have been fixed. The deficiency log is then updated by the CxA, noting the date and corrective action taken.

It is common for the CxA to oversee and ensure the adequacy of the O&M training in order to ensure that the ECMs and energy production systems are properly maintained and operated. Some ECMs, such as natural ventilation, daylighting, night time flushing, and use of building thermal mass, result in a building that behaves differently than a conventional building. It is important that the commissioning contractor, building maintenance staff, and occupants understand how the building or facility now works. For example, an energy management behavioral program for employees is one way to educate building and facility occupants.

Depending on the preference of the agency, the project developer/lender then assembles the Final Commissioning Report or a Systems Manual, as prescribed in the contract. At a minimum, a Final Cx Report should be provided, which typically includes:

- Commissioning summary report
- Project developer/lender-certified pre-functional checklists
- Completed manufacturers startup sheets

- Results of functional testing and verification of system performance
- Detailed operating procedures/sequences of operations
- Closed-out deficiency log
- Overview of training provided to O&M staff

Some customer/debtor's may prefer to receive a more comprehensive Systems Manual, which is required for LEED 37 certification. A Systems Manual typically brings together comprehensive project documentation, including:

- Project requirements or design intent of the parties to the project financing agreement
- Schematic system drawings
- Approved submittals
- Recommended record keeping procedures
- Maintenance procedures and schedules
- Test requirements for ongoing commissioning

Commissioning activities that typically extend beyond final Project Acceptance include deferred functional testing and warranty verification. Often, some functional testing may be postponed until seasonal conditions are appropriate to evaluate the system. When some functional testing has been deferred, acceptance of the project is conditional upon the success of the scheduled tests.

PACE Programs

A Property Assessed Clean Energy ("PACE") financing program is an innovative and cost effective method enabling local governments to finance renewable energy and energy efficiency projects on privately owned residential, commercial and industrial properties. PACE can be used to finance a wide variety of clean energy installations from insulation to solar PV panels, solar thermal systems, high efficiency furnaces and water heaters, energy efficient windows and in some program water conservation related equipment.[21]

In regions with PACE legislation in place, municipal governments offer a bond to investors and then take those funds and loan the money to consumers and businesses to purchase energy efficiency and renewable energy production systems on their real property. The loans are repaid over a typical term of 15-20 years through an annual assessment on their real property tax bill. Uniquely, the loan is attached to the property rather than in individual or company. Because PACE is funded through municipal bonds that are secured by the tax assessments on the real property, they create no liability to the city's funds.

All PACE financing programs work at the local municipal level. Although program elements vary to meet the needs of each community they do meet the state laws in their implementation. PACE programs in different communities have the following similarities:

- Real property owners within the financing district do not have to participate. If they do not want to participate through an energy efficiency upgrade or an energy production system on their property, they do not need to participate and therefore have no increase in their property taxes.
- Before a project is approved for funding, an energy audit is undertaken and only qualified contractors competent in the scope of the work can perform the installation of the system.
- The public entity underwriting the program establish, in law or public policy, a specific goal or objective.
- The public entity will provide the financing for the projects utilizing low interest rate municipal bonds and pass those low rates on to the home or commercial property owner.
- The borrower who receives funding under the PACE program will agree to accept a property tax assessment or charge for up to 20 years.
- The obligation is affixed to the property and is passed on to the new property owner if the property on which the energy project was performed is sold or transferred.
- The financing mechanism has a "senior" lien position on the real property.

> *"Take care of the earth and she will take care of you."*
>
> Author Unknown

Over 37,000 assessment districts levy tax assessments on over 5 million properties for parks, sidewalks, street lights, fire prevention, water and sewage systems and many others.[22] Many of these are "opt-in" plans. All municipal assessments such as seismic strengthening in California, septic tank replacement in Massachusetts, and sidewalks in Florida are not imposed broadly on residents. All municipal assessments are accepted by mortgage lenders and acknowledged in their standard mortgage underwriting documents.

PACE financing programs underwritten by real property tax assessments differ from the others in at least two ways:

1. PACE saves money for property owners because programs are designed to create annual energy savings that exceed annual assessment charges. Nearly all other tax based assessments increase a property owner's expenses with no offsetting money saving benefits.
2. PACE districts are voluntary. Only real property owners who opt-in and receive the decrease in energy costs are assessed. A municipality is not required to create the program if it elects not to.

Since the completion of the Berkeley pilot, there have been many developments related to PACE. Most importantly, the Federal Housing Finance Authority (FHFA), Freddie Mac and Fannie Mae have issued strict rulings against any PACE program that places a PACE loan in a superior position to a mortgage. Unless and until these issues are resolved, Berkeley and other public municipal entities will not be utilizing the PACE programs and concepts to help consumers that reside in their districts and who want solar systems financed through an assessed property tax program.

Some of the companies that can help set up and administer PACE programs for public entities are shown in Table 4-7.

Table 4-8 is a case study comparison of some typical PACE programs in the U.S.[23]

PACE enabling legislation has been adopted in 23 states and the District of Columbia. The program provides a cost effective method for real property owners to finance the installation of energy saving equipment, cuts pollution, creates jobs and easily transfers to new homeowners when homes change ownership. However, PACE financing for residential properties was dealt a serious blow in 2010 when Fannie Mae and Freddie Mac refused to back mortgages with PACE liens on them. We will discuss this issue below.

On May 7, 2010 the Department of Energy announced its guidelines for PACE financing programs. They give guidance and best practice guidelines to state and local governments (where permitted by law) to extend the use of land-secured financing districts to fund energy efficiency and renewable energy improvements on private property. The PACE programs attach the obligation to repay the cost of the capital asset improvements to the property and not to the individual borrower.

With the implosion of the housing markets and the challenging economic environment, the guidelines described below will help ensure that there is an extra layer of protection to both the borrowers and to the lenders who hold mortgages on the real properties with PACE tax liens. The guidelines are divided into two sections: Program Design Best Practice Guidelines and Assessment Underwriting Best Practice Guidelines.

A. ***Program Design Best Practice Guidelines***

a. *Expected Savings-to-Investment Ratio (SIR) Greater Than One*[24]

The principal rationale for PACE is to pursue a legally-defined "public purpose." That rationale would include environmental, health, and energy independence benefits. The assets that are financed should be designed to pay for itself over the life of the assessment. Presumably, the transaction would

Table 4-7: PACE Servicing Companies

Company	Website
Clean Fund	http://www.cleanfund.com
EcoCity Partners	http://www.ecocitypartners.com
Renewable Funding	http://www.renewfund.com
Renovate America	http://renovateamerica.com
Samas Capital	http://www.samascapital.com
Ygrene Energy Fund	http://yygrene-energy.com

Table 4-8

City	Program Launched	Median Family Income	Source of Capital	Financing Mechanism	Collection Mechanism	Eligible Measures	Credit Requirements	Security	Rate, Term & Max Amt	Who Processes App
Berkeley, CA	Nov 2008	$86K	"Micro" bond sold to financial partner	Special tax (Mello-Roos)	Property tax bill	Solar PV (pilot)	Clear title & good property tax payment history	Senior lien on property	7.75% 20 years $37,500	Third party
Palm Desert, CA	Oct 2008	$70K	City's general fund for Phase 1, then Redevelopment Agency bonds, now seek a financing partner for Phase III	Assessment (AB 811)	Property tax bill	Energy efficiency, solar thermal, solar PV	Clear title & good property tax payment history	Senior lien on property	7% Up to 20 yrs No max	City staff
Boulder County, CO	April 2009	$84K	County issues bonds	Assessment (HB 08-1350)	Property tax bill	Energy efficiency & variety of renew-ables	Clear title & good property tax payment history	Senior lien on property	Varies (6.68% for 1st round) 15 years $50,000	County staff with third party support
Babylon, NY	Aug 2008	$84K	Municipal solid waste revolving fund	Assessment (amended solid waste code)	Separate bill, transfers to property tax bill if delinquent	Energy efficiency, solar thermal, solar PV	Clear title & good property tax payment history	Senior lien on property	3% Term varies $12,000	City staff

improve the borrowers debt-to-income ratio and thereby increasing their ability to repay the PACE assessments and other debit, such as the mortgage payments. The three program design features that the DOE recommends to ensure that the expected SIR is greater than one are:

- An energy audit and modeling of expected savings to identify energy efficiency and renewable energy property improvement measures that are likely to deliver energy and dollar savings in excess of the financed costs over the assessment term.
- In lieu of audits, programs may choose to limit eligibility to those measures with well-documented energy and dollar savings for a given climate zone.
- Encourage energy efficiency improvements before renewable energy production systems. The economics of renewable energy production investments can be enhanced when they are packaged with the energy efficiency measures. The SIR should be calculated for the entire package of investments in aggregate, not individual measures.

> *"Don't blow it—good planets are hard to find."*
>
> Quoted in *Time*

b. *The Term of the Assessment Should Not Exceed the Useful Life of the Improvements*
This is intended to ensure that a property owner's ability to repay is enhanced throughout the life of the PACE assessment by the energy savings derived from the improvements. It is important to note that the useful life of the measure often exceeds the assessment term.

c. *Senior Mortgage Holders of Record Should Receive Notice When PACE Liens are Placed On The Property*[25]

d. *PACE Lien Non-Acceleration Upon Property Owner Default*
In states where non-acceleration of the lien is standard for other assessments, it should also be standard for PACE assessments. After a foreclosure, the successor owners are responsible for future assessment payments. Non-acceleration is an important mortgage hold protection because liability for the assessment in foreclosure is limited to any amount in arrears at the time—the total outstanding assessed amount is not due in full.

e. *The Assessment Should Be Appropriately Sized*
PACE assessments should generally not exceed 10% of a real property's estimated value (i.e. a property value-to-lien ratio of 10:1). In addition, because of the administrative requirements of administering PACE programs, assessments should generally not be issued for projects below a minimum cost threshold of approximately $2,500. PACE programs might also choose to set the maximum assessment relative to median home values in the area where the home is located.

f. *Quality Assurance and Anti-Fraud Measures*
Quality assurance and anti-fraud measure for all participants including property owners, mortgage holders, investors and local governments. Those measures should include:

- Only validly licensed auditors and contractors should be permitted to conduct energy audits and retrofits.
- Random inspections should be conducted on work and services performed
- Payments should be withheld on any work not properly performed
- Property owners should sign-off before payment is issued for the work

g. *Rebates and Tax Credits*
The amount of funding under a PACE program should be "net" of any expected direct cash rebates for the project.

h. *Participant Education*
Educational programs for all participants in a PACE program should be implemented. Programs should clearly explain and provide disclosures of the following:

- How the PACE financing program works
- Information on other financing options available to the borrower
- Disclosure on all program fees and who/how the costs will be paid
- Effective interest rate
- The effect that the PACE assessment will have on escrow payments required by the mortgager
- Disclosure on the effect that a default would have both financially and on the credit score of

the borrower

- Procedures on transferring the assessment to a new owner of the property if a sale occurs
- Options for and implications of including tax credits in the financed amount

i. Debt Service Reserve Fund

A reserve fund should be established for the investors reflecting expected default rates on the PACE program that covers late payments or nonpayment of the PACE assessments.

j. Data Collection

Programs should collect the data necessary to evaluate the efficacy of the PACE program that was implemented. Typical data collected would include: installed measures, investment amount, default and foreclosure data, expected savings by the borrower, and actual energy use before and after the project was implemented.

B. Assessment Underwriting Best Practices Guidelines

The governmental agency that is implementing the PACE program should design underwriting criteria to help reduce the risk of default and impairment to the properties mortgage holders. The guidelines should include the following:

a. Property Ownership

Check to make sure the applicant has clear title to the real property on which the energy project is being constructed and that the property is located within the jurisdiction of the financing district.

Check the property title for restrictions such as details about power of attorney, easements, subordination agreements, environmental issues and any outstanding defaults (both on taxes and to the mortgage holder). This is normally done through a title search by a title company or attorney.

b. Property-Based Debt and Property Valuation

- Estimated real property value should be in excess of any public or private debt on the property, including mortgages, home equity lines of credit, and the addition of the new PACE assessment.
- Avoid placing an additional tax lien on properties that are already in distress, have recently been in distress, or are at risk for distress.
- Obtain an estimated real property value by reviewing the assessed tax rolls or by an appraisal on the property. There should be current market data to substantiate implementation of the energy project.

c. Property Owner Ability to Pay

PACE programs attach the obligation to repay the cost of the energy project to the property and not to the individual borrower. This can be accomplished by:

- Having a SIR greater than one (see above) to maintain or improve the property owner's debt-to-income ratio.
- Make sure the property owner is current on the property taxes and has not been late more than once in the past 3 years, or since the purchase of the property if less than three years.[26]
- The property owner has not filed for or declared bankruptcy for seven years.

PACE Status Update

The Federal Housing Finance Agency (FHFA) regulates Fannie Mae, Freddie Mac, and the 12 Federal Home Loan Banks. On July 6, 2010, FHFA and the Office of the Comptroller of the Currency (OCC) concluded that PACE programs "present significant safety and soundness concerns" to the housing finance industry.[27]

This statement came after a year of discussions with state and federal agencies in which PACE has gone from receiving support from the White House, canonization as of Scientific American's "World Changing Ideas" and legislative adoption in 24 states to questionable relevance, at least in the residential sector.[28]

Whether PACE resumes its expansion as an innovative tool for financing energy efficiency and clean generation depends on outcomes in each of the three branches of government—discussion on PACE among federal agencies, litigation in federal court, and legislation in Congress—all highly uncertain.[29]

FHFA first raised concerns about PACE programs in June 2009.[30] In that letter, FHFA stated: " ... the (PACE) loan amount is repaid as part of the homeowner's real property tax assessment and the loans have a superior lien status to existing first mortgages. The effect is to impair the value of first mortgages to creditors and any subsequent holder of first mortgages." The agency suggested that PACE financing would increase homeowner debt burdens and "...could cause a greater probability of default." They also warned of a "possible systemic impact ... to the housing finance system." As a result, in early May of 2009, the expansion of the PACE finance mechanism among state and local governments came to an abrupt end. The regulators concluded that property owners that participate in senior-lien residential PACE programs will violate standard mortgage provisions and trigger a mortgage default. Typically, the tax liens created by assessments are senior to other obligations, like mortgages, and must be paid first in the event of foreclosure. The regulators reasoned the PACE assessments were, in effect, loans not assessments and so violated standard mortgage provisions requiring priority over any other loan. End result—no more PACE—at least for now.

So where is PACE going in the future? Obviously, there needs to be an interagency agreement and solution that provides sufficient assurances to mortgage lenders and to financial regulators. It appears that commercial transactions will survive in the short term. It is the residential transaction that needs the fix even though there has not been a clear demarcation between the two. One solution is a "subordinate-lien" PACE. But still, these subordinate-lien PACE programs face administrative, financing and legislative challenges.

The Department of Energy recently released a Status Update for Pilot PACE Financing Programs.[31] It states that:

> *"The DOE and Administration continue to support pilot PACE financing programs. Recovery Act grantees are not expressly prohibited from using funds to support viable PACE financing programs, however the practical reality is that residential PACE financing programs with a senior lien priority face substantial implementation challenges in the current regulatory environment. In light of the clear opposition from the regulators for PACE financing programs with a senior lien priority, prudent management of the Recovery Act compels DOE and Recovery Act grantees to consider alternatives to programs in which the PACE assessment is given a senior lien priority."*

Behind the scenes, there are vested interests in energy production "status quo" that are not in favor of PACE financing programs. Two of those are the coal industry and utility companies. The coal industry supplies over 50 percent of fuel now used for electricity generation and the utility companies can foresee a future hit to their bottom lines if the PACE program were to expand beyond the "pilot" stage. Additionally, existing private sector companies that are growing at a rapid rate such as SolarCity, SunRun and Sungevity could foresee a decline in their growth if the PACE programs were to expand and therefore would not be big advocates of the program. Underlying financing rates for a homeowner are much lower when a municipality passes on to the consumer their dramatically lower costs of capital in the form of municipal bonds as opposed to the cost of capital that a privately held company has.

Incentives and Rebates

Incentive and rebates come in many different forms, amounts, cover many different energy technologies and have different time periods in which they can be received. They are the second largest source of funds to pay for an energy project behind only federal tax incentives.

Table 4-9 shown below and provided by DSIRE (Database of State Incentives for Renewables and Efficiency) shows state by state, what the multiple financial incentives are for renewable energy projects and energy efficiency projects. This summary table provides a snapshot of government, utility, and non-profit financial incentives that promote renewables in the United States. This table allows viewers to quickly compare the number and types of incentives in each state.

The incentive keys for the table are:

F = Federal S = State/Territory
L = Local U = Utility P = Private

The following describes each of the incentive types:

- **Corporate Tax Incentives**

  Corporate tax incentives include tax credits, deductions and exemptions. These incentives are available in some states to corporations that purchase and install eligible renewable energy or energy efficiency equipment, or to construct green buildings. In a few cases, the incentive is based on the amount of energy produced by an eligible facility. Some states allow the tax credit only if a corporation has invested a minimum amount in an eligible project. Typically, there is a maximum limit on the dollar amount of the credit or deduction. In recent years, the federal government has offered corporate tax incentives for renewables and energy efficiency. (Note that corporate tax incentives designed to support manufacturing and the development of renewable energy systems or equipment, or energy efficiency equipment, are categorized as "Industry Recruitment/Support" in DSIRE.)

- **Grant Programs**

  States offer a variety of grant programs to en-

Table 4-9: Financial Incentives for Renewable Energy

State	Personal Tax	Corp. Tax	Sales Tax	Property Tax	Rebates	Grants	Loans	Industry Support	Bonds	Performance-Based Incentive
Alabama	1-S				1-U	1-S	2-S 2-U			2-U
Alaska				1-S		1-S	2-S			1-U
Arizona	4-S	2-S	1-S	2-S	8-U 1-L		1-U	1-S		
Arkansas					1-U		1-S 1-U	1-S		
California				1-S	7-S 45-U 5-L		1-S 1-U 3-L	1-S		1-S 1-L
Colorado			2-S 1-L	3-S	17-U 5-L	1-L	2-S 1-U 1-L			
Connecticut			2-S	1-S	3-S 1-U 1-L	2-S	3-S 1-U 1-P	2-S		
Delaware					1-S 3-U		1-S			1-S
Florida			1-S		18-U 5-L		1-S 6-U 3-L	1-L		2-U
Georgia	1-S	1-S	1-S		12-U 1-L	1-P	1-S 1-U 1-L 1-P			3-U
Hawaii	1-S	1-S		1-L	1-S 1-U		2-S 2-U 1-L			1-S
Idaho	1-S			1-S	2-U	1-P	1-S		1-S	
Illinois			1-S	2-S	2-S 9-U	3-S 1-L 1-P	2-S	1-S	1-S	1-S 1-P
Indiana	1-S			1-S	29-U		1-U			2-U
Iowa	1-S	2-S	1-S	3-S	21-U		2-S 2-U			1-U
Kansas	1-S	1-S		1-S	2-U		1-S	1-S		
Kentucky	1-S	1-S			1-S 11-U	1-S	2-S 1-U 1-L 1-P	1-S		2-U
Louisiana	1-S	1-S		1-S	1-S 1-U		2-S 1-L			
Maine			1-S		1-S	1-S	3-S 1-L 1-P			1-S
Maryland	2-S	2-S	4-S	4-S 10-L	4-S		5-S			1-S
Massachusetts	1-S	2-S	1-S	1-S	4-S 9-U 1-L	5-S	2-S 1-U 1-P	2-S		1-S
Michigan				2-S	6-U	1-S 1-L	4-S 2-L 2-P	5-S		1-U
Minnesota			2-S	1-S	52-U	1-S 2-U	7-S 2-U			1-S
Mississippi					6-U		1-S 2-U	1-S		2-U
Missouri		1-S		1-S	11-U		2-S 2-U 1-L			
Montana	3-S	1-S		3-S	4-U	1-U	1-S	2-S		
Nebraska	1-S	1-S	1-S	1-S	2-U		1-S			
Nevada			1-S	3-S	2-S 2-U		1-S 1-U			1-S
New Hampshire				1-S	3-S 7-U	1-S	4-S 1-P			
New Jersey			1-S	2-S	4-S		1-S	3-S		2-S
New Mexico	6-S	5-S	4-S	1-S	1-U		1-S	1-S	1-S	3-U
New York	2-S	1-S	3-S 1-L	2-S 1-L	8-S 7-U	2-S	3-S			2-S
North Carolina	1-S	1-S		2-S	8-U 1-L		3-S 3-U 1-L	1-S		5-U 1-P
North Dakota	1-S	1-S	3-S	2-S	4-U		2-U			
Ohio			1-S	2-S 2-L	8-U 1-P		3-S 1-U 1-L	1-S		1-S 2-U
Oklahoma		1-S		1-S	7-U		4-S 3-U	1-S		
Oregon	1-S	1-S		1-S	6-S 19-U	2-S 1-P	3-S 9-U	1-S		1-S 1-U
Pennsylvania				1-S	1-S 6-U	7-S 2-L	7-S 1-U 5-L	3-S		1-S
Rhode Island	1-S	1-S	1-S	2-S		1-S	1-S 1-P			1-S
South Carolina	2-S	2-S	1-S		5-U		1-S 4-U			1-S 3-U 1-P
South Dakota			1-S	2-S	6-U		1-S 2-U			
Tennessee			1-S	1-S	1-U	1-S	2-S 1-U	2-S		2-U
Texas		1-S		1-S 2-L	28-U 2-L	1-S 1-L	2-S 1-U	1-S		1-U
Utah	1-S	1-S	1-S		4-U			1-S		
Vermont		1-S	1-S	1-S	1-S	1-U	2-S 1-P			1-S 2-U
Virginia				1-S	1-S		2-S 1-U	3-S		2-U
Washington			1-S		12-U	1-P	9-U	1-S		1-S 3-U
West Virginia	1-S	1-S		1-S	1-U					
Wisconsin	1-S	1-S	1-S	1-S	7-S 5-U		2-S 2-L			3-U
Wyoming			1-S		7-U		1-S 1-U			
District of Columbia					1-S		1-S			1-S
Palau										
Guam										
Puerto Rico	1-S		2-S	1-S	1-S	1-S		1-S		
Virgin Islands						1-S	1-S			
N. Mariana Islands										
American Samoa										
Totals	41	38	44	75	493	52	203	39	3	68

courage the use and development of renewables and energy efficiency. Most programs offer support for a broad range of technologies, while a few programs focus on promoting a single technology, such as photovoltaic (PV) systems. Grants are available primarily to the commercial, industrial, utility, education and/or government sectors. Most grant programs are designed to pay down the cost of eligible systems or equipment. Others focus on research and development, or support project commercialization. In recent years, the federal government has offered grants for renewables and energy efficiency projects for end-users. Grants are usually competitive.

- **Green Building Incentives**

Green buildings are designed and constructed using practices and materials that minimize the impacts of the building on the environment and human health. Many cities and counties offer financial incentives to promote green building. The most common form of incentive is a reduction or waiver of a building permit fee. The U.S. Green Building Council's Leadership in Energy and Environmental Design (LEED) is a popular point-based certification program for green buildings. The LEED system awards points for site selection and development; material, energy and water efficiency; indoor air quality; innovation; and the application of renewable technologies. (Note that this category includes green building incentives that do not fall under other DSIRE incentive categories, such as tax incentives and grant programs.)

- **Industry Recruitment/Support**

To promote economic development and the creation of jobs, some states offer financial incentives to recruit or cultivate the manufacturing and development of renewable energy systems and equipment. These incentives commonly take the form of tax credits, tax exemptions and grants. In some cases, the amount of the incentive depends on the quantity of eligible equipment that a company manufactures. Most of these incentives apply to several renewable energy technologies, but a few states target specific technologies, such as wind or solar. These incentives are usually designed as temporary measures to support industries in their early years. They commonly include a sunset provision to encourage the industries to become self-sufficient.

- **Leasing Programs**

A handful of programs have been established by government agencies and utilities that allow homeowners, businesses, and other entities to lease energy-efficient equipment or renewable energy systems. In some cases, the customer may choose to purchase the system after a specified period of time. (Note that it is increasingly common for companies to lease energy equipment to customers. However, with the exception of incentives offered by utilities, DSIRE generally does not include incentives offered by businesses.)

- **Loan Programs**

Loan programs provide financing for the purchase of renewable energy or energy efficiency systems or equipment. Low-interest or zero-interest loans for energy efficiency projects are a common demand-side management (DSM) practice from electric utilities. State governments also offer low-interest loans for a broad range of renewable energy and energy efficiency measures. These programs are commonly available to the residential, commercial, industrial, transportation, public and/or non-profit sectors. Loan rates and terms vary by program; in some cases, they are determined on an individual project basis. Loan terms are generally 10 years or less. In recent years, the federal government has offered loans and/or loan guarantees for renewables and energy efficiency projects.

- **PACE Financing**

Property Assessed Clean Energy (PACE) financing (see prior pages) effectively allows property owners to borrow money to pay for renewable energy and/or energy-efficiency improvements. The amount borrowed is typically repaid over a period of years via a special assessment on the owner's property. In general, local governments (such as cities and counties) that choose to offer PACE financing must be authorized to do so by state law.

- **Performance-based Incentives**

Performance-based incentives (PBIs), also known as production incentives, provide cash payments based on the number of kilowatt-hours (kWh) or Btus generated by a renewable energy system. A "feed-in tariff" is an example of a PBI. To ensure project quality, payments based on a system's actual performance are generally more effective than payments based on a system's

> *"We do not inherit the earth from our ancestors, we borrow it from our children."*
>
> Native American Proverb

rated capacity. (Note that tax incentives based on the amount of energy produced by an eligible commercial facility are categorized as "Corporate Tax Incentives" in DSIRE.)

- **Personal Tax Incentives**

Personal tax incentives include income tax credits and deductions. Many states offer these incentives to reduce the expense of purchasing and installing renewable energy or energy efficiency systems and equipment. The percentage of the credit or deduction varies by state, and in most cases, there is a maximum limit on the dollar amount of the credit or deduction. An allowable credit may include carryover provisions, or it may be structured so that the credit is spread out over a certain number of years. Eligible technologies vary widely by state. In recent years, the federal government has offered personal tax credits for renewables and energy efficiency.

- **Property Tax Incentives**

Property tax incentives include exemptions, exclusions, abatements and credits. Most property tax incentives provide that the added value of a renewable energy system is excluded from the valuation of the property for taxation purposes. For example, if a new heating system that uses renewable energy costs more than a conventional heating system, the additional cost of the renewable energy system is not included in the property assessment. In a few cases, property tax incentives apply to the additional cost of a green building. Because property taxes are collected locally, some states have granted local taxing authorities the option of allowing a property tax incentive for renewables.

- **Rebate Programs**

States, utilities and a few local governments offer rebates to promote the installation of renewables and energy efficiency projects. The majority of rebate programs that support renewables are administered by states, municipal utilities and electric cooperatives; these programs commonly provide funding for solar water heating and/or photovoltaic (PV) systems. Most rebate programs that support energy efficiency are administered by utilities. Rebate amounts vary widely by technology and program administrator.

- **Sales Tax Incentives**

Sales tax incentives typically provide an exemption from, or refund of, the state sales tax (or sales and use tax) for the purchase of a renewable energy system, an energy-efficient appliance, or other energy efficiency measures. Several states have established an annual "sales tax holiday" for energy efficiency measures by annually allowing a temporary exemption – usually for one or two days – from the state sales tax.

Careful attention needs to be paid to how the IRS views state and local tax incentives—is it income, capital or a tax reduction? On March 2, 2011, the IRS issued appeals settlement guidelines on the tax consequences of state and local location tax (SALT) incentives received by corporate taxpayers. The guidelines provide clarity for corporate taxpayers on how tax incentives, including renewable energy grants and credits, as well as other climate change and sustainability incentives should be treated.

According to the guidelines, a SALT or similar tax incentive:

— Is not income under Section 61,
— Is not a contribution of capital under Section 118(a), and
— Therefore does not reduce a corporation's basis under Section 362(c).

The reasoning is that these tax incentives, whether in the form of an abatement, credit, deduction, rate reduction, or exemption, simply reduce the tax imposed by state or local governments.[32] State governments use incentives to encourage renewable energy generation, energy efficiency improvements and other similar environmental goals. SALT inducements may include one or more of the following:

— Tax rate reductions
— Tax abatements
— Tax credits
— Exemptions from income or property tax
— Tax credits for the creation of additional local jobs
— Utility Rate Discounts

A few utilities offer rate discounts to encourage residential energy efficiency. For homes that meet certain energy efficiency criteria, such as those established by the federal Energy Star program, the owner or tenant is awarded a discount on their electric bills.

DSIRE tracks renewable energy incentives and policies established by the federal government, state governments, U.S. territories, local governments, larger utilities and a few non-profit organizations. DSIRE categorizes these incentives and policies into two groups:

- **Financial Incentives** include a variety of tax incentives, grants, loans, rebates, industry recruitment/

support, green building incentives, performance-based incentives and other forms of incentives.

- **Rules, Regulations & Policies** include public benefits funds, renewable portfolio standards, net metering, interconnection standards, line-extension analysis, contractor licensing, equipment certification, solar/wind access policies, solar/wind permitting standards, construction & design standards (including building energy codes and energy standards for public buildings), mandatory utility green power options, generation disclosure policies and green power purchasing policies.

> *"An acre of windy prairie could produce between $4,000 and $10,000 worth of electricity per year—which is far more than the value of the land's crop of corn or wheat."*
>
> Denis Hayes, environmental activist

The federal incentives included in DSIRE are generally limited to those available on an ongoing basis to residents, businesses and/or other end-users. DSIRE does not include federal funding opportunities for research & development, demonstration projects, outreach or inter-governmental programs.

They also track relevant incentives and policies from all investor-owned utilities (electric and natural gas) in the United States. However, because there are thousands of electric cooperatives and municipal utilities across the country, DSIRE's scope is generally limited to incentives and policies established by electric cooperatives and municipal utilities with more than 30,000 customers. (If your utility is relatively small, contact the utility directly to find out if any incentives are available.)

DSIRE provides information on approximately 250 incentives and policies established by local governments (excluding municipal utility incentives and policies). However, because there are tens of thousands of municipalities and counties in the United States, DSIRE's scope is generally limited to local incentives and policies that are especially innovative, and to those established by municipalities and counties with the largest populations.

For more information on federal funding opportunities for research & development and demonstration projects related to renewable energy or energy efficiency, visit the following web sites:

- Grants: *http://www.grants.gov/*
- U.S. Department of Energy (DOE): *http://energy.gov/*
- U.S. Department of Agriculture (USDA): *http://www.usda.gov/wps/portal/usda/usdahome*
- U.S. Department of Housing and Urban Development (HUD): *http://portal.hud.gov/hudportal/HUD*
- U.S. Department of Transportation (DOT): *http://www.dot.gov/*
- U.S. Department of Commerce: *http://www.commerce.gov/*
- U.S. Environmental Protection Agency (EPA): *http://www.epa.gov/*
- U.S. Small Business Administration (SBA): *http://www.sba.gov/*

In addition to the table above, DSIRE also has tables for the following items:

1. Financial incentives for energy efficiency
2. Rules, regulations, and policies for renewable energy
3. Rules, regulations, and policies for energy efficiency

Finally, DSIRE's Quantitative RPS Data Project provides quantitative information about state renewables portfolio standards (RPS). In the DSIRE RPS Data Spreadsheet, state requirements are defined by year and by resource class and include other key data elements such as monetary penalties or alternative compliance payments, eligibility of new and/or existing facilities, the percentage of the state's electric load covered by the policy, comments to clarify data entries or assumptions, and an update memo to describe recent changes to the data. The DSIRE RPS Field Definitions document contains detailed descriptions of the data fields in the DSIRE RPS Data Spreadsheet and how they are organized. This project began in 2008 to support analysis efforts at the National Renewable Energy Laboratory (NREL).

Separately, Lawrence Berkeley National Laboratory (LBNL) has allowed DSIRE to publicly post the data that it has assembled on state level compliance with RPS mandates. The LBNL RPS Compliance Data Spreadsheet[33] details annual state RPS obligations (MWh) and RPS achievement (% of obligation) for both overall state standards and solar or distributed generation set asides. It also includes notes describing the sources of the data and how the calculations were made for each state.

New program summaries are added and existing summaries are updated as the DSIRE project staff become aware of new information. Government incentives

> *"The 'soft landing' that many people hope for—a voluntary change to solar energy and green fuels, energy-conserving technologies, and less overall consumption—is a utopian alternative that will come about only if severe, prolonged hardship in industrial nations make it attractive."*
>
> Joseph Tainter, U.S. anthropologist (2004)

and policies that are created or modified through the legislative process, such as tax incentives, are reviewed and updated as necessary—at least once per year. Other types of incentives and policies that are typically created or modified by other means, such as rebate programs and grant programs, are reviewed several times per year. Each program summary included in DSIRE indicates the date on which the program was last updated or verified. To get the latest changes to the DSIRE database, the reader should go to: *http://www.dsireusa.org*.

Therefore, to research the latest incentives and rebates, their amounts, RPS goals and achievements, and rules and regulations as they pertain to the renewable energy industry, one should consider this source as an extremely valuable tool to aid the reader in quantifying what rebates and incentives (and their rules and regulations) are available on a state by state basis. Doing so, will allow you to plug the appropriate amounts and timing into the financial analysis needed to adequately evaluate the returns and risks of the capital investment.

References

1. Sacks v. Commissioner, 69 F34d 982 (9th Circ 1995), rev'g, 64 T.C.M. 1003 (1992).
2. National Renewable Energy Laboratory, Technical Report NREL/TP-6A2-45551, May 2009
3. D. De Jager; M. Rathmann, "Policy instrument design to reduce financing costs in renewable energy technology projects." Prepared for the International Energy Agency-Renewable Energy Technology Deployment, Utrecht, October 2008. Available online at: http://www.iea-retd.org/files/retd_PIC0810_Main.pdf.
4. V. Dinica, "Support systems for the diffusion of renewable energy technologies-an investor perspective." Energy Policy, Vol. 34, No. 4, 2006, pp. 461-480.
5. Ernst & Young, "Renewable Energy Country Attractiveness Indices 2008, Quarter 1-2," July 2008
6. A. Klein; B. Pfluger; A. Held; G. Resch; T Faber, "Evaluation of Different Feed-in Tariff Design Options – Best Practice Paper for the International Feed-in Cooperation: 2nd edition." Karlsruhe, Germany: Fraunhofer Institute Systems and Innovations Research, October 2008
7. http://freeingthegrid.org/wp-content/uploads/2012/07/FreeingTheGrid2011.pdf
8. SRECTrade, Inc., 90 New Montgomery St, San Francisco, CA 94105, (877) 466-4606
9. Renewable Energy World, Effective SREC Market Design, May 2011, www.renewableenergyworld.com
10. A qualified source includes biomass, solar thermal, photovoltaic, wind, geothermal, fuel cells using renewable fuels, small hydroelectric generation of 30 megawatts or less, digester gas, municipal solid waste conversion, landfill gas, ocean wave, ocean thermal, or tidal current, and any additions or enhancements to the facility using that technology.
11. http://www.srectrade.com/blog
12. Ibid
13. Costing Green: A Comprehensive Cost Database and Budgeting Methodology, July 2004. Davis Langdon
14. United States Green Building Council
15. Navigant Consulting
16. Dr. Ryan Wiser, "Wind Power and the Production Tax Credit: An Overview of Research Results," Lawrence Berkeley National Laboratory, March 29, 2007.
17. Rick Nevin and Gregory Watson, "Evidence of Rational Market Valuations for Home Energy Efficiency," The Appraisal Journal, October 1998
18. Ben Hoen, et al, "An Analysis of the Effects of Residential Photovoltaic Energy System on Home Sales Prices in California," 2011
19. Ibid
20. Andrew J. Black, "Why is a Solar Electric Home Worth More?," July 2004
21. National Resources Defense Council, PACE Now, Renewable Funding LLC, and The Vote Solar Initiative: Property Assessed Clean Energy Programs White Paper, May 2010
22. http://pacenow.org
23. Merrian C. Fuller, Cathy Kunkel, Daniel M Kammen: "Guide to Energy efficiency & Renewable Energy Financing Districts for Local Governments," Renewable and Appropriate Energy Laboratory (RAEL), University of California, Berkeley, September 2009
24. SIR is the estimated savings over the life of the assessment, discounted back to present value using an appropriate discount rate, divided by the amount financed through PACE assessment.
25. Savings can include reduced utility bills as well as any payments for renewable energy credits or other quantifiable environmental and health benefits that can be monetized. The savings should be calculated on an annual basis and include annual escalators for future energy price increases.
26. A different standard may apply to non-residential properties.
27. Applicants that have purchased the property within three years have recently undergone rigorous credit analyses that would compensate for the short property tax payment history.
28. See: http://www.fhfa.gov/webfiles/15884/PACESTMT7610.pdf
29. Lawrence Berkeley National Laboratory, Environmental Energy Technologies Division, Clean Energy Financing Policy Brief, August 2010
30. bid
31. See: http://pacenow.org/documents/FHFA%20Letter.pdf
32. http://www1.eere.energy.gov/wip/pace.html
33. PricewaterhouseCoopers L.L.P., Sustainable Business Solutions, March 2011, www.pwc.com

Chapter 5

Internal Components of the Financial Analysis

"The devil is truly in the details" when it comes to financing renewable energy projects. When thinking about how best to structure the financing of an energy project, it is important to keep separate the three perspectives of a transaction—the cash, the tax, and the accounting. Tax and accounting calculations can be complicated because there are many different methods, taxing districts and practices. To understand the tax and accounting ramifications, an analysis of project finance structures must include many components—all of which become integral to the final economic analysis of the project. These include both internal and external components. The internal components that are addressed in this chapter comprise two major categories—accounting and tax.

INTERNAL COMPONENTS

Most of the internal components of a cleantech energy project financing structure can be broken down into two major categories—accounting decisions and requirements, followed closely by the tax treatments and elections. It must be understood that the two categories are mutually exclusive of each other. The elections and assumptions made for accounting reasons have little or no effect on the tax side. In all financial structuring and analysis, the book (accounting) treatment has nothing to do with how those same assets, liabilities, profits and losses, and supporting schedules are treated for the tax books. This is true for both the credit lender and for the debt obligor. It should also be noted that it is not necessary for either party to elect the same accounting or tax treatment of the project finance. In many, if not most cases, the credit lender will select one method of accounting and tax treatment while the debt obligor will select a totally different method.

To make matters even more complex, each of the two parties (credit lender and debt obligor) may elect to have each finance transaction treated different than another similar finance transaction simply because the facts and circumstances are slightly different. For example, a credit lender may elect to treat all transactions as operating leases or energy purchase contracts in its portfolio of receivables, or have certain of those "similar" transactions treated as a "loan" receivable on their books because of residual risk assumptions, length of the actual contracts or other business risk parameters.

In this chapter, we will first look at a listing of what the components are, and then each of the components will be addressed in detail. The detail will explain both the reason for the component and also the implications for both the credit lender and for the debt obligor.

Accounting

Accounting for cleantech project financing focuses on three essential types of information.

1. The timing of the revenue, expenses, profits and taxes
2. The balance sheet and income statement effects of the transaction structure
3. The yield (or cost/rate to the debtor) that will result from the transaction structure

For accounting, the following components need to be addressed:

- Accounting classification
  - Direct loan or capital lease
  - Operating lease or energy purchase agreement
- General ledger entries consisting of six major groups
  - Original booking information
  - Actual cash flows including when taxes are paid
  - The tax due
  - Totals that are spread over the life of the project using various allocation factors
  - Termination value calculations
  - Reconciliation
- Direct loan or capital lease accounting
  - Income allocation methods

- — Monthly income booked
  - — Tax provision methods
  - — Initial direct costs
  - — Tax timing differences
  - — Permanent tax differences
  - — After-tax book income
  - — Transactions and accounts
  - — Accounting yields
- Operating lease and PPA accounting
  - — Recognition of revenue
  - — Sources of revenue
  - — Expense elections and recognition
  - — Transactions and accounts
  - — Tax timing differences

Taxes

The complexity of the tax code in the U.S. is overwhelming. No one can be expert on a code that has grown from a length of an article in the New Yorker magazine when it was first enacted in 1913 to almost 2.2 million words today. Add to that number over seven million words of IRS regulations that interpret the code and even more legislative history, court decisions, rulings, notice and revenue procedures or guidance to enforce it. This book is not meant to be even a small interpretation of it. Rather, it will be focused on only the general aspects of the code that is meaningful to renewable energy projects. It will allow you, the reader, a great deal of creativity in the *"art of financing renewable energy projects in the U.S."*

Federal tax incentives provide the largest source of external help for all renewable energy projects. Some of the most important are based on tax credits and tax deductions. A tax credit is an actual reduction of tax liability (after-tax) and a tax deduction reduces taxable income (pre-tax). The difference is very significant. The two principal federal tax credits are the Investment Tax Credit (Business Energy Tax Credit) and the Production Tax Credit (Renewable Energy Production Tax Credit). Almost all renewable energy technology qualifies for either the investment or the production credit—no project is eligible for both. The Energy Improvement and Extension Act of 2008 expanded the number of qualifying technologies for both programs.

The Investment Tax Credit (ITC) was first suggested in late 1961 for the purpose of increasing economic growth (26 USC § 48). Since then, the credit percentage has increased, decreased and even been eliminated. It has also increased on certain types of renewable energy equipment (e.g., solar) over other more traditional revenue producing equipment such as forklifts, construction equipment, printing systems, etc. The credit was finally enacted in 1962. Congress felt that a tax subsidy would encourage domestic investment in capital goods and thereby allow American producers to compete favorably with the counterparts in the world who had the advantage of lower labor costs. It permits an immediate reduction in corporate income tax liability with no offsetting increase in future taxes (as does depreciation expense). It is important to understand that unless a taxpayer has an income tax liability, it is of no immediate value to that taxpayer. However, if the taxpayer does have income taxes due, it would provide immediate cash flow to the taxpayer in the amount that would otherwise be payable in the tax liability to the IRS.

> *"Renewable energy is proving to be commercially viable for a growing list of consumers and uses. Renewable energy technologies provide many benefits that go well beyond energy alone. More and more, renewable energies are contributing to the three pillars of sustainable development—the economy, the environment and social well-being—not only in IEA countries, but globally."*
>
> Benjamin J. Sovacool, Professor at Vermont Law School

The ITC is based on the capital cost of the equipment and is taken in the year that the capital asset is deemed placed in service (see page 35). The current ITC rate is 30% for commercial investment in certain renewable energy applications such as solar technologies, fuel cells and small commercial wind. A 10% ITC is available for technologies such as geothermal heat pumps, combined heat and power systems, and microturbines.

The Production Tax Credit (PTC) is based on the actual "energy output" of the system, is earned on a kilowatt-hour basis and is available beginning in the year in which the facility is placed in service. The PTC generally applies to the first 10 years of operation and is currently worth 2.2¢ per kWh for wind, geothermal electric, and closed loop biomass. Other qualifying technologies including small hydroelectric and open-loop biomass receive half the PTC rate.

The most important "tax deduction" offered by the federal government is the Modified Accelerated Cost Recovery System (MACRS) depreciation on the capital assets of the renewable energy project followed closely by the bonus depreciation (if available). The deduction provides for a five-year recovery at a 200% double declining balance method. In addition, in 2008 there was a first year bonus depreciation of 50%, 2009 brought forth a 100% bonus depreciation and 2012 dropped the rate

Table 5-1: ITC Credit Termination Date & Applicable Payment Percentage

Specified Energy Property	Credit Termination Date	Applicable Percentage of Eligible Cost Basis
Large Wind	January 1, 2014	30%
Closed-Loop Biomass Facility	January 1, 2014	30%
Open-Loop Biomass Facility	January 1, 2014	30%
Geothermal under IRC Sect 45	January 1, 2014	30%
Landfill Gas Facility	January 1, 2014	30%
Trash Facility	January 1, 2014	30%
Qualified Hydropower Facility	January 1, 2014	30%
Marine & Hydrokinetic	January 1, 2014	30%
Solar	January 1, 2017	30%
Geothermal under IRC Sect 58	January 1, 2017	10% [1]
Fuel Cells	January 1, 2017	30% [2]
Microturbines	January 1, 2017	10% [3]
Combined Heat & Power	January 1, 2017	10%
Small Wind	January 1, 2017	30%
Geothermal Heat Pumps	January 1, 2017	10%

[1] Geothermal property that meets the definitions of qualified property in both § 45 and § 48 is allowed either the 30% ITC credit or the 10% PTC credit but not both.

[2] For fuel cell property the maximum amount of the payment may not exceed an amount equal to $1,500 for each 0.5 kilowatt of capacity.

[3] For microturbine property the maximum amount of the payment may not exceed an amount equal to $200 for each kilowatt of capacity.

back down to 50%. If the ITC was taken when the asset was placed in service, the regulations required that the depreciable "basis" of the property be reduced by one half of the amount of ITC taken. For example, a project that had assets that received a 30% ITC, the depreciable basis was reduced by 15% (half the amount of the ITC received), resulting in a depreciable basis of 85% of the asset cost. The bonus depreciation was based on the 85% basis. After the bonus depreciation was taken in the respective year, the 200% DDB method of depreciation was taken on the remaining depreciable basis over the next five years.

Karlynn Cory from NREL put together an interesting table to show the value of the 50% and 100% bonus depreciations on a renewable energy project (the 50% bonus depreciation remains in place through the end of 2012). Her analysis compares the impact of the bonus schedules compared to the regular 5-year MACRS. Table 5-2 shows the levelized cost of energy (LCOE) for a 2 MW solar PV system with identical inputs except for the depreciation schedule. The LCOE (to the customer) using 50% and 100% bonus depreciation decreased by over 11% or 22%, respectively, compared to only the 5-year MACRS depreciation.

> *"Texas has long been known as the nation's largest energy producer, but we are equally proud of our distinction as the nation's leading energy innovator."*
>
> Rick Perry, governor of Texas

Clearly, the bonus depreciation has had a strong impact on the LCOE to the ultimate customer when those monetized tax attributes were passed through to the customer in a financing arrangement.

There are numerous types of state incentives on many renewable energy technologies and can include state corporate tax incentives, sales tax exemptions, property tax exemptions, rebates and grants, loans, and production incentives (for both electricity and thermal energy). It is important to remember that in all cases, state incentives come and go, have restrictions, and most have some sort of expiration date.

Table 5-2: LCOE of PV for Three Different Depreciation Schedules

	5-year MACRS	50% Bonus + MACRS	100% Bonus
LCOE (¢/kWh)	55.9	49.5	43.2
% decrease in LCOE		11.5%	22.7%

Some examples of state incentives are:

- Florida offers a renewable energy production tax credit of $.01 per kWh for certain renewable energy technologies that produce electricity.
- Texas provides a solar and wind energy device franchise tax deduction allowing two options for a corporation. They can either deduct the cost from its taxable capital base or deduct 10% of the cost from its taxable income.
- Washington State offers a sales and use tax exemption for many renewable energy applications including solar water heat, solar photovoltaic, and wind, providing for an exemption from sales tax for the equipment and installation costs of systems of at least 200 kW.
- Minnesota offers a sales tax exemption for certain solar technologies including solar water heat and solar photovoltaic as well as wind energy conversion systems.
- New York State has a solar, wind, and biomass energy systems property tax exemption offering a 15-year property tax exemption for many renewable energy applications.
- California exempts solar PV and solar thermal renewable energy technologies from all personal property taxes.
- The California Solar Initiative initially offered rebates of up to $2.50 per watt for commercial solar PV system of less than 50 kW. The utilities also offered performance based rebates (PBI). All the rebates are on a declining basis based on the total amount of energy systems installed in the state. In 2011, California also started a rebate program on solar thermal energy production systems. The amounts of the rebates are based on the SRCC[1] ratings of the systems thermal output levels.
- North Carolina has the Energy Improvement Loan Program that provides loans for certain types of renewable energy. Loan amounts may be up to $500,000 for a maximum term of 10 years. The interest rate can be as low as 1%.
- Iowa offers the Alternative Energy Revolving Loan Program, which provides 50% (maximum of $1,000,000) of the total loan required for certain renewable energy investments at no interest rate.
- New Jersey, Massachusetts, Connecticut and Rhode Island all have Renewable Energy Credits at multiple price levels that help meet the RPS goals in those states.

For taxes, the following components need to be addressed:

- Federal and state tax credits
- Depreciation
  - Conventions (full year, half year, mid-quarter, etc.)
  - First year depreciation
  - Asset life assumptions
  - Additional 1st year bonus depreciations (when applicable)
  - Capitalized cost (book value)
- Federal
- State
  - Depreciation methods (ACRS, DDB, SYD, etc.)
- Alternative minimum tax (AMT)
  - Depreciation preferences
  - Alternative minimum taxable income (AMTI)
  - Effect on Investment Tax Credit (ITC), Energy Tax Credits (ETC) and Production Tax Credits (PTC)
- Federal vs. state requirements
- Tax due dates

Additionally, the following items need to be negotiated, input and documented in the final finance agreement and reflected in the accounting, tax and yield analysis performed by both the credit lender and the debt obligor:

- Early buyout provisions
- Residual assumptions
- Economic compulsion test
- IRS and FASB guidelines and tests
  - Tax treatment (loan vs. true lease or service contract)
  - FASB 13
  - IRS §55-540, §75-21 and others
  - Uneven rent test
  - Free cash flow test
  - Minimum equity test
  - Maximum leverage test
  - Debtor investment test

  - Minimum risk test
  - Bargain purchase option test
  - Remaining economic life test
  - Remaining value test
  - Prepaid and deferred test
  - Present value calculations
  - Minimum guaranteed residuals
  - Pre-tax profit test
  - Reasonable cash flow test
- Constraints
  - Frequency of when payments are made (monthly, quarterly, annual, etc.)
  - Payments made in advance or in arrears
  - Holiday from payments periods
  - Floor and ceiling structures
  - Fluctuations in gross receipts (e.g., a PPA) when there are variations in sun, wind, tides or other sources of fuel for renewable energy generation projects
  - Leverage
  - Payment methods
- Proportional
- Saw-tooth (frequently used in energy financing projects)
- Annual proportional
- Maintain steps/dates and allow payments to float
  - Delayed equity
  - Rates and yields
- Present value rates
  - Cost-of-funds rate
  - Full term rate
  - Full term rate with residual
  - First borrowing loan interest rate
  - Implicit interest rate
  - Debtor's incremental borrowing rate
- Discounted cash flows
- Net present values
- Minimum ROA
- Maximum PV of debt payments
- Maximum leverage
- Uneven rent—both for early buy-out and extended terms
- Pre-tax
- After-tax
- ROI
- IRR
- Modified IRR
- Pre-tax cash flow (PTCF)
- Nominal after-tax MISF (multiple investment sinking fund)
- Nominal pre-tax IRR PTCF using MISF
- APR and simple interest
- Single investment sinking fund
- Pre-tax equivalent (PTE)
- Spread over index rate using 5 methods:
  1. Constant
  2. Fixed: average-life
  3. Fixed: term
  4. Internal cost-of-funds
  5. Variable/Floating
- ROE (return on equity)
  - Compounding elections
- Annually
- Composite
- Daily
- End-of-month
- Monthly
- Periodic
- Quarterly
- Semi-annually
  - Break-even residual computations
  - Defeasance net present value computations with consideration for:
  - Lockout period
  - Defeasing to the prepayment date vs. the maturity date
  - Benefits of prepayment rights
  - Defeasance deposit vs. defeasance collateral
  - Agencies vs. treasuries as defiance collateral
  - Successor debtor
  - 360 vs. 365 day calculations
- Interim or construction advances and structures
- Component replacement schedules
- Maintenance costs
- Insurance costs
- Other asset costs
- Termination values
- Stipulated loss values
- Tax credit recaptures

Each of these components present multiple opportunities to create highly structured financing agreements that provide for many elections that generate unique yields, marketing techniques, funding opportunities and true customized project financings for both the credit lender and the debt obligor. The final result presents a unique solution to a very complex financing mechanism for each energy project.

Leveraged Leases and Power Purchase Agreements

Most financial transactions in renewable energy systems are structured as either a leveraged lease or a power purchase agreement. The major distinction between the two for tax purposes is that a lease has its form of income "rentals" and a power purchase agreement has as its form of income "sale of energy" and is treated for tax purposes as a "service contract" by the IRS.

There is a lot of history in tax law for leveraged leases but very little for power purchase agreements. Looking at the rules for leveraged leases will give the reader a good insight as to the issues that would also be involved for power purchase agreements. Revenue Procedure 2001-28[2] provides guidelines that the IRS will use for advance ruling purposes in determining whether certain transactions purporting to be leases of tangible personal property are, in fact, leases for federal income tax purposes. Such leases generally involve three parties: a lessor, a lessee and a lender to the lessor. In general, these leases are net leases (meaning the lessee is responsible for all costs associated with the use of the equipment), the lease term covers a substantial part of the useful life of the leased property, and the lessee's payments to the lessor are sufficient to discharge the lessor's payments to the lender.

> *"We've embarked on the beginning of the last days of the age of oil. Embrace the future and recognize the growing demand for a wide range of fuels or ignore reality and slowly—but surely—be left behind."*
>
> Mike Bowlin, chairman and CEO of Arco (now BP)

Unless other facts and circumstances indicated a contrary intent, for advance ruling purposes only (guidelines the IRS would use "if" they were to rule on the legality of the finance structure), the IRS will consider the lessor in a leveraged lease transaction to be the owner of the property and the transaction a valid lease if *all* the guidelines described below are met.

- **Minimum unconditional "at risk" investment**

The lessor must have made a minimum unconditional "at risk" investment in the property (the "Minimum Investment") when the lease begins, must maintain such Minimum Investment throughout the entire lease term, and such Minimum Investment must remain at the end of the lease term. The Minimum Investment must be an equity investment (the "Equity Investment") that, for purposes of the revenue procedure, includes only consideration paid, and personal liability incurred, by the lessor to purchase the property. The net worth of the lessor must be sufficient to satisfy any such personal liability. In determining the lessor's Minimum Investment, the following rules will be applied:

— The amount is 20% of the equipment cost. The Minimum Investment must be *unconditional*. That is, after the property is first placed in service, the lessor must not be entitled to a return of any portion of the Minimum Investment through any arrangement, directly or indirectly, with the lessee, a shareholder of the lessee, or any party related to the lessee. The lease transaction may include an arrangement with someone other than the foregoing parties that provides for such a return to the lessor if the property fails to satisfy written specifications for the supply, construction, or manufacture of the property. This could occur on a renewable energy production system in some circumstances—particularly if the energy project is unproven technology and the prototype does not function as intended.

— The Minimum Investment must remain equal to at least 20 percent of the cost of the property at all times *throughout the entire lease term*. That is, the excess of the cumulative payments required to have been paid by the lessee to or for the lessor over the cumulative disbursements required to have been paid by or for the lessor in connection with the ownership of the property must never exceed the sum of (i) any excess of the lessor's initial Equity Investment over 20 percent of the cost of the property plus (ii) the cumulative pro rate portion of the projected profit from the transaction (exclusive of tax benefits—which in most cases would be substantial).

— Residual Investment. The lessor must represent and demonstrate than an amount equal to at least 20 percent of the original cost of the property is a reasonable estimate of what the fair market value of the property will be at the end of the lease term. This could be a concern on some types of renewable energy systems. For this purpose, fair market value must be determined (i) without including in such value any increase or decrease for inflation or deflation during the lease term, and (ii) after subtracting from such value any cost to the lessor for removal and delivery of possession of the property to the lessor at the end of the lease term. In addition, the lessor must represent and demonstrate that a remaining useful life of the longer of one year or 20 percent of the originally estimated useful life of the property is a reasonable estimate of what the remaining useful life of the property will be at the end of the lease term.

This provision could be met more easily if the lessor were to value the system in part or in whole based on the revenue from the REC values to be realized when the lease term expires. The longer the lease term, the more contributory this component would be.

- **Lease Term and Renewal Options**
  The lease term includes all renewal or extension periods except renewals or extensions at the option of the lessee at fair rental value at the time of such renewal or extension.

- **Purchase and Sale Rights**
  No member of the Lessee Group[3] may have a contractual right to purchase the property from the lessor at a price less than its fair market value at the time the right is exercised. When the property is first placed in service or use by the lessee, the lessor may not have a contractual right to cause any party to purchase the property. The lessor must also represent that it does not have any present intention to acquire such a contractual right. The effect of any such right acquired at a subsequent time will be determined at that time based on all the facts and circumstances. A provision that permits the lessor to abandon the property to any party will be treated as a contract right of the lessor to cause such party to purchase the property.

> *"There is no energy crisis, only a crisis of ignorance."*
>
> R. Buckminster Fuller, American systems theorist, architect, engineer, author, designer, inventor, and futurist

- **Investment by Lessee**
  1. *Permitted Investments.* No part of the cost of the property or the cost of improvements, modifications, or additions to the property ("Improvements"), may be furnished by any member of the Lessee Group. This means that the lessee cannot make a "down payment" or "cap cost reduction" in the leased renewable energy system.
  2. *Severable Improvements.* A member of the Lessee Group may furnish amounts to pay for the cost of an Improvement that is owned by a member of the Lessee Group, and is readily removable without causing material damage to the lease property ("Severable Improvement"), provided that such Improvement is not subject to a contract or option for purchase or sale between the lessor and any member of the Lessee Group at a price other than fair market value at the time of such purchase or sale. At the commencement of the term of the lease, a Severable Improvement to the leased property must not be required in order to render the leased property complete for its intended use by the lessee. However, property will be considered to be complete even though the lessee may add as Severable Improvements ancillary items of equipment of a kind that customarily are selected and furnished by purchasers or lessees of property of the kind subject to the lease. Thus, for example, to the extent an item of equipment such as the boiler for a leased, steam powered vessel otherwise constituted a Severable Improvement, the vessel would not, for purposes of this section, be considered complete without the boiler. On the other hand, a leased concentrating solar thermal system would be considered complete without items of equipment such as liquid storage vessels, monitoring equipment, or an energy management system that controls certain aspects of the use of the solar thermal system even though such items of equipment are to be added by the lessee.
  3. *Nonseverable Improvements.* A member of the Lessee Group may furnish amounts to pay for cost of Improvements that are not readily removable without causing material damage to the property ("Nonseverable Improvements") if they are described in subparagraph (a) below and the conditions of subparagraph (b) are met.

a) A Nonseverable Improvement below if either:
   I. It is furnished in order to comply with health, safety, or environmental standards of any government or governmental authority having relevant jurisdiction (or any industry-wide standard recognized by such government or governmental authority);

II. It does not increase the productivity (or capacity) of the leased property to more than 125 percent of its productivity (or capacity) when first placed in service (this could be a consideration on a lease of a renewable energy "production" system), or modify the leased property for a materially different use. For this purpose, separate units that are subject to one lease (e.g., ten solar panels subject to one lease) are each considered "the leased property"; or
III. The cost of the Nonseverable Improvement, when added to the cost of Nonseverable Improvements that previously have been made to the property (other than those described in subparagraph (I) above) does not exceed 10 percent of the cost of the property. For purposes of this subparagraph, the cost of a Nonseverable Improvement will be considered to be the actual cost multiplied by a fraction, the numerator of which is the Implicit Price Deflator for Fixed Nonresidential Investment (published by the Department of Commerce in the Survey of Current Business) for the year in which the property was placed in service, and the denominator of which is the Implicit Price Deflator for Fixed Nonresidential Investment for year in which the Improvement is made. Ordinary maintenance and repair does not constitute an Improvement.

b) The following conditions must be satisfied:
I. At the commencement of the term of the lease, a Nonseverable Improvement must not be required in order to complete the property for its intended use the by the lessee;
II. The Nonseverable Improvement must not cause the leased property to become limited use property within the meaning of section 5.02 of the revenue procedure; and
III. The furnishing of the cost of the Nonseverable Improvement must not constitute an equity investment by a member of the Lessee Group in the property. For this purpose, the lessee's right to use the Improvement during the lease term in which such improvement is made does not constitute an equity investment in the property. The furnishing of such cost will be considered an equity investment in the property if a member of the Lessee Group may receive compensation, directly or indirectly, for its interest in such Nonseverable Improvement. A member of the Lessee Group will be regarded as having made an equity investment in the property if, for example:
   - The lessor is obligated to purchase the Nonseverable Improvement or reimburse a member of the Lessee Group for the cost of the fair market value of the Nonseverable Improvement;
   - Any option price or renewal rental rate to a member of the Lessee Group is adjusted downward to reflect any portion of the cost of fair market value of the Nonseverable Improvement; or
   - The lessor is obligated to share with a member of the Lessee Group a portion of the proceeds of any sale or lease of the property to a third party.

4. Cost Overruns and Modifications. If the cost of property exceeds the estimate on which the lease was based, the lease may provide for adjustment of rent to compensate the lessor for such additional cost.
5. Maintenance and Repair. If the lease requires the lessee to maintain and keep the property in good repair during the term of the lease, ordinary maintenance and repairs performed by a member of the Lessee Group will not constitute an Improvement.

- **No Lessee Loans or Guarantees**
  No member of the Lessee Group may lend to the lessor any of the funds necessary to acquire the property, or guarantee any indebtedness created in connection with the acquisition of the property by the lessor. A guarantee by any member of the Lessee Group of the lessee's obligation to pay rent, properly maintain the property, or pay insurance premiums or other similar conventional obligations of a net lease does not constitute a guarantee of the indebtedness of the lessor.

- **Profit Requirement**
  The lessor must represent and demonstrate that it expects to receive a profit from the transaction, apart from the value of or benefits obtained from the tax deductions, allowances, credits, and other

tax attributes arising from such transaction. This requirement is met if:

1. *Overall Profit.* The aggregate amount required to be paid by the lessee to or for the lessor over the lease term plus the value of the residual investment referred to in section 4.01(3) of the revenue procedure exceed an amount equal to the sum of the aggregate disbursements required to be paid by or for the lessor in connection with the ownership of the property and the lessor's Equity Investment in the property, including any direct costs to finance the Equity Investment; and
2. *Positive Cash Flow.* The aggregate amount required to be paid to or for the lessor over the lease term exceeds by a reasonable amount the aggregate disbursements required to be paid by or for the lessor in connection with the ownership of the renewable energy property.

- **Uneven Rent Test**
  Leveraged lease transactions that satisfy the guidelines set forth in section 4 of Revenue Procedure 2001-28 and that contain uneven rent payments may be subject to section 467 and the regulations thereunder relating to the accounting treatment for certain leases with prepaid or deferred rent (see page 161).[4]

- **Limited Use Property**
  In general, section 4.01(3) of the revenue procedure requires the lessor to represent and demonstrate certain facts relating to the estimated fair market value and estimated remaining useful life of the property at the end of the lease term. This requirement is intended, in part, to assure that the lessor has not transferred the use of the property to the lessee for substantially its entire useful life. In the case of such "limited use" property, at the end of the lease term there will probably be no potential lessees or buyers other than members of the Lessee Group. As a result, the lessor of limited use property will probably sell or rent the property to a member of the Lessee Group, thus enabling the Lessee Group to enjoy the benefits of the use or ownership of the property for substantially its entire use life.[5]

- **Effective Date**
  The leveraged lease guidelines were issued and became effective on May 7, 2001.

REVENUE COMPONENTS

Here again, there are many different components that go into creating the "ideal" financing solution for all parties to the cleantech energy project. Most of them center on the potential "revenue" streams that are inherent in most energy projects. Typically, they can include components like:

- Rebates and incentives
  - Federal
  - State
  - Utility
  - Foundations
  - Other taxing entities
- When those rebates and incentives occur (they can occur separately or concurrently)
  - At inception
  - Over various terms
- Based on various factors
  - System costs
  - System performance
  - Who the energy user is

> *"The two most abundant forms of power on earth are solar and wind, and they are getting cheaper and cheaper..."*
>
> Ed Begley, Jr., American author and environmentalist

- Private sector
- Government
- Non-profit
- Affordable housing entity
  - Where the system is located
  - Type of technology generating or saving the energy
- Environmental attributes such as renewable energy credits (RECs)—sometimes known as "green tags"
- Energy efficiency credits—known as "white tags"
- Grants and match-fundings
- Type of project financing utilized
- Offsets producing savings
  - Electric
  - Gas
  - Water
  - Energy Conservation Measures (ECMs)
  - GHG (or carbon) reductions

Non-cash components such as:

- Government policies

— LEED™ (Leadership in Energy and Environmental Design) accreditation standards
— Title 24 building mandates
— Legislative mandates
— Federal Energy Policy Act of 2005 (EPAct)
— Energy Improvement and Extension Act of 2008 (EIEA)
— GHG emission reductions (AB32 in California and RGGI on the east coast of the U.S.)
— Renewable Portfolio Standards (RPS)
— Regulatory agencies (air, waste, water, health, etc.)
— Criteria pollutant mandatory emission reduction schemes
— Other federal, state and local government goals and mandates

> *"I believe that the average guy in the street will give up a great deal, if he really understands the cost of not giving it up. In fact, we may find that, while we're drastically cutting our energy consumption, we're actually raising our standard of living."*
>
> David R. Brower, environmentalist

- Securities regulations for publically held enterprises
- Litigation avoidance (the public as well as stockholder)
- Alternative regulatory compliance measures (ACMs)
- Insurance risk (terms and conditions)
- Accounting standards, reporting and disclosures
- Terms, conditions and covenants imposed by existing credit lenders
- Overall business risk mitigation measures and strategies
- Fuel cost risk strategies
- Multiple sources of energy savings from a single installed system—cogen and tri-gen technologies
- On-site distributed energy security risk reduction
- Back-up and stand-by energy alternative risk mitigation
- Multiple sources of debt retirement from a single installation
- Future FASB and IASB final guidelines

Obviously, there are also many external drivers that will either "create" new revenue sources or that would stop, eliminate or reduce potential revenue sources. One of the most volatile of these potential revenue sources is new or pending legislation at all levels of government including federal, state, county or city. In addition, it is not uncommon to see special taxing districts (such as utilities, water districts, economic development corporations and even quasi-public/private partnerships) impose their own "creations." In most cases, these are beneficial to the cleantech energy business. However, it can be detrimental as well, when existing revenue sources that a debtor was planning on to help pay for the energy asset is suddenly eliminated causing severe economic hardships or even total shutdown of the entire energy project.

Both the internal and external components described above (and described in more detail below) are used to test, analyze, structure, document and implement the ideal project finance on energy generation and efficiency systems. Virtually no component can be left undecided or on the table since each of these components is a critical tool in the properly structured project finance. Major accounting, tax and debt service ramifications will result from the proper use and leverage of each of the components that have been presented above. Chapter four presented in full all of the principal "external components" in renewable energy project financing structures. The remainder of this chapter will focus on the "internal components."

FINANCE COMPONENT DETAILS

To properly structure or analyze a project finance mechanism used to acquire energy assets, you need to understand not just what the component is, but also the end effect—both economically and legally. The details of each project finance component are defined and explained below so that "no stone is left un-turned" as the details are explored. Although there are circumstances where specific components are either not available (such as in tax credits) or constrained in some way, most of the major components described in the balance of this chapter need to be evaluated and elections made based on those parameters. Those elections are not only accounting and tax elections, but also elections on which party in the project finance will receive the benefit, or conversely, be responsible for the liability or strict performance as a result of the election(s) chosen.

Once those components are clearly defined, Chapter seven (Fundamental Financial Structuring Techniques and Examples), will present some sample cases on how each of the elections chosen, components utilized, and other variables to be applied in differing energy projects will cause major shifts in the final outcome of the project finance structure. Although volumes of information can be written (and in fact have been written) on each of the following components, this section will limit our discussions to those most often encountered in a detailed analysis of a commercially structured energy finance project and leave the more in-depth complex descriptions and analysis of those components to other authors.

I. Accounting Classification

In all cases, the accounting classification is the principal driver in determining the eventual proper form of legal structure that will result in the optimal benefit for both the project lender and the project debt obligor. A simple example of that is the determination by the two parties of who will be receiving the tax benefits under the proposed structure. If the project debt obligor seeks to retain those benefits for their own account, then a direct finance structure in the form of a commercial loan, chattel mortgage, capital lease, security agreement or other type of collateralized or un-collateralized finance structure would be utilized. Conversely, if the project debt obligor was not able to adequately utilize the tax attributes because of tax loss carry-forwards, AMT (Alternative Minimum Tax) obligations that could not be avoided, or other large capital asset acquisitions were going to be completed before the tax year end, then other types of finance structures would be more appropriate. Those would include an operating lease or some type of energy purchase agreement. By doing so, the parties would be able to properly allocate the tax attributes of the project to the party that would be best able to utilize them. Since tax benefits are a large part of most energy project financings, the additional yield to the party that holds and utilizes the attributes would be reflecting in the financing terms and conditions with the monetization of those attributes. If the project lender or owner would be retaining those tax attributes for their own account, it would not be uncommon to see actual payments to the project debt obligor being reduced by as much as 75% below that of a direct finance structure.

The real marketing reason so much time is spent structuring the transaction properly prior to the project financing commitment is that the two parties usually want off-balance sheet treatment (operating lease or executory contract like an energy purchase agreement) of the transaction. Structuring the transaction in this manner means that the project financing is not capitalized on the debtor obligor's balance sheet, the corresponding future liability is not recorded (but in most cases would be shown in the footnotes to the financial statements) and the debt would be a direct expense on the income statement. Off-balance sheet treatment is very important for most debt obligors who may want to borrow money, issue equity, acquire additional assets or want an effective tool to deal with covenants on existing debt obligations. In the end, if a structure is put in place that in any way transfers ownership to the debt obligor (actual, potential or effective), the transaction would be treated as a capital lease or contract. If the financial structure is for "usage" only, then the transaction would receive operating lease status and meet the financial structuring needs of most debt obligors as to the accounting treatment.

Financial ratios under an operating lease, energy purchase agreement or other type of FASB or IRS guideline structured transaction portrays the debt obligor as being financially healthier than ratios under a capital lease or direct finance transaction for the following principal reasons:

- Improved Liquidity
  - Current ratio
  - Quick or acid ratio
  - Net working capital
- Improved Solvency
  - Times-interest-earned
- Improved Financial Leverage
  - Debt-to-equity
  - Percentage debt
- Improved Profitability
  - Net profit margin
  - Asset turnover
  - Return on assets
  - Leverage factor
  - Return on equity
  - Earnings per share

If the transaction is classified as a capital lease or a direct finance (even though the contract says "Lease" in its form), the FASB requires that it be accounted for as a capitalized asset on the debt obligor's balance sheet. The capital lease accounting treatment will very closely resemble an installment purchase and payments are required to be broken out by principal and interest. The asset is shown on the balance sheet and a liability equal to the capitalized value of the financed equipment is also shown. Further, the capitalized asset is depreciated according to accepted accounting principles over either the contract term or the economic life of the asset. Payments paid are separated into principal and interest expense as though they are installment loan payments.

The two most critical decisions in this area are driven by rules established by either the Internal Revenue Service (IRS) for tax purposes or by the Financial Accounting Standards Board (FASB) for accounting purposes. Both of these regulatory agencies have equal weight in the two principal party's deciding how the project finance structure should be optimized. Additionally, new rules being promulgated and out for review from the International Accounting Standards Board (IASB) could conceivably dramatically change these historical accounting and tax treatments. Every single decision from this point forward in this chapter is driven by these two principal regulatory controlling agencies who will determine the final outcome of the proposed project finance structure!

In turn, the decisions made by the project lender and the project debt obligor will be totally governed by the long established guidelines promulgated and enforced by the two agencies. If there is to be no challenge to the elections made by the lender and obligor and to assure that the desired outcome will not be jeopardized (referred to as "safe harbor"), then those guidelines must be very carefully followed and the principals of those guidelines must be very carefully reflected in the final executed legal documents.

FASB has had numerous pronouncements over the past forty years that have been used to give accounting guidance as to how a project finance structure should be treated for accounting purposes. Most of the pronouncements have focused on the distinctions between an operating lease (or energy service contract for that matter) and a capital lease. Table 5-3 is a summary of the FASB pronouncements.[6]

There are many decisions that need to be made as the parties to the energy project structure is evaluated and implemented. Figure 5-1 is a general review of some of the principal elements in that process for a renewable energy project lender/investor.

Then, once the determination is made as to the type of a structure that most likely would be used in the transaction, the next step is to drill down to the next process of determining the most appropriate security instrument to be used. Figure 5-2 presents some of the most common instruments used in either a Direct Finance or in a Tax Leveraged Finance agreement.

If the parties want the transaction to be treated in a way that allows the project debt obligor to retain the tax ownership rights of the project financing structure (and thereby receive the principal tax attributes of depreciation and tax credits), the project would be financed under a "direct finance" method.

If the parties want the transaction to be treated in a way that provides for the lowest possible debt payments, then the proper finance structure would be a "tax leveraged finance" agreement or an "energy purchase agreement." The project lender would monetize the available tax attributes in the transaction and pass that value through to the project debt obligor in a debt structure that would have payments less than that in a direct finance method.

In both types of project financing, the project lender may or may not "leverage" the transaction by not providing 100% of the funds necessary to purchase the asset and instead borrowing up to 100% of the funds from a third party (commercial lender, private party, or some other entity). Obviously, FASB and IRS guidelines must be followed very closely to make sure the structure does not violate any of the guidelines. Generally speaking, if there is borrowing from third parties by the project lender to help finance the project, the yields can increase dramatically to that project lender—so long as the guidelines are adhered too.

Further decisions need to be made when the site host (debtor) is a non-taxpaying entity such as a government or non-profit. They have additional project finance options that could include a Municipal Bond, CREBs, Tax-Exempt Lease (with or without fiscal funding or non-appropriation provisions), Energy Saving Sharing Agreement or a Pre-paid Service Contract.

Income Allocation

The method of expensing the project on the project debt obligor's income statement will vary, depending upon the type of agreement entered into. The method of reporting the transaction on their balance sheet will also be a direct reflection of the type of financing chosen. These ramifications will be shown later in the general ledger entry section below.

Also, for the project lender, the income allocation methods and how the transaction will be recorded on their general ledger and shown on their balance sheet will be a reflection of the type of contract agreement entered into.

It should also be noted that after the income allocation method has been chosen, it can also elect to have the income commence in "advance" or in "arrears." In advance, the first period's income is earned when the asset is acquired. In arrears, the first period's income is earned 30 days after the asset is acquired. As a general rule, most direct finance transactions have income allocation in arrears. The tax leveraged finance transactions

Table 5-3: FASB Pronouncements

Pronouncement	Topic
Statement No. 13	Accounting for Leases
Statement No. 17	Accounting for Leases—Initial Direct Costs
Statement No. 22	Changes in the Provisions of Lease Agreements Resulting from Refunding of Tax-Exempt Debt
Statement No. 23	Inception of the Lease
Statement No. 26	Profit Recognition on Sales-Type Leases of Real Estate
Statement No. 27	Classification of Renewals or Extensions of Existing Sales-Type or Direct Financing Leases
Statement No. 28	Accounting for Sales with Leasebacks
Statement No. 29	Determining Contingent Rentals
Statement No. 77	Reporting by Transferors for Transfers of Receivables with Recourse
Statement No. 91	Accounting for Nonrefundable Fees and Costs Associated with Originating or Acquiring Loans and Initial Direct Costs of Leases
Interpretation No. 19	Lessee Guarantee of the Residual Value of Leased Property
Interpretation No. 21	Accounting for Leases in a Business Combination
Interpretation No. 23	Leases of Certain Property Owned by a Governmental Unit or Authority
Interpretation No. 24	Leases Involving Only Part of a Building
Interpretation No. 26	Accounting for Purchase of a Leased Asset by the Lessee During the Term of the Lease
Interpretation No. 27	Accounting for a Loss on a Sublease
Technical Bulletin No. 79-10	Fiscal Funding Clauses in Lease Agreements
Technical Bulletin No. 79-11	Effect of a Penalty on the Term of a Lease
Technical Bulletin No. 79-12	Interest Rate Used in Calculating the Present Value of Minimum Lease Payments
Technical Bulletin No. 79-13	Applicability of FASB 13 to Current Value Financial Statements
Technical Bulletin No. 79-14	Upward Adjustment of Guaranteed Residual Values
Technical Bulletin No. 79-15	Accounting for Loss on a Sublease not Involving the Disposal of a Segment
Technical Bulletin No. 79-16	Effect of a Change in Income Tax Rate on the Accounting for Leveraged Leases
Technical Bulletin No. 79-17	Reporting Cumulative Effect Adjustments from Retroactive Application of FASB Statement No. 13
Technical Bulletin No. 79-18	Transition Requirement of Certain FASB Amendments and Interpretations of FASB Statement No. 13
Technical Bulletin No. 85-3	Accounting for Operating Leases with Scheduled Rent Increases
Technical Bulletin No. 86-2	Accounting for an Interest in the Residual Value of a Leased Asset

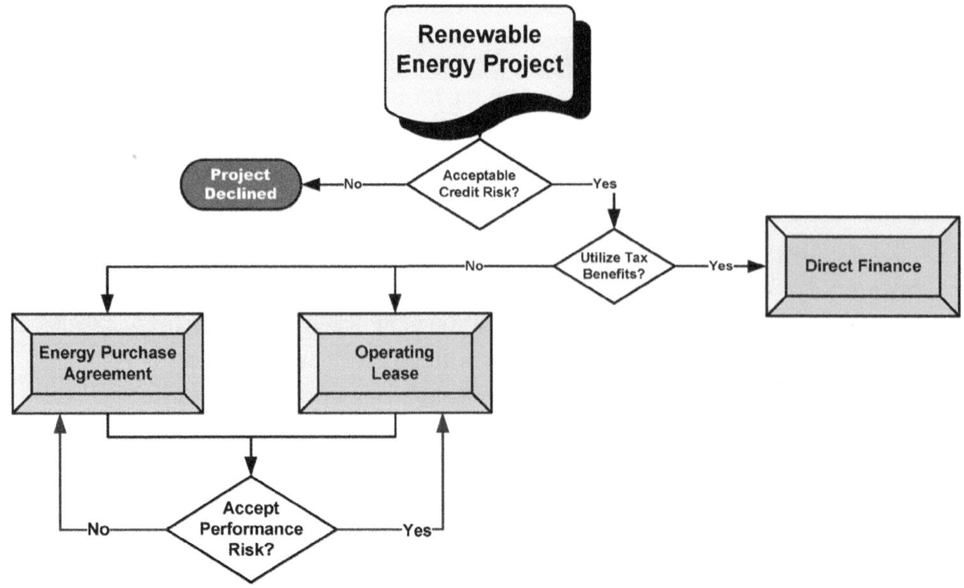

Figure 5-1: Project Finance Structure Decision Tree

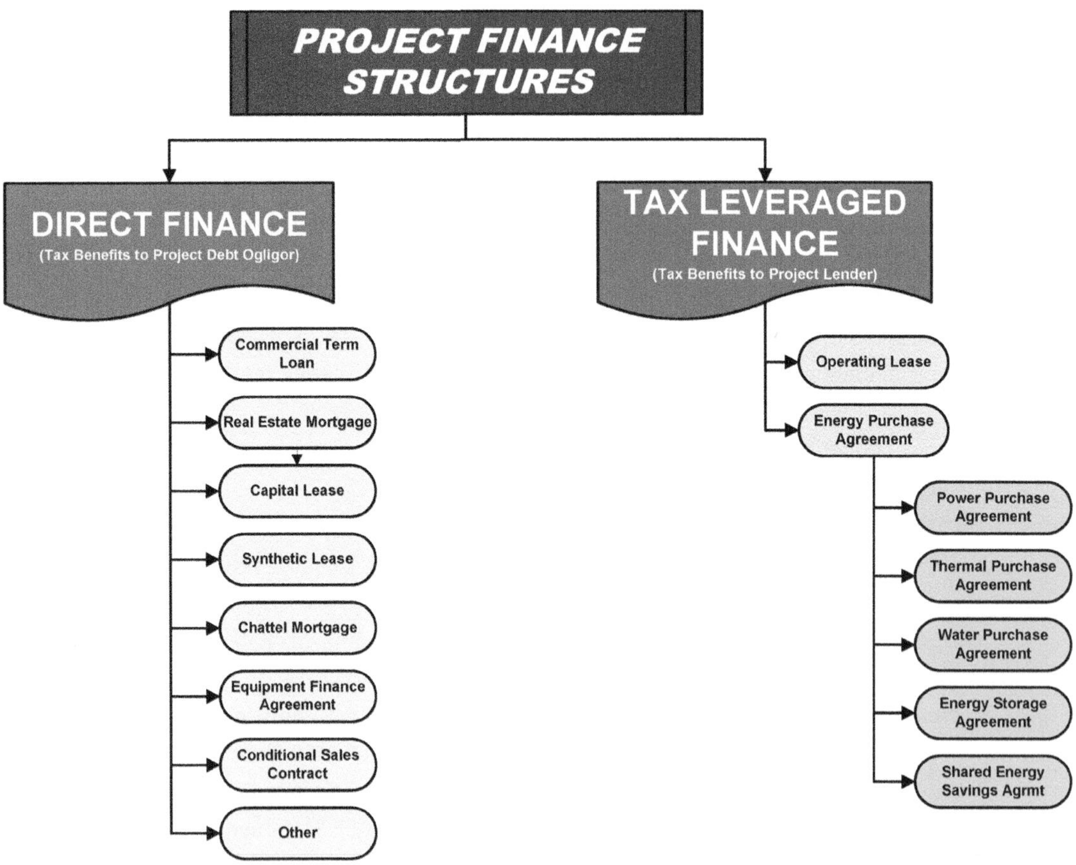

Figure 5-2: Project Finance Contract Instruments

will often choose to use the income in advance allocation method.

The various income allocation methods for both the project lender and the project debt obligor determine the way total cash and taxes are spread over the life of the project. Each month's allocation is the proportion of the total income recognized during that month. The income allocation is used to spread pre-tax income, state and federal taxes and state and federal income tax credits. The possible 12 different income allocation methods are as follows:

1) **Base Term Rate and Base Term Rate with Residual**
These methods calculate the rate that discounts the base payment or rent (and residual), excluding interim, to the equipment cost on the commencement date. The rate is called the "allocation rate." This rate is similar to the familiar "base term rate" rent statistic. The only difference, if any, arises because this rate uses monthly compounding while the base term rate uses periodic compounding (quarterly, semi-annual, etc.).

2) **Full Term Rate and Full Term Rate with Residual**
These methods are similar to the "base term rate" method described above. The only difference is that this method also includes the interim earnings and the equipment cost on the funding date as opposed to the commencement date.

3) **Cash (Pre-Tax Cash Flow)**
This is a very simple method. The pre-tax cash flow is divided by the total pre-tax cash flow to produce the income allocation. With this method, the book income will likely equal the pre-tax cash flow.

4) **Level Rate-of-Return (Pre-Tax)**
Reflects the "multiple investment (after-tax)" method for leveraged transactions.

5) **Internal Rate of Return (After Tax)**
This method calculates the rate that will present value, using monthly compounding, the after-tax cash flow to zero. The rate is similar to the familiar "internal rate-of-return." The only difference, if any, arises because this rate uses monthly compounding while the internal rate of return could use a different method of compounding (quarterly, semi-annual, etc.).

This rate is then applied to the monthly after-tax cash flow to calculate the monthly interest. The outstanding balance is calculated on the 30th of each month and interest is calculated monthly in arrears, also on the 30th. The monthly interest is then divided by the total interest to produce the monthly allocation factors.

6) **Level Rate-of-Return (pre-tax)**
This method calculates the rate that discounts the pre-tax cash flows to zero, using monthly compounding. This rate is then applied to the monthly pre-tax cash flow to calculate monthly interest. The outstanding balance is calculated on the 30th of each month and interest is calculated monthly in arrears, also on the 30th. The monthly interest is then divided by the total interest to produce the monthly allocation factors.

This method is recommended by FASB for non-leveraged transactions.

7) **Loan Lending (Direct Finance)**
If the transaction is classified for tax purposes as a direct finance agreement, then this method switches to the "full term rate with residual" method. Otherwise this method calculates the rate that discounts with monthly compounding the loan lending debt service payments, to the loan lending takedown. The rate is called the "allocation rate." The rate is calculated that discounts the total debt service less the takedown (converted to monthly) to zero. This rate is similar to the loan lending interest rate. The only difference, if any, arises because this rate uses monthly compounding.

The rate is then applied to calculate the monthly interest. The outstanding balance is calculated on the 30th of each month and interest is calculated monthly in arrears, also on the 30th. The monthly interest is then divided by the total interest to produce the monthly allocation factors.

8) **Multiple Investment (after-tax) used in Leveraged Accounting**
This method used the FASB 13 leveraged lease accounting yield (see the "Yield" section below). This yield produces monthly interest on the 30th of each month. (This interest is 0 for the months when the investment balance is 0.) The monthly interest is divided by the total interest to produce the monthly allocation factors.
For leveraged transactions, the method is recommended by FASB.

9) **Rule of 78's**
This method calculates the monthly allocation factors as the number of months remaining divided by the sum of the months. For example, in a 12-month transaction the sum of months is 1+2+3+4+5+6+7+8+9+10+11+12 = 78. The factor for month one is 12/78, the factor for month two is 11/78, and so on until the last month's factor of 1/78. The sum of these factors is 78/78, which is, of course, 1.

The start month for this method is the month when the asset is delivered. The last month is the month when the debt payments end. If there is more than one asset, then factors should be calculated for each asset delivery date and then weighted by the asset cost. If the monthly income is booked in arrears, the allocation factor for the start month is 0. If the monthly income is booked in advance, the allocation factor for the last month is 0.

This method produces very accelerated allocation factors. For example, in a 12 year transaction, 50.66% of the income is recognized in the first 3 years and 6 months of the transaction, and only 8.65% of the income is recognized in the last 3 years and 7 months of the transaction.

10) **Specified (External Adjustments)**
This method would use allocation factors that would be entered via certain selected elections. Although this would allow a great deal of "creativity" in income allocations, it would also be subject to careful scrutiny by both FASB and the IRS. Therefore, you should be prepared to have substantiating evidence to support your "specified" elections.

11) **Straight Line**
The method calculates a constant monthly allocation factor by simply dividing 1 by the number of months from the start month to the last month. This is perhaps the most "conservative" possible method of income allocation.

The start month for this method is the month when the asset is delivered. The last month is the month when the scheduled debt payments ends. If there is more than one asset, then factors should be calculated for each asset delivery date and weighted by the asset cost. If the monthly income is booked in arrears, the allocation for the start month is 0. If the monthly income is booked in advance, the allocation factor for the last month is 0.

12) **Yield Earnings**
This method uses the interest from a yield calculation. The interest amounts are then divided by the total interest to produce the allocation factors. With this method, you also can specify three characteristics about the yield: the methodology, the type (FASB 13, IRR, MISF), and the compounding. Depending on the compounding selection, the allocation factors may not be monthly. This method can be used to create custom allocation methods.

Monthly Income Booked

Each of the standard allocation methods of income allocation described above calculates the allocation factors on a monthly basis in arrears except the "Yield Earnings" method which uses the compounding specified in the yield definition. Using this method allows you to book the income in advance or pro-rate it as specified in your accounting controls.

If you specify "advance," each month's allocation factor is simply moved back in time one month. (However, with the "Yield Earnings" method, each allocation factor you establish would be moved to the date of the prior allocation factor.)

You can "pro-rate" an income allocation also. Typically you would set the numbers of days spread back. The normal date used is to set it to the month of the weighted average asset delivery date.

> *"Tradition is what you resort to when you don't have the time or the money to do it right."*
>
> Kurt Herbert Alder (1905-1988)

With all of the allocation methods except the "Yield Earnings" method, a constant is calculated as the number of days to be spread back divided by 30. This constant is the percentage of each month's allocation factor that is to be taken out of the current month and added to the previous month. Of course, the first month's factor is not split, as there is no preceding month. The first month's factor is, however, increased by the constant times the second month's factor. The last month's factor is only decreased by the constant factor.

In the above monthly book income calculations, the allocation method is either "Straight Line," "Level Rate of Return (Pre-Tax)," or "Multiple Investment (After-Tax)." If Tax Leveraged Financing structures are used, straight line is used when the transaction accounting method is straight line, multiple investment is used when the Tax Leveraged Financing structure accounting method used is multiple investment, and otherwise level rate-of-return method is used in Tax Leveraged Financing structures.

Tax Provision Method

In the Direct Finance method of project financing, there are two possible methods of calculating the state and federal tax provisions. You will need to choose the either the "Proportional" method or the "Times Tax Rate" method.

When you choose the "Proportional" method, then the total state and federal taxes paid are spread into the state and federal tax provisions proportionally to the pre-tax book income. This is not a recommended method to be used by most taxpayers.

The "Times Tax Rate" method is calculated as the pre-tax book income times the current state and federal tax rate. When you have changing state tax rates, then it is likely that the total state provisions do not equal the total states taxes paid. These differences can be accounted for in a transaction called "Permanent Basis Adjustment, State" as described below.

The federal tax provisions are calculated as the pre-tax book income less the state tax provisions times the current federal tax rate. When you have changing federal tax rates then it is likely that the total federal provisions do not equal the total federal taxes paid. These differences are accounted for in a transaction called "Permanent Basis Adjustment, Federal" as described below.

Initial Direct Costs (IDC)

There is an IDC component that is frequently used to follow FASB guidelines for accounting treatment. Only those costs incurred by the lender/project developer that are costs directly related to the origination of the project finance contract that result directly from and are essential to acquire the transaction, would not have been incurred had that transaction not occurred, and certain costs directly related to specified activities performed by the lender/project developer for that transaction.

Typical of those activities are:

- Evaluating the prospective customer's financial condition;
- Evaluating and recording guarantees;
- Evaluating and analyzing the finance structure and related costs, both present and future;
- Evaluating collateral, including engineering and construction risks;
- Evaluating related contracts and documents that secure the transaction;
- Performing site analysis;
- Performing emissions analysis;
- Performing environmental risk analysis;
- Performing component degradation analysis;
- Evaluating potential technologies and their relation to each other;
- Evaluating energy production or energy efficiency performance potential;
- Negotiating contract terms and conditions;
- Preparing and processing all documentation;
- Filing of all required documentation with regulatory agencies;
- Permits and licenses;
- Establishing maintenance schedules;
- That portion of the employee's total compensation and payroll-related fringe benefits directly related to time spent performing those activities for that transaction;
- Fees paid to third parties for origination, underwriting, marketing or analysis;
- Fees paid for project commissioning costs (see page 98);
- Tax, accounting or legal advisory services attributable to the specific project;
- Preparation of operating and maintenance manuals; and
- Closing the transaction.

IDC is calculated using the following steps:

1. Calculate projected gross monthly book income including all fees.
2. Calculate projected gross monthly book income excluding all IDC Fees.
3. The difference between the two gross monthly booked incomes is the IDC fee accounting.

The IDC fee accounting is loaded into the general ledger by a transaction called "IDC (FAS 91)." The debit account is called "IDC (FAS 91) debit" and the credit account is "Memo contra." The IDC fee is also brought into the calculations in the accounting group called "Initial Direct Costs."

Tax Timing Differences

Tax timing differences occur when the total federal/state tax provision does not equal the total state/federal taxes due. This happens whenever there are one or more changes in the federal/state tax rate. These differences are loaded into the GL with a transaction called "Permanent Basis Adjustment, Federal/State." The debit account is "Tax timing difference, federal/state" and the credit account is called "Deferred tax, federal/state."

The dates of the transactions are the last day that a particular rate applies. For example, if the federal rate changes from 35% to 30% on January 1st, 2010, then the adjustment is entered into the GL on December 30, 2009. If there are more than two rates then the adjustment is made on the last day that the first rate applies and then on the last day that every other rate applies, except than an adjustment is always made on the day before the last rate starts.

Permanent Tax Differences

Permanent tax differences occur when there are parameters that are not 100% taxable. For example, the asset has a depreciation basis of only 70%. These differences are loaded into the GL with a transaction called "Income Adjustment." The debit account is "Income adjustment, federal/state" and the credit account is "Memo contra, account."
The total federal/state difference is loaded into the GL proportional to the "Income Earned" account.

After-tax Book Income

The total after-tax cash flow is not loaded directly into the GL, but of course it can be derived from the GL as the net of several accounts. The "After-Tax Booked Income" may be calculated from the following accounts:

Table 5-4: After-Tax Book Income

+	Income earned
-	Tax provisions state
-	Tax provisions federal
+	ITC earned state
+	ITC earned federal
=	After-Tax Booked Income

II. General Ledger Transactions/Accounts *(Direct Finance)*

For a project lender using a Direct Finance structure, the GL Transaction and Accounts lists below show each type of transaction and the two accounts that are used by them. These lists are then summarized in a chart. Similar tables are used for Tax Leveraged Finance transactions.

a. **Book Transactions**
The transaction is initially booked on the "in-service" date, which is the first delivery date, or the first pre-tax cash flow, whichever is earlier. All of the book transactions are on the in-service date.

b. **Cash Transactions: Tables 5-7 through 5-10**

c. **Tax Due Transactions:**
There is a transaction to load the state taxes due and another to load the federal taxes due.

d. **Spread Transactions**
These transactions are calculated by using the allocation factors (which are usually monthly) over the entire transaction term.

e. **Other Transactions**

III. General Ledger Transactions/Accounts *(Tax Leveraged Finance)*

A project lender who is structuring the transaction as a Tax Leveraged Finance will use somewhat different GL entries. Income recognition will normally use one of two methods—straight-lined over the individual rental payments or over the whole contract term. The former straight-lines each rental amount over its accrual period. The latter straight-lines each interim rental amount over its accrual period and straight-lines the total base rent from the commencement date to the end of the rent. This control is also used for periodic expenses and periodic income.

i. **Transactions and Accounts**
Accounting for operating leases and energy purchase agreements (of all types) uses some, but not all, of the transactions and accounts used in the Direct Finance accounting, and adds several additional ones. (See Tables 5-11 and 5-12.)

ii. **Depreciation Transactions**
The book depreciation is entered in the "book" parameter of the GL. The default method most often used is "straight-line-to-end." With this method the monthly depreciation is calculated as the total depreciation less the salvage value (if any has been established) divided by the number of months from the book depreciation start date to the asset residual date. This monthly amount is loaded into the GL on the 30th of each month except the first and last months.

Table 5-5: Book Transactions

TRANSACTION	DEBIT ACCOUNT	CREDIT ACCOUNT
Book asset purchase	Income unearned	Equipment
Book fee	Income unearned	Fees payable
Book interest expense	Income unearned	Interest payable
Book interest income	Interest receivable	Income unearned
Book periodic expense	Income unearned	Periodic expense payable
Book periodic income	Periodic income receivable	Income unearned
Book rent	Rent receivable	Income unearned
Book residual	Residual receivable	Income unearned
Book ITC, federal	Taxes payable/receivable, federal	ITC unearned federal
Book ITC, state	Taxes payable/receivable, state	ITC unearned state

Table 5-6: Cash Transactions

TRANSACTION	DEBIT ACCOUNT	CREDIT ACCOUNT
Cash asset purchase	Equipment	Cash
Cash Fee	Fees payable	Cash
Cash interest paid	Interest payable	Cash
Cash interest received	Cash	Interest receivable
Cash loan takedown borrowing	Cash	Loans payable
Cash loan takedown lending	Loans receivable	Cash
Cash periodic expense	Periodic expense payable	Cash
Cash periodic income	Cash	Periodic income receivable
Cash principal paid	Loans payable	Cash
Cash principal received	Cash	Loans Receivable
Cash rent	Cash	Rent receivable
TRANSACTION	**DEBIT ACCOUNT**	**CREDIT ACCOUNT**
Cash residual	Cash	Residual receivable
Cash security deposit	Security deposit payable	Cash
Cash tax, federal	Taxes payable/receivable, federal	Cash
Cash tax, state	Taxes payable/receivable, state	Cash
Cash ITC, federal	Cash	Taxes payable/receivable, Federal
Cash ITC, state	Cash	Taxes payable/receivable, State

Table 5-7: Tax Due Transactions

TRANSACTION	DEBIT ACCOUNT	CREDIT ACCOUNT
Tax due, federal	Deferred tax, federal	Taxes payable/receivable, federal
Tax due, state	Deferred tax, state	Taxes payable/receivable, state

Table 5-8: Spread Transactions

TRANSACTION	DEBIT ACCOUNT	CREDIT ACCOUNT
Income recognized	Income unearned	Income earned
Permanent basis adjustment federal	Tax timing difference, federal	Deferred tax, federal
Permanent basis adjustment state	Tax timing difference, state	Deferred tax, state
Tax provision, federal	Tax provision, federal	Deferred tax, federal
Tax provision, state	Tax provision, state	Deferred tax, state
ITC recognized federal	ITC unearned federal	ITC earned federal
ITC recognized state	ITC unearned state	ITC earned state

Table 5-9: Other Transactions

TRANSACTION	DEBIT ACCOUNT	CREDIT ACCOUNT
IDC (FAS 91)	IDC (FAS 91) debit	Memo contra
Income adjustment	Income adjustment, federal	Memo contra, account
Income adjustment	Income adjustment, state	Memo contra, account
Income adjustment	Tax provision, federal	Deferred tax, federal
Income adjustment	Tax provision, state	Deferred tax, state
Reconcile	Reconcile	Income earned
Reconcile	Reconcile	Income unearned
Reconcile	Reconcile	Any other account

The first month gets the monthly amount divided by 30 times the number of days in the first month. It is loaded into the GL on the 30th of the first month. The last month gets the monthly amount divided by 30 times the number of days in the last month. It is loaded into the GL on the asset residual date.

iii. **Tax Timing Differences**

Tax timing differences are booked for Tax Leveraged Finance structures in the same manner as they are with Direct Finance structures as described above.

IV. **Loan Accounting**

In loan accounting, the transaction is booked as a loan, which means that the pre-tax cash flows are broken into a loan-equivalent stream of interest and principal payments. The interest is taxable, and there are no deductions for depreciation.

Table 5-10: General Ledger Transactions/Accounts (Direct Finance)

ACCOUNTS	Cash	Deferred tax, Federal	Deferred tax, state	Fees payable	Equipment	IDC (FAS 91) debit	Income adj, federal	Income adj, state	Income earned	Income unearned	Interest payable	Interest receivable	Loans payable	Loans receivable	Memo contra, account	Periodic expense payble	Periodic income receivable	Rent receivable	Residual receivable	Security deposit payable	Taxes pay/rec, federal	Taxes pay/rec, state	Tax provision, federal	Tax provision, state	Tax timing diff, federal	Tax timing diff, state
Book asset purchase					+					-																
Book fee				+						-																
Book interest expense										-	+															
Book interest income										+		-														
Book periodic expense										-						+										
Book periodic income										+							-									
Book rent										+								-								
Book residual										+									-							
Cash asset purchase	+				-																					
Cash fee	+			-																						
Cash interest paid	+										-															
Cash interest received	-											+														
Cash loan takedown borrowing	-												+													
Cash loan takedown lending	+													-												
Cash periodic expense	+															-										
Cash periodic income	-																+									
Cash principal paid	+												-													
Cash principal received	-													+												
Cash rent	-																	+								
Cash residual	-																		+							
Cash security deposit	+																			-						
Cash tax, federal	+																				-					
Cash tax, state	+																					-				
Tax due, federal		-																			+					
Tax due, state			-																			+				
Income recognized									+	-																
Permanent basis adj, federal		+																							-	
Permanent basis adj, state			+																							-
Tax provision, federal		+																					-			
Tax provision, state			+																					-		
IDC (FAS 91) debit						-									+											
Income adjustment							-								+											
Income adjustment								-							+											
Income adjustment		+																					-			
Income adjustment			+																					-		
TOTALS	ACTF	0	0	0	0	IDC fees	Federal income-PTCF	State income-PTCF	PTCF	0	0	0	0	0		0	0	0	0	0	0	0	Tax paid, federal	Tax paid, state		

Income Allocation Methods:

Loan Lending

With this method, monthly allocation factors are computed based on a stream of "artificial interest" payments. At the end of each month, the artificial interest that would be payable because of the preceding month's ending principal balance being outstanding for one month is considered earned income. In months when there is no actual cash payment made, that interest is refinanced as additional principal. In months when there is a cash payment made, that payment is likely to more than offset the would-be refinanced principal, reducing the outstanding principal. This method computes an artificial interest rate which causes the total artificial interest (income) to be equal to the actual total interest paid. That rate, which may be different from the actual interest rate on the note, is the income allocation rate. The monthly allocation factors, finally, are the artificial interest amounts divided by the total interest.

Level Rate of Return (Pre-Tax)

This method calculates the rate that discounts the pre-tax cash flows to zero, using monthly compounding.

This rate is applied to the monthly pre-tax cash flows to calculate the monthly interest. The outstanding balance is calculated on the 30th of each month, and interest is calculated monthly in arrears, also on the 30th. The monthly interest is then divided by the total interest to produce the monthly allocation factors.

V. Alternative Minimum Tax (AMT)

The tax issues involved when a taxpaying entity purchases any sort of renewable energy equipment is both complex and vary greatly from taxpayer to taxpayer. Solar energy projects in particular have many tax aspects that need to be considered—both in the context of economic benefits and in rapidly changing tax laws that frequently expire or are extended on both a federal and individual

Table 5-11: Operating Lease & Energy Purchase Agreement Additional

TRANSACTION	DEBIT ACCOUNT	CREDIT ACCOUNT
Load book basis	Book basis	Book basis
Cash asset purchase	Equipment	Cash
Depreciation	Income earned	Equipment
Depreciation, remaining	Income earned	Equipment
Book rent	Rent receivable	Income earned
Cash rent	Cash	Rent receivable
Book residual	Residual receivable	Income earned
Cash residual	Cash	Residual receivable
Book fee	Income earned	Fees payable
Cash fee	Fees payable	Cash
IDC (FAS 91)	IDC (FAS 91 debit	Memo contra, account
Book periodic expense	Income earned	Periodic expenses payable
Cash periodic expenses	Periodic expenses payable	Cash
Book periodic income	Periodic income receivable	Income earned
Cash periodic income	Cash	Periodic income receivable
Cash loan takedown borrowing	Cash	Loans payable
Cash principal paid	Loans payable	Cash
Cash loan takedown lending	Loans receivable	Cash
Cash principal received	Cash	Loans receivable
Book interest expense	Income earned	Interest payable
Cash interest paid	Interest payable	Cash
Book interest income	Interest receivable	Cash
Cash interest received	Cash	Interest receivable
Tax provision, state	Tax provision, state	Deferred tax, state
Tax provision, federal	Tax provision, federal	Deferred tax, federal
Cash tax, federal	Taxes payable/receivable federal	Cash
Cash tax, state	Taxes payable/receivable state	Cash
Cash ITC, federal	Cash	Taxes payable/receivable federal
Cash ITC, state	Cash	Taxes payable/receivable state
Tax due, federal	Deferred tax, federal	Taxes payable/receivable federal
Tax due, state	Deferred tax, state	Taxes payable/receivable state
Cash security deposit	Security deposit	Cash

Table 5-12: General Ledger Transactions/Accounts (Tax Leveraged Finance)

ACCOUNTS	Book basis	Cash	Deferred tax federal	Deferred tax state	Fees payable	Equipment	IDC (FAS 91) debit	Income earned	Income unearned	Interest payable	Interest receivable	Loans payable	Loans receivable	Memo contra, account	Periodic expense payable	Periodic income receivable	Rent receivable	Residual receivable	Security deposit payable	Taxes payable/receivable, federal	Taxes payable/receivable, state	Tax provision federal	Tax provision state
Load book basis	±																						
Cash asset purchase		+				-																	
Depreciation						+		-															
Depreciation remaining						+		-															
Book rent								+									-						
Cash rent		-															+						
Book residual								+										-					
Cash residual		-																+					
Book fee					+			-															
Cash fee		+			-																		
IDC (FAS 91) debit							-							+									
Book periodic expense								-							+								
Cash periodic expense		+													-								
Book periodic income								+								-							
Cash periodic income		-														+							
Cash loan takedown borrowing		-										+											
Cash principal paid		+										-											
Cash loan takedown lending		+											-										
Cash principal received		-											+										
Book interest expense								-		+													
Cash interest paid		+								-													
Book interest income								+			-												
Cash interest received		-									+												
Tax provision, state				+																			-
Tax provision, federal			+																			-	
Cash tax, federal		+																		-			
Cash tax, state		+																			-		
Tax due, federal			-																	+			
Tax due, state				-																	+		
Cash security deposit		+																	-				
TOTALS	0	ATCF	0	0	0	0	IDC Fees	PTCF	0	0	0	0	0		0	0	0	0	0	0	0	Tax paid, federal	Tax paid, state

state level.

The set of subjects covered in this section are not designed to be all encompassing of the tax considerations. Rather, it is presented only to cover some of the issues that need to be understood when deciding on the proper financing structure for a renewable energy project to a commercial or industrial business in the United States. Remember that individual states have sometimes conflicting state applications of the issues including reduced advantages or in other cases, increased incentives that are applicable on certain renewable energy systems.

A good example is the State of Oregon. Although every taxpayer purchasing a solar system in the United States in tax year 2008 is eligible for a 30% energy tax credit on new qualified solar systems, in Oregon the system would also qualify for a 50% state energy tax credit known as a BETC (Business Energy Tax Credit). The BETC is in addition to the federal credit but is different in other aspects.

The federal tax credit is earned by the taxpayer the day the system is fully commissioned and is deemed "placed in service." It is earned 100% immediately, and cannot be sold to a third party.

In the state of Oregon, the BETC is allowed to be earned at the rate of 20% per year over a 5 year period and is not allowed to be applied against state taxes owed by a taxpayer all in the first year. Additionally, the credit can be sold to a third party who then can use the credit against their own Oregon state tax liability. It should be noted that the Oregon State Department of Energy will actually assist you in finding a buyer for the BETC.

AMT creates a special problem for those who are looking to the most efficient way to maximize the economic benefits in a project financing. Under the Federal Energy Tax Act of 2005, the energy tax credits that are generated from a renewable energy project cannot be used to offset the AMT due by a taxpayer under EPAct 2005. This was changed in 2008 for tax years 2009 through 2016.

The AMT is an alternative method of calculating federal taxes due. After calculating the regular taxes due (ignoring AMT) and then followed by calculating the AMT taxes due, a company is required to use the *higher of the two* amounts for the amount of taxes due.

Regular taxes due are calculated as taxable income times the current tax rate. AMT income is the regular taxable income, *adjusted by preference items*, multiplied by the AMT tax rate, currently at 20%. When taxable income is positive and the preference adjustment that must be made are not significant, then AMT tax due will be lower than regular tax due, and therefore AMT will not apply. AMT mainly comes into play when regular taxable income is negative (since 20% of a negative number is higher than 35% of the number), or when the preference items are significant.

Calculation of the AMT and assessing the amount of tax due is performed by the steps shown in Figure 5-3.

The tax laws give preferential treatment to certain kinds of income and allow special deductions and credits for certain kinds of expenses. The alternative minimum tax attempts to ensure that anyone who benefits from these tax advantages pays at least a minimum amount of tax. The alternative minimum tax is applicable to individuals as well as for profit corporations and partnerships.

A commercial solar tax credit cannot be used to reduce a taxpayer's regular income taxes by more than 75% of what the taxpayer would otherwise pay, or below the taxpayer's alternative minimum tax amount, whichever is greater. [A corporation must pay, essentially, whichever amount is greater—its regular income taxes at a 35% rate (assuming the corporation is in the highest corporate tax rate), or its "alternative minimum taxes" at a 20% rate, but on a broader definition of taxable income as described below.] Therefore, companies that pay the minimum tax are unable to use energy tax credits—at least in the year they pay the AMT. The credits can be carried to another tax year. These limits are limits not only on use of commercial solar tax credits, but also on most other "business credits." Thus, the commercial solar tax credits in combination with other business credits cannot reduce a taxpayer's tax liability

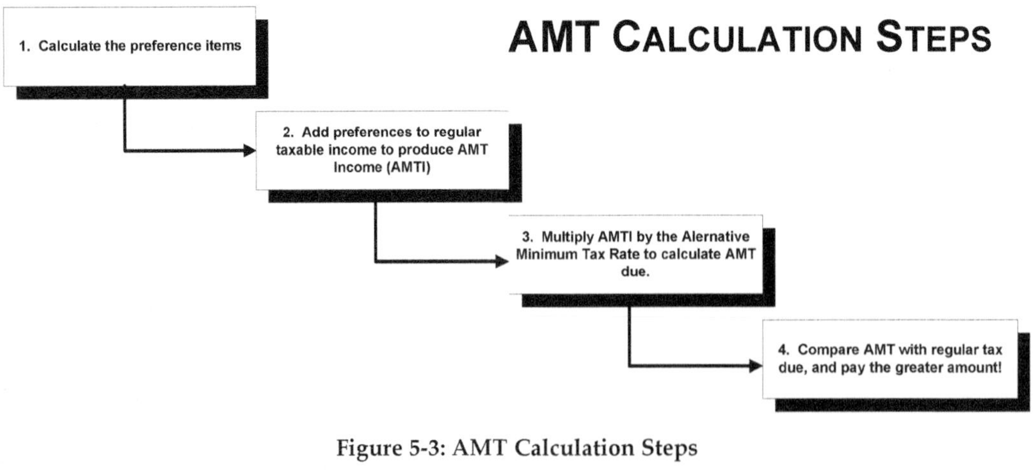

Figure 5-3: AMT Calculation Steps

in a given year below the AMT floor (prior to 2009).

The alternative minimum tax is a separately figured tax that eliminates many deductions and credits, thus increasing tax liability for a taxpayer who would otherwise pay less tax. The tentative minimum tax rates on ordinary income are percentages set by law. For capital gains, the capital gains rates for the regular tax are used.

A taxpayer may have to pay the alternative minimum tax if their taxable income for regular tax purposes plus any adjustments and preference items that apply are more than the exemption amount. The exemption amounts are set by law for each filing status and listed in the Form 6251 Instructions (if you are an individual) and Form 4626 if you are a corporation.

If you are liable for alternative minimum tax as an individual, you must complete Form 6251, Alternative Minimum Tax-Individuals. If you are not liable for alternative minimum tax this year but paid alternative minimum tax in one or more previous years, you may be eligible to take a special minimum tax credit against your regular tax this year. If eligible, you should complete and attach Form 8801, *Credit for Prior Year Minimum Tax-Individuals, Estates and Trusts*. Similar forms are applicable for corporations.

Some of the deductions and tax credits available from the purchase of renewable energy equipment are subject to the *preference items* defined under the Alternative Minimum Tax rules and should be carefully considered when deciding what the best project financing structure to use to pay for the equipment could be. It may be more advantageous to let a third-party lender/investor retain the tax benefits associated with solar equipment if you cannot utilize the benefits in the year of acquisition because of the AMT. The lender could provide longer term repayments than normal as a result.

It is the "preference items" that give rise to the greatest problems for a corporation in the normal course of business, and thereby creating the additional tax due in a given year. The corporate taxpayer needs to take a close look at the items that create the preference item and try to find ways to avoid the creation of as few preference items as possible. A more thorough description of the issue of preference items is described below (*see page 136*).

The tax law gives preferential treatment to some kinds of income and allows special deductions and credits for some kinds of expenses. Taxpayers who benefit from these provisions of the law may have to pay the additional AMT tax. It is a separate tax computation that, in effect, eliminates many deductions and credits and creates a tax liability for an individual or corporation who would otherwise pay little or no tax.

For 2003 and future years, the exemption amounts for figuring the AMT have increased. The amount depends on your filing status. You may have to pay AMT if your taxable income for regular tax purposes, combined with certain adjustment and tax preference items, is more than the exemption amounts below for individual taxpayers (different exemptions are in effect for corporate tax payers as shown later):

- $58,000 if you are married filing a joint return or a qualified widow(er),
- $40,250 if you are single or head of household, or
- $29,000 if you are married filing a separate return.

The adjustments and tax preference items include such things as: standard or certain itemized deductions, taxable state and local tax refunds, accelerated depreciation of certain property, intangible drilling costs, certain tax exempt interest and the difference between AMT and the regular tax gain or loss on the sale of property, treatment of incentive stock options and depletion allowances.

A valuable resource to use to determine if you are or will be subject to the AMT can be found by going directly to the IRS website and use a calculator they have provided. All you need to do is answer some basic questions and it gives you the result. The web site address is *http://apps.irs.gov/app/amt*.

All of the items below are preference items and will be eliminated from your deductions on your regular tax liability calculations and used to calculate your AMT. Once your tax liability is calculated under the AMT calculation, *you will be subject to paying the higher of your regular tax liability or the recalculated AMT tax liability*. By defining the items below as a preference item for AMT calculations, the AMT sets a limit on the amount these benefits can be used to reduce a taxpayer's total tax liability.

> *"Business? It's quite simple. It's other people's money."*
>
> Alexandre Dumas (1802-1870)

Recordkeeping is extremely important for any taxpayer subject to the AMT (most individual taxpayers who have $60,000 or more per year in income). For the AMT, certain items of income, deductions, etc., receive different tax treatment than for the regular tax. Therefore, you need to recalculate items for the AMT that you calculated for the regular tax. In some cases, you may wish to do this by completing the applicable tax form a second time. If you do complete another form, do not attach it to your tax return, but keep it for your records.

For the regular tax, some deductions and credits may result in carrybacks or carry-forwards to other tax years. Examples are investment interest expense, a net operating loss, a capital loss, a passive activity loss, and the foreign tax credit. Because you may have to refigure these items for the AMT, the carryback or carry-forward amount may be different for the AMT than for the regular tax. Your at-risk limits and basis amounts also may differ for the AMT. Therefore, you must keep records of these different amounts.

If you are a partner in a partnership or a shareholder in an S corporation, see Schedule K-1 and its instructions to figure your adjustments or preferences from the partnership or S Corporation to include on Form 6251.

See Form 8801, *Credit for Prior Year Minimum Tax—Individuals, Estates, and Trusts*, if you paid AMT for 2004, 2005 or earlier years or you had a minimum tax credit carry-forward on your 2004 or 2005 Form 8801. If you pay AMT for 2005 or 2006, you may be able to take a credit on Form 8801 for years 2006 and later. Similar rules hold true for tax years after 2006.

As an example of preference items that are subject to the AMT calculation:

- Taxes Paid—From Schedule A on the 1040, line 9 and includes any state and local general sales taxes you deducted.
- Home Mortgage Interest Adjustment (interest deductions taken on the 1040 that was used for purposes other than the principal mortgage)
- Investment interest
- Depletion allowances
- Net Operating Losses
- Interest from Private Activity Bonds exempt under the 1040 return
- Qualified Small Business Stock held more than 5 years before selling
- Exercise of Incentive Tax Options
- Estate and Trust income
- Adjustment from Large Partnership K-1
- Disposition of Property including casualty and theft losses
- Depreciation—difference between MACRS (200% DDB) and 150% DDB
- Passive Activity Losses (usually from a K-1 form)
- Certain loss limitations
- Certain mining costs
- Research and experimental costs
- Intangible drilling costs
- Certain charitable contributions of property
- Interest paid in a trade or business
- Section 179 expense
- Expense for business use of home
- Self-employed health insurance deduction
- Self-employed SEP, SIMPLE, and qualified plans deductions
- IRA deduction
- Alternative Tax Net Operating Loss Deduction (ATNOLD)

Since corporations are also subject to the AMT, the following should be noted if you are a corporation looking at a possible AMT issue. Generally, a corporation will need to calculate AMT on Form 4626 if either of the following apply:

- The corporation's taxable income or (loss) before the net operating loss (NOL) deduction plus its adjustments and preferences total more than $40,000 or, if smaller, it's allowable exemption amount.
- The corporation claims any general business credit (including the energy tax credit), the qualified electric vehicle credit, the non-conventional source fuel credit, or the credit for prior year minimum tax.

There is an exemption to filing the AMT calculations for small corporations. A corporation is treated as a small corporation exempt from the AMT for its current tax year beginning in 2004 if:

- The current year is the corporation's first tax year in existence (regardless of its gross receipts for the year), or
- Both of the following apply.
  - It was treated as a small corporation exempt from the AMT for all prior tax years beginning after 1997.
  - Its average annual gross receipts for the 3-tax-year period (or portion thereof during which the corporation was in existence) ending before its tax year beginning in 2004 did not exceed $7.5 million ($5 million if the corporation had only 1 prior tax year).

VI. The General Business Tax Credit—Including Energy Tax Credit

In order to provide some uniform rules about

dollar limitations, carrybacks and carry-forwards, and other technical details, many of the federal income tax credits available to businesses are lumped together and treated as components of the "general business credit." Specifically, the general business credit is composed of:

- the investment credit which is made up of the rehabilitation credit, the energy credit, and the reforestation credit
- the work opportunity credit (formerly the targeted jobs credit)
- the welfare-to-work credit
- the alcohol fuels credit
- the R & D credit
- the low-income housing credit
- the enhanced oil recovery credit
- the disabled access credit
- the renewable-resource electricity production credit
- the empowerment zone credit
- the Indian employment credit
- the employer FICA credit on tips
- the CDC credit

The order in which the components are claimed is important. If you plan to claim more than one of these credits for the year, you must claim them in the prescribed order, using Form 3800, General Business Credit. That way, if you exceed your credit dollar limit for the year, the credits further down the list will be the ones that are carried back or carried over to other years.

Dollar Limits on Credits

Your total general business credit for the year can't exceed your net income tax, minus the greater of (1) your tentative minimum tax, or (2) 25 percent of your net regular tax liability that is more than $25,000 ($12,500 for married taxpayer's filing separately). Your net income tax is your net regular tax liability plus your alternative minimum tax.

EXAMPLE:

An individual taxpayer's general business credit for the year is $30,000. Its net income tax is $27,500. Its tentative minimum tax, figured on Form 6251, is $18,487. The amount of general business credit it can take for the year is $9,013. This is the net income tax of $27,500 minus the larger of its tentative minimum tax, $18,487, or 25 percent of its net regular tax liability that is more than $25,000 (25% of $2,500 = $625). Since $18,487 is larger than $625, it subtracts $18,487 from $27,500 to arrive at $9,013.

Carrybacks and Carry-forwards

If the dollar limitations on the general business credit prevent you from claiming all of it in the year that it was earned (the "credit year"), you can generally carry it back to the year preceding the credit year, and forward to the following 20 years. Credits arising before 1998, could be carried back for the three years preceding the credit year, and forward to the 15 years following the credit year.

> *"Giving society cheap, abundant energy...would be equivalent of giving an idiot child a machine gun."*
>
> Paul Erhlich, U.S. biologist (1978), describing the possible impact of a future abundant source of energy, in light of the environmental damage already brought about by the existing form of cheap energy, fossil fuels

To claim a carryback, first, try to carry the credit back to the earliest allowable year preceding the credit year, observing your remaining dollar limit on credits for that year. If you can't use it up in that year, move on to the following year. This process is repeated until the credit is used up, or until the end of the carryover period—if any credit is still left, it can be deducted in the year following the last carryover year. Some credits have special rules under which they can't be carried back to a year before that particular credit was enacted into law and this is one reason why it's important to claim credits in the correct order.

If you have any carrybacks or carry-forwards from other credit years, figure your general business credit for this year in the following order: (1) any carry-forwards to this year, the earliest ones first; (2) the business credits for this year; and (3) any carrybacks to this year, the earliest ones first. As a result of this rule, in each year the oldest credits (and the ones closest to expiring) will always be used up first, and the newest credits become carryovers if the business credit limit is exceeded.

To claim a carryback, you must generally file an amended return (Form 1040X, Amended U.S. Individual Income Tax Return, or 1120X, Amended U.S. Corporation Income Tax Return) for the tax year to which you're carrying the credit. You can also apply for a quick refund of taxes for a prior year by filing Form 1045, Application for Tentative Refund, or Form 1139, Corporation Application for Tentative Refund. Either of these two forms is used to claim a tentative adjustment of tax from a general business credit carryback.

Depreciation in the Calculation of AMT

Although many items listed above are considered "Adjustments and Preference Items" under the AMT, the most critical item that affects the AMT calculation is depreciation on equipment in a business. This would include all cleantech renewable energy projects.

The Tax Reform Act of 1986 modified the previous Accelerated Cost Recovery System (ACRS). The name for the current depreciation system is Modified Accelerated Cost Recovery System (MACRS). Under this system, personal property placed in service after 1986 is grouped into eight recovery classes of property. The property is placed in these classes based on the Asset Depreciation Range (ADR) guidelines. These guidelines are stated in Revenue Procedure 87-56.

a. 3-Year Class—Property with an ADR life of 4 years or less and certain race horses. IRC sections 168(e)(1), (e)(3)(A)(i). Automobiles are not included in this class even though they have a 4-year ADR life.
b. 5-Year Class—Property with an ADR life of more than 4 years, but less than 10 years. IRC section 168 (e)(1). This includes automobiles, light trucks, computers and peripheral equipment, office machinery, property used in research and experimentation and breeding and dairy cattle. IRC section 168 (e)(3)(B).
c. 7-Year Class—Property with an ADR life of at least 10 years but less than 16 years. IRC section 168 (e)(1). It includes office furniture and fixtures.
d. 10-Year Class—Property with an ADR life of at least 16 years, but less than 20 years. IRC section 168(e)(1). This includes water transportation equipment and single purpose agriculture and horticultural structures. IRC section 168(e)(3)(D)(i).
e. 15-Year Class—Property with ADR life of at least 20 years, but less than 25 years. IRC section 168(e)(1). It includes certain depreciable improvements made directly to or added to land such as fences, roads, bridges, and shrubbery.
f. 20-year Class—Property with an ADR life of at least 25 years. IRC section 168(e)(1). It includes farm buildings and municipal sewage treatment plants.
g. Nonresidential Real Property—This is IRC section 1250 property that is not Residential Rental Property or property with an ADR life of less than 27.5 years. IRC section 168(e)(2)(B). The recovery period is 31.5 years for property placed in service before May 13, 1993, or 39 years for property placed in service after May 12, 1993.
h. Residential Rental Property—This class includes real property such as rental homes or structure if eighty percent or more of its gross rental income for the tax year is from dwelling units. IRC section 168(e)(2)(i). The ADR life for this property is 27.5 years.

Under MACRS, depreciation can be computed one of five ways. But first, two terms need to be identified. They are General Depreciation System (GDS) and Alternative Depreciation System (ADS). GDS uses the life per the eight main property classes. ADS uses the specific assigned class life per Revenue Procedure 87-56.

The five methods for computing depreciation under MACRS are:

1. 200-percent declining balance method over the GDS recovery period. This method switches to straight line in the year that it provides a greater deduction.
2. 150-percent declining balance method over the GDS recovery period. This method also switches to straight line when it provides a greater deduction.
3. Straight line (SL) using the GDS recovery period.
4. 150-percent declining balance over the ADS recovery periods, switching to straight line when that method provides a greater deduction.
5. Straight line using the ADS recovery period.

The declining balance methods provide greater deductions in the first years of service with lesser amounts at the end of the asset's life. By contrast, straight line provides equal deductions over the life of the asset. In addition, the GDS methods provide shorter periods for depreciation than do the ADS methods. Also, there are certain restrictions on which types of property can use which of the above methods.

While a method is prescribed for each type of property, the taxpayer may elect to use an alternative method. Table 5-13 summarizes the prescribed method and the alternative method available for each type of property.

For purposes of AMT, the taxpayer must use the 150-percent declining balance method with a half-year convention using the asset's ADR class life. IRC section 56(a)(1)(A). For real property, the taxpayer must use straight line using the ADR class life. IRC section 56(a)(1)(A). The ADR class life for all real property is 40 years. IRC section 168(g)(2)(c)(iii).

If the taxpayer elects the ADR method for regular

Table 5-13: Alternative Depreciation Methods

Recovery Class	Prescribed Methods	Alternative Methods
3-Year Class	200 % DB-GDS	150 % DB-ADS
5-Year Class (most renewable energy)	200 % DB-GDS	SL-GDS
7-Year Class	200 % DB-GDS	SL-ADS
10-Year Class (Non-Farm)	200 % DB-GDS	-
3-year Class	150 % DB-GDS	DB-ADS
5-Year Class	150 % DB-GDS	SL-GDS
7-Year Class	150 % DB-GDS	SL-ADS
10-Year Class (Farm)	150 % DB-GDS	-
15-Year Class	150 % DB-GDS	SL-ADS
20-Year Class (Nonfarm and Farm)	150 % DB-GDS	SL-GDS
Nonresidential and Residential Property	SL-GDS	SL-ADS

tax purposes, no adjustment would have to be made for AMT purposes. However, most taxpayers will use the accelerated methods which provide for maximum deductions in the assets' early years. Therefore, an adjustment will have to be made for AMT purposes. The adjustment will be the difference between the amount of depreciation claimed by the taxpayer and the amount of depreciation per the AMT SL-ADS method.

IRC section 356(a)(1)(A)(i) changes for property placed in service after December 31, 1998.

Taxpayers have to keep two depreciation tables—one for regular tax purposes and one for AMT purposes. These tables will also be necessary to compute the gain or loss if the asset is disposed of during the taxable year.

Use the tables in Revenue Procedure 87-57 to determine the applicable depreciation for each year in question. There are tables for depreciation for regular tax purposes and for AMT purposes.

For property placed in service after December 31, 1998, the taxpayer may elect to use AMT depreciation for regular tax purposes.

> ***Example***: The individual taxpayer is an independent court reporter. They purchase and place into service a new word processor on June 6, 1994, costing $6,500.
>
> *For regular tax purposes*, depreciation was computed as follows:
>
> **200-percent Declining Balance—5-Year Property**

Table 5-14: MACRS Depreciation at 200% DDB

Year	Basis	Percentage	Depreciation
1	$6,500	20%	$1,300
2	$6,500	32%	$2,080
3	$6,500	19.2%	$1,248
4	$6,500	11.52%	$749
5	$6,500	11.52%	$749
6	$6,500	5.76%	$374

For AMT purposes, depreciation is computed as shown in Table 5-15.

Table 5-15: Depreciation for AMT Purposes

Year	Basis	Percentage	Depreciation
1	$6,500	15 %	$975
2	$6,500	25.5 %	$1,658
3	$6,500	17.85 %	$1,160
4	$6,500	16.66 %	$1,083
5	$6,500	16.66 %	$1,083
6	$6,500	8.33 %	$541

Comparison of Depreciation, regular versus AMT is shown in Table 5-16.

Table 5-16: Comparing Regular MACRS Depreciation vs. AMT Depreciation

Year	Regular	AMT	AMT Adjustment
1	$1,300	$975	$325
2	$2,080	$1,658	$422
3	$1,248	$1,160	$88
4	$749	$1,083	($334)
5	$749	$1,083	($334)
6	$374	$541	($167)

Therefore, years 1, 2, and 3 will require a positive adjustment of $325, $422, and $88, respectively. Years

4, 5, and 6 will result in negative adjustments of ($334), ($334), and ($167), respectively.

Since regular depreciation is one of the components of taxable income, adding the depreciation preference to regular taxable income has the effect of swapping regular depreciation out and AMT depreciation in. Table 5-17 shows yet another way the depreciation preference works when considering the AMT on an asset cost of $1,000,000 (without any ITC).

AMT calculations for the debt obligor are slightly different than AMT calculations for the lender or project developer. In particular, the debt obligor does not have to worry about a book preference. However, the AMT calculations can have a significant effect of the debt obligor's cash flow when they are in an AMT position. This is because whether the debt obligor purchases the asset, rents the equipment under an operating lease, or purchases the energy under an energy purchase agreement, their taxable income will always be negative. So, rather than writing off their expenses at the current rate of 35%, the debt obligor can only write off his expenses at the 20% AMT rate.

Table 5-17: Example of MACRS Depreciation vs. AMT Depreciation Calculations

Period Ending	Regular Depreciation	AMT Depreciation	Depreciation Preference	Cumulative Depreciation Preference
Year 1	200,000	125,000	75,000	75,000
Year 2	320,000	218,750	101,250	176,250
Year 3	192,000	164,062	27,937	204,187
Year 4	115,200	140,625	(25,425)	178,762
Year 5	115,200	140,625	(25,425)	153,337
Year 6	57,600	140,625	(83,025)	70,312
Year 7	0	70,312	(70,312)	0
Totals	1,000,000	1,000,000	0	0

IRS regulations stipulate that AMT is not used if it is less than the regular tax due. Remember that AMT is used in calculating the total operations of the taxpayer, and is not applied on a transaction by transaction basis. This can also affect AMT on ITC. The federal ITC recognition is affected by the AMT. The annual federal ITC may not exceed the annual regular Tax Due minus 75% of the annual AMT. Again, this rule applies to the total operations of the taxpayer as a whole, and is *not applied to an individual transaction.*

If the taxpayer is allowed a deduction under IRC section 179, Election to Expense Depreciable Property, no AMT adjustment is required. If the IRC section 179 deduction is disallowed and regular depreciation is taken, this could affect AMT.

Leasing property under a qualified guideline operating lease or purchasing energy under an energy purchase agreement does not affect the AMT calculation. Lease (operating) or energy purchase payments are fully deductible for both regular and AMT purposes to the debt obligor.

In cases where purchasing the energy equipment directly would tip the taxpayer into an AMT position (primarily as a result of the depreciation preference issue), an operating lease or energy purchase agreement can suddenly become very attractive.

For the debt obligor in either an operating lease or energy purchase scenario, there are no preference items. Therefore, AMTI simply equals regular Taxable Income. Since the rent or energy purchase is a taxable expense, 20% of a negative Taxable Income will always be "higher" (more positive) than 35% of that numbers.

So, if the debt obligor is in an AMT position, then the AMT will be used in place of regular taxes due. Also, if the debt obligor purchases the energy equipment at the end of the contract term and begins depreciation, the same set of rules will again come into play for them. Nevertheless, when a taxpayer is in an AMT position, especially a border-line AMT situation, leasing or purchasing the energy produced from the asset tends to become more attractive. It must also be remembered that in all transactions, the monetization of the tax attributes by the lender or project developer will always be reflected in a lower debt payment stream to the debt obligor as compared to a direct finance structure where the debt obligor retains the tax attributes for their own account.

Qualifying Fixed Assets Under ARRA

Under the American Recovery and Reinvestment Act of 2009 (sections 1102 and 1603) taxpayers are entitled to claim an investment tax credit (or apply for a grant in lieu of the investment tax credit under ARRA) for investments in certain qualified energy facilities. The ITC available in those qualified energy facilities is based on the qualifying basis of the energy property. The energy properties that qualify for the credit or grant are defined under IRC sections 45 and 48 and include:

- Solar
- Wind
- Closed-loop biomass
- Open-loop biomass
- Small irrigation
- Geothermal
- Municipal solid waste
- Qualified hydropower
- Combined heat and power
- Microturbines
- Fuel cells

Over the years, there has been considerable disagreement on what qualifies under a "qualified facility" for purposes of the tax credit or grant. The qualifying basis for purposes of the credit or grant is determined under IRC section 38. Most would agree on the term "tangible personal property" but the conflict occurs when there are other related costs that might also qualify for inclusion in the asset basis. It is well known that a building or its structural components do not qualify but the IRS also states that anything that is an "integral part" of furnishing the energy does qualify. This can include certain structural components that look like or would normally be assumed to be a building and related structures. The service also gives good examples of what is or is not to be considered tangible personal property. In general, it is always wise to identify items that would qualify by employing third-party engineers, project managers and contractors.

> *"The release of atomic energy has not created a new problem. It has merely made more urgent the necessity of solving an existing one."*
>
> Albert Einstein

In a broad sense, eligible property is any component that is an "integral part of furnishing the energy." It is "integral" if it is used directly in the activity of producing energy or essential to the completeness of the activity. In a wind farm, items that would qualify would include the structural steel used to support low-voltage capacitors and disconnect switches. Low-voltage equipment is generally tangible personal property used in furnishing electrical energy. Though not part of the equipment cost itself, the equipment's structural steel support is "essential to the completeness of the activity" performed by the qualifying asset. This could also include "private access roads" that are essential to the completeness of the activity of the turbines. It would also include the substation low-voltage equipment such as switchgear housed in the substation building structure that receives the electricity from the wind collection system and "transfers" that electricity to the substation step-up transformer since that equipment is essential to the completeness of the activity of the wind collection assets.

Another example would be in a solar qualified system. Concrete foundation pads used to support the solar collectors is "other tangible property" and would include fencing required by ASHRAE guidance documents for safety purposes. Solar collectors are "tangible personal property" used in furnishing electrical energy. Though not part of the equipment cost itself, the equipment's concrete foundations are "essential to the completeness of the activity" performed by the underlying solar system.

A further example would be with boiler related steam piping. Steam piping used to transfer the steam generated from the boiler to the turbines is "other tangible property." The boiler is "tangible personal property" used in furnishing electrical energy. Though the piping is not generally part of the equipment cost itself, the steam piping is "essential to the completeness of the activity" performed by the equipment. A close corollary would be the totality of a solar thermal system used in an HVAC solar system. The collectors generate hot water in the range of 190° F to 250°F. The hot water is then utilized by an absorption chiller to make cold water that is used in a central plant for district heating and cooling system in various buildings to provide air conditioning. All of the piping, hot and cold water storage tanks, the absorption chiller and other related support components would qualify as tangible personal property in the qualified facility.

The IRS identifies qualified property for the grant program in its guidance documents that states qualified property would include:

- Storage devices
- Power conditioning equipment

- Transfer equipment
- Parts related to the functioning of those items

However, a taxpayer must be astutely aware of what are typical *non-qualifying costs*. Those would include:

- Operation and maintenance buildings and related site work
- Public roads and roads having a "dual use"
- Transmission property further defined as:
  — Substation "high-voltage" assets
  — Transmission lines, tower and grid interconnect
  — Any equipment beyond the transmission stage (such as transformers and distribution lines

When accounting for the costs in a qualified facility, there are generally four major "groups" of costs that can be included in the renewable energy project.

1. Major equipment purchases (such as turbines and solar collectors) with their associated to-site transportation costs and all costs associated with the installation of those assets.
2. Balance of Plant ("BOP") contracts. This most often refers to the general contractor and all sub-contractors.
3. Sub-station contract(s)
4. Other owner costs that could include:
   - Engineering and surveying
   - Owner project management
   - Outside consultants and analysis
   - Permitting
   - Energy generation monitoring and reporting assets
   - Design and development
   - Land
   - Commissioning and testing
   - Financing (interim construction financing costs as well as points and other underwriting costs to secure permanent financing)

The critical item that would support the inclusion of the above items in the qualified facility costs is to establish a proper cost accounting system. It is critical that an accounting system with the appropriate coding format and detailed schedule of values is in place during the project development stage. The taxpayer should integrate the engineers and project managers into the process of creating the accounting system. This will also assist in proactively accounting separately for the qualified property. The developer or lender(s) (who might take tax ownership in the project) should insist that the schedule of values within the BOP contract and the substation contract (or any other "construction" contract) adhere to the coding format. Then a direct link must be established that forms an "audit trail" from the invoice accounting system to the taxpayer's credit reporting forms or grant application.

The lack of a proper accounting system can easily result in failing to capture all qualifying costs and, therefore, less credit or grant to which the taxpayer would otherwise be entitled. The lack of a properly documented "audit trail" may lead to unfavorable determinations under an IRS audit.

When a taxpayer produces or creates a renewable energy project, the taxpayer will generally incur a great portion of the expenses before the product is ready to produce income. When this happens, the taxpayer is usually required to capitalize those expenses and recover (deduct) them over the period of time that the product is producing income. Section 263A of the IRC describes that process in detail. The total cost of creating the asset is required to be capitalized. This includes cost of researching, preparing, installation, permitting, engineering, etc. It also includes an allocation of indirect costs such as utilities, tools, clerical, management, rental of equipment, etc.

Allowable Capitalization Costs (IRC § 263A)

Generally, the renewable energy project owner will want to include as many direct development costs as possible in the asset acquisition costs and thereby gain the largest possible depreciable cost and maximum tax credit from that process.

The uniform capitalization (UNICAP) rules require the capitalization of all direct costs and certain indirect costs properly allocable to tangible personal property produced by the taxpayer. This would include the development of a renewable energy project. For purposes of the uniform capitalization rules, to "produce" means to construct, build, install, manufacture, develop, improve, create, raise or grow. In addition, § 263A(f) requires the capitalization of interest expense when the taxpayer produces certain tangible personal property.

How does § 263A identify the costs subject to capitalization? As a threshold requirement, one must determine whether the costs would, but for § 263A, be otherwise deductible. A cost that is not otherwise deductible may not be allocated to property produced or acquired for resale. In addition, any cost required to be capitalized under § 263A may not be included in inventory or charged to capital accounts or basis any earlier than the taxable year during which the amount is incurred.

Except as otherwise provided, direct and indirect costs that directly benefit or are incurred by reason of the performance of production or resale activities must be capitalized to the property produced or acquired for resale. For a RE project developer, the direct costs generally include direct material and direct labor. Examples of indirect costs required to be capitalized are:

- bidding costs (this would include all analysis work and written proposals)
- capitalizable service costs (including capitalizable mixed service costs)
- cost recovery allowances (however, remember depletion is only allocated to inventory produced and sold during the year)
- engineering and design
- employee benefit expenses
- handling costs
- indirect labor costs
- indirect material costs
- insurance
- interest (see special rules under § 263A(f) below)
- licensing and franchise costs
- officers' compensation
- permit fees
- environmental permit fees
- commissioning costs
- pension and other related costs
- purchasing costs
- quality control
- rent
- repairs and maintenance
- spoilage
- storage costs
- taxes
- tools and equipment
- utilities

Project developers must capitalize costs (other than interest) whether incurred before, during, or after the production period of property. Interest is only capitalized during the production period of property. Pre-production costs are subject to capitalization if the property is held for future production or if it is reasonably likely that the property will be produced at a future date. Thus, costs of storing raw materials and carrying costs of property held for development are required to be capitalized. Some issues may arise in determining the taxpayer's intent and the taxpayer's change in intent. Production period costs are costs incurred beginning on the date on which production of the property begins and ending on the date on which the property is ready to be placed in service or is ready to be held for sale. Post-production costs are costs incurred after the actual production and may include costs of storage, warehousing, insurance, materials, and handling.

Capitalization of Interest—IRC § 263A(f)

Interest is capitalized with respect to each unit of designated property. Interest is also capitalized during each computation period—the amount of interest that is capitalized is a function of two components:

- the amount of accumulated production expenditures; and
- the amount of outstanding debt on each measurement date

The taxpayer should also note that tax treatment of the capitalized costs are usually dramatically different than the accounting treatment of those same costs. The accounting treatment most often falls under what is referred to an "indirect cost." For accounting purposes, the eligible basis of property is determined in accordance with the general rules for determining the basis of property for federal income tax purposes and includes all items properly included in the depreciable basis, such as installation costs and the cost for transportation. Certain indirect costs, as part of the depreciable basis, are allocable to all or some of the direct costs of the project in accordance with the general rules for allocating indirect costs under Tax Regulation Section 263A. This often results in the treatment for tax purposes being different than for accounting treatment under Generally Accepted Accounting Procedures (GAAP):

- Capitalized Interest—capitalized to the project and allocable for tax
- Internal Salaries—capitalized to the project and allocable for tax

Section 263(a) and section 1.263(a)-1(a) of the Income Tax Regulations provide that no deduction is allowed for any amount paid out for new buildings or for permanent improvements or betterments made to increase the value of any property or estate. Section 1.263(a)-2(a) provides that capital expenditures include the cost of acquisition, construction, or erection of buildings, machinery and equipment, furniture and fixtures, and similar property having a useful life substantially beyond the taxable year.

Internal Revenue Code Section 263A also defines the term "produce" very broadly. Production activities include construct, build, install, manufacture, develop, or improve. However, the allocation of indirect costs must also be "reasonable." Examples of specific indirect cost allocations are:

- BOP Contractor (Balance of Plant) Management. The BOP contractor generally oversees the construction of all phases of the project with few exceptions.
- The BOP Contractor should provide the owner with a statement of allocation of Contractor Management costs among several general categories determined by the owner's accounting system.
- Capitalized Internal Salaries attributable to the project.
- The owner should provide an allocation of such salaries among several general categories determined by his accounting system such that:
  - — The allocation is reasonable; and
  - — The allocation can be "examined, on a test basis" by the independent accounting firm

It is important to note the different treatment as IRC Section 266 requires the taxpayer to file an election to capitalize interest, taxes and other carrying costs while IRC Section 263A does not.[7] Taxpayers involved in ITC transactions must file an IRC Section 266 election with their tax return to capitalize interest, taxes and other carrying charges to their energy property basis eligible for the ITC.[8]

Construction Environmental Compliance

Environmental compliance is rarely reasonably based on a cost proportionate allocation. More often than not, for a renewable energy project, the significant environmental compliance measures are due largely to the special nature of the project and, hence, the special components of the project. A strict cost proportionate allocation may understate the taxpayer's eligible basis.

> *"Almost every way we make electricity today, except for the emerging renewables and nuclear, puts out CO_2. And so, what we're going to have to do at a global scale is create a new system. And so, we need energy miracles."*
>
> Bill Gates, American business magnate, investor, philanthropist, and author

Moreover, because a taxpayer's renewable energy development project constitutes production of property within the meaning of section 263A(g)(1), a taxpayer is required to capitalize under section 263A the direct costs and a proper share of the allocable indirect costs associated with the development. In Von-Lusk v. Commissioner, 104 T.C. 207 (1995), the court held that certain expenses incurred by a real estate developer before actual physical work began on undeveloped land are subject to section 263A. The court found that the developer's activities, such as obtaining building permits and zoning variances, negotiating permit fees, and similar activities, represent the "first steps in the development of the property." The court further noted that the pursuit of building permits and zoning variances, negotiating permit fees, and similar activities "are ancillary to actual physical work on the land and are as much a part of a development project as digging a foundation or completing a structure's frame. The project cannot move forward if these steps are not taken."

As with any other business venture, if a renewable energy project is abandoned, the taxpayer can claim a deduction for the unrecovered basis. Abandonment requires that the taxpayer show intent to abandon and makes an affirmative act of abandonment in such a manner that the asset is not retrievable.

"Resources" Under Section 45 that Qualify for the Tax Credit

Under section 45(c) the term "qualified energy resources" means:

- wind
- closed-loop biomass
- open-loop biomass
- geothermal energy
- solar energy
- small irrigation power
- municipal solid waste
- qualified hydropower production

Section 45(c)(2) defines closed-loop biomass as any organic material from a plant which is planted exclusively for purposes of being used at a qualified facility to produce electricity.

Section 45(c)(3) defines open-loop biomass to mean:

(1) any agricultural livestock waste nutrients, or

(2) any solid, non-hazardous, cellulosic waste material or any non-hazardous lignin waste material which is segregated from other waste materials and which is derived from:

 (i) any of the following forest-related resources: mill and harvesting residues, pre-commercial thinning, slash (tops, branches, damaged trees, slabs, sawdust from milling operations), and brush,

(ii) solid wood waste material, including waste pallets, dunnage, manufacturing and construction wood wastes (other than pressure treated, chemically treated, or painted wood wastes), and landscape or right-of-way tree trimmings, but not including municipal solid waste, gas derived from the biodegradation of solid waste, or paper which is commonly recycled, or

(iii) agricultural sources, including orchard tree crops, vineyard, grains, legumes, sugar, and other crop by-products or residues. Such term shall not include closed-loop biomass or biomass burned in conjunction with fossil fuel (co-firing) beyond such fossil fuel required for startup and flame stabilization.

The term *"agricultural livestock waste nutrients"* means agricultural livestock manure and litter, including wood shavings, straw, rice hulls, and other bedding material for the disposition of manure. The term *"agricultural livestock"* includes bovine, swine, poultry, and sheep.

"Geothermal energy" means under section 45(c)(4) energy derived from a geothermal deposit (within the meaning of section 613(e)(2)).

Under section 45(c)(5) the term *"small irrigation power"* means power (a) generated without any dam or impoundment of water through an irrigation system canal or ditch; and (b) the nameplate capacity rating of which is not less than 150 kilowatts but is less than 5 megawatts.

"Municipal solid waste" for the purposes of section 45 has the meaning given the term "solid waste" under section 2(27) of the Solid Waste Disposal Act (42 U.S.C. § 6903).

Under section 45(c)(8) the term "qualified hydropower production" means:

(1) in the case of any hydroelectric dam which was placed in service on or before the date of the enactment of this paragraph [enacted Aug. 8, 2005], the incremental hydropower production for the taxable year, and

(2) in the case of any non-hydroelectric dam described in section 45(c)(8)(C), the hydropower production from the facility for the taxable year.

Under section 45(c)(7) the term "refined coal" means a fuel which:

(1) is a liquid, gaseous, or solid fuel produced from coal (including lignite) or high carbon fly ash, including such fuel used as a feedstock,

(2) is sold by the taxpayer with the reasonable expectation that it will be used for purpose of producing steam,

(3) is certified by the taxpayer as resulting (when used in the production of steam) in a qualified emission reduction, and

(4) is produced in such a manner as to result in an increase of at least 50 percent in the market value of the refined coal (excluding any increase caused by materials combined or added during the production process), as compared to the value of the feedstock coal.

"Facilities" Under Section 45 that Qualify for the Tax Credit

Wind Facility. The term "qualified facility" means any facility owned by the taxpayer that is original placed in service after December 31, 1993 and before January 1, 2013.[9]

Closed-Loop Biomass Facility. The term "qualified facility" means any facility (i) owned by the taxpayer which is originally placed in service after December 31, 1992, and before January 1, 2014, or (ii) owned by the taxpayer which before January 1, 2014, is originally placed in service and modified to use closed-loop biomass to co-fire with coal, with other biomass, or with both, but only if the modification is approved under the Biomass Power for Rural Development Programs or is part of a pilot project of the Commodity Credit Corporation as described in 65 Fed. Reg. 63052.

Open-Loop Biomass Facility. The term "qualified facility" means, with respect to a facility using open-loop biomass to produce electricity, any facility owned by the taxpayer which (i) in the case of a facility using agricultural livestock waste nutrients (a) is originally placed in service after the date of the enactment of this sub-clause and before January 1, 2014, and (b) the nameplate capacity rating of which is not less than 150 kilowatts, and (ii) in the case of any other facility, is originally placed in service before January 1, 2014. In the case of any facility described in above, if the owner of such facility is not the producer of the electricity, the person eligible for the credit allowable under section 45 (a) shall be the lessee or the operator of such facility.

Geothermal or Solar Energy Facility. The term "qualified facility" means any facility owned by the taxpayer that is originally placed in service after the date of the enactment ARRA and before January 1, 2014 (January 1, 2006, in the case of a facility using solar energy). Such term shall not include any property described in section 48(a)(3) the basis of which is taken into account by the taxpayer for purposes of determining the energy credit under section 48.

Small Irrigation Power Facility. The term "qualified facility" means any facility owned by the taxpayer that is originally placed in service after the date of the enactment of ARRA and before October 22, 2008.

Landfill Gas Facility. The term "qualified facility" means, with respect to a facility producing electricity from gas derived from the biodegradation of municipal solid waste, any facility owned by the taxpayer which is originally placed in service after the date of the enactment of ARRA and before January 1, 2014.

Trash Combustion Facility. The term "qualified facility" means any facility owned by the taxpayer that is originally placed in service after the date of the enactment of ARRA and before January 1, 2014. Such term shall include a new unit placed in service in connection with a facility placed in service on or before the date of the enactment of ARRA, but only to the extent of the increased amount of electricity produced at the facility by reason of such new unit.

Refined Coal Production Facility. The term "refined coal production facility" means a facility which is placed in service after the date of the enactment of ARRA and before January 1, 2010 with respect to any other facility producing refined coal, and facility placed in service after the date of the enactment of the American Jobs Creation Act of 2004 and before January 1, 2010.

Qualified Hydropower Facility. The term "qualified facility" means (a) in the case of any facility producing incremental hydropower production, such facility but only to the extent of its incremental hydropower production attributable to efficiency improvements or additions to capacity described in subsection (c)(8)(B) placed in service after the date of the enactment of ARRA and before January 1, 2014, and (b) any other facility placed in service after the date of the enactment of ARRA and before January 1, 2014. In the case of a qualified facility described in subparagraph (a) above, the 10-year period referred to in section 45(a) shall be treated as beginning on the date the efficiency improvements or additions to capacity are placed in service.

Indian Coal Production Facility. The term "Indian coal production facility" means a facility which is placed in service before January 1, 2009.

General Requirements to Claiming the Energy Tax Credits under Section 45

In general to claim the Section 45 credit, a taxpayer must sell electricity (or in the case of a refined coal facility, refined coal) that it produces to an unrelated person. A lessee or operator may claim the credit in lieu of the owner of a qualifying facility in the case of a qualifying open-loop biomass facility and in the case of a closed-loop biomass facility modified to co-fire with coal, to co-fire with other biomass, or to co-fire with coal and other biomass.

For a facility in which more than one person has an ownership interest, production from the facility is generally allocated among the owners in proportion to their respective ownership interest in the gross sales of the facility—IRC code section 45(e)(3) (2006). For a partnership, the section 45 credits attributable to the partnership may be passed through to and allocated among the partners in accordance with each partner's interest in the partnership at the time the section 45 credit arises (private letter ruling 200142018). If a partnership receipt (i.e., income) gives rise to the section 45 credit, and that receipt also gives rise to a valid allocation of partnership income, the partners' interest in the partnership with respect to the item of credit must be in the same proportion as the partners' respective distributive share of such income (private letter ruling 200318066). For more information on partnership accounting, see "Partnership Accounting Issues" (page 151) below.

> *"Our dependence on fossil fuels amounts to global pyromania, and the only fire extinguisher we have at our disposal is renewable energy."*
>
> Hermann Scheer (1944-2010)

Claiming the Section 45 Credit

In order to provide some uniform rules about dollar limitations, carrybacks and carry-forwards, and other technical details, many of the federal income tax credits available to businesses are lumped together and treated as components of the "general business credit" allowed under section 38. The section 45 tax credit is a component of the general business credit. It is important in which order the components of the general business tax credit are claimed. If a taxpayer plans to claim more than one of the credits in any tax year, the taxpayer must claim them in the prescribed order using Form 3800. The form allows taxpayer's to know that if the credit dollar limit is exceeded for a tax year, the credits further down the list are the ones that are carried back or carried over to other years. The section 45 tax credit is computed on Form 8835. For partners that receive the credit, the amount of credit allocated to each partner will be on the individual partner's Schedule K-1 (Form 1065).

Placed in Service Rules

One of the main requirements for qualification of a facility for the section 45 credit is that it be placed in service for tax purposes at the appropriate time. The Code and Regulations do not provide a definition of placed in service for the purpose of the section 45 credit. In a private letter ruling, the IRS looked to the depreciation and investment tax credit rules for guidance as to when a facility is placed in service for purposes of the section 45 credit (private letter ruling 200334031). Under the depreciation and investment tax rules, property is *placed in service in the tax year the property is placed in a condition or state of readiness and availability for a specifically designed function*—Treasury Regulation Section 1.46-3(d)(1)(ii) and section 1.167(a)-11(e)(1)(i). In general, the factors that are looked at in determining placed in service dates for facilities under section 45 (and section 48 equipment for that matter) are:

1. equipment must have been delivered and physical construction or installation on site must have been completed—other than minor punch list items;
2. approval of required licenses and permits;
3. taxpayer must have taken legal title and control of the equipment—passage of control of the facility to the taxpayer from the contractor/developer;
4. completion of critical tests or commissioning;
5. commencement of daily or regular operations; and
6. synchronization into a power grid for generating electricity to produce income.

Note that if a facility operates on a regular basis but does not produce the projected output it may still be considered placed in service.[10] If a facility is only operating on a test basis, it is not placed in service until it is available for service on a regular basis. However, property has been found to be placed in service despite the fact that it is not operating in certain situations when the fact that the facility is not operating is beyond the taxpayer's control.[11]

There is a disadvantage to placing the property in service too early. The placed in service date sets the beginning period for when the section 45 credit may be claimed. A facility does not have to achieve full contemplated output to be placed in service as long as it is in the process of increasing its production levels. For example, for many types of facilities (open-loop biomass facility, geothermal facility, small irrigation power facility, landfill gas facility, or trash combustion facility), the section 45 credit is currently available for only five (5) years. A few months spent improving production could reduce substantially the amount of the credit available over the five-year period. The available credit may be reduced below estimated levels; therefore, an owner of a facility has to be careful it is not using valuable time improving production. Unless an owner is approaching a placed in service deadline, the owner may want to wait to begin production and take other steps to be placed in service until it is comfortable that the facility will work and may want to wait to begin production until after additional facilities that could prevent operation at full capacity are constructed and placed in service.

Also in many cases, a developer, rather than the owner, will place a facility in service. The developer may not be able to benefit from the section 45 credit because it has insufficient income. The clock starts running for claiming the section 45 credit when a developer places a facility into service and does not start over on transfer to a new owner. As a result, a developer should try to transfer the facility to an owner who can benefit from the section 45 credit before, or as soon as possible after, placing the facility in service.

The date on which the facility is originally placed in service by the taxpayer is the important placed in service date. A subsequent transferee of a facility (including by a technical termination or reformation of a partnership under section 708 (Continuation of Partnership) will be able to claim the section 45 credit despite the fact that is it not the original owner, but the 5- or 10-year credit periods will continue to run from the date the facility was originally placed in service. Revenue Ruling 94-31, 1994-1 C.B. 16 (1994).

Once a facility is considered placed in service for purposes of the section 45 credit, the 5- or 10-year credit period, as the case may be, will continue to run even if changes are made to the facility as long as the value of the original property is more than 20% of the facility's total value. Therefore, if a facility is destroyed by fire and the original property remaining after the fire is less than 20% of the facility's total value, the rebuilt facility will be considered a new facility and the credit period will begin when the rebuilt facility is placed in service.

Section 45 Credit Limitations

1. **Component of the general business credit.**
The section 45 credit is a component of the general business credit of section 38 and is subject to the general business credit limitation (IRC code section 38(b)(8) (2006)). The general business credit cannot reduce the taxpayer's tax liability below a minimum threshold in any given year. The minimum threshold is the greater of (i) 25% of the excess of a taxpayer's regular income tax liability over $25,000 (calculated before taking the general business credit) or (ii) the taxpayer's tentative minimum tax. IRC code section 38(c)(1) (2006). Any section 45 credit that cannot be used (whether as a result of this limitation or otherwise) is allowed a one-year carryback period and a 20-year carryforward period. 26 U.S.C. § 39(a) (2006). (Also see AMT discussions above.)

2. **Phase-out of credit and inflation adjustments**
The section 45 credit is subject to a phase-out if the reference price (defined below) for electricity exceeds a certain threshold. The amount of the credit is reduced by an amount that bears the same ratio to the amount of the credit as the amount by which the reference price for the calendar year in which the sale occurs exceeds 8 cents, bears to 3 cents. IRC code section 45(b)(1) (2006). "Reference price" means, with respect to a calendar year, the Treasury Secretary's determination of the annual average contract price per kilowatt hour of electricity generated from the same qualified energy resource and sold in the previous year in the United States. IRC code section 45(e)(2)(C) (2006). For the section 45 credit to be phased out—even in part—for a year the reference price would have to exceed the 8 cents threshold price (which amount is adjusted for inflation).

IRC code section 45(e)(8)(B) contains a similar phase-out of the section 45 credit for refined coal. In that case as an example, the credit is reduced by an amount that bears the same ratio to the $4.375 per ton general rate (which amount is adjusted for inflation) as the amount by which the reference price of fuel used as feedstock for the calendar year in which the sale occurs exceeds an amount equal to 1.7 multiplied by the reference price for such fuel in 2002 bears to $8.75 (see Jobs Act Conference Report at 512). The reference prices for fuel used as feedstock are $31.90 per ton for calendar year 2002 and $36.36 per ton for calendar year 2005. Because the 2005 reference price of that fuel used as feedstock for refined coal does not exceed the $31.90 reference price of that fuel in 2002 multiplied by the inflation adjustment and 1.7, the credit phase-out provided in section 45(e)(8)(B) does not apply to refined coal sold during the calendar year 2005.

As noted above, each of the 1.5 cent per kilowatt hour credit amount (currently 1.9 cents per kWh), the $4.375 per ton of refined coal (now $5.486 per ton) and the reference price of fuel used as a feedstock is adjusted by an inflation factor. For electricity produced in open-loop biomass facilities, small irrigation power facilities, landfill gas facilities, and trash combustion facilities, section 45(b)(4)(A) requires the amount in effect under section 45(a)(1) (before rounding to the nearest 0.1 cent) to be reduced by one-half. Under the calculation required by section 45(b)(2), the credit for renewable electricity production for calendar year 2005 under section 45(a) is 0.9 cents per kilowatt hour on the sale of electricity produced by those facilities [2005 Tax Notes Today 138-31 (2005)]. The Treasury Secretary must by April 1 of each calendar year determine and publish in the Federal Register, the inflation adjustment factor and reference price for that calendar year. The inflation adjustment factor is based on a fraction the numerator of which is the GDP implicit price deflator for the preceding calendar year and the denominator of which is the GDP implicit price deflator for calendar year 1992. I.R.C. section 45(e)(2)(B) (2006).

3. **Credit reduced for grants, tax-exempt bonds, subsidized energy financing, and other credits.**
The amount of the section 45 credit that can be claimed is reduced to the extent that the facility is the beneficiary of other subsidies. The amount of the reduction is based on a fraction the numerator of which is the sum, for the tax year and all prior tax years, of:
   1) grants provided by the United States, a state, or political subdivision of a state;
   2) proceeds of an issue of state or local government obligations issued to provide financing for the project the interest on which is exempt from tax;
   3) the aggregate amount of subsidized energy financing provided (directly or indirectly) under a federal, state, or local program provided in connection with the project; and
   4) the amount of any other credit allowable for

any property that is part of the project; provided, however, the IRS recently confirmed that the amount of the federal credit allowable under section 45 shall not be reduced by an state tax credit also available for the facility; and

5) the numerator of which is the aggregate amount of additions to the capital account for the project for the tax year and all prior tax years. IRC code section 45(b)(3) (2006).

The amount of the reduction cannot exceed 50% of the amount of the credit. Also, the reduction does not apply to a facility owned by the taxpayer that before January 1, 2006, is originally placed in service and modified to use closed-loop biomass to co-fire with coal or other biomass, but only if the modification is approved under the Biomass Power for Rural Development Programs or is part of a pilot project of the Commodity Credit Corporation. IRC code section 45(d)(2)(A)(ii) (2006).

> *"First, once the renewable infrastructure is built, the fuel is free forever. Unlike carbon-based fuels, the wind and the sun and the earth itself provide fuel that is free, in amounts that are effectively limitless.*
>
> *Second, while fossil fuel technologies are more mature, renewable energy technologies are being rapidly improved. So innovation and ingenuity give us the ability to constantly increase the efficiency of renewable energy and continually reduce its cost.*
>
> *Third, once the world makes a clear commitment to shifting toward renewable energy, the volume of production will itself sharply reduce the cost of each windmill and each solar panel, while adding yet more incentives for additional research and development to further speed up the innovation process."*
>
> Al Gore, Our Choice, 2009

4. **No credit for tax exempt use**

If the renewable energy project is "leased" to the end user and that user is a tax exempt entity, no credit will be allowed. The IRS definition of a tax exempt entity includes any entity that has received a tax exempt status from the IRS (this would include all non-profits who have received a 501(c)(3) status, 501(c)(6) or other similar tax exemption certification) or any governmental entity that does not pay taxes. Developers and investors that wish to take advantage of the solar energy credits often are involved in contracts with tax-exempt and governmental entities including hospitals, school districts, and federal, state or other governmental agencies. These transaction are most often structured in a way that the developer of the project enters into a roof lease with the power recipient that permits the developer to locate its equipment (either electrical or thermal) on the power recipient's property. The roof lease is then accompanied by a power purchase agreement that sets forth the terms under which the developer or asset owner will sell the power generated by the system to the exempt entity.

The only way that a developer, investor or other owner of the renewable energy system can obtain the tax credit is by selling the power to the end user through a power purchase agreement (PPA) or structured as a service contract and *not* renting or leasing the equipment to the end user as is done under a lease agreement. IRC section 7701(e) contains the guidance for how this is accomplished. It lists various factors distinguishing service contracts (PPAs) from leases. The key issue is "safe harbor." A contract that purports to be a service contract and not a lease will be treated as a service contract *unless*:

- The service recipient (or related entity) operates or controls the renewable energy system
- The service recipient (or related entity) has a significant economic or possessory interest in the property
- The service recipient (or related entity) bears any significant financial burden if there is non-performance under the contract or other arrangement
- The service *provider* (or a related entity) receives any significant financial benefit if the operating costs of such facility or assets are less than the standards of performance or operation under the contract or arrangement
  - PLR (private letter ruling) 8749045 allows certain expenses to be passed through as long as electricity or other energy (such as thermal) is being provided
- The service recipient (or related entity) has an option to purchase, or may be required to purchase, all or part of the renewable energy system at a fixed or determinable price other than for fair market value

- The total contract price does not substantially exceed the rental value of the property for the contract period[12]

Section 7701(e) of the Code is a provision that was enacted under the Deficit Reduction Act of 1984 and has never been the subject of any proposed, temporary or final regulations, but has critical importance in many renewable energy transactions, especially in today's transactions involving solar energy credits.

Section 38 allows a credit against tax for solar energy credits determined under the investment credit rules of section 46. Section 46, in turn, allows an investment credit for certain types of energy property described in section 48, one of which is solar energy property. It is important to note that congress recently modified section 48 by extending through 2016 the 30 percent investment tax credit for solar energy property.[13]

Thus, in the context of a typical solar renewable energy system (and possible other equipment types) transaction with a governmental or other tax-exempt entity, the key question is whether the contractual arrangements between the owner of the assets and the power recipient amount to a "lease" of the property to the tax-exempt entity for U.S. federal income tax purposes. Bottom line on having a tax exempt customer in your contract is that *it must be documented* as a power purchase agreement (or in the alternative, a service contract or other type of "energy" purchase agreement) and not a "lease" if the developer or renewable system owner wants to receive the benefits of the section 48 tax credit!

There have been numerous House of Representatives reports that have helped clarify congresses intent when section 7701(e) of the Code was enacted. With respect to the "physical possession" rule:

> *Physical possession of property is indicative of a lease. Under the bill, property that is located on the premises of a tax-exempt entity, or located off the premises but operated by employees of a tax-exempt entity, is viewed as in the physical possession of the entity (and therefore not qualified to receive the tax credit by the owner). However, property is not in the physical possession of a tax-exempt entity merely because the property is located on land leased to the service provider by the tax-exempt entity.*[14]

As to the "control" rule, the House Reports states that:

> *The fact that the tax-exempt entity controls the property is indicative of a lease. Under the bill, a tax-exempt entity is viewed as controlling the property to the extent the entity dictates or has a contractual right to dictate the manner in which the property is operated, maintained, or improved. Control is not established merely by reason of contractual provisions designed to enable the tax-exempt entity to monitor or ensure the service provider's compliance with performance, safety, pollution control, or other general standards.*[15]

With respect to the "possessory or economic interest" rule, the House Report states that:

> *A contract that conveys a significant possessory or economic interest to a tax-exempt entity resembles a lease. Under the bill, the existence of a possessor or economic interest in property is established by facts that show (1) the property's use is likely to be dedicated to the tax-exempt entity for a substantial portion of the useful life of the property, (2) the tax-exempt entity shares the risk that the property will decline in value, (3) the tax-exempt entity shares in savings in the property's operating costs, or (5) the tax-exempt entity bears the risk of damage to or loss of the property.*[16]

The presence of any one of these factors indicates that this factor supports lease classification and thereby the owner not being able to benefit from the tax credit. With regard to the "substantial risk of non-performance" rule, the House Report states that:

> *Under a service contract arrangement, the service provider bears the risk of substantially diminished receipts or substantially increased expenditures if there is nonperformance under the contract by the service provider or any property involved. Under the bill, facts that establish that the service provider does not bear significant risk of nonperformance are indicative of a lease.*[17]

The House Report provides that "the concurrent use of… property to provide significant services to entities unrelated to the tax-exempt entity is indicative of a service contract" and also explains the "rental value" rule:

> *The fact that the total contract price (including expenses to be reimbursed by the tax-exempt entity) substantially exceeds the rental value of the property for contract period is indicative of a service contract. If the total contract price reflects substantial costs that are attributable to items other the use of the property subject to the contract, then the contract more closely resembles*

a service contract. Conversely, the fact that the total contract price is based principally on recovery of the cost of the property is indicative of a lease. A contract that states charges for services separately from charges for use of property is indicative of a lease.[18]

The House Report also gives examples of how to distinguish between a "lease" and a "service contract." The asset owner should look carefully at the "safe harbor" leasing provisions (*see page 165*) for additional help in properly structuring the lease transaction to meet IRS guidelines.

Partnership Accounting Issues

There are numerous code sections of the IRS regulations that can have a significant impact on all renewable energy transactions. Some of the more important ones are listed below.[19]

Section 704(c) of the IRS regulations apply when a partner contributes assets into the partnership at a fair market value (FMV) different than the tax basis of the asset in order to regulate the possible shifting of tax consequences among partners. A contribution defers the tax consequences that might be associated with the built-in gain or loss (the difference between its basis and FMV at the time it is contributed to the partnership). Section 505(c) requires built-in gain or loss to be eliminated over time through tax allocations that put the partners who contribute only cash to the partnership in the same (or similar) tax position as though the partnership had purchased contributed assets at FMV. Section 704(c) remedial, curative and traditional allocations methods are provided to resolve this disparity. The choice of method can affect economic results significantly.

Partnerships represent one of the complex parts of the U.S. tax code. Implementing the regulations represents one of the key challenges associated with modeling and tracking partnerships. The partnership tax code places requirements on a partnership's allocations of income and loss involving substantial economic effect, capital account, liquidation, deficit restoration obligations, minimum gain and contribution of assets. The section 704(c)[20] anti-abuse rules specifies than an allocation method is not reasonable if the contribution of property and the corresponding allocation of tax items are made with a view to shifting the tax consequences of built-in gain or loss among the partners in a manner that substantially reduces the present value of the partners' aggregate tax liability.

Under the ceiling rule (Reg. § 1.704-3(b)(1),[21] a partnership cannot allocate more income, gain, loss or deduction to its partners for a taxable year with respect to a property than the total partnership, gain, loss or deduction actually realized with respect to that property. For example, a partnership may not allocate more depreciation to a partner than may be claimed by the partnership, even though the partner may bear the capital account burden of a larger (book) allocation determined by the property's FMV upon its contribution. A partnership might be able to remedy problems caused by the ceiling rule by using the remedial allocation method.

A deficit restoration obligation (DRO) occurs when a partner's capital account balance plus its share of any minimum gain becomes negative.[22] Many partnership agreements do not obligate partners to pay a DRO Balance in cash to the partnership, but in many transactions, this obligation may be needed to support the tax code requirement for substantial economic effect.

DRO risk describes the potential cash payment a partner would have to make in the event of "liquidation." A DRO limit specifies the extent to which a partner allows DRO Balances. Increasing DRO amounts and duration can increase yield and DRO-related risk.

The gross income and expense reallocation method reduces a DRO by separately reallocating gross expenses and gross income between partners' capital accounts. The net income reallocation method requires less effort to model than the gross income and expense reallocation method.

Under IRC code section 702(a)(7) each partner determines the partner's income tax by taking into account separately the partner's distributive share of the partnership's other items of income, gain, loss, deduction or credit to the extent provided by regulations prescribed by the Treasury Secretary. Under Regulation section 1.702-1(a) the distributive share is determined under section 704 and Regulation section 1.704-1. Under section 704(a), a partner's distributive share of income, gain, loss, deduction, or credit is, except as otherwise provided in Chapter 1 of Subtitle A of Title 26, determined by the partnership agreement. Under section 704(b)) a partner's distributive share of income, gain, loss, deduction, or credit is determined in accordance with the partner's interest in the partnership, if (1) the partnership agreement does not provide for the partner's distributive share of income, gain, loss, deduction, or credit, or (2) the allocation to a partner under the agreement of income, gain, loss, deduction or credit lacks substantial economic effect.

Regulation section 1.704-1(b)(2) provides that the *two-part test* (I and II below) to determine substantial economic effect is (a) the allocation must have economic effect, and (b) the economic effect of the allocation must be substantial. In order for an allocation to have economic effect, it must be consistent with the underlying economic arrangement of the partners. This means that in the event there is an economic benefit or economic burden that corresponds to an allocation, the partner to whom the allocation is made must receive such economic benefit or bear such economic burden.

I. Economic Effect (Part one of two part test): The Big Three Requirements

An allocation of income, gain, loss, deduction or credit to a partner will have economic effect if, and only if, throughout the full term of the partnership, the partnership agreement provides:

1. For the determination and maintenance of the partners' capital accounts in accordance with the capital accounting rules that each partner's capital account is increased by:
   (i) the amount of money contributed by the partner to the partnership,
   (ii) the fair market value of property contributed by the partner to the partnership (net of liabilities that the partnership is considered to assume or take subject to), and
   (iii) allocations to the partner of partnership income and gain (or items thereof), including income and gain exempt from tax and income and gain described in paragraph (b)(2)(iv)(g) of section 1-704-1 (Adjustments to reflect book value), but excluding income and gain described in paragraph (b)(4)(i) of section 1-704.1 (allocations to reflect revaluations);

   and is decreased by:
   (iv) the amount of money distributed to the partner by the partnership,
   (v) the fair market value of property distributed to the partner by the partnership (net of liabilities that such partner is considered to assume or take subject to), and
   (vi) allocations to the partner of expenditures of the partnership described in section 705(a)(2)(B) (Expenditure not deductible in computing partnership taxable income and not properly chargeable to capital account), and
   (vii) allocations of partnership loss and deduction (or item thereof), including loss and deduction described in paragraph (b)(2)(iv)(g) of section 1.704-1 (adjustments to reflect book value), but excluding items described above and loss or deduction described in paragraphs (b)(4)(i) (allocations to reflect revaluation) or (b)(4)(iii) (excess percentage depletion in respect of an item of depletable property) of section 1.704-1; and
2. Liquidating distributions are made in accordance with the positive capital balances of the partners, as determined after taking into account all capital account adjustments for the partnership taxable year during which such liquidation occurs, by the end of such taxable year; and
3. If such partner has a deficit balance in his capital account following liquidation of his interest, such partner is unconditionally obligated to restore the amount of such deficit balance to the partnership by the end of such taxable year, which amount upon liquidation shall be paid to creditors of the partnership or distributed to other partners in accordance with their positive capital account balances (hereinafter referred to as the "Big Three").

The rationale for the Big Three should be apparent. Unless tax allocations of income or loss are accompanied by increases or decreases to the partner's capital accounts, there is no way to assure that the tax consequences will ever reflect the partners' economic business deal. For example, a special allocation of $100 of extra income can be respected for tax purposes only if the partners eventually will receive the economic benefit of that income. Since the partners' ultimate economic stakes in the partnership are measured by their capital accounts, all allocations (and other significant financial events in the life of the partnership) must be reflected in those capital accounts. The second and third requirements ensure the validity of the premise by requiring that the amounts partners will receive on liquidation are determined by their positive capital accounts. Because a negative capital account indicates that a partner is in debt to the partnership, the Regulations require that a partner must satisfy that debt (by restoring the deficit) on or before a liquidation.

Alternate Economic Effect Test

If the partnership agreement satisfies the first two requirements of the Big Three but fails to include an unconditional deficit make-up provision, the Regulations provide an alternate test for economic effect. This more flexible standard looks to both the effect of an allocation on a partner's capital account and the extent of any partial obligation by the partner to restore a deficit or make additional capital contributions to the partnership. An allocation under the alternate economic effect test will have economic effect to the extent that it does not create or increase a deficit in the partner's capital account (in excess of any limited deficit restoration obligation that the partner may have) and the agreement includes a provision known as a "qualified income offset."

The partnership agreement contains a "qualified income offset," if, and only if, it provides that a partner who unexpectedly receives an adjustment, allocation, or distribution as described in subsections (3)(a), (3)(b) and (3)(c) above, will be allocated items of income and gain in an amount and manner sufficient to eliminate a deficit balance as quickly as possible.

This test makes sense because even without an unlimited obligation to restore a deficit, a partner who receives an allocation of losses still suffers a corresponding economic burden as long as the allocation does not create a capital account deficit or exceed any additional amounts that the partner has agreed to contribute to the partnership in the future. If an allocation does create or increase a deficit (in excess of any limited deficit make-up obligation), the loss will be reallocated in accordance with the partners' interest in the partnership.

II. Substantiality (Part two of two-part test)

The second major test under the Regulations looks to whether the economic effect of an allocation is substantial both in the year of the allocation and over the life of the partnership. The economic effect of an allocation is substantial if there is a reasonable possibility that the allocation will affect substantially the dollar amounts to be received by the partners from the partnership, independent of tax consequences. Perhaps recognizing that this general rule is not very informative, the Regulations elaborate by stating that, notwithstanding the above rule, the economic effect of an allocation is not substantial if, at the time the allocation becomes part of the partnership:

1. after-tax economic consequences of at least one partner may, in present value terms, be enhanced compared to such consequences if the allocation was not contained in the partnership agreement, and

2. if there is a strong likelihood that the after-tax economic consequences of no partner will, in present value terms, be substantially diminished compared to such consequences if such allocation were not contained in the partnership agreement.

In other words, an allocation fails the substantiality test if its effect is to benefit one or more partners after taxes and not to affect adversely any other partner—in both cases, comparing the effect of the allocation to the result if no allocation had been contained in the partnership agreement. In determining the after-tax economic benefit or detriment to a partner, tax consequences that result from the interaction of the allocation with other tax attributes of the partner unrelated to the partnership must be taken into account.

> *"Affordable energy in ample quantities is the life blood of the industrial societies and a prerequisite for the economic development of the others."*
>
> John P. Holdren, U.S. physicist)

To illustrate the general rule, assume the AB general partnership invests in income producing securities. Partner A expects to be in the 30% marginal tax bracket in the current year and Partner B expect to be in the 15% marginal bracket. Assume further that the partnership faithfully satisfies the Big Three and thus all of its allocations will have economic effect. Finally assume that the partnership structures its investments so that it will earn relatively equal amounts of tax-exempt interest and taxable dividends and the partnership agreement allocates tax-exempt interest 90% to A and 10% to B and the dividends 100% to B. Although the allocation has economic effect, the substantiality test is failed at the time the allocation is made because A is expected to enhance his after-tax economic consequences as a result of the allocation, and there is a strong likelihood that neither A nor B will substantially diminish his after-tax consequences.

Allocations of Tax Credits

Pursuant to Regulation 1.704-1(b)(4)(ii), allocations of tax credits and tax credit recapture are not reflected by adjustments to the partners' capital accounts. Thus, such allocations cannot have economic effect under the first prong of the economic effect test that partner's capital accounts be maintained and determined by increasing (decreasing) the partner's capital account contributions made by the partner to the partnership (distributions made by the partnership to the partner), the fair market value of property contributed by the partner to the partnership (fair market value of property distributed by the partnership to the partner), allocations to the partner of partnership income and gain, expenditures of the partnership, and loss and deductions.

The tax credit and the tax credit recapture must be allocated in accordance with the partners' interest in the partnership as of the time the tax credit or tax credit recapture arises.

If a partnership expenditure (whether or not deductible) that gives rise to a tax credit in a partnership taxable year also gives rise to valid allocations of partnership loss or deduction (or other downward capital account adjustment) for the year, the partners' interests in the partnership with respect to such credit (of the cost giving rise to it) shall be in the same proportion as the partners' respective distributive shares of the loss or deduction (and adjustments). Identical principals apply in determining the partners' interest in the partnership regarding tax credits that arise from income of the partnership (whether or not taxable). If a partnership receipt gives rise to a tax credit, and that receipt also gives rise to a valid allocation of partnership income, the partners' interest in the partnership with respect to the item of credit will be in the same proportion as the partners' respective distributive share of such income.

Limitations on Losses, Deductions and Credits

There are three separate potential limitations on the amount of partnership losses that a partner may deduct on their individual return. These limitations and the order in which the partner must apply them are the basis rules, the at-risk limitations and the passive activity limitations.

A. **Basis Rules**

Generally, a partner may not claim his share of partnership loss (including a capital loss) to the extent the loss is greater than the adjusted basis of the partner's partnership interest at the end of the partnership's tax year. Any losses and deductions not allowed in any year because of the basis limitation can be carried forward indefinitely and deducted in a later year subject to the basis limitation for that year.

B. **At Risk Limitations**

Generally, if a partner has (a) a loss or other deduction from any activity carried on as a trade or business or for the production of income by the partnership, and (b) amount in the activity for you the partner is not at risk, the partner will have to complete Form 6198 to figure the partner's allowable loss.

The at-risk rules generally limit the amount of loss and other deductions that a partner may claim to the amount the partner could actually lose in the activity. These losses and deductions include a loss on the disposition of assets and the section 179 expense deduction. It is the responsibility of the partnership to identify on an attachment to a partner's Schedule K-1 the amount of any losses that are not subject to the at-risk limitations. The at-risk basis is capital contributions plus partner loans.

Partners are generally not at risk for amounts such as the following:

- Nonrecourse loans used to finance the activity, to acquire property used in the activity, or to acquire the partner's interest in the activity, that are not secured by the partner's own property (other than property used in the activity).
- Cash, property, or borrowed amounts used in the activity (or contributed to the activity, or used to acquire the partner's interest in the activity) that are protected against loss by a guarantee, stop-loss agreement, or other similar arrangement (excluding casualty insurance and insurance against tort liability).
- Amounts borrowed for use in the activity from a person who has an interest in the activity, other than as a creditor, or who is related, under IRC code section 465(b)(3), to a person (other than the partner) having such an interest.

Note to developers: fees are typically "non-qualified" debt.

C. **Passive Activity Limitations**

Section 469 provides rules that limit the deduction of certain losses and credits. Section 469 was enacted to restrict taxpayers from using deductions and other losses generated from certain passive investment activities to shelter income from other sources (such as a taxpayer's regular business income, compensation, dividends and interest). Section 469 disallows the current deductibility of losses and the use of credits from passive activities. The income and losses from each of a taxpayer's passive activities are first computed and then all are combined; in any taxable year, passive activity losses can be deducted only to the extent of the taxpayer's income from passive activities for that year. To the extent that losses from passive activities for the taxable year exceed the taxpayer's passive income, that excess may be carried forward and deducted (subject to the same limitations) against future net income from passive activities. Disallowed losses from a particular activity (but not credits) may be deducted in full on a taxable disposition of the entire activity. Section 469 does not forever disallow excess passive losses; it merely postpones them.

These rules apply to partners who:

1) Are individuals, estates, trusts, closely-held corporations or personal service corporations, and
2) Have a passive activity loss or credit for the tax year. Generally passive activities include trade or business activities in which the partner did not *materially* participate. A passive activity is any activity involving the conduct of any trade or business in which the taxpayer does not materially participate. Under section 469, a taxpayer materially participates in an activity only if he is involved on a regular, continuous and substantial basis in the operation of the activity. Therefore, only high-net-worth individuals with passive income could benefit and as a result, most investors are C corporations that can offset their active income.

The partner must determine if they materially participated in each trade or business activity held through the partnership. All determinations of material participation are made based on the partner's participation during the partnership's tax year. If the partner is an individual (either a general partner or a limited partner who owned a general partnership interest at all times during the tax year), the partner materially participated in any activity only if one or more of the following apply:

1) The partner participated in the activity for more than 500 hours during the tax year.
2) The partner's participation in the activity for the tax year constituted substantially all the participation in the activity of all individuals (including individuals who are not owners of interests in the activity).
3) The partner participated in the activity for more than 100 hours during the tax year, and the partner's participation in the activity for the tax year was not less than the participation in the activity of any other individual (including individuals who are not owners of interests in the activity) for the tax year.
4) The activity was a significant participation activity for the tax year, and the partner participated in all significant participation activities (including activities outside the partnership) during the year for more than 500 hours. A significant participation activity is any trade or business activity in which the partner participated more than 100 hours during the year and in which the partner did not materially participate under any of the material participation tests (other than this test 4).
5) The partner materially participated in the activity for any five (5) tax years (whether or not consecutive) during the ten (10) tax years that immediately precede the tax year.
6) The activity was a personal service activity and the partner materially participated in the activity for any three (3) tax years (whether or not consecutive) preceding the tax year. A personal service activity involves the performance of personal services in the fields of health, law, engineering, architecture, accounting, actuarial science, performing arts, consulting, or any other trade or business in which capital is not a material income-producing factor.
7) Based on all the facts and circumstances, the partner participated in the activity on a regular, continuous, and substantial basis during the tax year.

If a partner is a limited partner, the limited partner does not materially participate in an activity unless the limited partner meets one of the tests in paragraphs 1, 5, or 6 above. A limited partner's share of income received from the performance of services (by way of salary, guaranteed payment or allocation of partnership income) is not treated as income from a passive activity.

Conclusion

Owners (or operators/lessees in the case of open-loop biomass facilities and certain closed-loop biomass facilities) can receive an energy tax credit under section 45 of the Code from electricity it produces and sells in the United States to unrelated persons. If the owner of the qualified facility is a partnership, the partnership can allocate to its partners their share of the credit and income or loss that generated the credit in proportion to the partners' interest in the partnership. In order to claim the credit, the owner must complete and file a

Form 8835 and 3800 with the Internal Revenue Service. There are several limitations on the amount of the credit that can be claimed by the owner of the qualified facility, such as general business credit limitations (section 38), phase-out limitations (section 45), and reductions for grants, tax-exempt bonds, and other subsidies (section 45).

If a partnership owns the facility, allocations of income, gain, loss, deduction or credit as provided in the partnership agreement must have substantial economic effect as provided in Code section 704 and Regulation section 1.704-1. Allocations of tax credit cannot have substantial economic effect under Regulation section 1.704-1 because the credits are not reflected by adjustments to the partners' capital accounts. Therefore, credits must be allocated to the partners in accordance with the partners' interests in the partnership. If a partnership expenditure or receipt (income) gives rise to the tax credit, and gives rise to an allocation of partnership loss or income, the credit shall be allocated in the same proportion as the loss or income, if the allocation of loss or income has substantial economic effect under section 704. In order to determine if such allocations of tax credits to partners have substantial economic effect, it must be determined that the allocation of income or loss that the credit is related to has substantial economic effect.

Because of the restrictions on claiming the energy tax credits under section 45 and the requirements under partnership tax rules, careful consideration must be taken in setting up an entity to own a qualified facility and claim the energy tax credits under section 45 (and section 48 also).

5. Depreciation

Depreciation on an energy asset is one of the most important components when a taxpayer is looking to come up with the correct analysis of the financing project. There are over 30 methods of calculating depreciation. This section will first cover several "conventions" for calculating depreciation.

In calculating deprecation, many depreciation methods are affected by the first year Asset Depreciation Range (ADR) convention and the length of the first tax year, salvage value and end of depreciation treatment.

First Year of the Contract

The first year ADR conventions are:

1. *Facts and Circumstances*. Prorate the amount of depreciation allowed in the first year based on the Start Date.
2. *Full Year*. Take a full-year's worth of depreciation in the first year.
3. *Half Year*. Take a half-year's worth of depreciation in the first year
4. *Full-Half-Year*. Take a full-year's worth of depreciation for assets that deliver in the first half of the year, and a half-year's depreciation in the first year for asset that are delivered in the second half of the year.
5. *Full-Month*. Similar to "facts and circumstances," except that a full-month of depreciation is always taken in the month that the depreciation starts.
6. *Mid-Month*. Similar to "facts and circumstances," except that a half-month of depreciation is always taken in the month that the depreciation starts.
7. *Mid-Quarter*. Takes 1½ months of depreciation in the quarter in which the depreciation starts.
8. *Modified Half-Year*. Take a full year's worth of depreciation for assets that are delivered in the first half of the year, and no depreciation in the first year for assets that are delivered in the second half of the year.

The half-year, mid-quarter and modified half-year conventions are applied to the first tax year. If the first tax year is a short year (because the project finance agreement starts in the first fiscal year, and the first fiscal year is a short year), the depreciation method would be applied to that short year. The amount calculated will be less than with a full 12 month tax year. Note that this applies to "all" assets acquired by the taxpayer in that year.

Additional First Year Bonus Depreciation

At various times over the past decade, congress has allowed a special additional first year bonus depreciation on purchased assets for the taxpayer. This occurred in 2002 and again in 2008. Together, the 50% bonus depreciation plus the ½ year MACRS depreciation adds up to 60% of the net capitalized tax base in the first year if it was acquired in 2008. The American Recovery and Reinvestment Act (ARRA), enacted in February 2009, extended the bonus depreciation and increased the section 179 deduction. The Tax Relief, Unemployment Insurance Reauthorization, and Job Creation Act of 2010 (H.R. 4853) was signed into law by President Obama on

Dec. 17, 2010. That legislation included an extension of the Small Business Jobs and Credit Act of 2010's "bonus depreciation" allowance through the end of 2011. The bill temporarily increases bonus depreciation from 50 percent to 100 percent for investments placed in service after September 8, 2010 and through December 31, 2011.

MACRS allows tangible property to be depreciated on an accelerated basis according to a detailed schedule specified by the IRS. Combined with the additional first year bonus depreciation at 50%, Table 5-18 exemplifies the value as opposed to MACRS without the bonus depreciation (the higher the depreciation in the early years, the more valuable is the tax benefit).

Table 5-18: Value of Bonus Depreciation with MACRS Five Year Property

	Year 1	Year 2	Year 3	Year 4	Year 5	Year 6
MACRS	20.00%	32.00%	19.20%	11.52%	11.52%	5.76%
MACRS + 50% Bonus	60.00%	16.00%	9.60%	5.76%	5.76%	2.88%

The legislation allowed the taxpayer to expense applicable percentage (depending on the year of acquisition) of the net asset cost of acquired assets. This special first year depreciation was only good for tax year 2008 but as seen above, occurred again in future years to "stimulate" the economy. In addition to this first year bonus depreciation, the tax payer is still allowed the regular MACRS depreciation (on the net amount of the asset base after applying the bonus depreciation) on the energy generating asset during that first year (with the standard ½ year convention being applied). The bonus also applies to the alternative minimum tax depreciation. This massive amount of depreciation accounts for a significant tax advantaged return to a taxpayer acquiring a renewable energy asset as will be seen in the actual application of this component in later chapters. Be careful though—there are limitations on the bonus depreciation allowable.

The Economic Stimulus Act of 2008 included a 50% first-year 'bonus depreciation' provision for qualified renewable energy systems placed into service in 2008. This was extended for 2009 and 2010, and in December 2010, increased to 100% first-year bonus depreciation for qualified renewable energy projects placed in service after September 8, 2010 and before January 1, 2012. The bonus depreciation is still available in 2012, but reverted back to 50% from the 100% eligible basis. The bonus depreciation incentive is currently set to expire at the end of 2013.

Last Year of Depreciation

Any remaining depreciation (including salvage value) is taken on the residual date for a lender or project developer. The question is often asked as to why the remaining depreciation is taken. The answer is that the residual is considered as fully taxable when received. The last year of depreciation can be spread over the entire last year. This can be done in one of three ways:

1. Straight Line
2. Roll back to residual date
3. Roll up salvage to residual date (most common)

If there is a non-zero salvage value election made in setting up the method of depreciation election by the taxpayer, then the depreciation is calculated according to the method selected and the salvage value is not taken into depreciation until the asset is actually sold (the residual date).

Depreciation Methods

There are over 30 methods of calculating depreciation. The most common method for assets placed in service since January 1, 1987 is Double Declining Balance switching to Straight Line (DDB/SL), also known as "Modified ACRS" or "MACRS." There are a large amount of resources (including the IRS publications directly) that the reader can obtain on this component of the financial analysis and therefore they will not be covered here. However, the most common used in renewable energy generating assets is the 5 year MACRS method (which is effectively a six year method since only 50% of the first year's depreciation can be taken in the first year). Table 5-19 shows this method of depreciation.

Potential other depreciation methods not often taken include the following:

Table 5-19: MACRS 5-Year Depreciation Table

Year	Percent Allowed	Balance Remaining
1	20.00%	80.00%
2	32.00%	48.00%
3	19.20%	28.80%
4	11.52%	17.28%
5	11.52%	5.76%
6	5.76%	0.00%

- Accelerated Cost Recovery System Method:
  - ACRS 3 year
  - ACRS 5 year
  - ACRS 10 year
  - ACRS 15 year
- Declining Balance Method:
  - DB 150%
  - DB 175%
  - DB 200%
- Declining Balance Switching to Straightline Method
  - DB/SL 150%
  - DB/SL 175%
  - DB/SL 200%
- Declining Balance Switching to Sum of the Year's Digits Method
  - DB/SYD 150%
  - DB/SYD 175%
  - DB/SYD 200%
- Specified Depreciation
  - Specify the depreciation annually
  - Specify the depreciation annually but hold the dollar amount specified for depreciation fixed, so that it will not vary in proportion to the asset cost
  - Specify the depreciation daily
  - Specify the depreciation daily but hold the dollar amount specified for depreciation fixed, so that it will not vary in proportion to the asset cost
- Other Methods
  - Diminishing Value: A constant percentage of the remaining basis is taken each period.
  - Expensed: Takes the full amount of depreciation on the starting date (not likely to be approved by IRS under audit).
  - Interest: The interest amounts in an artificial P&I schedule
  - Japanese: Japanese method of depreciation
  - None: No depreciation will be taken
  - Operating: Straight line depreciation from the starting date through the residual date
  - Pickle: Pickle depreciation is straight line depreciation over the longer of the asset's class life, or 125% of the contract term
  - Principal: Principal portion of rent taken as depreciation
  - Straight Line Fixed: Straight line over the term entered
  - Straight Line to End: Straight line over the contract term
  - Sum of the Years Digits

Finance Structure Classification

All finance structures are classified by two major considerations.

- Tax purposes (IRS)
- Accounting purposes (FASB)

Depending upon the outcome desired by the lender/investor/project developer and the debt obligor, each of these have different rules of applicability. There are three caveats:

1. Just because a financial transaction is to be treated one way for tax purposes, doesn't mean that it will be treated the same way for accounting purposes
2. Just because the lender/project developer treats a transaction one way for tax purposes, the debt obligor is under no mandate to treat the transaction in the same manner. This is also true for accounting purposes.
3. Just because the principal parties to the transaction (lender/project developer and debt obligor) treat a transaction for either tax purposes or accounting purposes in a certain manner, it does not mean that third parties will also treat that finance structure in the same manner (and in many cases do not). Those third parties could include personal property tax assessors, sales tax regulators, energy utilities, state or other local governments, bankruptcy judges or administrators, and other judicial or legislative districts.

In all cases, both the IRS and FASB guidelines will need to be evaluated and applied to the transaction by each taxpayer—and independently of each other. The guidelines used to evaluate the transaction by both of these regulatory agencies are detailed below.

The results of the IRS tests (described in the guidelines) will determine if the transaction will be treated as either a true lease or true purchase of energy agreement, or classified as a conditional sale or direct finance transaction. This is also true for the FASB tests.

However, for the lender/investor/project developer, further classifications for FASB purposes are: 1) capital lease (also known as a direct finance lease); 2) operating lease; 3) leveraged lease; or 4) loan. In many transactions the present value test in FASB is the only test of significance for the proper accounting classification.

IRS Tax Treatment

The IRS tests determine whether "in the eyes of the IRS," a lease is a true lease or a conditional sale agreement. In a true lease, the lessor is entitled to depreciation benefits and recognizes the full rent as taxable income (as opposed to only the interest income in a conditional sale agreement). This would also apply to any type of energy purchase agreement (which is also known as an "executory contract" in the courts).

In a conditional sale, the lessee (debt obligor) is deemed the owner for tax purposes and would take depreciation and the lessor reports only the "interest" portion of the rent as income, not the full rent. This, by definition would never occur in an energy purchase agreement. The two principal tests that the IRS uses are based in part on the IRS Revenue Procedures 75-21 and 75-28.

FASB Accounting Treatment

FASB applies their own set of tests to the financing transaction that are independent of the IRS tests. Those tests will be described below, but will result in one of the following treatments:

- Operating
- Capital
- Capital: Leveraged
- Capital: Single Investor
- Capital: Loan

IRS Classification Tests
(for leases and applicable to other executory contracts such as power purchase agreements)

- *Pre-Tax Profit Test.* This determines whether the owner makes a profit on the transaction, apart from the tax benefits. This test (4.071 from the rulings) requires only that the total overall pre-tax profit be greater than zero. The overall pre-tax profit is the total pre-tax cash flow adjusted for the IRS residual. This is the same overall profit that is pro-rated in the minimum equity test. Inasmuch as the total profit used, there is no time value effect.

  A failure of this test may be corrected in two ways. The pre-tax cash flow can be increased, or the minimum IRS residual can be increased.

- *Cash Flow Test.* This determines whether adequate free cash flow is received throughout the project finance contract term. This test includes a specification for the minimum % of equity/year, which in most cases would need to default to 2%. Also, you will need to consider whether you want to include fees as part of the equity for this test. Including the fees in the equity makes it easier to pass this test.

  This test (4.072 from the rulings) requires that the total cash flows be reasonable. It is similar to the pre-tax profit test in that it is performed on the totals, so there is no time value effect.

  The total cash flow for this test is simply the total contract payments and periodic income minus debt service, minus periodic expenses, minus dependent fees. The question of whether or not it is reasonable is determined by a method that uses the total equity and the number of years in the contract term.

  The total equity is the total asset cost plus the total fees minus the total loans. The number of years in the contract term is the number of days between the in-service date and the end of payment accrual (not affected by advance or arrears) divided by 360.

  The total cash flow is divided by the number of years in the contract term to produce the cash flow per year. The beginning of the contract term is the commencement date (if there is an interim period, the commencement date or the weighted average delivery date, whichever comes first, is used). The end of the contract term is the end of the payment accrual. This annual cash flow is then divided by the total equity to calculate the annual cash flow as a percent of equity. This percentage is finally compared to the percentage you specific in IRS Classification as the Minimum % of Equity/Year. If the calculated value is less, the test fails; otherwise it passes.

  A failure of this test may be corrected by switching fees from the total cash flow to the equity; however, the test can always be passed by increasing the total cash flow or reducing the required percentage.

- *Minimum Equity Test.* This determines whether the minimum amount of equity is maintained throughout the contract term. The minimum equity is usually assumed to be 20%. This test (4.025 from the rulings) is only performed on certain test dates. On each test date the actual free cash accumulated to date is compared with the allowable free cash on the date specified by the test.

  The test dates are all payments, debt service, periodic income, periodic expense, and dependent fee payment dates. The dates prior to the commencement date can be excluded such as interim payments to be received during the construction/build-out phase, if desired.

- *Actual Free Cash.* The actual free cash is simply the payments plus other periodic income minus debt service, minus periodic expense payments, minus dependent fees, accumulated to the test date.
- *Allowable Free Cash.* The allowable free cash has two parts—a base and a pro-rata profit amount.

The base is a flat amount that applies to each date and is calculated as the total asset cost, plus the total fees, minus the total loan takedowns, minus the Minimum Equity Required percentage (usually 20% of the total asset cost).

The *pro-rate amount* is the total overall profit times a fraction. The total overall profit is the total pre-tax cash flow increased by the amount that the IRS residual exceeds the economic residual (or reduced by it, if the economic residual exceeds the IRS residual). The denominator of the fraction is the number of days from the start date of the minimum equity test to the date of the last rent. The minimum equity test start date is the earlier of the weighted average delivery date and the first pre-tax cash flow date. The numerator of the fraction is the number of days from the start date of the minimum equity test to the particular *test date*.

The pro-rata fraction is equal to 100% on the date of the last rent payment. (Note that this occurs at the start of the final rent period in an advance or flip structure.) If there is more debt service, periodic income, or periodic expense payments, the test continues beyond the last rent payment date. In that case, the fraction remains at 100% and the allowable free cash does not continue to increase.

The fees are included in the base of the allowable free cash rather than in the actual free cash. This method is conservative if there are any fees paid after the start date of the minimum equity test.

The total actual free cash at the end of the test will equal the total allowable free cash if the IRS residual is 20%.

A failure of this test may be corrected in two ways. First, the base can be increased by reducing the leverage. The base is used throughout the entire lease term and can therefore help the test pass on any date. The second way is to defer the actual free cash. This can be done by increasing the debt service or reducing the rent in the beginning of the lease.

- *Maximum Leverage Test.* In a leveraged lease (or an energy purchase agreement for that matter when a transaction is being structured to meet IRS tests for the equity partners), this determines whether the maximum amount of leverage is exceeded. The maximum can be specified, but normally would never exceed 80%.

- *The Debtor Investment Test.* This determines whether the debtor has exceeded an allowable amount of investment in the transaction, by comparing the total security deposit to a maximum amount. This amount is normally set at 10%.

- *Minimum Risk Test.* This determines the adequacy of the total amount of risk that the owner is bearing. That risk, computed as the total of the unguaranteed residual amounts, is compared to the true lease norm. The default in most transactions is 20%, but can vary.

- *Bargain Purchase Option Test.* This determines whether a purchase option, if present, constitutes a bargain, when compared to the FMV of the asset. (A bargain is considered to be any amount less that the FMV.) If *any single asset is a bargain* (even if the total of all purchase options is greater than the total of the FMVs), then the test is failed, and the transaction is classified a conditional sale.

- *Remaining Life Test.* This test (and the following remaining value test) is oriented toward used equipment that is re-leased. It analyzes whether a minimum of 20% of the economic life remains after the lease-end. If not, then this lease substantially consumes the value of the asset, making it a conditional sale. This test is performed on an asset-by-asset basis. Minimum remaining life (months) specifies the shortest period that must remain in the asset's useful life at the end of the lease, to pass this test. If a value is specified for this, that test is applied in addition to the test of the percentage of remaining life, which would normally default to 20% but could have a different election if desired by the taxpayer on a case-by-case basis.

- *Remaining Value Test.* This test determines whether a minimum of 20% of the value of the asset remains after the contract end. If not, then the contract substantially consumes the value of the asset, making it a conditional sale. This test is also performed on an asset-by-asset basis.

- *Prepaid and Deferred Test.* This test determines whether the cash rents and the rent allocations are correctly related throughout the lease term. Neither the cumulative cash nor cumulative allocation at the end of each calendar year may exceed the other, within 1 year. This test is documented following the main part of the uneven rent test (see next), when shifted (prepaid-deferred) rents are used.
- *Uneven Rent Test.* Note that the uneven rent test is not used to determine true lease status. Rather, it is used to see whether the rent needs to be leveled according to the Section 467 regulations. This test (4.081 and 4.082 from the rulings) determines whether the rent accruals (allocations) are adequately "smooth." This is done by computing the average annual rent, and then the minimum and maximum (typically 90% and 100%) allowable based on that average. Next each year's accrued rent is compared to this allowed range. If any year falls outside that range, the test fails. This could be problematic if a lessor/lender/investor would have a rent schedule that includes performance based or cash rebates received by the lessee and in turn paid to the lessor/lender/investor when received by the lessee as part of the rent schedule defined in the financing agreement. Therefore, if at all possible, the debt provider should schedule the rebates to be paid to them directly as opposed to having them part of the rent schedule.
- *Holiday.* A holiday is an initial period whose payments, if any, are excluded from the main uneven payment test. However, the annualized holiday payment must not exceed the average annual payment, calculated as the total rent (holiday and base payment) divided by the full term (holiday and base). The payment holiday may be up to 90 days in length, or in certain circumstances even longer. It may not, however, be longer than 10% of the contract term or 24 months. Also, the payment accruing to a given payment period may be paid as early as a year before the beginning of the calendar year of the period, or as late as a year after the end of the calendar year of the period.

FASB Accounting Classification Tests

The FASB classification process determines the appropriate accounting treatment, from the following alternatives: capital (leveraged), capital (single investor), operating/energy purchase agreement for the lessor, investor or project developer, and capital or operating/energy purchase for the debt obligor. The tests used to determine the classification include:

- Bargain purchase option
- Last quarter
- Economic life
- Present value (for both lender/project developer and debt obligor)

The first three apply to both the lender/investor/project developer and the debt obligor. The fourth, the present value test, is specified separately for lender/project developer and the debt obligor. If there are conflicts in the status determined, the first conclusive test decides.

1. *Bargain Purchase Option.* The bargain purchase option test compares each asset's purchase option amount, if one exists, to the fair market value (FMV) of that asset. The FMV is taken to be the residual value of the asset. A purchase option whose amount is less than the FMV is considered economically compelling, and therefore determines capital lease accounting. Such a compulsion on any single asset in the transaction decides that status, even if the total purchase option amount (across all assets) is more than the total FMV. Both parties need to be aware of this potential pit fall when establishing the financial structure of the project (see FMV description below). Therefore, make sure that the all assets in the renewable energy project have a FMV purchase option. This test would also include a transaction whereby the contract would automatically transfer ownership to the debt obligor at the end of the initial contract term.
2. *Last Quarter.* The last quarter test examines whether the transaction commences in the final quarter of each asset's economic life (think "used" equipment here). For this test, the economic life and the delivery date of the asset are used together to determine the start of the last quarter of the economic life. If the transaction commences after that date, then the asset's value has already been substantially consumed.
3. *Economic Life.* The economic life test compares the life of the asset to the contract term. If the contract consumes more than three-quarters of the life, it is considered to have consumed the substantial value of the asset, forcing capital asset accounting. (This criterion is not applied when the inception of the

contract occurs during the last 25% of the life of the asset financed.)

4. *Present Value (PV)*. The present value test (often called the 90% test) determines whether the PV of the minimum contract payments is 90% or more of the value of the equipment. (This criterion is not applied when the inception of the contract occurs during the last 25% of the life of the asset financed.) The test is performed separately for the lender/investor/project developer and the debt obligor. A PV of the minimum contract payments above the threshold indicates the contract substantially consumes the value of the asset and determines capital asset accounting. For the lender/investor/project developer, the minimum contract payments is the total rent to be received and any guaranteed portions of the residual value, discounted at the interest rate implicit in the contract (an implicit interest rate is one that is not explicit; in other words, the rate is not stated). For the debt obligor, the minimum contract payments is the total payments to be paid under the contract plus any debt obligor guarantee on the residual value, discounted at the debt obligor's incremental (the pre-tax coterminous rate that, at the inception of the contract, the debt obligor would have incurred to borrow over a similar term and conditions, the funds necessary to purchase the asset). This test excludes any executory costs. Executory costs are costs associated with the ownership of the asset such as insurance, property taxes and maintenance. Strategies used to meet operating lease guidelines (most often desired) would include the debt obligor using a higher discount rate. Conversely, the lender/project developer might in certain circumstances want to have the transaction classified as a capital lease and would therefore use a lower discount rate.

5. *Minimum Guaranteed Residual*. Using the implicit interest rate of the transaction, the minimum guaranteed residual (if one is provided for in the financing contract) is calculated by both parties to again determine the FASB accounting treatment and would be added to the above to determine the PV of the finance structure. The implicit rate in the transaction is the discount rate that, when applied to (1) the minimum contract payments (excluding executory costs) and (2) the unguaranteed residual value accruing to the benefit of the lender/project developer, causes the aggregate present value at the beginning of the contract term to be equal to the fair value of the leased property to the lender/investor/project developer at the inception of the contract, minus any ITC retained by the lender/project developer and expected to be realized by it.

   In fact, the implicit rate in the transaction is the internal rate of return (IRR) of the fair market value (less ITC), the minimal contract payments and the unguaranteed residual. This is the rate to be used as the lender/lessor/investor/project developer discount rate for purposes of the 90% test.

IRS Guideline Lease or Energy Purchase Agreement

A guideline lease/energy purchase agreement complies with all of the IRS requirements (or "guidelines") for a true lease; specifically, those set forth in Revenue Procedure 75-21, 75-28, 76-30 and 79-48. In general, these guidelines include, but are not limited to:

1. The contract term (including any extensions or renewals at a predetermined fixed rental) must not exceed 80% of the estimated useful life of the equipment at the commencement of the project transaction. Thus, the equipment must be projected to have an estimated remaining useful life equal to at least 20% of its original life at the end of the contract. These requirements limit the maximum term of the contract.

2. The equipment's estimated residual value (in constant dollars without adjustment for inflation or deflation) at the expiration of the contract term must, at contract commencement, be projected to equal at least 20% of its original value. This requirement also limits the maximum contract term.

3. Neither the debt obligor nor any related party can have a right to purchase the property from the lender/investor/lessor/project developer at a price less than its fair market value at the time of the purchase. Thus, the contract agreement cannot contain any option to purchase the equipment at a bargain purchase price. However, the debt obligor can be given a fair market value purchase option.

4. Neither the debt obligor nor any related party can pay, or guarantee payment of, any part of the price of the leased equipment. Simply put, the debt obligor cannot make any investment in the equipment. That's why tax-oriented financing is deemed to be 100% financing.

5. The equipment must not be "limited use" property. Equipment is limited use property if no one other than the debt obligor or a related party could use it

in a commercially feasible manner at the end of the contract term.

Tax Oriented Transaction

A tax-oriented transaction is a finance structure under which the debt provider will be treated by the IRS as the owner of the property for federal tax purposes and permitted to take tax benefits (e.g., depreciation deductions on the property and any available tax credits). All payments paid by a debt obligor under a tax-oriented transaction are deductible for federal tax purposes in its entirety. A tax oriented lease is sometimes referred to as "true lease." The transactions are also generally referred to as guideline leases (see above).

In a guideline lease (and by inference an energy purchase agreement), the lessor reports rental income and deducts related business expenses. The lessee deducts the rental payments. The IRS Commissioner, however, has on numerous occasions challenged purported lease agreements, arguing that a "sales" or "financing" transaction, rather than a "leasing" transaction, has actually occurred. When a lease is re-characterized as a sale, the lessee will be considered the owner of the leased property and, thus, lose the expense deduction for the rental payments, but have depreciation and other related expense deductions. The lessor will be treated as if he sold the leased property in a taxable transaction and recognizes gain and imputed interest income as rental payments are received. And since the lessor is no longer the owner of the leased property, no deduction for depreciation or other related expenses will be allowed. In order for the parties to avail themselves to the implicit tax benefits of a lease, the transaction must generally meet both common law economic substance and business purpose doctrines. However, due to the lack of a uniformly accepted bright-line test defining these doctrines, differing rules currently exist among the federal circuits. This has led to both taxpayer uncertainty and inconsistent tax results.

> *"The Stone Age did not end for lack of stone, and the Oil Age will end long before the world runs out of oil."*
>
> Ahmed Zaki Yamini, Saudi Arabian oil executive, former chief strategist for OPEC (1986)

There are two tests to determine economic substance. Economic substance is a doctrine in the tax law of the United States under which a transaction must have an economic purpose aside from reduction of tax liability in order to be considered valid. This doctrine is used to determine whether tax shelters, or strategies used to reduce tax liability, are considered "abusive" by the Internal Revenue Service. A transaction must have economic substance separate and distinct from the economic benefit achieved solely by tax reduction.[23]

- The transaction is rationally related to a useful nontax business purpose that is plausible in light of the taxpayer's conduct and economic situation.
- The transaction results in a meaningful and appreciable enhancement in the net economic position of the taxpayer (other than to reduce its tax).

In many cases, the lender/investor/project developer wants to make the payments at or below what the utility pricing is for the customer and will propose a financing structure to do so. Care must be taken to make sure that the payments are not construed as violating the economic substance guidance in that attempt. Tax attributes can be very high in some renewable energy transactions and the IRS can easily challenge the transaction claiming it does not have sufficient economic substance other than that of tax benefits. They will always ask whether the transaction had any practical economic effects other than the creation of income tax losses. The IRS will typically look at the transaction using a two prong test:

1. The subjective intent of the taxpayer entering into the transaction.
2. The objective economic substance of the transaction.

The IRS will look at the financing structure and require that the taxpayer must demonstrate that they were motivated by the opportunity to profit from the transaction, or at least had a valid business reason for entering into the transaction other than tax savings. In essence, the taxpayer must demonstrate that the transaction had a business purpose.

To ascertain that intent, the subjective portion of the guidance suggests considering:[24]

- whether a profit was even possible;
- whether the taxpayer had a nontax business reason to engage in the transaction;
- whether the taxpayer, or its advisors, considered or investigated the transaction, including market risk;
- whether the taxpayer really committed capital to the transaction;

- whether the entities involved in the transaction were entities separate and apart from the taxpayer and engaging in legitimate business before and after the transaction;
- whether all the purported steps were engaged in at arms-length with the parties doing what the parties intended to do; and
- whether the transaction was marketed as a tax shelter in which the purported tax benefits significantly exceeded the taxpayer's actual investment.

In order to satisfy the objective component, the taxpayer must demonstrate that the transaction resulted in a meaningful and appreciable enhancement in the net economic position of the taxpayer (other than to reduce its tax). One measure is whether there is a legitimate potential or realistic possibility for a pre-tax profit.[25] Since even seasoned and astute lenders or project developers occasionally lose money on a transaction, a transaction is not required to actually result in a profit in order for the taxpayer's transaction to have objective economic substance. The bottom line is that if the transaction was structured according similar to other transactions done in the industry by reasonable investors, it would in almost all cases pass muster and not be disqualified based on this component alone.[26]

Because of the high levels of tax attributes in renewable energy projects, there has been a concern that these projects might violate the historical economic substance doctrine used by the IRS. This concern has largely gone away after section 1409 of the Health Care and Education Reconciliation Act of 2010 was enacted. The Joint Committee of Taxation (JCT) looked at the issue and provided a technical explanation of section 1409 in footnotes. Those footnotes state that "if the realization of the tax benefits of a transaction is consistent with the congressional purpose or plan that the tax benefits were designed by Congress to effectuate, it is not intended that such tax benefits be disallowed."[27]

Some courts have recognized that a transaction has an economic objective if, in lieu of a reasonable possibility of profit, the taxpayer establishes that the transaction resulted in some other meaningful and appreciable enhancement in the net economic position of the taxpayer.[28] It is not enough for a transaction to have merely occurred. The transaction must have appreciably changed the taxpayer's net economic position before it will be given effect for tax purposes. One historical way the IRS used to determine if the transaction has no business substance other than that of a tax shelter is to uncover evidence to demonstrate that the taxpayer primarily planned the transaction for tax purposes. Such evidence had included:

- documents or other evidence that the transactions at issue were sold as tax shelters with limited consideration of the underlying economics of the transaction;
- evidence that the taxpayer, or its advisors, did not investigate the market risk prior to entering into the transaction;
- evidence that the independent parts making up the transaction were not entered into at arm's length, and
- evidence that a prudent investor would have or could have accomplished similar objectives using much simpler or more direct methods.

A direct source of such evidence regarding the taxpayer's contention of a nontax business purpose is written correspondence or other communication between the taxpayer and the promoter of a particular transaction, including, but of course not limited to, offering memoranda, letters identifying tax goals, and electronic messages. In-house communications at the offices of the taxpayer, the promoter, and any accommodating parties may also be useful. Indirect sources of evidence include correlations between tax benefits generated and tax benefits requested, and between the taxpayer's economic income and the tax benefits generated, particularly if it can be shown that the income to be sheltered was attributable to an unusual windfall, like the liquidation of stock options, or the sale of a business. Demonstrations of similarities of the nature and extent of tax benefits acquired by other clients of the promoter of the particular transaction under examination can be very important as well.

Bottom line is this: In appropriate cases, the IRS will use all of the tools at its disposal to combat abusive tax shelters, including the economic substance doctrine.[29]

Fair Market Value *(also see page 313)*

The fair market value of an asset is the price that an interested but not desperate buyer would be willing to pay and an interested but not desperate seller would be willing to accept on the open market assuming a reasonable period of time for an agreement to arise. Fair market value refers to the value which would be obtained in an arms-length transaction between an informed and willing buyer-user under no compulsion to buy and an informed and willing seller under no compulsion to sell. It also means the highest price, expressed in a dollar amount, that the property would bring, in an open and unrestricted market, between a willing buyer and a willing seller who are knowledgeable, informed, and prudent, and who are acting independently of each other.

Fair market value can often be determined by looking in an appraisers "bluebook" if the equipment value is shown there. One would usually need to know the date of manufacture, serial numbers, model numbers, condition of equipment, hours of use, etc. It is also often determined by looking at recent public auctions of the type of equipment in question. This is easy to do if the equipment has been around for a long time such as construction equipment, machine tools, medical systems, etc. It is not easy to do when trying to estimated future FMV on new technology like that often found in renewable energy projects.

Other times it is determined by each party selecting an appraiser of their choice, and then the two appraisers selecting a third appraiser to evaluate the value of the equipment. An average of the three appraisers results are then taken into consideration in determining the fair market value of the asset.

When fair market value is the issue, such value must be proved by a preponderance of the evidence. Although not required, an appraisal of the subject property is generally the best evidence to support value. It should be noted that an appraisal is not a letter of opinion that simply states the appraiser's opinion of the value of the subject property. Such opinion letters do not contain the data used by the appraiser and cannot be verified independently by the parties. An appraisal requires an examination of the three traditional approaches to value—the cost, income, and market approaches, if possible—and contains information on and analysis of the data relied on by the appraiser to form their opinion of value. Evidence of a recent sale of the equipment, recent sales of comparable equipment, or recent new costs of the subject equipment may be used. If an appraisal is relied on, testimony of the appraiser must be presented if the appraisal and opinion of value are to be given much weight.

Book value is an accounting term. Technically, it is simply the assets of the enterprise less its depreciated value, all at their values as stated on the books of the company. It's usually not an accurate measure of the real value of the asset. For that reason, it is seldom relevant.

Inception

Inception is defined as the date of either the agreement or the written commitment, if earlier. The commitment must be signed by both parties and very specifically set forth all of the provisions of the transaction. None of the principal provisions of the commitment can be left to further negotiations by the two parties.

> *"People do not want electricity or oil...but rather comfortable rooms, light, vehicular motion, food, tables, and other real things."*
>
> Amor Lovings, *Soft Energy Paths*, 1977, pp. 38-40

Noncancellable Term

The contract term for accounting and tax purposes is generally defined as the fixed non-cancellable term of the transaction, bargain renewal option periods, renewal periods subject to a nonrenewal penalty that reasonably assures extension, ordinary renewal periods during which the debt obligor guarantees the debt, ordinary renewal periods preceding a bargain purchase option and the lender/project developer-forced renewal periods. If a transaction is cancellable 1) only upon the occurrence of some remote contingency, 2) only with the permissions of the lender/investor/project developer, 3) only if the debt obligor enters into a new contract with the same lender/project developer, or 4) only upon payment by the debt obligor of a penalty in an amount such that continuation of the transaction appears, at inception, reasonably assured, is considered non-cancellable.

Safe Harbor Tax Treatment of Energy Systems

The partnership tax code, one of the most complex areas of the tax code, affects the majority of renewable energy financing deals done today. It presents many modeling choices that can have a profound impact on the transaction economics of the renewable energy project. There are three primary structures used for tax equity investments. They are:

1. **Partnership Flip Structure (Figure 5-4)**

This is the most frequently used since it is referenced in the Internal Revenue Service safe harbor leasing provisions and is explained in detail below. There are two phases in this structure. In the first phase, the tax equity investor is the primary project owner, retaining nearly all (99%) of the projects tax credit incentives and depreciation benefits. Then, after the flip, the primary ownership (95%) reverts back to the developer who receives most of the project's cash flows. There are important issues behind the economics of the partnership flip.

- Flip timing
- Discrepancy between the equity injection and cash flow split
- Equity contribution and syndication rate
- Debt

2. **Sale Leaseback Structure**

Under this structure, there is an initial sale of the asset by the developer, after which the tax equity investor becomes the project owner. The developer then leases the project from the investor, as the lessee, and the developer is charged with operating the project (and thus bears the operating expenses). At some point the lease terminates and the ownership can revert back to the developer given certain conditions. Issues that can influence the project economics are:

- Varying lease payments—required to meet the market economics mandated by the transaction
- Early buyout option—must meet certain IRS guidelines

3. **Inverted Lease Structure**

This is sometimes referred to as the 'lease pass-through' structure. It is almost the opposite of the sale leaseback in that the tax equity investor directs lease payments to the developer. The following issues are important for the financial modeling of the transaction using this method:

- Varying lease payments—required to meet the market economics mandated by the transaction
- Loss allocation
- Equity contribution and syndication rate
- Debt
- Developer equity
- Discrepancy of allocations

In October 2007, the IRS established safe harbor requirements for partnerships claiming IRC section 45 wind energy credits. It is widely believed that the same guidelines can be applied to all other renewable energy projects. The provisions apply to what is known as "partnership flip" structures. The partnership flip structure has now become an industry-recognized business model to finance the development of wind projects (and possibly other energy production facilities).

Tax equity in renewable energy projects is a complex undertaking. It is more complex than other policies for promoting renewables such as the 1603 Treasury grant or the feed-in tariff incentives that have become popular throughout Europe. It usually involves multiple parties including sponsors, developers, lending institutions and investors, with the switch of ownership midway through the projects lifecycle. This cannot be done without a complete understanding of the complex guidelines inherent in the U.S. revenue codes.

After the tax equity investor achieves its IRR, the allocations in the agreement "flip" such that nearly all of the income (loss), credits, and cash go to the developer and cash equity investors. This point in time is referred to as the "flip point," which is usually projected to occur approximately 10 years into the project—when the PTC period ends. This could occur sooner if the taxpayers elected the ITC in lieu of the PTC. Following the flip point, the developer typically has an option to purchase the tax equity investor's interest at fair market value.

In order to simplify the application of section 45[30] to partners and partnerships that own and produce electricity from qualified wind facilities, the IRS established safe harbor requirements under which it will respect the allocation of the section 45 wind energy production tax credits by partnerships in accordance with section 704(b).[31] The "Safe Harbor" (and therefore not subject to challenge by the IRS) is set forth in Revenue Procedure 2007-65. The Safe Harbor in section 4 of the revenue procedure applies to any partnership (the "Project Company") between a project developer (the "Developer") and one or more investors, as defined in section 4.01 (the "Investors"), with the Project Company owning and operating the project containing the qualified energy facilities ("Wind Farm" and for purposes of this definition the term does not include energy produced from such Wind Farm). In addition to the Project Company, the Developer, and the Investors, wind energy transactions typically involve lenders, land owners, a turbine supplier, a construction contractor, power purchasers, and a project operator. In order to qualify for the Safe Harbor, all of the requirements set forth in section 4 of the revenue procedure must be met.

Safe Harbor Section 4 (as defined in the IRC)

1) Investors Defined. Investors are partners in the Project Company whose investment return is reasonably anticipated to be derived from both § 45 credits and participation in operating cash flow.

2) Partners' Minimum Partnership Interest. The Developer must have a minimum one percent interest in each material item of partnership income, gain, loss, deduction and credit at all times during the existence of the Project Company. Each Investor must have, at all times during the period it owns a partnership interest in the Project Company, a minimum interest in each material item of partnership income and gain equal

Figure 5-4: General Flip Partnership Structure

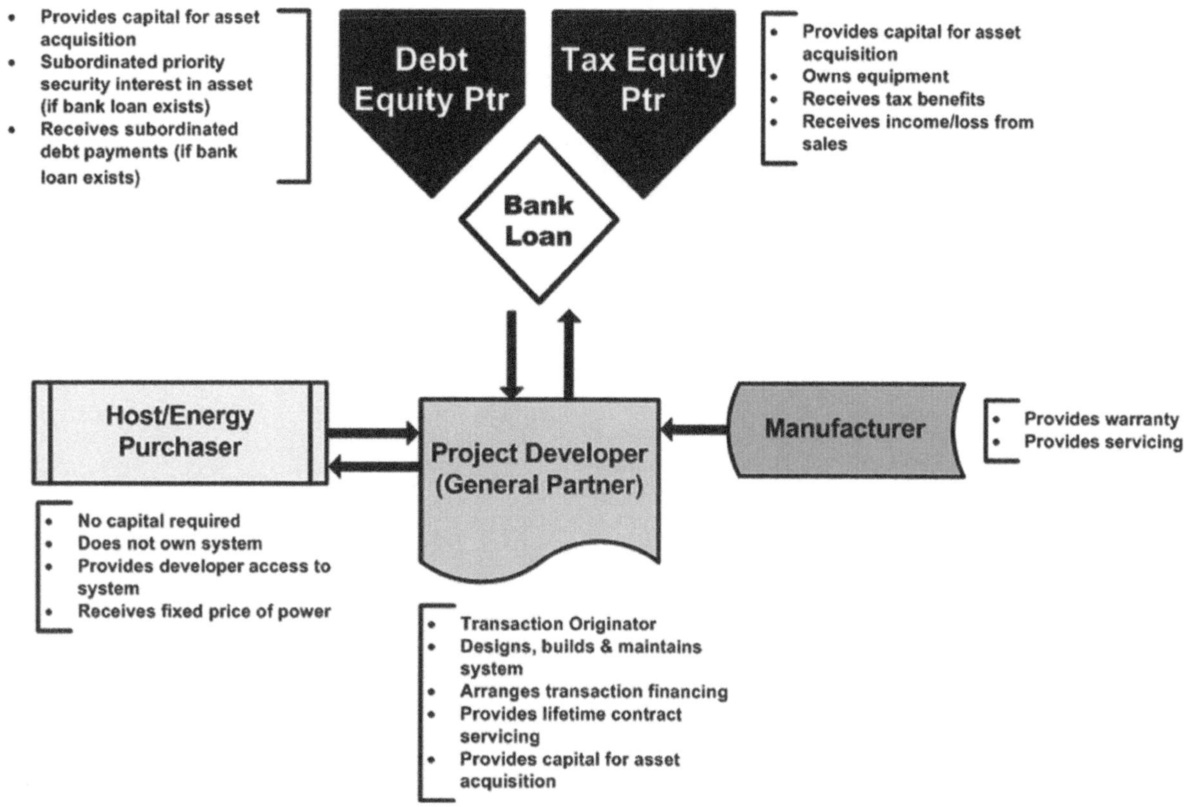

to 5 percent of the Investor's percentage interest in partnership income and gain for the taxable year for which the Investor's percentage share of income and gain will be the largest, as adjusted for sales, redemptions or dilution of its interest.

3) Investor's Minimum Unconditional Investment. On or before the later of the date the Wind Farm is placed in service or the date the Investor acquires its interest in the Project Company, the Investor must make a minimum unconditional investment in the Project Company (the "Investor Minimum Investment"). The Investor must maintain the Investor Minimum Investment throughout the duration of its ownership of its partnership interest in the Project Company, except that the Investor Minimum Investment can be reduced as a result of distributions of cash flow from the Project Company's operation of the Wind Farm or in connection with section 4.05. Contributions required to be made in the future will not be included in the Investor Minimum Investment until the contributions are actually made to the partnership. The Investor Minimum Investment must be equal to at least 20 percent of the sum of the fixed capital contributions plus reasonably anticipated contingent capital contributions required to be made by the Investor under the partnership agreement. The Investor must not be protected against loss of any portion of the Investor Minimum Investment through any arrangement, directly or indirectly, with the Developer, any other Investor, the turbine supplier or the power purchaser or any party related to the Developer, other Investors, turbine supplier or the power purchaser.

4) Contingent Consideration. At least 75 percent of the sum of the fixed capital contributions plus reasonably anticipated contingent capital contributions to be contributed by an Investor with respect to an interest in the Project Company must be fixed and determinable obligations that are not contingent in amount or certainty of payment.

5) Purchase Rights. Neither the Developer, the Investors nor any related parties may have a contractual right to purchase, at any time, the Wind Farm, any property included in the Wind Farm or an interest in the Project Company at a price less than its fair market value determined at the time of exercise of the contractual right to purchase, and provided further that the Developer (or any party related to the Developer) may not have a contractual right to purchase the Wind Farm or an interest in the Project Company earlier than 5 years after the qualified facility is first placed into service.

Any determination of the fair market value of the Wind Farm or an interest in the Project Company may take into account: (i) contracts or other arrangements creating rights or obligations (excluding power purchase agreements) only if such contracts or other arrangements creating rights or obligations are entered into in the ordinary course of the Wind Farm's business and are negotiated at arm's length with parties not related to the Project Company or Investors; and (ii) any power purchase contract only if such contract is entered into with parties not related to (within the meaning of § 45(e)(4)) to the Project Company.

6) Sale Rights. The Project Company may not have a contractual right to cause any party to purchase the Wind Farm or any property included in the Wind Farm, excluding electricity, from the Project Company. An Investor may not have a contractual right to cause any party to purchase its partnership interest in the Project Company.

7) Guarantees and Loans. No person may guarantee or otherwise insure the Investor the right to any allocation of the credit under § 45.

The Project Company must bear the risk that the available wind resource is not as great as anticipated or projected. The Developer, the turbine supplier, or any power purchaser may not provide a guarantee that the wind resource will be available at a certain level. A guarantee regarding wind resource availability may be provided by a third party not related to the Developer, the turbine supplier, any power purchaser, or any other project participant if the Project Company or an Investor directly pays the cost of or premium for such guarantee. For example, a weather derivative contract between the Project Company and an unrelated third party (such as an insurance company) is an acceptable guarantee.

A long-term power purchase agreement entered into between the Project Company and a party not related to the Project Company under § 45(e)(4) does not constitute a guarantee. However, a "Take or Pay" contract between related parties would constitute a guarantee and is not permissible. Any sale of electricity between related persons as defined in § 45(e)(4) will not qualify for the credit under § 45.

The Developer (or a party related to the Developer) may not lend any Investor the funds to acquire any part of the Investor's interest in the Project Company or guarantee any indebtedness incurred or created in connection with the acquisition of such Investor's interest in the Project Company.

8) Allocation of § 45 Production Tax Credits. The § 45 credit must be allocated in accordance with § 1.704-1(b)(4)(ii).

9) Separate Activity for Purposes of § 469. For purposes of the passive activity loss rules, under § 1.469-4(d)(4) each qualified facility will be treated as a separate activity for purposes of § 469 and that activity may not be grouped with any other activity, except other qualified wind facilities. Thus, generally, only entities not subject to § 469, and not individuals, will be able to offset non-project income with credits received as a passive investor in a partnership.

10) Definition of Related Party. Except as otherwise provided, for purposes of this revenue procedure parties are related if they bear a relationship to each other that is specified in § 267(b) or 707(b)(1).

This ruling and set of guidelines have had a huge impact on putting together energy projects in the U.S. They have made what was once thought to be a violation of IRS rules by partnerships to be accepted as long as all items in section 4 of the code have been met. Many historical renewable energy partnership structures were not set up using these guidelines.

During the first 5-7 years of a project investment, the limited partners get 99% of the investment tax credit, production tax credit, depreciation, operating losses (since the tax deductible items normally exceed the transaction revenue during the early years of the contract), etc. and the general partner only receives 1%. Then, the partnership revenue sharing will be able to change to the general partner receiving 95% of the revenue gains or losses (generally going positive after the 5-10 year initial partnership term) and the limited partners receiving 5% of the revenue gains or losses.

Revenue Procedure 2007-65 set forth the following example as a valid wind energy limited liability company classified as a partnership for federal tax purposes:

Example 1. The following is an example of a valid wind energy limited liability company that is classified as a partnership for federal tax purposes. Developer is a C corporation that owns and manages wind-based generation projects. Project Company is a limited liability company (LLC) that has been formed by Developer to develop, own and manage a renewable energy project that utilizes wind turbines to produce electricity from wind (the Project). Investor is a C corporation that invests in renewable energy projects primarily to benefit from § 45 credits. Developer has caused LLC to enter into, or has assigned to LLC, a number a contracts or agreements relating to the development of the Project.

Developer will own all of LLC during construction of the Project. Construction of the Project will be financed with $100x of construction financing. When construction of the Project is substantially complete, pursuant to a Membership Interest Purchase and Equity Capital Contribution Agreement, (1) Developer will contribute $15x to LLC, and (2) Investor will acquire newly issued membership interests from LLC in exchange for an upfront cash capital contribution in the amount of $10x which is 20% of Investor's total agreed capital contributions to LLC of $50x. Developer, as the developer of the Project, has not provided a guarantee to LLC or Investor regarding the level of the available wind resource at the Project or the amount of § 45 credits.

Pursuant to the limited liability company operating agreement (the "Operating Agreement"), Developer will have the right to manage LLC, subject to the right of Investor to consent to certain activities. Below is a chart and explanation that generally describes the distribution and allocation provisions applicable to Developer and Investor over various time periods.

Example 2. The facts are the same as in Example 1, except Investor is initially allocated 99.5% of LLC's gross income or loss and § 45 credits. Under these facts, the wind energy limited liability company's classification as a valid partnership would be closely scrutinized by the Service. Likewise, if any other provision of this safe harbor is not followed for any wind energy partnerships, the Service will closely scrutinize the validity of such purported partnerships.

In December 2007, the IRS issued further clarification of the guidelines with this statement:

	Developer			Investor	
Period	Cash	Gross Income/Loss and Section 45 Credits	Period	Cash	Gross Income/Loss and Section 45 Credits
Period 1 (inceptio n)	100%	1%	Period 1 (inception)	0%	99%
Period 2	0%	1%	Period 2	100%	99%
Period 3	95%	95%	Period 3	5%	5%

During Period 1, 99% of LLC's gross income or loss and the § 45 credits will be allocated to Investor, and 100% of LLC's cash flows will be distributed to Developer. Period 1 will continue until the earlier of (i) such time that Developer has received aggregate cash distributions in an amount equal to the aggregate contributions made by Developer (i.e., $15x) and (ii) a fixed outside date. Period 1 is expected to last four to six years. When Period 1 ends, Period 2 will begin.

During Period 2, 99% of LLC's gross income or loss and the § 45 credits will be allocated to, and 100% of LLC's cash flows will be distributed to Investor. Period 2 will continue until Investor has achieved an agreed after-tax internal rate of return (the "Flip Point"). Although the Flip Point might occur sooner, it is expected that the Flip Point will not occur until after the end of year 10 of the Project, at which time § 45 credits will no longer be available for the production and sale of electricity from the Project. Period 2 is expected to last four to six years. When Period 2 ends, Period 3 will begin. Moreover, upon the tenth anniversary of Investor's investment, Developer will have the option to purchase Investor's interest for its then-appraised fair market value. Assuming that option is not exercised, during Period 3, 5% of LLC's gross income or loss and § 45 credits will be allocated to, and 5% of LLC's cash flows will be distributed to, Investor; and 95% of LLC's gross income or loss and § 45 credits will be allocated to, and 95% of LLC's cash flows will be distributed to, Developer. Period 3 will continue for the remaining life of the Project.

> *This announcement revises Revenue Procedure 2007-65, 2007-45 I.R.B. 967, by adding the following language to Section 3: "The requirements set forth in this revenue procedure that must be satisfied in order to qualify for the Safe Harbor, however, are not intended to provide substantive rules and are not to be used as audit guidelines," and replacing "will not challenge" with "will respect" in Section 6.*

Then in 2009, the IRS issued a final clarification of the guidelines with this statement:

> *This announcement also replaces the following language from section 4.05:*
>
> "Neither the Developer, the Investors nor any related parties may have a contractual right to purchase, at any time, the Wind Farm, any property included in the Wind Farm or an interest in the Project Company at a price less than its fair market value determined at the time of exercise of the contractual right to purchase, and provided further that the Developer (or any party related to the Developer) may not have a contractual right to purchase the Wind Farm or an interest in the Project Company earlier than 5 years after the qualified facility is first placed into service," *with "The Developer, the Investor, or any related party may only have a contractual right to purchase the Wind Farm, any property included in the Wind Farm, or an interest*

in the Project Company (the Property) that satisfies the requirements of this section 4.05. The contractual right must be negotiated for valid non-tax business reasons at arm's length by parties with material adverse interests. The purchase price for the Property must either be a price that is not less than the fair market value of the Property determined at the time of exercise or, if the purchase price is determined prior to exercise, a price that the parties reasonably believe, based on all facts and circumstances at the time the price is determined, will not be less than the fair market value of the Property at the time the right may be exercised. Finally, the Developer (or any party related to the Developer) may not have a contractual right to purchase the Property earlier than 5 years after the qualified facility is first placed in service."

The revisions to the safe harbor provisions made by Announcement 2009-69 clarify that the failure to meet all of the safe harbor requirements will not subject the Project Company to close scrutiny and will make it easier to meet these requirements by relaxing the fair market value "determined at the time of exercise" rule. As a result, Announcement 2009-69 represents a significant and favorable development to the renewable industry. Moreover, developers of and investors in other renewable energy projects may also take some comfort in the recent announcement as they too often rely on Revenue Procedure 2007-65 when structuring their projects.

The Announcement replaces the requirement in section 4.05 of the Revenue Procedure that any purchase option be available only at fair market value determined at the time of exercise. Rather, the Announcement now provides that a purchase option in favor of the developer, the investors, and any related parties is permissible, provided (i) the option is "negotiated for valid non-tax business reasons at arm's length by parties with material adverse interests," and (ii) the option's purchase price either is a price that is not less than the fair market value of the property determined at the time of exercise or, if the purchase price is determined prior to exercise, a price that the parties reasonably believe, based on all facts and circumstances at the time the price is determined, will not be less than the fair market value of the Property at the time the right may be exercised.

This revision in the Announcement signals a major shift in the Service's approach to purchase options in renewable energy deals, allowing an option's purchase price to be fixed at the time of closing. This approach is consistent, however, with established case law in the leasing area.[32]

Lastly, the Announcement revises the statements in the Revenue Procedure relating to the application of the passive-activity limitations under section 469. As originally released, the Revenue Procedure suggested that, in the case of individual investors, any section 45 credits generated by a wind energy project would be available only to offset tax liability arising from that wind energy project and not with respect to tax liabilities arising from passive activities of the individual investor, generally. The Announcement renounces this position and specifically permits credits to offset non-project passive activity liabilities. The new language in section 4.09 of the Revenue Procedure now reads:

Generally, a taxpayer subject to § 469 may utilize passive activity credits from qualified wind facilities only to the extent of their tax liability allocable to passive activities, whether from qualified wind facilities or other sources.

Even if the Revenue Procedure does not apply, i.e., by reason of not meeting any other requirement of the guidance, the revised section 469 language appears consistent with the understood application of section 469 in the context of section 45 tax credits.[33]

The partnership looks at three principal items—project cost, revenue sources and expense or cost centers. These are then put into a cash flow analysis and based on the initial capital cost of the assets (also referred to as "Project Cost") a return is calculated based on when the cash outflows and revenue inflows occur over the project finance term. Exactly when those cash flows occur over the project life, and the tax effect of those multiple cash flows periods, provide the return to the project LLC.

Tax Equity Partner

The single largest benefit to the Tax Equity Partner is the Investment Tax Credit (ITC) or Production Tax Credit (PTC), followed closely by the depreciation deductions. Additionally, for tax year 2011, there were very large tax benefits to be derived from the expensing of the entire energy asset in 2011. This changed back to 50% expensing of the assets in 2012. At its peak in 2007, tax equity financing represented a $6 billion market. Yet, at other times, tax equity availability has been insufficient to support growth in the renewable energy sector and the Treasury cash grant has played a more significant role.

The ITC reduces federal income taxes for qualified tax-paying owners based on the capital investment of the renewable energy project. The ITC is set at 30%

of qualified capital expenditures and was recently extended through December 31, 2016 (WRI 2008; H.R. 2008, Section. 103). While the commercial ITC has never had a maximum amount, the 30% residential tax credit was capped at $2,000 until October 2008 when Congress removed the cap beginning January 2009. Additionally, only a limited number of entities can take full advantage of the 30% credit. Because the entities must pay federal taxes, not-for-profit businesses, state and federal government agencies, and all other businesses that do not have taxable profits are ineligible. The measure of taxes paid, in combination with the effective tax rate, serves as a high-level gauge for a tax equity investor's appetite for reducing their tax liabilities. The higher the effective tax rate, the greater the benefits achieved via tax equity investing. This could be true even more if the U.S. congress moves forward with increasing the tax rates for corporations as has been proposed by the current administration.

As described above, there are three primary structures used for the tax equity investment. They are the partnership flip, sale leaseback and inverted lease (or 'lease pass-through'). The most common used is the partnership flip structure.

There are a number of significant Tax Equity Partners in today's renewable energy market. Any corporate entity with a tax obligation could be considered a Tax Equity Partner in a renewable energy Flip Partnership LLP.[34] Many are brought to the portfolio through securities dealers that specialize in the placement of tax attributes to their corporate clients who are active in the purchase of tax credits (such as affordable housing tax credits, solar tax credits, etc.). The following banks and other entities have historically been active in the tax equity partner market for eligible renewable energy projects:

- Bank of America
- Credit Suisse
- JP Morgan
- Union Bank
- Key Bank
- Northern Trust
- PNC
- U.S. Bank
- Citibank
- GE EFS
- Morgan Stanley
- Google
- MetLife
- PG&E
- Sun Trust
- Wells Fargo

Only large institutional corporate entities with significant tax obligations can effectively utilize the large amounts of tax attributes available under a renewable energy project investment program. There are no legal restrictions to prevent the participation of non-financial entities. As an example, in recent year, utilities in California, as well as Google, have undertaken significant tax equity investments in renewable energy projects.

Barriers to non-institutional investors (primarily "passive-loss" and "at-risk" rules) make it challenging for individuals to take the ITC directly on their personal income taxes and therefore are not generally active. High net-worth individuals with large tax equity appetites are also generally excluded from forming or contributing to tax equity partnerships because of those rules.

As financial markets have become more stable after the financial crisis of 2008, and banks' taxable incomes have increased, the tax equity appetite of the institutional investors has improved, and more entities are coming back into the tax equity marketplace. The supply-demand imbalance and availability of tax equity players could be a constraint for the U.S. renewable energy sector in future years. Yet this could be mitigated as new players emerge for reasons such as an increase in effective marginal tax rates, corporate sustainability requirements, general business strategic plans, economics and even mandated environmental compliance mandates. Debt leverage is also becoming more available and the performance of tax equity projects is often enhanced with debt. The debt can come in the form of lending to the project itself, or, in the case of "back-leverage," to the developer involved in the energy project.

The combination of the energy ITC and the immediate expensing of the purchased assets in the first year (after reducing the tax basis by 50% of the ITC taken) create a very large tax benefit for the Tax Equity Partner immediately upon the acquisition of the assets. The example below is based on a $1 million cost of an energy production system (assuming a 35% federal tax rate) without considering the state tax value benefit:

ITC (or 1603 grant in lieu of ITC)—an after-tax benefit (equivalent to a pre-tax deduction of $461,538 at 35% tax rate)	$300,000
Immediate expensing of $850,000 tax basis (50% bonus election pre-tax) ($850,000 with the 100% bonus election!)	$510,000
Total pre-tax value of tax attributes at inception of energy project	$971,538

The tax benefits of ownership to the tax equity partner are received immediately when the assets are purchased. It is not necessary to wait until the filing of the following year's tax year to receive the benefits.

Given the strong language in the Revenue Procedure noting that the IRS will "closely scrutinize" flip projects that do not comply with the Safe Harbor provisions, stakeholders in all future projects, including those already in early stages of development, should take steps to make sure their partnership agreements meet all the Safe Harbor requirements. In summary, the following items would apply in any "safe harbor" partnership transaction to avoid challenges by the Internal Revenue Service and to provide tax certainty:

Minimum Partnership Interests

- The developer must have at least a 1% interest in all material partnership items
- Investor must have an interest in all material partnership items equal to at least 5% of the investor's maximum interest

Minimum Investment

- Investor must have invested at all times at least 20% of its total capital contributions
- At least 75% of contributions must be fixed
- Investor may not be protected against loss by developer or other persons related to the energy project
- Developer may not lend investor funds to invest or guarantee a loan to the investor

Purchase and Sale Rights

- Neither developer nor investor may have a right to purchase the project, any project assets or any interest in the project company at less than fair market value
- Developer many not have a right to purchase the project at any time earlier than 5 years after it is placed in service
- Neither the developer nor the project company may have any put rights

Guarantees and Loans

- No person may guarantee the investor the right to any allocation of section 45 credits
- The project company must bear the risk that the available renewable energy resources are not as great as anticipated or projected
- Third-party hedges (e.g., weather derivatives) are allowed
- Take or Pay contracts are not allowed

704(b) Allocation Rules

- Section 45 credits must be allocated in accordance with Treasury Regulation § 1.704-1(b)(4)(ii)
- This means production tax credits (and by inference, investment tax credits if the taxpayer chooses that election) must be allocated in the same manner as gross receipts from sales of electricity

Table 5-20 is an example of the capital accounts of a partnership prior to application of the Section 45 Credits (first two years).

As the various tax equity structures are evaluated, the following will be true for all:[35]

- Tax equity works. Returns can be attractive for both developers and investors.
- Size matters. Small projects will have a very difficult time finding tax investors who are interested in the transaction. The complexity of the tax code and variety of choices require more time to model and analyze than most small deal teams can afford (including closing costs).
- The investor and developer return profiles will differ. There are significantly different cash flows that lead to different rates of return.
- NPV and IRR analyses yield different answers to the optimization question.
- If there is a choice between ITC and PTC then choice will come down to the three 'P's—performance, perspective, and priorities.
- Structures outside of the partnership flip can accommodate other preferences.
- Structure selection may evolve into a tug of war between the two parties.
- Numbers don't tell the entire story.

The final structure selection may not be the ideal structure from the perspective of either the developer or the investor, but *it is the structure that gets the deal done.*[36]

Debt vs. Equity

There is always a continuing debate on whether a renewable energy project should take the debt route to finance a project or to walk down the tax equity route. Debt (institutional or private), managed well can be an effective vehicle to finance any project provided the tax attributes flow to the party as needed.

Debt is borrowing money from an outside source with the promise to return the principal, in addition to an agreed-upon level of interest.[37] Although the term tends to have a negative connotation, many startup developers turn to debt to finance the energy project to the extent possible. In fact, even the healthiest of corporate

Table 5-20: IRS Capital Accounts Example

IRS Section 704(B) Capital Accounts—Example			
Partnership Capital Account ($)	Initial Contribution	Year 1	Year 2
Beginning Capital Balance	100,000,000	100,000,000	75,200,000
Add: Additional Capital Contribution		-	-
Less: Cash Distributed to Partners		(8,800,000)	(9,000,000)
Subtotal (Before Current Year Allocations)		91,200,000	66,200,000
Taxable Income Allocation		(16,000,000)	(31,500,000)
Loss Reallocation		-	-
Total Taxable Income/Loss		(16,000,000)	(31,500,000)
Ending Tax Capital		**75,200,000**	**34,700,000**
Share of Recourse Debt		-	-
Share of Non-recourse Debt		31,400,000	30,500,000
Total Debt		**31,400,000**	**30,500,000**
Ending Tax Basis		**106,600,000**	**65,200,000**

balance sheet will include some level of debt. In finance, debt is also referred to as "leverage." The most popular source for debt financing is the bank, but debt can also be issued by a private company or individual.

<u>Advantages to Debt Financing</u>

- **Maintain Ownership.** When a developer or sponsor of a renewable energy project borrows from the bank or other lender, they are obligated to make the agreed-upon payments on time. But that is the end of the obligation to the lender. You can choose to run your business in any manner you choose without outside interference (although a lender may have restrictions on your ability to borrow additional funds through certain covenants you may be required to abide by as a condition to their lending you the money).
- **Tax Deduction.** This is a huge attraction for debt financing on renewable energy projects. In most cases, the principal (to the extent the proceeds are spent on allowable costs) and interest payments on a business loan are classified as a business expense, and thus can be deducted from the business income taxes. It helps to think of the government as a "partner" in the renewable energy project, with a 35 percent ownership stake (or whatever the businesses tax rate is). If you can cut the government out of the equation, then it's beneficial to your business.
- **Lower Interest Rate.** Furthermore, a renewable energy project asset owner should analyze the impact of tax deductions on the bank interest rate. If the bank is charging you 10 percent interest for your loan, and the government taxes you at 35 percent, then there is an advantage to taking a loan you can deduct. Take 10 percent (the loan rate) and multiply it by: 1-tax rate). In this case it is 10% times (1-35 percent), which equals which equals 6.5%. After your tax deduction for interest, you will be paying the equivalent of a 6.5 percent interest rate.

<u>Drawbacks to Debt Financing</u>

- **Repayment.** As mentioned above, your sole obligation to the lender is to make your payments. Unfortunately, even if your business fails, you will still have to make these payments. And if you are forced into bankruptcy, your lenders will have claim to repayment before any equity investors in the venture.
- **High Rates.** Even after calculating the discounted interest rate from your tax deductions, as explained above, you may still be faced with a high interest rate. Interest rates will vary with macroeconomic conditions, your credit history with the lender(s),

and your personal credit history (in most cases).

- **Impacts on Your Credit Rating**. It might seem attractive to keep bringing on debt when your project needs money (a practice known as "levering up"), but each loan will be noted on your credit rating. The more you borrow, the higher the risk to the lender, the higher interest rates you be forced to pay.
- **Cash and Collateral**. Even if you plan to use the loan proceeds to invest in the renewable energy assets, you will need to make sure the energy project will be generating sufficient cash flows by the time loan repayment starts. Also you will likely be asked to put up collateral on the loan that is above and beyond the underlying renewable energy project assets in case you default on the payments.

In many cases, there will likely be a combination of debt and equity financing in a renewable energy project. The question is: "What is the proper combination?" When deciding the right capital structure, both the realities of the market place plus the tax consequences will be employed. This is known as the debt/equity ratio. It is simply dividing the total debt amount of the project by your total equity put into the project either directly or through partners or investors. Everyone wants to see this number to get an accurate idea of how financially viable the project will be. The final consideration in this mix is 1) will the money be at a fixed or variable cost, and 2) what is expected life of the underlying assets, and 3) what is the expected net cash flows (after expenses) during the full expected life of the underlying capital assets?

FUTURE OF FINANCIAL REPORTING AND STANDARDS

Companies in emerging industries like renewable energy probably believe they have enough to worry about without dealing with the convergence of U.S. and international accounting standards. They couldn't be more challenged, however. The simple reasons behind convergence are to get the players in the world economy on the same page and avoid another financial meltdown like we saw in 2007-08. Because U.S. GAAP (Generally Accepted Accounting Principles) is significantly different than European accounting, FASB has been working with IASB to join the two accounting methods.

Now is the time for any renewable energy project creditor or developer to consider the implications of the International Accounting Standards Board (IASB, *www.iasb.org*) regarding the use of International Financial Reporting Standards (IFRS) that are soon to be adopted by the tax and accounting industry as well as the Securities and Exchange Commission (SEC). The United States has long worked with the Financial Accounting Standards Board (FASB), the AICPA (American Institute of Certified Public Accountants), and other trade groups in implementing their guidance's and promulgation's. Now that all countries are rapidly adopted international standards rather than just standards in the U.S., major consideration must be given to what these standards are, how they will affect the financial reporting of the future, and most importantly, how they will affect the financial analysis of renewable energy and energy efficiency projects. Although not all companies are publically regulated, it is best to adhere to the new standards as they are rolled out and adopted by AICPA, the SEC and others. If passed, these guidelines would significantly alter the way energy financing transactions are reported on financial balance sheets and could reduce the benefits of certain type of financing structures—including PPAs.

The IFRS is providing a single set of high-quality accounting standards that will play a pivotal role in investor protection and the efficiency and effectiveness of capital formation and allocation. As capital markets have become increasingly global, U.S. investors have a corresponding increase in international investment opportunities. As proposed, the IFRS will go into full effect in 2014 or 2015 although earlier adoption of the standards is advised by the SEC and others. This means converting (where appropriate) current financial reporting standards and formats to the new IFRS guidelines as soon as possible. Approximately 113 countries around the world currently require or permit IFRS reporting for domestic, listed public companies.[38]

Historically, lease accounting has been the best example for accounting bright lines and rules-based guidelines. The exposure draft (ED) creates a new accounting model for both lessees and lessors and eliminates entirely the concept of operating leases. If finalized, the ED would unite the FASB's and IASB's accounting for lease contracts in most of the significant areas. Essentially, all outstanding leases as of the date of initial application would be subject to the new lease accounting model—*there would be no grandfathering of existing leases*. This could also apply to other contractual obligations such as PPAs, EPAs and other similar energy contract instruments.

The two boards have been debating the accounting

guidelines being used since 2006. Many thought that the existing guidelines relied too heavily on bright lines and that the rules offered entities the opportunity to structure arrangements to get a desired accounting effect. This often resulted in economically similar transactions being accounted for differently.

The latest change the ED proposes is bringing all lease transaction onto balance sheets. Currently there is a difference between an operating lease and a capital lease. In an operating lease, the lessee has the right to use an asset and not assume the responsibility of ownership. Because of this lack of responsibility, the lessee does not have to put the asset on its balance sheet. The proposed rules would make all companies entering leases (or other energy agreements) record these transactions as assets and liabilities. Therefore, both parties in a lease or sale leaseback would have the energy system recorded on their balance sheets.

> *"This curious faith is predicated on the notion that we will soon develop unlimited new sources of energy: domestic oil fields, shale oil, gasified coal, nuclear power, solar energy, and so on. This is fantastical because the basic cause of the energy crisis is no scarcity: it is moral ignorance and weakness of character. We don't know how to use energy or what to use it for. And we cannot restrain ourselves. Our time is characterized as much by the abuse and waste of human energy as it is by the abuse and waste of fossil fuel energy."*
>
> Wendell Berry, author

Another significant proposed change redefines what constitutes a lease transaction; in particular, the difference between a lease and a service contract. This is important because PPAs are currently treated as service contracts. In most cases, a normal commercial PPA with the vast majority of energy fed to the host would be classified as leases. PPAs treated as leases, would be reported on a company's balance sheet, removing one of its major incentives for hosts—buying the energy produced by the project and outsourcing the risk of owning a renewable energy system.

One of the most significant areas that renewable energy project parties need to be concerned with is in the realm of revenue recognition. Revenue is an important number to users of financial statements in assessing a company's performance and prospects. However, revenue recognition requirements in US generally accepted accounting principles (GAAP) differ from those in International Financial Reporting Standards (IFRSs) and both are considered in need of improvement. The requirements in US GAAP comprise numerous standards—many are industry specific and some can produce conflicting results for economically similar transactions. This includes the subject of emissions inventory of a creditor or developer (including GHG and criteria pollutants). Although IFRSs contain fewer standards on revenue recognition, its two main standards have different principles and can be difficult to understand and apply beyond simple transactions.

The boards' objective is to improve the existing guidance in both IFRSs and US GAAP by developing a single revenue model that can be applied consistently regardless of industry. Applying the underlying principle proposed by the boards, a company would recognize revenue when it satisfies a performance obligation by transferring goods and services to a customer as contractually agreed. That principle is similar to many existing requirements and the boards expect that many transactions would remain unaffected by the proposals. However, clarifying that principle and applying it consistently to all contracts with customers would improve the comparability and understandability of revenue for users of financial statements.

Revenue recognition issues go beyond the financial statements and also impact the tax treatment of emissions components—a key ingredient in all renewable energy project transactions. Currently, there are no clearly defined methods established for either accounting or tax treatment (including state issues). Emissions trading schemes are designed to achieve a reduction of greenhouse gases through the use of tradable emission permits. The Board and the FASB are conducting a joint project to develop comprehensive guidance on the accounting for emissions trading schemes.

A list of some of the new standards currently under development that will affect energy efficiency and renewable energy projects worldwide are:

- Emissions trading schemes—affecting environmental components of the project
- Fair value measurement guidance (and inventory)—affecting the capitalized cost of the project and any measureable increase or decrease in the underlying asset's value of the term of the transaction
- Common control transactions and consolidation—affecting subsidiaries and related parties
- Financial statement presentation—particularly important to the debtor

- Government grants—could affect accounting and tax treatments of rebates and incentives
- Income taxes—reduce the differences between IAS 12 Income Taxes and the US standard, SFAS 109 Accounting for Income Taxes, and related US GAAP
- Leases—in all respects and types and is expected to result in a fundamental change in accounting for leases
- Liabilities—provides guidance on recognizing, measuring and disclosing liabilities that are not within the scope of other Standards
- Management commentary—a type of narrative report
- Revenue recognition—the new standard will replace the existing standards on revenue recognition
- Joint ventures—will affect both accounting and tax treatment issues
- Financial instruments—to clarify and enhance disclosures about fair value measurements and the liquidity risk of financial instruments
- Intangible assets (excluding goodwill)—recognition, measurement and disclosure or disclosure-only

An additional proposed change includes requiring more estimations as to the size of the asset and liability, estimations that often increase the dollar amount that will be showing up on the balance sheet. Currently, the contract's minimum requirements are used for sizing these numbers. For example, if a lease is written to be for 10 years, with two additional 5-year options to extend the lease term, then the lease is recorded as being 10 years long. However, the new rules would make companies:

- Estimate whether they will extend the lease and for how long;
- Estimate how much contingent rental payments will be accrued;
- Estimate what the residual value of the asset will be; and
- Estimate their discount rate.

The IASB and the FASB tentatively decided that the lease term should be defined, for both lessees and lessors, as follows:

"The lease term is the non-cancellable period for which the lessee has contracted with the lessor to lease the underlying asset, together with any options to extend or terminate the lease when there is a significant economic incentive for an entity to exercise an option to extend the lease, or for an entity not to exercise an option to terminate the lease."

Therefore, a company would now have to determine whether it plans on extending the lease at *inception*, what they expect contingent payments to be for the life of the lease, what the value of the asset will be at the end of the lease, and what the proper discount rate is for the transaction (and what it is based on). These decisions and their reasoning must be recorded in companies' financial statements, which should (theoretically) shed more light on a company's thought process and expectation for these transactions. However, it will also increase the recorded liability for the lease on a balance sheet and will force more judgment in calculating what those numbers will be.

Changes for Lessees

- Lessees will recognize a "right-of-use" asset and a liability for their obligation to make lease payments for all leases. "Off-balance sheet" leases and the concept of "lease classification" in the current accounting model will not exist for lessees.
- For leases previously classified as operating leases, rent expense will be replaced with amortization expense and interest expense. Amortization of the right-of-use asset will generally be on a straight line basis. However, interest expense will be front-end loaded.
- Under an expected-outcome approach, the lessee recognizes contingent rentals and residual value guarantees as part of the lease liability. The lessee bases its inclusion of rentals for renewal periods in the lease liability on the longest possible term that is *more likely than not to occur*.
- Unlike the current lease accounting model, the new model requires an assessment of whether there are new facts and circumstances that would significantly change the lessee's estimate of contingent rents and renewal periods as of each reporting period.
- The identification of non-lease components (e.g., maintenance costs in certain arrangements) will become more important under the new model.

- Total lease-related expense will be front-end loaded, unlike current operating lease treatment. Rising asset prices, or a lessee entering into an increased number of new leases, could result in net income remaining lower than the amount that would be achieved under current operating lease accounting—even as old leases expire.
- Because rental expense is not recorded under the new model, EBITDA will be higher than it is under current operating lease accounting.
- Lease payments will be treated as financing cash outflows in the statement of cash flows. Under current U.S. GAAP, operating lease rent payments are treated as an operating cash flow.

Changes for Lessors

- The proposed new accounting standard includes two accounting models for lessors. A lessor that retains exposure to significant risks or benefits associated with the underlying asset would apply the "performance obligation" approach. Otherwise, the lessor would apply the "derecognition" approach.
- Under the performance obligation approach, the leased asset remains on the lessor's books. The lessor records (1) a receivable for the expected lease payments, and (2) a corresponding performance obligation liability (essentially, deferred revenue).
- Under the derecognition approach, a portion of the leased asset is removed from the lessor's books. The lessor records (1) a receivable (and income) for the expected lease payments and (2) a residual asset representing the right to the underlying asset at the end of the lease term. Expense would be recognized for the portion of the leased asset that is removed from the lessor's books. Income and expense may be presented net depending on the lessor's business model.
- Under current accounting rules, the lessor takes the residual into income over the lease term. Under the proposed rules, the residual would not be recognized as income until realized.

Possible Impacts

Negative impacts of the proposed changes are abundant and include:

- A definite increase in accounting costs over the life of the lease, making lease transactions (and possibly energy service type contracts) more expensive.
- There may also be an increase in state and local taxes that are partially based on financial statements. Federal tax practices will remain unchanged. Therefore, there will be no additional federal taxes incurred, at least conceptually.
- Potential for more confusion or errors because the tax books will be even more different from the accounting books—at least for the first several accounting periods. The new model will result in additional temporary differences for income tax accounting purposes. In addition, state and local taxes will be affected when the computation (or impact) of taxes is based on U.S. GAAP amounts.
- It will more difficult for parties wishing to acquire a company or do a merger due to more assets and liabilities on a company's balance sheet.
- Companies may be perceived as having higher leverage. This has the potential to make debt more expensive.
- Debt/equity ratio will be higher due to an increase in total debt on the balance sheet. This could cause a problem for companies who have signed debt covenants and they will likely have to renegotiate them with their existing lenders.
- Return on equity will be lower due to a decrease in net income from higher amortization and interest expense.
- EBITDA (Earnings Before Interest, Taxes, Depreciation and Amortization) for lessees will be higher due to lease payments being treated as an interest expense rather than a rent expense.
- Expense recognition would be front-loaded because lease payments would be recognized the same way as interest expense (more interest at the start of the loan than at the end) rather than the straight-line expense recognition currently associated with most operating leases. This will have an effect on net income and the perception of whether a lease is economical in the earlier years of a transaction. This is irrespective of actual cash flows such as a PPA providing lower monthly payments that what is currently paid to a utility.
- Accounting systems will most likely need to be enhanced or updated to address the new standard—lease contract management systems will need to be more closely integrated with lease accounting systems. This will have a special impact on lessors

who will likely need to dramatically update their current asset management computer systems.

Scope

The only exceptions to the new proposed leasing guidelines are the assets clearly classified as "intangibles." This would include:

1. Leases for the right to explore for or use minerals, oils, natural gas, and similar non-regnerative resources.
2. Leases of biological assets, including timber.

Short-term leases will be treated differently than other leases of tangible personal property. A short-term lease is a lease that has a possible term of 12 months or less, including any options to renew. The parties will not be required to recognize lease assets or lease liabilities and thus recognize lease payments in profit or loss as rental income or expense on a straight-line basis over the lease term. The lessee or lessor would no longer make the decision on a lease-by-lease basis. Rather, they would make an accounting policy election on the basis of asset class. The ED (exposure draft) requires the disclosure of rental expense associated with short-term leases in each reporting period.

Specifications

The ED includes conditions for use in determining whether an arrangement contains a lease (e.g., power purchase agreements, supply contracts, take-or-pay contracts). If PPAs are treated like a lease, this could cause problems for existing contract holders and deter potential customers from entering new contracts—further adding costs and complexity. This would negate two of the PPA's most important value propositions by diminishing cost savings and no longer having these transactions as an "off balance sheet" item on the financial statements. Most accounting firms confirm a normal commercial PPA with the vast majority of energy fed to the host would be classified as leases. If PPAs are treated as leases this may prevent non-tax paying entities from being able to do third-party financing. Also, current federal law prohibits the use of the investment tax credit (ITC) when the renewable energy system is leased and a party to that lease is not allowed to claim the benefit, such as a government entity. Hence, PPA providers would not be able to claim the ITC on a transaction. Interestingly, the IRS has given guidance that the 1603 grant program would not follow this rule. Therefore, if the 1603 grant program is not extended in 2012 and beyond, it would be another reason for government entities and other non-taxpaying entities to not enter into PPA transactions on renewable energy systems.

> *"I know what I don't know. To this day I don't know technology, and I don't know finance or accounting."*
>
> Bernie Ebbers, Canadian Businessman

Additionally, the guidance requires lease accounting treatment if an arrangement conveys the right to *control the use of a specific asset.*[39] Many commentators on the ED expressed concern that this definition of a lease was too broad and that many service arrangements would be within the scope of the proposed lease guidance. The boards decided that the concept of control will be similar to that in the proposed revenue recognition project—that is, a contract would convey the right to control the use of a specified asset if the *customer has the ability to direct the use, and receive benefits from use, of that asset.*

An arrangement that conveys a *right to control the use of the underlying asset* is the case if any of the following conditions are met:

I. The purchaser in the arrangement has the ability or right to operate the asset or direct others to operate the asset (while obtaining more than an insignificant amount of the output of the asset).

II. The purchaser has the ability or right to control physical access to the asset (while obtaining more than an insignificant amount of the output of the asset).

III. There is only a remote possibility that parties other than the purchaser will take more than an insignificant amount of the output of the asset and the price that the purchaser will pay is neither fixed per unit of output nor equal to the current market price at the time of delivery.

To complicate the accounting further, special attention needs to be paid to contracts that contain *both* service and lease components. The proposed new accounting model requires that lease payments be allocated between the lease component (which would be accounted for under the lease standard) and the service component (which would be accounted for in accordance with other U.S. GAAP) when the service component is "distinct." The proposed accounting method states that the service component is distinct if the entity or another entity sells an identical or similar service separately or if the entity *could* sell the underlying service separately because it has a distinct function and a distinct profit margin. If the service component is distinct from the lease component, the entity will allocate payments between the service and lease components in accordance with the principles in the joint project on revenue recognition, *Revenue From Contracts With Customers*. However, if the lessee or lessor is unable to allocate the payments, the entire contract is accounted for as a lease. If the service component is not distinct from the lease component, the entire contract is accounted for as a lease.

> *"What do oil company executives, vampires and NASA bureaucrats all have in common? They fear solar energy."*
>
> Michio Kaku, theoretical physicist, professor, author

Inception Versus Commencement

The ED had proposed that a lease arrangement be measured as of the lease inception date and then recognized at lease commencement. The boards have tentatively decided that initial measurement and recognition will both be as of the date of commencement of the lease rather than at lease inception.

Lease Term

The ED states that the lease term is the "longest possible term that is more likely than not to occur." Therefore, if the lease contract includes renewal options or early termination options, determining the lease term will require the lessee to estimate the "probability" of occurrence *for each possible term* (lease renewal options). The ED lists considerations for a lessee in assessing the probability of each possible term, including, but not limited to:

- Contractual factors such as termination penalties (a contractual requirement for the lessee to incur substantial costs to restore the asset before returning it to the lessor) or level of lease payments (e.g., bargain renewal rates).
- Non-contractual factors such as the existence of significant leasehold improvements. For example, the lessee has installed significant leasehold improvements that would still have economic value when the option becomes exercisable or the facility is in a geographically desirable location with no other viable locations. This could certainly be problematical in many renewable energy projects.
- Market rentals for comparable assets.
- Whether the underlying asset is specialized or is crucial to the lessee's operations.
- Past experience of the entity or the entity's intentions including common industry practice.

The boards decided to require reassessment of the lease term when the "relevant factors" change so significantly that a lessee would have, or no longer have, a significant economic incentive to renew.

Lessee Accounting

The proposed draft of the new accounting model requires a lessee to use an expected-outcome approach to determine the lease payments required during the term of the lease. The expected outcome approach is described in the ED as "the present value of the probability-weighted average of the cash flows for a reasonable number of outcomes." Wow—sounds like something only an international regulatory body could come up with. The proposal does state that not every possible outcome has to be considered (in other words, the lessee only needs to consider the outcomes that it believes are "reasonable").

The ED specifically states that when determining the present value of the lease payments, the lessee must include contingent rents, residual value guarantees, and expected payments under termination penalties between the lessee and lessor. This is a significant change from the current lease accounting model, in which contingent rents are generally excluded from the calculation of minimum lease payments regardless of their probability of occurring. Under the proposed accounting model, contingent rents are now required to be estimated and recorded at the commencement of the lease.

The ED does include an exception for contingent rentals that depend on an index or rate. The ED states that the lessee would use forward rates or indices to determine the expected lease payments if such rates or indices are readily available. If forward rates or indices are not readily available, the lessee would use the prevailing rates or indices. In other words, the ED would not require a lessee to estimate future consumer price indices or prime rates (if the lease payments change in response to those rates). A similar application in a PPA contract would be applicable if the annual energy escalators would be based on an index or other unknown rate such as future utility rates.

Although purchase options are considered as part of the analysis in the determination of whether a lease contract represents the purchase or sale of the underlying asset, under the proposed model if a contract is determined to be within the scope of the accounting guidance, the purchase option would only be accounted for when it is exercised. The exercise price would not be considered a lease payment but part of the cost of acquiring the underlying asset.

After the commencement of the lease, the lessee will record amortization expense by amortizing the right-of-use asset on a systematic basis to the end of the lease term or over the useful life of the underlying asset if shorter. The lessee will record interest expense on the outstanding obligation by using the interest method to recognize the obligation at amortized cost.

The ED requires a lessee to reassess the carrying amount of the obligation each reporting period "if facts or circumstances indicate that there would be a significant change in the liability since the previous report period." If there is a change to the lease terms as a result of the reassessment, the lessee would recognize it by adjusting the obligation to make rental payments and right-of-use asset. Changes to the contingent rents, termination penalties, and any residual value guaranty would be recorded in the income statement if the change arises from current or prior periods. All other changes would be recorded as an adjustment to the right-of-use asset and the obligation to make rental payments.

A lessee would not amend the discount rate for changes in the expected lease term or when estimate of contingent rentals or residual value guarantees change unless the contingent rentals are contingent on variable reference interest rates, in which case the lessee would need to revise the discount rate for changes in the reference interest rates and recognize those changes in the income statement.

Any payments made by the lessee (advance rentals as an example) before commencement date should be accounted for as prepayments for the right-of-use asset. These repayments would then be added to the right-of-use asset on the commencement date.

Lastly, there is the issue in many renewable energy projects and contracts of lease incentive payments. These items must also now be treated in the initial measurement of the right-of-use asset (i.e., receipts for the lessor in the form of incentive grants, etc. would reduce the right-of-use asset).

Lessor Accounting

The proposed draft accounting standards under the ED describes two accounting models for lessors (and by inference, PPA providers). A lessor determines which model to apply to a particular lease contract (chosen on each individual lease) by determining whether the lessor retains exposure to significant risks or benefits associated with the underlying asset. The exposure to significant risks or benefits could occur either during the expected term of the lease contract (e.g., because of significant contingent rentals during the lease term, options to extend the lease, options to terminate or material non-distinct services provided under the lease contract) or after the term of the lease contract (e.g., when the lease term is not significant relative to the remaining useful life of the asset or a significant change in the value of the underlying asset at the end of the lease term is expected). A lessor that retains exposure to significant risks or benefits associated with the underlying asset would apply the performance obligation approach. Otherwise, the lessor would apply the derecognition approach. The determination of the application of the appropriate model to apply would be made at lease inception and not reassessed. The "credit risk" of the lessee *would not be considered* in the analysis of whether the lessor is exposed to significant risks or benefits associated with the underlying leased asset during the expected term of the current lease.

In general, the two modes are intended to accommodate an entity's business model, Figure 5-5 IASB Lessor Accounting Choices. An entity in the business of leasing an asset to multiple tenants over its economic life would typically follow a performance obligation approach. Manufactures and dealers of asset that use leasing as a tool to sell the asset, or banks that use leasing as a means to earn financing income, would typically apply the derecognition approach.

The lessor accounting model is based on the initial determination of whether the lessor is exposed to significant risks or benefits associated with the underlying asset.

Under the performance obligation approach, the underlying asset will remain on the lessor's books and the lessor will recognize (1) an asset for the right to receive lease payments plus any recoverable initial direct costs incurred by the lessor and (2) a lease liability at the present value of the lease payments. The lessor would recognize (1) lease income as the performance obligation is reduced over the lease term and (2) interest income on the receivable.

Under the derecognition approach, a portion of the leased asset is removed from the lessor's books. The lessor records (1) a receivable (and lease income) for the expected rental payments and (2) a residual asset

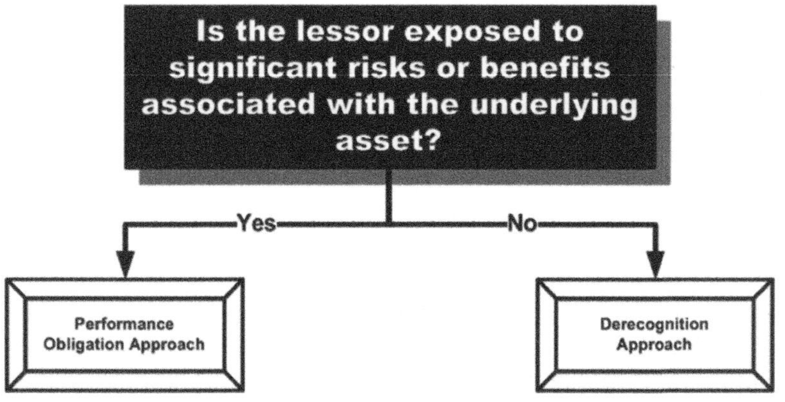

Figure 5-5. IASB Lessor Accounting Choices

representing the right to the underlying asset at the end of the lease term. Lease expense would be recognized for the portion of the leased asset that is removed from the lessor's books. Lease income and lease expense may be presented net depending on the lessor's business model. A lessor would classify lease income as revenue and lease expense as cost of sales "if that income and expense arise in the course of a lessor's ongoing, major or central activities."

1. **Performance Obligation Approach**

Under the performance obligation approach, the lessor will recognize, as of the date of commencement of a lease, () an asset for the right to receive lease payments plus any recoverable initial direct costs incurred by the lessor and (2) a lease liability at the present value of the lease payments. The lease liability represents the lessor's obligation to permit the lessee to use the underlying asset over the lease term.

The initial measurement of the asset for the right to receive lease payments and the performance obligation is based on the *longest possible lease term that is more likely than not to occur*. The ED states that the lessor determines the lease payments required during the term of the lease by using an expected outcome approach (similar to the approach used by the lessee). The rate the lessor charges the lessee is used to discount expected payments to their present value. Contingent rentals, residual value guarantees, and expected payments under termination penalties are included in the measurement (in the same manner as the lessee, the lessor would determine contingent rentals that depend on an index or rate by using forward rates if they are readily available; otherwise, the lessor would use the prevailing rate). However, the recognition threshold is higher for lessors because they can only include amounts related to contingent rentals and residual value guarantees if they can be "reliably measured." The initial measure of the asset for the right to receive lease payments would also include any recoverable initial direct costs incurred by the lessor. All amounts are initially measured as of the date of inception of the lease.

The ED requires that the asset representing the right to receive lease payments be amortized and that the lessor use the interest method to recognize interest income. To amortize the performance obligation to lease income, the lessor must use a systematic and rational approach, for example, hours of use or units produced—including energy produced by a renewable energy production system. If there is not a reliable method based on pattern of use, straight-line amortization should be used.

The lessor is required to reassess the expected lease payments (including the lease term, contingent rentals, termination options, and residual value guarantees) each reporting period if any new facts or circumstances indicate a significant change in the right to receive rental or sale of energy payments. If there is a change to the lease term as a result of this reassessment, the lessor would recognize it by adjusting the lease liability and the right to receive lease payments. Changes to the contingent rents, termination penalties, REC values, and residual value guarantees would be recorded in the income statement to the extent that the lessor has satisfied the related lease liability, or as an adjustment to the lease liability to the extent that the lessor has not satisfied the related lease liability. However, the lessor shall recognize any changes that would reduce the liability below zero in net income.

2. **Derecognition Approach**

The derecognition approach will result in the lessor's removing a portion of the carrying amount of the underlying asset from its books and recognizing income and expense upon lease commencement. The lessor will recognize an asset for the right to receive lease payments and a residual asset for the portion of the carrying amount of the underlying asset that represents the lessor's rights in the underlying asset that it did not transfer. Although the lessor recognizes income and expense upon lease commencement, the amount of upfront profit recognized may be different than that recognized under a sales-type lease under current U.S. GAAP. This is due to the ED's guidance related to contingent rentals, residual value guarantees, and other elements of lease contracts (including the calculation of the residual asset), which differ from current lease accounting guidance.

The lessor measures the asset for the right to receive lease payments (and a corresponding amount of revenue) the same way it performs its measurement under the performance obligation approach. The residual asset will be measured at an allocated amount of the carrying amount of the underlying asset, determined as of the date of inception of the lease. The portion of the underlying asset derecognized (and corresponding amount of expense) would be calculated as of the date of inception of the lease as follows:

$$\frac{\textit{Fair value of the right to receive lease payments}}{\textit{Fair value of the underlying asset}} \; X \;\; \textit{Carrying amount of the underlying asset}$$

The remaining portion of the underlying asset that is not derecognized would represent the residual asset. All amounts are initially measured as of the date of inception of the lease.

The lessor will use the interest method to amortize the receivable and recognize interest income. The residual asset would not be re-measured unless there is a change in lease term or the asset is impaired.

The lessor is required to reassess the expected lease payment (including the lease term, termination options, contingent rentals or energy units to be sold, future REC income and residual value guarantees) each reporting period if any new facts or circumstances indicate a significant change in the right to receive lease payments. If reassessment of the lease term results in a change in the residual asset, the ED requires the lessor allocate such change to the rights derecognized and to the residual asset and to adjust the carrying amount of the residual asset accordingly. Changes related to termination options, contingent rents, future REC income, and residual value guarantees that can be reliably measured would be recognized in the income statement.

As under the performance obligation approach, the lessor would not change its discount rate because of changes in lease term, or when amounts payable under contingent rentals vary, unless the rentals are contingent on variable reference interest rates, in which case the lessor would revise the discount rate for changes in the reference interest rates and recognize those changes in the income statement.

However, after defining the original ED above, it now seems that the decision is to adopt a "single" lessor account model—the receivable and residual method should apply to all leases.[43] This would be similar to the derecognition approach proposed in the ED. This model allows for profit recognition at lease commencement depending on whether the profit is reasonably assured. Under this model, the lessor will derecognize the underlying asset and recognize (1) a lease receivable measured as the present value of the lease payments (and presumably the future PPA or ESC energy payments) discounted at the rate the lessor charges the lessee and (2) a residual asset measured on an allocated cost basis, with the measurement depending on whether profit is reasonably assured. The lease receivable is subsequently amortized by using the effective interest method.

If profit is reasonably assured, the profit and residual asset will be measured as follows at lease commencement:

- Profit = (lease receivable + residual asset) – carrying amount of underlying asset.
- Residual asset = carrying amount of the underlying asset – [(present value of lease receivable ÷ fair value of the underlying asset) X carrying amount of the underlying asset)].

The residual asset is subsequently accreted by using the rate the lessor charges the lessee.

If profit is not reasonably assured, the profit will be recognized subsequently over the lease term and the residual asset on the commencement date of the lease will be measured as the difference between the carrying amount of the underlying asset and the lease receivable. The lessor would subsequently use a constant rate of return to accrete the residual asset to an amount equivalent to the underlying asset's carrying amount at the end of the lease terms as if it had been subject to depreciation.

If the right to receive lease payments is greater than the carrying amount of the underlying asset as of the lease commencement date, the lessor would recognize, at a minimum, the difference between those two amounts as profit on that date. No profit would be recognized at lease commencement if the carrying amount of the underlying asset is equal to its fair value and the right to receive lease payments is not greater than the carrying amount of the underlying asset.

> *"To me, the path to a sustainable energy future seems very obvious. We have to find a way to tap into a very small fraction of the sun's energy to convert it to a form suitable for supplying what are in fact the relatively small additional requirements of modern life...I think the technological challenge can be met. It remains to be seen whether the political and organizational challenges involved in recognizing and addressing the need to change from the status quo can also be met on a reasonable timescale."*
>
> Martin Green, scholar and author

Disclosures

The new proposed accounting standards would significantly increase the disclosures related to lease arrangements (and presumably PPAs or other energy service contracts).[44] An entity would be required to disclose quantitative and qualitative information that would enable users of the accounting information to understand the amount and timing of expected cash flows. Such information will include disclosure of terms of contingent rentals, renewal options, and residual value guarantees as well as information about changes in assumptions and judgments related to options, REC income, contingent rentals, residual value guarantees, and discount rates. Disclosures would need to be disaggregated to a level so that information provided is useful to the users of the financial statements. The ED would also require both lessee and lessor to provide a reconciliation between opening and closing balances for assets and liabilities related to the lease arrangement.

At their November 1, 2011, meeting, the FASB and IASB made certain tentative decisions that lessors that account for leases under the receivable and residual approach would be required to provide additional disclosures, including the following:

- A table of all lease-related income items that were recognized in the reporting period, disaggregated into (a) profit, recognized at lease commencement (split into revenue and cost of sales, if that is how the lessor has presented the amounts in the statement of comprehensive income); (b) interest income on the lease receivable; (c) interest income on the residual asset; (d) variable lease income; and (e) short-term lease income.
- Information about the basis and terms on which variable lease payments (contingent rentals and/or PPA and ESC receipts) are determined as required in paragraph 73(a)(ii) of the ED.
- Information about the existence and terms of options, including for renewal and termination required in paragraph 73(a)(iii) of the ED.
- A qualitative description of purchase options in leasing arrangements, including information about the extent to which the entity is subject to such agreements.
- A reconciliation of the opening and closing balance of the right to receive lease payments and residual assets.

In addition, the boards tentatively decided that a lessor is not required to disclose the initial direct costs incurred in the period, the weighted average or range of discount rates used to calculate the right to receive lease payments, or the fair value of the right to receive lease payments or the residual asset.

Enactment of New Accounting Standards

Changes are likely to be enacted sometime between 2014 and 2015 as it now appears even though continued feedback is being received. There is a great deal of debate whether "transparency" is better off after the implementation or not. If PPAs do become reclassified as leases, it may alter the financing landscape of the renewable energy sector thus stifling innovations in project financing.

Some items have still not had final decisions by the boards or put out in an ED and they include:

- Lessor—variable lease payment measurements
- Lessor—application of the "reasonably assured" notion for profit recognition
- Lessor—presentation and disclosure
- Lessor—transition issues related to existing leveraged leases
- Lessee—additional guidance on construction costs incurred by the lessee before the lease commencement date and prepaid rents
- Lessee—transition issues related to existing sale-

and-leaseback transactions

- Both—transition method
- Both—effective date
- Both—scope clarification for leases of inventory and internal-use software
- Both—guidance on how entities should calculate the discount rate when considering the use of a group discount rate and determining the yield on property
- Both—additional guidance on the concept of disguised fixed lease payments

CREDIT DECISION COMPONENTS

Many books have been written on this subject and this chapter will not attempt to re-write what can be obtained from those sources. Instead, it will look at this subject in light of the particular aspects of renewable energy and energy efficiency.

Underlying every single decision to invest in or lend money to an energy project is the absolute need to have a strong repayment source (customer) behind the decision to proceed. Yes, the quality of the underlying assets, the warranties of the equipment, the documentation and contracts that support the transaction and many other factors are important—but none (or even all them in aggregate) will take the place of a sound credit and financial analysis of the debtor.

Most every lender or investor will have some combination of three or more critical considerations when they make the decision to take a credit risk with the debtor or host. The most basic are often referred to as the "three C's of lending." Specifically, they are:

- Credit
- Collateral
- Capacity

Credit refers to both the financial strength as well as the historical credit history of the debtor or host. They must first have the financial strength to draw upon should their business take a nose dive or the economy in general declines such as occurred in late 2008 and on into 2009. Mostly, this refers to the net worth of the applicant. The company must have other assets that it could liquidate to meet the obligations under the project finance agreement. Most lenders and investors like to see a net worth that is at least three times the amount of the credit being extended under the project finance. For example, if the size of the project is $1 million, the net worth of the applicant should be at least $3 million. Many regulated institutional lenders like to see a net worth of at least 10 times the requested amount of the project.

The second "C" is referred to as collateral (see "Capital Assets and Collateral" below). Many of the technologies used in renewable projects do not have a long history of established "re-sale value." Should a debtor or host get into financial trouble, are unable to pay the obligations when they become due, and the lender or investor would need to take the underlying assets back (often called a "repossession"), the value of those assets to be sold in an open market to potential buyers becomes the second line of defense after adequate net worth and credit strength. Also, many of the renewable energy projects financed and invested in have a significant portion of the initial capitalized cost paid out to "soft costs" such as design, engineering, permits and installation—none of which can be re-captured if a repossession occurred and the assets were sold to an independent third party (either voluntarily or by legal action). The real truth is that in many cases, the assets have a much higher value remaining installed and operating, and then a new contract renegotiated with a potential new customer. In addition, it can be very costly to a lender or investor just to remove the project assets, repackage them, and to ship them to a warehouse, auction location or place for re-sale.

The third "C" is called capacity (see "Energy Accounting" below). This is simply the ability of the debtor or host to pay the obligations under the project finance agreement from historical and existing profits of the company. This can—and often does—include the energy savings realized from the project. Here again, lenders and investors like to see historical earnings (for at least three of the past five years) to pay the new obligation that are a minimum of three times the annual obligations under the renewable energy project. For example, if the annual debt obligations under the $1 million project above were $100,000 per year, the applicant should have a "net after tax" income (also known as disposable income) that is at least $300,000 per year. Regulated institutional lenders often like to see net profits for the year that are five or more times the annualized debt under the renewable energy project.

The conventional wisdom that has been historically used is that if the applicant can demonstrate at least two of the three "C's" defined above, then it would be a reasonable investment or loan risk and move forward with the project. Let's look at three possibilities of this thinking:

1. If the applicant has a good net worth and has historically paid all their bills on time to other creditors, and the company is making good money (historically) and has adequate cash flow, then one could ignore the collateral value of the underlying assets.
2. *or*: if the applicant has good net worth and the equipment has a very strong resale value should a repossession occur, then a lender or investor could ignore the fact that historical earnings have been "somewhat" weak or nonexistent for one year out of the past five.
3. *or*: if the applicant had good earnings that exceeded the industry norm and the equipment had great value, then most often an investor or lender could use those values to help offset the fact that the net worth of the company or the credit payment history may be somewhat suspect with other creditors (particularly "trade creditors").

Based on the above concepts, let's look a little deeper into the credit decision process.

Many lenders and investors will occasionally outsource the research and due diligence needed to a third party and then review the results with their own staff and professional advisors. When they do so, they will look at five or more other components of the credit decision process. This is particularly important when experiencing a major historical economic downturn. The attitude often taken is that sacrificing short-term profits and survival may outweigh long-term economic considerations and credit risks. This is also the time to look more carefully at outright supplier fraud and weakness of suppliers not being able to finish the construction and installation of the project assets because they ran out of money to do so (even though the investor or lender had advanced the required funds on a timely manner according to the construction schedule). The following steps (in addition to the three "C's" described above) could be considered prudent given the current economic circumstances:

1. Perform additional extensive diligence on all supplier and debtor or host creditworthiness. Third-party credit reports, as an example, are probably not sufficient. The lender/investor should take additional investigations by calling or visiting other creditors of the applicant in person. It is amazing the kind of comments and feedback you get when going directly to the suppliers and other long-term debt creditors the customer has.
2. Ask for a current aging of their payables and then call the major ones and a modest representation of the minor ones. The same can be done for the applicants receivables. Get the accounting list of accounts receivable of the applicant and call the principal ones, visit as many as appropriate in person and finally, run some standard credit reports on the most major customers that owe the applicant money. Make sure that the major ones are stable, pay other creditors on time, and have every intention to keep doing business with your applicant.
3. This step also suggests that the creditor obtain at least four years of historical financial statements plus an interim set of statements if the oldest is more than three months old (a lot can change in just 90 days). This includes the accountants' cover letter, balance sheet, income statement, source and application of funds statement, and complete footnotes. Once obtained, read and analyze them. If you don't have the expertise yourself to do so, have trusted third parties perform the evaluation and give you their opinions.
4. Scrutinize applicants in high-risk industries. Compare the applicant's recent performance to the industry norms and note any significant variances. Then, discuss the concerns you might have with the applicant's internal treasury group or their outside auditors and advisors. You may even consider requiring and obtaining an opinion letter from their accountants or legal counsel. This is an added cost for the applicant, but so long as the cost(s) are reasonable, the applicant should not have problems with the expenses that are customary.
5. Do adequate research on the applicant's competitors to make sure that your applicant's business strategy can adequately meet their competitor's strategies. Make sure they are meeting all mandates and reporting schedules they have with their regulators. Ascertain that they are not falling behind on any taxes and that there is adequate cash to meet the ongoing employment taxes and estimated tax payments when they become due. Check court records in the county and state in which they are domiciled to verify that there is no pending litigation against them or that they have not started litigation against any of their customers or competitors which could also lead to unknown future problems.
6. Finally, talk to the landlord if the applicant is leasing the premises. Verify when the current lease ex-

pires and whether there are renewal options under the lease agreement. Ascertain the likelihood of the applicant staying beyond the current lease term. This is critically important when the term of the project finance is longer than the remaining term (including the renewal option terms) of the property lease. When talking to the landlord, you might also question them about their future decisions to keep the property or if they are considering selling the property prior to the end of the project finance term. A new real property owner mid-term during the financing agreement could cause problems that are not acceptable to the project creditor.

Then there is always the technology and warranty risk's inherent in all renewable energy projects. Even seemingly legitimate manufacturers, engineers, vendors and suppliers can present warranty compliance risk. Always go to other projects that have been installed by those parties and verify that the equipment has been properly installed and commissioned, the technology is performing, outputs are meeting design parameters and that the responsible parties are maintaining and servicing the equipment as required. Verify that all needed repairs and modifications were performed on time, within budget and according to the terms of the warranties and other agreements. The creditor might also consider using an equipment or technology specialist to evaluate the performance, operations, viability and market appeal of the assets. In many cases, the meters and monitoring systems will also independently verify the performance and output expectations of the installed systems.

There are two additional "C's" that some creditors use in their evaluation of the credit risk on a project. They are "character" and "conditions." Character (reputation) is the prime determinate of a debtor's willingness to meet an obligation—often the most important element in any business relationship. Conditions refer to the economic environment and include systemic market risk and recession, high-risk industries and related businesses. This is of particular concern to most lenders and investors in today's negative economic climate and must be carefully considered before committing to any renewable energy project.

Being alert to the "conditions" precedent in the project will uncover potential fraud risks. In a down economy, short-term survival measures by third parties involved in the project can cause major problems as the project is completed and commissioned. Many lenders and investors hire a third party to conduct audits on the project as it moves through the various phases. This includes at inception when proposals of various technologies and systems are proposed to you or your customer. Don't just assume that the engineering or design done by a supplier is either accurate or properly sized to the project or that the technology chosen is best for you.

> *"Renewable energy also creates more jobs than other sources of energy—most of these will be created in the struggling manufacturing sector, which will pioneer the new energy future by investment that allows manufacturers to retool and adopt new technologies and methods."*
>
> Jay Inslee, former member of U.S. House of Representatives

Then, as the project is constructed, have your project manager, or third party you have hired, perform audits for correct installation procedures, proper permits, component quality, etc. (*see Commissioning page 98*). Often major problems can be averted early on when consistent auditing is being performed. This also means that if you are providing funds to the project during this stage, that those funds are not dispersed if all prior commitments haven't been met by the supplier, vendor, sub-contractor or other parties pursuant to the drawn-down schedule agreed to earlier. Without a physical inspection of the site and project, the project could get into trouble quickly. Also, don't assume that just because a prior job they did was completed satisfactorily by a contractor or supplier, that the same results will occur on the current project.

This is also the time to look carefully at bonding and completion issues on the project by your general contractor. In tough economic times, many contractors are no longer able to get bonding that they were able to obtain before. One can't be too careful. Yes, the costs associated with adequate insurance and bonding adds to the project costs. But, most projects can easily assume those costs and most lenders and investors are willing to have those costs included as part of the project costs. Doing so adds very little to the scheduled debt payments (since they are repaid over the entire term of the project finance) and certainly gives "peace of mind" to all parties.

Look carefully at your project plan and add the incremental steps described in this section to the plan. A thoroughly prepared project and construction plan is important to every project and with the "conditions" as they are today, every plan should be updated to reflect the realities of not just this project, but all projects you are the creditor on. That project plan needs to cover:

- Every single task properly defined from initial review as you consider the project, all the way through to final commissioning.

- Set realistic start and finish dates for each task.
- Assign personnel who will be responsible to assure that each task is performed on time and within budget.
- Make sure that the budget for each task has been agreed to by all parties to the project and that should a change need to be made (commonly known as a "change order"), that it is documented and agreed to in writing by all parties prior to implementing the change.
- Most tasks require proper sequencing and many are interdependent on other tasks being completed on time and within budget. Don't forget to adjust all other tasks according to the changes in the task being modified.
- Add resources to the project as required as the project is implemented. This includes adequate resources of people, equipment and materials.
- Distribute your people resources carefully so that no one person is overloaded and starts getting behind in their task responsibilities.

A time-constrained project is one in which the project finish date is the most important factor in your project plan. This is a very important issue in many renewable energy projects since there are major tax consequences (and therefore expected project yields) if projects are not completed by certain fall-dead dates. A time-constrained project is one in which the project finish date is the most important factor in your project plan. Although you still need to balance budget constraints and satisfy the project scope, the finish date reigns supreme as the primary priority. If your project plan calculates that your finish date will go beyond your all-important target finish date, focus on the critical path. Shorten the critical path and you bring in the finish date. Though you still need to balance budget constraints and satisfy the project scope, the finish date reigns supreme as the primary priority. This generally means that you have to be on top of the date constraints, task dependencies and task durations. Be prepared for the worst and plan adequately for the problems.

In the end, always do good due diligence, analyze the data received with advisors or third parties, and, most importantly, use common sense. Continually search for red-flags in the project to mitigate credit risk. Adhering to the five "C's" outlined above, will help you focus on the common sense credit decision needed.

In summary (and tongue in cheek), the following is some "advice from the devil"... 35 ways to get into trouble when extending credit as a lender or investor on an energy project:

1. **Rely on host customer projections for energy savings.** The energy audit that supports the project being financed was performed by the customer and not independently by you or your advisor. The debtor would never default just because the energy savings were not there to make the payments.
2. **Work alone.** With all your knowledge, skills and ingenuity you can save the debtor and his business. In you, this is doughty individualism—in others it is unmitigated egotism.
3. **Assume the supplier of the equipment and components will be in business when a warranty issue needs to be fixed.** You or your customer "never" select company's products that are not fail-proof and therefore all equipment will perform as intended over the entire term of the financial contract.
4. **Procrastinate.** If you wait long enough, any problem will go away or solve itself. This is wishful thinking for some, but there are so many more important things which call for your attention.
5. **Play it by ear.** There is no point in a planned attack on the problems or defaults at hand. Nothing works out perfectly anyway. Besides, there is always someone to help you out afterwards (including suppliers and engineers).
6. **Be the good guy.** Always give in to your customer's demands, no matter how unreasonable or unrealistic they are. It may be against your better judgment, but in the energy project investment/finance industry, you can't afford to offend anyone.
7. **Accept customer statements at face value.** Remember that credit is based on mutual trust. How can anyone doubt the customer when it is obvious they are so sincere.
8. **Jump on command.** Fast action is the hallmark of modern energy projects. You can consider the risks after you have approved and funded the project.
9. **Be patient.** If the debtor remains in business long

enough, you will receive sufficient income from the relationship to justify your present risk and efforts.

10. **Don't impose your standards on others**. A few third-rate accountants and engineers do improve with age. Verifying designs, drawings, permits, financial statements, energy savings and other time-consuming details is expensive when all you have to show for it is a project that would never default.

11. **Join the full-service club**. Anything other project developers, investors and lenders can do, you can do better. The fact that you don't know what you are doing doesn't count. The name of the game is beating the competition.

12. **Stick to the figures when making your credit decisions**. If the caliber of management with your customer is less than desirable, you can always install a good consultant in their business to straighten everything out.

13. **Specialize**. Concentrate on energy contract documents, credit and corporate finance. You can't afford to clog up your mind with economics, investment criteria, industrial trends, future energy costs, equipment knowledge, technology issues or competitor advantages. That is why you have experts.

14. **Place your faith in collected balances and earnings from the relationship with your customer**. What has happened in the past is clearly indicative of future success with the customer.

15. **Never worry about the real purpose behind an energy project request**. The corporate treasurer that works for your customer may be toying with the truth, but that is not your concern. Spend your time on figuring out the energy savings repayment source and trust that all payments and obligations will be met with that single important revenue source. That is really all that counts.

16. **Settle for what you have got**. You can never know all the facts in any energy project. That is known as making decisions under conditions of uncertainty. Accept it as way of executive life. It is very fashionable during these economic times.

17. **Stay at your desk**. No customer, advisor or supplier can ever accuse you of not being available to them. There is no need to go out and check on any assets pledged to you in this day and age—including a careful scrutiny of the project site. The Uniform Commercial Code was designed specifically to protect you from fraud and energy project miscalculations.

18. **Get the project on the books immediately**. You can pick up any loose ends on a follow-up basis. When you take good care of people, they won't let you down. And don't forget, your monthly and annual bonuses are based on "booked" transactions, not those "in the pipeline."

19. **Get the facts on paper in your spare time**. Tomorrow or the day after will do just fine. And even if those facts, figures, observations and conclusions never get written down they are locked in your bear-trap mind. You will always be around with answers—right?

20. **Remain flexible**. Energy project customers are entitled to change their minds. If you make a fetish of insisting that your customer's keep promises, honor commitments, and meet debt schedules, you will wind up with the reputation of being a hard-nose. Someone might not love you anymore.

21. **When trouble comes, move with caution and deliberation**. It takes a good deal of time to pull together everything you need to know. Things need to be well thought out before you act—particularly in the case of any sort of default under your contract with the customer. You don't want to be known as a panic-button pusher.

22. **Don't put much effort into diagnosing future renewal contracts**. This costs time and money. If it wasn't a good contract originally, you certainly wouldn't have put it on the books in the first place.

23. **Confine your relationship with your customer to contract and credit problems**. Leave criticism of the way he is running his business to others. That is why he has a CPA and/or a management consultant. This also means to not stick your nose into his business by offering other ways that he might save money on other potential energy efficiency projects.

24. **Limit your contacts with your customer to getting the transaction on the books and being paid at maturity**. Things will take care of themselves between times. And there is not much you can do until maturity anyway.

25. **Don't pester your customer with minor details such as insurance coverage, maintenance on the**

system, and monitoring to make sure all energy components are functioning properly. If the customer is smart enough to be able to get you to extend credit to him, he is certainly the kind of guy who will do common sense things over the term of the contract as well as making sure all payments are made promptly.

26. **Don't let a fuzzy picture of the customer's operation keep you from extending all the credit to them they ask for**. Things have a way of becoming clear with the passage of time. Before the contract is retired, you will learn a lot that you don't now know.
27. **Pick your contact in the customer's firm carefully**. Rely completely on the one person whom you trust and whose ability gives you confidence. They will keep you informed. You in turn will sleep nights because "no news is good news." As the principal contact goes so goes the company—and you will go right along with him.
28. **Honor your commitments**. If you promised to take care of the customer's energy needs, do it. The fact that they have soared out of proportion or that the financial statement has deteriorated a little is less important than maintaining your personal reputation with the customer.
29. **Put your faith in the future**. The past and the present are not important. Rely on future sales, future profits, future cash flow and the future economic climate in your customer's industry. Hope is the mother of all men—tomorrow will be better. You know—your customer told you so just last week.
30. **Develop a legalistic mind and put your faith in documents**. We pay lawyers good money to make sure all documents are correctly drawn in the best legal order. This project is not "unique" in any way and documents you have used in the past will do fine for this transaction also. What more protection could you ask for?
31. **Keep your costs well in mind**. Remember that checking and verifying with banks, trade suppliers, credit agencies, third-party energy analysts, and public authorities is expensive. There is some risk in short-cutting here, but the little savings do add up.
32. **Don't worry about taxes your customer might owe**. You can always have one of your banker friends lend your customer some extra money if the revenue agents get pushy.
33. **Determine that one important repayment source (energy savings) and then commit yourself**. If the energy savings isn't there to provide 100% of the debt obligation, you or your customer can think up a good alternative. And—if you can't—that is why we hire collection lawyers.
34. **Don't tie your customer up too tightly**. He needs freedom to move other assets in and out of this business (including the possibility of replacing your equipment) in the normal course of operations. If the situation gets a bit sticky later, you can obtain control of other assets the customer might have.
35. **Have confidence in yourself**. Your lending and investment policies, rules and procedures are only guidelines. They can't always be applicable to a specific problem. After all, the key to success is imagination and innovation. When you know you are right, it is hard to get into real trouble.

CAPITAL ASSETS AND COLLATERAL

The following questions need to be asked by the project developer, lender or investor as the energy project is reviewed:

- ☐ How do the specific components compare to components from other manufacturers of the same items? This implies comparing of performance, efficiency, warranties, serviceability, financial strength of the manufacturer to back the product, etc.
- ☐ In what order of preference would it rank with other models of the same component from different suppliers and vendors?
- ☐ Do the components meet the system design called out by the project engineers and do they comply with the requirements of the utility?
- ☐ How many other users are there where this equipment and system have been installed?
- ☐ Where are those users located should the assets need to be repossessed and quickly liquidated to a different user?
- ☐ Is there a market demand for this equipment (either new or used) and is that demand expected to continue for the functional life of the equipment?
- ☐ Are buyers for used assets of this type readily available?

- ❑ Are there used equipment dealers for these systems that would either purchase the system or assist in the refurbishing and remarketing of the equipment?
- ❑ How long has this technology and equipment been in the market?
- ❑ Has it met with creditable acceptance in its market?
- ❑ Has the equipment reached "commercial" status as opposed to a "pilot or experimental" status? This is also known as commercially viable (or "bankable" to lenders).
- ❑ Are the components manufactured domestically or from a foreign source?
- ❑ Has the debtor ever used this type of equipment before and are they knowledgeable in the operations and maintenance of the equipment?
- ❑ Would the system integrator, EPC contractor, supplier or vendor consider executing a "re-purchase or re-marketing agreement" if we found the need to repossess and sell the equipment? If so, what would the parameters of those obligations be?
- ❑ What would be a fair price for the used equipment and who would determine that price? Have there been recent auctions or liquidations of similar systems?
- ❑ Can the value of the system be determined at specific time intervals (3 year, 5 year, etc.)?
- ❑ Are their extensive decommissioning, shipping, storage and other re-marketing costs which could not be recovered on a resale?
- ❑ What were the "soft" costs when first purchased that could not be recovered such as installation, taxes, site preparation, design, engineering and permitting fees?
- ❑ Are there other "non-tangible" costs being paid for such as software, monitoring or service O&M agreements?
- ❑ What price has the equipment brought at recent public or private auctions?
- ❑ What is the "mark-up" of the assets?
- ❑ How long should the equipment last under either normal use or excessive use scenarios?
- ❑ What rate of tax cost recovery (depreciation) is generally used for this equipment?
- ❑ How much additional life or value would be realized if the equipment were to be "re-conditioned"?
- ❑ What is the extent of maintenance required to keep the system operating at peak performance?
- ❑ What is the expected downtime required for either scheduled or emergency maintenance?
- ❑ Who would have the expertise to perform that maintenance and are their secondary sources?
- ❑ Is the equipment subject to frequent or sudden breakdown and what is the extent of the potential risk?
- ❑ Are those repairs performed by the credit lender, debtor or third party?
- ❑ Would the equipment have to be moved to another location to make such repairs and what would the costs be associated with the transportation?
- ❑ Do repairs need to be performed by only factory trained technicians or parties with proper certifications or bonding requirements?
- ❑ Are their environmental risks associated with those potential repairs?
- ❑ Are spare parts readily available—of particular concern as the equipment gets older?
- ❑ Are there any new technologies on the "horizon" which could make the capital assets obsolete or less marketable?
- ❑ Is this equipment protected by patents and if so, how much longer does the patent have prior to termination?
- ❑ Are their potential risks from third parties (landlords, mortgage holders, etc.) who might claim an ownership risk in those capital assets?
- ❑ Is the equipment bolted to the ground, attached to the roof or other part of a building that could cause it to be classified as a "fixture"?
- ❑ Will any part of the energy system be lost or damaged should the equipment have to be forcefully removed?
- ❑ Does it take a skilled, certified or licensed operator to handle and run the equipment?
- ❑ Is it dangerous to operate the equipment?
- ❑ Are their safety or environmental concerns handling the removal, transportation or refurbishing of the energy system?
- ❑ Does the system come with all necessary safety devices and are they also removable?

- ❒ Does the system meet all OSHA or other regulatory agency requirements?
- ❒ What is the financial strength of the manufacturer(s)?
- ❒ Does the manufacturer have a reputation of honoring warranties or other agreements?
- ❒ Is the equipment standardized or is it manufactured to specification?
- ❒ Are attachments to the system standard or custom designed?
- ❒ If the system is made to specification, how readily can it be altered for use by others?
- ❒ Can the equipment be modified to meet various demands occasioned by changes in specifications, style or later modifications necessary to keep the equipment "state of the art"?
- ❒ Is the equipment part of a complex and integrated system of production or can it be operated as an independent unit?
- ❒ Does the energy system require certain fuels to operate, what are the sources of that fuel, and who has the obligation to pay for the fuel?
- ❒ Does the equipment have to be registered with any governmental body or utility?
- ❒ Are equipment licensing or use agreements transferable?
- ❒ Would the seller/dealer (including lender or project owner) have to be licensed or registered in order to sell the equipment?
- ❒ Does a "certificate of need" or other similar proof have to be obtained before someone can use the equipment?
- ❒ How much energy (electricity, natural gas, hydrogen, water, etc.) is required to use the equipment?
- ❒ Is there a more energy-efficient model or technology going to be introduced into the market soon that would make this system less desirable?
- ❒ Is the warranty on the system transferrable to a new owner or user?
- ❒ Is there a cost of transferring the warranty?
- ❒ Are there any general or specific lawsuits or litigation in process concerning the use of the equipment?
- ❒ Could the use of the equipment be considered "restraint of trade"?
- ❒ Does the system integrator, EPC contractor or supplier have a service department and what is their reputation? Is there limiting geographic areas for that service?
- ❒ Have all necessary city, county, state, federal and regulatory permits been obtained by all parties in order to install and use the energy system?
- ❒ Has the landlord of the premises approved both the installation and use of this equipment on the premises?
- ❒ How much will the debtor rely on the equipment for the operations of their business/plant?
- ❒ Is the energy essential to the business or just a "nice to have" item?
- ❒ Does the energy system help the debtor meet emission reductions or other environmental requirements that are mandated by regulatory agencies?
- ❒ Are complete manuals and product literature available for placement in the transaction permanent file?
- ❒ Do the system and all its components have independent serial numbers?
- ❒ Will the debtor allow you to put ownership and inventory control notifications on the system and its components?
- ❒ Are those notifications easily removable?
- ❒ Will the debtor allow you to advertise the completed installation to the market?
- ❒ Is the energy system easily assessable and does it require prior authorization to inspect or service? Have proper permits for that been obtained and are they transferable?

ENERGY ACCOUNTING

Managing energy costs in an enterprise, selling energy efficiency or energy generation systems and obtaining financing on energy projects all require detailed analysis that starts by knowing what energy costs are. Energy accounting provides feedback on how much energy various parts of a company uses on a historical basis. That information must then be communicated to facility staff, building occupants, energy project developers, multiple potential sources of rebates and incentives on energy saved or produced, stockholders, suppliers, design and engineering units and even funding sources that might be capable of funding the proposed energy project.

Energy accounting will help all parties to:

- **Record and attribute energy consumption and costs**. Energy costs depend on the amount consumed and its price. In an organization with many facilities, energy accounting makes it possible to compare energy use and cost among facilities, production units within a facility, and to monitor how energy use changes over time. By communicating this information all parties can get feedback on how their current energy systems are doing.
- **Troubleshoot energy problems and potential billing errors**. By consistently tracking energy use, everyone can identify problems. A sudden unexplained increase in consumption or decrease in energy production (from an energy producing system) sets off alerts to everyone involved to investigate the site for the cause.
- **Provide a basis for prioritizing energy capital investments**. Find out which facilities, processes or units of production have the highest energy costs, and consider targeting them for energy retrofits or other energy management efforts.
- **Substantiate the economics of a proposed new energy project**. If new energy related capital assets are going to be acquired either in energy saving projects or in energy production projects, they will need to have adequate and timely data to support the investment of capital.
- **Evaluate energy program success and communicate results**. Was expected energy savings or energy production actually realized from the energy project after its commissioning? Everyone that is a party to the project will need to communicate that information to those needing the accountability and facts—and to all levels of decision making management and operations.
- **Create incentives for energy management**. It is often difficult to get anyone in an organization to take the time and responsibility required for carrying out energy management activities because there is little incentive to take on the task. A maintenance director or site manager may not see much benefit in reducing energy costs if all of the savings revert to the general fund, or if lower energy bills only result in smaller allocations for utility costs in next year's budget.

  To remedy this "disconnect" between responsibility and benefits, many organizations have created incentives for energy cost management by sharing energy savings. Energy accounting makes it possible to set quantifiable energy cost reduction goals.

- **Budget more accurately**. Energy accounting gives a historical look at costs that will help an organization budget energy needs more realistically for the future. As a side benefit, it will help meet sustainability goals that many companies are required to have either as a result of securities reporting requirements or possible board of director's policies and goals for management.

Any energy accounting process begins with a complete energy audit of the business enterprise including interviewing management for the goals and priorities they might have. Often called an energy analysis or energy evaluation, the energy audit examines the ways energy is currently being used and identifies some alternatives for reducing those energy costs. An energy audit is a quantitative analysis of energy use. The audit also becomes a useful tool for determining resource use and environmental impacts. How much energy is needed at each point in a system and in what form that energy exists will also be measured in the audit process.

Every energy audit will:[45]

- Clearly identify the types and costs of energy use
- Produce an understanding of how that energy is being used—and possibly wasted
- Identify and analyze alternatives such as improved operational techniques and/or new equipment that could substantially reduce energy costs
- Perform an economic analysis on those alternatives and determine which ones are cost effective for the business or industry involved

Some aspects of energy accounting could include what is referred to as a Life Cycle Cost Analysis or LCCA. LCCA is a comprehensive evaluation methodology used to determine the most cost-effective of related or competing energy efficiency alternatives for incorporation into a new or remodeled building or facility. The methodology accounts not only for initial capital costs, but also maintenance and operations costs over the rated life of the alternatives.

Often, performing an LCCA is the most accurate means to fairly evaluate alternative designs that have greater up-front capital costs but lower long-term operating costs than the least-first-cost design. High energy- and water-efficiency technologies are often found to be more economically favorable than base-case standard technologies, even though there can be an initial cost premium associated with them. The LCCA brings the economic viability of implementing such technologies to the forefront. In such instances, the standard design with the least-first-cost will yield the highest life cycle cost when all operating factors are considered.

Typical factors involved in a LCCA are:

- Initial costs of standard vs. alternative design (including financing)
- Energy consumption and demand costs
- Energy utility rebates
- Water costs
- Recurring and non-recurring operations, maintenance and repair costs
- Capital replacements
- Residual or salvage value at end of rated life

As can be seen in this chapter, it is critical to understand the internal components inherent in every renewable energy project—tax, accounting (book and energy), credit analysis and technology due diligence. Without these critical reviews, any project is doomed to face multiple insurmountable challenges and likely to face ultimate failure.

> *"...the transition from coal, oil, and gas to wind, solar, and geothermal energy is well under way. In the old economy, energy was produced by burning something—oil, coal, or natural gas—leading to the carbon emissions that have come to define our economy. The new energy economy harnesses the energy in wind, the energy coming from the sun, and heat from within the earth itself."*
>
> Lester R. Brown, Plan B 4.0: Mobilizing to Save Civilization

References

01. U.S. Department of Energy, "The Smart Grid: An Introduction," Galvin Electricity Initiative
02. US Energy Information Administration (EIA), *International Energy Outlook* 2011
03. U.S. Department of Energy, 2009 *U.S. State Clean Energy Data Book*, October 2010
04. SEIA (Solar Energy Industries Association) 2012 Annual Report, www.seia.org
05. Timothy Hasset, "Harnessing Nature's Power," World Resources Institute, 2009
06. Ibid
07. Ibid
08. United States Department of Energy, Office of Budget, *Renewable Energy Characterizations*, 1997
09. http://www.usabiomass.org
10. http://www.geo-energy.org
11. American Wind Energy Association, www.awea.org
12. Sandia National Laboratories , *Renewables 2010 Global Status Report, 2010*, pp. 15-16
13. Timothy Hasset, *Harnessing Nature's Power*, World Resources Institute, 2009
14. M Bollinger, "Preliminary Evaluation of the Impact of the Section 1603 Treasury Grant Program on Renewable Energy Deployment in 2009," Lawrence Berkeley National Laboratory.
15. Ibid
16. U.S. Department of the Treasury, *Overview and Status Update of the §1603 Program*, October 31, 2011
17. M Bollinger, "Preliminary Evaluation of the Impact of the Section 1603 Treasury Grant Program on Renewable Energy Deployment in 2009," Lawrence Berkeley National Lab.
18. Federal Register, Vol. 71, No. 156, Monday, August 14, 2006
19. http://www.cleanedge.com
20. National Council on State Legislatures, http://www.ncsl.org
21. The price has now dropped to $245 in New Jersey and is $540 in Massachusetts.
22. Sacks v. Commissioner, 69 F34d 982 (9th Circ 1995), rev'g, 64 T.C.M. 1003 (1992).
23. National Renewable Energy Laboratory, *Technical Report NREL/TP-6A2-45551*, May 2009
24. D. De Jager; M. Rathmann, "Policy instrument design to reduce financing costs in renewable energy technology projects." Prepared for the International Energy Agency-Renewable Energy Technology Deployment, Utrecht, October 2008. Available online at: http://www.iea-retd.org/files/retd_PIC0810_Main.pdf.
25. V. Dinica, "Support systems for the diffusion of renewable energy technologies-an investor perspective." *Energy Policy*, Vol. 34, No. 4, 2006, pp. 461-480.
26. Ernst & Young, "Renewable Energy Country Attractiveness Indices 2008, Quarter 1-2," July 2008
27. A. Klein; B. Pfluger; A. Held; G. Resch; T Faber, "Evaluation of Different Feed-in Tariff Design Options – Best Practice Paper for the International Feed-in Cooperation: 2nd edition." Karlsruhe, Germany: Fraunhofer Institute Systems and Innovations Research, October 2008
28. http://freeingthegrid.org/wp-content/uploads/2012/07/FreeingTheGrid2011.pdf
29. SRECTrade, Inc., 90 New Montgomery St, San Francisco, CA 94105, (877) 466-4606
30. Renewable Energy World, *Effective SREC Market Design*, May 2011, www.renewableenergyworld.com
31. A qualified source includes biomass, solar thermal, photovoltaic, wind, geothermal, fuel cells using renewable fuels, small hydroelectric generation of 30 megawatts or less, digester gas, municipal solid waste conversion, landfill gas, ocean wave, ocean thermal, or tidal current, and any additions or enhancements to the facility using that technology.
32. http://www.srectrade.com/blog
33. Ibid
34. Costing Green: A Comprehensive Cost Database and Budgeting

Methodology, July 2004. Davis Langdon
35. United States Green Building Council
36. Navigant Consulting
37. Dr. Ryan Wiser, "Wind Power and the Production Tax Credit: An Overview of Research Results," Lawrence Berkeley National Laboratory, March 29, 2007.
38. Rick Nevin and Gregory Watson, "Evidence of Rational Market Valuations for Home Energy Efficiency," The Appraisal Journal, October 1998
39. Ben Hoen, et al, "An Analysis of the Effects of Residential Photovoltaic Energy System on Home Sales Prices in California," 2011
40. Ibid
41. Andrew J. Black, "Why is a Solar Electric Home Worth More?," July 2004
42. National Resources Defense Council, PACE Now, Renewable Funding LLC, and The Vote Solar Initiative: *Property Assessed Clean Energy Programs White Paper,* May 2010
43. http://pacenow.org
44. Merrian C. Fuller, Cathy Kunkel, Daniel M Kammen: "Guide to Energy efficiency & Renewable Energy Financing Districts for Local Governments," Renewable and Appropriate Energy Laboratory (RAEL), University of California, Berkeley, September 2009
45. SIR is the estimated savings over the life of the assessment, discounted back to present value using an appropriate discount rate, divided by the amount financed through PACE assessment. Savings can include reduced utility bills as well as any payments for renewable energy credits or other quantifiable environmental and health benefits that can be monetized. The savings should be calculated on an annual basis and include annual escalators for future energy price increases.
46. A different standard may apply to non-residential properties.
47. Applicants that have purchased the property within three years have recently undergone rigorous credit analyses that would compensate for the short property tax payment history.
48. See: http://www.fhfa.gov/webfiles/15884/PACESTMT7610.pdf
49. Lawrence Berkeley National Laboratory, Environmental Energy Technologies Division, *Clean Energy Financing Policy Brief,* August 2010
50. Ibid
51. See: http://pacenow.org/documents/FHFA%20Letter.pdf
52. http://www1.eere.energy.gov/wip/pace.html
53. PricewaterhouseCoopers L.L.P., *Sustainable Business Solutions,* March 2011, www.pwc.com
54. Galen Barbose, LBNL, (510) 495-2593
55. Solar Rating & Certification Corporation, www.solar-rating.org
56. Rev. Proc. 2001-28, 2001-1 CB 1156, 5/07/2001, IRC Sec(s). 167
57. within the meaning of § 318 of the Internal Revenue Code
58. IRC Section 1.467-3(c)(4)
59. See Rev. Rul. 55-541, 1955-2 C.B. 19 for an example
60. The Handbook of Equipment Leasing, Amembal & Isom, ISBN 0-945988-00-1
61. *Renewable Energy Tax Credit Handbook,* Novogradac & Company LLP, page 29
62. Ibid
63. Internal Revenue Bulletin: 2011-22
64. Sealy Power Ltd. V. Commissioner, 46 F.3d 382 (5th Cir. 1995); Revenue Ruling 84-85, 1984-1 C.B. 10.
65. Treasury Regulation 1.46-3(d)(2)(ii); Sears Oil Co. v. Commissioner, 359 Fed 191 (2nd Cir. 1966); SMC Corp v. United States, 675 F2d 113 (6th Cir. 1982).
66. IRC § 7701(e)(1)
67. PLR 111-343, Div B, Title 1, Sec 103 (October 3, 2008).
68. H. Rep. 98-432, at 1152 (emphasis added).
69. Ibid
70. PLR 8718016 (January 23, 1987).
71. Ibid
72. Ibid
73. Modeling Choices Impact Tax Equity Financing, Dennis Moritz, North American Windpower, www.nawindpower.com
74. Ibid
75. Ibid
76. Ibid
77. See Frank Lyon Co. v. U.S., 435 U.S. 561, 583-84 (1977).
78. Goldstein v. Commissioner, 364 F.2d 734 (2d Cir. 1966); Sacks, supra note 5; Winn-Dixie, Inc. v. Commissioner, 113 T.C. 254 (1999) aff'd, Winn-Dixie Stores, Inc. v. Commissioner, 254 F.3d 1313 (11th Cir. 2001), cert. denied, 535 U.S. 986 (2002); Rose, supra note 8; Casebeer v. Commissioner, 909 F.2d 1360 (9th Cir 1990); Newman v. Commissioner, 894 F.2d 560, 563 (2d Cir. 1990); Salina P'ship v. Commissioner, T.C. Memo 2000-352 (2000); Kirchman, supra note 10; Nicole Rose Corp. v. Commissioner, 117 TC 328 (2001); IES Industries Inc. v. Commissioner, 253 F.3d 350, 355-356 (8th Cir. 2001); James v. Commissioner, 899 F.2d 905 (10th Cir. 1990); Pasternak, supra note 7.
79. See, e.g., Gilman v. Commissioner, 933 F.2d 143, 146 (2d Cir. 1991).
80. Cherin v. Commissioner, 89 T.C. 986, 994 (1987).
81. *Renewable Energy Tax Credit Handbook 2010,* Novogradac & Company LLP, page 36
82. See Knetsch v. United States, 364 U.S. 361 (1960).
83. Donald L. Korb, Chief Counsel for the Internal Revenue Service, remarks at the 2005 University of Southern California Tax Institute presentation in Los Angeles, CA on January 25, 2005.
84. Section 45 provides the taxpayer with a production credit in the amount of 1.5 cents (adjusted for inflation) per kilowatt-hour of electricity produced by the taxpayer from qualified energy resources and at a qualified facility during the 10 year period beginning on the date the facility was originally placed in service, and sold to an unrelated person during the taxable year.
85. Section 404(b) provides that a partner's distributive share of income, gain, loss, deduction or credit is determined in accordance with the partner's interest in the partnership, if (i) the partnership agreement does not provide for the partner's distributive share of income, gain, loss, deduction or credit, or (ii) the allocation to a partner under the agreement of income, gain, loss, deduction or credit lacks substantial economic effect.
86. Hunton & Williams Client Alert, September 2009,
87. Ibid
88. There are restrictions that prevent certain types of non-taxpaying entities from participating as a tax equity partner. This includes real estate investment trusts (REITs) and municipal or cooperative utilities. Private sector utilities, however, do not have the restriction and can be a tax equity partner.
89. *U.S. Clean Energy—White Paper,* Bloomberg New Energy Finance, November 21, 2011.
90. Ibid
91. Daniel Richards
92. Some countries have enacted IFRS as national standards and require compliance to be stated with those national standards. In some cases, these national standards are identical to IFRS as issued by the IASB; in other cases, these national standards have been more narrow, yet consistent with IFRS as issued by the IASB; and, in yet other cases, these national standards may permit additional options that are inconsistent with IFRS as issued by the IASB, although companies may opt to apply standards so that they comply with IFRS as issued by the IASB. See http://www.iasplus.com/country/useias.htm .
93. S. Cerutti; J. Nickell; E. Putri, "Recap of Lease Redeliberation Results," Deloitte & Touche LLP, August 2011
94. Ibid
95. The ED defines "date of inception of the lease" as the "earlier of the date of the lease agreement and the date of commitment by the parties to the lease agreement."
96. The ED defines "the date of commencement of the lease" as the "date on which the lessor makes the underlying asset available for use by the lessee."
97. S. Cerutti; J. Nickell; E. Putri, "Recap of Lease Redeliberation Results," Deloitte & Touche LLP, August 2011
98. FASB Draws a Bright Line Through Operating Leases, Deloitte, August 17, 2010
99. Barney Capehart; Wayne Turner; William Kennedy, *Guide to Energy Management, Sixth Edition,* The Fairmont Press Inc, Lilburn, GA, USA

Chapter 6

Energy Efficiency Components of the Financial Analysis

Turmoil in the energy market over the past decade makes the benefits of energy efficiency more valuable than ever before as a way to control energy costs. The problem is that the term "energy efficiency" can mean different things to different people in different industries. Additional confusion surrounds the variety of activities that provide energy efficiency.

INTRODUCTION

"Energy Efficiency—the gift the keeps giving"

The services demanded of buildings—lighting, warmth in the winter, cooling in the summer, water heating, electronic entertainment, computing, lighting, refrigeration, and cooking—require significant energy use, about 40 quadrillion Btu (quads) per year.[1] The total utility bill for energy used by U.S. buildings topped $369 billion in 2005.[2] Energy efficiency is that action taken to reduce the amount of energy required to provide products and services across all market segments. Improvements in energy efficiency are most often achieved by adopting a more efficient technology or production process.

Manufacturers, consumers, commercial building owners, government at all levels and industrial facilities are struggling with volatile energy costs needed to meet those continued levels of energy consumption. While many decision makers anticipate a solution in the form of lower energy prices (certainly not a realistic view), others are investigating the merits of efficient practices and systems that reduce unnecessary energy consumption. Most often this will or should occur at the same time that a company is considering distributed energy generation on a renewable energy project. In most cases, an effective energy efficiency plan will reduce current energy needs between ten and twenty percent from existing levels. Then, given those reductions (and considering future energy growth needs) a professionally designed renewable energy system can be put together that encompasses the reductions that have taken place from the energy efficiency implementation. The dual approach—*energy efficiency combined with energy generation*—clearly makes the most cost effective way to controlling all future energy costs in a business.

The commercial sector is considerably more heterogeneous than residential buildings, encompassing hospitals, schools, offices, houses of worship, lodging, and the retail sector with its big box stores, enclosed malls, strip malls, grocery stores and fast food and sit-down restaurants. Each of these commercial sub-sectors is unique in its market structure, energy use, and energy intensity, and in the set of decision makers involved in design and construction projects. The two largest energy using sectors are offices and retail.

> *"Efficiency is doing things right; effectiveness is doing the right thing."*
>
> Peter Drucker, writer and management consultant

In 2003, there were 4.86 million commercial buildings in the United States, with an average size of 14,700 square feet. The U.S. adds about 1.6 billion square feet per year—nearly 110,000 buildings annually at the mean size, or roughly half a million buildings every five years.[3] The sheer magnitude of annual growth of the commercial sector provides a larger context in which to understand some of the important, but still relatively small, achievements in "green" buildings.

America's potential for increasing energy efficiency—that is, reducing energy use while delivering the same services—is enormous.[4] Technology exists today, or is expected to be developed before 2030, that could save about 30 percent of the energy used in the buildings, transportation, and industrial sectors while saving money. Nowhere can this be seen more dramatically than in the buildings sector. Residential and commercial buildings account for about 73 percent of the electricity used in the U.S. More efficient technologies for space heating and cooling, water heating, and lighting would likely provide most of this reduction. For the entire buildings sector, a cumulative investment of $440 billion in existing technology between 2010 and 2030 could produce an annual savings of $170 billion in reduced energy costs—and based on a sound financial investment strategy.

There are numerous barriers to deployment of more energy efficient technologies. Principal among them is the fact that most utilities profit when their customers use more energy and so are not rewarded for achieving increases in energy efficiency. But, there are policies currently being implemented in many states that could dramatically change those facts—mostly legislative mandates for energy efficiency deployment.

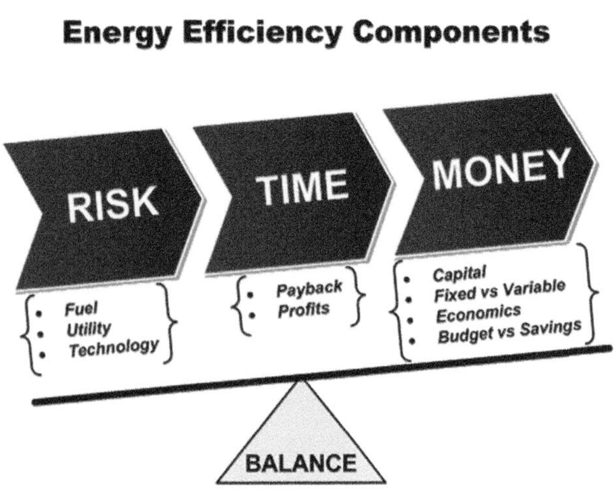

Figure 6-1: Energy Efficiency Components

Senior management at all levels face challenges of balancing risk, time and money in order to meet their corporate objectives. It takes a great deal of cooperation between departments, divisions and staff. It requires the concurrence of all staffing levels from operations and engineering to maintenance and finance in addition to the top leadership. In many cases, strong technical skills are required to properly analyze the projects. "Energy efficiency" is one of many issues that are competing for industry's time, resources, and leadership. In the end, implementing a cost effective energy efficiency program at the corporate level means that it must be part of a larger energy agenda including energy production and contribute to a broad industrial competitiveness and needs in areas such as economic development, demonstrating sustainability and astute corporate governance, disaster preparedness, and pursing new markets and revenues. Companies that achieve their sustainability goals recognize that energy efficiency, not supply chains or greenhouse gas emission reductions, is the top priority for their organization. Energy efficiency projects, particularly those within the organization's buildings and other facilities, offer a cost-effective way to achieve significant, quick and measureable improvement.

ENERGY EFFICIENCY

Energy efficiency (EE) is an investment, just as any other capital asset infrastructure is. The intent is to reduce energy consumption as an offset to rising energy demands. Energy efficiency is the low hanging fruit to return the cost of implementation quicker with less cost than any other energy project. Energy efficiency is a simple concept: consuming less energy to get the same amount of heat for the shower, light for the office and power for the factory. It is much less expensive, destructive and time-intensive to reduce demand through energy efficiency projects than to increase supply through the building of new power plants. Efficiency is all about doing the same—or more—with less. The by-products of good EE policies are decreased environmental demands, an economic development improvement and an increase in energy security. EE is truly the fastest way to address growing energy demands by consumers, industry and government.

Residential energy use per capita in the U.S. has remained fairly consistent over the past 40 years as can be seen in Figure 6-2 from the U.S. Energy Information Administration:

The biggest use of energy on the commercial side is in buildings as shown in Figure 6-3.

> *"There can be economy only where there is efficiency."*
>
> Benjamin Disraeli (1804 – 1881), British Prime Minister

Older commercial equipment that can be found in many businesses is not energy efficient. Energy audit programs should be implemented that are designed to encourage the use of high-efficiency space and water heating equipment, central air conditioning, lighting, motors, compressors and other measures in commercial

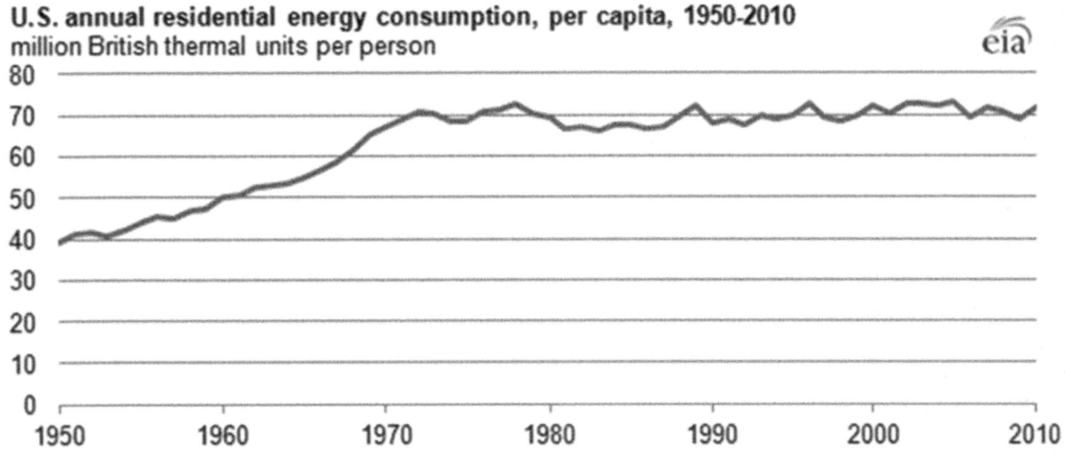

Figure 6-2: Annual Per Capita Energy Consumption

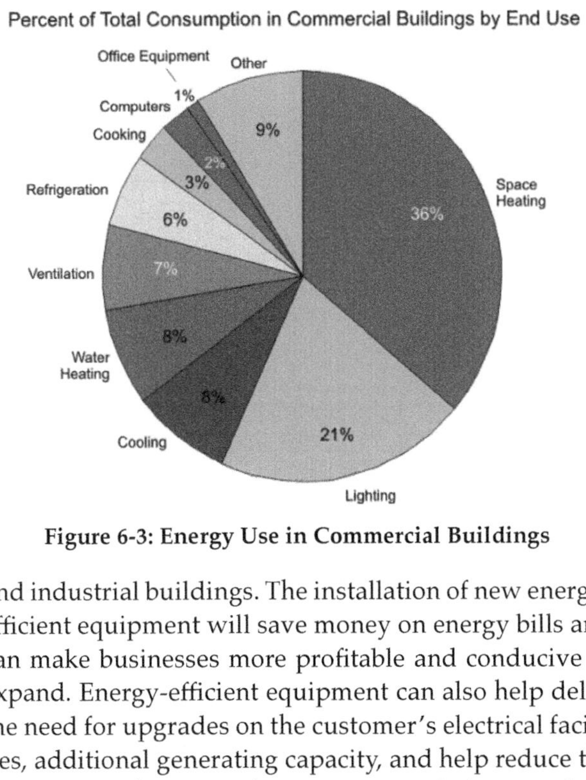

Figure 6-3: Energy Use in Commercial Buildings

and industrial buildings. The installation of new energy-efficient equipment will save money on energy bills and can make businesses more profitable and conducive to expand. Energy-efficient equipment can also help delay the need for upgrades on the customer's electrical facilities, additional generating capacity, and help reduce the demand on the natural resources needed to produce energy.

Most companies tend to resist implementing energy-efficient practices even though they recognize the energy savings that can be derived from such practices. They tend to look at energy as an on-going and uncontrollable cost of just being in business. Some go so far as getting an energy audit from a utility or other professional agency and still don't proceed with the immediate implementation of the recommendations made. One of the main reasons for the audit is nothing more than a good understanding of what is involved and finding a good management advocate within the organization to champion the process. With misunderstanding comes resistance. Most corporate management simply do not understand that in addition to saving money 1) immediately and 2) on a continuing basis, that there are other benefits that most energy auditors and staff don't adequately present that includes:

- Reducing fuel expense
- Providing a permanent hedge against assured future energy price escalations
- Increasing the reliability and productivity of existing equipment and facilities
- Demonstrating smart corporate governance
- Meeting existing and future mandated environmental regulations
- Enjoying faster production cycles and more consistent product quality
- Development of expanded markets and strategic business relationships
- Reducing exposure to environmental, health, and safety liabilities
- Increased efficiency from current staffing and workforce
- Meeting external demands by corporate customers to achieve sustainability goals
- Meeting demands by shareholders to set sustainability goals

However, the most often cited reason for not immediately implementing an energy efficiency program is simply "cost." Seldom has there been a budget allocation for these kinds of less urgent capital expenditures. Here again, renewable energy and energy efficiency project creditors, investors and developers can ride into the corporate board room and become a hero. In nearly all cases (unless there is a clearly demonstrated credit or financial risk with the customer) the cost of the equipment to achieve significant energy savings can be bundled into other parts of an energy project and financed over a significant time frame—and without capital outlay by the customer. Additionally, the savings from the energy efficiency component of the project can significantly help with the cash flow needed to acquire an energy "production" system such as solar PV, solar thermal, cogeneration and CHP applications, fuel cells, etc. The graph below is indicative of the results of combining an energy efficiency project with a renewable energy production project using an operating lease structure. The second graph is the same project but instead using a PPA finance structure.

Energy efficiency contributes 24% of the annual cash flow in the first year and increases to 39% in year 30 in this example—a significant financial contribution on either an operating lease or PPA basis. This assumes of course that the energy efficiency component will have 30-year useful life, as most energy efficiency components do.

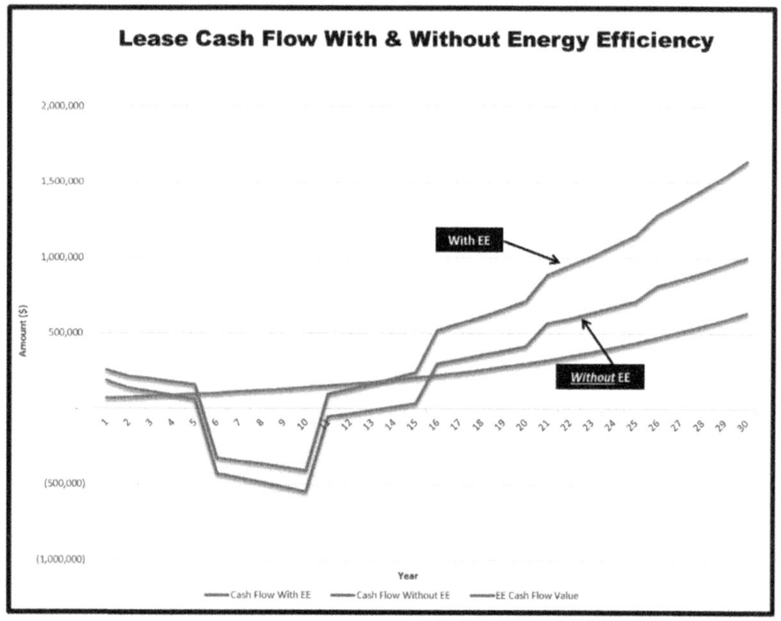

Figure 6-4: Operating Lease Financing Structure

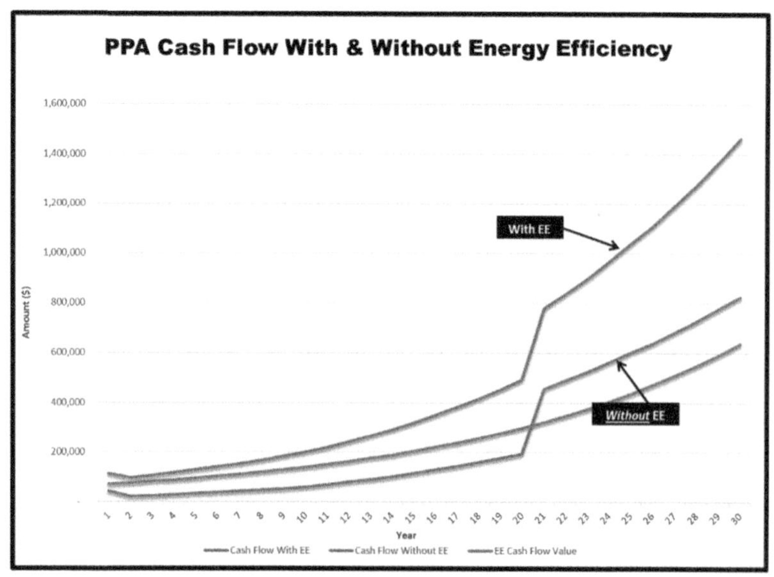

Figure 6-5: PPA Financing Structure

Reasons for Not Implementing EE

Often, the equipment and operations that benefits the most from energy efficiency improvements are large assets like HVAC systems, boilers, furnaces, air compressors, lighting and all types of motor driven devices. There are many smaller assets that also benefit and at a much lower capital replacement costs and includes pumps, fans and smaller motors. Unfortunately, the actual design of the overall operating system in a facility in which they are installed is not as easy to change. Often, lower level management doesn't suggest improvements simply because they feel it might reflect negatively on their maintenance and performance levels. Most departments work within the bounds of their responsibilities and often don't coordinate the larger needs of the facility.

Many companies continue to manage their energy programs like they have done for decades where energy costs were very stable with small annual increases, reliability of energy supplies was not questioned, and emissions from the use of energy was not an issue—or even measured. Today, things are dramatically different. Today's management face highly volatile and rapidly changing energy costs, a much more regulated utility industry with renewable portfolio standards that costs substantially higher to acquire and sell to their customers under mandated regulations, uncertain and constrained supplies and ever increasing emission controls and costs. With so many issues to manage, it is natural for executives to focus on core business concerns, delegating most other matters to subordinates who are not in a position to either make decisions or to implement a policy change of such magnitude. While executives are keenly aware of energy prices, they are usually unconcerned with "energy consumption" or "energy efficiency." Then, covering all the above, the company must often overcome organizational complexities and long-standing procedures that prevent action.

The old paradigm was characterized by the following perceptions:[6]

- "Energy is not our core business"
- "You're the engineer—you figure it out"
- "Low fuel price is the solution"
- "That's the way we've always done it"
- "We're not going to bust the budget under my watch"

Different groups within an organization are looking for different solutions.[7] Executives want solutions that are effective and durable (low risk), easy to implement (not time-intensive), and financially valuable (providing a quick and sizable financial return, with minimal or no capital investment.) The facility general managers want to reach their production targets on-time, ensure a high level of product quality, and minimize their expenses. They have no responsibility for general plant costs like energy and therefore have no incentive to save energy costs from the performance of the operations. Facility maintenance and engineering personnel are held accountable primarily for the reliability of plant equipment. Controlling cost of operating this equipment, including its energy consumption, is important but usually secondary unless energy expenses become noticeable at higher levels in the organization and only if an individual and that department alone caused that increased utility cost.

EE Solutions and Strategies

Research by the Alliance to Save Energy reveals five basic strategies for attaining industrial energy efficiency, and every company adopts at least one of these.[8]

1. Do nothing (the most frequent "strategy")
2. Switch fuels or fuel suppliers

> *"Perhaps the quickest, easiest, and most profitable way to reduce electricity use worldwide—thus cutting carbon emissions—is simply to change light bulbs. Replacing the inefficient incandescent light bulbs that are still widely used today with new compact fluorescents (CFLs) can reduce electricity use by three fourths. The energy saved by replacing a 100-watt incandescent bulb with an equivalent CFL over its lifetime is sufficient to drive a Toyota Prius hybrid car from New York to San Francisco."*
>
> Lester R. Brown. PLAN B 3.0:
> Mobilizing to Save Civilization (2008)

3. Implement easy, low-tech projects
4. Develop advanced technology capital projects (subject to capital budgets or financing alternatives)
5. Utilize continuous energy improvement mechanisms throughout the corporation

While management in a company today may be more aware of energy costs than ever before, their awareness of the techniques for controlling costs or implementing changes remains low. Often there is an on-going misguided belief that there will be new energy supplies and that will lower energy prices. A company's progress in becoming energy-efficient will depend on the energy management strategy that it devises to suit its unique circumstances. No one strategy fits all companies.

The ten most frequently heard management objections to energy efficiency projects are:

1. "We don't have the money for energy efficiency projects."
2. "We don't have the time."
3. "Programs take priority over maintenance."
4. "Energy projects interrupt our operations."
5. "I am held accountable for reliability, not efficiency."
6. "I would rather achieve efficiency by securing fuel at the lowest price."
7. "We are already as efficient as we can be."
8. "Doing nothing costs nothing."
9. "We need to cut the fat."
10. "The technology is too risky."

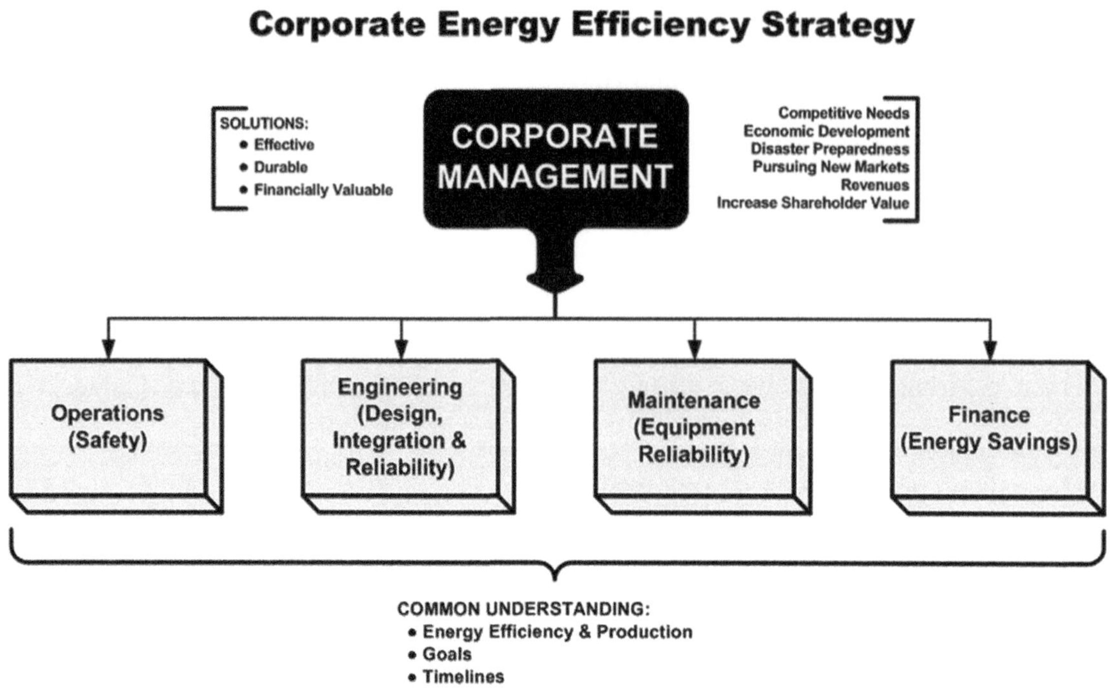

Figure 6-6: Energy Efficiency Strategy

While implementation times and priorities for energy efficiency programs will vary from company to company, so do earmarked rebates available from utility companies and other sources. Different states have different emphasis on increasing energy efficiency and its counterpart: demand management reduction programs. Potentially large incentives are available to implement energy efficiency programs but they vary greatly by utility and region. For a complete and current update on all that are available, visit *http://www.dsireusa.org*.

EE in the Commercial and Industrial Sector

The U.S. industrial sector energy consumption continues to decline gradually. In 2007, U.S. industrial sector energy consumption was 32.3 Quadrillion Btu (quads).[9] This was about 32% of total U.S. energy use in 2007 and considerably less than the record 1997 level of 35.3 quads. Excluding electric utility generation and transmission losses, net industrial energy use was 24.9 quads.

> *"The progress of science is characterized by the fact that more and more energy is utilized for human purposes, and that the transformation of the raw energies...is attended by ever-increased efficiency."*
>
> Wilheim Ostwald, German physical chemist (1907)

Industrial energy intensity is often used to gauge trends in the efficiency of energy use. Energy intensity refers to the amount of energy used to produce a unit of output (typically, Btu of energy per dollar of output or gross domestic product (GDP)). Over the past 10 years, trends in energy consumption and intensity include:

- Slowly declining industrial energy consumption as the economy continues to shift away from energy-intensive manufacturing industries.
- Nearly 20% improvement in energy intensity, which may stem from rising energy prices and increased concern about global warming.
- Overall increase in value added, which is the measure for productive services (such as labor and capital) that increase the value of materials being processed.

By law, the U.S. Department of Energy must set energy efficiency standards for equipment and appliances at the maximum level of energy efficiency that is technically feasible and economically justified. This includes new appliance efficiency standards. The potential types of energy efficiency measures (ECMs) that can be examined in the commercial and industrial sectors to determine the possible energy efficiency sources, priorities and cost effectiveness can include:

1. **Lighting Retrofits**
   - Fluorescent lighting
   - LED exit signs
   - Motion Sensors
   - PL Lamps
   - Electronic ballasts
   - Reflectors
   - Daylighting control systems

2. **Energy Management Systems (EMS) and Controls**
   - Energy management systems
   - Load reset/setback
   - Direct digital controls
   - Demand controls
   - Electric deregulation monitoring and control
   - HVAC and lighting controls
   - Management information tools
   - Software
     - — Scheduled start/stop
     - — Optimized start/stop
     - — Temperature compensated duty cycle
     - — Temperature compensated demand shed
     - — Night setback
     - — Temperature reset—chilled water, hot water, condenser water and supply temperature

3. **Mechanical and Electrical Retrofits/Installations**
   - Economizers (Air/Fluid)
   - HVAC Controls
   - HVAC Unit Change-outs (including CFC management)
   - Switch from package HVAC units to a central plant arrangement
   - Variable Frequency Drives
     - — Chilled water pumping
     - — Condenser water pumping
     - — Cooling tower fans
     - — Variable air volume (VAV) fan systems
     - — Chillers
   - Boiler/Steam Equipment
   - Fuel Conversion and Dual Fuel Systems
   - Cogeneration and Waste Heat Recovery Systems
   - Peak-Shaving and Distributed Generation (especially renewable energy systems)
   - Thermal Storage Systems (hot, cold & ice)
   - Gas/Thermal Cooling Technologies, e.g. absorption chillers
   - Air-side Recovery Systems
   - High Efficiency Motors

4. **Miscellaneous**
   - Steam Traps Replacement
   - Domestic Hot Water System Retrofits
   - Power Factor Correction
   - Utility Rate Analysis
   - Flush-less or Low-flush Toilets
   - Low Water Consumption Landscaping
   - Grey Water Recovery
   - Multiple Sustainable Building & Architecture Systems
   - Retro-commissioning of Existing Facilities
   - New Low-Energy Production Equipment
   - Energy Star Appliances

Energy efficient technologies, procedures and operating behaviors allow facilities to control the energy costs. Energy-efficient principles and activities also contribute to the mechanical integrity and reliability of energy-using equipment such as boilers, furnaces, air compressors, fans, pumps, and motor-driven systems. As a facility boosts the reliability of these assets, it offsets the risk of operational failure or "down-time." Reliable plant assets work longer and make more products, therefore helping the facility to achieve higher production targets and bring in more revenue.

Sara Hayes, a senior researcher at the American Council for an Energy Efficient Economy (ACEEE) has pointed out some components that are critical to a thorough understanding of energy efficiency.[10]

- The lack of national standards for measuring and verifying efficiency-driven savings has left states to develop their own. So now more than half of all states have efficiency targets and are measuring their progress toward meeting those goals. Utilities have also been documenting energy savings from efficiency measure for decades. In many cases, a utility's authority to collect revenues is based on its ability to verify, with substantial certainty, those savings. So utilities have invested significant resources into development methods that stand up to the scrutiny of regulators and ratepayers.

> *"What we need to do is really improve energy efficiency standards, develop in full scale renewable and alternative energy and use the one resource we have in abundance, our creativity."*
>
> Lois Capps, congresswoman from California

- An entire profession of energy program evaluators has developed over the last three decades. They use methods that are accepted in regulatory proceedings across the nation. When a new piece of equipment replaces an older version, the energy savings or losses can be accurately measured. While other factors such as the weather may affect total energy use, statistical methods can separate out these effects, pulling the wheat from the chaff.
- Efficiency is not a "demand/response" device that is simply switched on when needed. Rather, it is more of a "baseload" approach that, once put into practice or embedded in a device, continues to save energy whenever that device operates.
- Energy savings from efficiency are real and save Americans money. Since 1970, efficiency improvements have reduced U.S. energy costs by about $700 billion from what they would otherwise have been in 2005. And energy savings from efficiency measures in all sectors is predicted to be 16-30% of current consumption by 2025.

PUBLIC SECTOR ENERGY EFFICIENCY PROJECTS

This section addresses the special needs of public sector agencies such as city and county governments, public school districts, hospitals, and special districts, such as water and wastewater treatment districts. However, many of the same principals apply to the private sector.

Cost effectiveness is the principal component of the decision making process in public sector energy efficiency projects. Before financing an energy efficiency project, the public sector agency will want to determine if the project is cost effective. This can be done using one of the following methods:

Simple Payback

This is the time required to recapture the initial project costs from the energy and other cost savings. If you had a $200,000 project which produced an annual savings of $100,000, it would have a two-year "simple payback." Ideally, the faster the payback, the more attractive the project.

Simple payback is the most commonly used cost effectiveness criterion because it is easy to use and understand. If the payback is short relative to a project's useful life, simple payback is an adequate measure of cost-effectiveness. If the project payback is long, use of one of the other criterion, such as life-cycle costs, will give a more accurate picture of a project's value.

Net Present Value (NPV)

A project's net present value depends on its future costs and benefits measured in today's dollars. Costs such as maintenance or replacement of equipment/parts may vary each year. To calculate NPV, future costs and benefits need to be discounted using a reasonable discount or inflation rate. When using this criterion, the general rule-of-thumb is to select projects with a NPV of zero or greater.

Rate of Return/Return on Investment (ROI)

This is the percentage of an investment that is paid back each year. A $200,000 project that saves $100,000 each year has a 50 percent rate of return or return on investment (ROI). In business, a 10 percent ROI is considered good. Most energy-efficiency projects have an average 15 percent ROI.

Lifecycle Cost Analysis

This method evaluates all of a project's savings and costs over its lifetime. Included are salvage and maintenance savings as well as operating, maintenance, replacement, and disposal costs. If the NPV of the benefits is greater than costs, the project is considered cost-effective.

The most comprehensive and accurate measure of a project's cost-effectiveness is probably lifecycle cost, since it captures all savings and cost over a project's life. This method will involve more research and analysis than calculating simple payback. Each method has its advantages and limitations.

Options for Financing Energy Efficiency Public Sector Projects

The main ways of financing energy efficiency projects for the public sector (as it is with the private sector) are (1) self-financing; (2) loans; and (3) third-party financing (including PPAs).

Self-financing with Internal Funds

This is the least common form of acquiring assets for an energy efficiency project. Funds normally come from an annual budget or may be borrowed internally from enterprise accounts. However, there could be separate accounts for deferred maintenance or reserve accounts that might also be utilized for the self-financing. In most cases, these accounts would be repaid from the energy savings realized in the project. A key question that must always be asked before funds are utilized from these sources is: "Are the internal funds currently invested to earn a higher yield than the interest cost of financing an energy project?" If the answer is yes, the public entity might wish to seek outside financing for the project.

Loans

Generally, local agencies are forbidden from borrowing money for more than a year. Most state constitutions prohibit an elected board from creating indebtedness for the subsequent board without a vote of the electorate.

Although rules will vary from state to state, California laws are indicative of what is found in most other states. Energy efficiency projects financed by the California Energy Commission, have received a special exemption from the State Attorney General's Office. Under a 1984 Attorney General's ruling, energy efficiency projects that "pay for themselves" from energy cost savings do not constitute debt.

The California Energy Commission, the California Department of General Services, and the State Assistance Fund for Enterprise, Business and Industrial Development Corporation (SAFE-BIDCO) offer loan programs for public and nonprofit agencies. Commission loans target local governments, special districts and public and private non-profit schools and hospitals. The Department of General Services, Office of Energy Assessment (OEA), offers financing for state agencies, public universities, community college districts, and public K-12 schools through its Revenue Bond Program. SAFE-BIDCO, a nonprofit corporation, also offers loans to small commercial businesses and non-profit organizations for energy efficiency projects.

> *"I think the cost of energy will come down when we make this transition to renewable energy."*
>
> Al Gore, 45th Vice President of the U.S.

Third-party Financing

Governmental agencies cannot rely on budget appropriations alone to fund the energy efficiency and generation projects needed to meet their sustainability mandates. Funding options include energy savings performance contracts (ESPCs), utility energy service contracts (UESCs), power purchase agreements (PPAs), energy incentive programs, leasing and pooled bond financing. Carefully matching available funding options with specific situations can make the difference between a stalled, unfunded project and a successful project generating energy and significant cost savings. Utilizing these financing tools can stretch appropriations over many more projects.

Energy Savings Performance Contracts

ESPCs allow federal, state and local agencies to conduct energy projects with no upfront capital costs, minimizing the need for budget appropriations. An ESPC is a partnership between a governmental agency and an energy service company (ESCO). The ESCO conducts a comprehensive energy audit on the facility and identifies improvements to save energy. The ESCO then designs and constructs a project that meets the agency's needs and arranges the necessary funding. The ESCO guarantees the improvements will generate energy cost savings sufficient to pay for the project over the term of the contract. After the contract ends, all additional cost savings accrue to the agency. Depending on the governmental entity, terms of up to 25 years are allowed.

Utility Energy Service Contracts

UESCs are where an agency enters into a contract with local energy utilities to implement energy and water related improvements at their facilities. Agencies may fund the project with appropriations, or the utility may arrange funding to cover the capital cost of the project, which is repaid over the contract term from cost savings generated by the energy and water efficiency measures. The end benefits of UESCs are the ability to implement energy projects with no initial capital investments, minimal net costs, and time and resource savings. Performance guarantees are an option that can add additional value to a UESC project.

Power Purchase Agreements

On-site renewable PPAs allow governmental agencies to fund on-site renewable energy production projects with no upfront capital costs incurred. A developer installs a renewable energy system on agency property under an agreement that the agency will purchase the power generated by the system. The agency pays for the system by purchasing the energy produced by the system over the life of the contract. After installation, the developer owns, operates, and maintains the system for the life of the contract. The PPA price for the energy is typically determined through a competitive procurement process. Pricing usually starts out at 5-10% less than the power being purchased from the utility and increases incrementally over the term of the contract (up to 25 years) at a rate that is equal to or less than the increases from the utility. Therefore, there is an anticipated savings per year of 5-10% or greater over that of comparable power that is supplied by the local utility.

Energy Incentive Programs

Many utilities offer energy incentive programs. These services are offered at low or no cost to the agency and are generally funded by fees included in the utilities general rate structures. Demand response and load management programs are one form of incentive offering. In these programs, utility companies or regional transmission operators provide rate incentives and/or cash payments in exchange for curtailing energy demand during peak usage periods to increase system reliability and reduce the need for constructing new generation facilities.

Leasing

This is financing obtained through a lease-purchase contract with a lessor. These financing arrangements typically finance 100% of the assets and incorporate an option to purchase the equipment for a fixed amount at the end of the contract term. The two most common types of leases are finance leases and operating leases.

Financing leases are generally installment purchases of energy efficiency equipment. The lessee makes no capital outlay to purchase the equipment and receives all the savings from the project. The lessee is considered the owner of the equipment and may take depreciation on the equipment and deductions on the interest portion of the payments. Public agencies seldom see any advantage in this type of arrangement as they do not pay taxes.

Operating leases are an arrangement in which the lessor owns the equipment, which is leased or rented to the lessee for a monthly fee during the term. Under this arrangement it is the lessor who gets the tax benefits associated with the depreciation of the equipment. The lessor retains ownership of the equipment and it does not pass to the public agency upon expiration of the lease.

The public agency can purchase the equipment upon lease termination. This type of financing is most common for property that can be moved and less common for equipment which is a part of a building. The larger the project, the more often this type of leasing is utilized.

Municipal leases are available only to tax exempt entities like cities, counties, public school districts and special districts. Under this arrangement, the lessor does not have to pay taxes on the interest portion of the lessee's payments. Therefore, the lessor can offer a lower interest rate compared to other types of leases. Under the municipal lease structure, the public agency has the option to purchase the equipment at the end of the lease term. Municipal leases are commonly used among public agencies. These leases have the advantage of low interest rates, reducing overall project cost. Unlike bonds, municipal leases do not require voter approval. Municipal leases allow the lessee to lock-in an interest rate when the lease is entered.

Master lease agreements are "umbrella" contracts with general terms and conditions. This type of lease allows public agencies to fund many projects overtime. As the lessee makes individual purchases or begins individual projects, new leases or lease schedules are funded and appended to the master lease.

Certificates of Participation (COPs) are lease-purchase agreements that are divided and sold to multiple investors, similar to stocks. Since the risk of the project is distributed among the investors, this option generally offers a lower interest rate than other financing options. Since COPs are in the open market, they have to be registered with the Securities and Exchange Commission. Therefore, this option requires the participation of a financial advisor, bond counsel, issuer, underwriter, trustee and rating agencies. All of these parties and complexities add to the initial cost of utilizing this type of financing.

Lease revenue bonds are another leasing arrangement that is analogous to a certificate of participation. The difference is that instead of a corporation serving as lessor, a single government agency acts as lessor while the jurisdiction needing funding serves as lessee. The lessor government issues the bonds, enters into a lease with the lessee jurisdiction, and the lease revenues are pledged as repayment for the bonds.

Pooled Bond Financing

Pooled bond programs help reduce the cost of bond issuance. The bond transaction cost is spread among the borrowers to pay for a financial adviser, bond counsel, underwriter and trustee. In pooled bond arrangements, usually a small group of borrowers can pool their financing needs together and issue a single bond. Projects less than $500,000 are typically not accepted into these pools. The reason is the need to issue a large bond to make this option cost-effective. For projects in the multimillion dollar range, however, individual or pooled bonds may be a cost-effective and feasible option and could yield the lowest cost money.

Several local government associations and/or joint powers authorities in California (as a typical state) offer pooled bond programs. Examples include the California State Association of Counties, the Association of Bay Area Governments, the Financing Authority for Resource Efficiency in California and the California Municipal Utility Association.

Table 6-1 summarizes the features of the different financing options for public sector energy efficiency projects (using California as an example).

The Bond-PPA Hybrid[11]

The hybrid model is a financing option by which a public entity issues a government bond at a low interest rate and transfers that low-cost capital to a developer in exchange for a lower PPA price.

In this finance structure, a public entity (the administrator) issues a request for proposals (RFP) seeking a developer to build, operate, and own a renewable energy project on public buildings (local hosts). The administrator sells bonds to finance the development costs of the renewable energy project. The administrator then

Table 6-1: Features of Various Financing Options for Public Sector Energy Efficiency Projects

Financing Options	Interest Rates	Up-front Costs	Requires Voter Approval	Complex	Staff Time	Ownership	Project Size
Self Financing	NA	No	No	No	Low	Agency	Neutral
Municipal Lease	Low	No	No	No	Low	Lessor	Neutral
State Loan (CEC)*	Low	No	No	No	Low	Agency	Small to Medium
State Loan (EA)**	Low	No	No	No	Now	Agency	Neutral
COP	Low	Yes	No	Can be ***	High	Lessor	Medium to Large
Pooled Bonds	Low	Yes	No	Can be ***	High	Agency	Medium to Large

* CEC (California Energy Commission)

** EA (CA Department of General Services, Energy Assessments

*** Can be complex because of the need for a financial advisor, bond counsel, underwriter, trustee and other service providers.

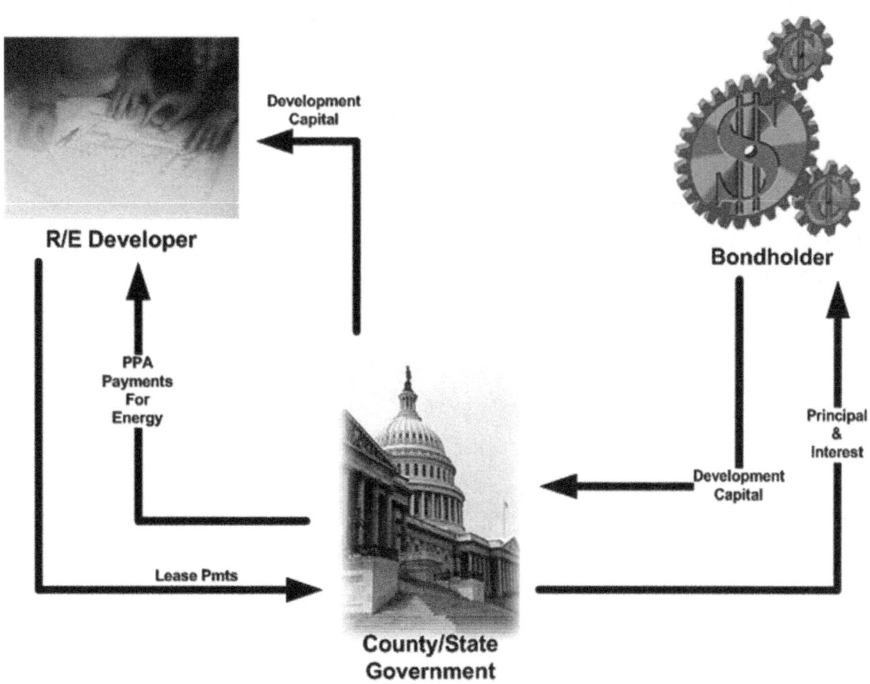

Figure 6-7: Cash Transfers in Bond-PPA Hybrid

enters into both a lease-purchase agreement with the winning bidder and a PPA (on behalf of the local hosts) to purchase the energy produced by the renewable energy system.

A word of caution for the use of this model: though most governmental bonds in the U.S. are sold to investors as tax-exempt investments, federal regulations require that bonds issued for private use must be taxable. Bonds issued for the purpose of the hybrid model are considered private use because the proceeds are used to fund a project owned by a private entity. Although the bonds must be issued as taxable investments, the good credit rating of the administrator will often make its borrowing rate less than that of the renewable energy project developer.

In this model, the developer makes lease payments that fully cover the bond payments. These lease payments are lower than the loan payments on funds that the developer would otherwise have borrowed. The cost savings means that between the low lease payments and the tax attributes, the developer can offer the administrator an attractive PPA price while still making a strong financial return. In addition, the administrator receives fixed energy costs under a long-term PPA contract and has no operating and maintenance responsibilities for the renewable energy system. Also, because the public entity is able to provide low-cost capital to the project and assuming financial risk, it has leverage to bargain for better PPA pricing. A potential downside of the hybrid model is that transaction costs could be higher than under either the self-ownership or third-party PPA models.

This model requires the financial contract between the administrator and developer to be structured as a capital lease, not a loan. For the purposes of state law, the administrator is considered the project owner/lessor, and the developer is the lessee. However, the terms of the lease-purchase agreement are such that all of the benefits and burdens of ownership are transferred to the developer. This means that for federal tax purposes, the developer owns the project and can take advantage of the investment tax credit (or U.S. Treasury cash grant if available). The National Tax Council issued an opinion for a developer stating that although the structure is a lease, tax ownership transfers to the developer. The administrator may structure lease repayment as annual amortized payments. The lease-purchase agreement includes annual fees to be paid to the government issuer for administration costs.

The developer and the administrator sign a PPA on behalf of the local hosts. One benefit of the hybrid model is that the public entity can negotiate its own terms and conditions and on a project by project basis.

The security agreement protects the administrator in the event of developer default. The security is provided in two forms: a performance and payment bond and a posted security:

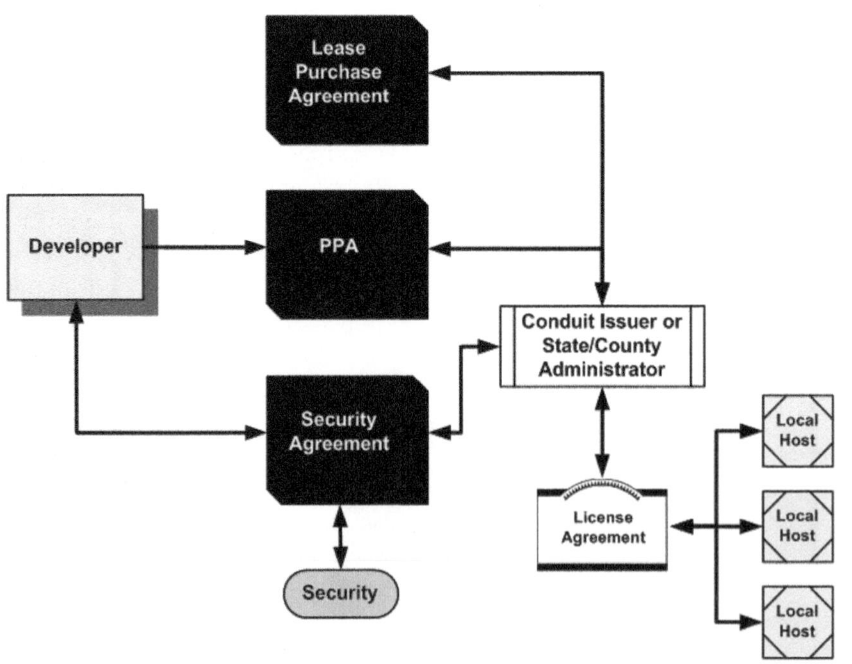

Figure 6-8: Contract Arrangements in Hybrid Model

- *Performance and payment bond*: The developer (or its contractor) must obtain a performance and payment bond for the project, which protects the administrator in the case of construction contract non-performance. The administrator is guaranteed compensation for monetary loss up to the amount of the performance and payment bond.

- *Posted security*: The developer must also post a form of security that ensures that the administrator can pay its bondholders. Projects that have used this model have developed a formula to establish an appropriate level for this security. It is sized according to what the administrator needs to protect them in the event that the developer walks away. This security protects the administrator up to the "deficiency amount." The deficiency amount is the sum that the administrator owes to the bondholders minus the sum owed to the developer in PPA payments for the energy already delivered and the sum of any revenues generated by the project:

Deficiency amount = ∑ bond principal + interest - ∑ PPA payments - ∑ additional revenues (e.g., SRECs)

The security requirement can be satisfied in a number of ways, including a parent or affiliate guarantee, a stand-by-letter of credit, a direct equity contribution, or by escrowing the 1603 cash grant (if it is available in the transaction). If a default on lease payments occurs after the project is built, the developer releases this security and forfeits all rights to the project. The administrator then becomes the project owner, with access to the energy produced by the project and any other revenues generated by the project (e.g., SRECs).

Though not necessary, a "conduit issuer"—an entity that issues debt on behalf of a state or local government—can be advantageous. A conduit issuer typically does not have an independent credit rating.[12] The use of a conduit issuer may be advantageous for the following reason: If an administrator issues its own bond via its general obligation taxing authority, the issuance is considered a direct obligation and counts towards the administrator's total debt load. On the other hand, a conduit issuance amounts to a guarantee obligation for the administrator. In contrast with a direct obligation, a guarantee obligation does not count against the total debt the administrator can assume.[13] Each state has unique laws that would govern the applicability of the bond-PPA hybrid model and professional counsel should be used in every case.

> *"There are no passengers on Spaceship Earth. We are all crew."*
>
> Marshall McLuhan, 1964

On-bill Financing

On-bill financing generally refers to a financial structure that is serviced by, or in partnership with, a utility company for energy efficiency improvements in a building, and repaid by the building owner on their monthly utility bill. Programs can be tailored to the industrial, commercial, and residential sectors. Underlying the structure is providing the debtor/utility customer the ability to repay the loan from the energy savings inherent in the project. Despite the benefits of energy efficiency investments, high upfront costs continue to be a significant barrier to leveraging retrofits to achieve potential monetary and energy savings across the building sector. On-bill financing has the power to attract capital from previously untapped sources because customers tend to prioritize their utility bill payments and this is viewed by some investors as a form of security.

The American Council for an Energy Efficient Economy reports that there are at least 20 states that now have utilities who have implemented or are about to implement on-bill financing programs for their customers. Challenges to the utility include the up-front costs to modify their existing billing systems and the administrative aspects of acting like a lender. They also must have access to capital, either their own or lines of credit or outside sources, that will support the program. On the other hand, such a financing program can leverage a utility's unique relationship with their energy customers to provide convenient access to funding for the energy efficiency project. There is also potential for a traditionally credit-constrained customer to gain access to financing through modified underwriting that takes bill payment history into account. The on-bill financing mechanism provides a clear link between energy use and savings, enabling a program participant to relate a reduction in energy consumption with the investments made through the loan program.

Some program administrators are also exploring the potential of bundling on-bill loans with other financial products, and creating a secondary market for capital.[14] The current perception is that on-bill loans are cost-effective, low risk, and would offer a modest return. It is possible, given appropriate risk assessment, that financial institutions could market low-risk securities comprised of bundled on-bill loans to a secondary market to augment available capital. However, there are also major barriers to tapping secondary markets such as uncertainty surrounding the behavior of energy efficiency as an asset class, uniformity of loan products, and lengthy returns on investment.

Major barriers to adoption include up-front costs to utilities with a need to modify their billing systems, a perception that utilities need to behave like a financial institution to participate in on-bill financing, risks of non-payment, handling transfer of property, finding capital to support the program, and addressing non-utility fuels.[15] On-bill programs have the potential to address gaps that have not been historically addressed by other energy financing mechanisms. With support from policymakers, they can do even more to provide cost and energy savings to a broad range of markets. However, on-bill programs are still generally in their infancy, and much additional work is needed to find the best ways to overcome barriers.[16]

In some states, there are specific loan programs available. California is one example. Through a program for cities, counties, public care institutions, public hospitals, public schools and colleges, and special taxing districts, it is administered by the California Energy Commission and is called the State Energy Program (SEP).

The first program is at an incredible rate of 1% interest. Eligible projects include:

- Automated energy management systems & controls
- Building insulation
- Energy audits and feasibility studies
- Energy generation including renewable technologies and CHP
- Heating and air conditional modifications
- Lighting systems
- Pumps and motors
- Streetlights and LED traffic signals
- Waste water treatment equipment

A second loan program is available at a 3% interest rate under a program called Energy Conservation Assistance Account (ECCA—and yes, it doesn't match the name). Loans for energy projects under ECCA must be repaid from energy cost savings within 15 years, including principal and interest (approximately 11 years simple payback). Simple payback is calculated by dividing the dollar amount of the loan by the anticipated annual energy cost savings. The loan term cannot exceed the useful life of loan-funded equipment. The repayment schedule is based on the estimated annual projected energy cost savings from the aggregated project(s), using energy costs and operating schedules at the time of loan approval. Loans will be amortized on the estimated annual energy cost savings achieved by the loan-funded project. Applicants are billed twice a year, in June and December, after the projects are completed. Loans must be repaid from energy cost savings or other legally available funds within a maximum term of 15 years, including principal and interest. Applications can be found at *http://www.energy.ca.gov/efficiency/financing*.

ENERGY AUDITS

The fact is, an energy user must find out where "they are" before they can determine where they want to go in cutting energy costs and installing energy generation systems that complement the energy efficiency components of the energy project. The map and journey of energy efficiency savings starts with an energy audit. When seeking a qualified auditor to perform the audit, it is suggested that you retain an energy engineer with special credentials such as CEA (Certified Energy Auditor) or CEM (Certified Energy Manager)—both are administered through the Association of Energy Engineers (AEE).[17]

The logical first step for an industrial or commercial facility seeking to control its energy costs is to secure an energy assessment/audit to identify the energy improvement opportunities. From less than one percent to five percent of your annual utility cost, a full energy audit will identify opportunities for developing a significant savings program that will far exceed the cost of the survey. The cost of any survey will vary based upon the size of the annual utility bills and buildings and the complexity of the energy systems and load centers in the facility. A complete energy audit consists of four coordinated sections and typically can be performed in four separate stages. Each stage can cost variable amounts depending on the complexity of the project or size of the facility being evaluated. The four distinct stages of an energy audit (includes identifying an EEM or Energy Efficiency Measure) are:

- **Screening Audit**. The screening audit in most cases is the simplest, cheapest and fastest quick review high-level assessment of the entire facility and is the starting point for the gathering of information task. It most often starts with a review of the facility's historic energy bill before a physical

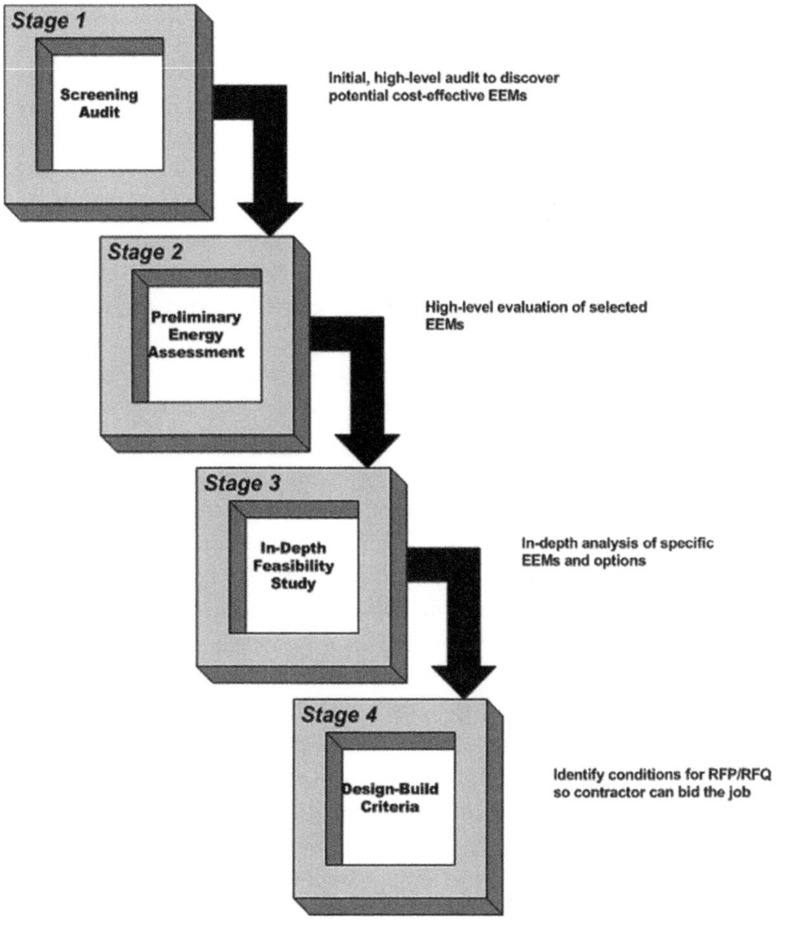

Figure 6-9: Energy Audit Stages

site visit. This is then followed by an actual visit to the site. The site visit allows the auditor to identify those ECMs (energy conservation measure) or EEMs (energy efficiency measures) that could identify potential cost-effective energy savings to the facility. The screening audit might cost nothing or as much as several thousand dollars per building depending on the complexity of the energy loads of the building.

- **Preliminary Energy Assessment (PEA).** This next stage entails reviewing the energy bills and design drawings of the facility and performing a high-level energy audit or report. The data collected from the energy bills and the data and observations collected from the site visit are compiled to identify and quantify potential energy savings and financial benefits of implementing the measures identified in the in screening audit. This assessment provides an analysis of all the measures selected and identified in the first stage. The analysis compares existing systems with potential replacement systems and equipment. The PEA is usually used to calculate "simple payback" periods for each measure to determine whether an In-Depth Feasibility Study (stage three) is required. The potential improvements can then be calculated in terms of both energy and cost savings. The costs of a typical PEA are often between 3 and 12 cents per square foot of each building at the site.

- **In-depth Feasibility Study.** After the preliminary cost-benefit analysis and estimates are established in the PEA of stage two, a more comprehensive assessment or evaluation of one or more specific measures is performed to fine tune the preliminary economic results. This is also where any renewable energy generation components of the project are defined and evaluated as to how they can be integrated into the energy project. It should be noted that an In-Depth Feasibility Study could be performed without the need for a Screening Audit or even a PEA if a client knows exactly what systems are to be examined for possible replacement or incorporated with the renewable energy generation components. The feasibility study explores options available to facility owners, lenders and project developers highlighting the economic benefits of differing system configurations.

Drilling down to specific items of equipment comes into the forefront of the audit at this point. Usually, additional field data (using data loggers and other tools) is collected to perform system energy simulations and to identify in detail the implementation logistics for the energy measures. Several different system options are usually compared with the existing baseline items of equipment that currently exist at the facility. The feasibility study also moves beyond a "simple payback" analysis and incorporates a "life cycle" analysis for each option. The financial analysis also calculates present worth and uniform annual costs for each possible energy measure. The costs for the feasibility study can run between $2,000 and $30,000 *per system* evaluated.

It is usually at this point that alternative financing options for the measures are evaluated and priced as described in the prior section of this chapter. Some lower cost projects might be paid for in cash while others would need financing over extended periods.

- **Design-Build Criteria**. This activity entails developing Design-Build Criteria, designing a potential RFQ (Request for Qualification) or RFP (Request for Proposal), evaluating the RFQ or RFP, assistance with the bidding process, overseeing the construction and implementation of the energy efficiency measures, and designing and performing acceptance tests and final commissioning of the energy project. This is completed for each of the energy measures that are selected for implementation and generally involves frequent visits to the facility to verify implementation logistics and quality control that will be needed during the construction process. This activity documents the details that will be used by the design-build general contractor, who in turn is responsible for both the final design and construction of the project. This stage defines for the contractor such things as the specific type and manufacturer of the equipment or system to be installed including the size, style, model and specifications. The document includes all of the information contractors need to bid on the project and describes in detail the "scope of work." This final stage could cost between $3,000 and $30,000 per system evaluated (and assumes a feasibility study is in place).

The four coordinated sections are integrated into each stage of the audit and include:

1. Site survey and data gathering
2. Establishing the load profile and usage data base
3. Performing a complete operations and maintenance review
4. Developing the final energy management program

To insure that you have an accurate audit, it is imperative that you engage the services of a qualified energy auditor as described above. This means you should only seek advice from architects, engineers and consultants who specialize in this area of auditing. Unlike conventional architects and HVAC designers who only design to meet code, these energy and environment professionals are familiar with optimal solutions and can better navigate, educate, and challenge codes and uninformed building officials while capitalizing on federal, state and regional transitional incentive programs that will help make "going green" a sustainable cost-efficient solution for the client.

Traditional energy assessments culminate in a written document. In addition to providing the raw data upon which the report is based including historical and current energy load centers and consumptions, it also summarizes a list of opportunities with the facilities major energy using equipment. This broad technical approach fails to explain the broader organization implications of energy use described in the previous section above. In a typical industrial facility or commercial building, energy choices usually have an impact on equipment reliability, staff safety, product quality and productivity. Therefore, that audit should provide potential benefits and answers for a wide range of staff and management, not just the equipment and systems operators. The energy assessment then becomes a "roadmap" for pursuing all available energy options—efficiency and generation alike. From that living energy roadmap document comes a strategic business plan for implementing energy improvements in a cost effective manner through a relationship between the energy auditor, facility staff and corporate management.

There are many firms that can provide energy assessments, but the content and quality of the assessments can vary widely. Most firms will perform the audit for a fee while some utilities and universities provide low- or no-cost audits. Often the utilities perform the audit (either directly or by paying a third party to perform the audit) for free as part of their commitment to lower energy use for their customers as required by their regulatory agencies such as public utility commissions who set tariffs and rules for the utilities in each region they provide their energy services.

An energy audit is the key to identifying energy-saving opportunities, analyzing those opportunities and then providing a report that quantifies the aspects and the economics (cost, savings, financial payback, useful life, warranties, emission reductions, safety benefits, warranties and rebates or incentives) of each ECM. The report is technical in nature and is led by a mechanical or industrial engineer that has the expertise and professional qualifications to perform the audit. The client then must decide when and if the company will act on any of the recommendations and in what priority order. The challenge for the auditor is to make the benefits clear and concise to all the users of the report. However, it is management that must follow on the implementation of the report. Remember, the assessment becomes a foundation for understanding how business performance improves with better energy decision making but is worthless if it doesn't lead to the implementation of the improvements.

The Alliance to Save Energy describes a world-class energy assessment in Table 6-2.[18]

The physical examination of the client's facility, two to three years of energy bills or costs and other energy-related records will require research and the cooperation of a number of staff at the clients business. It is not uncommon to see some reluctance from those asked to provide the records since they tend to see the process as disruptive and a threat to "things as usual." It can also be construed as a threat to their performance. The auditor will also be looking at the general mechanical condition of the energy equipment and systems, its age and repair histories, work capacities and tolerances, preventive maintenance schedules and history, and the possible use of other raw materials and processes that may be cost effective as energy costs are curtailed. In the end, the assessment will show the client not only what can be done to improve energy performance and to quantify the costs to do so, but also how to sustain the results over the long term.

The financial impact of the energy savings described in the audit has several components. The first and most widely understood (but not necessarily the most important financially) is "payback." Payback normally describes the number of years it takes for the cost of an investment to be recovered through the annual savings that it provides. That is, the capital cost divided by the energy savings per year equals the payback period—at least as it defined by many engineers

Table 6-2.

FEATURE	ASSESSMENT PARAMETERS
Goal	Identify, prioritize, and suggest alternative strategies for improving the client's business performance through more efficient energy choices.
Elements for Study	Energy-using equipment and technology plus: Organizational design and relationships Skills and training needs Operations and maintenance procedures Management commitment and communications needed to effectively capture and sustain potential energy savings
Client Participation	Preparation for an assessment requires input from the general manager plus leadership for engineering, finance, maintenance, procurement and operations. The client should designate an "energy champion" as the lead contact. Conduct of the assessment itself requires the participation of plant engineers, maintenance leaders and equipment operators. Presentation of assessment findings requires an audience of all the above.
Deliverable	An active, ongoing relationship keeps the client apprised of changes to the costs and benefits of potential energy improvements as market variables change. Communication may include: A written report on the initial assessment findings A presentation of findings to client staff Implementation scenarios that present different options for organizing recommended improvements Periodic updates of cost-benefit findings as market conditions change A spreadsheet template for modeling cost-benefit A listing of contacts for financial and technical assistance services Announcements that recognize implementation milestones, reminding key decision-makers of the progress made and what remains to be done
Outcome	The client pursues continuous energy improvement through a business plan that identifies what needs to be done, assigns goals and responsibilities, and provides a framework for tracking, evaluating and communicating progress.

and plant personnel. Unfortunately, no consideration is given to the actual "useful life" of the ECM. To make matters worse, many people reviewing the report, try to compare the payback period of what is basically a very long-term useful life of an infrastructure asset to that of a revenue producing asset such as a computer, forklift, printing press or other asset the client uses in their business to produce a product or service. This is a critically wrong comparison and should never be done. Most capital assets or equipment that are part of an ECM project have very long useful lives (much as an "infrastructure" asset) and the "payback" period should consider two very important factors:

1. The actual projected useful life of the asset
2. The actual cash used to acquire the asset (which for most cases is zero) when the total asset cost is financed through an energy project finance structure

A lot of management will place a payback "hurdle" term that must be met. That is not a problem so long as that ECM is categorized with other assets of like nature. This would include other infrastructure assets such as bathroom fixtures, lighting fixtures, electrical panels, piping and plumbing, roofs, etc. Doing so will point out that the payback is most often much more rapid than other infrastructure assets and in fact can often beat the payback period of even some revenue producing assets that a company might be considering the acquisition of.

Perhaps a better way to classify the ECM is in terms of key performance indicators (KPIs) of the business. This means expressing an energy savings in terms of a reduction in energy use (or cost) on a per unit, gallon, square foot, day-of-operation, or any unit relevant to a facility's operations. A KPI describes financial results per some basic unit of business activity. Some examples of these basic business activities may be:[19]

- Tons of product
- Barrels of product
- Thousand square feet of product
- Cases of product
- Hours of operation
- Heating or cooling degree day
- Units of service revenue produced
- Revenue per square foot or leased space

Potential energy efficiency projects can be classified in a number of ways.[20]

- Type of energy system—lighting, steam, production, HVAC, compressed air, etc.
- Investment impact—non-capital vs. capital investment and short vs. long payback
- Operational impact—distinguish between those that apply to current systems and procedures and those that will require capital investments or procedural changes
- Financing options—budget vs. borrowing vs. energy purchase agreements
- Time—organize both from implementation and from operational perspectives
- Risk—categorize per their relative risk of success or impact on operations
- Departmental Impact—categorize accordingly and by primary responsibility
- "Make-or-Buy"—distinguish between those projects that can be done internally vs. those that will need to be done by outside expertise

So what is the distribution of the typical energy efficiency projects that provide the greatest energy savings in a typical organization over a defined period? Figure 6-10 on a heating efficiency component project (as identified by the U.S. Department of Energy) provides the best visual answer.

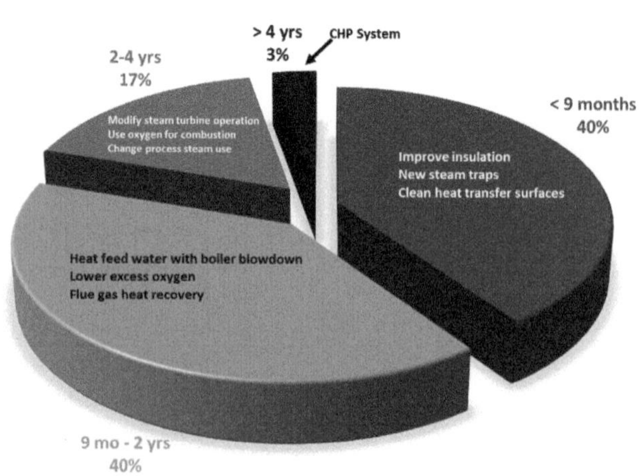

Figure 6-10: Greatest Energy Savings

An example of a full energy audit/assessment is included in Appendix 4.

ISO Standards

In the final analysis, it is an energy management system (EMS) that will determine the validity and operation of any energy system installed. Furthermore, that EMS will in most cases be subject to ISO 50001—a standard developed by the International Organization for Standardization (ISO). The ISO has a membership of some 160 national standards bodies from countries large and small, industrialized, developing and in transition, in all regions of the world. They have over 18,600 standards that have been developed for use by business, government and society with practical tools for all three dimensions of sustainable development: economic, environmental and social. An ISO International Standard represents a global consensus on the state of the art in the subject of that standard.

ISO 50001 for EMS establishes a framework for industrial plants; commercial, institutional, and governmental facilities; and entire organizations to manage energy. It is estimated that the standard could influence up to 60% of the world's energy use. Energy is critical to organizational operations and can be a major cost or organizations, whatever their activities. In addition to economic costs of energy to an organization, energy can impose environmental and societal costs by depleting resources and contributing to problems such as climate change—including compliance measures imposed by local air districts, state, and national environmental regulators. ISO 50001 is based on the management system model that is already understood and implemented by organizations worldwide. It provides a framework of requirements enabling organizations to:

- Develop a policy for more efficient use of energy
- Fix targets and objectives to meet the policy
- Use data to better understand and make decisions concerning energy use and consumption
- Measure the results
- Review the effectiveness of the policy
- Continually improve energy management

A principal ingredient that ties in closely to the comprehensive energy management policy of ISO 50001 is the measurement and verification tools mentioned above as it relates to most renewable energy projects. The financial structures that enable those projects to succeed and be repaid to the sponsor, developer and investors are all closely tied to a comprehensive EMS.

A complete description and implementation plan for ISO 50001 can be found at the ISO's website: *www.iso.org*.

TAX ATTRIBUTES OF ENERGY EFFICIENCY PROJECTS

Energy efficiency tax incentives first came about in the Energy Policy Act of 2005 and included many different tax incentives (*see Appendix 4*). The Energy Improvement and Extension Act of 2008, passed by Congress on October 3, 2008, significantly expands federal energy tax incentives on renewable energy projects. The new law extends the duration of existing credits for all renewable energy technologies to include solar energy, fuel cells, cogeneration projects and microturbines by eight years. In also increases the credit amounts for fuel cells; established new credits for small wind-energy systems, geothermal systems, and combined heat and power (CHP) systems; extends eligibility of credits to public utilities; and allows taxpayers to take the credit against the alternative minimum tax, subject to certain limitations.

The Energy Policy Act of 2005 included a new tax incentive for commercial building energy efficiency projects also. It established a tax deduction for expenses incurred for energy efficient building expenditures made under IRS section 179D. The deduction is limited to $1.80 per square foot of the property (cap), with allowances for partial deductions for improvements in interior lighting, HVAC and hot water systems, and building envelope systems. Additionally, there is no limit to the amount of these deductions available to the taxpayer.[21]

Section 1331 of the Energy Policy Act of 2005 provides that "energy-efficient commercial building property" is defined as property that is:

1. Installed on any building in the US that is within the scope of Standard 90.31-2001 energy standard for buildings.

2. Installed as part of (i) the interior lighting systems, (ii) the heating, cooling, ventilation, and hot water systems, or (iii) the building envelope.

3. Certified as being installed as part of a plan designed to reduce the total annual energy and power costs of interior lighting systems, heating, cooling, ventilation, and hot water systems of the building by 50% or more when compared to a reference building.

The deduction is equal to energy-efficient commercial building property expenditures made by the taxpayer, subject to a cap. The deduction is immediate for the year when the expenditure is made and the asset is placed in service (meaning 100% deductible when made and therefore not required to be depreciated over an extended period of time) and is limited to an amount equal to $1.80 per square foot of the property for which such expenditures are made. For tax purposes, "placed in service" generally means the time at which the property is ready for its intended use (see page 35). Without this tax benefit, any improvements of this type would historically have been required to be deducted over a 39-year period!

> *"Over its lifetime, each standard (13 watt) CFL will reduce electricity bills by roughly $30. And though a CFL may cost twice as much as an incandescent, it lasts 10 times as long. Since it uses less energy, it also means fewer CO_2 emissions. Each one reduces energy use by the equivalent of 200 pounds of coal over its lifetime."*
>
> Lester R. Brown. PLAN B 3.0: Mobilizing to Save Civilization (2008

Certain certifications requirements must be met in order to qualify for the deduction. Qualified computer software must be used to certify the savings. The software is based on the 2005 California Nonresidential Alternative Calculation Method Approval Manual. The intention is that the calculation method be fuel neutral—the same energy efficiency features qualify a building for the deduction, regardless of whether the heating source is a gas or oil furnace, or boiler, or an electric heat pump as an example. The calculation methods for certification may take into account the extent of commissioning (the initial operability of a system) in the building, and allow the taxpayer to take into account the amount of system performance that may exceed typical performance.

The IRS Notice 2006-52 requires inspectors of an installation to be engineers or contractors licensed in the jurisdictions where the building is sited. The inspections must also meet the guidelines of the National Renewable Energy Laboratory. In a unique application of the deduction, if the expenditure is made by a public entity (and therefore not a taxpaying entity) such as public schools, the deduction can be allocated to the person primarily responsible for designing the property in lieu of the public entity. Obviously, this would only be beneficial if the designer is a "for profit" entity.

The certification document that is signed by an engineer or contractor who is licensed must contain the information stipulated by the IRS and can be viewed at *http://www.irs.gov/pub/irs-irbs/irb06-26.pdf*. The taxpayer is not required to attach the certification to the tax return on which the deduction is taken but requires that the taxpayer maintain the certification is such books and records as are sufficient to establish the entitlement to the deduction claimed. The certification must contain all of the following:

1. The accurate name, address and telephone number of the qualified taxpayer.
2. The address of the building to which the certification applies.
3. A statement by the qualified certifier that one of the available and different deduction options are met. These statements are very descriptive in nature. The National Electrical Manufacturers Association (NEMA) can provide specific guidance on the certification statements.

The deduction described above is for a "whole building" deduction. In the case of a building that does not meet the whole building requirement of a 50 percent energy savings, a partial deduction is allowed with respect to each separate building system that comprises energy-efficient property and which is certified by a qualified professional as meeting or exceeding the applicable system savings targets established by the IRS (Secretary of Treasury).

The applicable systems savings targets established by the IRS as those that result in a total annual energy savings of 50 percent for the whole building, if each of the separate systems met the system target. In this case, the maximum allowable deduction is $0.60 per square foot based on the following separate building systems (in other words, the $0.60 applies to each independent component of the whole building but not to exceed $1.80 total):

1. Interior lighting system
2. Heating, cooling, ventilation, and hot water systems
3. Building envelope

Building owners and potential debtors of the energy project financing are encouraged under the law to focus first on lighting systems for two reasons. First, their ease and availability of upgrading, and second, the knowledge that achievement in energy efficiency that will be gained. In the case of a lighting system (including the retrofit of an existing system), the system energy savings target for the lighting systems is deemed to be met by are reduction in lighting power density of 40 percent (50 percent in the case of a warehouse) of the minimum requirements defined in ASHRAE/IESNA Standard 90.1-2001.

In the case of a lighting system that reduces lighting power density by 25 percent, a partial deduction of $0.30 per square foot is allowed. A pro-rated partial deduction is allowed in the case of a lighting system that reduces lighting power density between 25 and 40 percent. Certain lighting level and lighting control requirements must also be met in order to qualify for the partial interim lighting deductions. Then, for tax purposes, the basis of the property is reduced by the deduction amount and the remaining asset value is depreciated over its tax life for the class of property.

It is interesting to note that garages are eligible for deduction but churches are not. Furthermore, the person who gets the Commercial Building Tax Deduction is the person who owns the property for tax purposes. This is particularly important when structuring the financing for the creditor and debtor to know. It is a question of fact and the determination according to the IRS depends on the "arrangements" between the parties. Also, the deduction applies to all portions of the project costs to include labor and even recycling costs of the old system(s). Although weird (and seldom a significant cost component), exit signs cannot be considered part of the lighting project. Also, screw in Compact Fluorescent Lights cannot be used to reduce wattage for purposes of the deduction.

As it pertains to warehouse lighting projects, the requirement of 50 percent savings is strict and there is no allowance for the reduction down to 25 to 40 percent sliding scale availability as is found in other lighting projects.

In most energy efficiency projects, the tax deduction combined with the incentives and rebates offered by the utilities in each region become a significant reason why these types of ECMs are often included in the energy financing project. Frequently, they become a critical component of revenue sources to justify the project.

Now, as of tax year 2012, the IRS has changed energy savings percentage for partial Section 179D deductions (notice 2012-22). The energy savings percentages shown in Table 6-3 are available for property placed in service on or after February 24, 2012. The notice provides that until December 31, 2013, taxpayers may use either the energy savings percentages provided in the notice in 2008, or the energy saving percentages provided under the new Notice 2012-22.

> *"Today's green buildings use some 30% less energy than their comparable sized non-green counterparts (some save much more), and they're generally brighter, healthier, and more aesthetically pleasing. Often built with little or no additional up-front cost, green offices, for instance, payback not only in energy savings but also in greater employee retention, attendance, and productivity."*
>
> Ron Pernick and Clint Wilder,
> The Clean Tech Revolution, 2007 p. 21

COMBINED HEAT AND POWER (CHP)

CHP is a specific form of distributed energy generation (DG), which refers to the strategic placement of electric power generating units at or near customer facilities to supply on-site energy needs—electricity and thermal heat. CHP enhances the advantages of DG by the simultaneous production of useful thermal and power output (also called cogen or cogeneration), thereby increasing the overall efficiency.

CHP offers energy and environmental benefits over electric-only and thermal-only systems in both central and distributed power generation applications. CHP systems have the potential for a wide range of applications and the higher efficiencies result in lower emissions than separate heat and power generation. The advantages of CHP broadly include the following:

- The simultaneous production of useful thermal and electrical energy in CHP systems lead to increased fuel efficiency.

Table 6-3.

	Notice 2006-52	Notice 2008-40	Notice 2012-22
Interior lighting systems	16 2/3%	20%	25%
Heating, cooling, ventilation and hot water systems	16 2/3%	20%	15%
Building envelope	16 2/3%	10%	10%
Effective for property placed in service:	1/1/2006 to 12/31/2008	1/1/2006 to 12/31/2013	2/24/2012 to 12/31/2013

- CHP units can be strategically located at the point of energy use. Such onsite generation avoids the transmission and distribution losses associated with electricity purchased via the grid from central stations (typically utility companies).
- CHP is versatile and can be coupled with existing and planned technologies for many different applications in the industrial, commercial and residential sectors.

CHP is the sequential or simultaneous generation of multiple forms of useful energy (usually mechanical and thermal) in a single, integrated system. CHP systems will usually consist of a number of individual components—prime mover (heat engine), generator, heat recovery, and electrical interconnection—configured into an integrated whole. The type of equipment that drives the overall system (i.e., the prime mover) typically identifies the CHP system. Prime movers for CHP systems include reciprocating engines, combustion or gas turbines, steam turbines, microturbines, and fuel cells. These prime movers are capable of burning a variety of fuels, including natural gas, coal, oil, and renewable alternative fuels (biomass, landfill gas, digester gas, etc.) to produce shaft power or mechanical energy. Although mechanical energy from the prime mover is most often used to drive a generator to produce electricity, it can also be used to drive rotating equipment such as compressors, pumps, and fans. Thermal energy from the system can be used in direct process applications or indirectly to produce steam, hot water, hot air for drying, or chilled water for process cooling.

Typically, a standalone conventional power plant at a utility company would use 98 units of fuel to produce 30 units of electricity (31% efficiency), a standalone oiler will use 56 units of fuel to produce 45 units of steam (80% efficiency), and combined they would use 154 units of fuel to produce 75 units of energy (75% efficiency). A CHP system typically will only use 100 units of power to produce the same 75 units of energy—a savings of over 30% in fuel to produce the same amount of energy and a corresponding decrease in environmental emissions. Measures of efficiency are denoted either as lower heating value (LHV) or higher heating value (HHV) which includes the heat of condensation of the water vapor in the products. Most often, all efficiency measures are reported on an HHV basis.

Tables 6-4 and 6-5 provide a summary of CHP technology aspects.

Emissions

In addition to cost savings, CHP technologies offer significantly lower emissions rates compared to separate heat and power systems. The primary pollutants from gas turbines are oxides of nitrogen (NO_X), carbon monoxide (CO), and volatile organic compounds (VOCs) (unburned, non-methane hydrocarbons) all of which are referred to a "criteria" pollutants. Other pollutants such as oxides of sulfur (SO_x) and particulate matter (PM) are primarily dependent on the fuel used. Similarly, emissions of carbon dioxide are also dependent on the fuel used. Under various Green House Gas emission reduction rules being implemented across the U.S., these become important considerations in evaluating the financing alternative scenarios in the typical renewable energy project. Many gas turbines burning gaseous fuels (mainly natural gas) feature lean premixed burners (also called dry low-NO_X burners) that produce NO_X emissions ranging between 0.17 to 09.25 lbs/MWh with no post-combustion emissions control. Typically commercially available gas turbines have CO emissions rates ranging between 0.23 lbs/MWh to 0.28 lbs/MWh. Selective catalytic reduction (SCR) or catalytic combustion can further help to reduce NO_X emissions by 80% to 90% from the gas turbine exhaust and carbon-monoxide catalysts can help to reduce CO by approximately 90 percent. Many gas turbines sited in locales with stringent emission regulations (such as the South Coast Air Quality Management District in southern California) use SCR or other emission reduction technologies for after-treatment to achieve extremely low NO_X emissions.

> *"To truly transform our economy, protect our security, and save our planet from the ravages of climate change, we need to ultimately make clean, renewable energy the profitable kind of energy."*
>
> Barack Obama, address to Joint Session of Congress, Feb 24, 2009

Microturbines have the potential for low emissions. All microturbines operating on gaseous fuels feature lean premixed (dry low NO_X, or DLN) combustor technology. The primary pollutants from microturbines include NO_X CO, and VOCs. Other pollutants such as SO_x and PM are primarily dependent on the fuel used. The sulfur content of the fuel determines emissions of sulfur compounds, primarily. Microturbines are designed to achieve low emissions at full load and emissions are often higher when operating at part load.

Table 6-4: Summary of CHP Technologies

CHP Technology	Advantages	Disadvantages	Available Sizes
Gas turbine	High reliability. Low emissions. High grade heat available. No cooling required.	Require high pressure gas or in-house gas compressor. Poor efficiency at low loading. Output falls as ambient temperature rises. Emissions controls can be required.	• 500 kW to 250 MW
Microturbine	Small number of moving parts. Compact size & light weight. Low emissions. No cooling required.	High costs. Relatively low mechanical efficiency. Limited to lower temperature cogeneration applications.	• 30 kW to 250 kW
Spark ignition reciprocating engine **Compression ignition reciprocating engine (dual fuel pilot ignition)**	High power efficiency with part-load operational flexibility. Fast start-up. Relatively low investment cost. Can be used in island mode and have good load following capability. Can be overhauled on site with normal operators. Operate on low-pressure gas.	High maintenance costs. Limited to lower temperature cogeneration applications. Relatively high air emissions & may need emission control devices. Must be cooled even if recovered heat is not used. High levels of low frequency noise.	• <5 MW in DG applications • High speed (1,200 RPM) ≥4 MW • Low speed (102-514 RPM) 4-75 MW
Steam turbine	High overall efficiency. Any type of fuel may be used. Ability to meet more than one site heat grade requirement. Long working life and high reliability. Power to heat ratio can be varied.	Slow start up. Low power to heat ratio.	• 40 kW to 250 MW
Fuel Cell	Low emissions and low noise. High efficiency over load range. Modular design.	High costs. Low durability and power density. Fuels requiring processing unless pure hydrogen is used.	• 5 kW to 2 MW

Typical NO_X emissions for microturbine systems range between 4 ppm and 9 ppm or 0.08 lbs/MWh and 0.20 lbs/MWh. Additional NO_X emissions removal from catalytic combustion in microturbines is unlikely to be pursued in the near term because of the dry low NO_X technology and the low turbine inlet temperature. CO emissions rates for microturbines typically range between 0.06 lbs/MWh and 0.54 lbs/MWh.

Exhaust emissions are the primary environmental concern with reciprocating engines. The primary pollutants from reciprocating engines are NO_X CO, and VOCs. Other pollutants such as SO_x and PM are primarily dependent on the fuel used. The sulfur content of the fuel determines emissions of sulfur compounds, primarily SO_2. NO_X emissions from small "rich burn" reciprocating engines with integral 3-way catalyst exhaust treatment can be as low as 0.06 lbs/MWh. Larger lean-burn engines have values of around 0.8 lbs/MWh without any exhaust treatment; however, these engines can utilize SCR for NO_X reduction.

Emissions from steam turbines depend on the fuel used in the boiler or other steam sources, boiler furnace

Table 6-5: Summary of CHP Technologies Cost and Performance Characteristics

Summary Table of Typical Cost and Performance Characteristics by CHP Technology[22]					
Technology	**Steam Turbine[23]**	**Recip. Engine**	**Gas Turbine**	**Microturbine**	**Fuel Cell**
Power Efficiency (HHV)	15-38%	22-40%	22-36%	18-27%	30-63%
Overall Efficiency (HHV)	80%	70-80%	70-75%	65-75%	55-80%
Effective Electrical Efficiency	75%	70-80%	50-70%	50-70%	55-80%
Typical Capacity (MW_e)	0.5-250	0.01-5	0.5-250	0.03-0.25	.005-2
Typical Power to Heat Ratio	0.1-0.3	0.5-1	0.5-2	0.4-0.7	1-2
Part-load	OK	OK	Poor	OK	Good
CHP Installed Costs ($/kW$_e$)	430-1,100	1,100-2,200	970-1,300 (5-40 MW)	2,400-3,000	5,000-6,500
O&M Costs ($/kWh$_e$)	<0.005	0.009-0.022	0.004-0.011	0.012-0.025	0.032-0.038
Availability	Near 100%	92-97%	90-98%	90-98%	>95%
Hours to Overhauls	>50,000	25,000-50,000	25,000-50,000	20,000-40,000	32,000-64,000
Start-up Time	1 hr-1 day	10 sec	10 min – 1 hr	60 sec	3 hrs – 2 days
Fuel Pressure (psig)	n/a	1-45	100-500 (compressor)	50-80 (compressor)	0.5-45
Fuels	All	Natural gas, biogas, propane, landfill gas	Natural gas, biogas, propane, oil	Natural gas, biogas, propane, oil	Hydrogen, natural gas, propane, methanol
Noise	High	High	Moderate	Moderate	Low
Uses for Thermal Output	LP-HP steam	Hot water, LP steam	Heat, hot water, LP-HP steam	Heat, hot water, LP steam	Hot water, LP-HP steam
Power Density (kW/m^2)	>100	35-50	20-500	5-70	5-20
NO_x (lb/MMBtu)-not including SCR	Gas 0.1-.2 Wood 0.2-.5 Coal 0.3-1.2	0.013 rich burn with 3-way cat. 0.17 lean burn	0.036-0.05	0.015-0.036	0.0025-0040
$lb/MWh_{Total/Output}$ (not including SCR)	Gas 0.4-0./8 Wood 0.9-1.4 Coal 1.2-5.0	0.06 rich burn with 3 way cat. 0.8 lean burn	0.17-0.25	0.08-0.20	0.011-0.016

combustion section design, operation, and exhaust cleanup systems. Boiler emissions include NO_X SOX, PM and CO. The emissions rates in steam turbines depend largely on the type of fuel used in the boiler as seen in the above chart. A variety of commercially available combustion and post-combustion NO_X reduction techniques exist with selective catalytic reductions achieving reductions as high as 90%. Again, SO_2 emissions from steam turbines depend largely on the sulfur content of the fuel used in the combustion process.

Fuel cells have inherently low criteria emissions profiles because the primary power generation process does not involve combustion. The fuel processing subsystem is the only significant source of emissions as it converts fuel into hydrogen and a low energy hydrogen exhaust stream. The hydrogen exhaust stream is combusted in the fuel processor to provide heat, achieving emissions signatures of less than 0.019 lbs/MWh of CO, less than 0.016 lbs/MWh of NO_X and negligible SO_X without any after-treatment for emissions. Fuel cells are not expected to require any emissions control devices to meet current and projected regulations.

While not considered a pollutant in the ordinary sense of directly affecting health as the criteria pollutants do, CO_2 emissions do result from the use of fossil fuel-based CHP technologies. The amount of CO_2 emitted in any of the CHP technologies discussed above depends on the fuel carbon content and the system efficiency. The fuel carbon content of natural gas is 34 lbs carbon/MMBtu; oil is 48 lbs of carbon/MMBtu and ash-free coal is 66 lbs of carbon/MMBtu. Obviously, as the price of carbon reduction strategies continues to arise, the importance of reducing carbon emissions becomes greater and the benefits from using CHP and other renewable energy technologies becomes a greater economic consideration in properly evaluating the economics of the project finance structure.

Federal Tax Attributes

The Energy Improvement and Extension Act of 2008 provides for a 10% investment tax credit (ITC) for the costs of the first 15 megawatts (MW) of CHP property under section 48(a)(3) (A)(v) of the Internal Revenue Code of 1986. To qualify for the 10% ITC, the CHP system specifically must:

- Produce at least 20% of its useful energy as electricity and 20% in the form of useful thermal energy
- Be 60% efficient on a lower heating value basis
- Be smaller than 50 MW
- Be constructed by the taxpayer or have the original use of the equipment begin with the taxpayer
- Be placed in service before January 1, 2017

Again, the ITC may be used to offset the alternative minimum tax (as in other renewable energy projects) and the CHP system must be operational in the year in which the credit is first taken. The credit applies to eligible property placed into service after October 3, 2008. It is important to note that CHP property does not include "property used to transport the energy source to the facility or to distribute energy produced by the facility." Accelerated MACRS depreciation would also apply (five years) under section 168 of the IRC.

The act also amended sections 48(c)(1) and 48(c)(2) of the IRC in the following ways:

- Extending the existing 30% ITC for fuel cell property and the 10% ITC for microturbine property through December 31, 2016.
- Increasing the credit cap for fuel cell property from the $1,000 per kilowatt (kW) of capacity for qualified fuel cells to $3,000 per kW of capacity. The cap for microturbines was left unchanged at $200 per kW of capacity.

Eligible property includes:

- Fuel cells with a minimum capacity of 0.5 kW that have electric-only efficiencies of 30% or higher
- Microturbines up to 2 MW in capacity that have an electric-only efficiency of 26% or higher

MEASUREMENT AND VERIFICATION (M&V)

Whether prior to implementing the energy efficiency project or after the project has been completed, the measurement and verification process is critical to determining either the expected savings from which the project costs will be paid or measuring the final engineering, design and production performance of the installed assets. More importantly, if the finance structure calls for a percentage of the energy savings to be a part or all of the debt repayment, M&V is absolutely essential. Project investors must also have the ability to measure and verify the environmental attributes that are also a vital component to the overall yield (or conversely, the constraints) on the project finance.

M&V methods and processes are used to measure and verify, in a defined, disciplined and transparent way, the energy savings resulting from planned and defined changes to all or parts of the energy infrastructure of a specific facility or a group of specific facilities. M&V has a more focused purpose than traditional energy monitoring, accounting and analysis and requires additional discipline, rigor and transparency.

Investment in energy efficiency offers the largest and most cost-effective opportunity for private and public sector organizations to limit the financial, health and environmental costs of burning fossil fuels. Such investment opportunities in America are estimated to be in the order of hundreds of millions of dollars to tens of billions dollars per year. When organizations, public or private, invest in energy efficiency, their executives naturally want to know how much they have saved and how long their savings will last. If the installation had been made to generate energy, then measurements would be trivial—install a meter on the generation equipment. Unlike energy generation, the determination of energy savings is a challenge, and requires both accurate measurement and repeatable methodology, known as a *measurement and verification protocol* (M&V).

In America, as elsewhere, the long-term success of energy savings projects has been hampered by the inability of project developers and investors to agree on how the energy savings can be measured and verified to prove that the projects have been successful.

There are compelling incentives on both public and private sector facility owners/managers to increase the rigor and transparency of how they report on-going energy performance of their facilities. Reasons include:

- Increasing awareness of the economic, environmental, health and social costs of greenhouse gas emissions (GHG)
- Increasing compliance requirements from regulatory agencies to reduce GHG emissions
- Increasing pressures on budgets for real cost reductions in energy usage

- Increasing demands for performance measurement and accountability against targets and promised savings outcomes

Measurement and verification methods are used to measure and verify, in a defined, disciplined, rigorous and transparent way, the energy savings resulting from implementation of energy conservation measures, which have been planned and designed to improve the energy performance of a specific facility or group of specific facilities. This is done without regard to the energy performance of any facility other than the one at which a change in energy infrastructure is implemented. In the end, M&V provides certainty that reported results are real and verifiable—absolutely essential if certification of environmental attributes is required prior to the sale to third parties.

M&V Plan

The best way to proceed with a measurement and verification process is to develop a formal plan that all parties agree to. The M&V plan is central to an accurate accounting of the savings or production achieved and serves as the foundation for verification. The plan may be a single M&V protocol that addresses all of the energy production and ECMs at a facility or consist of multiple protocols that address specific ECMs or energy production systems. The M&V plan should be developed as part of the financing structure analysis and commitment and not an afterthought as the financing is implemented. No ECM or energy production should be finalized until it has been determined that there is a feasible and practical way of measuring and verifying the expected savings or production levels.

A well-conceived M&V plan should include many of the following components:

- A detailed description of the energy conservation measure or energy production system and their intended results.
- Identification of the upper and lower limits expected to be realized by the ECM or energy production system.
- Proper documentation of historical, and more importantly, the base-line year and conditions.
- Properly identifying any planned changes to the base-line data.
- Identifying the phases and/or timelines in which the ECM or energy production asset will be implemented.

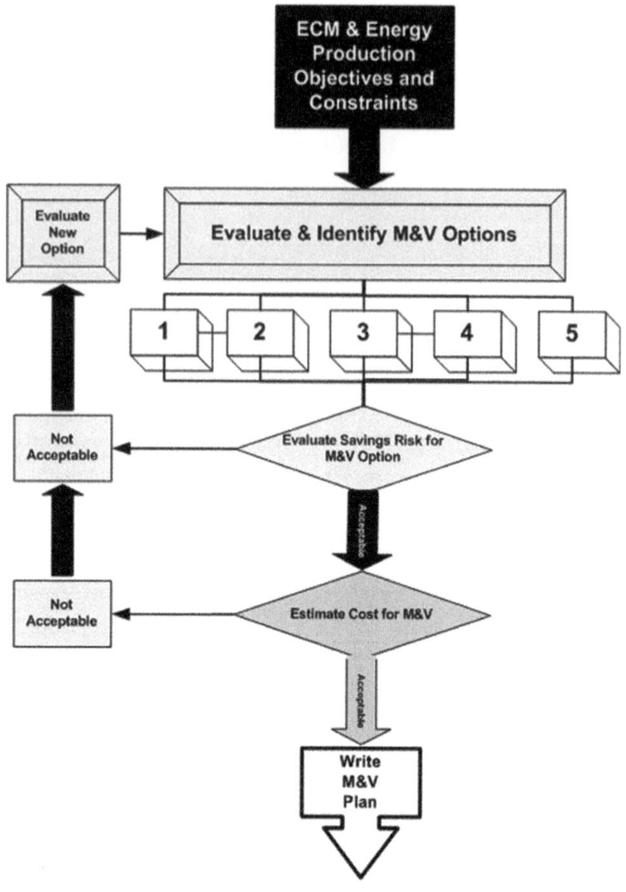

Figure 6-11: M&V Planning Flowchart

- Specifying the adjustments that will be made should savings or production expectations not be met.
- Determining the exact M&V protocols and in what measurement units the results will be documented.
- Documenting the procedures that will be used to make the measurements.
- Reaching an agreement on any software that will be used to analyze the data received.
- Documenting the accuracy of measurements, data capture and analysis.
- Agreeing to the parties that will be receiving the results of the M&V strategies.
- Agreeing to specific auditors that will verify the measurements and data, costs of such verification and when the results will be required.
- Procedures that will be implemented should adjustments to the ECM or production systems be required.

There are occasions when a particular ECM performance could be measured but it might be best to stipulate its operations instead. The savings could be verified by engineering calculations using short term or continuous post-retrofit measurements and stipulations. For example, you might be able to measure energy used by the old lighting system and the new lighting system (and therefore the savings) but you may need to stipulate the number of hours of use if the lights are controlled manually.

An objective of any M&V planning is to design the process to incur no more cost than needed to provide adequate certainty and verifiability in the reported savings. The issue is: "how much certainty is enough, and what is a reasonable cost?"

The value of savings or level of energy production for a specific project places limits on the expenditure that can be justified for M&V. Conversely, the number, type and complexity of ECMs in the project or levels of energy production increases the M&V effort and expenditure for a given level of savings certainty. Obviously, the more costly the project, the better the case for M&V. Clearly a project with constant load and operating hours is easier to deal with (and hence cheaper) than one with variable load, variable operating hours, and with non-ECM factors, (such as weather, occupancy or production levels).

In energy purchase agreements, it is essential that good M&V measures be employed since the output is the source for the billing of the energy produced and hence, the most significant revenue stream in the renewable energy project. The only question is what level of M&V is needed. Most project developers and lenders employ a comprehensive suite of M&V instrumentation along with the corresponding software and even some backup systems should the principal measurement component fail. Ancillary data such as temperature, barometric pressure, wind direction and speed, etc. are usually measured and recorded along with constant monitoring down to individual components such as panel and even cell production levels in the case of a solar PV system.

The acceptable level of uncertainty in a savings calculation or an energy production calculation is a function of the value of expected savings and the cost effectiveness of decreasing uncertainty through additional time, effort and cost.

The M&V process itself introduces uncertainties through:

- **Measurement and Instrumentation Errors**. The magnitude of instrumentation errors stated in manufacturer's specifications are typically small and not a major source of error. Errors can be introduced through improper use or if calibrations are not maintained.
- **Modeling Errors**. They are inherent in creating and using baseline models or other computational models, and can be introduced by factors such as omitting important terms from the model, assigning incorrect values for "known" factors, and extrapolating results outside their range of validity.
- **Sampling Errors**. These result from the fact that measurements were taken from a sample rather than the entire set of items under study.
- **Planned and Unplanned Assumptions**. These errors cover all the unquantifiable errors associated with stipulations, and other assumptions.
- **Insufficient Data Points**. This is particularly critical on a project encompassing energy production systems. For example, if production monitoring is done on a "string" of solar panels instead of at the individual panel level, it would be very difficult to see if an entire panel has failed since that individual panel is only one of an entire string of panels that is being monitored. And, since revenue is a direct function of the production from every panel, the project developer, system owner, or lender is hurting their bottom line from inadequate M&V procedures.

Much but not all of the savings uncertainty in ECMs can be quantified. The remaining unquantifiable uncertainty has to be assessed qualitatively. There are practical statistical techniques for combining the components of uncertainty and deriving and overall savings uncertainty. Quantified uncertainty should be expressed in a statistically meaningful way, by declaring both accuracy and confidence level.[24]

Finding the best balance between savings uncertainty and M&V cost is simply a question of risk management; there is no one "right" balance. M&V practices allow project performance risks to be understood, managed, and allocated among the parties. The accuracy and confidence level of the savings measurement is important for financial risk management.

There are two principal documents that provide guidelines for M&V.

1. IPMVP *International Performance Measurement and Verification Protocol: Concepts and Options for Determining Energy and Water Savings Volume I, EVO-100000-1.2007, Efficiency Valuation Organization*

Table 6-6: Risk, Responsibility and Performance Matrix for Measurement & Verification

Responsibility/Description	Proposed Approach
FINANCIAL	
1. **Interest Rates** Neither the project developer, lender or debtor have significant control over prevailing interest rates. Higher interest rates will increase the project cost, financing or project term, or both. The timing of the project documentation may have an impact on the available interest rate and final project costs.	
2. **Construction Costs** All parties play a role in the determination of the construction costs and defining a budget. However, ultimately the project developer or lender will play the most significant role. In a fixed-price design/build contract, the debtor assumes little responsibility for cost overruns. However, if construction estimates are significantly greater than originally assumed, the project developer or lender may find that the project or ECM is no longer viable and drop it before construction commences. In any design/build contract, the debtor loses some design control.	*Clarify design standards and the design approval process (including changes) and how costs will be reviewed.*
3. **M&V Confidence** All parties will need to assume partial responsibility in the M&V program/plan and energy savings or production determinations. The desired confidence will be reflected in the resources required for the M&V program/plan and all parties will need to consider the requirements prior to project finance document execution.	*Clarify how project savings are being verified (e.g., equipment performance, operational factors, energy use) and the impact on M&V costs.*
4. **Energy Related Cost Savings** The debtor and the project developer/lender will need to agree that the project will include savings from recurring and/or one-time costs. This may include one-time savings from avoided expenditures for projects that were scheduled but will no longer be necessary. This amount must become one of the components of a productive renewable energy financial project analysis. Recurring savings generally result from reduced O&M expenses. These O&M savings must be based on actual spending reductions.	*Clarify sources of non-energy cost savings and how they will be verified.*
5. **Delays** Both the customer and the project developer/lender can cause delays. Failure to implement a viable renewable energy project in a timely manner can cost the customer lost savings and the project developer/lender lost revenue. It can also add costs to the project in additional construction financing costs.	*Clarify schedule and how delays will be handled.*
6. **Major Changes in Facility** The customer/debtor controls major changes in facility use—including closure. This is a major concern for the project developer/lender and needs to be clearly addressed in the project documentation.	*Clarify responsibilities in the event of a premature facility closure, loss of funding, or other major change.*
OPERATIONAL	
1. **Operating Hours** The customer/debtor generally has control over the operating hours in an ECM. The energy production project is controlled by the source of the renewable energy—solar for example. Increases and decreases in operating hours can show up as increases or decreases in "savings" depending on the M&V method chosen. If the operating hours are to be stipulated, the baseline should be carefully documented and agreed to by both parties.	*Clarify whether operating hours are to be measured or stipulated and what the impact will be if they change.*
2. **Load** Equipment loads can change over time. The customer/debtor generally has control over hours of operation, conditioned floor area, intensity of use (e.g., changes in occupancy or level of automation). Changes in load can show up as increases or decreases in "savings" depending on the M&V method. If the equipment loads are to be stipulated, the baseline should be carefully documented and agreed to by both parties.	*Clarify whether equipment loads are to be measured or stipulated and what the impact will be if they change.*
3. **Weather** A lot of ECMs are affected by weather, which no one has control over. Should the customer/debtor agree to accept risk for weather fluctuations, it will be contingent upon aggregate payments not exceeding aggregate savings in most instances. It is not uncommon to see a floor or ceiling on the variations.	*Clearly specify how weather corrections will be performed.*
4. **User Participation** Many ECMs require user participation to generate savings (e.g., control settings). The savings can be variable, and the customer/debtor may not be	*Clarify what degree of user participation is needed and utilize*

Table 6-6 (*Cont'd*): Risk, Responsibility and Performance Matrix for Measurement & Verification

Responsibility/Description	Proposed Approach
willing to invest in these measures. If performance is stipulated, document and review assumptions carefully and consider M&V to confirm the capacity to save (e.g., confirm that the controls are functioning properly).	*monitoring and training to mitigate risk.*
PERFORMANCE	
1. **Equipment Performance** The project developer/lender has control over the design of the project and selection of the equipment and is responsible for the proper installation, commissioning, and performance of the system in most cases. This is particularly true in an energy purchase agreement contract but may not necessarily be true if the financing structure is a capital lease or direct loan where that risk is passed on to the customer/debtor directly. In most cases, the project developer/lender has the responsibility to demonstrate that the new improvements meet expected performance levels, including specified equipment capacity, standards of service, and efficiency.	*Clarify who is responsible for initial and long-term performance, how it will be verified, and what will be done if performance does not meet expectations.*
2. **Operations** Performance of the day-to-day operations activities is negotiable and can impact performance. However, in most cases, the project developer/lender (or the equipment manufactures) bears the ultimate risk regardless of which party performs the activity.	*Clarify which party will perform equipment operations, how the records will be maintained and who will maintain the records, the implications of equipment control, how changes in operating procedures will be handled, and how proper operations will be assured.*
3. **Preventive Maintenance** Performance of day-to-day maintenance activities is negotiable and can impact performance. However, in most energy production projects the project developer/lender will have the responsibility but in capital leases, direct loans and some operating leases, the customer/debtor will assume the responsibility.	*Clarify how long-term preventive maintenance will be assured, especially if the party responsible for long-term maintenance is not responsible for maintenance (e.g., the project developer/lender provides the maintenance checklist and reporting frequency). Clarify who is responsible for long-term maintenance to maintain operational performance throughout the contract term. Clarify what will be done if inadequate preventive maintenance affects performance.*
4. **Equipment Repair and Replacement** Performance of day-to-day repair and replacement of project developer/lender-installed equipment is negotiable. However, it is often tied to project performance. The project developer/lender bears the ultimate responsibility and risk regardless of which party performs the actual function.	*Clarify who is responsible for performing replacement of failed components or equipment replacement throughout the contract term. Specifically address potential impacts on performance due to equipment failure. Specify expected equipment life and warranties for all installed equipment and who will be providing the warranties. Discuss replacement responsibility when equipment life is shorter than the term of the contract.*

2. *ASHRAE Guideline 14-2002: Measurement of Energy and Demand Savings*, American Society of Heating, Refrigerating and Air-Conditioning Engineers

The potential to generate savings may be verified through spot/short-term metering and inspections conducted immediately before and immediately after installation. Annual (or some other regular interval) inspections must be conducted to verify that the proper equipment/systems are installed and the equipment/systems are performing to specification. If conditions have changed, additional performance period measurements or non-routine adjustments may be appropriate.

Collecting the Data

Collecting comprehensive baseline data is advised in all cases. All collected information and inputs need to be documented in a format that allows due-diligence review. Inadequate, disorganized, self-contradictory, or conflicting documentation are often the reasons a lot of potential quality ECM projects or even renewable energy generation projects are never finally consummated.

To obtain end-use data for consideration, building subsystem metering must be included in the project M&V activities for baseline and performance periods. The specific sub-systems selected for monitoring are in most cases the installed ECMs and related systems. For ECMs such as windows or insulation that cannot be monitored, the impacted HVAC system should be sub-metered. The model calibration will benefit the most from monitoring the energy end uses for which the least information is available.

Required data typically include:

- Utility bill records: Collect a minimum of 12 (and preferably 24, 36, or 48) consecutive months of utility bills for the months immediately before installation of the ECMs. The billing data should include meter read date, kWh consumption, peak electric demand, and heating fuel use (e.g., natural gas). Additional data in hourly and 15-minute formats may be required.
- Architectural, mechanical, and electrical drawings: as-built drawings are preferred.
- Site survey data: Comprehensive equipment and system data, typically collected during an investment grade audit, including:
  - — HVAC systems: primary equipment (e.g., chillers and boilers): capacities, number, model and serial numbers, age, condition, operating schedules, etc.
  - — HVAC systems: secondary equipment (e.g., air-handling units, terminal boxes): characteristics, fan sizes and types, motor sizes and efficiencies, design-flow rates and static pressures, duct-system types, economizer operation, and type of controls
  - — HVAC system controls, including location of zones, temperature set-points, control set-points and schedules, and any special control sequences
  - — Lighting systems: number and types of lamps, with nameplate data for lamps and ballasts, lighting schedules, etc.
  - — Building occupants: population counts, occupation schedules in different zones
  - — Other major energy-consuming loads: type (industrial process, air compressors, water heaters, elevators), energy consumption, schedules of operation
- Site survey data that may be required in addition to data normally collected during an audit include:
  - — Plug loads: summarize major and typical plug loads for assigning values per zone
  - — Building envelope and thermal mass: dimensions and type of interior and exterior walls, properties of windows, and building orientation and shading from nearby objects. Infiltration rates are important, but are often difficult to determine
  - — HVAC systems: ventilation air-flow rates can have a dramatic effect on energy use
- Short-term monitoring: The building energy management control system (EMCS) or data-logging equipment is set up to record system data as it varies over time. Typically, primary energy using systems and equipment involved in an ECM are monitored. This data may be required if particular subsystems (e.g., the chiller plant) needs to be accurately modeled in order to determine savings. The data reveals how variable loads change with building operating conditions such as weather, occupancy, daily schedules, etc.
- Spot measurements of specific equipment: The power draw on lighting, plug load, HVAC equipment, and other circuits should be recorded to determine actual equipment operating powers.

- Operator interviews: Building operators can provide much of the above listed information and also any deviation in the intended operation of building equipment.
- Weather data: For calibration purposes, representative site weather data are required for the period in question.
- Minimum code performance standards: For new construction projects and major renovations, minimum performance standards are often mandated for the baseline based on required codes. If standards must be referenced in the baseline, the minimum equipment efficiencies to represent the standards should be used.

The level of certainty and thus effort required to verify both a project's potential to perform and its actual performance will vary from project to project. The contract and/or the project-specific M&V plan should be prepared with serious consideration of what M&V requirements, reviews, and costs will be specified. Some key factors, outlined below, should be considered when choosing the M&V options and techniques to use for each Energy Savings Performance Contract (ESPC) project.

- Value of ECM in Terms of Projected Savings and Project Costs. The scale of a project, energy rates, term of the contract, comprehensiveness of energy conservation measures (ECMs), the benefit-sharing arrangement, and the magnitude of savings can all affect the value of the ECM or ESPC project. The M&V effort should be scaled to the value of the project so that the value of the information provided by the M&V activity is appropriate to the value of the ECM and the project itself.
- Complexity of ECM or System. More complex projects may require more complex (and thus more expensive) M&V methods to determine energy savings. In general, the complexity of isolating the savings is the critical factor. For example, a complicated chiller measure may not be difficult to assess if there are energy sub-meters and monitoring systems dedicated to the chiller system. When defining the appropriate M&V requirements for a given project, it is helpful to consider ECMs as being in one of the following categories (listed in order of increasing M&V complexity):
  - — Constant load, constant operating hours
  - — Constant load, variable operating hours
  - — Variable hours with a fixed pattern
  - — Variable hours without a fixed pattern (e.g., weather-dependent)
  - — Variable load, variable operating hours
  - — Variable hours or load with a fixed pattern
  - — Variable hours or load without a fixed pattern (e.g., weather-dependent)
- Number of Interrelated ECMs at a Single Facility. If multiple ECMs are being installed at a single site, the savings from each measure may be, to some degree, related to the savings resulting from other measures or other non-ECM activities at the facility. Examples include interactive effects between lighting and HVAC measures or between envelope improvements and a chiller replacement. In these situations, it may not be possible to isolate and measure one system in order to determine savings.
- Risk of Achieving Savings. The importance of the M&V activities is often tied to the confidence associated with the estimated energy or cost savings. An ECM with which the facility staff is familiar may, subjectively, require less M&V rigor than ECMs that are less well known. Similarly, unproven technologies may warrant additional attention. A simple method of estimating payment risk can be based on the estimated project value, technical uncertainty, and project sponsor experience. Such a method assumes that, as a starting point, all projects will be inspected to verify the project's potential to perform and estimate savings uncertainty and payment risk.

Often, the array of instrumentation installed and the measurements collected for M&V can be used for other purposes, including commissioning and system optimization. Data and systems are more cost-effective if they are used to meet several objectives, and not just those of the M&V plan. In addition, savings could be quantified beyond the requirements of the performance contract. This information could be useful for allocating costs among different tenants, planning future projects, or allocating research.

In general, the more rigorous the M&V, the more expensive it will be to determine energy savings. The factors that typically affect M&V accuracy and costs (some are interrelated) are:

- Level of detail and effort associated with verifying baseline and performance period surveys
- Sample sizes (number of data points) used for me-

tering representative equipment

- Duration and accuracy of metering activities
- Number and complexity of dependent and independent variables that are metered or accounted for in analyses
- Level of engineering required to conduct analyses
- Availability of existing data collecting systems (e.g., energy management systems)
- Contract term
- Level of accuracy needed in energy savings analyses

> *"The variability of sun, wind and so on, turns out to be a non-problem if you do several sensible things. One is to diversify your renewables by technology, so that weather conditions bad for one kind are good for another. Second, you diversify by site so they're not all subject to the same weather pattern at the same time because they're in the same place. Third, you use standard weather forecasting techniques to forecast wind, sun and rain, and of course hydro operators do this right now. Fourth, you integrate all your resources—supply side and demand side..."*
>
> Amory Lovins, American physicist

The M&V effort should be scaled to the value of the project so that the value of the information provided by the M&V activity is appropriate to the value of the project itself. Rule-of-thumb estimates put overall annual M&V costs at 1% to 10% of typical project cost savings. Often, some ECMs or energy production projects will entail greater M&V costs, but the overall M&V costs for the project are balanced by other ECMs or projects that do not require substantial annual activities.

For an M&V plan to be successful, the sensors used for baseline and performance period measurements must meet minimum accuracy requirements for the application and must be properly calibrated. If the accuracy of any instrument is less than suitable, the measurements may introduce unacceptable levels of error into the energy calculations. Instrumentation accuracy requirements should be sufficient to ensure that overall energy and cost estimates are reasonable. It is important to keep in mind that the inaccuracies introduced by the instrumentation will likely be the greatest source of uncertainty in calculated savings.

The Measurement and Verification Plan is a document that defines project-specific M&V methods and techniques that will be used to determine savings resulting from a specific performance contracting project. The plan may include 1) a single option that addresses all the measures installed at a single facility, or 2) several M&V options to address multiple measures installed at the facility.

In addition to providing accurate and conservative methods to calculate energy savings, a good M&V Plan is clear, consistent, and repeatable. In a long-term contract, it is very important to ensure that all assumptions, procedures, and data are recorded properly so they may be easily referenced and verified by others. The data included should be sufficient for a third party to implement or verify the M&V procedures. This is particularly important if the results of the measurements will be used to sell the emission attributes or savings to a third party as is done with Renewable Energy Credits or SRECs (Solar Renewable Energy Credits) in some states like New Jersey. Since these sources of potential revenue can be very important to the overall return on investment for the project developer/lender, it is important that they be measured accurately and recorded in formats that auditors are able to utilize to verify the quantities and types of emission attributes the project generates.

M&V activities include site surveys, energy measurements, metering of key variables, data analyses, calculations, quality assurance procedures, and reporting. All of these key components need to be adequately detailed in the M&V Plan.

It is commonly understood that ECMs and energy production systems interact with one another. Reduced lighting loads, for example, can reduce air conditioning energy consumption (a cooling bonus), but increase heating consumption (a heating penalty). Whole-building M&V approaches such as building simulation or utility billing analysis account for these types of interactive effects, whereas retrofit isolation M&V approaches do not. The M&V plan must properly account for interactive effects and avoid double-counting of savings, which can occur inadvertently if interactions are not carefully considered.

M&V Equipment

Many tools are available which help collect and analyze system-wide HVAC data, control data, and lighting performance data. Data may include power (kW), energy (kWh), and operating parameters such as temperature, humidity, pressure, flow rates, status, and lighting levels. Data can be collected through one-time measurements or can be recorded in user-defined intervals. Prices, applications, and complexity of these tools vary.

For data collection, storage, and reporting, there are two general categories of metering equipment for M&V activities: data loggers and energy management systems.

1. Data loggers range from simple battery-powered portable devices to more complex tools that can collect inputs from up to 30 transducers. The most simple portable data loggers collect information about a single variable (such as light fixture on/off status or amp draw from a motor). Others can capture multiple inputs (such as voltage, power factor, and amperage) and perform some calculations. Portable data loggers tend to be inexpensive per unit, but are more limited in applications. The downloading of data is usually done manually off site through a connection to a personal computer, although modem connections are sometimes used. Battery-powered portable loggers can offer non-intrusive monitoring within an occupied area, are relatively simple to use, and are inexpensive. More complex data loggers can collect information from a range of different inputs, conduct some analyses, prepare reports, and, typically through modems, download information for remote data collection. Permanently installed data loggers tend to be relatively expensive (when transducer and installation costs are included) and, if hard-wired, not very portable, which is an issue when only short-term measurements are required.

2. Energy management systems are used for controlling systems. These would logically be an excellent option since such systems are often already in place and have data collection, trending, and computing capability; however, caution should be exercised, as many systems are not designed for data storage and reporting, and many operators are not familiar with M&V requirements.

Measurement and Verification Goals

The goal of each M&V Plan is to reduce energy, water, and/or operations and maintenance (O&M) costs at project site. The M&V Plan should be designed to provide energy, water, and operating savings information in such a way that cost savings can be reasonably estimated.

For example, energy cost savings will be calculated using energy savings and the appropriate cost per unit of energy saved. In most cases, the unit cost of energy will be based on the servicing utility's energy rate schedules at the time the project is implemented. The unit cost of energy that will be used in calculating energy cost savings each year during the performance period must be defined in sufficient detail in the contract to allow savings to be calculated using each of the factors that affect cost savings. These factors include items such as (for electric bills) kWh saved, kW saved, power factor, kW ratchets, and energy rate tiers. If the rate uses time-of-use periods, the energy and demand savings may be calculated separately for each time-of-use period. More complex rates, such as demand ratchets, may require additional calculations. The savings calculations are straightforward.

Demand savings may be based on an average demand reduction or a maximum demand reduction. Average reduction in demand, which is typically not equal to the actual reduction in billing demand, is calculated as the kWh savings during the time period in question (usually the utility summer peak period) divided by the hours in the time period. Maximum reduction in demand is typically the reduction in the utility-metered maximum demand under terms and conditions specified by the servicing utility. For example, the billing peak may be based on the maximum building kW load measured in 15-minute intervals and coincident with the utility peak demand period. The maximum demand reduction is usually calculated to determine savings in utility peak demand charges. Thus, if utility demand savings are to be determined, each site must define 1) how the reduction will affect the utility bill and 2) how the demand reduction will be calculated for purposes of payments to the project developer/lender if the project finance structure is that of an energy purchase agreement.

When determining the value of the energy, caution should be exercised to ensure that a conservative estimate is used that will not overvalue savings. The marginal cost of energy (i.e., the actual cost for the last portion of energy used for each month) should be used, rather than average values. The marginal costs can be determined by reducing the utility usage by 1 kWh or 1 kW, for electricity, and then recalculating the bill. Because there can be many fixed fees, demand charges, and distribution charges, it is important that average values are not used and that only commodity-based charges are included.

O&M and other energy-related cost savings are allowable in most M&V plans, and are defined as reduction in expenses (other than energy cost savings) related to energy and water consuming equipment. Energy-related cost savings can result from avoided expenditures for operations, maintenance, equipment repair, or equipment replacement due to the ECM and renewable energy production project. This includes capital funds for projects (e.g., equipment replacement) that, because of the project, will not be necessary. Sources of energy-related savings include:

- Avoided current or planned capital expense
- Transfer of responsibility for O&M and/or equipment repair and replacement (R&R) to the project developer/lender
- Avoided renovation, renewal, or repair costs as a result of replacing old and unreliable equipment

Specific guidance on documenting and verifying O&M savings in federal projects was developed by a industry-government working group. The resulting document, *"How To Determine and Verify Operating and Maintenance (O&M) Savings in Federal Energy Savings Performance Contracts"*[25] serves as a good example of how best to approach the issue of O&M savings.

The general rule to follow is that any savings claimed from O&M activities must result in a real decrease in expenditures. O&M budget baselines cannot be based on what the customer/debtor should be spending for proper O&M; baseline expenditures must be based on what the customer/debtor is spending. The customer's O&M expenditures after implementation need to decrease for savings to be considered real.

References

1. U.S. Department of Energy, *Energy Efficiency Trends in Residential and Commercial Buildings*, July 2008
2. *http://buildingsdatabook.eren.doe.gov/docs/4.1.3.pdf*
3. Energy Information Administration, Annual Energy Outlook 2008, Table A5, "new additions" through the year 2010.
4. National Research Council. *America's Energy Future: Technology and Transformation: Summary Edition*. Washington, DC: The National Academies Press, 2009.
5. U.S. Energy Information Administration, *www.eia.gov*
6. *Executive Reactions to Energy Efficiency Report*, Alliance to Save Energy, June 2006, *www.ase.org*
7. Ibid
8. Ibid
9. U.S. Department of Energy, 2008 *Industrial Technologies Market Report*, May 2009
10. The American Council for an Energy-Efficient Economy is a nonprofit, 501(c)(3) organization that acts as a catalyst to advance energy efficiency policies, programs, technologies, investments, and behaviors. *http://www.aceee.org*
11. Claire Kreycik, "Financing Solar PV at Government Sites with PPAs and Public Debt," NREL, December 2011
12. M. Bailey; D. Choist; G.T. Magnatta, "Tax Exempt Bonds: The Role of Conduit Issuers in Tax Compliance." The Advisory Committee on Tax Exempt and Government Entities (ACT) White Paper, June 2011
13. S. Perlman, "Solar Power Purchase Agreements (PPA): Financing Options for Local Governments—Hybrid Option (Morris Model)," Webinar presented at the Council of State Governments, Eastern Regional Conference, February 2011
14. C. Bell; S. Nadel; S. Hayes, "On-bill Financing for Energy Efficiency Improvements: A Review of Current Program Challenges, Opportunities, and Best Practices," American Council for an Energy-Efficient Economy, Washington, D.C., 2011, *www.aceee.org*
15. Ibid
16. Ibid
17. *www.aeecenter.org*
18. Alliance to Save Energy, *World-Class Energy Assessments Report*, June 2006
19. Ibid
20. ibid
21. See IRS Bulletin Notice 2006-52 for complete administrative and procedural guidelines
22. Data are illustrative values for typically available systems. All costs are in 2007 US Dollars
23. For steam turbine, not the entire boiler package.
24. *A Best Practice Guide to Measurement and Verification of Energy Savings*, The Australian Energy Performance Contracting Association, 2004
25. *http://www1.eere.energy.gov/femp/pdfs/10_4_determineverifyom-savings.pdf*

Chapter 7

Fundamental Financial Structuring Techniques and Examples

Now that a complete understanding of the internal and external components, legislative, environmental and legal considerations have been explored, it is time to look at how each of these issues are applied in the real world of financing cleantech renewable energy and energy efficiency projects—"The Art of Financing." There are many different ways to analyze and then structure the financing of the project. This chapter will explore in detail some examples of the application of the principles presented in the prior chapters.

ANALYSIS OF THE PROJECT COMPONENTS

The ability to finance an energy project is the litmus test of the viability of any energy project. If it is financeable, the project developer will be able to build and operate the project with sufficient revenue sources to repay its capital investment and obtain an adequate return on that capital over a reasonable period of time. If any of the key components of an energy project is missing, the project will not get financed. There are many components that have interrelationships, and the ability of a project developer to put all the pieces of the project together is paramount. The components are all subject to change at any time as a project is structured, built and commissioned. This can create challenges, opportunities and disappointment. Fortunately, because there are so many components to a successful energy project finance, there can be many alternative ways to solve a problem project component using one or more of the remaining project components. Alternatively, if some components are uncertain, it may translate into risk premiums that could increase the cost of the finance or cause the financing to fail entirely.

This chapter will apply those components, evaluate the options, and present case examples of how project difficulties could be overcome with creative finance structuring by the project developer. We will explore these components as they are independently broken out in their respective categories that are defined as:

- Internal components
- External components
- Market components
- Technology components
- Legislative, regulatory, environmental and compliance components
- Legal components

The International Energy Agency (EIA) defines renewable energy as energy that is derived from natural processes that are replenished constantly. It its various forms, it derives directly or indirectly from the sun or from heat generated deep within the earth. Included in the definition is energy generated from solar, wind, biomass, geothermal, hydropower and ocean resources. Also included are bio-fuels, energy from waste sources and hydrogen derived from renewable resources.

In the real world, energy efficiency (EE) measures are often included in the financial analysis and structuring of most cleantech renewable energy projects. Chapter six described typical energy efficiency measures, how they are incorporated into the energy project, and the implications they have on the cash flows in the project.

In a broad overview of the analysis each project can be broken down into three principal items—project cost, revenue sources and expense or cost centers. These are then put into a cash flow analysis and based on the initial capital cost of the assets (also referred to as "Project Cost") a return is calculated based on when the cash outflows and revenue inflows occur over the project finance term. An accurate financial analysis of the energy project can be determined when those cash flows occur over the project life and the net tax effect of those cash flows have been determined.

Tables 7-1 through 7-4 provide an overview of the considerations that should be reviewed as each energy project is evaluated and the financing options chosen. The tables were prepared by SolarTech under a PIER funding grant from the California Energy Commission.

Table 7-1: Financing Options Characteristics

Characteristic	Description	Capital Expenditure	3rd Party Provided Financing	Operating Lease	Power Purchase Agreement
Ownership & Title	Who will hold title and be the tax-owner of the system?	Host	Host (with lien)	Lessor	PPA Provider
Payment Description	To whom does the user make payments and how are they calculated?	One cash payment at time of installation (construction financing to be negotiated).	Monthly payments, typically fixed, as determined by financing institution. Usually based on an amortization schedule.	Monthly, quarterly, semi-annual or annual payments, typically fixed, as determined by Lessor.	Monthly payment based on the kWh, therms or other energy measurement produced by the project and a contractually determined tariff, or energy unit. Tariff typically increases each year.
Term & Expiration Options	What are the legal requirements for ownership transfer, if any, at the expiration of the contract?	NA	Typically exceeds 75% of the useful life of the system. Debtor usually will own equipment at expiration of the contract.	5-15 years The assets may be purchased for fair market value at the expiration of the contract.	15-25 years. Usually there is no provision for ownership of the assets by the host at the expiration of the contract.
Energy Project Expertise or Experience	To what extent is experience with the technology required to complete and operate a system?	Responsibility falls with the Host/Owner	Responsibility falls with the Host/Owner unless an O&M contract is executed with supplier.	Responsibility is negotiated between the Host and Lessor.	PPA provider leverages previous project experience and responsibility for optimal energy production.
Transferability/ Assignment	Can Host of the facility (or the contract) be assigned?	Yes	Negotiable	Typically no. Not assignable without consent of Lessor and subject to credit approval.	PPA can be transferred after 6 years at which point Host may have option of taking ownership.

Table 7-1 (*Cont'd*): Financing Options Characteristics

Characteristic	Description	Capital Expenditure	3rd Party Provided Financing	Operating Lease	Power Purchase Agreement
Impact on Financial Statements	How does the asset or obligation affect the Host's financial statements?	Asset	Asset (+ Liability)	Operating expense subject to new IASB regulations.	Operating expense subject to new IASB regulations.
Contract Expediency	What complications may arise in execution of the contract?	Little to none with the exception of construction issues & possible warranty issues.	Host is responsible to secure financing; due diligence will vary with financing institution.	Contracts are standardized, fewer complications.	PPA provider must secure internal financing and then host must satisfy credit requirement of the PPA provider.
Monitoring & Maintenance	Who is responsible for monitoring production and ensuring proper system operation?	Host	Host	Host	PPA provider
Site Characteristics	What are the impacts of the Host's ownership (fee vs. leasehold) at the site?	Fee owner: Improvements may cause increase in tax liability; may require subordination agreement with current lien holders or mortgagors. Leasehold: Tenant will have to seek approval from landlord.	Fee owner: Improvements may cause increase in tax liability; may require subordination agreement with current lien holders or mortgagors. Leasehold: Tenant will have to seek approval from landlord. Lien may be placed against property (real and/or personal).	Fee owner: No impact Leasehold: Approval from landlord	Fee owner: May require subordination agreement with current lien holders or mortgagors. Leasehold: Approval from landlord

A central theme for every renewable energy project (and in fact, is the starting point as each transaction is analyzed and modeled) is deriving the expected energy savings. Without knowing the energy savings, it is impossible to determine if the project makes sense for the customer. The first step is looking at the historical energy costs with the existing systems in place (see energy audits on page 208). The second step is to find out the cost of a new system that will produce energy at a lower cost than the existing utility rates. And then the third step is structuring a payment on the capital assets cost by having a payment as much below the utility rates as possible (both at inception and also over the term of the contract).

Table 7-2: Financing Options Benefits

Benefit	Description	Capital Expenditure	3rd Party Provided Financing	Operating Lease	Power Purchase Agreement
Tax Credits	Who owns the ITC/Grant proceeds and what requirements exist?	Host (if allowable by the tax code)	Host (if allowable by the tax code)	Lessor	PPA Provider
Rebates & Incentives	Who owns the rebates, utility incentives, etc., what requirements exist, and what are the tax implications?	Host (if allowable)	Host (if allowable)	Lessor (but could be assigned to Host, supplier or other third party).	PPA Provider
Environmental Attributes	Who owns RECs, Green Tags, Carbon Credits, emission reduction credits, etc.?	Host	Host	Lessor but could be negotiated.	PPA Provider but could be negotiated.
Depreciation	Who can claim and benefit from federal and state accelerated depreciation?	Host (if allowable)	Host (if allowable)	Lessor	PPA Provider
Electric and other Energy Rates	What can the host expect in the form of reduced energy expenses for the useful life of the assets?	Reduction of current utility bill based on size & energy production from system.	Reduction of current utility bill based on size & energy production from system. Energy purchased from utility still subject to market volatility.	Reduction of current utility bill based on size & energy production from system (for the term of the lease). Energy purchased from utility still subject to market volatility.	Stable, predictable, contractually agreed upon energy rates. Energy purchased from utility still subject to market volatility.

However, to keep the monthly debt service as high as possible for a faster project repayment, the owner must structure the transaction looking to future energy costs from the customer's current provider and that takes some "guess work." Most energy production projects that require extensive financing have a payment stream that goes up each year but not faster than the projected energy costs that the utilities will be charging for that energy. This requires some good estimates and is usually based on historical rate increases. Each region is different as is the rate increases from the local utilities in those regions. Table 7-5 is a good starting point for estimating what the future energy costs from the utilities might look like and then propose a transaction

Table 7-3: Financing Options Costs

Cost	Description	Capital Expenditure	3rd Party Provided Financing	Operating Lease	Power Purchase Agreement
Capital Outlay	What are the cash requirement to commence construction and operation of the facility?	100% of the system cost	Down Payment (5-40%), negotiated with financing institution.	Minimal	Zero
Operations and Maintenance Expenses	Who is responsible for operating and maintaining the facility?	Host	Host	Host/Lessee	PPA Provider (costs are built into the tariff)
Insurance	Who is responsible for insuring the facility?	Host	Host	Host/Lessee	Negotiated (cost can be included in the tariff)
Transaction Costs	Who will be responsible for transaction costs?	Host	Negotiable	Host/Lessee	PPA Provider (costs are built into the tariff)
Equipment Replacement	Who will be responsible for equipment replacement?	Host	Host	Lessor	PPA Provider (costs are built into the tariff)
Removal Costs	Who will be responsible for equipment removal at contract expiration?	Host	Host	Lessor	PPA Provider (costs are built into the tariff)

debt stream that is at or below what is expected from the utilities, thus providing continued or increased savings to the customer over the term of the transaction. The table rate of escalation is over a 20-year period from the Energy Information Administration (EIA) "Average Price by State Provider, 1990-2010" and "average Retail Price of Electricity to Ultimate Customers by End-Use Sector, by State—Table 4.6.8"[1] Table 7-5 lists the yearly residential and commercial rates in nominal terms (the example is Florida).

As can be seen from Table 7-6, an asset owner receiving income from the sale of electricity on a renewable energy project in Florida, and knowing that the percent of rate escalation will have a measurable impact on the present value of the future energy production when that owner does their financial modeling on the transaction will provide for a better solution for the customer (and less financial risk for the owners of the renewable energy project).

PROJECT CASH WATERFALL

One simple way most investors and lenders use in evaluating the investment is to use what is referred to as a Project Waterfall Chart shown in Figure 7-1.

YIELDS

There are many different methods used to value the investment. All of them will look at a discounted value of the future cash flows but will evaluate the return based on a multitude of measures and all using different discount rates that are unique to their company. Often,

Table 7-4: Financing Options Risks

Risk	Description	Capital Expenditure	3rd Party Provided Financing	Operating Lease	Power Purchase Agreement
Energy Production Risk	What are the impacts to the Host if production does not meet projections?	Project IRR will be reduced due to decreased avoided electric costs.	Project IRR will be reduced due to decreased avoided energy costs. Cash flow may be negative.	Negative Cash Flow (in many cases, but not all)	Minimal. Host payment is tied directly to system production. Only loss is the difference in expected production multiplied by utility tariff (if higher than PPA tariff).
Warranty Risk	What is the impact to the Host if warranties are not honored?	Host incurs all risks of warranty failures.	Host incurs all risks of warranty failures.	None. Lessor assumes responsibility.	None. PPA Provider assumes responsibility.
Financing Risk	How will the risk of financing complications affect the Host?	NA	Financing typically approved by lending institutions. Current market conditions dictate credit availability.	Minimal. Projects are done deal by deal.	PPA Provider's history of performance with the technology in addition to market conditions may affect Host.
Technology Risk	What is the impact of the risk associated with technology failure?	Host incurs all technology risks.	Host incurs all technology risks.	Lessor incurs risks	PPA Provider incurs all risks
Construction Risk	What is the impact of the risks associated with construction (permitting, engineering, installation, etc.)?	Host must hold developer liable.	Host must hold developer liable.	Lessor must hold developer liable. No risk to Host.	PPA Provider must hold developer liable. No risk to Host.
Site Risk	What is the impact of site complications such as roof life or ground erosion?	Host is responsible.	Host is responsible with financing institution covenants.	Host/Lessee is responsible.	Negotiated between PPA Provider and Host.
Incentive or Rebate Risk	How will changes in incentives and rebates (local, state and federal) impact the Host?	Project IRR for Host may be affected.	Project IRR for host may be affected.	None. Lessor assumes responsibility.	None. PPA Provider assumes responsibility.
Utility Rate Risk	What is the impact if utility rates fall or rise?	Value of avoided cost of electricity rises or falls.	Value of avoided cost of electricity rises or falls.	Value of avoided cost of electricity rises or falls.	Value of avoided cost of electricity rises or falls.

Table 7-5: Utility Rate Escalations Over Last 20 Years (nominal) in Florida

Year	Residential	Commercial
1990	7.77	6.66
1991	7.91	6.77
1992	7.75	6.68
1993	7.99	6.69
1994	7.78	6.35
1995	7.82	6.39
1996	7.99	6.63
1997	8.08	6.62
1998	7.89	6.38
1999	7.73	6.22
2000	7.77	6.25
2001	8.59	7.08
2002	8.16	6.64
2003	8.55	7.13
2004	8.99	7.61
2005	9.62	8.16
2006	11.33	9.91
2007	11.22	9.75
2008	11.65	10.14
2009	12.30	10.86
2010	11.52	9.80

Table 7-6: CAGR of Utility Rates in Florida

Timeframe	Residential	Commercial
20 Year CAGR	1.99%	1.95%
10 Year CAGR	4.01%	4.60%
5 Year CAGR	3.67%	3.73%

these rates are referred as the "hurdle rate" of the project and in the generic sense, is the minimum rate of return they expect to receive before investing in the project. Chapter five covered many of the common terms used in a project analysis and they included:

- Return on Investment (ROI)
- Return on Equity (ROE)
- Return on Assets (ROA)
- Internal Rate of Return (IRR)
- Modified Internal Rate of Return (MIRR)
- Net Present Value (NPV)
- Future Value (FV)
- Nominal Interest Rate
- Effective Interest Rate
- Simple Payback Period (SPP—often used by a borrower or host)
- Cash on Cash (COC—normally excluding the tax effects of the investment)

There are many different "yields" that parties to a renewable energy project look at and use when they evaluate the investment against other potential investments—each evaluated and based on that parties own specific needs. To achieve specific yields for a party, it is common to re-allocate certain revenue streams and expenses to the various parties. The most important thing to remember is that each party has their own interpretation of what the "yield" is—and it will vary from organization to organization. The following is a quick review of some of the more commonly used yields (or rate of return):

Simple Payback (SPB)

The simple payback is often used with the renewable energy industry to calculate the time it takes for the purchaser of the renewable (energy efficiency) system to recoup their investment. This method analysis has limitations that must be understood before being relied upon.

Figure 7-1: Project Revenue Waterfall

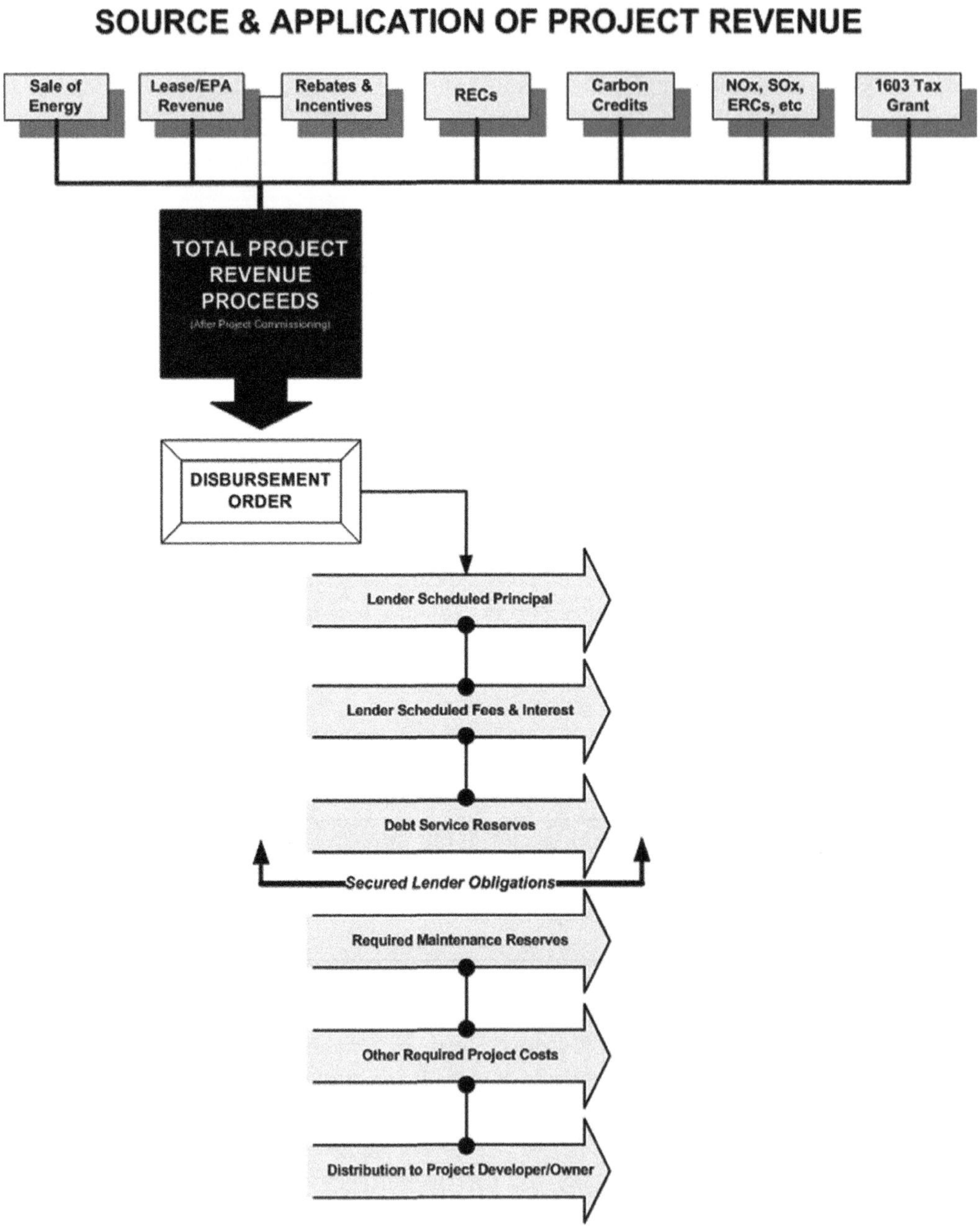

$$\text{Simple Payback} = \frac{\text{Initial Investment Cost}}{\text{Annual Operating Savings}}$$

Simple payback is just that, it does not include a discounted cash flow model, nor does it take into account risk, lost opportunity costs, O&M expenses, or asset degradation. The assumed utility costs per unit of energy (kWh as an example) is fixed during the payback period which is *never* the case. It is simply the initial upfront non-discounted net cost of the renewable energy project divided by the annual fixed non-discounted cash flow (annual unit cost of energy times the fixed utility rate). The end result is displayed in years or fractional years. Caution is warranted when using only a simple payback analysis of most renewable energy projects as owner's actual payback in years will often be longer once all of the other financial considerations are taken into account.

While it is interesting to know how much energy it takes to run a project or how much energy is generated from a RE production project, energy efficiency is about

> *"Tradition is what you resort to when you don't have the time or the money to do it right."*
>
> Kurt Herbert Alder (1905-1988)

savings—how quickly will the savings cover the product's purchase price? Calculation of simple payback can determine at what point this will occur through the realized electricity savings. Although simple payback does not take into account compounded savings, discount rates, inflation rates, or replacement costs, it is a very easy, commonly used, and sometimes useful tool.

Projects with simple paybacks less than 3 to 5 years should be implemented. Projects with paybacks greater than 10 years are "generally" not cost effective. Simple payback period ignores the impact of any cash flows that are received after the payback period—even though it is precisely those cash flows that determine the profitability of the investment.

Modified Payback (MPB)

A case can be made for a modified payback analysis which would allow a prospective renewable energy asset owner to determine when they would recoup their original investment. The modified payback would take into account many of the financial considerations that are excluded from SPB model. The MPB is fairly easy to calculate from the present value and NPV analysis results. It is the time in years it takes for the negative cash flow (as determined in the NPV and PV calculations) to be equaled by the present value of the positive cash flow.

This may produce multiple payback timeframes, since the initial investment may be recouped before one or more components in a renewable energy system is scheduled to be replaced. If this is the case, once that component is replaced a new investment cycle is started with a new payback timeframe determined. If the initial investment is not recouped before the component is replaced, then a single payback timeframe would be produced. The MPB timeframe will often be considerably longer than the SPB timeframe. However, it should be a more accurate presentation of the prospective energy asset owner's recoupment of their actual investment.

Prospective renewable energy system owner's may find that the cost to replace an old technology component near the end of the energy systems life cycle in a small number of cases may not make sense, and in fact it may make more sense financially to upgrade the entire energy system at that time using current technology as it is likely that efficiencies will have improved, costs will have come down and the life cycle timeframes will most likely have been extended.

Net Present Value (NPV)

The net present value is the sum of all positive and negative cash flows which are discounted to the present value. For the netting effect the negative initial cash flow is based on the prospective PV system purchaser's true cost once all tax credits, treasury grant, rebates, depreciation, bonus depreciation, taxes on rebate and loss of utility energy bill tax deductions (for commercial businesses) are factored in. In order to calculate the initial cost, a basic understanding of Internal Revenue Code sections 25D, 48, and other sections that directly relate to renewable energy projects is necessary. Review earlier chapters to ascertain the guidelines, options, opportunities and applications that are attributable to each specific energy project.

Internal Rate of Return (IRR)

An internal rate of return (IRR) calculation is related to the NPV calculation where the NPV equals zero and the discount rate at that point becomes the IRR. In general it is assumed that when comparing projects of equal duration and risk the project with the highest IRR should be chosen. Caution should be used with comparing a renewable energy project to other investment opportunities based solely on the IRR as a project with a large initial negative cash flow in the first year may produce a lower IRR compared to a project with a small initial negative cash flow. However, the project with the large initial negative cash flow may have a higher NPV upon reaching the end of its life cycle, and therefore a higher return in the number of dollars on capital invested.

There are issues associated with using IRR with energy projects. IRR assumes that the positive cash flow will be reinvested immediately at the IRR. This is often not the case since there is rarely another project with a comparable IRR waiting to be started on a monthly or annual basis. Another issue is that with multiple negative cash flows during a project life such as with an inverter replacement cost in a solar PV system during year 16, the IRR may return multiple values based on the negative and positive cash flows.

Due to this a modified internal rate of return (MIRR) might be a better approach for energy projects. If a high IRR is the sole reason for choosing to invest in a particular renewable energy project compared to investment vehicles with a low rate of return such as a certificate of deposit, then another look at the other financial analysis methods mentioned below may be warranted.

Modified Internal Rate of Return (MIRR)

The modified internal rate of return is just that—a modified version of the IRR which resolves two of the issues mentioned previously regarding the IRR as it relates to renewable energy projects. The first assumption is the potential for multiple rates of return due to multiple positive and negative cash flows, and second is the assumption that all positive cash flows will be reinvested at the stated IRR (which obviously is not often possible).

In the modified version, it is assumed that positive cash flows will be reinvested at a chosen fixed rate of return which is less than the MIRR, and negative cash flows are discounted to present value using the Weighted Average Cost of Capital [WACC] (or other owner defined discount rate), thereby producing a single rate of return which may more closely resemble the owner's financial situation.

Implicit Interest Rate (IIR)

An interest rate that is not explicitly stated. The interest rate is not stated in a transaction, but rather, the implicit rate can be determined by use of present value factors. Any transaction that involves a stream of payments that extend over multiple future periods must incorporate an interest rate, even if there is no rate stated in the transaction agreement, because there is a cost associated with delaying payments over a period of time, which is known as interest expense. It takes into account all the cash in-flows and out-flows and brings them down to a present value basis.

FASB 13 (1977) requires the lessor in a lease arrangement to compute the rate of interest implicit in the lease. This computation is required to determine whether the lease should be classified as an operating lease or a sales-type or direct financing lease.

Return on Investment (ROI)

Return on investment is a return calculated in percentage terms on the total investment. It can be calculated over a single annual period or annualized over multiple years. Sometimes it is also used in a more unconventional sense to show the total return over an investment timeframe. This unconventional use can be somewhat meaningless to an energy system owner. For example, if the total ROI is 50%, that may sound like a great investment. However, if that total return is over a 30-year timeframe and has not been annualized, then that may not be considered by some as a great ROI.

ROI calculations are difficult to perform accurately when multiple positive or negative cash flows are involved during an annual time period and become even more difficult if those positive or negative cash flows cannot be ascertained with absolute certainty. In the scenario where multiple positive or negative cash flows are involved then the MIRR may be more appropriate. The definition of the term in the broadest sense just attempts to measure the profitability of an investment and, as such, there is no one "right" calculation.

ROI is the ratio of money gained or lost (whether realized or unrealized) on an investment relative to the amount of money invested. The amount of money gained or lost may be referred to as interest, profit/loss, gain/loss, or net income/loss. The money invested may be referred to as the asset, capital, principal, or the cost basis of the investment.

$$ROI = \frac{(Gain\ from\ Investment - Cost\ of\ Investment)}{Cost\ of\ Investment}$$

Return on Equity (ROE)

Return on equity (ROE) measures the rate of return on the ownership interest (shareholders' equity) of the common stock owners. It measures a firm's efficiency at generating profits from every unit of shareholders' equity (also known as net assets or assets minus liabilities). ROE shows how well a company uses investment funds to generate earnings growth. ROEs between 15% and 20% are considered desirable. ROE is best used to compare companies in the same industry or similar renewable energy projects using the same technologies on a project by project basis. Return on equity measures a corporation's profitability by revealing how much profit a company generates with the money shareholders have invested. Investors usually look for companies with returns on equity that are high and growing.

$$ROE = \frac{Net\ Income\ (After\ Tax)}{Shareholder\ Equity}$$

Return on Assets (ROA)

ROA shows how profitable a company's assets are in generating revenue. Return on assets is an indicator of how profitable a company is before leverage, and is compared with companies in the same industry. Since the figure for total assets of the company depends on the carrying value of the assets, some caution is required for companies whose carrying value may not correspond to the actual market value. Return on assets is a common figure used for comparing performance of financial institutions (such as banks), because the majority of their assets will have a carrying value that is close to their actual market value. This number tells you what the company can do with what it has, i.e. how many dollars of earnings they derive from each dollar of assets they control. Can sometimes also be used in the same context as ROI (see above).

$$ROA = \frac{Net\ Income}{Total\ Assets}$$

Effective vs. Nominal Interest Rate

The nominal interest rate is the amount, in percentage terms, of interest payable. The effective interest rate, which measures the purchasing power of interest receipts, is calculated by adjusting the nominal rate charged to take inflation into account. It is the interest rate on a loan or financial product restated from the nominal interest rate as an interest rate with annual compound interest payable in arrears. The effective interest rate generally does not incorporate one-time charges such as front-end fees.

Pre-tax vs. After Tax

The final consideration in analyzing yields or returns on renewable energy projects is that of pre-tax vs. after-tax. Some owners have a real preference one way or the other. Therefore, any financial investment analysis that is performed on an energy system should do both. With significant tax changes that could possible occur before the project is commissioned or even after it is in operation could have a significant concern for the owner of the capital asset. Every model run should do so with various assumptions so that an owner could adequately assess the risk due to tax risk in the transaction. No financial model is perfect, and each model does contain flaws. However when presented together (the project evaluated using more than one of the above methods), a more accurate picture will emerge and allow a renewable energy system owner to make better informed decisions.

As the sample cleantech renewable energy projects are evaluated below, examples are given of how the outcome of each of these analysis methods presents very different results. In each case, it is "in the eyes of the beholder" that must always be remembered. That concept means that just because one party to the transaction evaluates the project returns one way, it is very seldom that another party to the project will use the same method. For example, a very simple analysis by a Host in an energy purchase agreement may only look at the transaction from a Cost of Capital (COC) basis and ask the question "will my energy costs be lower than my current energy costs from the utility?" They would also add value to that evaluation by considering the issue of fixed annual escalators from the power provider versus the unknown (but likely) annual increases for the energy from the utility. The investor or project developer may only take into consideration their ROI based on their net investment costs after rebates and incentives (on either a pre-tax or after-tax basis) with adequate analysis of the actual credit risk, technology risk and residual risk in the transaction. Both parties would come up with a completely different method of financial analysis with completely different results.

Another example is how different taxing authorities view the actual value of the underlying asset regardless of project costs. The federal and state income tax authorities would look at costs in mostly the same way but use different depreciation schedules and different length of time that the same asset would be depreciated and therefore the net asset value would be different between them. This of course would have no reflection of how the project costs would be shown on an accounting financial statement and what methods of depreciation or amortization would have been used to reflect the current project values on the balance sheet. The sales tax auditor who is looking at the project costs for sales or use tax purpose would have a totally different project cost than would the county or state personal property tax auditor using ad valorem tax guidelines.

All users of the energy produced by a renewable energy system will initially base their investment decision as part of its capital budgeting process. If the numbers don't make sense on that basis, the company will look to third-party ownership and then purchasing the power from that third party under a lease, power purchase agreement or some other contract basis if it makes more sense to do so.

> *"Never invest your money in anything that eats or needs repairing."*
>
> Billy Rose (1899-1966)

The following are the basic elements of the capital budgeting process:

- Estimating all of the cash flows associated with a project over its full life including costs (generating a negative cash flow) and revenue or cost savings (generating a positive cash flow). This information is sufficient to determine the simple cash payback, which measures how long it takes for the project to cover its initial capital costs.

- Identifying the company's WACC or other hurdle rate since many firms consider the time value of money in the capital budgeting process and do not rely only on the simple payback.
- Determining either:
  - The net present value (NPV) of the project cash flows based on its hurdle rate or the WACC, which may be adjusted for the relative risk of the project, or
  - The internal rate of return (IRR) of the cash flows.
- Analyzing the results where there is either a positive NPV or there is an IRR greater than the hurdle rate. Either would indicate an acceptable investment based on the estimated cash flow profile. In theory, all projects with positive NPV or IRR outcomes should be accepted, but since capital is constrained in many cases, there will be a priority ranking on projects that get implemented. Project "risk" also plays a critical role in the final selection process.

Estimating the cash flows of a capital asset investment project is the key building block in the capital budgeting process. While estimating cash flows for a renewable energy investment is similar to any other capital expenditure project, there are several unique elements. Those unique elements include accounting for federal and state incentive, avoided costs, carbon value, dispatch profile and net metering.

- **Avoided Cost.** If a company uses 100% of the energy from the deployment of an on-site renewable energy system, there is no incremental revenue from the project. Instead, cash flow is increased by the avoided cost of purchased energy. This is the case in most renewable energy projects that are actually constructed. Therefore, it is critical to estimate the future avoided cost of energy correctly when considering renewable energy projects. (See sample table on page 235.)
- **Carbon Value.** One of the factors that may have a significant impact on future energy costs is the cost of CO2 emissions in a carbon-constrained economy. A corollary to this element is regulatory compliance mandates on existing equipment that emits criteria pollutants such as NO_X, SO_X and volatile organic compounds. Many types of equipment (such as boilers) emit these pollutants and therefore face increasing requirements for emission reductions that can come from the installation of new renewable energy production systems. This is particularly true in on-site solar thermal applications. Legislation (AB32 in California as an example) can be a big driver in determining the priority of which capital project a company would implement.
- **Dispatch Profile.** Understanding the dispatch profile (e.g. the timing of electricity generation) of a renewable energy application relative to a company's electricity demand profile is critical to estimating projects cash flow. Projects that offer a good peak load shaving profile can reduce demand for purchased electricity when it is at its highest price or when demand response programs mandated by utilities kick into effect.
- **Net Metering.** Net metering is a valuable element in many renewable energy projects that produce so much energy at certain times that exceed the usage profile that the excess produced can be used at another time. When the site generates more electricity than it needs, the excess is fed into the grid and the electric meter runs backward, thereby offsetting energy purchases during other periods. This effectively allows the net-metered site to offset future grid purchases at retail prices. Solar thermal projects can do the same thing with systems that produce more hot water than needed and the excess is stored in large thermal storage tanks for use at a different time when the hot water is needed in a facility.

FINANCIAL ANALYSIS PRINCIPLES

Consistent throughout most all financial analysis models on renewable energy projects are some core input values that have to be considered to get an accurate return from the financing models used. Without these basic values, any result would not only be inaccurate but also be meaningless to the financing of an energy project. This would include projects for single owners, all equity partnership flips, a leveraged partnership flip structure, sale leaseback, lease structures in all their incarnations, and PPA or ESC structures including many different hybrid models. The results can be categorized into the following general areas of importance:

- **Cash flow results**:
  - — Timing and net effect of the revenue streams less the actual cash expenses—including tax benefits—over the term of the financing contract or useful life for the owner and user of the energy if there is no financing used.

- **Energy production results from the system (kWh):**
  - — Energy is the total amount generated by the system (electricity in our examples, but could be thermal value, etc.). In most cases engineering formulas can be used to convert therms from thermal energy systems into electricity values if needed.
  - — Normally needs to be run on an hourly basis and based on the source of the energy production over an annual basis. For example, wind and sun amounts vary considerably over the period of a year.
  - — System downtimes for maintenance also need to be considered.
  - — Degradation factors need to be considered as the production levels from the project will most likely decline over time. Most often the manufacturer of the components can provide real life expectations for this factor.

- **The economic energy value of the system ($):**
  - — The energy value of the project is the value of electricity that the project user avoids purchasing from their utility provider or in the case of a PPA or ESC, the revenue from the sale of the energy to the host including escalators for future years.
  - — This value changes dramatically both on a daily basis as well as on an annual basis since most utilities base their rate structures on both an hourly use and when during the year the electricity is being purchased from them. Some utilities also change the amount they charge based on the gross amounts purchased on a daily, monthly, quarterly or annual basis.

$$\textit{Energy Value} = \textit{Revenues with System} - \textit{Revenues without System}$$

- **Initial cost to build the system**:
  - — Interim construction financing costs
  - — Permanent debt fees and underwriting expenses
  - — Permits, engineering and design costs
  - — Component costs
  - — Construction costs
  - — Installation costs
  - — Bond and construction insurance costs
  - — Environmental fees
  - — Land acquisition fees
  - — Property improvement fees
  - — Interconnection fees with the utility
  - — Developer fees
  - — Placement fees
  - — Debt closing costs
  - — Equity closing costs
  - — Legal and due diligence costs
  - — Documentation fees
  - — Sales costs
  - — Initial accounting costs

- **Replacement Costs**:
  - — Component degradation or failure
  - — Upgrades to components when appropriate

- **Operating expenses over the useful life**:
  - — Operation and maintenance—will most likely vary from year to year
  - — Insurance
  - — Property taxes (would in most cases decline over time as the assessor devalues the system)
  - — Fuel (if appropriate)
  - — Net salvage value (revenue when received)
  - — Monitoring and measurement costs

- **Financing structures and costs**:
  - — Construction financing costs
  - — Annual credit line fees
  - — Debt restructuring costs
  - — Term debt balance

- **Principal reduction**
- **Interest expense**
- **Balloon payments**
- **Incentives to be received and the timing of those incentives**:
  - — Investment based incentive
  - — Cash incentive at inception of the project (could be a percentage of something or a flat amount)
  - — Capacity based incentives

— Performance based incentives (as the project produces energy) over various time periods
— Production tax credit (PTC)
— Investment tax credit (ITC)
— State tax credits
— State sales tax forgiveness
— Renewable energy credits
— Carbon credits
— Emission reduction credits

• **Federal tax effect: (effect on equity)**
— Depreciation—up to seven different classes
— Bonus depreciation
— Section 179 expensing opportunities
— Federal taxes due and timing
— Federal tax savings and timing

• **State tax effect: (effect on equity)**
— Depreciation
— State taxes due and timing
— State tax savings and timing

• **After tax cost and cash flow**:
— The after tax cash flow represents the project's net cash flow including the value of energy generated by the system.
— The effective tax rate calculation is:

Effective Tax Rate = Federal Tax Rate × (1-State Tax Rate) + State Tax Rate

• **Levelized cost of energy (LCOE):**
— See section below

• **Payback**:
— The payback period is the number of years that it takes for the cumulative payback expenses included in cash flows to switch from negative to positive. This could be a negative amount when the payback period is greater than the analysis period. The cumulative payback cash flow for each year is the sum of the current year's payback amount and the previous year's cumulative amount.

• **Misc**:
— Inflation rate
— Mandated lender (debt) reserve costs (less interest earned on reserves)
— Internal reserve costs (less interest earned on reserves)
— Sinking fund for certain component replacements
— Working capital reserves
— Weather predictions
— Utility rate structures
— System degradation on certain components

MATHEMATICAL EQUATIONS

For the mathematically "pure" readers, the following formulas comprise nearly all models and the results using those models.

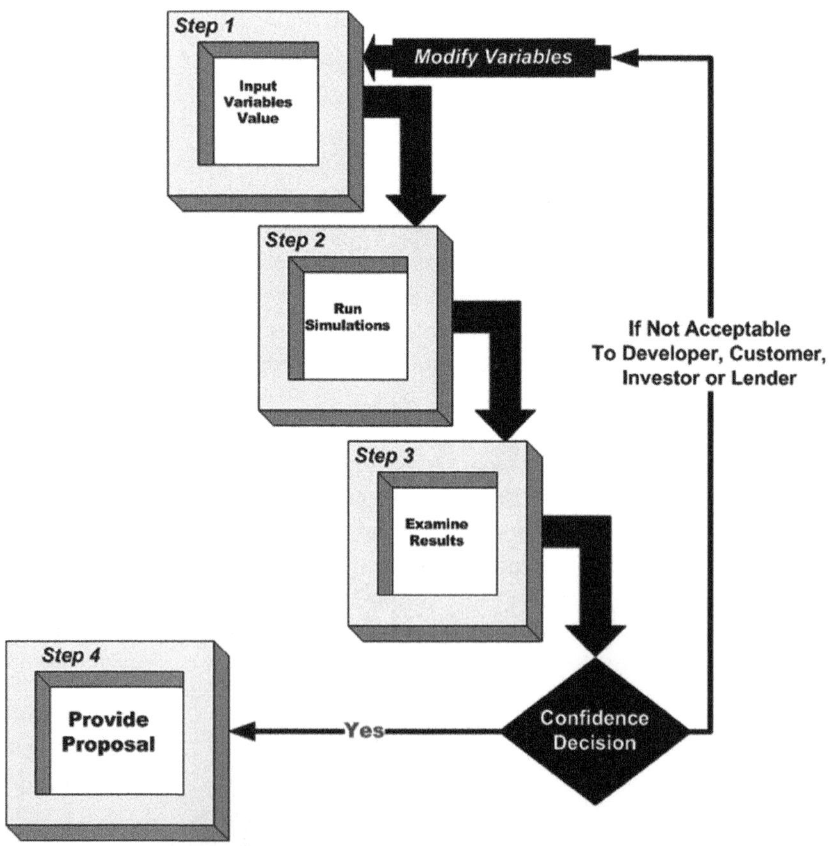

Figure 7-2: The Project Financial Analysis Decision

Project "pre-tax" cumulative IRR

- Pre-Tax Cash Flow in Year Zero = Issuance of Equity
- Pre-tax Cash Low in Year n>0 = Total Cash Flows from Operating Activities + Total Cash Flows from Investing Activities +Total Incentives
- The cumulative IRR in a given Year N is the discount rate that results in a value of zero for the present value of the discounted pre-tax cash flows up to Year N

$$Net\ Present\ Value\ (NPV) = \sum_{n=0}^{N} \frac{C_{PreTax,n}}{(1+IRR)^n} = 0$$

Project "after-tax" cumulative NPV

- The cumulative net present value in a given Year N is the sum of the present values of the pre-tax cash flows up to Year N
- $d_{nominal}$ is the nominal discount rate

$$Net\ Present\ Value\ (NPV) = \sum_{n=0}^{N} \frac{C_{PreTax,n}}{(1+d_{nominal})^n}$$

Total project "after-tax" returns

- After-tax Cash Flow in Year Zero = Pre-tax Cash Flow in Year Zero
- After-tax Cash Flow in Year One = Pre-tax Cash Flow in Year One + Total ITC + Total PTC + Project Tax Benefit
- After-tax Cash Flow in Year n>1 = Pre-tax Cash Flow in Year n + Total PTC + Project Tax Benefit

Project "after-tax" cumulative IRR

- The cumulative IRR in a given Year N is the discount rate that results in a value of zero for the present value of the discounted pre-tax cash flows up to Year N
- $C_{AfterTax}$ is the after-tax cash flow

$$Net\ Present\ Value\ (NPV) = \sum_{n=0}^{N} \frac{C_{AfterTax,n}}{(1+IRR)^n} = 0$$

Project "after-tax" cumulative NPV

- The cumulative net present value in a given Year N is the sum of the present values of the pre-tax cash flows up to Year N
- $C_{AfterTax,n}$ is the after-tax cash flow and $d_{nominal}$ is the nominal discount rate

$$Net\ Present\ Value\ (NPV) = \sum_{n=0}^{N} \frac{C_{AfterTax,n}}{(1+d_{nominal})^n} = 0$$

Compound Annual Growth Rate (CAGR)

- Often performed on a renewable energy system for a 25- to 30-year period to determine the current value of a system or to project the future value of a system
- May want to use the EIA data for the formula (see Table 7-6 on page 235)

$$CAGR = \frac{(starting\ electricity\ rate)^{\left(\frac{1}{\#\ of\ years}\right)}}{(ending\ electricity\ rate)} - 1$$

PROJECT LCOE (LEVELIZED COST OF ENERGY)

The levelized cost of energy in cents per kilowatt-hour accounts for a project's installation, financing, tax, and operating costs and the quantity of electricity it produces over its life. LCOE is a widely used term in the renewable energy sector. The levelized cost of energy (LCOE) allows alternative technologies to be compared when different scales of operation, different investment and operating time periods, or both exist. Analysts can use the LCOE to compare the option of installing a renewable energy system to purchasing electricity from an electric service provider, or to compare utility and commercial PPA projects with investments in energy efficiency, other renewable energy projects, or conventional fossil fuel projects. The LCOE captures the trade-off between typically higher-capital-cost, lower-operating-cost renewable energy projects, and lower-capital-cost, higher-operating-cost fossil fuel-based projects.

In the simplest form, LCOE is determined by dividing the project's total cost of operation by the energy generated. The total cost of operation should include all costs that the project incurs—including construction and operation—and may incorporate any residual value at the end of the projects life. That is:

$$LCOE = \frac{Total\ Life\ Cycle\ Cost}{Total\ Lifetime\ Energy\ Production}$$

The LCOE is that cost that, if assigned to every unit of energy produced (or saved) by the system over the analysis period, will equal the TLCC (total life cycle cost) when discounted back to the base year. LCOE is not recommended when selecting among mutually exclusive alternatives because differing investment sizes are not considered. The LCOE for commercial PPA and utility financing options includes a margin for profits defined by the internal rate of return. The LCOE depends upon your assumptions in:

- Annual electricity generated (or saved) for each year in the analysis period
- Degradation and availability assumptions
- Installation and operating costs
  - Initial investment or capital cost
  - O&M and other operating expenses
  - Financing costs
  - Insurance costs
  - State and federal income taxes
  - Property taxes (if applicable)
  - Sales tax (if included in gross receipts)
  - Return required on investment
  - Decommissioning or removal at end of project term
- Tax credits (including ITC, PTC and depreciation)
- Incentive payments both at inception and over the term of the project

Making comparisons between different LCOEs can become a quagmire. To get a true picture between different project LCOEs or technologies, the same factors must be included in each calculation. The smallest changes or assumptions can dramatically affect the end results—making the comparisons unrealistic and invalid.

Table 7-7 from the Energy Information Administration sets forth their estimated levelized cost of new generation resources (by technology) for plants going into operation by 2016 (costs are expressed in terms of net AC power available to the grid for the installed capacity).

As can be seen, the highest LCOE (based on technologies) are usually the technologies that received the highest rebates and incentives. It is with those rebates and incentives in mind, that the renewable energy technologies vs. the conventional technologies are able to achieve *grid parity*. Also, solar PV has one of the lowest transmission investments because most of those projects are installed on a "distributed" basis—the energy is used directly where it is produced and doesn't need to have transmission lines installed with the exception of a utility solar PV project.

The table shows cost for each "utility-scale" generation technology and are calculated based on a 30-year cost recovery period, using a real after tax weighted average cost of capital (WACC) of 7.4 percent. However, in the case where evaluating projects in GHG intensive technologies (like coal-fired plants) an additional 3% point increase in the cost of capital is added. Also these are national averages and the results could be substantially different on a regional basis (for example solar in

Table 7-7: Estimated Levelized Cost of New Generation Resources, 2016

Plant Type	Capacity Factor (%)	Levelized Capital Cost	Fixed O&M	Variable O&M (including fuel)	Transmission Investment	Total Systems Levelized Cost
Conventional Coal	85	65.3	3.9	24.3	1.2	94.8
Advanced Coal	85	74.6	7.9	25.7	1.2	109.4
Advanced Coal with CCS	85	92.7	9.2	33.1	1.2	136.2
Natural Gas-fired						
Conventional Combined Cycle	87	17.5	1.9	45.8	1.2	66.1
Advanced Combined Cycle	87	17.9	1.9	42.1	1.2	63.1
Advanced CC with CCS	87	34.6	3.9	49.6	1.2	89.3
Conventional Combustion Turbine	30	45.8	3.7	71.5	3.5	124.5
Advanced Combustion Turbine	30	31.6	5.5	62.9	3.5	103.5
Advanced Nuclear	90	90.1	11.1	11.7	1.0	113.9
Wind	34	83.9	9.6	0.0	3.5	97.0
Wind—Offshore	34	209.3	28.1	0.0	5.9	243.2
Solar PV	25	194.6	12.1	0.0	1.0	210.7
Solar Thermal (Electricity Only)	18	259.4	46.6	0.0	5.8	311.8
Geothermal	92	79.3	11.9	9.5	1.0	101.7
Biomass	83	55.3	13.7	42.3	1.3	112.5
Hydro	52	74.5	3.8	6.3	1.9	86.4

the southwest). With technologies that have significant fuel cost (spark spread), both fuel cost and overnight costs estimates will significantly affect the LCOE. And finally, investing in new or unproven technologies may be risky and investors should associate greater risk with these technologies—meaning either a higher rate of return is needed or a shorter repayment period would be required. There are many factors that influence whether to invest in a project other than LCOE. Those parameters are often financial but should also be qualitative or regulatory in nature (e.g., regions where air quality regulators mandate annual reductions in criteria pollutants such as NO_X or PM_{10}).

It is also a good idea to conduct a sensitivity analysis of the results with respect to the measured cost and benefits of the externalities. Many times the values assigned to specific externalities are provided as a range, and a sensitivity analysis on this range of values should be performed. In some cases, the inclusion of such costs and benefits will reinforce the results of the analysis in the absence of the costs and benefits. In these cases, they may be appropriate to exclude.

The introduction of a backup unit in a renewable energy system, such as a solar energy system, raises the issue of the size of the solar energy portion of the system and the solar fraction provided. To determine the optimal solar fraction, the life-cycle cost of the entire system (including backup) should be computed for different solar fractions and the results compared.

Salvage value is the value of an investment remaining at the end of the analysis period. For example, if an investment can be resold or recycled, a positive salvage value exists, and if the investment must be dismantled or destroyed, a negative salvage value exists. In most cases, salvage value is estimated as the resale value of the investment. Another method is replacing the cost of the investment with that of equal characteristics and conditions. Still another method is to equate salvage value to the unamortized portion of the original or replacement costs. For all economic measures, except payback, salvage value is treated as a revenue stream at the end of the evaluation life. Salvage value is not accounted for when calculating depreciation for tax purposes using an accelerated depreciation method.

> *"Your grandchildren will likely find it incredible, or even sinful, that you burned up a gallon of gasoline to fetch a pack of cigarettes."*
>
> Paul MacCready, American aeronautical engineer (1925-2007)

If the technology being analyzed leads to changes in the time of electricity use for a generic industrial or commercial customer, the implications of this usage pattern change should be investigated through a sensitivity analysis.[2] The impact of the change should be assessed by varying both the change in size and/or timing of peak demands, as well as by varying the rate structures and rates associated with energy and demand changes. For example, the effects of replacing a commercial chiller with a more efficient unit having electrical requirements 5 kW lower than its predecessor should be analyzed over a range of impacts on the commercial establishment's peak load (the high end of the range being 5 kW) and over a range of demand charges per kW representative of the utilities' rate structures in the region(s) of interest.

The "real" LCOE is a constant dollar, inflation-adjusted value and the "nominal" LCOE is a current dollar value. The choice of real or nominal LCOE depends on the analysis. Most long-term analyses are conducted in real (constant) dollars to account for many years of inflation over the project life, whereas most short-term analyses use nominal (current) dollars. Some energy sectors and industries prefer to use one form over the other. For example, when discussing LCOE for parabolic trough projects, analysts tend to use the nominal LCOE, while the U.S. Department of Energy uses the real LCOE in its comparative analysis of photovoltaic project costs. Be sure to use the *same form of the LCOE* when comparing costs for different alternatives.

Many times it is necessary to include the entire system in an analysis. For example, suppose the analyst must compare a wind system with a conventional peak-load generating system. These alternatives offer potentially different services, and in order for the comparison to make sense the entire utility system may have to be evaluated. The need to extend a system's boundary beyond the direct boundary may occur in end use markets as well as in utility investments. For example, a daylighting system will have different impacts on the space heating and cooling requirements of a building than those of a conventional lighting system. These different impacts can be addressed either by including the entire heating, ventilating, and air conditioning systems in the analysis (which may, in turn, require that the building shell be included) or, more simply, by including only the value of the impacts (determined exogenously from the lighting analysis). A dollar value credit or cost can be appended to the annual operating cost of the daylighting system to account for these space conditioning impacts.

The real LCOE is less than the nominal LCOE

whenever the inflation rate is greater than zero. Because the nominal discount rate used to compute the nominal LCOE includes inflation, inflation is effectively factored out of the nominal LCOE. If the inflation rate is zero, the real and nominal LCOE would be equal.

- **Project PPA Revenue**—the total PPA revenue is the project's annual revenue from electricity sales, not accounting the salvage value:
  Project PPA Revenue = Net Energy (kWh) × PPA Price (cents/kWh) ÷ 100 (cents/$)
- **Net Energy (kWh)**—the total amount of electricity generated by the system in AC kilowatt-hours for each year
- **NPV of PPA Revenue**—the present value of the annual PPA revenue streams over the analysis period used as the numerator of the LCOE equation:

$$NPV\ (Revenue) = \sum_{n=0}^{N} \frac{R_{PPA,n}}{(1 + d_{nominal})^n} = 0$$

  — Where $R_{PPA,n}$ is the revenue from electricity sales-tax cash flow, and $d_{nominal}$ is the nominal discount rate

- **NPV of net annual energy (nominal)**—the LCOE calculation requires a discounted energy term in the denominator. The value discounted using the nominal discount rate is for the nominal LCOE equation.
  — Where Q_n is the annual energy value described above, and $d_{nominal}$ is the nominal discount rate

$$NPV\ (Energy\ Nominal) = \sum_{n=0}^{N} \frac{Q_n}{(1 + d_{nominal})^n} = 0$$

- **Project Nominal LCOE**

Project Nominal LCOE = NPV (Revenue) ÷ NPV (Energy Nominal)

- **NPV of Net Annual Energy (real)**—the LCOE calculations requires a discounted energy term in the denominator. The value discounted using the real discount rate is for the real LCOE equation.
  — Where Q_n is the annual energy value described above, and d_{real} is the nominal discount rate.

$$NPV\ (Energy\ Real) = \sum_{n=0}^{N} \frac{Q_n}{(1 + d_{real})^n} = 0$$

- **Project Real LCOE**

Project Real LCOE = NPV (Revenue) ÷ NPV (Energy Real)

- It is important to note that if the system output (Q) or savings remains constant over time, the equation for LCOE can be reduced as follows:

LCOE = (TLCC/Q) × (UCRF)

Where:
TLCC = total life-cycle cost
Q = annual energy output or saved energy
UCRF = the uniform capital recovery factor, which is equal to:
$d(1+d)^N \div (1+d)^N - 1$ d = discount rate

SOFTWARE MODELS

In analyzing renewable energy projects the complexity as additional parameters added makes it imperative that software tools be used to get a complete understanding of the results of the investment. The software tools used in this chapter will include:

1. HP12C Financial Calculator
2. NREL's *System Advisor Model* (SAM)—*http://www.sam.nrel.gov*
3. *SuperTrump* from Ivory Consulting—*http://www.ivorycc.com*
4. Sandia National Laboratories *PV Value—http://pv.sandia.gov/pvvalue*
5. OnGrid from OnGrid Solar—*http://www.ongrid.net*
6. CREST from NREL—*https://financere.nrel.gov/finance/content/crest-model*

System Advisor Model (SAM)

The System Advisor Model (SAM) is a performance and financial model designed to facilitate decision making for people involved in the renewable energy industry including:

- Project managers and engineers
- Incentive program designers
- Technology developers
- Researchers

SAM makes performance predictions and cost of energy estimates for grid-connected power projects based on installation and operating costs and system design parameters that you specify as inputs to the model.

Projects can be either on the customer side of the utility meter, buying and selling electricity at retail rates, or on the utility side of the meter, selling electricity at a price negotiated through a power purchase agreement (PPA). The current version of the SAM includes performance models for the following technologies:

- Photovoltaic systems (flat-plate and concentrating)
- Parabolic trough concentrating solar power systems
- Power tower concentrating solar power systems (molten salt and direct steam)
- Linear Fresnel concentrating solar power systems
- Dish-Sterling concentrating solar power systems
- Conventional fossil-fuel thermal systems
- Solar water heating for residential or commercial buildings
- Large and small wind power projects
- Geothermal power and geothermal co-production
- Biomass power

In the analysis examples provided in this chapter, we will be looking only at solar PV projects.

SuperTrump

SuperTrump, the leading pricing software in the industry, is designed to provide ease of use and flexibility. It has the power to perform a broad spectrum of financial analyses and is being used successfully throughout all niches of the leasing industry, by lessors, lenders, lessees, advisors, brokers and syndicators as well as the banking and investment sectors.

SuperTrump performs financial analysis and optimization for true lease, loan, and lease vs. purchase transactions. It quickly and accurately calculates taxes, accounting entries, cash flows and termination values in investments ranging from simple single-investor leases, operating leases and straightforward loans to highly structured leveraged leases. A new energy system analysis module is now in beta testing. SuperTrump models domestic, international and offshore FSC structures, concurrent full-term and early-buyout optimizations, complex loans, real estate leases and portfolios.

In addition to the essential present value and yield calculations (MISF, FASB, ROA/ROE, IRR), FASB and IRS tests, AMT and regular tax calculations and general ledger entries, SuperTrump features:

- Simple input using common financial terms
- Single screen parameter data entry and statistics display
- Target capability for yield or PV adjusting rent, residual, fee, cost, etc.
- Linear programming rent and debt optimization, including prepaid/deferred, arrears/advance flip, EBO, economic compulsion test and individual loan constraints
- Data import into word processing, spreadsheet and database environments
- Over 200 standard reports

PV Value™

The photovoltaic energy valuation model spreadsheet tool was developed by Sandia National Laboratories and Solar Power Electric™. It is intended to help determine the value of a new or existing photovoltaic (PV) system installed on residential and commercial properties. It is designed to be used by real estate appraisers, mortgage underwriters, credit analysts, real property assessors, insurance claims adjusters and PV industry sales staff. For appraisers, the inputs specific to PV in the Residential Green and Energy Efficient Addendum[3] can be used as inputs to PV Value™ (see Appendix 4).

Valuing a PV system is done using an income capitalization approach, which considers the present value of projected future energy production along with estimated operating and maintenance costs that are anticipated to occur during the PV module power production warranty timeframe.

This tool was created with Microsoft Excel® 2007, and works with both Excel® 2007 and 2010. Use of the spreadsheet requires activating macros, ActiveX controls and data connections. A detailed user manual accompanies this tool and can be found in the download area.

OnGrid™

The OnGrid Tool is a solar sales calculator that accelerates Quoting & Proposal generation for Solar PV Systems. The Tool calculates optimal sizing, financial savings, system top-line pricing, and net cost after incentives. It then demonstrates payback, rate of return, property resale value, and cash flow. OnGrid puts these results into attractive customizable proposals, quotes & contracts to make a professional presentation and speed the close of the sale. The OnGrid Tool includes electric rates, incentives, state & federal tax calculations, and estimates system performance, including all performance factors and shading data.

DATA TOOLS, SOURCES AND CALCULATORS

Every financial analysis model requires the acquisition of current data to input into the model if accurate results are to be expected. Finding that data can be a substantial challenge. The following resources will help you find some of the data you will need.

System Advisor Model (SAM)[4]

Developed in 2006, the System Advisor Model (SAM) is a performance and financial model designed to facilitate decision making for people involved in the renewable energy industry.

Solar and Wind Energy Resource Assessment[5] (SWERA) Model

The availability of reliable, accurate, and easily accessible solar and wind energy resource data is critical—and it can greatly accelerate the deployment of these technologies. The Solar and Wind Energy Resource Assessment (SWERA) is a pilot project designed to compile such data in 13 developing countries and to facilitate investments in solar and wind energy projects. The Strategic Energy Analysis Center (SEAC) developed a Geo-spatial Toolkit, which uses a Geographic Information System (GIS) to easily access this data.

SunPath (Version 3.2)[6]

SunPath is a fully MS Windows-based implementation of the popular SUNPATH 2.0, an MS DOS application allows the user to select latitude and longitude coordinates for a site of interest and then determine the position in the sky of the center of the sun for any day of the year and time of day, or for a sequence of days and times.

Energy Data for Decision Makers

The National Renewable Energy Laboratory (NREL) is home to a wealth of data and tools that can be linked together to derive knowledge and expand decision-making capabilities. Their platform links energy communities and decision makers such as policymakers, researchers, technology investors, venture capitalists, and market professionals—with valuable energy data, information, analyses, tools, images, maps, and other resources.

Renewable Energy Data Book[7]

The Renewable Energy Data Book for 2011 provides facts and figures on energy in general, renewable electricity in the United States, global renewable energy development, wind power, solar energy, geothermal power, bioenergy, hydropower, advanced water power, hydrogen, renewable fuels, and clean energy investments.

Clean Energy Data Book for States[8]

The 2009 U.S. State Clean Energy Data Book provides a summary of the status of state-level energy efficiency and renewable energy (taken together as clean energy) developments and supporting policy implementation. It is intended as a reference book for those interested in the progress of the states and regions toward a clean energy economy. Although some national-scale data are given in the initial section, the data are mostly aggregated by states and region, and no data on federal- or utility-level policies are presented here.

Power Technologies Energy Data Book[9]

This report, prepared by NREL's Strategic Energy Analysis Center, includes up-to-date information on power technologies, including complete technology profiles. The data book also contains charts on electricity restructuring, power technology forecasts, electricity supply, electricity capability, electricity generation, electricity demand, prices, economic indicators, environmental indicators, and conversion factors.

Technology & Market Data Reports[10]

Market data are presented in individual reports for each technology area. Data include market penetration; industry trends; cost, price, and performance trends; policy and market drivers; as well as future outlook. Technology areas covered include geothermal, industrial, solar, vehicle, and wind technologies. Program areas covered include the Federal Energy Management Program (FEMP) and the Weatherization and Intergovernmental Program (WIP).

Open EI (Open Energy Information)[11]

An open data platform developed by NREL—with DOE support—that catalyzes the world's energy information and links data together in new ways using "linked open data." Energy information and data will now be at your fingertips to use, edit, add, download, and build valuable new analyses, tools, and decisions.

Database of State Incentives for Renewables and Efficiency (DSIRE)[12]

DSIRE is a comprehensive source of information on state, local, utility and federal incentives and policies that promote renewable energy and energy efficiency.

This source is constantly updated and provides the latest information on a state by state basis. Established in 1995, DSIRE is an ongoing project of the North Carolina Solar Center and the Interstate Renewable Energy Council (IREC). It is funded by the U.S. Department of Energy's Office of Energy Efficiency and Renewable Energy (EERE), primarily through the Office of Planning, Budget and Analysis (PBA). The site is administered by the National Renewable Energy Laboratory (NREL), which is operated for DOE by the Alliance for Sustainable Energy, LLC.

Renewable Energy Conversion[13]

The Renewable Energy Conversion estimator converts electricity from renewable sources into equivalent household energy needs and displaced emissions.

Photovoltaic Land Area Estimator[14]

The Photovoltaic Land Area Estimator estimates land area requirements for photovoltaic electricity based on user inputs.

Wind Power Land Area Estimator[15]

The Wind Power Land Area Estimator estimates land area requirements for wind electricity based on user inputs.

Energy-10[16]

ENERGY-10 software can identify the best combination of energy-efficient strategies, including daylighting, passive solar heating, and high-efficiency mechanical systems. Using ENERGY-10 at a project's start takes less than an hour and can result in energy savings of 40%-70%, with little or no increase in construction cost.

Energy Technology Cost and Performance Data[17]

Recent cost estimates for utility-scale and distributed generation (DG) renewable energy technologies are available across capital costs, operations and maintenance (O&M) costs, capacity factor, and levelized cost of energy (LCOE). Where available, links to utility-scale and DG data are available under the tab headings. The LCOE tab provides a simple calculator for both utility-scale and DG technologies that compares the combination of capital costs, O&M, performance, and fuel costs.

Geographic Information System[18]

This site provides dynamically generated maps of renewable energy resources that determine which energy technologies are viable solutions in the United States. The National Renewable Energy Laboratory analyzes the resources and inputs the data into the GIS—Geographic Information Systems.

PVWatts™ Grid Data Calculator (Version 2)[19]

PVWatts™ Grid Data calculator allows users to select a photovoltaic (PV) system location in the United States from an interactive map.

The Grid Data calculator uses hourly typical meteorological year weather data and a PV performance model to estimate annual energy production and cost savings for a crystalline silicon PV system. It allows users to create estimated performance data for any location in the United States or its territories by selecting a site on a 40-km gridded map. The 40-km Grid Data calculator considers data from a climatologically similar typical meteorological year data station and site-specific solar resource and maximum temperature information to provide PV performance estimation.

HOMER[20]

HOMER, the micropower optimization model, simplifies the task of evaluating design options for both off-grid and grid-connected power systems. When you design a power system, you must make many decisions about the configuration of the system: What components does it make sense to include in the system design? How many and what size of each component should you use? How do the costs and environmental impacts of different system designs compare? The large number of technology options, range of technology costs, and variable availability of energy resources make these decisions difficult to make. HOMER's optimization and sensitivity analysis algorithms make it easier to evaluate the many possible system configurations.

Hybrid2[21]

The Hybrid2 code is a user-friendly tool to conduct detailed long-term performance and economic analysis on a wide variety of hybrid power systems.

RET Finance[22]

RETFinance is a levelized cost-of-energy model, which simulates a detailed 20-year nominal dollar cash flow for renewable energy power projects including project earnings, cash flows, and debt payment to calculate a project's levelized cost-of-electricity, after-tax nominal Internal Rate of Return, and annual Debt-Service-Coverage-Ratios.

Regional Energy Deployment System (ReEDS)[23]

Regional Energy Deployment System (ReEDS) is a

multiregional, multi-time-period, Geographic Information System (GIS), and linear programming model of capacity expansion in the electric sector of the United States. The model, developed by NREL's Strategic Energy Analysis Center (SEAC), is designed to conduct analysis of the critical energy issues in today's electric sector with detailed treatment of the full potential of conventional and renewable electricity generating technologies as well as electricity storage. The principal issues addressed include access to and cost of transmission, access to and quality of renewable resources, the variability of wind and solar power, and the influence of variability on the reliability of the grid. ReEDS addresses these issues through a highly discretized regional structure, explicit accounting for the variability in wind and solar output over time, and consideration of ancillary services requirements and costs.

SERA (Scenario Evaluation, Regionalization & Analysis)[24]

The Scenario Evaluation, Regionalization and Analysis (SERA) model is a geospatially and temporally oriented infrastructure analysis model that determines the optimal production and delivery scenarios for hydrogen, given resource availability and technology cost. Given annual H2 demands on a city-by-city basis, forecasts of feedstock costs, and a catalog of available hydrogen production and transportation technologies, the model generates "blueprints" for hydrogen infrastructure build-out that minimize the overall net-present-value of capital, operating, and feedstock costs for infrastructure networks that meet the specified demand profiles. The model represents production facilities and pipelines at the level of individually geolocated components, while it treats truck and rail transportation at an aggregate level. Intra-urban locations of dispensing stations and of hydrogen production for stationary applications are generated using a geospatial statistical model that matches empirical distributions of such facilities.

Stochastic Energy Deployment System (SEDS)[25]

The Stochastic Energy Deployment System (SEDS) model is a capacity-expansion model of the U.S. energy market. The model uses five-year time periods from 2005 to 2050. SEDS can be operated either deterministically or stochastically. When operated deterministically, SEDS uses a single value instead of the input-probability distributions for the uncertain parameters. In this mode, the results are immediate and informative, in terms of how the model responds to different inputs and assumptions. When operated stochastically, SEDS uses Monte Carlo simulations to make a number of sweeps through the time period. In each sweep, the random variables are sampled using a Latin Hypercube approach that improves on a standard Monte Carlo simulation.

Biomass Feedstock Composition and Property Database[26]

Biomass Feedstock Composition and Property Database is the resulting data from analysis of more than 150 (as of 10/01) samples of potential biofuels feedstocks including corn stover, wheat straw, bagasse, switchgrass and other grasses, and poplars and other fast-growing trees.

Jobs and Economic Development Impact[27]

The Job and Economic Development Impact (JEDI) Models are easy-to-use, spreadsheet based tools that analyze the economic impacts of constructing and operating power generation and biofuel plants at the local and state level. First developed to model wind energy development impacts, JEDI has expanded to offer models that analyze the job and economic impacts of biofuel plants and concentrating solar power, coal and natural gas power plants.

Theoretical Ethanol Yield Calculator[28]

The Theoretical Ethanol Yield Calculator allows you to calculate the theoretical ethanol yield of a particular biomass feedstock, based on its sugar content.

Building Life-cycle Cost (BLCC)[29]

The BLCC Programs analyze capital investments in buildings. Includes EERC 2.0-11, the Energy Escalation Rate Calculator that computes an average annual escalation rate based on EIA energy price forecasts to calculate contract payments in ESPC and UESC projects.

DOE-2[30]

LBNL developed DOE-2 to be a hourly whole-building simulation software for commercial building architects and builders.

EnergyPlus[31]

The EnergyPlus Simulation Program helps building designers and owners save money, reduce energy and improve indoor air quality.

FEDS 6.0[32]

The Facility Energy Decision System (FEDS) provides a comprehensive integrated resource planning approach to selecting technologies with a minimum life-cycle cost. FEDS software makes assessments and analyzes energy efficiency in single or multiple buildings, including central energy plants and thermal loops. Users can quickly compare energy savings potential across different sites through multiple FEDS runs. It provides an easy-to-use tool for identifying retrofits, selecting minimum life-cycle costs, determining payback, and prioritizing options.

FRESA[33]

The Federal Renewable Energy Screening Assistant evaluates renewable energy options. The Federal Renewable Energy Screening Assistant (FRESA) helps Federal agencies analyze the use of renewable energy technologies for buildings and facilities. Although anyone can use FRESA, the software is targeted for use by the Federal sector.

Interactive Building Envelope Calculators[34]

ORNL developed the Web-based software, Interactive Building Envelope Calculators, for estimating the combined effects of envelope materials. The interactive calculators allow a user to enter values specific to construction type and location to determine the energy efficiency of your new or existing building.

SunAngle Professional Suite[35]

More sophisticated, robust, and well-documented version of SunAngle for people interested in better understanding the calculation methodology or developing their own solar angle calculation tools. The Professional Suite includes well-documented HTML/JavaScript and Microsoft Excel versions of SunAngle, plus a detailed technical manual explaining how to perform all of the underlying calculations.

PV-DesignPro[36]

Simulates photovoltaic system operation on an hourly basis for one year, based on a user selected climate and system design. PV-DesignPro is recommended for designs that include battery storage that can be both standalone systems with generator backup, or utility interconnected systems. Systems with no battery storage can be modeled using special instructions. The purpose of the program is to aid in photovoltaic system design by providing accurate and in-depth information on likely system power output and load consumption, necessary backup power during the operation of the system, and the financial impacts of installing the proposed system.

* * * * *

A more comprehensive listing of over 225 available software tools focused specifically on building energy applications can be found in Appendix 2.

FINANCIAL ANALYSIS STRUCTURING EXAMPLES

In each of the sample projects described below, it is important that each analysis incorporates the basic renewable energy project template to accurately review the financial results of the project. It is best if this can be presented in a template format that is common in each project so that the results can be accurately and fairly evaluated from project to project and from the viewpoint of the various parties. Financing for any project requires a demonstration of revenue the project is expected to generate. The model will need to take into account revenue from the sale of energy (or savings on energy if applicable) as well as revenue from other sources unique to renewable energy assets. This is true also on the expense side.

Each time a new renewable energy project is considered, a complete analysis of the project's cash flow using a range of assumptions is required for arranging debt funding, equity funding, and financial security from the future performance of the energy project. The amount of work and time to achieve an accurate financial result cannot be understated. Generally, more than one model is used to cross-check the results of another model. Different models focus on different aspects of financial modeling and frequently an analysis would want to use "pieces" of each model to make presentations to investors, customers, lenders and regulatory authorities.

> *"I'd put my money on the sun and solar energy.*
> *What a source of power! I hope we don't have to wait*
> *'til oil and coal run out before we tackle that."*
>
> Thomas Edison (1847-1931)

Renewable energy project finance is essentially the raising of capital for a new project using the security of future revenues that are combined with tax incentives to return the investment rather than utilizing a corporate balance sheet or other existing credit lines. As a result, it is likely that various components of each model will be used to "sell" the project's financial soundness to each of the parties. Until all parties to the project buy in, no project will move forward to closing. In the end, risk must be minimized and profits must be maximized.

The driving force in nearly every renewable energy project is finding a way that is satisfactory to the customer that will lower current and future energy costs below that which are now received from the utility. As you will see in the examples, that is not always easy and in some cases may not be achievable at all. Hence, most project structures begin with a targeted monthly payment that has an LCOE lower than what the customer now has. Then, the investor (developer, lender, PPA provider, etc.) needs to figure out a financing mechanism that can meet the customer's goal—lower cost of energy. Therein rests both the problem and the opportunity to artfully model one or more ways to achieve a finance structure that meets the customer's cash flow needs.

Therefore, the project model examples will for the most part, look at the solution through the eyes of the investor and not the borrower. Although some components are applicable to both (interest income and interest expense in a conditional sales contract), the examples given are structured from the investor viewpoint.

As we move forward throughout this chapter and look at different modeling tools and techniques, it is very important to know that when *the art of the financing* is applied to any renewable energy project it is the "details" that can make or break the success of any project. The "art" of financing techniques can be broken down into five distinct categories: accounting, tax, system design assumptions, revenue streams and external site specific parameters. We will only be looking at a solar PV system, but the concepts can be applied to all renewable technologies.

1. *Accounting* (see accounting details in prior chapters)

2. *Tax* (see tax details in prior chapters)

3. *System Design* (solar as an example)
   a. System size (watts)
   b. System cost
   c. Derate factor
   d. Degradation rate on other components
   e. Array type (fixed, single axis, dual axis)
   f. Array tilt (roof slope)
   g. Array azimuth (degrees)
   h. Mount type (roof, ground, carport, etc.)
   i. Energy production levels and when
   j. Key component replacement costs and frequency
   k. O&M parameters
   l. Monitoring
   m. Warranty costs and periods
   n. Projected productive life of system

4. *System Life Revenue Streams*
   a. Utility rebates
   b. SRECs or RECs
   c. Emission reduction credits
   d. Carbon credits

5. *External Site Specific*
   a. Current utility rates, schedules and demand response penalties
   b. Projected utility rate escalators
   c. Assumed general inflation rates
   d. Site preparation and structural support

The examples provided below are intended to facilitate a discussion related to selected tax concepts relevant to tax credit monetization financial models. The calculations in the examples are not intended to illustrate a project that complies or does not comply with the tax rules. In some cases, the examples deliberately

Project Description

Project Name: **Project Number:**

Technology: **Energy Type:** **State:**

Project Energy Size:

Project Acquisition Costs

Initial Project Cost: **Unique Cost Parameters:**

Finance Structure

Transaction Type:

Term of Structure: **Renewal Options:**

Purchase Rights, Terms & Amounts:

Fixed or Floating Rates: **Annual Escalator:**

Figure 7-3: Financial Analysis Parameters Template (*Continued*)

Residual Value Assumption:

Rebates & Incentives

Source #1:	Amount:	Parameters:
Source #2:	Amount:	Parameters:
Source #3:	Amount:	Parameters:
Source #4:	Amount:	Parameters:

Tax Guidelines Used

Tax Credit Amount: IRC Section 45: ☐ IRS Section 48: ☐

Grant in Lieu of Credit:

Depreciation: Bonus Depreciation:

IRS True Lease Test Met: IRS Un-even Rent Test Met:

Market Conditions

Current Energy Costs: Escalation Assumptions:

Unique Energy Costs:

Goal:

Environmental Parameters

Revenue Source: Current Value:

Future Value Assumptions:

Environmental Ownership: Revenue Distribution:

Green Branding:

Regulatory & Compliance Parameters

Subject Rules:

Current Cost of Permits & Offsets:

Future Rules—Federal:

Future Rules—State:

SEC Requirements:

Insurance Underwriting Issues:

Operating & Maintenance

Whose responsibility:

Fuel costs responsibility: Fuel Assumptions:

Insurance responsibility:

Future Costs:

Accounting Guidelines Used

Treatment: FAS 13 for Lessor: FAS 13 for Lessee:

Other

Description:

Equipment Parameters:

Equipment Description:

Support Equipment Description:

Soft Cost Description:

Principal Suppliers:

General Contractor:

Project Manager:

Risk Mitigation

Insurance:

Construction Period:

Permanent:

Provided By:

Maintenance:

Projected Maintenance Cost Per Year:

Fuel:

Other:

Projected Energy Production

Energy Type (kWh, Therms, etc):

Figure 7-3: Financial Analysis Parameters Template (*Continued*)

Amount Per Year:
Constraints:
Energy Production Estimates
Annual:
Performance Degradation Estimates
Annual:
Key Component Replacement Estimates
Description:
Energy Monitoring System
Description:

Figure 7-3: Financial Analysis Parameters Template (*Concluded*)

deviate from the tax rules to illustrate a concept for discussion purposes. Please consult your tax advisor when modeling the tax concepts discussed throughout the examples. The rules are very complex and each project's facts and circumstances are unique.

In all samples, the following general assumptions will be made (unless otherwise noted):

- Composite (federal and state) tax rate of: 40.7460%
- Project commencement date: July 1 of the current year
- MISF rate is 0% so as not to distort cash flow earnings
- 100% of the project cost development, engineering and construction are included in the project finance structure and that the borrower or host does not contribute any portion of the capitalized project costs
- The project will be a solar photovoltaic project
- Debtor's incremental borrowing rate is 10.0%
- Project sinking fund rate is 0.0%
- Economic cost of capital is 15.0%
- Income will be compounded at the end of the month
- ITC will not be included in pre-tax-cash-flow (PTCF) to calculate rate
- Title to asset will not automatically transfer to debtor at end of contract
- Payments from debtor are reasonably collectible
- The renewable energy assets are not limited use property
- Any down payment timing will be spread over funding period
- Alternative minimum tax (AMT) will not be considered
- The owner of the assets is not a foreign sales corporation (FSC)

Copies of printed reports that are significant for the readers understanding of each project are included in Appendix 3. Not every model variation will have reports since that would be too voluminous. However, the basic start of each project will have reports and then in the narrative of each project example below, I will examine possible changes or enhancements to the project analysis and summarize the results under that Project ID.

Project 1

Let's get started with a couple of the most basic financial models—simple payback and modified simple payback. This is the method some people would use because it is the easiest to provide a quick litmus test of the proposed project and doesn't need an understanding of accounting, taxes or legal components. It can be done using only a HP12C or other financial calculator. Most often this model is used when the owner of the asset pays cash for it and doesn't use a third party to finance the project. Then we will take the basic model and add two things to the mix—real project realities and lastly the results with the tax effects added (project 1-A) using SuperTrump.

Project 1 (Figure 7-4): Simple payback with user financing the project directly using no debt.

Note that there is no consideration given for:

- Escalation in energy costs over the five years
- No consideration for the tax effects
- No consideration of incentives or rebates
- No consideration for loss of income from cash investment that may have been possible putting the capital to use in another investment

PARAMETER	
System Cost	$1,000,000
Energy Savings	$200,000 per year
Simple Pay Back	5 years

Figure 7-4

a) Figure 7-5 assums the user had considered the indicated items for a modified simple payback answer.

b) Figure 7-6 assumes further: That energy costs (savings) escalate 10% per year (without compounding).

c) Figure 7-7: Looking at a simple net present value analysis on the same project assuming:

- The rebates and incentives were received at the fourth month (realistic)
- Energy savings are equal monthly over each year
- Looking only at a *"pre-tax"* analysis
- Assuming a 15% discount rate

NPV = $903,955 @ 15%

To get a NPV of $1,000,000, the project would only realize a 3% return.

PARAMETER	
System Cost	$1,000,000
Utility Rebate	100,000
ITC Tax Incentive	300,000
Net Cash Investment	$600,000
Energy Savings	$200,000 per year
Modified Pay Back	3.0 years

Figure 7-5

PARAMETER		Cumulative Cash Balance
System Cost	$1,000,000	(1,000,000)
Utility Rebate	100,000	
ITC Tax Incentive	300,000	
Net Cash Investment	$600,000	(600,000)
Energy Savings 1st Year	200,000	(400,000)
Energy Savings 2nd Year	220,000	(180,000)
Energy Savings 3rd Year	240,000	60,000
Total Savings	$660,000	
Modified Pay Back	2.75 years	

Figure 7-6

PARAMETER		Months	Cumulative Cash Balance
System Cost	(1,000,000)	1	(1,000,000)
Energy Savings (1st 3 months)	16,667/mo	1 - 3	(950,000)
Utility Rebate—4th month	100,000	4	(850,000)
ITC Tax Incentive—4th month	300,000	4	(550,000)
Energy Savings (9 months)	16,667/mo	4 - 12	(400,000)
Energy Savings 2nd Year	18,333/mo	13-24	(180,000)
Energy Savings 3rd Year	20,000/mo	25 – 36	60,000

Figure 7-7

Project 1-A: Start advancing into real project components

Using SuperTrump as a financial modeling tool would provide the following yield results (see Appendix 3 for Project 1-A yield and cash flow reports):

- Three-year project analysis period
- No compounding of assumed utility rate escalators
- All cash received (ITC and utility rebate) applied as equity
- No consideration for taxes—either rates or components such as depreciation
- The pre-tax effective rate and the after-tax effective rate would both be the same since no tax effects were considered in the project. Project rate would yield 5.433%
- The implicit interest rate would be -24.2968%

Project 1-B: Moving a bit further into a real world project basis utilizing the tax effects

Using SuperTrump as a financial modeling tool would provide the following yield results (see Appendix 3 for Project 1-B yield and cash flow reports):

- Federal tax rate is 35% (assuming maximum) and state tax rate (California as an example) is a flat 8.84% thereby providing for a weighted combined tax rate of 40.7460%
- The maximum federal tax bracket means the tax payer has a net taxable income of $18,333,333
- The ITC received would not be a fee receivable, rather it would have a significant tax effect as it would be applied against taxes due (federal)
- Federal MACRS depreciation would be taken with the 50% bonus depreciation in the first year
- Federal asset capitalized depreciation would be reduced by ½ of the ITC taken (85%)
- The project would have a minimum expected life of five years
- Utility rates (without compounding) would continue at 10% escalation per year
- The net results would now be:
  - — Cumulative pre-tax cash flow of $332,320
  - — Pre-tax effective yield of 53.2633%
  - — Pre-tax nominal yield of 46.8250%
  - — After-tax effective yield of 31.5606%
  - — After-tax nominal yield of 27.7457%
  - — Implicit Interest Rate of 21.8942%
  - — Total taxes saved of $166,008

As can be seen in just the first project looked at, there can be numerous results from the same given project. Project rates of return can be from a "payback" of five years in its simplest analysis to providing a phenomenal return of 53 percent! While many entities considering a renewable energy project will only want to look at the simple payback analysis, it is far from being even close to what the payback really is. In the real world there are things like taxes (both federal and state), accounting requirements, expected asset life cycle, etc. And, not all entities are taxed at the same rate or are located in the same state. Federal tax rates alone have 8 tax brackets ranging from 15% to 35% and state tax rates can have between one (as in California) to as many as ten tax brackets (Alaska).

Project 2 (see Appendix 3 for full reports)

CSC vs. Equipment Lease.

Under this project analysis, we will do a side by side comparison of financing a renewable energy project under a conditional sales contract (CSC) vs. a lease. This is a comparison that is commonly done on many energy projects. This is also the level where some degree of complexity can come into play since we are now working with tax attributes that could be monetized. Although not every permutation will be considered that has been detailed in earlier chapters, some of the basic ones will be analyzed. Where permitted, ITC could or could not be passed on to the lessee. Accounting issues as they pertain to balance sheet treatment (mostly by the lessee) also become a consideration.

The basic parameters used in this renewable energy project are:

- System cost: $1,000,000
- Federal tax rate: 35% (for lender—lessee may be the same)
- State tax rate: None
- Initial term: 60 payments
- Payments made: In arrears
- Down payment: None
- Project fees: Paid by lender and not charged to borrower
- Incremental Borrowing Rate: 10% (debtor)
- Utility rebate: Retained by debtor

Conditional Sales Contract

- Interest rate: 10%
- Balloon payment: None
- Payment amounts: Fixed
- Total interest: $274,822.68

Making the payments in advance instead of arrears has an insignificant difference in yield to the lender. All it would do is to add another hurdle in the eyes of the borrower and therefore not suggested. However, making the following changes would provide the following results:

1. Providing for a balloon payment of 20% ($200,000) would lower the payment to $18,664 from $21,247 and the yield would remain the same.
2. The after tax cash flow to the lender would increase from $178,635 to $207,908—an improvement of $29,273. The yield would not change—just the timing and therefore the amount. Some investors/lenders like this approach and it also benefits the borrower by having a lower payment each month.
3. If the energy savings were only $20,000 per month from the project, a lower payment would make for an easier closing proposal to the borrower. In most cases, the investor/lender would finance the balloon payment when it came due over a 12 to 24 month period—thereby providing positive cash flow to the borrower at all times.

Equipment Lease Contract

There are many different lease structures and there is no need to cover them all on this project model. We will use the same basic parameters as above but with following specifications on the basic lease contract.

- It will be booked as a true lease by the investor/lessor/lender
- 30% Federal ITC is received by the investor/lessor/lender
- Capitalized asset cost for depreciation is $850,000 (cost reduced by 50% of ITC taken)
- Payments in arrears
- Payments variable for term (equal to utility savings)
- No state taxes considered—federal only at 35%
- No purchase option at the end of the lease term other than FMV for lessee

Results:

1. MISF pre-tax yield of 34.1220% and after-tax yield of 22.1793%
2. IRR pre-tax yield of 7.1585% and after-tax IRR of 4.6531%
3. The challenge at this point is to get the payments below the utility savings and still keep the yield to investor the same. This could be done using one of the following options on the lease:
   a. With a target payment of 10% under the utility savings and keeping the term the same, the investor could accept a lower yield: MISF pre-tax yield would drop to 27.5749%, the MISF after-tax yield would drop to 17.9367%, pre-tax IRR would drop to 2.917% and after tax IRR would drop to 1.8945%. Depending on the investor, this may or may not be acceptable but would get the customer closer to accepting the proposal.
   b. With a target of 10% under the utility savings, the residual assumption could change to $141,300 (14% of system cost).
   c. With a target of 10% under the utility savings, the term could be extended for six months (10% longer than original term) at $22,500 per month.
   d. Customer could make a refundable security deposit in the amount of $350,000.
4. Any number of the above combinations plus other options could be employed. There is no one solution and the goal at this point is to get the investor into thinking of solving the customer's demand for lower utility payments by using one or more structuring tools to do so.

Project 3 (see Appendix 3 for full reports)

Lease vs. Purchase Analysis (see Figure 7-8)

Lease vs. Purchase analysis calculates the cash flows (including tax payments or benefits) from the leasing scenario and from the purchase scenario independently, and then compares the present value of the two sets of cash flows at a given rate or rates. The rates entered are used in this present value calculation. Since the rates entered here are directly applied to after-tax cash flows it should be viewed as an after-tax rate.

There can be many different evaluations but the example included will give just one set of parameters to consider. In this case, the purchase option is more favorable than the lease option. The primary reason is that the payment structures are the same on both and there was no monetization value provided for the tax attributes by the investor/lessor (an obvious mistake no lessor should make).

Project 4 (see Appendix 3 for full reports)

Basic Energy Production Asset Analysis

From Project 4 through the remainder of the projects we will be looking at, a much more in-depth analysis based on the technology parameters will be ad-

	Present Value					Purchase		Lease		
period ending	compound period after-tax cash flow	pre-tax discount rate (not used)	after-tax discount rate (used)	days	after-tax discount factor	after-tax cash flows	present value	after-tax cash flows	present value	difference
Dec-30-12	-688,834.30	15.3846	10.0000	164	0.955622	-640,500.00	-652,120.54	-48,334.30	-47,421.31	604,699.23
Dec-30-13	-39,634.00	15.3846	10.0000	360	0.864982	95,200.00	85,331.63	-134,834.00	-123,336.86	-208,668.49
Dec-30-14	-90,711.70	15.3846	10.0000	360	0.782939	57,120.00	46,342.77	-147,831.70	-122,418.12	-168,760.90
Dec-30-15	-126,562.30	15.3846	10.0000	360	0.708677	34,272.00	25,168.31	-160,834.30	-120,567.86	-145,736.17
Dec-30-16	-139,562.00	15.3846	10.0000	360	0.641459	34,272.00	22,781.10	-173,834.00	-117,965.38	-140,746.48
Dec-30-17	-97,195.70	15.3846	10.0000	360	0.580822	17,136.00	10,311.38	-114,331.70	-72,270.14	-82,581.52
total	-1,182,500.00			1,964		-402,500.00	-462,185.35	-780,000.00	-603,979.68	-141,794.33

Figure 7-8

dressed. We will start looking at just a few and build to a complete analysis looking at all the variables. In our examples, we will again be considering solar PV technology but the same principals apply to all other renewable energy technologies.

The first financial modeling tool to be used is PV Value™[37] (an Excel spreadsheet) which was developed jointly by Sandia National Laboratories, Solar Power Electric™ and the U.S. Department of Energy. It is a very basic model intended to help determine the value of a new or existing photovoltaic (PV) system installed on residential and commercial properties.

It is important to note that two otherwise similar solar PV systems of equal size and cost that are installed at a different tilt and orientation from each other, installed at different locations in the U.S., and which also have different amounts of shading, will not necessarily produce equal amounts of energy, and in some cases may have dramatically different annual energy production figures. The annual energy production figures is what determines the true value of a solar PV system at any given location. Valuing a PV system is done using an income capitalization approach, which considers the present value of projected future energy production along with estimated operating and maintenance costs that are anticipated to occur during the PV module power production warranty timeframe. The model's core belief is that the value of the income stream is related to energy production, existing utility electricity rates, future utility escalation rates, discount rate and O&M expenses over its remaining useful lifetime. The limitation of the modeling tool is that it is only valid for grid-tied PV systems with net metering. Additionally, the model does not take into consideration the tax attributes of depreciation and ITC, or the future values of RECs, SRECs, utility rebates, etc. The free modeling tool can be downloaded from Sandia. A manual and a video on how to use the model is included.

Figure 7-9: Solar PV Resource Map

A modeling tool like PV Value™ can provide the investor with the "first cut" on whether the project costs and estimated output over a 25-year term can substantiate the investment. This modeling tool can be used as the "starting" point for basic data that will be used as inputs into other financial models. It is a good basic modeling tool since it uses exact locations, current FMA discount factors, proper derate factors and other important criteria. The "value" of the energy system output does not necessarily correlate to what the system is being sold for, rather it estimates the "value" of the system based on the economics of the system production expectations. With basic input by the analyst, the model will produce the following key information regarding the proposed system:

- Appraised range of value estimate—low, medium and high—for the system
- kWh Production per year by the system
- Energy value per year ($) of the system
- Accumulated energy present value with O&M expenses
- Over a 25-year time frame
- Residential, commercial or user defined rate from utility based on zip code ¢/kWh (current version does not include "time of use" rates)
- Utility escalation rates (historical)
- Estimated inverter replacement cost
- Uses FNMA 30-year fixed 60-day rate for discount—can be user defined also
- Applies a derate factor on the solar PV system
- User can select results for fixed, single or dual axis array type

In this example we have used a 250 kW solar PV system that was installed in zip code 92868 (California). The results can be seen in the Appendix 3 and are summarized here:

1. The existing utility, SCE, sells power at $0.14 per kW
2. The commercial escalation rate is 1.24
3. Annual energy production from the system is 369,382 kWh
4. The economic value of the system per year starts at $51,454
5. The estimated value of the system is:
   a. Low of $724,200
   b. Medium of $779,207
   c. High of $840,831

Using this model, let's look at a solar PV system installed at four different locations and the results in Table 7-8 (assuming same size and configured commercial system [250 kW] in all four locations):

As can be seen, there is a wide variety of system values predicated on where the solar PV project is located from this model. The value ranges from $0.92 cents per watt to $9.39 cents per watt. Now you can see why everyone wants to move to Hawaii, set up business and become an investor in solar PV projects (excluding the climate and beaches). It also shows that without massive state subsidies to help cover the construction costs extremely few projects would be built. Remember, this model doesn't take into consideration any tax considerations and is based solely on the economic value of the systems in each location. The key uses of the model would 1) as a tool to develop parameters for input into other financial modeling software, and 2) to ascertain what selling prices by developers and system integrators of completed systems would be worth to investors.

The model can be tweaked to change certain assumptions also. For example (using the project shown in Appendix 3):

- Installing the system with a two axis tracker would raise the value of the system 33% to $1,035,364. However, it would also add to the developers cost and also to the O&M and component replacement costs.
- Raising the estimated utility escalation rate from 1.24 to 2.5 (assuming you could provide hard core evidence for this assumption) would raise the value of the system 51% to $1,180,172 without a

Table 7-8: PV Value™ Results of Four Systems in Various Locations

Location	Current Utility Rate (¢)	Utility Escalation Rate	Energy Produced (annual)	Energy Value (annual)	System Value (average)
Orange, CA	.14 per kW	1.24	369,382 kWh	$51,454 per year	$779,207
Portland, OR	.06 per kW	2.45	253,052 kWh	$15,107 per year	$229,849
St. Paul, MN	.07 per kW	1.44	297,551 kWh	$20,724 per year	$295,035
Kapalua, HI	.28 per kW	4.94	364,681 kWh	$101,600 per year	$2,347,441

corresponding increase in construction costs.

- Raising the derate factor by five basis points (assuming your engineer and system designed could substantiate the increase in a written report) to .82 would cause energy production to increase and therefore raise the value of the system 7% to $833,573.

Project 5 (see Appendix 3 for full reports)

Energy Production and Cost Savings (PVWatts™)

PVWatts™ is an online calculation tool used for estimating the energy production and cost savings grid connected PV systems at locations around the world. PVWatts™ is used by a wide spectrum of people, including those wanting to get an initial, high-level understanding of PV potential to those wanting to generate an hourly output for a site. Two versions of PVWatts™ are available. Version 1 allows a user to select a location from a map or text list of pre-determined locations throughout the world. Version 2 allows users to select any location in the United States.

The PVWatts™ Viewer is an interactive map providing access to multiple data sets which link directly to their corresponding PVWatts™ Calculators, allowing the user to determine energy production and cost savings of grid-connected solar photovoltaic (PV) systems. Both calculators are accessible through the viewer by querying their corresponding data layers, which feature weather data in the form of specific locations (239 TMY2 sites in the United States and 76 international) as well as a 40km x 40km grid which covers the United States.

The model provides for two map views—street view and satellite base map.

Inputs include:

- The user first selects a location from a map or text list of pre-determined locations throughout the world (for Version 1) or from any location in the US (for Version 2).
- The user then inputs the following data for the location and system being considered:
  - DC rating (in kW)
  - DC to AC derate factor
  - Array type (fixed tilt, 1- or 2- axis tracking)

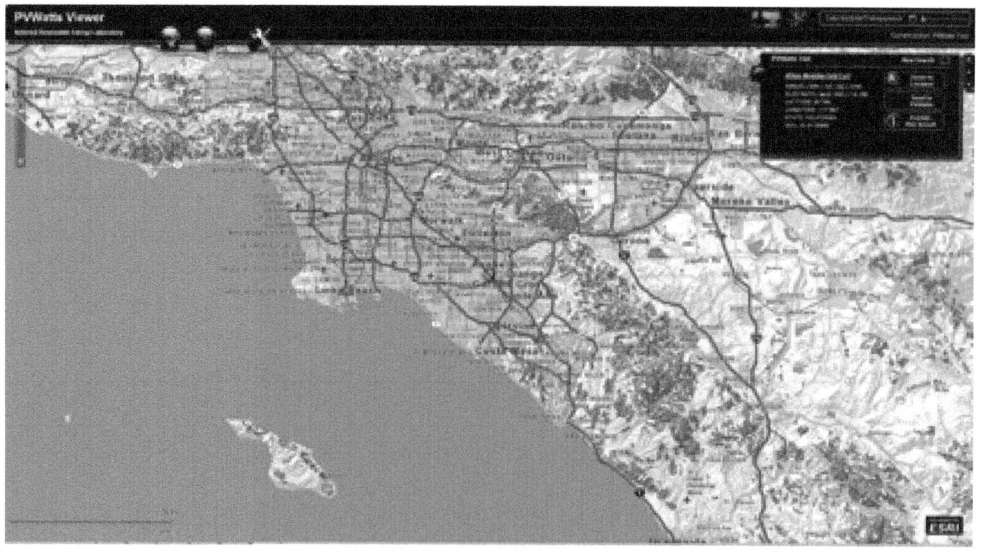

Figure 7-10: PVWatts™ Street Map View

Figure 7-11: PVWatts™ Satellite View Map

— Array tilt (in degrees)
— Array azimuth (in degrees)
— Cost of electricity (in cents/kWh)

- Default values are provided for all of these inputs, should the user need to use those.

Outputs include:

- The tool outputs the following location-specific information:
  — latitude
  — longitude
  — elevation
- It outputs the following PV system information on a monthly basis:
  — Average solar radiation (kWh/m2/day)
  — AC energy (kWh/month)
  — Energy value ($/month)
- Annual numbers are also provided for three outputs:
  — Average solar radiation (kWh/m2/day)
  — AC energy (kWh/year)
  — Energy value ($/year))

The user is also able to output hourly performance data (AC power (W)) for many typical meteorological year (TMY) datasets.

Using the basic same data as in Project 4 above, the results shown in Tables 7-9 and 7-10 occur:

Input:

Table 7-9

Station Identification	
City:	Orange
State:	California
Latitude:	33.8° N
Longitude:	117.7° W
PV System Specifications	
DC Rating	250.0 kW
DC to AC Derate Factor	0.77
AC Rating	192.5 kW
Array Type:	Fixed Tilt
Array Tilt:	33.8°
Array Azimuth	180.0°
Energy Specifications	
Cost of Electricity:	14.0 ¢/kWh

Output:

Table 7-10

		Results	
Month	Solar Radiation (kWh/m²/day)	AC Energy (kWh)	Energy Value ($)
1	4.59	25,467	3,565.38
2	5.17	26,013	3,641.82
3	5.84	32,245	4,514.30
4	6.18	32,707	4,578.98
5	6.40	34,767	4,867.38
6	6.48	33,599	4,703.86
7	6.63	34,946	4,892.44
8	6.83	35,936	5,031.04
9	6.33	32,478	4,546.92
10	5.57	30,033	4,204.62
11	5.09	27,128	3,797.92
12	4.36	24,359	3,410.26
Year	5.79	369,679	$ 51,755.06

When compared to the model results in Project 4, it can be seen that there is little difference between the two. Most often, this modeling tool will be used to provide input into other software programs such as SuperTrump or PV Value™. The advantage is that instead of a total for the year as shown in Project 4, this model provides monthly outputs. Obviously, this is a precursor to evaluating the energy value of the system for the first year, since in most finance projects it would be a short year (system not operating for a full 12 months). Also, for more sophisticated analysis where the utility has higher rates they charge in the summer than the winter months, the value would increase since the system is producing more energy during the months when the utility rates are highest. Utilities in many states also have "tier" rates that increase from a base line as the user uses more electricity. These tiers can be as low as .14¢/kWh to as high as .35¢/kWh in the higher energy usage tiers and therefore the value of the system would increase as the higher tiers are reduced for the user. This becomes an extremely important "artful" parameter to use in finance project proposals and could easily drive down the cost to the customer and still maintain the higher PPA rates needed to secure the final project yields to the investor.

Project 6 (see Appendix 3 for full reports)
Using PV Watts and PV Value™ for Energy Production Parameters (SuperTrump)

This project will build on the output from the two prior projects that calculated the amount of energy expected to be produced by the solar PV system. That data will be put into the SuperTrump financial model and various sets of parameters will be looked at to achieve a proposal on the renewable energy project.

The following *assumptions* will be used:

- The projected production on a monthly basis and the commercial pricing of .14¢/kWh as a value will be used to calculate the monthly payments (SCE is the utility in Orange, CA per the PV Value™ model above).
- The payments will have an annual escalation factor of 2.50
- The finance structure could be either a tax lease or a PPA
- The derate on the modules is 0.77% per year (as in the PV Value™ model)
- The contract term will be 10 years (120 monthly payments)
- Residual value assumption is a 5% salvage value ($50,000)
- REC value is $10 (1 MW of production) in first year
- REC value escalation is 10% annually
- O&M costs are $20 per kWh per year (no escalation)
- Utility rebate of 5% of asset cost
- Annual energy production first year is 362,187 kWh

The *results* are:

- Over a ten-year period, the finance structure would be almost the same value as is the utility rate to the customer (assuming no demand charges and a fixed monthly energy cost with only 1 tier).
- The yields are:
  - MISF effective pre-tax of 2.8765%
  - MISF effective after-tax of 1.7044%
  - Implicit interest rate of -2.5617%
  - IRR pre-tax-cash-flow rate of -7.1646%
  - IRR after-tax rate of -4.2453%

As can be seen from the results, this structure would not be very attractive to either the investor (too low of a yield) or the customer (energy costs are same as from the utility). Therefore, let's look at some "art" out of using the financing model:

Options:

When selecting options, try to modify only one at a time to begin with (as is done below). Then, if specific results have not been achieved, try changing more than one variable as needed. Changing too many variables at one time can distort results beyond what is needed. Try changing as follows:

1. Extend the contract five more years to 15 years would bring the MISF effective pre-tax yield to 9.9958% —an increased yield of over 3.47 times the original yield for an offsetting increase in term of only 50%. Still no benefit to the customer though.
2. Extend the contract ten more years to 20 years would bring the MISF effective pretax yield to 13.4616%—an increased yield of over 4.68 times the original yield by doubling the original contract term from ten to 20 years (normal term for most projects of this scale including PPA structures). Still no benefit to the customer though.
3. Add a residual of 20% (probably a very conservative estimate) at the end of the 10-year agreement (instead of the 5% assumed above) would raise the MISF effective pre-tax yield from 2.8765% to 7.0551%—a 2.45 fold increase whereas, using a more realistic value of 40% at the end of the 10-year agreement, would raise the yield to 11.2004%.
4. Increase the escalation rate (payments) from 2.5% per year to 3.00% per year would raise the yield 115% to 3.3116% (MISF pre-tax effective).
5. Increase the REC escalation rate from 10% to 20% per year over the 10-year period would raise the yield to 3.9926% (MISF pre-tax effective).
6. Real life example...Lower the amount of how much will be charged for the energy system production by various amounts and at the same time increasing the amount of revenue expected over future years for the REC values.
   a. Start by lowering the energy cost to the customer 20%. Instead of charging the same rate as the utility (.14¢/kWh), lower starting energy cost to just .1120¢/kWh.
   b. Increase the estimated residual value from 5% to 20% of the original system cost—a conservative number that is realistic.
   c. Have the monthly payment escalator go up 3% per year starting in the 2nd year.
   d. The term of the contract is 20 years.
   e. Assume the cost of O&M will go up 20% starting in the 10th year

Results:

- A real win-win for both the investor and the customer

- A great value for the customer—most contracts only offer a 10% or less reduction below the current utility costs for the same amount of energy.
- Yield to investor now is (with a composite tax rate of 40.7460%):
  - — MISF Pre-tax Effective of 13.2011%
  - — MISF After-tax Effective of 7.8222%
  - — IRR Pre-tax Effective of 3.5625%
  - — Implicit interest rate of 5.9948%

Installed capacity (kW)		250
	total	per kW
Cash Flow Statement		
cash in:		
lease rentals	1,146,477	4,585.9080
specified TV	0	0.0000
residual	200,000	800.0000
principal	0	0.0000
interest	0	0.0000
periodic income	190,925	763.7011
fees	50,000	200.0000
subsidy	0	0.0000
total cash in	1,587,402	6,349.6091
cash out:		
principal	0	0.0000
interest	0	0.0000
debt service	0	0.0000
asset cost	1,000,000	4,000.0000
loan borrowing	0	0.0000
fees	0	0.0000
sales tax	0	0.0000
capitalized fees	0	0.0000
dependent fees	0	0.0000
periodic expenses	110,000	440.0000
total cash out	1,110,000	4,440.0000
pre-tax cash flow	477,402	1,909.6091
federal solar grant	300,000	1,200.0000
taxes paid (saved)	247,022	988.0893
after-tax cash flow	530,380	2,121.5198

Figure 7-12: Cash Flow Statement of 20 Years

As can readily be observed from this model, it is abundantly clear that the more parameters you have to manipulate, *the more creative your solution*! By carefully tweaking one or more parameters—or tweaking a combination of parameters—allows the investor to produce multiple proposals to a customer. Now, instead of just a single proposal, the customer would have a choice from multiple proposals from you. This is a much sought after benefit by end-users.

Project 7 (see Appendix 3 for full reports)

Cost of Renewable Energy Spreadsheet Tool (CREST)

The Cost of Renewable Energy Spreadsheet Tool (CREST) is an economic cash flow model designed to enable PUCs and the renewable energy community assess projects, design cost-based incentives (e.g., feed-in tariffs), and evaluate the impact of tax incentives or other support structures. CREST is a suite of three analytic tools, for solar (photovoltaic and solar thermal), wind, and geothermal technologies, respectively.

The model is a product of a 2009-2010 partnership between the National Renewable Energy Laboratory (NREL), the U.S. Department of Energy (DOE) Solar Energy Technologies Program (SETP), and the National Association of Regulatory Utility Commissions (NARUC). The model was developed by Sustainable Energy Advantage (SEA) under the direction of NREL.

The primary intended uses include:

- Estimating the cost of energy (COE) from a range of solar, wind, and geothermal electricity generation projects for the purpose of informing the setting of cost-based incentive rates
- Gaining an understanding of the economic drivers of renewable energy projects, which lead to the calculated COE
- Understanding the relative economics of generation projects with differing characteristics, such as project size, resource quality, location (e.g., near or far from transmission) or ownership (e.g., public or private).

COE is the minimum revenue per unit of production needed for the modeled renewable energy project to meet its equity investors' assumed minimum required after-tax rate of return. The CREST model includes the flexibility to analyze:

- Ownership by either a taxable (private sector investor) or non-taxable (government, non-profit, or cooperative) entity
- Financing based on equity-only or a specified proportion of equity and debt, subject to minimum debt service coverage requirements (DSCRs)
- A range in the level of detail for capital and operating cost inputs
- All of the most commonly available federal and state renewable energy incentives to ensure that modeling results produce a COE net of other available incentives.

The CREST model also allows the user to easily conduct sensitivity analyses, including variations in:

- Incentive payment durations
- Assumed project revenue for the remainder of a generator's expected life following the end of the incentive payment term
- The ability of equity investors to efficiently utilize tax incentives.

Model Output

CREST model results can be calculated as either a constant fixed price (sometimes referred to as the "nominal levelized price") or an escalating payment stream. The primary output is the modeled project's COE. The COE is the year-one price in cents per kilowatt-hour (¢/kWh) necessary for the project to meet all expenses and debt service obligations (if applicable), as well as the equity investors' minimum required after-tax rate of return. At the model user's discretion, the COE can be calculated to assume an escalation rate (applied to all or a portion of the initial rate) over time. In calculating the COE, the CREST model includes the option to specify both a percentage of the tariff subject to escalation and the associated tariff escalation rate. The results can be used to inform a range of cost-based incentives, including FIT rates.

The secondary output is the modeled project's levelized cost of energy (LCOE). The LCOE is a single, fixed, non-escalating value over the incentive's payment duration. The escalating stream of payments generated by the COE and the constant stream of payments generated by the LCOE have the same net present value (NPV) when discounted at the same required rate of equity return. Policymakers can refer to the LCOE output if policy objectives favor a single, fixed price per kilowatt-hour for the life of the cost-based tariff. If the tariff rate escalation factor is set to zero, then the calculated COE and LCOE values will be equal. Developers, policymakers, and all other model users must understand, however, that while the LCOE may result in the same after- tax IRR as an equivalent escalating year-one COE, the two scenarios would have dramatically different cash flow implications for the project.

In addition to the COE and LCOE, annual summaries are also provided for revenues, operating expenses, debt service, reserves, pre-tax cash flow, taxable income, tax benefit or loss, after-tax cash flow, cumulative cash flow, after-tax IRR, and DSCR. Those annual figures are provided to promote the transparency and credibility of the discounted cash flow calculations as reasonably realistic metrics and to facilitate collaboration among the stakeholders using this information.

Again, we are building on the prior models and expanding into new areas using the CREST model. The basic assumptions used in this model and project are shown in Table 7-11.

Using Table 17-11 for the inputs with the CREST model produces the following output:

Net Year-One Cost of Energy (COE) = 16.15 ¢/kWh
Net Nominal Levelized
Cost of Energy (LCOE) = 16.15 ¢/kWh

Table 7-11

Input Data	
Selected Technology	Photovoltaic
Nameplate Capacity	250 kW dc
Net Capacity Factor, Yr 1	22.1%
Production, Yr 1	484,948 kWh
Annual Degradation	.5% per year
Project Useful Life	25 years
Total Installed Cost	$4.00 /Watt dc
Total System Cost	$1,000,000
Fixed O&M Expense, Yr 1	$24.00/kW-yr dc
O&M Cost Inflation	2.0% per year
Percent Debt	40%
Debt Term	18 years
Debt Interest Rate	6.50%
Lender's Fee (% of total borrowing)	3.0%
Percent Equity	60%
Target After-Tax Equity IRR	12.00%
Weighted Average Cost of Capital	8.74%
Owner a taxable entity?	Yes
Federal Tax Rate	35%
State Tax Rate	8.5%
Effective Tax Rate	40.53%
ITC	30%
ITC Amount	$282,000
First Equipment Replacement	Year 10
First Replace Cost	$0.235/watt dc
Second Equipment Replacement	Year 20
Second Replace Cost	$0.235/watt dc
Initial Debt Service Reserve	$19,160
# of months of O&M Expense	6
Initial O&M and WC Reserve	$3,844
Interest on All Reserves	1.0%
Bonus Depreciation	Yes
Bonus Depreciation Percentage	50%

An annual project cash flow is included in Appendix 3. Figure 7-13 shows graphs from that analysis.

Sample Options:

1. Changing the targeted investor yield to 16% from 12% would bring the LCOE to 19.00 ¢/kWh
2. Lowering the targeted investor yield to 9% from 12% would bring the LCOE to 14.45 ¢/kWh
3. Increasing the price per watt for the system cost from $4.00 to $4.50 would bring the LCOE to 17.85 ¢/kWh

Here again it can be seen that changing the variable parameters one at a time or in various combinations allow for creative (artful) proposals with this project as was the case in the other projects above.

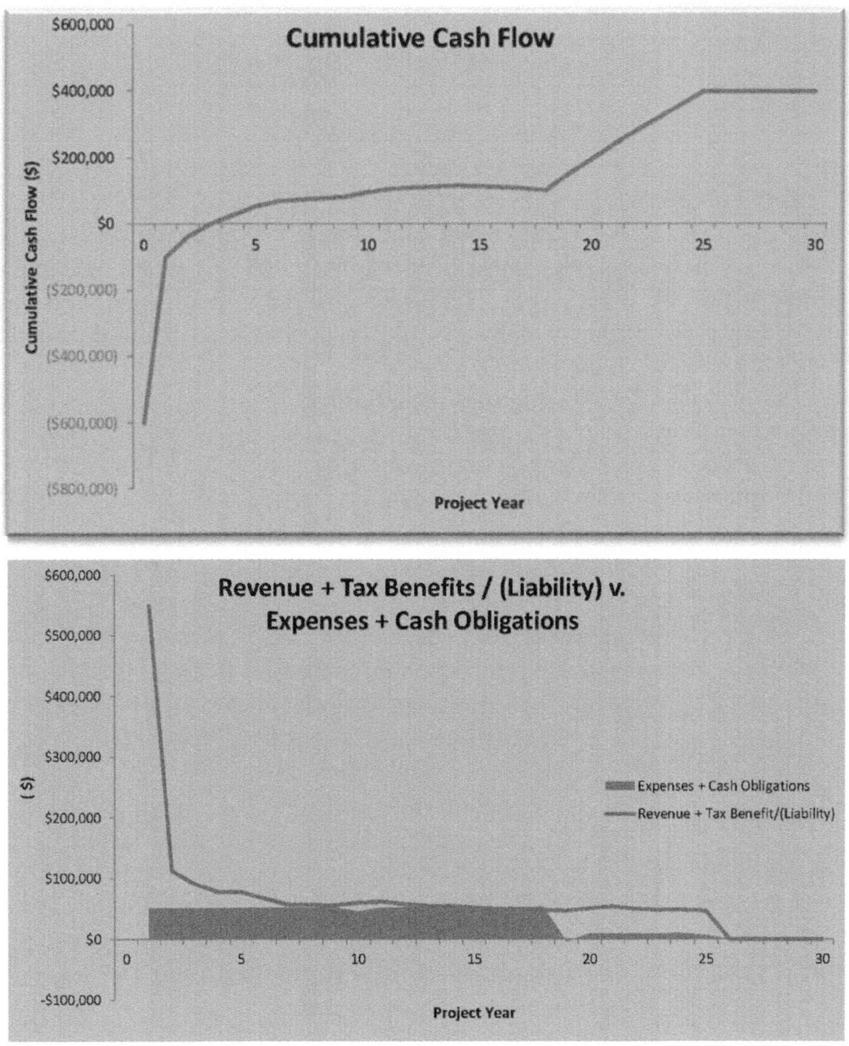

Figure 7-13

Project 8 (see Appendix 3 for full reports)

Complete System Based Financial Analysis (SAM)

The System Advisor Model (SAM)[38] is a performance and financial analysis model designed to facilitate decision making for people involved in the renewable energy industry. SAM makes performance predictions and cost of energy estimates for grid-connected power projects based on installation and operating costs and system design parameters that the user specifies as inputs to the model. Projects can be either on the customer side of the utility meter, buying and selling electricity at retail rates, or on the utility side of the meter, selling electricity at a price negotiated through a power purchase agreement (PPA).

The first step in using the model is to choose the technology and financing options for the project. Next, you provide project location information, the specifications regarding the equipment in the system, the cost of installing and operating the system, and financial and incentives assumptions.

At that point you can run simulations and examine the results. A typical analysis involves running simulations, examining results, revising inputs, and repeating that process until you understand and have confidence in the results.

SAM displays modeling results in tables and graphs, ranging from the metrics table displaying levelized cost of energy, first year annual production, and other single-value metrics, to the detailed annual cash flow and hourly performance data that can be viewed in tabular or graphical form. A built in graphing tool displays a set of default graphs and allows for the creation of custom graphs. Graph sliders make it easy to visually examine the effect of changing input variables in graphs and tables without changing values on the input pages. All graphs and tables can be exported in various formats for inclusion in reports and presentations, and also for further analysis with spreadsheet or other software.

SAM's performance model makes hour-by-hour calculation of

power system's electric output, generating a set of 8,760 hourly values that represent the system's electricity production over a single year. The current version of SAM includes performance models for the following renewable technologies:

- Photovoltaic systems (flat-plate and concentrating)
- Parabolic trough concentrating solar power systems
- Power tower concentrating solar power systems (molten salt and direct steam)
- Linear Fresnel concentrating solar power systems
- Dish-Sterling concentrating solar power systems
- Conventional fossil-fuel thermal systems
- Solar water heating for residential or commercial buildings
- Large and small wind power projects
- Geothermal power and geothermal co-production
- Biomass power

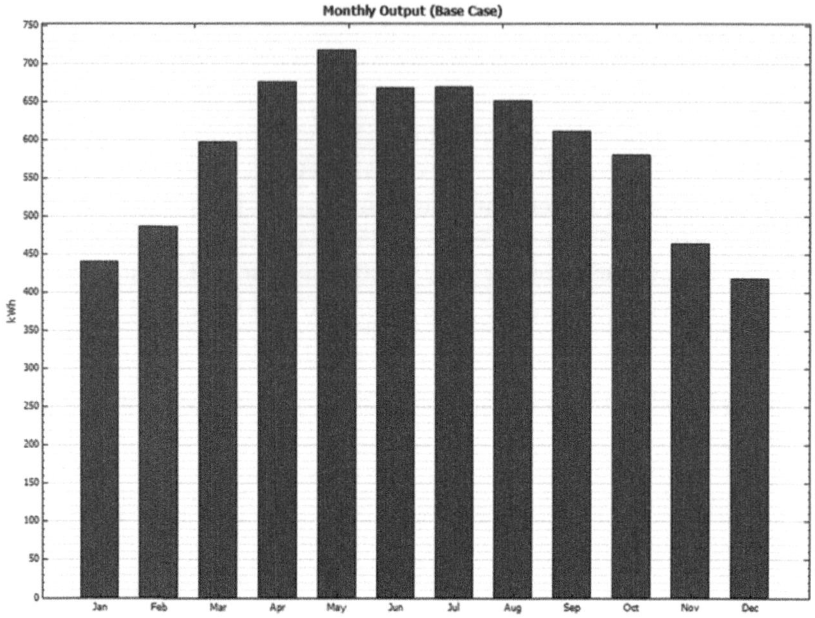

Figure 7-14: Monthly Output Graph

SAM's financial model calculates financial metrics for various kinds of power projects based on a project's cash flows over an analysis period that you specify. The financial model uses the system's electrical output calculated by the performance model to calculate the series of annual cash flows.

SAM includes financial models for the following types of projects:

- Residential rooftop (retail electricity rates)
- Commercial rooftop (retail rates or power purchase agreement)
- Utility-scale (power purchase agreement)
  - Single owner
  - Leveraged partnership flip
  - All equity partnership flip
  - Sale leaseback

Residential and commercial projects are financed through either a loan or cash payment, and recover investment costs by selling electricity through either a net-metering or time-of-use pricing agreement. For these projects, SAM reports the following metrics:

- Levelized cost of energy
- Revenue with and without renewable energy system
- After-tax net present value
- Payback period

Utility and commercial PPA projects are assumed to sell electricity through a power purchase agreement at a fixed price with optional annual escalation and time-of-delivery adjustment factors. For these projects, SAM calculates:

- Levelized cost of energy
- PPA price (electricity sales price)
- Internal rate of return
- Net present value
- Debt fraction or debt service coverage ratio

The financial model can account for a wide range of incentive payments and tax credits, including:

- Investment-based incentives (IBI)
- Capacity-based incentives (CBI)
- Production-based incentives (PBI)
- Investment tax credits (ITC)
- Production tax credits (PTC)
- Depreciation (MACRS, straight-line, custom)

The following options are for analyses that investigate impacts of variations and uncertainty in assumptions about weather, performance, cost, and financial parameters on model results:

- Parametric analysis: Assign multiple values to input variables to create graphs and tables showing the value of output metrics for each value of the input variable.

- Sensitivity analysis: Create tornado graphs by specifying a range of values for input variables as a percentage.
- Optimization: Find the value of input variables that result in either a maximum or minimum value of an output metric.
- Statistical: Create histograms showing the sensitivity of output metrics to variations in input values.
- P50/P90: For locations with weather data available for many years, calculate the probability that the system's total annual output will exceed a certain value.

Project 8: Residential Project for Consumer Homeowner

For this sample project analysis, we will look at a residential flat-plate PV solar system in Phoenix, AZ. The user input data variables shown in Table 7-12 form the bases of the project and as can be seen, is a very comprehensive set of parameters that allows for the in-depth analysis we could expect. Because of all the variables, the art of designing creative financing structures can be

Table 7-12

Input Data	
System location	Phoenix, AZ
Latitude	33.4333°
Longitude	-112.017°
Direct normal radiation	2,518.6 kWh/m^2
Average annual ambient temperature	22.5°C
Real discount rate	10.80%
Nominal discount rate	13.57%
Federal tax rate	28.0%
State tax rate	7.0%
Net salvage value	$0.00
Loan type	Standard
Loan rate	4.95%
WACC	13.57%
Federal tax credit (ITC)	30%
State tax credit	None
Production tax credit	None
Payment Incentives	None
Annual system degradation	5%
System availability	100%
System size	4.0 kW dc
Modules per string	9
Strings in parallel	2
Inverters	1
Total modules	18
Nameplate capacity	3.78243 kW dc
Total area	22.3922 m^2
Inverter capacity	4.0 kW dc
Tracking	Fixed

Input Data	
Utility	Arizona Public Service
Utility rate	Residential E-12
Annual rate escalator	2.5%
Analysis period	30 years
Inflation rate	2.5%
Tilt	20%
Derate factor	90%
Module costs	$8,737.41
Inverter cost	$2,880.00
Balance of system costs	$4,954.98
Installation labor	$4,009.38
Total capital cost	$20,581.77
Engineering costs	$1,400.00
Total installed cost	$21,981.77
Cost per watt dc	$5.81
Annual O&M cost	$200.00 per year
Fixed cost by capacity	$25.00/kW/year
Shading	None
Modules	SunPower SPR-210-Blk
Module efficiency	16.89%
Module maximum power	210.135 Wdc
Module material	c-Si
Cells per module	72
Inverter manufacturer	SMA America
Inverter model	SB4000US
Inverter voltage	240 volt

fully explored. See Appendix 3 for graphs and charts showing the results of the analysis.

Based on the above user variable parameters on the simple residential solar PV system we can now analyze the project and view the results.

Output Metrics

- Net annual energy: 6,987.47 kWh
- LCOE nominal: 38.4078
- LCOE real: 31.5132
- 1st year revenue with system: $ 1,676.99
- After-tax net present value: - $4,809.14
- Payback period: 10.2014 years
- Capacity factor: 21.0885
- 1st year kWh/kW: 1,847.35
- System performance factor: .778553
- Analysis period: 31 years
- Array derated DC (kWh) annual: 7,286.32 kWh
- Engineering cost per kW: $ 0.370132
- Installation cost per kW: $ 1.06
- Inverter cost per kW: $ 0.761415
- Balance of system cost per kW: $ 1.31
- Module cost per kW: $ 2.31
- Federal ITC: $ 6,594.53

Note: There is no depreciation providing after-tax benefits since the project is to a consumer/individual tax payer and they do not qualify for depreciation expense.

Project 9 (see Appendix 3 for full reports)

Commercial PPA (SAM)

For this sample project analysis, we will look at a commercial PV solar system in Los Angeles, CA done under a PPA finance structure. The project is a 20 MW system under a 20-year PPA and has a single axis tracker system.

Based on the above user variable parameters on the commercial PPA solar PV system we can now analyze the project and view the results.

Output Metrics

- Net annual energy: 39,685,669 kWh
- PPA price: 13.70 ¢/kWh
- LCOE nominal: 13.70 ¢/kWh
- LCOE real: 11.16 ¢/kWh
- After-tax IRR: 15.00%
- After-tax net present value: $ 4,658,743.22
- PPA price escalation: None
- Debt fraction: 50%
- DC to AC capacity factor: 22.7%
- System performance factor: 0.88
- 1st year kWhac/kWdc 1,984
- Analysis period: 20 years
- Installation cost per kW: $ 0.48
- Inverter cost per kW: $ 0.375794
- Balance of system cost per kW: $ 0.43
- Module cost per kW: $ 2.05
- Federal ITC: $ 29,060,890.36

Multiple graphs and charts of the project are shown in Appendix 3. Many of the input data parameters can be modified showing different simulations—all of which would provide different results. Table 7-13 shows one example where we changed the PPA from a fixed amount (13.70¢/kWh) over the term of the agreement to a starting rate of 12.00¢/kWh with an annual escalator of 2.5%. The principal changes are highlighted from the optimization simulation #1.

Certainly, this would be very attractive to the customer purchasing the power but the question also is would this be attractive enough for the investor? As different simulations are run, it is likely that numerous possible options could be arrived at—some more attractive for one or the other party.

SAM provides a wide array of possible simulations from a base case, great sensitivity simulations under different cases, and good reporting (including graphs, charts and spreadsheets) that runs very quickly on both a Windows and Mac OS. Data, graphs, charts and tables can all be output to the clipboard, CSV format, PDF, and sent directly to Excel (Windows only).

Finally, SAM provides five options for modeling Utility Market projects. These become even more complex but with the software provided they are manageable and have a great deal of flexibility when used with guidelines and regulations provided in prior chapters of this book. Those options are:

1. **All Equity Partnership Flip and Leveraged Partnership Flip.** These two options are two-party projects that involve equity investments by a project developer and a third-party tax investor. The tax investor has sufficient tax liability from its other business operations to utilize any tax benefits (tax credits and depreciation deductions) fully in the years in which the project generates the benefits. The project sets up a limited liability entity, and once the project begins generating and selling electricity, all of the project's net cash flows and tax benefits are passed through this entity to its owners (see page 165). The project allocates a majority of the cash and tax benefits to the tax investor when the project begins operation and until the tax investor receives a pre-negotiated after-tax IRR,

Table 7-13

Input Data	
System location	Los Angeles, CA
Latitude	33.9333^0
Longitude	$- 118.4^0$
Direct normal radiation	1,800.0 kWh/m^2
Average annual ambient temperature	16.7^0C
Elevation	32 m
Wind speed	3.6 m/s
Analysis period	20 years
Inflation rate	2.5%
Real discount rate	5.2%
Nominal discount rate	7.83%
Federal tax rate	35.0%
State tax rate	8.84%
Sales tax rate	8.75%
Property tax rate	None
Net salvage value	$0.00
Insurance	0.5% of installed cost
Construction loan	$94,970,229.95
Construction loan rate	7.0%
Balance of system cost	$ 8,599,929.31
Installation labor cost	$ 9,599,921.09
Installer margin/overhead	$ 16,199,866.85
Contingency	None
Total system direct cost	$ 82,915,190.25
Permitting & environmental	$ 4,599,962.19
Grid interconnection	$ 199,998.36
Sales tax on direct cost	$ 7,255,079.15
Total indirect cost	$ 12,055,039.69
Total installed cost	$ 94,970,229.95
Installed cost per watt dc	$ 4.75

Input Data	
Construction debt fraction	50%
WACC	9.57%
Minimum required IRR	15%
PPA price	0.15 ¢/kWh
PPA escalation rate	None
Federal depreciation	5 yr MACRS
State depreciation	5 yr MACRS
Federal ITC	30%
Incentives	None
Total modules	65,528
Total area	106,876 m^2
Nameplate capacity	20,000 kW dc
Total inverter capacity	20,313 kW ac
Tracking	Single axis
Module soiling derate	95%
Pre-inverter derate	95.5598%
Post-inverter derate	99%
Total derate factor	89.874%
Land area	66.0228 acres
Module costs	$ 40,999,663.00
Inverter costs	$ 7,515,810.00
O&M fixed cost by capacity	$20.00/kW/year
Shading	None
Modules	SunPower
Module model	SPR-305-WHT
Module efficiency	18.71%
Maximum module power	305.211 Watt dc
Module material	c-Si
Inverter manufacturer	Solaran
Inverter model	333-3159000
Inverter AC voltage	480 volt
Annual system degradation	0.5%
System availability	100%

also known as the flip target. Once the flip target is reached, a majority of the cash and any remaining tax benefits are allocated to the developer.

2. **Sale Leaseback.** The Sale Leaseback option is another two-party structure that involves a tax investor purchasing 100% of the project from the developer and then leasing it back to the developer. This structure differs from the partnership flip structures in that the tax investor and the developer do not share the project cash and tax benefits (or liability). Instead, each party has its own separate cash flow and taxable income. The purchase price paid by the tax investor is equal to the total project cost, less a lease payment and the value of working

capital reserve accounts. The developer typically funds the reserve accounts to insure it has some financial exposure. The tax investor receives lease payments from the developer and any ownership-related incentives such as the tax credits, incentive payments, and the depreciation deductions. The developer operates the project and keeps any excess cash flow from operations, after payment of all operating expenses and lease payments. This provides the developer with an incentive to operate the project as efficiently as possible.

3. **Single Owner and Independent Power Producer (IPP).** In this option, one entity owns the project and has sufficient tax liability to utilize the tax benefits. This structure is less complicated from the Partnership Flip and Sale Leaseback structures because there is no need to allocate cash and tax benefits to different partners. The owner may be either the original developer or third-party tax investor that purchases the project from the developer.

Table 7-14 summarizes the difference between one of five options.

Conclusion

The nine projects described above provide a wide range of options in artfully crafting financial solutions to renewable energy projects. Not all projects require the detailed solutions that others might need and the modeling tools used are an example of any project structuring that could benefit from these software tools. Volumes of books could be written looking at all the different combinations of user defined variables and techniques associated with each simulation and outputs desired. The best way to see results is to get immersed directly. Many of the models are free while others require purchase. Also, many models take data produced from other models to populate the user defined variables. You can see that there is certainly no single best model or single best approach to how many variables need to be run to achieve the desired results for that perfect proposal to the customer, investors, lenders and developers.

ADMINISTRATIVE, BILLING AND ASSET MANAGEMENT

Congratulations! A lot of work has been done on your clean renewable energy project to this point. You have analyzed the financial returns, provided numerous proposals to the customer, negotiated all the tax, accounting and ownership issues, performed all the required due diligence on the credit of the customer as well as the project itself, presented and negotiated numerous sets of documents and were finally able to execute the transaction structure and the documents that support that structure, found equity partners, found interim construction lenders, negotiated and executed credit lines for the permanent financing leverage portion of the transaction, found the right EPC partner to construct the project, finalized all design and engineering conditions, obtained all permits, negotiated and executed the interconnection agreement with the utility, performed all necessary commissioning on the project, paid off the interim construction lender, put in place the

Table 7-14: Summary of Key Attributes in Advanced Structures

Metric	Base	Opt. 1
Net Annual Energy	39,685,669 kWh	39,685,669 kWh
PPA price	12.00 ¢/kWh	9.75 ¢/kWh
LCOE Nominal	14.37 ¢/kWh	11.83 ¢/kWh
LCOE Real	11.71 ¢/kWh	9.51 ¢/kWh
After-tax IRR	15.12 %	8.02 %
Pre-tax min DSCR	1.00	0.77
After-tax NPV	$ 6,176,987.75	$ 957,185.70
PPA price escalation	2.50 %	2.50 %
Debt Fraction	50.00 %	50.00 %
DC-to-AC Capacity Factor	22.7 %	22.7 %
First year kWh ac/kW dc	1,984	1,984
System Performance Factor	0.88	0.88
Total Land Area	66.02 acres	66.02 acres

final permanent financing if needed, paid all the suppliers, met all environmental mandates, put in place all M&V system components, obtained proper insurance endorsements and think that now the battle is over and you have won the war—wrong.

Although not all encompassing, this section of the chapter will address some of the key attributes of a good administrative, billing and physical asset management system. A good management software solution would encompass both contract administration and also asset administration. Most management systems are provided on a "module" basis whereby the user can acquire functionality in different areas as needed.

Acquiring ownership in a renewable energy asset is just the beginning of a 10- to 40-year asset management task. Once the energy capital asset is acquired, it now must be managed over an extended period of time by administrative, legal, accounting and tax personnel. Maintaining records for the inevitable audits, O&M requirements, tax reports and billing functions requires a significant investment of time, money and management oversight. Any software solution must be able to support the administrative functions of asset management over the entire lifecycle of the assets regardless of the type of contract structure employed on the project. All information must be maintained at the asset level and at the same time be able to assemble that information on both a contract level and a customer level.

This task cannot be done without additional software. Although there are a number of software companies who have historically provided these tools on other managed assets, none have been currently modified to meet the unique needs of the renewable energy finance sector. Most will require that you use existing modules that they have developed over many years in the traditional asset management industry like leasing and loans. This is slowly changing and many are now working overtime to add to important features to their asset and "contract" management tool sets. They must do this to meet the needs of the renewable energy industry investment protocols and to meet the needs of the IASB accounting mandates as described in earlier chapters.

Traditional lease and loan accounting systems cater to banks, captives and independent industry types. The renewable energy market adds the PPA (electric, thermal, etc.) as another form of billing tracking and invoice generation. Usage based software systems are in the market such as copy machines, but the unique characteristics of the PPA and other metered processing joined with the need for interfaces to the generated energy require a specialized form of billing functions.

All asset management software systems must tract, support and inform senior management in three distinct increments—seeking the customer, building the project and servicing the asset for the life of the asset. This is often expressed as "cradle to grave" energy asset management.

During the "seek" step, the developer/investor is looking at many different potential projects. It is precisely at this point that the project management function begins by tracking possible customers, providing proposals with multiple solutions, working with one or more potential suppliers (including EPC contractors)—all with the goal of getting a letter of commitment from the customer. This step is followed by the credit and documentation phase where the developer/investor performs all necessary

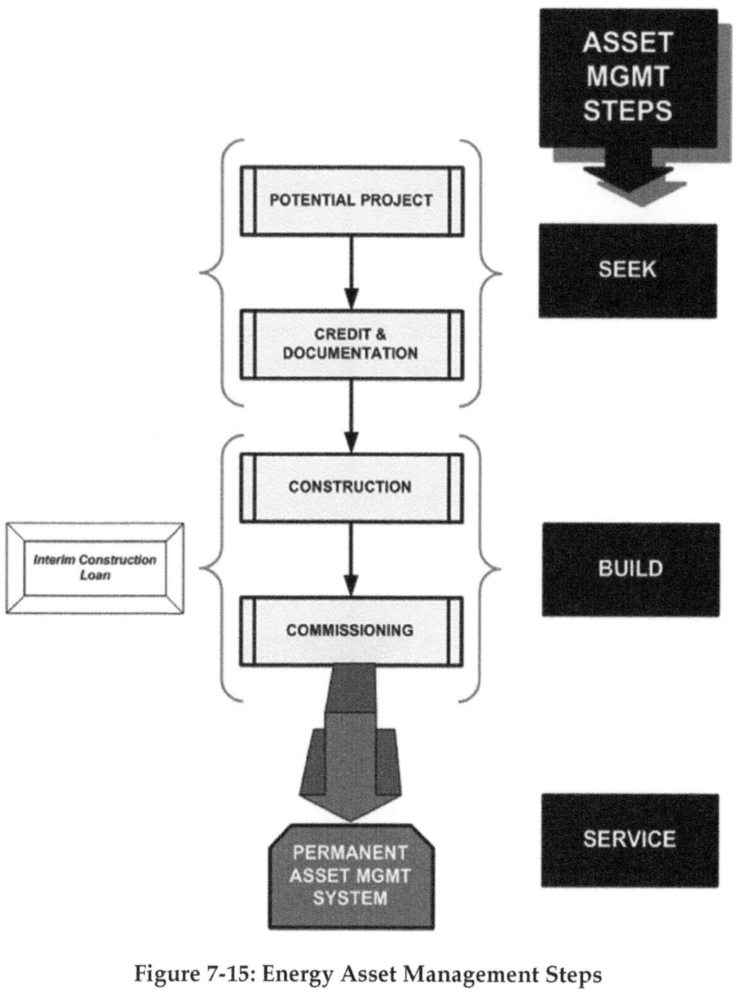

Figure 7-15: Energy Asset Management Steps

due diligence on the credit worthiness of the customer. This is of course necessary to evaluate the credit risk of the transaction as well as to make sure that it meets the qualification guidelines of the permanent lender (if one is involved in the structure) and for the equity partner. Normally this step could take up to six or more weeks and will culminate in the preparation of all legal documents that will need to be executed.

Assuming that the contract and all supporting documentation has been executed, it is at this point that many more details of the actual assets in the project start taking place and need to be tracked. This "build" stage also in most cases would require an interim lender to provide financing for the developer/investor during the construction phase. All final supplier price negotiations, issuance of purchase orders, signing of contracts with the EPC or general contractor, final design and engineering is performed, permits are pulled, final agreements reached with utilities for interconnection to the grid (if needed) are executed and draw downs on the interim construction financing are started. Active project management by the soon to be "owner" of the assets is needed during this step and would normally include detailed project timelines, milestones and multiple "change-orders." All of this information must be carefully entered into the asset management software system since all future performance of the energy system will be measured against what is finally constructed and commissioned.

The third step is the actually booking of the "as built" assets and permanent lenders enter the picture along with the equity partner(s). It is vitally critical that the system is properly set up on the owner's accounting and tax books since all future servicing of the energy project assets will be a direct result of the accuracy of this input.

As you will recall from the prior chapters, there are two distinct sets of books that will need to be set up and maintained on the assets comprising the energy project—tax and book. To recap some of the key points of the "tax" set of books:

- The federal tax books are set up for two primary purposes—depreciation and investment tax credit. Assuming that the full 30% investment tax credit is taken on a qualifying asset, the federal book cost of the asset is reduced by half of the amount of ITC taken (15%) and therefore the "depreciable basis" of the asset for federal purposes is 85% of the actual final construction/asset acquisition costs. Bonus depreciation is taken if available under section 179. MACRS depreciation is then applied to the remaining book value of the assets over a total period of six years (technically five years plus the remaining half of the first year depreciable basis).
- The state tax books are set up to allow for state depreciation and where available, any state tax credits allowed. The asset depreciable basis is normally 100% of the construction/asset acquisition cost with no reduction in basis for tax credits taken. Normally the assets are then depreciated over a longer term (of up to 15 years) depending upon the state in which the owner of the assets is domiciled. Therefore, the federal and state depreciable asset costs and the term and rate of depreciation will normally vary significantly from the federal books.
- Depending upon the state in which the system is located, the sales or use tax elections will dictate how and when these items will have tax applied to them. Keep in mind that there may be multiple taxing authorities on the asset acquisition or the receipt of the rents or PPA charges. Not only are state level taxes applicable, but in many taxing jurisdictions county, city and other taxing authorities will need to have periodic reports prepared and

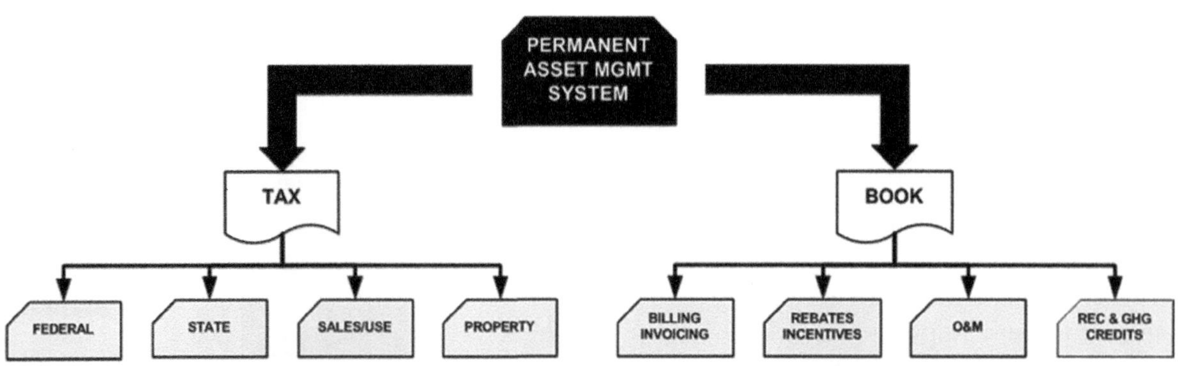

Figure 7-16: Permanent Asset Management System Components

submitted over the entire life of the assets. These rates will change frequently and therefore any asset management system will need to interface to another specific tax system that directs the main asset management system on what rates need to be applied each time cash is received from the customer or equipment is purchased by the energy system owner.

- Property tax assessors view each asset purchased through different "glasses" than do federal and state taxing authorities. It is not uncommon in some energy projects, to see equipment "traded-in" and thus having a lower acquisition cost for the owner of the energy system when they are newly purchased or new equipment is "upgraded" under an existing contract. Therefore, the "asset acquisition cost" may be less than the "original cost" of the new system. Property tax assessors are particularly watchful for these types of asset acquisitions and if the actual price prior to the trade-in is not shown on the return, it is likely that under audit (and they will be coming) additional assessments will occur and a larger than expected tax liability will be realized by the asset owner(s). Additionally, each property tax assessor will have their own guidelines (and for the most part "unpublished") for the expected life of personal property along with a minimum amount that they will allow for "salvage value." Still other states (or for that matter, certain counties) will allow certain types of renewable energy systems to not be taxed for personal property tax purposes. Carefully review the state regulations where the equipment will be physically located to determine the proper reporting procedures. You should check the DSIRE database for the latest updates.[39]

The accounting books are kept (as explained in earlier chapters) under a totally different set of procedures than are the tax books. The primary categories for the "accounting books" are:

Billing and Invoicing

The billing and invoicing management side of a project is nearly identical regardless if the transaction was booked as an operating lease, power purchase agreement, sale leaseback, finance lease or other similar type of structure. Let's look at some of the more important aspects of what this responsibility encompasses.

1. The ability to manage renewable energy assets on both a book and a tax basis

2. Invoicing must be flexible and allow for billing by:
   - Individual assets
   - All assets under a single contract
   - All assets at a specific physical location
   - All assets under contract to each customer
   - All assets by acquisition date
   - All assets by energy category (e.g., electric, thermal, energy efficiency, etc.)
   - All assets by county, state or other taxing jurisdiction
   - Assets measured by specific meters at a facility
   - Meter and inverter reporting associated to a third-party tracking system
   - Daily and/or hourly downloads of energy production
   - Annual energy production output for REC and GHG emission credits sold to third parties
   - Periodic changes to billing rates:
     i. Pursuant to the contract
     ii. Pursuant to the time of year
     iii. Pursuant to time of production—or time of use by the host
     iv. Floor and ceiling billing ability—monthly, quarterly, semi-annual, annual, seasonal or even by total production or use over the life of the assets

   All of the above must be able to be produced in detail to the invoice going to the customer if needed

3. Don't forget that other items will periodically need to be added to an invoice for such items as:
   - Specific taxes
   - O&M charges
   - Insurance
   - Returns
   - Warranty costs or deductions
   - Utility chargebacks or incentives
   - Swaps—changing out a non-performing component or asset for another with a different acquisition cost, description and serial numbers
   - Terminations
   - Stipulated loss values as detailed in the energy contract
   - Tax credit recapture events

4. Bill interest and/or interim rent for each progress payment
   - Manage open-ended interim billing, prior to contract commencement:

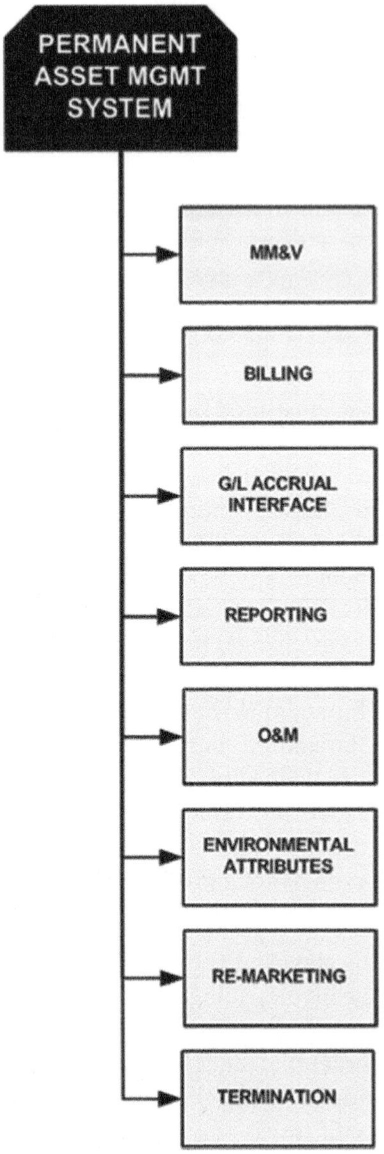

Figure 7-17. Permanent Asset Management Systems

   i. Charge interest/interim rent on progress payments as assets are built
   ii. Charge interest/interim rent on fully delivered assets as others are installing

5. Supplier purchase order and invoice management
6. Variable rates with the ability to establish a ceiling and floor
7. Fixed or floating rates with multiple indexes
8. Billing reflecting dramatic changes over the year based on actual energy production

Asset Description

Some of the specific fields of information that need to be tracked on each asset includes:

- Manufacturer
- Model
- Serial number
- Detailed and a summary description of the energy asset
- Date of acquisition
- Delivery date
- Contract start date
- Date of acceptance by the customer
- Federal and state "in-service" date
- Original system cost
- Trade-in or cap reduction amounts
- Investment tax credit amounts (federal, state or other)
- Property tax cost
- Federal and state tax depreciation methods
- Federal and state depreciation terms
- Book depreciation method and term
- Equipment physical location (including state, county and city)
- Legal description of real property where assets are located
- Projected book and tax life
- Metered source interface (third-party)
- Measurement and verification of production protocol
- REC, ERC and GHG environmental attributes
- All tracking of expiration or renewal dates such as:
  — UCC-1
  — Environmental attribute commitments
  — Energy contract expiration
  — O&M contracts
  — Insurance
  — Dealer holdbacks or subsidies
- Serial number changes
- Location changes
- Asset swaps
- Asset upgrades
- Meter swaps
- Contract amendments
- Renewal and remarketing information
- Assets in warehouse (off contract assets)
- Asset status or disposition
  — Returned
  — Repossessed
  — Sold
  — Scrapped
  — Re-financed

Asset Profitability

Getting a return on your assets is the primary reason to own them. Asset profitability reports take all the above data and show the energy project owner how the assets are performing on their entire portfolio—including drilling down to specific assets. Some of the reporting an owner would need includes:

- Profitability by asset
- Profitability by model
- Profitability by salesperson
- Profitability by supplier/vendor
- Profitability by region, county, state, etc.
- Sales by number of assets
- Sales by dollar volume
- Year to year asset growth
- Asset residual management
- Asset inventory turnover

Environmental Attributes

The asset management system needs to be able to:

- Group the energy production from each location to an asset record
- Prepare reports for multiple parties that have an interest in the production including auditors, customers, third parties and regulatory agencies
- Track purchasers of the environmental attributes and attribute contract expiration dates
- Billing of sold environmental attributes to the purchasers of those attributes

Other Functions

There are significant additional accounting and administrative functions that depend on the level of management needs.

- Collection and repossession management
- Status tracking
- Inventory control
- Warehouse management
- Warranty tracking
- Recycle/e-waste
- Returns/RMA
- Residual forecasting
- Integration with standard third-party loan and lease analysis software systems
- Total portfolio aggregations broken down by:
  - — Date of acquisition
  - — Remaining contract terms
  - — Asset classifications
  - — Regional distributions
  - — Environmental credits sold to third parties
  - — Risk classifications of many different categories
- Credit facility management
- Track total credit exposure on customer across relationships
- Integration with credit bureaus
- Integration with corporate general ledger
- Integration with third-party sales and use tax systems
- Support for dealer/vendor/supplier private branding application processing
- Funding techniques, sources, participations, and syndications
- Integration with income tax software systems
- Vendor participation and management
- Sales, use and property tax integration and reporting

As can be seen from this chapter, it is clear that the "life cycle" of a renewable energy project starts with the financial analysis and doesn't end until the asset is fully managed over the it's useful life—including final asset disposition. That is a very long time and would normally cover multiple generations of energy users, energy sellers and asset managers. Renewable energy projects have a very long useful life and the owner(s) of those assets must be ready for extensive management functions for a long period.

References

1. http://www.eia.doe.gov/cneaf/electricity/epa/average_price_state.xls
2. W. Short; D. Packey; T. Holt, "A Manual for the Economic Evaluation of Energy Efficiency and Renewable Energy Technologies," National Renewable Energy Laboratory, March 1995
3. http://www.appraisalinstitute.org/education/downloads/AI_82003_ReslGreenEnergyEffAddendum.pdf
4. http://sam.nrel.gov
5. http://swera.unep.net
6. http://www.fsec.ucf.edu/en/research/buildings/fenestration/software.htm
7. http://www.nrel.gov/docs/fy13osti/54909.pdf
8. http://www.nrel.gov/docs/fy11osti/48212.pdf
9. http://www.nrel.gov/analysis/power_databook
10. http://www.nrel.gov/analysis/market_re_data.html
11. http://en.openei.org/wiki/Main_Page
12. http://www.dsireusa.org
13. http://analysis.nrel.gov/databook2003/convert.asp
14. http://www.nrel.gov/analysis/power_databook/calc_pv.php

15. http://www.nrel.gov/analysis/power_databook/calc_wind.php
16. http://www.nrel.gov/buildings/energy10.html
17. http://www.nrel.gov/analysis/tech_cost_data.html
18. http://www.nrel.gov/gis/data.html
18. http://www.nrel.gov/rredc/pvwatts/grid.html
20. http://www.homerenergy.com
21. http://www.ceere.org/rerl/projects/software/hybrid2
22. http://analysis.nrel.gov/retfinance/login.asp
23. http://www.nrel.gov/analysis/reeds
24. http://en.openei.org/wiki/Scenario_Evaluation,_Regionalization_%26_Analysis_%28SERA%29
25. http://www.lumina.com
26. http://www.afdc.energy.gov/biomass/progs/search1.cgi
27. http://www.nrel.gov/analysis/jedi
28. http://www1.eere.energy.gov/biomass/ethanol_yield_calculator.html
29. http://www1.eere.energy.gov/femp/information/download_blcc.html
30. http://gundog.lbl.gov/dirsoft/d2whatis.html
31. http://apps1.eere.energy.gov/buildings/energyplus
32. http://www1.eere.energy.gov/femp/information/download_feds.html
33. https://www3.eere.energy.gov/femp/fresa
34. http://www.ornl.gov/sci/roofs+walls/calculators/index.html
35. http://apps1.eere.energy.gov/buildings/tools_directory/software.cfm/ID=454/pagename=alpha_list
36. http://apps1.eere.energy.gov/buildings/tools_directory/software.cfm/ID=96/pagename=alpha_list
37. http://energy.sandia.gov/?page_id=8047
38. SAM can be downloaded for free at https://sam.nrel.gov/
39. www.dsireusa.org

Chapter 8

Legal Components

The proper structuring of a renewable energy project is not complete without a careful understanding of the legal documentation components and analysis of how best to select the legal structure of the project. Once the external and internal factors have been defined, the pricing model developed, and the type of finance vehicle to be used, the final step will be to select a legal structure for the business entity that will execute the finance structure model, prepare all project documentation and fund the renewable energy project. Although it is in many cases the final step, the importance of this step should not be taken lightly. It is this step that codifies all of the previous decisions made by the project developer, lender or investor.

OVERVIEW

While there is an overall pattern to project documentation, each transaction is different and must encompass the components of the financial negotiations that have occurred between the creditor and the debtor. Whether the creditor is a "lessor," "lender," "energy provider" or other entity and the debtor is a "lessee," "borrower," "host provider" or other entity, a security instrument and supporting documents must be prepared, executed, filed and enforced if a renewable energy project is to be funded. No two transactions will be the same or require the same documents completed in the same way.

Before a single document is drafted, negotiated and executed, the complete financial analysis of the project must be completed by all the parties, and the details of the transaction defined and allocated. Those negotiated components of the transaction then must be documented to each party's satisfaction. Generally, the larger the project, the more detailed and complex the documentation would be. On smaller transactions, documentation would be more boilerplate in nature but on larger transactions, the documentation would normally require the use of outside legal counsel to properly reflect the needs and intent of all the parties.

This chapter will explore first the legal structures of the business entity itself that will provide funding for the renewable energy project and then be followed by some of the most common types of principal documents and supporting documentation needed to finalize the financing of the renewable energy project.

HISTORICAL TAX EFFECTS

Over the years there have been many different legal structures put together to maximize the cash flows, minimize tax liabilities and to meet accounting requirements by lenders and investors who are involved in project financing of capital equipment. The "preferred" legal structure has changed to meet the pronouncements of the IRS and to meet the rules and regulations of new tax acts and accounting guidelines as they have been enacted. Generally speaking, if the lender or investor is a corporation, there are very few pitfalls to overcome. However, if the lender or investor in a renewable energy project is an individual investor or group of investors who are taxed at the individual level as is found in limited partnerships, sole proprietorships or subchapter S corporations (all of which are taxed at the individual level and not the operating entity level), then much more attention must be paid to exactly how such entities would be structured. For the most part, C corporations (a business entity taxed at the corporate level) avoid many of the tax issues that arise with tax payers at the individual level.

This eventually becomes the Achilles heel of many renewable energy finance projects because most renewable energy projects have a large tax component to the financing structure that is put together to meet the needs of the market place and to leverage the tax attributes so that the debt payment stream on the project reflects the needs and preferred interests of all parties. The debtor is looking to realize the lowest payment possible in many projects and does this by allowing the lender/investor to keep the tax attributes for their account, monetize those attributes, and then pass the resulting lower payment structure through to the project in the lowest debt payments possible.

The primary issue faced by individual taxpayers is that of how best to monetize the tax attribute components. The legal structure of the lender/investor(s) is the key in doing so. It was the 1986 tax reform act that dramatically changed the way that financing structures could be set up. Congress realized that, although totally legal, individual tax payers who had very high amounts of ordinary income (including high salaries) were investing in projects that were throwing off large amounts of losses and those losses were being used to offset their ordinary taxable income and thereby paying little or no taxes. Those losses came primarily from non-cash deductions such as depreciation and amortization and, to a limited extent, interest deductions from borrowings they obtained to get into the project. In many cases, the borrowing was for 100% of the project cost and the loans were either totally non-recourse or limited recourse to the borrower who used those funds to acquire the underlying project assets. It was perceived by both legislators and the general public at large that such extremes were abusive of the generous tax laws of the time and unfair to other taxpayers who were not able to be involved in these types of projects and were thereby paying a disproportionate share of taxes.

> *"...if we get the right kind of energy, there are endless amounts. I think we should be developing every kind of alternative fuel that is available to us. That includes hydrogen to soybeans, from solar to wind. Whatever we can find that is going to help us clean up the environment we should be working really hard on developing."*
>
> Morgan Freeman, American actor, film director, aviator and narrator

This perception also applied to tax credits that arose when the projects involved the acquisition of qualified equipment and machinery where investment tax credits (ITC) were generated and utilized by the project financier taxpayer. Just prior to the passage of the 1986 tax reform act, there was an ITC of 10% of the asset cost available to offset any taxes owed by the taxpayer. This amount was in addition to the other pre-tax deductions of depreciation, interest, and operating costs which generated losses in most projects during the earlier years of the investment. Again, the ITC was put in place by Congress for a very clear purpose—that of stimulating the economy in general. But, on top of the operating losses generated in the financing of these assets during the first several years, the ITC was of even more importance to the taxpayer who financed the asset acquisitions. ITC tax credit was a credit against actual taxes owed (no matter the revenue source on which the tax was owed), and not a pre-tax deduction. It was also received immediately by the taxpayer when they acquired the asset(s) and therefore provided an instantaneous offset to any current tax liability the taxpayer might have had.

The 1986 tax reform act made the following three major changes—particularly as it is applied to individual tax payers:[1]

1. "At-risk" rules were established that prevented a taxpayer from writing off more losses on an investment than that which they were "at-risk" for.
2. Losses from a "passive activity" could only be used to offset income from a passive activity and not offset income from ordinary sources or revenue such as salaries.
3. Tax credits could only be used to offset taxes owed on passive activity income and not that of other ordinary income.

To fully understand the currently preferred method of financing renewable energy projects today known as "flip partnerships," a more detailed understanding of the three changes needs to be examined and put into perspective. The combination of the three changes has made it very difficult for most if not all "individual taxpayers" to realize the full tax potential of being involved in the financing of renewable energy projects.

Three separate limits apply to a partner's or shareholder's distributive share of a loss from a partnership or S corporation, respectively. The limits determine the amount of the loss each partner or shareholder can deduct on his or her own return. These limits and the order in which they apply are:

1. The adjusted basis of:
   a. The partner's partnership interest, or
   b. The shareholder's stock plus any loans the shareholder makes to the corporation,
2. The at-risk rules, and
3. The passive activity rules.

At-risk Rules

The at-risk limits apply to individuals (including partners and S corporation shareholders), estates, trusts, and certain closely held corporations (other than S corporations).

The at-risk rules limit an individual taxpayer's losses from most investment activities to the amount they have at risk in the investment or activity. You treat any loss that is disallowed because of the at-risk limits as a deduction from the same activity in the next tax year. Obviously, this is a serious occurrence for any taxpayer that was hoping to use business losses from an activity in the current tax year. The usefulness of a loss in future years instead of the current tax year greatly diminishes its value to the taxpayer. Additionally, if your losses from an at-risk business activity are allowed, they are subject to recapture in later years if the amount you are at risk is reduced to below zero. Lastly, a taxpayer must apply the at-risk rules before the passive activity rules discussed below.

Losses from a business operation are limited to the amount of money you can actually lose in the business. The IRS defines a loss as the excess of allowable deductions from the activity for the year (including depreciation or amortization allowed or allowable and disregarding the at-risk limits) over income received or accrued from the activity during the year. Income does not include income from the recapture of previous losses. You are subject to at-risk rules if you are filing Schedules C, E, or F. For example, if you are a member of a partnership and are reporting a loss from the Partnership K-1 on your Schedule E, your loss is limited to the amount of money you can actually lose in the partnership. If you invested $100,000 in the partnership, then you can actually lose only up to $100,000. If any part of your investment in the business is not at-risk, you must complete Form 6198 to calculate your allowable loss.

In a Subchapter S corporation (organized as a corporation with shareholders, but taxed at the individual shareholder level), each shareholder has an amount at-risk. This is the amount of money the shareholder stands to lose from their investments or loans to the company. A shareholder's amount at-risk is calculated as follows:

Adjusted Stock Basis + Adjusted Loan Basis
= Amount At-Risk

Each shareholder's stock basis and loan basis will be adjusted for their pro-rata share of losses even if those losses are suspended because of the at-risk rules. It is therefore very important for the S-Corporation and its shareholders to track adjusted stock basis and adjusted loan basis accurately and meticulously. The same concept applies to general partnerships, limited partnerships and limited liability corporations, all of which are taxed at the individual level and not at the business entity level by the IRS.

A shareholder's or partner's capital or equity account needs to reflect the taxpayer's investments and current basis in the business entity's equity or liabilities. A taxpayer is invested in the business to the extent that they have made an equity investment, advanced a loan or guaranteed a loan (or portion thereof) by a third party to the company.

Shareholder's or partner's equity is reflected in the capital account. This account should show the dollar amount of cash investments, and/or value of property donated to the business entity. The capital account is adjusted from time to time to reflect additional equity investments. Additionally, the capital account is adjusted at the end of the year to reflect each shareholder's or partner's pro-rata share of income and expenses.

For the at-risk rules, a corporation is a closely held corporation if at any time during the last half of the tax year, more than 50% in value of its outstanding stock is owned directly or indirectly by or for five or fewer individuals. To figure if more than 50% in value of the stock is owned by five or fewer individuals, apply the following rules:

1. Stock owned directly or indirectly by or for a corporation, partnership, estate, or trust is considered owned proportionately by its shareholders, partners, or beneficiaries.
2. An individual is considered to own the stock owned directly or indirectly by or for his or her family. Family includes only brothers and sisters (including half-brothers and half-sisters), a spouse, ancestors, and lineal descendants.
3. If a person holds an option to buy stock, he or she is considered to be the owner of that stock.
4. When applying rule (1) or (2), stock considered owned by a person under rule (1) or (3) is treated as actually owned by that person. Stock considered owned by an individual under rule (2) is not treated as owned by the individual for again applying rule (2) to consider another the owner of that stock.
5. Stock that may be considered owned by an individual under either rule (2) or (3) is considered owned by the individual under rule (3).

The activities covered by the at-risk rules are very broad. However, the activity most important to that of renewable energy project financing is leasing (or other types of financing) of section 1245 property. Section 1245 property is defined by the IRS as property that is subject to depreciation or amortization and is:

- Personal property
- Property used in manufacturing, production, extraction or furnishing transportation, communication, *electrical or thermal energy*, gas, water, or sewage disposal services

There is a very important exception for equipment financing by a closely held corporation (see above). If a closely held corporation is actively engaged in equipment financing, the equipment financing is treated as a separate activity not covered by the at-risk rules. A closely held corporation is actively engaged in equipment financing (leasing, PPA contracts, etc.) if 50% or more of its gross receipts for the tax year are from that activity. Equipment financing means the leasing, purchasing, servicing, energy sales, and selling of equipment that is section 1245 property. "Active participation" in the activity is also a critical component when considering the at-risk rules. Active participation depends on all the facts and circumstances. Factors that indicate active participation include making decisions involving the operation or management of the activity, performing services for the activity, and hiring and discharging employees. Factors that indicate a lack of active participation include lack of control in managing and operating the activity, having authority only to discharge the manager of the activity, and having a manager of the activity who is an independent contractor rather than an employee.

Your amount of money you are at risk in any activity includes:

- The money and adjusted basis of property you contribute to the activity, and
- Amounts you borrow for use in the activity if:
  - You are personally liable for repayment, or
  - You pledge property (other than property used in the activity) as security for the loan.

You are at risk for amounts borrowed to use in the activity if you are personally liable for repayment. You are also at risk if the amounts borrowed are secured by property other than property used in the activity. In this case, the amount considered at risk is the net fair market value of your interest in the pledged property. The net fair market value of property is its fair market value (determined on the date the property is pledged) less any prior (or superior) claims to which it is subject. However, no property will be taken into account as security if it is directly or indirectly financed by debt that is secured by property you contributed to the activity. You are not considered at risk for amounts protected against loss through non-recourse financing, guarantees, stop loss agreements, or other similar arrangements. Nonrecourse financing is financing for which you are not personally liable. If you borrow money to contribute to an activity and the lender's only recourse is to your interest in the activity or the property used in the activity, the loan is a nonrecourse loan.

> *"I believe that the U.S. can and should be a global leader in the development of alternative energy sources."*
>
> Barrack Obama, President of the United States

However, certain borrowed amounts could be excluded. Even if you are personally liable for the repayment of a borrowed amount or you secure a borrowed amount with property other than property used in the activity, you are not considered at risk if you borrowed the money from a person having an interest in the activity or from someone related to a person (other than you) having an interest in the activity. This does not apply to:

- Amounts borrowed by a corporation from a person whose only interest in the activity is as a shareholder of the corporation,
- Amounts borrowed from a person having an interest in the activity as a creditor, or
- Amounts borrowed after May 3, 2004, secured by real property used in the activity of holding real property (other than mineral property) that, if nonrecourse, would be qualified nonrecourse financing.

"Related persons" include:

- Members of a family, but only an individual's brothers and sisters, half-brothers and half-sisters, spouse, ancestors (parents, grandparents, etc.), and lineal descendants (children, grandchildren, etc.);
- Two corporations that are members of the same controlled group of corporations determined by applying a 10% ownership test;
- The fiduciaries of two different trusts, or the fiduciary and beneficiary of two different trusts, if the same person is the grantor of both trusts;
- A tax-exempt educational or charitable organiza-

tion and a person who directly or indirectly controls it (or a member of whose family controls it);

- A corporation and an individual who owns directly or indirectly more than 10% of the value of the outstanding stock of the corporation;
- A trust fiduciary and a corporation of which more than 10% in value of the outstanding stock is owned directly or indirectly by or for the trust or by or for the grantor of the trust;
- The grantor and fiduciary, or the fiduciary and beneficiary, of any trust;
- A corporation and a partnership if the same persons own more than 10% in value of the outstanding stock of the corporation and more than 10% of the capital interest or the profits interest in the partnership;
- Two S corporations if the same persons own more than 10% in value of the outstanding stock of each corporation;
- An S corporation and a regular corporation if the same persons own more than 10% in value of the outstanding stock of each corporation;
- A partnership and a person who owns directly or indirectly more than 10% of the capital or profits of the partnership;
- Two partnerships if the same persons directly or indirectly own more than 10% of the capital or profits of each;
- Two persons who are engaged in business under common control; and
- An executor of an estate and a beneficiary of that estate.

To determine the direct or indirect ownership of the outstanding stock of a corporation, apply the taxpayer needs to review the following rules.

1. Stock owned directly or indirectly by or for a corporation, partnership, estate, or trust is considered owned proportionately by or for its shareholders, partners, or beneficiaries.
2. Stock owned directly or indirectly by or for an individual's family is considered owned by the individual. The family of an individual includes only brothers and sisters, half-brothers and half-sisters, a spouse, ancestors, and lineal descendants.
3. Any stock in a corporation owned by an individual (other than by applying rule (2)) is considered owned directly or indirectly by the individual's partner.
4. When applying rule (1), (2), or (3), stock considered owned by a person under rule (1) is treated as actually owned by that person. But, if a person constructively owns stock because of rule (2) or (3), he or she does not own the stock for purposes of applying either rule (2) or (3) to make another person the constructive owner of the same stock.

Remember also, that any capital you have contributed to an activity is not at risk if you are protected against economic loss by an agreement or arrangement for compensation or reimbursement. For example, you are not at risk if you will be reimbursed for part or all of any loss because of a binding agreement between yourself and another person (such as a general partner).

Adjusted-basis Rules

A shareholder (in a Subchapter S company) or partner in a partnership may advance money to the business entity as a loan. Loans to the company or partnership may be short-term loans (to be repaid in one year or less) or long-term loans (to be repaid in more than one year). They could also be loans from a bank or other lender in which the shareholder or partner has guaranteed a portion of or all of. Those shareholders or partners may take a tax deduction in the current year for losses in excess of their stock or partnership basis, but only to the extent they have loan basis for which they are at-risk if the loan is not repaid.

Loan basis, and adjusted loan basis, is calculated as follows:

+	Initial amount loaned or personally guaranteed from another party
+	Additional amounts loaned to the company
+	Deferred interest that is capitalized (added to the loan) instead of being repaid
–	Amount of loan principal repaid
–	Amount of loan principal forgiven by the shareholder or partner
–	Amount of loan principal converted to stock or equity
–	Share of net loss in excess of adjusted stock or equity basis
=	Adjusted basis of business entity debt at end of the year for the at-risk rules

Passive Activity Income

Passive activity income includes all income from passive activities and generally includes gain from disposition of an interest in a passive activity or property used in a passive activity.

Passive activity income does not include the following items:

- Income from an activity that is *not* a passive activity.
- Portfolio income. This includes interest, dividends, annuities, and royalties not derived in the ordinary course of a trade or business. It includes gain or loss from the disposition of property that produces these types of income or that is held for investment. The exclusion for portfolio income does not apply to self-charged interest treated as passive activity income.
- Personal service income. This includes salaries, wages, commissions, self-employment income from trade or business activities in which you materially participated, deferred compensation, taxable social security and other retirement benefits, and payments from partnerships to partners for personal services.
- Income from positive section 481 adjustments allocated to activities other than passive activities. (Section 481 adjustments are adjustments that must be made due to changes in your accounting method.)
- Income or gain from investments of working capital.
- Income from an oil or gas property if you treated any loss from a working interest in the property for any tax year beginning after 1986 as a non-passive loss. This also applies to income from other oil and gas property the basis of which is determined wholly or partly by the basis of the property in the preceding sentence.
- Any income from intangible property, such as a patent, copyright, or literary, musical, or artistic composition, if your personal efforts significantly contributed to the creation of the property.
- Any other income that must be treated as non-passive income.
- Overall gain from any interest in a publicly traded partnership.
- State, local, and foreign income tax refunds.
- Income from a covenant not to compete.
- Reimbursement of a casualty or theft loss included in gross income to recover all or part of a prior year loss deduction, if the loss deduction was not a passive activity deduction.
- Alaska Permanent Fund dividends.
- Cancellation of debt income, if at the time the debt is discharged the debt is not allocated to passive activities under the interest expense allocation rules.

Passive Activity Losses

The passive activity loss rules were enacted as part of the Tax Reform Act of 1986. Congress perceived that private investors (individuals, estates, trusts, and personal service corporations) were abusing the tax system by taking "tax" losses on activities that they did not materially participate in. They wanted to prevent the use of losses from activities in which an investor could offset their wages, interest and dividend income. Often the ownership and financing of renewable energy systems generate losses in the early years of the transaction that far exceeds the income from the transaction. Historically, private investors would enter into ownership positions on tangible personal property (such as renewable energy systems) with very little actual cash investment and take the losses from the venture to a point that no taxes were actually paid by the taxpayer even though wages and interest income had been received in very large amounts.

> *"For a successful technology, reality must take precedence over public relations, for Nature cannot be fooled."*
>
> Richard P. Feynman, American physicist

Therefore, as a practical matter, "private" investors (those that are not for-profit C corporations) cannot utilize the tax attributes that most renewable energy projects generate unless they have large amounts of passive "income." Passive income are items like investment interest, royalties from other assets the taxpayer owns, pensions, and other revenue from a "trade or business activities in which they did not materially participate." This is precisely why so many projects in the renewable energy sector are structured so that other eligible parties who have either passive income or qualified business income can offset those income streams with the tax attributes thrown off in the renewable energy project.

In general, there are two kinds of passive activities:

1. Trade or business activities in which you do not materially participate during the year.
2. Rental activities, even if you do materially participate in them, unless you are a real estate professional.

A rental activity is a passive activity even if you materially participated in that activity, unless you materially participated as a real estate professional. An activity is a rental activity if tangible property (real or personal) is used by customers or held for use by customers, and the gross income (or expected gross income) from the activity represents amounts paid (or to be paid) mainly for the use of the property. It does not matter whether the use is under a lease, PPA, energy service agreement or some other arrangement. However, remember the exception to this rule for active leasing activities on section 1245 property described above. This exemption could be useful when evaluating the appropriate business entity legal structure. The taxpayer will be required to show a preponderance of evidence to utilize this exemption.

An additional component of current tax law that will help the taxpayer seeking an exemption from the passive activity rules is if the taxpayer "materially participates" in the trade or business activity. Material participation tests include the following:

1. You participated in the activity for more than 500 hours.
2. Your participation was substantially all the participation in the activity of all individuals for the tax year, including the participation of individuals who did not own any interest in the activity.
3. You participated in the activity for more than 100 hours during the tax year, and you participated at least as much as any other individual (including individuals who did not own any interest in the activity) for the year.
4. The activity is a significant participation activity, and you participated in all significant participation activities for more than 500 hours. A significant participation activity is any trade or business activity in which you participated for more than 100 hours during the year and in which you did not materially participate under any of the material participation tests, other than this test.
5. You materially participated in the activity for any 5 (whether or not consecutive) of the 10 immediately preceding tax years.
6. The activity is a personal service activity in which you materially participated for any 3 (whether or not consecutive) preceding tax years. An activity is a personal service activity if it involves the performance of personal services in the fields of health (including veterinary services), law, engineering, architecture, accounting, actuarial science, performing arts, consulting, or any other trade or business in which capital is not a material income-producing factor.
7. Based on all the facts and circumstances, you participated in the activity on a regular, continuous, and substantial basis during the year.

A closely held corporation or a personal service corporation is treated as materially participating in an activity only if one or more shareholders holding more than 50% by value of the outstanding stock of the corporation materially participate in the activity.

Limited partners take notice. If you owned an activity as a limited partner, you generally are not treated as materially participating in the activity. However, you are treated as materially participating in the activity if you met test (1), (5), or (6) under Material participation tests, discussed earlier, for the tax year.

You are not treated as a limited partner, however, if you also were a general partner in the partnership at all times during the partnership's tax year ending with or within your tax year (or, if shorter, during that part of the partnership's tax year in which you directly or indirectly owned your limited partner interest).

You can use any reasonable method to prove your participation in an activity for the year. You do not have to keep contemporaneous daily time reports, logs, or similar documents if you can establish your participation in some other way. For example, you can show the services you performed and the approximate number of hours spent by using an appointment book, calendar, or narrative summary.

S-Corporation shareholders and partners in partnerships or LLCs are subject to the passive activity rules. These rules govern to what extent a loss is currently deductible by the individual taxpayer. If the business entity is engaged in the rental property (either real or personal property) business, then shareholders or partners must meet the stringent "active participation" tests in order to deduct rental losses in full. If a taxpayer cannot meet the active participation tests (described below), then business entity rental losses are deductible only to the extent the taxpayer has passive activity income. Additionally, if an S-Corporation or partnership is engaged in any business but the shareholder or partner does not actively participate in the business, then S-Corporation or partnership losses are deductible only to the extent the shareholder or partner has passive activity income in this business entity or in other combined business entities that are considered as "passive" in nature.

Active participation is not the same as material participation. Active participation is a less stringent standard than material participation. For example, you may be treated as actively participating if you make management decisions in a significant and bona fide sense. Management decisions that count as active participation include approving new customers, deciding on finance terms, approving expenditures, and similar decisions.

Passive activity income includes passive income from S-Corporations, partnerships, trusts, interest, dividends, and other investment income. A loss is the excess of allowable deductions from the activity for the year (including depreciation or amortization allowed or allowable and disregarding the at-risk limits) over income received or accrued from the activity during the year. Income does not include income from the recapture of previous losses.

Passive Activity Deductions

Passive activity deductions include all deductions from activities that are passive activities for the current tax year and all deductions from passive activities that were disallowed under the passive loss rules in prior tax years and carried forward to the current tax year. They also include losses from dispositions of property used in a passive activity at the time of the disposition and losses from a disposition of less than your entire interest in a passive activity.

Passive activity deductions do not include the following items:

- Deductions for expenses (other than interest expense) that are clearly and directly allocable to portfolio income.[2]
- Qualified home mortgage interest, capitalized interest expenses, and other interest expenses (other than self-charged interest) properly allocable to passive activities.
- Losses from dispositions of property that produce portfolio income or property held for investment.
- State, local, and foreign income taxes.
- Miscellaneous itemized deductions that may be disallowed because of the 2%-of-adjusted-gross-income limit.
- Charitable contribution deductions.
- Net operating loss deductions.
- Percentage depletion carryovers for oil and gas wells.
- Capital loss carrybacks and carryovers.
- Deductions and losses that would have been allowed for tax years beginning before 1987 but for basis or at-risk limits.
- Net negative section 481 adjustments[3] allocated to activities other than passive activities.
- Casualty and theft losses, unless losses similar in cause and severity recur regularly in the activity.
- The deduction for one-half of self-employment tax.

Passive Activity Tax Credits

You can subtract passive activity tax credits only from the tax on net passive income. Passive activity credits include the general business credit and other special business credits, such as the credit for fuel produced from a nonconventional source and solar tax credits. Credits that are more than the tax on income from passive activities are carried forward. This restriction can also be of great concern to any potential lender or investor in a renewable energy project and must be taken into consideration when structuring the optimal legal structure. Any loss (or carry-forward to future tax years) would dramatically affect the net yield of the finance structure to the lender or investor.

Additionally, un-allowed passive activity credits, unlike un-allowed passive activity losses, cannot be claimed when you "dispose of your entire interest in an activity." However, to determine your gain or loss from the disposition, you can elect to increase the basis of the credit property by the amount of the original basis reduction for the credit, to the extent that the credit was not allowed because of the passive activity limits. Also, you cannot elect to adjust the basis for a partial disposition of your interest in a passive activity.

BUSINESS ENTITY STRUCTURES

Proper business entity structuring will allow the lender/investor taxpayer to realize those attributes without a challenge from the IRS. Selecting the proper legal structure of the business entity that will finance the renewable energy project comes after all other components of the project have been defined and negotiated as described in the earlier chapters. Although there is no "one size fits all" structure, many of the financial components and considerations will inevitably lead the lender or investor towards certain choices.

Perhaps the most used legal business structure currently being used in project finance transactions today is the "flip" partnership. Historically, section 45 of the IRC (which broadly addresses the tax credits available on renewable energy projects) was adopted in 1992. It was originally limited to wind and closed-loop biomass projects. Poultry litter was added in 2000. Many partnership structures were developed over the years to take advantage of the tax credits made available under section 45, primarily in the wind industry. IRC section 45K was added to adjust the tax credits for inflation so that investors didn't lose the present value of the credits simply because rising inflation rates made the credits less useful. Section 45 was expanded again in 2004 to include additional renewable energy project types. As the tax credits became more widely known and different legal structures were being set up to address the available credits, taxpayers were looking for more assurances from the IRS as to what was going to be the types of acceptable structures that would not be challenged by them. The IRS announced a "no rule" position on section 45 credits and partnerships in 2006 (notice 2006-88). Then finally, in October 2007, they issued guidelines for a "safe harbor" in partnership flip structures that applied specifically to wind partnerships.

The IRS issued guidelines, if followed, will allow a "safe harbor" for taxpayers selecting a flip partnership and that the structure will not be challenged by the IRS. Section 45 equipment relates to energy produced by the renewable wind projects where there are tax credits generated from the energy produced the equipment in the project. It applies to partners and partnerships that own and produce electricity from qualified wind facilities. However, the general consensus is that a taxpayer following the guidelines established under those section 45 safe harbor rules would be covered if the qualified facility were other renewable energy facilities such as solar PV, solar thermal, geothermal, bio-mass, etc. The Safe Harbor is set forth in Revenue Procedure 2007-65 ("Rev. Proc. 2007-65") and will apply to transactions entered into on or after that date (see page 165).

The Safe Harbor provisions apply to any partnership between a project developer and one or more investors where the partnership owns and operates a qualified energy facility. To receive "safe harbor" protection accorded by Rev Proc 2007-65, the provisions must be carefully followed with no deviation unless you are willing to risk possibly not having the partnership qualify for the obvious benefits. There are a number of key requirements found in the Revenue Procedure including:

- The Investors in the partnership must have a reasonable expectation of a return on their investment from a combination of both the tax credits and the cash flow of the project finance structure.[4]
- The project developer (in most cases the general partner) must have a minimum 1% interest in each material item of partnership income, gain, loss, de-

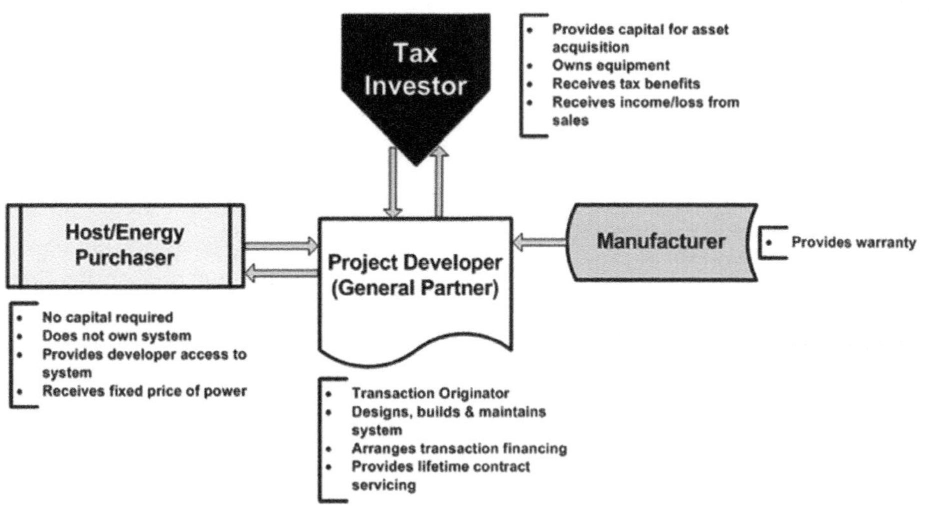

Figure 8-1: Flip Parties

duction and credit at all times during the existence of the business entity.

- Each Investor must have a minimum interest during the period of ownership in each material item of partnership income and gain equal to 5% of the Investor's percentage interest in partnership income and gain for the taxable year for which the Investor's percentage share of income and gain will be the largest, as adjusted for sales, redemptions or dilution of its interest. Absolute compliance in some years may raise issues when attempting to adhere to rules of section 704(b) which refers to regulations relating to the capital account maintenance rules. These regulations expand the rules regarding a partnership's right to adjust capital accounts to reflect unrealized appreciation and depreciation in the value of the partnership assets. Section 704(b) of the Internal Revenue Code provides that a partner's distributive share of income, gain, loss, deduction, or credit is determined in accordance with the partner's interest in the partnership if the partnership agreement does not provide as to the partner's distributive shares of these items, or the allocation to a partner of these items under the agreement does not have substantial economic effect. Under the capital account maintenance rules of §1.704-1(b)(2)(iv), partnership property is generally reflected on the partnership's books at historic cost, rather than at fair market value.
- The Investor must make a minimum unconditional investment (equal to at least 20% of the sum of the fixed capital contributions plus reasonably anticipated contingent capital contributions) on or before the date an interest in the business entity is acquired. This minimum investment must be maintained throughout the duration of the Investor's ownership of its partnership interest in the business entity, except that the minimum investment can be reduced as a result of distributions of cash flow from the business entity's operation of the qualified energy project. Contributions required to be made in the future will not be included in the minimum investment until the contributions are actually made to the business entity.

> *"We can create a more sustainable, cleaner and safer world by making wiser energy choices."*
>
> Robert Alan Silverstein, utopian author

- The Investor must not be protected against loss of any portion of the minimum investment through any arrangement, directly or indirectly, with the Developer, any other Investor, the equipment supplier(s) or the power purchaser or any party related to any such party.
- At least 75% of the sum of the fixed capital contributions, plus reasonably anticipated contingent capital contributions, to be invested in the business entity must be fixed and determinable obligations of the Investor that are not contingent in amount or certainty of payment. This requirement must be satisfied without engaging in any discounting of future contributions.
- No one connected with the business entity, including related parties, may have a contractual right to purchase the qualified energy project, any property included in the project or an interest in the business entity at a price less than its fair market value determined at the time of exercise of the contractual right to purchase. In addition, the Developer (or any related party) may not have a contractual right to purchase the qualified energy project or an interest in the business entity earlier than five years after the qualified facility is first placed into service. The requirement also outlines what contracts of the business entity may be taken into account in determining fair market value. Most transactions have granted the Developer a fair market value purchase option at the equivalent of the flip point. Although it is highly unlikely or impossible for the flip point to be achieved by year 5, to comply with this five-year requirement, the Developer must not even possess the right.
- The business entity may not have a contractual right to require any party to purchase the qualified energy project or any property included in the project (excluding electricity) from the business entity. An Investor may not have a contractual right to cause any party to purchase its partnership interest in the business entity. Frequently, a business entity will have a contract to sell renewable energy credits or the like. The Safe Harbor does not address whether such credits are property included in the qualified energy project.
- No person may guarantee or otherwise insure the Investor the right to any allocation of the tax credits.

- The business entity must bear the risk that the available energy resource is not as great as anticipated or projected. However, a guarantee regarding energy resource availability may be provided by a third party not related to the Developer, the equipment supplier, any power purchaser or any other project participant if the business entity or an Investor directly pays the cost of or premium for such guarantee. A long term power purchase agreement between the business entity and a party not related to the business entity also does not constitute a guarantee—presumably even if such agreement is in the nature of a "take or pay."
- The Developer (or a related party) may not lend any Investor the funds to acquire any part of the Investor's interest in the business entity or guarantee any indebtedness incurred or created in connection with the acquisition of such Investor's interest in the business entity. This does not, however, prevent an Investor from borrowing funds from a third party to invest in the business entity.
- The tax credits must be allocated in accordance with Treasury Regulations section 1.704-1(b)(4)(ii), i.e., the tax credits must be allocated in the same manner as the gross income from the sales of electricity.[5]
- The Investor(s) interest can never be less than 5% of its original equity position in the business entity throughout the term that it remains a party to the business entity.

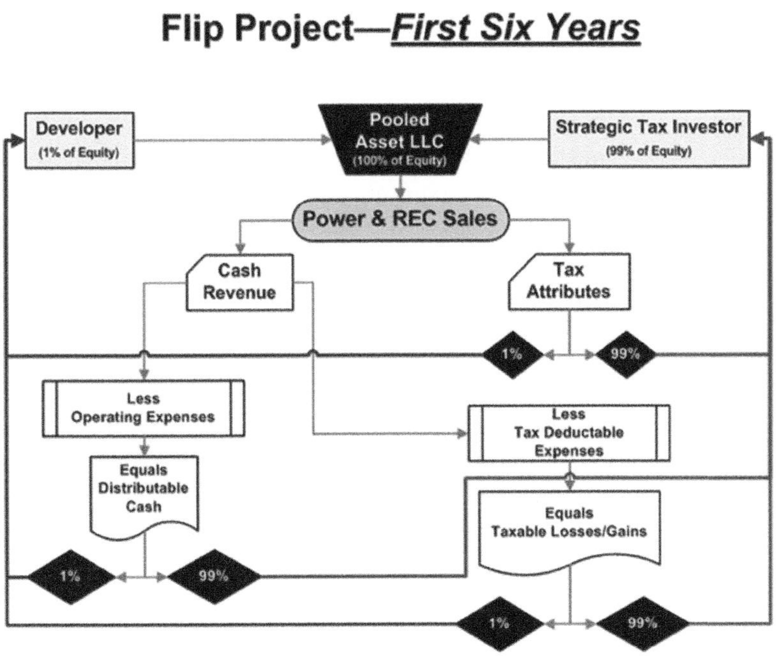

Figure 8-2: Initial Equity Positions

The goal of a business entity being structured such that investors receive the majority of the income (or losses) and tax credits during the early years of a project and the Project Developer (most often the General Partner) during the later part of the project finance term is best shown in Figures 8-2 and 8-3.

Then, after the Investors have received most of the tax benefits (and related profits/losses during those years), the business entity equity positions "flip." The Project Developer now receives 95% of income/losses from the project and the Investor receives 5% of the income/losses.

The exact time when the flip equity positions occur will depend on the type of the energy project, the term of the financing, the cash flow streams projected, component replacement costs, projected maintenance expenditures and other similar factors. Also, when the projects are funded will play a role. If there are multiple renewable energy projects that the business entity will invest in, some of them may require funding over a period of two or more tax years. Generally speaking, most Project Developers will try to limit all projects to a single tax year if possible. If more projects are available for funding, the Project Developer may set up a new business entity to accommodate the realities of the marketplace.

In most projects, there will be three distinct periods of equity ownerships established under the operating agreement (LLC) or partnership agreement (LLP). During the first period the Investor(s) will be allocated 99% of the gross income or loss and the tax credits and the Project Developer will be allocated 1% of the gross income or loss and the related available tax credits. Period One will continue until the earlier of (i) such time that the Developer has received aggregate cash distributions made by the developer and (ii) an outside date. Period One will usually last between four and six years.

- 99% of the projects income or losses as well as the tax credits will be distributed to the Investor(s).

- 1% of the projects income or losses as well as the tax credits will flow to the Project Developer.
- This period will end once the Investor has achieved an agreed after-tax internal rate of return (the "Flip Point"). The flip point may not occur until after the end of year 10 of the Project—depending upon the cash flow stream in the underlying project finance structure.

During period two, 95% of the projects gross income or losses and cash flows will be distributed to the Project Developer and 5% to the Investor(s). Period two can continue indefinitely as long as the underlying assets continue to be on the books of the business entity.

Most operating agreements also provide that the Project Developer, upon the tenth anniversary of its investment, will have the option of purchasing the Investor(s) interest for its then appraised fair market value. If this option is exercised, then during Period two, the Project Developer will be the sole equity holder in the business entity and be allocated 100% of the project's gross income or losses.

Most renewable energy project financing structures have four distinct stages.

1. Initial Stage—Generally financed by the Project Developer out of their own funds.
2. Equipment Deposit Stage—Generally financed by the Project Developer out of their own funds or through credit lines that have been put in place for the benefit of the Project Developer.
3. Construction Stage—Generally financed by the Project Developer out of their own funds or through credit lines that have been put in place for the benefit of the Project Developer for the precise purpose of construction and installation.
4. Operating Stage—Construction financing is replaced by a combination of the tax equity investors, debt providers or the Project Developer.

Since almost all tax benefits, particularly the tax credit benefits, in a renewable energy project are available only on "new" assets purchased and not used assets, it is imperative that the Project Developer does not take title to the equipment directly. The permanent financing must be provided by the business entity that underlies the project and title to the equipment must flow to that entity directly. Care should be taken to make sure that these guidelines are carefully adhered to and doing so also prevents an additional state sales tax event for sale to a second entity on the underlying asset.

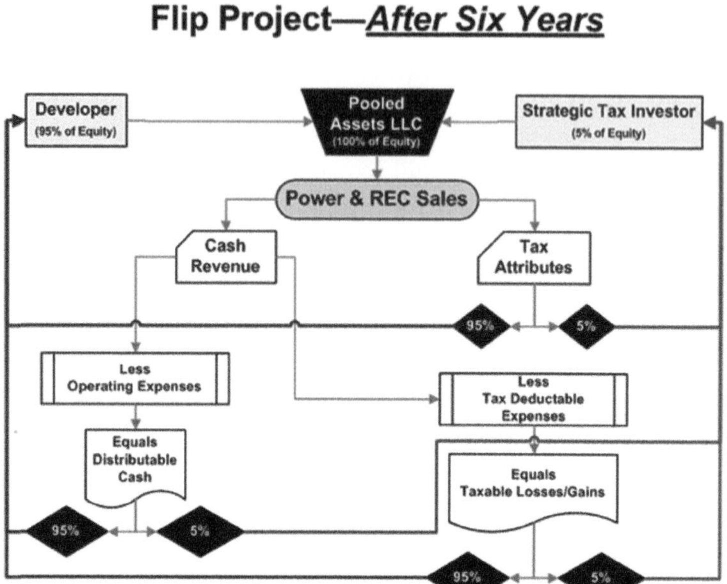

Figure 8-3: Subsequent Equity Positions

In most flip structures, the Project Developer has two types of fees that they charge to the business entity. The first is a "development" fee that is charged to the business entity when it enters into the project finance. This fee generally covers the costs of development, due diligence on both the credit side and also the engineering side of the project, filing fees, commissions, permitting costs, documentation costs, etc. This amount can either be paid at inception and included as part of the acquisition costs of the project or charged over the term of the financing. The second is a "management" fee that is paid to the Project Developer over the term of the contract and covers the Project Developers costs of providing on-going administrative services to the business entity in the form of billing, collections, maintenance costs, insurance, accounting, tax preparations, etc. These fees must be reasonable or they will not be allowed under audit and create additional problems for the investor(s).

If there is any debt in the project, those costs would need to be paid prior to cash distributions to any of the equity holders. Some projects may make economic and tax sense to have between 20% and 55% of the project costs be provided by third-party lenders. In most cases, the third-party lender would require that a first lien position be provided to them on the underlying assets as security for their loan advance to the project. They will also require a first lien position on the cash flows in the project, assignment of contract rights, and pledges of equity shares. Additionally, most lenders require their debt be paid over a shorter period of time than that of the underlying finance structure would be.

Where the Project Developer has contributed capital to the business entity to fund the gap between the total development costs and the amount of the Investor's capital contribution, under Revenue Ruling 2007-65 the Developer's capital contribution can be returned as a priority cash flow item prior to the 99-1 sharing ratio described above during Phase One and Phase Two. The Project Developer could borrow outside the business entity to obtain this capital, generally pledging to the lender as collateral the Developer's interest in the business entity.

A common question is "why would the Project Developer or the Investor(s) elect to use debt when funding their equity in the project?" Briefly, the answers are:

- Improve liquidity
- Improve profits from the project development
- Husband Developer capital
- Reduce equity risk
- Recycle Developer capital
- Enable marginally economic projects
- Third-party risk validation

Cash flows to the business entity come from four principal sources.

1. The payments required under the financing structure put into place for the renewable energy project.
2. Executory rental payments found in an operating lease
3. Payments for the energy delivered to the host party under an energy purchase agreement
4. The sale of renewable energy credits, emission offsets, carbon (GHG) credits, or other types of emission credits. The credits could be received on an annual basis or on a one time basis if the credits are sold "in perpetuity" at some point over the term of the energy project.

The cash returns to a tax equity investor can vary widely, as some energy projects produce significant cash flow while others do not. In most cases, the tax equity investor only wants to remain in the project for the duration of the tax benefits or until they receive the expected rate of return on their investment (often called the "hurdle rate"). In many cases, the Project Developer would purchase the Investors interest in the project at that point. The return to the investors is a combination of the tax credits, depreciation losses and the cash flows they receive. An IRR is calculated based on these three benefits. Therefore proper financial modeling of the project is very critical for each project as is described in detail throughout this book.

Table 8-1 suggests just some of the many different ways that a qualified renewable energy project could be structured.

BUSINESS ENTITY TAXATION

Innovations in U.S. finance, many of them in private equity partnerships, have boosted the U.S. economy and even smoothed out business cycles. Great profits have been earned from brilliant new financial products such as those described in this book, and one of those new flows of income is called carried interest.

Carried interest is not interest in the sense of an interest-bearing savings account. It is a share in a partnership. The person claiming that interest is the manager or general partner, and the carried interest is calculated as a percentage of the profits generated by the investment they manage. When the investment project has a capital gain, the manager's percentage is treated as a gain to him, taxed like an ordinary capital gain on the sale of real estate or stock. Critics say this particular income source does not fit the correct definition of capital gain and should be taxed as wages.

If a firm organizes as a regular corporation, called a C-Corporation, the income it produces is taxed twice by the federal government. The firm must pay the federal corporate income tax, usually at the statutory rate of 35 percent, and then when it distributes after-tax gains to its shareholders, those people must pay individual income taxes on their gains, usually at a 15-percent rate. This is a major reason why most renewable energy projects are structured as limited liability companies or partnerships.

Other business forms such as renewable energy project partnerships are exempt from the corporate income tax, and all the company profits are "passed through" to its owners, who are then taxed at the ordinary individual rate. Hence the generic name "pass-

Table 8-1: Possible Finance Structures

FINANCING STRUCTURE	PROJECT CAPITAL STRUCTURE	EQUITY INVESTORS	DESCRIPTION
Corporate	All equity	Strategic Investor	Assumes Developer is able to utilize tax benefits (no flip)
Strategic Investor Flip	All equity	Developer and Strategic Investor	Strategic Investor contributes almost all of the equity and receives a *pro-rated* percentage of the cash and tax benefits prior to a return-based flip in the allocations
Institutional Investor Flip	All equity	Developer and Institutional Investor	Institutional Investor contributes most of the equity and receives *all* of the tax benefits and, after the developer has recouped its investment, *all* of the cash benefits, until a return-based flip in the allocations.
Pay-As-You-Go ("PAYGO")	All equity	Developer and Institutional Investor	Similar to the Institutional Investor flip but with the Institutional Investor injecting equity only as the tax credits are generated, rather than at the outset of the project (as in PTCs in a wind project)
Cash Leveraged	Equity & debt	Developer and Strategic Investor	Similar to the Strategic Investor flip, but including commercial debt leverage, with the loan size based on the amount of cash flow from power sales
Cash & Tax Credits Leveraged	Equity and debt	Developer and Strategic Investor	Similar to the Strategic Investor flip, but including commercial debt leverage, with the loan size and amortization profile based on the amount of cash flow from energy sales *plus* current tax credit or a monetization of the PTCs from a wind project
Back Leveraged	All equity (but Developer uses debt outside of the project)	Developer and Institutional Investor	Similar to the Institutional Investor flip, but with the Developer leveraging its equity stake in the project using commercial debt

through entities" for these business forms. Although the top individual tax rate is 35 percent—the same as the top corporate rate—avoiding double taxation can be a great boon to entrepreneurs.

Unfortunately, tax sense, not business sense, sometimes drives the essential business decision of the type of business entity that needs to be set up for renewable energy projects. One of the principal components of taxation in an energy project investment is the taxation of the carried interest by the general partner or investment manager. Carried interest (or "carry" in finance), is a share of the profits of an investment that is paid to the investment manager in excess of the amount that the manager contributes to the partnership. More specifically, taxation of carried interest has been an issue since the mid-2000s, particularly as the compensation earned by certain investors increased along with the sizes of the projects. Historically, carried interest has been treated as a capital gain for tax purposes. The reason for this treatment is that a manager would make a substantial commitment of his own capital into the fund and carried interest would represent a portion of the manager's return on that investment. While hedge funds typically trade their investments actively, private equity firms tend to hold their investments for many years as they do in the renewable energy sector. As such, the capital gains typically qualify as long term capital gains, which receive favorable tax treatment in the U.S. Critics of this tax treatment seek to disaggregate the returns directly related to the capital contributed by the manager or general partner from the carried interest allocated from the other investors in the partnership to the partnership general partner or manager.

Because the manager/general partner is compensated with a profits interest in the renewable energy project, the bulk of their income from the fund is taxed, not as compensation for services, but as a return on investment. Typically, when a partner receives a profits interest (commonly referred to as a "carried interest"), the partner is not taxed upon receipt, due to the difficulty of ascertaining the present value of an interest in future profits. Instead, the partner is taxed as the partnership earns income. Investors in energy projects, however, typically invest for a long term, with the result that income earned by the project is long-term capital gain, taxable to individuals at a maximum 15% rate. Because the profits share typically is the bulk of the manager's compensation and because this compensation can reach, in the case of the most successful projects, enormous figures, concern has been raised, both in the U.S. Congress and in the media, that managers are taking advantage of tax loopholes to receive what is effectively a salary without paying the ordinary 35% marginal income tax rates that an average person would have to pay on such income. The issue of favorable tax rates for carried interest had even become a hot issue during the 2012 Republican Primary race for President, because the bulk of candidate Mitt Romney's income was carried interest.

For example, if a renewable energy project is structured as a limited partnership, the limited partners receive a certain return on their investments and the general partner, who is the fund manager, receives the carried interest. Carried interest exists despite the fact that the general partner does not contribute capital to the partnership—it encourages him/her to make profitable investment decisions for the partnership. Unlike management fees, carried interest has historically been viewed as generating a capital gain rather than income. As a consequence carried interest is viewed as a vital component, not only in the establishment of renewable energy project structures, but as an important tool in the recruitment and retention of key staff in project management firms.

> *"Energy will be the immediate test of our ability to unite this Nation, and it can also be the standard around which we rally. On the battlefield of energy we can win for our Nation a new confidence, and we can seize control again of our common destiny."*
>
> Jimmy Carter, former U.S. President

Just as carried interest is the chief means of aligning the interests of general partners and limited partners, "vesting" of carried interest is the means of aligning the interests of individual investment professionals and the general partner, ensuring that they have an incentive to remain active throughout the long life of a renewable energy project. The vesting period and the pace of the vesting can vary widely. In the majority of cases, vesting is tied loosely to the investment period of the renewable energy project from which the carried interest is derived. Note that carried interest is allocated and vested with respect to each separate project managed by a manager. Vesting in a tax pass-through entity should take into account adjustments to past and future allocations of income and loss and how vesting affects both past and future distributions of proceeds. The issues involved in allocation and vesting of carried interest are numerous and complex and should be approached with great care. Carried interest structures are more like private wealth management structures and often complex. Consult with tax and legal advisors who are specialists in this area of taxation and project structuring.

PROJECT DOCUMENTATION

See Appendix 1 for forms referenced in this section.

Renewable energy project financing (and energy efficiency project financing is some cases) is relatively new in the project finance world, often tends to be technology specific, is a hybrid of other types of traditional commercial finance methods that have long been used, and in many cases have some amount of leverage involved. Hence, additional lenders are involved that can further complicate the type and amount of documentation involved in the project finance transaction. Therefore, no two transactions will require the same documents completed in the same way.

No matter what type of transaction finance is finally negotiated, all principal financial instruments will have five general areas that will need to be covered in the final drafted agreement.

1. A detailed description of the type of transaction that is being agreed to. This would include the "how much, how long and payment schedule." It would define any additional funding on the project such as interim or construction advances the creditor would provide and any future funding the creditor has agreed to.
2. Conditions precedent. This covers issues and components that must be accomplished or exist prior to advances under the agreement.
3. Debtor's covenants and representations. Statements made and agreed to by the debtor at inception of the agreement and that will exist throughout the term of the agreement.
4. Default. What constitutes a default, how a default is cured and what rights the creditor has should the debtor default in any of the covenants.
5. Boilerplate. Waivers, notices, jurisdiction, etc.

When a creditor in the project finance is obtaining a lien upon personal property or fixtures as collateral for their extension of credit or investment in the project, the interest in the collateral (project assets) is called a "security interest." The document that creates a security interest is a "security agreement" or "security instrument" and can come in many different varieties. Typical in a renewable energy project would be a direct loan, chattel mortgage, capital lease, operating lease or some type of energy purchase agreement. Although each have their own specific terms reflecting the intent of the parties, many of the contents and clauses of the instrument used are similar, to include the supporting documents. Supporting much of the drafting required is the Uniform Commercial Code (UCC) described more fully below. A valid security agreement under the UCC requires five specific items:

1. The agreement must be in writing
2. The agreement must be signed by the debtor
3. The agreement must contain a description of the collateral
4. Contain a specific grant of a security interest
5. Describe the obligations that it secures

In fact, a valid security agreement could be as simple as "I, John Adams, hereby grant to ABC Renewable Energy Project Creditor, a security interest in a 250 kW solar system to secure the operating lease that I am executing. s/John Adams." However, the UCC and commercial law allows the creditor to say more and it is best to do so. A well-drafted security agreement will cover at least the following:

- Description of the agreement and the obligation(s) it secures
- Date agreement is executed
- *Accurate* names and addresses of both debtor and creditor
- Grant of a specified security interest
- Detailed description of the collateral—be specific and include everything including engineering, drawings, permits and manuals, together with all accessions, substitutions and replacements
- Representations and warranties
- Events of default and acceleration provisions
- Rights and remedies
- General provisions (boilerplate)
- Signatures of both debtor and creditor

In a renewable energy project finance transaction, the creditor who is the owner or secured party in the underlying project assets may borrow up to 80% of the equipment cost on a non-recourse, partial recourse or full recourse basis. Hence, the term "leveraged." The owner, who may invest as little as 20% of the project cost, will realize tax benefits from the investment tax credit and depreciation deductions on 100% of the project cost. For example, $1 million in equity could be leveraged to obtain up to $5 million in equipment being placed into the project. Renewable energy project finance structures, in all of the various incarnations, is an extremely valuable supplement to conventional financing techniques. The final execution requires a sophisticated evaluation of the project finance structure and careful planning of all the tax, accounting and economic components of that structure which are culminated in the careful drafting of the documentation that reflects the intent of all the parties to the project.

Although there are numerous critical issues and components that flow into the preparation of project finance documentation, there are some key considerations that are always in the forefront when drafting all of the documents inherent in renewable energy project finance transactions and remain in the forefront of concerns at inception and over the remaining term of the contract.

1. Proper title vesting—ownership issues
2. Perfected and continuous security interest
3. Tax basis and resulting tax benefit dispositions
4. Adequate economic return debt payment structures
5. Residual risk management

Although there are many other considerations that are important and described more fully in the remainder of this chapter, the above five key considerations will most often take precedent in executing a properly documented project finance structure. Letter rulings from the Internal Revenue Service are for the most part something of the past and not being issued anymore. Therefore, ownership and tax issues are components of the project that require the most care when drafted and negotiated between the parties.

A complete documentation checklist is normally prepared by the creditor. It would include every detail of the project, the documentation required, who the parties would be, key dates of execution, filing requirements and dates, timeframe for issuance of the various documents, key investigation and inspection parties, and other types of due diligence procedures. The checklist is used as a starting point and then modified to meet the needs of each individual project. The checklist will normally describe the document and then have columns for "required," "received" or "waived."

The first document normally needed would be the commitment letter (prepared by the project finance team) between the creditor and debtor.

Commitment Letter

In the majority of the cases, the parties will spend a great deal of time defining all of the components to the project finance, reach an agreement on the disposition of those components and then describe those understandings in a commitment letter from the lender/project developer to the debtor. The terms and conditions stated in the commitment letter should careful reflect the numerous questions, factual and legal, that have been reviewed by the parties. Those parties could include those beyond the principal creditor and debtor and may in many cases require multiple commitment letters to each of the parties that have been involved in the successful negotiations of the project. These other parties could include escrow companies, suppliers, construction firms, engineering and architectural firms, environmental consulting firms, off-take parties, fuel suppliers, rebate providers and REC purchasers.

Perhaps the most important item in the commitment letter is the correctness of the debtors' exact, correct and current name. The importance of this requirement cannot be over-emphasized—whether obtained through debtor's counsel opinion letter (sample in Appendix 1), by-laws or other corporate or governmental records. In addition, the following items would normally be covered in the commitment letter:

- Full legal name of any guarantors
- Name of the underwriter
- Name of the creditor
- A complete equipment description
- Total asset cost
- Names of all equipment suppliers and vendors
- Name of installation company and any sub-contractors
- Exact location where assets will be located
- Description of all monitoring equipment and reporting needed
- Support equipment, software, spare parts, etc
- System performance requirements
- Type of finance structure being utilized
- Expected documentation closing date
- Exact term and payments proposed
- Security deposit or other fund requirements
- Environmental attribute ownerships
- Tax attribute ownerships
- Warranties
- Early termination provisions
- Renewal options
- Return provisions
- Purchase options
- Event of loss provisions
- Insurance requirements
- Filing requirements
- General default provisions
- Assignment provisions
- Contract transfers over the term
- Use and maintenance provisions
- Appraisal requirements
- Non-interference provisions
- Additions, modifications and improvements
- Documentation requirements
- Funding conditions
- Commitment fees
- Transaction expenses

> *"Alternative energy is a future idea whose time is past. Renewable energy is a future idea whose time has come."*
>
> Bill Penden (1977)

- Final funding requirements and dates
- Pricing assumptions
- Engineering drawings
- Host site requirements
- Roof or grounds lease details
- Indemnification provisions
- Stipulated loss values
- Certifications of legal structures
- Environmental warranties and disclosures
- List of external documents required
- Debtor's counsel opinion letter
- Establishment of capacity and authority

Uniform Commercial Code

All renewable energy and energy efficiency projects need to be carefully documented using proper due diligence regardless of the type of document used (e.g., operating lease, energy purchase agreement, etc.) to fund the project. In nearly all cases, the transaction should be documented following standard accepted procedures and paying particular attention to Article 9 of the Uniform Commercial Code. The Uniform Commercial Code (UCC or the Code) is one of a number of uniform acts that have been promulgated in conjunction with efforts to harmonize the law of sales and other commercial transactions in all 50 states within the United States of America. The Uniform Commercial Code (UCC) is a set of suggested laws relating to commercial transactions. The UCC was one of many uniform codes that grew out of a late nineteenth-century movement toward uniformity among state laws. The UCC is the longest and most elaborate of the uniform acts and promulgates a uniform set of laws that govern how commercial laws are to be interpreted and applied. The administration of the UCC has an important impact on the economy and upon the rights of the public, in all states of the United States. The volume of international, interstate & multistate transactions pursuant to the UCC requires that the administration of the UCC be conducted in a manner that promotes both local and multi-jurisdictional commerce by striving for uniformity in policies and procedures among the various states. The project to be financed should be viewed as a "secured" transaction and documented accordingly under the UCC. Article 9 of the code gives the creditor (lender or investor) guidance in how this should be executed. The most important measure is to obtain a perfected security interest.

Perfected Security Interest

The first goal of the creditor is take make sure that the all documentation reflects that the creditor will be granted a security interest in the project using the underlying assets as the security. The second goal is to "perfect" that interest using carefully designed rules that all states have adopted for the recording of that secured interest. Failure to follow these rules could allow the creditor to be in an "unsecured" position and having the equipment subject to another creditors secured interest. Therefore, to obtain rights against third parties, the secured party creditor must insure that their security agreement, or an acceptable substitute, is placed in the public record.

There are many different "titles" to the equipment that a creditor could hold and might include tax title, security title, production title, accounting title, emissions title, renewable energy credit title, GHG or carbon credit title, energy tax credit title, etc. The first title that needs to perfected is the security interest title. It is from the perfection of that title that all other titles flow and are perfected. Holding a valid and perfected security interest also means that should the debtor fail to meet their obligations under the contract you have prepared and which they have executed (default), you can cause the collateral (assets purchased or financed on the project) to be sold and the proceeds from the sale applied on the debt owed to you. If you do not have possession of the underlying collateral, you may take possession of it (repossession) so long as you do not breach the peace.

A valid security interest means that your rights in and to the collateral are enforceable against the debtor. A valid and perfected security interest places your rights in the collateral ahead of the debtor's trustee in bankruptcy's rights. Also, if your valid and perfected security interest or interest is prior in time to any other perfected security interests or to any lien, your rights in the collateral will be ahead of almost everybody. If there are some other security interest or lien claimants ahead of you, you will, of course, still have to face the property resolution of the conflicting claims between you and those other claimants. A good example of this type of interest would be a landlord or mortgage holder interest since you might be placing the project assets on their property. In that case, additional documentation would be needed in the form of waivers by either or both of those parties who might prevent you from removing the assets from the facility. The landlord or mortgage holder would normally claim that because the equipment is "attached" to their property, that it belongs to them and not to you. Without a specific waiver to the contrary, such claims by other debtor claimants could cause the Project Developer to have serious contract enforcement problems. Obviously, your position as a secured creditor is much better than that of an unsecured creditor with respect to the trustee in bankruptcy or other creditors of your debtor and also with respect to obtaining payment of your debt if your debtor subsequently becomes unwilling or unable to pay you.

> *"Water flows uphill towards money."*
>
> Anonymous, saying in the American West, quoted by Ivan Doig in Marc Reisner, Cadillac Desert, 1986)

When describing the equipment in a UCC-1 filing statement, it is best to use the most detailed description as possible—just as is done in the securing instrument of the project finance. In fact, most creditors will use the same asset or equipment list for both sets of documents—the security instrument and the UCC-1. Most energy project creditors, in addition to the actual equipment description, use the phrase. "...and all now owned or hereafter acquired or created, and all parts, accessories, accessions, and additions thereto or replacements therefore." As an additional word of caution, make sure that the attachment to the UCC-1 filing where the assets or equipment are described, has been properly recorded with the UCC-1 statement by the filing officer and the filing has been returned to the creditor. It would be a major deficiency in the execution of a properly drafted set of project finance documents if this small detail were not followed up on.

Should you decide later to leverage your project financing by borrowing money from another party to finance a portion or all of the project, you will not be able to do so without a prior perfected security interest that is available under Article 9 of the UCC. Most lenders will not accept an assignment of the documentation or advance funds under your agreement without also making sure that there has been a timely filing of the perfected security interest.

Article 9 serves two purposes. The first is to create a single, unitary security device known as a security interest. The document you create reflects the agreement that the creditor and debtor have agreed to and is called a security agreement. This can be an operating lease agreement, energy purchase agreement or some other agreement. The second purpose of Article 9 is to simplify the perfection procedures by establishing a single notice system for perfecting your security interests in the assets. This is done by filing a special document called a UCC-1 with the Secretary of State. The timely filing of the UCC-1 assures the creditor of a security interest in the asset(s) being used as collateral in the transaction.

Security interest[6] is defined in the code as an "interest in personal property which secures payment or performance of an obligation." However, it is not an encumbrance on real property. Security interests created under Article 9 are consensual security interests[7]. The consensual security interest to which Article 9 applies include not only security interests created under Article 9, but also security interests arising under the Article on Sales (Article 2) which is described in more detail below. This means that even though a Creditor's interest arose under Article 2, once the Debtor has possession, the Creditor's interest will be protected only if the Creditor has a written security Agreement and has perfected interest by filing or otherwise.

Although neither an operating lease nor energy purchase agreement would require a filing under Article 9 to perfect a Creditor's interest, most creditors do so as a preponderance of caution. A capital lease, conditional sales contract, chattel mortgage or other type of direct financing structure does require a perfected security interest and the creditor should always do so. Remember that the UCC filing system follows the rule of "first in time, first in right." This means that whatever creditor files the UCC-1 first on a specified item of equipment has the rights to that collateral over the rights of subsequent filings by other creditors of the debtor. In general then, the filing party (normally the creditor) will have a position that is junior to any creditor that filed before they did but would be senior to any creditor filing after their filing.

The final key element to perfecting the security interest in the underlying assets of the renewable energy project is to make sure that the filing occurs within 10 business days of receiving title to the equipment from the equipment suppliers (commonly called a "purchase money security interest"). The UCC is somewhat vague in that it is not clear if filing has to occur within 10 days of the debtor 1) receiving the equipment, 2) the creditor getting official title from the seller, or 3) the actual security interest agreement being finalized between the parties to the transaction.[8] In any event, failure to do so could subject your lien interest to that of other secured lien holders of the debtor. Therefore, make sure that the security interest is perfected by a timely filing of the UCC-1 document. A copy of the form is included in the Appendix 1.

It is important that filing instructions be followed explicitly. Misspelling of names, address errors, etc. may not nullify the value of your filing bit it is a chance that should be avoided. Also, don't forget to include all of the correct fees when sending the form into the proper authority for recording. Article 9 permits a secured party to file a UCC-1 financing statement consistent with the language of the security agreement without any authentication by the debtor. Therefore, be sure that whatever security agreement is used (lease, energy purchase agreement or other agreement) that there is a clause allowing the secured party to file a UCC-1 without the signature of the Debtor.

A filing which is made in good faith in an improper place or not in all of the places required is nevertheless effective with regard to any collateral as to which the filing complied with the requirements of Article 9 and is also effective with regard to collateral covered by the financing statement against any person who has knowledge of the contents of such financing statement. Also, a filing which is made in the proper place continues effective even though the debtor's residence or place of business or the location of the collateral or its use, whichever controlled the original filing, is subsequently changed. It is a good idea to file the UCC-1 with both the Secretary of State and the county recorder's office of where the equipment will be located.

All UCC-1 filings expire at the end of five years from the date of filing. Therefore, it is important that the creditor set up a tickler file to amend the original filing every five years that the project is still in effect. The form needed to amend or extend the original filing through a continuation filing is UCC-2. A continuation statement may be filed by the secured party within six months prior to the expiration of the five year period. Any such continuation statement must be signed by the secured party, identify the original statement by file number and state that the original is still effective.

The final UCC document filed occurs when the obligation has been paid in full and the secured party wishes to release their secured interest in the underlying asset of the project finance. This form is a UCC-3. It can be filed within one month of release of the security interest or within ten days following written demand of the debtor. This form can only be signed by the secured party or their assignee.

Article 2A of the Uniform Commercial Code[9]

Uniform Commercial Code (UCC) Article 2A—Leases, governs true leases of goods. It was added to the Uniform Commercial Code in 1987, and amended in 1990. It was the first article added to the UCC after its original promulgation in 1951, and responded to the enormous increase in the use of leases that began in the 1970's. Leasing became used in that time as a method of financing transactions in goods. In finance leases, lessor and lessee became analogous to creditor and debtor in these kinds of transactions.

Uniform Commercial Code Article 2A is a set of laws relating to personal property leasing. Any type of a lease including a capital lease (finance lease) or an operating lease should carefully follow this section of the UCC. Virtually every form of equipment lease used by major leasing company's state that it is governed by the laws of one of the states which has adopted Article 2A. Article 2A makes many changes in existing Article 9 law which are beneficial to both lessors and lessees. These changes, essentially, standardize state law so that the lessor is unable to select favorable quirks in the law of its home state.

In a true lease, the lessor gives possession and right to use the goods to the lessee for a fixed period of time in return for rent. The title to the property and a meaningful residual interest remain with the lessor. A "finance lease" is a true lease in which the lessor is not the fundamental supplier of the goods leased, but leases goods to lessees as a means of financing their acquisition from the supplier. UCC Article 2A governs finance leases as true leases, but treats them differently in some respects from other true leases. For example, UCC 2A provides an implied warranty of quality, but since the lessor in a finance lease is not the source of the goods, the warranty does not run directly to the lessor. The lessor passes through warranties given by the supplier under other law (principally a sale warranty of fitness) to the lessee. UCC 2A provides for priority of lessor interests for finance leases, analogous to the concept of priority between creditors in secured transactions under UCC Article 9. Great care was taken to establish finance leases as a separate financing category from secured transactions so that no doubt as to the method of establishing priority for any transaction would arise.

It should always be remembered that Article 2A supports provisions commonly found in equipment

> *"The sunlight...that strikes Earth's land surface in two hours is equivalent to total human energy use in a year. While much of that sunlight becomes heat, solar energy is also responsible for the energy embodied in wind, hydro, wave, and biomass, each with the potential to be harnessed for human use. Only a small portion of that enormous daily, renewable flux of energy will ever be needed by humanity."*
>
> Christopher Flavin in Worldwatch Institute (2008)
> Building a Low-Carbon Economy

leases, under which a lessee has no right to require the lessor to repair or replace defective equipment or to withhold rents while defective equipment is being repaired. This "hell or high water" protection applies only to lessors who are not in fact, the manufacturer or other vendor of the leased equipment. If the lease from such a lessor qualifies, it will be a UCC-2A "finance lease." The so-called "hell or high water" provisions have long been a standard of the finance lease industry. They obligate the lessee to make all payments and perform all obligations of the lease agreement despite any setoff, abatement, defense or counterclaim that they may have against the lessor, manufacturer or other entity for any reason whatsoever. Article 2A has established the concept of a "finance lease" under which the lessee's promises become irrevocable and independent upon the lessee's acceptance of the equipment being leased. That promise by the lessee is not subject to cancellation, termination, or modification without the consent of the lessor or its assignee.

Other provisions of Article 2A make it clear that the lessor may assign the lease to a third party, who will take the lessor's right to receive rent, but none of its obligations, notwithstanding contrary language of the lease. If so stated in the lease, some assignments could create a default by the lessor, giving the lessee right to damages; even this would not affect the ability of the assignee to enforce provisions of the lease against the lessee.

Whenever possible, it is a good idea for the lessor to have a lease that conforms to the Article 2A provisions of the UCC.

Principal Security Agreement/Instrument

Depending upon the legal structure selected by the parties to the renewable energy project (loan, capital lease, operating lease, energy purchase agreement, etc.), the following components are required in nearly all contracts that are drafted and executed:

- Contract number and date of contract
- The proper legal names of the parties, their addresses, contact information, etc.
- A complete description of the equipment (usually on a separate document called an "equipment or asset schedule"
- The original term of the contract and the payment schedule with amounts and dates
- The debtor's inspection and acceptance of the asset(s) or equipment
- Disclaimer of warranties and limitation of liability
- Issues affecting installation, maintenance, repair and replacement
- Unconditional obligation to pay rent or charges
- Representations and warranties of debtor
- Representations and warranties of creditor
- Rights of assignment
- Risk of loss and damage
- Insurance requirements and obligations
- Indemnification
- Liens and taxes
- Results of debtor's failure to perform
- Identification of assets as "personal property"
- Physical location of assets
- Ownership and title provisions (including REC title, tax title, etc.)
- Use of assets provisions
- Surrender of assets
- Events of default and specified remedies
- Creditor's suspension of obligations
- Special terms
- Attorneys' fees
- Miscellaneous provisions
  — Effect of Waiver
  — Notices
  — Security Interest
  — Applicable law
  — Arbitration provisions
  — Financial statement requirements
  — Severability
  — Headings
  — Substitutions and alterations
  — Entire agreement

A copy of a sample standard lease and energy purchase agreement is included in Appendix 1.

Landlord's Waiver, Mortgage Waiver and Fixture Filing

A number of states allow the landlord to have a lien against the assets of a tenant located on the premises. This can create a number of problems for a secured creditor under a renewable energy project finance. Frequently, a landlord might seek to recover unpaid rents at the expense of a creditor's interest in their assets that they have a security interest in to the detriment of that secured creditor. As a result, most secured energy project creditors will ask the landlord to waive or subordinate his rights.

A related document would be a "fixture filing" under the UCC (filed in the county where the asset(s) of the energy project are located) and is filed for the same reasons—protecting the secured creditor against any claims by the landlord or in some cases, the mortgage lender of the real property. A fixture is an item of personal property that (as in many renewable energy projects) becomes so affixed to real property that it could become treated as part of the real property. Usually, the courts will rely on the "intent" of the parties to the transaction if there is a dispute. A creditor needs to secure its interest in the project property by perfecting a fixture filing (using a standard UCC-1 document) with the addition of a legal description of the real property upon which the asset(s) will be placed and the name of the legal record owner of the real property. The signatures must be notarized and the form recorded in the official records of the county where the real property is located.

If the debtor owns the real property and has a loan on the real property with a mortgage lender, it would be most appropriate to also have a mortgage waiver signed by the mortgage lender(s). The purpose is the same as the landlord waiver and fixture filing described above. A copy of a sample Mortgagee Waiver is included in Appendix 1.

The landlord waiver, fixture filing and mortgage waiver must all be filed in the records of the county where the equipment is located. Doing so, provides assurance to the secured creditor that neither the landlord or the mortgage lender will claim an interest in the equipment and that they will allow the creditor to enter the premises to repossess or sell the equipment upon default by the tenant/debtor. It would also be an advantage to the secured creditor if the landlord or mortgage lender advised the project creditor if a default does occur to them, and that the landlord notifies the secured project creditor if they sell the premises and to notify his successor of the waiver. By properly filing the waiver and fixture filing in the county, an encumbrance will appear on the real property records showing the interest of the secured project creditor. Nearly all renewable energy projects involve assets that could easily be considered a "fixture" by a landlord or mortgage lender and unless a waiver is obtained and duly recorded, an energy project creditor could easily find themselves in court trying to defend their interests in the underlying assets of the project—whether the debtor is directly in default to the project creditor or not.

As a final note on these three specific documents, don't forget to get the signatures of all parties notarized and that an exact legal description of the real property is located on the document or the county recorder's office will have the documents returned for corrections prior to an effective filing. A sample copy of a landlord waiver is included in the Appendix 1.

Guaranty

Guarantees can come from many different parties. That would include personal guaranties from principals of a debtor, cross guaranty from related companies, and a guaranty from third parties including landlords, suppliers and other parties who might be involved in the renewable energy project or who might have a vested interest in the energy project in some manner. Most guaranties follow the same guidelines and a sample "Personal Guaranty" is included in Appendix 1. Also included in Appendix 1 is an "Authorization to Add" additional obligation's to an existing guaranty.

A guaranty is an agreement by which one party assumes the responsibility of assuring payment or fulfillment of another's debts or obligations. A guaranty can be absolute or conditional. It can also be limited or unlimited in scope. Most guaranties should also be drafted as "joint and several" despite the objections that may be raised by some guarantors. It is also considered prudent by drafters of guaranty's that should a corporation guaranty a debt of another entity, that a corporate resolution to authorize the guaranty also be obtained in addition to the guaranty itself.

The issue of "consideration" should also be considered when accepting a guaranty from any party. Normally, a guaranty by a third party who derives no direct benefit for offering a guaranty of a debtor should be avoided. Always document the credit file with a reason for the acceptance of a guaranty by a guarantor in the project. A guarantor can use the defense that they did not receive any consideration or value for the guaranty if a creditor enforces the guaranty. Additionally, make sure that every guarantor in a transaction be kept informed of any delinquency in the project finance. Courts can frown on a creditor demanding payment by a guarantor if they have not received notice that the primary debtor is delinquent its obligations to the creditor.

Consumer Leasing Act

The Consumer Leasing Act (Act),[10] commonly known as Regulation M of the Federal Reserve Board, became effective September 24, 1998 and is tied closely to the "Truth in Lending Act." It is federal legislation that mandates how leasing costs and terms are disclosed to consumers. Although most renewable energy projects are "commercial" in nature, some transactions can be with "consumers" (such as a lease of a solar system on the roof of a personal residence). If this is the case in a specific transaction, then the creditor should be aware of the provisions of the Consumer Leasing Act and be prepared to make the proper disclosures contained in that Act and to have documents drafted that reflect the provisions of the Act.

> *"Clearly, we need more incentives to quickly increase the use of wind and solar power; they will cut costs, increase our energy independence and our national security and reduce the consequences of global warming."*
>
> Hillary Rodham Clinton, speech at Cleantech Venture Forum VIII, Oct 25, 2005

The Act defines a "consumer lease" as a contract for the use of personal property by a person primarily for personal, family, or household purposes, for a period exceeding four months and for a total contractual obligation not exceeding $25,000, whether or not the lessee has the option to purchase or otherwise become the owner of the property at the expiration of the lease. However, even if the transaction is for more the $25,000, which is often the case on renewable energy projects, and could be used even "partly" by a consumer, it would be wise for the creditor to adhere to the provisions of the Act to avoid challenges to the agreement at some point in the future as the contract matures.

The Act requires that numerous items be disclosed to the debtor prior to execution of the lease contract. The disclosures must be clear and conspicuous, or more precisely, reasonably understandable. For example, the disclosures must be presented in a way that does not obscure the relationship of the terms to each other. In addition, although no minimum type size is required, the disclosures must be legible. A sample disclosure statement is included in *Appendix 1*.

The disclosure needs to be given to the lessee together with a dated statement that identifies the lessor and the lessee and with the following items:

- An accurate and complete description of the property to be leased
- Amount due at lease signing or delivery
- Payment schedule and total amount of periodic payments
- Other charges (that are not included in the periodic payments) itemized by type and amount
- Total of all payments to be made over the term of the contract
- Payment calculation that provides:
  - — Gross capitalized cost
  - — Capitalized cost reduction
  - — Adjusted capitalized cost
  - — Residual value
  - — Depreciation and any amortized amounts
  - — Rent charge
  - — Total of base periodic payments
  - — Lease payments with a description of the number of payment periods
  - — Base periodic payment (total payments divided by number of payment periods)
  - — Itemization of other charges that are part of the periodic payment
  - — Total periodic payments including base periodic payment and any other charges that are part of the periodic payment
- Early termination
  - — Conditions and disclosure of charges
  - — Early termination notice
- Maintenance
  - — Statement of responsibilities
  - — Wear and use standard
  - — Notice of wear and use standard
- Purchase Option
  - — End of lease term
  - — During lease term
- Statement referencing non-segregated disclosures
- Liability between residual and realized values
- Right of appraisal
- Liability at end of lease term based on residual value
  - — Rent and other charges
  - — Excess liability
  - — Mutually agreeable final adjustment
- Fees and taxes
- Insurance
  - — Through the lessor
  - — Through a third party
- Warranties or guarantees
- Penalties and other charges for delinquency
- Security interest

- Limitations on rate information

Then, if the original lease term has expired and the parties wish to renew the lease for an additional term, the renegotiation requires new disclosures. This could include renegotiation, extension or assumption but are not required if:

- there is a reduction in the rent charge;
- the deferment of one or more payments (whether or not a fee is charged);
- the extension of a lease for not more than six months;
- a substitution of lease property with property that has a substantially equivalent or greater economic value;
- the addition, deletion or substitution of leased property in a multiple-item lease, provided the average periodic payment does not change by more than 25 percent; or
- an agreement resulting from a court proceeding.

There are also significant disclosures required on any advertising used (advertisement includes messages inviting, offering, or otherwise generally announcing to prospective customers the availability of consumer leases, whether in visual, oral, print or electronic media). The advertising disclosure requirements are onerous and should be carefully reviewed by the creditor and their counsel prior to using this medium to solicit transactions. For example, the creditor needs to provide a toll free number for the consumer to call, disclosure of all items defined above, etc. Some states have additional disclosures that need to be followed if the leased property will be located in that state.

Lastly, the Act also applies to an "arranger" of a lease (such as a supplier, system integrator, lease broker or underwriter, project developer, etc.). To "arrange" for the lease of personal property means to provide or offer to provide a lease that is or will be extended by another person under a business or other relationship pursuant to which the person arranging the lease (a) receives or will receive a fee, compensation, or other consideration for the service or (b) has knowledge of the lease terms and participates in the preparation of the contract documents required in connection with the lease.

Other Standard Documents and Requirements

Although there many additional or unique documents that would be appropriate in a particular renewable energy project finance, some of the more common documents or supporting items are:

- Copies of the debtor's articles of incorporation, bylaws, certificate of partnership, partnership agreement, LLC operating agreement, etc. This would also encompass all modifications or amendments to those documents. Don't just get the items for your credit file, but carefully review them for possible issues that need to be resolved or supported through other documents.
- Preliminary title report on the real property where the assets of the renewable energy project will be placed. The report will show correct ownership of the real property, correct legal description and all current lienholders. This information will be needed in many of the standard documents that will be executed. For example, the correct owner will be needed in all documents concerning the "landlord"; legal description will be needed for landlord waivers, mortgage waivers, roof leases, engineering and permitting, etc. The exact names of the lienholders, trustees and assignees will be needed for mortgage waivers and other documents that have a reference to real property issues. Another example is the identification of potential third parties who may have mineral rights, access rights, and other types of encumbrances on the property whose permissions may be needed in certain types of renewable energy project documents.
- Corporate Resolution to Borrow or Enter into Agreement (see sample Corporation Resolution to Lease in Appendix 1)
- Certificate of Secretary on Corporate Resolution (see sample in Appendix 1)
- Subordination and Pledge Agreement
- Hypothecation Agreement
- Lease Purchase or Renewal Option (*see sample in Appendix 1*)
- Purchase Order (*see sample in Appendix 1*)
- Power of Attorney
- Pre-Construction Scoping Analysis (*see sample in Appendix 1*)
- Disclaimer of Ownership (*see sample in Appendix 1*)
- Confidentiality and Non-Disclosure Agreement (*see sample in Appendix 1*)

- Master Renewable Energy Certificate Purchase & Sale Agreement (see Appendix 1)
- Lease Security Deposit Agreement (*see sample in Appendix 1*)
- Equipment Delivery and Acceptance (*see sample in Appendix 1*)

Miscellaneous Issues and Concerns

- Usury (in some states)—both on original terms and also on default charges
- Insurance—both liability and comprehensive collateral coverage
- Prepayments, early termination and stipulated loss values
- Acceleration clause
- End of contract provisions and notice by debtor to creditor of intentions
- Return provisions by lessee (very critical in any type of equipment lease)
- Obligations by creditor after a default and repossession and a sale of assets in a "commercially reasonable manner"
- Deficiency obligations by debtor after a repossession

ENVIRONMENTAL FACTORS

Environmental laws have had a profound effect on commercial transactions in recent years. This is particularly true regarding commercial facilities in the United States. Less well known has been the effect of these laws on business financial transactions. In most cases, these laws become the responsibility of the facility or equipment owner and hence, the applicability for anyone who would be the owner of an asset. In renewable energy projects, this indirect contingent risk could be both detrimental as well as beneficial. For example, if the project would be a landfill gas project using methane to provide fuel to a co-generation project or to power a I/C engine and compressor system that sends the gas down a pipeline to a third party for purchase, there could be multiple environmental exposures that a project developer might face. This same exposure could present itself in a biofuel or waste to energy project. Although tangential in nature, the detrimental risk would still exist and would have to be addressed and either mitigated in some manner or eliminated entirely. Even the simple construction of a solar project by a project developer could turn into an environmental disaster during the installation phase if an accident would occur that was the responsibility of the energy provider.

However, there are significant beneficial factors as well in nearly every single renewable energy project. Whether that is in the form of RECs, carbon credits, emission offsets, NO_X credits on a solar thermal project, GHG reductions or even particulate matter reductions from a renewable energy project replacing a peaker turbine plant, many positive environmental benefits flow from the financing of a typical cleantech renewable energy project. The project developer needs to recognize these positive factors and then use all available marketing tools to gain both a public relations benefit and to market the financial value in any manner possible.

Transactional environmental law must be combined with environmental law, corporate law and contract law in a synchronized event that accurately balances risk with reward. This also means that the effective application of environmental transactions principles in project finance needs to incorporate relevant scientific and engineering practices, such as the depth and extent of environmental audits (both at inception of the project and over the term of the project as well) that would be carried out in the transactional context. This would include the design and engineering of the system, installation, commissioning, and operations for the life of the underlying assets.

Historically, no financial transactions involved environmental considerations until late in the 20th century. Now environmental laws affect a broad spectrum of business transactions in the United States and the impact of the laws will continue to grow in importance. Companies and individuals are now held liable under environmental laws such as CERCLA (Comprehensive Environmental Response, Compensation and Liability Act—"Superfund"), Superfund Amendments and Reauthorization Act of 1986 (SARA), The Environmental Planning and Community Right-to-Know Act (EPCRA), Resource Conservation and Recovery Act (RCRA), Clean Air Act, Clean Water Act, Toxic Substances Control Act (TSCA), Federal Water Pollution Control Act, Federal Insecticide, Fungicide, and Rodenticide Act (FIFRA), Safe Drinking Water Act (SDRA), and many other acts and laws. Additionally, other regulatory agencies such as the Securities and Exchange Commission (SEC), the International Accounting Standards Board (IASB) require disclosures to stockholders and the public. In California, AB32 mandates the public reporting of all green-house gas emissions to the Climate Control Action Registry (CCAR)—both historically and every year into the future (*see Appendix 1 for sample report*).

> *"We've embarked on the beginning of the last days of the age of oil. Embrace the future and recognize the growing demand for a wide range of fuels or ignore reality and slowly—but surely—be left behind."*
>
> Mike Bowlin, chairman and CEO of Arco (now BP)

Environmental law that affects the financing of renewable energy projects is made up of no less than nine major federal statues and many other state and local laws. It is the assortment and interaction of all of the federal, state and local laws that makes documentation of renewable energy project financings such a challenge. These challenges are not just a nuisance, they are a necessity if the project developer or lender is going to be prepared to achieve the level of commercial documentation necessary to protect themselves and have an enforceable set of documentation but also to have a project eligible for additional financing from third parties through the secondary market that most projects will attempt to achieve. These laws create many rights and responsibilities for all parties in the energy project and each party will attempt to maximize the attributes for their own benefit during the documentation process. Ultimately, no project will achieve final funding if everyone involved in the project doesn't feel that they are assuming an acceptable business risk. Extensive negotiations can result in some projects never closing if one or more parties feel that the risk to them is greater than the benefits they would receive if the project were to close. Environmental risks, simply because of their potentially very large "unknown" quantity, often create the largest stumbling block in the project finance.

In nearly all cases, strict liability is imposed by the environmental laws, rules and regulations which create joint and several liability with other parties whose acts may have contributed to the violations and harm, and may also be retroactive past the date of enactment of the statute which imposed the liability. Simply put, this means that an owner, operator, or other responsible party may be liable for the acts of others who are now insolvent or who are no longer in business. The generic term used for this concept by the regulators is called "Potentially Responsible Parties" or simply PRPs. The fact that anyone could be held jointly or severally liable for not only their own actions but also the actions of others in a project, can create a potentially high cost of compliance for all. Each party will try their best to have all other parties in the transaction to indemnify themselves from others actions. This is normally none through properly drafted indemnification agreements and the purchase of insurance from insurers who are expected to be around for the duration of the project. This is no time to cut corners and go with insuring entities who don't have the financial depth and resources to provide adequate coverage at some distant time in the future if needed.

There are four classes of PRPs who may be liable to perform a cleanup or to pay costs incurred by a regulatory agency or other parties who may claim that you are liable.

1. The current owner(s) and operator(s) of the facility or project. It is not necessary that a party be both owner and operator. Either capacity will be adequate to bestow liability on you.
2. Persons who owned or operated the facility at the time of environmental damage.
3. Persons who, by contract or otherwise, arranged for the disposal or treatment of hazardous substances, transportation of hazardous substances, or for the creation, disposal or treatment of the substance—whether a result of that persons direct actions or indirectly because that person "may" have had something to do with the environmental damage. This is the "catch all" that can get almost anyone caught up in the liability action that could occur.
4. Any person who transported an environmentally damaging substance to a facility and who selected the facility.

Although each of the above PRP descriptions is usually used in the context of CERCLA, they can be applied whenever there is an environmental action that causes liability to anyone associated with that action. The standard of liability is such that the liability of a PRP is strict liability. Strict liability means that a person may be responsible for performing a cleanup of contaminated property without regard to negligence, intent, or other fault. "Strict" liability also means that parties can be held liable merely because they fall within one of the statutory classes of responsible parties and without regard to fault. There are only three statutory defenses to CERCLA liability (and by extension, that of other environmental statutes): an act of God, an act of war, an act or omission of a third party, other than an employee or agent of the PRP, or other than one whose act or omission occurs in connection with a contractual relationship, existing directly or indirectly, with the PRP (commonly referred to as the "third-party" defense). It is the third-party statutory defense that is most often sought to be achieved in documenting the renewable energy project.

Project developers, financial institutions and other lenders to a renewable energy project who take a security interest in property or the underlying personal property assets can easily be caught up in the search for PRPs by government agencies that are looking for "deep pockets." The Environmental Protection Agency (EPA) has promulgated an interpretive rule to exempt secured creditors from this liability and to clarify the types of transactions that will or will not subject a secured lender to environmental liability. This is covered in section 101(20)(A) of CERCLA and is generally known as EPA Policy Number 4 and became effective on April 29, 1992, in 57 Fed. Reg. 18,344 (4-CFR Part 300). In 1995, the EPA and the Department of Justice (DOJ) issued further clarification with Policy on CERCLA Enforcement Against Lenders and Government Entities that Acquire Property Involuntarily. This was later withdrawn and replaced with the Asset Conservation, Lender Liability, and Deposit Insurance Protection Act in 1996. Section 2502 of that Act amends CERCLA's secured creditor exemption and also addresses lender liability under RCRA. In the end, the document is intended solely as guidance for employees of the U.S. Environmental Protection Agency. It is not a rule and does not create any legal obligations. Whether and how EPA applies this policy in any given case will depend on the facts of the case.

> *"The effects of rising temperature are pervasive. Higher temperatures diminish crop yields, melt the mountain glaciers that feed rivers, generate more-destructive storms, increase the severity of flooding, intensify drought, cause more-frequent and destructive wildfires, and alter ecosystems everywhere."*
>
> Lester R. Brown, U.S. environmental analyst

Lenders that have failed to conduct due diligence or which were not thorough in protecting their security interests have inherited huge environmental liabilities under CERCLA. As a preponderance of caution then, the most important thing that a project developer, lender or investor can do is to perform a thorough environmental audit of the project as part of the due diligence procedures when documenting the financing of the renewable energy project. This audit would include soil, air, and occasionally, employee safety and health. The three elements formulated as a result of that environmental audit of the project are:

1. Indicia of ownership
2. Ownership be held primarily to protect security interest
3. Prohibition of secured creditors from participating in the active management of a facility

It is the third element that must be carefully reviewed when an energy purchase agreement or operating lease agreement is the financial vehicle used to secure the project finance. This is particularly true in case of default and the secured creditor takes aggressive actions to protect their collateral, not realizing that it could affect their potential liability for environmental damages by doing so. The EPA has identified four areas where a secured creditor may conduct "acceptable loan management" activities without violating the exemptions afforded a secured lender.

1. Before the transaction takes place, or at the inception of the transaction
2. During the tenure of the transaction
3. While undertaking a financial workout with a defaulting debtor
4. At foreclosure and when preparing the facility (or project) for sale or liquidation

In practice, the 1996 Act expressly identifies certain actions that will not qualify as participating in the management of the debtor. They are:

- holding, abandoning or releasing a security interest;
- including environmental covenants or warranties in a credit or security agreement;
- monitoring or enforcing, or altering, restructuring or renegotiating, the terms and conditions of the credit extension or security agreement;
- conducting one or more inspections of the facility;
- requiring a response action "or other lawful means of addressing the release or threatened release of a hazardous substance";
- providing financial or other advice or counseling seeking to mitigate, prevent or cure default or

diminution in value; and

- exercising other legal remedies for the breach of a credit or security agreement.[11]

This means that you can take an active role in protecting your collateral. In the end, however, it is vitally important that the secured creditor does not take an active role in the actual management of the company or facility of their debtor. The operative phrase is "participating in the management." The caveat is that CERCLA's secured creditor exemption is not absolute protection from environmental liability. Environmental liability still could attach to a secured creditor in several ways.

1. Even if protection is available to the secured creditor, it may not be available to a third party. This is especially problematic if the secured creditor wants to transfer their interest under a loan agreement or if selling the foreclosed property to someone else. As a result, the value of the underlying collateral could be reduced by at least the amount necessary to remediate any contamination.
2. The CERCLA lender liability exemption only insulates the lender as a PRP.
3. This does not cover the lender under the Clean Air Act, Clean Water Act, and other laws. It is available only under CERCLA rules and regulations.
4. It does not cover the secured creditor where they directly or indirectly caused the contamination because of their own acts or omissions—liability could still attach.

Some of the environmental strategies that a secured lender might want to employ to reduce their risk from an environmental risk perspective could include:

1. Avoid "participation in management" of your debtor—at inception, over the term of the project, or in active liquidation of the underlying assets.
2. Conduct pre-funding environmental diligence audits, environmental audits at reasonable times over the term of the project, and prior to liquidation of the assets—either through normal termination or default (see Appendix 1).
3. Evaluate what strategic options are available to you for limiting liability to include indemnification agreements and insuring the environmental risk through third parties.
4. Observe good environmental management of the underlying assets of the renewable energy project throughout the term by performing adequate periodic inspections of your collateral.
5. Keep good records. This would include written inspection results, remote monitoring of the project, pictures, governmental permits and engineering drawings including any changes or modifications to the equipment.

A good starting point to evaluate a potential renewable energy project site is to do an initial "pre-construction" project scoping site analysis. A sample form is included in *Appendix 1*. This would then be followed up with an environmental audit as described in the following section. The pre-construction analysis would normally be performed on every project regardless of the type of financing structure that would ultimately be negotiated and executed. It takes a careful look at the general site and identifies some of the potential challenges that a project could encounter as the project is constructed. Some of the parameters it identifies are:

- Potential problems from existing operations at the site (or nearby operations) that could cause future impairment to the project assets. These could include such issues as spray painting that would cause paint to drift onto a solar array or fundamental structural issues on the building that would prevent the renewable energy production system from being installed.
- Determining if there are existing electrical, structural, plumbing or other drawings that would help determine the best installation of the equipment.
- Ascertain current utility usages that would point out the energy savings that would be derived from the proposed project. It would also determine potential energy efficiency components that could be integrated into the project.
- Determine security and emergency criteria that the proposed project could or would need to be designed for.
- Determine current load centers and review any existing or proposed energy management systems or technologies the customer might be employing in the near future.
- Review of site specific parameters such as:
  - Electrical panels, transformers, voltages, subpanel locations, etc.
  - Gas delivery pipe sizes (needed for any co-

generation project using natural gas as a fuel source)
  - Current roof age, material, available square footage, roof condition, pitch, direction and any limitations that might exist
  - Environmental issues such as shading, parking, security fencing, site access, or right of way concerns
  - Space availability on where the project assets will be placed and any environmental risks or restrictions

- Other project parameters that would include:
  - Customer credit and financial condition information
  - Identifying all current operating permits
  - Identifying all agencies that would need to issue permits for the project—both construction and operations
  - Wind risks (including strength, direction and dust issues)
  - Safety, labor, noise, geo-technical or landscaping issues
  - Bonding requirements needed

ENVIRONMENTAL AUDITS

An environmental audit is the systematic examination of the interactions between any business operation and its surroundings. This includes all emissions to air, land, and water; legal constraints; the effects on the neighboring community, landscape and ecology; and the public's perception of the operating company in the local area. An environmental audit does not stop at compliance with legislation. Nor is it a 'green-washing' public relations exercise. Rather it is a total strategic approach to the organization's activities.

Investors, project developers and lenders are concerned about environmental responsibility. They want to know about potential hazards and future environmental liabilities of companies. Even accounting firms are required during an audit to assess contingent liabilities, including environmental risks. Environmental audits are intended to quantify environmental performance and environmental position. In this way they perform an analogous function to financial audits. An environmental audit report ideally contains a statement of environmental performance and environmental position, and may also aim to define what needs to be done to sustain or improve on indicators of such performance and position.

Mattsson and Olsson (p. 178) say that there are three types of audit:[12]

1. Liability audit
2. A management audit
3. A functional audit (sometimes called an activity or issues audit)

Liability audits assess compliance with legal obligations. Management audits verify that an Environmental Management Strategy meets its stated objectives. An activity audit may investigate a specific area such as energy or water use.

The value of environmental auditing is as a tool that helps minimize current or future liability, avoid compliance costs with new projects, and identify opportunities for reducing risks and improving economic returns on the renewable energy projects that are being financed. Indirectly, the audit can also identify potential revenue sources from the project by reducing emissions that may have an economic value to the debtor or other third party that would be willing to purchase the emission reductions or offsets.

Audit criteria may be compliance requirements such as regulations or may be management practices that benefit the environment. In either case, an audit provides information on the operational status of an organization compared to management's environmental performance expectations. For example, if management expects the organization to be in compliance with regulations, an audit will provide information on whether compliance has been achieved or not, and if not, what specific measures are required to achieve compliance.[13]

> *"Oil is like a wild animal. Whoever captures it has it."*
>
> Jean Paul Getty, U.S. industrialist, founder of
> Getty Oil Company (1986; quoted by biographer Robert Lenzner)

A key to establishing the secured lender exemption under environmental regulations is the "all appropriate inquiry" requirement. The statute doesn't define what that inquiry needs to consist of. It does, however, provide a flexible standard of "good commercial or customary practice."[14] Currently, the "all appropriate inquiry" phrase is generally considered to mean an environmental audit. The audit will ascertain the issues needing to be addressed between the parties that will make the transaction workable for all concerned. Additionally, the audit will provide a thorough investigation into the environmental condition of the property itself or the property on which the project will be located before acquisition of the interest so that the secured creditor will not inadvertently acquire more than they bargained for.[15] The environmental audit will cover all types of property including both real property and personal property.

In a broad sense, initial environmental audits will generally be covered in what the industry classifies as the three phases of an audit that could be performed. Phase One, the simplest, will usually cover the following:

- Physical inspection of the property
- Examination of the title records of the property
- Examination of the records of federal, state or local government environmental agencies
- Examination of aerial photographs of the property
- Interview with persons familiar with the property regarding its present and past uses

If Phase One identifies actual contamination or if contamination is suspected, a Phase Two audit would be performed to determine the nature and extent of the environmental concern. In this phase, actual samples would be taken, analyzed and a report of the findings prepared. Phase Two would in many cases also provide the parties with possible remediation procedures.

Phase Three consists of the actual development of specified remedial action plans. In each Phase, additional costs can be expected with a Phase Two and Phase Three audit costing significantly more than just a Phase One audit. Most secured creditors who have identified problems with the property in Phase One of an environmental audit elect to cancel the project and not move forward simply because of the higher costs involved in further audits and implementing the specified remediation procedures. Alternatively, the debtor or another third party could pay for the added costs in Phase two or three provided it made economic sense based on the size of the project and the related costs.

The secured lender must take into consideration not just the environmental issues at inception of the project, but based on the facility and operations where the project will be physically located, what additional environmental risks could result over the term of the project. The secured party must also consider the final disposition of the underlying assets in the project finance when the project finance term is completed. If the underlying assets in any way can be contaminated or if the asset contaminated other property (real or personal) over the term of the project finance, costs of remediation and further environmental audits need to be considered. If those projected costs exceed certain realistic thresholds, the project should be abandoned prior to accepting those future added costs. Here again, a proper risk environmental assessment is required and appropriate decisions made prior to entering into the project finance.

Included in *Appendix 1* are several environmental audit checklists that can provide a basis for more detailed checklists that should be developed by every secured creditor who invests in both renewable energy projects and energy efficiency projects since both require a careful review of existing and potential new future environmental risks that a project finance might face. Appendix 1 includes a general checklist, detailed audit checklist and a creditor environmental checklist.

ENVIRONMENTAL CONTRACT PROVISIONS

Regardless of the outcome of the environmental audit, there are always a number of contractual provisions that should always be included in any project documentation for the protection of the secured creditor (project developer, lender, investor or other secured party). The purpose of those provisions is to define the responsibility between the owner of project asset(s) and the lessee, energy purchaser, engineering firms, installers, suppliers or other party who may have an interest in the project development and operation. Those provisions need to cover any environmental condition known to exist or that may be discovered or occur subsequent to the transaction. The indemnification, release of liability or any other covenant or agreement assigning liability between the asset owner and the debtor or other parties is only effective between those parties. It would not affect any potential liability that the owner of the asset may have to the EPA or any other federal, state or local regulatory agency.

The transfer of the environmental liability to the parties other than the owner of the asset(s) is not easy to achieve. Most of the environmental liability transfer occurs through specific representations, warranties and indemnifications. Although the purpose and wording of the provisions can vary widely, the basics of those provisions are as follows:

- ***"As Is" Provisions.*** The owner of the project asset(s) provides a provision that the asset is being used (in the case of a lease) or being placed on the property for the production of energy (in the case of an energy purchase agreement) in an "as is" condition, and the owner of that asset makes no representations or warranties regarding the condition of the asset(s). In most cases, the provision states that the "user" (as in the case of a lease) or "purchaser of the energy" (as in the case of an energy purchase agreement) has had an opportunity to investigate the environmental condition of the asset(s) to ascertain that it will not produce any environmental contamination or hazardous substances or emissions as a result of operating the equipment. Although the effectiveness of this type of a provision can be limited under some circumstances, it should never-the-less be incorporated into all project finance documentation. A typical provision might have the following language:

Owner of the Asset(s) makes no covenant, representation, or warranty as to the suitability of the Asset(s) or as to the physical condition thereof for any purpose whatsoever. Debtor acknowledges that it has inspected the property, observed its physical characteristics and existing condition, and has been afforded the opportunity to conduct such investigation and study on and of the Asset(s) as it deems necessary for the purpose of acquiring the Asset(s), use of the Asset(s), or placement of the Asset(s) on the premises, and Debtor hereby waives any and all objections to or claims with respect to any and all physical characteristics and existing condition of the property, including, without limitation, any hazardous materials or emissions in, at, on, under, or related to the Asset(s). Debtor further acknowledges and agrees that the Asset(s) to be acquired, used or placed on the Debtor's premises is to be sold, conveyed to, used, or placed on the premises in its present condition, "as is," and with all faults, known or unknown, and Debtor hereby assumes the risk that adverse past, present, or future characteristics, use and conditions may not have been revealed by the Debtor's inspection or investigation of the Asset(s).

- ***Limitation on Creditor's Obligations***. The creditor may also wish to include limitation on its responsibility for claims of third parties arising out of the use of the Asset(s) by or for the benefit of the Debtor. Many potential claimants could arise in the future either because of the direct environmental damage caused by the asset(s) or the spread of the damage to adjoining property owners. It could also include claims for personal injuries by third parties who are exposed to the environmental contamination (whether real or perceived) and even claims of regulatory agencies for possible penalties and remediation costs. Those claims have the potential of being very significant and the secured creditor cannot overlook those risks in a project finance transaction. A typical provision might have the following language:

Notwithstanding the foregoing Section ____, (the general liability section of the agreement), the liability of Creditor hereunder with respect to Environmental Conditions, whether for remediation or claims asserted against either Creditor, Debtor, or both, shall collectively be limited to the sum of $XXX million dollars ($XXX,XXX,XXX.00); provided, however, that this limitation shall not apply if any claim by a third party or any governmental agency arises solely as a result of any negligent act or omission of Creditor, its employees, consultants, or contractors during the performance of the Environmental Conditions required of Creditor herein, or the use of the equipment by Debtor or Creditor as contemplated under this agreement. In addition thereto, in the event a third party obtains judgment of joint and several liability against both Creditor and Debtor based upon the Environmental Conditions or the use of the Asset(s) herein, either Debtor or Creditor may request and obtain apportionment between Debtor and Creditor of such joint and several liability from a court of competent jurisdiction, and such apportionment shall be made on the basis of this Agreement.

- ***Debtor's Release to Secured Creditor***. In nearly all cases, the secured Creditor will seek to obtain a release of all liability regarding environmental conditions on the asset(s) at time of closing, other than for those conditions that have been identified through environmental audits and that may require remediation before or even after closing. This would also include the use of the asset(s) over the term of the transaction. Most Debtor's do not want to release Creditor's from any and all liability that may result from unknown conditions and therefore such general release provisions may be difficult to obtain. A sample provision may have the following language:

Debtor, for itself and its agents, affiliates, successors and assigns, hereby releases and forever discharges Creditor, its agents, affiliates, successors and assigns from any and all rights, claims and demands at law or in equity, whether known or unknown at the time of this agreement, which Debtor has or may have in the future, arising out of the physical, environmental, economic or legal condition of the Asset(s). Debtor specifically waives the provisions of Section 1542 of the California civil code ("Section 1542") and any similar law of any other state, territory or jurisdiction. Section 1542 provides: A general release does not extend to claims which the Creditor does not know or suspect to exist in his favor at the time of executing the release, which if known by him must have materially affected his settlement with the Debtor. Buyer specifically acknowledges the Buyer has carefully reviewed this subsection and discussed its importance with legal counsel and that the provisions of this subsection are a material part of this Agreement.

The Debtor should specifically acknowledge this provision by either signing the provision under a separate agreement or acknowledging the provision by its signature next to the actual provision in the agreement.

- ***Definition of "Environmental Condition."*** When a Creditor prepares project documentation they should be careful to make sure that all parties agree on what an "environmental condition" and a "hazardous substance" means. Be careful that any definition also incorporates any specific state or local regulatory agency listing of the substances or descriptions of what constitutes an environmental condition since they could be different than the federal descriptions. A typical provision might have the following language:

  "Environmental Condition" shall mean the presence on the property of any "hazardous substance" as that term is defined in any federal, state, county or municipal statue, ordinance, regulation, rule, order, judgment, or decree, including, without limitation, (i) the Comprehensive Environmental Response, Compensation and Liability Act of 1980, as amended; the Resource Conservation and Recovery act of 1976, as amended; the Clean air Act; the Water Pollution Contract Act (the Clean Water Act); the Toxic Substances Control Act, the Safe Drinking Water Act, and the Insecticide, Fungicide and Rodenticide Act, as amended, and the state counterparts of those laws; (ii) any material or substance which is now listed in the United States Department of Transportation Hazardous Materials Table (49 C.F.R. §172.101); (iii) a chemical listed by the State of California EPA Office of Environmental Health Hazard Assessment; and (iv) any contaminant, oil, petroleum product or by-product, radioactive material or by-product, any mining waste, toxic substance, hazardous waste, radioactive waste, or other material, the removal of which is required or the existence or management of which is prohibited, penalized, or regulated by any federal, state, or local government agency, authority, or unit.

  Chemicals used for "everyday uses" are excluded and shall mean the normal use of (i) fuel oil and natural gas for heating; (ii) lubricating, cleaning, coolant, and other compounds customarily used in building maintenance; (iii) materials routinely used in the day-to-day operations of an office project, such as copier toner; (iv) consumer products; (v) materials reasonably necessary and customarily used in construction and repair of the Asset(s) in this project finance; and (vi) fertilizers, pesticides and herbicides commonly used for routine office landscaping.

There are many other provisions that are used in renewable energy project finance documentation concerning environmental issues and could include some of the following:

- Representations and warranties by Debtor in the actual use of the asset(s)
- Representation and covenant regarding compliance with all environmental laws
- Representations and covenants regarding receipt of notices and actions from regulatory agencies
- Exclusion of certain chemicals for routine maintenance from definition of "hazardous substances"
- Creditor's access rights to property for environmental assessments
- Debtor's representations and warranties regarding wetlands, flood plain and special geologic conditions on where the asset(s) will be physically placed
- Debtor's obligations for any remediation of environmental conditions at inception or over the term of the contract or agreement
- Right of entry by Creditor for maintenance or modifications on environmental conditions
- Right of entry by creditor for maintenance or modifications originating from adjoining property or premises

- Contacts with environmental agencies
- Standards for remediation
- Responsibility for permits, manifests and other regulatory documents
- Selection of remedial contractor
- Accounting records for remediation action
- Use of property during remediation
- Completion of remedial work
- Use of hazardous substances by Debtor on the premises where the asset(s) is located
- Landlord's compliance with environmental laws
- Hazardous discharges on the premises where the asset(s) are located including environmental complaints by third parties
- Reporting by Debtor of government notices it receives
- Any environmental events that would cause a default in the underlying project documents by the Debtor
- Testing and monitoring for environmental conditions and defining who has the responsibility

In addition to the above general provisions found in the project finance security agreement, judicious secured creditors would prepare a complete separate document called an "Environmental Indemnity Agreement" as part of the overall project documents (sample is included in Appendix 1). It is intended to be supplemental to other documents evidencing the project finance and the security interest in the project asset(s). It should contain a broad indemnification from the Debtor to the Creditor and relates the indemnity to the underlying debt obligation, so that an act of default in the environmental agreement would concurrently constitute an act of default in the principal project security agreement.

The liability created by CERCLA, RCRA, TSCA and other environmental rules, regulations and statutes, can be very encompassing. The liability is like a mile-long trawler fishing net—it is wide, deep and dangerous to anything that gets caught up in it. No creditor can ignore "the net." Regulators and private third parties alike are always looking for other parties to whom they can allocate a portion of the liability for the expense of cleaning up and remediating an environmental occurrence. The best way to avoid or minimize and environmental liability is to:

— Conduct an environmental audit prior to entering into the financing of the project;

— Include warranties, representations, and indemnities in all transactions documents regarding environmental condition of the property where the project's asset(s) will be placed;

— Use caution performing any type of activities that could be classified as a "management" function during any type of actions under a default of the project;

— Consider a judicial action rather than a foreclosure action (if appropriate);

— Limit collection activities to only essential activities;

— Look into establishing a holding company to acquire title;

— Perform ongoing appropriate environmental audits at each stage of the collection activities;

— Sell and divest of the foreclosed property (if appropriate) quickly after obtaining physical possession; and

— Make sure that your collection and repossession activities do not release any hazardous substances.

ENVIRONMENTAL ATTRIBUTES

As described in earlier chapters, the environmental attributes of a renewable energy project can have significant economic value. Whether the creditor or the debtor can claim them is a direct reflection of the finance structure, the clauses in the security agreement, and any separate supporting documents that are executed. As a general rule, the environmental attributes will always accrue to the benefit of the title holder of the asset in the same manner as are the tax attributes. However, unlike the tax attributes (on a federal level) which cannot be assigned to other parties, the environmental attributes can be assigned. The assignment could be to the debtor or any other third party to the transaction and that assignment would be evidenced by a formal agreement between the owner of the environmental attributes and the party to whom the owner wishes to transfer those attributes to.

The first issue is a proper definition in the project documents that clearly defines exactly what the attribute(s) are. The California Public Utilities Commission has a good definition that they have adopted and which could be applied to most renewable energy projects.

> *"Environmental Attributes" or "Green Attributes" means any and all credits, benefits, emissions reductions, offset and allowances, howsoever entitled, attributable to the generation from the Unit(s), and its displacement of conventional energy generation. Environmental Attributes include but are not limited to any Renewable Energy Credits as well as: (1) any avoided emissions of pollutants to the air, soil or water such as sulfur oxides (SO_x), nitrogen oxides (NO_X), carbon monoxide (CO), and other pollutants (this would include particulate matter (PM), volatile organic compounds (VOC), etc.); (2) any avoided emissions of carbon dioxide (CO_2), methane (CH_4), nitrous oxide, hydrofluorocarbons, perfluorocarbons, sulfur hexafluoride and other greenhouse gases (GHGs) that have been determined by the United Nations Intergovernmental Panel on Climate Change, or otherwise by law, to contribute to the actual or potential threat of altering the Earth's climate by trapping heat in the atmosphere; and (3) the reporting rights to these avoided emissions such as Green Tag Reporting Rights or Renewable Energy Credits. Green Tag Reporting Rights are the right of a Green Tag Purchaser to report the ownership of accumulated green tags in compliance with federal or state law, if applicable, and to a federal or state agency or any other party at the Green Tag Purchaser's discretion, and include without limitation those Green Tax Reporting Rights accruing under section 1605(b) of the Energy Policy Reporting Act of 1992 and any present or future federal, state or local law, regulation or bill, and international or foreign emissions trading program. Green Tags are accumulated on MWh basis and one Green Tag represents the Environmental Attributes associated with one (1) MWh of energy. Green Attributes or Environmental Attributes do not include (i) any energy, capacity or reliability or other power attributes from the Unit(s), production tax credits associated with the construction or operation of the energy projects and other financial incentives in the form of credits, reductions or allowances associated with the project that are applicable to a state or federal income taxation obligation, (iii) fuel-related subsidies or "tipping fees" that may be paid to Seller to accept certain fuels, or local subsidies received by the generator for the destruction of particular pre-existing pollutants or the promotion of local environmental benefits, or (iv) emission reduction credits encumbered or used by the Unit(s) for compliance with local, state or federal operating and/or air quality permits. If Seller's Unit(s) is a biomass or landfill gas facility and Seller receives any tradable Green Attributes or Environmental Attributes based on the greenhouse gas reduction benefits or other emission offsets attributed to its fuel usage, it shall provide Buyer with sufficient Green or Environmental Attributes to ensure that there are zero net emissions associated with the production of electricity from such a facility.*

Similar language can be drafted and employed where the renewable energy project is producing therms or Btus of heat from a renewable energy solar thermal project, co-generation energy project or any other type of energy project where Green or Environmental Attributes are available and inherent in the project finance agreement.

BANKRUPTCY CONSIDERATIONS

Careful and fast actions by the secured creditor needs to implemented if the renewable energy project transaction becomes involved in a bankruptcy proceeding caused by the debtor. The first action starts before the transaction has been executed and requires careful skill in the drafting of the language in the principal security agreement (lease, loan, energy purchase agreement, etc.). Proper drafting reflects two major considerations—perfecting the creditor's security interest in the projects asset(s) against other creditors and making sure that the documentation reflects the correct tax purposes and positions of the parties to the agreement. No creditor wants the transaction re-classified as a loan instead of an operating lease or energy purchase agreement by a bankruptcy court and then face the real possibility of losing the tax attributes that were built into the economic return to creditor. Even worse, the underlying asset could be lost to another creditor or even to the trustee of the court if actions taken (or for that matter, not taken) by the creditor were incorrect when the project documentation was drafted and executed. If the secured creditor cannot enforce its rights to the underlying asset, the terms of the security agreement underlying the project finance, from the secured party's viewpoint, then are rewritten at the worst possible time.

> *"Capitalism without bankruptcy is like Christianity without hell."*
>
> Frank Borman, Astronaut

Under the new federal bankruptcy codes recently enacted, the power of the bankruptcy court not only to stay the enforcement of your contracts default remedies and right to repossession but to allow the debtor to continue used the assets or collateral in violation of the terms of your security agreement can be very detrimental. And, given the possibility of a "cram down" in the event of a confirmed plan of re-organization, secured creditors need to give additional weight to credit risk decisions and to the economic viability of debtor to repay its obligation over the term of the security agreement.

The anticipated economic yield on the transaction could be significantly diminished in a bankruptcy proceeding if rulings of the court go against the secured creditor. A creditor's equity in the value of the underlying assets may be reduced or eliminated entirely if the court were to reduce or eliminate payments or other debt obligations owed to the creditor at the time of the debtor's filing. This could occur concurrently with the automatic stay provisions of the bankruptcy code that is always placed into effect by the filing of the action by the debtor. In almost all cases, it is best to always "just say no" to any requests by the debtor or the court regarding your project finance transaction and attempt to enforce the terms and conditions of the security agreement as you drafted it.

Of particular importance is the distinction of having your transaction viewed as either a "true" lease or executory energy purchase agreement versus being recast as a transaction intended as a "security instrument." Depending upon the circumstances, the classification of a creditor as a lessor or seller of energy may dramatically affect rights and remedies that were drafted and executed between the parties at the inception of the project finance. Most secured creditors wish to have the agreement be classified as an "executory" agreement (Bankruptcy Code section 365(a)) meaning that the parties to the agreement have not yet performed all their duties as stipulated in the agreement. Put another way, if either side stopped performing the contract it would be an actual breach of contract. For example, in a lease, the lessee has to pay rent and lessor has to provide equipment. Another example, in an energy purchase agreement, the energy provider must create the energy from the underlying project assets and the energy purchaser must pay for that energy when it is generated. An executory contract definition can best be described using that definition by suggested by Professor Vern Countryman.[16]

> *"Civilization is in no immediate danger of running out of energy or even just out of oil. But we are running out of environment—that is, out of the capacity of the environment to absorb energy's impacts without risk of intolerable disruption."*
>
> Vijay Vaitheeswaran, Indian journalist (2002

A contract under which the obligation of both the debtor and the other party to the contract are so far unperformed that the failure of either to complete performance would constitute a material breach excusing the performance of the other.

In most cases, a true lease/operating lease and an energy purchase agreement would be considered to be an executory contract or agreement. Executory contracts and agreements are treated differently from general unsecured claims in a bankruptcy court in three important ways.

- First, a debtor (or a bankruptcy trustee) gets to decide whether to agree to perform or refuse to perform its obligations under an executory contract. In bankruptcy parlance, agreeing to perform translates to "assumption" of the contract and refusing to perform translates to "rejection" of the contract.
- Second, while the debtor is thinking about what to do, the secured party to an executory contract will have to keep on performing as if no bankruptcy had been filed.
- Third, if the debtor assumes the executory contract and wants to keep using the asset or benefits from the use of the asset, the debtor has to pay ("cure") in full any payment or other defaults and show that it can actually perform in the future too. Additionally, if the debtor wants to assume and assign the executory contract to someone else, commonly a buyer of its assets, at a minimum the debtor has to cure any defaults and the new buyer has to show that it can actually perform under the contract in the future.

Another important consideration in the drafting of the proper financial instrument that secures the renewable energy transaction is to: 1) make sure that the terms of the transaction call for immediate termination upon repossession of the assets after default although such repossession is not an election of remedies and the creditor retains its right to obtain monetary damages, and 2) that there should be no grace periods for curing defaults that have not expired at the time of the filing of a bankruptcy petition are automatically extended for sixty days after an "order for relief" or, if it occurs later, to the end of such grace period, including any suspension of such period occurring on or after commencement of the case.[17] In general, the project documents should provide that defaults will take place immediately upon occurrence of the particular event of default, with immediate termination of the transaction or conversion to a month-to-month or "at will" tenancy, and a grace period only to reinstate the transaction, so that the right to cure the default is then a condition subsequent to termination or modification of the transaction and not a condition precedent.

Section 101(4) of the bankruptcy Code also states that a claim by a creditor includes any right to payment, liquidated or not, fixed or contingent, matured, disputed, equitable, secured or unsecured. It also includes a right to an equitable remedy for breach of performance under the properly drafted executory documents in the project finance if such a breach gives rise to a right of payment to the creditor. Thus, all legal obligations of the debtor, no matter how remote or contingent, would accrue to the properly secured project creditor. This classification as a secured creditor with an executory contract (and not one viewed by the court as a "disguised" asset loan or finance agreement) provides the project creditor with the ultimate protection in a bankruptcy proceeding. The basic important distinction is that in a true lease or energy purchase agreement the creditor retains all risks and benefits as to the value of the asset at termination of the agreement. If the transaction were re-classified from an executory contract to one in the nature of a "security" finance agreement (loan, conditional sales contract, chattel mortgage, etc.), the payments would be looked at as consisting of interest and principal and the creditor would be at a distinct disadvantage. Legislative history of the bankruptcy code also recognizes the criteria for the true lease vs. security interest distinction under the UCC in addition to citing the criteria of FASB 13 and various SEC regulations (see prior chapters).

A properly drafted "liquidated damage" clause (which is not unreasonable, penal in nature, or unconscionable) would in most cases also be enforceable to establish the project creditor's claims for the entire amount of its damages and not be subject to section 502(c) of the Code which disallows any right to payment arising from a right to an equitable remedy for breach of performance.

Additionally, if the project financing transaction is not assumed by the debtor or the court after "an order for relief" has been granted or the stipulated rental if the lease is assumed, the claims by the creditor for the use of the assets between the time the bankruptcy filing occurred and the order for relief was granted, are classified as administrative expenses under section 503(b) of the Code and are entitled to priority status for payment above other creditor's claims.

The "automatic stay" that goes into effect the minute the bankruptcy proceeding is filed affects the creditor, regardless of the ultimate decision by the court as to whether the transaction will be classified as an executory contract or not. However, the court can grant the creditor ex parte relief from any stay under section 362(f) if such relief is necessary to prevent irreparable damage to the interest of an asset if such interest will suffer such damage before there is an opportunity for notice and a hearing. That relief can often be obtained (although sometimes limited in nature) for the necessary protection, maintenance, or preservation of the asset. Good examples would be attempted sales by the debtor, lack of guard service, improper or illegal use, failure to maintain insurance, lack of appropriate maintenance procedures, or the immediate threat of any such types of acts or omissions. Another example would be the failure to use the energy produced by the system and causing the asset to overheat, prematurely fail, cause damage to other equipment, etc. Obtaining immediate relief from the automatic stay is very important to the project creditor should a bankruptcy filing occur.

Furthermore, section 362(d) (2) of the Code provides that the court "shall grant relief from the automatic stay against an asset on request of the secured party" after notice and a hearing, if the debtor does not have an "equity in such property" and that property is not necessary for an effective reorganization. This protection—available for the project creditor who has a properly drafted executory contract—is highly valuable when putting pressure on the debtor to assume or reject your contract. Most debtors, after looking at their alternatives, will quickly realize that if the asset would be returned to the creditor, their utility costs would immediately skyrocket and be much higher than the costs of keeping the renewable energy generation system on the premises and assuming the contract as provided for in the Code.

A determination by the bankruptcy court that the project contract is in the nature of a security agreement would preclude relief for the automatic stay unless the court also finds that the value of the collateral (see Fair

Market Value below) is less than the amount of the secured debt, resulting in no economic equity for the debtor. Here again, it is the project creditor who has a valid executory contract who comes out the winner. The project creditor in its filing for relief from the automatic stay needs to urge the court in its filing that:

1. The debtor furnish clear evidence that it *must* use the asset to continue operating; and
2. That debtor demonstrates a *high* degree of likelihood that it can be reorganized within a reasonable period of time.

In general, the creditor is allowed possession of the asset if the debtor does not agree to perform all of its obligations under the contract within sixty days after commencement of the case, cure all existing defaults within such sixty-day period and cure all post-bankruptcy defaults within thirty days after such default or within such sixty-day period, whichever occurs later. The lesson to be learned is to file for relief from the automatic stay immediately upon learning of the bankruptcy filing.

"Adequate protection" is another important consideration should the project creditor find itself in a bankruptcy proceeding where the underlying asset(s) it has as an owner or for security under the project finance structure, is being addressed by the court. A project creditor may be provided adequate protection by periodic cash payments to the extent of the decrease in the value (see Fair Market Value below) of the creditor's interest in such property, an additional or replacement lien to the extent of the decrease in such value, or such other relief as will result in the realization by the project creditor of the "indubitable equivalent" of the value of its interest in such property. This opens the door for a potential increase in the pricing of the energy being sold to the debtor in the case of an energy purchase agreement or some other such equitable economic value being granted by the court. The secured project creditor should promptly reapply for relief from the stay and request additional conditions of adequate protection in the event of any subsequent deterioration of the project assets or of the debtor's financial condition.

In summary, the burgeoning growth of the cleantech renewable energy project finance market has resulted in an awareness of the conflicting rules of law and the bankruptcy rules are certainly no exception. The project creditor must in all cases promptly secure good bankruptcy counsel both in the drafting of the project finance documents and also anytime that a bankruptcy proceeding is commenced by a debtor. The preservation of the project creditor's rights and claims are paramount in any court proceeding, especially the bankruptcy court. Time is of the essence in such events, and no delay in affirmative actions taken should ever be allowed—protect your creditor rights and your underlying project assets!

FAIR MARKET VALUE (FMV) OPTIONS

The goal of most operating leases and energy purchase agreements is to realize the best economic return using tax attributes, revenue over the term of the agreement plus a salvage value for the underlying asset at termination of the agreement or a future date after one or more agreement renewal periods. In equipment financing transactions that have historically covered computers, medical systems, printing equipment, machine tools, construction equipment, etc.—all of which have an estimated marketable useful life of 15 years or less (in the case of computers, a term of three years or less)—estimating the fair market value at the end of a finance term of seven years or less was not rocket science. In fact, the value of much of those types of equipment could easily be established by published books that clearly stated values of equipment over time or even public auctions where the equipment values were established by the prices paid for the equipment by successful bidders.

Estimating some future fair market value for many types of renewable assets is much more difficult for three reasons. First, the asset can frequently have a useful life of thirty to fifty years or longer. In the case of solar photovoltaic systems, the warranty from the manufacturer is 25 years and could be even longer. Add to that, the "useful" life of the asset which common sense dictates a term of a minimum of twice the warranty period, and then a creditor faces many wide choices of issues that need to be addressed when considering the "fair" market value over such an extended term.

Secondly, in a practical sense the renewable assets have never had a book published that gives values for the various assets on used equipment because no market has ever existed. It probably won't be long before some systems may be up for auction either because the asset may have been repossessed by the creditor or the asset has been returned to the creditor after the initial term of the agreement has been completed in the normal course of business. But, because most financing terms on renewable assets are between ten and twenty years initially, and most project finance agreements have not yet been in existence that long, there just has not been any reliable method of getting a good estimate on the value of the equipment 10-20 years or more down the road on assets that have a useful life far exceeding the original term of financing.

Thirdly, in the case of renewable energy systems that generate either electricity or thermal energy, the value is in the comparison of utility costs in future years to the costs of how much those same kilowatt hours or thermal units cost as a result of the asset that has been financed. It is an accepted fact that utility costs for electricity and fuel (natural gas, fuel oil, etc.) for heating will continue to accelerate over the next thirty years as fuel costs to the utilities continue to increase and the supply of fossil fuels they need to supply the commodities to the consumer continue to decline. Electricity costs have continued to climb at over 5% per year in most of the United States and the costs of fuel for heating (and other industrial applications) have been rising even faster than that of electricity. Therefore, that value of one unit of energy produced by a renewable energy generating asset continues to become more and more valuable to the owner as the asset continues to produce over the useful life of that asset. Conceivably, the system could go up in "fair market value" over the useful life and not decline at all. On the other hand, if a radically new technology were to develop that made an energy generating asset become obsolete simply because it could produce that much more power per square foot of available area of production than the existing renewable energy system, the existing older system could lose nearly all of its value. That scene is not likely in the short term but could occur over the longer useful life of the RE asset.

Therefore, since a considerable economic risk in energy producing assets is taken by a creditor in most transactions, that economic value in the future plays a critical role in realizing the expected overall economic return to the risk taking creditor. This is not the case, however, if the transaction were simply structured as a loan or other type of secured credit structure where the future value risk of the asset has been accepted by the debtor and not assumed by the creditor.

The correct definition of fair market value is "the price that an interested but not desperate buyer would be willing to pay, and an interested but not desperate seller would be willing to accept on the open market assuming a reasonable period of time for an agreement to arise." Therefore, the fair market value should mean and refer to the value, as reasonably determined by creditor, which would be obtained in an arms-length transaction between an informed and willing buyer-user under no compulsion to buy and an informed and willing seller (the creditor and secured party) under no compulsion to sell. It is the highest price, expressed in a currency, an asset would bring, in an open and unrestricted market, between a willing buyer and a willing seller who are knowledgeable, informed, and prudent, and who are acting independently of each other.

> *"Quality in a product or service is not what the supplier puts in. It is what the customer gets out and is willing to pay for. A product is not quality because it is hard to make and costs a lot of money, as manufacturers typically believe. This is incompetence. Customers pay only for what is of use to them and gives them value. Nothing else constitutes quality."*
>
> Peter Drucker (1909-2005)

I.R.S. Revenue Ruling 59-60 provides that Fair Market Value is the price that would be demanded and paid in a sale involving a willing buyer under no compulsion to buy and a willing seller under no compulsion to sell, assuming both buyer and seller have reasonable knowledge of the relevant facts about the asset. Revenue Ruling 59-60 has been around for 40 years and has stood the test of time when it comes to the fundamental principles of valuing a business, equipment, for divorce or any other purpose. The text of IRS ruling 59-60 is as follows:[18]

> *"In valuing the stock of closely held corporations, or the stock of corporations where market quotations are not available, all other available financial data, as well as all relevant factors affecting the fair market value must be considered for estate tax and gift tax purposes. No general formula may be given that is applicable to the many different valuation situations arising in the valuation of such stock. However, the general approach, methods, and factors which must be considered in valuing such securities are outlined."*

It should be noted (as stated in earlier chapters), that book value is an accounting term as opposed to FMV which is a true realistic economic term determined as stated above. Technically, book value is simply the assets of the company less their depreciated value, all at their values as stated on the books of the company. It's usually not an accurate measure of the real value of the asset. For that reason, it's seldom relevant.

In the end and to avoid the potential of a properly structured set of project finance documents being disallowed by the IRS from intent of the parties to the project finance transaction simply because an option to the purchase the financed assets at some point of time in the future at either a specified amount (or even with a "floor" or "ceiling" definition) or at anything less than true fair market value as defined by the IRS is just not worth the risk for the creditor or the debtor. If anticipated returns were to be put at risk because a transaction is re-classified by the IRS as other than a true lease or other intended structure and the tax attributes lost because of that event, it would be extremely detrimental to the creditor or investor and even to the debtor.

Bankruptcy courts also carefully consider any purchase option by a debtor other than fair market value to be indicative of a "disguised" sales finance agreement and the project creditor would lose the protection afforded to them under the executory contract statutes. If that were to occur, the court would consider the financed asset as belonging to the estate of the debtor and allow any equity in the asset to go to the benefit of the other creditors, and not to the creditor whose intent was to keep any equity in the asset for their own account and not that of the bankruptcy estate or other creditors (secured or unsecured).

PRODUCT LIABILITY

Product liability has always been a "in the back of my mind" problem for any creditor involved in the purchase (resulting in an "ownership" position) and receiving a subsequent economic return on their investment from a debtor who will directly use the equipment (as in the case of a direct equipment finance agreement), who will "rent" the equipment from the owner of the assets (as in the case of an operating lease agreement), or who will purchase the energy being produced by the underlying project assets (as in the case of an energy purchase agreement). This would include negligence, warranty, and strict liability in tort. There would naturally be a distinction between a "merchant-lessor" who might be a seller of the equipment as part of its normal business activities as well as financing the sale under a lease arrangement, an energy project developer who is involved in the design, selection and installation of an energy system that will be used to sell the energy produced by the project to the energy purchaser/debtor, and the finance lessor who simply finances the transaction under a capital finance lease structure.

Whether a transaction is a "true lease," "energy purchase agreement," or a "security interest finance" transaction under Article 9 of the Uniform Commercial Code (or even tax liability and accounting treatment) has no bearing on product liability. Instead the courts have looked to the criterion of "superior knowledge of the goods" of a merchant in the assets as the prerequisite to a nonconsensual product liability decision. It is the debtor's reliance of the merchant's superior knowledge of the goods that makes liability appropriate. Here again, it is proper drafting of all project documents that can be a critical difference as to how the creditor will be treated for product liability claims by the debtor (or third parties as they may exist).

U.C.C. § 2-104(1) states: A "merchant" means a person who deals in goods of the kind or otherwise by his occupation holds himself out as having knowledge or skill in peculiar to the practices or goods involved in the transaction or to whom such knowledge or skill may be attributed by his employment of an agent or broker or other intermediary who by his occupation holds himself out as having such knowledge or skill. Clearly, this can raise particular concerns for the project developer or creditor who becomes the secured creditor under an energy purchase agreement. The liability of merchants under an implied warranty theory in non-sales areas such as leases and bailments dates back more than 150 years.[19]

Warranties to fitness are regarded by law as an incident of a transaction because one party to the relationship is in a better position than the other to know and control the condition of the chattel transferred and to distribute the losses which may occur because of a dangerous condition the chattel possesses if a party were to be injured. These factors make it likely that the party acquiring possession or use of the asset, or benefit from the "product of the asset" (as in the case of an energy purchase agreement), will assume it is in a safe condition for use and therefore refrain from taking precautionary measures themselves.[20] Superior knowledge is the basis for liability for the merchant-lessor or energy provider. The lack of such knowledge precludes liability for a creditor that is a finance lessor or is acting as a lender under a loan or other type of equipment security agreement.[21] Whether a transaction is a true lease (or an energy purchase agreement) or a transaction in the nature of a security interest depends upon the subjective intent of the parties, objective determination of which has generated an abundance of confusion. Whether a transaction is a true lease or a transaction with a security interest is not determinative of product liability. Rather, the test is whether the creditor is a "merchant" or "finance" creditor. It should be noted that UCC section 9-217 says that the mere existence of a security interest or authority given to the debtor to dispose of or use the collateral does not impose contract or tort liability upon the secured party for the debtor's acts or omissions.

There are a number of theories of liability that should be considered when drafting the renewable energy project finance documents. The first is negligence. For example, under an energy purchase agreement where the energy provider provides full maintenance and sells the energy to the debtor would generally be considered as a "merchant." Although the energy provider would be responsible for securing their own warranties on the assets, they may not be guilty of "negligence" if someone was injured on the energy system. The basic question often boils down to whether one who endorses a product for his own economic gain, and for the purpose of encouraging and inducing the public to acquire the benefit of the installed assets may be liable to an energy purchaser (or other third party) who is injured because it is defective and not as represented in the endorsement.[22] Damages from negligence that results in physical harm could be established if:

1. A party negligently gives false information to another if that party reasonable relies upon such information.
2. Such negligence may consist of failure to exercise reasonable care in ascertaining the accuracy of the information or in the manner in which that information is communicated.

In the end as it regards negligence, the creditor can rest somewhat comfortably knowing that the plaintiff must prove that the creditor was negligent in the care, maintenance, or other services provided and in the selection of the product, inspection of the product or total misrepresentation of the product itself. The creditor cannot be held to a higher standard than "reasonable care."

The second theory of liability under common law is in the area of warranty. Warranties may be both expressed and implied. A finance lessor would be immune for the warranty of merchantability by definition since the debtor selected the equipment and not the creditor. The fitness warranty would only be applicable through an expressed warranty by the creditor. Contrast this with that inherent to an energy provider under an energy purchase agreement. All of the risk of the warranty of merchantability and warranty of fitness on the equipment rests solely with the creditor. If the equipment doesn't perform and therefore doesn't provide the energy that could be sold to the debtor, the debtor simply uses more energy from the current utility provider and it is the creditor who has financial losses. Warranties of any nature are simply inapplicable in the rendition of services such as would occur under an energy purchase agreement contract. When there is no superior knowledge of the creditor, with respect to either selection or maintenance of equipment, there should be no warranty liability. [23]

Therefore, the biggest concern is when the transaction is to be classified as an operating lease by the parties. Clearly, the courts have upheld that a finance lessor or traditional equipment lender is not liable under any of the warranty theories. It is also quite clear that the energy provider under an energy purchase agreement assumes all of the risk of warranties since that creditor would be the only party injured if the equipment warranties didn't keep the creditor whole on the equipment fitness or merchantability provisions. That leaves only the operating lease type creditor in question. That true lease lessor (also known as the operating lease lessor) would have the debtor/lessee sign disclaimers in their project finance documentation. The disclaimer of implied warranties in a lease agreement is governed by Article 2 of the UCC as it is in sales.[24] Additionally, the lease agreement in most cases requires that payments must continue in the event that the equipment fails to perform as expected or represented.[25] This disclaimer is often found in the "hell or high water" provision signed by the debtor when they accept the equipment and authorize the creditor to pay the supplier(s) of the equipment. Therefore, the debtor's rights under the warranty provisions of the agreement are essentially against the manufacturer who must cure all defaults of the warranty liability. The debtor's obligations to the creditor of the project finance will continue unabated and without interruption as a result of any warranty liability theories.

> *"A nation that can't control its energy sources can't control its future."*
>
> Barack Obama, The Audacity of Hope: Thoughts on Reclaiming the American Dream)

Obviously, the simple solution to product liability issues is to purchase product liability insurance when appropriate. The creditor, whether a merchant in the case of an energy purchase agreement or a finance lessor or lender in other transactions, could negotiate is own product liability coverage or, better yet, endorsements to the policies of the suppliers of the equipment (get the actual certificate of endorsement in all cases) with the right to notice of cancellation and the opportunity cure the primary insured's defaults. An umbrella liability coverage policy would also be appropriate in many cases. See Uniform Commercial Code above for additional insight on applicability to product liability issues.

TAXES

There are a number of different tax obligations that a creditor faces in drafting and subsequently servicing a renewable energy project finance transaction. Of course, there are the standard taxes known as income taxes or the taxes on the profits of a business entity. However, there are a number of other tax issues that need to be addressed. Those other tax issues can be different from state to state. The discussions below apply to the state of California, but are examples of the issues involved in other states also and should be considered when drafting and servicing the project contract.

Sales Tax

Each project finance transaction is usually subject to sales taxes when the underlying assets of the project are purchased, the importation of the equipment into the taxing jurisdiction for rental purposes, or the collection of rental or energy production payments. More specifically, the collection of a tax on rental or sale of energy payments is commonly called a "use" tax. Most sales tax jurisdictions define an equipment lease or similar agreement (this would include a PPA agreement) as, "a contract under which a person secures for a consideration the temporary use of tangible personal property, which may not be on his premises, and is operated by or under the direction or control the person, lessee or their employees." Beyond that very simple definition, however, all other issues concerning sales and use taxes can become radically different, depending upon the taxing authority.

It is important to note that just because lease income and equipment acquisition costs are treated certain ways for federal, state or county property tax purposes, doesn't mean they will be treated the same for sales or use tax purposes.

Adding to the complexity in sales tax components is the overwhelming changes each year in the sales tax rates within the U.S. Since every new or existing renewable energy project would have sales tax components either initially or over the term of the project it would be wise for senior management to carefully track those changes. Most projects could have multiple tax rates and taxing entities. The average combined U.S. sales and use tax rate for 2010 hit a new record average of 9.64 percent. Tables 8-2 and 8-3 summarize the sales tax rate changes from 2003-2011 and average U.S. sales tax rates in 2011.[26]

Project owners are faced with an array of taxing entities and the names that are attached to each assessment vary: sales tax, use tax, transaction tax, privilege tax and gross receipts tax are but a few. Also, each taxing authority has a unique method of measuring, timing, assessing, and requiring the project owner to report those assessments. New rules and regulations are passed at a record pace (see above) and renewable energy asset owners are expected to comply. Making tax management an early and integral part of every financial transaction can yield some significant cash, tax and earnings benefits, as well as improving internal controls associated with the financial reporting of income taxes (including costs of audits).

A creditor who executes a lease, PPA or other energy related agreement of any nature as the preferred type of transaction has three *options*:

Table 8-2: Sales Tax Rate Changes 2003-2011

Type of Change	2003	2004	2005	2006	2007	2008	2009	2010	2011
State Rate Changes	5	4	3	3	2	5	8	3	3
County Rate Changes	104	188	144	118	181	275	215	68	70
City Rate Changes	183	248	298	281	279	280	240	191	188
District Tax Changes	4	5	30	12	31	30	15	20	23
New Taxing States	0	0	0	5	0	0	0	0	0
New Taxing Counties	66	32	21	67	46	8	9	9	5
New Taxing Cities	194	130	110	86	137	98	101	51	57
New District Taxes	45	41	63	73	112	101	119	213	113
Total	601	648	669	642	788	797	707	555	459

Table 8-3: Summary of Average U.S. Sales Tax Rates by Year

Year	State Average Rate	County Average Rate	City Average Rate	District Average Rate	Combined Average Rate
2003	4.7585	1.4335	1.6045	0.9530	8.7495
2004	4.7618	1.3933	1.6118	0.9415	8.7084
2005	5.2818	1.4187	1.6195	0.9330	9.2530
2006	5.3219	4.4242	1.6290	0.9172	9.2923
2007	5.3182	1.4194	1.6364	0.9249	9.2989
2008	5.3839	1.5275	1.6402	0.9212	9.4728
2009	5.4781	1.5387	1.6502	0.9133	9.5803
2010	5.5224	1.5451	1.6598	0.9163	9.6436
2011	5.4880	1.5301	1.6698	0.9165	9.6044

1. Pay the sales tax on the equipment to the supplier when purchased.
2. Provide the supplier with a state sales tax resale certificate that exempts the lessor or owner from paying the sales tax to the supplier, but instead obligates the lessor or owner to pay the sales tax to the Franchise Tax Board (the sales tax regulatory authority in the case of the state of California) on its own quarterly sales tax return.
3. Don't pay the sales tax on the acquisition price of the equipment at all. Instead, the lessor or owner would charge a "use tax" on the total rental payments or energy payments billed and received (including all other charges that are billed).

If the remitter elects either Option #2 or #3, they must obtain the necessary "resale" certificates from each tax jurisdiction in which a potential tax would be payable. This can be quite a burden since it could include permits at the state and county levels in addition to possibly the city level of every location where an energy system is located. The remitter might then be required to post performance bonds (normally requested when new permits are issued) and they would have to file quarterly reports in each and every one of those jurisdictions where equipment is located. These reports are required every quarter that a valid re-sale certificate is in the remitter's possession *whether or not taxes are due.*

Because of the resulting compliance, audit (and they will come...) and staffing costs needed to meet those basic requirements, most smaller owners of energy systems elect to pay the sales tax to the supplier or EPC contractor when the equipment is purchased, thereby eliminating a major cost center in their operations.

In any of the above cases, an additional sales tax would be due when the equipment is finally sold at the expiration of the contract term. The tax would be based on the actual sales price at the time that the equipment is eventually sold. This would again be paid by the creditor on their quarterly tax return for the period in which the final sale occurred.

A lessor must be careful to ascertain whether there are also certain "local" taxes also due which can occur in some cities and counties throughout the U.S. To make the issue even more complicated, some taxing authorities have a tax rate that varies or is tiered, depending on the gross receipts collected over the tax period and is irrespective of the actual tax the lessor is charging and collecting from the individual lessee.

The cautious asset owner's next hurdle is called a "timely election." It is not only necessary to make the choices, but it is important to do so quickly for each transaction. Generally, the election must be made on the return for the reporting period in which the equipment first enters service (commissioned), and once the election is made, *it is irrevocable for the entire contract term* of that transaction. When an asset owner has a single debt obligation covering equipment from several suppliers to be delivered in two or more different quarters, the taxing method election chosen in the first reporting quarter constitutes an irrevocable election. That election applies to the transaction in subsequent quarters.

If the equipment owner wishes to utilize Option #1, the equipment acquired must be placed in service in *substantially the same form as when it was acquired.* This is known as the "same form rule." The purpose of this rule is to prevent energy system owners from acquiring equipment at a low cost, making major modifications to the equipment to raise its value, and then receiving revenue from the debtor at a much higher price (thereby avoiding the payment of sales tax on the higher value of the asset). In this situation, the energy system owner is required to select Option #3, collecting taxes on the gross receipts method.

Many creditor trade associations have challenged the gross rental receipts definitions in the courts but have met with little success, as have attempts to pass legislation to exclude such obviously "double taxed" items as property tax payments made by the debtor to the creditor from being assessed as gross receipts. As unfair as it may seem at times, items such as license, royalty, advance rentals, charges designated as fees or interest, property tax payments paid the debtor, "mandatory charges" which could include warranty extensions or maintenance contracts, and delivery charges must still be included in the gross receipts calculations. Late charges and some license fees such as those charged by the Department of Motor Vehicles could still be exempt. Check carefully with your advisors.

Another misunderstood, and therefore problem-laden area, is that of an assignment of the contract to a third party. Most energy system owners will at some time during the contract assign the transaction to a funding source (either with recourse, non-recourse or partial recourse) at various times, and it is the manner in which that assignment occurs that can result in major sales tax assessments.

Taxing authorities have attempted to attack a creditor's assignment of a contract as a "sale," and therefore, it being classified as a taxable event. If that attack is upheld, the "sale" is taxed based on the *gross unpaid rents or future receipts assigned*. Many initial contract creditor's (and therefore the capital asset owner) have faced major tax assessments because their transaction assignment had terms wording in them such as "sell," "sale," or "assignment of all right, title and interest" instead of, or in addition to, the *required word*, such as simply "assign" or "hypothecate." Usually, it is the funding source who insists on that kind of working, often unaware of the tax problem they are creating. It is import for energy system owners to point out to the funding source or third party that the resulting tax would have to be collected *from the funder* by the assigning party, which results in more reasonable wording requirements.

Assignors (the energy system owner) must also be aware that it is not the intent of the parties that taxing authorities focus on (unlike the courts), but rather the document verbiage itself. This focus has been an ongoing battle ground between industry trade associations and state auditors and likely will not change until new regulations are drafted.

This issue alone can cause major adverse tax assessment for an assigning energy system owner under audit. California lessors in particular should be aware that auditors consider three major types of assignments and assess taxes differently on each:

1. Assignment of a right and creation of a security interest (the best for the assigning party).
2. Assignment of the contract with transfer of right, title, and interest for security purposes.
3. Assignment of the contract and all right, title, and interest thereto as a sale.

Parties acquiring the contract (and possible ownership rights in the equipment) must be aware that when the third type of assignment occurs, the assignee (funding source) has assumed the position of the energy system assignor. When the tax being collected is measured by the gross receipts method, the assignee is required to hold a seller's permit and is *obligated* to collect, report and remit the sales or use tax to the proper taxing authority.

Items that sales and use tax auditors look at include:

- What is the extent of recourse or continuing financial liability of the assignor to the assignee?
- Was sales tax paid at contract inception or is use tax being assessed on the gross receipts?
- Does the assignor retain a residual position in the equipment after the initial contract term is being assigned?
- Are residuals pledged to secure the underlying financial obligations that the assignor has to the assignee?
- Is the assignment for "security purposes" only?
- What federal tax treatment did the assignor elect in its federal income tax return regarding the assignment of the transaction?

Another concern that an energy system owner might have regarding sales and use tax payable in the state of its domicile is where the equipment is located outside the state in which they are located. In most cases, there would be no sales or use tax due in the owner's state. However, the owner of the energy system would probably need to obtain an ongoing sales/use tax permit in the taxing jurisdiction where the *equipment is physically located*. Taxes due in that district will have to be collected, reported, and remitted to that out-of-state jurisdiction. Moreover, even an "occasional" transaction involving tangible personal property in another tax jurisdiction are being scrutinized by increasing aggressive local taxing authorities desirous of generating revenue for their own district. Therefore, getting the appropriate tax permits in each state or district in which an energy system owner might have equipment physically located is usually desirable.

In *early contract termination* situations, caused either by default or early contract termination, court cases in many states have upheld the position that all proceeds from an early termination are taxable at the time the event occurs. This includes all unpaid rental payments (less discounts, if any), sale of the assets, etc. It makes no difference whether sales tax was paid on the equipment at contract inception, or whether use tax was collected on the revenue stream. Many energy system owners get into problems here in computing their tax obligation, assuming incorrectly that since tax was paid on the equipment when acquired, the only tax that needs to be collected at termination is that on the purchase price option amount or residual balance due as was collected from the debtor. In fact, the system owner must collect sales tax on the *gross payoff* of the contract, not just the residual. There are steps that could be taken to avoid this and one way is to make sure that there are two distinct actions. One is for the payment of the discounted future rental or revenue stream and the second transaction (preferably at a later date) for the actual sale of the equipment. Again, it is suggested that legal or tax counsel be consulted when an early contract termination occurs. Also, if personal property taxes are due to be reported at the time of contract termination, don't forget to include those upcoming assessments in the termination calculations.

> *"The best way to make a fire with two sticks is to make sure that one of them is a match."*
>
> Will Rogers, U.S. humorist and commentator (1879-1935)

The energy system owner must keep sales and use tax records for at least four years, unless the taxing entity specifically authorizes their earlier destruction. This retention period may be even longer if you need to prove the acquisition details of the capital assets to an auditor (who typically audits three years of records at a time—not just a single year). These records should include all gross receipts from the sale or use of the tangible personal property, original invoices on the purchase of the assets, any termination payments and when they occurred, all records of the actual sale of equipment at end of the contract term and all schedules of work papers used in connection with the preparation of the sales tax returns.

Energy system asset owners who wish to be successful over the long term must take steps to establish internal guidelines that dictate what elections are taken and when they are taken. They must also review their assignment documents (if used) with each funding source and make sure that all taxes have been properly assessed on early terminations, regardless of the contract inception tax options elected. Policies regarding sales and use tax treatments on your contract should be carefully reviewed at least annually with both tax and legal counsel to assure that documentation adequately reflects the true intent of the parties to each transaction. Lenders and other funding sources also should take steps to assure that they will not become liable for future sales or use tax assessments that are not being adequately paid or accounted for by the owner assignor in the event of the untimely closing of the assignor's business.

Personal Property Taxes

In the U.S., the property tax is an ad valorem tax (meaning that a tax is imposed on the basis of value) that an owner of an asset pays based on the value of the property being taxed. There are three types of property taxes: land, improvements to land (e.g. buildings) and personal property (generally considered "movable" property). Renewable energy projects involve the later—personal property. Forms of property tax assessments and the valuations vary widely between taxing jurisdictions. Tangible personal property is any property, except land or improvements, that may be seen, weighed, measured, felt, or touched, or which is in any other manner perceptible to the senses. This includes additions, improvements, replacements or items that are considered "fixtures." Often, these taxes are called the "unsecured taxes" of a taxing jurisdiction.

In most cases, property taxes are assessed at the local government or county level. The county then gives a pro-rata share to each city or other taxing jurisdiction within the county. What is taxable, when the tax reporting and tax payment is due, and the taxation rates vary widely between jurisdictions. The property tax is given as a percentage and is often called a "mill levy." A mill is one-thousandth of a dollar. The taxing authority will multiply the assessed value of the property times the mill rate and then divide by 1,000. The taxes collected fund budgets for schools, police, fire stations, hospitals, garbage disposal, sewers, road and sidewalk maintenance, parks, libraries, and miscellaneous expenditures.

The assessor often will use one of three methods of determining the value of a renewable energy system:

- Market/Comparable Sales
- Cost
- Income Capitalization

Generally speaking, the range of annual personal property taxes is between .5% and 5% of the assessed value of the asset. The amount will go down some over time as the value of the personal property decreases in value—usually because of age. However, the amount of decrease can be very different between taxing authorities even on the identical item of equipment. You can always appeal the value given by the tax assessor, but unless there are very extenuating circumstances, most taxpayers will not win in an appeal attempt. Valuation can often be subjective by the taxing authority. The assessor will value the property at 100% of the current market value (which will likely change over time). Market, or true and fair value, is the amount that a willing and unobligated buyer will pay a willing and unobligated seller.

The good news in many renewable energy projects is that many times the assets are exempted from personal property taxes. This is particularly true on solar systems. Thirty states allow for the exemption of solar systems from property taxes. However, if the asset(s) of the renewable energy project are being located in a state that does not allow an exemption from property taxes, it could have an effect of the yield in the project. This effect can be mitigated by having the debtor be responsible for the property tax. Alternatively, the creditor could include the cost of the annual property taxes in their financial analysis when preparing the project finance proposal.

The owner of the asset is required to file an annual property tax statement with the taxing authority where the asset is located. Tangible personal property is taxable where it has established "permanent situs" (location), regardless of where the owner lives. Each state has different dates on which the tax is reportable and due. Some are January 1 of each year while others are April 1 of each year and others dates can apply depending upon the state. Most forms require the same basic data (in addition to the owner's information):

- Name of the debtor or business name where the asset is sited
- Exact physical address of the asset location
- Exact description of the asset
- Date the asset was purchased
- Date the contract started
- Date the contract will end
- Purchase price of the asset
- Any trade-in or down payment the owner received when purchasing the asset
- Whether the asset was new or used when acquired
- Repayment terms of the contract with debtor if applicable (as in a capital or operating lease) including the periodic payment amounts
- Who is obligated by the contract to pay the tax (e.g. lessor or lessee)
- Personal property category (e.g. solar PV, solar thermal, co-generation, fuel cell, etc.)
- Mailing address of the debtor if different than the situs address

Normally, it takes the taxing authority up to sixty days to prepare and mail the tax statement to the owner. Shortly thereafter (usually within 60 days of the billing), the tax will be due to the tax collector. The amount of tax due becomes a lien on the asset. The lien is in effect from the time the assessor makes the assessment until the taxes are paid. For example, an assessor values personal property in June, and the lien is in effect until the taxes are paid on August 1. If the tax remains unpaid, the treasurer may place a lien on the owner's other real and personal property. The lien follows the property. This means that a new owner can be held liable if the previous owner does not pay the tax. Personal property taxes not paid by the due date are subject to interest and penalties in addition to the tax that was due.

The tax collector doesn't care whether the creditors agreement with the debtor states that the tax is payable by the debtor. The collector will look directly to the "owner" of the asset both to file the return and to pay the taxes. Often, as in a typical operating lease agreement, the lessee doesn't pay the lessor in a timely manner but the lessor, as owner of the asset, is still responsible for paying the tax when due—whether collected by them or not from the lessee. On large projects, this could cause a significant cash flow problem for the creditor. It is wise to carry cash reserves in transactions where there could be a property tax due and one or more of the debtor's don't pay the tax to the creditor when due.

> *"Sir, I do not know, but someday you will tax it."*
>
> Michael Faraday, English scientist noted for research in electricity (1791-1867)

Renewable energy project asset owners have long complained that the property tax on business equipment is inconsistent, arbitrary, and inefficient. A deep divide exists between taxpayers and tax agencies concerning the fundamental fairness of the application of the personal property tax. In particular, the role of obsolescence as a factor in depreciation is the subject of an ongoing debate between taxpayers and assessors. For purposes of valuing business equipment, the concept of "useful life" should include economic and technological obsolescence, as well as physical deterioration but often doesn't. In fact, some equipment may have a negative value, because the cost to get rid of it or remove it exceeds the value. Most assessors will still carry any asset at a minimum value of 20% of the original assessed value, no matter how old or useful the equipment is. In the end, most parties including the assessors agree that the compliance costs are out of proportion to the tax generated from these businesses.

Most owners of assets under renewable energy projects should also be extra careful when evaluating whether property taxes apply when the debtor is a "non-taxpaying entity" such as found with governments, universities, cities, etc. Check carefully with the assessor in the county where the equipment is located to ascertain whether it should be reported or not. Using California as an example, the value of PV equipment that is subject to local assessment is excluded from the real property's value (Cal rev & Tax Code § 73). The exclusion has no specified time limit, but lasts only until there is a change in ownership of the PV property, at which point the property would be reassessed and may increase in value. ABX1-15 enacted in 2011 clarified that sale-leasebacks and other structures commonly used to finance PV systems do not trigger a reassessment.[27] The same property, if owned by a utility however, would be assessed by the state (and not the local taxing district) using a composite of all three accepted valuation methodologies. Centrally-assessed properties are not eligible for the exclusion described above.[28] Similar discrepancy can be found regarding the personal property tax application on SREC receipts (using the income approach of assessments) to a system owner. As can be seen, there are many traps for the unwary renewable system owner that varies within a state as well as between states. As a result, there is significant disparity in the level of property tax policies on renewable energy projects—hence, owner beware.

The applicability of personal property taxes to renewable energy projects, and solar in particular, is a complex, arbitrary and changing set of laws. Great caution needs to be taken by the investor/project owner since using the wrong assumption could easily wipe out much if not all of a projects projected return. Some of these states also have policies that allow local governments to opt-in or opt-out of providing an exemption or special assessment.[29] Also, remember that just because something is exempt from property taxes this year, doesn't mean they will be exempt next year!

Lastly—be prepared for audits. These can come from every jurisdiction that a return is filed. Often these will come from the jurisdictions where the largest valuation of assets resides. Although it can vary, most jurisdictions have rules that if more than a certain dollar amount of assets are reported on property tax returns in that jurisdiction, they assessor is required to perform an audit every three to four years. When the audit comes, it will always cover more years than just the most recent tax year or reporting period. The owner will have to provide proof of all items reported in the property tax filing to include copies of invoices, cancelled checks, copies of project contracts, debt agreements, UCC-1 filings, billing statements, etc.

MARKET DISRUPTION

A creditor to a renewable energy project may want to consider incorporating a "Market Disruption" clause in the underlying project security agreement or provide a separate supporting document. Such a clause may be very critical in a financial market that is experiencing a significant disruption in historical operations as is often seen in a financial crisis and severe economic disorder. Frequently, a creditor is relying on funding to the project that is coming from specific financial market mechanisms and should that funding source not be available at the time of final funding for a project, the clause would allow a creditor to substitute another funding source for the project with a resulting change in the rates (and sometimes the terms and conditions) of the contract. The invocation of the clause would allow the creditor to increase the rate in the agreement to reflect the actual cost of funds to the creditor. The clause is intended for use by parties that envision pricing certain project finance transactions based on an index or other third-party price source and, as a result, wish to provide for an alternative basis for determining the Contract Price should the relevant index or price source be disrupted, substantially altered or no longer published.

SUBORDINATION, NON-DISTURBANCE AND ATTORNMENT

When a creditor finances renewable energy projects, they must be cognizant of two issues that could dramatically affect the performance of the contract they have negotiated—tenants' rights relative to present and future property financing issues and priority of the project finance instruments relative to existing and future tenants' rights. Those tenant rights could have a profound effect on how—and even if—the creditor will be able to collect the amounts due under the project financing terms and conditions. Generally, the rights of a landlords' lender upon some "future financing," as the landlord may view it, or upon foreclosure of landlord's property are just not top priorities in the minds of either the landlord or the tenant when a real property lease is negotiated. Astute parties to the real property lease or roof lease terms and conditions (as in the case of an energy purchase agreement in a renewable energy project), will ensure that they will focus on the rights of affected third parties to carefully consider the benefits that all can gain from doing so. The subordination, non-disturbance and attornment agreement (SNDA) is the document that the landlord, tenant and creditor under the energy project finance transaction often employ to resolve how the rights and obligations will be addressed. A lot will depend on the amount of money that is spent on "tenant improvements"—certainly the case when considerable sums are spent on assets found in the typical renewable energy project. The SNDA agreement can often be hotly negotiated, depending upon the bargaining positions of the respective parties. The bargaining position of a tenant can be greatly enhanced when the tenant presents the financial commitment they and the project creditor are making in improving the value of the property and premises.

The typical SNDA is an agreement between a lender and a tenant in which the tenant acknowledges that the their lease is subordinate to the landlord's mortgage, and as long as the tenant is not in default under its lease, the tenant will not be disturbed if the landlord defaults under the mortgage. The goal of the energy project creditor is to be sure that no party could invalidate the existing facility lease with the landlord during the term of the energy project financing which would have the real possibility of major economic problems for the creditor. This term should also consider not only the original term of the project finance but also any possible renewal or contract extension terms that may arise. The energy project creditor must realize that the mortgage lender's goal is to ensure that any favorable leases on the real estate will continue and at the same time to retain the freedom to terminate a below-market or other problem lease in case of foreclosure of the property. If the creditor's debtor were to be perceived by the mortgage lender to fall into one of these categories, that lender may try to cancel the lease with the debtor of the energy project and in turn cause serious problems for the renewable project creditor.

The SNDA will address how and when the rights of a tenant will be subordinate to the rights of lenders or, at lenders' option, senior to the rights of current or future real property lenders. The SNDA will assure a tenant that their rights to the premises will be preserved (non-disturbed) on certain conditions within their control, even if the landlord defaults on its loan to the mortgage holder and the mortgage holder forecloses on the real property. This is important for all project creditors. The "attornment" part of the SNDA assures a creditor that the tenant will attorn to the mortgage holder that they will continue as a tenant of the new landlord or a purchaser following a foreclosure. It would be a serious blow to a creditor in project finance if their debtor, a tenant, were forced to vacate the premises if a mortgage lender were to foreclose on the landlord and end up with the real estate through the foreclosure proceeding. About half the states of the U.S. allow the mortgage holder to pick and choose the leases it wants to retain upon foreclosure. In states where a tenant's rights of occupancy are not clearly recognized in the event of a foreclosure, the tenant should almost always insist that the current lender enter into a non-disturbance agreement even if there is no requirement by a creditor on a renewable energy project. This will mean that the tenant's rights will be automatically protected as to the rights of any possible future lender which might take its interest subject to a tenant's occupancy, but which did not enter into an agreement of subordination, non-disturbance and attornment.

> *"We know how to fix the problems in America because we have the owners manual."*
>
> SOURCE: *The Huffington Post* 2012-04-09

It is not uncommon that a new lender to a landlord to require current tenants who have signed leases with the landlord to sign a "subordination and attornment" agreement when the new financing is finalized. What is left out is the "non-disturbance" component. A tenant and their creditors' (as found in the case of renewable energy project financiers) want to be assured that the new lender will agree that the tenant need not fear the loss of use of the premises. By this mechanism, the real property lender retains the lease despite a foreclosure. Be aware, however, that occasionally the landlord's mortgage lender may use this opportunity to require additional provisions governing the relationship with the tenant. Typical "additional" provisions requested could include:[30]

- The tenant's waiver of claims against the lender for landlord defaults that occurred under the lease prior to foreclosure;
- The tenant's waiver as to the mortgage lender of any offsets or defenses that the tenant may have against any prior landlord;
- An agreement that the tenant will give the lender notice of any default under the lease and will permit the lender some additional time to cure the default;
- A prohibition against any assignment or subleasing without the lender's prior written consent;
- A statement that the mortgage lender will not be responsible to return any security posted with the prior landlord unless actually received by the lender; and
- A statement that the mortgage lender will not be bound by lease amendments and rent reductions made without the lender's prior approval

Another simple document that astute lenders frequently require in conjunction with the SNDA is an Estoppel Certificate. An estoppel certificate is ordinarily a simple form requesting information regarding the lease term, amount of rent, and the amount of the security deposit. The estoppel may also ask the tenant to confirm that the lease is still in effect and that neither the tenant nor the landlord is in default under the lease. If the debtor is a tenant of the facility where the assets of the energy project will be physically located, the estoppel certificate will serve as an independent confirmation for the credit file that the tenant is not in default under the current plant lease with the landlord. The estoppel should have a statement that provides a recitation of the reasons why the creditor needs the certificate, language that the creditor will rely on the tenant's statements in the certificate and a statement that the tenant is aware of the fact that the creditor is relying on the certificate to provide funding on the renewable energy project by giving the creditor assurances that it should rely on the assurances they are providing in the estoppel certificate. A sample Estoppel Certificate is in *Appendix 1*.

In the end, the bargaining power of the parties will determine the exact advantages or disadvantages in the terms that end up in the final negotiations. It is important for both the creditor and the debtor in the renewable energy project to inform the mortgage holder (and the landlord if applicable) that the assets being placed on the property will add a considerable amount to the property value that is serving as the collateral for the note under the mortgage. The increase in the property value will add significant leverage in the negotiations of the SNDA. Two sample SNDAs are included in *Appendix 1*.

INSURANCE

Insurance on the underlying assets of a renewable energy project is obviously a key requirement of any project finance documentation. The costs of the underlying assets are very high and it is paramount that adequate insurance coverage be provided as part of the properly structured transaction. The creditor must protect its investment. Depending upon the final finance structure, one or more parties will be required to provide insurance on the equipment over the term of the finance contract.

There are two key components of the insurance requirements. First, there needs to be adequate insurance covering the types of risks inherent in the finance structure, and secondly that the creditor's interest in the underlying insurance policies be recognized by the insurers. The easiest of the two requirements is the insurers knowing of the creditor's interest in the proceeds of the policies. In most finance structures other than an energy purchase agreement, the debtor will be mandated to provide adequate all risk insurance coverage on the asset(s). Although it is possible for the creditor to provide the coverage if they wished to or, if requested by the debtor, to have the creditor select an insurance provider on the debtor's behalf. Any costs associated with that coverage would then be built into the financing terms so that the costs would be covered. A copy of a sample Insurance Coverage Request is found in *Appendix 1*.

There are two basic types of coverage that most creditors would seek to have in effect. The first is casualty coverage and the second is liability coverage. In most cases, the same insurer would provide both coverage's as part of a general insurance policy. There are times when in addition to the basic coverage, a lender may elect to secure coverage that exceeds the basic coverage and in fact could obtain blanket excess coverage that would cover all finance transactions they enter into.

All insurers are willing to provide a certificate of insurance to the creditor when requested to do so by the debtor. In addition, they will provide the creditor with a form called "438 BFU." The 438 BFU form (called a Lender's Loss Payable Endorsement—copy in Appendix 1) is a standard form that all insurers use when requested. It states the terms of the coverage and agrees to provide the creditor with a notice in advance of the expiration date or with notice of default for non-receipt of a paid premium. It is highly recommended that the creditor get this endorsement and then set up a proprietary tickler procedure for follow-up. This is a rather simple task to perform and should never be overlooked by the creditor whose assets could be at risk for loss without it.

Occasionally, other types of insurance coverage could be requested by a prudent creditor. For example, life insurance on one or more principals who would generally be personal guarantors in the project or specialized environmental insurance to coverage perceived environmental risks. This list could be quite extensive and must be evaluated by costs and the related marketing and pricing ramifications.

It is not uncommon to see larger companies providing self-insurance for all or a portion of the risk coverage the creditor seeks. Again, be careful that there is a commitment by the insurer or a trustee (in the case of self-insurance) of notices of expiration or loss of coverage for any reason whatsoever.

Most insurance clauses in a financing or project finance documents should be effective for liability coverage in addition to the casualty loss possibility. The liability protection is there for a possible claim by a third party resulting from an injury from the projects assets. This is easily accomplished by the creditor and debtor being named as joint beneficiaries and any payment upon a possible loss is then simplified.

Two final considerations regarding insurance under the renewable energy project finance are the amounts of coverage and the deductions. Generally, common sense sets these parameters unless there are extenuating circumstances. Be sure that any casualty coverage be for the full replacement value, and nothing less. Insurance companies like to insure only for the depreciated value which is a major concern for the creditor. Since in most cases, the assets are depreciated in six years or less on many renewable energy projects, and yet the assets have a life expectancy of fifty years or more it is very conceivable that with a project financing term of ten years a critical shortfall in insurance proceeds could occur without a creditor insisting on a full replacement value stipulation.

> *"Not only will atomic power be released, but someday we will harness the rise and fall of the tides and imprison the rays of the sun."*
>
> Thomas Alva Edison, U.S. inventor (1921)

In light of complete company failures by some insurers in today's market, it would be advisable to carefully review the strength of the insurer prior to accepting coverage. It does little good to have uncollectable coverage if the insurer goes out of business at any time during which coverage must be in place. The creditor should add this concern to their documentation checklist under the insurance section.

Finally, if the project is funded under an energy purchase agreement where the creditor played a critical or significant role in the selection of the assets or even in the engineering or design of the final system, it would be prudent to carry products liability coverage. Courts have not been unknown to have placed liability on the creditor for a product causing damage in some manner. The issue here is the creditor as a "merchant" and is discussed earlier in this chapter.

PROJECT CONSTRUCTION

Engineering, Procurement and Construction (EPC)

This is the contract that is normally executed between the energy project developer and the construction company who has been chosen to build the project. This instrument is what enables the construction contractor to purchase the required materials and components of the energy system, and then to construct the system. The principal contractor (often called the "general" contractor) will sub-contract many of the components of the system out to other specialty contractors. This is normally done at a "fixed" price. It is the contractor that takes the risk for performance, scheduling and budget.

Frequently, in energy projects, the contractor is known as the "integrator"—particularly in renewable energy generation projects. As an EPC contractor they will design, obtain permits, arrange for government rebates for the owner, negotiate interconnection agreements with the utility, order components, design the component integration, arrange for all necessary subcontractors to install the energy system and do the final commissioning of the project after it is completed. All warranties on the components are fulfilled through the integrator.

The system owner or developer would use an EPC contract for a number of reasons as opposed to building the project themselves including:

- Move the design and installation risk away from themselves
- Insulate the owner/developer from changes in component and construction costs
- Provides a single point of contact for all project progress
- Provide a third party to engineer, permit and commission the project
- Fixes the finished project cost with any over-runs accruing for the account of the EPC provider
- Eliminates labor issues that might arise
- Eliminates environmental issues that might arise during the construction of the project

Usually, the EPC contract is paid in mutually agreed upon installments that are based on certain project task completions or milestones. Many of those dates can occur as a result of components being delivered to the project site and having to be paid for by the EPC contractor. Coordination with utility companies, subcontractors, government permitting offices, public regulators, insurance companies, lender's providing construction financing and modifications needed (including engineering and design) as the project is built out or the scope of the project changes. Projects that are finished on time and with minimal problems are always a result of good communication between all parties to the project. A more comprehensive evaluation and insight to EPC agreements is published by Mayer Brown: "Worlds Apart: EPC and EPCM Contracts: Risk issues and allocation," by Phil Loots and Nick Henchie, November 2007.

A typical EPC contract would include the following elements in the agreement:

- Name of developer and/or integrator
- Site host and site address
- Effective date of the contract
- Estimated permit submittal date
- Estimated procurement and construction start date
- Scheduled substantial completion date
- Complete description of the project and detailed list of components
- What the contract price is and when the payments under the contract will be made
- Who the utilities are at the host site
- What the estimated annual energy production will be from the project
- List of all applicable incentive sources and who will receive the incentives

Additionally, there are usually many attachments to the EPC agreement that could include:

- Site access
- Scope of work
- Specifications and submittals
- Project schedule
- Progress payment schedule
- Commissioning schedule
- Data acquisition (monitoring) system
- Integrator form documents
- Shading study if applicable
- Warranties
- Insurance requirements
- Approved products/components

The EPC contract is usually unique to a specific project and not a generic document. However, all of the contracts would include the standard recitals, definitions, default provisions and their remedies, dispute resolution, waivers, severability, confidentiality and survival sections. Because of the complexity of this document, it is highly suggested the legal counsel be obtained by all parties and having counsel be the lead in contract negotiations.

PERMITTING

Energy projects will require a great deal of permitting before they are started or finished, will include building and environmental permits, and can take anywhere from 10 days to 5 or more years to obtain. Without a comprehensive permitting plan for the project, it will never be built. Lenders and investors in particular will require all permitting to be in place before a single dollar is committed to the energy project. Although there is a lot of puffery and commitments to "expedited permit process" by agencies, departments, utilities and regulators the reality is that such a concept is highly elusive. Granted, smaller projects are permitted quicker and with less coordination than larger projects but all energy projects will need to be permitted before they can move forward with obtaining required funding, project construction and operations. The key difference between small and large energy project permitting is that often smaller projects cannot absorb engineering review costs that might be required by a permitting agency.

Figures 8-4 and 8-5 are pre-construction and final inspection (with utility interconnection process) flow charts that are very simplified examples of a small energy project. Large energy projects require significantly more sophisticated processes.

Often, permits can be required to be obtained periodically even after the project is built to be sure they are being operated safely and within environmental guidelines (often called "operating" permits). The continuing permits after project completion and commissioning can come from local municipalities as well as federal and state regulators. This would include Title V permits from the Environmental Protection Agency (EPA), air permits from local and state air emissions agencies, CO_2 reporting to state and federal agencies, solid waste operating permits, rainwater runoff permits, OSHA permits, etc. Therefore, just because the project is "built" with permits, it doesn't mean that permitting ends after project commissioning.

For PV energy production projects, the Solar America Board for Codes and Standards published a complete whitepaper and report entitled: Expedited Permit Process for PV Systems: A standardized Process for the Review of Small-Scale PV Systems and written by Bill Brooks, P.E. of Brooks Engineering.

Large scale energy projects will require an even more complex set of permitting. There are many books and reports published regarding specialized energy projects and it is suggested that these be reviewed as part of any specific energy project and don't forget to consult with your legal counsel on this project documentation component.

CONCLUSION

There have been hundreds of books written on commercial documentation from a financing perspective over the last dozen decades. Commercial law, bankruptcy law, IRC codes and interpretations, FASB and IASB guidelines, environmental laws, energy concepts, new asset titles and rights, and many other factors are continuously changing. Courts, SEC, accounting boards, insurance companies and other peripheral entities are constantly reinterpreting and re-evaluating contracts, intent of parties, and societal perceptions of "fairness," "transparency" and "obligations to future generations." As a result, no book written on a specific type of financing like renewable energy can ever be current or inclusive of all the issues—directly or indirectly.

There have been many books, white papers, doctoral thesis' and court opinions recorded. It would not appropriate to give an extensive list of all the resources that are available to readers when evaluating this subject. However, I would suggest that if you are interested in reading more comprehensively, you might consider looking into the following books (besides the obvious search on the subjects via the internet).

1. The Handbook of Leasing—Techniques and Analysis by Terry Isom and Sudhir Amembal (ISBN 0-89433-157-4)

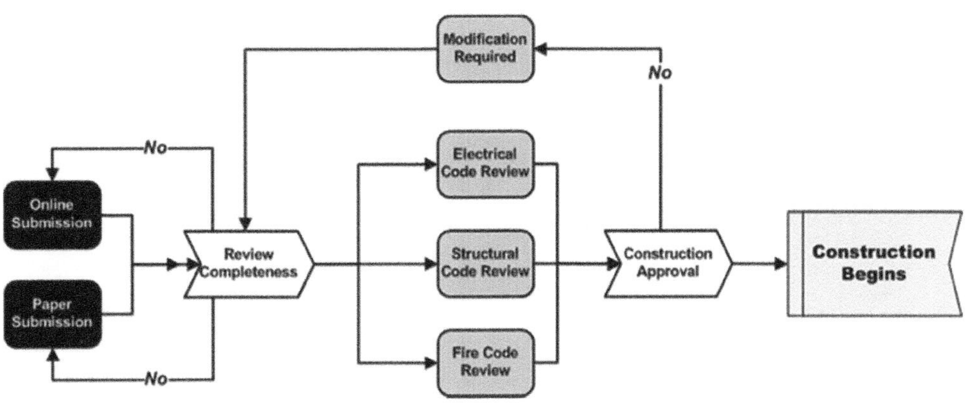

Figure 8-4: Final Inspection & Utility Interconnection Process

2. The Handbook of Equipment Leasing by Amembal & Isom (ISBN 0-945988-00-1)
3. Operating Leases—The Complete Guide by Sudhir Amembal (ISBN 0-9673948-0-5)
4. Many publications by the Practicing Law Institute, Matthew Bender, Clark Boardman, and other legal publishers.

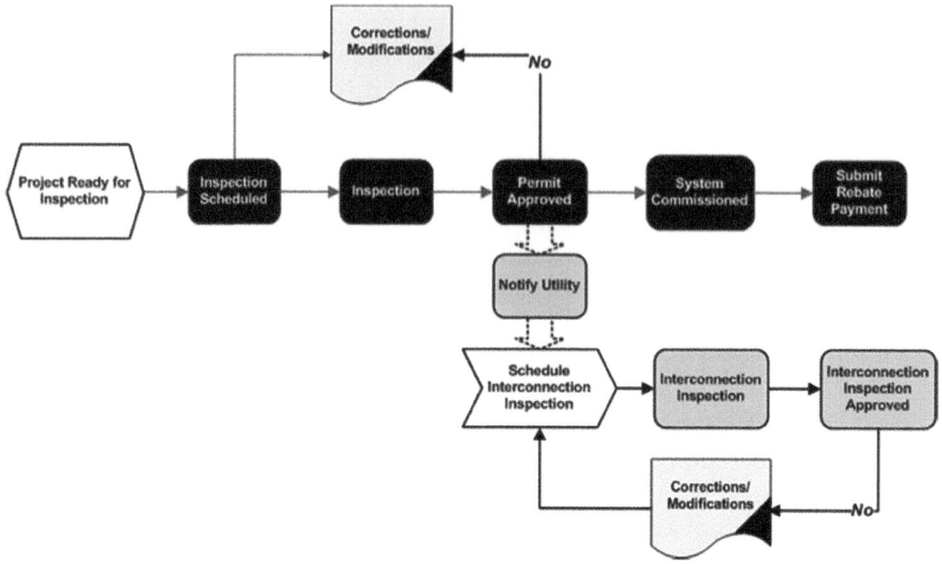

Figure 8-5: Pre-construction Permitting Process

References

1. See *http://www.irs.gov/pub/irs-pdf/p925.pdf* for the full IRS guidance document.
2. Income from investments, dividends, interest, royalties and *capital* gains. Portfolio income does not come from passive investments and is not earned through normal business activity. Typically, income from interest on money that has been loaned does not count as portfolio income.
3. Section 481 adjustments are adjustments required due to changes in accounting methods.
4. It should be noted that the Investor(s) could pay most (up to 80%) of its funds on a pay-in schedule of up to 10 years under the regulation, but at least 75% of the Investor(s) reasonably expected investment must be fixed and determinable and not contingent. The 20% investment must be invested at the "in-service date" of the assets or sooner.
5. Section 45 (originally adopted in 1992) of the Internal Revenue Code anticipates that the owner of a project many have more than owner—like most LLP or LLC flip partnerships have. The tax credits would then be shared by the owners in direct proportion to their respective equity interests.
6. Section 1-201 (37) of the Uniform Commercial Code provides:
7. "Security Interest" means an interest in personal property or fixtures which secures payment or performance of an obligation. The retention or reservation of title by a seller of goods notwithstanding shipment or delivery to the buyer (Section 2-401) is limited in effect to a reservation of a "security interest." The term also includes any interest of a buyer of accounts or chattel paper which is subject to Article 9. The special property interest of a buyer of goods on identification of such goods to a contract for sale under Section 2-401 is not a "security interest," but a buyer may also acquire a "security interest" by complying with Article 9. Unless a lease or consignment is intended as security, reservation of title hereunder is not a "security interest" but a consignment is in any event subject to the provisions on consignment sales (Section 2-326). Whether a lease is intended as security is to be determined by the facts of each case; however, (a) the inclusion of an option to purchase does not of itself make the lease one intended for security, and (b) an agreement that upon compliance with the terms of the lease the lessee shall become or has the option to become the owner of the property for no additional consideration or for a nominal consideration does make the lease one intended for security.
8. See UCC §9-313
9. See *http://www.law.cornell.edu/ucc/2A/overview.html* for a complete copy of Article 2A of the Uniform Commercial Code.
10. Title 15 U.S.C. 1601, 1640, 1667 et seq. § 1601.
11. 42 U.S.C. § 9601(20)(F)(iv).
12. B. Mattsson and P. Olsson 2001. 'Environmental audits and life cycle assessment'. in Dillon, M.; Griffith eds. *Auditing in the Food Industry—From Safety and Quality to Environmental and Other Audits*, Woodhead Publishing
13. *The Small Business Source Book on Environmental Auditing*, United States Environmental Protection Agency, EPA 233-B-00-003, May 2000
14. CERCLA §107(b)(3), 42 U.S.C. §9607(b)(3) (1980)
15. Richard H. Mays, "Environmental Laws: Impact on Business Transactions," The Bureau of National Affairs, Inc., 1992, Page 51
16. Countryman, *Executory Contract in Bankruptcy*: 57 Minn. I. Rev. 439, 460 (1973).
17. *Equipment Leasing-Leveraged Leasing*, 2nd Edition, Practicing Law Institute, page 104
18. Revenue Ruling 54-77, C.B. 1954-1, 187, superseded.
19. *See* Hoisting Engine Sales Co. v. Hart, 237 N.Y. 30, 142 N.E. 342 (1923)
20. 45 N.J. at 446, 212 A.2d at 775
21. Hawkland, "The Impact of the Uniform Commercial Code on Equipment Lease," 1972 U. Ill. L.F. 446
22. 276 Cal. App. 2d 680, 81 Cal. Rptr. 519 (1969)
23. Northwest Collectors, Inc v. Gerritsen, 64 Wash. 2d 690
24. *See, e.g.*, Todd Equipment Leasing Co. v Milligan, 395 A.2d 818 (Me. 1978)
25. *See, e.g.*, Citicorp Leasing, Inc. v. Allied Institutional Distribs., Inc., 454 F. Supp. 511 (W.D. Okla. 1977)
26. Vertex, Berwyn, PA., *www.vertexinc.com*
27. California State Board of Equalization, *Draft Guidelines for Active Solar Energy Systems New Construction Exclusion*, 2011
28. David Yeung, California Board of Equalization, Personal Communication, February 28, 2012
29. Database of *State Incentives for Renewables and Efficiency, State Property Tax Incentives for Solar Projects*, 2012, *http://www.dsireusa.org/userfiles/image/summarymaps/solarpropertytaxmap.gif*
30. Douglas J. Sanderson, "Subordination, Non-disturbance and Attornment Agreements: Meeting the Legitimate Goals of Landlords, Tenants and Lenders; Negotiation Techniques," McCandlish & Lillard, P.C., Fairfax, Virginia

Chapter 9

Investing in Climate Change

Global climate change and the components of that change have become a significant concern to government, companies and citizens alike. The single largest solution to the problem is found in the massive reduction of CO_2 emissions from the burning of fossil fuels worldwide. This includes transportation sources, stationary sources (power plants) and even that of agriculture. The single most effective tool that can be used to reduce CO_2 emissions is the replacement of use of fossil fuels with that of renewable energy sources. This chapter will provide an overview of history of carbon emissions and an analysis of what can be achieved in carbon emission reductions through the effective use of renewable energy generation methods.

HISTORY OF CARBON EMISSIONS

The need to act now to adapt to climate change and to find ways to mitigate the effects being felt around the world is urgent. Evidence has shown that the amount of carbon in the atmosphere has reached an 800,000 year high.

Global climate change and GHG emissions are all about opportunities for renewable energy project developers and financing entities and minimizing risks for the potential clients of energy projects. There has been unprecedented activity in US regulation and legislation on climate change since January 2009. The high level of activities are occurring on both a federal level and also a state level and suggests many new activities for the renewable energy sector. Opportunities abound with many more coming to light on a weekly basis. The operative words are "*be prepared!*" The opportunities exist and are being further promulgated for offsets and other incentives of every type. Investing in renewable energy projects where the underlying assets have GHG reduction attributes associated with them is an investment strategy just now being realized and exploited. To a large extent, an analysis of forthcoming legislation on climate change needs to be viewed by comparing the changes to what has occurred in Europe over the past seven years since it is highly likely that the monumental changes coming will parallel the European structure.

Talk about a fast-track legislative process, take into consideration the following:

- **April 2, 2007**: U.S. Supreme Court's decision in *Massachusetts v. EPA*, 549 U.S. 497 (2007), concluded that greenhouse gases meet the Clean Air Act definition of an air pollutant and instructed EPA to regulate CO_2 as a pollutant.
- **March 10, 2009**: EPA's proposed GHG reporting rule was signed, in accordance to *FY 2008 Consolidated Appropriations Act* (H.R. 2764; Public Law 110-161). EPA issued the rule pursuant to its authority under the Clean Air Act. The proposed rule received over 17,000 written comments!
- **April 17, 2009**: EPA's Proposed *Endangerment* and *Cause or Contribute Findings* for GHG under the Clean Air Act was signed.
- **September 22, 2009**: EPA's final GHG reporting rule was signed.
- **January 1, 2010**: EPA mandatory reporting of GHG emissions begin.

The principal responsible parties for GHG reporting are the same individuals that most project developers and lenders would deal with directly in putting together a renewable energy project.

- Corporate Environment, Health, and Safety (EH&S)
- Facility Operations/Management
- General Counsel
- Finance and Treasury

However, with the potential for carbon allowances and offset credits to be traded in ways similar to other commodity instruments (under the proposed cap-and-trade program), requirements for internal controls may be comparable to existing internal control requirements for financial data and reporting. Such controls may be required to meet future commodity and carbon market regulations, as well as management and disclosure requirements under Sarbanes-Oxley or even new reporting requirements under International Accounting Standards Board (IASB) regulations for accounting.

> *"Some of our businesses use more energy than others, but our strategy everywhere is the same... first, reduce our use of energy as much as possible. Then, switch to renewable sources of power where it makes economic sense. And, over time, as a last resort, offset the emissions we can't avoid."*
>
> Rupert Murdoch, Founder, Chairman, CEO of News Corporation

Currently, there are three different possible reporting criteria, depending where the company is located. A reporting company could be subject to one or up to three. This includes California under AB32, RGGI in the northeast U.S. and now the EPA federal reporting requirements. It is possible that in some cases, as the federal reporting requirement is implemented the other regulators may to allow respondents to comply with the federal requirements and no longer enforce their own regulations. This is sure to cause a period of confusion and added compliance costs to industry. It is clear that reporting automation and scalability will be the key in adapting to multi-jurisdictional reporting and the various disclosure requirements. As the carbon reporting markets develop, requirements for internal controls over the carbon data may be comparable to existing internal control requirements for the reporting of financial data. It is apparent that a robust third party audit and verification industry will be developed to meet this need.

The six gases covered in the regulation are:

- CO_2 (Carbon Dioxide)
- CH_4 (Methane)
- N_2O (Nitrous Oxide)
- SF_6 (Sulfur Hexafluoride)
- HFC (Hydroflurocarbons)
- PFC (Perfluorocarbons) and other fluorinated gases

The EPA regulation is expected to cover over 10,000 facilities or 85% of the GHG emissions in the U.S. and most of those will have their emissions coming from stationary combustion sources. Surprisingly, the three largest industries are cement and lime manufacturing, and the livestock industry that has copious amounts of manure as a by-product (think methane gases). The threshold for being included in the regulated list is any company emitting 25,000 metric tons of CO_2 equivalent (e) per year. The reporting is on an annual basis with initial date collection beginning on January 1, 2010. The first annual reports will need to be submitted to the EPA on March 31, 2011 for the 2010 year.

The cleanest fossil fuel, natural gas, emits about half as much CO_2 per unit of energy as coal does when burned for electricity generation. While the U.S. natural gas resource base is only about 9 percent of the world total, some 85 percent of the natural gas consumed in the United States is produced domestically, and much of the rest comes from Canada. In recent years, natural gas production from conventional resources has declined. But production from unconventional resources, such as coal beds, tight gas sands (rocks through which flow is very slow), and natural gas shales has increased. Higher natural gas prices in 2007 and 2008 led to expanded drilling from unconventional sources. This expansion increased total U.S. gas production by about 9 percent in 2008 after a decade of its being roughly constant. The result has been stable natural gas prices for several years now and likely will remain fairly stable over the next decade.

Putting the reporting threshold into layman terms, 25,000 metric tons of annual CO_2e is equivalent to:[1]

- Approximately 4,600 passenger vehicles
- 58,000 barrels of oil consumed
- Energy use of approximately 2,300 homes
- Burning approximately 130 railcars' worth of coal
- Approximately 1 million propane cylinders used for home BBQs

All documentation must be retained for 3 years including:

- Data used to calculate the GHG emissions for each unit, operation, process and activity and must be categorized by fuel or material type
- Documentation of the processes and methods used to collect data for GHG emissions calculations
- Documentation of GHG emissions calculations and methods used
- Identification of key facility personnel responsible for collection of the emissions data
- A written GHG Monitoring Plan

- Annual GHG reports
- Missing data computations
- Results of all required certification and quality assurance tests of monitoring systems used to provide data for the annual GHG report
- Maintenance records for monitoring instrumentation

Facilities and suppliers can cease reporting of their annual GHG emissions if: a) after five consecutive years of emissions below 25,000 metric tons CO_2e/year, b) after three consecutive years of emissions below 15,000 metric tons CO_2e/year, or c) if the GHG-emitting processes or operations are shut down.

There is a great deal of uncertainty as events are unfolding in the climate change arena. The uncertainty is both in the regulatory world as well as the legislative world including:

- Uncertainty as to the timing of the regulations and legislation
- Uncertainty as to the scope of the regulations and legislation

Uncertainty as to the pricing of the carbon emissions and the resultant energy pricing to the cost of the carbon emissions reductions. This uncertainty then creates the concern of the compliance costs to industry. These costs will include first of all the costs of going back historically to ascertain what your potential emissions were in 1990 (or some other date selected by the regulators) and then secondly, the costs of reducing current and future emissions down to the 1990 level. Add to that, the natural growth and accommodating that growth through a strategy of emission reductions first to the 1990 level by 2020 or some other date and then even further in subsequent years as will be mandated. To get to those targeted levels means huge reduction in energy costs (since a very large component of a company's carbon footprint comes from the use of electricity and natural gas or propane) by some other less emitting technology for that energy—which is highly likely to be multiple forms of renewable energy generation "on site" rather than off the grid or pipeline. Hence, the opportunity exists for RE developers, lenders and investors to build many more energy project assets. However, the window of opportunity may be limited in some areas such as landfill methane and coal-bed methane projects.

Any energy project that builds assets that can throw off emission offsets and garner other incentives will be very attractive to invest in. These are basic carbon reduction strategies that will be able to be leveraged in the project finance structure and will need to be analyzed carefully. That strategy must start with a "carbon footprint audit" to establish the baseline needed. That then needs to be expanded by looking at the technologies and policies that will be used to reduce the customer's carbon footprint to levels it must achieve under a regulatory scheme or legislative mandate. Part of that carbon footprint reduction strategy is the analysis each customer will use to compare their carbon footprint to their competitors and be used for green-branding bragging rights. This point is very important to senior management but not necessarily true for the facilities manager or engineering team. The latter are much more concerned with the regulatory compliance picture and not the green bragging rights aspect.

> *"As (oil) peaking is approached, liquid fuel prices and price volatility will increase dramatically, and, without timely mitigation, the economic, social, and political costs will be unprecedented."*
>
> Robert Hirsch, U.S. author and energy consultant (2005; in a U.S. Department of Energy study known as the Hirsch Report).

The questions always are what are the abatement options, what offsets are needed, and what incentives are available to be utilized when project capital cost budgets are formulated? Where will the sources of solutions for those questions come from?

Regulated entities—the targeted customer base of project developers, lenders and investors—have a great deal at risk during this major shift towards addressing the world climate change concerns. Along with risk come the inevitable opportunities for those customers. Early adopters of employing mitigating measures will have hidden assets that can be leveraged through: a) new carbon reducing energy projects, b) banking the emission reductions for use in later years as production levels rise in the company, and c) selling the excess emission offsets and credits to other parties at a profit. Many new energy projects now being developed recognize the impact that the forthcoming regulations and legislation will have on the project itself and are seeking ways to use the attributes derived from the project in some economic manner.

When people speak of "carbon credits," they mean one of two things:

1. "GHG *allowances*"—They are part of a mandatory cap-and-trade program to reduce emission levels (i.e., European Union Emissions Trading Scheme under the Kyoto Protocol). Some call these allowances a "license to pollute" but are actually a license to emit certain gases—either criteria pollutants such as NO_X, SO_X, etc. or non-criteria pollutants (those that are not dangerous to your health) such as CO_2 (carbon dioxide).
2. "GHG *offsets*"—Created by GHG emission reductions or sequestration of emissions in a sector *not covered by a cap-and-trade program*. These are often referred to as an "abatement" program.

Carbon credits are a key component of national and international attempts to mitigate the growth in concentrations of greenhouse gases (GHGs). One Carbon Credit is equal to one ton of Carbon. Carbon trading is an application of an emissions trading approach. Greenhouse gas emissions are capped and then markets are used to allocate the emissions among the group of regulated sources. The idea is to allow market mechanisms to drive industrial and commercial processes in the direction of low emissions or less "carbon intensive" approaches than are used when there is no cost to emitting carbon dioxide and other GHGs into the atmosphere. Since GHG mitigation projects generate credits, this approach can be used to finance carbon reduction schemes between trading partners and around the world. There are multiple types of carbon credits (with their own acronyms), some are more fungible than others (including the fact that some are fungible in some regimes but not others), and they can include:

> *"Coal, in truth, stands not beside, but entirely above all other commodities. It is the material energy of the country—the universal aid—the factor in everything we do."*
> William Stanley Jevons, English economist (1865).

- AAUs (Kyoto Protocol)—Assigned Amount Units—Carbon credits which can be traded, sold, or bought at the discretion of the holder. The AAUs are redeemable for the emission of one metric ton of carbon. AAUs can be used or stored at any time. AAUs are not to be bought, sold, or traded from a non-ratifying country.
- EUAs (EU Emission Trading System)—European Union Allowance—Each allowance carries the right to emit one ton of carbon dioxide.
- CERs (Kyoto Protocol Clean Development Mechanism)—Certified Emission Reductions—A credit generated under Kyoto's Clean Development Mechanism (CDM) for the reduction of emissions of greenhouse gases equal to one ton of CO_2 -equivalent. They are designed to be used by industrialized countries to count toward their Kyoto targets but can also be used by EU companies and governments as offsets against their emissions under the EU Emissions Trading Scheme. These are "offset" credits.
- VERs (CERs or ERUs that have not yet been verified, certified or issued by the UN)—Verified Emission Reduction—The general name given to carbon offset credits in the voluntary carbon market. These are tradable credits for greenhouse emission reductions generated to meet voluntary demand for carbon credits by organizations and individuals wanting to offset their own emissions. These also are "offset" credits.
- ERUs (Kyoto Protocol Joint Implementation)—Emission Reduction Unit—Tradable credits generated from activities to reduce greenhouse emissions in industrialized countries, particularly those of the former Soviet-bloc, under the Kyoto Protocol's Joint Implementation (JI) mechanism.
- Others:
  — Voluntary credits (also called VERs)
  — RGGI, California or other regional credits
  — Credits from any new US legislation

There are both "mandatory" markets (generally found in a cap-and-trade program) and "voluntary" market for these carbon credits. The mandatory exists for companies who must reduce their emissions and will buy credits they need for continued operations and production levels or sell any excess credits they hold to other companies who may need them for their own compliance obligations. The voluntary market exists for those companies who want to project a "carbon neutral" image from their operations. Companies buy the credits because they want to, not because they "have to."

The size of the mandatory market in 2008 was about $120 billion. Most of that market was in Europe. The size of the voluntary market was only about $800 million. The size of the mandatory market will go up many fold if mandates are put into place in the United

States as is now being proposed at all levels of government. If the U.S. puts programs in place, there will be many additional types of carbon credits generated which will then be able to be sold and bought by the participants.

There are a number of gases that have a major impact on global climate change. They are known as the "Kyoto 6" gases. Table 9-1 shows the GHG value relative to 1 ton CO_2 equivalent of those gases that are often found in most companies with manufacturing facilities. Those potency of these gases are shown as a CO_2e (equivalent) or simply GWP or Global Warming Potential. Regulators will use the CO_2e as the unit of measure for setting limits under a cap-and-trade scheme.

As can be seen from Table 9-1, any energy project that also reduces emissions from those gases on a scale greater than CO_2 provides a significant market opportunity for new RE projects that can reduce those CO_2 equivalents. This opportunity can also be used as an additional source of revenue to enhance yield in the potential renewable energy project if the offsets or credits could be sold to an interested third party—of which there is an abundance world-wide. Astute project developers, lenders and investor (and the occasional debtor or host) recognize this opportunity and incorporate it into their financial analysis. An example of this revenue strategy can be found in Chapter 7. Remember, 1 ton of CO_2 equivalent is the same anywhere it is emitted—this is the principle of an "offset."

Part of the attempt to control GHG emissions can be found in the applicability of the Renewable Portfolio Standards (RPS) in individual states. RPSs require that renewable energy sources such as wind, solar, biomass and geothermal make up a certain portion of retail electricity supply sold to utility customers by a certain date. Thirty-five states and Washington, DC, have enacted some form of RPS—all of them with differing requirements. The RPS is one of the most important state-level policies promoting renewable energy development in the United States. The Waxman-Markey bill that is now pending on the federal side, if passed, will introduce a national RPS standard that will apply to all 50 states. It is important to note that the Renewable Energy Credit or REC under the Waxman-Markey bill will be a completely separate credit market from the GHG allowance market or offset markets described above.

As can be seen, rules vary across states and no two policies are exactly the same. The RPS encourages renewable energy developers to provide competitively priced generation to utilities to meet their targets or provide an opportunity for a utility to purchase generation projects to meet their RPS compliance goals. As a example, looking at the 12 U.S. states in the Western Electricity Coordinating Council (WECC), 10 have RPSs (including the El Paso region of Texas, which is part of the WECC). Targets vary from 5 percent (in Texas) to 33 percent (in California) and target dates range from 2015 to 2025. California's three large IOUs collectively served 19.6% of their 2012 retail electricity sales with renewable power.

These RPS mandates are now creating a very strong market demand for deploying renewable energy technologies and great opportunities for renewable energy developers to help meet these state mandates. Based on a Black & Veatch analysis,[3] the amount of incremental renewable energy generation that must be added to meet WECC states' RPS demands by their target dates is over 100,000 gigawatt-hours a year. California's requirement is the largest, requiring approximately 60,000 GWh/yr of incremental generation.

> *"The activist is not the man who says the river is dirty. The activist is the man who cleans up the river."*
>
> Ross Perot, U.S. businessman and ran for U.S. President

Table 9-1: GHG Equivalency[2]

Green House Gas	Global Warming Potential (GWP)
CO_2	1
Methane	21
Nitrous Oxide	310
HVC-134a	1,300
HFC-23	11,700
HFC-152a	140
HFC-125	2,800
SF_6	23,900

Table 9-2: Renewable Portfolio Standards by State

State	RPS Mandate/Goal
Arizona	15% by 2025
California	20% by 2012 33% by 2020
Colorado	20% by 2020 (IOUs) 10% by 2020 (co-ops and large MOUs)
Connecticut	23% by 2020
Delaware	20% by 2019
District of Columbia	20% by 2020
Hawaii	20% by 2020
Illinois	25% by 2025
Iowa	105 MW
Maine	40% by 2017
Maryland	20% by 2022
Massachusetts	15% by 2020
Michigan	10% by 2015
Minnesota	25% by 2025
Missouri	15% by 2021
Montana	15% by 2015
Nevada	20% by 2015
New Hampshire	23.8% by 2025
New Jersey	22.5% by 2021
New Mexico	20% by 2020 for IOUs 10% by 2020 for co-ops
New York	24% by 2013
North Carolina	12.5% by 2021 IOUs 10% by 2018 MOUs & co-ops
North Dakota	10% by 2015 (goal)
Ohio	25% by 2025
Oregon	25% by 2025 for large utilities 5% to 10% by 2025 for smaller utilities
Pennsylvania	8% by 2020
Rhode Island	16% by 2019
South Dakota	10% by 2015 (goal)
Texas	5,880 MW by 2015
Utah	20% by 2025 (goal)
Vermont	10% by 2013 (goal)
Virginia	12% by 2022 (goal)
Washington	15% by 2020
Wisconsin	10% by 2015 (goal-varies by utility)

Whether these goals can be met is debatable. They can only be met if there are sufficient financial resources deployed through astute renewable energy developers and that there are adequate transmission lines to deploy them (assuming that a substantial portion of the new renewable energy generation will come from facilities designed for utility size generation and not the distributed generation model).

In addition, there are currently two bills working their way through congress regarding federal legislation on renewable portfolio standards(RPS)—also known as renewable energy standards (RES) in the bills. The first bill is the house bill H.R. 2454 (Waxman-Markey) and is known as the "American Clean Energy and Security Act." The second bill is the senate bill 1462 (Bingman) and is known as the "American Clean Energy Leadership Act of 2009." Although there are some differences between the two bills, there are more similarities than there are differences. Both bills have an exemption for utilities that generate less the 4 million megawatt hours of electricity per year. Resources that qualify such as wind, solar, etc. are nearly identical in both bills as are the non-qualifying resources such as new nuclear, new hydro, fossil-fueled facilities, etc. The house bill RES requirements are:

- Requires 6 percent of electricity to come from renewables by 2012 (3 percent by 2011 in the senate bill)
- Requires 20 percent of electricity to come from renewable by 2020 (15 percent by 2021 in the senate bill)
- Up to 5% can come from energy efficiency (up to 4% of the 2021 senate objective)
- Federal government must purchase 6% of total energy consumption by 2012 and 20% by 2020
- Solar water heating qualifies towards the RES
- Both bills have an "Alternative Compliance Penalty" (ACP) for utilities who cannot meet the RES. $25 per MWh adjusted for inflation in the house version and $21 per MWh adjusted for inflation on the senate side.
- Both bills utilize Renewable Energy Credits as a tool for meeting the mandates

Similar federal bills are likely to be forthcoming each new year as until something is finally passed in both houses and signed by the President.

CARBON CAPTURE AND STORAGE (CCS)[4]

Carbon capture and storage (CCS) has an essential role in reducing global greenhouse gas emissions. As part of a portfolio of low-carbon technologies, CCS is needed to stabilize atmospheric greenhouse gas concentrations at levels consistent with limiting projected temperature rises to 2°C by 2050, as recommended by the United Nations Intergovernmental Panel on Climate Change.

The specific challenge for the CCS industry is to demonstrate the entire chain at commercial scale—incorporating CO_2 capture from large point sources, CO_2 compression and then transportation and injection into suitable storage sites or for a use that results in permanent emissions abatement.

Fossil fuels are considered the most dependable, cost-effective energy source in the world. The availability of these fuels to provide clean, affordable energy is essential for domestic and global prosperity and security well into the 21st century. However, a balance is needed between energy security and concerns over the impacts of concentrations of greenhouse gases (GHGs) in the atmosphere – particularly carbon dioxide (CO_2).

Estimated costs for sequestering up to 500 million tons of carbon per year—an amount that would offset up to one-third of current annual U.S. carbon emissions—range from \$30 to \$90 per ton.[5] On a per-ton basis, these costs are comparable to those estimated for other climate change mitigation options such as fuel switching or energy efficiency. A sequestration program on this scale would involve large expanses of land and significant upfront investment; as such, it would almost certainly require a phased approach over a number of years and careful attention to policy details to ensure efficient implementation.

Near the end of 2011, there were eight large-scale projects in operation around the world and a further six under construction.[6] Three of these projects have recently commenced construction. Importantly, these include a second power project, Boundary Dam in Canada, and the first project in the United States that will store CO_2 in a deep saline formation, the Illinois Industrial Carbon Capture and Sequestration (ICCS) project. The total CO_2 storage capacity of all 14 projects in operation or under construction is over 33 million tons a year. This is broadly equivalent to preventing the emissions from more than six million cars from entering the atmosphere each year.

> *"We need to push ourselves to make as many reductions as possible in our own energy use first ... and that takes time. But we must do this quickly—the climate will not wait for us."*
>
> Rupert Murdoch, Founder, Chairman, CEO of News Corporation

So why hasn't carbon capture and storage been adopted worldwide?

"Two major challenges stand in the way of carbon sequestration reaching its full potential," said Sally Benson, professor (research) of energy resources engineering at Stanford University. "One is the high cost of capturing CO_2. The other is an overall lack of confidence in the capacity, safety and permanence of sequestration in deep geological formations." CO_2 storage could be implemented in oil and gas reservoirs, deep formations with salt water, and deep coal beds. Specific sites would have to be selected, engineered, and operated with careful attention to safety. In particular, the deep subsurface rock formations selected to hold the CO_2 must allow the injection of large quantities at sufficient rates and must also be layered geologically so as to prevent, over centuries to millennia, the upward migration of injected CO_2.

Current surveys suggest that the storage available within 50 miles of most of the major U.S. sources of CO_2 would be more than enough to handle emissions for many decades, and that up to 20 percent of current emissions could be stored at estimated costs of \$50 per ton of CO_2 or less. However, given the large volumes involved, the challenge should not be underestimated. Remember, the compliance cost provides absolutely no revenue stream for the facility. At typical densities, a single 1-GW coal-fired plant would have to inject about 300 million standard cubic feet of CO_2 *per day*, a flow for which the volume would equal that of the petroleum produced from a large oil field.

> *"To truly transform our economy, protect our security, and save our planet from the ravages of climate change, we need to ultimately make clean, renewable energy the profitable kind of energy."*
>
> Barack Obama, Address to Joint Session of Congress, February 24, 2009

Too little is known now to determine which power generation technologies and which CO_2 sequestration options would be best for electricity production after 2020 if carbon emissions are constrained. The reliable cost and performance data needed for both carbon capture and carbon storage can be obtained only if full-scale demonstration facilities are constructed and operated. Such demonstrations could convince suppliers, manufacturers, investors, and other private-industry interest that power plants incorporating advanced technologies and storage facilities could be built and operate cost-effectively. The variety of coal types and the myriad conversion options for coal, natural gas, and biomass fuels will require a diverse portfolio of CO_2 capture demonstrations. Similarly, it will be necessary to operate a number of large-scale storage projects in a variety of subsurface settings to evaluate the options and their costs, risks, environmental impacts, legal liabilities, and regulatory and management issues.

For two reasons, 2012 will be a milestone for carbon capture and sequestration (CCS) technologies, marking the beginning of its practical utilization.[7]

First: The next step of the ongoing international climate change talks will be hosted by Qatar, which, with Saudi Arabia, has long pushed to have CCS included among approved technologies for carbon reduction under the European Union cap and trade scheme. (CCS can be used to make electricity cleaner, not only from coal, but also from heavy petroleum residues.) At last year's talks, they finally succeeded, with more details to be hammered out in the coming months.

And secondly: The very first U.S. power purchase contract was just signed for coal power with CCS from a coal plant. It will also sell the carbon dioxide. (Perhaps this kind of CCS should be called Carbon Capture, Sequestration and Sale (CCSS) because one way to make CCS more cost effective is not merely store the carbon dioxide, but to sell it.)

CAP-AND-TRADE

The concept of a cap-and-trade program had its nexus in the Kyoto Protocol. It was designed such that the total emissions from all sources would:

1. Be required to reduce emissions to 1990 levels by 2012
2. Further reduce emissions to 20% of 1990 levels by 2050

These are very aggressive targets that could be extremely costly to business. It starts with all large emitters having a "cap" each year of the emissions that they are allowed to produce. They will then have to reduce their emissions according to a defined level each year (often called a "hair-cut") until the ultimate emission level has been achieved. At the end of each year, the source will have to give up enough allowances or purchase offsets to attain their mandated goal of emission levels. There is a patchwork of rules and regulations on a regional basis on when and how this will be achieved. Four of the most significant schemes are RGGI, AB32 in California, MGGA (Mid-Western Greenhouse Gas Accord), and WCI (Western Climate Initiative) and each have their own scheme that is being implemented and enforced (see later section). The following figure shows how those schemes are generally put into effect and how the emissions are expected to be reduced over time.

There will be great opportunities for RE project developers, lenders and investors in these markets as they are implemented. The pricing per ton for carbon emissions can vary widely. For example, in the RGGI market, the value is about $4 per ton while in the EU they have a value of over $20 per ton.

The European Union Emissions Trading System (EU ETS) is an active cap-and-trade market that has

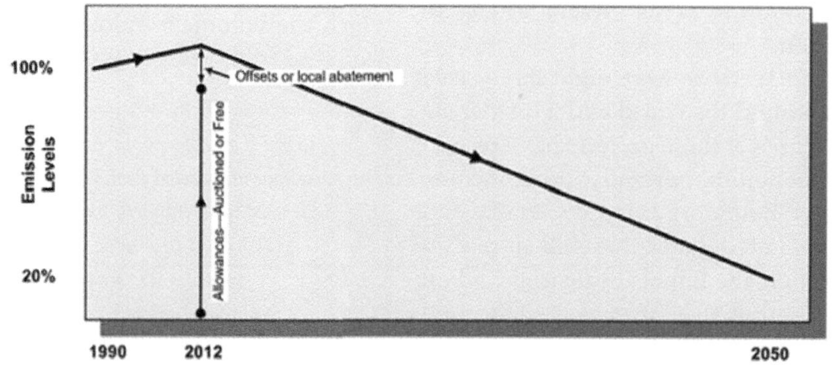

Figure 9-1: Cap & Trade Programs

been working since January 1, 2005 and has 27 member countries. It is the scheme that is most often referred to as new regulations are adopted and legislation is being promulgated. The system has a goal of reducing carbon emissions to a level of 8% below 1990 levels by 2012. There are 10,000 facilities in the system and the trading market value now is exceeding $100 billion per year. The current facilities are primarily manufacturing firms but after 2012, they are expected to also bring in the aviation industry and aircraft flying into Europe from around the world.

In Canada, the Government of Ontario has recently introduced framework legislation to allow for the implementation of a greenhouse gas emissions cap-and-trade system in the province. The bill amends the Ontario Environmental Protection Act to more clearly permit regulations to be passed to establish the scope of a cap-and-trade program, the creation, use, distribution, and trading of allowances and offsets, the establishment of monitoring and reporting requirements, and, perhaps most notably, to support emission trading across jurisdictions. The proposed amendments, if passed, would better enable the province to develop a cap-and-trade program for greenhouse gases that can be integrated with other systems and other jurisdictions including the Western Climate Initiative in the U.S., Quebec, and a possible future North American federal trading system.

The global size of the carbon trading market is shown in the Table 9-3.

The total GHG emissions worldwide in 2008 were 27 billion tons. The sources of GHG emissions can be broken down as follows:

- 34% from electricity production
- 28% from transportation
- 19% from manufacturing

Table 9-3: Global Carbon Emissions

Region	Emissions (Bn Tons of CO_2E)	% of Total
United States	6	22%
China	6	22%
EU	4	15%
Asia	3	11%
Russia	3	11%
Rest of World	2	7%
India	1	4%
Japan	1	4%
Australia/NZ	0.5	2%
Canada	0.5	2%

- 8% from agriculture
- 6% from commercial
- 5% from residential

It is highly likely that from a timing perspective, whatever form of legislation is finally enacted in the United States, the regulation will go into full implementation on January 1, 2013. However, if legislation is delayed for any reason, this could slip by one or two years. The legislation will cover clean energy, energy efficiency, and the GHG programs described in this section. The key provisions of any legislation passed would probably encompass:

- A cap-and-trade program that would be mandated for all sources that have emissions greater than 25,000 tons per year of CO_2e. This is the same size of emissions now existing for the EU trading system that is already in place.

> *"Today, there are also buyers and sellers of all these energy commodities, just like there are buyers and sellers of food commodities and many other commodities."*
>
> Kenneth Lay (1942 – 2006), former CEO of Enron

- Command-and-control regulations administered by the Environmental Protection Agency (EPA) *would be imposed* on all sources that have emissions less the 25,000 tons per year but more than 10,000 tons per year that effectively mandate the same levels of reduction but without the ability to participate in the cap-and-trade program. These regulations would likely take a bit longer to be implemented than the cap-and-trade program since they would be very prescriptive in nature and likely face many technical, policy and procedural challenges from the regulated community.
- There will likely be a separate cap-and-trade program for hydroflurocarbon (HFCs) emissions. The program will be a more rapid step-down in emission levels because of the level of potency of these gases.
- 50-65% emission reductions from "new" coal fired power plants that are built.
- Allowances under the legislation:
  — 10-15% will be auctioned off (with the money

going to the government in the form of a carbon tax equivalent and creating a large revenue source for them) in the early years.
    - There will be some free allocations for some sources and as incentives for other sources to implement carbon reduction projects.
- Banking of emission credits for use in future years and borrowing against future emission credits (which would have to be paid back) will be available in some manner that will have to be determined.
- Offset emissions will be allowed.
    - Up to 2 billion per year of which ½ will be from domestic offsets and ½ from international offsets
    - Sources can use up to 30% of their compliance obligations with the offsets (15% domestic and 15% international)
    - All projects must be approved by the EPA
    - Credits generated from CDM projects elsewhere in the world may be eligible
- Highly likely that there will be a federal RPS
    - A goal of 6% in 2013 and 20% in 2020. This could potential cause a great deal of problems for utilities in some states that rely heavily on coal power production and do not have good natural renewable energy resources such as wind, solar, geo-thermal or wave/tide. There may be some credits available from energy efficiency savings in the mix. Also, it will allow some states (such as California) who have higher RPS levels to use those levels instead of the federal levels.
    - There may be "extra" credit for distributed generation sources such as roof mounted solar PV or solar thermal but the energy generated from those sources would likely to have to be used directly at the site where it is generated and not transmitted for use elsewhere. As an example, instead of just 1 credit for a megawatt of power from the grid, the solar PV would be eligible for 2 additional credits for a total of 3 credits! Again, a tremendous potential opportunity for any RE project as a potential high revenue generation source for the project economics.
- Other possible incentives and opportunities for building assets under the programs could include:
    - Carbon capture and sequestration
    - More DOE funding and loan guarantees for low emission and clean energy projects
    - Energy efficiency incentives and not just energy generation incentives
    - Clean vehicle technologies
    - Energy storage technologies

> *"There is one forecast of which you can already be sure: someday renewable energy will be the only way for people to satisfy their energy needs. Because of the physical, ecological and (therefore) social limits to nuclear and fossil fuel energy use, ultimately nobody will be able to circumvent renewable energy as the solution, even if it turns out to be everybody's last remaining choice. The question keeping everyone in suspense, however, is whether we shall succeed in making this radical change of energy platforms happen early enough to spare the world irreversible ecological mutilation and political and economic catastrophe."*
>
> Herman Scheer, Energy Autonomy: The Economic, Social and Technological Case for Renewable Energy

Looking to the next several years, it is highly likely that there will be a potential shortage of U.S. based offsets. The market size could reach $2 trillion per year by 2020—an incredible number. Energy prices and carbon prices could be depressed for some time if the economic downtown continues. In the end, you can be assured that the legislative and regulatory momentum is building and all RE project developers, lenders and investors need to take advantage of the opportunities these actions are providing. But, beware, there could overlapping federal and state schemes that could cause confusion in the market and even uneven values for the carbon credits (if you look at the EU mechanisms as an example) that could bottom and peak many times before there is a more "stable" market pricing.

Cap-and-trade systems won't be a panacea for the United States to solve its carbon emissions challenges. However, it is highly likely that the opportunities for building assets for RE project developers, lenders and investors will be great. Any cap-and-trade system is likely to be an extraordinary political event that pits regions of the country and producers of energy against one another. So there's going to be a huge amount of political infighting between the existing state and proposed federal programs as to how the programs will work, what the levels of the reductions will be, when they will be implemented and what businesses and industry sectors will be regulated and forced into the schemes.

One can argue that the aggressive and mandatory reductions in greenhouse gas emissions tied to global warming are unrealistic in the short term—particularly given the current economic downtown and the added costs that any carbon reduction scheme would impose on society already beleaguered with loss of revenue and increased expenses. But, it should be recognized that as new pollution-cutting technologies commonly emanating from RE energy projects and cleantech find their way into mainstream energy production methodology, the policies will become even more ambitious.

Many think that the best system would be a carbon tax where the regulated community would all pay a tax on the basis of carbon emissions—with all the proceeds flowing to the government coffers and just putting an increased cost burden on everyone. In any case, changes are coming and the opportunities for investing in cleantech will be everywhere.

The Obama-Biden "Energy for America" plan recognizes the potential for dire consequences resulting from climate change caused by GHG emissions. The plan sets ambitious goals to reduce GHGs by 80 percent by 2050. It has massive goals to invest in alternative and renewable energy, end our addition to foreign oil, address the global climate crisis, and create millions of new green energy jobs. The plan also calls for a commitment to make the Research and Experimentation Tax Credit permanent. Despite the positive steps taken by the current administration, the overall energy policy goals are extremely ambitious, and it is questionable whether the programs outlines so far will be able to meet them. Perhaps even more of a concern, the faltering economy complicates discussions about investment in clean energy and reducing GHG emissions and most importantly the "timing" in which all of the plans and goals will be implemented. Most say that the President must strike a balance between stimulating the economy in the next few years and investing in the long-term future of the environment.

> *"Remember when atmospheric contaminants were romantically called stardust?"*
>
> Lane Olinghouse, author

AB 32—CALIFORNIA

In 2006, the California legislature passed and Governor Schwarzenegger signed AB 32, the Global Warming Solutions Act of 2006, which set the 2020 greenhouse gas emissions reduction goal into law. It establishes a first-in-the-world comprehensive program of regulatory and market mechanisms to achieve real, quantifiable, cost-effective reductions of greenhouse gases (GHG). AB 32 was authored by then-Assembly Member Fran Pavley and Assembly Speaker Fabian Nunez (D-Los Angeles). AB 32 requires the California Air Resources Board (CARB) to develop regulations and market mechanisms to reduce California's greenhouse gas emissions to 1990 levels by 2020 (the equivalent of taking approximately 28 million cars off the nation's roads), representing a 25% reduction statewide, with mandatory caps beginning in 2012 for significant emissions sources. The bill provides the Governor the ability to suspend the emissions caps for up to one year in the case of an emergency or significant economic harm. The program can be thought of as "direct" regulation of greenhouse gas production. As a result, no new source of electricity generation in California can have GHG emission levels higher than a natural-gas, combined-cycle power plant. Interestingly, peaking power plants are exempt from the "performance" standards of the regulation but still must comply with the emission reductions and limits. The bottom line is that there is a chilling effect on new power plant generation facilities—with the exception of the renewable energy projects (which have no emissions at all ...).

The cap-and-trade portion of the program places an upper limit on statewide greenhouse gas emissions. This is the first program of its kind in the United States. The program will take effect beginning in 2012, with a limit placed that year that will be reduced by two percent each year through 2015 and three percent each year from 2015 to 2020. The rules apply first to utilities and large industrial plants, and in 2015 will begin to be applied to fuel distributors as well, eventually totaling 360 businesses at 600 locations throughout the State of California. Free credits will be distributed to businesses to account for about 90 percent of overall emissions in their sector, but they must buy allowances, or credits, to account for additional emissions. Interestingly, the bill was challenged by Proposition 23 on the November 2010 ballot, which aimed to suspend AB 32 until state unemployment stayed below 5.5% for four consecutive quarters. The proposition was defeated by a wide margin.

The law's cap-and-trade measure, which was scheduled to begin on January 1, 2012, will now go into effect on January 1, 2013. The companies that will be covered under the program will have another year to comply before they are required to reduce emissions under the program. While compliance will be delayed by a year, the total amount of emission reductions required remain the same. After extensive stakeholder input, research and analysis, CARB decided to implement a cap-and-trade program as one of 70 separate measures to cut emissions. Cap-and-trade has been used many times before to successfully reduce pollution, and will complement other regulations like building, vehicle and appliance energy efficiency standards. Since cap-and-trade places an absolute limit (a cap) on the amount of pollution that can be released and creates a price for carbon emissions (through trading), the program as a whole creates a strong economic incentive to cut pollution quickly and at the lowest possible cost.

The program was designed to help businesses transition smoothly to a low-carbon economy over the next decade and reward those that reduce emissions fastest. Since industrial companies that are forced to participate in the program will not have to pay for most of their emissions permits (allowances) at the program start, the 360 regulated companies will still be competing on an even playing field against those in states and nations that don't have a price on pollution according to CARB. Additional features will help keep costs down and maintain competitiveness. One such feature is the ability to use offsets (state-certified pollution reductions from economic sectors—such as agriculture and forestry—that are not directly covered by the program). Conceptually, this could include reductions from implementing other carbon reduction strategies by installing renewable energy production systems or even purchasing renewable energy credits or other carbon reduction credits from third parties. Another program feature to contain costs is an allowance reserve (a "rainy-day" pool of allowances) that becomes available if prices go up yet does not compromise the environmental integrity of the program.

Initially, the program will be using a free allowance structure instead of selling them through an auction mechanism as has been done elsewhere. Giving away free allowances at the start of the program protects businesses from incurring significant compliance costs. Some businesses use large amounts of energy or face stiff competition from producers outside the state and free allowances affords them time to invest in efficiency improvements. With a free allowance structure at the beginning, regulators are able to soften the impact to businesses of their compliance obligations while protecting consumers from increased costs. But within a couple of years of program commencement, these large industrial users of energy will need to find other ways to reduce their emission footprints and that would probably include to a great extent finding new renewable energy sources that do not have emissions associated with them. This is yet another great example of how renewable energy production projects (and the attendant need for financing of those projects) will be playing an increasingly important role in the future (in California initially and probably expanding on a national level in the not to distant future). Renewable energy projects might be able to obtain GHG offset credits if CARB fully adopts market-based programs that recognize wind and solar (and to some extent other renewable sources like geothermal) as "displacing" a certain level of CO_2 emission from average combustion levels. The program as a whole requires at least 50 % of reductions come from regulated businesses and high-quality offsets can only be used to meet 8 % of compliance obligations.

Currently, there are only four official compliance offset protocols that have been approved with others in the process:

1. U.S. Forest and Urban Forest Project Resources—*http://www.arb.ca.gov/cc/capandtrade/protocols/usforestprojects.htm*
2. Livestock Projects—*http://www.arb.ca.gov/regact/2010/capandtrade10/coplivestockfin.pdf*
3. Ozone Depleting Substances Projects—*http://www.arb.ca.gov/regact/2010/capandtrade10/copodsfin.pdf*
4. Urban Forest Projects—*http://www.arb.ca.gov/regact/2010/capandtrade10/copurbanforestfin.pdf*

The regulation will result in a 25% reduction in GHG emissions in California compared with currently projected levels. The climate change documentation uses the unit of million metric tons (MMT) of carbon dioxide equivalents (MMT CO_2) to describe the magnitude of greenhouse gas (GHG) emissions or reductions. However, most of us have little "feel" for this unit of measure. Reducing 1 MMT of CO_2 emissions is equivalent to:

- Avoiding the total emissions from 1.5 state-of-the-art 500 megawatt (MW) combined-cycle gas-fired power plants for one year (500 MW is a typical power plant size in California and there are a total of 965 power plants ranging in size from 0.1 MW to

2,545 MW)

- Converting a typical 500 MW power plant burning coal to two state-of-the-art 500 MW combined cycle gas-fired power plants and running for one year (i.e., the efficiency gains are great enough to reduce CO_2 emissions while generating twice the electricity)
- 216,000 passenger cars not driven for one year (in 2005, about 14 million passenger cars were operated on California roads)
- 179,000 passenger cars and light trucks not driven for one year (in 2005, over 21 million passenger cars and light trucks were operated on California roads)
- 114 million gallons of gasoline saved (California consumes about 16 billion gallons of gasoline per year)
- 2.3 million barrels of oil saved (California consumes about 320 million barrels of oil per year)
- 13,400 tanker trucks of gasoline saved
- One year of electricity use by 128,000 average U.S. households
- One year of electricity use by 193,000 average California households
- Replacing 1.5 million less efficient refrigerators by Energy Star refrigerators
- The energy savings in one year from replacing 13 million standard light bulbs with compact fluorescent lamps
- Every adult under 65 in California walking up one floor instead of taking an elevator each workday
- 26,000,000 tree seedlings grown for 10 years
- 833,000 acres of pine or fir forests absorbing CO_2 for one year
- 556,000 tons of waste being recycled instead of going to a landfill in California
- 110,000 round trips around the world by one typical passenger car (traveling at the equator)
- 1 MMT CO_2 has the same volume as the air in about 500 Empire State Buildings (under standard conditions of pressure and temperature)
- 1 MMT CO_2 has the same volume as the air in about 200,000 hot air balloons (under standard conditions of pressure and temperature)

Mandatory Reporting Requirement under AB 32

Who:

Any source or category of source whose emissions are at a level of significance such that its participation in the program will enable the state air resources board (ARB) to effectively reduce greenhouse gas emissions and monitor compliance with the statewide greenhouse gas emissions limit described in the regulation. The ARB is to consult with the Public Utilities Commission in the development of the regulations as they affect electricity and natural gas providers in order to minimize duplicative or inconsistent regulatory requirements. The regulation applies to all electric retail providers in California, and to *operators of the following facilities*:

- Cement plants
- Petroleum refineries
- Hydrogen production facilities (emitting more than 25,000 metric tons per year of CO_2)
- Electric generation facility rated ≥ 1 megawatt (MW), including hybrid generating facilities. Excludes facilities that are solely:
  - — Nuclear
  - — Hydroelectric
  - — Wind
  - — Solar
- Cogeneration facilities ≥ 1MW
- Any individual facility (except a hospital identified as SIC 8069 and school identified as SIC 8299) within California that emits 25,000 metric tons or more per year of CO_2 resulting from stationary combustion sources.
- Any individual facility within California that emits greater than or equal to 25,000 metric tons per year of CO_2 from stationary fuel combustion sources, and is not required to report under the regulation, *shall report all indirect energy purchased and consumed!*

What:

- The company or organization having operational control of a facility (known as the facility operator) must report emissions for the facility
- Must report all emissions from stationary combustion sources:
  - — Direct CO_2
  - — Direct N_2O
  - — Direct CH_4
- Must report each of the GHGs separately for:
  - — Each fuel used
  - — Each process unit
- Combustion of biomass-derived fuels must be

separately identified, calculated and reported.

- All fugitive emissions must be identified, calculated and reported separately on each process.
- Must report separately the production, sale, disbursement, purchase or acquisition of 50 lbs. or more of sulfur hexafluoride (SF_6), any hydrofluorocarbon (HFC), or any perfluorocarbon (PFC)
- Operators of all facilities or retail provider (except electric generating facilities) must separately calculate and report consumption of purchased or acquired electricity, heat, cooling or steam.

Reporting Schedule:

- Electric power generation facilities and co-generation facilities operational as of January 1, 2008
- First report is due April 30, 2009.
- Must be updated annually and submitted by April 30 of each year for the previous year.
- Cement plants, petroleum refineries, hydrogen plants, general stationary combustion facilities, electric retail providers, and electric power generation facilities must report no later than August 31, 2009, and every year thereafter on August 31 for the previous year.

Verification Schedule:

- Annual reports must be verified by an accredited verifier
- Data must be verified
- Must include verification opinion
- Due August 31 of each reporting year
- Petroleum refineries, hydrogen plants, electric retail providers, general stationary combustion facilities engaged in operating oil and gas field properties, and electric power generation facilities (including co-generation) reports are due by December 31 of each reporting year

Cement manufacturing plants, and electric power generation or co-generation facilities not operated by a retail provider with nameplate generating capacities <10MW or combusting only biomass-derived fuels can be verified triennially after the initial report due on December 31, 2009. General stationary combustion facilities, except facilities engaged in operating oil and gas field properties can submit triennial reports after the initial report.

Emissions Data Report:

The following information is required in each report:

- Facility name, identification number, mailing address, location, and other specified information
- Description of the reporting organization including SIC and NAICS codes
- Person responsible for reporting and contact information
- Reporting period covered
- Direct GHG emissions
- Indirect energy use
- Quantification must be separate for each GHG and must include emissions occurring during routine maintenance, start-ups, shutdowns, upsets and downtime
- Indirect electric and thermal energy consumed for electricity, heat, steam, cooling or hydrogen
- Efficiency metrics as specified in individual sector requirements
- Signed and dated statement that the report meets all the requirements of the regulation
- Signed and dated statement that the statements and information contained in the emissions data report are true and accurate and must include all information on the certifying official

Operators and retail providers must maintain an effective greenhouse gas estimation program to ensure that the emissions data calculations are transparent and independently verifiable. The program must:

- Establish
- Document
- Implement
- Maintain effective data acquisition and handling activities for the estimation and report of the greenhouse gas emissions. These activities include measuring, monitoring, analyzing, recording, processing and calculating parameters in order to be able to report on the greenhouse gas emissions.
- The operator or retail provider must ensure that the annual emissions report is not materially misstated nor contain a material non-conformity. The operator or retail provider shall include internal audits, quality assurance, and quality control for the reporting program and the data reported. Bottom line—this is a permanent "program" that is required by the facility and is as important as accounting, tax, legal, Secretary of State, SEC, Sarbanes Oxley, AQMD or other mandatory reporting requirements of a company.

Upon request by the Air Resources Board, the operator or retail provider must provide to CARB any data used to develop annual emissions data reports.

The information submitted as part of the emissions data report must allow for replication of the determination of emissions by the verifier or other third party and *all information must be retained for seven years* after the submission of the report. Included in the information retention is:

1. The list of all source streams included in the emission estimates
2. The activity data used for calculation of the *emissions for each source steam*, categorized by process and fuel or material type
3. Documentation of the process for collecting of activity data for the facility and its source streams
4. Any GHG emissions calculations and methods used
5. All emission factors used for emission estimates and documentation for tem
6. Any facility or other input data used for emission estimates
7. Documentation of biomass fractions for specific fuels
8. Record of electric power purchase and sale transactions
9. The activity data, emissions, or other data submitted to the ARB under the regulation
10. The annual emissions data report
11. Any other information that is required for the verification of the annual emissions report

For measurement based methodologies, the following information must also be retained for at least seven years after the submission of the emissions data report:

1. List of all emission sources monitored
2. The data used for the uncertainty analysis of emissions from each emissions source, *categorized by process*
3. Quality assurance and quality control information including measurement blanks as applicable
4. The data used for the corroborating calculations
5. A detailed technical description of the continuous measurement system (CEM or "Continuous Emission Monitoring") including the documentation of the approval from the competent authority
6. Raw and aggregated data from the continuous measurement system including documentation of changes over time, the log-book on tests
7. Down-times, calibrations, servicing and maintenance
8. Documentation of any changes of continuous measurement systems

Confidentiality:

The following information is public information that *may not be claimed as confidential*:

1. Direct greenhouse gas emissions by source type (stationary, process, fugitive) at the facility level, emissions by greenhouse gas type, and energy use that enables the estimation of indirect emissions by ARB
2. Reported sector-specific performance metrics as required

Enforcement:

- Any person who commits a violation of the regulation is subject to the penalty provisions specified in section 38580 of the Health and Safety Code
- $25,000 to $250,000 fine and/or up to nine months in jail
- If defendant is a corporation, the fine could be up to $1 million
- Failure to meet any requirement of the regulation or failure to submit any information required by the regulations will constitute a single, separate violation of the regulation *for each day* until the requirement is satisfied or the information is submitted
- False reporting of any information submitted to CARB will constitute a single, separate violation of the requirement of the regulation for each day after the information has been received by CARB
- Late submittal of an emissions data report or verification reports will constitute a single, separate violation of the requirements of the regulation for each day that the information has not been submitted beyond the specified reporting dates
- At the end of each three-year compliance period, all companies will have to hold allowances equal to their emissions

- Emissions reports and results from allowance auctioning and trading will be publicly available. CARB will oversee the program with assistance from sister agencies like the California Energy Commission and local air districts. These agencies have several decades of experience successfully enforcing efficiency standards and air quality regulations. State and local agencies will have the authority to investigate and exact penalties for non-compliance.

Severability:

Each part of the regulation is deemed severable, and in the event that any provision of the regulation is held to be invalid, the remainder of the regulation shall continue in full force and effect.

Cost of Implementation Fees:

In general, fuel suppliers and some large industrial sources will report and/or pay the fee. There will be approximately 285 initial fee payers in the following industries:

- Large natural gas distributors and large users of natural gas
- Refineries
- Suppliers and importers of gasoline and diesel fuel
- Electricity importers and in-state generating facilities
- Facilities that combust coal and petroleum coke
- Cement manufacturers

The battle that will be fought as the program becomes fully implemented is between "command and control" methods of enforcement and that of "market mechanisms"—essentially known as "Cap-and-Trade." Command and control enforcement strategies have a number of negative issues including i) decreased flexibility, ii) higher costs of compliance for the regulated companies, and iii) the higher costs of compliance increases political resistance to GHG reduction goals. Market mechanisms (e.g., emissions trading) have i) greater flexibility, ii) a lower cost of compliance, iii) achieves the same GHG reductions, iv) encourages technological innovation, and v) has a proven track record. Market-based compliance mechanism is an "option" available to the regulators under AB 32 but is not required in the regulation. The market-based compliance mechanism, if used, must have the same GHG reductions, over the same period, as does the command-and-control method of enforcement. The first auction of the so-call energy "allowances" was scheduled for August of 2012. Allowance futures are already trading on at least one private exchange. That first auction in August of 2012 is expected to generate an astounding $1 billion in revenue with more to follow in subsequent years and the program is fully implemented. At this point, it is not clear what will happen to this money but once the politicians get involved, a significant portion is likely to go into the state's general coffers—the state is known to have a huge budget deficit. Some predictions are that in future years, the auction could reach as high as $14 billion. Eventually, these costs will fall on the backs of the residents of the state as most will be passed through to them in various ways. In the end, the regulated companies will need to purchase future allowances from a shrinking—and presumably increasingly more expensive—pool.

Cap-and-Trade has been used successfully with other regulatory agencies in the U.S. (South Coast Air Quality Management District in southern California as an example) and other countries such as in Europe with the Kyoto agreements.

The "cap":

- An overall cap on emission levels is set
- The regulatory agency establishes a certain number of allowances
- The allowances (rights to emit emissions) are distributed or sold to the sources of emissions such as factories, plants, etc.
- The GHG emission sources subject to the cap are required to surrender an allowance for every unit (e.g., metric ton) of CO_2 they emit
- As annual caps on GHG emissions are ratcheted down, the regulatory agency will distribute fewer allowances to sources of emissions

The "trade"

- If one company needs more emission allowances to cover its emissions in a year, it can purchase (i.e., "trade") additional allowances from entities that have more allowances than they need.

RGGI—NORTHEAST US

The Regional Green House Gas Initiative (RGGI) is a regulated trading scheme that started in 2009. It is now operating and the only regulated community in the scheme are utility power plants. It was the first fully functional mandatory program in place in the United States. It is the first market-based regulatory program in the United States to reduce greenhouse gas emissions. RGGI is a cooperative effort among the ten states of Connecticut, Delaware, Maine, Massachusetts, Maryland, New Hampshire, New Jersey, New York, Rhode Island, and Vermont. Together, these states have capped and will reduce CO_2 emissions from the power sector 10 percent by 2018.

States sell nearly all emission allowances through auctions and invest proceeds in consumer benefits: energy efficiency, renewable energy, and other clean energy technologies. As a result, RGGI is spurring innovation in the clean energy economy and creating green jobs in each state. Regional Greenhouse Gas Initiative, Inc. is a 501(c)(3) non-profit corporation created to support development and implementation of the Regional Greenhouse Gas Initiative (RGGI).

Its mission statement is to:

- RGGI, Inc.'s exclusive purpose is to provide administrative and technical services to support the development and implementation of each Participating State's CO_2 Budget Trading Program. RGGI, Inc.'s activities include:
  - Development and maintenance of a system to report data from emissions sources subject to RGGI, and to track CO_2 allowances
  - Implementation of a platform to auction CO_2 allowances
  - Monitoring the market related to the auction and trading of CO_2 allowances
  - Providing technical assistance to the participating states in reviewing applications for emissions offset projects
  - Providing technical assistance to the participating states to evaluate proposed changes to the states' RGGI programs

> *"In an underdeveloped country, don't drink the water; in a developed country, don't breathe the air."*
>
> *Changing Times* magazine.

RGGI, Inc. has no regulatory or enforcement authority. All such sovereign authority is reserved to each participating state.

A report[8] released in February 2011 shows that, overall, the states that participated in the first RGGI control period are investing 80 percent of CO_2 allowance proceeds, which now total more than $952 million, in strategic energy programs:

- **52 percent** to improve energy efficiency;
- **11 percent** to accelerate the deployment of renewable energy technologies;
- **14 percent** to provide energy bill payment assistance, including assistance to low-income ratepayers;
- **1 percent** for a wide variety of greenhouse gas reduction programs, including programs to promote the development of carbon emission abatement technologies, efforts to reduce vehicle miles traveled, and programs to increase carbon sequestration.

The report is based on each state's plan for the investment of CO_2 allowance proceeds and on evaluations of strategic energy programs.

These investments are reducing CO_2 emissions and generating important consumer benefits, including lower energy bills, greater electric system reliability and more jobs. Evaluations of several energy efficiency and renewable energy programs in the RGGI Participating States show $3-$4 in benefits for every $1 invested.

The Value of CO_2 Allowances

A key design element of RGGI is the distribution of CO_2 allowances through quarterly, regional CO_2 allowance auctions. Building on the experiences of earlier cap-and-trade programs, which distributed allowances to regulated entities for free, the RGGI participating states each chose to auction the majority of their CO_2 allowances and invest the proceeds in consumer benefit programs. Table 9-4 shows the percentage of CO_2 allowances offered through auction by each state, as well as the percentage of CO_2 allowances offered for sale directly to certain qualifying emitters at a fixed price of $2.00 per allowance, as specified in each state's regulations. Across all ten RGGI states, approximately 86 percent of CO_2 allowances are offered at auction and approximately 4 percent of CO_2 allowances are offered for sale at a fixed price.

Auctioning CO_2 allowances provides three important benefits in the context of a cap-and-trade system. First, auctions ensure all parties have access to CO_2 allowances under uniform terms. Second, auctions realize the value of CO_2 allowances for investment in strategic energy programs that reduce CO_2 emissions, save con-

Table 9-4: CO_2 Allocation by State in RGGI

State	Initial Annual CO_2 Allowance Budget	Percent Offered through Auctions	Percent Offered for Sale at a Fixed Price
Connecticut	10,695,036	77%	13%
Delaware	7,559,787	60%	n/a
Maine	5,948,902	80%	n/a
Maryland	37,503,983	80%	n/a
Massachusetts	26,660,204	98%	n/a
New Hampshire	8,620,460	69%	n/a
New Jersey	22,892,730	74%	25%
New York	64,310,805	94%	n/a
Rhode Island	2,659,239	99%	n/a
Vermont	1,225,830	99%	n/a
Total	**188,076,976**	**86%**	**4%**

sumers money, and create jobs. Third, reinvestment of auction proceeds in energy efficiency and renewable energy programs allow cap-and-trade programs to address CO_2 emissions at both the supply side (power plants) and the demand side (energy use), delivering emission reductions at lower cost.

Overall, the RGGI participating states are investing the vast majority of CO_2 allowance proceeds in programs to improve energy efficiency and accelerate the deployment of renewable energy technologies. These investments deliver triple benefits – to the environment, consumers, and the economy.

Harnessing the power of renewable energy sources, such as solar, wind, and geothermal, is central to developing a clean energy economy. However, renewable energy generation projects often confront market barriers associated with higher up-front costs and access to capital. To overcome these barriers, the RGGI participating states are investing 11 percent of CO_2 allowance proceeds to support the deployment of renewable energy technologies. The vast majority of the programs provide grants and low- or no-interest loans for on-site renewable energy generation systems on homes, businesses, and public buildings, and in commercial and industrial settings.

On-site renewable energy generation systems, such as solar, geothermal, and wind, have several unique benefits compared to conventional large-scale power plants. By generating clean, renewable electricity at the point of use, renewable energy generation sys-

Table 9-5: CO_2 Allowance Proceeds by State Through Dec 31, 2010

State	Proceeds— Auctions 1-10	Other Proceeds	Total Allowwance Proceeds
Connecticut	$44,900,580	$441,094	$45,341,674
Delaware	$18,858,578	n/a	$18,858,578
Maine	$23,544,204	n/a	$23,544,204
Maryland	$147,530,363	n/a	$147,530,363
Massachusetts	$123,229,478	n/a	$123,229,478
New Hampshire	$28,215,274	n/a	$28,215,274
New Jersey	$90,913,275	$11,310,356	$102,223,631
New York	$282,272,683	n/a	$282,272,683
Rhode Island	$12,340,209	n/a	$12,340,209
Vermont	$5,701,535	n/a	$5,701,535
Total	**$777,506,180**	**$11,751,450**	**$789,257,630**

tems reduce demand for conventional grid electricity, depressing wholesale electricity prices and improving overall electric system reliability. These investments also reduce CO_2 emissions and, in some cases, generate excess power that consumers can sell back to the grid for a profit.

> *"We are entering a new era, one of rapid and often unpredictable climate change. In fact, the new climate norm is change. The 25 warmest years on record have come since 1980. And the 10 warmest years since global recordkeeping began in 1880 have come since 1996."*
>
> Lester R. Brown, U.S. environmental analyst

The most current event concerning RGGI occurred in May 2011 when Governor Christie pulled the state out of RGGI and promised to ban coal fired utility generation facilities in the state. Branding the RGGI a failure, Christie told a press conference that the state will withdraw from the program "in an orderly fashion" by the end of the year, coinciding with the end of RGGI's first compliance period. He said the program's allowances were never expensive enough to change behavior, and that New Jersey has brought its carbon emissions below its 2020 goal as a result of market forces rather than cap-and-trade. "Because states such as Pennsylvania are not RGGI members it's just possible that by making the cap too stringent, clean New Jersey plants would be forced to close only to be replaced by power from dirty Pennsylvania coal plants," Christie added. "It doesn't make any sense environmentally or economically."

This action by Governor Christie is a good example of how difficult it really is to have a comprehensive energy policy that is not national in scope. Consistency on a national level is what is required to be effective, not a state-by-state or region-by-region basis. Historically, attempts to implement a national GHG legislation have failed. Assuming that at some time in the future a federal cap and trade program does emerge, pre-emption of state programs and its consequences will need resolution. All federal attempts to date have had a component that pre-empts states environmental requirements. This runs counter to long-established principles of federal legislative policy. The Clean Water Act, the Clean Air Act, and other foundational enactments of federal environmental protection all provide a set of federal requirements, but generally preserve a state's authority to impose more stringent local requirements. A federal plan could override both RGGI and AB32 in California (*see page* 339).

There are some who suggest that RGGI and other state GHG programs be pre-empted by a federal cap-and-trade program. The reasons given are that an effective national trading system requires a consistent set of standards; it would be inefficient and unfair to expect businesses to meet multiple standards as to what counts as a tradable allowance.[9] They suggest that one certain consequence is that the RGGI states' existing revenues from auctioning RGGI allowances would disappear. So would the programs those revenues have financed unless replacement dollars are found.[10]

> *"There's so much pollution in the air now that if it weren't for our lungs there'd be no place to put it all."*
>
> Robert Orben, American comedy and speech writer

References

1. Source: U.S. Environmental Protection Agency Final Rule Mandatory Reporting of GHG, October 2009
2. EPA, *Inventory of U.S. Greenhouse Gas Emissions and Sinks*: 1990-2003, EPA 430-R-05-003 (Final Version: April 2005), Table ES-1
3. Josh Finn and Ryan Pletka, "Are Western RPS Standards Technically Feasible," January 5, 2010
4. National Academy of Sciences, National Academy of Engineering, National Research Council, *Overview and Summary of America's Energy Future: Technology and Transformation*, National Academies Press, 2010
5. Robert Stavins & Kenneth Richards, "The Cost of U.S. Forest-Based Carbon Sequestration," Pew Center on Global Climate Change, January 2005
6. *The Global Status of CSS*: 2011, Global CSS Institute, October 4, 2011
7. Susan Kraemer, EarthTechling, February 2, 2012
8. *Investments of Proceeds from RGGI* CO_2 Allowances, RGGI, Inc., February 2011
9. Ralph Child; David O'Connor; Colin Van Dyke, "Why RGGI Should Die and State GHG Regulation Should Thrive," Mintz Leven Cohn Ferris Glovsky and Popeo PC, 2010.
10. Ibid

Chapter 10

The Future

The forces shaping the future of renewable energy project financing are technological, financial, political, legal, new accounting rules and tax uncertainty. The current economic downturn has put pressure on every level of government, utilities and regulators to "hold the line." This has occurred in the past and will continue to occur many times into the future. Energy projects and the financing of those projects is no exception.

As the future of global energy markets is debated around the world, there are two principal concerns that summarize all discussions—climate change and whether the world has sufficient energy resources to fuel continued economic growth. We have to ponder these issues based on historical trend data and then utilize those trends to estimate the energy future of tomorrow while always being aware of the risks that accompany those predictions. Energy intensity (defined as energy consumption per unit of GDP) lies at the very heart of the America's energy future and the risks that temper the results.

The International Energy Agency is very bullish on its energy forecast for the world in its recently published report entitled *Medium-Term Renewable Energy Market Report 2013*[1]. They expect energy production from wind to double and solar to triple in six years. The report includes the two graphs shown in Figures 10-1 and 10-2, encapsulating their world outlook from renewable energy production by 2018.

Energy risks are accentuated these days. There is fuel risk, regulatory risk, political risk, commodity pricing risk, tax risk, climate risk and the risk of embracing the wrong technology or putting in place energy technology that could soon be outdated. The continuing combination of these forces is hugely complex and vital to understanding the future of financing renewable projects in the future.

The funding requirement to achieve global renewable energy ambitions is epic in scale. Renewable energy as a sector must pull in more capital than ever before, at a time when investment needs for other energy infrastructure are booming, and just as funding capacity from banks, corporates and capital markets is the lowest

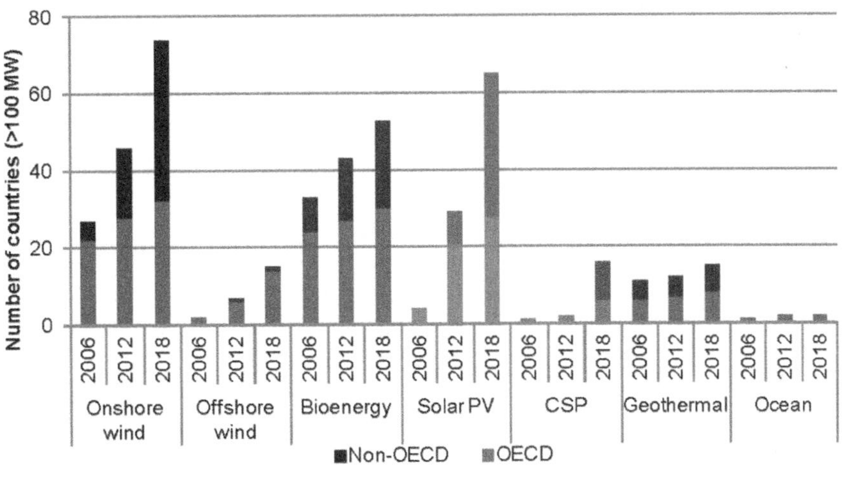

Figure 10-1: IEA-Number of Countries With Non-hydro Renewable Capacity Above 100 Megawatts (MW)

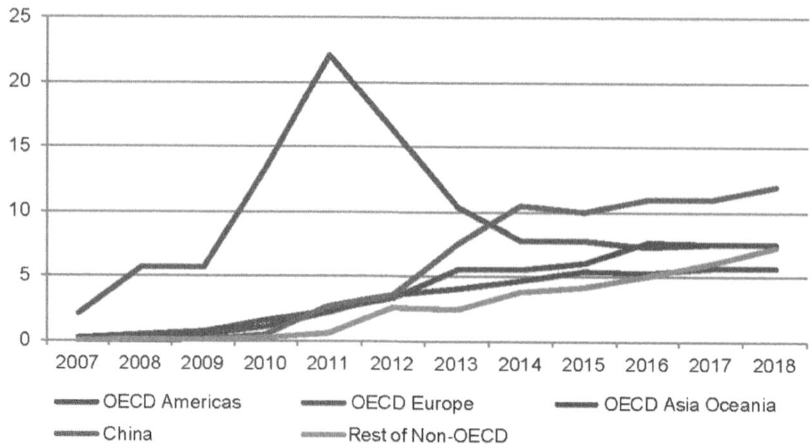

Figure 10-2: Solar PV Annual Additions by Region (GW)

it has been in the past decade.[2] For the first time ever, China has passed the U.S. on the Ernst & Young May 2011 All Renewables Index.[3] And, for the first time in 2011, renewable energy sources provided more energy than the nuclear sector by hitting 11.73 percent of U.S. energy production.[4]

The PEW Charitable Trust reports that the global clean energy economy has experienced truly remarkable growth in just the past few years with the United States leading G-20 members in venture capital and private equity investments associated with technology innovation.[5]

- Globally, clean energy investments have increased 230 percent since 2005.
- Investment by nearly all G-20 members grew by more than 50 percent over the past five years.
- Despite a worldwide recession, global clean energy investments reached $162 billion in 2009.
- G-20 members accounted for more than 90 percent of worldwide clean energy finance and investment.
- More than 250 gigawatts of renewable energy generating capacity have been installed around the world, producing six percent of global energy.

Continued government support for alternative energy is up in the air. This includes production tax credits and investment tax credits. The production tax credits for wind, geothermal, hydropower and a couple of other renewables are set to expire at the end of 2013. The PTC has been extended four times since it was first enacted in 1992—but was allowed to sunset on three occasions. Today's reality in Washington is that any new funds or tax credits (including renewing existing ones) congress might provide will need to be offset by equal cuts elsewhere—concepts known as "pay-for" and "pay-as-you-go." Adding to the uncertainty of continued incentives for renewable energy was the financial failure of Solyndra, EnerDel and Beacon Power.

> *"The best way to make a fire with two sticks is to make sure that one of them is a match."*
>
> Will Rogers, U.S. humorist and commentator (1879 – 1935)

With the two major political parties in the U.S. in continuous election-year mode and a stalemate in terms of which party will win future elections, there is little chance of significant energy legislation in 2014. However, most expect renewable energy to do well as state governments continue to lead the way with higher renewable portfolio standards, increased energy efficiency mandates and continued rebates and incentives. Numerous states are creating new specific credits or "set-asides" to emphasize certain types of renewable energy. Perhaps the best known is the SREC or solar renewable energy credit in some states. Other credits include offshore renewable energy credits (OREC), zero emissions renewable energy credits (ZREC) and low emissions renewable energy credits (LREC). In fact, all of these types of renewable energy credits will become increasingly more valuable in the future. The National Renewable Energy Laboratory (NREL) says that by

2015, states will need 150 TWh of green energy to meet RPS requirements. This is nearly a three-fold increase from the current level of 65 TWh that now exists.

Mega mergers will continue at an unprecedented rate in the U.S. A good example is the proposed merger of Progress Energy and Duke Energy that will create the largest utility in America. The megalith will span six states and serve 7 million customers. Its generation muscle will amount to 57 gigawatts. The Exelon-Constellation deal is another example.

There is a growing sense of national urgency about the role of energy in long-term U.S. economic vitality, national security, and climate change. The U.S. has the resources to combat this energy challenge; the dilemma is to identify which solutions will be right for our country, and how to address the massive technological and social changes to come. Since the industrial revolution 200 years ago, we have depended on fossil fuels. Our ability to begin backing off on the reliance on this fuel source is paramount to our continued growth as a nation. Renewables form a major part of our energy needs and the financing of that mega shift in technology is the biggest change the U.S. faces. Energy efficiency will play a role in meeting that challenge but let's face it, any efficiency savings will soon be eaten up by higher consumption per capita.

Table 10-1: Share of Fuel 1990 – 2030[6]

	1990	2030
Renewables*	0.4	6.3
Nuclear	5.6	6.0
Hydroelectric	6.0	6.8
Coal	27.3	27.7
Natural Gas	21.8	25.9
Oil	38.9	27.2

(% Shares of World Energy Use)

* Renewable energy includes biofuels

According to a recent issue of the "Monthly Energy Review" by the US Energy Information Administration (IEA), with data through September 30th, 2011, renewable energy sources continued to expand rapidly while substantially outpacing the growth rates of fossil fuels and nuclear power. Renewable energy sources, including wind, solar, biomass and geothermal, accounted for 24.93% of all new U.S. electrical generating capacity installed in the first six months of 2013 for a total of 2,144 MW, according to the Federal Energy Regulatory Commission's latest Energy Infrastructure Update report. Hence, renewables provided more *new* generating capacity than did coal and nuclear power combined. Renewable sources now account for nearly 16% of total installed U.S. operating generating capacity. "Notwithstanding the recession of the past four years, renewable energy sources have experienced explosive rates of growth that other industries can only envy," said Ken Bossong, Executive Director of the SUN DAY Campaign.[7] It is estimated that by 2035 the U.S. will use 31% more electricity than we do today and certainly renewable energy will play a significant role in supplying that need.

Tax equity is set to reclaim a pivotal role in renewables finance with the expiration of the American Recovery and Reinvestment Act (ARRA) Section 1603 Grant program in December 1011.[8] With the conclusion of the Grant, developers have to resort to tax equity to monetize the established IRC Sections 45 and PTCs and investment tax credits (ITCs) to entice outside project equity. However, demand for tax equity may outstrip the traditional supply provided by established tax equity investors. The supply/demand imbalance could result in increasing tax equity yields making development more challenging.

Utilities are being ordered to use renewable sources before electricity from fossil fuels that they sell to their customers. On January 12, 2012 the California Public Utilities Commission (CPUC) voted unanimously to strengthen a key clean energy policy in California called the Loading Order. The Loading Order sets a priority list for electricity sources. California's utilities must first employ energy efficiency and conservation to meet customer demand; then energy from renewable sources such as wind, solar and geothermal. *Only after* all those supplies are exhausted may the utilities purchase power from fossil fuel plants. You can expect to see very similar regulations go into effect in most states over the next decade. The utilities historical decisions—to deploy massive new power plants and transmission infrastructure—will be changing. The utilities have built or are building numerous large, natural gas power plants while falling behind on the clean energy mandates. According to the California Energy Commission (CEC), the state has about 30 percent more power than needed on peak energy days, and the CPUC anticipates they will be 60 to 80 percent over-built by 2020 should current trends continue. The new mandates to supply clean energy from renewable energy sources will dramatically change this trend.

Renewable energy provided by solar PV technology is continuing to gain strength despite the recession.

> *"The solar-power market offers perhaps one of the greatest opportunities among its clean-tech peers. Not only is the worldwide solar market growing by 30% to 50% per year, but the same technologies that enabled the semiconductor and computer revolution are now being leveraged in the solar market."*
>
> Ron Pernick and Clint Wilder,
> The Clean Tech Revolution, 2007 p. 20

Helping is the Department of Interior's proposed Solar Energy Zones (17 in total) in the Southwestern U.S. They were designed to speed development of solar on federal lands. The proposed Riverside East zone is the largest of the zones (147,910 acres). As of August 2011, 7 solar project applications were pending in the proposed SEZ, and 2 projects had been authorized within the SEZ. However, nothing is always as easy as it is supposed to be. The Riverside county governing board imposed a "Sun Tax" (Board Policy B-29) that would effectively charge an annual fee of $450 per acre on any large utility scale PV project. That case is now in litigation. It is likely that it may be declared as an invalid tax but not without a costly legal challenge by the developers in the Solar Energy Zone.

There also is a large of amount of growth over the past several years in residential solar PV installations and this trend is likely to continue. And, it is not just wealthy home owners. In fact, the vast majority of the new PV installations on private residences have been on medium income homes. It is important to note that attractive financing mechanisms are what have driven this market also. According to Environment California's Research & Policy Center, the falling price of solar PV and soft-cost reductions is likely to mean installed residential solar systems could reach $5.25 per installed watt by 2014. With continued net-metering, that level would be at grid parity in the state.

The U.S. venture capital sector continues to invest heavily in cleantech companies. Total investment in 2011 remained flat in terms of deals at $4.9 billion (down 4.5% in terms of capital invested compared to 2010) according to Ernst & Young LLP. However, this represents a 29% increase from the $3.8 billion raised in 2009. Companies in the revenue generation stage of development accounted for 60% of dollars invested, up from 50% in 2010. Total dollars invested in companies at this stage of development reached $3.5 billion, a 31% annual increase. The VC's continue to look very favorably on the cleantech sector and will likely continue with their commitments well into the future. It is expected that California will continue to lead that charge.

In late 2011, Bloomberg New Energy Finance (BNEF. New York, New York, U.S.) released a new report discussing some of the parameters that cleantech will need to be keenly aware of in the future. Their head of analysis for North America, Michel Di Capua stated that "There is life after the expiration of the Treasury

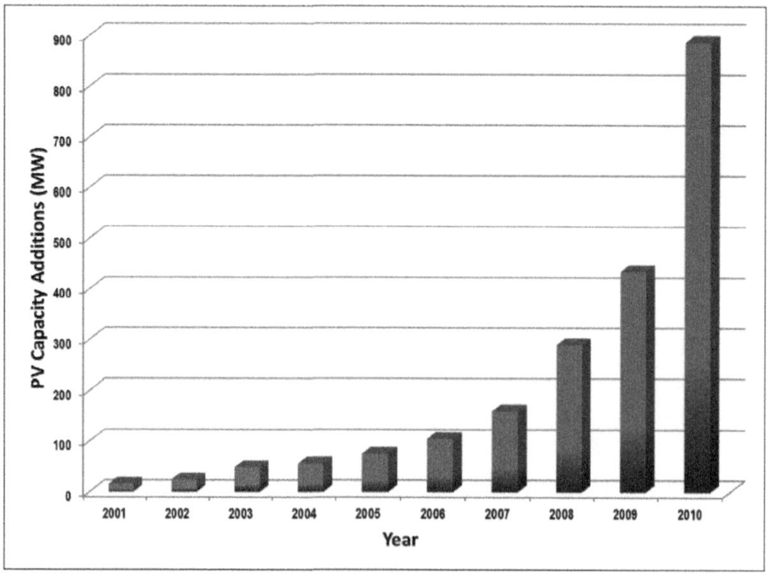

Figure 10-3: U.S. Grid-tied Solar PV Capacity Additions, in MW, 2001-2010—Source: SEIA[9]

cash grant program." The report stated that the U.S. renewable energy sector will need to find new sources of tax equity if it is to meet market demand for project finance, predicting that the total market for tax equity could reach more than USD 7 billion in 2011. The report continues by stating that there is a "vast" pool of potential incremental tax equity available, as the 500 largest companies in the United States paid more than USD 137 billion in taxes in 2011. The report[10] was commissioned by Reznick Group and depicts the outlook for US renewable financing in 2012 and beyond and delves into the economics of tax equity, focusing on the applications and comparative advantages of the various tax equity structures. The report noted that:

- Growth in the US renewable sector has been largely driven by the availability of tax equity or its temporary substitute in the aftermath of the financial crisis, the 1603 cash grant.
- Alternative sources of tax equity may need to emerge to meet market demand for project finance.
- There is life after the death of the cash grant.
- The three primary tax equity structures (described in earlier chapters) offer distinct advantages to developers and tax equity investors.
- The economics of these structures can be attractive.
- The choice of investment versus production tax credits (ITC vs. PTC) comes down to the three 'P's: performance, perspective and priorities.
- The optimal tax equity structure depends on the project characteristics... but perfect optimization may be a pipedream.

> *"Nature provides a free lunch, but only if we control our appetites."*
>
> William Ruckelhaus, Business Week, June 18, 1990

Energy has long played a key role in our nation's national security, economic prosperity, and environmental quality. As a nation, we are paying increased attention about how we are producing and consuming energy. New energy technologies that have come on-line in the past two decades are welcome but are unlikely to be sufficient to meet the nation's energy challenges. They will, however, provide significant alternatives and options to us. Political instability in primary energy-producing regions around the world, rapidly rising global demand for energy (especially in developing countries) and a growing awareness of the impact of fossil fuel use on global climate change have contributed to a new sense of urgency about the role of energy. Those future costs will be very large for projects of all sizes, from simple lighting replacements to huge energy generation facilities. The implications for central plant energy production with the attendant power transmission and distribution will be affected greatly by the concept of distributed energy generation at the very source of its consumption. The transformation of traditional patterns of energy supply and use is inevitably complicated.

Domestic U.S. oil and gas reserves are being depleted. Nuclear plants and to an even greater extent, coal fired plants, are rapidly reaching (or in many cases have already reached) their expected plant lives. Renewing or replacing those assets will take decades and require investments totaling several trillion dollars. Our electrical energy production system as currently configured is unsustainable over the long run. Prices for the fossil fuels we use to power plants and transportation have been volatile. Over the past 2 years alone, petroleum ranged from $32 to $147 a barrel and natural gas from $4 to $13 per thousand cubic feet.

California

California, representing the world's eighth largest economy, has certainly become the leading state in America for addressing our future energy needs and providing regulatory guidance and political will to seriously address solutions to the energy challenges. In California, renewable energy is king as projects large and small push the sector to ever greater heights. What has happened in California will soon be followed in many of the other states in the U.S. The state has adopted ambitious environmental and energy related policy goals, including reducing statewide greenhouse gas emissions to 1990 levels by 2020 and further reductions to 20% of 1990 levels by 2050. The California legislature has also enacted legislation that mandates all investor owned utilities to provide 30% of the power they sell to their customers to come from renewable energy sources by 2020. These goals will need to be accomplished by making sure the utilities provide the energy with safety and reliability—without compromising just and reasonable rates. The five principal agencies that will need to work together as a "California" team to implement the strategies required to attaining those goals (and by reference required in some form or other in most states) are:

1. California Environmental Protection Agency (CalEPA)

2. California Air Resources Board (CARB)
3. California Public Utilities Commission (CPUC)
4. California Independent System Operator (California ISO)
5. California Energy Commission (CEC)

Achieving California's goals depends on state leaders engaging California citizens, utility customers, businesses, and stakeholders including non-governmental organizations and local governments.[11] Renewable energy is California's supply-side resource of choice, followed by combined heat and power (CHP) and distributed generation (DG) as well as the cleanest and most-efficient conventional generation (mostly natural gas fueled facilities). These five agencies have created an integrated Clean Energy Future Implementation Plan for California that clearly identifies the key actions needed to achieve their goals.

The transformation of California's building infrastructure will be well underway by 2020. Strategies for realizing 100 percent of achievable cost-effective energy efficiency will include progressively more stringent building and appliance standards, incentive programs, innovative financing mechanisms (as described in prior chapters), targeted research, development and demonstration efforts, new business models, technical assistance, targeted marketing, education and outreach. Statewide implementation of smart grid technologies (now well underway by all California IOU utilities providing over 80% of the power to residents and companies in the state), as well as electric rate design reform, will provide additional opportunities for customers to install behind the meter resources and utility-level enabling technologies in response to a price signal or usage information.[12] Feed-in-tariffs and other procurement strategies will be expanded to address impediments to wholesale DG and CHP, including transaction costs, developer experience, financing, interconnection processes, local permitting, and operational impacts on the distribution system. The five agencies are targeting a significant fraction of renewable supply resources to have dispatch capabilities, such as the capability to decrease (and possibly increase) their output of energy in response to either dispatch instructions or automated control signals.

> *"The real measure of your wealth is how much you'd be worth if you lost all power and energy sources."*
>
> Gene Beck, Author

Energy storage will be a significant feature of the cleaner power system. As a result of agency support for storage technology pilot studies, increased utility-scale and aggregated smaller scale storage technologies (such as batteries, flywheels, compressed air energy storage, pumped, hydroelectric energy storage, capacitors and thermal energy storage) will be available to help facilitate integration of intermittent wind and solar renewable resources; shift renewable production to times of higher value and demand; and provide grid operators with ancillary services such as regulation and spinning reserve. A key component to all of these strategies, of course, is the financing of these infrastructure energy projects. California agencies are targeting 1,000 megawatts of additional storage capacity to be brought onto the system by 2020.

Adding additional impetus to the ultimate energy solution, California has just set terms for new a new massive energy storage mandate. In September 2013, the California Public Utilities Commission released a long-awaited proposal that will mandate an unprecedented 1.3 GW of energy storage to support the state's power grid by 2020. The 81-page proposed decision from CPUC Commissioner Carla J. Peterman[13] establishes a new regulatory scheme in which utilities, third-party storage providers and customer-owned storage assets can play an integrated role in the state's future energy storage plans. Importantly, the rules would limit the utilities from owning more than 50 percent of the total amount of energy storage to be procured by the three large investor owned utilities (Southern California Edison, San Diego Gas & Electric and Pacific Gas and Electric).

The proposal calls for utilities to consider all forms of ownership including utility-owned, third-party owned, customer-owned and joint ownership. The decision establishing the target requires the utilities to comply starting on January 1, 2014—truly a "fast track" implementation. The proposal specifically excludes pumped hydro storage projects of 50 megawatts or more from being considered in the mandate. That means that battery-based storage, thermal energy storage, compressed-air energy storage fuel cells and other technologies will be utilized to fulfill the requirements.

> *"It's good stuff, but it's expensive, and we have to find business cases."*
>
> Stephen Berberich of the California ISO, referring to the difficulties in building out grid-scale energy storage

This is truly an exceptional *new* opportunity for renewable energy project developers, investors, lenders and energy users to capitalize on. It is the ultimate energy solution envisioned by the state of California: Energy Efficiency + Renewable Energy Generation + Energy Storage = OPPORTUNITY. There are sure to be new state tax incentives and rebate mechanisms established to drive and encourage this mandate—all benefiting the readers of this book. And remember: as California goes, so eventually will most of the states in the U.S.

The Nation

America's Energy Future: Technology and Transformation[14] is a report that explores potential technology pathways for fundamentally transforming U.S. patterns of energy supply and demand. The report study findings found the following:

> *"The human species has begun the most important infrastructure shift in its history, melding energy with information technology and new ideas, blending technical with social breakthroughs, creating one astonishment after another and then merging them into still more. And this crucial next decade, even the next few years, is when most of the big bets will be placed."*
>
> Amory Lovins in his book, Reinventing Fire

- **Energy efficiency potential**. The deployment of existing energy efficiency technologies is the nearest-term and lowest-cost option for moderating the U.S. consumption of energy.
- **Electricity supply options**. The United States has many promising options for obtaining new supplies of electricity and changing its supply mix during the next two to three decades, especially if renewable electric-power technologies, carbon capture and storage (CCS), and evolutionary nuclear technologies can be deployed at sufficient scale. Renewable energy sources could provide an estimated additional 500 terawatt-hours (TWH) of electricity per year by 2020 beyond current production of electricity from renewable energy sources.
- **Modernizing the nation's power grid**. Expansion and modernization of the nation's power grid—the electric power transmission and distribution systems—are urgently needed. This would cost (in 2007 dollars) $175 billion and $50 billion respectively for concurrent expansion and modernization of the transmission of the transmission system, and $470 billion and $170 billion respectively for concurrent expansion and modernization of the distribution system.
- **Continued dependence on oil**. Petroleum will continue to be an indispensable energy fuel through at least 2035.
- **Reduction of GHG**. Substantial reductions in greenhouse gas emissions from the electricity sector are achievable over the next two to three decades.
- **Technology research, development and demonstration**. R&D is needed to fill the pipeline with new technologies. To meet this need, both the public and private sectors will need to perform extensive research, development and demonstration over the next decade.
- **Barriers to accelerated deployment**. Formidable barriers could delay or even prevent the accelerated deployment of the energy-supply and end-use technologies. Policy and regulatory actions, as well as other incentives, will be required to overcome these barriers—a principal one being that of finding available capital and investment sources to finance the new technologies.

The United States is the 2nd largest energy consumer in terms of total use in 2010. The U.S. ranks seventh in energy consumption per-capita after Canada and a number of small countries. Not included is the significant amount of energy used overseas in the production of retail and industrial goods consumed in the U.S. The state with the lowest per capita energy use is California.

The majority of this energy is derived from fossil fuels: in 2009, EIA data showed 37% of the nation's energy came from petroleum, 21% from coal, and 25% from natural gas. Nuclear power supplied 9% and renewable energy supplied 8%, which was mainly from hydroelectric dams although other renewables are included such as wind power, geothermal and solar energy. Energy consumption has increased at a faster rate than energy production over the last fifty years in the U.S. (when they were roughly equal). This difference is now largely met through imports. That United States has and continues to get most of its electrical production from conventional thermal power plants. Most of these are coal; however, the 1990s and 2000s have seen a significant increase in natural gas and other kinds of gas powered plants.

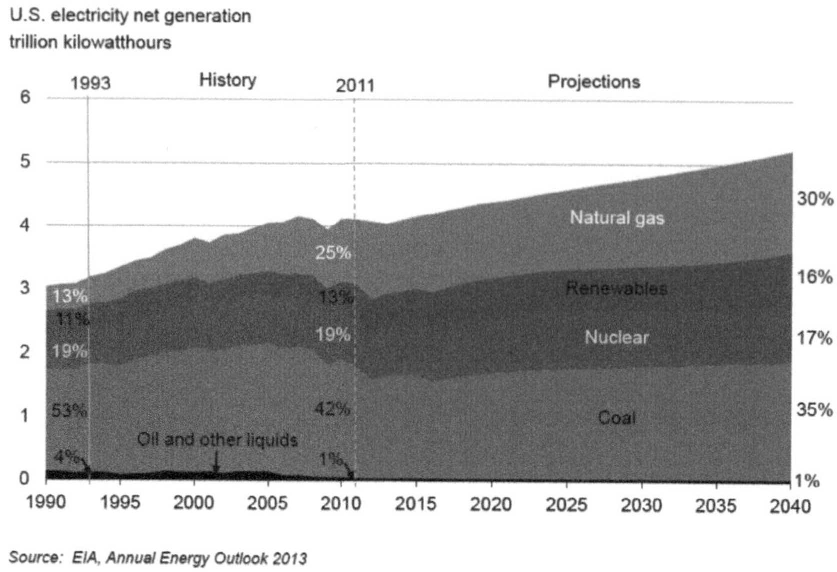

Figure 10-4: Electrical Production in the United States

Renewable energy sources that are geothermal, biomass, wind power and solar energy combined only produce 2.4% of total electrical production in the U.S. The percentage of the total market for renewable energy growth is very large and expected to grow at compound annual growth rates exceeding 20% per year for the foreseeable future.

The industrial sector has long been the country's largest energy user, currently representing about 33% of the total. Energy efficiency mandates combined with the decline of economic growth starting in 2008 caused the energy consumption in the U.S. to drop from historical levels. The U.S. ranks ninth in energy consumption per-capita after Canada and a number of small countries (see below).

In the most rigorous analyses undertaken to date, two recently released resource assessments, show that waves and tidal currents off the nation's coasts contain enough energy to provide a significant portion our nation's total annual electricity usage.

In 2009, China overtook the U.S. in total energy consumption expressed in million tons of oil equivalent (Mtoe). Worldwide consumption of energy in 2012 is shown in Figure 10-3.

Compare this when compared to actual *per capita* consumption as shown in Figure 10-6.

Table 10-2:
Electrical Production in the United States for 2012

Power Source	Percent of Annual Production
Coal	37%
Natural Gas	30%
Nuclear	19%
Hydropower	7%
Biomass	1.42%
Geothermal	0.41%
Solar	0.11%
Wind	3.46%
Petroleum	1%
Other	<1%

Source: EIA

> *"Energy consumption matters both to our environment and our economy."*
> John Baldacci, American politician

The United States uses about 4,000 terawatt hours (TWh) of electricity per year. The reports find that the nation's waves and tides could potentially produce up to 1,420 TWh annually. The wave and tidal resource assessments, combined with preliminary results from ongoing DOE assessments of ocean current, ocean thermal, and hydropower opportunities, indicate that water power can potentially provide 15% of our nation's electricity by 2030. The West Coast, including Alaska and Hawaii have especially high potential for wave energy development while significant opportunities also exist along the East Coast, which have strong tides that could be tapped to produce energy.

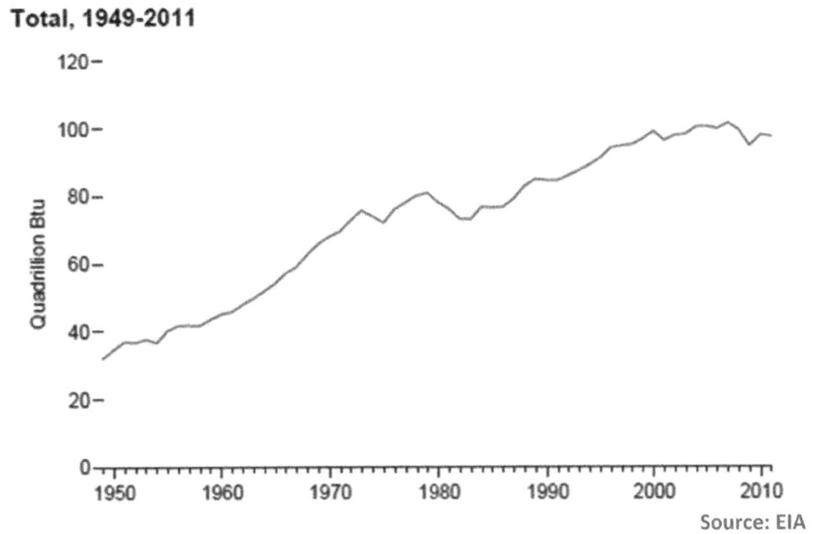

Figure 10-5: U.S. Energy Consumption 1949-2011

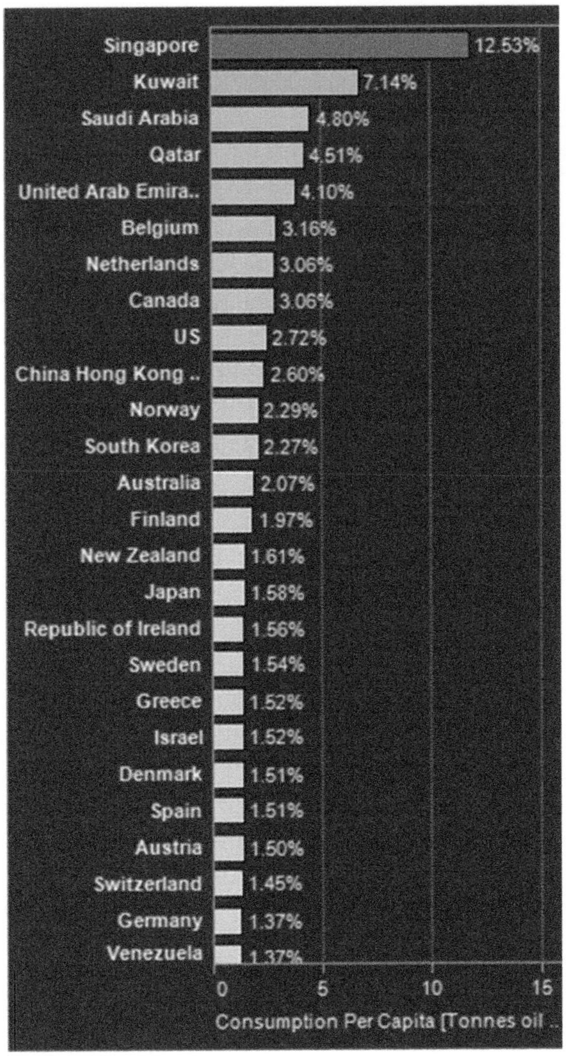

Table 10-3:
Worldwide Energy Consumption by Country (2012)

Country	Mtoe
China	2,713
United States	2,152
India	774
Russia	725
Japan	457
Germany	314
Brazil	281
South Korea	244
Canada	256
France	251

Source: Enerdata

The top five companies using renewable energy will likely continue to be the leaders for the next several years. They are:

1. Intel Corporation
   88% of total electrical consumption
2. Kohl's Department Stores
   101% of total electrical consumption
3. Whole Foods Market
   100% of total electrical consumption
4. City of Houston, TX
   34% of total electrical consumption

Figure 10-6:
World Energy Consumption Per Capita in 2012

5. Starbucks
52% of total electrical consumption

Some people talk about the clean energy economy as if it's a hypothetical future development, but the fact is that it's already here and poised for tremendous growth in the coming years. According to a recent study[18] by the Brookings Institution, today's clean economy employs some 2.7 million workers across a diverse array of industries. Sectors such as solar energy and green construction have seen strong job gains over the past few years.

In 2005, nonresidential green building construction was a $3 billion dollar industry in the United States. By last year, the value of that industry had soared to somewhere between $43 billion and $54 billion – a gain of at least 1400 percent in the midst of a recession. McGraw Hill[19] estimates that by 2015, that market will rocket to a value somewhere between $120 billion and $145 billion. Those gains buck the general trend of the construction industry, which has struggled in recent years. In fact, the U.S. Green Building Council[20] projects that these green construction projects will support 3.3 million workers between 2009 and 2013, up from just over 1 million in the eight years prior.

The U.S. Energy Information Administration just released its Annual Energy Outlook 2012 report. Projections in the Annual Energy Outlook 2012 (AEO2012) Reference case focus on the factors that shape U.S. energy markets in the long term, under the assumption that current laws and regulations remain generally unchanged throughout the projection period. The AEO2012 Reference case provides the basis for examination and discussion of energy market trends and serves as a starting point for analysis of potential changes in U.S. energy policies, rules, or regulations or potential technology breakthroughs.

Some of the highlights in the AEO2012 Reference case include:

- ***Projected growth of energy use slows over the projection period, reflecting an extended economic recovery and increasing energy efficiency in end-use applications***
  Projected transportation energy demand grows at an annual rate of 0.2 percent from 2010 through 2035 in the Reference case, and electricity demand grows by 0.8 percent per year. Energy consumption per capita declines by an average of 0.5 percent per year from 2010 to 2035. The energy intensity of the U.S. economy, measured as primary energy use in British thermal units (Btu) per dollar of gross domestic product (GDP) in 2005 dollars, declines by 42 percent from 2010 to 2035.

- ***Domestic crude oil production increases***
  Domestic crude oil production has increased over the past few years, reversing a decline that began in 1986. U.S. crude oil production increased from 5.1 million barrels per day in 2007 to 5.5 million barrels per day in 2010. Over the next 10 years, continued development of light oil, in combination with the ongoing development of offshore resources in the Gulf of Mexico, pushes domestic crude oil production in the Reference case to 6.7 million barrels per day in 2020, a level not seen since 1994. Even with a projected decline after 2020, U.S. crude oil production remains above 6.1 million barrels per day through 2035.

> *"We are taking challenges and turning them into opportunities by developing homegrown, local energy production to become independent from foreign sources."*
>
> Mitch Daniels, governor of the state of Indiana

- **With modest economic growth, increased efficiency, growing domestic production, and continued adoption of nonpetroleum liquids, net petroleum imports make up a smaller share of total liquids consumption**
  U.S. dependence on imported petroleum liquids declines in the AEO2012 Reference case, primarily as a result of growth in domestic oil production by more than 1 million barrels per day by 2020; an increase in biofuels use to more than 1 million barrels per day crude oil equivalent by 2024; and modest growth in transportation sector demand through 2035. Net petroleum imports as a share of total U.S. liquid fuels consumed drop from 49 percent in 2010 to 36 percent in 2035 in AEO2012. Proposed fuel economy standards covering vehicle model years 2017 through 2025 that are not included in the Reference case would further reduce projected liquids use and the need for liquids imports.

- ***Natural gas production increases throughout the projection period***
  Much of the growth in natural gas production is a result of the application of recent technological advances and continued drilling in shale plays

with high concentrations of natural gas liquids and crude oil, which have a higher value in energy equivalent terms than dry natural gas. Shale gas production increases from 5.0 trillion cubic feet in 2010 (23 percent of total U.S. dry gas production) to 13.6 trillion cubic feet in 2035 (49 percent of total U.S. dry gas production).

- ***U.S. production of natural gas is expected to exceed consumption early in the next decade***
  The United States is projected to become a net exporter of liquefied natural gas (LNG) in 2016, a net pipeline exporter in 2025, and an overall net exporter of natural gas in 2021. The outlook reflects increased use of LNG in markets outside of North America, strong domestic natural gas production, reduced pipeline imports and increased pipeline exports, and relatively low natural gas prices in the United States compared to other global markets.

- ***Use of renewable fuels and natural gas for electric power generation rises***
  The natural gas share of electric power generation increases from 24 percent in 2010 to 27 percent in 2035, and the renewables share grows from 10 percent to 16 percent over the same period. In recent years, the U.S. electric power sector's historical reliance on coal-fired power plants has begun to decline. Over the next 25 years, the projected coal share of overall electricity generation falls to 39 percent, well below the 49-percent share seen as recently as 2007, because of slow growth in electricity demand, continued competition from natural gas and renewable plants, and the need to comply with new environmental regulations.

- ***Total U.S. energy-related carbon dioxide emissions remain below their 2005 level through 2035***
  Energy-related carbon dioxide (CO2) emissions grow by 3 percent from 2010 to 2035, to a total of 5,806 million metric tons in 2035. They are more than 7 percent below their 2005 level of 5,996 million metric tons in 2020 and are still below the 2005 level at the end of the projection period. Emissions per capita fall by an average of 1 percent per year from 2005 to 2035, as growth in demand for transportation fuels is moderated by higher energy prices and Federal corporate average fuel economy (CAFE) standards, and as electricity-related emissions are tempered by efficiency standards, State renewable portfolio standard (RPS) requirements, competitive natural gas prices that dampen coal use by electricity generators, and the need to comply with new environmental regulations. Proposed fuel economy standards covering model years 2017 through 2025 that are not included in the Reference case would further reduce projected energy use and emissions.

Economic Growth

The future of energy projects will be closely tied to historical events. This is particularly true as it relates to economic growth after a recession. Recovery from the 2008-2009 recession is expected to show the slowest growth of any recovery since 1960. Table 10-4 compares average annual growth rates over a five-year period following U.S. recessions that have occurred since 1960 (U.S. EIA).

The recessions highlighted in the table are those which the annual GDP percentage change was nega-

> *"Renewable energy provides 18 percent of total net electricity generation worldwide. Renewable energy generators are spread across the globe, and wind power alone already provides a significant share of electricity in some regions: for example, 14 percent in the U.S. state of Iowa, 40 percent in the northern German state of Schleswig-Holstein, and 20 percent in the nation of Denmark. Some countries get most of their power from renewables, including Iceland (100 percent), Brazil (85 percent), Austria (62 percent), New Zealand (65 percent), and Sweden (54 percent)."*
>
> Christopher Flavin, former president of Worldwatch Institute

Table 10-4: Average Annual Growth Rates over a Five-year Period Following Post-1960 Recessions

Recession Ending	Real GDP	Real Consumption	Real Investment	Nonfarm Employment	Unemployment Rate
1975	3.7%	3.2%	7.3%	3.3%	-3.3%
1982	4.5%	4.7%	7.5%	2.6%	-8.6%
1991	3.3%	3.4%	8.5%	2.0%	-4.6%
2009	2.5%	2.1%	9.4%	1.0%	-3.5%

tive when compared with the previous year's annual value of GDP. The 2001 recession was not included even though it technically qualified as a recession (where two successive quarters showed negative economic growth). The 2001-2002 recessions showed a slowdown in annual GDP growth but did not show negative growth.

The EIA projects non-hydro renewable energy to grow from just under 3% today, to over 12% by 2035. This is real good news for the sector. It also means that in the next 20 years, growth will exceed four times what it is today. That calls for a huge amount of energy project financing to accommodate that type of an expansion and hence providing exciting opportunities for energy project developers, sponsors and lenders. Other organizations claim that the non-hydro sources could provide 10 percent of the nation's electricity generation by 2020 and 20 percent or more by 2035.

Wind and solar power currently have the highest growth rates as renewable resources for electricity generation. Although wind power represented less that 1 percent of total electricity generation in 2007, from 1997 to 2007 it experienced a 25.6 percent compounded annual rate of growth. In 2008, another 8.4 GW of capacity was added, for a total capacity of approximately 25 GW. Despite the economic downturn, 2.8 GW of new wind power generation capacity was installed in just the first quarter of 2009 alone.[21]

Central-utility generation of electricity from concentrating solar power (CSP) and photovoltaics (PV) combined to supply 600 GWh in 2007. This level has been approximately constant since 1990. However, it does not account for the increase in residential and other small-PV installations, the fastest-growing sector in solar electricity use. The use of solar PV in the U.S. has grown at a compounded annual rate of more than 40 percent from 2000 to 2005. Solar PV is a distributed generation source, with the electricity generated in the place where it is used. As such, it competes against retail electricity prices, not wholesale electricity prices. Therefore, if the retail electricity prices continue to increase (as they have across nearly all geographic regions) and more utilities adopt "time-of-day" pricing, which charges the highest rate during the middle of the day, solar PV could become even more cost competitive. However, the consumer of the solar power must still be connected to the grid (in most cases) in order to receive their electric needs when the sun is not shining.

Consistent and long-term policies and commitment from policy makers, government agencies and regulatory bodies (including tax and accounting) is essential to encouraging investment in renewable technologies and allowing renewable generation to reach its potential. Legislators and other government policy makers cannot continue to use the "on-again, off-again" policies of the past. Production tax credits, investment tax credits, depreciation methods, incentive and rebate programs all contribute to having a full future energy investment policy but not when they are not deployed consistently over many years. Investments in energy infrastructure projects are long-term commitments by developers, investors, lenders and users. Government policies must mirror those commitments.

> *"Drill for oil? You mean drill into the ground to try to find oil? You're crazy."*
>
> Reported comment to Col Edwin L. Drake from an investor when he asked to support his venture to drill the first commercial oil well in the U.S. (1859)

Perhaps the greatest immediate threat to the renewable energy industry was the termination of the treasury 1603 grant program on December 31, 2011. Although it could be re-introduced again in some form later, there is no clear indication that it will be. And, if the worst predictions are accurate, the cost of tax equity—even for the best projects sponsored by the strongest developers—may increase substantially. This would most certainly drive up the cost of financing renewable energy projects since the 1603 grant provided significant economic value to many renewable power projects.

On the plus side however, tremendous revenues on renewable energy projects can be expected to come from the sale of the renewable energy credits, carbon credits and emission reduction credits on both existing and future energy projects. The U.S. carbon market is estimated to grow to $1 trillion by 2020 and credits from renewable energy projects will be a significant portion of that market.

Energy Tax Provisions

Certainly, favorable tax provisions are a major driver for future renewable energy projects and a number of key provisions are due to expire at the end of 2012, 2013, 2016 and beyond. At this point it is largely unknown as to what will ultimately become of the favorable expiring energy tax provisions.

The current Obama administration is seeking to modify a number of energy tax incentives under their FY 2013 budget proposal which include:

- Extend PTC, grant

Table 10-5: Energy Tax Provisions Expiration

Incentive	Expiration Date
December 31, 2012	
Production tax credit (PTC)—wind section 45	December 31, 2012
Investment tax credit (ITC) in lieu of PTC—wind section 49	December 31, 2012
Cellulosic biofuels producer credit—section 40	December 31, 2012
Bonus depreciation for cellulosic biofuel plant property—section 168(l)	December 31, 2012
Indian coal credit—section 45	December 31, 2012
December 31, 2013 and Beyond	
PTC for biomass, geothermal, waste, hydropower, marine/hydrokinetic—section 45	December 31, 2013
ITC in lieu of PTC for biomass, geothermal, hydropower, marine/hydrokinetic—section 48	December 31, 2013
Energy efficient commercial buildings deduction—section 169(D)	December 31, 2013
Refinery expensing—section 179(C)	December 31, 2013
Fuel cell vehicles—section 30(B)	December 31, 2014
ITC for all property except for non-heat pump geothermal property—section 48	December 31, 2016 (solar ITC credit amount reduces to 10% after December 31, 2016)
Residential energy efficient property credit—section 24(D)	December 31, 2016

- Refundable credits
- $5 billion for 48C credits
- Convert 179D deduction into tax credit
- New and expanded vehicles credits
- Extension of 100% expensing

Conclusion

The renewable energy technologies and their respective financing alternatives described in this book will help to create a more secure and sustainable U.S. energy system. This assumes that there is a committed governmental strategy and national willingness to encourage efforts to accelerate renewable energy deployment. Both the public and the private sector will need to coordinate their efforts and commitment to achieve America's future energy needs. We have many new and promising technologies to make sure this happens. Both industry and the government must adopt a "portfolio" approach to developing and subsequent deployment of these renewable energy technologies. One thing that can be certain is: *future energy costs from traditional fossil fuel sources will continue to rise and costs from renewable technologies will continue to decline.* This can only be accomplished if, we as a nation, are committed to adopting a national comprehensive energy policy to meet our goals for sustainability, economic prosperity, security, and environmental quality.

It is essential that we **start now**.

References

1. *Medium-Term Renewable Energy Market Report 2013*: Market trends and projections to 2018, International Energy Agency, 2013
2. *Renewable Energy Country Attractiveness Indices*, Ernst and Young, May 2011
3. Ibid
4. U.S. Energy Information Administration
5. B. MacGillis and N. Grayson, PEW Charitable Trusts, Washington, D.C., March 24, 2010
6. British Petroleum PLC, *The BP Energy Outlook 2030*, London, January 2012
7. The SUN DAY Campaign is a non-profit research and educational organization to promote sustainable energy technologies as cost-effective alternative to nuclear power and fossil fuels. *http://www.sustainableenergycoalition.org/*
8. Ernst & Young, *Renewable Energy Country Attractiveness Indices*, February 2012
9. Solar Energy Industries Association and GTM research, *U.S. Market Insights 2010 Year in Review and First Quarter 2011-Executive Summary* *www.seia.org*
10. Bloomberg New Energy Finance, *US Clean Energy-White Paper*, November 21, 2011

11. *California's Clean Energy Future*, CEC-100-2010-002
12. Ibid
13. *http://www.photon.info/newsletter/document/80324.pdf*
14. National Research Council, *America's Energy Future: Technology and Transformation: Summary Edition*. Washington, DC: The National Academies Press, 2009
15. *Mapping and Assessment of the United States Ocean Wave Energy Resource*, 2011 Technical Report, Electric Power Research Institute, 3420 Hillview Ave, Palo Alto, CA
16. *Assessment of Energy Production Potential from Tidal Streams in the United States*, Final Project Report, Georgia Tech Research Report, June 29, 2011
17. EPA Green Power Partnership, October 2011
18. Mark Muro; Jonathan Rothwell; Devashree Saha, "Sizing the Clean Economy, A National and Regional Green Jobs Assessment," The Brookings Institution, 1775 Massachusetts Av NW, Washington, DC 20036-2188, Metropolitan Policy Program, 2011
19. *Green Outlook 2011: Green Trends Driving Growth*, McGraw Hill, 2011
20. *Green Jobs Study*, Booz Allen Hamilton, 8283 Greensboro Drive, McLean, VA 22108-3838
21. National Research Council, *America's Energy Future: Technology and Transformation: Summary Edition*, Washington, DC: The National Academies Press, 2009.
22. Carbon TradeEx America

Appendix 1

Sample Forms

There is no perfect set of forms used in documenting a renewable energy project. Each creditor or investor will have a basic set for forms they use and most will customize each of their standard forms used for each individual transaction. Additionally, the creditor or investor will use various forms as each individual project dictates—some in every project and some only in certain circumstances. Each of the forms discussed or reproduced in this book are regularly used in renewable energy projects. Each of them have been modified by me over the years from standard commercial documentation uses and revised to meet the needs of projects that are focused on renewable energy projects in the United States.

As a caveat, remember that no creditor should ever adopt a form for use without understanding it completely and having your own counsel review it for general use as well as for specific unique transactions you are contemplating entering into. That would include not only the language used, but also why a particular phraseology was selected. Additionally, anyone using a form should also learn to conform the models given here to the peculiarities of their own transaction and to the state and local laws of the jurisdiction where the energy project is physically located.

The scope of all the forms given here are reflective of commercial transactions only. They should not be used for consumer transactions (with the exception of the Consumer Solar Lease Transaction Disclosure). There are many laws that apply specifically to consumer transactions and this book does not seek to cover the multiplicity of laws covering consumer or commercial business transactions.

DISCLAIMER

The information provided in this Appendix is presented solely for educational and research purposes and to provide helpful information on the subjects discussed. The information is for general guidance on matters of interest only. The author and publisher are not offering the contents as legal, accounting, or other professional services advice. There is absolutely no assurance that any statement contained in any form or documents is true, correct or precise. While best efforts have been used in preparing the forms, the author and publisher make no representations or warranties of any kind and assume no liabilities of any kind with respect to the accuracy or completeness of the contents and specifically disclaim any implied warranties of merchantability or fitness of use for a particular purpose. Neither the author nor the publisher shall be liable for any loss or damage of whatever nature (direct, indirect, consequential, or other) whether arising in contract, tort or otherwise, which may arise as a result of your use of (or inability to use) this information, or from your use of (or failure to use) the information provided. Every company is different and the advice and strategies contained herein may not be suitable for your situation. Forms should be used as a guide and modified to meet the laws in your state. Laws may have changed, been modified or overturned by subsequent development since the document was created. The information provided is, at best, of a general nature. You should never delay seeking legal advice, disregard legal advice, or commence or discontinue any legal action because of information herein. Nothing in this Appendix or this book should be construed as an attempt to offer or render a legal opinion or otherwise engage in the practice of law. You should seek the services of competent professional's including legal, accounting, tax, or other advisors before using any of the forms or documents.

Listing of Sample Forms:

- ☐ Agreement to Apply Federal Grant to Asset Cost
- ☐ Application for Section 1603 Federal Grant
- ☐ Assignment Notice of Payment Under Section 1603 Grant
- ☐ Assignment of Deposit Account
- ☐ Assignment of Lease
- ☐ Authorization to Add
- ☐ Certificate of Secretary on Corporate Resolution
- ☐ Confidentiality and Non-Disclosure Agreement
- ☐ Consumer Solar Lease Transaction Disclosure Information
- ☐ Corporate Resolution to Lease
- ☐ Credit Authorization Release
- ☐ Creditor Environmental Audit Checklist
- ☐ Debtor's Attorney's Opinion Letter
- ☐ Disclaimer of Ownership
- ☐ Energy Purchase Agreement
- ☐ Environmental Audit Checklist
- ☐ Environmental Indemnity Agreement
- ☐ Equipment Acceptance Notice and Delivery Certificate
- ☐ Estoppel Certificate
- ☐ General Environmental Audit Checklist
- ☐ Guaranty-Personal
- ☐ Insurance Coverage Request
- ☐ Landlord Waiver
- ☐ Lease Purchase Option
- ☐ Lender's Loss Payable Endorsement
- ☐ Letter of Intent
- ☐ Memorandum of Solar Site License & Lease
- ☐ Mortgagee Waiver and Consent
- ☐ Mutual Non-Disclosure Agreement
- ☐ Notice of Assignment of Section 1603 Payment Under ARRA
- ☐ Operating Lease Agreement
- ☐ Performance Bond
- ☐ Pledge Agreement
- ☐ Pre-Construction Project Scoping Analysis
- ☐ Purchase Order
- ☐ PV System Plan Check Worksheet
- ☐ Renewable Energy Environmental Audit Checklist
- ☐ Section 1603 Accountant Certification Report
- ☐ Security Deposit Agreement
- ☐ Service Agreement on Project Assets
- ☐ Subordination, Attornment, Non-Disturbance and Assignment Agreement
- ☐ Subordination, Non-Disturbance, and Attornment Agreement

Agreement to Apply Federal Grant to Asset Cost

Payments for Specified Energy Property In Lieu of Tax Credits
Under the
AMERICAN RECOVERY AND REINVESTMENT ACT OF 2009

TERMS AND CONDITIONS

The parties to this agreement are ____________ (Applicant) and ____________. The parties hereby agree that proceeds from Section 1603 of the American Recovery and Tax Act of 2009 (ARRA) will be applied towards the purchase of the assets described in the renewable energy project. The proceeds are subject to the terms and conditions described below as required under Section 1603 of the Act.

1. **Authority**
   Section 1603 of the American Recovery and Reinvestment Tax Act of 2009 (Section 1603) authorizes the United States Department of the Treasury (Treasury) to make payments to persons who place in service specified energy property provided certain conditions are met.

2. **Eligibility**
   a. The applicant is the owner or lessee of specified energy property that qualifies for funds under Section 1603 and is the original user of the property.
   b. The applicant is not a federal, state or local government, or any political subdivision, agency or instrumentality thereof; an organization that is described in section 501(c) of the IRC and is exempt from tax under section 501(a) of the IRC; or an entity referred to in section 54(j)(4) of the IRC.
   c. The applicant is not a partnership or pass-thru entity that has a person described in section 2.c above as a direct or indirect partner (or other holder of an equity or profits interest) unless this person only owns an indirect interest in the applicant through a taxable C corporation.
   d. The applicant is not a foreign person or entity unless it is a foreign person or entity that qualifies for the exception in section 168(h)(2)(B) of the IRC.

3. **Ongoing Representations and Obligations**
   a. The applicant understands that Treasury is relying on the accuracy of the information contained in the application in making determinations with respect to the applicant's eligibility for a Section 1603 payment. If the applicant determines that any information included on or with the application was materially inaccurate or incorrect, the applicant must immediately inform Treasury. If Treasury determines, as a result of this information, that the applicant does not qualify for funds or that the applicant received funds in excess of the amount to which the applicant was entitled, the applicant must immediately return the funds to Treasury.
   b. The applicant understands that none of the applicant's obligations herein terminate upon the sale or other disposition of the property to an eligible entity.

4. **Production and Investment Tax Credit**
   a. The applicant will not claim a tax credit under section 45 or section 48 of the IRC with respect to the property described in the application.

5. **Reporting**
   a. The applicant shall provide periodic reports as required by Treasury. A project performance report is required on an annual basis for a period of five years after the property was placed in service. Annual performance reports are due no later than 21 days following the end of the reporting period. The first reporting period begins on the date the property is placed in service.

b. On an annual basis, the applicant must provide a project performance report including the following elements:
Name of applicant
Current owner of property
Treasury application number
Name of project
Location of project: city/county, State, zip code
Number of jobs retained
Annual production (in kilowatt hours, MMBtus, or horsepower as applicable)
Installed nameplate capacity (in kilowatts, MMBtus, or horsepower as applicable)

c. The applicant shall submit any other reports that Treasury deems necessary to comply with American Recovery and Reinvestment Act guidance.

6. **Recapture**

a. The applicant shall certify to Treasury on an annual basis for a period of five years from the date the property was placed in service that the property has not been disposed of to a disqualified person and that the property continues to qualify as specified energy property (as that term is used in Section 1603). Annual certifications shall be submitted at the same time as the performance report described in Section 5 above.

b. If the property is disposed of to a disqualified person and/or ceases to qualify as a specified energy property (hereinafter "disqualifying event") within five years from the date the property is placed in service the applicant must repay funds to the Treasury as follows: 100% of the funds must be repaid if the disqualifying event takes place within one year from the date the property is placed in service; 80% of the funds must be repaid if the disqualifying event takes place after one year but before two years from the date the property is placed in service; 60% of the funds must be repaid if the disqualifying event takes place after two years but before three years from the date the property is placed in service; 40% of the funds must be repaid if the disqualifying event takes place after three years but before four years from the date the property is placed in service; and 20% of the funds must be repaid if the disqualifying event takes place after four years but before five years from the date the property is placed in service.

c. Any amount subject to recapture becomes a debt owed to the United States payable to the General Fund of the Treasury and enforceable by all available means including enforcement by the United States Department of Justice against any assets of the applicant entity. Debts arising under these rules are not considered tax liabilities.

7. **Maintenance of and Access to Records**

a. The applicant must maintain project, financial, and accounting records sufficient to demonstrate that Section 1603 funds were properly obtained in accordance with the Section 1603 program and these Terms and Conditions. The Treasury, as the awarding office, the cognizant Treasury inspector general, and the Comptroller General of the United States, or any of their authorized representatives, shall have the right of physical access to the applicant's facilities and to any pertinent books, documents, papers, or other records (electronic and otherwise) of the applicant and each partnership and pass-thru entity that directly or indirectly owns an interest in the applicant which are pertinent to the Section 1603 payment, in order to conduct audits, examinations, and evaluations.

8. **Disallowance**

a. If the applicant materially fails to comply with any term of the award, whether stated in a Federal statute or regulation, program guidance, these Terms and Conditions, or a notice of award, Treasury may take any remedial action that is legally available including disallowing all or a part of the Section 1603 payment. Any payment that is disallowed must be returned to the Treasury.

b. In taking an enforcement action, Treasury will provide the applicant with the opportunity for a hearing, appeal, or other administrative proceeding to which the applicant is entitled under any statute or regulation applicable to the action involved.

c. The applicant must immediately report any indication of fraud, waste, abuse, or potentially criminal activity pertaining to Section 1603 funds to Treasury and the cognizant Treasury inspector general.

9. Information Sharing

a. The applicant agrees that any information provided to the Treasury in the application, attachments, supporting documents, reports or otherwise in connection with its application under Section 1603 may be shared with other federal agencies, including the Internal Revenue Service, as needed by those agencies to conduct official agency business. Notwithstanding the foregoing, bank account information and proprietary information will not be shared unless required by law.

b. The applicant acknowledges that Treasury may publicly release the name of the applicant; the type, location, and description of the property that is the subject of the application; and the amount of funding provided.

SIGNATURES

Under penalties of perjury, we declare that we have examined these Terms and Conditions, agree to them, and will ensure that they will be followed. Each party declares that they are an authorized official of the respective party and are authorized to bind the applicant to these Terms and Conditions.

Applicant:

Name	Title
Phone	Email
Signature	Date signed

________________:

Name	Title
Phone	Email
Signature	Date signed

Application for Section 1603 Federal Grant

PAYMENTS FOR SPECIFIED RENEWABLE ENERGY PROPERTY IN LIEU OF TAX CREDITS

This is one of two parts of the application package for payment under the Section 1603 program. The other document is the signed Terms and Conditions. All applicants must submit this application form before October 1, 2011. Applicants who place a qualified property in service during 2009 or 2010 should submit the application form and the Terms and Conditions form at the same time after the property has been placed in service. Applicants who have begun construction of a qualified property during 2009 or 2010 and have not yet placed the property in service by the date of application, should submit only this application (not the Terms and Conditions) before October 1, 2011 to demonstrate that construction began during 2009 or 2010. Once the qualified property is placed in service, the applicant should submit both an updated application form and the signed Terms and Conditions document, indicating the identification number (issued by Treasury) of the applicant's preliminary submission.

While there are directions in this application, they are not a substitute for reading and understanding the Program Guidance, Terms and Conditions, Section 1603 of the American Recovery and Reinvestment Tax Act of 2009, and Sections 45 and 48 of the Internal Revenue Code.

Section 1: Applicant Eligibility

1A. Type of Applicant – check the box or boxes which describe the applicant. Governments, 501(c) organizations, 54(j)(4) entities, partnership or pass-thru entities with any government /501(c)/54(j)(4) entity as a partner (or other holder of an equity or profits interest), and in some cases foreign persons and entities are not eligible for Section 1603 payments.

- ☐ Federal, State, or local government or any political subdivision, agency, or instrumentality thereof – do not continue with application
- ☐ Organization described in section 501(c) of the Internal Revenue Code and exempt from tax under section 501(a) of such Code – do not continue with application
- ☐ Entity referred to in paragraph (4) of section 54(j) of the Internal Revenue Code – do not continue with application
- ☐ Partnership or pass-thru entity with a government or any political subdivision, agency, or instrumentality thereof, 501(c) organization, or 54(j)(4) entity as a direct or indirect partner (or other direct or indirect holder of an equity or profits interest) unless such person only owns an indirect interest in the applicant through a taxable C corporation – do not continue with application.
- ☐ Foreign person or entity not qualifying for the exception in section 168(h)(2)(B) of the Internal Revenue Code with respect to the property – do not continue with application
- ☐ Foreign person or entity qualifying for the exception in section 168(h)(2)(B) of the Internal Revenue Code with respect to the property
- ☐ Sole proprietorship
- ☐ Joint venture
- ☐ Partnership
- ☐ Domestic C corporation
- ☐ Domestic S corporation
- ☐ Cooperative organization described in section 1381 of the Internal Revenue Code
- ☐ Real Estate Investment Trust (REIT)
- ☐ Other (specify here):

1B. Applicant's Interest in the Property – check the appropriate box.

- ☐ Applicant is owner of the property.

☐	Applicant is lessee of the property (include waiver from owner as described in the Program Guidance and in Section 6 of this Application).
☐	Applicant is not the owner or lessee of the property – do not continue with application.

Section 2: Property Information

2A. Depreciation and Use of Property – check the box or boxes which describe the property.

☐	Property is depreciable or amortization is allowed in lieu of depreciation.
☐	Property is not depreciable or amortization is not allowed – do not continue with application.
☐	Property is public utility property within the meaning of section 168(i)(10) of the Internal Revenue Code.

2B. Property Identification – enter information about the location of the property.

Name	Street Address/County
City	State & Zip Code

2C. Property Placed in Service – enter the date on which the property was placed in service. See Program Guidance for a definition of placed in service date. If applying for multiple units of property that the applicant is treating as a single, larger unit of property and the units have different placed in service dates, enter the date the first and last units were placed in service. If property is not yet placed in service, skip to Section 2D below.

Date property placed in service – skip to Section 3.

2D. Date Construction Began – for properties not yet placed in service, enter the date on which construction began. See Program Guidance for a definition of beginning of construction and the credit termination date by which time the project must be placed in service.

Construction of the property began on this date.

Construction of the property has not begun – do not continue with this application.

2E. Expected Placed in Service Date – for properties not yet placed in service, enter the anticipated date when the property will be placed in service. See Program Guidance for dates by which specific properties must be placed in service to be eligible for Section 1603 funds.

Anticipated date the property will be placed in service.

2F. Narrative Description of Beginning of Construction – for properties not yet placed in service, describe what construction activities have taken place. Limit to 2,500 characters.

Section 3: Applicant Information

3A. Applicant – enter information about the entity that placed the property in service/began construction. If applicant did not or will not originally place the property in service do not continue with this application.

Business Name	Street Address

Phone Number	City
Employer Identification Number (EIN)	State & Zip Code
DUNS Number	Website Address

3B. Contact Person – enter information for the person to be contacted about this application.

Name	Organization Affiliation
Phone & Fax	E-mail Address

3C. Previous Applications – check the box indicating whether the applicant has submitted any applications previously for Section 1603 payments for this property.

☐ No Applications submitted previously for Section 1603 payments for this property.

☐ Applications submitted previously for this property or property at this same location; enter Treasury application number issued for the applications here:

Section 4: Property Description

4A. Specified Energy Property – check the box or boxes which describes the type of specified energy property. See Program Guidance for a further explanation of each type.

☐ Specified properties eligible under Section 45 of Internal Revenue Code

☐ Wind Facility – uses wind to produce electricity (wind turbines with capacity of 100kW or less may also qualify below as small wind energy property but only one payment is allowed with respect to the property).

☐ Closed-loop Biomass Facility (other than a facility described in the box below) – uses organic material from a plant grown exclusively for purposes of being used to generate electricity. If a portion of fuel is not closed-loop biomass, give the percentage of fuel, on an annual basis, that is closed-loop biomass:

☐ Facility modified to use closed-loop biomass to co-fire with coal, other biomass, or both. Modification must be approved under the Biomass Power for Rural Development Program or be part of a pilot project of the Commodity Credit Corporation. Give the percentage of fuel, on an annual basis, that is closed-loop biomass:

☐ Open-loop Biomass Facility (cellulosic waste material) – uses solid, non-hazardous, cellulosic waste material or any lignin material derived from qualified sources described in section 45(c)(3)(ii) of the Internal Revenue Code to produce electricity. If a portion of fuel is not open-loop biomass of this type, give the percentage of fuel, on an annual basis, that is open-loop biomass of this type:

☐ Open-loop Biomass Facility (livestock waste nutrients) – uses agricultural livestock waste nutrients to produce electricity and has a nameplate capacity rating of not less than 150 kW. If a portion of fuel is not agricultural livestock waste nutrients, give the percentage of fuel, on an annual basis, that is agricultural livestock waste nutrients:

☐ Geothermal Facility – uses geothermal energy to produce electricity.

☐ Landfill Gas Facility – uses gas derived from the biodegradation of municipal solid waste to produce electricity.

☐ Trash Facility – uses municipal solid waste to produce electricity and is not a landfill gas facility.

☐ Hydropower Facility (incremental hydropower) – produces incremental hydropower production as a result of efficiency improvements and additions to capacity to which the incremental hydropower production is attributable. The baseline and incremental increase in energy production must be certified by FERC.

☐ Hydropower Facility – hydropower producing facility installed on a qualifying non-hydroelectric dam. The property must be licensed by FERC and meet all other applicable environmental, licensing, and regulatory requirements

☐ Marine and Hydrokinetic Renewable Energy Facility – uses marine and hydrokinetic renewable energy to produce electricity and has a nameplate capacity rating of at least 150 kW.

☐ **Specified properties eligible under Section 48 of Internal Revenue Code**

☐ Solar Electricity Property – uses solar energy to generate electricity.

☐ Solar Thermal Property – uses solar energy to heat or cool (or provide hot water for use in) a structure, or to provide solar process heat (property used to generate energy for heating a swimming pool ineligible).

☐ Solar Lighting Property – uses solar energy to illuminate the inside of a structure using fiber-optic distributed sunlight.

☐ Geothermal Property – equipment used to produce, distribute, or use energy derived from a geothermal deposit.

☐ Fuel Cell Property – fuel cell power plant that has a nameplate capacity of at least 0.5 kW of electricity using an electrochemical process and an electricity-only generation efficiency greater than 30%.

☐ Microturbine Property – stationary microturbine power plant that has a nameplate capacity of less than 2,000 kW and an electricity-only generation efficiency of not less than 26% at International Standard Organization conditions.

☐ Combined Heat and Power System Property – system that uses the same energy source for the simultaneous or sequential generation of electrical power, mechanical shaft power, or both, in combination with the generation of steam or other form of useful thermal energy ad that meets all of the following requirements:

1. System produces at least 20% of total useful energy in the form of thermal energy which is not used for electrical or mechanical power (report thermal production in section 4D of this application)
2. System produces at least 20% of total useful energy in the form of electrical or mechanical power (or combination) (report electrical and/or mechanical production in section 4D of this application).
3. System energy efficiency percentage exceeds 60% (unless system uses open or closed loop biomass (see Guidance) for at least 90% of the energy source). Specify energy efficiency percentage%: _____ and, if applicable, % of energy source from open or closed loop biomass: _____
4. System does not exceed 50 MW or a mechanical energy capacity in excess of 67,000 horsepower or an equivalent combination of electrical and mechanical energy capacities (report system capacity in section 4D of this application).

☐ Small Wind Energy Property – uses a turbine with nameplate capacity of not more than 100 kW to generate electricity.

☐ Geothermal Heat Pump Property – uses the ground or ground water as a thermal energy source to heat a structure or as a thermal energy sink to cool a structure.

4B. Narrative Description of Property – give a summary description of the property that is suitable for publication. Limit the summary to 2,500 characters. If applying for multiple units of property that are being treated as a single, larger property, so indicate in the narrative.

4C. Use of Energy - enter information in one of the two boxes to describe how the energy produced is being/will be used.

Energy produced has been/will be sold. ☐
Enter the name and address of the buyer.

Energy produced has not been/will not be sold. ☐
Describe how it is/will be used. Limit to 2,500 characters. ______

4D. Energy Generated by the Property – fill in the appropriate column depending on whether the property generates electrical, mechanical, or thermal energy (or combination) for the capacity and production of the property. This section is not applicable to solar illumination properties and geothermal heat pump properties. For properties not yet placed in service or that have not operated for a full year, enter the estimated production. kW=kilowatt(s), kWh=kilowatt hour(s), MMBtu=one-million British Thermal Units, hp=horsepower.

	Electrical	Mechanical	Thermal
Installed nameplate capacity	☐ kW	☐ (must specify whether kW, MMBtu, or hp)	☐ MMBtu/hr
Estimated annual production	☐ kWh	☐ (must specify whether kWh, MMBtu, or hp)	☐ MMBtu

4E. Jobs Created/Retained by the Property – enter the estimated number of direct jobs created/retained by the property. Direct jobs are those created/retained in the project, not by suppliers who make the materials used in the project.

	Construction stage	Operational stage
Full—time jobs (at least 35 hours per week)		
Part-time jobs (less than 35 hours per week)		

Section 5: Cost Basis and Request for Payment

5A. Cost Basis and Applicable Percentage – enter the qualified cost basis of the property and the applicable percentage to calculate the request for payment. The applicable percentage is either 30% or 10% depending on the type of energy property. See Program Guidance to determine the correct percentage to apply. For properties not yet placed in service, skip to Section 6B.

☐	Qualified cost basis as shown in supporting documentation.
☐	Applicable percentage (enter either 30% or 10%)
☐	For Fuel Cell Property – if the applicable percentage times the qualified cost basis exceeds an amount equal to $1,500 for each 0.5 kW of capacity, enter an amount equal to $1,500 times each 0.5 kW of capacity
☐	For Microturbine Property – if the applicable percentage times the qualified cost basis exceeds an amount equal to $200 for each kW of capacity, enter an amount equal to $200 times the number of kW of capacity

5B. Request for Payment – from the calculation in 5A, enter the amount of request for payment. For properties not yet placed in service, skip to Section 6B.

$0.00	Amount of request for payment.

Section 6: Documentation

6A. Documentation for Properties Placed In Service – for properties placed in service attach documentation: to establish that the property has been placed in service as claimed in Section 3C of this application; to demonstrate that the property has met the requirements shown in Section 4 of this application; and to support costs claimed in Section 5 of this application. Check the boxes in the chart below to show that the documentation is provided. See Program Guidance for information on acceptable documentation to establish that a property is placed in service and meets the eligibility requirements and to support costs. If the applicant is a lessee (as indicated in Section 1B), attach a waiver, as described in the Program Guidance, from the owner. For properties not yet placed in service, skip to Section 6B.

☐	Documentation to support eligibility of the specified energy property is attached.
☐	Documentation to support costs is attached.
☐	Documentation to establish that property is placed in service is attached.
☐	Owner's waiver, if applicant is a lessee (as indicated in Section 1B), is attached – otherwise enter NA for not applicable.

6B. Documentation for Properties Not Yet Placed In Service – for properties not yet placed in service attach documentation to verify that construction has begun. Check the box in the chart below to show that the documentation is provided. See Program Guidance for information on acceptable documentation to establish that construction has begun.

☐	Documentation to establish that construction has begun is attached.

Section 7: Signature of Applicant

Under penalties of perjury, I declare that I have examined this application and to the best of my knowledge and belief, it is true, correct, and complete. I declare that I am the applicant or an authorized official for the applicant. Further, I agree the information in this application can be disclosed to the Internal Revenue Service.

Name	Title	
Phone	Email	
	Signature	Date Signed

Assignment of Payments Made Under Section 1603 of Division B of The American Recovery and Reinvestment Act of 2009

I. Conditions on Assignment

Recipients of payments made under the 1603 Program may assign the payment to a financial institution provided:

(1) the payment is $1,000 or more

(2) the payment is assigned to a bank, trust company or other financing institution, including any Federal lending agency;

(3) The assignment covers all amounts payable and is not subject to further assignment except that any assignment may be made to one party acting as agent or trustee for two or more parties who are participating in the financing;

(4) The assignee files a written Notice of Assignment of the payment together with a true copy of the instrument of assignment with Treasury (see instructions below)

II. How to Accomplish the Assignment

The assignee must provide to Treasury a Notice of Assignment signed by the assignee and a true copy of the instrument of assignment. These documents must be submitted at the time the applicant completes an application for a property that has been placed in service. Documents may be submitted by email to: *1603Assignments@do.treas.gov*. The Notice of Assignment must include the Treasury Application Number (TAN) provided to the applicant by Treasury at the time the application is submitted. Assignees who provide a valid Notice of Assignment along with a true copy of the instrument of assignment will receive an email notification from Treasury acknowledging receipt.

Applicants must ensure, as a condition of any such assignment, that the assignee register in the Central Contractor Registry (CCR) *www.ccr.gov*. A payment cannot be issued to an assignee that is not registered in the CCR.

Assignment Notice of Payment Under Section 1603 Grant

This Notice refers to Treasury Application Number (TAN) ____________________ submitted by (*name of applicant*) ______________________________ to the United States Department of the Treasury for payment under Section 1603 of Division B of the American Recovery and Reinvestment Act of 2009.

The payment due or to become due under the application described above has been assigned to the undersigned under the provisions of the Assignment of Claims Act of 1940, as amended, 31 U.S.C. 3727, 41 U.S.C. 15.

A true copy of the instrument of assignment executed by the above named applicant on (*date*)______________ is attached.

The payment due or to become due under the application described above should be made payable to the undersigned assignee, provided the undersigned is registered in the Central Contractor Registry.

____
Name of Assignee

____
DUNS number of Assignee

____
Address of Assignee

____
Signature of Authorized Representative of Assignee

____
Title of Authorized Representative

Assignment of Deposit Account

THE UNDERSIGNED does hereby assign to Lessor, ___________________, funds of any nature which we now have or may hereafter invest as security for our obligations or indebtedness, contingent or otherwise. It is understood and agreed between the parties hereto that the amount covered by this assignment shall not exceed the total indebtedness of the undersigned, contingent or otherwise, to said Lessor.

IT IS FURTHER UNDERSTOOD AND AGREED between the parties hereto that this assignment shall terminate at such time as all indebtedness and lease obligations of the Lessee shall be paid in full.

Date: ____________________ Your Town, California

____________________ Witness: _________________

____________________ Witness: _________________

Receipt of Passbook Number ___________ and/or Certificate Number __________ is hereby acknowledged.

LESSOR: ________________________________

By:____,

Title: ____________________________________

Assignment and Security Agreement

1. **Identification of Parties.** THIS AGREEMENT made and entered into on the date indicated below is intended to set forth the rights and responsibilities of the parties hereto, being ________________________(hereinafter "Assignor") and ________________________ (hereinafter "Assignee").

2. **Assignment and Security Interest**. For value received, Assignor does hereby assign to Assignee all of its right, title and interest in that certain Lease Number__________, and the proceeds thereof, between Assignor and ______ ________________________ (hereinafter "Lessee"), under date of______________________.

Remaining Lease Term:		months
Payment Amount:	$	
Discounted Rate:		Percent (%)
Amount Advanced:	$	

This Assignment is for the purpose of securing Lessee's obligation to pay all rentals, taxes, late charges, collection fees, attorney fees and any and all other monetary obligations pursuant to the terms of the Lease. Assignor also assigns to Assignee solely as security for performance of the Lease by Leseee, all of its right, title and interest in and to the equipment (including all substitutions, replacements, additions, attachments and proceeds thereof) subject to the Lease. Assignor further assigns solely as security for performance of the Lease by Lessee, all of its right, title and interest in and to any additional agreements with Lessee or third parties, including but not limited to any purchase orders, guarantees, insurance policies, delivery and acceptance notices, addendums to Lease, security agreements, mortgages or their interests in real property, powers of attorney and any and all other agreements and documents related to the Lease assigned. All of the foregoing, including but not limited to the equipment, shall be collectively referred to as the "Collateral."

3. **Effective Date of Assignment.** It is agreed that this Assignment shall be of no effect until accepted and executed by Assignee at Assignee's offices.

4. **Consideration**. As consideration for this Assignment, Assignee will pay to Assignor an amount equal to the monthly rental specified in the Lease multiplied by the remaining number of months in the term of the Lease, less such discount as is agreed upon by Assignor and Assignee.

5. **Reassignment**. In the event and at such time as Lessee has performed each and every of its obligations as required by the Lease and provided that Assignor is not in default of any of its obligations to Assignee arising out of this agreement or any any other agreement between Assignor and Assignee, Assignee will reassign to Assignor all right, title and interest in and to the Collateral, without any warranty of any kind, express or implied, and without recourse. In the event of a reassignment, it is understood that Assignee will not, under any circumstances, be responsible for any expenses involved with regard to the equipment or the return thereof, and Assignee will further have no responsibility to deal with or control the equipment following reassignment.

6. **Assignor Representations and Warranties**. Assignor makes the following representations and warranties with regard to the Lease and the equipment subject thereto:

a. Assignor is the owner of the Lease and the equipment subject thereto. Title of Assignor is absolute with no encumbrances of any kind other than the leasehold interest of the Lessee pursuant to the Lease. Assignee's assignment and grant of a security interest therein to Assignor is not and will not be encumbered by any pre existing, superseding, superior or inferior interest of any kind.

b. The Lease is a bona fide obligation of the Lessee and any Co Lessees and is valid and enforceable according to its terms. Any guarantees thereof are bona fide obligations of the guarantors and are valid and enforceable according to their terms. All agreements provided in connection with this transaction have been duly executed by the appropriate parties, who have been duly authorized to execute same. All agreements are enforceable in accordance with their terms and are not presently in default.

c. The Lease is for business or commercial purposes only and not for agricultural, personal, family or household purposes.

d. All of the equipment described in the Lease has been delivered to and accepted by Lessee, and Lessee has designated its satisfaction therewith in form satisfactory to Assignee.

e. The Lease is the sole and complete agreement by and between Assignor and Lessee, and there are no other lease agreements between Assignor and Lessee or any other party with respect to the equipment.

f. Lessee's obligations, including but not limited to the duty to pay rent and other monetary obligations, are not subject to any known defense, setoff or counterclaim of any kind.

7. **Scope of Assignor Liability**. This assignment is a non-recourse assignment by Assignor to Assignee and upon default by Lessee in the payment or performance of its obligations under the Lease, Assignee shall have recourse solely against the Collateral; provided, however, in the event that Assignor breaches any duty, warranty, representation or other obligation in this agreement Assignor shall refund to Assignee in cash and on demand an amount equal to the then existing value of the remaining rentals, determined by discounting future payments at the same rate of discount used to determine the original amount paid by Assignee for the assignment. In such event, the Collateral shall be reassigned to Assignor, without any warranty of any kind, express or implied. Alternatively, Assignor, at its election, may pay to Assignee all payments due under the Lease and perform all obligations of the Lease as each comes due.

8. **Foreclosure of Assignee's Security Interest**. In the event that Lessee files a petition in bankruptcy, Assignee's security interest in the Collateral shall be deemed immediately foreclosed, and agrees to give written notice of the petition to the Assignor. In the event that the Lease is in default, as determined by Assignee in Assignee's sole discretion, Assignee shall have the right to foreclose its security interest in the Collateral immediately and agrees to give written notice to Assignor of such action. In the event that Assignee forecloses its security interest Assignor shall have no further right, title or interest in the Collateral whatsoever, except pursuant to Assignee's exercise of its rights pursuant to Paragraph 7, but shall nevertheless cooperate with and assist Assignee in its enforcement, collection and recovery efforts. In the event that the proceeds of foreclosure exceed Lessee's liabilities under the Lease and Assignee's expenses (including reasonable attorney's fees, whether or not suit is instituted), Assignor shall receive such excess.

9. **Audit; Endorsement**. Assignor agrees that Assignee may, upon reasonable notice, audit Assignor's books and records relating to the assigned transaction and may sign and endorse in Assignor's name any checks, drafts, money orders, notes or other remittances received on account of the assigned transaction.

10. **No Assignor Modification; No Waiver.** Assignor shall have no authority to, and will not, without Assignee's prior written consent, accept collections, repossess or consent to the return of the equipment described in the Lease, or modify, settle or adjust the terms of the Lease or related agreements, or cancel or terminate the Lease or related agreements. Assignee's knowledge now or hereafter of any breach of or non compliance with the provisions of this Agreement shall not constitute a waiver by Assignee of any of Assignee's rights with respect to such breach or non compliance. Assignee's waiver of any provision of this Agreement in one instance shall not constitute a waiver in any other instance.

11. **Successors and Assigns**. This Agreement shall be binding upon the heirs, administrators, executors or other successors or assigns of the parties hereto.

12. **Entire Agreement; No Oral Modification**. This instrument constitutes the entire agreement between Assignor and Assignee. No provision of this Agreement shall be modified unless in writing and signed by an authorized

representative from the executive offices of both parties.

13. **Severability**. Assignor and Assignee intend this Assignment to be a valid and enforceable legal instrument, and no provision of this Assignment which may be deemed unenforceable shall in any way invalidate any other provision or provisions of this Assignment, all of which shall remain in full force and effect.

14. **Assignment**. Assignor shall not, without Assignee's prior written consent, assign this Agreement or any of its obligations pursuant to this Assignment. Assignee may freely assign its right and obligation hereunder, in whole or in part, at any time, providing written notice is given to Assignor and the new party agrees to be bound by the terms and conditions of this agreement as well as the Master Purchase Agreement incorporated herein.

15. **Indemnification**. Notwithstanding anything to the contrary in this Agreement, Assignor shall indemnify Assignee against any claims, actions, damages or liabilities, including all attorney fees and costs, whether or not suit is instituted, arising out of or connected with the assigned transaction or this Agreement caused by Assignor's actions, without limitation. This indemnification shall survive any termination, cancellation or other cessation of this Agreement.

16. **Choice of Law and Venue; Attorney Fees**. This Assignment shall not be effective until signed by Assignee at its office. This Assignment shall be considered to have been made in the State of ____________ and shall be interpreted in accordance with the laws and regulations of the State of ____________, county of ____________________. Assignor agrees to ______________ jurisdiction in any action, suit or proceeding arising out of this Assignment, and concedes that it, and each of them, transacted business in the State of ____________ by entering into this Agreement. In the event of legal action to enforce the terms of this Assignment, Assignor agrees that venue may be laid in ____________ County, State of ____________. If enforcement action is taken by Assignee to enforce any term of this Assignment, the prevailing party in any such action shall be entitled to a reasonable attorney fee, including attorney fees incurred at trial, on appeal and review, or incurred without actions, suits or proceedings, together with all costs and expenses incurred in pursuit thereof.

AGREED TO by and between the undersigned parties on ________________________

ASSIGNOR: ______________________________
Address: ____

By:

Title: ____________________________

ASSIGNEE: __________________________
Address: ____

By:

Title: ____________________________

Authorization to Add to Lease or Guaranty

I (we) authorize____________________________, its successors and/or assigns, to add to my (our) Guaranty and/or Equipment Lease number________, any amounts necessary to pay off, bring current any senior lienholder(s), including delinquent taxes or tax sale(s), or other amounts that may be advanced for the benefit of Trustor(s) or ________________________, its successors and/or assigns, as may be required by ________________________________ for real estate pledged by Trustor(s) as collateral for the Guaranty and/or Equipment Lease Agreement.

I (we) authorize ____________________________, its successors and/or assigns, to add to my (our) Guaranty and/or Lease Agreement any amounts necessary to keep fire/flood/earthquake insurance premiums paid current for the real estate pledged by Trustor(s) as collateral for the Guaranty and/or Equipment Lease Agreement.

I (we) understand that ______________________, its successors and/or assigns, requires sufficient fire/flood/earthquake insurance coverage for property(ies) located at ____________________________ at all times.

DATE:

LESSEE:	TRUSTOR(S):
By: ____________________________	____________________________
By: ____________________________	____________________________
By: ____________________________	____________________________
By: ____________________________	____________________________

Certificate of Secretary As to Adoption of Resolutions

(Corporate Guarantor)

The undersigned, ________________ (Corporate Secretary), hereby certifies:
That he/she is now, at all times herein mentioned has been, the duly elected, qualified and acting Secretary of ________________, a duly organized and existing corporation, and in charge of the minute book and corporate records of said corporation; that the following is a full, true and correct copy of certain resolutions adopted by the Board of Directors of said corporation at a meeting thereof duly held on ________________ at which meeting a quorum of said Board was at all times present and acting; and that said resolutions have not been modified nor rescinded and are at the date of this certificate in full force and effect.

WHEREAS ________________ has requested ________________ ("Lessor") to enter into a certain Equipment Lease Agreement and/or other agreement or agreements extending financial accommodation and Lessor is willing to execute said Equipment Lease Agreement and/or agreements and consummate the transactions now or hereafter contemplated thereby only on the condition that this corporation guaranty payment of and performance by Customer of all terms and conditions on its part to be performed under said Equipment Lease Agreement and/or other agreement or agreements, all other undertakings of Customer to Lessor in connection therewith and all other undertakings in which obligations run from Customer to Lessor; and

WHEREAS the Board has caused a copy of the proposed Continuing Guaranty of Indebtedness to be presented to this meeting.

NOW, THEREFORE, BE IT RESOLVED: That this corporation enter into that certain Continuing Guaranty of Indebtedness in favor of Lessor and dated ________________, substantially in the form presented to this meeting.

RESOLVED FURTHER: That the President, ________________, and the Secretary, and each of them, is hereby authorized and directed to execute, acknowledge and deliver in the name of and on behalf of this corporation said Continuing Guaranty of Indebtedness and to execute and deliver any other documents and to take any further action which may be necessary or be by such officer deemed appropriate in order to carry out the purposes of the foregoing.

RESOLVED FURTHER: That the Secretary of this corporation be and he/she hereby is authorized and directed to execute, acknowledge and deliver a certified copy of these resolutions to Lessor and any other person or agency which may require copies of these resolutions.

RESOLVED FURTHER: That Lessor is authorized to act upon these resolutions until written notice of the revocation thereof is delivered to Lessor, such revocation in no way to affect the guaranty of said obligation of Customer to Lessor with relation to agreements entered into prior to delivery of such notice of revocation.
IN WITNESS WHEREOF, the undersigned has executed this Certificate the ____ day of ________________, 20____.

Secretary: ________________

Confidentiality and Non-Disclosure Agreement

Renewable Energy Creditor (REC), a ________________ corporation having its principal place of business at ____, and ABC Company ("ABC"), a ______________________ corporation having an address at ________________________________, enter into this Non-Disclosure Agreement ("Agreement") as of __________________. In this Agreement, references to "REC" or "ABC" shall include each company's respective principal owners. Each party hereto is a "Party" and the parties hereto are, collectively, the "Parties."

Each disclosing Party, in each instance the "Disclosing Party," is prepared to furnish to each receiving Party, in each instance, the "Receiving Party," and the Receiving Party's Representatives, certain information that is confidential, proprietary or not generally available to the public, subject to the confidentiality obligations, use and disclosure restrictions, and other conditions contained in this Agreement. References in this Agreement to the Parties include each Party's Representatives. As used in this Agreement (either before or after this definition), the "Representatives" of a Party shall mean its directors, officers, employees, agents or advisors, including without limitation its attorneys, accountants, consultants, bankers, and financial advisors.

1. Undertaking of Confidentiality. The Receiving Party agrees to keep strictly confidential any information it receives from any Disclosing Party concerning the following proposed project: installation of photovoltaic solar energy systems, and the structuring of appropriate financing and energy contracts for ____ (the "Project"), and any derivative information prepared by or for the Receiving Party or the Receiving Party's Representatives based on that information (collectively referred to as the "Confidential Information"), and to observe all use and disclosure restrictions and other conditions contained in this Agreement with respect to the Confidential Information. For purposes of this Agreement, (i) disclosure of the Confidential Information will mean communication of the Confidential Information in any manner, including the dissemination of such information orally, electronically, or in writing, (ii) disclosures of the Confidential Information by the Disclosing Party's Representatives will be considered a disclosure of such information by the Disclosing Party, and (iii) receipt of the Confidential Information by the Receiving Party's Representatives will be considered a receipt of such information by the Receiving Party.

2. Confidentiality as to the Disclosing Party's Information and Non-Circumvention. The Receiving Party agrees to observe all use and disclosure restrictions and other conditions contained in this Agreement with respect to any written, oral (if promptly confirmed in writing) or electronic information provided by the Disclosing Party to the Receiving Party relating to the Project. ETF agrees not to pursue, without written approval from OEC, any of the specifically disclosed solar project opportunities or possible sites, clients, installers or panel suppliers disclosed to it by OEC. OEC agrees not to pursue, without written approval from ETF, any of the specifically disclosed financing or lease suppliers or similar resources disclosed to it by ETF. The foregoing shall be for the term of this Agreement.

3. Definition of Confidential Information. The "Confidential Information" includes (i) any engineering data, descriptions, maps, models, interpretations, evaluations and reports regarding the Project provided by the Disclosing Party to the Receiving Party under this Agreement; (ii) any operational, regulatory, legal, commercial, contractual, financial, tax or other related or unrelated information regarding the Project provided by the Disclosing Party to the Receiving Party under this Agreement; and (iii) all notes, analyses, compilations, studies, interpretations or other documents or derivative information prepared by or for the Receiving Party or the Receiving Party's Representatives which contain, reflect or are based upon, in whole or in part, the information furnished by the Disclosing Party to the Receiving Party under this Agreement. The term Confidential Information includes information in whatever form it may exist, whether oral (if promptly confirmed in writing), written, graphic, or electronic, and information prepared by the Disclosing Party, the Disclosing Party's Representatives or otherwise.

4. Exclusions from Confidential Information. The term "Confidential Information" does not include (i) informa-

tion that is or becomes generally available to the public other than as a result of a disclosure by the Receiving Party or its Representatives as a result of breach of this Agreement, (ii) information that the Receiving Party possesses prior to that information being provided to the Receiving Party under this Agreement, unless that information came into the Receiving Party's possession as a result of a breach of a contractual, legal or fiduciary obligation of confidentiality to the Disclosing Party, (iii) information that becomes available to the Receiving Party on a non-confidential basis from a source other than the Disclosing Party or his representative, provided that such source is not known by the Receiving Party to be bound by a contractual, legal or fiduciary obligation of confidentiality to the Disclosing Party or any other party with respect to such information, or (iv) information developed independently developed by the Receiving Party.

5. General Use and Disclosure Restrictions. The Receiving Party agrees that the Receiving Party and its Representatives will use the Confidential Information solely for the purpose of evaluating the Project, and that, except as expressly provided in this Agreement, the Receiving Party and its Representatives will not use the Confidential Information for any other purpose or disclose the Confidential Information in any manner without the prior written consent of the Disclosing Party, which may be withheld for any reason including convenience. The Receiving Party may disclose any of the Confidential Information to those of the Receiving Party's Representatives who need to know such information for the purpose of evaluating the Project.

6. Disclosures Required by Law. Notwithstanding any other provisions of this Agreement, the Receiving Party may disclose, without liability to the Disclosing Party, any part of the Confidential Information the Receiving Party is required to disclose by law, rule, or regulation, or by order or request of a court or other governmental entity claiming to have jurisdiction or in connection with any legal proceeding. The Receiving Party agrees, subject to applicable law, rule, regulation and legal process, to notify the Disclosing Party immediately after the Receiving Party learns any such disclosure of the Confidential Information will be required to allow the Disclosing Party to seek appropriate protection of the Confidential Information.

7. Disclosure of Negotiations. The Receiving Party agrees, subject to applicable law, rule, regulation and legal process, not to disclose to any other person that it has received the Confidential Information, that discussions or negotiations are occurring concerning the Project, or any of the terms, conditions or other facts with respect to the Project, including the status of the negotiations. The term "person" as used in this Section 7 shall be broadly interpreted to include the media and any corporation, partnership, group, individual or other entity not considered a Representative of the Disclosing Party or the Receiving Party, but shall exclude any governmental or judicial entity.

8. Copying of Confidential Information. The Receiving Party agrees that, without the prior written consent of the Disclosing Party, which may be withheld for any reason including convenience, the Receiving Party and its Representatives will not copy any of the Confidential Information except for the purposes set forth in this Agreement. "Copy" as used in this Section 8 shall not include the electronic transmission of Confidential Information as may be permitted hereunder.

9. Destruction of Confidential Information. If the Disclosing Party and the Receiving Party do not enter into an agreement with respect to the Project within twelve (12) months of the date first set forth above, then the Receiving Party upon the Disclosing Party's written request must (i) promptly return to the Disclosing Party all Confidential Information received from the Disclosing Party, (ii) promptly destroy all other Confidential Information in the possession of the Receiving Party or its Representatives, or (iii) inform the Disclosing Party within ten (10) days after receiving the Disclosing Party's request to return or destroy the Confidential Information that the Receiving Party has complied with the foregoing requirements of this Section 9. Notwithstanding the destruction of the Confidential Information, the Receiving Party and its Representatives will continue to be bound by the confidentiality obligations, use and disclosure restrictions, and other conditions of this Agreement for the term of the Agreement. Notwithstanding the foregoing, upon providing written notice to the Disclosing Party, the Receiving Party may retain one legal archival copy of the Confidential Information, including materials prepared from the Confidential Information, provided that such party and its Representa-

tives continue to be bound by its obligations hereunder.

10. No Obligation to Conclude Project. The Disclosing Party and the Receiving Party acknowledge and agree that, unless and until a definitive agreement regarding the Project has been executed, neither the Disclosing Party nor the Receiving Party will be under any legal obligation to enter into any such agreement and neither the Disclosing Party nor the Receiving Party will have any liability to the other based on any assertion of detrimental reliance or any other legal or equitable theory of recovery. For purposes of this Section 10, a definitive Project agreement shall not include a letter of intent or any other preliminary written agreement or offer. The Disclosing Party and the Receiving Party further acknowledge and agree that the Disclosing Party has the right, in its sole discretion, to reject any and all bids or proposals made by the Receiving Party regarding the Project, and to terminate discussions and negotiations about the Project at any time without liability to the Receiving Party or any other Party prior to entering into definitive agreements regarding the Project. Each Party will bear its own evaluation, consultant, legal, and other expenses associated with any evaluation, discussions, and negotiations concerning the Project.

11. Right of Assignment. This Agreement may not be assigned by any Party without the other Parties' prior written consent, which may be withheld for any reason including convenience.

12. Complete Agreement and Amendment. This Agreement is the complete agreement among the Parties regarding the matters contained in this Agreement and supersedes any prior understandings and written or oral agreements among the Parties, if any, regarding the exchange of information by the Parties and the Project. No amendment, change or modification of this Agreement will be valid unless it is in writing and signed by a duly authorized Representative of each Party.

13. Governing Law. This Agreement shall be governed by and construed in accordance with the laws of the state of ____________________.

14. Term. The confidentiality obligations of this Agreement with respect to the Confidential Information will expire and be of no further force and effect two (2) years from the date first set forth above.

15. Remedies. The Receiving Party acknowledges the competitive value of the Confidential Information and the damage to the Disclosing Party that could result if the Confidential Information is disclosed to third parties. The Receiving Party also acknowledges the value of the information provided by the Disclosing Party to the Receiving Party and the potential damage to the Disclosing Party if the Receiving Party circumvents the Disclosing Party. Accordingly, each Party hereto agrees that both injunctive relief and monetary damages, alone or in combination, are appropriate remedies for any breach of this Agreement.

16. No Partnership. The Parties agree that no partnership, agency, joint venture, employment, or fiduciary relationship shall be deemed to exist or arise between them with respect to this Agreement.

17. Counterparts and Facsimile Execution. This Agreement may be executed in counterparts, each of which shall be deemed to be the original instrument for all purposes, but all of which taken together will constitute only one agreement. A facsimile transmission or photocopy of an executed counterpart of this Agreement will have the same force and effect as an executed original counterpart of this Agreement.

18. Covenant of Good Faith and Fair Dealing. The Parties hereby agree to deal with one another fairly and in good faith during the term of this Agreement.

The Parties respectively execute this Agreement by their duly authorized Representatives as of the date first written above.

Renewable Energy Project Creditor

By: ______________________________

Name:

Title:

Date:

ABC Company

By: ______________________________

Name:

Title:

Date:

TRANSACTION DISCLOSURE INFORMATION

(CONSUMER SOLAR LEASE)

Date: ______

Lessee: ______ **Lessor:** ______

Equipment Description: ______

Amount Due at Lease Signing: ______

Documentation Fee ______

Refundable Security Deposit $______

Other: ______ $______

Total Due: $______

Monthly Payments: Your first monthly payment of ______ is due ______, followed by ______ payments of ______ due on the ______ day of each month thereafter. The total of all payments you will have made by the end of the lease term is______. If you do not renew the lease at the end of the original lease term defined above or purchase the equipment pursuant to the terms described below, you will be responsible for returning the equipment in good working order to a place designated by the Lessor at your cost.

Your monthly payment is determined as shown below:

Gross Capitalized Cost The agreed upon value of the solar system including components: $______
If you need an itemization of this amount, check this box: □

Capitalized Cost Reduction $______

Adjusted Capitalized Cost $______

Residual Value □ Fair Market Value (see below) □ Fixed price in the amount of $______

Depreciation and any Amortized Amounts $______

Rental Charge $______

Total of Base Rental Charges Depreciation, any amortization and rental charges $______

Number of Months in Original Lease Term

Base Monthly Lease Rental ______

Sales or Use Tax ______

Total Monthly Payment $______

Early Termination You may have to pay a substantial charge if you terminate this lease early. The actual charge will depend upon when the lease is terminated. The earlier you end the lease, the greater this charge will be.

Initial: ______

Options at End of Lease Term

1. Return the equipment to the Lessor pursuant to the terms and conditions below
2. Purchase the equipment as stated in "Residual Value" above
3. Renew the lease for an amount agreed upon between Lessor and Lessee

Initial: ______

Determination of Fair Market Value

The price that an interested but not desperate buyer would be willing to pay and an interested but not desperate seller would be willing to accept on the open market assuming a reasonable period of time for an agreement to arise.

Fair market value shall mean and refer to the value, as reasonably determined by Lessor, which would be obtained in an arms length transaction between an informed and willing buyer-user under no compulsion to buy and an informed and willing seller under no compulsion to sell.

Highest price, expressed in a dollar amount, that the property would bring, in an open and unrestricted market, between a willing buyer and a willing seller who are knowledgeable, informed, and prudent, and who are acting independently of each other.

Often determined by looking in an appraisers "bluebook" if the equipment value is shown there. Usually need to know the date of manufacture, serial numbers, model numbers, condition of equipment, hours of use, etc.

Often determined by looking at recent public auctions of the type of equipment in question.

Other times it is determined by Lessee and Lessor each selecting an appraiser of their choice, and then the two appraisers selecting a third appraiser to evaluate the value of the equipment. Then, an average of the three appraisers is taken into consideration in determining the fair market value of the equipment.

When fair market value is the issue, such value must be proved by a preponderance of the evidence. Although not required, an appraisal of the subject property is generally the best evidence to support value. It should be noted that an appraisal is not a letter of opinion that simply states the appraiser's opinion of the value of the subject property. Such opinion letters do not contain the data used by the appraiser and cannot be verified independently by the parties. An appraisal requires an examination of the three traditional approaches to value — the cost, income, and market approaches, if possible — and contains information on and analysis of the data relied on by the appraiser to form his opinion of value. Evidence of a recent sale of the equipment, recent sales of comparable equipment, or recent new costs of the subject equipment may be used. If an appraisal is relied on, testimony of the appraiser must be presented if the appraisal and opinion of value are to be given much weight.

I.R.S. Revenue Ruling 59-60 provides that Fair Market Value is the price that would be demanded and paid in a sale involving a willing buyer under no compulsion to buy and a willing seller under no compulsion to sell, assuming both buyer and seller have reasonable knowledge of the relevant facts about the asset. Book value is an accounting term. Technically, it is simply the assets of the enterprise less its depreciated value, all at their values as stated on the books of the company. It's usually not an accurate measure of the real value of the asset. For that reason, it's seldom relevant.

Insurance Insurance is required to be maintained on the equipment. Physical damage coverage is required for fire, extended coverage, vandalism, and malicious mischief for the full value of the equipment (see "Gross Capitalized Cost" above) with a maximum deductible of $1,000.00 per occurrence. Liability insurance coverage is required with minimum amounts of $100,000 and $300,000 for bodily injury and $50,000 property damage.

□ Lessor will provide the coverage above.
□ Lessee will provide the coverage above. *Initial*: _____

Maintenance

□ Lessor will provide all maintenance and servicing on the equipment.

□ Lessee will provide all maintenance and servicing on the equipment. *Initial*: _____

Warranties All manufacturer warranties are for the benefit of the Lessor and Lessee. Lessor provides no warranties of any nature—express or implied.

Early Termination and Default

□ The lease may be terminated before the end of the original lease term. The amount owing by the Lessee to the Lessor is the unpaid balance of the lease. There is no prepayment penalty.

□ The lease may be terminated before the end of the original lease term. The amount owing by the Lessee to the Lessor is the unpaid balance of the lease plus the following:

- If the lease is terminated within the first 12 months after start of the lease, an additional cost equal to 30% of the "Gross Capitalized Cost" shown above.
- If the lease is terminated between the 12th and 24th month after start of the lease, an additional cost equal to 25% of the "Gross Capitalized Cost" shown above.
- If the lease is terminated between the 24th and 36th month after start of the lease, an additional cost equal to 20% of the "Gross Capitalized Cost" shown above.
- If the lease is terminated between the 36th and 48th month after start of the lease, an additional cost equal to 15% of the "Gross Capitalized Cost" shown above.
- If the lease is terminated between the 48th and 60th month after start of the lease, an additional cost equal to 10% of the "Gross Capitalized Cost" shown above.
- If the lease is terminated between the 60th and 72nd month after start of the lease, an additional cost equal to 5% of the "Gross Capitalized Cost" shown above.
- If the lease is terminated after the 72nd month after start of the lease, there is no additional cost other than the outstanding balance of the lease.

Note: In any of the above options, in addition to any other amounts shown, there will always be a processing fee to terminate the lease early equal to 2% of the "Gross Capitalized Cost" shown above. ***Initial***: _____

Security and Environmental Interests The lessor reserves all security and environmental interests in the leased equipment to secure performance of the terms and conditions of the lease agreement.

Tax Attributes All tax attributes in the equipment are for the account of:

- ☐ The account of the Lessee
- ☐ The account of the Lessor

Initial: _____

Transfer of Lease to Another Party The lease agreement may transferred to another party with the approval of the lessor. The approval is subject to credit approval by the lessor of the new party and such approval will not be unreasonably withheld by the lessor. Any such transfer requires the new party to execute new lease documentation and there will be a $500.00 fee charged for any such transfer. The lessee may also elect to terminate the lease early and purchase the equipment as defined above. If the new party does not meet the necessary credit requirements of the lessor or does not wish to enter into a new lease agreement with the lessor, the lessee will be required to terminate the lease pursuant to the above terms and conditions and either return the equipment to the lessor (see below) or purchase the equipment as defined above. ***Initial***: _____

Supplier:
The lessee, acting on their own, has selected the above supplier(s). The supplier of the equipment has made the following disclosures upon which the lessee has relied upon:

- The estimated annual energy output of the solar system selected is _____ kilowatt-hours
- The estimated annual cost of the power produced by the system is _____ per kilowatt-hour
- The lessee has received in writing a full description of all maintenance and servicing required on the system to achieve peak performance levels
- The estimated useful life of the equipment will exceed the warranty of the system by an amount equal to a minimum term of 150% of the warranty period which is
- The warranty on the equipment and components including the installation is the sole responsibility of the supplier(s)

Equipment Return Provisions All the Equipment shall remain personal property (it being the intent of the parties that the Equipment shall not become fixtures) and the title shall remain with the Lessor exclusively. Upon the termination or expiration of this Lease, or any extension thereof, Lessee shall forthwith, at its own cost and expense, return the Leased Equipment to the Lessor at an address designated by Lessor in the same condition as when received by Lessee, reasonable wear and tear resulting from proper use thereof alone excepted. All replacement parts, additions and accessories incorporated in or affixed to (and including the definition of) the Equipment, whether before or after commencement of this Lease, all manuals and spare parts, shall also be returned to Lessor and shall become the property of the Lessor. The Lessee shall also pay to the Lessor such sum as may be necessary to cover replacement for all damaged, broken, out of calibration or missing parts of the Equipment.

Initial: _____

Late Payments The charge for late payments is 10% of the scheduled monthly lease payment.
Record of Notice on Real Property AB 2863 requires that a notice be recorded on the title of the real property on which the equipment is located.

Official Fees and Taxes The total estimated amount you will pay for official fees, and taxes over the term of your lease, whether included with your monthly payments or assessed otherwise: $ ______

Initial: _____

Other Important Terms and Conditions See your lease documents for additional detailed information on defaults, early termination, purchase options, maintenance responsibilities, warranties, late charges, insurance and security interest terms and conditions.

Corporate Resolution to Lease

RESOLVED, that this corporation, ________________ lease from ______________, hereinafter referred to as Lessor, such items of personal property, and upon such terms and conditions, as the officer or officers hereinafter authorized, in their discretion, may deem necessary or advisable.

RESOLVED FURTHER, that ____________ the _____________ acting together with _____________ of this corporation (the officer or officers, or officers acting in combination, authorized to act pursuant hereto, being hereinafter designated as "authorized officers") be, and they hereby are, authorized, directed and empowered, in the name of this corporation, to execute and deliver to Lessor and Lessor is requested to accept, any lease that may be required by Lessor in connection with such leasing of personal property.

RESOLVED FURTHER, that the authorized officers be, and they hereby are, authorized, directed and empowered, in the name of this corporation, to do or cause to be done all such further acts and things as they shall deem necessary, advisable, convenient, or proper in connection with the execution and delivery of any such lease and in connection with or incidental to carrying of the same into effect, including, without limitation on the scope of the foregoing, the execution, acknowledgment, and delivery of any and all instruments and documents which may reasonably be required by Lessor under or in connection with any such lease.

RESOLVED FURTHER, that Lessor is authorized to act upon this resolution until written notice of its revocation is delivered to Lessor, and that the authority hereby granted shall apply with equal force and effect to the successors in the office of the officers herein named.

I, ____________, Secretary of ______________, a corporation, incorporated under the laws in the State of __________, do hereby certify that the foregoing is a full, true and correct copy of resolutions of the Board of Directors of the said corporation which was duly and regularly called and held in all respects as required by law, and the by laws of the said corporation, at the office thereof on the ____day of_________________________, 20____, at which meeting a majority of the Board of Directors of said corporation was present and voted in favor of said resolution.

I further certify that said resolutions are still in full force and effect and have not been amended or revoked and that the specimen signatures appearing below are the signatures of the officers authorized to sign for this corporation by virtue of the said resolutions.

IN WITNESS WHEREOF, I have hereunto set my hand as such Secretary, and affixed the corporate seal of the said corporation, this ____day of______________________________, 20____.

AUTHORIZED SIGNATURES:

X________________________________, Title ____________

X________________________________, Title ____________

X ________________________________
(Secretary of Corporation)

AUTHORIZATION

TO WHOM IT MAY CONCERN:

Re: ______________________________

I hereby give my full and unrestricted authorization to release any and all information concerning my (our) account relationship(s) to include all closed accounts, open accounts, paying habits, related account information, open or proposed credit lines, etc. on both a personal as well as a company basis. This form may be reproduced or photocopied and the copy shall be as effective an authorization as the original which I have signed.

My signature hereby certifies that I authorize all parties to take all steps necessary to fully investigate the credit worthiness of the company and the principals whose signature appears below including credit bureau reports.

Respectfully,

X____

X____

X____

X____

Date: ________________________

If your application for business credit is denied, you have the right to a written statement of the specific reasons for the denial. To obtain the statement, please contact ________________________ at________________________________, within 60 days from the date you are notified of our decision. We will send you a written statement of reason(s) for denial within 30 days of receiving your request for the statement.

NOTICE: The Federal Equal Credit Opportunity Act prohibits creditors from discriminating against credit applicants on the basis of race, color, religion, national origin, sex, marital status, or age (provided the applicant has the capacity to enter into a binding contract); or because all or part of the applicants income derives from any public assistance program or because the applicant has in good faith exercised any right under the Consumer Credit Protection Act. The federal agency(s) that administers compliance with this law is the Federal Trade Commission, Equal Credit Opportunity, Washington, D.C. 290580; the Federal Deposit Insurance Agency, Washington, D.C.; the Comptroller of the Currency, Consumer Examinations Division, Washington, D.C. 20219; as well as other agencies.

Renewable Energy Project

CREDITOR ENVIRONMENTAL AUDIT CHECKLIST

***<u>GENERAL INFORMATION</u>*:**

Applicant: **Contact Person:** **NACIS Code**

Site Location: **Telephone:**

Legal Owner of Property:

Size of Property: **Age of Property:**

***<u>PROCESS OPERATIONS</u>*:**

Principal Products: **Volume:**

Processes Used:

Chemicals Used: **How Used:**

***<u>WASTEWATER SOURCES</u>*:**

What Are Sources?

Flow Volume & Characteristics:

How Managed/Treated (past & present):

On-site Treatment? ☐ Yes ☐ No **Describe:**

Where is Discharge?

Disposition of Sludges:

Permit Status: **From Whom?** **SPCC Plan:**

Spill History:

Agency Contact: **Notice of Violation(s) & Disposition:**

Compliance Schedules:

AIR EMISSION SOURCES:

Title V Facility: ☐ Yes ☐ No What Are Sources?

Volume & Characteristics:

Emission Controls:

Emission Points:

Permits & Status of Each:

Monitoring Requirements:

Notices of Violations(s) & Disposition:

Agency Contact:

Special Rules of Concern:

SOLID/HAZARDOUS WASTES:

What Are Sources?

Quantities & Characteristics:

Treatment, Storage & Disposal (past and present):

On-site/Off-site Disposal (past and present):

RCRA Permits:

Compliance Reports:

Notices of Violations & Dispositions:

Compliance History:

Agency & Contact:

***FUELS MANAGEMENT*:**

Fuels Used & Historical Volumes:

Describe Storage Methods & Volumes:

***PCB EQUIPMENT*:**

Location(s):

Size: **Type:**

Inspection Report(s):

***ASBESTOS*:**

Location(s): **Amount(s):**

Disposition(s):

***UNDERGROUND TANKS (PAST & PRESENT)*:**

Location(s):

Size: **Ages:**

Construction Materials: **Contents:**

Testing Results & Dates:

Monitoring Types: **Monitoring Results:**

Removed When/How/By Whom:

Inspection Reports:

THIS QUESTIONNAIRE WAS COMPLETED BY:

Name: ______

Title: ______

Company: ______

Address: ______

Telephone: ______

Date: ______

Debtor's Attorney Opinion Letter

Date:

Renewable Energy Project Creditor

Address

City, State & Zip

Attn: **Reference:**

Gentlemen:

We have acted as legal counsel to ____________________, a ______________________ (hereinafter the "company"), in connection with the _________________________ to be provided by you on a renewable energy project to be located at ___ ___________________________________, and described as contract number ___________, and are rendering this opinion at the request of the Company and acknowledge that you intend to rely upon this opinion letter.

As a basis for the opinions set forth herein, we have reviewed all of the documents to be executed in connection with the above described transaction, including without limitation the following:

-
-
-
-
-

In addition, we have examined originals, photocopies, faxed or certified copies of all such corporate records, all such agreements, communications, and other instruments, certificates of public officers and corporate officers, and all other such documents and have made such inquiry as we have deemed relevant and necessary as a basis for the opinions hereinafter set forth.

Based on the foregoing, it is our opinion that:

1. The Company has been duly incorporated and organized, and is existing as a corporation in good standing under the laws of the State of __________________. The Company has the corporate power and authority to own its properties and assets, to conduct its business as now conducted; and based upon representations made to us by officers of the Company, the Company is not required to qualify to do business as a foreign corporation any other jurisdictions. The Company has not changed its name or been the surviving corporation in a merger or acquired any business.
2. The execution, delivery and performance of the Project Documents by the Company will not violate any law or the terms s of the incorporation documents or bylaws of the Company.
3. The Company has the corporate power and authority to enter into and execute the Project Documents, and to perform the transactions set forth therein, and the Project Documents have been duly authorized, executed, and delivered and the transactions contemplated therein have been duly authorized.
4. The Project Documents constitute valid and legally binding obligations of the Company and are enforceable against the Company in accordance with their respective terms.
5. We are aware of no claim, litigation, or proceeding, pending, threatened against, or otherwise affecting the Company which involves the possibility of any judgment or liability not fully covered by insurance or which may result in a material adverse change in the condition, financial or otherwise, of the Company.

Respectfully,

ABC Law Firm

By: ______________________ Title: ______________________

Disclaimer of Ownership

The undersigned (the "Lessee") proposes to be the Lessee of certain equipment from Renewable Energy Project Creditor (the "Lessor") pursuant to an Equipment Lease between Lessor and Lessee bearing Lease No. _______ executed by the Lessee on _________________ (the "Lease"). The equipment covered by the Lease is hereinafter referred to as the "Equipment."

The Equipment will be purchased by Lessor from _________________ (the "Vendor"). Lessee has made a Cap Reduction Payment to the Vendor as part of the original purchase order, and it is contemplated that, upon Lessor's receipt of all necessary documentation and satisfaction of all conditions to Lessor entering into the Lease, Lessor shall pay the Vendor(s) the remaining balance of the purchase price and receive a bill of sale from the Vendor covering a 100% interest in the Equipment.

The Lessee, being satisfied that its payments under the Lease are based only upon Lessor's payment to the Vendor and not Lessee's Cap Reduction Payment, hereby consents to the Vendor transferring the entire ownership in the Equipment to the Lessor, and, effective on the actual transfer of the Equipment to Lessor, disclaims any ownership interest or right in the Equipment except those the Lessee has by virtue of being the Lessee under the Lease.

Dated: ______________________, 20____.

Lessee: ____________________________

By: ________________________________

Title: ______________________________

SUMMARY OF TERMS AND CONDITIONS

Name of Customer CONFIDENTIAL

Summary of Terms

Energy Purchase Agreement
for
Customer Name

This Confidential Summary of Terms provides for a Energy Purchase Agreement (EPA) by EPA Provider of a new Solar Energy System (the "Equipment"). The capitalized cost of the solar energy system amount shall not exceed $1,000,000.00.

1.	***Energy Purchaser***	**Customer Name**
2.	*Guarantor(s)*	
3.	*Arranger & Underwriter*	ABC Energy Provider, Inc.
4.	*Owner EPA Provider (Energy Provider)*	EPA Provider will purchase and own the Equipment and sell the energy produced from the Equipment to Energy Purchaser on the terms and conditions set forth herein. EPA Provider will have final authorization for credit approval and will be the only party to guaranty full funding of the transaction.
5.	*Equipment*	A Solar Energy System as per attached Annex B. Each a "Unit" and collectively, the "Equipment." An unconditional Equipment acceptance must be signed by Energy Purchaser prior to payment of Equipment invoice to equipment provider.
6.	*Equipment Cost*	Fair market value (to be defined in the EPA) of the Equipment on an installed basis, subject to appraisal acceptable to EPA Provider, which shall not exceed $1,000,000.00 ("EPA Provider's Cost")
7.	*Suppliers & Vendors*	The EPA Provider has the sole responsibility of selecting the suppliers, vendors, auditors, engineers and installers of the Equipment. All performance guarantees are the sole responsibility of the providers of the system.
8.	*Equipment Location*	To be selected by Energy Purchaser and supplied to EPA Provider. All engineering, design, construction, installation and permits are the responsibility of the EPA Provider. Subject to Paragraph 7, the Energy Purchaser shall appoint its own project manager. A copy of the engineering blueprints (with final corrections) will be provided to the Energy Purchaser upon final completion of the project installation if requested. The Equipment will be installed and located at Energy Purchaser's City, State facility. Energy Purchaser will provide site rights to EPA Provider which extend through the estimated useful life of the Equipment. Site rights shall be in form and substance acceptable to the EPA Provider. It is currently anticipated that such site rights will be granted pursuant to an easement and Site Lease in form and substance acceptable to EPA Provider.
9.	*Monitoring & Reporting*	The Energy Purchaser agrees to have computerized monitoring, reporting and record-keeping systems put in place that will remotely monitor the Equipment performance 24 hours per day. The Energy Purchaser also agrees to allow periodic inspection and adjustments if required of the monitoring system by vendors appointed by the EPA Provider. The Energy Purchaser shall provide annual financial operating reports to EPA Provider on or prior to April 15 of each year. In addition, if requested by EPA Provider, Energy Purchaser shall provide to EPA Provider quarterly unaudited financial statements within 60 days after the end of each of the first three fiscal quarters of Energy Purchaser; provided that so long as such financial statements are publicly available to EPA Provider, Energy Purchaser shall be deemed to have satisfied such requirement.

10.	*Optional System Support Items*	All items required to engineer, design, permit, install, monitor and operate the Equipment will be included in the Energy Purchase Agreement provided with this proposal, subject to satisfaction of any tax and appraisal constraints. This may include such items as energy audits, design and engineering, permits and fees, shipping, installation, spare parts, inspections, emission source testing, maintenance contracts and other similar items. Any optional items must be approved by the EPA Provider prior to final approval and documentation of the transaction.
11.	*System Performance*	All performance guarantees are the sole responsibility of the providers of the Equipment or EPA Provider and EPA Provider will furnish all maintenance and insurance on the Equipment.
12.	*Transaction Structure*	EPA Provider's Equipment cost will be financed under a single Energy Purchase arrangement as follows: Energy Purchaser will assign its purchase contract(s) (if any) for the Equipment to EPA Provider and EPA Provider will sell the energy produced by the delivered Equipment to Energy Purchaser under a Energy Purchase Agreement (the "EPA"), on the terms and conditions set forth therein and outlined here. Subject to satisfaction (or waiver in EPA Provider's sole discretion) of customary conditions to Equipment acquisition and installation (including those set forth in Paragraph 34 below), on the scheduled funding dates set forth in Annex A hereto (each a "Funding Date"), EPA Provider will fund the applicable portion of EPA Provider's Cost of the Equipment set forth opposite such Funding Date directly to the system suppliers, vendors, contractors or others. The EPA will be a net contract in which the EPA Provider will be responsible for all costs, insurance (other than property damage), taxes, impositions and expenses required in connection with the operation, maintenance, acquisition and ownership of the Equipment. EPA Provider will retain legal title, tax title, environmental title and all other ownership rights of the Equipment during the entire term of the EPA. As provided in Paragraph 17, certain environmental attributes of the Equipment will accrue for the benefit of EPA Provider.
13.	*Document Closing Date*	The documentation for the transaction is intended to be executed on or about September 1, 2013 (the "Document Closing Date").
14.	*EPA Term*	The base term of the EPA shall commence on or after the final Funding Date and upon the Equipment being placed in service and shall end on the 20th anniversary ("Base Term"). If Energy Purchaser elects to renew the EPA as provided in Paragraph 21 "Renewal," the EPA Term shall also include the Renewal Term for not less than all the Equipment under the EPA.
15.	*Base EPA Payment Schedule*	Base EPA Payments will be due in amounts as specified in EPA Provider's schedule and as shown in Annex A. All payments will be made in arrears (due and payable on each monthly payment date specified in the EPA. The Payment Rates are based on the following assumptions: (a) Tax Attributes EPA Provider expects the transaction to have the following income tax attributes: (i) EPA Provider will be entitled to (A) all Federal and/or State energy tax credits, (B) 5 year MACRS depreciation allowance deductions with respect to the Equipment; and (C) amortize any Transaction Costs (which may include the Commitment Fee and certain other costs set forth in Paragraph 10, if such Commitment Fee and other costs may be included in Equipment Cost for tax and accounting purposes) paid by EPA Provider on a straight line basis over the Base Term; (ii) All items of income and expense will be reported and treated on a calendar year and an accrual basis and as derived from sources within the United States;

(iii) No inclusions in EPA Provider's income except scheduled monthly installments of energy produced, any fees provided for herein, any early termination payment or purchase option payment and casualty value following an event of loss, any interest on amounts paid other than when due, any amounts required to be paid on an after-tax basis and any amount giving rise to a deduction of equal amount of the same character in the same year as the inclusion; and

(iv) The Equipment will be ready for its intended use at the commencement of the Base Term (no later than December 1, 2013).

(b) Transaction Pricing Assumptions

The Base EPA Payment Rates assume commencement of the Base Term of 240 months. Any Interim Payments will be charged at the Base EPA Payment daily equivalent.

The Base EPA Payment Rates, termination values and stipulated loss values and dates will be adjusted to reflect (a) the actual commencement of the Base Term; (b) actual Transaction Costs financed through the EPA; (c) upward or downward movements in the Index Rate before the commencement of the Base Term and (d) the effect of Federal or state tax law enacted or proposed (including new or changed regulations, announcements and judicial precedent) before the commencement of the Base Term. All adjustments will be computed, first to preserve EPA Provider's economics and second to minimize the Energy Purchaser's net present value of the EPA Payments.

16.	*Security Deposit*	None
17.	*Environmental Ownership*	The environmental ownership of the Equipment will remain with the EPA Provider throughout the base term of the EPA and all renewals thereafter. The Renewable Energy Credits (RECs), emission attributes and any state rebates attributable to the Equipment will also accrue to the benefit of the EPA Provider.
18.	*Indemnities*	(a) General Indemnities.

Energy Purchaser will indemnify, defend and hold Energy Provider and its officers, directors, agents, employees, successors and assigns (the "EPA Provider Indemnitees") harmless (on an after-tax basis) from and against any and all costs, expenses, liabilities, losses, damages, claims, taxes, actions and suits (including legal fees and expenses) (each a "Claim") in a manner customary for transactions of this type including, without limitation, those arising out of or relating in any way to the selection, manufacture, engineering, design, ownership, use, lease, maintenance, operation, acceptance or rejection of the Equipment, the EPA or any related documents or the site (including any Claim for clean up or remediation of any hazardous materials or other environmental liability) or any failure on the part of the Energy Purchaser to comply with its obligations in connection with the EPA transaction, including those arising out of or relating to the active or passive negligence of the Energy Purchaser, any strict liability of any Energy Provider Indemnitee in tort or otherwise, subject to customary exclusions to be agreed upon in the Energy Purchase Agreement.

(b) Income Tax Indemnity.

Energy Purchaser will make customary representations, including a representation as to the eligibility of the Equipment for federal energy credits, to support the foregoing Tax Attribute assumptions and, subject to customary exclusions, to be agreed upon in the EPA, will indemnify Energy Provider on an after tax basis against any loss of the benefit of the Tax Attributes resulting from the acts, failures to act, omissions, or misrepresentations of or breaches by Energy Purchaser.

(c) Additional Environmental Covenants and Indemnification

Energy Purchaser agrees to comply with all Federal and State OSHA and other requirements relative to the work to be performed in the installation of the Equipment. If the Energy Purchaser's facilities where the Equipment is to be installed contain hazardous materials, including asbestos bearing materials and any such materials are encountered, Energy Purchaser shall have no obligation to remove or remediate them and Energy Purchaser shall indemnify, defend and hold the Energy Provider Indemnitees harmless from any and all Claims arising out of or relating thereto.

(d) Project Supervision

Without limiting Paragraph 7 above, Energy Provider shall not have any duty or authority to direct, supervise or oversee any contractors of Energy Purchaser or their work or to provide the means, methods or sequence of their work or to stop their work. Energy Provider shall only be responsible for its own employees and contractors. Energy Provider shall not be liable for the failure of Energy Purchaser's contractors or others to fulfill their responsibilities, and Energy Purchaser hereby agrees to indemnify, defend and hold the Energy Provider Indemnitees harmless against any claims arising out of any such failures.

(e) Contests; Scope

Energy Purchaser will be given certain customary contest and appeal rights, and the indemnities will contain certain exceptions, in each case to be negotiated between the Energy Purchaser and Energy Provider.

---

19. *Warranties*

During any period when no EPA Event of Default exists, all warranties of any nature regarding the system proposed and received by Energy Provider from suppliers, contractors, vendors or any other party will be utilized by the Energy Provider for the benefit of the Energy Purchaser to ensure the performance of the system.

---

20. *Early Termination*

There is no provision in the proposed EPA for early termination. The Energy Purchaser must allow the equipment to be installed and serviced for the entire duration of the original EPA term of 240 months and to pay for all energy produced by the system during that term.

---

21. *Renewal Option*

So long as no event of default shall have occurred and be continuing, at the expiration of any Base Term or any Renewal Term, as applicable, upon 360 days prior written notice, Energy Purchaser may renew the EPA of all, but not less than all, of the Equipment for a renewal term of up to 60 months in duration (the "Renewal Term"); provided that the length of the Renewal Term must satisfy tax and accounting constraints (e.g., Renewal Term does not exceed 75% of the useful life of the Equipment or extend to a period in time on or after which the uninflated residual value is less than 20% of the Equipment Cost) pursuant to the EPA renewal schedule found in Annex A. If Energy Provider has not been notified by Energy Purchaser per the above, so long as no EPA Event of Default then exists, the EPA will automatically be renewed for the period defined in Annex A.

---

22. *Purchase Option*

End-of-Term Purchase Option

For all, but not less than all, of the Equipment on the last day of any Base Term or the Renewal Term, Energy Purchaser may, with 360 days prior written notice, purchase all of the Equipment for its then fair market value on an in-place in-use basis (to be defined in the EPA) but not less than 20% of the Energy Provider's Cost of the Equipment. If not agreed to by Energy Provider and the Energy Purchaser, fair market value will be determined by averaging the appraisals obtained from:

- An appraiser selected by Energy Provider
- An appraiser selected by Energy Purchaser
- An appraiser mutually selected by the above two appraisers

All appraisers selected must be certified by, accredited with and be an active member of The American Society of Appraisers and accredited in the valuation of Machinery and Equipment and experienced in the valuation of solar energy systems. Energy Purchaser shall bear the cost of all appraisals referenced in this Paragraph 22.

---

23. *Event of Loss*

An Event of Loss with respect to a Unit means the occurrence of any of the following events: (i) destruction, damage beyond repair, total loss, constructive total loss, or rendition of the Unit or the site permanently unfit for normal use as contemplated by the EPA; or (ii) the condemnation, confiscation or seizure of the Unit or the site in whole or in any significant part, or requisition of title to, or use of, any significant part of the Unit or the site for a period in excess of three (3) consecutive months.

Upon the occurrence of an Event of Loss, so long as no EPA Event of Default then exists, the Energy Purchaser shall substitute, repair or restore the Unit subject to the Event of Loss to its condition immediately prior to the occurrence of the Event of Loss, in which case the Unit shall continue under the EPA and the monthly payments payable under the EPA for energy production shall not be reduced. The proceeds of any insurance or condemnation will be applied against the casualty value or the expense of such substitution, repair or restoration, as applicable, unless a default under the EPA has then occurred and is continuing. Any excess insurance proceeds with respect to insurance policies maintained by the Energy Purchaser will be paid to the Energy Purchaser and the Energy Provider, as their interests may appear, unless a EPA Event of Default has then occurred and is continuing, in which case, all such excess insurance proceeds will be paid to Energy Provider. During the continuance of any EPA Event of Default, at Energy Provider's option, Energy Purchaser shall either substitute, repair or restore the Unit subject to the Event of Loss or the Energy Purchaser shall pay to Energy Provider the stipulated loss value specified in the EPA and all energy production payments and other amounts then due and payable under the EPA and upon such payment to Energy Provider, the EPA shall terminate and Energy Provider shall be entitled to the return of all of the Equipment in accordance with Paragraph 24, other than with respect to condition of the Unit subject to the Event of Loss.

---

24. *Equipment Return*

Return; Location; Condition

Upon receipt of such written notice, Energy Provider shall have the right to continue to locate and use the Equipment at the Site for a period of not more than 120 days from the expiration date of the EPA or to uninstall the solar energy systems as described below.

Energy Purchaser shall permit the free storage of the Equipment for a period not to exceed 120 days following termination of the Base Term or any Renewal Term if Energy Provider does not elect to use the Equipment at the Site.

Energy Provider, at its expense, will cause the Equipment to be removed.

---

25. *Assignment; Sublease*

Energy Purchaser may not assign or sublease any interest under the EPA or the Units without the prior written consent of Energy Provider except that, if no EPA default or event of default exists, Energy Purchaser may sublease to a wholly owned subsidiary without Energy Provider's consent, so long as Energy Purchaser remains fully liable under the EPA during the term of such sublease. However, Energy Purchaser will give written notice to Energy Provider of any such event. The EPA and any assignment or sublease will expressly provide that it is subject and subordinate to Energy Provider's interests in the EPA and Equipment.

---

26. *Transfers*

After the Document Closing Date, the Energy Provider may transfer its interest or assign its interest, without the consent of Energy Purchaser, to a qualified entity which is not a competitor of Energy Purchaser, it being acknowledged and agreed that any transferee of Energy Provider which is a financial institution, insurance company, a bank or a leasing company or any affiliate of any of the foregoing which provides EPA or other financing, shall not be deemed to constitute a competitor of the Energy Purchaser, and provided that such entity agrees in writing to be bound by the EPA to the same extent as the transferring Energy Provider.

---

27. *Use; Maintenance*

Energy Purchaser acknowledges that the Equipment will be maintained in good operating condition by Energy Provider and Energy Provider shall maintain, refurbish, rebuild and repair the Equipment so as to keep it in accordance with the Manufacturer's suggested maintenance recommendations, and, (i) in accordance with applicable law or regulations (ii) in good operating condition (ordinary wear and tear excepted), (iii) in accordance with customary industry standards and in any event in accordance with standards no lower than the highest of those applied by Energy Provider on similar equipment owned by it, (iv) in compliance with the terms of all relevant contracts (including, without limitation, insurance policies and Manufacturer's suggested maintenance standards and warranty requirements) and (v) free of all liens and encumbrances other than customary Energy Provider's liens agreed to in the EPA. Energy Provider shall solely bear any expense incurred as may be required to maintain the Equipment.

Energy Provider shall allow the use of the Equipment only in the manner for which it was designated and intended by the Manufacturer. The Equipment shall be installed, used, operated and maintained in compliance with all federal, state and local laws, rules, regulations and permits.

Energy Provider at its sole discretion may, from time to time, inspect the Equipment and perform maintenance of the Equipment during normal business hours. Copies of all maintenance contracts and records will be provided to Energy Purchaser at their request. All parts, which are lost, destroyed, or deemed unfit for use, shall be replaced at Energy Provider's sole expense. Title to all replacement parts shall vest with Energy Provider.

28.	*Appraisal*	Appraisals shall be obtained when required by the Energy Provider as provided for under the EPA or upon sale of the Equipment to Energy Purchaser pursuant to Paragraph 22 above.
29.	*Insurance*	Energy Purchaser will be required to maintain, at all times, insurance in amounts, with deductibles, and from insurance companies, reasonably acceptable to Energy Provider. Such insurance shall specify Energy Provider as an additional insured for occurrences arising out of Energy Purchaser's use and operation of the Equipment on liability policies, and as loss payee as Energy Producer's interest may appear. Prior to the execution of the EPA, Energy Provider will have had the opportunity to review and approve the insurance companies and insurance coverage that will be provided by Energy Purchaser.
30.	*Events of Default*	The EPA will contain customary defaults for a transaction of this type, subject to customary grace periods where applicable, including, without limitation: failure to make payments when due; failure to observe or perform any of the covenants, conditions, or agreements of the EPA; bankruptcy and insolvency, defaults and misrepresentations and a cross-default to Energy Purchaser's material indebtedness.
31.	*Non-Interference*	Energy Provider will covenant that it will not disturb or otherwise interfere with, or cause any disturbance of or other interference with, Energy Purchaser's quiet use and enjoyment of the Equipment to produce energy under the EPA, unless a EPA Event of Default has occurred and is continuing.
32.	*Additions, Modifications & Improvements*	The Energy Provider shall have the right to make changes, additions, modifications or improvements ("Modifications") to the Equipment that it deems necessary or desirable. Energy Provider will be required to make modifications which are required by law or by any governmental or regulatory authority having jurisdiction over the Equipment or the EPA, subject to customary contest rights agreed to in the EPA. Any such mandatory modifications, and any other modifications which cannot be removed without adversely affecting the value, utility or remaining economic useful life of the Equipment ("Non-severable modifications"), shall be deemed to constitute "Equipment" under the EPA and shall be the property of Energy Provider.
33.	*Documents*	The EPA will be a new contract, evidencing the unconditional obligation of Energy Purchaser to pay for all energy produced without set off, reduction or delay whatsoever associated with the Equipment. The EPA will contain additional provisions not outlined herein but usual in EPA transactions, including but not limited to: representations and warranties; rights of Energy Provider to have access to the equipment and requiring Energy Purchaser and/or Guarantor(s) to deliver periodic financial statements to Energy Provider and to pay costs and interest at a specified rate on any payments not received when due. Financial covenants, if any, to be determined and agreed upon in the EPA and supporting documents (including UCC-1 filings, landlord or mortgage waivers, fixture filings, corporate resolutions, etc.) will contain a cross-default provision relating to other material indebtedness of the

		Energy Purchaser. Energy Provider's counsel will prepare all documents.
34.	*Funding Conditions*	Energy Provider's obligation to enter into the EPA is subject to customary conditions including (but not limited to) the following: (1) Conditions to Closing: a. Receipt of the executed EPA and other transaction documents, appropriate closing certificates, evidence of insurance, corporate authorizations and good standing certificates; b. Receipt of a favorable legal and tax opinions of counsel of Energy Provider; c. All representations and warranties being true and correct; e. Payment of applicable fees and transaction costs; d. Receipt of such other documents as Energy Provider may reasonably require. e. No default or casualty shall have occurred, and no material adverse effect with respect to Energy Purchaser shall have occurred. f. Receipt of all documentation and other information required by regulatory authorities under applicable "know your customer" and similar regulations, including but not limited to the Patriot Act. (2) Conditions to each Funding: a. Evidence that Energy Provider has a first priority perfected security interest and is named on the certificate of title for the Equipment (subject to no liens other than any permitted liens agreed to in the EPA); b. Receipt of evidence that Energy Purchaser has adequate insurance in conformity with the EPA; c. Receipt of customary closing certificates and opinions, including bring-down certificates of Energy Purchaser with respect to representations and warranties and absence of defaults; d. Receipt of a bill of sale or invoice for the Units of Equipment to be delivered, signed by Energy Purchaser with customary warranties acceptable to Energy Provider; e. No event exists that would constitute a default or event of default under the EPA or any other basic document and no material adverse effect with respect to Energy Purchaser shall have occurred; f. No funding will occur after December 31, 2013 (see Paragraph 37 below); g. Receipt of such other documents as Energy Provider may reasonably require; and, h. All documents must be satisfactory to Energy Provider.
35.	*Commitment Fee*	A non-refundable Underwriter Commitment Fee of 1.0% of Equipment Cost (the "Commitment Fee") shall be paid to Underwriter as a condition precedent to the Document Preparation by Energy Provider.
36.	*Transaction Expenses*	All legal fees and other transaction costs of Energy Provider in connection with negotiation and preparation of transaction documents, ("Transaction Costs"), will be for the account of Energy Purchaser if the transaction does not close.
37.	*Final Funding Date*	Installation and commissioning of the equipment including all funding must occur prior to or on December 31, 2013. Should each of the foregoing not occur by that date, the Energy Provider will not be under any obligation to do the final funding on the proposed transaction and any advances made for the benefit of the Energy Purchaser will be immediately due payable in full to the Energy Provider, together with all interest, and other fees, costs and expenses then due and payable to the Energy Provider.

Any commitment of the Energy Provider to fund any amounts or enter into any definitive documentation for the transactions contemplated by this Summary of Terms and Conditions is subject to (a) Energy Provider's completion of and satisfaction in all respects with the results of Energy Provider's business, legal, tax, accounting, environmental and other due diligence investigation, (b) execution and delivery of definitive documentation in form and substance satisfactory to Energy Provider, (c) Energy Provider obtaining all internal credit and corporate approvals necessary for the transactions contemplated hereby and (d) satisfaction of other customary conditions precedent, including those specified in Paragraph 34 above.

Renewable Energy Project
Environmental Audit Checklist

Applicant Name: ____________________
Property Owner: ____________________
Property Address: ____________________

Note: See "Terminology" at end of this checklist

Item	*Answer*	*Question*
1.		*What are the past and present uses of the Property? Include all buildings and operations, such as foundry, metal plating, power plant, laboratories, etc.*
2.	☐ Yes ☐ No	Is the property or any adjoining property used for an industrial use? What are the past and present industrial processes conducted on the site?
3.	☐ Yes ☐ No	To the best of your knowledge, has the property or any adjoining property been used for an industrial use in the past?
4.	☐ Yes ☐ No	Is the property or any adjoining property used as a gasoline station, motor repair facility, commercial printing facility, dry cleaners, photo developing laboratory, junkyard or landfill, or as a waste treatment, storage, disposal, processing, or recycling facility?
5.	☐ Yes ☐ No	To the best of your knowledge, has the property or any adjoining property been used as a gasoline station, motor repair facility, commercial printing facility, dry cleaners, photo developing laboratory, junkyard or landfill, or as a waste treatment, storage, disposal, processing, or recycling facility?
6.	☐ Yes ☐ No	Are there currently, or to the best of your knowledge have there been previously, any damaged or discarded automotive or industrial batteries, or pesticides, paints, or other chemicals in individual containers of greater than five gallons in volume or fifty gallons in the aggregate, stored on or used at the property or at the facility?
7.	☐ Yes ☐ No	Are there currently, or to the best of your knowledge have there been previously, any industrial drums (typically 55 gallon) or sacks of chemicals located on the property or at the facility?
8.	☐ Yes ☐ No	Has fill dirt been brought onto the property which originated from a contaminated site or which is of an unknown origin?
9.	☐ Yes ☐ No	Are there currently, or to the best of your knowledge have there been previously, any pits, ponds or lagoons located on the property in connection with waste treatment or waste disposal?
10.	☐ Yes ☐ No	Is there currently, or to the best of you knowledge has there been previously, any stained soil on the property?
11.	☐ Yes ☐ No	Are there currently, or to the best of your knowledge have there been previously, any registered or unregistered storage tanks (above or underground) located on the property?
12.	☐ Yes ☐ No	Are there currently, or to the best of your knowledge have there been previously, any vent pipes, fill pipes or access ways indicating a fill pipe protruding from the ground on the property or adjacent to any structure located on the property?
13.	☐ Yes ☐ No	Are there currently, or to the best of your knowledge have there been previously, any flooring, drains, or walls located within the facility that are stained by substances other than water or are emitting foul odors?
14.	☐ Yes ☐ No	If the property is served by a private well or non public water system have contaminants been identified in the well or system that exceed guidelines applicable to the water system or has the well been designated as contaminated by any government environmental/health agency?
15.	☐ Yes ☐ No	Does the Owner or Occupant of the property have any knowledge of environmental liens or governmental notification relating to past or current violations of environmental laws with respect to the property or any facility located on the property?
16.	☐ Yes ☐ No	Has the Owner or Occupant of the property been informed of the past or current existence of hazardous substances or petroleum products or environmental violations with respect to the property or any facility located on the property?

17.	☐ Yes ☐ No	Does the Owner or Occupant of the property have any knowledge of any environmental site assessment of the property or facility that indicated the presence of hazardous substances or petroleum products on, or contamination of, the property or recommended further assessment of the property?
18.	☐ Yes ☐ No	Does the Owner or Occupant of the property know of any past, threatened, or pending lawsuits or administrative proceedings concerning a release of any hazardous substance or petroleum products involving the property by any Owner or Occupant of the property?
19.	☐ Yes ☐ No	Does the property discharge waste water on or adjacent to the property other than storm water or into a sanitary sewer system?
20.	☐ Yes ☐ No	To the best of your knowledge, have any hazardous substances or petroleum products, unidentified waste materials, tires, automotive or industrial batteries or any other waste materials been dumped above grade, buried and/or burned on the property?
21.	☐ Yes ☐ No	Is there a transformer, capacitor or any hydraulic equipment for which there are any records indicating the presence of PCBs?
22.		***What environmental permits does the owner or tenant have (or had in the past) or has applied for? Provide copies of such documentation.***
23.	☐ Yes ☐ No	Are there logs of soil borings taken on the property, geotechnical reports from past design or construction work, or monitor well logs for the property?

GOVERNMENT RECORDS & HISTORICAL SOURCES INQUIRY

Do any of the following federal government record systems list the property or any property within the circumference of the area noted below:

24.	☐ Yes ☐ No	National Priorities List within 1.0 mile /1.6 Km?
25.	☐ Yes ☐ No	CERCLIS List within .5 mile / .8 Km?
26.	☐ Yes ☐ No	CERCLIS List within .5 mile / .8 Km? CERCLIS List within .5 mile / .8 Km?
27.	☐ Yes ☐ No	Do any of the following state record systems list the property or any property within the circumference of the area noted below?
28.	☐ Yes ☐ No	List maintained by state environmental agency of hazardous waste sites identified for investigation or remediation that is the state agency equivalent to NPL within approximately 1.0 mile /1.6 Km?
29.	☐ Yes ☐ No	Leaking Underground Storage Tank (LUST) List within .5 mile / .8 Km?
30.	☐ Yes ☐ No	Solid Waste/Landfill Facilities within .5 mile / .8 Km?
31.	☐ Yes ☐ No	Based upon a review of fire insurance maps or consultation with the local fire department serving the property, all as specified in the Guide, are any buildings or other improvements on the property or on an adjoining property identified as having been used for an industrial use or uses likely to lead to contamination of the property?

THIS QUESTIONNAIRE WAS COMPLETED BY:

Name: ____________________

Title: ____________________

Company: ____________________

Address: ____________________

Telephone: ____________________

Date: ____________________

TERMINOLOGY

Materials

1. "Materials" means any liquid, solid, or semisolid substances, including raw materials, commercial products, chemicals, wastes and fuels.
2. Use of the term "materials" is intended to encompass broadly all "hazardous substances" as governed by the Comprehensive Environmental Response, Compensation and Liability Act (CERCLA).
   a. "Hazardous substances" as covered by CERCLA include hazardous wastes, certain air pollutants, toxic water pollutants, and other types of substances which may be harmful to the environment or human health. Materials which may create an immediate hazard, such as explosives, corrosives, and highly toxic chemicals, are included on the list, as well as carcinogens, pesticides, and other chemicals which may have a chronic impact on health or the environment.
   b. Common "hazardous substances" include:
      i. Solvents
      ii. Degreasers
      iii. Acidic or basic solutions
      iv. Hydraulic fluids and coolants especially those contaminated through use
      v. Used oils
      vi. Asbestos
      vii. Paint or ink wastes and thinners
      viii. Ignitable materials
      ix. "PCB" fluids—fluids containing polychlorinated biphenyls, commonly used as dielectric fluid in electric transformers and capacitors
      x. Materials containing arsenic, barium, mercury, cadmium, lead, chromium, selenium, and silver
      xi. Pesticides
3. What is covered by the term "release"?
   a. CERCLA defines a "release" as: any spilling, leaking, pumping, pouring, emitting, emptying, discharging, injecting, escaping, leaching, dumping or disposing into the environment (including land, air, surface water and groundwater).
   b. The term "release" is extremely broad, including intentional as well as unintentional or accidental occurrences.

Environmental Indemnity Agreement

THIS INDEMNITY AGREEMENT is made as of the ____ day of ____________, 2___, by and between ________________, a ________________, having an office at ________________ ("Indemnitor"), in favor of ________________, a ________________ having an office at ________________, its successors and assigns ("Indemnitee").

WHEREAS, ________________ ("Debtor") is the fee owner (or tenant as appropriate) of that certain real property located in the City of ____________, County of ____________ and State of ________________, known as ________________ and more particularly described in Exhibit A attached hereto (said real property, together with any real property hereafter encumbered by ________________ (Lease, Contract of Sale, Energy Purchase Agreement, etc), being herein collectively referred to as "Land"; the Land, together with all structures, buildings and improvements now or hereafter located on the Land, (being collectively referred to as the "Property"); and

WHEREAS, Indemnitee is prepared to enter into ________________ (describe the contract), to be evidenced by a certain agreement known as the ____________, given by Debtor to Indemnitee and secured by, among other things certain Asset(s) as described more fully in the ____________, made by Debtor to Indemnitee which will encumber the Property; and

WHEREAS, as a condition to entering into the ________________, Indemnitee requires Indemnitor to provide certain indemnities concerning Hazardous Materials (as hereinafter defined) and Asbestos (as hereinafter defined); and

WHEREAS, to induce Indemnitee to consummate the above described transaction, Indemnitor has agreed to enter into this agreement.

NOW THEREFORE, in consideration of the premises and other good and valuable consideration, the receipt and sufficiency of which is hereby acknowledged, Indemnitor hereby represents, warrants and covenants to Indemnitee as follows:

1. Indemnitor represents and warrants that (i) to the best of Indemnitor's knowledge, after due inquiry and investigation, (a) there are no Hazardous Materials or Asbestos on the Property, except those in compliance with all applicable federal, state and local laws, ordinances, rules and regulations, and (b) no owner or occupant nor any prior owner or occupant of the Property has received any notice or advice from any governmental agency or any source whatsoever with respect to Hazardous Materials or Asbestos on, from or affecting the Property; and (ii) to the best of Indemnitor's knowledge, no property adjoining the Property is being used, or has ever been used at any previous time, for the disposal, storage, treatment, processing or other handling of Hazardous Materials or Asbestos except as disclosed in the Environmental Report.

2. Indemnitor covenants that (i) the Property shall be kept free of Hazardous Materials and Asbestos, except for those Hazardous Materials necessary for the operation of the Property provided that Indemnitor complies with all applicable federal, state and local laws, rules and regulations and (ii) neither Indemnitor nor any occupant of the Property shall use, transport, store, dispose of or in any manner deal with Hazardous Materials or Asbestos on the Property, except for those Hazardous Materials necessary for the operation of the Property provided that such materials are used, transported, stored and disposed of in compliance with all applicable federal, state and local laws, ordinances, rules and regulations. Indemnitor shall comply with, and ensure compliance by all occupants of the Property with, all applicable federal, state and local laws, ordinances, rules and regulations, and shall keep the Property free and clear of any liens imposed pursuant to such laws, ordinances, rules or regulations. Indemnitor shall conduct and complete all investigations, studies, sampling, and testing, and all remedial actions necessary to clean up and remove any Hazardous Materials and Asbestos from the Property in accordance with all applicable federal, state, and local laws, ordinances, rules and regulations.

3. (a) Indemnitor covenants and agrees at its sole cost and expense, to protect, defend, indemnify and hold Indemnitee, its directors, officers, shareholders, employees, agents, successors, assigns and attorneys harmless from and against any and all losses (including diminution in the value of the Property), liabilities, obligations, claims, damages, penalties, causes of action, fines, costs and expenses, including without limitation, litigation costs (including, without limitation, attorneys' fees, expenses, sums paid in settlement of claims and any such fees and expenses incurred in enforcing this Agreement or collecting any sums due hereunder), other than those arising solely from the willful misconduct of Indemnitee (collectively, the "Indemnified Claims"), directly or indirectly imposed upon or incurred by or asserted against Indemnitee, its directors, officers, shareholders, employees, agents, successors, assigns and attorneys arising out of or in connection with (1) any violation of laws, orders, rules, regulations, requirements, guidelines or demands of any local, state or federal

governmental agency or other authority which are based upon or in any way related to Hazardous Materials or Asbestos including, without limitation, attorney and consultant fees, investigation and laboratory fees, court costs, and litigation expenses; (2) any lawsuit brought or threatened, settlement reached, or government order relating to such Hazardous Materials or Asbestos; (3) the use, generation, refining, manufacture, transportation, transfer, production, processing, storage, handling, or treatment of any Hazardous Materials or Asbestos, on, under, from, or affecting the Property or any other property; (4) the presence, disposal, dumping, escape, seepage, leakage, spillage, discharge, emission, pumping, emptying, injecting, leaching, pouring, release, or threatened release of any Hazardous Materials or Asbestos on, under, from, or affecting the Property or any other property; (5) any remedial action, or imposition of standards of conduct, including the clean-up, encapsulation, treatment, abatement, removal and/or disposal of any Hazardous Materials or Asbestos on, under, from or affecting the Property or any other property to the extent required by any federal, state or local law, ordinance, rule, order, regulation, guideline or demand of applicable governmental authority; (6) any personal injury (including wrongful death) or property damage (real or personal) arising out of or related to such Hazardous Materials or Asbestos; or (7) a material misrepresentation or material inaccuracy in any representation or warranty or a material breach of or failure to perform any covenant made by Indemnitor in this Agreement.

(b) Indemnitor understands and agrees that its liability to Indemnitee shall arise upon the earlier to occur of (1) the discovery of, or the threat or suspected presence of, any Hazardous Materials or Asbestos on, under or about the Property, whether or not the Environmental Protection Agency, any other federal agency or any state or local environmental or other agency or political subdivision or any court, administrative panel or tribunal has taken or threatened any action in connection with the presence, or threatened or suspected presence, of any Hazardous Materials or Asbestos or (2) the institution of any Indemnified Claims, and not upon the realization of loss or damage. Indemnitor shall also indemnify and hold harmless Indemnitee from and against all loss, costs, damages, or expenses (including, without limitation, attorneys' fees) arising out of the enforcement of this Agreement, Or the assertion by any Indemnitor of any defense to its obligations hereunder.

4. The term "Hazardous Materials" as used in this Agreement shall include, without limitation, (a) radon gas, urea formaldehyde foam insulation, transformers or other equipment which contain dielectric fluid containing levels of polychlorinated biphenyls in excess of federal, state or local safety guidelines, whichever is most stringent; (b) any chemical, material or substance, other than Asbestos, including, without limitation, gasoline, petroleum products, explosives, radioactive materials or related or similar materials or any other substance or material defined as or included in the definition of "hazardous substances," "hazardous wastes," "hazardous materials," "extremely hazardous wastes," "restricted hazardous wastes," "toxic substances" or "medical wastes" or words of similar import under any applicable local, state or federal law, similar import under any applicable local, state or federal law, ordinance, rule or under the regulations adopted or publications promulgated pursuant thereto, including, but not limited to, the Comprehensive Environmental Response, Compensation and Liability Act of 1980, as amended, 42 D.S.C. §9601, et. seq.; the Hazardous Materials Transportation Act, as amended, 49 D.S.C. §1801, et. seq.; the Resource Conservation and Recovery Act, as amended, 42 D.S.C. §690l, et. seq.; the Federal Water Pollution Control Act, as amended, 33 U.S.C. §1251, et. seq.; (c) laboratory wastes and medical wastes, including without limitation, contaminated clothing, body fluids, contaminated medical instruments and equipment, catheters, used bandages, gauzes, needles and other sharps; and (d) any other chemical, material or substance, other than Asbestos, exposure to which is prohibited, limited or regulated by any governmental authority. The term "Asbestos" as used in this Agreement shall mean any asbestos or material containing asbestos.

5. This Agreement, the payment of all sums due hereunder and the performance and discharge of each and every obligation, covenant and agreement of Indemnitor contained herein, are, and shall be deemed to be, secured by the ______________________.

6. The liability of Indemnitor under this Agreement shall in no way be limited or impaired by, and Indemnitor hereby consents to and agrees to be bound by, any amendment or modification of the provisions of the Other Security Documents to or with Indemnitee by Indemnitor or any person who succeeds Indemnitor or Debtor as owner of the Property. In addition, the liability of Indemnitor under this Agreement shall in no way be limited or impaired by (i) any extensions of time for performance required by any of the Other Security Documents, (ii) any sale or transfer of all or part of the Property, (iii) except as provided herein, any exculpatory provision in any of the Other Security Documents limiting Indemnitee's recourse to property encumbered by the ________________ or to any other security, or limiting Indemnitee's rights to a deficiency judgment against Indemnitor or Debtor, (iv) the accuracy or inaccuracy of the representations and warranties made by Indemnitor or Debtor under any of the Other Security Documents or herein, (v) the release of Indemnitor or any other per-

son from performance or observance of any of the agreements, covenants, terms or condition contained in any of the Other Security Documents by operation of law, Indemnitee's voluntary act, or otherwise, (vi) the release or substitution in whole or in part of any security for the ________________, or (vii) Indemnitee's failure to record the ________________ or file any UCC financing statements (or Indemnitee's improper recording or filing of any thereof) or to otherwise perfect, protect, secure or insure any security interest or lien given as security for the ______________; and, in any such case, whether with or without notice to Indemnitor and with or without consideration.

7. The obligations and liabilities of Indemnitor under this Indemnity shall survive any termination, satisfaction, assignment, entry of a judgment of foreclosure or delivery of a deed in lieu of foreclosure of the ______________.

8. Any amounts payable to Indemnitee under this Agreement shall become immediately due and payable and, if not paid within thirty (30) days of written demand therefore, shall bear interest at the rate of __________ percent (__ %) from the earlier to occur of (i) the date payment is made or loss or damage is sustained by Indemnitee or (ii) the date Indemnitor's liability shall arise pursuant to paragraph 3(b) hereof, until paid.

9. Indemnitor hereby waives (i) any right or claim of right to cause a marshalling of Indemnitor's assets or to cause Indemnitee or other Indemnitee to proceed against any of the security for the ________________ before proceeding under this Agreement against Indemnitor; (ii) and relinquishes all rights and remedies accorded by applicable law to Indemnitor's or guarantors, except any rights of subrogation which Indemnitor may have, provided that the indemnity provided for hereunder shall neither be contingent upon the existence of any such rights of subrogation nor subject to any claims or defenses whatsoever which may be asserted in connection with the enforcement or attempted enforcement of such subrogation rights including, without limitation, any claim that such subrogation rights were abrogated by any acts of Indemnitee or other Indemnitee; (iii) the right to assert a counterclaim, other than a mandatory or compulsory counterclaim, in any action or proceeding brought against or by Indemnitee or other Indemnitee; (iv) trial by jury in any action or proceeding brought by Indemnitor or Indemnitee or other Indemnitee or in any counterclaim asserted by Indemnitee or other Indemnitee against Indemnitor or in any matter whatsoever arising out of or in any way connected with this Agreement; (v) notice of acceptance hereof and of any action taken or omitted in reliance hereon; (vi) presentment for payment, demand of payment, protest or notice of nonpayment or failure to perform or observe, or other proof, or notice or demand; and (vii) all homestead exemption rights against the obligations hereunder and the benefits of any statutes of limitations or repose. Notwithstanding anything to the contrary contained herein, Indemnitor hereby agrees to postpone the exercise of any rights of subrogation with respect to any collateral securing the Loan until the Loan shall have been paid in full.

10. Indemnitor shall take any and all reasonable actions, including institution of legal action against third-parties, necessary or appropriate to obtain reimbursement, payment or compensation from such persons responsible for the presence of any Hazardous Materials or Asbestos at, in, on, under or near the Property or otherwise obligated by law to bear the cost. Indemnitee shall be and hereby is subrogated to all of Indemnitor's rights now or hereafter in such claims.

11. Indemnitor represents and warrants that:
    a. Indemnitor has the full corporate power and authority to execute and deliver this Agreement and to perform its obligations hereunder; the execution, delivery and performance of this Agreement by Indemnitor has been duly and validly authorized; and all requisite corporate action has been taken by Indemnitor to make this Agreement valid and binding upon Indemnitor, enforceable in accordance with its terms;
    b. Indemnitor's execution of, and compliance with, this Agreement are in the ordinary course of business of Indemnitor and will not result in the breach of any term or provision of the charter or by-laws of Indemnitor or result in the breach of any term or provision of, or conflict with or constitute a default under or result in the acceleration of any obligation under, any agreement, indenture or loan or credit agreement or other instrument to which Indemnitor or the Property is subject, or result in the violation of any law, rule, regulation, order, judgment or decree to which Indemnitor or the Property is subject;
    c. There is no action, suit, proceeding or investigation pending or threatened against Indemnitor which, either in anyone instance or in the aggregate, may result in any material adverse change in the business, operations, financial condition, properties or assets of Indemnitor, or in any material impairment of the right or ability of Indemnitor to carry on its business substantially as now conducted, or in any material liability on the part of Indemnitor, or which would draw into question the validity of this Agreement or of any action taken or to be taken in connection with the obligations of Indemnitor contemplated herein, or which would be likely to impair materially the ability of Indemnitor to perform under the terms of this Agreement;

d. Indemnitor does not believe, nor does it have any reason or cause to believe, that it cannot perform each and every covenant contained in this Agreement;
e. No approval, authorization, order, license or consent of, or registration or filing with, any governmental authority or other person, and no approval, authorization or consent of any other party is required in connection with this Agreement;
f. This Agreement constitutes a valid, legal and binding obligation of Indemnitor, enforceable against it in accordance with the terms hereof.

12. No delay on Indemnitee's part in exercising any right, power or privilege under this Agreement shall operate as a waiver of any such privilege, power or right.

13. Each party hereto shall, within five (5) business days of receipt thereof, give written notice to the other party hereto of (i) any notice or advice from any governmental agency or any source whatsoever with respect to Hazardous Materials or Asbestos on, from or affecting the Property, and (ii) any claim, suit or proceeding, whether administrative or judicial in nature ("Legal Action"), brought against such party or instituted with respect to the Property, with respect to which Indemnitor may have liability under this Agreement. Such notice shall comply with the provisions of paragraph 15 hereof.

14. Indemnitee shall, at all times, be free to independently establish to its satisfaction and in its absolute discretion the existence or nonexistence of any fact or facts the existence or nonexistence of which is a condition of this Agreement.

15. All notices, demands, requests, consents and other communications which are required or permitted to be given herein shall be in writing and shall be deemed given when postmarked, addressed and mailed by first class mail to the address as set forth below of the party to whom such notice is to be given, or to such other address as Indemnitor or Indemnitee, as the case may be, shall in like manner designate in writing:

If to Indemnitor:

Attention:

With a copy to:

Attention:

If to Indemnitee:

Attention:

With a copy to:

or at such other address of which it shall have notified the party giving such notice in writing, as aforesaid.

16. Indemnitor covenants and agrees (i) that in any action or proceeding brought by Indemnitee against Indemnitor under this Agreement, the Supreme Court of the State of ______________ for the County of ______________, or, in a case involving diversity of citizenship, the United States District Court for the __________ District of ______________, shall have jurisdiction over any such action or proceeding; (ii) that service of any summons and complaint or other process in any such action or proceeding may be made by registered or certified mail directed to Indemnitor to its address at __________________ ______________, Indemnitor hereby waiving personal service thereof; and (iii) that within thirty days after such mailing Indemnitor so served shall appear or answer to any summons and complaint or other process, and should Indemnitor so served fail to appear or answer within said thirty-day period, said Indemnitor shall be deemed in default and judgment may be entered by Indemnitee against the said party for the amount as demanded in any summons and complaint or other process so served.

17. The terms of this Agreement are for the sole and exclusive protection and use of Indemnitee. No party shall be a third-party beneficiary hereunder, and no provision hereof shall operate or inure to the use and benefit of any such third party.

18. Capitalized terms used herein and not specifically defined herein shall have the respective meanings ascribed to such terms in the ________________________________.

19. This Agreement may be executed in several counterparts, each of which counterparts shall be deemed an original instrument and all of which together shall constitute a single agreement of Indemnity. The failure of any party hereto to execute

this Agreement, or any counterpart hereof, shall not relieve the other signatories from their obligations hereunder.

20. This Agreement may not be modified, amended, waived, extended, changed, discharged or terminated orally or by any act or failure to act on the part of Indemnitee, but only by an agreement in writing signed by the party against whom enforcement of any modification, amendment, waiver, extension, change, discharge or termination is sought.

21. All pronouns and any variations thereof shall be deemed to refer to the masculine, feminine, neuter, singular or plural as the identity of the person or persons referred to may require. Without limiting the effect of specific references in any provision of this Agreement, the term "Indemnitor" shall be deemed to refer to Indemnitor and each person or entity comprising Indemnitor from time to time, as the sense of a particular provision may require, and to include the heirs, executors, administrators, legal representatives, successors and assigns of Indemnitor, all of whom shall be bound by the provisions of this Agreement. Each reference herein to Indemnitee shall be deemed to include its successors and assigns, to whose favor the provisions of this Agreement shall also inure.

22. If Indemnitor consists of more than one person or entity, the obligations and liabilities of each such person or entity hereunder shall be joint and several.

23. Anyone or more parties liable upon or in respect of this Agreement may be released without affecting the liability of any party not so released.

24. The rights and remedies herein provided are cumulative and not exclusive of any rights or remedies which Indemnitee has under the ____________________________, or the Other Security Documents or would otherwise have at law or in equity.

25. If any term, condition or covenant of this Agreement shall be held to be invalid, illegal or unenforceable in any respect, this Agreement shall be construed without such provision.

26. This Agreement shall be governed and construed in accordance with the laws of the State of ________________________ and the applicable laws of the United States of America.

IN WITNESS WHEREOF, this Agreement has been executed by Indemnitor and Indemnitee, and is effective as of the day and year first above written.

INDEMNITOR:

By:

INDEMNITEE:

By:

Equipment Acceptance Notice & Delivery Certificate

Re: LEASE #

All the items of equipment subject to the Lease dated ____________________, 2____, between us, as Lessee, and you, as Lessor, have been received by us and (if required) have been installed.

The undersigned acknowledges that: (1) the undersigned has fully inspected the Equipment, has heretofore been delivered to the undersigned by Vendor(s); (2) the said Equipment is in full compliance with the terms of the Lease Agreement pertaining thereto; (3) said Equipment has not been delivered to the undersigned, nor installed, on a trial basis; (4) said Equipment is in good condition (operating and otherwise) and repair; and (5) the undersigned accepts said Equipment, as is and where is. The undersigned confirms that you have made no warranty or representation, express or implied, of merchantability, fitness, design, condition, workmanship or otherwise of the Equipment.

It is further understood that Renewable Energy Project Creditor as Lessor shall not be responsible for any third party service contracts or other agreements, unless specifically included in Lease Contract; that default of such agreements (if any) shall in no way affect our responsibility for payment of Lease Agreement in accordance with the terms thereof.

WE ACKNOWLEDGE THAT WE MAY NOT, WITHOUT YOUR PRIOR WRITTEN APPROVAL, ADD TO, OR DELETE FROM, OR SUBSTITUTE OTHER ITEMS OF EQUIPMENT FOR, THE ABOVE ITEMS, OR MAKE ADJUSTMENTS WITH THE SUPPLIER(S) OR RELOCATE THE EQUIPMENT. WE HAVE REVIEWED AND APPROVED THE PURCHASE ORDER/SUPPLY CONTRACT, RECEIVED ALL WARRANTIES FROM THE SUPPLIER AND APPROVED ALL LEASE DOCUMENTS.

SUPPLIER: This Acceptance must be signed by Lessee and returned to us before your invoice can be paid.

LESSEE: Do not sign until you actually receive the equipment in good order and condition and installed.

THIS ACCEPTANCE RELATES TO A NON CANCELLABLE LEASE

DATE: ________________

LESSEE: ____

The undersigned affirms that they are a duly authorized corporate officer, partner or proprietor of the above name Lessee.

X ______________________________ **TITLE:** ____________________________

Estoppel Certificate

To: **Renewable Energy Project Creditor (the "Creditor")**

RE: **Tenancy at ______________________________ (the "Leased Premises")**

The Undersigned (the "Tenant"), as tenant under a lease dated __________________ (the "Lease"), between the Landlord, ____________________________________, and the Tenant respecting the Leased Premises, hereby certifies to the Creditor and the Landlord and acknowledges that the Creditor and the Landlord are relying upon the following in connection with the Premises:

1. The term of the Lease commenced on __________________, of a lease term of ____________________, and terminates on ________________________ of the lease term (as in the Lease).
2. The Tenant is in possession of the Leased Premises in accordance with the terms of the Lease. The Lease Premises are comprised of ______________ square feet.
3. The Lease has not been altered or amended since its execution and is in full effect and force.
4. The minimum of base rent is presently $_____________ per _________ and all rent has been paid to date in accordance with the terms of the Lease.
5. The amount of prepaid rent or security deposit currently held by the Landlord is $______________.
6. The Tenant is not claiming any deduction, abatement or set-off of any rent payable, nor any counterclaim of defense against the enforcement of its obligations to be performed under the Lease.
7. There is no existing default or breach of the Lease on the part of the Landlord of which the Tenant has notice.
8. There is no agreement between the Tenant and the Landlord, other than that contained in the Lease, pertaining to the obligations of the Landlord and the rights of the Tenant relating to the use and occupation of the Leased Premises or the Property by the Tenant.
9. The Tenant acknowledges that the Tenant is to continue to make rental and other payments to the Landlord in accordance the terms of the Lease and that it has not received any notice of assignment of the Lease or the rents payable thereunder except as herein contained.
10. The Tenant further acknowledges that the Tenant will, if possession is taken under, or any proceedings are brought for possession under or the foreclosure of, or in the event of the exercise of the power of sale under the mortgage, attorn to the Mortgagee, its assignee or the purchaser upon any such foreclosure, sale or other proceeding and will recognize the Mortgagee, its assignee, or the purchaser as the landlord under the Lease, provided that the Mortgagee, its assignee or the purchaser, as the case may be, agrees not to disturb the Tenant's possession under the Lease as long as the Tenant performs its obligations thereunder and hereunder.

Dated: __________________________________

Tenant: ________________________________

By: ____________________________________

General Environmental Audit Checklist

Requirement	Question	Verification Method
The organization shall define and document the scope of its environmental management system.	Where has the organization defined and documented the scope of its environmental management system?	Review the documented scope statement.
Top management shall define the organization's environmental policy and ensure that, within the defined scope of its environmental management system, it is communicated to all persons working for or on behalf of the organization?	What is the organization's environmental policy? What does it mean to you in the work that you do?	Ask employees in different levels and functions what their understanding is of the environmental policy and how it applies to their work. Take a stratified sample. Assess degree of understanding, e.g. through informal tallying of the number of employees whose understanding is excellent, fair/good, or inadequate. Include contractors working on-site or persons working off-site whose work activities are associated with the organization's significant environmental aspects.
The organization shall ensure that the significant environmental aspects are taken into account in establishing, implementing and maintaining its environmental management system.	How has the organization taken into consideration its significant environmental aspects in establishing, implementing and maintaining its environmental management system?	Review the main elements of the management system. Assess whether adequate consideration has been given to significant environmental aspects . Review especially the setting of objectives and targets, training, communication, operational control, emergency preparedness and response, and monitoring and measurement.
The organization shall establish and maintain a procedure(s) to determine how these requirements apply to its environmental aspects.	How has the organization determined the applicability of environmental legal and other requirements to its activities, products and services?	Ask management to describe a process for assessing the applicability of legal requirements and other requirements to its activities, products and services.
The organization shall ensure that any person(s) performing tasks for	How does the organization assess the competence of	Look for an analysis, by significant aspect, of the

REQUIREMENT	QUESTION	VERIFICATION METHOD
it or on its behalf that have the potential to cause significant environmental impact(s) identified by the organization is (are) competent on the basis of appropriate education, training or experience, and shall retain appropriate records.	personnel performing tasks which can cause significant environmental impacts? How does the organization know which employees, or other persons working for it or on its behalf, can have significant impacts on the environment? What associated records are retained?	types of personnel associated with the work, and trace the organization's determination of competence. Look for the establishment by the organization of criteria of performance, and for evidence that personnel are assessed against those criteria. Include suppliers and subcontractors, as appropriate. Look for consequences of the assessment of personnel, such as implementation of training programs, educational development, and skill enhancement, and associated record keeping.

Continuing Guaranty

For valuable consideration, the undersigned ("Guarantors") jointly and severally unconditionally guarantee and promise to pay ______________________________ ("Lessor"), or order, on demand, in lawful money of the United States, any and all Indebtedness of ______________________________ ("Lessee") to Lessor.

The word "Indebtedness" is used herein in its most comprehensive sense and includes any and all advances, debts, obligations and liabilities of Lessor or any one or more of them heretofore, now, or hereafter made, incurred or created, whether voluntary or involuntary and however arising, whether due or not due, absolute or contingent, liquidated or unliquidated, determined or undetermined, and whether Lessee may be liable individually or jointly with others, or whether recovery upon the Indebtedness may be or hereafter becomes barred by any statute of limitations, or whether the Indebtedness may be or hereafter becomes otherwise unenforceable.

1. Liability

The liability of Guarantors shall not exceed at any on time the sum of the total rental payments defined in Equipment Lease Number ______, a copy of which is acknowledged, together with all lease charges, other obligations defined in the Lease and interest upon the Indebtedness. Notwithstanding the foregoing, Lessor may permit the Indebtedness of Lessee to exceed Guarantors' liability. Any payment by Guarantor shall not reduce their maximum obligation hereunder, unless written notice to that effect is actually received by Lessor at or prior to the time of such payment.

2. Continuing Guaranty

This is a continuing guaranty relating to any Indebtedness, including that arising under successive transactions which shall either continue or from time to time renew the Indebtedness whether or not any prior Indebtedness has been satisfied. This guaranty shall not apply to any new Indebtedness created after actual receipt by Lessor of written notice of its revocation. Said written revocation shall not apply to extensions or renewals of Indebtedness in existence at the time of receipt of the written revocation. Notwithstanding the full payment of any Indebtedness, this guaranty shall remain in effect or be reinstated with respect to such Indebtedness if, in connection with bankruptcy, insolvency or similar proceedings filed by or against the Lessee, a court enters an order of judgment compelling or requiring the Lessor to return any or all payments made with respect to such Indebtedness.

3. Obligations of Guarantors are Independent

The obligations hereunder are independent of the obligations of Lessee, and a separate action or actions may be brought and prosecuted against Guarantors whether action is brought against Lessee or whether Lessee is joined in any such action or actions; and Guarantors waive the benefit of any statute of limitations affecting their liability hereunder or the enforcement thereof to the extent permitted by law. Any partial payment by Lessee or other circumstance which operates to toll any statute of limitations as to Lessee shall operate to toll the statute of limitations as to Guarantors.

4. Authority to Modify Indebtedness

Guarantors authorize Lessor, without notice or demand and without affecting their liability hereunder or under any other document related to the Indebtedness to which any of the Guarantors is a party, from time to time to (a) renew, compromise, extend, amend, waive, restructure, refinance, release, accelerate or otherwise change the terms of the Indebtedness or any part thereof, including increase or decrease in the Indebtedness or the rate of interest or lease service charges thereon; (b) accept new or additional documents, instruments or agreements relative to the indebtedness; (c) consent to the change, restructure or termination of the corporate structure of Lessee and correspondingly restructure the Indebtedness; (d) take and hold security or additional guarantees for the payment of this guaranty or the Indebtedness guaranteed, and amend, alter, exchange, substitute, transfer, enforce, waive, subordinate, terminate or release any such security; (e) apply such security and direct the order or manner of sale thereof as Lessor in its discretion may determine; (f) release or substitute any one or more of the endorsers or guarantors; and (g) accept partial payment on the Indebtedness.

5. Waiver of Rights and Defenses

Guarantors waive any right to require Lessor to (a) proceed against Lessee or any other person or company; (b) proceed against or exhaust any security held from Lessee; or (c) pursue any other remedy in Lessor's power whatsoever. Lessor may, at its election, exercise any right or remedy it may have against Lessee or any security held by Lessor, including without limitation the right to foreclose upon any such security by judicial or nonjudicial sale, without affecting or impairing in any way the liability of Guarantors hereunder except to the extent the Indebtedness has been paid, and Guarantors waive any defense arising out of the absence, impairment or loss of any right of reimbursement or subrogation or other right or remedy of Guarantors against Lessee or any such security, whether resulting from such election by Lessor, or otherwise. Guarantors waive any defense arising by reason of any disability of other defense of Lessee or by reason of the cessation from any cause whatsoever of the liability of Lessee. Until all Indebtedness of Lessee to Lessor shall have been paid in full, even though such Indebtedness is in excess of Guarantors' liability hereunder, Guarantors shall have no right of subrogation, and waive any right to enforce any remedy which Lessor now has or may hereafter have against Lessee, and waive any benefit of, and any right to participate in any security now or hereafter held by Lessor. Guarantors waive all presentments, demands for performance, notices of non-performance, protests, notices of protest, notices of dishonor, and notices of acceptance of this guaranty and of the existence, creation, or incurring of new or additional Indebtedness.

Guarantor(s) hereby expressly waiver all antideficiency protections, including, but not necessarily limited to, California Code of Civil Procedure Sections 580 d (i.e., the protection against an antideficiency judgment)) and 726 (i.e., requiring the Lessor to proceed against the real property security first), and acknowledges that if a deficiency (i.e., the entire outstanding lease balance was not paid off and the equipment returned) to the Lessor on the lease obligation being guaranteed after the Lessor completes a nonjudicial foreclosure of the real property security, the Lessor may, because of this waiver, bring a legal action against the Guarantor(s) and obtain a judgment in favor of Lessor and against Guarantor(s) to recover that deficiency.

6. Information About Lessee's Financial Condition

Guarantors assume the responsibility for being and keeping themselves informed of the business, operation and financial condition of Lessee and of all other circumstances bearing upon the risk of nonpayment of the Indebtedness which diligent inquiry would reveal, and agree that absent a request for such information by Guarantors, Lessor shall have no duty to advise Guarantor of information, matter, fact or thing now or hereafter known to it regarding such condition of any such circumstance.

7. Liens and Setoff

In addition to all liens upon, and rights of setoff against the moneys, securities or other property of Guarantors given to Lessor by law, Lessor shall have a lien upon and a right of setoff against all money, securities and other property of Guarantors now or hereafter in the possession of or on deposit with Lessor, whether held in a general or special account or deposit, or for safekeeping or otherwise; and every such lien and right of setoff may be exercised without demand upon or notice to Guarantors. No lien or right of setoff shall be deemed to have been waived by any act or conduct on the part of Lessor, or by any neglect to exercise such right of setoff or to enforce such lien, or by any delay in so doing; and every right of setoff and lien shall continue in full force and effect until such right of setoff or lien is specifically waived or released by an instrument in writing executed by Lessor.

8. Acceleration

If this Continuing Guaranty is secured by a deed of trust, the deed of trust contains the following statement (Due on Sale clause);

Upon default by Trustor in payment of any indebtedness secured hereby or in performance of any agreement hereunder, or in the event Trustor or any successor in interest to Trustor in the property sells, conveys, alienates, assigns or transfers said property, or any part thereof, or any interest therein, or becomes divested of Trustor's title or any interest therein in any manner or way, whether voluntary or involuntary, Beneficiary shall have the right, at its option, to declare said lease, note and any other indebtedness or obligation secured hereby, irrespective of maturity dates specified in any lease, note or written agreement evidencing the same, immediately due and payable without notice or demand, and no waiver of this right shall be effective unless in writing and signed by Beneficiary.

9. Subordination

Any Indebtedness of Lessee now or hereafter held by Guarantors is hereby subordinated to the Indebtedness of Lessee to Lessor; and such Indebtedness of Lessee to Guarantor if Lessor so requests shall be collected, enforced and received by Guarantors as trustees for Lessor and paid over to Lessor on account of the Indebtedness of Lessee to Lessor but without reducing or affecting in any manner the liability of Guarantor under the other provisions of this guaranty.

10. Waiver of Right of Subrogation

Notwithstanding anything to the contrary contained herein or in any other document to which any of the Guarantors is a party, Guarantors hereby expressly waive any and all rights to subrogation, reimbursement, exoneration, contribution, setoff or any other rights that could accrue to a surety against a principal, to a guarantor against a maker or obligor, to an accommodation party against the party accommodated, or to a holder or transferee against a maker, and which any of the Guarantors may have or hereafter acquire against Lessee or any other person in connection with or as a result of Guarantors' execution, delivery and/or performance of this guaranty or any other document to which any of the Guarantors is a party, whether or not such claim, remedy or right arises in equity, or under contract, statute or common law. Guarantors shall not have or assert any such rights against Lessee or their successors and assigns or any other person (including any surety), either directly or as an attempted setoff to any action commenced against any of the Guarantors by any Lessee (as Lessee or in any other capacity), Lessor or any other person. Guarantors hereby acknowledge and agree that this waiver is intended to benefit Lessee and Lessor and shall not limit or otherwise affect Guarantors' liability under this guaranty, under any other document to which any of the Guarantors is a party, or the enforceability hereof or thereof. In furtherance, and not in limitation, of the preceding waiver, Guarantors agree that any payments made by them under this guaranty shall be deemed a contribution to the capital of Lessee or other obligated party and any such payment shall not cause Guarantor to become creditor of Lessee or other such party.

11. Benefit to Guarantor

Guarantor represents and warrants that there is an express benefit, either directly or indirectly, to Guarantor in executing this guaranty, which offsets their liability to Lessor under this guaranty.

12. Transfer of Guaranty

This guaranty shall, without further reference, pass to and may be relied upon and enforced by any successor or assignee of Lessor and any transferee or subsequent holder of any of the Indebtedness.

13. Authority of Officers

Where any one or more of Lessees are corporations or partnerships it is not necessary for Lessor to inquire into the powers of Lessee, or the officers, directors, partners or agents acting or purporting to act on their behalf, and any Indebtedness made or created in reliance upon the professed exercise of such powers shall be guaranteed hereunder.

14. Attorneys' Fees

Guarantors agree to pay a reasonable attorneys' fee and all other costs and expenses which may be incurred by Lessor in the enforcement of this guaranty.

15. Recourse to Separate Property

Any married person who signs this guaranty hereby expressly agrees that recourse may be had against his or her separate property for all his or her obligations under this guaranty.

16. Rights Cumulative

The rights, powers and remedies given to Lessor by this guaranty are cumulative and shall be in addition to and independent of all rights, powers and remedies given Lessor by virtue of any statute, rule of law, or any agreement between Guarantors and Lessor or between Lessee and Lessor. Any forbearance or failure or delay by Lessor in exercising any right, power or remedy hereunder shall not preclude the further exercise thereof; and every right, power and remedy of the Lessor shall continue in full force and effect until such right, power or remedy is specifically waived by an instrument in writing signed by Lessor.

17. Successors and Assigns

The guaranty shall bind Guarantors successors and assigns. Lessor may without notice assign the guaranty in whole or in part.

18. Applicable Law

This Agreement shall be governed by, and construed in accordance with, the laws of the State of ____________________.

19. Joint and Several

The obligations of Guarantors hereunder are joint and several.

20. Section Headings

The section headings used in this guaranty are for convenience of reference only and shall not limit or otherwise affect this guaranty.

21. Singular, Plural

In all cases where there is but a single Lessee or a single Guarantor, then all words used herein in the plural shall be deemed to have been used in the singular where the context and construction so require; and when there is more than one Lessee named herein, or when this guaranty is executed by more than one Guarantor, the word "Lessees" and the word "Guarantors" respectively shall mean all and any one or more of them.

IN WITNESS WHEREOF the undersigned Guarantors have executed this guaranty ____________________, 2_____.

Guarantors: ____

By: ______________________________ By: ______________________________________

Insurance Coverage Request

TO:

Agents Name: Policy #:
Company Name:
Address:
Telephone Number: FAX Number:

FROM:

Lessee:
Address:

LEASE #: **Date:**

November 21, 2013

Gentlemen:

We have entered into a lease agreement with Renewable Energy Project Creditor for the lease of certain equipment described in the attached schedule that has a value of $___________.

The equipment will be located at the above address with the exception of:

This is a net lease and we are responsible for the insurance cost. Please see that we have immediate coverage and notify Renewable energy Project Creditor at once in the form of a Binder or a Certificate of Insurance. Both should include therein the standard 10 day notice of cancellation to the Lessor or Loss Payee.

PHYSICAL DAMAGE Insurance is to be provided for fire, extended coverage, vandalism and malicious mischief for the full value of the equipment with a maximum deductible of $1,000.00 per occurrence on Form 438BFU. *Renewable Energy Project Creditor* is to be named as Loss Payee at the address show below as well as the following party as their interest may appear:

LIABILITY: Coverage should be written with minimum limits of $100,000 and $300,000 for Bodily Injury and $50,000 property damage. *Renewable Energy Project Creditor* is to be named as Additional Insured.

If you have any questions, please do not hesitate to call our insurance department at ________________.
Thank you,

LESSEE: X **Title:**

RECORDING REQUESTED BY:
Renewable Energy Project Creditor
1234 S Any Street
Your Town, CA 92866

AND WHEN RECORDED, MAIL TO:
Renewable Energy Project Creditor
1234 S Any Street
Your Town, CA 92866

Waiver and Consent By Real Property Owner(s)

THIS WAIVER AND CONSENT is made and entered into between Renewable energy Project Creditor (hereinafter referred to as "Secured Party") and: ______________________________ (hereinafter referred to as "Owner"), whether one or more, and affects the real property in the city of__________________, County of ______________, State of__________________, described as:
[Legal description of real property]

and commonly known as ____ (hereinafter referred to as the "Premises").

This Waiver and Consent is executed to induce Secured Party to enter into or refrain from terminating an Equipment Lease Agreement dated __________________________ (hereinafter referred to jointly as "Agreements") with: ___________________________ (hereinafter referred to as "Debtor"), which Agreements, among other things were given by Debtor to Secured Party for the purpose of securing payment of the purchase price of the "Goods," a copy of which is attached hereto and made a part hereof, and/or of all obligations and performance of all duties now or hereinafter owing be Debtor to Secured Party, of every kind and description. This Waiver and Consent does not amend any of the terms and conditions of the Agreements and reference thereto is made for further particulars.

By the Agreements, Secured Party shall sell or lease, or has sold or leased or lent credit or monies or has loaned credit or monies against the security of merchandise, equipment, furniture, furnishings, fixtures, machinery and tools, together with all additions, substitutions, replacements, improvements and repairs to same (hereinafter referred to as "Goods") to debtor, which Goods are or shall be located on and may be affixed to the Premises or improvements thereon.

SECURED PARTY AND OWNER AGREE THAT:

1. Notwithstanding and provision of the lease between Owner and Debtor, pertaining to the premises or any of the provisions of the ____________________ Uniform Commercial Code, including, without limitation, §9102(l)(c) thereof, the __________________ Uniform Commercial Code shall govern the rights between them pertaining to the Goods.

2. The Goods shall be and remain Personal Property notwithstanding the manner of their annexation to the Premises, their adaptability to the uses and purposes for which the Premises are used and the intentions of the party making the annexation.

3. Any rights which Owner may claim to have in and to the goods no matter how arising, shall be second and subordinate to the rights of Secured party therein.

4. Owner consents to the installation of the Goods on the premises, agrees that the Secured party may do to and with the Goods any or all of the acts below enumerated, and grants Secured Party a license to enter into possession of the Premises to do any or all of the following to said Goods: assemble, have appraised, display, operate, sever, remove, maintain, prepare for sale or lease, repair, lease, transfer and/or sell (at Public Auction(s) or Private Sale(s), the Goods, or any part thereof.

5. The Waivers and Consents herein granted shall continue until such time as Secured Party has been paid the full purchase price of the Goods and/or all obligations and expenses (including, without limitation, reasonable attorney's fees) have been paid

and all covenants and conditions as more specifically enumerated in the Agreements have been fully performed.

6. In the event Debtor breaches any of the terms and conditions of said lease between Debtor and Owner, Owner shall notify Secured Party in writing not less than fifteen (15) days of said breach. Further, Secured Party shall have the right to access the Premises for the purposes described in Paragraph 4 above, for a period of up to ninety (90) days (at Secured Party's discretion), following Owner's placing Secured Party in possession of the Premises, or abandonment of the Premises by Debtor, whichever occurs later. All structural damage to the Premises caused by the removal of the Goods shall be repaired by Secured Party at its expense in a commercially reasonable manner.

7. This Waiver and Consent shall be interpreted under the laws of the State of ______________________ and shall inure to the benefit of and be binding upon the successors, heirs and assigns of Owner and Secured Party.

Dated: ____, 19 _____

Renewable Energy Project Creditor ("Secured Party")	**LANDLORD ("Owner"):** ______________________________
By:______________________________	**By:**______________________________
Title:______________________________	**Title:**______________________________

(THIS DOCUMENT MUST BE EXECUTED BEFORE A NOTARY PUBLIC AND THE PROPER NOTARIAL ACKNOWLEDGEMENTS ATTACHED.)

First Amendment to Equipment Lease Schedule

THIS FIRST AMENDMENT is made as of ______________________ by and between Renewable Energy Project Creditor ("Lessor"); and __________________________ ("Lessee").

WITNESSETH

WHEREAS, the Lessor and Lessee are parties to a certain Equipment Lease dated __________________ ("Equipment Lease") and a certain Equipment Lease Schedule No. _________________ (the "Schedule"); and

WHEREAS, the parties hereto desire to amend certain of the terms of the Schedule as hereinafter provided;

NOW, THEREFORE, in consideration of the premises and the mutual obligations hereinafter contained, and for other good and valuable consideration, the receipt whereof is hereby acknowledged, the parties hereto agree as follows:

1. Notwithstanding any provision contained in the Equipment Lease or the Schedule to the contrary, upon expiration of the lease term set forth in the Schedule (the "Initial Lease Term") and payment by Lessee of all rentals and obligations set forth in the Schedule, and provided that no Event of Default (as defined in the Equipment Lease) shall have occurred and be continuing, Lessee, at its option, may purchase all of Lessor's right, title and interest in and to all, but not less than all, of the equipment described in and covered by the Schedule (the "Equipment") for a purchase price equal to the greater of (a) the then fair market value of the Equipment determined as hereinafter provided, or (b) ____________________ In order to exercise such option, Lessee shall notify Lessor in writing of Lessee's intention to exercise such option at least ninety (90) days prior to the expiration of the Initial Lease Term and shall deliver to Lessor on or before the expiration of the Initial Lease Term the appraisal referred to in paragraph 2 hereof and payment of the purchase price in cash or by certified or bank cashier's check.

2. For the purposes of paragraph 1 hereof, the "fair market value" of the Equipment shall be determined by an independent third party appraiser selected by Lessee. The appraiser's report shall be in writing and delivered to Lessor in accordance with the preceding paragraph. All fees and expenses of the appraiser shall be paid by Lessee.

3. If the Lessee for any reason does not purchase the Equipment in accordance with paragraph 1 hereof, the lease term set forth in the Schedule applicable to the Equipment shall automatically and without further action on the part of the Lessor or Lessee be extended for an additional term of twelve (12) months at a monthly rental of ________________________, with the first such rental being due and payable by Lessee 30 days after the scheduled expiration of the original lease term. Upon termination of the extended lease term, the Lessee shall be obligated to return the Equipment to Lessor in accordance with the terms of the Equipment Lease.

4. Except as amended hereby, the Equipment Lease and the Schedule shall remain in full force and effect, and are in all respects hereby ratified and affirmed.

IN WITNESS WHEREOF, the parties hereto have caused this instrument to be executed by their duly authorized officers as of the day and year first above written.

LESSOR:	**LESSEE:**
Renewable Energy Project Creditor	______________________________
By:__________________, President	**By:____________________, __________**

Lender's Loss Payable Endorsement

1. Loss or damage, if any, under this policy, shall be paid to the Payee named on the first page of this policy, its successors and assigns, hereinafter referred to as "the Lender" in whatever form or capacity its interest may appear and whether said interest be vested in said Lender in its individual or in its disclosed or undisclosed fiduciary or representative capacity, or otherwise, or vested in a nominee or trustee of said Lender.

2. The insurance under this policy, or any rider or endorsement attached thereto, as to the interest only of the Lender, its successors and assigns, shall not be invalidated nor suspended: (a) by any error, omission, or change respecting the ownership, description, possession, or location of the subject of the insurance or the interest therein, or the title thereto; (b) by the commencement of foreclosure proceedings or the giving of notice of sale of any of the property covered by this policy by virtue of any mortgage or trust deed; (c) by any breach of warranty, act, omission, neglect, or non-compliance with any of the provisions of this policy, including any and all riders now or hereafter attached thereto, by the named insured, the borrower, mortgagor, trustor, vendee, owner, tenant, warehouseman, custodian, occupant, or by the agents of either or any of them or by the happening of any event permitted by them or either of them, or their agents, or which they failed to prevent, whether occurring before or after the attachment of this endorsement, or whether before or after a loss, which under the provisions of this policy of insurance or of any rider or endorsement attached thereto would invalidate or suspend the insurance as to the named insured, excluding herefrom, however any acts or omissions for the Lender while exercising active control and management of the property.

3. In the event of failure of the insured to pay any premium or additional premium which shall be or become due under the terms of this policy or on account of any change in occupancy or increase in hazard not permitted by this policy, this Company agrees to give written notice to the Lender of such non-payment of premium after sixty (60) days from, and within one hundred and twenty (120) days after, due date of such premium and it is a condition of the continuance of the rights of the Lender hereunder to be paid the premium due within ten (10) days following receipt of the Company's demand in writing therefore. If the Lender shall decline to pay said premium or additional premium, the rights of the Lender under this Lender's Loss Payable Endorsement shall not be terminated before ten (10) days after receipt of said premium written notice by the Lender.

4. Whenever this Company shall pay to the Lender any sum for loss or damage under this policy and shall claim that as to the insured no liability therefore exists, this Company, at its option, may pay to the Lender the whole principal sum and interest and other indebtedness due or to become due from the insured, whether secured or unsecured, (with refund of all interest no accrued), and this Company, to the extent of such payment, shall thereupon receive a full assignment and transfer, without recourse, or the debt and all rights and securities held as collateral thereto.

5. If there be any other insurance upon the within described property, this Company shall be liable under this policy as to the Lender for the proportion of such loss or damage that the sum hereby insured bears to the entire insurance of similar character on said property under policies held by, payable to and expressly consented to by the Lender. Any Contribution Clause included in any Fallen Building Cause Waiver or any Extended Coverage Endorsement attached to this contract of insurance is hereby nullified, and also any Contribution Clause in any other endorsement or rider attached to this contract of insurance is hereby nullified except Contribution Clauses for the compliance with which the insured has received reduction in the rate charged or has received extension of the coverage to include hazards, other than fire and compliance with such Contribution Clause is made a part of the consideration for insuring such other hazards. The Lender upon the payment to it of the full amount of its claim, will subrogate this Company (pro rata with all other insurers contributing to said payment to all of the Lender's rights of contribution under said other insurance).

6. This Company reserves the right to cancel this policy at any time, as provided by its terms, but in such case this policy shall continue in force for the benefit of the Lender for ten (10) days after written notice of such cancellation is received by the Lender and shall then cease.

7. This policy shall remain in full force and effect as to the interest of the Lender for a period of ten (10) days after its expiration unless an acceptable policy in renewal thereof with loss thereunder payable to the Lender in accordance with the terms of this Lender's Loss Payable Endorsement, shall have been issued by some insurance company and accepted by the Lender.

8. Should legal title to and beneficial ownership of any of the property covered under this policy become vested in the Lender or its agents; insurance under this policy shall continue for the term thereof for the benefit of the Lender but, in such event, any privileges granted by this Lender's Loss Payable Endorsement which are not also granted the insured under the terms and conditions of this policy and/or under other riders or endorsements attached thereto shall not apply to the insurance hereunder as respects such property.

9. All notices herein provided to be given by the Company to the Lender in connection with this policy and this Lender's Loss Payable Endorsement shall be mailed to or delivered to the Lender or its office or branch described on the first page of this policy.

Letter of Intent

In order to be a valid and enforceable agreement, a document must contain certain essential legal provisions and must not leave either undecided or to be determined at some time in the future any aspect of such essential legal provisions. If these essential elements are not present, then the document is not a binding one and is often referred to by courts as an "agreement to agree" or a letter of intent, both of which are not enforceable as contracts.

Parties to a transaction sometimes intentionally create a letter of intent as an expression of what they intend to agree upon should certain circumstances arise. The document may even be made expressly non-binding until such other circumstances do in fact arise but even if there is no express statement to that non-binding effect, the document will not be binding and thus not enforceable until those circumstances arise. Thus, the letter of intent is essentially a legally worthless document. It is not clear to me the reason any party would ever bother to create such a document and yet I have seen it used on many occasions. If parties to a transaction intend to bind each other, then they should create a binding contract, not a letter of intent. If the parties to a transaction do not intend to bind each other, then why bother creating a document that is not binding?

However, sometimes one of the parties prepares a document believing it to be a valid and enforceable agreement only to find, after expensive litigation, that it was not a binding agreement at all but merely a non-binding, non-enforceable agreement to agree, letter of intent.

A recent case points out the issues related to this latter type situation. In *Richie Co. LLP vs. Lyndon Insurance Group, Inc.*, a federal case out of the Eighth Circuit interpreting Minnesota law, the Court was called upon to decide if a document was a binding obligation or merely an unbinding letter of intent, agreement to agree. Although the case dealt with an interpretation of Minnesota law, the same general principles of contract law are applicable in most states, although you should consult with an attorney in your state.

The summary of the facts in that case is as follows: the plaintiff, Richie, had a previously existing contractual relationship with another entity, Mechanical Breakdown Protection, Inc. ("MBPI") and proposed, on April 16, 1999, in a writing called "letter of agreement," which writing was signed by all parties, an agreement with the defendant Lyndon, that the defendant would pay Richie on terms that were "substantially identical" to the terms in the MBPI agreement. The April 16, 1999 writing set forth certain terms regarding payment to Richie, which terms were to be included in a "subsequently-drafted 'Service Contract Agreement.'" This "Service Contract Agreement" was to be entered into within 180 days after the defendant acquired a specific company, called FPC. That event took place on March 6, 2000. However, the Service Contract Agreement was never entered into.

The plaintiff sued, claiming that the defendant breached the April 16, 1999 "agreement" [my quotes] by failing to enter into that said Service Contract Agreement. The defense was, in part, that the said April 16, 1999 "agreement" was not in fact an agreement at all but a non-binding agreement to agree in the future. The defense also stated that the plaintiff never presented any such Service Contract Agreement to the defendant nor did the parties ever act on the terms of any such Service Contract Agreement.

The Court held that the April 16, 1999 "agreement" was not an agreement at all but a non-binding letter of intent and agreement to agree. The Court stated:

> *A letter creating an agreement to negotiate in good faith in the future is not enforceable where the parties have contemplated that the agreement is not the complete and final agreement governing the transaction at issue.*

The Court also stated:

> Furthermore, where the parties have agreed that an "agreement to negotiate" or letter of intent, in its entirety, is not a binding legal agreement, Minnesota courts have refused to enforce an individual provision of the letter as a freestanding "contract" promise.

The Court stated further:

> *However, the parties need not agree on every point, but only that the parties' intent as to fundamental terms be reasonably certain [citing a case]. But where substantial and necessary terms are left open for future negotiation, the purported contract is void.* [citing a case].

The Court discussed a similar case in which certain terms, terms that might otherwise be essential to contract formation, were in fact set forth but the "agreement" also stated that "the parties shall enter into a definite purchase agreement which shall be drafted by the buyers within 30 days." That court held and this Court agreed that such "agreement" was not a binding agreement but merely an agreement to agree and that the setting forth of such definitive terms was merely a "summary of negotiations."

In the instance of this case, the Court said that the April 16, 1999 document was not a binding obligation but merely a non-binding letter of intent and agreement to agree. The Court pointed to the language of the document itself which stated that the defendant "will enter" into the above-mentioned service agreement. Thus "will enter" was the same as "shall enter" in the above-discussed case.

The Court stated further:

> *That language [in the cited case], like the language in the April 16, 1999 letter, spoke of future actions and agreements contemplated but not yet completed by the parties, and showed that the letter "was not the complete and final agreement the parties contemplated would govern" but "merely created an agreement to negotiate in good faith."*

Such language clearly manifests an intention to do something essential at a later date…thus the document is not a binding contract but merely an unenforceable agreement to agree and a non-binding letter of intent.

Note: while there may be other legal causes of action a plaintiff might legally pursue in this situation, such other legal causes of action were not discussed in this case and thus are not addressed in this article.

Conclusion

Result: plaintiff loses, defendant wins. In truth, both sides lost since the cost and time consumption involved in pursuing both the trial and appeal must have been enormous. I have been at both the negotiation table and the litigation table and the former is significantly less expensive than the latter.

In general terms and not in reference to the above specific case, if you intend to have your project be a success, then plan for success. (Most people say that this is what they want but in fact seem to operate contrary to those statements). Otherwise, all you are doing is putting yourself in a lose-lose situation. If the project is a failure, you lose. If the project is a success and your legal foundation is not proper, you may find that the other party, not you, ends up making all the money or you may open yourself up for more claims and expenses than you can even imagine and in which event, you lose because you pay all your profits to lawyers and/or damages to the offended parties.

What kind of a way is that to run a business? Remember, "help me is almost always cheaper than fix me."

RECORDING REQUESTED BY

Name

AND WHEN RECORDED MAIL TO:
Name
Documentation Department
Street Address
City, State & Zip

Assessors Parcel Number: SPACE ABOVE THIS LINE FOR RECORDER'S USE ONLY

Memorandum of Lease

THIS MEMORANDUM OF LEASE (this "Memorandum") is made and effective as of ——, by and between Landlord Legal Name a Type of Entity in the State of State, with an address at Complete Address ("Landlord"), and Licensee/Lessee Legal Name a Type of Entity in the State of State, with an address at Complete Address ("Licensee/Lessee").

RECITALS

A. Landlord and Licensee/Lessee entered into that certain Solar Site License and Lease Agreement ("Lease"), pursuant to which Landlord leased to Licensee/Lessee a portion of the real property ("Property") situated in the city of City, county of County, state of State, as more particularly described on **Exhibit A** attached hereto and hereby made a part hereof (the "Premises"), which Premises is depicted on **Exhibit B** attached hereto and hereby made a part hereof (the "Premises Site Plan"), all on and subject to the terms, covenants and conditions contained in the Lease.

B. Pursuant to the Lease, Licensee/Lessee plans to install or have installed and to operate a photovoltaic power system with the specifications described on **Exhibit C** attached hereto and hereby made a part hereof (the "System").

C. Landlord and Licensee/Lessee desire to enter into this Memorandum, and to record the same in the public land records of the county in which the Premises is located, for the purpose of giving public record notice of the Lease pertaining to the Premises and Premises Site Plan, and acknowledgement of Licensee/Lessee's exclusive ownership of the System.

ACKNOWLEDGEMENTS AND AGREEMENTS

NOW, THEREFORE, in consideration of the foregoing premises and other good and valuable consideration, the receipt and sufficiency of which are hereby acknowledged, the parties hereby acknowledge and agree as follows:

1. **Lease**. The parties now enter into this Memorandum, and the same shall be recorded in the public land records of the county in which the Property is located, for the purpose of giving public record notice of the Lease and Licensee/Lessee's exclusive ownership of the System.

2. **Term**. The initial term of the Lease is for twenty (20) years and includes an option for renewal.

3. **Effect of Lease**. This Memorandum is subject, in all respects, to the Lease and the terms and provisions thereof. Neither this memorandum nor any term or provision hereof shall limit, alter, vary, modify, or amend, in any manner or respect, the Lease or any term or provision thereof.

4. **Counterparts**. This Memorandum may be executed in one or more counterparts, each of which shall be an original and all of which together shall be a single instrument.

◆ **[Signature Page to Follow]** ◆

IN WITNESS WHEREOF, the parties are authorized and have executed this Solar Site License and Lease Agreement on the day and year first above written.

<u>LANDLORD</u>
Landlord Name

By: ____________________________
Name: Persons Name
Title: Title of Person Signing

LICENSEE/LESSEE
Licensee/Lessee Name

By: ____________________________
Name: Persons Name
Title: Title of Person Signing

STATE OF ________________________)
) ss.
COUNTY OF ______________________)

On this ____ day of ______________, 20__, before me, a Notary Public in and for the State of ______________, personally appeared ____________________, personally known to me (or proved to me on the basis of satisfactory evidence) to be the person who executed this instrument, on oath stated that he/she was authorized to execute the instrument, and acknowledged it as the____________________ of ___________, to be the free and voluntary act and deed of said party for the uses and purposes mentioned in the instrument.

IN WITNESS WHEREOF, I have hereunto set my hand and official seal the day and year first above written.

____
NOTARY PUBLIC in and for the State of______________________
residing at______________________________________
My appointment expires______________________________
Print Name______________________________________

STATE OF ________________________)
) ss.
COUNTY OF ______________________)

On this ____ day of ______________, 20__, before me, a Notary Public in and for the State of ______________, personally appeared ____________________, personally known to me (or proved to me on the basis of satisfactory evidence) to be the person who executed this instrument, on oath stated that he/she was authorized to execute the instrument, and acknowledged it as the____________________ of ___________, to be the free and voluntary act and deed of said party for the uses and purposes mentioned in the instrument.

IN WITNESS WHEREOF, I have hereunto set my hand and official seal the day and year first above written.

____
NOTARY PUBLIC in and for the State of____________________
residing at______________________________________
My appointment expires__________________________
Print Name______________________________________

****

EXHIBIT A
TO
MEMORANDUM OF LEASE

LEGAL DESCRIPTION

****

EXHIBIT B
TO
MEMORANDUM OF LEASE

PREMISES SITE PLAN

****

EXHIBIT C
TO
MEMORANDUM OF LEASE

DESCRIPTION OF THE SYSTEM

Mortgagee's Waiver and Consent

Lessor: Renewable Energy Project Creditor Mortgagee: ______________________________

1. **General**. This Mortgagees' Waiver and Consent is entered into between the undersigned lessee ("Lessee") and Mortgagee. Lessee and Lessor have entered into, or are about to enter into, an agreement whereby Lessor has acquired or will acquire a security interest or other interest in certain of Lessee's personal property, which Lessor has leased or will lease to Lessee, including without limitation the equipment listed on Exhibit A (collectively, the "Collateral"). Some or all of the Collateral may be affixed or otherwise become located on the premises set forth below ("Premises"). Mortgagee is the holder of a mortgage ("Mortgage") encumbering the real estate located at ______________________________ as particularly described below as PREMISES below. The Mortgaged Premises are owned by Obligor. To induce Lessor to extend the Lease to Lessee against such security interest in the Collateral and for other valuable consideration, Mortgagee hereby agrees with Lessor and Lessee as follows.

2. **Disclaimer of Interest**. Mortgagee hereby consents to Lessor's security interest (or other interest) in the Collateral and disclaims any and all interest, title, liens and claims which Mortgagee now has or may hereafter acquire in and to the Collateral by virtue of its interest in the Premises. Mortgagee agrees that any lien or claim it may now have or may hereafter have in the Collateral will be subordinate at all times to Lessor's security interest (or other present or future interest) in the Collateral and will be subject to the rights granted by Mortgagee to Lessor in this Agreement.

3. **Collateral Is Personal Property**. All of the Collateral may be kept, installed, maintained, used and operated on the Premises, and shall remain personal property notwithstanding the manner of the attachment of such Collateral to the realty and shall not become fixtures.

4. **Entry Onto Premises**. In the event of default by Lessee under its obligations to Lessor, Lessor may: (i) abandon the Collateral on the Premises; (ii) assemble the Collateral and conduct an auction thereof on the Premises; or (iii) remove the Collateral from the Premises in accordance with the terms hereof. Mortgagee and Lessee grant to Lessor the right to enter upon the Premises for the purpose of removing the Collateral from the Premises or conducting sales of the Collateral on the Premises. The rights granted to Lessor in this Agreement will continue until a reasonable time after Lessor receives notice in writing from Mortgagee that Lessee no longer is in lawful possession of the Premises. If Lessor enters onto the Premises and removes the Collateral, Lessor agrees with Mortgagee not to remove any Collateral in such a way that the Premises are damaged, without either repairing any such damage or reimbursing Mortgagee for the cost of repair.

5. **Miscellaneous Provisions**. The following miscellaneous provisions are a part of this Agreement: This Agreement shall extend to and bind the respective heirs, personal representatives, successors and assigns of the parties to this Agreement. The covenants of Lessee and Mortgagee respecting subordination of the claim or claims of Mortgagee in favor of Lessor shall extend to, include, and be enforceable by any transferee or endorsee to whom Lessor may transfer any claim or claims to which this Agreement shall apply. Lessor need not accept this Agreement in writing or otherwise to make it effective. This Agreement shall be governed by and construed in accordance with the laws of the Commonwealth of Pennsylvania. If Mortgagee is other than an individual, any agent or other person executing this Agreement on behalf of Mortgagee represents and warrants to Lessor that he or she has full power and authority to execute this Agreement on Mortgagee's behalf. Lessor shall not be deemed to have waived any rights under this Agreement unless such waiver is in writing and signed by Lessor. Without notice to Mortgagee and without affecting the validity of this Consent, Lessor may do or not do anything it deems appropriate or necessary with respect to the Lease, any obligors on the Lease, or any Collateral for the Lease; including without limitation extending, renewing, rearranging, or accelerating any of the Lease indebtedness. This Consent shall inure to the benefit of the successors and designs of Lessor and shall be binding upon the heirs, successors and assigns and personal representatives of Lessee and Mortgagee.

6. **Amendments**. This Agreement constitutes the entire understanding and agreement of the parties as to the matters set forth in this Agreement. No alteration of or amendment to this Agreement shall be effective without the prior written consent of Lessor.

7. **No Waiver By Lessor**. Lessor shall not be deemed to have waived any rights under this Agreement unless such waiver is given in writing and signed by Lessor. No delay or omission on the part of Lessor in exercising any right shall operate as a waiver of such right or any other right. A waiver by Lessor of a provision of this Agreement shall not prejudice or constitute a waiver of Lessor's right otherwise to demand strict compliance with that provision or any other provision of this Agreement. No prior waiver by Lessor, nor any course of dealing between Lessor and Mortgagee, shall constitute a waiver of any of Mortgagee's obligations as to any future transactions. Whenever the consent of Lessor is required under this Agreement, the granting of such

consent by Lessor in any instance shall not constitute continuing consent to subsequent instances where such consent is required and in all cases such consent may be granted or withheld in the sole discretion of Lessor.

8. **Severability**. If a court of competent jurisdiction finds any provisions of this Agreement to be illegal, invalid, or unenforceable as to any circumstance, that finding shall not make the offending provision illegal, invalid, or unenforceable as to any other circumstance. If feasible, the offending provision shall be considered modified so that it becomes legal, valid and enforceable. If the offending provision cannot be so modified, it shall be considered deleted from this Agreement. Unless otherwise required by law, the illegality, invalidity, or unenforceability of any provision of this Agreement shall not affect the legality, validity or enforceability of any other provision of this Agreement.

IN WITNESS WHEREOF, the undersigned parties have executed this Agreement as of the date first set forth above.

LESSEE:	**MORTGAGEE:**
By: ______________________	By: ______________________
Name: ______________________	Name: ______________________
Title: ______________________	Title: ______________________

PREMISES LEGAL

ADDRESS:

____

Mutual Non-Disclosure Agreement

Mutual Non-Disclosure Agreement, effective as of ______________________, 20____ (this "**Agreement**"), is entered into by and between Renewable Energy Project Creditor, a __________________ ("**REPC**") and ABC Company, a ________________ (the "**Company**").

In order to pursue the mutual business purpose of a possible transaction or relationship between REPC and the Company and/or their affiliates (the "**Transaction**"), both REPC and the Company recognize that there is a need to disclose to one another certain information in respect of itself and/or its affiliates. All such information, delivered by or on behalf of one party and/or its affiliates (the "**Disclosing Party**") to the other party (the "**Receiving Party**") and/or its Representatives (as defined below), whether furnished before or after the date of this Agreement and regardless of the manner in which it is furnished, together with all analyses, compilations, studies or other documents or records prepared by the Receiving Party and/or its Representatives to the extent such analyses, compilations, studies, documents or records contain, otherwise reflect, or are generated from such information, is referred to herein as "Evaluation Material." In consideration of the opportunity to consider such **Evaluation Material**, both parties hereby agree as follows:

1. The Evaluation Material will be used by the Receiving Party solely for the purpose of evaluating the Transaction. Such Evaluation Material will be kept strictly confidential by the Receiving Party, except that the Evaluation Material or any portion thereof may be disclosed to affiliates, directors, officers, employees, advisors, attorneys, agents, controlling persons, potential bidding partners and financing sources or other representatives (each, a "**Representative**," and collectively, the "**Representatives**") of the Receiving Party who need to know such information for the purpose of evaluating the Transaction and who agree to treat the Evaluation Material in accordance with the terms of this Agreement.

2. The term "Evaluation Material" does not include information which (i) is or becomes generally available to the public other than as a result of the breach of the terms of this Agreement by the Receiving Party and/or any of its Representatives, (ii) is or has been independently acquired or developed by the Receiving Party and/or any of its Representatives without violating any of the terms of this Agreement, (iii) was within the Receiving Party and/or any of its Representatives' possession prior to it being furnished to the Receiving Party and/or any of its Representatives by or on behalf of the Disclosing Party pursuant to the terms hereof or (iv) is received from a source other than the Disclosing Party and/or any of its Representatives; provided that, in the case of (iii) and (iv) above, the source of such information was not known by the Receiving Party to be bound by a confidentiality obligation to the Disclosing Party or any other party with respect to such information.

3. In the event that the Receiving Party or any of its Representatives receives a request to disclose all or any part of the Evaluation Material under the terms of a subpoena or order issued by a court of competent jurisdiction or under a civil investigative demand or similar process, (i) the Receiving Party agrees to promptly notify the Disclosing Party of the existence, terms and circumstances surrounding such a request and (ii) if the Receiving Party or its applicable Representative is in the opinion of its counsel compelled to disclose all or a portion of the Evaluation Material, the Receiving Party or its applicable Representative may disclose that Evaluation Material that its counsel advises that it is compelled to disclose and will exercise reasonable efforts to obtain assurance that confidential treatment will be accorded to that Evaluation Material that is being so disclosed.

4. Unless otherwise required by law, or unless otherwise provided in a final definitive agreement regarding the Transaction when, as and if executed, both parties and their respective Representatives will not, without the prior written consent of the other party, disclose to any person (other than Representatives of the parties hereto who need to know such information for the purpose of evaluating the Transaction and who agree to treat such information in accordance with the terms of this Agreement) any of the terms or conditions of the Transaction.

5. Nothing in this Agreement shall divest the Disclosing Party of any of its right, title or interest in and to any Evaluation Material. Within five (5) days after being so requested by the Disclosing Party, the Receiving Party and its Representatives shall destroy or return all Evaluation Material furnished to the Receiving Party and/or any of its Representatives by the Disclosing Party. Except to the extent a party is advised by counsel that such destruction is prohibited by law, the Receiving Party and its Representatives will also destroy all written material, memoranda, notes, copies, excerpts and other writings or recordings whatsoever prepared by the Receiving Party and/or its Representatives based upon, containing or otherwise reflecting any Evaluation Material. At the request of the Disclosing Party made at the time of its request for the destruction of Evaluation Material, any destruction of materials shall be certified to the Disclosing Party in writing by an authorized officer of the Receiving Party supervising such destruction.

6. The Receiving Party acknowledges and agrees that neither the Disclosing Party nor any of its Representatives are making any representation or warranty as to the accuracy or completeness of any of the information furnished hereunder to the Receiving Party or any of its Representatives and each of the Receiving Party and the Disclosing Party further acknowledges and agrees that no party has any obligation to the other party or any of its Representatives to authorize or pursue with the other party the Transaction. Each of the Receiving Party and the Disclosing Party may at any time terminate any discussions or negotiations regarding the Transaction that may be taking place, and only those terms and conditions of the Transaction, if any, which are made in a final definitive agreement, when, as and if executed, will have any legal effect.

7. Both parties agree that money damages may not be a sufficient remedy for any breach of the terms of this Agreement by the Receiving Party or any of its Representatives, and that, in addition to all other remedies at law or in equity to which the Disclosing Party may be entitled, the Disclosing Party may be entitled to specific performance and injunctive or other equitable relief as a remedy for any such breach.

8. The validity and interpretation of this Agreement shall be governed by, and construed and enforced in accordance with, the laws of the State of California applicable to agreements made and to be fully performed therein (excluding the conflicts of laws rules).

9. If it is found in a final judgment by a court of competent jurisdiction (not subject to further appeal) that any term or provision hereof is invalid or unenforceable, (i) the remaining terms and provisions hereof shall be unimpaired and shall remain in full force and effect and (ii) the invalid or unenforceable provision or term shall be replaced by a term or provision that is valid and enforceable and that comes closest to expressing the intention of such invalid or unenforceable term or provision.

10. To the extent that any Evaluation Material may include materials subject to the attorney-client privilege, work product doctrine or any other applicable privilege concerning pending or threatened legal proceedings or governmental investigations, each party hereto understands and agrees that both parties hereto and their respective Representatives have a commonality of interest with respect to such matters and it is the desire, intention and mutual understanding of both parties hereto that the sharing of such Evaluation Material is not intended to, and shall not, waive or diminish in any way the confidentiality of such Evaluation Material or its continued protection under the attorney-client privilege, work product doctrine or other applicable privilege. All Evaluation Material provided by either party hereto that is entitled to protection under the attorney-client privilege, work product doctrine or other applicable privilege shall remain entitled to such protection under those privileges, this Agreement, and under the joint defense doctrine.

11. The Disclosing Party understands that the Receiving Party and/or its Representatives may currently or in the future be developing information internally, or receiving information from other parties, that may be similar to the Evaluation Material furnished by or on behalf of the Disclosing Party. In addition, the Disclosing Party understands that the Receiving Party and/or its Representatives may have, or in the future may enter into, relationships with third parties having pre-existing relationships with the Disclosing Party and/or its Representatives. Provided that each party complies with its obligations contained herein, and except as otherwise expressly provided herein, this Agreement shall not in any way limit, restrict or preclude either party from pursuing any of its present or future business activities or interests or from entering into any agreement or transaction with any person, regardless of whether such business activities or interests are competitive with the business activities and interests of the other party and regardless of whether the subject matter of any such agreement or transaction is in any way similar to or different from the Transaction and/or the Evaluation Material evaluated by the parties.

12. Neither party hereto shall assign in whole or in part its rights or obligations under this Agreement without the express written consent of the other party. This Agreement shall be binding upon and shall inure to the benefit of each of the party's successors and permitted assigns.

13. This Agreement embodies the entire agreement and understanding of the parties hereto and supersedes any and all prior agreements, arrangements and understandings relating to the matters provided for herein. No alteration, waiver, amendment, change or supplement hereto shall be binding or effective unless the same is set forth in writing signed by a duly authorized representative of each party.

14. For the convenience of the parties, any number of counterparts of this Agreement may be executed by the parties hereto. Each such counterpart shall be, and shall be deemed to be, an original instrument, and all such counterparts taken together shall constitute one and the same agreement.

15. The term of this Agreement shall be three (3) years from the date hereof.

IN WITNESS WHEREOF, this Agreement has been duly executed on the date first written above.

Renewable Energy Project Creditor

By: ______________________________
Name:
Title:

ABC Company

By: ______________________________
Name:
Title:

Notice of Assignment

IRC SECTION 1603 ENERGY GRANT PAYMENT

To: [Name of Contracting Officer at Specified Government Agency or third party]

DUNS Number of 3rd Party if applicable: ______________________________

This has reference to Treasury Application No.__________ dated _______________, entered into between ______________________ [Applicant's name and address] and ___________________________________ [Government agency, name of office, and address], for _____________________________ [Describe nature of the Section 1603 payment].

Moneys due or to become due under the IRC Section 1603 payment described above have been assigned to the undersigned under the provisions of the Assignment of Claims Act of 1940, as amended, 31 U.S.C. 3727, 41 U.S.C. 15.

A true copy of the instrument of assignment executed by the Contractor on __________ [Date], is attached to the original notice.

Payments due or to become due under this Section 1603 payment should be made to the undersigned assignee.

Please return to the undersigned the three enclosed copies of this notice with appropriate notations showing the date and hour of receipt, and signed by the person acknowledging receipt on behalf of the addressee.

Very truly yours,

__________________________ DUNS Number: ________

[Name of Assignee]

By ____

[Signature of Signing Officer of Assignee]

____

[Title of Signing Officer of Assignee]

____

[Address of Assignee]

Acknowledgement

Receipt is acknowledged of the above notice and of a copy of the instrument of assignment. They were received _________(a.m.) (p.m.) on __________, 20___.

____

[Signature]

____

[Title]

____

On behalf of

____

[Name of Addressee of this Notice]

Performance Bond

KNOW ALL PERSONS BY THESE PRESENTS:

THAT WHEREAS, ________________________________ ("Purchaser") has awarded to ____________________ ____________________ as Principal a contract dated the _____ day of _________, (the "Contract"), which Contract is by this reference made a part hereof, for the work described as follows:

AND WHEREAS, Principal is required to furnish a bond in connection with the Contract, guaranteeing the faithful performance thereof.

NOW, THEREFORE, we, the undersigned Principal and ____________________ as Surety are held and firmly bound unto the Purchaser in the sum of ________________________________ dollars ($_________), to be paid to the Purchaser or its successors and assigns; for which payment, well and truly to be made, we bind ourselves, our heirs, executors, administrators, successors, and assigns, jointly and severally, firmly by these presents.

THE CONDITION OF THIS OBLIGATION IS SUCH, that if Principal, or its heirs, executors, administrators, successors, or assigns approved by the Purchaser, shall promptly and faithfully perform the covenants, conditions, and agreements of the Contract during the original term and any extensions thereof as may be granted by the Purchaser, with or without notice to Surety, and during the period of any guarantees or warranties required under the Contract, and shall also promptly and faithfully perform all the covenants, conditions, and agreements of any alteration of the Contract made as therein provided, notice of which alterations to Surety being hereby waived, on Principal's part to be kept and performed at the time and in the manner therein specified, and in all respects according to their true intent and meaning, and shall indemnify, defend, protect, and hold harmless the Purchaser as stipulated in the Contract, then this obligation shall become and be null and void; otherwise it shall be and remain in full force and effect.

No extension of time, change, alteration, modification, or addition to the Contract, or of the work required thereunder, shall release or exonerate Surety on this bond or in any way affect the obligation of the bond; and Surety does hereby waive notice of any such extension of time, change, alteration, modification, or addition.

Whenever Principal shall be and declared by the Purchaser to be in default under the Contract, Surety shall promptly remedy the default, or shall promptly:

1. Undertake through its agents or independent contractors, reasonably acceptable to the Purchaser, to complete the Contract in accordance with its terms and conditions and to pay and perform all obligations of Principal under the Contract, including without limitation, all obligations with respect to warranties, guarantees, and the payment of liquidated damages, or, at Surety's election, or, if required by the Purchaser.

2. Obtain a bid or bids for completing the Contract in accordance with its terms and conditions, and, upon determination by the Purchaser of the lowest responsible bidder, arrange for a contract between such bidder and the Purchaser and make available as work progresses (even though there should be a default or a succession of defaults under the contract or contracts of completion arranged under this paragraph) sufficient funds to pay the cost of completion less the balance of the Contract Sum, and to pay and perform all obligations of Principal under the Contract, including, without limitation, all obligations with respect to warranties, guarantees, and the payment of liquidated damages; but, in any event, Surety's total obligations hereunder shall not exceed the amount set forth in the third paragraph hereof. The term "balance of the Contract Sum," as used in this paragraph, shall mean the total amount payable by the Purchaser to the Principal under the Contract and amendments thereto, less the amount paid by the Purchaser to Principal.

3. Surety's obligations hereunder are independent of the obligations of any other surety for the performance of the Contract, and suit may be brought against Surety and such other sureties, jointly and severally, or against any one or more of them, or against less than all of them without impairing the Purchaser's rights against the others.

No right of action shall accrue on this bond to or for the use of any person or corporation other than the Purchaser or its successors or assigns.

Surety may join in any arbitration proceedings brought under the Contract and shall be bound by any arbitration award.

In the event suit is brought upon this bond by the Purchaser, Surety shall pay reasonable attorney's fees and costs incurred by the Purchaser in such suit.

Correspondence or claims relating to this bond shall be sent to Surety at the address set forth below.

IN WITNESS WHEREOF, we have hereunto set our hands this ___ day of ____________, 20___.

Principal: ____________________________ **Surety:** ____________________________________

By: _________________________________ **By:** ____

Printed Name: _______________________ **Printed Name:** ______________________________

Title: ________________________________ **Title:** ____

Address and Contact information for notices to Surety: _____________________________________

____

Pledge Agreement

THIS AGREEMENT is made this _____ day of ____________________, 20____, by and between ABC Company (PLEDGEE) 123 South Any St, Orange, CA 92868-1625 and ________ (PLEDGOR) at ________.

PLEDGOR wishes to have PLEDGEE purchase equipment from time to time for the purpose of leasing to ; and

PLEDGEE is unwilling to purchase equipment and enter into such lease(s) for the lease of certain equipment unless PLEDGOR enters into this PLEDGE AGREEMENT.

THEREFORE, for good and valuable consideration given by PLEDGEE to PLEDGOR, and in order to induce PLEDGEE to purchase such equipment from time to time and lease it to PLEDGOR, and in consideration thereof and of the promises and agreements herein contained, it is agreed as follows:

1. **THE PLEDGE.** As collateral security for the payment and performance by PLEDGOR of all of its obligations to PLEDGEE, whether now existing or hereafter arising, direct or indirect, liquidated or unliquidated, absolute or contingent, due or not due, including but not limited to the obligations of PLEDGOR to PLEDGEE under any Lease Rental Agreement(s) now and hereafter entered into between them and in consideration of the promises, PLEDGOR, by these presents does hereby pledge, transfer and assign to PLEDGEE, its successors and assigns, that certain:

   and all renewals, extensions and substitutions therefor and the proceeds thereof (COLLATERAL), which said COLLATERAL has been concurrently delivered and endorsed to PLEDGEE or its assignee. PLEDGOR warrants that the COLLATERAL is free and clear of all liens and encumbrances and that PLEDGOR has the right to pledge, transfer and assign same without the consent of any other party. PLEDGOR authorizes PLEDGEE to extend or renew the COLLATERAL or substitute like COLLATERAL or instruments in the same amount for it on its maturity having a rate and term agreed to by PLEDGEE in its discretion. So long as no default has occurred hereunder, interest shall be for the account of and may be paid to PLEDGOR.

2. **THE TERM.** The term hereof shall be for months at which time PLEDGEE shall release all of its rights under the COLLATERAL in favor of PLEDGOR provided PLEDGOR is not then nor had been previously in default of any payment or of any of the other terms and conditions of the lease or of the PLEDGE AGREEMENT, in which case the term of this PLEDGE AGREEMENT shall be for the full term of the lease or for a shorter term at PLEDGEE's discretion.

3. **REMEDIES.** In the event of non-performance or non-payment by PLEDGOR of any of its obligations or liabilities to PLEDGEE, then, upon five (5) days written notice to PLEDGOR of PLEDGEE's intention to redeem or sell and of the time and place of such redemption and sale, and without advertisement or other notice or demand whatsoever to or upon PLEDGOR, all and each of which demands, advertisements and/or notices of intention are expressly waived, PLEDGEE at its option and in its sole discretion may sell, assign, redeem, transfer, cause to be reissued in its own name, hold same absolutely free from any claim or right whatsoever kind, or otherwise dispose of at a time and location of its choice, at such price(s) as PLEDGEE may deem best, and or all of the collateral including any interest which may have accrued thereon. Such notification as hereinabove stated shall be conclusively deemed to be reasonable under the California Uniform Commercial Code as it may now or hereafter be in effect. PLEDGOR irrevocably authorizes PLEDGEE in its own name or in the name of PLEDGOR to demand, apply for withdrawal, receive and give acquittance for any and all monies and claims for monies hereby pledged, transferred and assigned, and to exercise any and all rights and privileges and receive all benefits accorded by the COLLATERAL and to execute any and all instruments required therefor. PLEDGEE shall apply the proceeds of any disposition required therefor. PLEDGEE shall apply the proceeds of any disposition of the COLLATERAL to the expenses of collection of such proceeds and shall apply the balance to the payment of the obligations of PLEDGOR to PLEDGEE. Any surplus over and above the amount necessary to satisfy the obligations of PLEDGOR to PLEDGEE shall be paid over to PLEDGOR.

4. **VENUE.** This agreement shall be governed by the laws of the State of California.

IN WITNESS WHEREOF, the undersigned hereby set their hand and seals as to the aforesaid date.

PLEDGOR:	**PLEDGEE:** ABC Company
BY:______________________________	BY:______________________________
TITLE:____________________________	TITLE:

BANK ACKNOWLEDGEMENT

WE DO HEREBY ACKNOWLEDGE receipt of $_____________________________ to be placed in a Certificate of Deposit, No:_____________________________ and to be held by us in accordance with the terms and conditions of the PLEDGE AGREEMENT hereinabove stated.

BANK: _____________________________________

BY:_____________________________________

TITLE:__________________________________

DATE:___________________________________

Project Name: **Date:**

Principal Contact: **Tele:**

Pre-Construction Project Scoping

Address of the property:
What is the property zoning?
Who is the owner of the building?
Name, address, and contact of mortgage holder:
Loan Number:
How long has the current occupant been in the building?
Current use of the building:
When was the building constructed?
If the building was constructed prior to 1979, has there been an asbestos inspection? 0 Yes 0 No
What is the current use of the adjacent buildings?
Are there any electrical transformers or capacitors on the property? ☐ Yes ☐ No
Is there any evidence of leakage or damage around them? ☐ Yes ☐ No
Who owns the transformers or capacitors?
Has an environmental audit, study or report been conducted regarding the property? ☐ Yes ☐ No
Are there activities on the property which produce air emissions (e.g., spray booth painting, printing, venting, mechanical exhaust, etc.)? ☐ Yes ☐ No
Describe:
Are site sketches available? ☐ Yes ☐ No
Describe:
Are mechanical, civil, electrical, elevation or other types of plans available? ☐ Yes ☐ No
Describe:

Insurance

Is there general liability insurance on the property? ☐ Yes ☐ No
Who is the carrier?
Name, address and contact information of the broker:

Current Operations

Electricty:

- ☐ Usage history for last two years
- ☐ Utility Name: Contact: Tele:
  Account #: Contract: ☐ Yes ☐ No
  Rate Structure:

Gas:

- ☐ Usage history for last two years
- ☐ Utility Name: Contact: Tele:
  Account #: Contract: ☐ Yes ☐ No
  % Usage for domestic hot water:
  % Usage for process heat:
  % Usage for HVAC:
  Heat temperatures needed:
  Date current contract expires:

Water:

- ☐ Usage history for last two years
- ☐ Utility Name: Contact: Tele:

Account #: Contract: ☐ Yes ☐ No

% Usage for domestic hot water:

% Usage for processes:

Security/Backup:

Method/Type:

Total wattage: Compliance Mandates:

Max Expected Days Needed:

Principal Internal Contact: Tele:

Load Centers:

Method	Type	Capacity (kw)	Age	Annual Maintenance Cost
Generator				
UPS				
Fuel Cells				
Batteries				
Other				

Item	#	Size	Location	Mfg'r	Type & Voltage	Model	Age	Annual Maintenance Cost
Space A/C								
Space Heat								
Boilers								
Hot Water Tanks								
Other #1								
Other #2								

Existing Energy Management System:

Age: Manufacturer:

Describe:

Site Specific Parameters

Electricity:

Voltages: Load/Amperage:

Main Panels: Sub-panels:

Meters: Lighting:

Gas:

Delivery Pipe Size: Meter:

Other—Describe:

Roof:

☐ Flat ☐ Sloped Approximate pitch: Direction:

Material: Condition:

Age: Total Available Sq Ft:

Structural Support:

Use Limitation Issues:

Estimated remaining life of roof:

Building Structure:

Construction Type: Age of Building:

Stories: Total Sq Ft:

Office Sq Ft: Production Sq Ft: Warehouse Sq Ft:

Principal Structure Use: ☐ Commercial ☐ Industrial ☐ Mixed ☐ Residential

Access: ☐ Rail ☐ Truck Dock ☐ Large Truck ☐ Other:

Overhead Restrictions:

Foundation: Equipment Location Pad:

Environmental Parameters:

☐ Urban ☐ Rural Zoning:

Topography: ☐ Flat ☐ Hillside Distance from truck highway:

Total site sq ft: Special Notes:

Parking Total spaces: # Covered: # Underground:

Trees, shrubs, other buildings:

Other obstacles:

Security fencing: ☐ Yes ☐ No

Describe:

Road Access:

Right of Way Issues:

Known Environmental Risks:

Existing Energy Savings Devices:

☐ T8 Lights ☐ Motion Sensors ☐ Zone Controls ☐ Load Shedding Controls

☐ Insulation ☐ Crawl Space Fans ☐ Other:

New Equipment Space Availability:

☐ Covered ☐ Open ☐ Roof ☐ Ground

Amount: Distance from load:

Other Important Site Specific Parameters:

Other Project Parameters

Last building appraisal: Copy available: ☐ Yes ☐ No
Time company has been in business: At this location:
D&B #: Credit Rating:
Primary Bank: Contact: Telephone:
Type of Business:
Business Structure: ☐ Private for profit company ☐ Non-profit ☐ Government
☐ Corporation ➲ Taxed as: ☐ C Corp ☐ Subchapter S
☐ Partnership ☐ Sole Proprietorship ☐ Other

Key Officers/Principals:
Existing permits:
City: County:
Water District: Sanitation:
Air District:
# of Active: Title V Facility: ☐ Yes ☐ No
Variances Existing:

Describe all available rebates, incentives, grants, etc that will be used in the construction of this project:

Has an energy audit been performed or scheduled to be performed? ☐ Yes ☐ No
Is the facility owned by the project user? ☐ Yes ☐ No
Mortgage holder name and telephone number:
Landlord name and telephone number:

Surrounding Area:
Type of usage: Emission discharges:
Fire Risk:
Air Risk:
Flood Risk:
Future use: Other restrictions/risks:

Solar Availability:
Describe:

Wind Parameters:
Frequency: Dominant Direction:
Max Strength: Normal Strength:
Dust Issues: Chemical Issues:

Safety Issues:
Labor Issues:
Noise Issues:
GeoTechnical:
Landscape:
Other Contractors/Sub-contractors:

Bonding Requirements: ☐ Yes ☐ No
Describe:

Other Critical Project Parameters

Purchase Order

LEASE #: ____________ PURCHASE ORDER #: _________

SELLER/VENDOR:	***SHIP TO LESSEE:***

DESCRIPTION OF EQUIPMENT:

ITEM	*DESCRIPTION*

1. Invoices in duplicate must be mailed on date of shipment to Lessor at address shown below.
2. Show our purchase order on all invoices, crates, packing lists, etc.
3. All shipping costs must be prepaid by Seller and invoiced to Lessee.
4. Unless otherwise specified, this purchase order is for new equipment.
5. This purchase order is subject to cancellation if the equipment covered is not unconditionally accepted by Lessee or all lease documentation is not completed to the satisfaction of the Lessor.

INVOICES CANNOT BE HONORED UNLESS FULL EQUIPMENT DESCRIPTION INCLUDING SERIAL NUMBERS, APPEAR THEREIN.

THIS PURCHASE ORDER IS SUBJECT TO THE TERMS AND CONDITIONS ENCLOSED HEREIN AND MADE A PART HEREOF.

LESSEE ACKNOWLEDGEMENT:

1. Lessor is purchasing above *at my request*.
2. All warranties *of any nature* are the responsibility of the above supplier.

Lessee: **By:**

____

Seller: **By:**

____

Lessor: Renewable Energy Project Creditor **By:**

____

1234 S Any Street
Your Town, CA 92866

TERMS AND CONDITIONS OF PURCHASE

1. **NO CHANGES AUTHORIZED.** This purchase order must be accepted as written. Any increase in price, change in quantities or quality of merchandise ordered, or any other changes or terms or conditions of this order shall not be binding on the Buyer (also known as Lessor) unless such change is agreed to in writing. Delivery must be in accordance with the conditions on the purchase order, and unless otherwise specifically noted thereon, vendor is to deliver the merchandise F.O.B. common carrier; destined as thereon indicated. It shall be incumbent upon the seller to provide all shipping insurance and pay for the costs of same.

2. **NO CHARGES AUTHORIZED.** No charges for crating, boxing, packing or drayage, or for unloading, assembly or installing any merchandise will be allowed or payable unless specified on the reverse side hereof.

3. **INSPECTION AND REJECTION.** All merchandise shall be received subject to Buyer's as well as Lessee's inspection and rejection, either before or after delivery thereof. The place and time of inspection shall be determined by Buyer. Merchandise which is defective or otherwise not in accordance with this purchase order may be returned for credit and vendor shall assume all transportation and handling charges in connection therewith. Rejected merchandise shall not be replaced except upon Buyer's specific instructions in writing to that effect.

4. **RISK OF LOSS.** Vendor shall bear all risk of loss of any merchandise covered by this purchase order until physically delivered at the designated place, and shall also bear all risk of loss on rejected merchandise.

5. **DELIVERY TO BE MADE TO LESSEE.** The person, firm or corporation to which the merchandise covered by this purchase order is to be delivered (as indicated on the enclosed purchase order) has leased said merchandise from the Buyer, and is hereinafter referred to as "Lessee." Lessee is authorized on behalf of the Buyer to receive delivery of such merchandise, to inspect and to accept or reject same.

6. **REJECTION BY LESSEE.** If Lessee shall reject or refuse to accept any merchandise pursuant to this purchase order, Buyer, shall be deemed relieved of any liability to vendor under such purchase order as to such merchandise and all obligations of Buyer hereunder as to such merchandise shall, upon such rejection or refusal, be deemed those of Lessee, with the same force and effect as if Lessee, instead of Buyer, had placed this purchase order as to such merchandise; and vendor in such event, shall look only to Lessee with respect to any liability or obligation hereunder.

7. **NO ASSIGNMENT BY VENDOR.** Vendor agrees not to assign this purchase order, without the prior written consent of Buyer. In the absence of such consent, no such assignment shall be effective, and, at Buyer's option, shall effect a cancellation of all Buyer's obligations hereunder.

8. **CANCELLATION BY BUYER.** This purchase order may be canceled by the Buyer in the event the Lessee is not authorized to enter into the Lease, or the person signing the Lease on behalf of the Lessee is not authorized so to do, or, in the event that the vendor or any of its agents make any representations to the Lessee inconsistent with the terms or conditions of the lease, upon which the Lessee reasonably relies.

9. **PATENTS.** Vendor agrees to indemnify, protect and hold harmless Buyer, its successors or assigns and the Lessee and its successors and assigns against all claims, demand, damages, costs or expenses (including attorneys fees) for actual or alleged infringement of any patent, trademark or copyright covering any merchandise or software purchased hereunder or the use thereof.

10. **FAIR LABOR ASSURANCE.** Vendor warrants and represents that the goods ordered hereby have been produced in compliance with the requirements of the Fair Labor Standards Act of 1938, as amended.

11. **IRS SECTION 199.** Vendor acknowledges that the equipment and services identified on the face of this Purchase Order will be the sole property of Renewable Energy Project Creditor as defined by the Internal Revenue Service under Section

199 of the Internal Revenue Service regulations and any benefits accruing from such ownership will be for the sole account of Renewable Energy Project Creditor.

12. **WARRANTIES BY VENDOR**. Vendor warrants that the merchandise ordered hereunder will be fit and sufficient for the purpose intended; that it will conform to the specifications, drawings or samples, if any, furnished or adopted by the Buyer and Lessee and will be merchantable, of good quality and free from defects in material or workmanship. No part or parts made according to buyer's design will be sold to any other person, firm or corporation. The foregoing is in addition to and not in lieu of any and all other warranties express or implied. All warranties shall run to enure for the benefit of and be enforceable by both buyer and its Lessee, jointly and separately.

13. **EXCUSABLE DELAYS**. Vendor will not be responsible for delays or defaults in delivery if occasioned by unforeseeable cause beyond the control and without the fault or negligence of the Vendor; and Buyer shall not be responsible for failure to receive or take delivery if occasioned by any like cause on it's or Lessee's part.

14. **FREIGHT**. If the Buyer has not indicated any preference for the method of shipment, then the merchandise shall be shipped in the cheapest way, and the Buyer may charge back transportation charges in excess of the cheapest rate of shipment.

15. **UCC ARTICLE 2 A**. This purchase order shall be deemed to satisfy all requirements of the Uniform Commercial Code Article 2 A as amended.

16. **OTHER**. All quantity, cash, rebates of any nature or other discounts granted by the Seller/Vendor as a direct or indirect result of the purchase herein ordered shall be paid to Lessor. Vendor represents and warrants that no payments have been made to the Lessee nor has the Lessee received any other consideration as a direct or indirect result of the purchase herein ordered unless the amount of such payment or the value of such consideration is deducted from the gross invoice price. This purchase order shall be deemed to have been accepted by you in accordance with its terms unless you have otherwise informed us in writing within 10 days after the date hereof. This Purchase Order supersedes any purchase order which might previously have been received by you from the Lessee. By your acceptance of this Purchase Order, you warrant to us that you own the equipment referenced and that title will pass from you to us free of any liens or encumbrances. Seller acknowledges that the right of the parties under this Purchase Order shall be governed by the laws of the State of ______________ and was entered into in ________ County.

PV SYSTEM PLAN CHECK WORKSHEET

Supplied Diagrams

- ☐ Will a basic site diagram be supplied with the permit package?
  Identify location of major equipment identified on plan.

- ☐ Is a one-line diagram supplied with the permit package?
  - Array configuration shown
  - Array wiring identified
  - Combiner/junction box identified
  - Conduit from Array to PV Power Source Disconnect identified
  - Equipment grounding specified
  - Disconnect specified
  - Conduit from inverter to disconnect to panel identified
  - System grounding specified
  - Point of connection attachment method identified

Inverter Information

- ☐ Are cut sheets provided for Inverter?
- ☐ Inverter model number
- ☐ Is inverter listed for utility interactivity?
- ☐ Maximum continuous output power at 40o C
- ☐ Input voltage range of inverter

PV Module Information

- ☐ Are cut sheets provided for PV modules?
- ☐ Are the modules listed (on an approved list)?
- ☐ Open-circuit voltage (Voc) from listing label
- ☐ Maximum permissible systems voltage from listing label
- ☐ Short-circuit current (Isc) from listing label
- ☐ Maximum series fuse rating from listing label
- ☐ Maximum power at Standard Test Conditions (Pmax on Label)
- ☐ Voltage at Pmax from listing label
- ☐ Current at Pmax from listing label

Array Information

- ☐ Number of modules in series
- ☐ Number of parallel source circuits
- ☐ Total number of modules
- ☐ Operating voltage (number of modules in series X module voltage at Pmax)
- ☐ Maximum system voltage (NEC 690.7)
- ☐ Short-circuit current (NEC 690.8)

Wiring and Overcurrent Protection

- ☐ Wire type is 90o wet rated
- ☐ Conductor ampacities are sufficient
  - Maximum PV source circuit current
  - Minimum PV source circuit conductor ampacity
  - Minimum PV output circuit conductor ampacity

- Minimum inverter output circuit conductor ampacity

- ☐ Source Circuit Overcurrent protection is sufficient
  - If inverter is not listed for no backfeed current, does each source circuit have overcurrent protection in compliance with the listed maximum series fuse?
  - If inverter is listed for no backfeed current, Overcurrent protection is not necessary if only two parallel strings are connected to the inverter
- ☐ Overcurrent protection on Inverter Output Circuit is sufficient
- ☐ Point of connection meets provisions of NEC 690.64
- Point of connection panel busbar rating

Roof Information (for rooftop systems)

- ☐ Are the conductors from the PV Array run through a facility? If yes, what method will be used to address the protection issues?
- ☐ Weight of array for roof systems (pounds per square foot—include mounting hardware)
- ☐ Age of building (roof structure) If building is under 30 years old and array weight is less than 5 lb/sq ft, then engineering calculations unnecessary for roof loading)
- ☐ If roof structure is over 30 years old, describe structural elements:
  - Rafter composition (wood, steel, etc.)
  - Size of rafters (e.g. 2″ x 6″)
  - Span of rafters (e.g. 14′)
  - Spacing of rafters (e.g. 24″)
- ☐ Indentify roofing type (e.g. composition shingle, masonry tile, shake, etc.)
- ☐ Is the detail of PV panel mounting attachment to the roof-framing members provided?
- ☐ Identify method of sealing roof penetrations (e.g. flashing, sealed with urethane caulk, etc.)

Ground Mounting Structure (for ground-mounted structures)

- ☐ Weight of Array (pounds per square foot—including mounting hardware)
- ☐ Are the details of the Array supports, framing members, and foundation posts and footings provided?
- ☐ Is the information on mounting structure(s) construction provided? If the mounting structure is unfamiliar to the local jurisdiction and is more than six feet above grade, it may require engineering calculations.
- ☐ Is the detail on module attachment method to mounting structure provided?

Public Emissions Summary Report

CRIS: Climate Registry Information System

Entity Emissions Summary Report (Public)

02/05/08 16:00:44

General Entity Information

Entity Name	ABC Manufacturing
Address	3570 Las Vegas Boulevard Las Vegas, NV 89109 United States
Website	www.ABCmanufacturing.com
Phone Number	(909) 555-1234
Email Address	cgutierrez@ABC.com
Entity Contact	Gutierrez, Carla
Entity Type	Industry
Description	Small manufacturer of bowling balls and other gaming equipment. Serving customers across North America.

VERIFIED EMISSIONS INFORMATION

Reporting Protocol:	General Reporting Protocol (January 2008)
Reporting Year:	2003
Consolidation Methodology:	Operational Control and Equity Share
Base Year:	2004

Operational Control

Direct Emissions (metric tons)	CO_2e	CO_2	CH_4	N_2O	HFCs*	PFCs	SF_6
Mobile Combustion	790.29	790.29	0.00	0.00	0.00	0.00	0.00
Stationary Combustion	675,282.90	675,282.90	0.00	0.00	0.00	0.00	0.00
Process Emissions	0.00	0.00	0.00	0.00	0.00	0.00	0.00
Fugitive Emissions	0.00	0.00	0.00	0.00	0.00	0.00	0.00
TOTAL DIRECT	676,083.19	676,083.19	0.00	0.00	0.00	0.00	0.00

Indirect Emissions (metric tons)	CO_2e	CO_2	CH_4	N_2O
Purchased Electricity	7,931.79	7,931.79	0.00	0.00
Purchased Heating	0.00	0.00	0.00	0.00
Purchased Cooling	0.00	0.00	0.00	0.00
Purchased Steam	0.00	0.00	0.00	0.00
TOTAL INDIRECT	7,931.79	7,931.79	0.00	0.00

Estimated Emissions (metric tons)	CO_2e	CO_2	CH_4	N_2O	HFCs*	PFCs	SF_6
TOTAL ESTIMATED EMISSIONS	0.00	0.00	0.00	0.00	0.00	0.00	0.00

Optional Emissions (metric tons)	CO_2e	CO_2	CH_4	N_2O	HFCs*	PFCs	SF_6
TOTAL OPTIONAL	131.72	131.72	0.00	0.00	0.00	0.00	0.00

* HFCs and PFCs are classes of greenhouse gases that include many compounds. These columns may reflect the total emissions of multiple HFC and PFC compounds, each of which has a unique Global Warming Potential (GWP). Emissions of each gas are first multiplied by their respective GWP and then summed in the total CO2-equivalent column.

Equity Share

Direct Emissions (metric tons)	CO_2e	CO_2	CH_4	N_2O	HFCs*	PFCs	SF_6
Mobile Combustion	790.29	790.29	0.00	0.00	0.00	0.00	0.00
Stationary Combustion	675,282.90	675,282.90	0.00	0.00	0.00	0.00	0.00
Process Emissions	0.00	0.00	0.00	0.00	0.00	0.00	0.00
Fugitive Emissions	0.00	0.00	0.00	0.00	0.00	0.00	0.00
TOTAL DIRECT	676,083.19	676,083.19	0.00	0.00	0.00	0.00	0.00

Indirect Emissions (metric tons)	CO_2e	CO_2	CH_4	N_2O
Purchased Electricity	7,931.79	7,931.79	0.00	0.0
Purchased Heating	0.00	0.00	0.00	0.00
Purchased Cooling	0.00	0.00	0.00	0.00
Purchased Steam	0.00	0.00	0.00	0.00
TOTAL INDIRECT	7,931.79	7,931.79	0.00	0.00

Estimated Emissions (metric tons)	CO_2e	CO_2	CH_4	N_2O	HFCs*	PFCs	SF_6
TOTAL ESTIMATED EMISSIONS							

Optional Emissions (metric tons)	CO_2e	CO_2	CH_4	N_2O	HFCs*	PFCs	SF_6
TOTAL OPTIONAL	131.72	131.72	0.00	0.00	0.00	0.00	0.00

* HFCs and PFCs are classes of greenhouse gases that include many compounds. These columns may reflect the total emissions of multiple HFC and PFC compounds, each of which has a unique Global Warming Potential (GWP). Emissions of each gas are first multiplied by their respective GWP and then summed in the total CO2-equivalent column.

VERIFICATION INFORMATION

Verifying Organization:	DNV Certification, Inc.
Lead Certifier Name:	Toshikazu Otsuka
Verifier Opinion:	Complete and Accurate
Comment:	

OPTIONAL INFORMATION

Information in this section is voluntarily provided by the participant for public information, but is not required and thus, not certified under Registry protocols.

Supporting Documentation

Document Name	Document Description	Document Type	Status	Date Added
ABC Manufacturing Annual Report.doc		Annual Report	Public	10/05/07

THE COMMITTMENT AGREEMENT

for California' s Solar Electric Incentive Programs

Pursuant to Senate Bill 1

Existing commercial buildings that apply for incentives for solar energy systems are required to have an energy audit performed on the building and receive an energy performance (benchmark) rating during the application/design phase of the project. Although it is recommended that all existing commercial buildings be retro-commissioned, buildings that are 100,000 square feet or greater that receive an energy performance rating of less than 75 are required to go through a retro-commissioning process to receive solar energy system incentives.

Retro-commissioning (RCx) is a thorough and systematic process for improving an existing commercial building's performance. Cost effective operational and maintenance improvements and sometimes energy efficiency measures are identified that will ensure that the building operates efficiently, performs optimally, provides a safe and comfortable work environment, and meets owner or occupant needs and expectations. A 2004 study of 106 retro-commissioning projects by Lawrence Berkeley National Lab demonstrated that retro-commissioning can pay for itself in energy cost savings (in addition to improved performance comfort) in 0.2 to 2.1 years.[1]

The building owner/operator/manager that is applying for incentives for a solar energy system is required to implement all cost effective measures recommended in the RCx assessment that result in an improved energy performance rating. Ideally, the RCx assessment and recommended repairs, adjustments and other energy efficiency measures will be completed prior to or in conjunction with the installation of the solar energy system. However the repairs, adjustments and measures identified in the RCx assessment can be implemented up to one year after completion of the installation of the solar energy system. In this case, the building owner/operator/manager is required to complete, sign and submit this Commitment Agreement along with their Solar Energy System Incentive Application that commits the building owner/manager to completing the recommended repairs, adjustments and energy efficiency measures identified in the RCx assessment by the date indicated.

Please complete, and sign the following Commitment Agreement. Specify the date by which the repairs, adjustments or measure change-outs are planned to be completed. Submit the signed Commitment Agreement, a copy of the energy audit and Information and Disclosure form with the Solar Energy System Incentive Application to the program administrator. Submit a copy of the final retro-commissioning report to the Program Administrator when the retro-commissioning process is complete.

COMMITTMENT AGREEMENT

To be completed by the Building Owner/Manager. Please initial each item, fill in the blanks and sign below:

____ I certify that I am the owner/operator/manager (circle one) of the commercial building located at ____________________ ____________________________________, and I am applying for incentives for a solar energy system.

____ I certify that the building that is to receive the solar energy system was benchmarked on ______________________ by ______________________________ and received an energy performance (benchmark) rating of _________________.

____ If the energy performance rating is below 75, I certify that the retro-commissioning assessment will be completed on ____________________________ on the building that is to receive the solar energy system.

____ I certify that all cost effective measures identified as likely to improve the energy performance rating will be implemented, and will be completed by ________________________________. I will submit a copy of the retro-commissioning report to the PV program administrator when the work is complete.

____

(signature) *(title)* *(date)*

____

Payments for Specified Energy Property In Lieu of Tax Credits Independent Accountant Requirements

Applicants requesting payments of **$1 Million or more** for a specified property shall submit an independent accountants' examination opinion attesting to the accuracy of costs claimed as part of the basis of the property. The examination is to be conducted in accordance with AT Section 101, Attest Engagements (Statements on Standards for Attestation Engagements 10, as amended) established by the American Institute of Certified Public Accountants (AICPA). **Attachment A is the required examination report and an illustrative report of management asserting their compliance.**

Applicants requesting payments of less than $ 1 Million and whose eligible cost basis is more than $500,000 for a specified property may submit, in lieu of an examination report, with their application, a report of Agreed Upon Procedures (AUP) prepared by an independent accountant in accordance with AT Section 201, Agreed Upon Procedure Engagements (Statements on Standards for Attestation Engagements 10, as amended) of the AICPA. The Department of the Treasury's objective in having the AUP performed is to obtain independent procedures and findings as to whether the project costs and the eligibility of the costs are in accordance with the general rules for determining the basis of property for federal income taxes as further described in Section V of the "Program Guidance for the Payments for Specified Energy Property in Lieu of Tax Credits under the American Recovery and Reinvestment Act of 2009." **Attachment B has the procedures to be performed by the independent accountant and an illustrative AUP report.**

ATTACHMENT A

[Applicants requesting payments of $ 1 Million or more]

[CPA LETTERHEAD]

INDEPENDENT ACCOUNTANTS' REPORT

Applicant Company Name

Applicant Company Address

We have examined management's assertion, included in the accompanying Report of Management on Eligible Cost Basis, that the eligible cost basis for the qualified property relating to [*identify asset*] of *Applicant Company* in the amount of $XX,XXX,XXX has been determined in accordance with the general rules for determining the basis of property for federal income tax purposes, as further described in Section V of the Program Guidance for the Payments for Specified Energy Property in Lieu of Tax Credits under the American Recovery and Reinvestment Act of 2009. *Applicant Company's* management is responsible for the assertion. Our responsibility is to express an opinion based on our examination.

Our examination was conducted in accordance with attestation standards established by the American Institute of Certified Public Accountants and, accordingly, included examining, on a test basis, evidence supporting management's assertion and performing such other procedures as we considered necessary in the circumstances. We believe that our examination provides a reasonable basis for our opinion.

[Additional paragraph(s) may be added to emphasize certain matters relating to the attest engagement, the assertion or the subject matter.]

In our opinion, management's assertion referred to above is fairly stated, in all material respects based on the general rules for determining the basis of property for federal income tax purposes, as further described in Section V of the Program Guidance for the Payments for Specified Energy Property in Lieu of Tax Credits under the American Recovery and Reinvestment Act of 2009.

[This report is intended solely for the information and use of the management [and the audit committee] of the Company and the Department of Treasury and is not intended to be and should not be used by anyone other than these specified parties.]

[Signature of CPA firm]

[License number and State if report is signed by an individual CPA rather than a firm]

[Date]

REPORT OF MANAGEMENT ON ELIGIBLE COST BASIS

[Month] XX, 20XX

Department of the Treasury

Management of [XYZ Company] (the "Company") is responsible for establishing and maintaining adequate internal controls to provide reasonable assurance to the Company's management and *[insert parties charged with governance, such as the Board of Directors or the Managing Member]* that the accounting records supporting the eligible cost basis for qualified property are valid, complete and accurate, and that the costs included in the eligible cost basis of such assets have been determined in accordance with the criteria set forth below.

The cost basis of property eligible for the Payments for Specified Energy Property in Lieu of Tax Credits pursuant to Section 1603 of the American Recovery and Reinvestment Act of 2009 (the "ARRA") relating to the construction of the *[specify asset type; e.g., wind energy facility]* (the "qualified property") of the Company at *[project name]* in the amount of $XX,XXX,XXX has been determined in accordance with the general rules for determining the basis of property for federal income tax purposes as further described in Section V of the Program Guidance for Specified Energy Property in Lieu of Tax Credits under the ARRA [and in the paragraph[s] below].

[Additional description of the property or cost basis, including any significant interpretations, necessary for understanding the qualified property]

[Name and title of chief executive officer]

[Name and title of chief financial officer]

[Name and title of chief compliance officer]

ATTACHMENT B

[Alternative Agreed Upon Procedures report for entities requesting payments of less than $ 1 Million and whose eligible cost basis is more than $ 500,000]

[CPA LETTERHEAD]

Independent Accountants' Report on Applying the Agreed-Upon Procedures For Payments for Specified Energy Property in Lieu of Tax Credits Under the American Recovery and Reinvestment Act of 2009

(Applicant Name) and United States Department of the Treasury

We have performed the procedures enumerated in the appendix attached, which were agreed upon by (insert applicant name) and the United States Department of the Treasury to assist you in evaluating the specified property costs and the eligible cost basis for the payment requested under Section 1603, Division B, of the American Recovery and Reinvestment Act of 2009. The management of (the applicant/company name) is responsible for the accuracy of the reported costs and determining the eligible basis for the property. This agreed-upon procedures engagement was conducted in accordance with AT Section 201, Agreed Upon Procedure Engagements (Statements on Standards for Attestation Engagements 10, as amended) of the American Institute of Certified Public Accountants. The sufficiency of these procedures is solely the responsibility of those parties specified in this report. Consequently, we make no representation regarding the sufficiency of the procedures described below either for the purpose for which this report has been requested or for any other purpose.
Our procedures, and the results of those procedures, are set forth in the attached appendix to this report.

We were not engaged to, and did not conduct an examination of the specified property costs and the eligible cost basis, the objective of which would be the expression of an opinion. Accordingly, we do not express such an opinion. Had we performed additional procedures, other matters may have come to our attention that would have been reported to you.

This report is intended solely for the information and use of (Applicant name) and the United States Department of the Treasury, and is not intended to be and should not be used by anyone other than these specified parties.

(Signature) CPA

License number and State

Date

Payments for Specified Energy Property in Lieu of Tax Credits Under the AMERICAN RECOVERY AND REINVESTMENT ACT OF 2009

Independent Accountant Report on Agreed Upon Procedures

Principal Information Requests: While not intended to be a complete listing of all information that may be requested by the independent accountant, the applicant should provide the independent accountant with the following information:

1. A copy of all documentation to be submitted in support of the application.
2. A listing of all invoices and associated purchase orders, contracts and payment advices as considered relevant to the cost basis [if not provided in (1) above]. The listing should also indicate the nature of costs associated with each invoice, for example, purchase of solar panels, payment for construction labor, etc. and dates incurred.
3. A detailed calculation of cost basis linked to actual accounting records [if not provided in above].

Agreed Upon Procedures ("AUP") to be performed by the Independent Accountant

Section 1: Testing Cost Eligibility

1. From the information obtained (request 1), determine the location and definition of the specified property.
2. From the information obtained, review the classification of costs to determine whether the costs are related to the specified property.
3. Review management's detailed calculation of costs (information request 3) to determine that such costs are in accordance with the requirements of Section 1603, specifically consider the following areas as explained in the program guidance:
   (a) Used Parts.
   (b) Costs are for tangible property (not including a building) which is an integral part of the facility.
   (c) Only specified energy property is taken into account.
   (d) Qualified property that generates electricity excluding any electrical transmission equipment.
   (e) Specific property requirements.
   (f) Lessee and Lessee in a Sale-Leaseback.

4. Review the detailed calculation of costs (information request 3) to determine that such costs are in accordance with IRC Section 1012. Determine if there are any adjustments to basis which may need to be disallowed such as depreciation. Also determine if all depreciable basis costs such as installation costs and freight costs were included in the cost basis.

5. Inquire of management if there are any federal grants, state grants or rebates that reduce cost basis. They reduce the cost basis only if they are not taxable income to the applicant. Obtain a management representation.

Section 2: Testing Costs

1. Accuracy Testing –From the detailed listing of costs (information request 2), select a sample of costs representing at least 30% of the total costs listed and at least 15% of the total number of invoices. From the samples selected, agree the descriptions and costs to actual invoices, POs, contracts and payment advices to determine the accuracy of the listing and whether such costs were actually incurred for the specified property.
2. Completeness Testing - Perform a two-way check as follows:
   (a) From the sample tested above, trace all permitted items to the detailed calculation of cost basis (information request 3).
   (b) Identify any individual material costs in the detailed calculation of cost basis that were not sampled and trace such costs to the detailed listing. Determine whether such costs actually exist and are permissible.

3. Inquire of management to determine that accrual basis of accounting was considered to identify all costs associated with the cost basis.
4. Reasonableness Testing –Taking into consideration all of the information obtained and procedures performed, consider whether the detailed calculation of cost basis appears to be reasonable.

Section 3: Conclusion

1. If the accountant became aware of any potential discrepancies, request management to investigate and, if appropriate, correct such discrepancies to the accountant's satisfaction.

(2) Obtain a representation letter from management regarding the information obtained and oral representations made throughout the engagement.

Prepare an Agreed Upon Procedures Report and attach the accountant's procedures and findings.

DATE: ____________________

LEASE NO: ______________

Supplement to Lease Agreement

Security Deposit

WHEREAS, Renewable Energy Project Creditor (hereinafter "Lessor"), and __________________________ (hereinafter "Lessee") have entered into an Equipment Lease Agreement and related documents thereto (hereinafter "Lease") of even date herewith;

NOW THEREFORE, in further consideration for entering into said Lease, Lessee agrees to deposit with Lessor a Security Deposit in the amount of __________________________________ Dollars ($_________). Lessor shall retain this Security Deposit, in addition to any other security that Lessee may have given to secure the performance by Lessee of its obligations under said Lease. This Security Deposit shall be non-interest bearing. If Lessee shall default in the performance of any of its obligations as may be more specifically set forth in said Lease and related documents thereto, Lessor may, at Lessor's option, apply this Security Deposit or any portion thereof, to the curing of that default. Any such application by Lessor shall not constitute a defense to Lessor's acceleration of the balance of rents and other charges reserved in said Lease and related documents thereto, or to any other action by Lessor arising out of any default or any failure of Lessee to perform its obligations under said Lease and related documents thereto. Upon demand by Lessor, Lessee shall immediately restore this Security Deposit to its full amount.

This Security Deposit cannot be assigned or transferred by Lessee without the prior written consent of Lessor and any attempted assignment or transfer thereof shall be void, shall not be binding upon Lessor, and shall constitute an event of default under the Lease and related documents thereto. Any assignment of said Lease and related documents thereto by Lessee, for which Lessor's prior written consent is obtained, shall constitute an assignment of Lessee's interest in this Security Deposit, unless the terms of Lessor's consent expressly provides otherwise.

Lessor hereby agrees that upon full payment of all rents and any other amount due under said Lease and related documents thereto, and full performance of all terms and conditions of said Lease and related documents thereto, together with the return of the equipment, said Security Deposit will be returned to Lessee. If Lessee has executed a Purchase Option in favor of Lessor, Lessee agrees that upon full payment of all rents and other amounts due under said Lease and related documents thereto, and full performance of all terms and conditions of said Lease and related documents thereto, Lessee agrees that Lessor will credit the proceeds of this Security Deposit against sums due under the Purchase Option. Sums held in excess of those due under the Purchase Option will be returned to Lessee.

It is agreed that no modification of this Security Agreement shall be binding upon the parties, either of them, unless such modification shall be in writing and executed by the parties hereto. This agreement shall be governed by, and construed in accordance with the laws of the State of _________________________.

ATTEST:

LESSOR: Renewable Energy Project Creditor

BY: _______________________________________

LESSEE: __________________________________

BY: _______________________________________

ABC RENEWABLE ENERGY EQUIPMENT SUPPLIER
AND
ABC LESSOR/PROJECT DEVELOPER

SERVICE AGREEMENT TERMS AND CONDITIONS
for
SOLAR PHOTOVOLTAIC ROOF MOUNTED ENERGY SYSTEM

This Service Agreement ("Agreement") by and between __________________ ("Owner"), and __________________, a ______________ corporation ("Service Provider") applies to the ______________________________ purchased by the Owner and located at the Site.

1.0 Definitions

The following terms shall have the meaning set forth below:

1.1 "Acceptance" means the successful completion of the ___________________________ acceptance test at the Owner's Site, including completion and cosigning of the Commercial Closure Documents.

1.2 "Balance of Plant" or "BOP" means all components of the Plant other than the ___________________________, as specified by Service Provider from time to time in its ____________ Specifications.

1.3 "Consumables" shall mean the ____ which are specified in the Service Provider's maintenance manual and necessary for the Power Plant to perform its functions. Specifically excluded from the definition of "Consumables" are Utilities.

1.4 "______________________" or "Plant" A ______________________ power plant utilizing Service Provider's ________________________ technology.

1.5 "Effective Date" means the date on which the Term commences as provided in this Agreement.

1.6 "Excluded Service" shall mean any activity regarding the Power Plant or component thereof, which may be required due to: (i) any Force Majeure event; (ii) breach of contract, negligence, willful misconduct or otherwise of Owner or Owner's agents, contractors, employees or persons acting on behalf of Owner, their agents, or contractors; (iii) act or omission of any third party; (iv) failure of Owner or Owner's agents, contractors, employees or persons acting on behalf of Owner to operate the Power Plant in strict accordance with Service Provider's and other manufacturer's specifications, instructions and manuals, but excluding the negligence, acts or omissions of Service Provider or its agents; or (v) changes to any law, ordinance, regulation or order of governmental authority having jurisdiction over the Power Plant and/or its maintenance and repair that become effective after the Effective Date of this Agreement.

1.7 "Facility" shall mean the connections, interfaces, and supporting equipment for the Plant, including the support system, slab or pedestal on which the Plant is located, electrical distribution system, and equipment connected to the Plant's interface points but excluding the Plant itself.

1.8 "Force Majeure" shall mean any event beyond the reasonable control of the party affected, including, without limitation, any act of God, act (or failures to act) of governmental authorities or public enemy, strike, work stoppage or other labor disturbance, delays in transportation, utility outage, war (declared or undeclared), strikes or other labor disturbances, military conflicts, terrorist acts (foreign or domestic) epidemics, civil unrest, blockade, riot, public unrest, lightning, fire, violent storm, flood, unforeseeable geological condition, drought, adverse or severe weather, explosion, earthquake, delays in transportation, government order or restraint, whether of a similar or dissimilar nature, which event (i) could not have been reasonably anticipated by the affected party, and (ii) cannot be reasonably avoided or circumvented by the affected party and as to Service Provider, acts (or omissions) of Owner including failure to promptly: (a) provide Service Provider with information and approvals necessary to permit Service Provider to proceed with work immediately and without interruption, (b) comply with the terms of payment, or (c) provide Service Provider with such evidence as Service Provider may request that any permit has been issued.

1.9 "________________" refers to that portion of the ______________ Power Plant, which performs the conversion of sun energy to electricity using photovoltaic cells.

1.10 "Repair" or "Repairing" shall mean in relation to any item of the Power Plant, the repair or replacement, at Service Provider's option, utilizing repair measures determined by Service Provider, of a part or parts of any damage to, or malfunction or breakdown of such Power Plant.

1.11 "Site" means the location where the ______________________ under this Contract are to be located, which address is ______________________.

1.12 "Specifications" mean the Solar Power Plant Specifications attached to this Agreement as Appendix 1.

1.13 "Taxes" are defined as: All taxes, duties, fees, or other charges of any nature (including ad valorem, consumption, excise, franchise, gross receipts, property, import, license, stamp, storage, transfer, use, sales, or value-added taxes and any and all items of withholding, deficiency, penalty, addition to tax, interest or assessment related thereto). Products exported from the United States are presumed to be exempt from Taxes levied within the United States.

1.14 "Utilities" shall mean air, water, wastewater, fuel and ______________________ required to operate the Power Plant.

2.0 Division of Responsibilities

2.1 Service Provider Responsibilities

2.1.1 General Scope: Service Provider shall; (a) provide either new or remanufactured parts, in its sole discretion, as available, in performing its obligations hereunder, and upon replacement, Owner shall take title to such replaced parts or components; (b) provide all special Power Plant tooling necessary to perform its obligations under Agreement; and (c) coordinate maintenance activities with Owner in accordance with Service Provider's customary procedures. This Agreement requires that Service Provider's specifications and instructions including, without limitation, the various specifications appended to this Agreement as Exhibits or, in the absence thereof, generally accepted operating practices of the electric power industry, be strictly adhered to.

2.1.2 Preventative Maintenance: Service Provider shall be responsible for providing technical service, parts and Consumables associated with preventative maintenance as specified in the Service Provider's ______________________ Maintenance Manual. Preventative Maintenance as used herein shall mean in relation to any component of the Plant, the minor inspection, major inspection, part cleaning, replacement, and performance of other scheduled maintenance with respect thereto, in order to keep the Power Plant that has been otherwise operated and maintained by Owner pursuant to the terms of this Agreement as set forth in Service Provider's Operations and Maintenance Manuals, in good working order.

2.1.3 Unplanned Maintenance: Service Provider shall be responsible for providing Repair of the Balance of Plant in accordance with this Agreement whenever during the Term such Repair is determined by Service Provider to be necessary. Service Provider shall use reasonable efforts to effect immediate and remote diagnostics upon notification to Service Provider by Owner of a malfunction of the Power Plant. Upon Service Provider's determination that a malfunction of the Power Plant cannot be remedied remotely, Service Provider shall use reasonable efforts to dispatch service personnel to the Site after notification of malfunction subject to the availability of necessary labor, components and tooling.

2.1.4 Power Plant Performance: Service Provider warrants to Owner that for the Term, the Power Plant Output, as determined using onboard instrumentation and Service Provider's standard testing protocols with corrections to measured performance, shall decline no more than 5% from the corrected output ("Guaranteed Output") determined at the time of Acceptance ("Acceptance Output" herein). Should the Plant fail to perform in accordance with the foregoing warranty, Service Provider shall correct the failure such that the output of the Power Plant is greater than 95% of the Acceptance Output or provide a pro rata reduction in the Service Fees, based on the shortfall (kW) from the Guaranteed Output, for the years in which the shortfall occurs. It is understood that if the Power Plant fails to produce the Guaranteed Output in any year during the Term and if the Power Plant exceeded such Guaranteed Power Plant Output in any other year, then the Power Plant Output shall be the average of the Power Plant Output in the year(s) in excess and the Power Plant Output in the year in which the shortfall occurs.

2.1.5 Owner's Responsibilities: Owner shall (a) maintain the qualification and safety of the Facility and the Power Plant and their operations; (b) properly maintain the Facility; (c) provide one analog phone line and high-speed access link to the Power Plant for remote monitoring; (d) supply unrestricted access to the Power Plant and the Facility and shall make available at the Site, office space, phones, fax machines, water, air conditioning, sanitary facilities, potable water, site security, and safety equipment for Service Provider's on-site personnel; (e) maintain all the permits, including emissions and licenses necessary to operate the Facility and the Power Plant, (f) provide for the care, custody, and insurance of parts and Modules while on site; (g) strictly comply with Service Provider's procedures, manuals and instructions and in the absence thereof with generally accepted operating practices of the electric power industry; (h) provide operators, waste water facilities, start-up power and support all Service Provider-required Power Plant testing; (i) provide Utilities in accordance with Service Provider's specifications, (j) provide onsite storage of replaced Consumables; (k) remove and properly dispose of replaced Consumables and other wastes materials in accordance with applicable federal, state and local regulations; (l) determine electrical connection point arc flash rating and hazard category; (m) provide equipment arc flash labeling and (n) provide Service Provider with necessary performance and production data to determine conformance with Service Provider's specification(s).

2.2 Upgrades: If at any time during the Term, Service Provider develops an upgrade, which may improve Power Plant performance, Service Provider will make such upgrade available to Owner on mutually agreeable terms and conditions.

3.0 Exclusions

3.1 Service Provider shall not be responsible for removal or replacement of structures or parts of any Facility required to perform Service Provider's services under this Agreement. Any such services are Excluded Services.

3.2 Service Provider's obligations set forth herein are conditioned upon (i) Owner's proper storage, installation, operation and maintenance of the Solar Power Plant and conformance with the instruction, operations and maintenance manuals (including revisions thereto) provided by Service Provider and/or its subcontractors, as applicable and (ii) Owner's satisfactory repair or modification pursuant to Service Provider's instructions or approval. Owner shall keep proper records of operation and maintenance during the Term. These records shall be kept in the form of logsheets and copies shall be submitted to Service Provider upon its request. Any such services are Excluded Services.

3.3 This Agreement does NOT cover Repairs to the Power Plant required due to Excluded Services, unless otherwise agreed by Service Provider on a case-by-case basis. Such Repairs and Consumables, materials and labor required due to Excluded Services, shall be at Owner's expense.

3.4 This Agreement does NOT cover Repairs to the Power Plant if Owner or its vendors, suppliers, employees or agents makes any changes, modifications or alterations to the Power Plant or its components without the written approval of Service Provider. Unapproved changes, modifications or alterations may void Service Provider's obligations hereunder.

4.0 Term, Termination and Suspension

4.1 Term: This Agreement will commence upon Acceptance and will conclude ______ months following such date, (herein referred to as the "Term"). Each year during the Term shall comprise twelve consecutive months commencing on the date of Acceptance or on the anniversary thereof. Subject to mutual agreement as to the Service Fees, and provided the Owner is not then in default, Owner may extend the Term for one _____ month increment by Notice to Service Provider in writing at least ninety days prior to the expiration of the Term.

4.2 Suspension and Termination: In the event either party to this agreement fails to materially comply with the provisions of this Agreement and upon the other party's failure to cure such noncompliance within thirty (30) days of receipt of Notice thereof by the other party, the other party may, at its option suspend or terminate this Agreement. Notwithstanding any provision herein, neither party shall not be deemed in default of its obligations under this Agreement resulting from a suspension of work under this paragraph nor shall that party's suspension operate as a waiver, release or forfeiture of any other remedy or right of either party hereunder. If either party suspends the work on this Agreement, hereunder, and the other party does not remedy the situation after 90 days of suspension, or within any shorter period of time as specified in writing, that party shall be entitled to terminate this Agreement for cause. In addition, either party may terminate this Agreement upon ten (10) days Notice for non-payment of amounts due or should the Service Provider to perform it's obligation under this Agreement.

4.3 Complete Term: It is understood that the Service Provider's obligations under this Agreement and pricing hereunder are based on the full ___ month Term.

5.0 Delays

5.1 Neither Party shall have any liability or be considered to be in breach or default of its obligations under this Agreement to the extent that performance of such obligations is delayed or prevented, directly or indirectly due to Force Majeure. The Party claiming Force Majeure shall notify the other party of such claim in writing. The date of performance shall be extended for a period equal to the time lost by reason of delay, plus such additional time as may be reasonably necessary to overcome the effect of such excusable delay.

5.2 If delay excused by this Article extends for more than one hundred and eighty (180) days and the parties have not agreed upon a revised basis for continuing the work at the end of the delay, including adjustment of the Service Fee, then either party upon thirty (30) days written notice, may terminate this Agreement with respect to any unperformed or uncompleted services.

5.3 In the event that this Agreement is terminated pursuant to Paragraph 5.2 and prior to its completion, charges for the terminated portion payable by Owner to Service Provider shall be the price of all products supplied as of the date of termination. The selling price of those products for which unit prices are not designated or for which Seller does not have published prices shall be determined in accordance with Seller's standard accounting practices. Seller's termination charges shall not exceed the total Service Fee under this Agreement as reduced by the amounts of payments otherwise made. For purposes of this Paragraph, all equipment, materials, supplies, components, services, engineering, design and data, in other words, all work which Service Provider has contracted to perform hereunder, or any part or parts thereof, are referred to as "products."

6.0 Limitations

6.1 Limited Warranty: This Agreement sets forth Owner's exclusive remedies for all claims of any kind arising out of the performance or breach of this Agreement, installation, Repair or use of any Power Plant or based on failure of or defect in the Power Plant, whether such claim, however instituted, is based on contract, indemnity, warranty, tort (including negligence), strict liability or otherwise. *THE FOREGOING WARRANTIES ARE EXCLUSIVE AND ARE IN LIEU OF ALL OTHER WARRANTIES AND GUARANTEES WHETHER WRITTEN, ORAL, IMPLIED OR STATUTORY. NO IMPLIED STATUTORY WARRANTY OF MERCHANTABILITY OR FITNESS FOR A PARTICULAR PURPOSE SHALL APPLY TO THE EQUIPMENT, ITS INSTALLATION OR REPAIR OR REPLACEMENT.*

6.2 General Limitation of Liability

6.2.1 Notwithstanding anything to the contrary herein, each Party's total liability hereunder with respect to any and all claims of any kind, whether arising in contract, warranty, tort (including negligence), strict liability, indemnity, or otherwise, arising out of the performance or breach of this Agreement, installation, Repair or use of any Power Plant or a failure of or defect in the Power Plant shall be limited to the Service Fees, as hereinafter defined.

6.2.2 Each party (Indemnitor) agrees to indemnify and hold harmless the other party (Indemnitee) from and against any and all losses, obligations, liabilities, damages, claims which may be asserted against or sustained or incurred by the Indemnitee arising out of or related to any breach of any of the representations, warranties, agreements and covenants made by Indemnitor in this Agreement; or any wrongful and negligent act of Indemnitor.

6.2.3 Each Party's liability under this Agreement shall terminate upon expiration of the Term.

6.2.4 In no event, shall any failure of the Power Plant to perform, any defect in the Power Plant or breach of this Agreement or any claim, whether arising on breach of contract, tort (including negligence), strict liability, indemnity, or otherwise, render either Party or its subcontractors or suppliers liable to the other Party for lost profits or loss of revenues, loss of use of the Power Plant or any associated equipment, cost of capital, cost of substitute equipment, facilities, services or replacement power, downtime costs, claims of the other Party's customers for such damages, or for any special, consequential, incidental, indirect or exemplary damages and each Party shall indemnify the other against such claims.

6.2.5 If Service Provider furnishes Owner with advice or assistance concerning any products, systems or work which is not specifically required pursuant to Service Provider's Specifications, the furnishing of such advice or assistance will not subject Service Provider to any liability, whether in contract, indemnity, warranty, tort (including negligence), strict liability or otherwise.

6.2.6 The provisions of this Article shall prevail over any conflicting or inconsistent provisions contained in any of the documents comprising this Agreement, except to the extent that such provisions further restrict the other party's liability.

7.0 Commercial Payment Terms

7.1 During the Term, Owner shall pay Service Provider a Service Fee of ______________ payable in __________ installments of _________________. Owner shall pay Service Provider the first installment of the Service Fee to Service Provider with Owner's execution of this Agreement. Owner shall pay Service Provider subsequent installments of the Service Fee within ten (10) days of the end of each ____________ thereafter during the Term.

7.2 During the Term, the Service Fee specified in this Agreement shall be adjusted annually in accordance with the following adjustment formula:

Where:

S1 = the adjusted price to be paid by Owner.

S0 = the price specified in herein.

P = the "Producer Price Index less Food and Energy" as determined by the U.S. Department of Labor, Bureau of Labor Statistics. P for each annual adjustment shall be the then most current index available at the time of invoicing.

CI = the most current index available on the execution date of this Agreement.

Should the Index specified above be discontinued or significantly modified, the nearest equivalent Index shall be substituted. All adjustments shall be calculated to the nearest 1/10th of 1%.

7.3 Excluded Services provided by Service Provider will be priced at Service Provider's then current pricing and will be subject to Service Provider's standard terms and conditions at the time Service is provided.

7.4 In the event that any payment due from Owner under this Contract is not paid within 15 days of when due, Owner shall pay Service Provider interest on such overdue payment during a period commencing on such due date until the date that such overdue payment is actually made to Service Provider, the annual rate of interest being equal to three percent (3%) above the highest commercial prime rate as published in the Wall Street Journal on the day the payment first became due. Nothing in this paragraph shall prevent Service Provider from exercising any right it has under this Agreement.

8.0 Intellectual Property and Confidentiality

8.1 Ownership of Intellectual Property: Owner acknowledges that all Intellectual Property rights in and relating to the Solar Power Plant, whether developed by or for Service Provider prior to or after the date of this Agreement, are and shall remain the property of Service Provider or its third party licensors. Owner may use Service Provider's Trademarks to refer to the Solar Power Plant, provided that all such uses receive prior written approval by Service Provider.

8.2 Proprietary Information: During the Term of this Agreement, it may be necessary for a party to provide proprietary or confidential information to another Party. The Parties agree to protect such information in accordance with the Confidentiality Agreement signed between the Parties on ____________.

8.3 Software and Other Intellectual Property Integrity. Owner shall not, and shall not permit its employees, subcontractors, facility operators, site owners or agents to reproduce, distribute, transmit or modify the software provided by the Service Provider or other intellectual property, except that Owner shall be permitted to use and operate such software and intellectual property in connection with the operation and use of the Plant hereunder; nor shall Owner, its employees, subcontractors, facility operators, site owners or agents reverse engineer or decompile the software or other intellectual property for any purpose, or permit others to do so.

8.4 In the event Owner wishes to transfer title to, or control of, the Solar Power Plants to a third party, Owner agrees that in addition to any other applicable provision of this Agreement, and as a condition of, and prior to any such transfer of title or control, Owner shall, in a writing to Service Provider, obligate such third party to be bound by the provisions of this Article to the same extent as Owner is obligated.

9.0 Choice of Law

This Agreement shall be governed by and construed in accordance with the laws of the State of ________________ without regard to the conflict of laws provisions thereof.

10.0 Disputes

Any action, dispute, claim or controversy of any kind (collectively described hereinafter as "disputes") between Owner and Service Provider arising out of or pertaining to this Agreement shall be resolved in accordance with the following:

10.1 The Parties shall attempt to amicably resolve such dispute by discussion between the respective project managers within fifteen (15) working days.

10.2 If unsuccessful, the Parties shall elevate the dispute to the senior division or group executives for resolution within an additional fifteen (15) working days or such additional term as the Parties mutually may agree.

10.3 In the event the Parties are unable to resolve the dispute by the methods set forth above, the dispute shall be resolved by a court of competent jurisdiction in ____________________________.

10.4 Notwithstanding the above, in the event of (i) non-payment by Owner within thirty (30) days of receipt of a valid invoice or (ii) financial insolvency, imminent insolvency or loss of project funding, Service Provider may, at its option, stop work, terminate for breach and initiate suit for collection of outstanding balances without compliance with the above paragraphs of this Article; or Service Provider may stop work, invoice Owner in advance for all remaining payments due under this Agreement, and Service Provider shall continue performance of this Agreement upon receipt of such payments, with appropriate schedule adjustments needed for any delay.

11.0 Insurance

Each Party shall maintain the following insurance coverage written with carriers authorized to insure risks at the Site location, with the other Party named as additional insured, providing thirty (30) days written notification of cancellation:

11.1 Workers' Compensation providing statutory limits and coverage and Employer's Liability, in an amount not less than one million dollars ($1,000,000) policy limit; and;

11.2 Commercial General Liability covering bodily injury (including death) and property damage in an amount not less than five million dollars ($5,000,000) per occurrence; including Premises Operations, Contractual Liability, Products and Completed Operations, and Broad Form Property Damage.

11.3 Commercial Automobile Liability in an amount not less than five million dollars ($5,000,000) combined single limit per accident, covering all owned, non-owned, leased, rented or hired autos used in connection with the performance of this Agreement.

12.0 Taxes and Duties

Owner shall be responsible for, and shall pay directly when due and payable, any and all Taxes. If Owner deducts or withholds Taxes from the payments, the Owner will make the Service Provider whole such that the sum of all payments equals the Service Fee. If the Service Provider is required to pay Taxes, the Owner shall, promptly upon presentation of the Service Provider's invoice for such Taxes, pay to the Service Provider an amount equal to the Taxes or alternatively, Owner shall provide Service Provider with a tax exemption certificate acceptable to the taxing authority.

Owner agrees to furnish, when requested by the Service Provider, without charge, evidence of tax or duty exemption acceptable to the taxing or customs authorities. Furthermore, if Owner arranges for export shipment, Owner agrees to provide Service Provider without charge, an export bill of lading.

13.0 Assignment

Either Party ("Assignor") may assign its rights and obligations hereunder, in part or in whole, to a third party ("Assignee") only with the express written consent of the other Party, which shall not be unreasonably withheld. Upon the effective date of said assignment, all of the rights and obligations of the Assignor under this Agreement shall vest solely in such Assignee. Each Party agrees to execute such documents as may be necessary to effect the assignment.

14.0 Notices

Any notices or invoices required or permitted under this Agreement shall be in writing and personally delivered or sent to the address of each Party as set forth below, or to such other address as either Party may substitute by written notice to the other in any manner expressly provided for herein.

Service Provider: Owner:

ABC Renewable Energy Equipment Supplier
Attn: John Doe
Director, Installed Systems
123 S Any Road
Your Town, CA 92229

Fax:	Fax:
Phone:	Phone:

15.0 General Clauses

15.1 This Agreement, together with its exhibits and appendices, constitutes the entire and only agreement between the parties relating to the subject matter hereof and supersedes and cancels all agreements, negotiations, commitments and representations in respect thereto made prior to commencement of this Agreement and may not be released, discharged, abandoned, changed or modified in any manner except by an instrument in writing of concurrent or subsequent date signed by duly authorized officers or representatives of each of the parties hereto.

15.2 Any oral or written representation, warranty, or course of dealing not contained or referenced herein shall not be binding on either Party. Each Party agrees that it has not relied on or been induced by any representations of the other Party not contained in this Agreement.

15.3 The provisions of this Agreement are for the benefit of the Parties hereto and not for any other person or entity except as specifically provided herein.

15.4 The invalidity, in whole or in part, of any Article or Paragraph thereof shall not affect the validity of the remainder of such Article or Paragraph of this Agreement.

15.5 Capitalized terms, unless expressly stated otherwise, shall have the meanings specified herein. The singular includes the plural and the neuter shall include the feminine and masculine gender, and vice versa, as the context requires. "Includes" or "including" means "including, without limitation."

15.6 The failure of either Party to strictly enforce any of the terms, covenants or conditions of this Agreement, or to exercise any of its rights, shall not be construed or deemed as a waiver or relinquishment of any term, covenant, condition or right with respect to previous or further performance under this Agreement.

15.7 This Agreement shall take precedence over any other documents, attachments or specifications referred to herein, including the Terms and Conditions of any Owner Purchase Order referred to herein or attached hereto.

15.8 The provisions of Article 8 shall survive termination of this Agreement.

IN WITNESS WHEREOF, the Parties hereto have caused this Agreement to be duly executed by their duly authorized representatives as of the day and year first above mentioned.

______________________________, **Owner** **Service Provider:** ______________________

By ______________________________ By ______________________________

Typed Name: ______________________________ Title:

Date:

Title: ______________________________

Date: ______________________________

Exhibit 1– Service Provider Optional Services

The following options are available for an additional annual fee. The Monitoring option includes the Data Access option.

1. Data Access: Power Plant data shall be made available to Service Provider through ______________________________ .

2. Monitoring: Service Provider shall provide remote monitoring capability for Power Plant operations. Service Provider shall maintain communication systems to provide the ability to contact first response providers within a reasonable period of time. Power Plant data will be made available through ______________________.

3. Response: Service Provider shall respond to Power Plant alarms within a reasonable time after receipt of notice of such alarms either from Owner or by remote monitoring and shall restore the Power Plant to normal operation in accordance with Service Provider's Operations Manual.

APPENDIX 1

Service Provider's Specifications

The following specifications are incorporated herein by reference.

1.
2.

ENGINEERING, PROCUREMENT AND CONSTRUCTION AGREEMENT

(Source: SolarTech)

Developer: Integrator:

Site Host: Site Address:

Contract Effective Date:

Estimated Permit Submittal Date:

Estimated Procurement and Construction Start Date:

Scheduled Substantial Completion Date:

Solar Energy Generating Facility (SEGF) Abstract: [Mirrors Attachment B Project Overview paragraph]

Contract Price:

Utility: Est. Annual Energy Production ________ kWh-yr1

Incentive Program:

Estimated Incentive Amount:

This Engineering, Procurement and Construction Agreement ("Contract") is made and entered into as of the Contract Effective Date by and between ___________________, a _____________ ("Integrator"), and ________________, a _____________ ("Developer"), for the purposes of providing a turnkey, engineered and constructed Solar Energy Generating Facility (as defined below). Integrator and Developer may singularly be identified as "Party" and collectively as "Parties." The attachments listed below as being attached are attached hereto and fully incorporated herein.

ATTACHMENTS TO CONTRACT

	Attachment Title	Attached	Not Applicable/ Not Attached
A	Site Access	☒	☐
B	Scope of Work	☒	☐
C	Specifications and Submittals	☒	☐
D	Project Schedule	☒	☐
E	Progress Payment Schedule	☒	☐
F	Commissioning Schedule	☒	☐
G	Data Acquisition System Requirements	☒	☐
H	Integrator Form Documents	☒	☐
I	Shading Study Guidelines	☒	☐
J	Warranties	☒	☐
K	Insurance Requirements	☒	☐
L	Approved Products	☒	☐

[Signature Page Follows]

IN WITNESS WHEREOF, and intending to be legally bound, the Parties hereto subscribe their names to this Contract by their duly authorized officers as of the Contract Effective Date above.

Developer

[DEVELOPER NAME]

a ________________

By: ______________________________

[PRINTED NAME]

[TITLE]

Address: __________________________

____

Telephone: _____________________

Integrator

[INTEGRATOR NAME]

a ________________

By: ______________________________

[PRINTED NAME]

[TITLE]

Address: __________________________

____

Telephone: _____________________

Integrator's License Number: _______________

License Type: ____________

GENERAL TERMS AND CONDITIONS
CONTRACT RECITALS

WHEREAS, Developer and Site Host have entered into a Power Purchase Agreement ("PPA") and Site Lease Agreement ("Lease") pursuant to which Developer will own and operate a solar photovoltaic system (as further defined in Section 1 below, the "Solar Energy Generating Facility" or "SEGF") located on the Site, and sell to the Site Host all electricity generated by the Solar Energy Generating Facility for the term specified in the PPA;

WHEREAS, Integrator is a full-service, licensed contracting services company with the financial and technical capabilities to provide services to Developer including, but not limited to, engineering, procurement, project and construction management, construction and installation, commissioning, testing, verification and warranty coverage of the Solar Energy Generating Facility and training as to its operation and maintenance; and

NOW, THEREFORE, Developer and Integrator hereby agree as follows:

SECTION 1. DEFINITIONS

For purposes of the Engineering Procurement and Construction Contract, and its Attachments, the defined terms herein shall have the meaning set forth as follows:

1.1 **Applicable Laws**: "Applicable Laws" shall mean all laws, building codes, rules, regulations, or orders of any federal, state, county, local, or other governmental body, agency, or other authority having jurisdiction over Solar Energy Generating Facility and/or the performance of the Work.

1.2 **Applicable Permits**: "Applicable Permits" shall mean all permits, waivers, authorizations, or licenses issued or required to be issued by any federal, state, county, local, or other governmental body, agency, or other authority having jurisdiction over the Solar Energy Generating Facility and/or performance of the Work.

1.3 **Application for Payment**: "Application for Payment" shall mean an invoice from the Integrator for a Milestone Payment, which shall be accompanied by an executed conditional progress payment lien waiver and release from Integrator and each applicable subcontractor and supplier, substantially in the form provided in **Attachment H** and any supporting documentation necessary to evidence Integrator's achievement of the applicable Project Milestone(s).

1.4 **Application for Substantial Completion**: "Application for Substantial Completion" shall mean the application for Substantial Completion that will be submitted by Integrator to Developer as contemplated by **Section 12.1**.

1.5 **Certificate of Substantial Completion**: "Certificate of Substantial Completion" shall mean the written notice executed by Developer and the Integrator in accordance with **Section 12.1**. Such fully executed certificate shall be conclusive evidence that the Work is Substantially Complete.

1.6 **Certificate of Final Completion**: "Certificate of Final Completion" shall mean the written notice executed by

Developer pursuant to **Section 12.2**. A fully executed Certificate of Final Completion shall be conclusive evidence that Final Completion of the Work has been achieved.

1.7 **Change**: "Change" shall mean any material addition to, deletion from, or other modification to the quality, function, or intent of the Work, including without limitation any such addition, deletion, or other modification that constitutes a material change to the Scope of Work.

1.8 **Change Order**: "Change Order" shall mean a written document signed by both Integrator and Developer that authorizes Integrator to perform a Change to the Scope of Work. The Change Order shall modify the Scope of Work and shall identify: (1) the Change to the Scope of Work; (2) any additional compensation or reduction in compensation to be paid to Integrator to perform such Change; and (3) any extensions of Time to the Project Schedule to perform such Change.

1.9 **Commissioning**: "Commissioning" shall mean the set of tests and procedures performed on the Solar Energy Generating Facility as described in **Attachment F**.

1.10 **Commissioning Engineer**: The "Commissioning Engineer" shall be Developer or a representative designated by Developer to evaluate and certify the capabilities of the Solar Energy Generating Facility.

1.11 **Construction Documents**: "Construction Documents" shall mean the final designs, drawings and other materials, that describe the technical requirements for the installation of all the materials and equipment pursuant to this Contract and that are used for the Work.

1.12 **Contract**: "Contract" shall mean this Engineering Procurement and Construction Agreement and all Attachments attached hereto which are incorporated herein, as the same may be amended or modified from time to time in accordance with the provisions hereof, including any Change Orders executed in accordance with this Contract.

1.13 **Contract Amount**: "Contract Amount" shall mean the amount of compensation that shall be paid by Developer to Integrator for performing the Work in accordance with the Scope of Work attached hereto as **Attachment B** and in accordance with the Specifications and Submittals, attached hereto as **Attachment C**, as such amount may be increased or decreased in accordance with Change Orders.

1.14 **Contract Documents**: "Contract Documents" shall mean this Contract, the Construction Documents, the Submittals, and any amendments thereto.

1.15 **Contract Effective Date**: "Contract Effective Date" shall mean the date so noted on the first page of this Contract.

1.16 **Contract Term**: The "Contract Term" shall commence on the Contract Effective Date and end on the last day of the Performance Term, unless terminated earlier in accordance with the terms hereof.

1.17 **Data Acquisition System (DAS)**: "Data Acquisition System" or "DAS" shall mean the Solar Energy Generating Facility monitoring and metering system described in **Attachment G.**

1.18 **Energy Delivery Point**: "Energy Delivery Point" means the point or points of tie-in between the Solar Energy Generating Facility and the Site Host's electrical switchgear.

1.19 **Engineering Design Package**: "Engineering Design Package" shall mean the materials defined in **Attachment C** and further described in **Attachment B.**

1.20 **Environmental Attributes**: "Environmental Attributes" means, collectively, all environmental and other attributes that differentiate the Solar Energy Generating Facility or the energy output of the Solar Energy Generating Facility from energy generated by certain other generation units, fuels or resources, including those attributable to the avoidance of environmental impacts on air, soil, water or climate, such as the emission of any oxides of nitrogen, sulfur or carbon or of mercury, or other gas or chemical, soot, particulate matter or other substances attributable to the Solar Energy Generating Facility or the compliance of the Solar Energy Generating Facility or the energy output with the law, rules and standards of the United Nations Framework Convention on Climate Change (the "UNFCCC") or the Kyoto Protocol to the UNFCCC or crediting "early action" with a view thereto, or laws or regulations involving or administered by the Clean Air Markets Division of the Environmental Protection Agency or successor administrator or any local, state or federal entity given jurisdiction over a program involving transferability of environmental attributes and right to report to any federal, state, or local agency or authority or other party that Developer or Site Host owns the environmental attributes associated with the energy output of the Solar Energy Generating Facility.

1.21 **Environmental and Financial Incentives**: "Environmental and Financial Incentives" means all rights, credits (including tax credits), rebates, benefits, reductions, offsets, and allowances and entitlements of any kind, howsoever entitled or named (including carbon credits and allowances and renewable energy certificates), whether arising under federal, state or local law, international treaty, trade association membership or the like arising from the Environmental Attributes of the Solar Energy Generating Facility or the energy output or otherwise from the development or installation of the Solar Energy Generating Facility or the production, sale, purchase, consumption or use of the energy output. Without limiting the forgoing, Environmental and Financial Incentives includes the right to apply for (and entitlement to receive) incentives under any applicable state rebates or incentive programs and the right to claim federal income tax credits under Sections 45 or 48 of the Internal Revenue Code of 1986, as amended.

1.22 **Estimated Annual Energy Production**: "Estimated Annual Energy Production" shall mean Developer's estimated number of kWh that the Solar Energy Generating Facility shall produce in the first year based on performance modeling using industry standard tools and assumptions.

1.23 **Estimated Incentive Amount**: "Estimated Incentive Amount" shall mean the amount in U.S. Dollars indicated as such on the first page of this Contract.

1.24 **Final Completion**: "Final Completion" shall be deemed to have occurred when (a) Developer agrees in writing that 100% of the Work as identified in the Scope of Work and Specifications and Submittals has been completed to the satisfaction of Developer, Developer's agent, and/or Developer's designated 3rd Party Commissioning Engineer; and/or (b) a Certificate of Final Completion has been issued to Integrator.

1.25 **Force Majeure**: "Force Majeure" shall mean those events beyond the control of the affected Party and which by the exercise of due diligence such Party could not reasonably have been expected to avoid and which it has been unable to overcome despite the exercise of reasonably diligent efforts, including, without limitation, acts of God and the public enemy; relocation or construction of transmission facilities or the shutdown of such facilities for the purpose of necessary repairs; permanent or temporary relocation of the Solar Energy Generating Facility and/or the Support Structure, including due to re-roofing in all circumstances; natural disasters; fire; civil disobedience, sabotage; restraint by court order or public authority (whether valid or invalid), and/or inability to obtain or keep in force the necessary governmental or Site Host authorizations, permits, licenses, certificates or approvals, in each case, if not caused by the fault of the Party asserting the Force Majeure.

1.26 **Hazardous Substances**: "Hazardous Substances" shall mean any hazardous, toxic, or dangerous wastes, substances, chemicals, constituents, contaminants, pollutants, and materials and any other carcinogenic, liquids, corrosive, ignitable, radioactive, reactive, toxic, or otherwise hazardous substances or mixtures (whether solids, liquids, gases) now or at any time subject to regulation, control, remediation, or otherwise addressed under Applicable Laws; (i) any "hazardous substance" as defined by the Resource, Conservation and Recovery Act of 1976 (42 United States Code ("U.S.C."), Section 6901 et seq.), as amended, and regulations promulgated thereunder; (ii) any "hazardous, toxic or dangerous waste, substance or material" specifically defined as such in U.S.C. Section 9601 et seq., as amended and regulations promulgated thereunder; and (iii) any hazardous, toxic or dangerous waste, substance, or material as defined in any so-called "superfund" or "superlien" law. For purposes of this Contract, Hazardous Substances shall also include without limitation any pesticide, or any insecticide, fungicide or rodenticide as described in the Federal Insecticide, Fungicide, and Rodenticide Act, 7 U.S.C. Section 136 et seq.

1.27 **Independent Engineer**: "Independent Engineer" shall be the 3rd Party Engineer hired by Developer or Developer's project investors, to certify the Estimated Annual Energy Production of the SEGF and to validate the construction completeness, quality, O&M plans and budgets and system performance prior to Final Completion.

1.28 **Interconnection Agreement**: "Interconnection Agreement" shall mean an agreement entered into by and between Developer or Site Host (as appropriate) and the Utility which agreement shall provide for (i) the Solar Energy Generating Facility to be interconnected with the Utility's electricity distribution system, (ii) for energy to flow from the Solar Energy Generating Facility to such system and (iii) for energy to flow from such system to the Site, as applicable, under the provisions of the Utility's tariff.

1.29 **Lease**: "Lease" has the meaning set forth in the first recital in the General Terms and Conditions of this Contract.

1.30 **Load**: "Load" shall mean the total electric consumption as measured by the aggregate of all meters at delivery points serving the Site.

1.31 **Materials**: "Materials" means any articles, apparatus, goods, materials, products, items, data, documents, supplies, equipment, component parts and assemblies, or any other substances, parts, or any combination thereof used, consumed, furnished or installed by Integrator or any subcontractor as part of the Work, including the materials identified in the Scope of Work attached hereto as **Attachment B**.

1.32 **Network Access Point**: "Network Access Point" shall mean the RJ45 jack into which the DAS may be plugged and which provides direct access to the Internet, either via the Host's network, or via a 3rd Party service such as DSL, cable or cellular data modem.

1.33 **Party or Parties**: "Party" or "Parties" shall mean Integrator, Developer, each or both of them, as the context may require pursuant to the terms and conditions of this Contract.

1.34 **Performance Term**: "Performance Term" shall mean the period of time starting on the effective date of this agreement and commencing through the System Warranty Period as detailed in **Section 5.**

1.35 **Power**: "Power" shall mean the total quantity of all actual electric power, both energy and capacity generated by the Solar Energy Generating Facility including all Environmental Attributes and Environmental and Financial Incentives.

1.36 **PPA**: "PPA" or "Power Purchase Agreement" has the meaning set forth in the first recital in the General Terms and Conditions of this Contract.

1.37 **Price and Performance Ratios**: "Price and Performance Ratios" shall mean those ratios as further provided in **Attachment E,** that establish the baseline for comparisons of the Solar Energy Generating Facility to other projects and to provide a means of determination of a fair and equitable structure for changes to the Contract Price should Change Orders impact the project's internal rate of return.

1.38 **Project Milestone**: "Project Milestone" shall mean that portion of the Work required to be completed and verified prior to submittal of an Application for Payment in accordance with Section 4 and further described in **Attachment E.**

1.39 **Project Schedule**: "Project Schedule" means the schedule for the Work, as further detailed in Section 9.1.

1.40 **Punchlist**: "Punchlist" shall mean a list provided by Developer and Site Host to Integrator of items of unfinished Work that do not preclude Developer's beneficial use of the Solar Energy Generating Facility and can be completed within thirty (30) days, or a reasonable period if there are mutually agreed upon externalities that preclude such thirty-day period, and without material interference with Developer's operations.

1.41 **Retainage**: "Retainage" has the meaning set forth in Section 4.1.

1.42 **Site**: "Site" shall mean that area or areas where the materials and equipment for the Solar Energy Generating Facility (as described in the Scope of Work) shall be installed and/or used to perform the Work.

1.43 **Site Host**: "Site Host" shall mean the entity, which is the landlord under the Lease and the offtaker under the PPA, as identified on the first page of this Contract.

1.44 **Scheduled Substantial Completion Date**: "Scheduled Substantial Completion Date" means the date identified on the first page of this Contract, as such date may be extended in accordance with the terms of this Contract.

1.45 **Scope of Work**: "Scope of Work" shall mean the Work to be performed hereunder by Integrator, and/or Integrator's subcontractors, pursuant to the Scope of Work (as amended by Change Orders), attached hereto as **Attachment B,** and in accordance with the terms and conditions of this Contract.

1.46 **Solar Energy Generating Facility**: "Solar Energy Generating Facility" ("SEGF") shall mean the entirety of the solar generating system, its electrical and mechanical components, mounting or tracking components, inverter(s), modules, meter(s), monitoring components, conduit, and other elements installed in the nature of the Work as further described in **Attachment B** and in accordance in specifications described in **Attachment C.**

1.47 **Specifications**: "Specifications" shall mean such references, materials, methods, design and engineering requirements, safety requirements and other such standards of workmanship and materials as described in **Attachment C.**

1.48 **Submittals**: "Submittals" shall mean all documents required to be provided to Developer by Integrator as described in **Attachment C.**

1.49 **Substantial Completion**: "Substantial Completion" or "Substantially Complete" shall mean the stage in the progress of the Work or portion of the Work, where the Solar Energy Generating Facility is substantially and materially complete and has been fully designed, constructed and equipped in accordance with the Scope of Work and the Specifications, and is ready to be used for its intended purpose and this milestone shall be deemed achieved when the Commissioning Tests have been completed successfully in accordance with **Attachment F.**

1.50 **Substantial Completion Date**: "Substantial Completion Date" shall mean the date stated in the Certificate of Substantial Completion.

1.51 **Support Structure**: "Support Structure" shall mean the rooftop, ground-based or floating mounting system, elevated structure or tracking system that will hold the solar modules of the Solar Energy Generating Facility on the Site, and all supports thereto.

1.52 **Time**: "Time" shall mean the time period within which Integrator shall complete the Work in accordance with the Project Schedule.

1.53 **Utility**: For purposes of this Contract, the parties agree that the "Utility" is the entity so identified on the first page of this Contract.

1.54 **Utility Interconnection Approval**: "Utility Interconnection Approval" shall have the meaning written approval by the Utility to interconnect and operate the SEGF in parallel to the Utility's grid.

1.55 **Work**: "Work" shall mean the design, engineering, permit attainment, procurement, construction and installation of the Solar Energy Generating Facility and all other services to be provided by Integrator hereunder, in accordance with the terms hereof, including the Scope of Work and Specifications and Submittals.

SECTION 2. PERFORMANCE OF THE WORK

2.1 **Performance of Work.** Integrator shall perform the Work in accordance with the provisions of this Contract. Such Work shall be performed in an expeditious manner that is consistent with the standard of care of highly skilled contractors performing work similar in scope (and geographic location) to the Work. Integrator shall ensure that all Work is performed in accordance with applicable equipment manufacturers' requirements, including all requirements necessary to preserve and maintain in effect any and all warranties and, if applicable, any performance guarantees with respect to such equipment. Integrator shall perform the Work in accordance with all workmanship and materials specifications and safety requirements as defined in Attachment C.

SECTION 3. DEVELOPER OBLIGATIONS

3.1 **Data Acquisition System Interconnectivity Requirements.** Developer shall be responsible for obtaining for the benefit of the Solar Energy Generating Facility, at Developer's sole cost and expense, the Internet communication service necessary for the operation of the Data Acquisition System, up to a defined Network Access Point, which requirements are more specifically detailed on Attachment G attached hereto.

3.2 **Site Host Information.** Developer shall use commercially reasonable efforts to cause Site Host to provide the following documents and to perform the following acts within ten (10) calendar days of Integrator's request therefor:

(a) Furnish all surveys or other information in Site Host's possession that describe the physical characteristics, legal limitations, and utility locations in and around the Site;

(b) Disclose any prior environmental review documentation and all known information in Site Host's possession concerning subsurface conditions, including without limitation the existence of any known Hazardous Substances, in or around the general area of the Site where the Work will be performed pursuant to the Scope of Work;

(c) Supply Integrator with all relevant information in Developer and Site Host's possession, including any structural or other relevant as-built drawings and photographs, of prior construction undertaken in the general area of the Site where the Work will be performed; and

(d) Obtain any and all easements, zoning variances, planning approvals, including any resolution of any environmental impact issues, and any other legal authorizations regarding utilization of the Site reasonably necessary for the execution of the Work.

3.3 **Integrator Assistance**

Developer shall also do the following:

(a) Attend the regularly scheduled progress meetings and participate as needed regarding scheduling of work.

(b) Participate in the job inspection walk-through(s) with Integrator and the subcontractor(s) to determine Substantial Completion. Upon approval of the physical aspects of the Work, and verification of the receipt of all required submittals, sign the Certificate of Substantial Completion.

(c) Provide knowledgeable staff to participate in the training programs, which will be scheduled in advance for proper coordination.

(d) Perform a final walk-through of the project to determine Final Completion status of the physical aspects of the Work.

(e) Upon receipt of the Submittals, verification of Punch List completion, and approval of the completion of the entire Scope of Work as listed in Attachment B according to the Specifications as listed in Attachment C, including training, sign a Certificate of Final Completion for the Work.

3.4 **Expeditious Manner.** All obligations of Developer hereunder shall be undertaken in an expeditious manner (and otherwise in accordance with the terms of the Contract) such that Integrator is not unreasonably delayed in its performance of the Work hereunder.

3.6 **Point of Contact; Response Periods.** Developer shall designate a single-point representative with whom Integrator shall consult on a reasonable, regular basis and who is authorized to act on Developer's behalf for all purposes in connection with this Contract and the Work, other than amendment of this Contract. Developer may from time to time change the designated representative by providing notice thereof to Integrator. Except as otherwise provided herein, Developer's representative shall render decisions in a timely manner (in no event longer than ten (10) business days) with regard to any documents submitted by Integrator and to other requests made by Integrator in order to avoid unreasonable delay in the orderly and sequential progress of the Work.

SECTION 4. PAYMENTS

Developer agrees to pay Integrator in accordance with Attachment E and this Section 4.

4.1 **Milestone Progress Payments.** As Project Milestones are achieved, after the appropriate Notice To Proceed has been issued, Integrator shall submit to Developer its Application for Payment based upon the payment milestone(s) achieved and calculated in accordance with the progress payment schedule in **Attachment E.** Developer shall review and respond to each Application for Payment within five (5) calendar days after Developer's receipt thereof ("Approval Date"). If such Application for Payment is approved by Developer, Developer shall pay the amount invoiced by Integrator in such Application for Payment within fifteen (15) days from the Approval Date ("Due Date"), less a ten percent (10%) retainage amount ("Retainage"). Applications for Payment shall be deemed approved if Developer fails to approve or dispute such before the Approval Date. If Developer fails to pay an approved invoice by the Due Date, Developer shall be liable for interest on the outstanding amount at a rate of 10% per annum.

4.2 **Final Payment.** Integrator shall deliver the final Application for Payment within thirty (30) days after Final Completion, which shall be accompanied by a final payment conditional lien waiver and release substantially in the form provided in **Attachment H** from Integrator and each subcontractor and supplier. In addition to any other amounts owed by Developer to Integrator hereunder, Developer shall release the balance of the Retainage to Integrator with the final payment hereunder (the "Final Payment").

4.3 **Disputed Invoices/Late Payments.** If Developer disputes any Application for Payment, or part thereof, or any supporting documentation related thereto, or otherwise disputes any Request for Payment, Developer shall make full payment to Integrator when required in **Section 4.1** above, less any portions of the Application for Payment amount in dispute, and shall provide to Integrator a written explanation of the basis for the dispute and the amount of the Application for Payment being withheld related to the dispute, no later than the Approval Date.

4.4 **Unconditional Lien Waivers.** Within fifteen (15) days after receipt of each progress payment, if so requested by Developer, and the Final Payment, Integrator shall provide (and shall cause its suppliers and subcontractors, and their subcontractors to provide) to Developer an unconditional lien waiver and release (related to progress payment or Final Payment as applicable) substantially in the form provided in Attachment H.

4.5 **Dated Down Copies of Lien Waivers and Releases.** Within fifteen (15) calendar days after Developer's request therefor, Integrator shall provide (and shall cause its subcontractors and suppliers to provide) to Developer additional lien waivers and releases (dated as of the date requested by Developer) with regard to payments previously made by Developer hereunder for the purpose of assisting Developer with any debt or equity financing for the Solar Energy Generating Facility.

SECTION 4. WARRANTY/LIMITATION OF LIABILITY

4.1 **System Warranty.** Integrator warrants and guarantees to Developer that, for the duration of the period commencing on the date of the Certificate of Substantial Completion and continuing for a period of ten (10) years from such date (the "System Warranty Period"), all Work will be substantially free from defects in design, workmanship, materials and Equipment. This warranty does not warrant a specified level of energy output in the Solar Energy Generating Facility. Any such warranty shall be as set forth in a separate degradation warranty of the PV module supplier.

4.2 **Manufacturer's Warranties.** Integrator shall, for the protection of Developer, use commercially reasonable efforts to obtain from all vendors and subcontractors from which Integrator procures machinery, equipment or materials or services, warranties and guarantees with respect to such machinery, equipment, materials or services, which shall be made available to Developer to the full extent of the terms thereof. Integrator shall at all times perform its construction, installation, commissioning, operation or maintenance activities in a manner consistent with all such warranties and shall not perform any actions that may violate or void such warranties. All applicable manufacturers' warranties that can be should be extended to ten (10) years if the standard warranty is not ten (10) years in length. A list of all applicable manufacturers' warranties is attached hereto as **Attachment J.**

4.3 **Repair or Replacement.** The sole and exclusive remedy for proven defects under the warranty described in Section 5.1 shall be replacement of the defective Work at Integrator's sole cost and expense. At Integrator's option, an alternative remedy shall be prompt rework or repair of the equipment and/or component to remove any defect at Integrator's sole cost and expense. Developer shall give Integrator prompt written notice as soon as practicable following discovery of any defects. Integrator shall have no responsibility under the warranty described in **Section 5.1** for any consumable items, including, but not limited to fuses, batteries, lubricants and filters.

4.4 **Warranty Claim.** Developer may request inspection of the Solar Energy Generating Facility by making a claim under this warranty. To make a claim, Developer must:

(a) Identify a performance threshold warning or a fault condition in the Solar Energy Generating Facility.
(b) Conduct preliminary troubleshooting in accordance with the Operations and Maintenance Manual.
(c) Contact Integrator Service Manager or designated support person.
(d) Perform reasonable troubleshooting of the Solar Energy Generating Facility requested by the Integrator Service Manager or designated support person.
(e) Notify Integrator in writing, through paper or electronic correspondence, including electronic mail, that service is requested in response to a claim under this warranty.

5.6 **Integrator Response.** *Integrator will respond to a claim under this warranty by acknowledging receipt of a written service request within twenty-four (24) hours following receipt of a service request and providing Developer with an action plan to remedy the defect within seventy-two (72) hours following receipt of the service request. Integrator will complete repair or replacement of the defect in accordance with the action plan no later than the (10) days following receipt of the written service request subject to the availability of replacement parts from Integrator's third-party supplier. If it is determined that the Developer's written service request is excluded or limited under Section 5.6 or provisions elsewhere in Contract, Developer will be liable for any reasonable labor and material expenses incurred by Integrator. In this case, Integrator will invoice Developer for any reasonable labor or material expenses incurred.*

5.7 **Warranty Exclusions.** The warranty provided herein does not cover damage, malfunctions or service failures caused by:

(a) Failure to follow Integrator's operation or maintenance instructions as defined in the Operations and Maintenance Manual.
(b) Repair, modification, or movement of the Solar Energy Generating Facility or components thereof by someone other than a service technician approved by Integrator.
(c) Abuse, misuse, or negligent acts.
(d) Damage or deteriorated performance of the Solar Energy Generating Facility caused by electrical surges, lightning, fire, flood, extreme weather, pest damage, accidental breakage, actions of third parties and other events or accidents outside Developer's reasonable control and not arising under normal operating conditions.

5.8 **Warranty and Guarantee Limitations.** *EXCEPT FOR THE WARRANTY IN THIS SECTION 5, DEVELOPER EXPRESSLY*

AGREES THAT INTEGRATOR MAKES NO OTHER WARRANTIES OR GUARANTEES IN CONNECTION WITH THE SALE AND INSTALLATION OF EQUIPMENT AND MATERIALS PROVIDED HEREUNDER WHETHER EXPRESS OR IMPLIED, ORAL OR WRITTEN. INTEGRATOR SPECIFICALLY DISCLAIMS ANY IMPLIED WARRANTIES OF MERCHANTABILITY OR FITNESS FOR A PARTICULAR PURPOSE.

SECTION 6. GOVERNMENTAL PERMITS AND APPROVALS; COORDINATION

6.1 **Permits and Approvals.** Integrator will obtain all permits and approvals required for the construction, installation, and start-up and operation of the Solar Energy Generating Facility and the performance the Work hereunder, to include but not limited to municipal building, planning, fire marshal, architectural or design review, landlord or other association or CC&R approvals, nighttime operations, or any other specialty permits, in each case, when and as required for the performance of the Work in accordance with the Project Schedule. Developer will provide reasonable cooperation and assistance to Integrator in obtaining all such permits and approvals.

6.3 **Coordination During Installation.** Developer and Integrator shall cooperate with each other in an effort to coordinate the activities of Integrator and Integrator's subcontractors and suppliers with those of Developer, its employees, agents and contractors.

6.4 **Coordination for Special Inspections.** Integrator shall coordinate the inspections of any governmental or independent entities with jurisdiction over the Solar Energy Generating Facility as well as any inspections required by the Independent Engineer, Utility, insurance company representative, incentive program representative, manufacturers' representative, etc.

6.5 **Incentive Programs.** If requested, Integrator shall prepare and submit to the applicable agencies, on behalf of Developer and/or Site Host (as applicable), or assist Developer in doing so directly, all applications, proof of progress submittals, or claim forms and documentation necessary for any Environmental or Financial Incentives; provided that Developer shall have the opportunity to review, comment on, and approve all such applications and documentation prior to submission by Integrator. If Developer shall decide to prepare and submit such documents, Integrator will coordinate and cooperate in the timely completion of said documents.

SECTION 7. OWNERSHIP OF CERTAIN PROPERTY

7.1 **Ownership of Certain Proprietary Property Rights.** Developer shall not, by virtue of this Contract, acquire any interest in any formulas, patterns, devices, trade secrets, secret inventions or processes, copyrights, patents, other intellectual or proprietary rights, or similar items which are the property of Integrator, whether or not used or provided to Developer in connection with the Solar Energy Generating Facility; provided, that Integrator hereby grants to Developer a perpetual, irrevocable royalty-free license for any and all software or other intellectual property rights necessary for Developer to operate, maintain, improve or repair the Solar Energy Generating Facility in a manner that will yield maximum energy output from the Solar Energy Generating Facility; provided, further, that in no event shall Developer use such items for the benefit of any other project or share any such items with any third parties, except as may be necessary for the efficient operation of the Solar Energy Generating Facility.

7.2 **Ownership of Environmental and Financial Incentives and Environmental Attributes.** Developer shall own, and may assign or sell in its sole and absolute discretion, all right, title and interest in all Environmental Attributes and/or Environmental and Financial Incentives associated with or resulting from the development and installation of the Solar Energy Generating Facility or the production, sale, purchase or use of the energy output of the Solar Energy Generating Facility including, without limitation, all Environmental and Financial Incentives and Environmental Attributes.

SECTION 8. LOCATION AND ACCESS

Developer shall provide space at the Site for the performance of the Work, and the installation, storage, and operation of any equipment and materials. As described in Attachment A, Developer shall provide Integrator with the right to access the Site, to the extent that the Site Host has granted to Developer the right to access the Site in the Lease, in order for Integrator and subcontractors to perform the Work during regular business hours, or such other reasonable hours as may be requested by Integrator and acceptable to Developer and Site Host. Integrator acknowledges it has familiarized itself with the Lease and Developer's access rights thereunder (including any restrictions in connection therewith) and that such access rights are sufficient to enable Integrator to perform the Work in accordance with this Contract.

SECTION 9. PROJECT IMPLEMENTATION - GENERAL

9.1 **Project Schedule.** The initial Project Schedule is attached hereto as Table 1 in **Attachment D**. Such schedule is preliminary in nature and shall be adjusted by mutual agreement of the Parties during the construction documentation phase of the Work. Upon such mutual approval thereof, the adjusted Project Schedule shall replace the existing Project Schedule in **Attachment D**.

9.2 **Project Meetings/Status Updates.** Integrator will meet with Developer regularly to review equipment, scope of work, and installation plans that relate to the design, engineering and construction of the Solar Energy Generating Facility.

SECTION 10. FINAL DESIGN AND PERMITTING PHASE

10.2 **Commencement of SEGF.** Upon Developer's issuance of a written Notice to Proceed ("Notice to Proceed" or "NTP"), Integrator shall prepare any necessary designs, drawings, and specifications, as well as feasibility and configuration assessments, environmental assessments, and other inspections of the Site. Integrator shall deliver draft design drawings and specifications to Developer for review and approval, which shall not be unreasonably withheld. Developer shall diligently review and respond to each submission by Integrator in an effort to finalize the Construction Documents as quickly as reasonably possible. If Developer fails to respond within ten (10) calendar days of receipt of any Construction Document, it shall be deemed to have approved the applicable Construction Documents.

10.4 **Notice to Proceed to Permit Application Submittal.** Upon Developer's approval of Construction Documents, Developer shall within ten (10) calendar days issue a Notice to Proceed to Permit Application Submittal which shall release the final design for permit submittal. Once a Notice to Proceed to Permit Application Submittal is issued, Developer shall not unreasonably withhold its consent to any modifications thereto that may be requested by any governmental or quasi-governmental agency with jurisdiction over the SEGF and/or the Work, excepting any changes that materially affect the tilt, azimuth or number of photovoltaic modules, or other aspects of the original design that may affect the Contract Price or the Estimated Annual Energy Production or Price and Performance Ratios. The Parties expressly agree that Developer's approval of any plans, designs, drawings, specifications or any other items hereunder shall in no way relieve Integrator of its obligations under this Contract

10.6 **Notice to Proceed to Procurement and Construction.** Upon Developer's approval of Construction Documents, Developer shall issue a Notice to Proceed to Procurement and Construction which shall provide approval to proceed to procurement and construction. Upon receipt of the Notice to Proceed to Procurement and Construction, Integrator shall facilitate, or cooperate with Developer in its efforts to facilitate, a kick-off meeting with the Site Host, Developer, Integrator, and any other relevant parties.

SECTION 11. PROCUREMENT AND CONSTRUCTION PHASE

11.1 **General Provisions.** Upon receipt of the Notice to Proceed to Procurement and Construction and after securing all necessary permits, Integrator shall commence the construction of the Solar Energy Generating Facility in accordance with the final Construction Documents. The construction shall be performed by Integrator and/or one or more licensed subcontractors qualified to perform the Work. The construction shall be performed in accordance with all Applicable Laws and Applicable Permits, and all manufacturer requirements for the maintenance of all applicable warranties. Prior to beginning construction, Integrator shall provide Developer with a copy of Integrator's safety plan, as well as an evaluation and appropriate documentation of the safety record of any licensed subcontractor that will be performing work on the Solar Energy Generating Facility.

11.2 **Integrator's Responsibilities During Procurement and Construction Phase.** As an independent contractor to Developer, Integrator will be responsible for providing, or causing to be provided by Integrator's subcontractor(s), all labor, materials, equipment, tools, transportation, security and other facilities and services necessary for the proper execution, construction, and completion of the Work as defined in the Scope of Work and any Change Orders. Integrator shall purchase, in advance of commencement of the Work, all necessary materials and supplies necessary for the performance of the Work. Integrator will also be responsible for all means, methods, techniques, sequences, and procedures employed for the construction required by the final Construction Documents.

11.3 Integrator shall use its best efforts to coordinate construction activities and perform the Work to minimize disruption to Site Host's operations at the Site. Integrator shall provide at least fourteen (14) calendar days written notice to Site Host of any planned power outages that will be necessary for the construction. Integrator shall cooperate with Site Host in scheduling such outages, and Developer agrees to cause Site Host to provide its reasonable approval of any scheduled outage.

11.4 Integrator shall be responsible for initiating and maintaining safety precautions and programs in connection with the Work. Integrator shall take reasonable precautions for the safety of, and shall provide reasonable protection to prevent damage, injury, or loss to: (1) employees of Integrator and subcontractors performing Work under this Contract; (2) Integrator's property and other materials to be incorporated for the Solar Energy Generating Facility, under the care, custody, and control of Integrator or its subcontractors; and (3) other property at or adjacent to the Site not designated for removal, relocation, or replacement during the course of construction.

11.5 Integrator shall maintain in good order at the Site copies of the Scope of Work, all Change Orders, this Contract, one record copy of all drawings, specifications, product data, samples, manufacturer's installation, operation & maintenance manuals, and other pertinent construction-related documents.

11.6 Integrator shall provide weekly progress photographs to Developer in digital format.

11.7 If the Solar Energy Generating Facility is in whole or in part ground mounted, or materials are to be stored on-site, then prior to the arrival of equipment and materials at the Site, the Integrator shall install a 6'0" fenced secured area and provide 24-hour security for the storage of such equipment and materials. The size and location of the secured area shall be subject to the approval of Developer and the Site Host, which approval shall not be unreasonably withheld, conditioned or delayed.

11.8 During the construction phase of the Work, Integrator shall conduct all Commissioning tests that are scheduled to occur prior to Substantial Completion in accordance with the terms of the Commissioning Schedule attached hereto as Attachment F. Integrator shall provide notice to Developer of any scheduled test(s) of installed equipment, and Developer and/or its designees shall have the right to be present at any or all such tests conducted by Integrator, any subcontractor, and/or manufacturers of the equipment. Integrator shall be responsible for correcting and/or adjusting all deficiencies in the Solar Energy Generating Facility and equipment operations that Integrator provided and installed that may be observed during equipment commissioning procedures.

11.9 Integrator shall organize and conduct regularly scheduled progress meetings throughout the installation period during which Integrator shall update Developer as to the status of the Solar Energy Generating Facility, including cost and scheduling matters. Such meetings shall occur as frequently as may be reasonably requested by Developer and may occur telephonically if requested by Developer.

11.10 **Independent Review by Developer.** Any independent review of the construction shall be undertaken at Developer's sole expense, and it shall be performed in a timely manner so as to not unreasonably delay the orderly progress of Integrator's Work. Neither any independent review of the construction by Developer nor any approval provided by Developer under this Contract shall relieve Integrator of any of its obligations or responsibilities hereunder.

11.11 **Changes.**

(a) Developer may request by Change Order any Change in the Work, whether such Changes are modifications, accelerations, alterations, additions or deletions. All such Changes shall be made in accordance with this Section 11.4 and shall be considered, for all purposes of this Contract, as part of the Work. Integrator shall perform all Changes to the Work included in Change Orders issued by Developer in accordance with this Section 11.4

(b) It is the desire of the Parties to keep changes to the work and to the construction of the support structure at a minimum; but the Parties recognize that such changes may become necessary and agree that they shall be handled pursuant to this Section. Integrator requested Changes and/or modifications to the Scope of Work shall be authorized by a written Change Order signed by both Developer and Integrator. To clarify, work pursuant to such a Change Order shall begin only upon Integrator's receipt of Developer's signed change order. The Change Order shall state the change and/or modification to the Scope of Work, any additional compensation to be paid, or extension of time, if needed, to Integrator to perform such changes and/or modifications. Integrator will use its reasonable efforts to continue other portions of the work not affected or impacted by such proposed Change Order until such time as the Change order is resolved.

(c) Changes to the Estimated Annual Energy Production or Price and Performance Ratios will require an amendment to the Contract Amount in such an amount that the Price and Performance Ratios are maintained in such a way that the amended Contract Amount divided by the amended Estimated Annual Energy Production will be equal to or lower than the original ratio described in Attachment E.

11.12 **Minor Changes to Scope of Work.** Integrator shall have authority to make minor changes without obtaining Developer's prior approval, provided that any such minor changes (i) do not change the total Contract Amount, (ii) do not materially impact the Project Schedule (including Integrator's ability to achieve Substantial Completion on or before the Scheduled Substantial Completion Date), and (iii) are consistent with the intent of the final Construction Documents. Integrator shall promptly inform Developer, in writing, of any such minor changes made during the course of the Work and shall make available to Developer at the Site a set of as-built drawings that will be kept current to show those minor changes. For clarification purposes, minor changes do not include any changes to agreed-upon manufacturer or type or quantity of modules, inverters, tracker, balance of system components, DAS system, or other aspects that would impact the Estimated Annual Energy Production or Price and Performance Ratios.

11.13 **Hazardous Substances.** Integrator shall promptly provide written notice to Developer if Integrator observes any Hazardous Substance, as defined herein, at or around the Site during the course of construction or installation of any equipment that have not been addressed as part of the Scope of Work. Integrator shall comply with all Applicable Laws in connection with the use, handling, and disposal of any Hazardous Substances in the performance of its Work. Integrator shall indemnify, defend, and hold Developer harmless from and against any and all claims and costs of whatever nature, including but not limited to, consultants' and attorneys' fees, damages for bodily injury and property damage, fines, penalties, cleanup costs, costs associated with delay or work stoppage, and third party claims that in any way result from or arise from such Integrator owned or generated hazardous materials and substances, except for liabilities due to Developer's, or its agents representatives, and employees', negligence or willful misconduct in handling, disturbance, or release of Hazardous Substances. This indemnification shall survive any termination of this Contract.

SECTION 12. PROJECT COMPLETION

12.1 **Application for Substantial Completion.** When Integrator considers the Work to be Substantially Complete in accordance with the Contract Documents, Integrator shall issue to Developer an Application for Substantial Completion, together with a Punchlist prepared by Integrator for Developer's approval, which Punchlist shall identify the items of remaining Work to be completed prior to Final Completion. Developer shall, within fifteen (15) business days of receipt of the Application for Substantial Completion and Punchlist, review the Work for the sole purpose of determining that it is Substantially Complete and in conformance with the Scope of Work, final Construction Documents and any Change Orders and review the Punchlist to confirm its accuracy. In connection with such review, Developer may (a) engage Developer's Commissioning Engineer to evaluate the Solar Energy Generating Facility for compliance with the requirements for Commissioning and to review and evaluate the proposed Punchlist, and/or (b) give written notice to Integrator of additional actions necessary before the Work is Substantially Complete and/or any necessary modifications to the Punchlist. Upon receipt of notice from Developer that the Work is not Substantially Complete or that the Punchlist needs modifications, Integrator shall promptly complete any incomplete items, remedy defective items and/or make such modifications to the Punchlist (as applicable), after which Integrator shall submit a revised Application for Substantial Completion, together with the Punchlist (revised as necessary). Developer shall re-inspect all Work completed or remedied by Integrator, and cause Developer's Commissioning Engineer to perform its Commissioning evaluation and review of the Punchlist within five (5) business days of Developer's receipt of such revised Application for Substantial Completion and Punchlist. Upon Developer's determination that the Work is Substantially Complete and the Punchlist is in final form, Developer shall deliver a Certificate of Substantial Completion to Integrator.

12.2 **Final Completion.** When Integrator considers the Work, including the Punchlist, to be fully complete in accordance with the Scope of Work, Integrator shall notify Developer that Integrator has achieved Final Completion of the Work and that the Work is ready for final inspection. Developer shall inspect the Work to verify the status of Final Completion within five (5) business days after its receipt of Integrator's certification that the Work is ready for inspection. If Developer determines that any Work is incomplete and/or defective, Developer shall promptly notify Integrator in writing of such incomplete and/or defective work, itemizing and describing such remaining items with reasonable particularity. Integrator shall promptly complete any incomplete items or remedy defective items after which Integrator shall provide written notice to Developer that the Work is fully complete. Developer shall re-inspect all work completed or remedied by Integrator within five (5) business days of Integrator's notice that the Work is fully complete. When Developer agrees that Integrator has achieved Final Completion of the Work in accordance with the Scope of Work and Contract Documents, which shall not occur prior to Developer's receipt of a completed Operations and Maintenance manual from the Integrator (which includes module and inverter warranty cards signed by Developer), Developer shall give Integrator written notice of acceptance of the Work and Final Completion and shall issue a Certificate of Final Completion to Integrator. At such time, Developer shall pay Integrator any remaining Contract Amount due and Retainage withheld by Developer.

SECTION 13. INDEMNIFICATION/INSURANCE

13.1 **Indemnification.**

(a) Integrator shall fully indemnify, hold harmless, and defend Developer, its officers, employees, and agents (collectively, the "Indemnified Party") from and against any and all actions, claims, demands, damages, disability, losses, expenses (including, but not limited to, reasonable attorneys' fees and other defense costs) and liabilities of any nature (including, but not limited to property damage and personal and bodily injury, sickness and disease) to the extent caused by Integrator's (i) breach of any obligation, representation or warranty contained herein, and/or (ii) negligence or willful misconduct (including any such breach, negligence or willful misconduct by Integrator's officers, employees, subcontractors and agents) except to the extent caused by Developer's sole negligence.

(b) Developer shall fully indemnify, hold harmless, release and defend Integrator, its officers, employees, and agents (collectively, the "Indemnified Party") from and against any and all actions, claims, demands, damages, disability, losses, expenses (including, but not limited to, reasonable attorneys' fees and other defense costs) and liabilities of any nature (including, but not limited to property damage and personal and bodily injury, sickness and disease) to the extent caused by Developer's (i) breach of any obligation, representation or warranty contained herein, and/or (ii) negligence or willful misconduct (including any such breach, negligence or willful misconduct by Developer's officers, employees, subcontractors and agents) except to the extent caused by Integrator's sole negligence.

13.2 **Indemnity Against Intellectual Property Infringement.** Integrator shall defend, indemnify and hold harmless Developer, its contractors and affiliates against all liabilities, claims, losses, damages and expenses (including attorneys' fees and court costs) arising from any claim or legal action for unauthorized disclosure or use of any trade secrets, or of patent, copyright or trademark infringement arising from Integrator's performance that either (a) concerns any equipment, materials, supplies, or other items provided by Integrator under this Contract, (b) is based upon or arises out of the performance of the Work by Integrator or any subcontractor or (c) is based upon or arises out of the design or construction and use of any item or unit specified by Integrator under this Contract. Developer shall provide Integrator with reasonably prompt notice of any claim or legal action relating to the foregoing. The indemnification obligations in this Section 13.2 shall survive the termination/completion of this Contract.

13.3 **Integrator Insurance.** Integrator shall maintain until Final Completion, the insurance coverage outlined in **Attachment K,** and all such other insurance as required by applicable law. Evidence of coverage will be provided to Developer on an annual basis, prior to policy expiration, via a certificate of insurance.

SECTION 14. FORCE MAJEURE

Neither Party shall be considered to be in default and shall be excused in the performance of any material obligation under this Contract (other than the obligation to make payments) when a failure of performance shall be due to an event of Force Majeure. Such excuse from failure of performance shall be solely for the duration and to the extent of such event of Force Majeure. Neither Party shall be relieved of its obligation to perform if such failure is due to causes arising out of its own negligence or due to removable or remediable causes which it fails to remove or remedy within a reasonable time period. Either Party rendered unable to fulfill any of its obligations under this Contract by reason of an event of Force Majeure shall give notice of such fact to the other Party within ten (10) days after it becomes aware that such Force Majeure event will (or may) have an impact on such Party's performance under this Contract.

SECTION 15. EVENTS OF DEFAULT

15.1 **Events of Default by Developer.** Each of the following events or conditions shall constitute an "Event of Default" by Developer:

(a) Any failure by Developer to perform or comply with the terms and conditions of this Contract (other than a payment default), including breach of any covenant contained herein, if such failure continues for fifteen (15) calendar days after notice to Developer demanding that such failure to perform be cured; provided that if such cure cannot be effected in fifteen (15) calendar days, then such fifteen (15) calendar day period shall be extended for a reasonable period of time (not to exceed 30 days), provided (i) any such failure or breach is reasonably susceptible to being cured within 60 days and (ii) Developer has commenced to cure such failure within the initial 15-day period and diligently and continuously prosecutes such cure to completion; or

(b) Any representation or warranty made by Developer in this Contract is false or misleading in any material respect when made; or

(c) Any failure by Developer to pay any undisputed amount to Integrator which is not paid within ten (10) business days of written notice from Integrator that the undisputed amount is past due.

15.2 **Events of Default by Integrator**. Each of the following events or conditions shall constitute an "Event of Default" by Integrator:

(a) Any failure by Integrator to perform or comply with the terms and conditions of this Contract (other than a payment default), including breach of any covenant contained herein, if such failure continues for thirty (30) calendar days after notice to Integrator demanding that such failure to perform be cured; provided, that if such cure cannot be effected in thirty (30) calendar days, then such thirty (30) calendar day period shall be extended for a reasonable period of time (not to exceed 60 days), provided (i) any such failure or breach is reasonably susceptible to being cured within 60 days and (ii) Integrator has commenced to cure such failure within the initial 30-day period and diligently and continuously prosecutes such cure to completion; or

(b) Any representation or warranty made by Integrator in this Contract was false or misleading in any material respect when made; or

(c) Any lien is placed upon the Solar Energy Generating Facility, the Site, the Work or any equipment by Integrator or any subcontractor, laborer, or supplier of Integrator, which is not removed by Integrator within twenty (20) business days of Integrator's receipt of notice from Developer of the existence of such lien; provided that Integrator shall not be required to remove such lien unless Integrator has been duly paid for undisputed Work in accordance with this Contract (including Attachment E).

SECTION 16. REMEDIES UPON DEFAULT

16.1 **Remedies upon Default by Developer.** If an Event of Default by Developer occurs, Integrator will be entitled to obtain any available legal or equitable remedies including recovery of amounts due and unpaid by Developer and/or damages, consisting of Integrator's out-of-pocket costs, and reasonable overhead and profit losses incurred by reason of such Event of Default, but excluding any consequential damages.

16.3 **Remedies Upon Default by Integrator.** If an Event of Default by Integrator occurs, Developer shall be entitled to obtain any available legal or equitable remedies including recovery of amounts due and unpaid by Integrator and/or damages, consisting of Developer's out-of-pocket losses incurred by reason of such Event of Default but excluding any consequential damages.

16.5 **Liquidated Damages.** Integrator acknowledges that Developer will incur damages if Integrator fails to meet its performance obligations under this Agreement; particularly if Integrator fails to perform its obligations timely or fails to comply with security requirements during construction, Developer may incur damages that are difficult to ascertain and Integrator agrees to pay the following liquidated damages. The parties agree that the amounts set forth below are reasonable estimates of Developer's actual damages for each case of Integrator's non-performance and Integrator agrees to pay such amounts within ten (10) days after written request from Developer and allows Developer, in the alternative, to deduct such amounts from any amount otherwise due Integrator under this Agreement.

1. In the event Substantial Completion is delayed beyond the Scheduled Substantial Completion Date due to any failure by Integrator to perform or comply with the terms and conditions of this Contract, Integrator shall pay Developer an amount equal to [__] for each day of delay ***[Use Note: harmonize with schedule options in Attachment D and avoid duplication of damages described in part (b)].***
2. In the event Substantial Completion is delayed beyond the Scheduled Substantial Completion Date due to any failure by Integrator to perform or comply with the terms and conditions of this Contract, including breach of any covenant contained herein, and Developer loses, partially or entirely, any Environmental or Financial

Incentive due to such delay, Integrator shall pay to Developer, in addition to any amounts stated elsewhere in this Agreement, the Estimated Incentive Amount, or a portion thereof, if the loss of Environmental or Financial Incentives is partial.

SECTION 17. ASSIGNMENT

17.1 **Consent Requirements.** Neither Party shall assign this Contract or any of its rights hereunder without the prior written consent of the other Party, which consent shall not be unreasonably withheld or delayed. Notwithstanding the foregoing, Developer may, without the consent of Integrator (and without relieving itself from liability hereunder), (i) transfer, pledge or assign this Contract as security for any financing and/or to an affiliated special purpose entity created for financing or tax credit purposes related to the Solar Energy Generating Facility and the Support Structure; (ii) transfer or assign this Contract to any person or entity succeeding to all or substantially all of the assets of Developer, provided, however, that any such assignee shall agree to be bound by the terms and conditions hereof; or (iii) assign its rights under this Contract to a successor entity in a merger or acquisition transaction, provided, however, that any such assignee shall agree to be bound by the terms and conditions hereof. Any assignment made in contravention of this clause shall be void and unenforceable.

17.2 **Lender Assignments.** With respect to an assignment pursuant to clause (i) in the second sentence of Section 17.1 above, Integrator acknowledges and agrees that, upon receipt of written direction by a financing-transaction assignee or secured party of Developer ("Lender"), and notwithstanding any instructions to the contrary from Developer, Integrator will recognize Lender, or any third party to whom Lender has assigned the rights of Developer under this Contract, as the proper and lawful customer under this Contract and such Lender (or assignee of Lender) shall be fully entitled to receive the rights and benefits of Developer hereunder so long as Lender (or its assignee) performs the obligations of Developer hereunder and Integrator shall tender performance of any and all other covenants to be performed by Integrator under this Contract to and for the benefit of Lender (or Lender's assignee) and as the Lender (or Lender's assignee) may direct in the future. Integrator shall be protected and shall incur no liability in acting or proceeding in good faith upon any written notice and direction from Lender or which Integrator shall in good faith believe to be from Lender. Integrator shall be under no duty to make any investigation or inquiry as to any statements contained or matters referred to in any such notice and direction. Integrator further agrees that it shall provide such additional cooperation as Developer may reasonably request in connection with Developer's efforts to obtain financing for the Solar Energy Generating Facility, including execution of such written consents and acknowledgements as may be reasonably requested by Developer or its financing parties for purposes of giving effect to the provisions of this Section 17.2 and Section 17.3.

17.3 **Lender Consent.** Integrator shall provide reasonable cooperation and further Assurances in connection with Developer's efforts to obtain debt or equity financing for the Solar Energy Generating Facility. Without limiting the foregoing, within ten (10) business days after Developer's written request, Integrator shall execute and deliver to Developer a written consent substantially in the form as to be provided by Developer and acceptable to Developer's Lender.

SECTION 18. SUBCONTRACTORS

18.1 **Authority to Subcontract.** Integrator may delegate its duties and performance under this Contract, and shall have the right to enter into agreements with any subcontractors and other service providers to perform the Work hereunder; provided, however that such delegations do not relieve Integrator from liability or its obligations to Developer under this Contract. Prior to the start of construction on the Site, Integrator shall submit to Developer a list of subcontractors and vendors for Developer's prior review and approval, which review and approval shall not be unreasonably withheld, delayed or conditioned. The approval or rejection of any subcontractor or vendor by Developer shall not relieve Integrator of any of its responsibilities under this Contract nor shall it be the basis for additional charges to Developer. Integrator shall bind every subcontractor to the terms and provisions of this Contract to the extent applicable to the subcontractor's work.

18.2 **Prompt Payment of Subcontractors.** Integrator shall promptly pay when due all amounts payable to its subcontractors for labor and materials furnished in the performance of this Contract and shall ensure that the Solar Energy Generating Facility and the Site remain free of any liens arising through Integrator and/or any of its subcontractors.

18.3 **Subcontractor Liens.**

(a) To the fullest extent permitted by law, Integrator shall be subcontractors' and vendors' sole payment recourse for labor, materials, supplies or other charges.

(b) In the event that any lien related to labor, materials, supplies or other charges is filed against the Site Host, the Site, the Solar Energy Generating Facility or SEGF by any Subcontractor, then Integrator, at no cost or expense to the Owner, shall not later than five (5) days after written notice from Developer: (i) pay the claimant thereof and obtain a discharge thereof from the claimant, or cause the lien to be discharged by filing a surety bond or making a deposit of funds as required by law; and (ii) take any and all other steps which may be necessary to resolve and discharge any such Lien.

(c) Integrator shall indemnify and hold harmless Developer from and against all loss, damage and claims due to any and all liens or claims filed by any of the subcontractors. Integrator shall, at the Owner's option and at Integrator's own cost and expense, defend Developer against any and all loss, damage and claims resulting from any lien or suit filed by any subcontractor.

18.4 **Responsibility**. Integrator shall, at all times, be responsible for the negligent acts, errors and/or omissions of its subcontractors and agents. Nothing in this Contract shall constitute any contractual relationship between Developer and any subcontractor or in any way obligation Developer to pay, or to be responsible for the payment of, any sums to any subcontractors.

SECTION 19. DISPUTE RESOLUTION

19.1 **Good Faith Negotiations.** If any question, dispute, difference or claim arises out of or in connection with this Contract, including any question regarding its existence, validity, performance or termination (a "Dispute"), of which either Party has notified the other, senior management personnel from both Developer and Integrator shall meet and diligently attempt in good faith to resolve the Dispute for a period of thirty (30) days following one Party's written request to the other Party for such a meeting. If, however, either Party refuses or fails to so meet, or the Dispute is not resolved by negotiation during such 30-day period, the provisions of Section 19.2 below shall apply. Integrator shall continue to perform the Work during the period of any dispute resolution.

19.2 **Dispute Resolution.** Any Dispute that is not settled to the mutual satisfaction of the Parties within the applicable notice or cure periods provided in this Contract or settled pursuant to Section 19.1 above shall be resolved by arbitration between the Parties conducted in San Francisco, California, in accordance with the Commercial Arbitration Rules of the American Arbitration Association in effect on the date that a Party files its demand for arbitration under this Section. The submitting Party shall submit such Dispute to arbitration by filing a written demand for arbitration with the American Arbitration Association and providing a copy to the other Party. The Parties shall select a single neutral arbitrator with contract dispute resolution experience and an understanding of the contemporary solar photovoltaic power industry and photovoltaic systems. If the Parties cannot agree on a single neutral arbitrator within fifteen (15) business days after the written demand for arbitration is provided, then the arbitrator shall be selected by the American Arbitration Association. Once an arbitrator has been selected, the parties may then commence with and exchange requests for documents in accordance with Rule 34 of the Federal Rules of Civil Procedure. No other form of discovery, including but not limited to interrogatories, requests for admissions, or depositions shall be permitted. The arbitrator shall conduct a hearing for as long as the arbitrator deems reasonably necessary and the Parties shall be entitled to submit expert testimony and/or written documentation in such arbitration proceeding. The hearing must take place within six (6) months of the filing of the arbitration demand. The decision of the arbitrator shall be final and binding upon the Parties and shall be set forth in a reasoned opinion, and any award may be enforced by either Party in a court of competent jurisdiction. For purposes of enforcement of the award, the Parties consent to the personal jurisdiction and venue of the State and Federal Courts within the City and County of San Francisco, California. Any award of the arbitrator shall include interest from the date of any damages incurred for breach or other violation of this Contract, and from the date of the award until paid in full, at the rate of one percent (1%) per month. Each Party shall bear its own cost of preparing and presenting its case; provided, that the Parties agree that the prevailing Party in such arbitration shall be awarded its reasonable attorney's fees, expert fees, expenses and costs incurred in connection with the Dispute. The cost of the arbitration, however, including the fees and expenses of the arbitrator, shall initially be shared equally by the Parties, subject to reimbursement of such arbitration costs and attorney's fees and costs to the prevailing Party.

19.3 **Arbitrator Confidentiality Obligation.** The Parties shall ensure that any arbitrator appointed to act under this Section will agree to be bound to the confidentiality provisions of Section 312 hereof with respect to the terms of this Contract and any information obtained during the course of the arbitration proceedings.

SECTION 20. REPRESENTATIONS AND WARRANTIES

20.1 **Each Party warrants and represents to the other that:**

(a) It has all requisite power, authority, licenses, permits, and approvals, to legally and validly execute and deliver this Contract and perform its obligations hereunder;

(b) The execution, delivery, and performance of this Contract have been duly authorized by, or are in accordance with, each Party's respective governing entity, and this Contract has been duly executed and delivered for it by the signatories so authorized, and it constitutes its legal, valid, and binding obligation;

(c) Its execution, delivery, and performance of this Contract will not breach or violate, or constitute a default under any contract, Lease or instrument to which it is a Party or by which it or its properties may be bound or affected; and

(d) It has not received any notice, nor to the best of its knowledge is there pending or threatened any notice, of any violation of any applicable laws, ordinances, regulations, rules, decrees, awards, permits or orders which would materially and adversely affect either Party's ability to perform hereunder.

20.2 **Integrator warrants and represents to Developer that:**

(a) Integrator has examined and carefully reviewed this Contract;

(b) Integrator has inspected the Site and become generally familiar with the general, local and site conditions that may affect the supply of the Solar Energy Generating Facility and the performance of the Work;

(c) Integrator has all the required skills and capacity necessary to perform or cause to be performed the Work in a timely and professional manner, utilizing sound engineering principles, project management procedures and supervisory procedures, all in accordance with prudent industry practices;

(d) Integrator is familiar with applicable law, regulations, and interconnection standards relevant to the performance of its obligations under this Contract; and

(e) Integrator will promptly notify Developer in writing of all conflicts, errors, ambiguities or discrepancies that Integrator discovers in the Contract Documents.

20.3 **Integrator has the appropriate licenses issued by the State in which the Site is located to perform its obligations under this Contract.**

20.4 **Developer warrants and represents to Integrator that:**

Developer has performed, or has caused to be performed, all necessary due diligence to determine suitability of the Site for the Solar Energy Generating Facility including without limitation any structural, soils, or civil analyses or reports. If any of these reports are completed after execution of this Contract, and the information gained in these reports necessitate a change order, Developer will be responsible for incurring the costs of any such change order.

SECTION 21. TITLE; DELIVERY; RISK OF LOSS

21.1 Title to all Work including Materials, constituting a Project Milestone, shall pass to Developer upon the time of payment therefor by Developer. All such Work and Materials shall be free and clear of any liens, claims, unsatisfied demands, notices of intention, stop notices, unsatisfied judgments, security interests, or other encumbrances in favor of Integrator or any other Person or entity. Such passing of title shall not be deemed to constitute the Owner's acceptance of non-conforming Work, including Materials. The transfer of title hereunder shall in no way affect the risk of loss provisions hereof or Integrator's responsibility for, and its obligation to take proper steps and precautions to protect all Materials and other portions of the Work until delivery of the turnkey SEGF to Developer in accordance with Section 21.2 below.

21.2 Notwithstanding the foregoing, Integrator shall deliver the turnkey SEGF on, and retain care, custody and control and risk of loss of any equipment, supplies and components furnished by Integrator hereunder until the Substantial Completion Date. Prior to such date, the Integrator shall bear the risk of loss for any Work and Materials delivered and be responsible for and obligated to replace, repair or reconstruct, all at its expense and as promptly as possible, any portion or all of the Work that is lost, damaged or destroyed (including any damage or loss that has occurred as the result of Force Majeure) prior to the Substantial Completion Date, except to the extent of intentional misconduct or gross negligence on the part of Developer. Developer shall bear the risk of loss and full responsibility from and after the Substantial Completion Date, except to the extent of intentional misconduct or negligence on the part of Integrator, its employees, representatives, agents or subcontractors.

SECTION 22. TERMINATION

22.1 **Termination for Cause.** Subject to Section 16.3 hereof, if there is an Event of Default by either Party under this Contract, pursuant to the provisions of Section 15, then in addition to the remedies provided for in Section 16, the non-defaulting Party may terminate this Contract by providing three (3) business days' notice to the defaulting Party in the case of a monetary Event of Default and ten (10) business days' notice to the defaulting Party in the case of a non-monetary Event of Default. Upon termination of this Contract, each Party shall promptly return to the other all papers, materials, and property of the other held by such Party in connection herewith. Each Party shall also assist the other in the orderly termination of this Contract and the transfer of all aspects hereof, tangible and intangible, as may be necessary for the orderly, non-disrupted business continuation of each Party. Notwithstanding anything to the contrary elsewhere in this Agreement or otherwise, in the event Integrator terminates this Agreement, Integrator shall remain obligated to deliver all Work performed until effective date of termination to Developer in accordance with the Project Schedule and shall be entitled to payment for all Work satisfactorily performed. Notwithstanding the foregoing, in the event there are more than two occurrences of: (i) any person operating any equipment in conjunction with the Work without having received proper training or having been issued a required license for such equipment operation; or (ii) any person working on the Site in conjunction with the Work without having received proper safety instructions and briefings (as indicated by a safety briefing sticker affixed to the helmet), the Developer shall have the right to terminate this Agreement with immediate effect.

22.2 **Termination for Convenience.** Developer shall have the right to terminate this Contract for any reason or no reason upon notice in writing to Integrator. If this Contract is terminated pursuant to this Section 22.2, Integrator shall be entitled to payment for all Work satisfactorily performed and costs incurred, including, but not be limited to material procurement obligations, restocking fees, return fees associated shipping costs, in accordance with this Contract up to the date of termination. Additionally, Developer shall pay Integrator (a) all direct project costs incurred as of the date of termination plus 15% and (b) all expenses related to terminating the project related to terminating the project and leaving the site in a safe condition (including but not limited to costs incurred with terminating vendor agreements and subcontracts) plus 15%.

22.3 **Suspension of Work.** Developer shall have the right to suspend the Work for any period of time (not to exceed 120 days in the aggregate); provided in all events, Integrator shall be entitled to an extension (day for day) of the Scheduled Substantial Completion Date as a result of such suspension.

SECTION 23. CONSTRUCTION OF CONTRACT

This Contract is the result of arms-length negotiations between two sophisticated parties and ambiguities or uncertainties in it shall not be construed for or against either Party, but shall be construed in a manner that most accurately reflects the intent of the Parties when such Contract was executed.

SECTION 24. BINDING EFFECT

Except as otherwise provided herein, the terms and provisions of this Contract shall apply to, be binding upon, and inure to the benefit of the Parties hereto and their respective heirs, legal representatives, successors, and permitted assigns.

SECTION 25. INDEPENDENT CONTRACTOR

Parties hereto agree that Integrator, and any agents and employees of Integrator, its subcontractors and/or consultants, in the performance of this Contract, shall act in an independent capacity and not as officers, employees, or agents of Developer.

SECTION 26. NO WAIVER

The failure of Integrator or Developer to insist upon the strict performance of the terms and conditions of this Contract shall not constitute or be construed as a waiver or relinquishment of either Party's right to thereafter enforce the same in accordance with this Contract.

SECTION 27. SEVERABILITY

In the event that any clause or provision of this Contract or any part thereof becomes or shall be declared by a court of competent jurisdiction invalid, illegal, void, or unenforceable, this Contract shall continue in full force and effect without said provisions, provided that no such severability shall be effective if it materially changes the benefits or obligations of either Party hereunder.

SECTION 28. ENTIRE AGREEMENT; AMENDMENT

This Contract, when executed, together with all Attachments, shall constitute the entire agreement between the Parties;

and this Contract cannot be amended, modified, or terminated except by a written instrument, executed by both Parties hereto; provided, however, if Integrator has been notified that Developer has assigned any of its rights, duties or obligations under this Contract to a Lender, then the prior written consent of Lender shall be required as well.

SECTION 29. APPLICABLE LAW

This Contract and the construction and enforceability thereof shall be governed and construed in accordance with the laws of the State of California, without regard to conflicts of laws principles.

SECTION 30. NOTICE

Any notice required or permitted hereunder shall be deemed received (i) on the day on which such notice is delivered personally, (ii) on the third business day after deposit in the U.S. Mail; provided such notice is sent by certified mail with a return receipt request and postage prepaid or (iii) the following business day if deposited with a recognized overnight carrier, to the address shown below or to such other persons or addresses as are specified by similar notice.

If to Developer:
[____________]
[____________]
[____________]
Attn: [____________]
Phone: [____________]
Facsimile: [____________]

with a copy to:

[____________]
[____________]
[____________]
Attn: [____________]
Facsimile: [____________]

If to Integrator:
[____________]
[____________]
[____________]
Attn: [____________]
Phone: [____________]
Facsimile: [____________]
with a copy to:
[____________]
[____________]
[____________]
Attn: [____________]
Facsimile: [____________]

SECTION 31. HEADINGS

Headings and subtitles used throughout this Contract are for the purpose of convenience only, and no heading or subtitle shall modify or be used to interpret the text of any section.

SECTION 32. CONFIDENTIALITY; PUBLICITY

All non-public information (including the existence and terms of this Contract) provided by either Party to the other or which is identified by the disclosing Party in writing as confidential or proprietary information shall be treated in a confidential manner and shall not be disclosed to any third party without the prior written consent of the non-disclosing Party, which consent shall not be unreasonably withheld. All Integrator publicity activities regarding this Contract or the Solar Energy Generating Facility shall require the prior written consent of Developer, which consent shall not be unreasonably withheld after the Substantial Completion Date. Notwithstanding the preceding, this Section and the restrictions herein contained shall not apply to any data or documentation, which is:

(a) Disclosed or required to be disclosed pursuant to state or federal law, an order or requirements of a regulatory body or a court, after five business days notice of such intended disclosure is given by the disclosing Party to the non-disclosing Party or if five business days notice is not practical, then such shorter notice as is practical;
(b) Disclosed by a Party to an affiliate of such Party or in connection with an assignment permitted by Section 17; or
(c) Is, as of the time of disclosure, public knowledge without the fault of the disclosing Party.

SECTION 33. NON-DISCRIMINATION

33.1 Integrator's Obligations. Integrator shall not unlawfully discriminate, harass, or allow harassment against any employee or applicant for employment because of sex, race, color, ancestry, religious creed, national origin, physical disability (including HIV and AIDS), mental disability, medical condition (cancer), age (over 40), marital status, and denial of family care leave. Integrator shall ensure that the evaluation and treatment of its employees and applicants for employment are free from such discrimination and harassment, and shall comply with the provisions of the Fair Employment and Housing Act (Government Code Section 12990 (a-f) et seq.) and the applicable regulations promulgated thereunder (California Code of Regulations, Title 2, Section 7285 et seq.). The applicable regulations of the Fair Employment and Housing Commission implementing Government Code Section 12990 (a-f), set forth in Chapter 5 of Division 4 of Title 2 of the California Code of Regulations, are incorporated into this Contract by reference and made a part hereof as if set forth in full].

SECTION 34. SURVIVAL

Sections 1, 2, 4, 4, 7, 10.6, 12, 13, 14, 16, 18, 19, 20, 21, 22, 23, 24, 25, 26, 27, 28, 29, 30, 31, 32, 33, 36 and the attachments hereto that are referenced in such Sections shall survive termination of this Contract and shall survive final payment to Integrator following Final Completion.

SECTION 22. COOPERATION

22.1 Upon the receipt of a request from the other Party, each Party shall execute such reasonable additional documents, instruments, estoppels, and assurances and take such additional actions as are reasonably necessary and desirable to carry out the terms and intent hereof. Neither Party shall unreasonably withhold, condition or delay its compliance with any reasonable request made pursuant to this Section.

22.2 Without limiting the generality of the foregoing, Integrator will provide Developer promptly upon Developer's written request all documents reasonably necessary for Developer to file and/or complete any application for Environmental and Financial Incentives and qualification of the SEGF as a "Qualified Facility" under pertinent rules and regulations of the Federal Energy Regulatory Commission or any other governmental authority.

ATTACHMENT A

SITE ACCESS

Developer will provide Integrator access to the Site to the extent permitted to Developer by Site Host under the Lease and in accordance with the terms of the Lease and this Contract.

Other than as indicated on the project plans, or listed below, /no additional restrictions on the Integrator exist.
[DESCRIBE ANY OTHER OBLIGATIONS FOR INTEGRATOR FROM PPA OR LEASE]

ATTACHMENT B

SCOPE OF WORK

PROJECT OVERVIEW

[ALL MATERIAL DETAILS, SIZE, MATERIALS, EXPECTED PRODUCTION, RATIOS, ETC. RELATED TO THE SEGF, PRIMARILY FROM THE ENGINEERING DESIGN PACKAGE AND INTERNAL DEVELOPER DOCUMENTATION]

1. **Turnkey Services**

Integrator will provide stamped electrical, structural or other required engineering drawings, secure all required permits, procure all necessary materials and install the photovoltaic modules, electrical wiring and components including inverters, electrical connection to the existing site host electrical infrastructure, and construction of mounting structures on which the photovoltaic modules are installed. Integrator shall commission the Solar Energy Generating Facility and support the interconnection process with the Utility. Integrator shall provide comprehensive on-site construction management for the Solar Energy Generating Facility and overall project management for the Work.

Integrator shall perform the Work, in accordance with practices generally accepted in the industry, all applicable laws, government approvals and permitting requirements, and quality control and inspections so that the Solar Energy Generating Facility (i) meets or exceeds all requirements of applicable laws, government approvals and licenses and the Solar Energy Generating Facility is installed in accordance with manufacturer's specifications or by methods otherwise approved by the manufacturer; (ii) complies with all requirements of the Interconnection Agreement; (iii) meets or exceeds the warranties and guarantees set forth in Section 5; (iv) are safe and adequate for their intended purpose and conditions; (v) are free from defects; (vi) is comprised of equipment which is new and of good quality when installed, designed and manufactured and of a grade in accordance with generally accepted national standards for the design, manufacture and quality of such equipment; and (viii) meets or exceeds all requirements for any applicable federal, state or other rebates and incentives.

2. **Feasibility Inspection and Assessment**

Prior to the execution of this Contract will have conducted feasibility and configuration assessments, environmental assessments, and other inspections of the Site to determine that the Site can support the installation of the Solar Energy Generating Facility, without further modification to the Site itself. Copies of all reports shall be provided to Developer. Required reports include without limitation:

(a) Third party Structural Report for all rooftop systems or elevated arrays.

(b) Third party Phase I Environmental Assessment for all ground-mounted systems or Negative Declaration

(c) Title Report showing any easements, CC&Rs, etc.

(d) Site electrical service capacities

Integrator will have prepared an Engineering Design Package for use by the Parties in project modeling and the development of this Contract. All preliminary engineering and installation drawings shall be consistent with prevailing construction standards, codes, and compliance. The system design will comply with all applicable laws and regulations. The preliminary design, drawings and materials shall be based on Developer's Approved Products as provided in Attachment L and adhere to Developer's SEGF Specifications consistent with Attachment C, including all Pre-Contract Submittals.

3. **Access to Site**

Developer will work with the Site Host to make available to Integrator access to the Site for the purposes set forth herein; provided however, that Integrator acknowledges that the Integrator's employees, agents, contractors and representatives shall abide by all requirements of Site Host for the access and security of the Site.

4. **Use of Site**

Integrator agrees not to do or permit to be done in or about the Site, nor to bring or keep or permit to be brought or kept in or about the Site, anything which is prohibited by or will in any way conflict with any legal requirements or which is prohibited by the standard form of fire insurance policy, or which will in any way increase the existing rate of (or otherwise affect) fire or any other insurance on the Site or any of its contents. Integrator agrees not to commit or suffer to be committed any waste in or upon the Site.

5. **Construction and Installation**

Prior to beginning construction, Integrator shall also provide Developer with a copy of Integrator's safety plan, as well as an evaluation and appropriate documentation of the safety record any licensed subcontractor that will be performing work on the Solar Energy Generating Facility. Integrator will apply for all permits necessary for development, construction, ownership and operation of the Solar Energy Generating Facility. Copies of all applicable permits shall be provided to Developer five (5) business days or less after they are obtained or completed, in all cases before a Notice to Proceed to Procurement and Construction will be issued. Developer and Site Host (if applicable) will review and approve the documents prior to commencement of construction.

Integrator will assemble, construct, and install with its own forces and/or with subcontractors the following Work:

a) Prepare the site. On ground mount systems including but not limited to drainage required by the civil engineering plan, and remove excess debris. On roof mount systems including but not limited to pre-installation removal from the roof surface of all existing items that might cause membrane puncture if stepped on.

b) Integrator will coordinate with Developer and Site Host when trenching is performed, when laydown areas are determined, when major shipments are planned, or any other activities that might impact the Site Host's business operations.

c) AC and DC Wiring, Junction Boxes, Shutoffs, Conduit, trenching

d) Modules, mounting system/solution, roof sealing and repairs (if appropriate), foundation work, elevated structure, tracker controllers, actuators, etc.

e) Inverters, switchgear and transformers and accompanying supports and/or concrete pads

f) Temporary security fence (6 feet tall), to be removed at end of construction; Permanent fencing and bollards if required.

g) Install the balance of the remotely accessible Data Acquisition System including Revenue Grade Metering

Developer, at its sole discretion, may randomly select up to twenty (20) modules of each type of photovoltaic modules used in the System for delivery to a third-party for quality verification testing. The costs of such verification testing shall be the responsibility of Developer.

6. Material Purchase

Integrator will purchase and furnish to the Site the following material without limitation and as appropriate per the Specifications:

a) Miscellaneous Structural or Module Mounting components

b) Components (Nuts, Bolts, Clamps, Conduit, Grounding Lugs, etc.)

c) Photovoltaic Modules

d) All AC and DC wiring

e) DC Junction Boxes

f) AC and DC shutoffs

g) Inverters and applicable shading structure

h) Electric Switchgear as needed

i) Transformers as needed

j) Meteorological Station

k) Remotely accessible Data Acquisition Systems including Revenue Grade Metering

l) All materials related to drainage required by the civil engineering plan as appropriate

m) All security components including fencing, cameras, perimeter monitoring, etc. as required.

n) All other components, parts, products and materials to complete the construction of the SEGF in accordance with the Contract.

The material will arrive on to the Site as to not delay the completion of the project. Integrator will provide flash test data for all modules to Developer upon procurement of modules.

If the Solar Energy Generating Facility is in whole or in part ground mounted, or materials shall be stored on-site during construction, prior to the arrival of equipment and materials at the Site, the Integrator shall install a fenced secured area and provide 24-hour security for the storage of such equipment and materials, such secured area to be approved by Developer, such approval not to be unreasonably withheld or delayed.

Integrator will be responsible for all storage and receiving of all freight at the Site in a secure manner to be approved by Developer, such approval not to be unreasonably withheld or delayed.

7. Substantial Completion

Prior to Substantial Completion, Integrator will perform the following tasks without limitation:

(a) The portion of the Work sufficient to consider the Solar Energy Generating Facility to be mechanically and electrically complete in accordance with the Contract Documents.

(b) Issuance of an Application for Substantial Completion to Developer.

8. Commissioning and Utility Interconnection Approval

(a) Commission the completed system in accordance with the Commissioning Tests and Procedures in Attachment F to verify that the system is functioning as expected within acceptable parameters and as designed at a nameplate capacity and first year of operation production capacity adjusted for actual weather conditions consistent with the Solar Energy Generating Facility Abstract on the first page of this Contract.

(b) Facilitate completion or execution of any Incentive related documents

(c) Prior to receipt of an Application for Substantial Completion executed by Developer, Integrator shall not contact the Utility to facilitate interconnection. Integrator will actively coordinate with Utility in preparation for and completion of the facilities' interconnection, as confirmed by the receipt of written approval from the Utility to operate or parallel the Solar Energy Generating Facility on the Utility's grid.

(d) Issuance of a Certificate of Substantial Completion by Developer to Integrator.

9. Final Completion

Prior to Final Completion, Integrator will perform the following tasks without limitation

(a) Complete all tasks described on the Punchlist.

(b) Site final clean up.

(c) Train Developer in the operation, and recommended O&M, of the Solar Energy Generating Facility

(d) Provide Developer with copies of all O&M manuals and warranties for System. Any and all O&M manuals for the System shall include warranty cards for all System equipment signed by Developer.

(e) Provide Final As-Built documents and all other required Submittals.

(f) Train Developer and Site Host's designee on emergency shut down procedures as well as standard inverter restart procedures.

ATTACHMENT C

SPECIFICATIONS AND SUBMITTALS

1.01 GENERAL

1.02 PRE-CONTRACT SUBMITTALS

A. The Integrator shall submit a comprehensive proposal to Developer prior to the execution of the Engineering, Procurement and Construction Agreement, which shall include the following documents, collectively the Engineering Design Package:

a. A Preliminary Design, including system layout detailing the tilt and azimuth of all modules, the location of all modules and the inverter(s), and all other major electrical or mechanical equipment.

b. A Preliminary Bill of Materials detailing solar module, inverter, and all other major components make and model number

c. A shading study using the [SolMetric SunEye](or comparable software), which includes a reference site map detailing the location of each reading per Developer's Shading Study Guidelines, per **Attachment I.**

d. Site security plan

e. Certification that Integrator has 7 day per week service and support capabilities, such that service notifications by Developer will be received and acted upon per Section 5 of this Contract.

f. For rooftop systems, Integrator is to note that structural blocking, if required, is included in the project cost, however structural improvement of the Host existing structure is not. Any requirement for structural improvement of the existing structure in order to accommodate the loads imposed by the SEGF must be separately identified. If the Integrator does not state that structural improvement is necessary with the proposal, the cost of that structural improvement is agreed by both parties to be included in the cost of the project.

g. For ground-mount systems, Integrator is to note that grading, landscaping, fencing, security, geotechnical investigation and any environmental studies have been included in their proposal.

h. Separate single-lines for SEGF electrical and SEGF DAS

i. Product data sheets and copies of all key product manufacturers' warranties

j. Detailed description of the existing Site electrical service panel and Utility meter(s) number(s).

k. For rooftop systems, Integrator shall detail the plan to preserve the Site Host's existing roof membrane warranty

1.03 REFERENCES

A. All components shall be designed, manufactured and tested in accordance with the latest applicable standards of NEMA, ANSI, NEC and UL.

B. In addition to the codes cited in Section 16010 of the Construction Specification Institution, specific requirements for individual components of the solar system include but are not limited to the guidelines shown herein.

C. The Work shall be designed and installed in accordance with the latest edition of all applicable codes, standards, and recommendations of the following agencies:

(a) ANSI-American National Standards Institute.

(b) ASCE-American Society of Civil Engineers

(c) ASME-American Society of Mechanical Engineers

(d) CAL OSHA-California / Occupational Safety and Health Administration

(e) CBC-California Building Code and/or Building Code for the State in which the Site is located

(f) CEC-California Energy Commission

(g) ETL-Electrical Testing Laboratories.

(h) IEEE-Institute of Electrical and Electronic Engineers

(i) ICEA-Insulated Cable Engineer's Association.

(j) IAEI-International Association of Electrical Inspectors.

(k) IPMVP- International Performance Measurements and Verification Protocol.

(l) NFPA-101-National Fire Protection Association. (Life Safety Code)

(m) NEMA-National Electrical Manufacturers Association.

(n) NESC-National Electrical Safety Code.

(o) NETA-National Electrical Testing Association.

(p) NEC -National Electrical Code

(q) UL-Underwriters Laboratories

1.04 DESIGN / ENGINEERING REQUIREMENTS

A. Engineering

1. Integrator is responsible for all project engineering. Specifically, the integrator is required to obtain the following before a Notice to Proceed to Permit Application Submittal will be issued:

a. If this is a ground mount system, a study, recommendations and stamp and sign off from a licensed structural and geotechnical engineer.

b. If this is a stand-alone elevated system, a study, recommendations and stamp and sign off from a licensed structural engineer and geotechnical engineer.

c. If this is a roof top system, a structural review including calculations and engineering approval stamp and sign off from a licensed structural engineer. This includes mechanical base anchorage details for mechanical equipment bearing engineer's seal and signature.

d. In all cases, electrical, civil, geotechnical, structural and other engineering designs are to be we-signed and stamped by a licensed engineer.

e. Voltage drop of less than or equal to 2.0% for the entire system (AC and DC circuits). Each run (Modules to combiners boxes, combiner box to DC Disconnects, etc) will be individually calculated, Conductor Type, Current at Max Power, Voltage at Max Power, Estimated Length of Line (one-way) and associated Voltage Drop will be shown in a table.

f. There should be separate single lines for the array, the monitoring system data communications and power, and for the tracking system power (and data communications if the tracker is being monitored separately) if applicable.

g. In all cases above, the studies and prints designed there from are to be stamped and wet-signed by the engineer as Engineer of Record.

h. In all cases engineers are to be properly licensed by the State where the Site is located.

i. Structural engineers are to specify grade of steel used in all support structures. Mill certifications showing the identification of the steel to be used on the project and the quality thereof shall be provided to Developer. Mill certifications shall be checked by Integrator prior to accepting delivery of any steel.

j. Integrator is responsible for the complete and totally functional operation of the DAS System. Any labor, communications devices, wiring and or other materials shall be included in the integrator's base price. It is explicitly understood by all parties that the Integrator is responsible for the workmanship and timely completion of any and all subcontractors that are necessary for the successful completion of this project.

k. Engineers must visit the Host Site to ascertain site conditions, accuracy of provided drawings and feasibility of design. Integrator is responsible to know what is actually in place no matter what provided drawings say. Integrator is responsible for the upgrades to the existing electrical system required to accommodate the SEGF installation, and is to include those changes in both their price and their design drawings.

B. Design Requirements

1. Proposed systems will have a shade free window between the hours of 10 am and 2pm (solar time) on the winter solstice.
2. Minimum inter-row spacing and setback guidelines for roof mounts and ground mounts will be in accordance with Developer Shading Study Guidelines. **Attachment I.**
3. A site audit will be required to confirm the location of existing rooftop or ground mount obstructions. The length, height and width of each obstruction as well as its location within the array must be detailed and included within the design. Stay out zones shall then be calculated and incorporated into the drawing set.
4. 10 degree minimum module tilt, 40 degree max module tilt, unless otherwise approved by Developer.
5. Southern orientation with an azimuth between 150 and 210 degrees unless otherwise approved by Developer
6. All DC wire, other than panel-to-panel wire in a string and grounding conductors, will be located in conduit. No direct sun exposure of USE-2 will be allowed.
7. The data acquisition (DAS) will be designed to meet the specifications as detailed in **Attachment G.**
8. Power and communications lines out to the combiner boxes will be located in a separate conduit from the high voltage DC
9. Conduit will be supported on a UV resistant polyethylene foam or synthetic rubber. Wood supports are not permitted.
10. The Location of the revenue meters will be identified on the preliminary and final plans and as close to the Energy Delivery Point with the Site Host's switchgear as possible.
11. The exact layout, number and type of PV Panels must be shown clearly in the Construction Documents. Tables should be added on each page re-capitulating numbers of combiner boxes, modules, etc. as a check on count.
12. Unless otherwise approved by Developer in advance, module shall be grounded with hardware per **Attachment L.**

13. Inverters shall be protected by at least 3 bollards per location where they are in the judgment of Developer at risk for collision damage. Inverter pads shall be a minimum of 6"concrete reinforced at 12" intervals with #5 rebar unless otherwise directed by the structural engineer. Inverter pads shall be fenced with a 7' chain link fence, with a locking gate. Locks to be provided by Developer.
14. Unless located indoors, or against the northern wall of a site, Inverters shall be protected by an enclosure structure from direct sun and the elements.
15. No signs or nameplates will be posted on the SEGF until approved by Developer except for those required by NEC or the AHJ or Developer. Integrator brand or contact information is not allowed on any signs, except for temporary construction signage.
16. Roof penetrations flashing and sealing are to be designed in accordance with and with the advice of the Host's roofer or roofing consultant. Host roof warranties shall be preserved.
17. On ground mount systems, all conduits shall be buried according to NEC or AHJ.
18. All conduits shall enter enclosures from below and be made watertight by sealing with silicone sealing compound.
19. All junction boxes, condolets, etc., are to be sealed with a silicone sealing compound and made watertight.
20. If not present before project has been started, and unless otherwise approved in advance by Developer, a water line will be constructed to a point adjacent of the array and a hose bib installed so that the array may be easily cleaned.
21. All conduit shall be run underground for a ground mount system.
22. All fencing shall be slat filled with a color that is the closest match to the adjacent building, where applicable, or color as appropriate to minimize visual impact.

1.05 SUBMITTALS PRIOR TO PERMIT SUBMITTAL, PROCUREMENT AND CONSTRUCTION

A. The following information shall be submitted to Developer as a prerequisite to receiving a Notice to Proceed to Permit Application Submittal:

1. Detailed site plan with detailed solar array layout including inverter location(s), monitoring and security
2. All required engineers' reports, signed and stamped.
3. A fully signed and wet stamped set of design prints, including cover and index, with any changes from the preliminary design clouded following the guidelines below:

EPC Drawing Requirements

Title Page

Information on the title page shall include, but not be limited to the following:

- System size: This shall include kWdc and kWac.
- Area of installation: Area, in square feet on rooftops, or acres on ground mounts, of area that the installation encompasses.
- Estimate of length of wire used: This shall include all of the wiring used on the system-side of the meter (i.e. home run wiring, DC wiring from combiner boxes to the inverters & AC wiring from inverters to the meters).
- Module part numbers and quantities.
- Inverter part numbers and quantities.

Single Line Diagrams/layout page

The single line diagrams shall accurately depict the physical electrical connections (i.e. quantity, type, and size of conductors, quantity, size, and type of conduit) between all electrical equipment used in the system. Information on the single line diagrams shall include, but not be limited to the following items:

- Modules per string.
- Number of strings for each combiner box.
- String map per array or subarray

- Depiction of the wiring and fusing in all disconnects.
- Wire size and quantity used for every run.
- Total wire length (inside a footnote box or similar notation)
- Conduit size and quantity of wires in each conduit for every run.
- All fuses sizes.
- Monitoring Data Communications and power

Grounding system design including connection points and conductor size

All electrical equipment shall be depicted, including their capacity/rating, manufacturer, part number, quantity and reference designator where applicable. Examples of equipment shall include but not be limited to the following:

- Modules
- Inverters
- Combiner Boxes
- Wire (gauges and quantity)
- Transformers
- Switchgear
- DC & AC Disconnects
- Fuses
- Data Acquisition System (DAS)
- Main Switchboard
- Meters
- Distribution Panels
- MET (Meteorological) Stations

Layout Page

- Tie-in locations

General Drawing Requirements

The Engineering Design Package shall also include, but not be limited to the following items:

- Array layout with location of equipment and tie-in relative to array
- Electrical equipment pad layout
- Locations of conduit runs
- Torque values for terminal hardware
- String Layout page showing the string, combiner box, disconnect, and inverter layout using a structured naming system
- A list of those changes made from the original proposal with the reasons therefor.
- Complete electrical calculations including voltage drops at each run.
- Updated Bill of Materials with the make and model number of the following equipment; solar modules, inverters, isolation transformers, AC/DC load break disconnect switches, grounding hardware, monitoring components, and all other material equipment.
- Full details of the mounting system including wind and seismic considerations and calculations
- Array wiring diagrams, wiring diagrams for the non-array part of the job, single lines,
- Electrical Physical Equipment Layout showing combiner boxes and all wiring and equipment required for Monitoring system including revenue meters. All such diagrams to have electrical equipment called out by make and model number. All wires to be called out by size and utility.
- Book with product data sheets on all equipment to be used on the array to include switches and fuses.

B. The following information shall be submitted to Developer as a prerequisite to receiving a Notice to Proceed to Procurement and Construction:

1. Microsoft Project or equivalent construction schedule (providing Gantt chart output) showing milestones, equipment order and delivery dates, and staffing requirements. Specific milestones such as conduit installation completion, material required arrival times, Interconnection date, and commissioning timeline, shall be highlighted.
2. Integrator shall develop a complete working plan of the site, showing material storage, a lay-down and layout yard, site office, etc. This plan shall be reviewed by the Developer Construction Manager. Integrator shall obtain a signed approval thereof from the Host.
3. Integrator shall develop and submit as a part of this package a complete work plan taking into account such issues as
   a. Access and mobilization
   b. Crane locations and traffic control
   c. Method of installation
   d. Staffing
   e. Site-specific safety plan – Integrator will develop a site specific OSHA approved safety plan and submit it to Developer for review prior to the start of construction. Safety meetings will be held once a week with all Integrator employees and subcontractors employees attending. Printed names will be taken of those attending the meeting. No individual will start work on the site without having attended a safety briefing on the dangers and protocols of the site. Records of this training will be kept and provided to Developer Construction Manager for his review. No individual will operate a piece of equipment on which they have not had certification training. Certification shall be carried on the operator at all times.
   f. Integrator shall procure and submit as a part of this package any and all permits or other approvals required by Authorities Having Jurisdiction, to include but not limited to: municipal building, planning, or architectural or design review, landlord or other CC&R approvals, nighttime operations, or any other specialty permits. Integrator is to include all such permit costs in their turnkey Contract Price.
   g. Integrator will specifically include any meter replacement costs or other electrical service upgrade costs required by the local utility or AHJ.
   h. For ground mounted systems, Integrator shall supply an erosion control plan, weed abatement plan, and security plan for the site. Such plans shall include estimated costs for contracted services to execute the plan(s). If no such plans are required a negative statement in the cover letter is required.
   j. The submittals will be reviewed by Developer. Approval or denial shall be delivered within 14 days.

1.06 SUBMITTALS FOR COMPLETION

Submittals for Substantial Completion

1. Completed inverter warranty registration cards and all other equipment that requires warranty registration.
2. Signed off permit final inspection card(s) by AHJ
3. Fuse list prepared on 8-1/2 x 11 sheets, - list by make and model number of which fuse is used where, with a notation as to exactly where the spare fuse box is located.
4. Signed Utility Interconnection Approval(s) from Utility and Final Signed Interconnection Agreement from Utility and Host.
5. Completed meter configuration form with meter calibration documents
6. Module flash test reports and serial numbers
7. Integrator Service Manger contact information,
8. Internet access IT network access configuration documentation,
9. Completed Developer Commissioning Report.
10. Operations and Maintenance Manual including Integrator's and manufacturers of warranted products specific preventive maintenance recommendations for all aspects of the SEGF

Submittals for Final Completion

1. The as-built drawing set will be the final drawing submittal and will be modified for the changes made during the construction process. Changes shall be clouded and a printed list of such changes shall be delivered with the drawings
2. The as-built drawing set will include a string map showing the location of each string within the array. Each module within each string will be labeled with is associated serial number on the as-built, or on a separate printed page clearly identifying modules per string. The serial numbers of the performance meters, combiner boxes and inverters will also be called out. The Modbus ID for each inverter will be called out.
3. Completed Punch List from Host, signed by Host as completed.

1.07 REGULATORY REQUIREMENTS

A. All electrical equipment supplied for this project shall bear a UL, CSA, ETL or UR label. Copies of the listing shall be supplied if Developer requests.

1.08 DELIVERY, STORAGE, ACCESS, AND HANDLING.

A. Equipment shall be stored and handled in accordance with manufacturer's requirements

B. Material received shall be identified by serial number, a report prepared and that report including make, model and serial numbers of the material and equipment received (if applicable) shall be forwarded to Developer Construction Manager.

C. Upon arrival modules shall be reported by serial number, and those serial numbers and the flash test data there for shall be forwarded to Developer Construction manager forthwith.

D. Integrator shall be responsible to fully inspect shipments for damage and report damage to both the Manufacturer and Developer. Further, Integrator is required to file claim upon shipper if any is needed.

1.09 PRODUCTS - APPROVED MANUFACTURERS and PRODUCTS

Only products identified in Attachment L shall be used in the construction of the Solar Energy Generating Facility, unless otherwise approved in writing by Developer. Components not listed in Attachment L shall meet the specifications below:

1.10 ENCLOSURES

A. Enclosures shall be NEMA 4x unless otherwise approved in advance by Developer. If the Site is within 1 mile of any body of water or 2 miles from any body of salt water, enclosures shall be NEMA 4x in stainless steel. All enclosures exposed to the elements shall be NEMA 4x.

B. All enclosures will be detailed prior to Final Completion to insure that any scratches, etc. are properly covered with paint as appropriate.

1.11 CONDUIT

A. Conduit shall be schedule 80 where PVC allowed

B. Conduit shall be rigid type where called for by Code.

C. In no case shall conduit be less than that called for by NEC

D. EMT

1.12 WIRE

A. Integrator shall use USE-2 type conductors for all conductors not in conduit

B. When in conduit conductors shall be USE-2 or THWN-2 (Thermoplasic Heat and Water Resistant Nylon Coated wire is permitted)

C. All connectors and conductors on the DC side will be rated for 600 Volts per design specification all conductors shall be sized per the most current NEC code, and line loss of no greater than 2%.

D. All conductors used for communication will be shielded cable with a drain.

1.13 FASTENERS AND WIRE MANAGEMENT

A. Plastic zip ties are not an acceptable wire management technique

B. Stainless steel zip ties or stainless steel wire clips may be used

C. Break-away or other theft-deterrent security fasteners in stainless steel shall be used to fasten modules to arrays. Submit desired fastener type with design documents.

D. All exposed USE-2 wire will be secured every 3.5′ minimum

1.14 FUSES

A. Integrator shall prepare a list of all fuses used in the installation, by make and model number. They shall then purchase at least 10 of each and provide these fuses in a standard enclosure box to be mounted at the largest inverter onsite. In the box is to be a clean, laminated list showing the fuse make and model number and where used in the installation. A copy of this list shall be provided as one of the close out documents.

B. Fuses for disconnects to be current limiting UL class J, RK1 or RK5 and of the appropriate voltage, delay or non-delay characteristic, and current rating to provide complete short circuit and overload protection per NEC sections regarding component selection.

C. Fuses located in the combiner boxes protecting PV string branch circuits shall be UL listed 600V DC rated, be in "finger-safe" type fuse holders providing load break disconnect capabilities when changing fuses. Midget fuses and fuse holders used in these circuits must be fully DC rated and adequate DC short circuit withstands and let-through capability must be provided for all power situations including "back-fed" conditions.

1.15 NAMEPLATES

A. All equipment, panels, boxes and associated equipment shall be clearly labeled with engraved phenolic nameplates. Unless otherwise approved by Developer in advance, nameplates shall be red background with 3/8" or greater white letters. Integrator shall submit the proposed nameplates with desired labeling for approval prior to installation.

B. Install engraved signs as in "A" above for instruction or warning identifying that a solar PV system is operational on the premises at appropriate locations and that there is potentially multiple power sources on the premises – submit wording and location

C. Provide identification of all DC power circuits on switches and clearly identifies individual module strings in DC combiner boxes. Use appropriate wire color codes (i.e. Red & Black) for negative and positive circuits.

D. PV Panels must include serial numbers in such a position as to be easily visible when installed.

E. Signage will include signage called out in article 690 of the 2008 NEC and the CA Fire Marshall Draft PV Specifications.

1.16 FACTORY TESTING

A. Any equipment – such as inverters – that is required to be factory tested by ANSI, NEMA and or UL standards shall be accompanied by the results of those factory tests, and further those results will be submitted as a part of the close out documents.

1.17 EXECUTION / CONSTRUCTION

A. Redlines shall be maintained on a not more-than-weekly basis. Final redlines shall be completed in a reasonable amount of time following the AHJ does final inspection and sign off.

B. Integrator shall work to the Construction Plan. Deviation from this plan shall be discussed with Developer Construction Manager before such deviation is undertaken.

C. Integrator shall verify all clearances in the field prior to construction, and is solely responsible therefor.

D. Integrator shall verify UL labeling of equipment prior to installation. Any equipment that has been installed and thereafter is determined to be not UL approved should meet alternative listing requirements such as CSA, ETL, or UR. In all cases NEC and AHJ rules shall apply.

E. Modules shall have their serial numbers recorded as they are installed grouped and listed by string.

F. If modules are delivered with power tolerance binning or other specific module power rating, they shall be installed in such a manner to minimize module mismatch on each string.

G. Integrator shall have mandatory pre-job safety briefing for all employees and sub-contractor employees on their first day on site. Hard Hat stickers shall be issued as a proof of briefing attendance.

H. Integrator shall have weekly safety meetings with all onsite construction personnel – both its own and sub-contractors' personnel. Attendance at these meetings is mandatory. Integrator shall record attendance and subject of meeting.

I. Integrator shall maintain a clean and workmanlike site. Loose debris shall not be tolerated at any time.

J. Correctly torque all such equipment or assemblies requiring torque and mark torqued bolts to designate status of having been torqued. The Developer Construction Manager or Developer's 3rd Party Engineer may at any time request a test of marked bolts. Failure of a bolt designated as torqued to show that torque may require all assemblies to be re-torqued in the presence of a 3rd party inspector – such inspector to be paid for by Integrator.

K. There is to be no metal cutting on the roof, with the exception of conduit, which shall be cut over a carpet or like filing collector and taken off the roof in a unit at the end of the project. In no instance shall metal filings blow or otherwise end up on the surface of any module.

L. Roof is to be loaded in a manner prescribed by the structural engineer so as not to overload any particular point on the roof.

M. Integrator is responsible for any Host Site damage.

N. Integrator is responsible for all site security, and is to provide a site security plan to be approved by Developer.

O. Backup power, if required by Host, is to be provided by Integrator during shutdowns.

P. Modules, inverters and electronic equipment shall be housed in containers until such time as they are installed.

Q. If Inverter manufacturers, ERI and other such manufacturers can provide factory trained technical representatives for the installation and start up of their systems Integrator shall use said resources.

R. Integrator shall be responsible for coordinating inspections by AHJ and third party engineers hired by investors and/or banks.

S. Integrator is solely responsible for obtaining Permits, paying Permit Fees and obtaining final permit inspection and sign off.

T. Damage to host customer's facility and or the solar energy facility shall be reported to Developer within 24 hours with photographs.

U. Integrator is responsible for providing construction power on all remote sites. The cost for this in included in the Contract Price.

V. Integrator is responsible for providing drinking water and sanitation facilities for all workers on all remote sites. The cost for this in included in the Contract Price.

W. All cut edges of galvanized strut or other support structure materials shall be cold galvanized.

X. All enclosures shall be have paint touched up to cover all scratches and other wear and tear that may have occurred during construction.

ATTACHMENT D

PROJECT SCHEDULE

Upon the Contract Effective Date, Integrator will develop, with input from Developer, a master Project Schedule using Microsoft® Project, or equivalent. The project team will establish a weekly construction meeting at which time the work of the previous week will be reviewed, and a three-week look ahead will be coordinated. The Project Schedule will be updated every two weeks. At this time, Integrator estimates the permitting, issuing of subcontractor contracts, design/engineering, mobilization, construction, and commissioning/ turnover phases.

1. The Work and the Solar Energy Generating Facility [shall] be completed in accordance with the Project Schedule. The preliminary schedule shown below shall be finalized during the completion of the Construction Documents. Such finalized

Project Schedule shall then completely replace Attachment D, Table 1 in its entirety. Any and all subsequent changes to such finalized Project Schedule shall require the prior written approval of Developer, in its sole and absolute discretion.

2. Integrator [shall][will use best efforts to] complete the Work by Scheduled Substantial Completion Date.

3. Integrator will make all reasonable, diligent efforts to obtain all permits, clearances, Interconnection Agreement, etc. necessary for performance and completion of the Work.

A preliminary schedule is shown below.

Table 1. Anticipated Key Engineering and Construction Dates

[To be developed on a project-by-project basis.]

ATTACHMENT E

PROGRESS PAYMENT SCHEDULE

The Milestone Schedule below shall be used to determine project progress payments. Upon completion of all Work necessary to achieve a Milestone, an Application for Payment may be submitted by Integrator to Developer. All Applications for Payment will be submitted to:

[____________]
Attn: [____________]
[____________]
[____________]
Phone: [____________], Facsimile: [____________]
Email: [____________]

Applications for Payment will utilize an agreed upon form. Upon verification by Developer of such Work and Milestone achievement, approval and payment will be made as described in Section 4.1 above.

1. Contract Amount.

1.1. As full and complete payment for the turnkey Solar Energy Generating Facility and Integrator's other obligations under the Contract Documents, Developer shall pay to Integrator in the manner specified in Section 4, and Integrator shall accept as payment in full by Developer for the delivery of the Solar Energy Generating Facility and its other obligations under the Contract Documents the following sum:

______________ US Dollars ($).

1.2 Price and Performance Ratios.

a. The Contract Amount is based on the delivery of a Solar Energy Generating Facility providing ______kW-DC-STC of peak power.
b. The Estimated Annual Energy Production of the Solar Energy Generating Facility during the first year of operation is ___________kWh-AC-yr1.
c. The resulting contract price ratios are: ________ $/W-DC-STC and _________$/kWh-AC-yr1.
d. The contract performance ratio is: _______kWh-AC/kW-DC-STC.

2. Solar Energy Generating Facility Progress Milestone Payments

Milestone Progress Payments scheduled as follows:

Table 1

Milestone Number	Description	Percentage of Contract Price
1	Notice to Proceed	5
2	Approved Notice to Proceed to Permit Application Submittal	5
3	Approved Notice to Proceed to Procurement and Construction	5
4	Procurement Partial for Down Payments	25
5	Construction 1	20
6	Construction 2	15
7	Construction 3	15
8	Substantial Completion	10
9	Final Completion	Change Orders and Retainage

ATTACHMENT F

COMMISSIONING SCHEDULE

Overview:

Integrator technical personnel, with the assistance of the equipment manufacturer(s) as needed, will perform a complete commissioning of the Solar Energy Generating Facility following the Commissioning procedures outlined in this Attachment as well as other standard tests, inspections, safety and quality checks, and documented on the form below. All testing and commissioning will be conducted in accordance with the manufacturer's specifications. Developer reserves the right to have the testing and Commissioning results verified by the Commissioning Engineer.

These Commissioning testing procedures for photovoltaic systems and major components are intended to determine system performance to the specification. The tests are designed to verify that the system, as installed, is safe for personnel as well as equipment, and to establish or verify system operation. The tests shall be used to determine actual post-construction operational, performance, and safety characteristics.

SOLAR ENERGY FACILITY COMMISSIONING RESULTS

Host Customer Name ______________________ Site Name ______________________

SEGF Address (City, State, Zip) ______________________

SEGF Size (kW DC-STC) ______________________

Utility and Host meter number______________________

Commissioning report submitted by______________________

Integrator ______________________

Time and date of commissioning____

Weather at time of commissioning____

Record and document inverter serial number and inverter location________________________

This checklist is a guide to establish post construction SEGF operation, performance and safety. The local authority having jurisdiction (AHJ) or inspector has the final say on what is or is not acceptable. Local codes may modify the requirements of the NEC. This list should be used in conjunction with Article 690 and other applicable articles. If article 690 differs from other articles of the NEC, Article 690 takes precedence.

PV ARRAY – GENERAL

Complete each item on the checklist below, check the box to the left of the item when it is complete.

- ☐ Verify that all combiner fuses are removed and that no voltage is present at the output of the combiner box
- ☐ Recheck that fuses are removed and all switches are open
- ☐ Check that non-current carrying metal parts are grounded properly (array frames, metal boxes, etc. are connected to the grounding system)
- ☐ All debris has been removed from roof or ground
- ☐ Photos of all sub-arrays and all inverters
- ☐ Inspect all roof penetrations and wall penetrations (ensure conduits and structural brackets are properly sealed/waterproofed)
- ☐ Ensure code compliant labels and safety signs specified in the plans are in place
- ☐ Check that all home runs are properly identified at the inverter back to the CB's
- ☐ Check that combiner boxes are properly labeled
- ☐ Check source strings in DC combiner box are in the proper order and make sure labeling is clearly visible
- ☐ Verify that all AC and DC disconnect switches are in the open position
- ☐ Check that the solar modules are secured to the mounting system
- ☐ Visually inspect the array for cracked modules
- ☐ Check to see that all wiring is neat and well supported

REPETITIVE SOURCE CIRCUIT STRING WIRING

- ☐ Verify that the both the positive and negative string connectors are identified properly with permanent wire marking
- ☐ Repeat this sequence for all source circuit strings
- ☐ VERIFY POLARITY OF EACH SOURCE CIRCUIT STRING in the DC String Combiner Box (place common lead on the negative grounding block and the positive on each string connection—pay particular attention to make sure there is NEVER a negative measurement)
- ☐ **WARNING: IF POLARITY OF ONE SOURCE CIRCUIT STRING IS REVERSED, THIS CAN START A FIRE IN THE FUSE BLOCK RESULTING IN THE DESTRUCTION OF THE COMBINER BOX AND POSSIBLY ADJACENT EQUIPMENT. REVERSE POLARITY ON AN INVERTER CAN ALSO CAUSE DAMAGE THAT IS NOT COVERED UNDER THE EQUIPMENT WARRANTY**
- ☐ Verify open-circuit voltage of each source circuit string is within proper range according to manufacturer's installation manual and number each string and note string position on as-built drawing. (Record the string voltage in the attached Appendix, provide one attachment per combiner)
- ☐ Retighten all terminals in the DC String Combiner Box

WIRING TESTS

- ☐ Check the AC line voltage(s) at the main AC disconnect and record the voltage here:

  ____

- ☐ If installation contains additional AC disconnect switches, repeat the voltage check on each switch working from the main service entrance to the inverter AC disconnect switch, closing each switch after the test is made except for the final switch before the inverter (it is possible that the system only has a single AC switch)
- ☐ Check an electrical connection between the ground and the conductive surface of the PV modules. Perform test with a multi-meter or 100 mA dc source. If the resistance is less than 1 Ω, then the ground is considered good

INVERTER STARTUP TESTS

- ☐ Be sure that the inverter is off before proceeding with this section
- ☐ Test the continuity of all DC fuses to be installed in the DC string combiner box, install all string fuses, and close fuse switches in combiner box
- ☐ Check open circuit voltage at DC disconnect(s) switch(s) to ensure it is within proper limits according to the manufacturer's installation manual and record the voltage here:

  ____

- ☐ If installation contains additional DC disconnect switches, repeat the voltage check on each switch working from the PV array to the inverter DC disconnect switch, closing each switch after the test is made except for the final switch before the inverter (it is possible that the system only has a single DC switch)

  ____

- ☐ At this point, consult the inverter manual and follow proper startup procedure (all power to the inverter should be off at this time)
- ☐ Confirm that the inverter is operating and record the DC operating voltage here:

  ____

- ☐ Cross check that the power output shown on the inverter is the same as on the supplied performance meter within a + or – 2% tolerance

Inverter kW ______________ Performance Meter kW ______________

ONSITE MONITORING SYSTEM COMMISSIONING

(Go to performance metering enclosure and CT location for this section)

- ☐ Check CT's are orientated in the correct direction and take a picture, the black wire's from the CT's should be facing towards the Utility service panel
- ☐ CT's manufacturer ____________________________
- ☐ CT serial numbers A__________ B__________ C__________
- ☐ Meter manufacturer and serial number (Ex: Shark or ION)

  ____

- ☐ Remove the **meter calibration report** from the monitoring enclosure for delivery to Developer with this report
- ☐ Power Factor (PF)________ (If the Power Factor is negative then one or more of the CT's are installed backwards)
- ☐ Watts (W)__________ Hz __________ Amps ________
- ☐ Volts L-N A________ B________ C________
- ☐ Volts L-L A________ B________ C________
- ☐ If Static IP: IP Address__________ Subnet __________ Gateway__________

ONLINE SYSTEM COMMISSIONING Check that the following field devices are communicating and the data feedback is accurate:

- ☐ Go to http://www.[______________________]
- ☐ Login to the system provider's website
- ☐ Generation Meter - Check kW output of system is accurate
- ☐ Environment - Check that the feedback from the weather station sensors is accurate
- ☐ Inverter Monitoring
- ☐ DC Monitoring

SYSTEM TEST

1. Digital Irradiance Meter (Ex: Daystar Solar Meter)
2. Infrared Thermometer (Ex: Extech 42512)
3. Solar Module(s) Data Sheet(s)

STEP 1: Calculating System Derate Factor

Developer uses the PV WATTS on-line calculator to determine the overall DC to AC derate factor to estimate the instantaneous expected power output. Because the PV Watts overall DC-to-AC derate factor is determined for STC, a component derate factor for temperature is not part of its determination and must be applied while onsite.

1. Field cell temp. (C) _____ - STC cell temp. (C) _______ = Temp. Differential (C) _________

   Note: Take field cell temp reading toward the interior of the module
2. Temp. diff.(C) _____x Module Pmax temp. Coefficient (C) _______ = Temp derate (%) ____

   Note: Module Pmax temp. Coefficient can be found on the module data sheet
3. 1.00 – Temp De-rate _________ = Decimal Temp De-rate ____________

   Note: Convert Temp De-rate % to a decimal Ex: Temp. derate of 8% = .08)
4. PV Watts De-rate ________ x Decimal Temp De-rate________= System de-rate_______

   Note: The PV WATTS De-rate is supplied by your assigned Developer Project Manager

STEP 2: Irradiance at the Time of Commissioning

1. Irradiance ____________W/m2 (Irradiance sensor should be placed in the same plane as the modules)
2. **% of peak irradiance** _____________ divide **irradiance** by 1000 W/m2 and record the value here: (Ex: 692 W/m2 ÷ 1000 W/m2 = 0.692 or 69.2 %

STEP 3: System Performance at Time of Commissioning

1. System size STC kW __________x System de-rate ______ = **Estimated AC kW** _________

2. Measured AC kW___________ ÷ % of peak irradiance______ = **Corrected AC kW** ________

STEP 4: Comparison of Corrected and AC KW

Corrected AC kW __________ ÷ Estimated **AC kW** ___________ = ______________%

The **Estimated AC kW** value is the expected output of the PV system at 1000 W/m2. The **Corrected AC kW** must be 90% or higher of the **Estimated AC kW**. If it is less than 90%, the PV system is either shaded, dirty, miss-wired, fuses are blown, or the modules or inverter are not operating properly.

APPENDIX 1

SYSTEM DATA – COMPLETE ONE FORM FOR EVERY DC STRING COMBINER BOX

Combiner Box # ______________________

Combiner box serial number # ______________

Inverter ______________________

Operating Voltage ______________________

String No.	Open Circuit Voltage (Volts DC)	Operating Current (Amps)	Ambient Temp (C)	Irradiance Watts/m2
1				
2				
3				
4				
5				
6				
7				
8				
9				
10				
11				
12				

ATTACHMENT G

DATA ACQUISITION SYSTEM REQUIREMENTS

1.1 Solar Energy Generating Facility Data Acquisition System(s) shall be supplied by [______________], and will include the following components:

A. Data Logger/Internet Gateway

B. Revenue Grade Energy Meter – Energy Meters will be on Developer's Approved Products, **Attachment L.**

C. Weather Station - The location of each of the below listed sensors will be approved by Developer. All weather station communication cables will be, at a minimum, #22AWG twisted pair with shielding and drain wire.

a. Two Solar Irradiation Sensors; one for global horizontal solar radiation and one for the plane of array solar radiation. Sensors will be mounted away from shadows, reflective surfaces, and sources of artificial irradiation. Irradiation sensors will be installed in the middle of the array.

b. Ambient Temperature Sensor with solar radiation shield. The sensor will be located in an open space no closer then four times the height of any surrounding obstructions.

c. PV Cell Temperature Sensor – Sensor will be mechanically attached to the back of a reference solar module. The sensor will be located within the interior of the module towards the center point. The sensor will not be located at the edge of the module or on the surrounding mounting system. The selected reference module should be located at the center point of the array.

d. Wind Speed Sensor – The wind sensor should be installed in the middle of the array at array height.

D. External Device Communication

a. Inverter Monitoring (Some Inverters will have to be ordered with communication kits pre-installed from the manufacturer, consult the supplier from 1.1 above for inverter specific specifications).

E. DC String Level Monitoring – Combiner boxes will be on Developer's Approved Products, **Attachment L**

1.2 Basic Monitoring Service – These services are provided by service provider in 1.1 above. Ongoing costs for monitoring services are included in the Operations and Maintenance Agreement, which is an agreement that is separate from this agreement. The Monitoring Service Agreement will be signed by and between Developer and [________________].

A. Energy Meter monitoring

B. Weather Data monitoring

C. Inverter Monitoring

D. String Monitoring

E. Reporting

F. Performance Alarm Handling

G. System Log Book

1.3 Internet Uplink – Developer must have a secure, reliable, internet uplink to remotely monitor its SEGF's. The below communication options are available. The communication solution options will be reviewed and approved by both Developer and [service provider from 1.1 above] prior to any hardware purchase.

A. Host Local Area Network

B. Dedicated line for dial up

C. Cellular Data Service

D. Broadband Satellite

ATTACHMENT H

INTEGRATOR FORM DOCUMENTS

Invoice

Date	
Developer Number	
Order Number	
Job Number	
Invoice Number	
Net Terms	10 days

Bill To: **Job Address:** [DEVELOPER NAME] [____________________] [____________________] Attn: [_______________] Phone: [_____________] Facsimile: [_____________] Email: [________________]	[Project Name] [Site Address] [Milestone Number]

Remit To:

[wiring instructions or
Street
City, State, Zip]

Billing Amount:
10% Retention Withheld:
Retention Due: __________
Subtotal: $ __________
Misc:
Tax:
Pay This Amount: $ __________

CONDITIONAL WAIVER AND RELEASE UPON PROGRESS PAYMENT

Upon receipt by the undersigned of a payment or a check from [XXX Project Entity] in the sum of $________ payable to [______________] and when the payment is effective or the check has been properly endorsed and has been paid by the bank upon which it is drawn, this document shall become effective to unconditionally and irrevocably waive and release any mechanic's lien, stop notice, or bond right the undersigned has on the job of [XXX Project Entity] located at ________________ [Job Description] (the "Project") to the following extent.

This release covers a progress payment for labor, services, equipment, or material furnished to [XXX Project Entity] through ________________ [Date] only and does not cover any retentions retained before or after the release date; extras furnished before the release date for which payment has not been received; extras or items furnished after the release date. Rights based upon work performed or items furnished under a written change order which has been fully executed by the parties prior to the release date are covered by this release unless specifically reserved by the claimant in this release. This release of any mechanic's lien, stop notice, or bond right shall not otherwise affect the contract rights, including rights between parties to the contract based upon a rescission, abandonment, or breach of the contract, or the right of the undersigned to recover compensation for furnished labor, services, equipment, or material covered by this release if that furnished labor, services, equipment, or material was not compensated by the progress payment. Before any recipient of this document relies on it, said party should verify evidence of payment to the undersigned. If the undersigned has filed with a public agency a U.C.C. Financing Statement evidencing a security interest in equipment delivered or installed in connection with the Project, the undersigned agrees to promptly execute and file with such public agency any documents necessary to terminate the effectiveness of such U.C.C. Financing Statement.

Dated: ______________________________ ______________________________

Developer

By ______________________________

(Title)

CONDITIONAL WAIVER AND RELEASE UPON FINAL PAYMENT

Upon receipt by the undersigned of a payment or a check from [XXX Project Entity] in the sum of $________ payable to [____________] and when the check has been properly endorsed and has been paid by the bank upon which it is drawn, this document shall become effective to unconditionally and irrevocably waive and release any mechanic's lien, stop notice, or bond right the undersigned has on the job of [XXX Project Entity] located at ________________________ (the "Project").

This release covers the final payment to the undersigned for all labor, services, equipment, or material furnished on the job, except for disputed claims for additional work in the amount of $________. Before any recipient of this document relies on it, the party should verify evidence of payment to the undersigned. If the undersigned has filed with a public agency a U.C.C. Financing Statement evidencing a security interest in equipment delivered or installed in connection with the Project, the undersigned agrees to promptly execute and file with such public agency any documents necessary to terminate the effectiveness of such U.C.C. Financing Statement.

Dated: ______________________________ ______________________________

Developer

By ______________________________

(Title)

UNCONDITIONAL WAIVER AND RELEASE UPON PROGRESS PAYMENT

The undersigned has been paid and has received a progress payment in the sum of $________ for labor, services, equipment, or material furnished to [XXX Project Entity] on the job located at ________________ [Job Description] (the "Project") and does hereby unconditionally and irrevocably waive and release any mechanic's lien, stop notice, or bond right that the undersigned has on the above referenced job to the following extent.

This release covers a progress payment for labor, services, equipment, or materials furnished to [XXX Project Entity] through ________________ [Date] only and does not cover any retentions retained before or after the release date; extras furnished before the release date for which payment has not been received; extras or items furnished after the release date. Rights based upon work performed or items furnished under a written change order which has been fully executed by the parties prior to the release date are covered by this release unless specifically reserved by the claimant in this release. This release of any mechanic's lien, stop notice, or bond right shall not otherwise affect the contract rights, including rights between parties to the contract based upon a rescission, abandonment, or breach of the contract, or the right of the undersigned to recover compensation for furnished labor, services, equipment, or material covered by this release if that furnished labor, services, equipment, or material was not compensated by the progress payment. If the undersigned has filed with a public agency a U.C.C. Financing Statement evidencing a security interest in equipment delivered or installed in connection with the Project, the undersigned agrees to promptly execute and file with such public agency any documents necessary to terminate the effectiveness of such U.C.C. Financing Statement.

Dated: ________________________________ ________________________________

Developer

By ________________________________

(Title)

NOTICE: THIS DOCUMENT WAIVES RIGHTS UNCONDITIONALLY AND STATES THAT YOU HAVE BEEN PAID FOR GIVING UP THOSE RIGHTS. THIS DOCUMENT IS ENFORCEABLE AGAINST YOU IF YOU SIGN IT, EVEN IF YOU HAVE NOT BEEN PAID. IF YOU HAVE NOT BEEN PAID, USE A CONDITIONAL RELEASE FORM.

UNCONDITIONAL WAIVER AND RELEASE UPON FINAL PAYMENT

The undersigned has been paid in full for all labor, services, equipment, or material furnished to [XXX Project Entity] on the job located at ____ [Job Description] (the "Project') and does hereby unconditionally and irrevocably waive and release any right to a mechanic's lien, stop notice, or any right against a labor and material bond on the job, except for disputed claims for extra work in the amount of $_________. If the undersigned has filed with a public agency a U.C.C. Financing Statement evidencing a security interest in equipment delivered or installed in connection with the Project, the undersigned agrees to promptly execute and file with such public agency any documents necessary to terminate the effectiveness of such U.C.C. Financing Statement.

Dated: ________________________________ ________________________________

Developer

By ________________________________

(Title)

NOTICE: THIS DOCUMENT WAIVES RIGHTS UNCONDITIONALLY AND STATES THAT YOU HAVE BEEN PAID FOR GIVING UP THOSE RIGHTS. THIS DOCUMENT IS ENFORCEABLE AGAINST YOU IF YOU SIGN IT, EVEN IF YOU HAVE NOT BEEN PAID. IF YOU HAVE NOT BEEN PAID, USE A CONDITIONAL RELEASE FORM.

****

ATTACHMENT I

Shading Study Guidelines

****

ATTACHMENT J

WARRANTIES

[List of manufacturers' warranties on a project-by-project basis]

Panel Manufacturer Warranty

Inverter Manufacturer Warranty

Other Equipment Manufacturer Warranties

****

ATTACHMENT K

INTEGRATOR INSURANCE

Integrator Insurance. Integrator shall maintain until Final Completion, the insurance coverage outlined in (i) through (ix) below, and all such other insurance as required by applicable law. Evidence of coverage will be provided to Developer on an annual basis, 30 days prior to policy expiration, via a Certificate of Insurance naming Developer and Site Host as an additional insured and certificate holder. All Insurance Carriers will be rated A-VIII or better by A.M. Best and Company.

(i) Workers' Compensation/Employers Liability. Limits as follows:

* Workers' Compensation – Statutory Coverage.
* Employers Liability – Bodily Injury by accident $1,000,000 each accident

Bodily Injury by disease $1,000,000 each employee

Bodily Injury by disease $1,000,000 policy limit

(ii) Commercial General Liability including Contractual Liability insurance with limits of :

* $1,000,000 per occurrence for Bodily Injury and Property Damage
* $5,000,000 General Aggregate - other than Products/Completed Operations
* $2,000,000 Products/Completed Operations Aggregate
* $100,000 Fire Damage

Coverage to be written on an Occurrence form per location basis, without endorsements that limit the policy terms with respect to: (1) the definition of an Insured Contract, (2) provisions for severability of interest, (3) explosion, collapse, underground hazard.

(iii) Auto Liability insurance for owned, hired and non-owned vehicles with limits of $1,000,000 per accident.

Coverage to be written on an Occurrence form per location aggregate limit. Coverage terms and limits to apply excess of the primary per occurrence and/or aggregate limits provided for in the Commercial General Liability, Auto Liability and Professional Liability policies. Coverage terms and limits to also apply in excess of those required for Employers Liability.

(vii) Builder's Risk insurance limits as follows:

* Property limit to be purchased on a replacement cost basis at the full construction contract amount including an agreed upon sub-limit for "soft cost." Coverage will be written on a "special" form cause of loss and include an agreed amount endorsement containing no co-insurance provisions or deduction for depreciation with deductible of no more than $10,000 and include a limit for loss of business income due to delay in start-up. Boiler and Machinery coverage will be purchased if required for any "hot-testing" of equipment. Developer and/or Host

Developer may require additional coverage under this section as required by industry standard to insure against losses caused by Flood, Earthquake, Terrorism or Windstorm for projects in locations exposed to these perils.

* No exclusion for faulty workmanship, design or material
* No deductible greater than $25,000

(viii) Policy Endorsements.

* The insurance specified in clause 15.3 above shall contain waivers of subrogation rights against Developer.
* The insurance provided for Builder's Risk, Commercial General Liability and Excess Liability shall:
    (a) include Developer and Site Host as an additional insured with respect to Work performed under this Contract, and

    (b) provide that the insurance is primary coverage with respect to all insureds and shall not be considered contributory insurance with any insurance policies of Developer

****

ATTACHMENT L

APPROVED PRODUCTS

Approved PV Modules

Because of the absolute requirement for long-term vendor support, high reliability and competitive pricing, Developer's SEGFs are built using established [crystalline silicon][thin film] PV technologies, provided by established PV manufacturers.

Developer's Approved PV Module Manufacturers

- [__________________]

Developer's General Guidelines for PV modules

- Advanced PV technologies (thin-film, concentrating PV, etc.) are not used by Developer at this time.
- All modules must be included on any required rebate-related approved module list as well as on the California Energy Commission's (CEC's) List of Eligible Photovoltaic Modules.

Developer's Specific Requirements for PV modules

Approved Inverter Hardware

The choice of power inverters is one of the most impacting decisions of a photovoltaic system design, for inverters consume power, are complex solid-state systems and are typically the one component of a SEGF most likely to experience failure. Developer's SEGF design preferences focus on smaller numbers of large inverters vs. large numbers of small inverters. All inverters must be included on any required rebate-related approved module list as well as on the California Energy Commission's List of Eligible Inverters.

Developer's Approved Inverter Manufacturers

- [__________________]

All inverters must have minimum of 10-year warranty coverage.

Inverter Manufacturer Preventative Maintenance and Support Services

Developer highly values preventative maintenance support services provided by inverter manufacturers, as well as comprehensive and highly responsive repair service offerings. In addition, as Developer will be monitoring our inverters' performance remotely, we require that the inverters utilize an open interface and documented protocols for third party monitoring software.

Approved Mounting Hardware

Developer desires to ensure that each Solar Energy Generating Facility is built with the highest level of structural integrity possible while at the same time minimizing the impact on its Site Host's buildings or land. Developer must be able to remove a SEGF easily if needed, and requires the ability for its Site Host to accomplish maintenance without unnecessary difficulty. On rooftops, Developer strives to minimize roof penetrations whenever possible and to minimize structural static and dynamic loading forces; thus, we encourage SEGF design with liberal seismic and wind force assumptions. Developer requires the strongest, least impacting and most reliable module mounting design possible.

Rooftop Mounting Systems

- [_________________]

Rooftop Mounting Rail Solutions

- [_________________]

Ground Mount Fixed Array Mounting Solutions

- [_________________]

Single Axis Tracker Solutions

- [_________________]

Elevated Array Solutions

- [_________________]

In some instances the proposed location of the array will require the use of elevated mounting structures. Elevated mounting structures should be designed and built with the sole intention of mounting PV modules on a site where the array must be elevated to access the solar resources.

Unlisted Mounting and Tracking Systems

Mounting or tracking solutions or systems not listed may be submitted to Developer for review and approval. Developer requires that all mounting solution descriptions clearly identify the mounting hardware, any engineering services related to the mounting solution, and details related to the number of roof penetrations required and the plan to seal and warrant the roof. Mounting solution costs should always take into consideration all of these elements to ensure an equitable comparison. Proposed mounting systems or tracking solutions should be supplied with full specifications, warranty details, etc.

Approved Data Acquisition System (DAS)

- [_________________]

Performance Monitoring and Reporting Service Provider

- [_________________]

Inverter Monitoring

- [_________________]

Approved DC String-Level Monitoring Combiner Box Manufacturers

- [_________________]

Weather Station Requirements

- Module temperature sensor
- Irradiance sensor (one mounted in-plane with modules)
- Wind speed sensor

- Ambient temp sensor

Internet Connection

- Developer must have a secure, reliable, Internet uplink to remotely monitor its SEGFs.

Energy Meters

- [____________________]

Approved DC Safety Switches

- [____________________]

Approved Grounding Lugs

- [____________________]

RECORDING REQUESTED BY AND
WHEN RECORDED MAIL TO:

SUBORDINATION, ATTORNMENT, NON-DISTURBANCE AND ASSIGNMENT AGREEMENT

THIS SUBORDINATION, ATTORNMENT, NON-DISTURBANCE AND ASSIGNMENT AGREEMENT (this "Agreement") is made as of the ____day of ______________, 20___, by and among ___________________, a ________________ ("ABC"), to be indexed as a grantor; __________________, a ________________________ ("XYZ"), to be indexed as a grantor and as a grantee; and ____________________________________, a ____________________(together with its successors and assigns as beneficiaries of the Deed of Trust described below, "Lender"), to be indexed as a grantor and as a grantee.

Recitals:

A. By Deed of Trust dated _________________________, recorded in Book _____________, at Page ________________ in the records of _________________ County, State of _________________________(the "Deed of Trust") between the ABC and Lender, ABC deeded certain property to Trustees, in trust for the benefit of Lender as more particularly described therein. The property secured by the Deed of Trust is described on Exhibit A attached hereto and made a part hereof (the "Property").

B. By a Master Rooftop Lease Agreement by and between ABC and XYZ dated _________________, ______, ("MRLA"), by which, among other things, ABC assigned to XYZ and XYZ assumed all Rooftop Licenses (as defined therein) upon and subject to the terms, covenants and conditions set forth in said MRLA.

C. Pursuant to certain provisions of the MRLA, including without limitation Sections ___ and ___, ABC is required to use its best efforts to procure, and XYZ needs ABC to procure and has certain remedies if ABC is unable to procure, among other things, the consent of Lender to said MRLA and Lender's execution of this Agreement.

D. The parties desire and intend, by this Agreement, that Lender subordinate certain of its rights under the Deed of Trust to the rights of and for the benefit of XYZ; that XYZ and ABC acknowledge that XYZ's payment obligations to ABC under the MRLA shall be assigned hereby to Lender to the same extent as other leases upon the Property; that XYZ agrees to attorn to the purchaser of the Property at foreclosure of the Deed of Trust in the event of such foreclosure, or to the Lender in the event of collection of the rents owing from XYZ to ABC by the Lender; and that XYZ is willing to agree to attorn if Lender and such purchaser will recognize XYZ's rights under the MRLA to the extent hereinafter indicated.

E. All capitalized words and terms that are used, but not defined, herein shall have the meanings ascribed to them in the MRLA.

NOW THEREFORE, for and in consideration of the sum of One Dollar ($1.00) paid in hand by each of the parties hereto to the other, receipt whereof is acknowledged, and for and in consideration of the Recitals set forth above, which are incorporated herein by this reference, and the terms, covenants and conditions herein made, the parties agree as follows:

1. ABC and Lender hereby confirm to XYZ that the Deed of Trust is in full force and effect and that as of the date of this Agreement, there is no event of default under the Deed of Trust by ABC.

2. Subject to the provisions hereof, the lien and provisions of the Deed of Trust shall be subject and subordinate to the terms, covenants and conditions of the MRLA, for the period of the initial term of the MRLA and any renewals or extensions thereof and for such period following its expiration or termination as XYZ has the right to receive any payments from Rooftop Tenants thereunder.

3. XYZ hereby is authorized to exercise all its rights under the MRLA, free of any interests, rights of consent, assignments of rents, or other involvement or rights of, from or on behalf of Lender. Specifically this authorization shall include, without limitation, all rights, title and interest in and to Licenses with Rooftop Tenants, whether now existing or created hereafter, being free of any interests of Lender. XYZ shall be free to enter into, terminate, and compromise contracts with Rooftop Tenants, and to pledge, hypothecate, assign and otherwise deal with Rooftop Tenants and their Licenses, all without any involvement or interest of Lender. XYZ acknowledges, however, that its payment obligations to ABC under the MRLA shall be collaterally assigned hereby to Lender to the same extent as the rental obligations of tenants under other leases

upon the Property are assigned to Lender.

4. If the interest of ABC in the Property shall be transferred to and owned by Lender by reason of foreclosure or other proceedings brought by it, or by deed in lieu of foreclosure or any other manner, or if Lender otherwise shall assume possession of the Property, XYZ shall be bound to Lender under all of the terms, covenants and conditions of the Deed of Trust for the balance of the term thereof remaining and any extensions or renewals thereof which may be effected in accordance with any option therefor in the Deed of Trust, with the same force and effect as if Lender had been the original grantor under the Deed of Trust, subject, however, to the provisions of this Agreement. XYZ does hereby attorn to (a) Lender as its landlord when Lender is in possession of the Property, (b) a receiver appointed in any action or proceeding to foreclose the Deed of Trust, (c) any party acquiring title to the Property and (d) any successor to ABC. Said attornment shall be effective and self-operative without the execution of any further instruments on the part of any of the parties hereto immediately upon Lender's succeeding to the interest of ABC in the Property. The respective rights and obligations of XYZ and Lender upon such attornment, to the extent of the then remaining balance of the term of the Deed of Trust and any such extensions and renewals, shall be and are the same as now set forth therein. Upon request, XYZ will execute a written attornment agreement in favor of Lender at such time as Lender succeeds to ABC's interest in the Property, provided that Lender in any such agreement shall acknowledge the subordination of its lien, and the non-disturbance provisions of this Agreement, as provided in this Agreement.

5. So long as no event of default has occurred which has continued to exist for such period of time (after notice, if any, required by the MRLA) as would entitle ABC under the MRLA to terminate the MRLA or would cause, without any further action of ABC, the termination of the MRLA, the MRLA shall not be terminated, nor shall XYZ's use, possession or enjoyment of, or its rights in and to, the Property be interfered with, nor shall the rights of XYZ granted by the MRLA be affected in any other manner, in any foreclosure or any action or proceeding instituted under or in connection with the Deed of Trust or, in case Lender takes possession of the Property, pursuant to the provisions of the Deed of Trust.

6. If Lender shall succeed to the interest of ABC under the MRLA, Lender shall not be (a) liable for any act or omission of any prior landlord (including ABC), (b) subject to any offsets or defenses which XYZ might have against any prior landlord (including ABC), (c) bound by any rent, security deposit or additional rent which XYZ might have paid for more than one month in advance to any prior landlord (including ABC), (d) bound by any amendment or modification of the MRLA made without Lender's consent or (e) except for acts or omissions occurring during Lender's period of actual or legal possession, bound to XYZ beyond the date on which it shall transfer title to the Property to a third party.

7. At any time after an event of default has occurred under the Deed of Trust and XYZ has received written notice thereof from or on behalf of Lender, XYZ shall make payments under the MRLA directly to Lender. Receipt of Lender's written certification that such an event of default has occurred shall be the only condition to XYZ's making payments directly to Lender, and XYZ shall not be required to investigate or verify the nature or extent of any default. ABC, by its execution of this Agreement, irrevocably consents to such direct payment by XYZ and agrees to hold XYZ harmless for the application of any payments so made.

8. XYZ agrees to certify to Lender from time to time, on reasonable written notice, as to whether the MRLA is in effect and whether there are any defaults thereunder.

9. All notices hereunder must be in writing and, unless otherwise provided herein, shall be deemed validly given if sent by certified mail, return receipt requested, postage prepaid, by overnight delivery via a nationally recognized delivery service or by personal delivery against receipt, addressed as follows (or to any other address which the party to be notified may designate by proper notice to the other party). Such notices shall be deemed effective upon the earlier of (i) actual receipt by the addressee thereof, (ii) one (1) business day after deposit thereof with a nationally recognized delivery service, or (ii) three (3) days after deposit thereof with the United States mail. Should ABC, XYZ or Lender have a change of address, the other party shall immediately be notified as provided in this Section of such change.

XYZ:

With a copy to:

and with a copy to: Any Successor to XYZ of which ABC receives notice.

ABC:

With a copy to:

Bank:

With a copy to:

10. The words "foreclosure" and "foreclosure sale" as used herein shall be deemed to include the acquisition of ABC's estate in the Property by voluntary deed (or assignment) in lieu of foreclosure. The word "Lender" shall include the Lender herein specifically named and any of its nominees, successors, and assigns, including anyone who shall have succeeded to ABC's interest in the Property by, through or under foreclosure of the Deed of Trust, or by voluntary deed.

11. All of the terms, covenants and conditions hereof shall run with the land and shall be binding upon, and inure to the benefit of, the parties hereto and their respective successors and assigns.

IN WITNESS WHEREOF, this Agreement has been signed and delivered as of the date and year first set forth above.

****

EXHIBIT A

Legal Description:

****

RECORDING REQUESTED BY AND
WHEN RECORDED MAIL TO:

SUBORDINATION, NON-DISTURBANCE AND ATTORNMENT AGREEMENT

THIS AGREEMENT, is made as of ________________, by __________________________ ("Tenant"), a ______________________ organized under the laws of the state of ________________, having its principal office at ____________________________, city of ______________, state of ___________, and ______________________ __________ ("Lender"), having its principal office at ____________________________, city of __________________, state of ______________, with reference to the following facts:

RECITALS:

A. Pursuant to a lease dated ______________________________ (the "Lease"), between ________________ ("Landlord"), and Tenant, Landlord leased to Tenant certain space (the "Premises") in the building located at ________________________________, which property is more particularly described in the Mortgage (as hereinafter defined) (the "Property");

B. Lender has made a loan (the "Loan") to Landlord, which Loan is evidenced by a note and secured, inter alia, by a first lien instrument in favor of Lender covering the property and upon the terms and conditions described therein, which is recorded in the Office of the County Recorder for ________________ County (said instrument and all amendments, modifications, renewals, substitutions, extensions, consolidations and replacements thereto and thereof, as applicable, are hereinafter collectively referred to as "Mortgage");

C. It is a condition precedent to obtaining the Loan that (i) the Mortgage be and remain at all times a first lien or charge upon the Property prior and superior to the Lease, (ii) Tenant specifically subordinate the Lease to the lien or charge of the Mortgage and (iii) Tenant attorn to the Lender and its successors and assigns in the event of the foreclosure or other proceeding to enforce the Mortgage;

NOW, THEREFORE, in consideration of the mutual benefits accruing to the parties hereto and for other valuable consideration, the receipt and sufficiency of which are hereby acknowledged, and in order to induce Lender to enter into the above-referenced Loan, Lender and Tenant hereby agree as follows:

1. **Subordination**. The Lease and any extensions, renewals, replacements, consolidations or modifications thereof, and the right, title and interest of the Tenant in and to the Premises, and all rights of the Tenant thereunder, are and shall be subject and subordinate to the Mortgage and lien and terms thereof.

2. **Lender's Exercise of Remedies.** In the event of (a) the institution of any foreclosure, trustee's sale or other like proceeding, (b) the appointment of a receiver for the Landlord or the Property, (c) the exercise of rights to collect rents under the Mortgage or an assignment of rents, (d) the recording by Lender or its successor or assignee of a deed in lieu of foreclosure for the Property, or (e) any transfer or abandonment of possession of the Property to Lender or its successor or assigns in connection with any proceedings affecting Landlord under the Bankruptcy Code, 11 U.S.C. §101 et seq. (with any such foreclosure, recording of a deed in lieu of foreclosure, or transfer or abandonment of the Property referred to in the preceding clauses (a) through (e) is hereinafter called a "Transfer," and Lender or any successor or assignee of Lender taking title to the Property in connection with a Transfer is hereinafter called the "Transferee"), such Transferee shall not: (i) be liable for any damages (including, without limitation, consequential damages) or other relief or be subject to any offsets, defenses or counterclaims of any kind attributable to any event, act, omission or default under the Lease, including, but not limited to, a breach of any representation or warranty under the Lease, of Landlord or any prior landlord under the Lease, except for any continuing event, act or omission of which Lender has been provided notice as described in paragraph 4 below, and if any such offset or defense is expressly provided for in the Lease, (ii) be bound by any prepayment by Tenant of more than one month's installment of rent unless such prepayment is expressly required in the Lease or has been specifically approved in writing by Lender, or be liable or responsible for any security deposit or other sums which Tenant may have paid under the Lease unless such deposit or other sums have been physically delivered to Transferee, or (iii) be bound by any modification or amendment of the Lease after the date hereof, or waiver of any terms of the Lease unless the same shall have been approved in writing by Lender.

3. **Attornment and Non-Disturbance.** Provided (a)Tenant complies with this Agreement, (b) Tenant is not in default under the terms of the Lease and no event has occurred which, with the passage of time or the giving of notice or both, would constitute a default under the Lease, and (c) the Lease is in full force and effect, except as set forth in

Paragraphs 2 and d and e of this Agreement, any default under the Mortgage and any proceeding to foreclose the same will not disturb the Tenant's possession under the Lease and the Lease will not be affected or cut off thereby, and not withstanding any such foreclosure or other Transfer of Property to Transferee, Transferee will recognize the Lease and will accept the attornment of Tenant thereunder.

Tenant shall attorn to Transferee, including Lender if Lender becomes a Transferee, as the landlord under the Lease. Said attornment is subject to the limitation of Transferee's obligations set forth in Paragraph 2 above and shall be effective and self-operative without the execution of any further instruments upon Transferee's succeeding to the interest of the Landlord under the Lease. Tenant and Lender shall, however, confirm the provisions of this paragraph in writing upon request by either of them.

4. **Lender's Right to Cure.** Notwithstanding anything to the contrary, in the Lease or this Agreement, Tenant shall provide Lender with written notice of any default of Landlord under the Lease (which can be a copy of the notice provided to the Landlord) if such default is of such a nature as to give the Tenant a right to terminate the Lease, to reduce rent thereunder or to credit or to offset any amounts against future rents, and will not seek to terminate the Lease or reduce the rent or credit or offset against rent or claim a partial or total eviction until giving such notice and providing Lender a period of thirty (30) days beyond the time available to Landlord under the Lease in which to cure the breach or default by Landlord, provided however, as to any breach or default by Landlord the cure of which requires possession and control of the Property or Premises and thereafter cure the breach or default with reasonable diligence, or obtain the appointment of a receiver pursuant to any court proceeding, or otherwise, and give such receiver a reasonable period of time in which to cure the default. Lender shall have no obligation to cure (and shall have no liability or obligation for not curing) any breach or default by Landlord, except to the extent that Lender agrees otherwise in writing.

5. **Miscellaneous.**

   a. This Agreement shall be binding upon and shall inure to the benefit of the parties hereto, their successors and assigns; provided, however, that in the event of the assignment or transfer of the interest of Transferee, all obligations and liabilities of Transferee under this Agreement shall terminate, and thereupon all such obligations and liabilities shall be the responsibility of the party to whom Transferee's interest is assigned or transferred; and provided further that the interest of Tenant under this Agreement may not be assigned or transferred except to the extent the assignment of Tenant's interest in the Lease is permitted under the Lease.

   b. Tenant acknowledges that it has notice that the Lease and the rent and all other sums due thereunder have been assigned to the Lender as part of the security for the note secured by the Mortgage and upon written notice from the Lender of a default under the Mortgage, Tenant shall pay its rent and all other sums due under the Lease directly to Lender, and Landlord, by its execution hereof, hereby direct Tenant to make such payments to Lender.

   c. Tenant acknowledges and agrees that it shall not terminate the Lease in the event of a default by Landlord unless Tenant provides Lender written notice and an opportunity to cure as described in Paragraph 4 above. In addition, Tenant agrees that it shall not terminate or cancel the Lease by agreement with the Landlord without Lender's prior written consent, unless such right to terminate or cancel is expressly set forth in the Lease. Tenant shall pay to Lender any and all termination fees or other consideration to be paid to Landlord in connection with such termination or cancellation and Landlord, by its execution thereof, hereby directs Tenant to make such payments or provide such other consideration to Lender.

   d. Tenant covenants and acknowledges that it has no right or option of any nature whatsoever, whether pursuant to the Lease or otherwise, to purchase the Property or the real property of which the Property is a part, or any portion thereof or any interest therein and to the extent that Tenant has had, or hereinafter acquires any such right or option, the same is hereby acknowledged to be subject and subordinate to the Mortgage and is hereby waived and release as against Transferee.

   e. This Agreement is the whole and only agreement between the parties hereto with regard to the subordination of the Lease to the lien or charge of the Mortgage. This Agreement may not be modified in any manner or terminated except by an instrument in writing by the parties hereto.

   f. This Agreement shall be deemed to have been made in the state where the Property is located and the validity, interpretation and enforcement of this Agreement shall be determined in accordance with the laws of such state.

   g. In the event of any legal action or proceeding is commenced to interpret or enforce the terms of, or obligations arising out of this Agreement, or to recover damages for the breach thereof, the party prevailing in any such action or proceeding shall be entitled to recover from the non-prevailing party all reasonable attorneys' fees, costs and expenses incurred by the prevailing party.

   h. Any notices or communications required or permitted to be given or made hereunder shall be deemed to be so given or made when in writing and delivered in person or sent by United States registered or certified mail, postage prepaid, or by nationally recognized overnight courier service, directed to the parties at the following addresses or such other addresses as they may from time to time designate in writing.

Lender:

Tenant:

Notices or communications mailed in the United States mail shall be deemed served on the third business day following mailing, notices or communications served by hand or by overnight courier shall be deemed served upon receipt.

i. This document may be signed in counterparts which together shall be deemed to be one and the same document. The signature pages from any such counterpart may be attached to another such counterpart to form one complete set of signatures for this document.

j. The parties hereto represent and warrant that their respective signatories to this Agreement have been duly authorized by the Tennant, Landlord and Lender, as applicable.

IN WITNESS WHEREOF, this Agreement has been signed and delivered as of the date and year first set forth above.

TENANT: ______________________________

BY: ___________________________________, TITLE: ______________________________

LENDER: ______________________________

BY: ___________________________________, TITLE: ______________________________

LANDLORD: ______________________________

BY: ___________________________________, TITLE: ______________________________

As to Paragraphs b and c: ____

____

Pricing Assumptions*

- The 5-year U.S. swap rate to be used as Index Rate *www.federalreserve.gov/Releases/H15/.*
- Energy Price Rates based upon an Equipment Cost of $1,000,000.00. Energy Purchase Pricing Amounts are shown below.
- Energy system size is 999.99 Watt DC
- Advance payments consisting of none
- Estimated annual energy production is 999.99 kWh per year
- Estimated daily sunlight hours of 4.75 hours per day

*Estimated costs of approximately $15,000.00 for documentation, security filing fees, legal and other miscellaneous expense is included in EPA pricing and is exclusive of Commitment Fee in Paragraph 35 above.

The capitalized cost of the energy system amount shall not exceed $1,000,000.00. All costs exceeding the above capitalized system amount, will not be paid by Energy Provider. Customer Name will need to pay all costs exceeding the $1,000,000.00 directly to Name of Supplier/Dealer or to other parties as appropriate.

<u>Energy Purchase Payment Schedule for Original EPA Term of 240 Months</u> (Based on capitalized energy system cost of $1,000,000.00):

<u>Note</u>: Rebate(s) of $999,999.00 that will be received by Energy Purchaser from Southern California Edison will occur on or before 90 days after EPA Commencement Date and will be paid in kind to Energy Provider on or before 90 days after EPA Commencement Date.

<u>Renewal Option Schedule for 60 Months:</u>

Term (Months)	Monthly Energy Purchase Price	Estimated Annualized Monthly Payment
First 12	$.0000 per kWh	$0.00 per month
Following 12	$.0000 per kWh	$0.00 per month
Following 12	$.0000 per kWh	$0.00 per month
Following 12	$.0000 per kWh	$0.00 per month
Following 12	$.0000 per kWh	$0.00 per month
Following 12	$.0000 per kWh	$0.00 per month
Following 12	$.0000 per kWh	$0.00 per month
Following 12	$.0000 per kWh	$0.00 per month
Following 12	$.0000 per kWh	$0.00 per month
Following 12	$.0000 per kWh	$0.00 per month
Following 12	$.0000 per kWh	$0.00 per month
Following 12	$.0000 per kWh	$0.00 per month
Following 12	$.0000 per kWh	$0.00 per month
Following 12	$.0000 per kWh	$0.00 per month
Following 12	$.0000 per kWh	$0.00 per month
Following 12	$.0000 per kWh	$0.00 per month
Following 12	$.0000 per kWh	$0.00 per month
Following 12	$.0000 per kWh	$0.00 per month
Following 12	$.0000 per kWh	$0.00 per month
Following 12	$.0000 per kWh	$0.00 per month
Following 12	$.0000 per kWh	$0.00 per month
Following 12	$.0000 per kWh	$0.00 per month
Following 12	$.0000 per kWh	$0.00 per month
Following 12	$.0000 per kWh	$0.00 per month
First 12	$.0000 per kWh	$0.00 per month
Following 12	$.0000 per kWh	$0.00 per month
Following 12	$.0000 per kWh	$0.00 per month
Following 12	$.0000 per kWh	$0.00 per month
Following 12	$.0000 per kWh	$0.00 per month

SUMMARY OF TERMS AND CONDITIONS

Name of Customer CONFIDENTIAL

ANNEX B

To

CONFIDENTIAL SUMMARY OF TERMS

EQUIPMENT

Insert description of energy system

Appendix 2

Software Tool Programs for Building Energy Projects[2]

For additional software tools on energy go to
http://apps1.eere.energy.gov/buildings/tools_directory/about.cfm

Tool	Applications	Free	Recently Updated
1D-HAM	Solves one-dimensional coupled heat, air and moisture transport problems in a multi-layered porous wall. 1D-HAM is based on finite difference technique with explicit forward differences in time. Analytical solutions for the coupling between the computational cells for a given air flow through the construction are used. Moisture is transferred by diffusion and convection in vapor phase. No liquid water transport occurs. Heat is transferred by conduction, convection and latent heat. Climatic data are supplied through a data file with a maximum resolution of values per hour over the year. The program accounts for surface absorption of solar radiation. http://www.buildingphysics.com		
3E Plus	Industrial energy management tool to simplify the task of determining how much insulation is necessary to use less energy, reduce plant emissions and improve process efficiency. The 3E Plus insulation thickness computer program is designed for facility managers, energy/environmental managers, industrial process engineers, and the industrial industry, the program is a valuable tool for determining the return on investment of an insulation upgrade on pipes, ducts, tanks, and boilers. http://www.pipeinsulation.org	☑	
AAMASKY	Analysis of component and total heating, cooling, and lighting energy consumption attributable to skylights in commercial buildings, as well as peak demand impacts. Also provides hourly and monthly patterns of illumination levels from daylighting. The American Architectural Manufacturers Association's AAMASKY (AAMA SKYlight) consists of a Skylight Design Guidelines Handbook containing worksheet-based calculations, as well as a software spreadsheet that allows much more rapid determination of skylight impacts; all required data for analysis in ten U.S. climates is provided. Directly applicable to simple diffusing skylight designs for most types of commercial buildings. Helps achieve compliance with performance-based building codes. With experience, can be used for some types of sloped glazing and atrium designs.		
Acuity Energy Platform	Agentis delivers energy efficiency software applications to businesses to improve energy management. Agentis partners with electric utilities to combine commercial and industrial energy use data with company demographics and provide business users with best practice comparisons to similar businesses, and personal recommendations of efficiency improvements and usage optimization that will save money and resources. Utilities can educate and engage their customers with energy- and cost-saving recommendations, while still meeting state-efficiency mandates. http://www.agentisenergy.com		
AEPS System Planning	The Alternative Energy Product Suite (AEPS) System Planning tool is a software application for the design, modeling, and simulation of electrical power systems with an emphasis on renewable energy sources (solar, wind, and hydro). The application calculates power generation, consumption, and storage for modeled systems. Power		

[227] U.S. Department of Energy

Tool **Applications**

Tool	Applications	Free	Recently Updated
	and cost data can be analyzed to optimize the modeled system based on user objectives and priorities. http://www.alteps.com		
AFT Fathom	AFT Fathom is a general-purpose pipe network analysis tool that can be used to simulate any incompressible fluid flow problem. Fathom is widely used to design chilled water and hot water systems, fire suppression systems, water distribution, chemical process plants, and HVAC duct systems. Fathom includes extensive built-in databases of fluids (liquids and gases), pipe materials, pipe fittings, and insulation materials. Fathom includes integrated heat transfer capabilities to model piping heat transfer and heat exchangers. http://www.aft.com		
AFT Mercury	AFT Mercury is a general-purpose pipe network optimization tool. AFT Mercury combines a proven pipe network analysis tool (AFT Fathom) with state-of-the-art optimization tools to allow designers to optimize pipe and component selection for lowest initial cost or lowest Life Cycle Cost (LCC) for a pipe or duct systems. Applied Flow Technology has demonstrated that optimization can reduce the energy usage and total life cycle cost by 20-50% for a variety of pumping systems. http://www.aft.com		
AGI32	3D lighting design and rendering software package for electric lighting and daylight analysis. AGI32 produces full-color renderings and predictive lighting system calculations simultaneously for all applications of electric lighting and daylighting in interior and exterior design projects. AGI32 displays dramatic calculation and rendering speeds making repetitive visualizations realistic, and dramatically shortening the conceptual part of the design process. Complex architectural environments are easily created internally, or externally created 3D environments can be imported via DWG or DXF format files. A comprehensive library of manufacturersï¿½ lighting product data is included. http://www.agi32.com		
AIRWIND Pro	Computes building air conditioning cooling and heating loads, in either Imperial or SI units, for projects drawn directly on-screen, with any number of walls, in any number of rooms, arranged at any angle, with any mix of construction materials and fenestration, organized into any number of zones and located anywhere in the world. Automatic and correctly weighted energy profiling at 30-minute intervals for every day of the year. Dynamically links to correctly weighted air conditioning equipment selection programs. http://us.mistralassociates.com		
AnTherm	Calculates temperature distributions, heat flows and (optionally) vapor diffusion flows in building structures - particularly those with thermal heat bridges. AnTherm (Analysis of Thermal behavior of Building Construction Heat Bridges) is designed for the technically qualified designer by providing thorough and reliable evaluation of thermal performance in accordance with current European standards (EN ISO). http://www.kornicki.com/antherm/EN		
Apache	Software tool for thermal design & energy simulation related to buildings. In design mode, APACHE covers the calculation of heating, cooling and latent room loads, the sizing of room units, internal comfort analysis and codes/standards checks. In simulation mode, APACHE performs a dynamic thermal simulation using hourly weather data. Linked modules deal with the performance of HVAC plant and natural ventilation. APACHE is a component of the IES Virtual Environment, an integrated computing environment encompassing a wide range of tasks in building design. http://www.iesve.com		
ArchiWIZARD	Thermal calculation software performs hourly simulations of buildings to provide mechanical, energy, and architectural engineers or architects with accurate estimates of a building's energy needs and input and output data structures tailored to facilitate architects', engineers', and design department work. http://www.archiwizard.fr/en		

Tool	Applications	Free	Recently Updated
Athena Model	Practical, easy-to-use decision support tool that provides high quality environmental data and assists with the complex evaluations required to make informed environmental choices. Our goal is to encourage the selection of material mixes and other design options that will minimize a building's potential life cycle environmental impacts and foster sustainable development. While there is a growing desire to put the environment on an equal footing with cost and other conventional design and product performance criteria, the task is by no means simple. It requires current, reliable and comparable environmental data in readily usable forms. The notion of Life-Cycle Assessment (LCA) has been generally accepted within the environmental research community as the only legitimate basis on which to compare alternative materials, components and services. http://www.athenasmi.ca	☑	
AUDIT	Calculates monthly and annual heating and cooling costs for residential and light commercial buildings. Virtually any type of cooling and heating system can be simulated by AUDIT including standard DX, evaporative, air source heat pumps, water source heat pumps, and all types of fossil fueled furnaces and boilers (both modulating and on/off controlled). An optional version of AUDIT with appliance capabilities can calculate appliance and hot water energy use as well. AUDIT uses monthly bin weather data and full load cooling hours in its calculations. Weather data for hundreds of cities throughout the world are built-in to AUDIT and additional weather data can be easily added. http://www.elitesoft.com		
Autodesk Green Building Studio	Seamlessly links architectural building information models (BIM) and certain 3-D CAD building designs with energy, water, and carbon analysis. Autodesk Green Building Studio enables architects to quickly calculate the operational and energy implications of early design decisions. The Autodesk Green Building Studio web service automatically generates geometrically accurate, detailed input files for major energy simulation programs. Green Building Studio uses the DOE-2.2 simulation engine to calculate energy performance and also creates geometrically accurate input files for EnergyPlus. Key to the integrated interoperability exhibited is the gbXML schema, an open XML schema of the International Alliance of Interoperability's aecXML Group. By using gbXML-enabled applications, Green Building Studio web service users are able to eliminate redundant data entry and dramatically reduce the time and expense traditionally associated with whole-building energy simulation analyses. http://usa.autodesk.com/adsk/servlet/pc/index?id=11179508&siteID=123112	☑	
AWDABPT	Provides dynamic temperature simulation of 1- to 15- room buildings, shelters, and cabinets over the course of 20 days. Useful for accommodation of heat dissipating equipment. Cooling or power plant failure and later restoration can be simulated. Includes indicative external bush/forest fire mode. http://www.awdabpt.com.au		
Awnshade	Calculates the unshaded fraction of a rectangular window for any given solar position coordinates relative to the window. Calculations are made for window shading configurations including awnings with or without side walls or overhangs of arbitrary dimensions above the window. Awnshade can also calculate the unshaded fraction for a sequence of solar positions. It calculates the effective unshaded fraction of diffuse sky irradiance or illuminance incident on the window, assuming uniform sky radiance/luminance, and the effective ground-reflected unshaded fraction. Includes the capability for handling cases in which shadows of the side of the awning/overhang cross the top of the window. http://www.fsec.ucf.edu/en		

Tool	Applications	Free	Recently Updated
BE$T	Multi-project energy savings and calculation tool for electric motors. The BE$T software can analyze the energy saving between three motors even if the motors incorporate variable frequency drives. It is ideal for quick energy efficiency calculations as well as large projects. http://www.baldor.com		
BEAVER	WINDOWS environment for the ESPII Fortran program which estimates the energy consumption of buildings using the ASHRAE Response Factor Method. BEAVER building energy simulation provides for user friendly input of data, processing and viewing of the results. http://members.ozemail.com.au/~acadsbsg		
BEES	Powerful technique for selecting cost-effective, environmentally preferable building products. BEES (Building for Environmental and Economic Sustainability) is based on consensus standards and designed to be practical, flexible, and transparent. BEES reduces complex, science-based technical content (e.g., over 400 environmental flows from raw material acquisition through product disposal) to decision-enabling results and delivers them in a visually intuitive graphical format. The Windows-based decision support software, aimed at designers, builders, and product manufacturers, includes actual environmental and economic performance data for nearly 200 building products (both generic and brand-specific). http://www.nist.gov/el/economics/BEESSoftware.cfm	☑	
Benchmata	BENCHMATA is an advanced system that can help utility companies, municipalities, local and state governments, and energy billing companies to automatically benchmark their customer's energy usage in ENERGY STAR® Portfolio Manager. It is the first commercially available system powerful enough to automate any organization's energy benchmarking needs. Software can put your organization on the fast track for bulk benchmarking of your customers in ENERGY STAR Portfolio Manager. http://www.benchmata.com		
BinMaker Pro	Creates summaries of U.S. hourly weather data for 239 cities. BinMaker PRO exports the resulting electronic files for use in spreadsheets, or other computer analysis programs. http://www.interenergysoftware.com		
BLCC	Provides comprehensive economic analysis of proposed capital investments that are expected to reduce long-term operating costs of buildings or buildings systems. BLCC5 and BLCC4 are the main programs in a set of six National Institute of Standards computer programs that are especially useful for evaluating energy and water conservation projects in buildings. The programs calculate Lowest Life-Cycle Cost, Net Savings, Savings-to-Investment Ratio, Adjusted Internal Rate of Return, and Payback Period. http://www1.eere.energy.gov/femp/information/download_blcc.html	☑	
BSim	Package of easy-to-use and flexible programs for evaluating the indoor climate and energy conditions as well as the designing of the heating, cooling and ventilation plants. The BSim package comprise the programs: SimView (user interface and graphic model editor), tsbi5 (simultaneous thermal and moisture building simulation tool), XSun (dynamic solar and shadow simulation and visualization), SimLight (daylight calculation tool), SimDXF (CAD import facility) and SimPV (building integrated PV-system calculation). http://en.sbi.dk		
BTU Analysis Plus	Heat load calculation program that performs comprehensive heat load studies with hardcopy printouts of the results. The BTU Analyst Plus program is designed for general heating, air-conditioning, and commercial studies. http://www.etreesw.com/ETSSWHome.htm		
Building Design Advisor	Software environment that supports the integration of multiple building models and databases used by analysis and visualization tools, through a single, object-based representation of building components	☑	

Tool	Applications	Free	Recently Updated
	and systems. BDA (Building Design Advisor) acts as a data manager and process controller, allowing building designers to benefit from the capabilities of multiple analysis and visualization tools throughout the building design process. http://gaia.lbl.gov/BDA		
Building Energy Analyzer	Provides quick economic analysis for commercial and industrial buildings. Building Energy Analyzer (BEA) estimates annual and monthly loads and costs associated with air-conditioning, heating, on-site power generation, thermal storage, and heat recovery systems for a given building and location. http://www.interenergysoftware.com		
Building Energy Modelling and Simulation: Self-Learning Modules	Provides a novel way to learn about building energy modeling and simulation. The self-learning courseware is available on the Web. http://www.bwk.tue.nl/bps/hensen/courseware/Class-mod+sim/sim_theory.htm	☑	
Building Greenhouse Rating	Provides assessments of the greenhouse intensity of office buildings by awarding a star rating on a scale of one to five. Buildings identified by the Australian Building Greenhouse Rating scheme with a high star rating will be more energy efficient and cheaper to run, and will result in lower greenhouse gas emissions. Separate components of the building can be rated - a base building rating measures the performance of those services provided by the building manager/landlord; and a tenancy rating measures the services for which the tenant is responsible. A whole building rating measures the combined effect. http://www.abgr.com.au	☑	
Building Performance Compass	Building Performance Compass analyzes commercial and multi-family building energy use patterns in a simple, easy-to-use Web-based interface. Using building details and energy data from the building's utility bills, it is unique in its ability to benchmark and compare all buildings, whether residential or commercial. http://www.psdconsulting.com/software/buildingperformance		
BuildingAdvice	BuildingAdvice™ is a user-friendly, Web-based platform designed to assess building energy performance and identify and quantify energy savings opportunities. Target buildings are in the 5k-200k sq. ft. range, with scalability up to 1mm sq. ft. The platform combines 1) portable wireless sensor packages for capture of real-time building data, 2) automated entry of weather data, 3) manual entry of basic building information, and 4) proprietary EnGen™ energy modeling software. http://www.airadvice.com		
BuildingSim	BuildingSim allows users to model a building and analyze the heating and cooling energy costs in any climate. Users can create any building—from a one-room apartment up to a 100+ floor skyscraper--and account for everything from window coverings to shade trees. BuildingSim uses actual hourly weather data from over 90 climates around the world to numerically solve the full thermodynamic differential equations every minute of the year, giving the user the actual energy use down to the cent. http://paragonrobotics.com/en-US-IE.html#website/home/en-US.html	☑	
C-MAX	Modularized software that systematically allows user to conduct industrial & commercial systems analysis to help evaluate options that could reduce the cost of owning, operating, and maintaining a facility; achieving energy conservation goals, and evaluate non-energy benefits. It could be used in a new and existing facility design, engineering, and specification preparation. It allows unlimited what-if case analysis of the following systems: centrifugal pumps, centrifugal compressors, fans and blowers, positive displacement compressors, and piping network. Other modules include: Energy Conservation Measure (ECM), Life Cycle Costing, Non-Energy Benefits,		

Tool	Applications	Free	Recently Updated
	Performance Charting, Utility, and Chemical/Physical Properties. http://www.unicade.com/cmax		
CAMEL	Calculates the design heating and cooling loads and associated psychrometrics for air conditioning plant in buildings. CAMEL is one of the leading air conditioning load estimation programs used in Australia and New Zealand. The calculations are based on the AIRAH/IHRACE Application Manual DA9 "Air Conditioning Systems, Load Estimation & Psychrometrics" which incorporates the cooling load estimation techniques and data developed by the Carrier International Corporation with considerable extensions and refinements to these methods and data, developed by ACADS-BSG. It models buildings in the Southern and Northern Hemisphere. http://members.ozemail.com.au/~acadsbsg		
Carbon Estates	Carbon Estates is a Web-based energy efficiency benchmarking and virtual simulation tool designed specifically for the built environment. It enables users to save money, reduce carbon, and comply with Carbon Reduction Commitment, a mandatory government scheme in the United Kingdom that is responsible for abating carbon emissions from buildings. http://www.co2estates.com		
CATALOGUE	Listings of windows and doors, including all products certified under the Canadian Window and Door Manufacturers Association program. CATALOGUE filters products (e.g., by operator type, frame material), and ranks products (e.g., ER value, U-value). Users can view and compare products (e.g., according to ABC values, construction type, performance characteristics). CATALOGUE is being linked with the compliance software for the Canadian National Energy Code (Houstrad and Buildtrad) and with the building simulation programs HOT2000 and ENERPASS. http://www.enermodal.com	☑	
CELLAR	Calculates the heat loss to the ground from a rectangular building with a foundation of the cellar type with constant insulation thickness at the floor and the wall. Both the heat loss variation during the year, including the peak effect, and the accumulated heat loss during the heating season is calculated. The effect of a sudden cold-spell may be analyzed. http://www.buildingphysics.com		
CHVAC	Quickly and accurately calculates the maximum heating and cooling loads for commercial buildings. CHVAC allows an unlimited number of zones which can be grouped into as many as 100 air handling systems. CHVAC automatically looks up all CLTD cooling load and correction factors necessary for computing loads. In addition, the programs can look up outdoor design weather data for over 1500 cities located around the world. There is also provision for editing the weather data as well as adding data for other cities. Comprehensive reports list the general project data, detailed zone loads, air handler summary loads, outside air loads, total building loads, building envelope analysis, tonnage requirements, CFM air quantities, chilled water flow rates (if applicable), and complete psychometric data with entering and leaving coil conditions. http://www.elitesoft.com		
CLIMATE 1	Global climate data atlas consisting of a data base and a software for data access and visualization. The data base contains more than 1200 station data sets distributed all over the globe. Station data consist of 16 monthly mean data sets: Temperature: mean, min., max., extreme min. and max. rel. humidity, precipitation: mean, min., max., day maximum, days with precipitation, potential evaporation, global radiation, sunshine hours, wind speed and direction. Once a station is selected, its data are displayed graphically on the screen, and the data can be exported for other applications. http://www.climate1.de		
Climate Consultant	Free, easy-to-use, graphic-based computer program that displays climate data in dozens of ways useful to architects, builders,	☑	

Tool	Applications	Free	Recently Updated
	contractors, and homeowners, including temperatures, humidity, wind velocity, sky cover, and solar radiation in both 2-D and 3-D graphics for every hour of the year in either Metric or Imperial units. Climate Consultant 3.0 also plots sun dials and sun shading charts overlaid with the hours when solar heating is needed or when shading is required. The psychrometric chart analysis shows the most appropriate passive design strategies in each climate, while the new wind wheel integrates wind velocity and direction data with concurrent temperatures and humidities and can be animated hourly, daily, or monthly. Because energy codes require slightly different types of buildings in each climate zones, it is important for people who are designing, constructing, or maintaining these buildings to understand the unique attributes of their climate and how it impacts their building's energy consumption. http://www.energy-design-tools.aud.ucla.edu		
Climawin 2005	Thermal calculation software to determine compliance with French building thermal regulations. CAD building files(DWG, DXF, IFC) can be imported to the calculations. http://www.bbs-slama.com		
CoDyBa	CoDyBa is used to analyze dynamic hygrothermal performance of building elements when subjected to any kind of climate conditions. The tool helps the user conduct studies of heating and cooling strategies, air conditioning or ventilation options, and insulating materials. The main objective is to forecast the energy consumption, temperature, and humidity evolution range. http://www.jnlog.com/codyba1_en.htm	☑	
COLDWIND Pro	Computes coldroom and freezer refrigeration loads, in either Imperial or SI units, for projects drawn directly on-screen, with any number of walls, in any number of rooms, arranged at any angles, with any mix of insulation materials, organized into any number of zones and located anywhere in the world. Automatic and correctly weighted energy profiling at 30-minute intervals for every day of the year. Dynamically links to correctly weighted refrigeration equipment selection and balancing programs. http://www.mistralassociates.com		
COMcheck	Designed to streamline the energy code compliance and approval process and is focused on the needs of those who design, build, and enforce building codes for commercial and high-rise residential building projects. The software addresses the enforceable provisions in commercial building energy codes based on ASHRAE/IESNA Standard 90.1-1989/1999 and IECC 1998, 2000 and 2001 that are applicable to commercial and high-rise residential projects, including building envelope, lighting, HVAC, and service water heating requirements. http://www.energycodes.gov	☑	
COMFIE	Performs hourly simulations of buildings, in order to provide mechanical, energy and architectural engineers or architects with accurate estimates of a building's energy needs and temperature profiles. The zone models of COMFIE are based upon a finite volume method on which a modal reduction technique is applied. The output comprises the yearly and hourly heating loads, hourly and mean temperatures in the thermal zones. http://www-cenerg.ensmp.fr/english/themes		
COMIS	Air flow distribution model for multizone structures; takes wind, stack and HVAC into account; allows for crack flow, flow through large openings, and single-sided ventilation. Includes pollution transport model. http://www-epb.lbl.gov/comis	☑	
Commodity Server	An energy database server and presentation system developed with a general time series database server and user interface. Designed by a developer with over 10 years utilities experience. http://www.yankeerino.com		

Tool	Applications	Free	Recently Updated
COMSOL	COMSOL Multiphysics slashes the metric of greatest value to computational scientists - time to solution. It is based on partial differential equations (PDEs) - the fundamental equations that describe the laws of physics. Through multiphysics and mathematical modeling, we transform any coupled PDEs into a form suitable for numerical analysis and solve it using the finite element method with high-performance solvers. http://www.comsol.com		
Construction R-value Calculator	This online calculator calculates the R-value of a large number of common wall and roof constructions given a specified level of insulation. It uses the isothermal planes method to account for thermal bridging of framing material. http://www.design-navigator.co.nz/CRC.php	☑	
CONTAM	Multi-zone (nodal) airflow and contaminant transport analysis program. CONTAM consists of two components ï¿½ a graphical user interface (GUI) and a simulation engine. The GUI is centered on a SketchPad that provides for the input of building topology via a set of drawing tools geared towards producing schematic representations of building floor plans. Drawing tools are used to draw walls, ducts and simplified control networks as well as to create iconic representations of building elements including flow paths, source/sinks and occupants. These drawing tools were designed to provide a robust means to create a well-formed multi-zone description of a building to be used by the simulation engine. http://www.bfrl.nist.gov/IAQanalysis	☑	
Cool Roof Calculator	Many reflective roof coatings and membranes are now available for low-slope roofs. These coatings help to reduce summer air-conditioning loads, but can also increase the winter heating load. The Cool Roof Calculator will estimate both how much energy you'll save in the summer and how much extra energy you'll need in the winter. Cool Roof Calculator provides answers on a 'per square foot' basis, so you can then multiply by the area of your roof to find out your net savings each year. http://www.ornl.gov/sci/roofs+walls/facts/CoolCalcEnergy.htm	☑	
Cool Room Calc	It requires a minimum of input data to be entered that are sufficient for most frequent tasks occurred in practice. The program can be used both by professionals and non-specialists in the field of air conditioning technology. The program works with dual units of measurement (SI and I-P). http://www.leshenko.com.ru/en		
CPF Tools	CPF Tools is the market-leading software for solar installers connecting sales, system design and financing. http://www.cleanpowerfinance.com/products/software/cpf-tools		
CtrlSpecBuilder	Free, on-line tool to help engineers write bid specifications for HVAC Control projects. CtrlSpecBuilder (Control Specification Builder) prepares open (non-proprietary and not sole-source) specifications based upon ASHRAE Guideline 13-2000, Specifying Direct Digital Control Systems. User options make it simple to include new technologies such as BACnet and Web-based controls in the specifications, and to specify energy saving options such as demand limiting, optimal start, and setpoint optimization. https://www.ctrlspecbuilder.com	☑	
Cymap Electrical	Cymap Electrical consists of an integrated CAD-based Electrics and Lighting design for internal, emergency, external, and daylighting, which include Part L Efficacy compliance, switching proximity indicator, and Fire Alarm Audibility check. This integrates with the Cymap Mechanical programs for building loads and regulation compliance. Low-voltage wiring design from the transformer through to final circuits with LV_HV discrimination capabilities. Can export small power and lighting to an integrated stand-alone wiring cable sizing and design program. http://www.cadline.co.uk		

Tool	Applications	Free	Recently Updated
Cymap Mechanical	Cymap uses the CIBSE quasi-dynamic analysis method to calculate building energy loads. CIBSE uses the admittance procedure and allows heating and cooling systems to be sized with a CAD model. It includes gas pipe sizing and hot and cold water system design (including HW returns that use CIBSE or BSEN 6700). The integrated QuickPlan CAD module, a materials properties calculator, shadows this program and the psychrometrics program. It has UK SAP and iSBEM and Cyprus iSBEM-CY capabilities. http://www.cadline.co.uk		
D-Gen PRO	Screening tool designed for economic analysis and determining economic feasibility of distributed power generation. D-Gen PRO quickly and easily evaluates the cost-effective application of on-site and distributed power generation. D-Gen PRO uses climate data from over 700 locations and it has a capability of creating new climate locations. D Gen PRO quickly performs economic analysis of life cycle cost savings, payback, internal rate of return, average cost of on-site generated kWh, monthly utility costs. D Gen PRO consists of improved on-site generation modeling capabilities (weekend operation, part load efficiency, thermal recovery, automatic generator deployment) and enhanced rate-handling capability. http://www.interenergysoftware.com		
Data Center Efficiency Savings Calculator	42U's Data Center Efficiency Savings Calculator helps IT Professionals and C-level management understand the short- and long-term savings that can be achieved by improving the energy efficiency of their data center infrastructure. Efficiency savings are financial (Capital expense [CAPEX] and operating expense [OPEX]) and environmental because carbon dioxide (CO2) emissions are reduced. The calculator is designed to help determine savings for any size data center, computer room, server room, or wiring closet. http://www.42u.com		
Daylight	An easy to use daylighting program. Daylight program calculates the daylight factor distribution in a room at the workplane. User interface is similar to a CAD program allowing user to resize and move windows with mouse. Window and wall properties can be changed and average DF and UxA values are automatically calculated. It should not take more than one minute to become proficient in using the Daylight program. http://www.archiphysics.com	☑	
DAYSIM	Free RADIANCE-based daylighting analysis software to predict the annual daylight availability and electric lighting use in arbitrary buildings for manual and automated lighting and blind controls. http://www.daysim.com	☑	
Degree Day .Net	Website that generates heating and cooling degree days for locations worldwide. Degree days are commonly used in calculations relating to building energy consumption. Once you have chosen a weather station (of which there are thousands available) and specified the degree days you want (e.g. what base temperature, do you want them broken down in daily, weekly or monthly format), Degree Days.net will calculate your degree days, and give them to you as a CSV file that you can open directly in a spreadsheet. http://www.degreedays.net	☑	
Degree Day Forecasts	Quick and easy web-based tool that provides free 14-day ahead degree day forecasts for 1,200 stations in the U.S. and Canada. Degree Day Forecasts charts show this year, last year and three-year average. Historical degree day charts and energy usage forecasts are available from the same site. http://www.energycap.com	☑	
Degree Day Reports	Quick and easy web-based tool that provides free historical degree days for 1,200 stations in the U.S. and Canada, 1994 to present. Degree Day Reports charts show mean daily temperature, cumulative heating and cooling degree days, and monthly comparison of any two years. Optional report (provided via email) compares month-by-month	☑	

Tool	Applications	Free	Recently Updated
	degree days for any two years and any balance point temperature. Degree day forecasts (next 14 days) and energy use forecasts are available from the same site. http://www.energycap.com		
Delphin	Delphin is a comprehensive numerical simulation tool for the combined heat, moisture, and matter (e.g. salt) transport in porous building materials. It is mostly applied to calculate transient processes in building envelopes and construction details, and predict condensation problems and durability risks in general. http://www.bauklimatik-dresden.de/delphin/index.php?aLa=en		
Design Advisor	Web suite of building energy simulators that model energy, comfort, and daylighting performance, and give estimates of the long-term cost of utilities. The simulations restrict flexibility in order to offer users greater ease-of-use and speed. The tool can be quickly mastered by non-technical designers, and runs fast enough to allow them the scope to experiment with many different versions of a design during a single sitting. The immediate feedback that the site provides makes it useful in the conceptual phase of design, when architects cannot afford to invest large amounts of time to rule out any particular idea. The emphasis of the energy model is on the envelope system of the building, and includes simulations of high-technology windows such as double-skin facades. Energy-load estimates are based on a library of climate data for 30 different cities around the world. http://designadvisor.mit.edu	☑	
DesignBuilder	User-friendly modeling environment where you can work (and play) with building models. It provides a range of environmental performance data such as: energy consumption, internal comfort data and HVAC component sizes. Output is based on detailed sub-hourly simulation time steps using the EnergyPlus simulation engine. DesignBuilder can be used for simulations of many common HVAC types, naturally ventilated buildings, buildings with daylighting control, double facades, advanced solar shading strategies etc. http://www.designbuilder.co.uk		
DIALux	A light planning program for calculation and visualization of indoor and outdoor lighting systems. DIALux can import from and export to all CAD programs (DXF, DWG, SAT,...) and has photorealistic visualization with an integrated ray tracer. More than 66 free electronic catalogues and photometric files (IES, EULUMDAT, CIBSE...) can be read in. It is available in 25 languages. DIALux is undergoing continuous refinement. The latest standards are always taken into consideration as well as planning regulations and customs of the specific country. DIALux can calculate daylight, interior and exterior lighting, road lighting and emergency lighting. It includes an easy to handle DIALux Light for simple projects and the possibility to create movies directly from the lighting design. http://www.dial.de/DIAL/en/dialux-international-download.html	☑	
DOE-2	Hourly, whole-building energy analysis program calculating energy performance and life-cycle cost of operation. Can be used to analyze energy efficiency of given designs or efficiency of new technologies. Other uses include utility demand-side management and rebate programs, development and implementation of energy efficiency standards and compliance certification, and training new corps of energy-efficiency conscious building professionals in architecture and engineering schools. http://simulationresearch.lbl.gov		
DOLPHIN	Calculates the pressure loss of a series of ducts and fittings to enable the fan pressure for a ductwork system to be determined. The user enters the ducts starting from the fan and working down towards a selected terminal. For each duct entered the fittings are selected and the program then calculates the pressure loss in each length of duct		

Tool	Applications	Free	Recently Updated
	and each fitting. Supply ducts and fittings are entered on one screen and return ducts are entered on a second screen. http://members.ozemail.com.au/~acadsbsg		
DONKEY	Determines the size of a duct network using the static regain, constant pressure gradient, or balanced pressure drop method. Duct sizes can also be fixed and the program handles rectangular, round or oval ducts. DONKEY can calculate duct leakage and heat loss/gain and automatically locate balancing dampers throughout the duct system. http://members.ozemail.com.au/~acadsbsg		
Duct Calculator	Provides access to duct calculation and sizing capabilities either as a standalone Windows program or from within the Autodesk Building Mechanical, the new HVAC-oriented version of AutoCAD. Based on the engineering data and procedures outlined in the ASHRAE Fundamentals Handbook Calculation Methods, Duct Calculator features an advanced and fully interactive user interface. Slide controls for air flow, velocity, friction and duct size provide real-time, interactive feedback; as you spin one, the others dynamically respond in real time. When used with Autodesk Building Mechanical, Duct Calculator streamlines the design process by automatically re-sizing whole branches of ductwork. http://www.marinsoft.com/home.htm		
DUCTSIZE	Quickly calculates optimal duct sizes using either the static regain, equal friction, or constant velocity method. Data entry can be accomplished manually or taken graphically from either Drawing Board or AutoCAD. Duct sizes can be calculated on a round, rectangular, and flat oval basis. Noise levels and required attenuation are printed for each runout duct. http://www.elitesoft.com		
e-Bench	Desktop computer tool for comprehensively measuring the energy, utility and environmental efficiency of a facility or process and comparing it to established benchmarks. http://www.energyts.com		
e-Sankey	ean software tool for drawing Sankey diagrams. Sankey diagrams are used to visualize energy flows in process systems with colored arrows whose width is proportional to the flow quantity. http://www.e-sankey.com/en		
E-Z Heatloss	Calculates residential building heating and cooling loads based on ACCA Manual J7. You enter the data required, the program does all the calculation and prints a complete report of the results. http://www.thomasandassoc.com		
E.A.S.Y. - Energy Accounting System for Your Buildings	E.A.S.Y. is an energy accountability system designed for municipalities, government entities, and commercial buildings. E.A.S.Y. uses electric, gas, and water data to prioritize individual facilities on documented performance-based energy consumption and total billing characteristics. The data cannot only be used for pinpointing where energy conservation efforts may be cost and emissions effective but also as a business forecasting and accounting tool for determining future cost projections based on past billing history, the consumer price index, or projected values for future rates. Different rate structure comparisons are also available. Information on multiple facilities can be 'ranked in energy, economic, and emissions terms in many different categories recognized by the business and energy professional. http://www.the-kelly-group.com		
EBS	Streamlines utility billing and cost allocation processes, while greatly improving the reliability and accuracy of information. EBS (eDNA Billing System) was designed to meet the complex utility accounting and reporting needs of a large organization with 100s or 1,000s of buildings and accounts often spread across multiple campus locations. EBS uses a highly flexible cost allocation structure ensuring direct access to meter, account, building, and defined group cost and consumption information. http://www.instepsoftware.com		

Tool	Applications	Free	Recently Updated
ecasys	Large scale, low income, program management, web application. ecasys is best suited for use within an energy agency to gather disparate applications and processes together; or, for use in a Utility, to monitor the energy programs that they fund. Using a standard Internet Explorer browser, you can access the backend, fully relational SQL database from anywhere with an Internet connection. http://www.fundamentalenergy.com		
EcoAdvisor	Interactive, online multimedia training and decision support tool for sustainable commercial buildings. EcoAdvisor is highly graphically oriented and highly interactive. When fully developed, it will engage the user via numerous animations and interactions such as mouse-overs, 'more info' drill-down options, radio button choices, sliders, drag-and-drop exercises, fill-in-the-blank exercises, and goal-oriented, problem-solving exercises. The current beta version contains several examples of graphic animations and user-interactions. Interactive multimedia is highly cost-effective compared with instructor-led learning for users can learn 40% faster than in classroom situations, and each user can learn at his/her own pace. http://www.ecoadvisor.com	☑	
EcoDesigner	EcoDesigner enables architects to quickly and efficiently evaluate design alternatives based on energy consumption, carbon footprint and monthly energy balance. Using EcoDesigner architects can easily analyze, at an early stage, their design for energy efficiency. Providing valuable feedback on the building's energy performance means the architect can make better decisions on how to conform to regulations and satisfy the interests of the client and the operator of the building. http://www.graphisoftus.com		
ecoInsight Energy Audit & Analysis Software	ecoInsight Energy Audit & Analysis software revolutionizes the way energy audits are conducted by providing professionals with mobile audit capabilities (on the iPad), integrated product pricing, and performance information and sales proposal generation tools. Information about building equipment, energy use, and occupant information is collected through a mobile device, making the information usable immediately for analysis, collaboration, and proposal generation. http://www.ecoinsight.com		
eDNA	Data historian software that collects, stores, displays, and reports real-time operational and engineering information from all operational assets. eDNA processes and stores real time data directly from electronically enabled utility meters, plant information systems, and building control systems, regardless of the source of the data (eDNA is vendor agnostic). The system stores this data in its original time stamped resolution in a highly compressed format allowing years to decades of high resolution data to be stored online and instantly accessible for analysis. Weather data can be collected and correlated with utility consumption for a complete view of energy needs. http://www.instepsoftware.com		
EE4 CBIP	Designed to demonstrate a building's compliance to the requirements of the Commercial Building Incentive Program (CBIP) performance path approach. EE4 CBIP is offered by Natural Resources Canada's Office of Energy Efficiency to building owners and developers for the design and construction of new commercial and institutional buildings that use 25% less energy than similar buildings built to the requirements of the Model National Energy Code for Buildings (MNECB). EE4 CBIP may also be used to perform non-compliance energy analyses and thus to predict a building's annual energy consumption, and to assess the impact of design changes to the building. Alternatively, EE4 CBIP can be used to determine a building's heating and cooling loads for equipment sizing. EE4 CBIP calculations	☑	

Tool	Applications	Free	Recently Updated
	are based on an approved version of DOE-2.1E http://canmetenergy.nrcan.gc.ca/buildings-communities/2218		
EED	Program for borehole heat exchanger design. Its easy of use, short learning curve, quick calculation times and inherent databases make EED a useful tool in everyday engineering work for design of ground source heat pump system (GSHP) and borehole thermal storage. In very large and complex tasks EED allows for retrieving the approximate required size and layout before initiating more detailed analyses. Even for very small plants EED values the effort to do a calculation instead of using rules of thumb is worthwhile. http://www.buildingphysics.com		
EEM Suite	Enables large companies to proactively monitor, analyze and manage energy costs and consumption. EEM Suite combines analysis and reporting tools; real-time, event-driven alerts; and Web-based enterprise visibility into a single solution so users can control their energy costs and usage. EEM Suite leverages meter, billing, production, real-time price, rate and weather information to drive significant energy and water reductions. http://www.mckinstry.com		
EffTrack	Collects, stores, and analyzes water cooled centrifugal and screw chiller operating data to determine performance, diagnose causes of inefficiency, and recommend corrective action. EffTrack notifies plant contacts via email if problems occur. Plant operators and facility managers can review the hourly updated information by logging in to EffTrack from any computer with Internet access. By following the EffTrack recommendations for improvement, plant operators can significantly lower the chiller kW/ton and plant kWh consumption. These savings are identified and measured in the EffTrack reports. http://www.efftec.com		
ENER-WIN	Energy design tool for large commercial buildings. Performs whole-building energy analysis for 8760 hours/year for up to 98 zones and 20 different wall and window types. Calculates transient heat flows, HVAC loads, daylighting, energy consumption, demand charges, life-cycle costs, and floating temperatures in unconditioned zones. Input is through a sketching interface. Weather data from included database of 1500 cities. Graphical output is in form of bar charts and graphs. Tabulates peak zone loads and air quantities. http://pages.suddenlink.net/enerwin		
EnerCop Energy Benchmarking and Accounting Software	EnerCop Energy Benchmarking & Accounting software delivers energy information solutions across a common platform to all parts of the organization. It enables collaborative, informed decisions about the energy cost center and gives the finance department accurate tools to manage energy budgets, accruals, and variances. It also providing facilities and operations managers with timely energy performance benchmarked data to validate and prioritize resources at unit-level operations. EnerCop provides a comprehensive energy and carbon (energy-based) profile of an organization's building portfolio and is the only comprehensive software solution that customizes benchmarking to the specific metrics that drive energy use for each industry. http://www.enercop.com		
Energy Estimation Software with Carbon Footprint Calculation	Energy Estimation Software for Fan and Pumping Applications estimates energy savings achieved when using a variable frequency drive instead of conventional control methods for fan and pumping applications. The results can be viewed in graphical format and text format and the software has built-in functions to generate an energy estimation report especially designed for consultants. http://www.baseblock.com/PRODUCTS/demosoftware.htm		
Energy Expert	Self-training software that creates a "smart model" of a building using interval data and hourly weather data and compares daily energy		

Tool	Applications	Free	Recently Updated
	consumption against this norm. The Energy Expert will tell you whether a facility over-consumed, under-consumed or used about the right amount of energy the prior day. Notification emails (or text messages) trigger immediate analysis and investigation to track down the cause of over-consumption. This results in faster response to fix problems and minimize energy cost variances. http://www.energyworksite.com/corporate		
Energy Lens	Enables the rapid analysis of half-hourly energy consumption data in Excel. Energy Lens facilitates the creation of charts and figures from half-hourly data, making it easy to determine energy consumption patterns, to identify and quantify energy waste, and to track energy performance. Energy Lens is commonly used by energy professionals for the analysis of their clients' half-hourly data, typically with the aim of helping them to save energy. Energy Lens is also popular as an energy management solution for businesses that want to cut their energy bills without investing a lot of time into the process. http://www.energylens.com		
Energy Profile Tool	A customizable, commercially available energy analysis tool. Users enter information about their facilities to receive detailed profiles of the energy use, as well as benchmark comparison results. The tool helps identify opportunities to reduce energy and costs, and take the next steps to long-term savings. http://www.energyprofiletool.com/subscription/default.asp		
Energy Usage Forecasts	Quick and easy web-based tool that provides free 14-day ahead energy usage forecasts based on the degree day forecasts for 1,200 stations in the U.S. and Canada. The user enters the daily non-weather base load and the usage per degree day weather factor; the tool applies the degree day forecast and displays the total energy usage forecast. Helpful FAQs explain the process and describe various options for the calculation of the base load and weather factor. Historical degree day reports and 14-day ahead degree day forecasts are available from the same site. http://www.energycap.com		
EnergyCAP Enterprise	Designed to be the foremost energy information software available for total integration and management of an organization's diverse utility bill and energy management needs. Enterprise options offer the full range of capabilities: bill tracking, manual and EDI entry, interface to A/P for bill payment, ENERGY STAR® automated data submittal, work flow system for user-defined bill approval processes, automatic bill auditing system, correct "to-the-penny" rate schedules, interval data tracking and analysis, tracking of production (or any other independent variables), greenhouse gas emissions tracking, cost avoidance calculations (M&V), submeter tracking, virtual meter formulas, tenant re-billing, and more. http://www.energycap.com		
EnergyCAP Professional	Software for domestic public school districts (see EnergyCAP Enterprise for other organizations) that need straightforward utility bill tracking, energy management reports and calculation of the cost avoidance attributable to energy management activities. A typical Professional client has 50 to 1,000 utility accounts, pays $500,000 to $10 million a year and is primarily used from one energy management or utilities management office. http://www.energycap.com		
EnergyPeriscope	EnergyPeriscope is a professional-level performance estimating and financial analysis engine. Use it to create financial performance reports for single- or multiple-technology energy solutions. EnergyPeriscope accommodates retrofit applications, new construction buildings, and "Energy Farms" for selling PV- or wind-generated electricity. Model PV, solar water heating, solar pool/spa heating, solar hydronic radiant floor systems, wind turbines and energy efficiency projects. http://www.energyperiscope.com		

Tool	Applications	Free	Recently Updated
EnergyPro	EnergyPro is composed of an interface, which includes a building tree, a set of libraries, and a database of state-certified equipment directories. Although EnergyPro provides fifteen different types of calculations, users can purchase only the modules that pertain to the type of work they do. http://www.energysoft.com		☑
EnergyWitness	EnergyWitness™ is an operational system based on data from all available sources, knowledge of building operations and analysis, and the technology to support the system. In combination, the elements define the science of building operations and provide a platform. http://www.intdatsys.com		
ENERPASS	Detailed building energy simulation program for residential and smaller commercial buildings. ENERPASS calculates the annual energy use for space heating, cooling, lighting, water heating and fan energy. The calculations are performed on an hourly basis using hourly measured weather data. ENERPASS can model up to seven building zones and provides hourly temperature and humidity predictions for each zone. A wide range of HVAC systems can be modeled including make-up air units, heat recovery ventilators, rooftop units, VAV, four-pipe fan coil, and dual duct. The program uses full screen data entry in an easy-to-use format. A typical building model can be generated in one to two hours. In IEA validation studies ENERPASS results compare favorably with other hourly based computer programs. http://www.enermodal.com		
ENFORMA	Includes the MicroDataLogger portable data acquisition equipment and HVAC and Lighting Analyzer software. ENFORMA is designed to cost-effectively gather data and convert it into information about building performance. ENFORMA provides a unique solution that can gather the data at a minimal cost and help you determine solutions to typical building problems. This detailed diagnostic information is the key that allows you to improve upon your current services or expand into new business opportunities. ENFORMA solutions typically result in projects with paybacks of less than one year. http://www.archenergy.com		
EQUER	Performs yearly simulations of a building life cycle, in order to provide mechanical, energy and architectural engineers or architects with environmental indicators (e.g., global warming, acidification and eutrophication potentials, and exhaust of natural resources). The Swiss Oekoinventare database and other data collected in the European REGENER project are used for material fabrication and other processes (energy, water, waste, transport). EQUER is linked to the energy simulation tool COMFIE. Replacement of components at the end of their life is automatically accounted for. http://www-cenerg.ensmp.fr/english/themes/cycle/index.html		
eQUEST	eQUEST® is a widely used, time-proven whole building energy performance design tool. Its wizards, dynamic defaults, interactive graphics, parametric analysis, and rapid execution make eQUEST uniquely able to conduct whole-building performance simulation analysis throughout the entire design process, from the earliest conceptual stages to the final stages of design. eQUEST's simulation engine, DOE 2.2, is also time-proven, well known, and widely used. http://www.doe2.com		
Evergreen LED	Evergreen LED has developed a unique energy savings calculator software tool to precisely calculate the energy savings, carbon savings, cost savings, and ROI on LED and energy-efficient lighting projects for commercial and residential use. http://www.ledlightsupply.com		
EZ Sim	Quick spreadsheet tool equivalent to sophisticated engineering analysis. EZ Sim lets you use utility bills to calibrate a simulation of a commercial facility in an interactive graphic window. Once it matches		

Tool	Applications	Free	Recently Updated
	your bills, the simulation model can provide reliable estimates of potential conservation savings. The calibration process reveals how energy is used within the facility, helping diagnose why there is excessive consumption or poorly functioning building components. http://www.ezsim.com		
EZDOE	An easy to use IBM PC version of DOE-2. EZDOE calculates the hourly energy use of a building and its life-cycle cost of operation given information on the building's location, construction, operation, and heating and air conditioning system. Using hourly weather data and algorithms developed by Lawrence Berkeley National Laboratory, EZDOE takes into account complex thermal storage effects of various building materials. In addition, it can also accurately simulate the operation of all types of heating and cooling plants including ice water thermal storage and cogeneration systems. Up to 22 different air handling systems each with multiple control options are supported. http://www.elitesoft.com		
FASER	Energy information management and analysis software. Identify utility bill errors, system problems and recover overcharges using FASER's Energy Alarm bill-checking engine. Interface with accounting and reduce bill-processing costs using the FASER AP Link module. Audit the cost avoidance of demand side management projects and performance contracts. Powerful 1000 plus utility rate schedule library for rate comparison using actual metered history. http://www.faser.com		
FEDS	Provides a comprehensive method for quickly and objectively identifying energy improvements that offer maximum savings. FEDS (Facility Energy Decision System) makes assessments and analyzes energy efficiency of single buildings, multiple buildings, or all buildings of an entire facility. It provides an easy-to-use tool for identifying energy efficiency measures, selecting minimum life-cycle costs, determining payback, and enabling users to prioritize retrofit options and compare alternative financing options (site funding, leases, loans, ESPCs). http://www.pnl.gov/feds		
FENSIZE	Calculates the thermal transmittance (U-factor), solar heat gain coefficient (SHGC), and visible transmittance (VT) of a window, curtain wall, skylight, or other fenestration product. FENSIZE greatly simplifies and speeds up calculation of overall window performance by combining thermal performance of glazing, spacer and frames and calculating overall performance on the fly. http://www.fenestration.com/index.php		
FENSTRUCT	Analyzes structural performance of fenestration products. The calculations are done using industry standard procedures in AAMA 103. FENSTRUCT is a database driven library of cross sections and dies. FENSTRUCT's main screen includes list of all standard cases specified in AAMA 103 standard document, as well as some common special cases. Additional special cases can be added per manufacturer's request. FENSTRUCT works and outputs in both sets of units, IP and SI. http://www.fenestration.com/index.php		
Flownex	Flownex is a systems and subsystems simulation tool used to design and optimize closed and open loop flow and heat transfer systems with any number of branching flows and inlets and outlets. Such systems include ventilation systems, water, and gas distribution systems, boiler designs, and complete power generation cycles. http://www.flownex.com		
foAudits	foAudits is a mobile auditing toolset to capture and report on information using templates that you maintain. You can download your customer list and audit templates to the mobile to create a customized work environment for auditors, inspectors, and contractors. (See the		

Tool	Applications	Free	Recently Updated
	site for information on HERS and NEAT-style audits.) foAudits supports a variety of inputs, including QR codes, bar codes, checkboxes, text input, numeric fields, collapsible memo fields, date fields, dropdown boxes, user-defined lists, buttons, and pop-up helpe. foAudits data are stored in a SQL Web-based server engine such as SQL Server or Oracle. http://www.foaudits.com		
FRAME4	Uses two-dimensional finite-volume analysis to evaluate heat transfer through complex building components. FRAME is part of the FRAMEplus toolkit for analysis of windows, doors, walls, roofs and below-grade assemblies. Users draw building components as assemblies of cross-sections. Any interior or exterior environmental condition can be applied. .DXF files and VISION4 files can be imported to speed up data entry. Results are displayed graphically and are used to determine heat transfer, potential for thermal bridging and surface condensation. The FRAME4 simulations (when combined with VISION) are an equal alternative to testing to determine the U-value and solar heat gain coefficient of windows and doors. The U.S. National Fenestration Rating Council and Canadian Standard Association recognize FRAME as the only acceptable computer program to determine heat transfer through opaque portions of windows, doors and curtainwalls. http://www.enermodal.com		
FSEC 3.0	A detailed whole-building and component analysis program; includes heat, moisture and contaminant transport simulation. Both detailed and simplified moisture models are available. Recent enhancements include models for radon transport and pressure driven airflows in buildings and systems. Primarily developed as a tool for research, design and development of innovative cooling and dehumidification systems. Developed by the Florida Solar Energy Center, FSEC 3.0 uses the finite element method for distributed modeling. http://www.fsec.ucf.edu/en		
Gas Cooling Guide PRO	Provides a wealth of information about gas cooling technologies and allows evaluating the performance and economic viability of particular pieces of equipment. Gas Cooling Guide PRO (GCG PRO) is a valuable analysis and reference tool for energy utilities, gas cooling equipment manufacturers, HVAC engineers, and others responsible for the technical assessment, economic evaluation, or selection of HVAC equipment for commercial buildings. http://www.interenergysoftware.com		
GenOpt	A generic multi-parameter optimization program for system optimization. It automatically determines the values of user-selected design parameters that lead to the best operation of a given system. Optimizes a user-selected objective function, such as a building's calculated annual energy use. It also offers an interface for easily implementing your own optimization algorithms into its library. http://gundog.lbl.gov/GO/index.html	☑	
GLASTRUCT	Analyzes structural performance of glass and glazing systems. The calculations are done using industry standard ASTM E1300-02. GLASTRUCT's main screen includes support for single or double glazed units, glass thicknesses up to 22 mm, laminated glass, heat strengthened glass, etc. GLASTRUCT calculates glazing load resistance and deflection and also displays Pass/Fail criteria. Calculations are done for short and long load durations, which are determined from the wind loading or other static and dynamic loadings. http://www.fenestration.com/index.php		
GLHEPRO	GLHEPRO performs three different tasks: (1) Simulation (for up to 100 years) of ground loop heat exchangers to determine monthly average and peak heat pump entering and exiting fluid temperatures, as well as power consumption of the heat pump. (2) Determination of the		

Tool	Applications	Free	Recently Updated
	required borehole depth to meet user-specified minimum and maximum heat pump entering fluid temperatures. (3) Sizing of hybrid ground source heat pump (HGSHP) systems by determination of the required borehole depth and necessary supplemental heat rejecter (cooling tower, fluid cooler) or heat extractor (boiler) size. http://www.hvac.okstate.edu/glhepro		
GPM PV+	GPM PV+ is a tool to manage, benchmark, and analyze any kind of renewable energy plant. This tool is mainly used with GreenPowerMonitor metering devices, but can be used with a large spread of data sources. http://www.greenpowermonitor.com/en		
Ground Loop Design	Ground Loop Design is a versatile ground source heat pump system design program that helps the trained geothermal HVAC designer/engineer size equipment, determine the correct lengths of bore or pipe required for commercial projects, optimize the piping configuration for balanced flow and optimal heat transfer, and calculate the annual and lifetime energy/operating/emissions costs associated with the design. http://www.gaiageo.com		
HEAT Energy Audit Tool	A management information system that not only compiles data in the field, but produces the reports you need for vendors, inventory control, auditing, invoicing and more. HEAT Energy Audit Tool is flexible, Windows-based software that is customizable. Produce invoices and reports for multiple funding sources. Develop custom reports as well. And it accommodates all commonly used energy fuels. http://www.hancocksoftware.com		
Heat Pump Design Model	Research tool for use in the steady-state simulation and design analysis of air-to-air heat pumps and air conditioners. The program can be used with most of the newer HFC refrigerants as well as with HCFCs and CFCs. The standard vapor-compression cycle is modeled with empirical representations for compressor performance and first-principle region-by-region modeling of the heat exchangers. http://www.ornl.gov/~wlj/hpdm	☑	
HEAT2	Calculates two-dimensional transient and steady-state heat conduction within objects that can be described in a rectangular grid. http://www.buildingphysics.com		
HEAT3	Three-dimensional transient and steady-state heat conduction within objects that can be described in a rectangular grid. HEAT3 can be used for analyses of thermal bridges, heat transfer through corners of a window, heat loss from a house to the ground, to mention a few applications. Arbitrary thermal properties and initial temperatures can be specified. HEAT3 can handle such internal modifications as heat sources and internal boundaries of prescribed temperature. http://www.blocon.se		
HEED	This user-friendly energy design tool shows how much money you can save by making changes to your home. It also shows how much greenhouse gas (including CO2) it accounts for, and its annual total energy consumption. HEED (Home Energy Efficient Design) works equally well for remodeling projects or designing new buildings. http://www.energy-design-tools.aud.ucla.edu	☑	
HOMER	Evaluates design options for both off-grid and grid-connected power systems for remote, stand-alone, and distributed generation (DG) applications. HOMER's optimization and sensitivity analysis algorithms allow you to evaluate the economic and technical feasibility of a large number of technology options and to account for variation in technology costs and energy resource availability. HOMER models both conventional and renewable energy technologies. https://analysis.nrel.gov/homer	☑	
HOT2000	Easy-to-use energy analysis and design software for low-rise residential buildings. Utilizing current heat loss/gain and system	☑	

Tool	Applications	Free	Recently Updated
	performance models, the program aids in the simulation and design of buildings for thermal effectiveness, passive solar heating and the operation and performance of heating and cooling systems. http://canmetenergy.nrcan.gc.ca/buildings-communities/2218		
HPSIM	Detailed, fundamentals-based, steady-state simulation model of an air-to-air heat pump operating on the vapor-compression-cycle principle and charged with single-component refrigerant. HPSIM (Heat Pump SIMulation) includes tube-by-tube modeling of plate-fin air-to-refrigerant heat exchangers. http://www.nist.gov/el	☑	
HVAC Solution	Software that allows users to graphically design and specify HVAC equipment. Pick familiar objects like boilers, pumps, fan coils and air handlers and using drag and drop methods, connect them to form a HVAC system. Once your system is designed, HVAC Solution will automatically spit out equipment schedules and export your schematic to a DXF file. Small projects and large, the software greatly simplifies the design and specification of HVAC equipment. Run different scenarios to find the most cost effective or energy efficient system for your building. http://www.hvacsolution.com		
HVACSIM+	Simulation model of a building HVAC (heating, ventilation, and air-conditioning) system plus HVAC controls, the building shell, the heating/cooling plant, and energy management and control system (EMCS) algorithms. The main program of HVACSIM+ (HVAC SIMulation PLUS other systems employs a hierarchical, modular approach and advanced equation solving techniques to perform dynamic simulations of building/HVAC/control systems. The modular approach is based upon the methodology used in the TRNSYS program. http://www.nist.gov/el	☑	
Hydronics Design Studio	Software that assists in analyzing the thermal and hydraulic performance of modern hydronic heating systems in residential and light commercial buildings. The Hydronics Design Studio - Professional Version software consists of twelve modules that perform tasks such as heating load analysis, series baseboard circuit analysis, piping heat loss estimating, expansion tank sizing, radiant circuit analysis, injection mixing simulation, buffer tank simulation, and fuel cost comparisons. http://www.hydronicpros.com		
I-BEAM	Educational software and building management tool that integrates indoor air quality (IAQ), energy efficiency and building economic concepts. I-BEAM provides comprehensive guidance for managing and assessing IAQ in offices, schools, universities and various public and institutional facilities. http://www.epa.gov/iaq	☑	
IDA Indoor Climate and Energy	A tool for simulation of thermal comfort, indoor air quality and energy consumption in buildings. The mathematical models in IDA ICE are described in terms of equations in a formal language, NMF. This makes it easy to customize the models for the needs of a particular project. Advanced users can do this themselves by using the IDA Simulation Environment (IDA SE). http://www.equa.se		
INDUS	Sizes air-duct networks. INDUS can handle both supply and extract systems, and can size the ducts according to the following design procedures: constant friction, constant-velocity or static-regain. The network can be made up from branches of any combination of duct sectional shapes, and sizing limits can be imposed for each branch in the network (such as fixed size, maximum depth, maximum velocity). INDUS can be used for sizing systems from scratch, or as a check on an existing system, when duct sizes and flow rates are specified. It accounts for the effects of diversity in VAV systems, and for supply systems automatically accounts for duct-heat pick up and the consequent volume-flow changes through the system. The system can be balanced using dampers only, or by resizing non-index runs.		

Tool	Applications	Free	Recently Updated
	Dampers are always placed to minimize the number required. http://www.iesve.com		
kW-Field	kW-Field is a tablet-based touch screen field tool for professionals conducting commercial and industrial energy audits. http://www.kwhours.com		
LESO-COMFORT	Evaluation of thermal comfort during a selected period (e.g. during the hottest part of summer), using a classical dynamic simulation computer code connected to the LESO-COMFORT code itself. The program uses the data already defined for LESOSAI, and only a very few additional data have to be introduced by the user. http://leso.epfl.ch		
LESO-SHADE	Calculation of shading factors on any facade or surface (e.g. a window) of a building, caused by the surrounding obstacles (other buildings, trees, walls, etc.). The calculated shading factor can be tabulated either hour by hour, or as a monthly average. The definition of the geometry (studied building and surrounding) is done using a graphical and user-friendly interface. http://leso.epfl.ch		
LESOCOOL	Calculates the airflow rate by stack effect, as well as the cooling potential and the overheating risk in a naturally or mechanically ventilated building, showing the temperature evolution, the air flow rate and the ventilation heat transfer. It take into account convective and radiative heat gains. http://leso.epfl.ch		
LESOKAI	Computes the static and dynamic thermal transmission properties of simple building components, estimates the risk of water vapour condensation and mould growth, and checks if the component complies with the Swiss SIA 180 standard. It also allows the calculation of optimal thickness in terms of energy or cost. Calculations are performed according to the most recent European standards. Included is a comprehensive materials data base. Lesokai 4 is part of the LESO series, and has the same user interface as Lesosai. http://leso.epfl.ch		
LESOSAI	Computes the energy use of a building according to the hourly and/or monthly simplified models described in the European standard EN ISO 13790 and in Swiss standard, the energy needs contained in the French standard RT2005, in the Luxembourg Standard, and in the Italian DLGs 192. It computes transmission and ventilation heat loss as solar gains from windows, sunspaces, double-skin facade, window solar collector and transparent insulation walls. It can handle several zones and rooms at various set point temperatures and helps size peak heating power (EN 12831, SIA384.201) and the cooling needs (EN ISO 13790). http://leso.epfl.ch		
LifeCycle	LifeCycle provides a framework for you to take account of different costs, including capital costs, running costs, annual maintenance and replacement costs. LifeCycle calculates the Net Present Value (NPV) for the particular option, based on inflation rates and the anticipated life of the building. You can then compare different design strategies in terms of NPV. http://www.iesve.com		
LightPro	Easy-to-use tool for placing and editing luminaires within rooms in the 3D building model, and for managing databases of luminaires and lamps. Once luminaires have been placed, you can use FlucsPro to perform lighting analyses to investigate lighting levels on the working plane or any other surface in the room. You can also use RadianceIES software to perform sophisticated 3D lighting simulations, generating glare or lux information and high quality images. LightPro contains a large database of luminaires and lamps, and also enables you to add or import other luminaire data. http://www.iesve.com		
LISA	Streamlined Life Cycle Analysis (LCA) decision support tool for construction. It was developed in response to requests by architects	☑	

Tool	Applications	Free	Recently Updated
	and industry professionals for a simplified LCA tool to assist in green design. LISA stands for LCA in Sustainable Architecture. http://www.lisa.au.com		
LoopDA	The Loop Equation Design Method has been proposed for sizing ventilation airflow components of natural and hybrid ventilation systems. While the approach has been demonstrated on a limited basis, the method has been automated in order to better evaluate its reliability under a more controlled, i.e., less error-prone, environment. LoopDA is a computer program developed by NIST that implements the Loop Equation Design Method of sizing the openings of naturally ventilated buildings. The tool, referred to as LoopDA for Loop Design and Analysis, is integrated with an existing multi-zone analysis tool CONTAM. LoopDA provides the designer of natural ventilation systems with an environment in which to perform and document the process of designing the opening sizes of natural ventilation systems and analyzing the system behavior under a variety of operating conditions. http://www.nist.gov/el		
Louver Shading	Louver Shading lets you visualize the annual shading performance of a louver shading system, such as slatted window blinds or a trellis. The tool accepts a location and the dimensions of the louver system as inputs, and produces a chart depicting the amount of shade it produces for each hour of the day, for each month of the year. http://www.susdesign.com	☑	
Maintenance Edge	Maintenance Edge is a suite of online Software as a Service (SaaS) facility management tools that gives control and management over buildings without a capital investment. Maintenance Edge enables you to combine work order, planned maintenance, work order wireless, and critical alarms with the option of adding inventory. http://www.facilitydude.com		
MC4Suite 2009	Mc4Suite 2009 contains all features for complete design with no additional software needed. Mc4Suite 2009 uses an AutoCAD platform offering complete compatibility with .dwg file format.s Import pre-existing architectural plans for a quick start. Graphical interface with EnergyPlus, hydronic and thermal system sizing, plumbing design, layout, snow and ice melting system design, radiant heating and cooling systems, heat loss - cooling loads (based on ASHRAE standards), hydraulic calculation for fire protection systems (based on NFPA standards, and 3-D mechanical room design. Solar BIM, solar water heating system design. http://www.mc4software.com		
METEONORM 6	Comprehensive meteorological reference, incorporating a catalogue of meteorological data and calculation procedures for solar applications and system design at any desired location in the world. METEONORM 6 is mainly a climate database combined with a weather generator. http://meteonorm.com		
METRIX4	Tool for monitoring energy usage and verifying cost savings from energy conservation measures. Metrix4 establishes baseline and target usage patterns, which can be used toï¿½track building performance. Metrix4 uses specific algorithms to test for correlation between energy usage and weather data or other variables that you can define (such as occupancy or production). http://www.abraxasenergy.com/metrix4		
MHEA	Analyzes energy use and evaluates possible weatherization retrofit measures of existing manufactured homes. State weatherization assistance programs and their subgrantees use MHEA (Manufactured Home Energy Audit) to determine appropriate weatherization retrofit measures for low-income manufactured homes. Energy consumption is calculated using the variable-based degree day method. The MHEA software was developed by the National Renewable Energy		

Tool	Applications	Free	Recently Updated
	Laboratory and is supported by Oak Ridge National Laboratory. http://www.ornl.gov		
Microflo	CFD simulation system for assessing building airflow, air quality and thermal performance. Microflo solves the 3D non-isothermal continuity, momentum, energy and species conservation equations incorporating the k-e turbulence model using finite difference method. Microflo is part of the IES Virtual Environment by which the CFD simulation is coupled dynamically with the full building thermal simulation. The difference in time constants between the building structures and air volumes is handled based on the integrated approach concept. http://www.iesve.com		
MOIST	Program to predict combined transfer of heat and moisture in multi-layer building construction. Inputs hourly weather data from diskette and predicts the moisture content and temperature of the construction layers as a function of time of year. Can be used to develop guidelines and practices for controlling moisture in walls, flat roofs, and cathedral ceilings. http://www.nist.gov/el/highperformance_buildings/performance/moist.cfm	☑	
MotorMaster+	Windows-based version of MotorMaster, with additional features to help energy coordinators at industrial facilities implement an effective energy management program. MotorMaster+ contains a motor inventory module, where motor nameplate data is stored and linked to utility, facility, plant and process information. It includes a field measurement and operating data storage repository. Also, descriptor searches may be performed to target inefficient or energy-intensive motors and motor-driven processes, and those which operate under abnormal or suboptimal conditions. Batch analyses can be run for new motor purchases, rewinds, or changeouts of operable motors with energy-efficient replacements. Life cycle costing, energy accounting, and program evaluation features are included. http://www1.eere.energy.gov/manufacturing/tech_deployment/software_motormaster.html	☑	
NewQUICK	Thermal design and simulation tool capable of calculating loads and energy consumption. NewQuick can predict hourly air temperatures and relative humidities, which makes it a valuable tool in the passive design of building envelopes. Complete load and energy analysis of a building can further be executed in order to design an efficient air-conditioning system (HVAC). The simulation tool executes dynamic thermal calculations for realistic 'real life' temperature and load predictions. The building model integrates natural ventilation, internal load (convective and radiative), occupant load and evaporative cooling models. The simulation tool includes the modelling of external shading devices, interior mass, direct solar heat gains and ground contact surfaces. http://www.newquick.com		
OnGrid Tool	The OnGrid Tool is an Excel-based application assisting in PV system sizing, pricing and quoting. It enables solar installers to gather a customer's utility and site information quickly and efficiently. It calculates optimum system size, electricity bill savings, system incentives, and system net costs. It then calculates various economic benefit factors and produces a variety of proposals, quotes, and. The OnGrid Tool includes rates, incentives, and tax calculations, and estimates system performance, including all performance factors and shading data. http://www.ongrid.net		
Opaque	Draws a detail of wall or roof sections, calculates U-value, timelag, and decrement factor. It plots temperature drop through the section. Draws 2-D daily and 3-D annual plots of outdoor and sol-air temperatures, normal and total surface radiation, and heat flow through the envelope.	☑	

Tool	Applications	Free	Recently Updated
	It was originally called SOLAR-3. http://www.energy-design-tools.aud.ucla.edu		
OptiMiser	OptiMiser is a PC-based and Web-distributed software tool that provides next-generation residential energy analysis for auditors, weatherization programs, and homeowners. OptiMiser evaluates a full range of near-optimal solutions for home energy efficiency retrofits, providing accurate and actionable reports of estimated savings and cost. OptiMiser represents an innovative paradigm shift in audit software that enables an auditor to quickly complete a thorough, accurate energy audit. http://optimiserenergy.com		
OptoMizer	OptoMizer is a turnkey lighting retrofit software solution for the commercial industry that provides the tools necessary to perform a full, accurate, and detailed lighting audit. It supports an unlimited number of projects and audits, full physical parts tracking and pricing, existing and design luminaire configurations, occupancy schedules, and detailed space data to support space-by-space audits. http://www.fdlabs.com		
Overhang Annual Analysis	Allows users to visualize the shading performance of a window overhang for an entire year. Overhang Annual Analysis tool accepts a location and the dimensions of the window and overhang as inputs, and produces a chart depicting the amount that the overhang shades the window for each hour of the day, for each month of the year. http://susdesign.com/overhang_annual	☑	
Overhang Design	Provides instant, graphical feedback on the extent to which an overhang shades a window or other aperture. http://www.susdesign.com		
Panel Shading	Panel Shading lets you optimize the geometry of rows of flat-plate solar collectors (PV or solar thermal) by visualizing on an annual basis how much the rows shade each other each hour of the day, each month of the year. The tool accepts a location and the dimensions of the panels and environment as inputs, and produces a chart depicting the degree to which the panels are shaded each hour. By adjusting the panel dimensions, tilt, and spacing, shading can be minimized during critical periods. http://www.susdesign.com	☑	
Pervidi	Manages preventative maintenance activities for HVAC and building systems, in order to provide mechanical, energy and architectural engineers with (a) easy to use process and system to record, track and manage preventative maintenance and capture readings for their building systems; (b) reporting and analysis tools to improve equipment utilization, minimize breakdown, and improve operational efficiencies. Pervidi utilizes sophisticated software, combined with wireless mobile handheld products to record, track, and manage readings and maintenance activities. http://www.pervidi.com		
PHOENICS	Comprehensive general purpose computational fluid dynamics program. PHOENICS simulates fluid movement and heat transfer for a wide variety of applications. http://members.ozemail.com.au/~acadsbsg		
PHPP	PHPP calculates energy demand for buildings. It is compatible with international norms (ISO 13790) and well validated with dynamic simulation tools as well as with measured data. It is especially adapted to high-performance buildings and can be used to prove Passive House requirements. The planning package comprises many tools specifically useful for the design of high-performance buildings. http://www.passivhaustagung.de/Passive_House_E/PHPP.html		
Physibel	Suite of heat and mass transfer programs. http://www.physibel.be		

Tool	Applications	Free	Recently Updated
Pipe Flow Expert	Application for designing and analyzing pipe networks where the flows and pressures must be balanced to solve the system. http://www.pipeflow.co.uk/public/control.php		
Pipe-Flo	Flow analysis software used to design, optimize, troubleshoot and simulate the operation of piping systems of any size or configuration. PIPE-FLO provides a total picture of the piping system including the flow and pressures in pipelines, along with the interaction of pumps, control valves, and flow meters. http://www.eng-software.com		
Pisces	Sizes hot or chilled-water circuits. PISCES accounts for single or two-pipe systems, reverse-return systems or any mixture of these circuit types. When sizing single-pipe systems, a local allowance is made for gravity effects for the flow through the radiator section. PISCES can be used for sizing systems from scratch, or as a check on an existing system, when pipe sizes and flow rates are specified. Different pipe materials, lagging properties and surface emissivities can also be specified. The circuit can be balanced using valves only, or by resizing non-index paths in the network. Velocity limits can be defined for the system, and if required, certain pipes in the system can be fixed in size. http://www.iesve.com		
PocketControls	Allows building operators get data from and send commands to an energy management system. With PocketControls the system can be controlled remotely, from a handheld Pocket PC, using wireless cellular communication technology. http://www.abraxasenergy.com		
Polysun	Polysun 4 is renewable energy system simulation software for planners and installers of energy systems. Polysun 4 helps users to configure and optimize solar and heat pump systems. Generated reports facilitate communication and marketing tasks. Polysun 4 makes system design simple and professional. Reliable yield-forecasts generated from integrated meteorological data create trust and promote understanding. Detailed models of the systems within the simulation software serve as the foundation for targeted system optimization and system comparisons. Polysun 4 accelerates the planning process; provides reliable yield forecasts; enables easy optimization of existing and new systems; provides relevant information when applying for subsidies; easily generates PDF reports for customers. http://www.solarconsulting.us/polysun.html		
Popolo Utility Load Calculation	Popolo Utility Load Calculation is a collection of classes for calculating various heat transfer phenomena. The routines have been written from scratch in C#, and present a modern Applications Programming Interface (API) for .NET Framework programmers, allowing wrappers to be written for very high level languages. It contains classes to calculate solid conduction, convective heat transfer near wall surfaces, air ventilation, radiative heat balance of wall surfaces, transmitted solar radiation through a window, and so on. Users should build up these classes to simulate a whole complex building system. http://www.hvacsimulator.net/index.php/Main_Page		
PRISM	Transforms run-of-the-mill billing data into statistically sound savings estimates. With PRISM (PRInceton Scorekeeping Method), utilities and energy analysts can systematically estimate total savings from a conservation or demand-side management program, for large samples of houses or buildings participating in the program, and for comparison groups as well. Enhanced model tuning and data pruning produce reliable savings estimates and statistics. http://www.princeton.edu/~marean		
Prophet Load Profiler	Internet-enabled software that empowers business energy customers to manage energy and reduce costs. Valuable to facility managers, energy managers and energy service companies, the Prophet web-based service delivers real-time and near-real-time energy information		

Tool	Applications	Free	Recently Updated
	on energy consumption and demand for any size facility. A number of facilities can be managed using consumption data gathered in 15 minute, 30 minute, 60 minute, daily, weekly and monthly intervals. Users can immediately view and analyze data with an eye toward load shedding, cost avoidance strategies, energy budget management, utility cost validation and energy forecasting. http://www.automatedenergy.com		
PsyCalc	PsyCalc is an electronic psychrometric calcultion tool that operates over a wide range of temperatures, moisture content and pressures. With two inputs, psychrometric properties and pressure, PsyCalc returns eleven key properties. PsyCalc contains Climatic Design Information, licensed from ASHRAE (1997 Fundamentals Chapter 26) presented in an easy to use interface with additional calculation features. PsyCalc includes a mixing airstream calculator for air flow rates up to 1,000,000 cfm. PsyCalc operates in English or SI units and can be used to convert values from one system to the other. PsyCalc includes many usability features such as saving and printing your work, saving user defaults and use of minimal screen space. http://www.linric.com		
PsyChart	PsyChart is a standalone Windows program that does complete moist air state calculations. It has a graphical interface with a component pallet of all common air-conditioning processes. You can add and link any processes on a graphic chart to form complete air-conditioning systems. Air states can be dragged around the chart and the process are automatically updated. http://www.coolit.co.za		
Psychrometric Analysis	Provides complete psychrometric analysis, displaying systems directly on the psychrometric chart. Psychrometric Analysis Reports include psychrometric chart with plot, notes, etc.; state point and process report and psychrometric flow chart diagram. Weather data and/or bin data is provided for cities throughout the world and can be displayed on the chart as data or bins, or can be displayed in a user defined data table for importing into other programs. Psychrometric Analysis supports both IP and SI units along with 13 different languages with one button click. http://www.handsdownsoftware.com	✓	
PUtility Psychrometric	The name of software is "PUtility Psychrometric". It is utility software which calculates moist air state and draws a psychrometric chart. Users can plot their data on the chart by giving the value of dry-bulb temperature and absolute humidity through a CSV formatted file. PUtility Psychrometric can give a graphic representation of comfortable air state with drawing region. Which PMV takes a specific value. Diagrams can be exported to vector image files (EMF). "PUtility Psychrometric" is released under GPL, and all the source codes can be freely downloaded from the Web site. http://www.hvacsimulator.net/index.php/Main_Page		
PV-DesignPro	Simulates photovoltaic system operation on an hourly basis for one year, based on a user selected climate and system design. PV-DesignPro is recommended for designs that include battery storage that can be both standalone systems with generator backup, or utility interconnected systems. Systems with no battery storage can be modeled using special instructions. The purpose of the program is to aid in photovoltaic system design by providing accurate and in-depth information on likely system power output and load consumption, necessary backup power during the operation of the system, and the financial impacts of installing the proposed system. http://www.mauisolarsoftware.com		
PVSYST	Software for the study, sizing, simulation and data analysis of complete PV systems. It is suitable for grid-connected, stand-alone and DC-grid (public transport) systems, and offers an extensive		

Tool	Applications	Free	Recently Updated
	meteorological and PV-components database. It includes a CAO tool for detailed shading analysis. PVSYST offers an ergonomic approach, with greenline guide, and several project levels. http://www.pvsyst.com		
PYTHON	WINDOWS-based program that analyses water piping systems for air conditioning applications. PYTHON Air Conditioning Heating and Cooling Piping Systems Design provides for the analysis of hot and chilled water closed loop systems and also open loop systems such as condenser water piping systems. PYTHON can however also handle any other fluid by entry of the fluid density, viscosity and specific heat. The program handles systems with primary and secondary circuits and is based on the methods and data in the AIRAH/IHRACE Application Manual Air Conditioning Water Piping (DA16). PYTHON includes all the fittings and associated pressure loss data in this manual readily accessible through drop down lists. http://members.ozemail.com.au/~acadsbsg		
Quick Calc	Online indoor lighting fixture-estimating tool. Quick Calc allows users to perform accurate quantity and footcandle calculations based upon pre-loaded IES photometric files and the information that users provide. After putting in requested information, the space being illuminated can be viewed in a flat plane or an isometric 3D plan. Printing capabilities have been included in the program to make it easier to share the information. Quick Calc includes indoor lighting fixture photometric files related to the ExceLine product line. http://www.exceline.com	☑	
QwickLoad	QwickLoad uses the ASHRAE TFM (Transfer Function Method) algorithms combined with a screen interface that provides building load calculations. It includes a Duct Sizing Program and supports IP and SI units. QwickLoad Residential 7.0 provides heat gain and heat loss calculations for up to 10 zones. QwickLoad Commercial 7.0 provides heat gain and heat loss calculations for up to 500 zones. Zones and plenums can be added or deleted with one button click. Intuitive screens for entering building information. Default is automatically displayed. Construction types for roofs, walls, partitions, windows, shade types, and scheduling control. Complete air-conditioning and heating system control and supply, return, heating and cooling duct static pressure specification. http://www.qwickload.com		
Radiance	Advanced lighting simulation and rendering package; calculates spectral radiance values (illuminance & color) and spectral irradiance (illuminance & color) for interior and exterior spaces considering electric lighting, daylight and interreflection. Used by architects and designers to predict illumination, visual quality and appearance of design spaces. Used by researchers to evaluate new lighting and daylighting technologies and study visual comfort and similar quantities related to the visual environment. http://radsite.lbl.gov/radiance/HOME.html	☑	
Radiance Interface	Provides an interface to Radiance which can accurately simulate the visible radiation in a space. Radiance is a powerful lighting simulation program that synthesises images from the 3D geometric model of the building. Radiance/4D+ is available for both daylight and electrical lighting simulation and provides photo-realistic images of the illuminated model. The simulation results can be displayed as photo-realistic images; lux values at user selected positions in the simulation 'frame', lux and daylight factors contours; glare factors and comfort indices. http://www.iesve.com		
RadOnCol	Provides radiation levels on a solar flat plate collectors based on: collector location (latitude); collector orientation (azimuth angle and tilt	☑	

Tool	Applications	Free	Recently Updated
	angle). RadOnCol (Radiation On Collector) provides hour by hour collected energy, or month by month collected energy for full sunshine conditions. http://www.builditsolar.com		
RadTherm	Thermal modeling program intended for comprehensive heat management design and analysis. RadTherm has powerful capabilities to solve transient solutions for 2D or 3D models in a natural environment, including the effects of direct, diffuse, and reflected solar radiation, thermal radiation, natural or forced convection, and conduction. RadTherm is equipped with everything but YOUR geometry: pre-processing/ set-up, a solver, and post-processor/ viewer. http://www.thermoanalytics.com		
REM/Design	User-friendly, yet highly sophisticated, residential energy analysis and code compliance software which eliminates the uncertainty and guesswork from energy design and code compliance decisions. Developed specifically with the needs of homebuilders, remodelers, energy consultants and designers in mind, REM/Design calculates heating, cooling, hot water, lights and appliance loads, consumption and costs for single and multi-family designs in over 250 North American cities. http://www.archenergy.com		
REScheck	A flexible approach for demonstrating compliance with the thermal shell requirements of the Council of American Building Officials (CABO) Model Energy Code (MEC), 1992, 1993, and 1995 editions as well as the 1998 and 2000 editions of the International Energy Conservation Code (IECC). Appropriate for thermal shell trade-off calculations in typical single-family and multifamily residential buildings. Allows quick comparison of different insulation levels to select a package that works best for the building. Determines compliance by comparing the total heat loss (represented as UA) through the building envelope to the heat loss through an equivalent code building. Automatically generates the forms that must be submitted for the plan review. http://www.energycodes.gov	☑	
RESEM	A simulation-based tool developed to allow the DOE Institutional Conservation Program (ICP) staff and participants to reliably determine the energy savings directly attributable to ICP-supported retrofit measures implemented in a building. RESEM (Retrofit Energy Savings Estimation Model) calculates long-term energy savings directly from actual utility data, with corrections for weather and use variations between the pre-retrofit and post-retrofit utility data collection periods. http://btech.lbl.gov/tools/resem/resem.htm	☑	☑
RESFEN	A program to help consumers and builders pick the most energy-efficient and cost-effective window for a given application. RESFEN calculates the heating and cooling energy use and associated costs as well as the peak heating and cooling demand for specific window products. Users define a problem by specifying the house type (single story or two story), geographic location, orientation, electricity and gas cost, and building configuration details (such as wall type, floor type, and HVAC systems). Window options are defined by specifying the window's size, shading, and thermal properties: U-factor, Solar Heat Gain Coefficient, and air leakage rate. RESFEN calculates the energy and cost implications of the windows compared to insulated walls. The relative energy and cost impacts of two different windows can be compared against each other. http://windows.lbl.gov/software/resfen/resfen.html	☑	
RETScreen	Software for evaluating energy production and savings, costs, emission reductions, financial viability and risk for various types of Renewable-energy and Energy-efficient Technologies (RETs). The software (available in multiple languages) also includes product, project, hydrology and climate databases, a detailed user manual, and	☑	

Tool	Applications	Free	Recently Updated
	a case study based college/university-level training course, including an engineering e-textbook. http://www.retscreen.net/ang/home.php		
ShadowFX	Amethyst ShadowFX is a sun and shadow analysis program for architects, designers and town planners. With the program, you can generate shadow profiles cast by buildings and other objects for any latitude, longitude and time of year. http://www.shadowfx.co.uk		
SkyVision	Calculates the overall optical characteristics (transmittance, absorptance, reflectance and Solar Heat Gain Coefficient) of conventional and tubular skylights, performance indicators of skylight/room interfaces (well efficiency and coefficient of utilization), indoor daylight availability (daylight factor and illuminance) and daily/annual lighting energy savings. SkyVision accounts for the skylight shape and glazing, geometry of the indoor space (curb, well, room), skylight layouts, lighting and shading controls, site location and sky/ground conditions. http://www.nrc-cnrc.gc.ca/eng/programs/irc/ie.html	☑	
SLAB	Calculates the heat loss to the ground from an evenly insulated rectangular slab on the ground. Both the heat loss variation during the year, including the peak effect, and the accumulated heat loss during the heating season are calculated. The effect of a sudden cold-spell may be analyzed. http://www.buildingphysics.com		
Solar Rater	Solar Rater app for Android devices makes it easy to determine the solar energy potential for any location on Earth, and calculates the appropriate size for a photovoltaic (PV) system at that location. http://www.earthscienceagency.com/software/android/solarrater		☑
SOLAR-2	Plots sunlight penetrating through a window with any combination of rectangular fins and overhangs. Also plots hour-by-hour 3-D suns-eye view 'movie' of the building. Prints annual tables of percent of window in full sun, radiation on glass, etc. http://www.energy-design-tools.aud.ucla.edu	☑	
SOLAR-5	Displays 3-D plots of hourly energy performance for the whole building or for 9 schemes and any of 40 different components. SOLAR-5 also plots heat flow into/out of thermal mass, and indoor air temperature, daylighting, output of the HVAC system, cost of electricity and heating fuel, and the corresponding amount of air pollution. It uses hour-by-hour weather data. It contains an expert system to design an initial base case building for any climate and any building type that an architect can copy and redesign. Contains a variety of decision-making aids, including combination and comparison options, color overlays, and bar charts that show for any hour exactly where the energy flows. http://www.energy-design-tools.aud.ucla.edu	☑	
SolArch	Design tool for architects familiar with passive solar energy. It includes a thermal performance calculator, a design element checklist, and excel spreadsheets database with useful Solar Architecture parameters (e.g. thermal properties). http://www.kahl.net/solarch	☑	
SolarDesignTool	SolarDesignTool is a Web site that allows people to design solar electric grid-tied systems online. http://get.solardesigntool.com/		
SolarShoeBox	Simple to use interface for EnergyPlus. Creates a rectangular model (shoebox) of a direct gain passive solar building. http://www.archiphysics.com	☑	
SPARK	An object-oriented program that allows the user to quickly build models of complex physical processes by connecting equation-based calculation modules from an object library. SPARK (Simulation Problem Analysis and Research Kernel) creates an executable simulation program from this network ready to be run. http://simulationresearch.lbl.gov	☑	
SPOT	Quantifies existing or intended electric lighting performance, evaluate annual daylighting characteristics and help establish the optimal photo	☑	

Tool	Applications	Free	Recently Updated
	sensor placement in a given space relative to annual performance and annual energy savings. The Sensor Placement and Optimization Tool, or SPOT, was developed with classroom daylighting in mind, but can be used for all types of spaces. http://www.archenergy.com/SPOT		
STREAM	STREAM, a computational fluid dynamics (CFD) software program developed in 1984, has been used in a wide variety of commercial applications. STREAM can calculate the phenomena related to HVAC (airflow, heat transfer--including radiation and solar radiation, humidity, condensation, contamination distribution, and air quality indexes--for all sizes of buildings. http://www.cradle-cfd.com		
SunAngle	Calculates solar angles based on location, date, and time. It's useful in passive solar building design, PV and solar thermal system design and analysis, and other applications such as photography. http://www.susdesign.com/sunangle		
Suncast	Performs solar shading and insolation analysis and can generate images and animations. Suncast uses sun tracking and hidden surface algorithms to generate and view shadow data for all internal and external surfaces of the model. Suncast generates shadows from any sun position defined by date, time, orientation, site latitude and longitude and can investigate: external obstruction and self-shading of a building; solar mapping through windows; solar radiation on external and internal surfaces; and the effects of changing orientation of the building. http://www.iesve.com		
SunPosition	Calculates time series of sun angles (such as solar altitude and solar azimuth) for a given location and outputs them as text files that can be imported into spreadsheets and solar energy analysis programs. Sun Position is highly customizable: you can have it calculate angles for one specific day, once a month for one year, once a week, daily, etc., and in a given day calculate the angles once a day, hourly, every 15 minutes, etc. Its primary purpose is to assist architects and solar designers perform energy analysis calculations. http://www.susdesign.com		
SUNREL	Aids in the design of single- or multizone energy-efficient buildings where the loads are dominated by the dynamic interactions between the building's envelope, its environment, and its occupants. SUNREL is especially well suited for passive solar buildings and includes algorithms for Trombe walls, advanced glazings, schedulable window shading, active-charge/passive-discharge thermal storage, and natural ventilation. The program is a true simulation model based on time steps of one hour or less. The model representation of the building is a thermal network solved with forward finite differencing among other techniques. http://www.nrel.gov/buildings/sunrel		
Sunspec	Calculates clear sky direct beam and diffuse sky solar spectral irradiances and the sum of these two spectra for sun positions and atmospheric conditions specified by the user. Sunspec version 1.0 also calculates the spectral irradiances incident on an arbitrarily tilted plane due to the direct beam, diffuse sky, and ground reflections. Sunspec integrates these spectra to determine the total irradiances, illuminances, and luminous efficacies for each component. Version 2.0 is in preparation and should be available by late-1997. Version 2.0 will be mouse-driven with user friendly I/O. http://www.fsec.ucf.edu/en		
TAPS	Allows users to size hot and cold water services by specifying the properties of pipe work branches connected to one another via nodes. As an option, you can also specify a secondary return pipe work system in the same manner, and TAPS will size the pipe work and the pump required to provide the required flow around the return circuit. Different types of cold-water supply can be specified, such as gravity feed or pressurized. The user can also specify items such as different		

Tool	Applications	Free	Recently Updated
	pipe materials, lagging properties and surface emissivity. Both the outflow circuit and the secondary return circuit are balanced by resizing the non-index runs. Velocity limits can be defined for the system, and if required, the dimensions of certain pipes in the system can be fixed. http://www.iesve.com		
Tariff Analysis Project	There are many software solutions that determine the energy savings due to some new technology, but virtually no solutions exist that determine the precise economic impact of these technologies. The Tariff Analysis Project, TAP, is a comprehensive data warehouse of utility tariffs and query tools designed to accurately and precisely calculate utility bills. TAP consists of a growing library of 100s of tariffs from over a hundred utilities which have been stored using a generic data format that is compatible with a variety of tariff structures. http://minotaur.lbl.gov/tariffs	☑	
TAS	Software package for the thermal analysis of buildings. TAS includes a 3D modeler, a thermal/energy analysis module, a systems/controls simulator and a 2D CFD package. There are also CAD links into the 3D modeler as well as report generation facilities. It is a complete solution for the thermal simulation of a building, and a powerful design tool in the optimization of a buildings environmental, energy and comfort performance. http://www.edsl.net/main		
Tetti FV	Program for the simulation, design and calculation of grid connected photovoltaic systems. The system components are loaded from the system database. Tetti FV is a simple and efficient system design for all photovoltaic system configurations. http://www.studioiesl.com		
Therm	Analysis of two-dimensional heat transfer through building products. Includes a graphical user interface that allows users to draw cross sections of fenestration and other building products, which can then be analyzed by an automatic mesh generator and finite-element heat transfer algorithms. Results are displayed graphically. http://windows.lbl.gov/software/therm/therm.html	☑	
TREAT	Performs hourly simulations for single family, multifamily, and mobile homes. Comprehensive analysis tool includes tools for retrofitting heating and cooling systems, building envelopes (insulation and infiltration), windows and doors, hot water, ventilation, lighting and appliances, and more. Weather normalizes utility bills for comparison to performance of model. Highly accurate calculations which consider waste heat (baseload), solar heat gain, and fully interacted energy savings calculations. Create individual energy improvements or packages of interactive improvements. Also performs load sizing. http://www.psdconsulting.com/software/treat		
TRNSYS	An energy simulation program whose modular system approach makes it one of the most flexible tools available. TRNSYS (TRaNsient SYstem Simulation Program) includes a graphical interface, a simulation engine, and a library of components that range from various building models to standard HVAC equipment to renewable energy and emerging technologies. TRNSYS also includes a method for creating new components that do not exist in the standard package. This simulation package has been used for more than 30 years for HVAC analysis and sizing, multizone airflow analyses, electric power simulation, solar design, building thermal performance, analysis of control schemes, etc. http://sel.me.wisc.edu/trnsys		
United Resources Group Lighting Conservation	Comprehensive lighting software designed to analyze existing lighting systems and provide alternative systems that will offer energy-savings retrofit options with corresponding total wattage reduction, percent reduction, kilowatt hour savings, maintenance savings, net air conditioning savings, and a corresponding cost and dollar savings total with payback. http://www.urgenergy.com		

Tool	Applications	Free	Recently Updated
UrbaWind	UrbaWind is an automatic CFD software solution for wind modeling in the built environment. This tool is dedicated to work-oriented applications: natural ventilation, wind energy, and pedestrian wind comfort. The local wind statistics (speed and direction) of any place in the world is integrated in the software. The outputs are user friendly and can be visualized in 3D. http://www.meteodyn.com		
UtilityTrac	UtilityTrac™ enables the user to audit, track and analyze utility usage in order to better understand the impact on energy consumption, identify energy conservation opportunities, track carbon footprint, and apply for ENERGY STAR® certification. http://www.facilitydude.com		
VIP+	Whole-building energy analysis program calculating hourly energy performance for a full year. VIP+ can also be used for economical and environmental calculations. http://vip.strusoft.com		
VIPWEB	Extremely easy energy analysis program calculating hourly energy performance for a full year on the web. Can also be used together with VIP+. http://vip.strusoft.com	☑	
Virtualwind	Virtualwind is a 3-D wind flow modeling and visualization software solution. It empowers users to quickly predict, understand, and convey complex wind flow phenomena in urban, suburban, and rural environments. Virtualwind wraps its advanced wind flow technology in user interfaces that are intuitive and natural. Complex wind and dispersion phenomena are simulated with our easy-to-use 3-D visualization tools. http://virtualwind.com		
VISION4	Models the combined optical and thermal performance of glazing systems and provides information on the energy flow and temperatures which result from imposed environmental conditions. VISION4 is part of the FRAMEplus Toolkit for the thermal analysis of windows, walls and doors. VISION4 can also calculate the velocity field within window glazing cavities to better predict condensation resistance. VISION4 simulations (when combined with FRAME) are an equal alternative to testing to determine the U-value, condensation resistance and solar heat gain coefficient of windows and doors. http://www.enermodal.com		
Visual	Comprehensive lighting analysis software engineered for demanding interior and exterior applications. Visual lighting design software integrates an advanced 3-D modeling environment with an intuitive interfaceï¿½providing a unique and powerful extension of the design process. Professional presentation capabilities enable you to quickly develop, analyze, and modify advanced lighting designs. Visual performs direct and interreflected component calculations and provides the ability to quickly compose professional presentations. http://www.visuallightingsoftware.com/	☑	
VisualDOE	A Windows interface to the DOE-2.1E energy simulation program. Through the graphical interface, users construct a model of the building's geometry using standard block shapes, using a built-in drawing tool, or importing DXF files. Building systems are defined through a point-and-click interface. A library of constructions, fenestrations, systems and operating schedules is included, and the user can add custom elements as well. http://www.archenergy.com/products/visualdoe		
Visualize-IT Energy Information and Analysis Tool	Designed to explore, summarize and analyze time series interval data. Visualize-IT has been developed specifically for electric and gas load data, but it is equally useful as a general purpose data visualization tool for other time series measurements such as weather, industrial process control, and water quality. http://www.rlw.com/Default.aspx		
WaterAide	Comprehensive residential, commercial and industrial water audit software package. WaterAide can evaluate a broad range of water saving opportunities. Savings can include domestic hot water energy		

Tool	Applications	Free	Recently Updated
	savings, in addition to water bill savings, if desired. http://www.energynewengland.com		
Window	Calculates thermal performance of fenestration products; heat transfer analysis method consistent with the rating procedure developed by the National Fenestration Rating Council (NFRC). http://windows.lbl.gov/software/window/window.html	☑	
Window Heat Gain	Calculates the solar heat gain through vertical windows in temperate latitudes. http://www.susdesign.com/windowheatgain		
WindPro	Fully integrated modular-based software package with outstanding interactive graphics and superior documentation. Used by 2,000 companies worldwide. http://www.windpro.com		☑
WUFI-ORNL/IBP	Advanced hygrothermal model that solves the coupled heat, and moisture transport in building envelope systems such as walls and roofs. The model is joint development between the Oak Ridge National Laboratory and the Fraunhofer Institute in Building Physics (IBP). WUFI-ORNL/IBP is an easy-to-use, menu-driven program for use on a personal computer which can provide customized solutions to moisture engineering and damage assessment problems for various building envelope systems. http://www.ornl.gov/sci/btc/apps/moisture	☑	

Appendix 3
Financial Modeling Reports

Project 1: Yield Summary on Modified Payback (SuperTrump)

CASH FLOWS

asset cost	1,000,000.00	100.000000
fees received	400,000.00	40.000000
equity	600,000.00	60.000000
utility savings	660,000.00	66.000000
total cash in	660,000.00	66.000000
equity	600,000.00	60.000000
total cash out	600,000.00	60.000000
pre-tax cash flow	60,000.00	6.000000
taxes paid	0.00	0.000000
after-tax cash flow	60,000.00	6.000000

STATISTICS

composite tax rate 0.0000
Tax treatment .... Conditional sale
FAS 13 for lessor (default) .... Capital: single investor (DFL)
FAS 13 for lessee .... Capital

	pre-tax effective	pre-tax nominal	after-tax effective	after-tax nominal
MISF (per)	5.4330	5.3022	5.4330	5.3022
IRR PTCF (per)	5.4330	5.3022	5.4330	5.3022

PV on Jul-01-12 of Min Lease Pmts @ IBR at 10.0000% 564,749.47 56.474947
on Jul-01-12 of Rent & Guar Res @ IIR at -24.2968% 1,000,000.00 100.000000

average-life of investment .... 13.5792 months

implicit interest rate .... -24.2968
Full term rate without residual .... -24.2968
with residual .... -24.2968
Customer rate .... -24.2968

Assets

cost	delivery	funding	residual	% cost	date	description
1,000,000.00	Jul-01-12	Jul-01-12	0.00	0.0000	Jul-01-15	"Project 1 Example"

Fee Income

#	Cash: amount	% of cost	date paid	equity		Amortization: start date	method	term	salvage	convention
1	100,000.00	10.000000	Nov-01-12	No	Fed		None			
2	300,000.00	30.000000	Nov-01-12	No	Fed		None			

1: "Utility Rebate"; accounting .... Cash; lessee obligation, non-financed

2: "ITC"; accounting .... Cash; lessee obligation, non-financed

commencement date Jul-01-12

		#	timing	from	to	1st pmt	type	amount	% of cost
"Energy Savings" payments (36)	660,000.00	12	mon arr	Jul-01-12 →	Jul-01-13	Aug-01-12	payment	16,667.00	1.666700
		12	↓ ↓	Jul-01-13 →	Jul-01-14	Aug-01-13	↓	18,333.00	1.833300
		12		Jul-01-14 →	Jul-01-15	Aug-01-14		20,000.00	2.000000

Taxes

Month fiscal year ends .... Dec
First year tax payments .... Level on remaining dates

Federal

tax calculation method .... Accrual (Arr Only)
tax estimation method .... Level

start date	rate	thru	paid	percent
		Mar	Apr	25.0000
		Jun	Jun	25.0000
		Sep	Sep	25.0000
		Dec	Dec	25.0000

Project 1: Cash Flow Report (SuperTrump)

period ending	utility savings -	equity -	fees =	pre-tax cash flow =	after-tax cash flow	cumulative after-tax cash flow
Jul-30-12	0.00	1,000,000.00	0.00	-1,000,000.00	-1,000,000.00	-1,000,000.00
Aug-30-12	16,667.00	0.00	0.00	16,667.00	16,667.00	-983,333.00
Sep-30-12	16,667.00	0.00	0.00	16,667.00	16,667.00	-966,666.00
Oct-30-12	16,667.00	0.00	0.00	16,667.00	16,667.00	-949,999.00
Nov-30-12	16,667.00	0.00	-400,000.00	416,667.00	416,667.00	-533,332.00
Dec-30-12	16,667.00	0.00	0.00	16,667.00	16,667.00	-516,665.00
	83,335.00	1,000,000.00	-400,000.00	-516,665.00	-516,665.00	
Jan-30-13	16,667.00	0.00	0.00	16,667.00	16,667.00	-499,998.00
Feb-30-13	16,667.00	0.00	0.00	16,667.00	16,667.00	-483,331.00
Mar-30-13	16,667.00	0.00	0.00	16,667.00	16,667.00	-466,664.00
Apr-30-13	16,667.00	0.00	0.00	16,667.00	16,667.00	-449,997.00
May-30-13	16,667.00	0.00	0.00	16,667.00	16,667.00	-433,330.00
Jun-30-13	16,667.00	0.00	0.00	16,667.00	16,667.00	-416,663.00
Jul-30-13	16,667.00	0.00	0.00	16,667.00	16,667.00	-399,996.00
Aug-30-13	18,333.00	0.00	0.00	18,333.00	18,333.00	-381,663.00
Sep-30-13	18,333.00	0.00	0.00	18,333.00	18,333.00	-363,330.00
Oct-30-13	18,333.00	0.00	0.00	18,333.00	18,333.00	-344,997.00
Nov-30-13	18,333.00	0.00	0.00	18,333.00	18,333.00	-326,664.00
Dec-30-13	18,333.00	0.00	0.00	18,333.00	18,333.00	-308,331.00
	208,334.00	0.00	0.00	208,334.00	208,334.00	
Jan-30-14	18,333.00	0.00	0.00	18,333.00	18,333.00	-289,998.00
Feb-30-14	18,333.00	0.00	0.00	18,333.00	18,333.00	-271,665.00
Mar-30-14	18,333.00	0.00	0.00	18,333.00	18,333.00	-253,332.00
Apr-30-14	18,333.00	0.00	0.00	18,333.00	18,333.00	-234,999.00
May-30-14	18,333.00	0.00	0.00	18,333.00	18,333.00	-216,666.00
Jun-30-14	18,333.00	0.00	0.00	18,333.00	18,333.00	-198,333.00
Jul-30-14	18,333.00	0.00	0.00	18,333.00	18,333.00	-180,000.00
Aug-30-14	20,000.00	0.00	0.00	20,000.00	20,000.00	-160,000.00
Sep-30-14	20,000.00	0.00	0.00	20,000.00	20,000.00	-140,000.00
Oct-30-14	20,000.00	0.00	0.00	20,000.00	20,000.00	-120,000.00
Nov-30-14	20,000.00	0.00	0.00	20,000.00	20,000.00	-100,000.00
Dec-30-14	20,000.00	0.00	0.00	20,000.00	20,000.00	-80,000.00
	228,331.00	0.00	0.00	228,331.00	228,331.00	
Jan-30-15	20,000.00	0.00	0.00	20,000.00	20,000.00	-60,000.00
Feb-30-15	20,000.00	0.00	0.00	20,000.00	20,000.00	-40,000.00
Mar-30-15	20,000.00	0.00	0.00	20,000.00	20,000.00	-20,000.00
Apr-30-15	20,000.00	0.00	0.00	20,000.00	20,000.00	0.00
May-30-15	20,000.00	0.00	0.00	20,000.00	20,000.00	20,000.00
Jun-30-15	20,000.00	0.00	0.00	20,000.00	20,000.00	40,000.00
Jul-30-15	20,000.00	0.00	0.00	20,000.00	20,000.00	60,000.00
	140,000.00	0.00	0.00	140,000.00	140,000.00	
TOTAL	660,000.00	1,000,000.00	-400,000.00	60,000.00	60,000.00	

Project 1-A: Yield Summary on Modified Payback with Tax Effect (SuperTrump)

CASH FLOWS

asset cost	1,000,000.00	100.000000
fees received	100,000.00	10.000000
equity	900,000.00	90.000000
utility savings	1,200,000.00	120.000000
total cash in	1,200,000.00	120.000000
equity	900,000.00	90.000000
total cash out	900,000.00	90.000000
pre-tax cash flow	300,000.00	30.000000
taxes paid	-166,008.00	-16.600800
after-tax cash flow	466,008.00	46.600800

STATISTICS

composite tax rate	40.7460
IRS true lease tests	passed
IRS un-even rent	failed
Tax treatment	True tax lease
FAS 13 for lessor (default)	Capital: single investor (DFL)
FAS 13 for lessee	Capital

	pre-tax effective	pre-tax nominal	after-tax effective	after-tax nominal
MISF (per)	53.2633	46.8250	31.5606	27.7457
IRR PTCF (per)	11.5511	10.9812	6.8445	6.5068

PV on Jul-01-12 of Min Lease Pmts @ IBR at 10.0000%	925,751.30	92.575130
on Jul-01-12 of Rent & Guar Res @ IIR at 21.8942%	700,000.00	70.000000
average-life of investment	19.8951 months	

implicit interest rate	21.8942
Full term rate without residual	6.9339
with residual	6.9339
Customer rate	6.9339

Payments

12@	16,667.00	12@	20,000.00	12@	23,333.00
12@	18,333.00	12@	21,667.00		

Assets

cost	delivery	funding	residual	% cost	date	description
1,000,000.00	Jul-01-12	Jul-01-12	0.00	0.0000	Jul-01-17	"Project 1 Example"

	Depreciation start date	Depreciation method	term	salvage	convention	ITC percent	ITC date
Fed	Jul-01-12	MACRS (DB/SL 200)	5.000	0.000	Half-year	30.0000	Jul-01-12
basis	85.0000	Additional first year	50.0000				
State	Jul-01-12	MACRS (DB/SL 200)	5.000	0.000	Half-year		

Fee Income

Cash amount	% of cost	date paid	equity
100,000.00	10.000000	Nov-01-12	No

"Utility Rebate"
accounting .... Cash
lessee obligation, non-financed

	Amortization start date	method	term	salvage	convention
Fed		None			
State		None			

Energy

commencement date Jul-01-12

"Energy Savings"
payments (60) 1,200,000.00

#	timing		from	to	1st pmt	type	amount	% of cost
12	mon	arr	Jul-01-12	Jul-01-13	Aug-01-12	payment	16,667.00	1.666700
12			Jul-01-13	Jul-01-14	Aug-01-13		18,333.00	1.833300
12			Jul-01-14	Jul-01-15	Aug-01-14		20,000.00	2.000000
12			Jul-01-15	Jul-01-16	Aug-01-15		21,667.00	2.166700
12			Jul-01-16	Jul-01-17	Aug-01-16		23,333.00	2.333300

Project 1-A: Cash Flow Report on Modified Payback with Tax Effect (SuperTrump)

	Dec-30-12	Dec-30-13	Dec-30-14	Dec-30-15	Dec-30-16	Dec-30-17	TOTAL
STATE TAX STATEMENT							
Revenues:							
Utility Savings	100,002	210,000	229,998	250,002	270,000	139,998	1,200,000
Total Revenue	100,002	210,000	229,998	250,002	270,000	139,998	1,200,000
Expenses:							
Depreciation	200,000	320,000	192,000	115,200	115,200	57,600	1,000,000
Total Expenses	200,000	320,000	192,000	115,200	115,200	57,600	1,000,000
Taxable Income	(99,998)	(110,000)	37,998	134,802	154,800	82,398	200,000
Taxes Due	(8,840)	(9,724)	3,359	11,916	13,684	7,284	17,680
Taxes Paid (saved)	(8,840)	(9,724)	3,359	11,916	13,684	7,284	17,680
FEDERAL TAX STATEMENT							
Revenues:							
Utility Savings	100,002	210,000	229,998	250,002	270,000	139,998	1,200,000
Total Revenue	100,002	210,000	229,998	250,002	270,000	139,998	1,200,000
Expenses:							
Depreciation	510,000	136,000	81,600	48,960	48,960	24,480	850,000
State Tax Due	(8,840)	(9,724)	3,359	11,916	13,684	7,284	17,680
Total Expenses	501,160	126,276	84,959	60,876	62,644	31,764	867,680
Taxable Income	(401,158)	83,724	145,039	189,126	207,356	108,234	332,320
Taxes Due	(140,405)	29,303	50,764	66,194	72,574	37,882	116,312
ITC Due	300,000	0	0	0	0	0	300,000
Taxes Paid (saved)	(440,405)	29,303	50,764	66,194	72,574	37,882	(183,688)
CASH FLOW STATEMENT							
Cash In:							
Utility Savings	83,335	208,334	228,331	248,335	268,334	163,331	1,200,000
Total Cash In	83,335	208,334	228,331	248,335	268,334	163,331	1,200,000
Equity	1,000,000	0	0	0	0	0	1,000,000
Fees	(100,000)	0	0	0	0	0	(100,000)
Total Cash Out	900,000	0	0	0	0	0	900,000
Pre-Tax Cash Flow	(816,665)	208,334	228,331	248,335	268,334	163,331	300,000
Total Taxes Paid (saved)	(449,245)	19,579	54,123	78,110	86,259	45,166	(166,008)

Project 2: Yield Summary on Conditional Sales Contract (SuperTrump)

Cash Flows

loans lending	1,000,000.00	100.000000
interest received	274,822.68	27.482268
principal received	1,000,000.00	100.000000
total cash in	1,274,822.68	127.482268
equity	1,000,000.00	100.000000
total cash out	1,000,000.00	100.000000
pre-tax cash flow	274,822.68	27.482268
taxes paid	96,187.94	9.618794
after-tax cash flow	178,634.74	17.863474

Statistics

composite tax rate 35.0000

	pre-tax effective	pre-tax nominal	after-tax effective	after-tax nominal
MISF (per)	10.3288	10.0240	6.7137	6.5156
IRR PTCF (per)	10.4713	10.0000	6.8063	6.5000

average life of loan: lending	32.9787 months
Full term rate without balloon	10.4713
with balloon	10.4713
Customer rate	10.4713
payment statistics displayed	effective

Loans Lending

		#	timing	from	to	rate	type	amount	% of loan
funding	1,000,000.00				Jul-01-12		funding	-1,000,000.00	-100.00000
interest	274,822.68	60	mon arr	Jul-01-12 →	Jul-01-17	10.0000	payment	21,247.04	2.124704
payments	1,274,822.68								

Taxes/Lender

Month fiscal year ends .... Dec
First year tax payments .... Level on remaining dates

Federal

tax calculation method .... Accrual (Arr Only)
tax estimation method .... Level

start date	rate	thru	paid	percent
Jan-01-07	35.0000	Mar	Apr	25.0000
		Jun	Jun	25.0000
		Sep	Sep	25.0000
		Dec	Dec	25.0000

period ending +	interest received =	taxable income =>	tax DUE =>	tax PAID
Dec-30-12	48,367.74	48,367.74	16,928.71	16,928.71
Dec-30-13	84,412.09	84,412.09	29,544.23	29,544.23
Dec-30-14	66,553.02	66,553.02	23,293.56	23,293.56
Dec-30-15	46,823.87	46,823.87	16,388.36	16,388.36
Dec-30-16	25,028.83	25,028.83	8,760.09	8,760.09
Dec-30-17	3,637.13	3,637.13	1,273.00	1,273.00
total	274,822.68	274,822.68	96,187.94	96,187.94

CSC Cash Flow Statement

	Dec-30-12	Dec-30-13	Dec-30-14	Dec-30-15	Dec-30-16	Dec-30-17	total
Federal Tax Statement							
revenues:							
interest	48,368	84,412	66,553	46,824	25,029	3,637	274,823
total revenue	48,368	84,412	66,553	46,824	25,029	3,637	274,823
taxable income	48,368	84,412	66,553	46,824	25,029	3,637	274,823
taxes due	16,929	29,544	23,294	16,388	8,760	1,273	96,188
taxes paid (saved)	16,929	29,544	23,294	16,388	8,760	1,273	96,188
Cash Flow Statement							
cash in:							
principal	65,654	169,143	186,854	206,420	228,035	143,893	1,000,000
interest	40,582	85,822	68,110	48,544	26,929	4,836	274,823
debt service	106,235	254,965	254,965	254,965	254,965	148,729	1,274,823
total cash in	106,235	254,965	254,965	254,965	254,965	148,729	1,274,823
equity	1,000,000	0	0	0	0	0	1,000,000
total cash out	1,000,000	0	0	0	0	0	1,000,000
pre-tax cash flow	(893,765)	254,965	254,965	254,965	254,965	148,729	274,823
total taxes paid (saved)	16,929	29,544	23,294	16,388	8,760	1,273	96,188
after-tax cash flow	(910,693)	225,420	231,671	238,576	246,204	147,456	178,635
cumulative after-tax cash flow	(910,693)	(685,273)	(453,602)	(215,026)	31,178	178,635	

CSC Income Statement & Balance Sheet

	Dec-30-12	Dec-30-13	Dec-30-14	Dec-30-15	Dec-30-16	Dec-30-17	total
Income Statement							
+ pre-tax earnings	48,368	84,412	66,553	46,824	25,029	3,637	274,823
- federal income tax provision	16,929	29,544	23,294	16,388	8,760	1,273	96,188
= net income	31,439	54,868	43,259	30,436	16,269	2,364	178,635
Federal Deferred Tax							
+ tax due	16,929	29,544	23,294	16,388	8,760	1,273	96,188
- income tax provision	16,929	29,544	23,294	16,388	8,760	1,273	96,188
+ interest receivable	234,241	148,420	80,309	31,765	4,836	0	
+ principal receivable	934,346	765,203	578,349	371,928	143,893	0	
- unearned income, pre-tax	226,455	142,043	75,490	28,666	3,637	0	
= lease assets	942,133	771,580	583,169	375,028	145,092	0	
+ cash	(910,693)	(685,273)	(453,602)	(215,026)	31,178	178,635	
= total assets	31,439	86,307	129,566	160,002	176,271	178,635	
Liabilities							
+ income earned	48,368	132,780	199,333	246,157	271,186	274,823	
- federal tax provision	16,929	46,473	69,766	86,155	94,915	96,188	
= retained earnings	31,439	86,307	129,566	160,002	176,271	178,635	
+ current federal tax	0	0	0	0	0	0	
= total liabilities	31,439	86,307	129,566	160,002	176,271	178,635	

Project 2: Yield Summary on Lease Contract (SuperTrump)

Cash Flows

asset cost	1,000,000.00	100.000000
rent	1,200,000.00	120.000000
total cash in	1,200,000.00	120.000000
equity	1,000,000.00	100.000000
total cash out	1,000,000.00	100.000000
pre-tax cash flow	200,000.00	20.000000
taxes paid	-177,500.00	-17.750000
after-tax cash flow	377,500.00	37.750000

Statistics

composite tax rate	35.0000
tax treatment (default)	True tax lease
FAS 13 for lessor (default)	Capital: single investor (DFL)
FAS 13 for lessee	Capital
implicit interest rate	21.8942

	pre-tax effective	after-tax effective
MISF (per)	34.1220	22.1793
IRR PTCF (per)	7.1585	4.6531
ROA	18.5129	12.0334

(lev = 85.000 borr & lend = 5.000)

PV on Jul-01-12 of Rent at 10.0000%	925,751.30	92.575130
payback from Jul-01-12	3.0833 years	
Full term rate without residual	7.1585	
with residual	7.1585	
payment statistics displayed	effective	

Assets

cost	delivery	funding	residual	% cost	date	description
1,000,000.00	Jul-01-12	Jul-01-12	0.00	0.0000	Jul-01-17	"Solar PV Energy Project"

	Depreciation start date	method	term	salvage	convention	Tax Credit percent	date	recapture
Fed	Jul-01-12	MACRS (DB/SL 200)	5.000	0.000	Half-year	30.0000	Jul-01-12	60.000 months

basis .... 85.0000 Additional first year 50.0000

Rents

commencement date Jul-01-12

		#	timing	from	to	1st pmt	type	amount	% of cost
payments (60)	1,200,000.00	12	mon arr	Jul-01-12 → Jul-01-13		Aug-01-12	payment	16,667.00	1.666700
		12		Jul-01-13 → Jul-01-14		Aug-01-13		18,333.00	1.833300
		12		Jul-01-14 → Jul-01-15		Aug-01-14		20,000.00	2.000000
		12		Jul-01-15 → Jul-01-16		Aug-01-15		21,667.00	2.166700
		12		Jul-01-16 → Jul-01-17		Aug-01-16		23,333.00	2.333300

Taxes/Lessor

Month fiscal year ends .... Dec
First year tax payments .... Level on remaining dates

Federal

tax calculation method .... Accrual (Adv & Arr)
tax estimation method .... Level

start date	rate	thru	paid	percent
Jan-01-12	35.0000	Mar	Apr	25.0000
		Jun	Jun	25.0000
		Sep	Sep	25.0000
		Dec	Dec	25.0000

Project 2: Cash Flow Summary on Lease Contract (SuperTrump)

	Dec-30-12	Dec-30-13	Dec-30-14	Dec-30-15	Dec-30-16	Dec-30-17	total
FEDERAL TAX STATEMENT							
Revenues:							
Lease Rentals	100,002	210,000	229,998	250,002	270,000	139,998	1,200,000
Total Revenue	100,002	210,000	229,998	250,002	270,000	139,998	1,200,000
Expenses:							
Depreciation	510,000	136,000	81,600	48,960	48,960	24,480	850,000
Total Expenses	510,000	136,000	81,600	48,960	48,960	24,480	850,000
Taxable Income	(409,998)	74,000	148,398	201,042	221,040	115,518	350,000
Taxes Due	(143,499)	25,900	51,939	70,365	77,364	40,431	122,500
ITC Due	300,000	0	0	0	0	0	300,000
Taxes Paid (saved)	(443,499)	25,900	51,939	70,365	77,364	40,431	(177,500)
CASH FLOW STATEMENT							
Cash In:							
Lease Rentals	83,335	208,334	228,331	248,335	268,334	163,331	1,200,000
Total Cash In	83,335	208,334	228,331	248,335	268,334	163,331	1,200,000
Equity	1,000,000	0	0	0	0	0	1,000,000
Total Cash Out	1,000,000	0	0	0	0	0	1,000,000
Pre-Tax Cash Flow	(916,665)	208,334	228,331	248,335	268,334	163,331	200,000
Total Taxes Paid (saved)	(443,499)	25,900	51,939	70,365	77,364	40,431	(177,500)

Project 2: Income and Balance Sheet on Lease Contract (SuperTrump)

	Dec-30-12	Dec-30-13	Dec-30-14	Dec-30-15	Dec-30-16	Dec-30-17	total
Income Statement							
+ pre-tax earnings	33,718	60,215	48,845	35,228	19,206	2,788	200,000
- federal income tax provision	20,652	36,882	29,917	21,577	11,763	1,708	122,500
+ federal ITC earned	50,578	90,322	73,267	52,843	28,809	4,182	300,000
= net income	63,643	113,655	92,194	66,494	36,251	5,263	377,500
Federal Deferred Tax							
+ tax due	(143,499)	25,900	51,939	70,365	77,364	40,431	122,500
- ITC due	300,000	0	0	0	0	0	300,000
- income tax provision	(29,925)	(53,441)	(43,350)	(31,265)	(17,045)	(2,475)	(177,500)
– deferred tax	(413,574)	79,341	95,289	101,630	94,409	42,906	0
–> cumulative deferred tax	(413,574)	(334,234)	(238,945)	(137,315)	(42,906)	0	
Assets							
+ rent receivable	1,116,665	908,331	680,000	431,665	163,331	0	
- unearned income, pre-tax	166,282	106,067	57,222	21,994	2,788	0	
= lease assets	950,383	802,264	622,778	409,671	160,543	0	
+ cash	(473,166)	(290,732)	(114,340)	63,630	254,600	377,500	
= total assets	477,218	511,532	508,438	473,301	415,143	377,500	
Liabilities							
+ income earned	33,718	93,933	142,778	178,006	197,212	200,000	
- federal tax provision	(29,925)	(83,366)	(126,715)	(157,980)	(175,025)	(177,500)	
– retained earnings	63,643	177,299	269,493	335,986	372,237	377,500	
+ current federal tax	0	0	0	0	0	0	
+ deferred federal tax	413,574	334,234	238,945	137,315	42,906	0	
– total liabilities	477,218	511,532	508,438	473,301	415,143	377,500	

Project 3: Yield Summary on Lease vs. Purchase Analysis (SuperTrump)

Preferred	PURCHASE
Equipment at end of financing	Keep (forever)
FAS Class	CAPITAL lease
Lease, tax treatment	True tax lease
Break-even discount rate	17.965573%

Purchase

asset cost	1,000,000.00	100.000000
equity	1,000,000.00	100.000000
equity	1,000,000.00	100.000000
total cash out	1,000,000.00	100.000000
pre-tax cash flow	-1,000,000.00	-100.000000
taxes paid	-597,500.00	-59.750000
after-tax cash flow	-402,500.00	-40.250000
PV ATCF at 10.0000% (AT)	-462,185.35	-46.218535
advantage	141,794.33	14.179433

Lease

rent	1,200,000.00	120.000000
pre-tax cash flow	-1,200,000.00	-120.000000
taxes paid	-420,000.00	-42.000000
after-tax cash flow	-780,000.00	-78.000000
PV ATCF at 10.0000% (AT)	-603,979.68	-60.397968
PV of MLP at 10.0000%	925,751.30	92.575130

Full term rate		
	without residual	6.9339
	with residual	6.9339
	all-in	6.9339

Taxes

Month fiscal year ends .... Dec
First year tax payments .... Level on remaining dates

Federal

tax calculation method .... Accrual (Arr Only)
tax estimation method .... Level

start date	rate	thru	paid	percent
Jan-01-07	35.0000	Mar	Apr	25.0000
		Jun	Jun	25.0000
		Sep	Sep	25.0000
		Dec	Dec	25.0000

State

tax calculation method .... Accrual (Arr Only)
tax estimation method .... Level

start date	rate	thru	paid	percent
Jan-01-07	0.0000	Mar	Apr	25.0000
		Jun	Jun	25.0000
		Sep	Sep	25.0000
		Dec	Dec	25.0000

Assets

delivery	description
Jul-01-12	"Solar PV Renewable Energy System"

LEASE PARAMETERS

Rents

commencement date Jul-01-12
payments (60) 1,200,000.00
associated with all assets

#	timing		from	to	1st pmt	type	amount	% of cost
12	mon	arr	Jul-01-12 →	Jul-01-13	Aug-01-12	payment	16,667.00	1.666700
12	↓	↓	Jul-01-13 →	Jul-01-14	Aug-01-13	↓	18,333.00	1.833300
12			Jul-01-14 →	Jul-01-15	Aug-01-14		20,000.00	2.000000
12			Jul-01-15 →	Jul-01-16	Aug-01-15		21,667.00	2.166700
12			Jul-01-16 →	Jul-01-17	Aug-01-16		23,333.00	2.333300

PURCHASE PARAMETERS

Assets

cost	delivery	funding
1,000,000.00	Jul-01-12	Jul-01-12

	start date	Depreciation method	term	salvage	convention	Tax Credit percent	date	recapture
Fed	Jul-01-12	MACRS (DB/SL 200)	5.000	0.000	Half-year	30.0000	Jul-01-12	60.000 months
basis 85.0000								

Lease ID .... Project #3

Project 3: Lease vs. Purchase Present Value Comparison—After-tax Cash Flows (SuperTrump)

	Present Value					Purchase		Lease		
period ending	compound period after-tax cash flow	pre-tax discount rate (not used)	after-tax discount rate (used)	days	after-tax discount factor	after-tax cash flows	present value	after-tax cash flows	present value	difference
Dec-30-12	-688,834.30	15.3846	10.0000	164	0.955622	-640,500.00	-652,120.54	-48,334.30	-47,421.31	604,699.23
Dec-30-13	-39,634.00	15.3846	10.0000	360	0.864982	95,200.00	85,331.63	-134,834.00	-123,336.86	-208,668.49
Dec-30-14	-90,711.70	15.3846	10.0000	360	0.782939	57,120.00	46,342.77	-147,831.70	-122,418.12	-168,760.90
Dec-30-15	-126,562.30	15.3846	10.0000	360	0.708677	34,272.00	25,168.31	-160,834.30	-120,567.86	-145,736.17
Dec-30-16	-139,562.00	15.3846	10.0000	360	0.641459	34,272.00	22,781.10	-173,834.00	-117,965.38	-140,746.48
Dec-30-17	-97,195.70	15.3846	10.0000	360	0.580822	17,136.00	10,311.38	-114,331.70	-72,270.14	-82,581.52
total	-1,182,500.00			1,964		-402,500.00	-462,185.35	-780,000.00	-603,979.68	-141,794.33

Project 4: PV Value™ Estimate of System Costs and Production Values (over 25 years)

SOLAR POWER ELECTRIC — Sandia National Laboratories

PV Value™ Photovoltaic Energy Valuation Model v. 1.0

Solar Resource Calculation	
Zip Code	92868
System Size in Watts	250,000
Derate Factor (online calculator)	0.770
Commissioning report # is required to override default derate factor	
Commissioning Report #	
Module Degradation Rate	0.5
Array Type	Fixed
Array Tilt (unchecked = latitude)	0.0
Array Azimuth (default = South)	180
Calculate PV Production	kWh Produced/Year: 369,382

Discount Rate Calculation	
Basis Points (low)	50
Basis Points (high)	200
Basis Points (average)	125
Choose Net Yield Rate	FNM 30-Year Fixed 60-day
Update FNM Rate	3/23/2012
	Rate is Out of Date
FNM 30-Year Fixed 60-day	3.67
Discount Rate (low)	4.17
Discount Rate (high)	5.67
Discount Rate (average)	4.92

Electricity Rate Inputs	
Click button to update location — Current Utility Reported Electricity Rate	*Southern California Edison Co.*
☐ Residential Rate from PVWATTS -> ¢/kWh	
☑ Commercial Rate from PVWATTS -> ¢/kWh	14.00
☐ User Defined (enter -> adjacent cell) -> ¢/kWh	
Utility Escalation Rates for	California
☐ Residential Escalation Rate from EIA (1990-current)	
☑ Commercial Escalation Rate from EIA (1990-current)	1.24
☐ User Defined (enter -> adjacent cell)	

Operation & Maintenance Inputs	
15-Year O&M Expenses as a function of the system size	
☑ 15-Year O&M Expenses -> ¢/W	35
☐ User Defined (enter -> adjacent cell) -> ¢/W	
Estimated Inverter Replacement Cost	$42,547.77
System Age and Remaining Lifetime	
Module Warranty/Years	25
Age of System/Years	0
Remaining Energy/Years	25
Is this a Lease to Purchase option?	☐ Click for Lease Option Valuation

User Input
User Input Override
Calculated Value

Appraisal Range of Value Estimate	
Low	$724,200.55
Medium	$779,207.85
High	$840,831.02

Present Value Estimate of Accumulated Energy Production

Year	KWh Production /YR	Energy Value /YR (low DR)	Accumulated Energy Present Value with O&M Expenses (low DR)	Energy Value /YR (average DR)	Accumulated Energy Present Value with O&M Expenses (average DR)	Energy Value /YR (high DR)	Accumulated Energy Present Value with O&M Expenses (high DR)
1	367,535	$51,454.85	$51,454.85	$51,454.85	$51,454.85	$51,454.85	$51,454.85
2	365,688	$49,755.42	$101,210.27	$49,399.77	$100,854.62	$49,049.16	$100,504.01
3	363,841	$48,110.89	$149,321.16	$47,425.55	$148,280.17	$46,754.75	$147,258.77
4	361,994	$46,519.51	$195,840.67	$45,529.06	$193,809.23	$44,566.52	$191,825.29
5	360,147	$44,979.61	$240,820.28	$43,707.27	$237,516.50	$42,479.60	$234,304.89
6	358,300	$43,489.53	$284,309.81	$41,957.27	$279,473.77	$40,489.34	$274,794.24
7	356,453	$42,047.70	$326,357.51	$40,276.27	$319,750.04	$38,591.30	$313,385.54
8	354,606	$40,652.58	$367,010.09	$38,661.59	$358,411.63	$36,781.25	$350,166.79
9	352,759	$39,302.68	$406,312.77	$37,110.62	$395,522.25	$35,055.15	$385,221.94
10	350,912	$37,996.57	$444,309.34	$35,620.90	$431,143.15	$33,409.13	$418,631.08
11	349,066	$36,732.84	$481,042.18	$34,190.04	$465,333.19	$31,839.52	$450,470.60
12	347,219	$35,510.15	$516,552.34	$32,815.73	$498,148.92	$30,342.81	$480,813.41
13	345,372	$34,327.19	$550,879.52	$31,495.78	$529,644.70	$28,915.63	$509,729.04
14	343,525	$33,182.69	$584,062.21	$30,228.05	$559,872.75	$27,554.79	$537,283.83
15	341,678	$32,075.41	$616,137.62	$29,010.51	$588,883.26	$26,257.24	$563,541.07
16	339,831	$31,004.18	$604,594.04	$27,841.20	$574,276.89	$25,020.06	$546,013.36
17	337,984	$29,967.85	$634,561.88	$26,718.23	$600,894.91	$23,840.47	$569,853.83
18	336,137	$28,965.28	$663,527.17	$25,639.78	$626,534.69	$22,715.81	$592,569.64
19	334,290	$27,995.41	$691,522.58	$24,604.13	$651,138.82	$21,643.55	$614,213.19
20	332,443	$27,057.20	$718,579.78	$23,609.59	$674,748.41	$20,621.28	$634,834.47
21	330,596	$26,149.61	$744,729.39	$22,654.55	$697,402.96	$19,646.69	$654,481.15
22	328,750	$25,271.68	$770,001.07	$21,737.46	$719,140.42	$18,717.57	$673,198.72
23	326,903	$24,422.46	$794,423.53	$20,856.84	$739,997.26	$17,831.83	$691,030.55
24	325,056	$23,601.02	$818,024.55	$20,011.26	$760,008.52	$16,987.46	$708,018.01
25	323,209	$22,806.47	$840,831.02	$19,199.34	$779,207.85	$16,182.55	$724,200.55

Energy value assumes a discount rate based on the adjusted Fannie Mae 15 or 30 year fixed rate 60 day commitment (or custom rate), 21 year Utility Escalation Rate from EIA data, current utility rate and estimated 15 year O&M expenses.

Project 5. Solar Lease Using PVWatts™ and PV Value™ Output Data for Energy Parameters (SuperTrump)

Cash Flows

asset cost	1,000,000.00	100.000000
fees received	50,000.00	5.000000
equity	950,000.00	95.000000
rent	554,960.42	55.496042
periodic income	56,141.21	5.614121
residual	50,000.00	5.000000
total cash in	661,101.63	66.110163
equity	950,000.00	95.000000
periodic expenses	50,000.00	5.000000
total cash out	1,000,000.00	100.000000
pre-tax cash flow	-338,898.37	-33.889837
taxes paid	-385,587.53	-38.558753
after-tax cash flow	46,689.16	4.668916

Statistics

composite tax rate	40.7460
IRS true lease tests	Passed
tax treatment	True tax lease
FAS 13 for lessor (default)	Capital: single investor (DFL)
FAS 13 for lessee	Operating
implicit interest rate	-2.5617

	pre-tax		after-tax	
	effective	nominal	effective	nominal
MISF (per)	2.8765	2.8543	1.7044	1.6913
IRR PTCF (per)	-7.1646	-7.4112	-4.2453	-4.3914

PV on Jul-01-12 of Min Lease Pmts @ IBR at 10.0000%	345,554.42	34.555442
on Jul-01-12 of Rent & Guar Res @ IIR at -2.5617%	635,383.80	63.538380

average life of investment	34.8706 months
Full term rate without residual	-10.4658
with residual	-8.4032
Customer rate	-10.4658

Assets

cost	delivery	funding	residual	% cost	date	description
1,000,000.00	Jul-01-12	Jul-01-12	50,000.00	5.0000	Jul-01-22	"Solar PV System"

	Depreciation						Tax Credit		
	start date	method	term	salvage	convention	percent	date	recapture
Fed	Jul-01-12	MACRS (DB/SL 200)	5.000	0.000	Half-year	30.0000	Jul-01-12	60.000 months
basis		85.0000						
State	Jul-01-12	DB/SL 200	10.000	0.000	Half-year			

Fee Income

Cash					Amortization				
amount	% of cost	date paid	equity		start date	method	term	salvage	convention
50,000.00	5.000000	Jul-01-12	No	**Fed**	Jul-01-12	Expensed			
"Utility Rebate"				**State**	Jul-01-12	Expensed			

accounting .... Cash
lessee obligation, non-financed

Rents

commencement date Jul-01-12

"solar revenue"
payments (120) 554,960.42

#	timing		from	to	1st pmt	type	amount	% of cost
1	mon	arr	Jul-01-12	Aug-01-12	Aug-01-12	payment	4,533.88	0.453388
1			Aug-01-12	Sep-01-12	Sep-01-12		5,006.26	0.500626
1			Sep-01-12	Oct-01-12	Oct-01-12		5,093.55	0.509355
1			Oct-01-12	Nov-01-12	Nov-01-12		4,559.55	0.455955
1			Nov-01-12	Dec-01-12	Dec-01-12		4,230.93	0.423093
1			Dec-01-12	Jan-01-13	Jan-01-13		3,660.99	0.366099
1			Jan-01-13	Feb-01-13	Feb-01-13		3,419.66	0.341966
1			Feb-01-13	Mar-01-13	Mar-01-13		3,501.82	0.350182
1			Mar-01-13	Apr-01-13	Apr-01-13		3,599.37	0.359937
1			Apr-01-13	May-01-13	May-01-13		4,349.03	0.434903
1			May-01-13	Jun-01-13	Jun-01-13		4,677.65	0.467765
1			Jun-01-13	Jul-01-13	Jul-01-13		4,723.86	0.472386
1			Jul-01-13	Aug-01-13	Aug-01-13		4,611.44	0.461144
1			Aug-01-13	Sep-01-13	Sep-01-13		5,091.91	0.509191
1			Sep-01-13	Oct-01-13	Oct-01-13		5,180.69	0.518069
1			Oct-01-13	Nov-01-13	Nov-01-13		4,637.55	0.463755
1			Nov-01-13	Dec-01-13	Dec-01-13		4,303.31	0.430331
1			Dec-01-13	Jan-01-14	Jan-01-14		3,723.62	0.372362
1			Jan-01-14	Feb-01-14	Feb-01-14		3,478.16	0.347816
1			Feb-01-14	Mar-01-14	Mar-01-14		3,561.72	0.356172

Page 1

1	mon	arr	Mar-01-14	→ Apr-01-14	Apr-01-14	payment	3,660.95	0.366095
1			Apr-01-14	→ May-01-14	May-01-14		4,423.43	0.442343
1			May-01-14	→ Jun-01-14	Jun-01-14		4,757.67	0.475767
1			Jun-01-14	→ Jul-01-14	Jul-01-14		4,804.67	0.480467
1			Jul-01-14	→ Aug-01-14	Aug-01-14		4,690.33	0.469033
1			Aug-01-14	→ Sep-01-14	Sep-01-14		5,179.02	0.517902
1			Sep-01-14	→ Oct-01-14	Oct-01-14		5,269.32	0.526932
1			Oct-01-14	→ Nov-01-14	Nov-01-14		4,716.89	0.471689
1			Nov-01-14	→ Dec-01-14	Dec-01-14		4,376.93	0.437693
1			Dec-01-14	→ Jan-01-15	Jan-01-15		3,787.32	0.378732
1			Jan-01-15	→ Feb-01-15	Feb-01-15		3,537.67	0.353767
1			Feb-01-15	→ Mar-01-15	Mar-01-15		3,622.66	0.362266
1			Mar-01-15	→ Apr-01-15	Apr-01-15		3,723.58	0.372358
1			Apr-01-15	→ May-01-15	May-01-15		4,499.10	0.449910
1			May-01-15	→ Jun-01-15	Jun-01-15		4,839.06	0.483906
1			Jun-01-15	→ Jul-01-15	Jul-01-15		4,886.87	0.488687
1			Jul-01-15	→ Aug-01-15	Aug-01-15		4,770.57	0.477057
1			Aug-01-15	→ Sep-01-15	Sep-01-15		5,267.62	0.526762
1			Sep-01-15	→ Oct-01-15	Oct-01-15		5,359.46	0.535946
1			Oct-01-15	→ Nov-01-15	Nov-01-15		4,797.58	0.479758
1			Nov-01-15	→ Dec-01-15	Dec-01-15		4,451.81	0.445181
1			Dec-01-15	→ Jan-01-16	Jan-01-16		3,852.11	0.385211
1			Jan-01-16	→ Feb-01-16	Feb-01-16		3,598.19	0.359819
1			Feb-01-16	→ Mar-01-16	Mar-01-16		3,684.63	0.368463
1			Mar-01-16	→ Apr-01-16	Apr-01-16		3,787.28	0.378728
1			Apr-01-16	→ May-01-16	May-01-16		4,576.07	0.457607
1			May-01-16	→ Jun-01-16	Jun-01-16		4,921.84	0.492184
1			Jun-01-16	→ Jul-01-16	Jul-01-16		4,970.47	0.497047
1			Jul-01-16	→ Aug-01-16	Aug-01-16		4,852.18	0.485218
1			Aug-01-16	→ Sep-01-16	Sep-01-16		5,357.73	0.535773
1			Sep-01-16	→ Oct-01-16	Oct-01-16		5,451.15	0.545115
1			Oct-01-16	→ Nov-01-16	Nov-01-16		4,879.66	0.487966
1			Nov-01-16	→ Dec-01-16	Dec-01-16		4,527.97	0.452797
1			Dec-01-16	→ Jan-01-17	Jan-01-17		3,918.01	0.391801
1			Jan-01-17	→ Feb-01-17	Feb-01-17		3,659.74	0.365974
1			Feb-01-17	→ Mar-01-17	Mar-01-17		3,747.66	0.374766
1			Mar-01-17	→ Apr-01-17	Apr-01-17		3,852.07	0.385207
1			Apr-01-17	→ May-01-17	May-01-17		4,654.36	0.465436
1			May-01-17	→ Jun-01-17	Jun-01-17		5,006.05	0.500605
1			Jun-01-17	→ Jul-01-17	Jul-01-17		5,055.50	0.505550
1			Jul-01-17	→ Aug-01-17	Aug-01-17		4,935.19	0.493519
1			Aug-01-17	→ Sep-01-17	Sep-01-17		5,449.39	0.544939
1			Sep-01-17	→ Oct-01-17	Oct-01-17		5,544.40	0.554440
1			Oct-01-17	→ Nov-01-17	Nov-01-17		4,963.14	0.496314
1			Nov-01-17	→ Dec-01-17	Dec-01-17		4,605.43	0.460543
1			Dec-01-17	→ Jan-01-18	Jan-01-18		3,985.04	0.398504
1			Jan-01-18	→ Feb-01-18	Feb-01-18		3,722.35	0.372235
1			Feb-01-18	→ Mar-01-18	Mar-01-18		3,811.78	0.381178
1			Mar-01-18	→ Apr-01-18	Apr-01-18		3,917.97	0.391797
1			Apr-01-18	→ May-01-18	May-01-18		4,733.98	0.473398
1			May-01-18	→ Jun-01-18	Jun-01-18		5,091.69	0.509169
1			Jun-01-18	→ Jul-01-18	Jul-01-18		5,141.99	0.514199
1			Jul-01-18	→ Aug-01-18	Aug-01-18		5,019.62	0.501962
1			Aug-01-18	→ Sep-01-18	Sep-01-18		5,542.62	0.554262
1			Sep-01-18	→ Oct-01-18	Oct-01-18		5,639.26	0.563926
1			Oct-01-18	→ Nov-01-18	Nov-01-18		5,048.04	0.504804
1			Nov-01-18	→ Dec-01-18	Dec-01-18		4,684.22	0.468422
1			Dec-01-18	→ Jan-01-19	Jan-01-19		4,053.21	0.405321
1			Jan-01-19	→ Feb-01-19	Feb-01-19		3,786.03	0.378603
1			Feb-01-19	→ Mar-01-19	Mar-01-19		3,876.99	0.387699
1			Mar-01-19	→ Apr-01-19	Apr-01-19		3,985.00	0.398500
1			Apr-01-19	→ May-01-19	May-01-19		4,814.97	0.481497
1			May-01-19	→ Jun-01-19	Jun-01-19		5,178.79	0.517879
1			Jun-01-19	→ Jul-01-19	Jul-01-19		5,229.95	0.522995
1			Jul-01-19	→ Aug-01-19	Aug-01-19		5,105.49	0.510549
1			Aug-01-19	→ Sep-01-19	Sep-01-19		5,637.44	0.563744
1			Sep-01-19	→ Oct-01-19	Oct-01-19		5,735.73	0.573573
1			Oct-01-19	→ Nov-01-19	Nov-01-19		5,134.40	0.513440
1			Nov-01-19	→ Dec-01-19	Dec-01-19		4,764.36	0.476436
1			Dec-01-19	→ Jan-01-20	Jan-01-20		4,122.56	0.412256
1			Jan-01-20	→ Feb-01-20	Feb-01-20		3,850.80	0.385080
1			Feb-01-20	→ Mar-01-20	Mar-01-20		3,943.31	0.394331
1			Mar-01-20	→ Apr-01-20	Apr-01-20		4,053.17	0.405317

Page 2

#	timing		from	to	1st pmt	type	amount	% of cost
1	mon	arr	Apr-01-20	May-01-20	May-01-20	payment	4,897.34	0.489734
1			May-01-20	Jun-01-20	Jun-01-20		5,267.39	0.526739
1			Jun-01-20	Jul-01-20	Jul-01-20		5,319.43	0.531943
1			Jul-01-20	Aug-01-20	Aug-01-20		5,192.83	0.519283
1			Aug-01-20	Sep-01-20	Sep-01-20		5,733.88	0.573388
1			Sep-01-20	Oct-01-20	Oct-01-20		5,833.85	0.583385
1			Oct-01-20	Nov-01-20	Nov-01-20		5,222.24	0.522224
1			Nov-01-20	Dec-01-20	Dec-01-20		4,845.86	0.484586
1			Dec-01-20	Jan-01-21	Jan-01-21		4,193.08	0.419308
1			Jan-01-21	Feb-01-21	Feb-01-21		3,916.68	0.391668
1			Feb-01-21	Mar-01-21	Mar-01-21		4,010.77	0.401077
1			Mar-01-21	Apr-01-21	Apr-01-21		4,122.51	0.412251
1			Apr-01-21	May-01-21	May-01-21		4,981.12	0.498112
1			May-01-21	Jun-01-21	Jun-01-21		5,357.50	0.535750
1			Jun-01-21	Jul-01-21	Jul-01-21		5,410.43	0.541043
1			Jul-01-21	Aug-01-21	Aug-01-21		5,281.67	0.528167
1			Aug-01-21	Sep-01-21	Sep-01-21		5,831.97	0.583197
1			Sep-01-21	Oct-01-21	Oct-01-21		5,933.66	0.593366
1			Oct-01-21	Nov-01-21	Nov-01-21		5,311.58	0.531158
1			Nov-01-21	Dec-01-21	Dec-01-21		4,928.76	0.492876
1			Dec-01-21	Jan-01-22	Jan-01-22		4,264.82	0.426482
1			Jan-01-22	Feb-01-22	Feb-01-22		3,983.68	0.398368
1			Feb-01-22	Mar-01-22	Mar-01-22		4,079.39	0.407939
1			Mar-01-22	Apr-01-22	Apr-01-22		4,193.04	0.419304
1			Apr-01-22	May-01-22	May-01-22		5,066.34	0.506634
1			May-01-22	Jun-01-22	Jun-01-22		5,449.15	0.544915
1			Jun-01-22	Jul-01-22	Jul-01-22		5,502.99	0.550299

Periodic Expense

		#	timing		from	to	1st pmt	type	amount	% of cost
"O&M Costs" payments	 50,000.00	10	ann	arr	Jul-01-12	Jul-01-22	Jul-01-13	payment	5,000.00	0.500000

Periodic Income

		#	timing		from	to	1st pmt	type	amount	% of cost
"REC" payments (120)	 56,141.21	1	mon	arr	Jul-01-12	Aug-01-12	Aug-01-12	payment	323.85	0.032385
		1			Aug-01-12	Sep-01-12	Sep-01-12		357.59	0.035759
		1			Sep-01-12	Oct-01-12	Oct-01-12		363.83	0.036383
		1			Oct-01-12	Nov-01-12	Nov-01-12		325.68	0.032568
		1			Nov-01-12	Dec-01-12	Dec-01-12		302.21	0.030221
		1			Dec-01-12	Jan-01-13	Jan-01-13		261.50	0.026150
		1			Jan-01-13	Feb-01-13	Feb-01-13		244.26	0.024426
		1			Feb-01-13	Mar-01-13	Mar-01-13		250.13	0.025013
		1			Mar-01-13	Apr-01-13	Apr-01-13		257.10	0.025710
		1			Apr-01-13	May-01-13	May-01-13		310.64	0.031064
		1			May-01-13	Jun-01-13	Jun-01-13		334.12	0.033412
		1			Jun-01-13	Jul-01-13	Jul-01-13		337.42	0.033742
		1			Jul-01-13	Aug-01-13	Aug-01-13		353.49	0.035349
		1			Aug-01-13	Sep-01-13	Sep-01-13		390.32	0.039032
		1			Sep-01-13	Oct-01-13	Oct-01-13		397.13	0.039713
		1			Oct-01-13	Nov-01-13	Nov-01-13		355.49	0.035549
		1			Nov-01-13	Dec-01-13	Dec-01-13		329.87	0.032987
		1			Dec-01-13	Jan-01-14	Jan-01-14		285.43	0.028543
		1			Jan-01-14	Feb-01-14	Feb-01-14		266.62	0.026662
		1			Feb-01-14	Mar-01-14	Mar-01-14		273.02	0.027302
		1			Mar-01-14	Apr-01-14	Apr-01-14		280.63	0.028063
		1			Apr-01-14	May-01-14	May-01-14		339.08	0.033908
		1			May-01-14	Jun-01-14	Jun-01-14		364.70	0.036470
		1			Jun-01-14	Jul-01-14	Jul-01-14		368.30	0.036830
		1			Jul-01-14	Aug-01-14	Aug-01-14		385.85	0.038585
		1			Aug-01-14	Sep-01-14	Sep-01-14		426.05	0.042605
		1			Sep-01-14	Oct-01-14	Oct-01-14		433.47	0.043347
		1			Oct-01-14	Nov-01-14	Nov-01-14		388.03	0.038803
		1			Nov-01-14	Dec-01-14	Dec-01-14		360.06	0.036006
		1			Dec-01-14	Jan-01-15	Jan-01-15		311.56	0.031156
		1			Jan-01-15	Feb-01-15	Feb-01-15		291.02	0.029102
		1			Feb-01-15	Mar-01-15	Mar-01-15		298.01	0.029801
		1			Mar-01-15	Apr-01-15	Apr-01-15		306.32	0.030632
		1			Apr-01-15	May-01-15	May-01-15		370.11	0.037011

Page 3

1	mon	arr	May-01-15	→ Jun-01-15	Jun-01-15	payment	398.08	0.039808
1			Jun-01-15	→ Jul-01-15	Jul-01-15		402.01	0.040201
1			Jul-01-15	→ Aug-01-15	Aug-01-15		421.16	0.042116
1			Aug-01-15	→ Sep-01-15	Sep-01-15		465.04	0.046504
1			Sep-01-15	→ Oct-01-15	Oct-01-15		473.15	0.047315
1			Oct-01-15	→ Nov-01-15	Nov-01-15		423.55	0.042355
1			Nov-01-15	→ Dec-01-15	Dec-01-15		393.02	0.039302
1			Dec-01-15	→ Jan-01-16	Jan-01-16		340.08	0.034008
1			Jan-01-16	→ Feb-01-16	Feb-01-16		317.66	0.031766
1			Feb-01-16	→ Mar-01-16	Mar-01-16		325.29	0.032529
1			Mar-01-16	→ Apr-01-16	Apr-01-16		334.35	0.033435
1			Apr-01-16	→ May-01-16	May-01-16		403.99	0.040399
1			May-01-16	→ Jun-01-16	Jun-01-16		434.52	0.043452
1			Jun-01-16	→ Jul-01-16	Jul-01-16		438.81	0.043881
1			Jul-01-16	→ Aug-01-16	Aug-01-16		459.71	0.045971
1			Aug-01-16	→ Sep-01-16	Sep-01-16		507.61	0.050761
1			Sep-01-16	→ Oct-01-16	Oct-01-16		516.46	0.051646
1			Oct-01-16	→ Nov-01-16	Nov-01-16		462.31	0.046231
1			Nov-01-16	→ Dec-01-16	Dec-01-16		428.99	0.042899
1			Dec-01-16	→ Jan-01-17	Jan-01-17		371.20	0.037120
1			Jan-01-17	→ Feb-01-17	Feb-01-17		346.74	0.034674
1			Feb-01-17	→ Mar-01-17	Mar-01-17		355.07	0.035507
1			Mar-01-17	→ Apr-01-17	Apr-01-17		364.96	0.036496
1			Apr-01-17	→ May-01-17	May-01-17		440.97	0.044097
1			May-01-17	→ Jun-01-17	Jun-01-17		474.29	0.047429
1			Jun-01-17	→ Jul-01-17	Jul-01-17		478.97	0.047897
1			Jul-01-17	→ Aug-01-17	Aug-01-17		501.79	0.050179
1			Aug-01-17	→ Sep-01-17	Sep-01-17		554.07	0.055407
1			Sep-01-17	→ Oct-01-17	Oct-01-17		563.73	0.056373
1			Oct-01-17	→ Nov-01-17	Nov-01-17		504.63	0.050463
1			Nov-01-17	→ Dec-01-17	Dec-01-17		468.26	0.046826
1			Dec-01-17	→ Jan-01-18	Jan-01-18		405.18	0.040518
1			Jan-01-18	→ Feb-01-18	Feb-01-18		378.47	0.037847
1			Feb-01-18	→ Mar-01-18	Mar-01-18		387.56	0.038756
1			Mar-01-18	→ Apr-01-18	Apr-01-18		398.36	0.039836
1			Apr-01-18	→ May-01-18	May-01-18		481.33	0.048133
1			May-01-18	→ Jun-01-18	Jun-01-18		517.70	0.051770
1			Jun-01-18	→ Jul-01-18	Jul-01-18		522.81	0.052281
1			Jul-01-18	→ Aug-01-18	Aug-01-18		547.72	0.054772
1			Aug-01-18	→ Sep-01-18	Sep-01-18		604.78	0.060478
1			Sep-01-18	→ Oct-01-18	Oct-01-18		615.33	0.061533
1			Oct-01-18	→ Nov-01-18	Nov-01-18		550.82	0.055082
1			Nov-01-18	→ Dec-01-18	Dec-01-18		511.12	0.051112
1			Dec-01-18	→ Jan-01-19	Jan-01-19		442.27	0.044227
1			Jan-01-19	→ Feb-01-19	Feb-01-19		413.11	0.041311
1			Feb-01-19	→ Mar-01-19	Mar-01-19		423.04	0.042304
1			Mar-01-19	→ Apr-01-19	Apr-01-19		434.82	0.043482
1			Apr-01-19	→ May-01-19	May-01-19		525.39	0.052539
1			May-01-19	→ Jun-01-19	Jun-01-19		565.08	0.056508
1			Jun-01-19	→ Jul-01-19	Jul-01-19		570.67	0.057067
1			Jul-01-19	→ Aug-01-19	Aug-01-19		597.85	0.059785
1			Aug-01-19	→ Sep-01-19	Sep-01-19		660.14	0.066014
1			Sep-01-19	→ Oct-01-19	Oct-01-19		671.65	0.067165
1			Oct-01-19	→ Nov-01-19	Nov-01-19		601.23	0.060123
1			Nov-01-19	→ Dec-01-19	Dec-01-19		557.90	0.055790
1			Dec-01-19	→ Jan-01-20	Jan-01-20		482.75	0.048275
1			Jan-01-20	→ Feb-01-20	Feb-01-20		450.93	0.045093
1			Feb-01-20	→ Mar-01-20	Mar-01-20		461.76	0.046176
1			Mar-01-20	→ Apr-01-20	Apr-01-20		474.62	0.047462
1			Apr-01-20	→ May-01-20	May-01-20		573.47	0.057347
1			May-01-20	→ Jun-01-20	Jun-01-20		616.81	0.061681
1			Jun-01-20	→ Jul-01-20	Jul-01-20		622.90	0.062290
1			Jul-01-20	→ Aug-01-20	Aug-01-20		652.57	0.065257
1			Aug-01-20	→ Sep-01-20	Sep-01-20		720.56	0.072056
1			Sep-01-20	→ Oct-01-20	Oct-01-20		733.12	0.073312
1			Oct-01-20	→ Nov-01-20	Nov-01-20		656.27	0.065627
1			Nov-01-20	→ Dec-01-20	Dec-01-20		608.97	0.060897
1			Dec-01-20	→ Jan-01-21	Jan-01-21		526.93	0.052693
1			Jan-01-21	→ Feb-01-21	Feb-01-21		492.20	0.049220
1			Feb-01-21	→ Mar-01-21	Mar-01-21		504.02	0.050402
1			Mar-01-21	→ Apr-01-21	Apr-01-21		518.07	0.051807
1			Apr-01-21	→ May-01-21	May-01-21		625.96	0.062596
1			May-01-21	→ Jun-01-21	Jun-01-21		673.26	0.067326

Page 4

1	mon	arr	Jun-01-21	→	Jul-01-21	Jul-01-21	payment	679.91	0.067991
1			Jul-01-21	→	Aug-01-21	Aug-01-21		712.30	0.071230
1			Aug-01-21	→	Sep-01-21	Sep-01-21		786.51	0.078651
1			Sep-01-21	→	Oct-01-21	Oct-01-21		800.23	0.080023
1			Oct-01-21	→	Nov-01-21	Nov-01-21		716.33	0.071633
1			Nov-01-21	→	Dec-01-21	Dec-01-21		664.71	0.066471
1			Dec-01-21	→	Jan-01-22	Jan-01-22		575.16	0.057516
1			Jan-01-22	→	Feb-01-22	Feb-01-22		537.25	0.053725
1			Feb-01-22	→	Mar-01-22	Mar-01-22		550.16	0.055016
1			Mar-01-22	→	Apr-01-22	Apr-01-22		565.48	0.056548
1			Apr-01-22	→	May-01-22	May-01-22		683.26	0.068326
1			May-01-22	→	Jun-01-22	Jun-01-22		734.89	0.073489
1	↓	↓	Jun-01-22	→	Jul-01-22	Jul-01-22	↓	742.15	0.074215

Taxes/Lessor

Month fiscal year ends .... Dec
First year tax payments .... Level on remaining dates
Residual is taxed over .... Entire year

Federal

tax calculation method .... Accrual (Adv & Arr)
tax estimation method .... Level

start date	rate	thru	paid	percent
Jan-01-07	35.0000	Mar	Apr	25.0000
		Jun	Jun	25.0000
		Sep	Sep	25.0000
		Dec	Dec	25.0000

State

tax calculation method .... Accrual (Adv & Arr)
tax estimation method .... Level

start date	rate	thru	paid	percent
Jan-01-07	8.8400	Mar	Apr	25.0000
		Jun	Jun	25.0000
		Sep	Sep	25.0000
		Dec	Dec	25.0000

Page 5

Project 6: Cash Flow Report Federal & State with ITC (SuperTrump)

	Dec-30-12	Dec-30-13	Dec-30-14	Dec-30-15	Dec-30-16	Dec-30-17	Dec-30-18	Dec-30-19	Dec-30-20	Dec-30-21	Dec-30-22	total
STATE TAX STATEMENT												
Revenues:												
Lease Rentals	27,086	51,820	52,706	53,608	54,525	55,458	56,407	57,372	58,353	59,351	28,274	554,960
Residual	0	0	0	0	0	0	0	0	0	0	50,000	50,000
Subsidy & periodic income	1,935	3,845	4,197	4,582	5,001	5,459	5,958	6,504	7,099	7,749	3,813	56,141
Total Revenue	29,020	55,665	56,904	58,190	59,526	60,917	62,365	63,875	65,452	67,100	82,087	661,102
Expenses:												
Depreciation	100,000	180,000	144,000	115,200	92,160	73,728	65,536	65,536	65,536	65,536	32,768	1,000,000
Fees	(50,000)	0	0	0	0	0	0	0	0	0	0	(50,000)
Periodic Expenses	2,500	5,000	5,000	5,000	5,000	5,000	5,000	5,000	5,000	5,000	2,500	50,000
Total Expenses	52,500	185,000	149,000	120,200	97,160	78,728	70,536	70,536	70,536	70,536	35,268	1,000,000
Taxable Income	(23,480)	(129,335)	(92,096)	(62,010)	(37,634)	(17,811)	(8,171)	(6,661)	(5,084)	(3,436)	46,819	(338,898)
Taxes Due	(2,076)	(11,433)	(8,141)	(5,482)	(3,327)	(1,575)	(722)	(589)	(449)	(304)	4,139	(29,959)
Taxes Paid (saved)	(2,076)	(11,433)	(8,141)	(5,482)	(3,327)	(1,575)	(722)	(589)	(449)	(304)	4,139	(29,959)
FEDERAL TAX STATEMENT												
Revenues:												
Lease Rentals	27,086	51,820	52,706	53,608	54,525	55,458	56,407	57,372	58,353	59,351	28,274	554,960
Residual	0	0	0	0	0	0	0	0	0	0	50,000	50,000
Subsidy & periodic income	1,935	3,845	4,197	4,582	5,001	5,459	5,958	6,504	7,099	7,749	3,813	56,141
Total Revenue	29,020	55,665	56,904	58,190	59,526	60,917	62,365	63,875	65,452	67,100	82,087	661,102
Expenses:												
Depreciation	170,000	272,000	163,200	97,920	97,920	48,960	0	0	0	0	0	850,000
Fees	(50,000)	0	0	0	0	0	0	0	0	0	0	(50,000)
Periodic Expenses	2,500	5,000	5,000	5,000	5,000	5,000	5,000	5,000	5,000	5,000	2,500	50,000
State Tax Due	(2,076)	(11,433)	(8,141)	(5,482)	(3,327)	(1,575)	(722)	(589)	(449)	(304)	4,139	(29,959)
Total Expenses	120,424	265,567	160,059	97,438	99,593	52,385	4,278	4,411	4,551	4,696	6,639	820,041
Taxable Income	(91,404)	(209,902)	(103,155)	(39,249)	(40,067)	8,531	58,087	59,464	60,902	62,404	75,448	(158,940)
Taxes Due	(31,992)	(73,466)	(36,104)	(13,737)	(14,023)	2,986	20,331	20,812	21,316	21,841	26,407	(55,629)
ITC Due	300,000	0	0	0	0	0	0	0	0	0	0	300,000
Taxes Paid (saved)	(331,992)	(73,466)	(36,104)	(13,737)	(14,023)	2,986	20,331	20,812	21,316	21,841	26,407	(355,629)
CASH FLOW STATEMENT												
Cash In:												
Lease Rentals	23,424	51,757	52,643	53,543	54,459	55,391	56,339	57,302	58,283	59,280	32,539	554,960
Residual	0	0	0	0	0	0	0	0	0	0	50,000	50,000
Subsidy & periodic income	1,673	3,821	4,171	4,553	4,970	5,425	5,921	6,463	7,055	7,700	4,388	56,141
Total Cash In	25,097	55,579	56,814	58,096	59,429	60,816	62,260	63,766	65,337	66,980	86,928	661,102
Equity	1,000,000	0	0	0	0	0	0	0	0	0	0	1,000,000
Fees	(50,000)	0	0	0	0	0	0	0	0	0	0	(50,000)
Periodic Expenses	0	5,000	5,000	5,000	5,000	5,000	5,000	5,000	5,000	5,000	5,000	50,000
Total Cash Out	950,000	5,000	5,000	5,000	5,000	5,000	5,000	5,000	5,000	5,000	5,000	1,000,000
Pre-Tax Cash Flow	(924,903)	50,579	51,814	53,096	54,429	55,816	57,260	58,766	60,337	61,980	81,928	(338,898)
Total Taxes Paid (saved)	(334,067)	(84,899)	(44,246)	(19,219)	(17,350)	1,411	19,608	20,224	20,866	21,538	30,546	(385,588)

Project 7: NREL Cost of Renewable Energy Spreadsheet Tool (CREST)

Annual Project Cash Flows, Returns & Other Metrics

Project Year	Tariff or Market Value ¢/kWh	Revenue $	Operating Expenses $	Debt Service $	Reserves $	Pre-Tax Cash Flow $	Federal Taxable Income $	State Taxable Income $	Federal Tax Benefit/ (Liability) $	State Tax Benefit/ (Liability) $	After Tax Cash Flow $	Cumulative Cash Flow $	After Tax IRR %	Debt Service Coverage
0											($599,657)	($599,657)		
1	16.15	$78,582	($6,000)	($38,320)	($6,528)	$27,734	($464,240)	($464,240)	$430,673	$39,460	$497,867	($101,790)	-16.97%	1.72
2	16.15	$78,255	($6,120)	($38,320)	($6,528)	$27,288	($83,378)	($83,378)	$26,702	$7,067	$61,077	($40,713)	-6.12%	1.71
3	16.15	$77,931	($6,242)	($38,320)	($6,528)	$26,841	($31,209)	($31,209)	$9,995	$2,653	$39,489	($1,224)	-0.17%	1.70
4	16.15	$77,609	($6,367)	($38,320)	($6,528)	$26,394	$336	$336	($107)	($29)	$26,258	$25,034	3.10%	1.69
5	16.15	$77,288	($6,495)	($38,320)	($6,528)	$25,946	$926	$926	($296)	($79)	$25,571	$50,604	5.69%	1.68
6	16.15	$76,970	($6,624)	($38,320)	($6,528)	$25,498	$24,827	$24,827	($7,951)	($2,110)	$15,436	$66,041	6.97%	1.67
7	16.15	$76,653	($6,757)	($38,320)	($6,528)	$25,048	$48,770	$48,770	($15,618)	($4,145)	$5,285	$71,325	7.36%	1.65
8	16.15	$76,338	($6,892)	($38,320)	($6,528)	$24,599	$49,505	$49,505	($15,854)	($4,208)	$4,537	$75,862	7.65%	1.64
9	16.15	$76,026	($7,030)	($38,320)	($6,528)	$24,148	$50,303	$50,303	($16,109)	($4,276)	$3,763	$79,625	7.87%	1.63
10	16.15	$75,388	($7,171)	($38,320)	$0	$29,898	$39,102	$39,102	($12,522)	($3,324)	$14,052	$93,676	8.59%	1.78
11	16.15	$74,753	($7,314)	($38,320)	($6,528)	$22,591	$32,686	$32,686	($10,468)	($2,778)	$9,345	$103,021	8.99%	1.59
12	16.15	$74,446	($7,460)	($38,320)	($6,528)	$22,138	$41,258	$41,258	($13,213)	($3,507)	$5,418	$108,439	9.19%	1.58
13	16.15	$74,140	($7,609)	($38,320)	($6,528)	$21,683	$46,918	$46,918	($15,025)	($3,988)	$2,670	$111,109	9.28%	1.57
14	16.15	$73,837	($7,762)	($38,320)	($6,528)	$21,228	$48,170	$48,170	($15,426)	($4,094)	$1,707	$112,816	9.33%	1.55
15	16.15	$73,535	($7,917)	($38,320)	($6,528)	$20,771	$52,914	$52,914	($16,946)	($4,498)	($673)	$112,143	9.31%	1.54
16	16.15	$73,235	($8,075)	($38,320)	($6,528)	$20,313	$57,967	$57,967	($18,564)	($4,927)	($3,179)	$108,964	9.23%	1.53
17	16.15	$72,937	($8,237)	($38,320)	($6,528)	$19,853	$59,760	$59,760	($19,138)	($5,080)	($4,364)	$104,600	9.13%	1.52
18	16.15	$72,641	($8,401)	($38,320)	($6,528)	$19,392	$61,495	$61,495	($19,694)	($5,227)	($5,529)	$99,071	9.00%	1.51
19	16.15	$72,251	($8,569)	$0	$12,632	$76,314	$63,275	$63,275	($20,264)	($5,378)	$50,672	$149,743	9.93%	N/A
20	16.15	$71,537	($8,741)	$0	$0	$62,796	$50,639	$50,639	($16,217)	($4,304)	$42,274	$192,017	10.49%	N/A
21	16.15	$70,887	($8,916)	$0	$0	$61,971	$42,968	$42,968	($13,760)	($3,652)	$44,558	$236,575	10.95%	N/A
22	16.15	$70,532	($9,094)	$0	$0	$61,438	$50,158	$50,158	($16,063)	($4,263)	$41,112	$277,687	11.29%	N/A
23	16.15	$70,180	($9,276)	$0	$0	$60,904	$54,136	$54,136	($17,337)	($4,602)	$38,965	$316,652	11.55%	N/A
24	16.15	$69,829	($9,461)	$0	$0	$60,368	$53,600	$53,600	($17,165)	($4,556)	$38,647	$355,299	11.77%	N/A
25	16.15	$69,461	($9,651)	$0	$3,844	$63,654	$56,427	$56,427	($18,071)	($4,796)	$40,787	$396,086	11.96%	N/A
26														
27														
28														
29														
30														

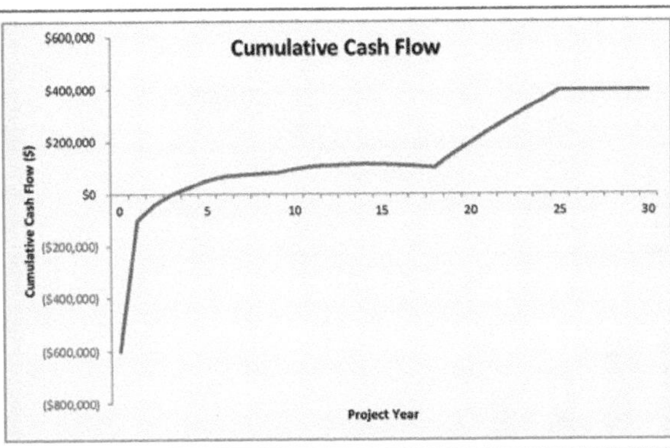

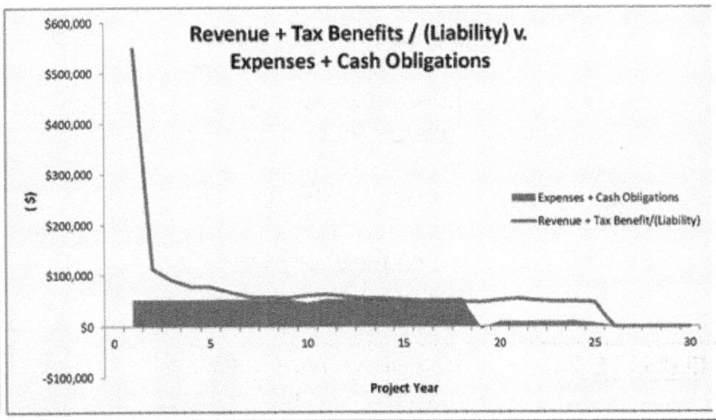

Project 8: System Advisor Model (SAM) Residential Flat Plate Analysis

SAM Photovoltaic System Report

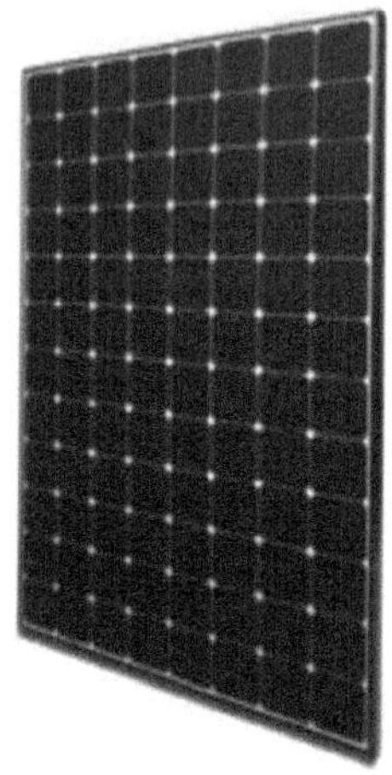

This report summarizes important system characteristics and results.

Important Metrics

LCOE (nominal): 38.4078 cents/kWh
LCOE (real): 31.5132 cents/kWh
Annual Generation: 6987.47 kWh
Net Present Value: $ -12743.2
Capacity factor: 21.0885 %

System Information

Nameplate Capacity: 3.78243 kWdc

Cost Information

Total installed: $ 21981.8
Per capacity: 5.81155 $/Wdc

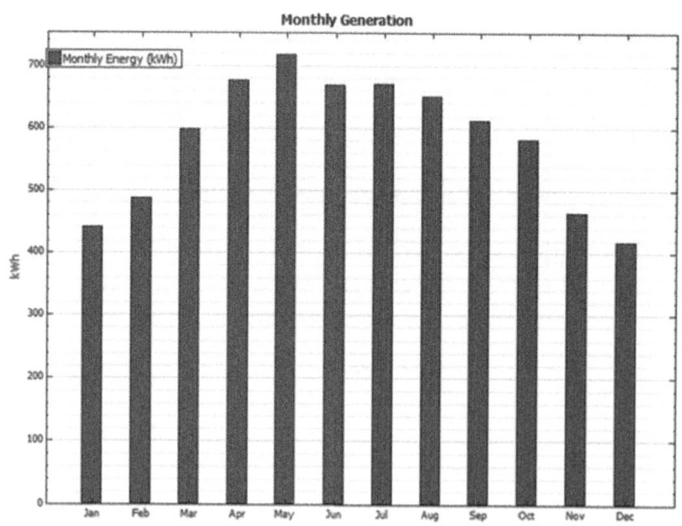

Project 9: System Advisor Model (SAM) Commercial Power Purchase Agreement Analysis

SAM Photovoltaic System Report

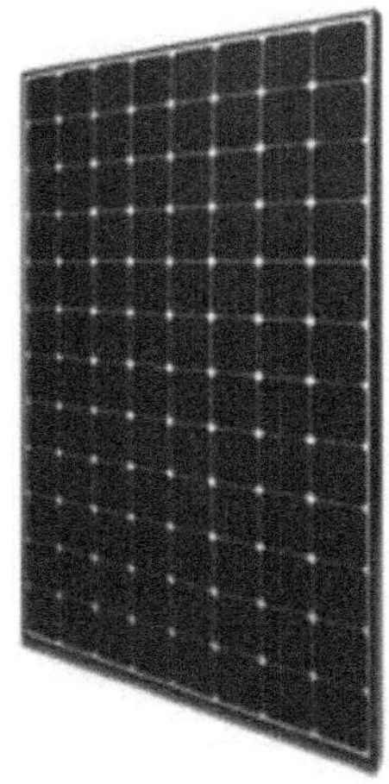

This report summarizes important system characteristics and results.

Important Metrics

LCOE (nominal): 13.7 cents/kWh
LCOE (real): 11.1595 cents/kWh
Annual Generation: 3.96857e+007 kWh
Net Present Value: $ 4.65874e+006
Capacity factor: 22.6518 %

System Information

Nameplate Capacity: 19999.8 kWdc

Cost Information

Total installed: $ 9.49702e+007
Per capacity: 4.74855 $/Wdc

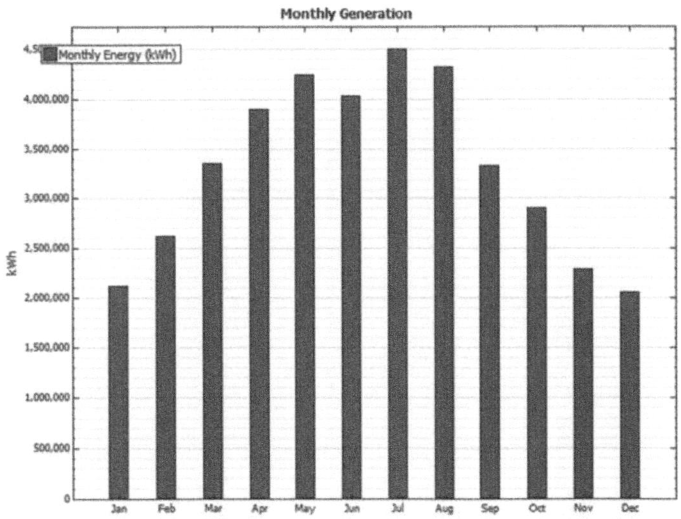

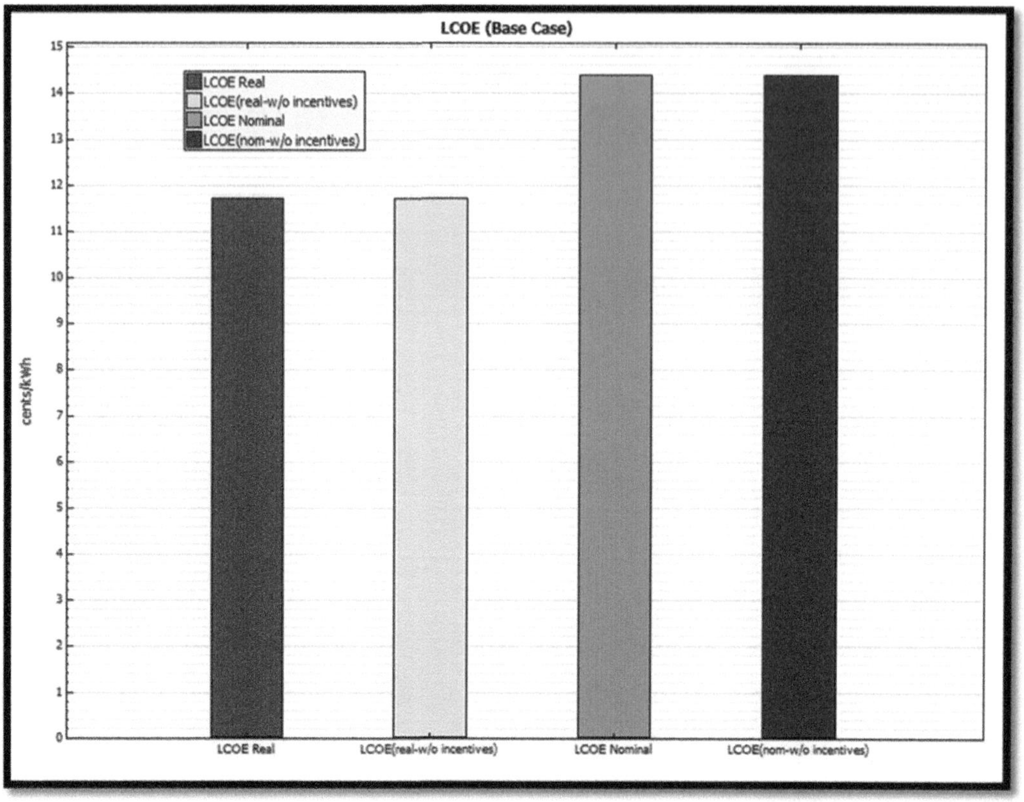
LCOE (Base Case)
LCOE Real
LCOE(real-w/o incentives)
LCOE Nominal
LCOE(nom-w/o incentives)
cents/kWh
0
1
2
3
4
5
6
7
8
9
10
11
12
13
14
15
LCOE Real
LCOE(real-w/o incentives)
LCOE Nominal
LCOE(nom-w/o incentives)

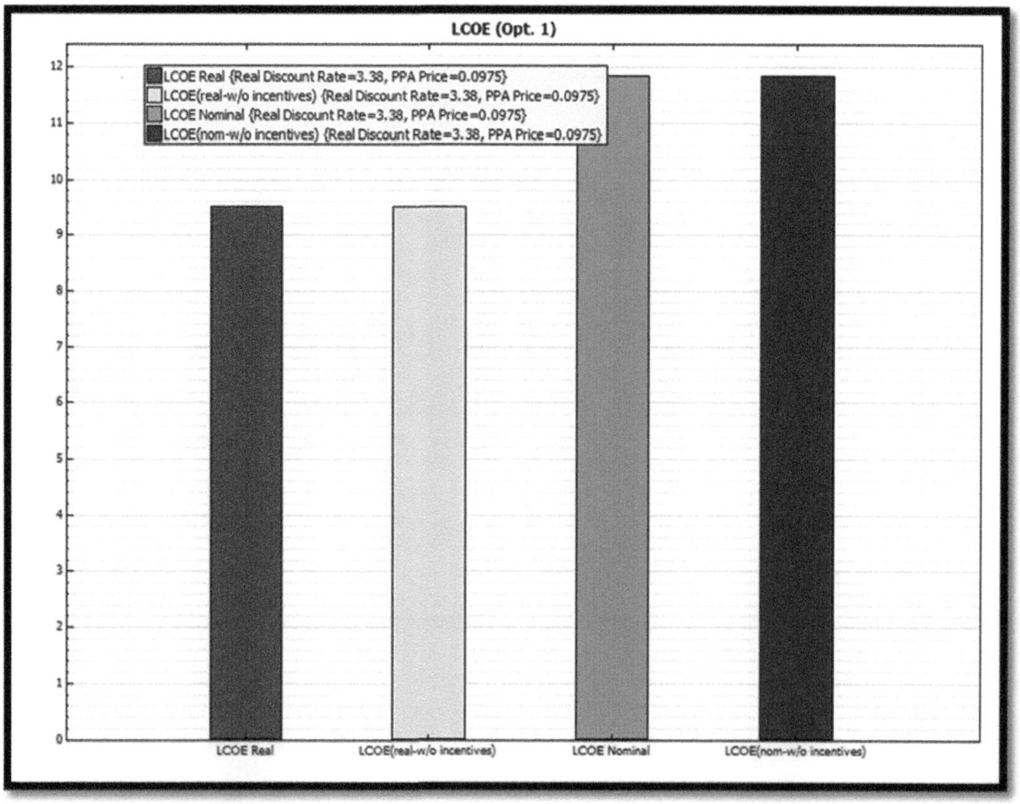
LCOE (Opt. 1)
LCOE Real {Real Discount Rate=3.38, PPA Price=0.0975}
LCOE(real-w/o incentives) {Real Discount Rate=3.38, PPA Price=0.0975}
LCOE Nominal {Real Discount Rate=3.38, PPA Price=0.0975}
LCOE(nom-w/o incentives) {Real Discount Rate=3.38, PPA Price=0.0975}
0
1
2
3
4
5
6
7
8
9
10
11
12
LCOE Real
LCOE(real-w/o incentives)
LCOE Nominal
LCOE(nom-w/o incentives)

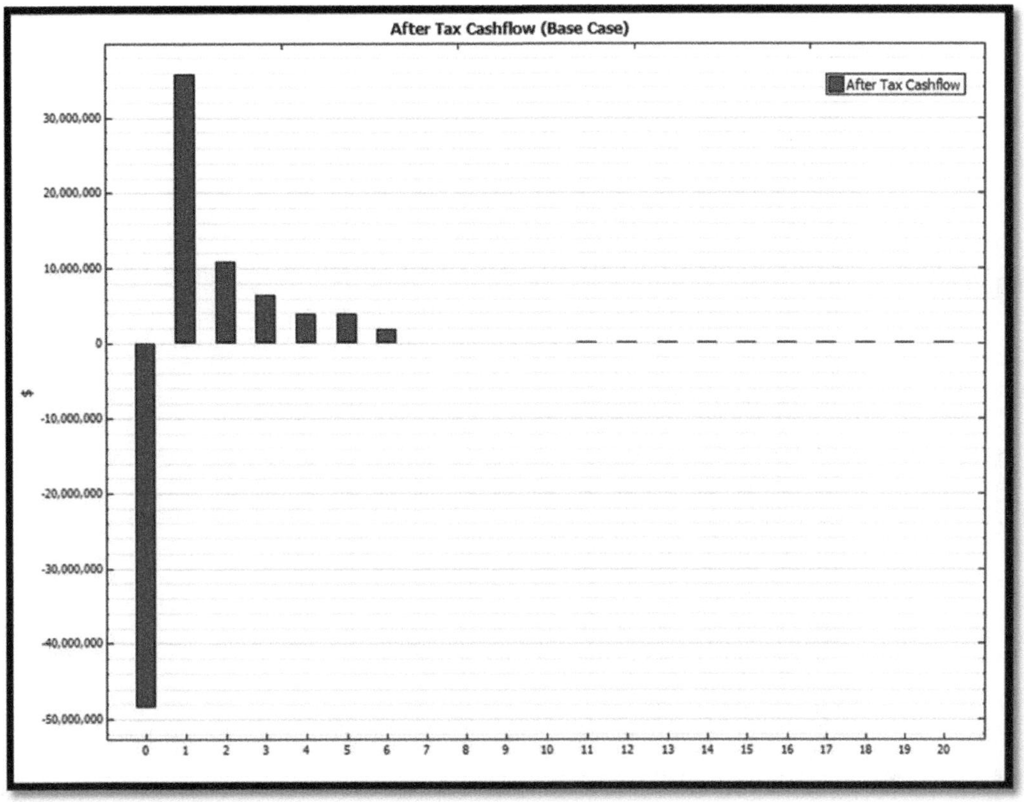
After Tax Cashflow (Base Case)
After Tax Cashflow
30,000,000
20,000,000
10,000,000
0
-10,000,000
-20,000,000
-30,000,000
-40,000,000
-50,000,000
$
0 1 2 3 4 5 6 7 8 9 10 11 12 13 14 15 16 17 18 19 20

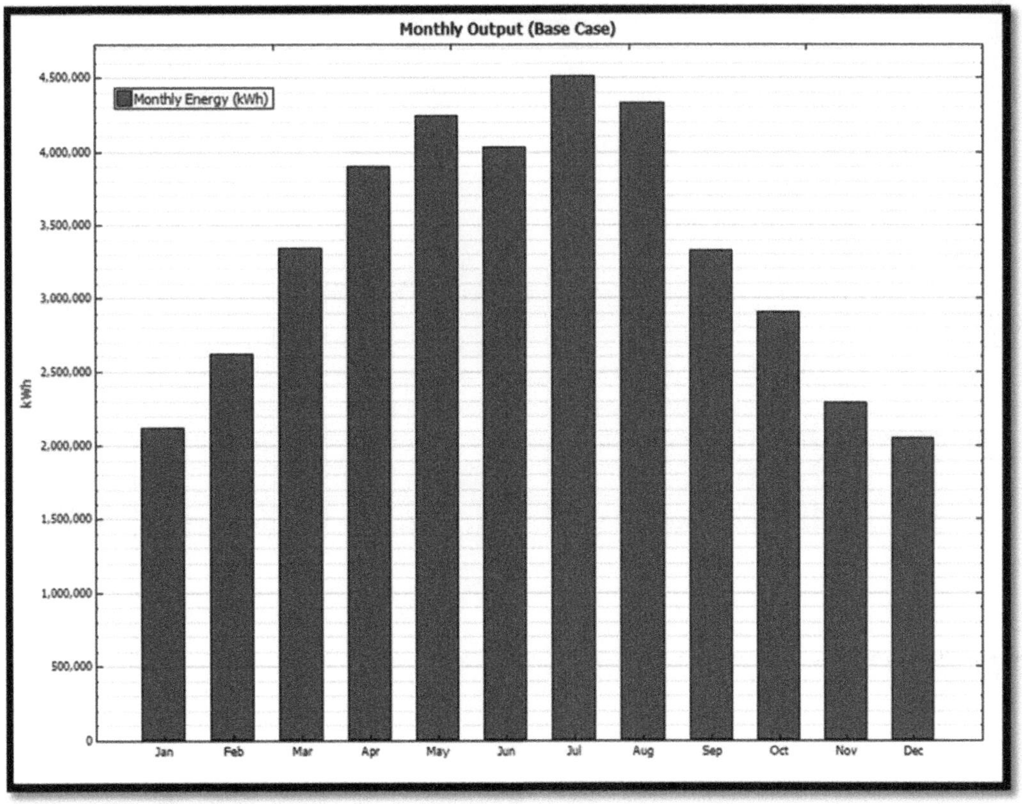
Monthly Output (Base Case)
Monthly Energy (kWh)
4,500,000
4,000,000
3,500,000
3,000,000
2,500,000
2,000,000
1,500,000
1,000,000
500,000
0
kWh
Jan Feb Mar Apr May Jun Jul Aug Sep Oct Nov Dec

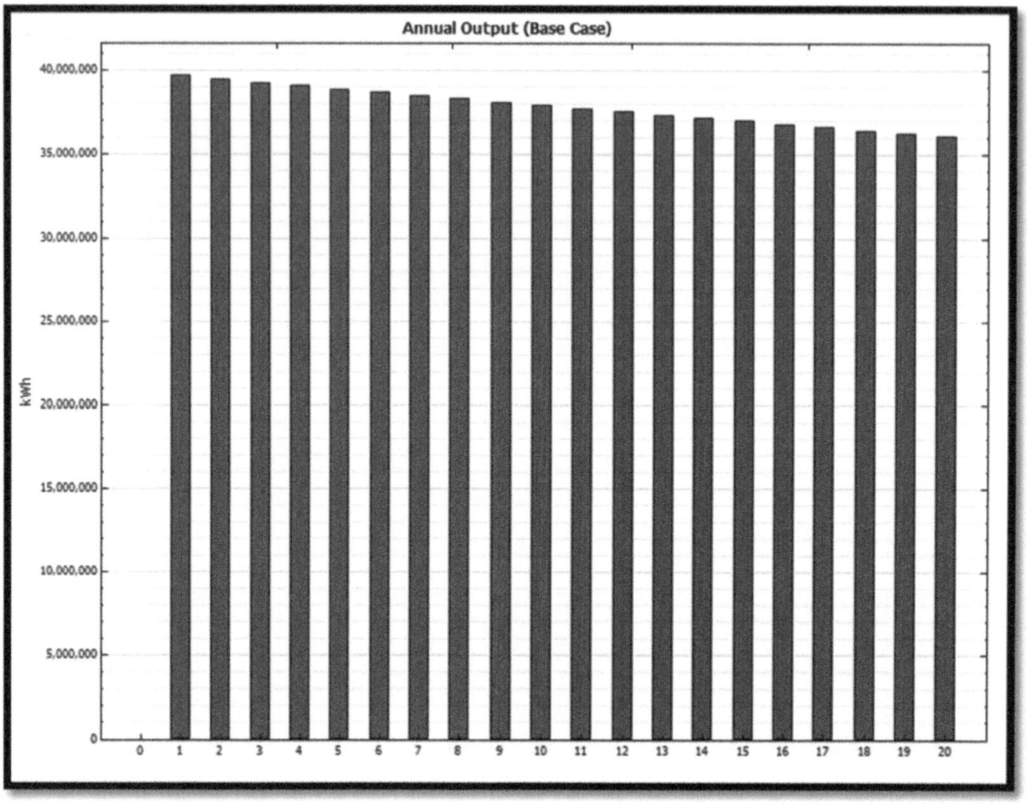
Annual Output (Base Case)
kWh
40,000,000
35,000,000
30,000,000
25,000,000
20,000,000
15,000,000
10,000,000
5,000,000
0
0
1
2
3
4
5
6
7
8
9
10
11
12
13
14
15
16
17
18
19
20

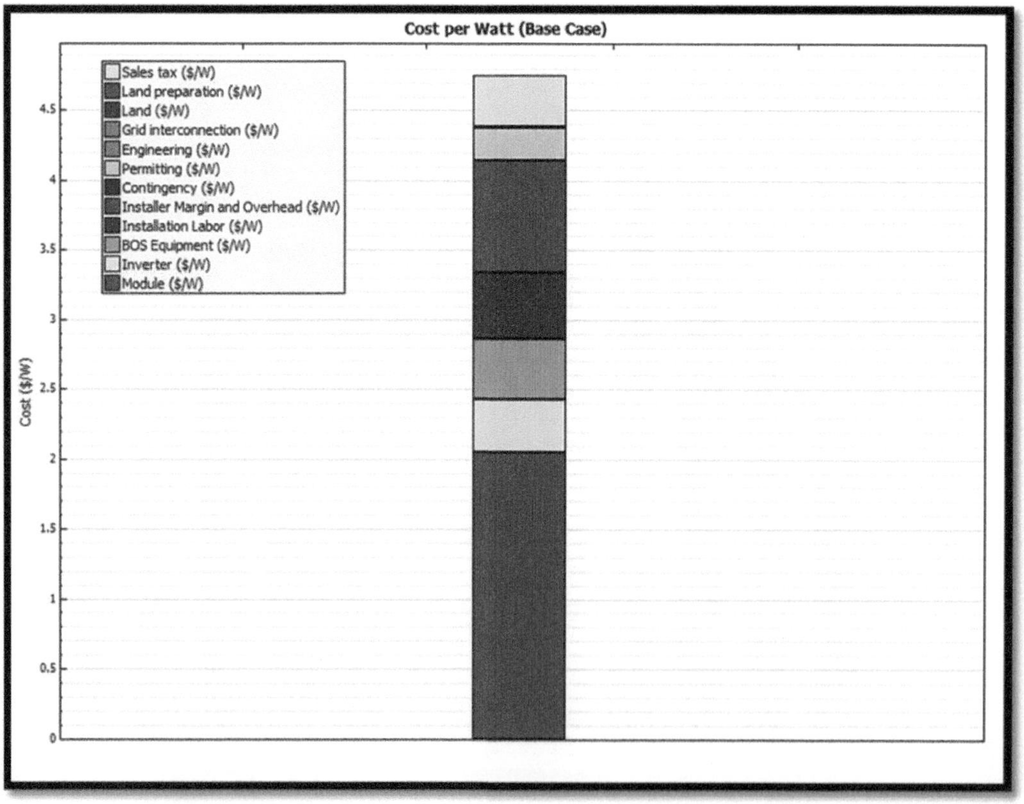
Cost per Watt (Base Case)
Cost ($/W)
Sales tax ($/W)
Land preparation ($/W)
Land ($/W)
Grid interconnection ($/W)
Engineering ($/W)
Permitting ($/W)
Contingency ($/W)
Installer Margin and Overhead ($/W)
Installation Labor ($/W)
BOS Equipment ($/W)
Inverter ($/W)
Module ($/W)
4.5
4
3.5
3
2.5
2
1.5
1
0.5
0

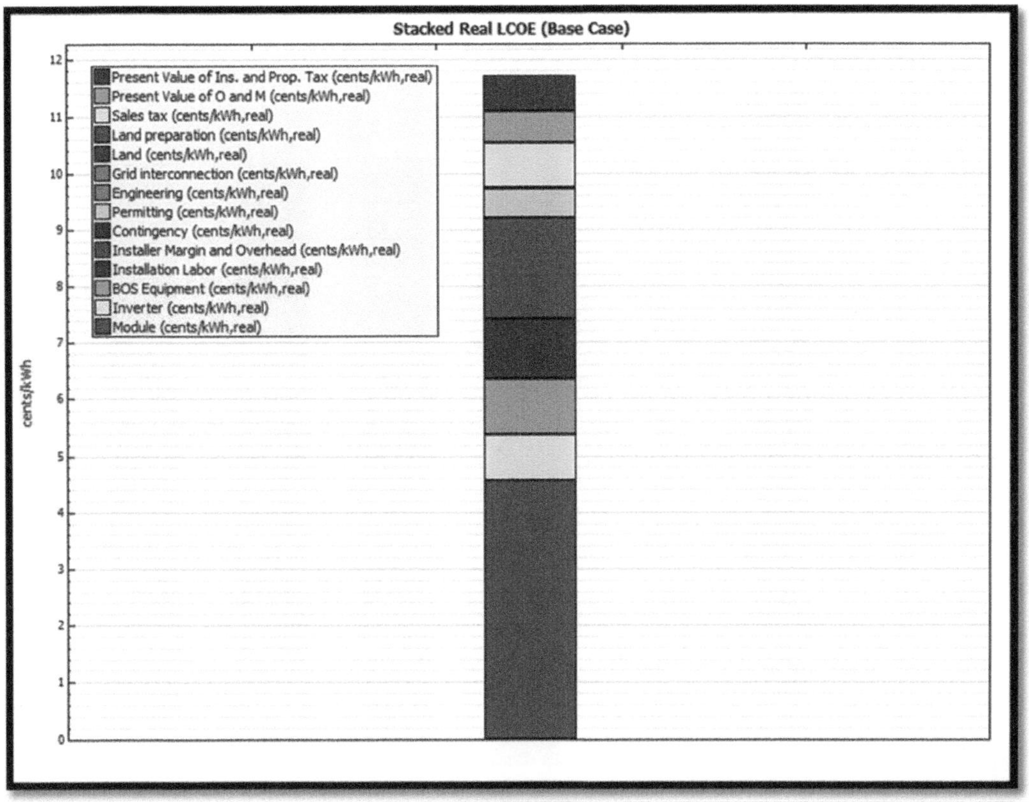
Stacked Real LCOE (Base Case)
Present Value of Ins. and Prop. Tax (cents/kWh,real)
Present Value of O and M (cents/kWh,real)
Sales tax (cents/kWh,real)
Land preparation (cents/kWh,real)
Land (cents/kWh,real)
Grid interconnection (cents/kWh,real)
Engineering (cents/kWh,real)
Permitting (cents/kWh,real)
Contingency (cents/kWh,real)
Installer Margin and Overhead (cents/kWh,real)
Installation Labor (cents/kWh,real)
BOS Equipment (cents/kWh,real)
Inverter (cents/kWh,real)
Module (cents/kWh,real)
cents/kWh
0
1
2
3
4
5
6
7
8
9
10
11
12

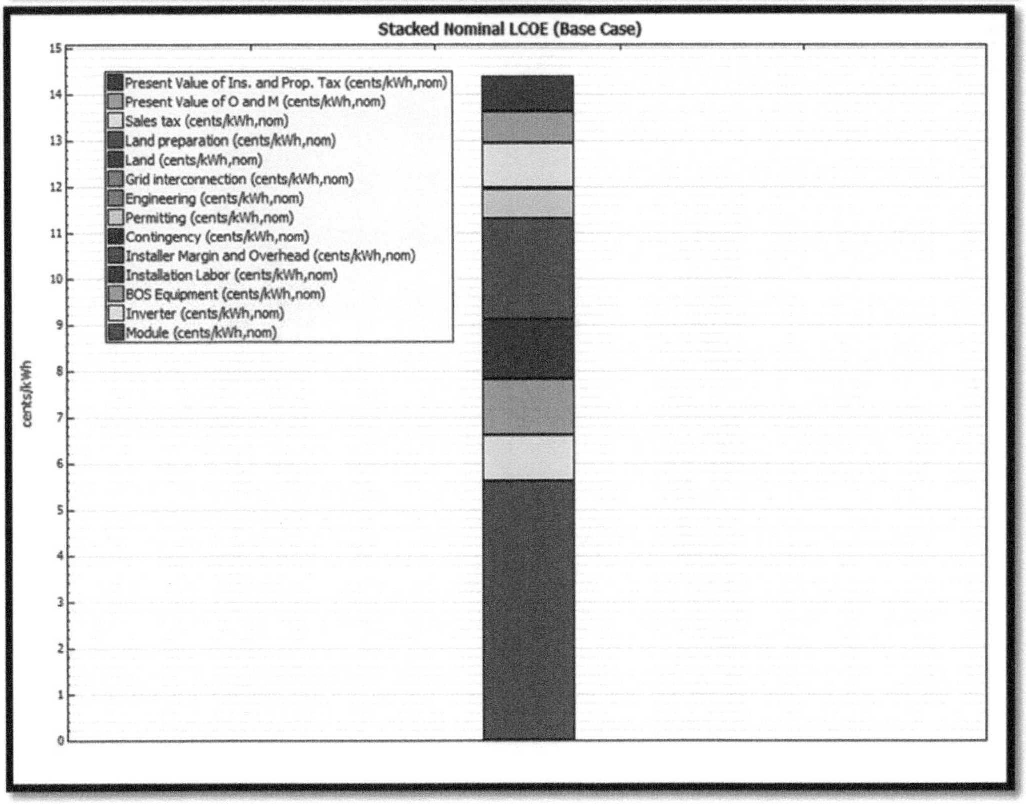
Stacked Nominal LCOE (Base Case)
Present Value of Ins. and Prop. Tax (cents/kWh,nom)
Present Value of O and M (cents/kWh,nom)
Sales tax (cents/kWh,nom)
Land preparation (cents/kWh,nom)
Land (cents/kWh,nom)
Grid interconnection (cents/kWh,nom)
Engineering (cents/kWh,nom)
Permitting (cents/kWh,nom)
Contingency (cents/kWh,nom)
Installer Margin and Overhead (cents/kWh,nom)
Installation Labor (cents/kWh,nom)
BOS Equipment (cents/kWh,nom)
Inverter (cents/kWh,nom)
Module (cents/kWh,nom)
cents/kWh
0
1
2
3
4
5
6
7
8
9
10
11
12
13
14
15

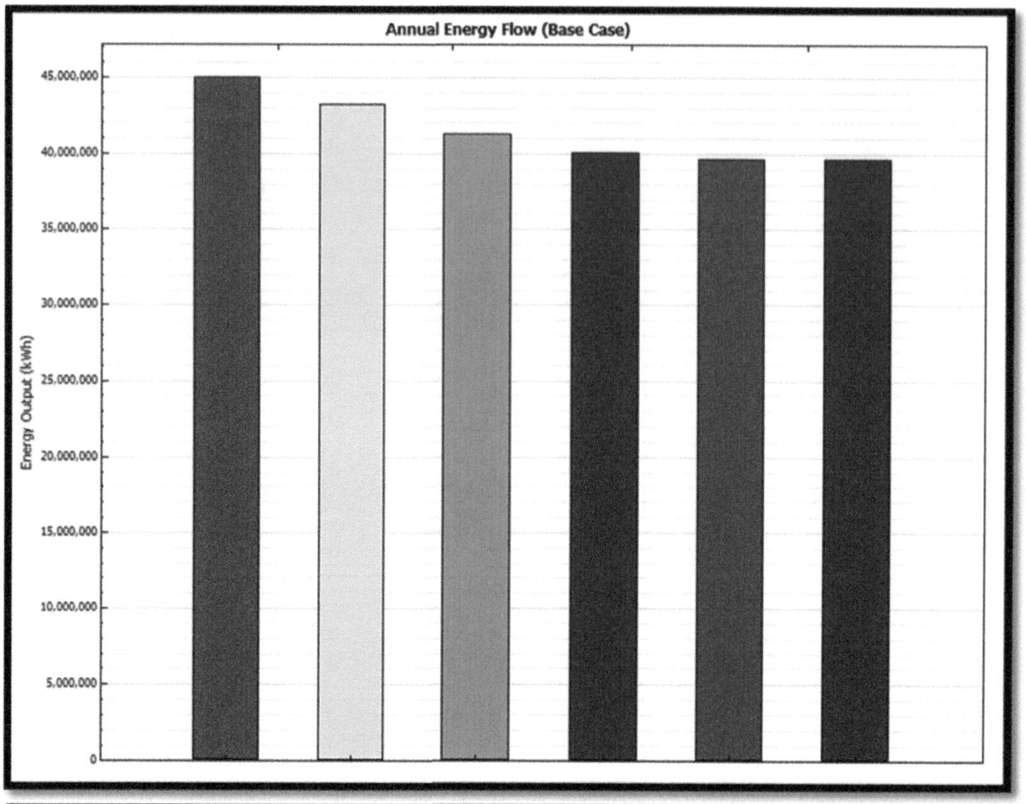
Annual Energy Flow (Base Case)
Energy Output (kWh)
45,000,000
40,000,000
35,000,000
30,000,000
25,000,000
20,000,000
15,000,000
10,000,000
5,000,000
0

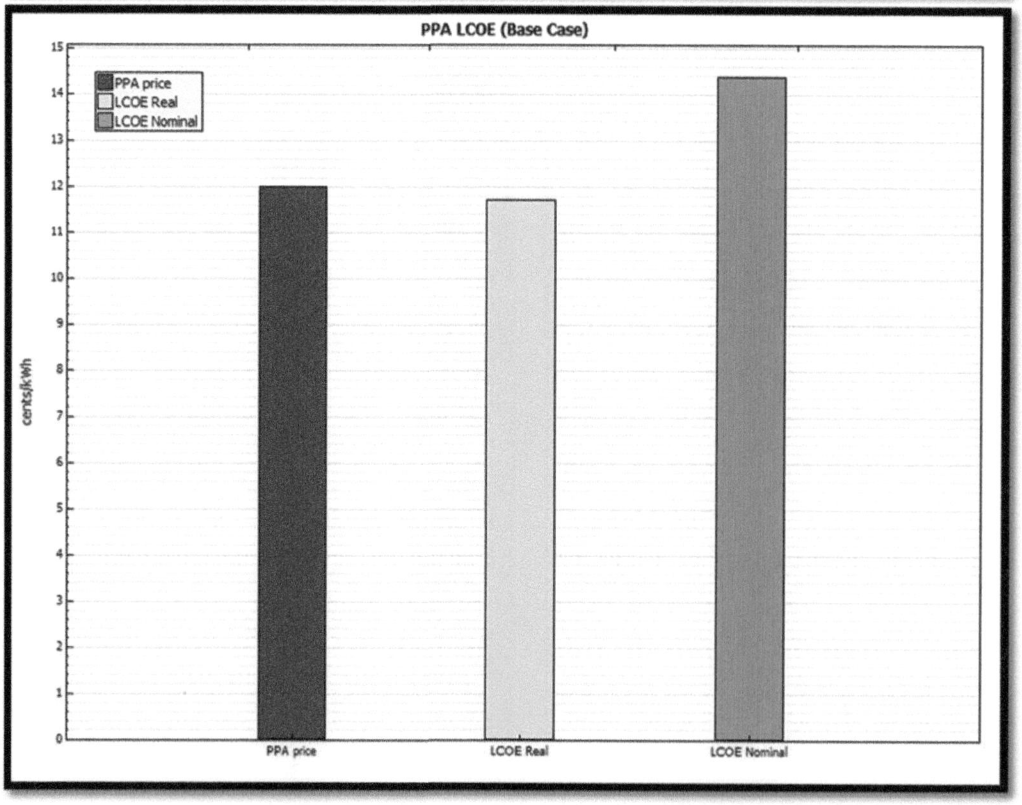
PPA LCOE (Base Case)
cents/kWh
PPA price
LCOE Real
LCOE Nominal
PPA price
LCOE Real
LCOE Nominal

Appendix 4

Supporting Material

1. U.S. Renewable Energy Resource Maps *(see this page)*
2. Average Retail Price of Electricity to Ultimate Customers by End-Use Sector, by State *(see page 565)*
3. Summary of Energy Efficiency Tax incentives in the Energy Policy Act of 2005 *(see page 567)*
4. Insurance Requirement for Interconnection *(see page 568)*
5. Residential Green and Energy Efficient Appraiser Addendum *(see page 569)*
6. Conversion Tables for Measures and Weights *(see page 572)*
7. Energy Audit Sample *(see page 573)*

U.S. Renewable Energy Resource Maps (NREL)

U.S. Renewable Resources

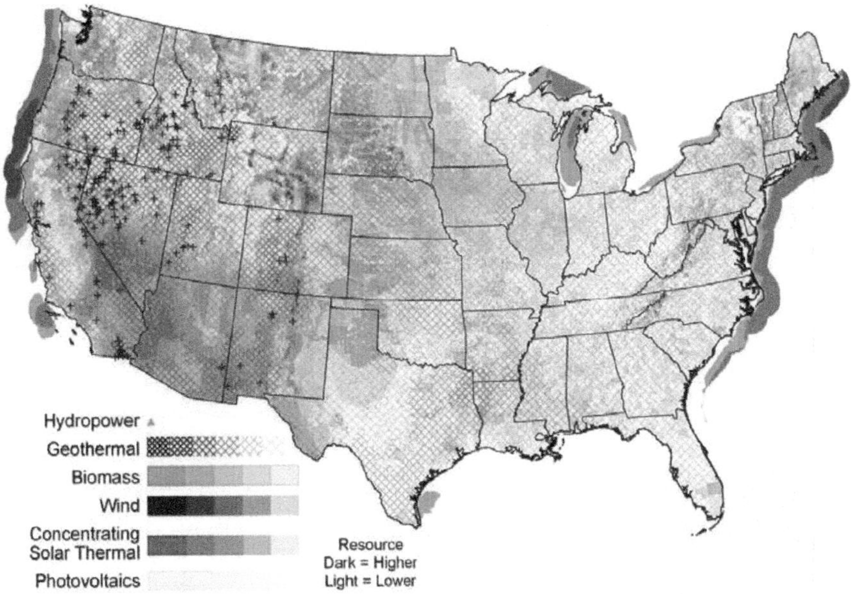

Including Power Transmission Lines

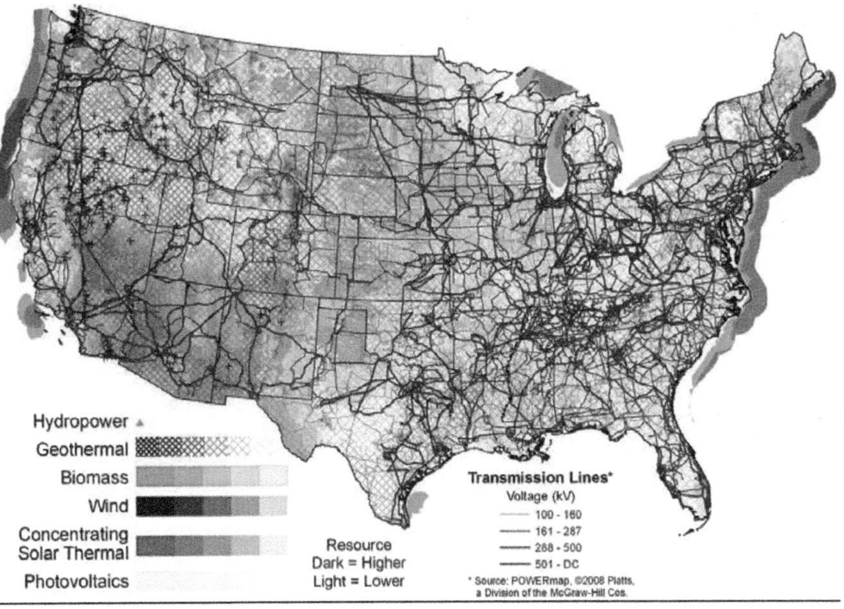

U.S. RENEWABLE ENERGY RESOURCE MAPS (NREL)

PV Solar Resources

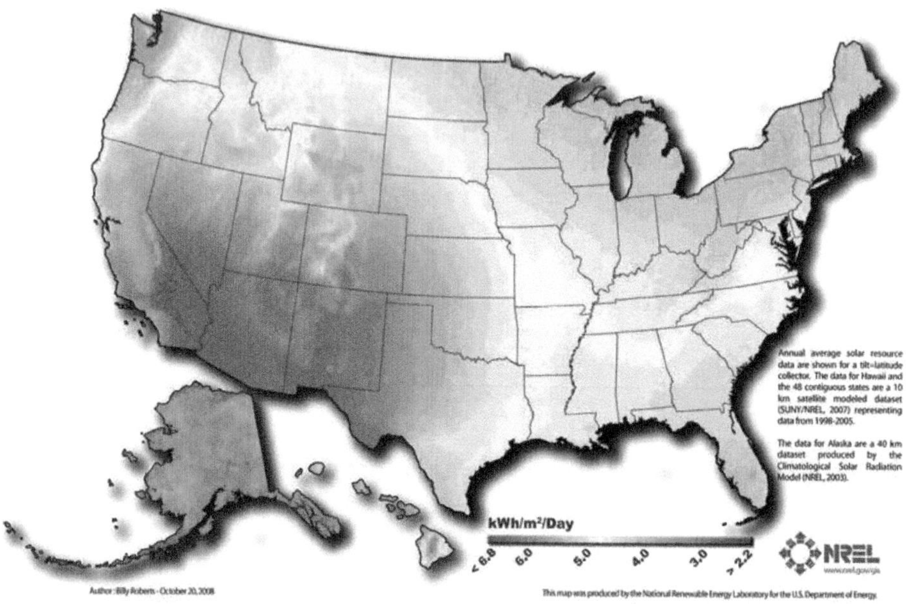

Concentrating Solar Resources

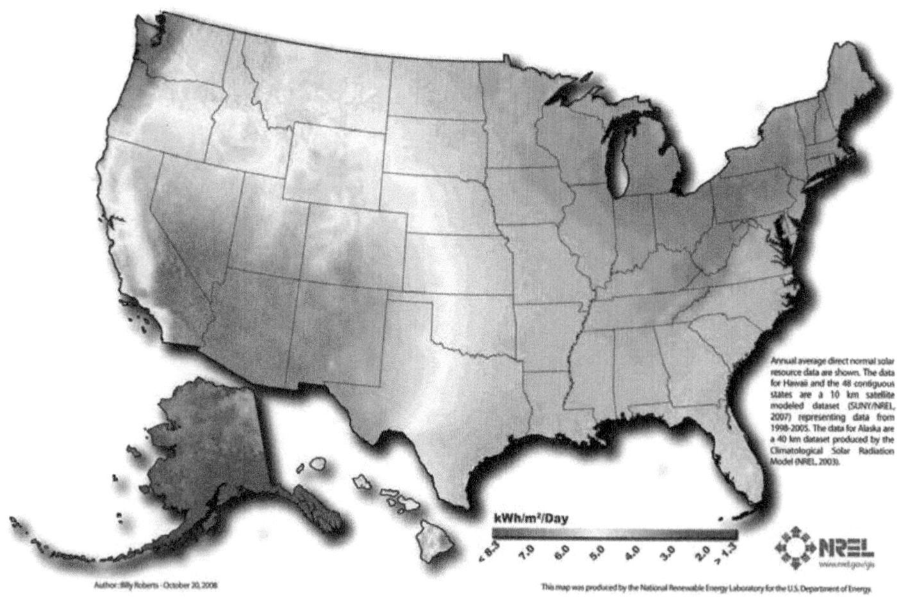

Wind Resources

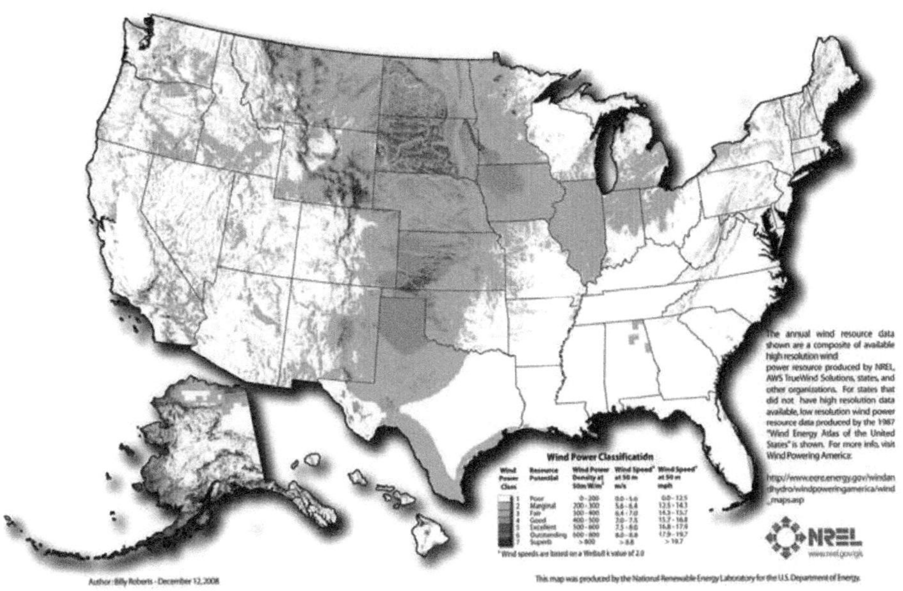

Biomass Resources

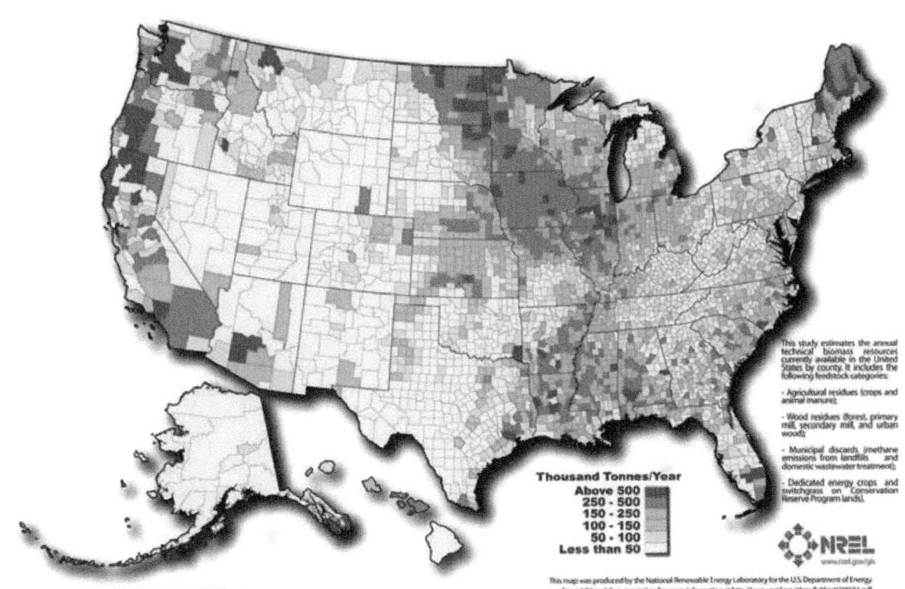

AVERAGE RETAIL PRICE OF ELECTRICITY TO ULTIMATE CUSTOMERS BY END-USE SECTOR, BY STATE

(Cents per Kilowatthour)

Census Division and State	Residential		Commercial[1]		Industrial[1]	
	2011	2010	2011	2010	2011	2010
New England	**15.98**	**16.24**	**14.33**	**14.72**	**12.68**	**12.98**
Connecticut	18.11	19.25	15.48	16.45	13.37	14.5
Maine	15.41	15.71	12.27	12.51	8.9	9.17
Massachusetts	14.82	14.59	14.45	14.53	13.55	13.71
New Hampshire	16.54	16.32	14.02	14.26	12.32	12.75
Rhode Island	14.45	15.92	12.49	13.11	11.31	11.82
Vermont	16.28	15.57	13.95	13.44	9.86	9.53
Middle Atlantic	**15.86**	**15.81**	**13.66**	**13.93**	**8.17**	**8.4**
New Jersey	16.24	16.57	13.48	13.89	11.5	11.81
New York	18.3	18.74	15.83	16.31	7.8	8.78
Pennsylvania	13.38	12.7	10.04	10.1	7.74	7.66
East North Central	**11.78**	**11.41**	**9.48**	**9.36**	**6.59**	**6.53**
Illinois	11.81	11.52	8.64	8.88	6.46	6.82
Indiana	10.06	9.56	8.74	8.38	6.25	5.87
Michigan	13.12	12.46	10.32	9.81	7.36	7.08
Ohio	11.44	11.32	9.6	9.73	6.21	6.4
Wisconsin	13.06	12.65	10.43	9.98	7.34	6.85
West North Central	**10.13**	**9.64**	**8.23**	**7.87**	**6.09**	**5.86**
Iowa	10.5	10.42	7.9	7.91	5.21	5.36
Kansas	10.63	10.03	8.79	8.25	6.73	6.23
Minnesota	10.97	10.59	8.58	8.38	6.51	6.29
Missouri	9.78	9.08	8.04	7.5	5.95	5.5
Nebraska	9.3	8.94	8.04	7.63	6.26	6
North Dakota	8.56	8.13	7.58	7.21	6.25	5.81
South Dakota	9.34	8.97	7.77	7.55	6.3	6.07
South Atlantic	**11.27**	**10.96**	**9.52**	**9.29**	**6.75**	**6.66**
Delaware	13.74	13.8	10.62	11.36	9.05	9.57
District of Columbia	13.4	14.01	12.92	13.42	6.86	7.78
Florida	11.67	11.44	9.99	9.76	8.85	8.85
Georgia	11.07	10.07	9.92	9.06	6.64	6.22
Maryland	13.44	14.32	11.34	11.75	8.81	9.57
North Carolina	10.29	10.12	8.18	8.16	6.06	6.17
South Carolina	11.13	10.5	9.35	8.9	5.96	5.74
Virginia	10.68	10.45	7.93	7.65	6.61	6.66
West Virginia	9.4	8.79	8.14	7.66	6.18	5.86
East South Central	**10.11**	**9.58**	**9.73**	**9.34**	**6.18**	**5.83**
Alabama	11.3	10.67	10.47	10.18	6.33	6.01
Kentucky	9.09	8.57	8.41	7.88	5.31	5.05
Mississippi	10.14	9.87	9.48	9.32	6.57	6.32

Tennessee	9.83	9.23	10.12	9.66	7.12	6.58
West South Central	**10.55**	**10.67**	**8.66**	**8.78**	**6.06**	**6.12**
Arkansas	9.05	8.86	7.55	7.31	5.65	5.44
Louisiana	9.06	8.98	8.47	8.5	5.71	5.84
Oklahoma	9.51	9.14	7.63	7.45	5.51	5.35
Texas	11.27	11.6	8.96	9.19	6.34	6.44
Mountain	**10.57**	**10.49**	**8.83**	**8.75**	**6.11**	**6.13**
Arizona	11.07	10.97	9.5	9.47	6.58	6.63
Colorado	11.26	11.04	9.42	9.13	7.12	6.9
Idaho	7.9	7.99	6.41	6.64	5.16	5.15
Montana	9.77	9.16	9.13	8.55	5.25	5.49
Nevada	11.61	12.36	9	9.78	6.66	7.37
New Mexico	11.04	10.52	8.93	8.57	6.11	6.01
Utah	8.97	8.71	7.35	7.15	5.11	4.93
Wyoming	9.14	8.77	7.72	7.42	5.4	4.98
Pacific Contiguous	**12.74**	**12.31**	**12.14**	**11.58**	**7.92**	**7.47**
California	15.24	14.75	13.81	13.1	11.01	9.8
Oregon	9.6	8.87	8.19	7.59	5.5	5.41
Washington	8.33	8.04	7.54	7.37	3.97	4.07
Pacific Noncontiguous	**27.48**	**23.22**	**24.4**	**20.45**	**24.99**	**19.88**
Alaska	17.57	16.26	14.94	13.95	15.53	14.14
Hawaii	34.68	28.1	32.38	25.93	28.4	21.94
U.S. Total	**11.8**	**11.54**	**10.32**	**10.19**	**6.89**	**6.77**

[1] See Technical notes for additional information on the Commercial, Industrial, and Transportation sectors.

Notes: • See Glossary for definitions. • Values for 2010 are final. Values for 2011 are preliminary estimates based on a cutoff model sample. See Technical Notes for a discussion of the sample design for the Form EIA-826. • Utilities and energy service providers may classify commercial and industrial customers based on either NAICS codes or demands or usage falling within specified limits by rate schedule. • Changes from year to year in consumer counts, sales and revenues, particularly involving the commercial and industrial consumer sectors, may result from respondent implementation of changes in the definitions of consumers, and reclassifications. • Retail sales and net generation may not correspond exactly for a particular month for a variety of reasons (i.e., sales data may include imported electricity). • Net generation is for the calendar month while retail sales and associated revenue accumulate from bills collected for periods of time (28 to 35 days) that vary dependent upon customer class and consumption occurring in and outside the calendar month. • Totals may not equal sum of components because of independent rounding.

Source: U.S. Energy Information Administration, Form EIA-826, "Monthly Electric Sales and Revenue Report with State Distributions Report."

SUMMARY OF ENERGY EFFICIENCY TAX INVENTIVES IN THE ENERGY POLICY ACT OF 2005

ACE3

Summary of Energy Efficiency Tax Incentives in the Energy Policy Act of 2005

Product	Eligibility Level	Units	Amount of Incentive	Years Covered	Notes
Existing homes and other non-business applications					$500 per taxpayer cap for existing home credits
Central air conditioners (split systems)	15	SEER	$300 if meets SEER & EER	2006 & 2007	For list of qualified products, go to the Consortium for Energy
	12.5	EER			Efficiency Product Directory-
Central air conditioners (package systems)	14	SEER	$300 if meets SEER & EER	2006 & 2007	www.ceehvacdirectory.org/continue.html
	12	EER			Look for "Residential Tier 2" Air Conditioners
Heat Pumps (air cooled)	15	SEER	$300 if meets SEER, EER & HSPF	2006 & 2007	See CEE list (link above) for products that meet 15 SEER and
	13	EER			9 HSPF. There is no way to identify equipment that meets 13 EER
	9.0	HSPF			without contacting the manufacturer/distributor (or contractor).
Group-source heat pumps					All Energy Star labeled Geothermal Heat Pumps qualify for credit
Closed loop	14.1/3.3	EER/COP	$300	2006 & 2007	System must also provide water heating.
Open loop	16.2/3.6	EER/COP	$300	2006 & 2007	System must also provide water heating.
Direct expansion (DX)	15/3.5	EER/COP	$300	2006 & 2007	System must also provide water heating.
Water heaters (non-business applications)					See GAMA Web site for list of qualifying products:
Electric	2.0	EF	$300	2006 & 2007	www.gamanet.org/gama/inforesources.nsf/vContentEntries/Product+Directories?OpenDocument
Gas and oil	0.8	EF	$300		
Gas and oil furnaces and boilers					See GAMA Web site (link above) for list of qualifying products.
High combustion efficiency equipment	95%	AFUE	$150	2006 & 2007	Can earn either one or both incentive with the same unit.
High electric efficiency equipment	Meets CEE spec		$50	2006 & 2007	CEE spec requires electricity use to be <=2% of site use.
Envelope improvements to existing homes					
Insulation, exterior doors, duct sealing and infiltration reduction	Meet 2000/2003 IECC + supplements		10% up to $500	2006 & 2007	Includes duct sealing and infiltration reduction. All Energy Star windows and doors qualify for credits.
Windows and skylights	Same as above		10% up to $200	2006 & 2007	Credits cover cost of components only, and do not include
Pigmented metal roofs	Meet Energy Star spec		10% up to $500	2006 & 2007	costs of onsite prep, assembly or installation.
Appliances					All appliance incentives go to manufacturer, not consumer;
Refrigerators					manufacturers are expected to reduce prices accordingly.
Save 15-19.9% relative to federal standard	Look to left		$75	2006	
Save 20-24.9% relative to federal standard	Look to left		$125	2006 & 2007	
Save 25% or more relative to federal standard	Look to left		$175	2006 & 2007	
Clothes washers	1.72 MEF, 8.0 WF		$100	2006 & 2007	
Dishwashers	2007 Energy Star		$32.31	2006 & 2007	
New homes					Incentives go to the builder, not the homebuyer.
Site-built or manufactured homes	50%	savings	$2,000	2006 - 2008	Savings relative to 2004 IECC.
Manufactured homes	30%	savings	$1,000	2006 - 2008	Savings relative to 2004 IECC.
	or meets Energy Star			2006 - 2008	
Commercial buildings					Max. is $0.60/sq.ft. per system or $1.80/sq.ft. for whole bldg.
Whole building	50%	savings	Deduction of $1.80/sq.ft.	2006 - 2008	Savings relative to ASHRAE 90.1-2001.
Lighting, HVAC or envelope	50%	savings	Deduction of $0.60/sq.ft. per system	2006 - 2008	Savings relative to ASHRAE 90.1-2001.
Lighting savings of at least 25%	25-50%	savings	Sliding scale: $.30/sq.ft. for 25% svgs	Unclear	Term of this provision depends on Treasury rulemaking.
Fuel cells and microturbines					
Fuel cells (business or individual credit)	30%	efficiency	30% up to $1000/kW	2006 - 2008	Systems >=0.5 kW for business credit. No size floor or efficiency requirements for individual credit.
Microturbines (only business credit)	26%	efficiency	10% up to $200/kW	2006 - 2008	Systems < 2000 kW.
Passenger vehicles	Complicated formula -- see http://aceee.org/press/0508hybridtaxcr.htm				
Heavy-duty vehicles	Complicated formula -- see www.aceee.org/transportation/hdhybtaxcred.htm for more information				

Key: AC= air conditioner; AFUE= annual fuel utilization efficiency; ASHRAE = American Society of Heating, Refrigerating & Air-Conditioning Engineers; CEE = Consortium for Energy Efficiency; COP= coefficient of performance; EER= energy efficiency ratio; EF= energy factor; HP= heat pump; HSPF= heating season performance factor; IECC= International Energy Conservation Code; kW= kilowatt; MEF= modified energy factor; SEER= seasonal energy efficiency ratio; WF= water factor.

Prepared by the American Council for an Energy-Efficient Economy, updated February 2008.

INSURANCE REQUIREMENTS FOR INTERCONNECTION

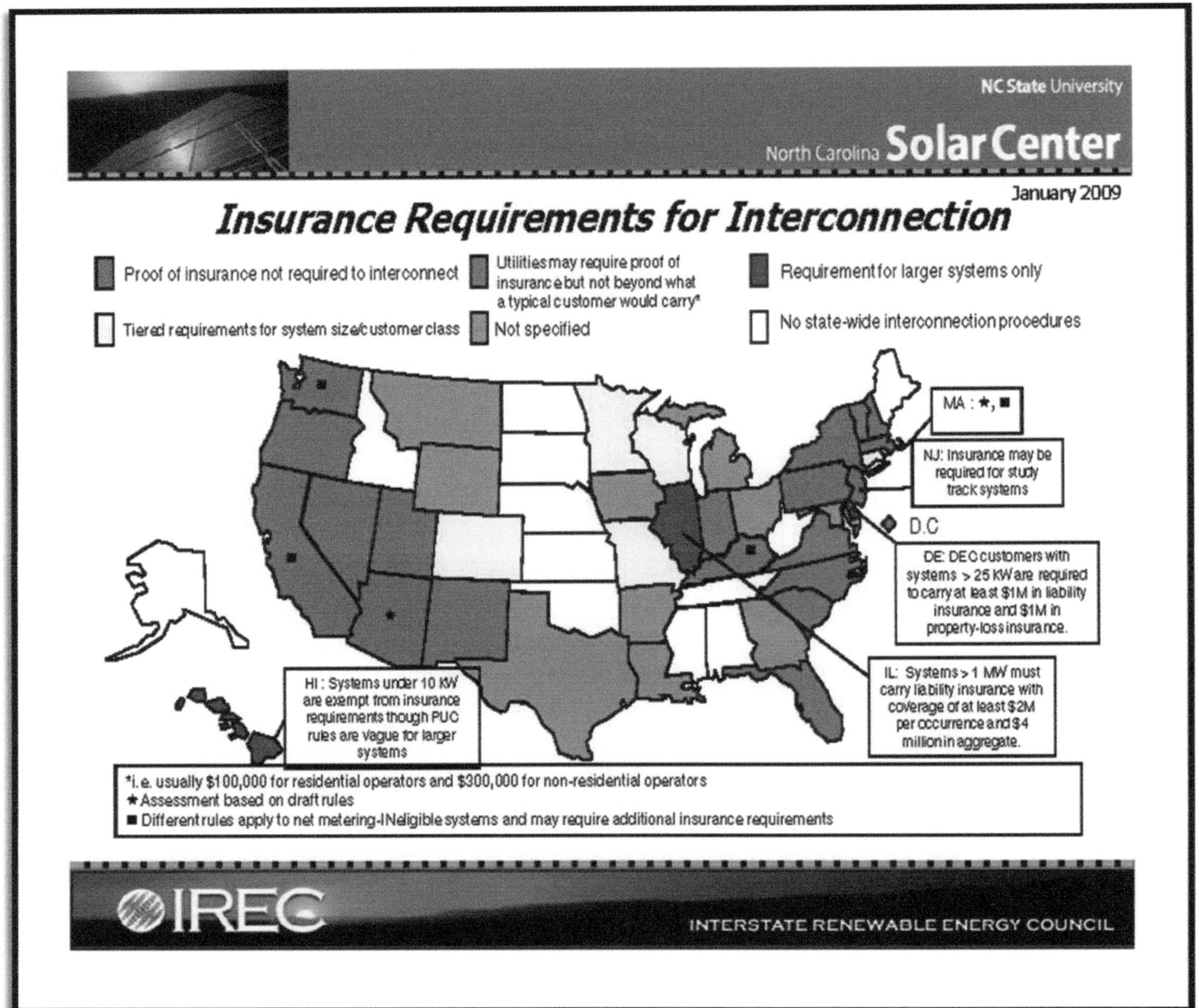

RESIDENTIAL GREEN AND ENERGY EFFICIENT APPRAISER ADDENDUM

AI Reports®
Form 820.03*

Client File #:		Appraisal File #:	

Residential Green and Energy Efficient Addendum

Client:
Subject Property:
City: State: Zip:

Additional resources to aid in the valuation of green properties and the completion of this form can be found at http://www.appraisalinstitute.org/education/green_energy_addendum.aspx

ENERGY EFFICIENT ITEMS

The following items are considered within the appraised value of the subject property:

Insulation	☐ Fiberglass Blown-In ☐ Foam Insulation ☐ Cellulose ☐ Fiberglass Batt Insulation ☐ Other (Describe): ☐ Basement Insulation (Describe): ☐ Floor Insulation (Describe):	R-Value: ☐ Walls ☐ Ceiling ☐ Floor
Water Efficiency	☐ Reclaimed Water System (Explain): ☐ Cistern - Size: Gallons ☐ Rain Barrels - #: ☐ Rain Barrels Provide Irrigation	Location:
Windows	☐ ENERGY STAR® ☐ Low E ☐ High Impact ☐ Storm ☐ Double Pane ☐ Triple Pane ☐ Tinted	☐ Solar Shades
Day Lighting	☐ Skylights - #: ☐ Solar Tubes - #: ☐ ENERGY STAR Light Fixtures	☐ Other (Explain):
Appliances	ENERGY STAR Appliances: ☐ Range/Top ☐ Dishwasher ☐ Refrigerator ☐ Other: Water Heater: ☐ Solar ☐ Tankless (On Demand) Size: Gal.	Appliance Energy Source: ☐ Propane ☐ Electric ☐ Natural Gas ☐ Other (Describe):
HVAC (Describe in Comments Area)	☐ High Efficiency HVAC – SEER: ☐ Heat Pump ☐ Thermostat/Controllers ☐ Programmable Thermostat ☐ Wind ☐ Radiant Floor Heat	☐ Passive Solar ☐ Geothermal
Energy Rating	☐ ENERGY STAR Home ☐ HPwES (Home Performance with ENERGY STAR) ☐ Other (Describe):	☐ Indoor Air PLUS Package ☐ Energy Recovery Ventilator Unit ☐ Certification Attached
HERS Information	Rating: Date Rated:	Monthly Energy Savings on Rating: $
Utility Costs	Average Utility Cost: $ per month based on:	☐ Dashboards - #:
Energy Audit	Has an energy audit/rating been performed on the subject property? ☐ Yes ☐ No ☐ Unknown If yes, comment on work completed as result of audit.	
Comments		

*NOTICE: The Appraisal Institute publishes this form for use by appraisers where the appraiser deems use of the form appropriate. Depending on the assignment, the appraiser may need to provide additional data, analysis and work product not called for in this form. The Appraisal Institute plays no role in completing the form and disclaims any responsibility for the data, analysis or any other work product provided by the individual appraiser(s).

AI Reports® AI-820.03 Residential Green and Energy Efficient Addendum June 2011

Client:		Client File #:	
Subject Property:		Appraisal File #:	

Solar Panels

The following items are considered within the appraised value of the subject property:

Description	Array #1 ☐ Leased ☐ Owned	Array #2 ☐ Leased ☐ Owned	Array #3 ☐ Leased ☐ Owned	Array #4 ☐ Leased ☐ Owned
KW				
Age of Panels				
Energy Production Kwh per Array				
Source for Production				
Location (Roof, Ground, Etc.)				
If Roof/Slope for Array				
Azimuth per Array				
Age of Inverter(s)				
Name of Utility Company:	Cost per Kwh charged by Company: $ /Kwh			
Comments (Discuss incentives available for new panels, condition of current panels, and any maintenance issues)				

Green Features

The following items are considered within the appraised value of the subject property:

Certification	Year Certified:	Certifying Organization:	☐ Reviewed on site	☐ Certification attached to this report
Rating	Score:	☐ LEED® Certified: ☐ Silver ☐ Gold ☐ Platinum ☐ Other:		
		☐ ICC-700 *National Green Building Standard* Certified: ☐ Bronze ☐ Silver ☐ Gold ☐ Emerald		
		Certifying Organizations Green Score Range - High Score: Low Score:		
Additions	Explain any additions or changes made to the structure since it was certified:			
	Do changes require recertification to verify rating is still applicable? ☐ Yes ☐ No			
Comments				

*NOTICE: The Appraisal Institute publishes this form for use by appraisers where the appraiser deems use of the form appropriate. Depending on the assignment, the appraiser may need to provide additional data, analysis and work product not called for in this form. The Appraisal Institute plays no role in completing the form and disclaims any responsibility for the data, analysis or any other work product provided by the individual appraiser(s).

AI Reports® AI-820.03 Residential Green and Energy Efficient Addendum June 2011

Client:		**Client File #:**	
Subject Property:		**Appraisal File #:**	

Location - Site

The following items are considered within the appraised value of the subject property:

Walk Score	Score:	Source:	
Public Transportation	☐ Bus - Distance: Blocks	☐ Train - Distance: Blocks	☐ Subway - Distance: Blocks
Site	Orientation - front faces: ☐ East/West ☐ North/South	Landscaping: ☐ Xeriscaped ☐ Zero Impact ☐ Natural	
Comments			

Incentives - Amount of Incentive and Terms

The following items are considered within the appraised value of the subject property:

Federal	
State	
Local	
Source	
Comments	

*NOTICE: The Appraisal Institute publishes this form for use by appraisers where the appraiser deems use of the form appropriate. Depending on the assignment, the appraiser may need to provide additional data, analysis and work product not called for in this form. The Appraisal Institute plays no role in completing the form and disclaims any responsibility for the data, analysis or any other work product provided by the individual appraiser(s).

AI Reports® AI-820.03 Residential Green and Energy Efficient Addendum June 2011

CONVERSION TABLES FOR MEASURES AND WEIGHTS

United States to Approximate Metric Equivalent

To Convert From	To	Multiply By
Inches	Centimeters	2.540
Inches	Millimeters	25.40
Square Inches	Square Centimeters	6.452
Square Inches	Square Millimeters	645.2
Feet	Meters	0.3048
Square Feet	Square Meters	0.09290
Yards	Meters	0.9144
Square Yards	Square Meters	0.8361
Ounces (avdp)	Grams	28.35
Troy Ounces	Grams	31.10
Pounds (avdp)	Kilograms	0.4536
Long Tons	Metric Tons	1.016
Short Tons	Metric Tons	0.9071
Fluid Ounces	Milliliters	29.57
Quarts	Liters	0.9464
Gallons	Liters	3.785
Bushels	Liters	35.24
Cubic Feet	Cubic Meters	0.02832
Cubic Yards	Cubic Meters	0.7646
Ounces per Square Yard	Grams/Square Meter	33.91

Metric to Approximate United States Equivalent

To Convert From	To	Multiply By
Centimeters	Inches	0.3937
Millimeters	Inches	0.03937
Square Centimeters	Square Inches	0.1552
Square Millimeters	Square Inches	0.01552
Meters	Feet	3.281
Meters	Yards	1.094
Square Meters	Square Feet	10.76
Square Meters	Square Yards	1.195
Grams	Ounces (avdp)	0.03527
Grams	Troy Ounces	0.03215
Kilograms	Pounds (avdp)	2.205
Metric Tons	Long Tons	0.9842
Metric Tons	Short Tons	1.102
Milliliters	Fluid Ounces	0.03381
Liters	Quarts	1.057
Liters	Gallons	0.2642
Liters	Bushels	0.02838
Cubic Meters	Cubic Feet	35.31
Cubic Meters	Cubic Yards	1.308
Grams per Square Meter	Ounces/Square Yard	0.0295

SAMPLE ENERGY AUDIT REPORT

FINAL REPORT
ASSESSMENT OF ENERGY SAVING OPPORTUNITIES
CLIENT

TABLE OF CONTENTS

Page

LIST OF APPENDICES

EXECUTIVE SUMMARY

*This report presents the results of an assessment of the energy saving opportunities for the **CLIENT** facility in XXXX This assessment was performed via Framework Agreement with **CLIENT** the parent corporation of XXXX. The objectives of the assessment were to help identify and prioritise energy savings opportunities that could be implemented with minimal cost, as well as identifying longer term capital projects for which a business case can be formulated (payback ≤ 3 years). More capital intensive, longer return items are briefly identified but are not the focus of this assessment.*

The XXXX site has a total building floor area of 85,000 ft^2 and dates from 1960, with later extensions. There are approximately 110 people employed at the site working a single-shift, 5 days per week, with shifts as needed on evenings and Saturdays. The main activities onsite are the manufacture of actuators and controls systems for the oil and gas, process and HVAC industries.

The site uses around 3,200 MWh of energy (gas and electricity) per year, at a cost of around $213,000/ year. The energy use and cost are summarised in the table below:

Utility	Energy Consumption		Cost	
	kWh/year	**%**	**$/year**	**%**
Electricity	1,405,200	44%	142,191	67%
Gas	1,791,925	56%	70,600	33%
Total Energy	**3,197,125**	**100%**	**212,791**	**100%**

** All energy values are in terms of delivered energy. Costs include delivery charges and tax.*

During the survey a number of technical measures were identified that would potentially reduce these energy costs. Many of these have very attractive financial returns, with return on investment of up to 100% for the best performing projects.

The individual projects identified are summarised in the Action Plan on the following page. Measures identified include:

- *Identification and repair of compressed air leaks;*
- *Reduction of the space heating temperature setpoints to more reasonable levels;*
- *Installation of electronic condensate drain traps in the compressed air distribution system;*
- *Substitution of compressed air tools for direct electric driven tools where practical;*
- *Upgrading of the compressed air sequence controller to a modern electronic sequence controller;*
- *Installation of variable speed drives (also known as variable frequency drives or inverters) on the Titan air rotation unit and the Torrit dust extraction systems; and*

- *Replacement of old T12 lighting in the factory and offices with modern high frequency fluorescent lighting and addition of occupancy control in certain areas.*

If all the prioritized measures shown in the Action Plan are implemented, the total un-aggregated savings represent a 16% reduction in annual energy consumption with a resulting 18% annual reduction in cost, or approximately $38,000/year in direct cost savings. If the measures are implemented in parallel, the totals may be reduced, as certain measures will reduce the impact of others. In this case the aggregated energy saving is estimated to be around 14%, with cost savings of 15%. The overall capital cost (including marginal cost items) is estimated to be just under $91,000, thus achieving an overall payback of 2.4 years, and an overall return on investment of 42%.

At the request of the site management, energy management practices were also reviewed. Although no quantification of potential has been given in this report, it is our opinion that further savings could be made through improving energy management practices, good housekeeping and increasing employee awareness of energy issues.

ACTION PLAN

PRIORITY	DESCRIPTION OF MEASURE	ESTIMATED ANNUAL SAVINGS		ESTIMATED COST ($)	RETURN ON INVESTMENT (over 5 years)	PAYBACK PERIOD (years)
		($/year)	(kWh/year)			
1	Reduce space heating setpoint	8,940	226,980	0	N/A	Immediate
2	Repair compressed air leaks	3,050	30,110	<500	N/A	Immediate
3	Install electronic compressed air condensate drain traps	300	3,010	300	100%	1.0
4	Substitute compressed air hand tools for direct electric-driven tools (where possible)	3,050	30,110	5,000	61%	1.6
5	Upgrade compressed air sequence controller	1,520	15,050	3,000	51%	2.0
6	Install VSD on Titan air rotation unit	2,760	27,300	6,750	41%	2.4
7	Install VSDs on Torrit Dust Collection systems	4,400	43,440	13,500	33%	3.1
8	Add occupancy control to lighting	3,720	36,760	12,600	30%	3.4
9	Replace T12 lighting with high frequency T5 fluorescent lighting	10,330	102,120	48,960	21%	4.7
	TOTAL	**$38,070**	**514,880**	**$90,610**	**42%**	**2.4**

1.0 INTRODUCTION

1.1 Background

The **CLIENT** XXXX dates from 1960 with additions in 1979 and 1996, and comprises around 85,000 ft^2 of manufacturing and office space. The facility manufactures actuators and controls systems for the oil and gas, process and HVAC industries.

was requested by **CLIENT** Corporate to undertake an energy assessment of the **CLIENT** XXXX facility to identify potential energy saving opportunities.

The survey was undertaken over the period February 7-8, 2007, by XXXX, Senior Consultant from . During the survey discussions were held with the following XXXX personnel:

- XXXXXX.

would like to acknowledge the assistance of these and other XXXX personnel who assisted during the survey period.

1.2 Objectives for the Visit

The objectives of this assessment were to help identify and prioritise energy savings opportunities that could be implemented with minimal cost, as well as identifying longer term capital projects for which a business case can be formulated (payback period < 3 years). More capital intensive and/or longer return items are briefly identified but are not the focus of this assessment.

The Scope of Work determined was to comprise the following tasks:

- Desk-based analysis of historical energy consumption data.
- Site visit consisting of a walk-through of all areas, plant rooms and an analysis of control systems, along with operation and maintenance practices. To involve discussions with maintenance, energy and environmental personnel regarding the management of energy at the site.
- Brief overview of energy management practices to date.
- Formulation of an Action Plan detailing potential measures to reduce energy consumption, including calculations of associated costs and paybacks. Measures to be divided into no costs, low cost and capital cost measures.
- Production of an energy assessment report. Follow up and feedback will be conducted via email and telephone discussions.

1.3 Site Details

The facility manufactures actuators and control systems under three brand names as follows:

XXXX

The main production activities are manual and CNC turning, milling and grinding. There are also welding operations and 2 furnaces for annealing and stress relief. These are rated at 2,462,400 BTU/hour (720 kW) and 984,960 BTU/hour (288 kW) respectively. The larger of the furnaces is used infrequently. Other operations at the site include shot blasting and painting. There are 3 dust extraction units serving the welding area, the sandblast cabinet and the carpentry shop.

The total building floor area is approximately 85,000 ft^2 (7,897 m^2), including 13,000 ft^2 (1,208 m^2) of office space.

The original factory was constructed around 1960. A steel span building was added in 1979 and a second steel span building to connect the two was added in 1996.

The factory space is heated by 2 large direct gas-fired air handling units (known as air rotation units). These also provide positive pressurization in the factory space. The unit serving the main valve assembly area is by Titan, and the unit serving the Bettis Valve area is by Healtex. The Bettis Valve area also has 3 indirect gas-fired convector heaters and a number of gas-fired U-tube radiant heaters. The Fabrication Shop (east Building) is heated by gas-fired radiant tube heaters. Under normal conditions the Healtex unit is not used, relying instead on the convector and radiant heaters. All air handling units, convector and radiant heaters are controlled by local thermostats. Some of these have been enclosed to prevent unauthorized adjustment.

The offices are heated or cooled by 4 roof-mounted air handling units with indirect gas-fired heaters and direct expansion cooling coils. These units were not readily accessible for inspection during the survey due to the weather conditions. Office heating and cooling is controlled by local wall-mounted digital controllers.

The production area is supplied with compressed air at 97 psi (6.7 bars) by 3 Quincy fixed speed screw compressors operating under cascade pressure control. Compressed air is used for paint spraying and shot blasting, operation of air-powered hand grinders and other handtools, and for blowing away chips and swarf with hand-held blow guns regulated to 30 psi (2 bar).

Lighting in the main production areas is by a combination of metal halide lamps rated at 400 W each and fluorescent lighting comprising 4 or 8 foot T12 (1½ inch diameter) battens in twin fittings. Lighting in the fabrication shop is by metal halide lamps rated at 250 W each with some 8 foot T12 fittings.

Lighting in office areas is by T12 fluorescent tube fittings.

1.4 Energy Procurement and Related Charges

Electricity is purchased from XXXX. The electricity market in this area has not been deregulated. The average unit cost, including all transmission charges is $0.1012 /kWh.

There is no electricity metering onsite, other than the supply company's meter.

Gas is supplied by XXXXX at $0.0394 /kWh. There is a main meter for gas supplied to the site. There is no further sub-metering of gas supplies.

1.5 Operating Hours and Shift Patterns

The facility operates 8.5 hours per day on a single shift, 6:30 a.m. to 3:00 p.m., Monday through Friday. Overtime is typically 1 to 2 hours per day, plus a half day on Saturdays. Office hours are typically 8:00 a.m. to 5:00 p.m., Monday through Friday only. There are around 110 personnel employed at the site.

1.6 Risks and Uncertainties

All costs and savings stated in this report are based on the data available at the time of the visit and can only be taken as indications at this stage. Further work may be required to develop this information in greater depth before any financial or commercial commitment is made.

It should be noted that there is no sub-metering of electricity and gas at the site, and therefore the detailed breakdown of gas and electricity use presented in this report has been estimated based on the installed equipment capacity and estimated utilization figures. These figures have also been taken as the basis of certain potential energy saving measures listed in the Action Plan, and, as this breakdown of energy use may not be accurate, caution should be taken when using these figures.

1.7 Limitations

While reasonable steps have been taken to ensure that the information contained within this report is correct, certain information may be incomplete, inaccurate or may have become out of date. Accordingly, makes no warranties or representations of any kind as to the content of this assessment of initial energy saving opportunities report or its accuracy except to the extent that the information provided to is accurate.

Nothing in this report is intended to be or should be interpreted as an endorsement of, or recommendation for, any supplier, service or product.

2.0 CURRENT ENERGY USE

2.1 Site Energy Consumption and Cost

The data provided below is based on the 2006 Calendar year (January through December 2006). The annual energy consumption for the site is approximately 3,197 MWh, purchased at a cost of just under $213,000.

Utility	Energy Consumption		Cost	
	kWh/year	%	$/year	%
Electricity	1,405,200	44%	142,191	67%
Gas	1,791,925	56%	70,600	33%
Total Energy	**3,197,125**	**100%**	**212,791**	**100%**

* *All energy values are in terms of delivered energy. Costs include delivery charges and tax.*

From the above data the average unit costs for electricity and gas are $0.1012/kWh and $0.0394/kWh respectively. Note that the electricity costs include standing charges and demand charges that are not expected to change due to any of the proposed energy efficiency measures.

2.1.1 Electricity

Electricity accounts for approximately 44% of total annual energy demand within the factory, and 67% of energy costs.

Consumption data is only available in monthly periods. More frequent monitoring is currently not available. The monthly electricity consumption figures over the last 3 years are given in Figure 1 below.

Figure 1
XXXXX – Monthly Electricity Profile 2004 to 2006

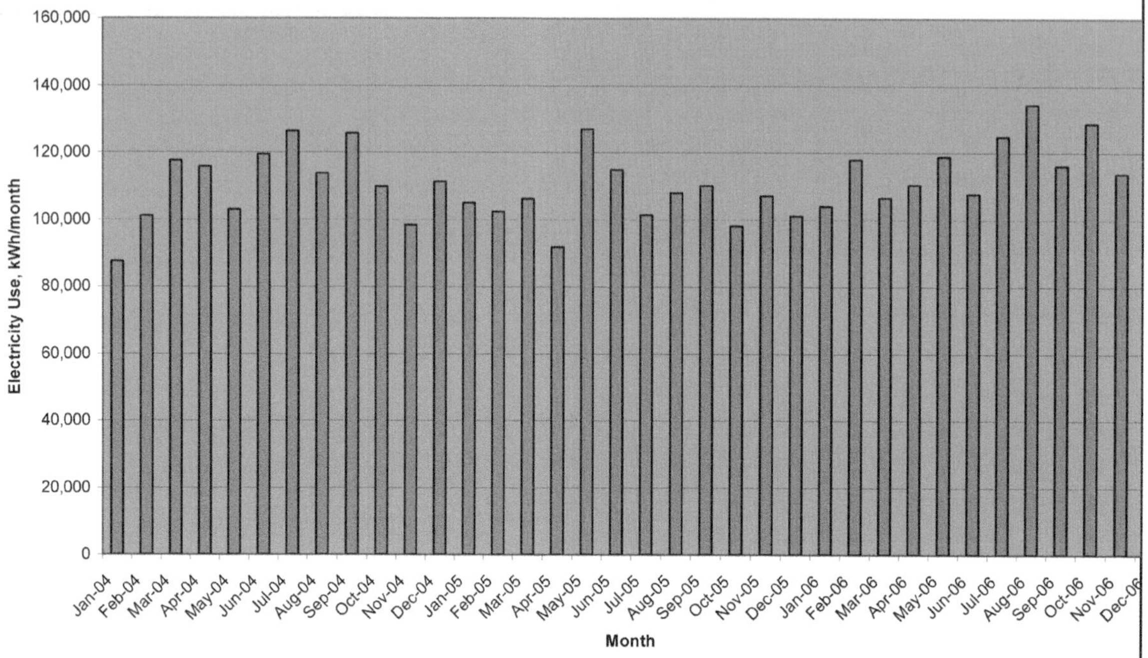

The profile shows slight seasonal variation, with higher peaks in summer time, which could be due to seasonal factors such as increased air conditioning load, increased production activity in summer time, or reduced activity in winter (e.g. the effect of Christmas holidays/shut down).

The main areas of electricity usage are:

- Machining (manual and CNC lathes, milling and grinding machines);
- Welding;
- Lighting;
- Compressed air generation;
- Ventilation;
- Dust extraction; and
- Cooling.

The breakdown of electricity consumption has been estimated using known quantities (such as lighting load and air compressor duty) and estimates, and is shown in Figure 2 below. It is emphasized that this is an estimate only and should be backed up by measurement before it can be treated reliably.

Figure 2
XXXXX – Estimated Breakdown of Electricity Use

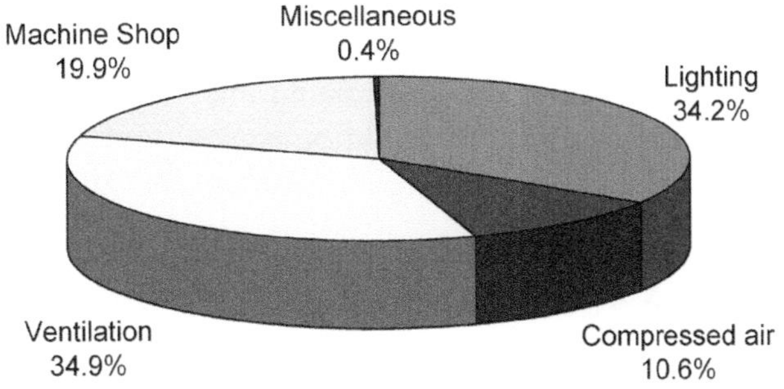

The miscellaneous electricity use would include domestic hot water generation, IT and office equipment, etc.

2.1.2 Gas

Gas accounted for 56% of energy use in 2006, but only 33% of costs. Gas is used almost entirely for space heating in the factory and office areas, with some supplementary uses such as the gas-fired stress relief furnace and the annealing furnace. The latter is a large consumer, but is rarely used.

The monthly gas use for the 3 year period January 2004 to December 2006 is shown in Figure 3 below.

Figure 3
XXXX – Monthly Gas Use 2004 to 2006

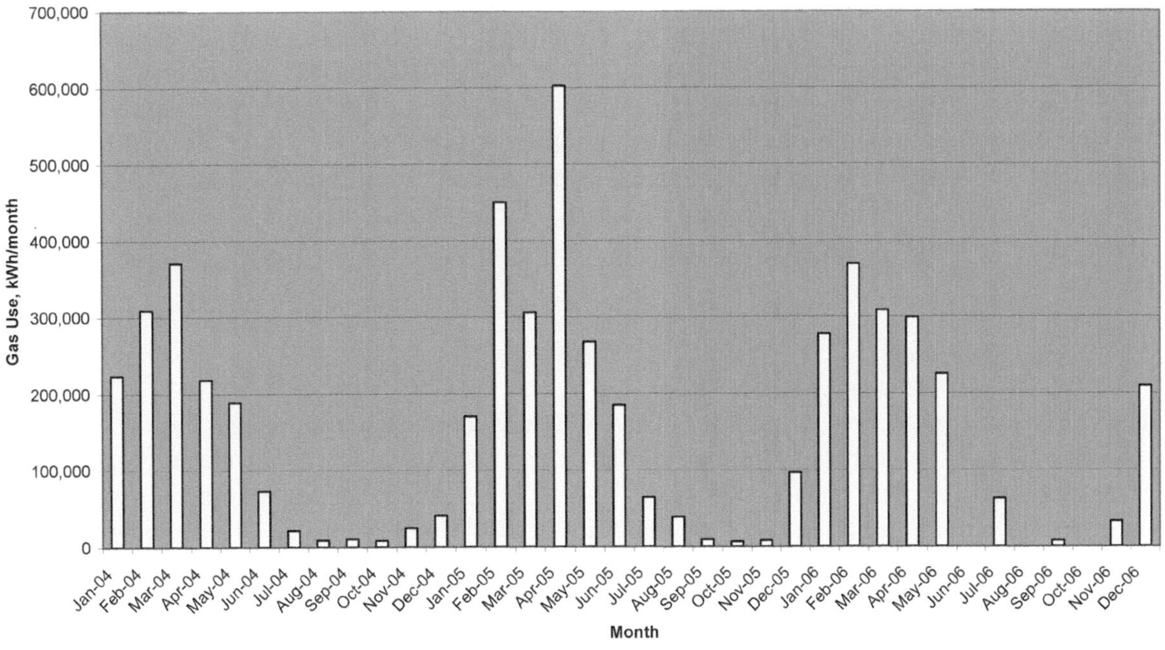

There is a very small gas use over the summer period. This may be attributable to the operation of the stress relief furnace, which operates all year round. The peak seen in April 2005 is almost certainly due to a late meter reading. Note that the data appears to be offset by at least 1 month due to the effect of billing in arrears.

The breakdown of gas consumption has been estimated and is shown in Figure 4 below. It is emphasized that this is an estimate only and should be backed up by measurement before it can be treated reliably.

Figure 4
XXXX – Breakdown of Gas Use

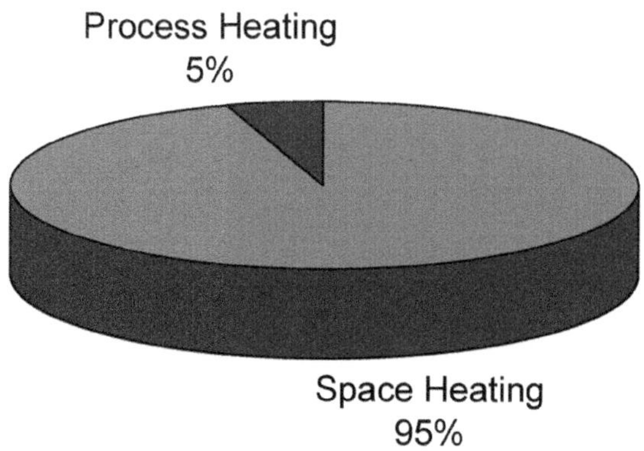

3.0 ENERGY MANAGEMENT PRACTICES

3.1 Introduction

There are often good savings to be achieved through improvement of energy management practices in business. By focusing on a controllable resource like energy, practices can be optimized and waste reduced or eliminated. This is often difficult to achieve in practice, and can require some investment in resources as well as sustained effort, however capital costs are usually low and returns are often excellent if applied correctly. carried out a brief assessment of energy management practices, using an assessment tool (the Energy Management Matrix) developed to help identify weaknesses in the energy management structure. The Energy Management Matrix is shown in Appendix A for reference, and the key findings are listed below.

3.2 Energy Policy

There is no energy Policy at the site. The implementation of a site energy policy is strongly recommended as a good way to underline the importance of good energy management to both employees and external stakeholders (e.g. local authorities/regulators, customers, shareholders, etc.), and to provide a platform for a program of energy improvements. The policy should be designed to cover all the key areas of importance, such as:

- Setting the direction ("Mission Statement");

- Reasons for action/impact (e.g. cost management, emissions reduction, etc.);
- Responsibility (chain of command);
- Targets/commitments;
- Measurement of progress and feedback;
- Investment measures; and
- Continuous improvement.

3.3 Responsibility

Currently there is no clearly-defined chain of command for energy issues.

Energy bills are currently received and paid by the Finance/Accounts function, but there is no linkage with other parts of the site management.

The site's Environment, Safety, and Health Coordinator also has responsibility for the main site services (i.e. heating, lighting, ventilation, etc.) so might be an obvious choice from a technical perspective, although there is also a need for input from someone in the plant management team to provide the necessary authority and to interface with the senior management on energy issues. There is also a need for someone to take a lead on training and awareness issues.

It is recommended that the role of local Energy Manager be formalized as part of the EHS responsibility, with support from the site management team. At this level of expenditure (around $200,000/year), it should form 10 to 20% of a full-time person's resource. It should be recognized that there are several issues to be covered, including management and reporting of consumption information, monitoring and negotiation of energy contracts, technical/engineering input to energy-related projects, and training/awareness projects. These roles may be split between several job functions, under the management of a single individual.

3.4 Information Systems

At present there is very little information available on energy usage. There are single meters for gas and electricity. These are under the ownership of the respective gas and electricity suppliers. Invoices are received by Finance and paid with no further scrutiny or passing on of information to others within the company (e.g. maintenance or engineering).

It is recommended that XXXX start to take its own electricity and gas meter readings on a weekly basis. Consideration should also be given to installation of further sub-meters (e.g. to record the consumption of individual switch boards and major energy users) (e.g. the air compressor). There may also be a case for installation of sub-meters on the process gas users (i.e. the stress relief and the annealing furnaces). recommends a weekly meter reading regime, with data collated on a spreadsheet. This simple regime will help the company to understand how and where energy is used, and can be developed over time into a more sophisticated system as understanding grows.

3.5 Awareness and Motivation

There is a need to improve employees' understanding of energy use and the cost to the company. This can help to reduce costs, once employees start to understand that energy used at work is not free and that their actions have an impact on energy usage and costs, and therefore profitability and, ultimately, job security. An awareness campaign should be planned starting with some simple awareness raising messages, such as a notice board summarising annual and monthly costs. This can be developed over time into a more sophisticated campaign, telling employees how energy savings can be achieved through them, and feeding back progress, particularly where successes have been achieved.

3.6 Investment

At present there is no specific plan for investment in energy efficiency projects. Projects have been considered in the past (e.g. lighting replacement), but discounted on financial grounds. With energy costs rising, now is a good time to re-visit these projects.

Investment criteria were discussed at the energy survey kick-off meeting, and the VP Finance stated that energy projects should meet the normal investment criteria of a Return on Investment (ROI) of greater than 35 to 40% over 10 years. There is a second financial hurdle in that projects must have a simple payback of less than 3 years. In this report we have calculated ROI for the identified projects to show that most of the identified projects exceed these criteria. Those that

4.0 ENERGY SAVING OPPORTUNITIES

The energy saving measures in Section 4.1 are given where there is a reasonable level of data available to indicate the potential savings and capital expenditure. It is by no means exhaustive but is based on opportunities with good payback, low capital outlay, and relatively simple installation.

4.1 Technical Recommendations with Estimated Energy Savings and Costs

1 REDUCE SPACE HEATING SETPOINT			
Cost Saving ($/year)	**Energy Savings (kWh/year)**	**Cost ($)**	**Payback in Years (ROI, %)**
8,940	226,980	0	Immediate (N/A)

Detail:	Reduce space heating temperature set point from current levels to 68°F.
Rationale:	The factory space is heated by the Titan air rotation unit, 3 gas-fired convector heaters and a number of gas-fired U-tube radiant heaters. All have local thermostatic control. The set points of these were not all visible, but of those that were, the set temperature ranged between 60 and 75°F (20 to 24°C), with an average of 71°F (22°F). This is considered slightly on the high side, especially considering that the external ambient air temperature during the time of the survey was something in the region of 9°F/-12°C.

	Typical recommended temperatures for a manufacturing environment with light manual work would be around 61 to 66°F (16 to 19°C). Setting the temperature to say 68°F (20°C) would save around 13% of space heating gas consumption. Reducing it further to 66°F would save 21%. This saving has been calculated at 68°F. A number of the thermostats are fitted with anti-tamper covers. These are generally a good idea, and the remaining thermostats should be similarly fitted with covers, ensuring that there is adequate airflow around the sensor.
Risks:	Possible staff dissatisfaction (is it reasonable to expect to be able to work in a t-shirt when it is 9°F outside?).
Next Step:	1. Fit tamper-proof covers to thermostats and reduce setpoints to 68°F (or lower if possible).

2	**REPAIR COMPRESSED AIR LEAKS**		
Cost Saving ($/year)	**Energy Savings (kWh/year)**	**Cost ($)**	**Payback in Years (ROI, %)**
3,050	30,110	<500	Immediate

Detail:	During the site survey, a substantial number of air leaks were identified around the factory. These should be repaired under routine maintenance.
Rationale:	Compressed air leaks represent wasted energy, and can often be in the region of 10 to 30% of the air compressors total output. In this case, the savings have been assessed at 20% of compressed air costs, but could be greater.
Risks:	None
Next Steps:	1. Carry out a compressed air leak survey and repair program. 2. Set up a planned preventative maintenance regime to tackle air leaks in future. 3. Encourage employees to report air leaks as they occur (leak tagging system).

3	**INSTALL ELECTRONIC COMPRESSED AIR CONDENSATE DRAIN TRAPS**		
Cost Saving ($/year)	**Energy Savings (kWh/year)**	**Cost ($)**	**Payback in Years (ROI, %)**
300	3,010	300	1.0 (100%)

Detail:	Fit electronic compressed air drain traps to the receiver condensate drain and the oil separator drain, plus any other drain applications on the compressed air distribution system.
Rationale:	The condensate drain on the air receiver is controlled by a timed solenoid valve, set to open for 30 seconds every 15 minutes. Whilst this is a reasonable and widely used solution to the issue of condensate build up, modern electronic drain traps can optimize this process, by sensing the level of condensate build up and opening only when necessary. The drain on the oil separator is a manual valve that is cracked open slightly to continually discharge oil. Unfortunately this also results in a continuous discharge of compressed air. Again, an electronic drain trap would optimize this process. There may be other suitable applications for improved traps around the compressed air distribution system, and a survey should be undertaken to identify further applications.

Risks:	None
Next Steps:	1. Obtain quotes for electronic condensate traps and install. 2. Identify other applications in compressed air distribution system.

4	**SUBSTITUTE COMPRESSED AIR HAND TOOLS FOR DIRECT ELECTRIC-DRIVEN TOOLS (WHERE POSSIBLE)**		
Cost Saving ($/year)	**Energy Savings (kWh/year)**	**Cost ($)**	**Payback in Years (ROI, %)**
3,050	30,110	5,000	1.6 (61%)

Detail:	Avoid use of compressed air powered hand tools where possible, substituting mains or battery powered tools where possible. Other practices to be avoided include unnecessary use of air blow off guns where hand brushes could be used instead.
Rationale:	Compressed air is an inefficient source of motive power, with only around 10% of the total energy input emerging as useful power, with the remainder lost in poor generation efficiency or leaks. Compressed air tends to be used for convenience only, or because that's the way it's always been done. Reducing use of compressed air by means of substitution by direct electrically powered tools can result in substantial savings.
Risks:	None
Next Step:	1. Carry out a study to determine where air is used and for what purposes, and examine feasibility of substitution by electric tools.

5	UPGRADE COMPRESSED AIR SEQUENCE CONTROLLER		
Cost Saving ($/year)	**Energy Savings (kWh/year)**	**Cost ($)**	**Payback in Years (ROI, %)**
1,520	15,050	3,000	2.0 (51%)

Detail:	Consider replacement of existing cascade controller by a modern electronic air compressor sequence controller.
Rationale:	There are 3 air compressors of identical capacity. These are connected into a common header with an air receiver. Air is then taken from the air receiver to the site ring main. The setpoint for the compressed air control system is set at 95 psi, with the pressure sensor taken from the ring main. The air in the receiver is held at 125 psi, and reduced to 95 psi via a reducing valve.
	The compressors are controlled by a "cascade" control system, which brings on additional compressors as the system pressure falls. Because there are 3 pressure switches, each with its own control band, this can result in compressed air being generated at a much higher pressure than is necessary, especially at periods of low air demand. An electronic sequence controller gets round this by varying the control setpoint with demand to minimize the generation pressure, and has other advantages in terms of rotation of compressors (if the compressors were of different capacities an electronic control could match the demand to the appropriate sized compressor or combination of compressors to maximize efficiency, but this point is not relevant with identically sized compressors).
Risks:	None
Next Step:	1. Obtain quotes for electronic compressor sequence controller and proceed if favorable.

6	INSTALL VSD ON TITAN AIR ROTATION UNIT		
Cost Saving ($/year)	**Energy Savings (kWh/year)**	**Cost ($)**	**Payback in Years (ROI, %)**
2,760	27,300	6,750	2.4 (41%)

Detail:	Install a variable speed drive (VSD, also known as an inverter or variable frequency drive, VFD) on the fan motor on the Titan Air Rotation unit and open the flow control damper fully. The existing pressure feedback loop that controls the damper position could be adapted to provide speed control input to the VSD.

Rationale:	At present the air pressure in the production area is controlled by the Titan Air Rotation unit. A pressure sensor sends a signal to the unit which opens or closes the flow control damper in the base of the unit according to whether the pressure falls or rises. At the time of the survey the damper was visually inspected and appeared to be almost fully closed. When the pressure drops, for example if one of the loading bay doors is opened, the damper will open to allow more air to flow through the system. This is fundamentally inefficient, as, under all conditions the fan motor runs at full speed (in fact there is some fall in amps drawn by the motor under low load, but it is not a linear relationship and the motor will draw perhaps 70% of full power with the damper almost closed). The more efficient way to do this would be to fully open the damper (the damper can remain in place as back up but would not be used under normal operation) and to fit a VSD to the fan motor, taking a speed control input (usually a 0 to 10 V signal) from the pressure sensor that controls the damper at present.

	Because there is a cube law relationship between air flow rate (as determined by the motor speed and hence the fan speed) and the power drawn by the motor, a small reduction in speed means a much larger reduction in power. Theoretically, with a flow rate equivalent to that achieved by the damper being almost fully closed (assume 80%), the actual power drawn by the fan motor would be less than 1 HP. For the purposes of this calculation we have assumed that the damper is closed only 50%. This is the way most modern air handling units with variable flow conditions are now controlled.
Risks:	None. VSDs are now reliable and should pose no additional maintenance or reliability risks. VSDs can introduce harmonics into the electrical distribution system and so should be fitted with an inline filter.
Next Step:	1. Obtain quotes for installation of VSD on Titan unit and proceed if favourable. Under some circumstances, VSD suppliers might be willing to install the equipment on a trial basis, thus reducing the risk to EPM. This should be investigated with the supplier. ***Note that there may be Federal tax breaks or other incentives (including those offered by energy suppliers) for investment in motor energy efficiency projects.***

7	INSTALL VSDS ON TORRIT DUST COLLECTION SYSTEMS		
Cost Saving ($/year)	**Energy Savings (kWh/year)**	**Cost ($)**	**Payback in Years (ROI, %)**
4,400	43,440	13,500	3.1 (33%)

Detail: Install variable speed drives (VSDs, also known as inverters or variable frequency drives, VFDs) on the fan motors on each of the Torrit dust extraction cyclones and open flow control dampers fully.

Rationale: There are 3 dust extraction cyclones serving the welding area, the sandblast cabinet and the carpentry shop. These are located on the outside of the factory (North Wall, East Building) and were not accessible for inspection during the survey due to the adverse weather conditions.

It is understood that all 3 units are fitted with manual flow control dampers and that these are set to roughly 75% open.

In this type of system the flow control damper is normally set to achieve the desired flow rate at the extraction point while allowing the cyclone to operate efficiently.

The use of a damper is fundamentally inefficient, as the fan motor continues to run at full speed (in fact there is some fall in amps drawn by the motor, perhaps to 85% to 90% of full power with the damper 25% closed).

The more efficient way to do this would be to fully open the damper (the damper can remain in place as back up but would not be used under normal operation) and to fit a VSD to the fan motor, and setting the VSD to the required speed to provide the right amount of flow at the extraction point, whilst allowing the cyclone to operate efficiently.

Because there is a cube law relationship between air flow rate (as determined by the motor speed and hence the fan speed) and the power drawn by the motor, a small reduction in speed means a much larger reduction in power. Theoretically, with a flow rate equivalent to that achieved by the damper being 25% closed, the power drawn by the fan motor would decrease by around 58%.

It is important that the damper setting on each of the dust extraction units is confirmed as it affects the economics of this project. The more closed the dampers are, the greater the savings will be.

Risks: None. VSDs are now reliable and should pose no additional maintenance or reliability risks. VSDs can introduce harmonics into the electrical distribution system and so should be fitted with an inline filter.

Next Step:	1. Obtain quotes for installation of VSD on Torrit units and proceed if favourable. This could initially be trialled on one unit only, and repeated if successful. Under some circumstances, VSD suppliers might be willing to install the equipment on a trial basis, thus reducing the risk to EPM. This should be investigated with the supplier. ***Note that there may be Federal tax breaks or other incentives (including those offered by energy suppliers) for investment in motor energy efficiency projects.***

8	ADD OCCUPANCY CONTROL TO WORKSHOP LIGHTING (IN CONJUNCTION WITH RECOMMENDATION 9 ONLY)		
Cost Saving ($/year)	**Energy Savings (kWh/year)**	**Cost ($)**	**Payback in Years (ROI, %)**
3,720	36,760	12,600	3.4 (30%)

Detail:	Install passive infra red (PIR) occupancy sensors to turn off lighting when personnel are not present. Back ground lighting levels should be maintained and emergency escape routes should be left illuminated.

	NOTE: This recommendation is not suitable for implementation with the existing metal halide factory lighting due to the re-strike periods on this type of lamp. The economics may only be viable if implemented in conjunction with Recommendation 9.
Rationale:	At present, workers are responsible for switching off lighting in their work areas (both factory and offices) when they leave, with any remaining lights being switched off by the cleaning crew. This can result in lights being left on for an unnecessarily long time, or even on constantly, depending on how diligent the workers are. Substantial savings could be achieved by turning off lighting when not required. Installation of automatic PIR controls eliminates the "human factor" and guarantees the savings will be achieved.
Risks:	Ensure that background lighting levels are maintained, and that general circulation areas and emergency escape routes are not affected. Ensure that sensors have a clear view of the work area to prevent unwanted or dangerous loss of light.
Next Step:	1. Obtain quotes for suitable controls, in conjunction with new fluorescent lighting systems discussed in Recommendation 9. ***Note that there may be Federal tax breaks or other incentives (including those offered by energy suppliers) for investment in lighting energy efficiency projects.***

9	REPLACE T12 LIGHTING WITH HIGH FREQUENCY T5 FLUORESCENT LIGHTING		
Cost Saving ($/year)	**Energy Savings (kWh/year)**	**Cost ($)**	**Payback in Years (ROI, %)**
10,330	102,120	48,960	4.7 (21%)

Detail: Replace existing 4 and 8 foot T12 fluorescent lamps by T5 high frequency low bay fittings.

Rationale: Factory lighting is provided by approximately 120 metal halide lamps (400 W in the main production area and 250 W in the fabrication shop) and around 400 4 or 8 foot T12 fluorescent tubes in twin tube fittings.

Office lighting is provided by around 420 4 foot or 1½ foot T12 (1½ inch diameter) fluorescent tubes in 3 tube fittings.

The T12 fittings are very inefficient compared to modern T8 (1 inch diameter) or T5 (5/8 inch diameter) tubes with high frequency control gear. In addition, T12 replacement tube costs are likely to be high, leading to possible maintenance savings.

Modern fluorescent lighting with high frequency controls also offers superior control options, including instant re-strike, meaning that the light fittings can be used in conjunction with PIR occupancy controls (see *Recommendation 8*). High frequency lighting can also be dimmed (providing a dimmable ballast is specified), meaning that lighting could be set back to a background level, rather than switched off when occupants were not present.

Tube life is also extended.

It is recognised that the economics of this project do not meet the financial criteria specified by EPM/Shafer. The economics would improve once the non-energy benefits of reduced maintenance costs (tube replacement costs and labor) are included, and these should be factored into the calculations.

Also, there may be capital or grants available or tax breaks that could reduce capital costs. These should be investigated.

Risks: None

Next Step: 1. Obtain quotes for replacement of lamps and proceed if favorable.

Note that there may be Federal tax breaks or other incentives (including those offered by energy suppliers) for investment in lighting energy efficiency projects.

APPENDIX A

ENERGY MANAGEMENT MATRIX

Level	Energy Policy	Organising	Training	Performance Measurement	Communication	Investment
4	Energy policy, Action Plan and regular review have active commitment of top management	Fully integrated into management structure with clear accountability for energy consumption	Appropriate and comprehensive staff training tailored to identified needs, with evaluation	Comprehensive performance measurement against targets with effective management reporting	Extensive communication of energy issues within and outside of organisation	Resources routinely commited to energy efficiency in support of business objectives
3	Formal policy but no active commitment from top management	Clear line management accountability for consumption and responsibility for improvement	Energy training targeted at major users following training needs analysis	Weekly performance measurement for each process, unit, or building	Regular staff briefings, performance reporting and energy promotion	Same appraisal criteria used as for other cost reduction projects
2	Un-adopted Policy	Some delegation of responsibility but line management and authority unclear	Ad-Hoc internal training for selected people as required	Monthly monitoring by fuel type	Some use of company communication mechanisms to promote energy efficiency	Low or medium cost measures considered if short payback period
1	An unwritten set of guidelines	Informal, mostly focused on energy supply	Technical staff occasionally attend specialist courses	Invoice checking only	Ad-Hoc informal contacts used to promote energy efficiency	Only low or no cost measures taken
0	No explicit energy Policy	No delegation of responsibility for managing energy	No energy related staff training provided	No measurement of energy costs or consumptions	No communication or promotion of energy issues	No investment in improving energy efficiency

APPENDIX B

DETAILS OF ENERGY SAVING OPPORTUNITIES

Compressed Air Savings Calculations

Compressor					
Motor size	50	HP			
	37.5	kW			
Motor Efficiency	90%				
	41.7	kW			
Load Factor	60%	(from observation)			
Off-load power	30%				
Average power	30.0	kW			
Runs	96.5	hours/week			
	52	weeks			
	5,018	hours/year			
Total energy	150,540	kWh/year		15,235	
				$	
Reduce air leaks	10%		15,054	1,523	
	20%		**30,108**	**3,047**	Estimated
	30%		45,162	4,570	

Electronic sequence control

Air comps generate at					Differential	
#1	135	psi	9.3	bar	1.4	bar
#3	132	psi	9.1	bar	20	psi
#2	115	psi	7.9	bar		
System supply at	95	psi	6.6	bar		
Saving:	5%	per	10	psi		
Saving %:	10%					
	15,054	kWh/year				

Compressed Air Electronic Drain Traps

Oil separator
Drain is cracked open
Condensate drain - time solenoid 30 seconds every 15 minutes

Save	2%	
	3,011	kWh/year
Cost	300	

Substitution of end users

Save	20%	
	30,108	kWh/year
Cost	5,000	

Ventilation and Dust Extraction Savings Calculations

	Motor Size HP	kW	Efficiency	Power Input kW	Run Hrs/day	Days/ week	Weeks/yr	Hours/ yr	kWh/ year
Titan Unit	30	22.5	0.9	20.0	24	7	52	8,736	174,720
Heatex Unit (2 speed)	20	15	0.9	2.1	24	7	10	1,680	3,500
Spray Booth 1	5	3.75	0.9	4.2	6	5.5	52	1,716	7,150
Spray Booth 2	5	3.75	0.9	4.2	6	5.5	52	1,716	7,150
Spray Booth Input		2.2	0.9	2.4	6	5.5	52	1,716	4,195
Man Cooler Fans		2.5	0.9	2.8	6	5.5	52	1,716	4,767
Fume Extracts	60	45	0.9	40.0	8	5.5	52	2,288	91,520
Office AHU 1	5	18	0.9	20.0	16	6	52	4,992	99,840
Office AHU 2	3	18	1.9	9.5	16	6	52	4,992	47,293
Office AHU 3	1.5	18	2.9	6.2	16	6	52	4,992	30,985
Office AHU 4	1	18	3.9	4.6	16	6	52	4,992	23,040
Total									**494,159**

VSD on Titan Unit

Power Input (throttled)	20.0	kW
Gross Power Input	25.00	kW
VSD Speed reduction	50%	
Power Input (VSD)	3.1	kW
Power Inout as % of full power	13%	
Saving	27,300	kWh/year

VSD on Torrit Cyclones

Power Input (throttled)	36.0	kW
Gross Power Input	45.00	kW
VSD Speed reduction	25%	
Power Input (VSD)	19.0	kW
Power Input as % of full power	42%	
Saving	43,436	kWh/year

Lighting Savings Calculations

Factory	**No Lamps**	**W/tube**	**Control Gear**	**Total Load**	**No Fittings**	**Installed Cost per Fitting**	**Capex $**
8' T12s	376	95	15%	41.1	188	170	31,960
4' T12s	22	34	15%	0.9	11	120	1,320
400 W Metal Halides	70	400	15%	32.2			
250 W Metal Halides	52	250	15%	15.0			
Total	**520**			**89.1**			
No fittings							
	4,862	hours/year					
Total Energy Use	433,147	kWh/year					

Offices	No Lamps	W/tube	Control Gear	Total Load	No Fittings	Installed Cost per Fitting	Capex $
Office Areas	348	34	15%	14	116	120	13,920
Corridors	66	18	15%	1	22	80	1,760
Total	**414**			**15**			
					Total		48,960
	3,432	hours/year					
Total Energy Use	51,387	kWh/year					
Total All Lighting	484,534	kWh/year					

Replace Factory T12s with HF T5s

Total Load	42	
Total Energy	203,904	kWh/year
T5 Savings	40%	
Saving	81,561	kWh/year

Replace Office T12s with T5s

Total Load	15	
Total Energy	51,387	kWh/year
T5 Savings	40%	
Saving	20,555	kWh/year

PIR Controls	Say	80%	of lighting can be PIR controlled (circulation areas remain lit 24/7)		
	Save	30%			
Factory use	122,342	kWh/year			
Office Use	30,832	kWh/year			
			No Fittings	Installed Cost per Fitting	CapEx $
Total	153,175	kWh/year			
Saving	36,762	kWh/year	315	40	12,600

References

1. Mills, E, H. Friedman, T. Powell, N. Bourassa, D. Claridge, T. Haasl, and M.A. Piette. "The Cost–Effectiveness of Commercial-Buildings Commissioning," Lawrence Berkeley National Laboratory, 2004.
2. U.S. Department of Energy

Index

For Product Safety Concerns and Information please contact our EU representative GPSR@taylorandfrancis.com Taylor & Francis Verlag GmbH, Kaufingerstraße 24, 80331 München, Germany

Batch number: 10723924

Printed by Printforce, the Netherlands